The National Interest and the Human Interest
An Analysis of U.S. Foreign Policy

Written under the auspices of the Center of International Studies, Princeton University. A list of other Center publications appears at the back of this book.

The National Interest
and the Human Interest

An Analysis of U.S. Foreign Policy

ROBERT C. JOHANSEN

PRINCETON UNIVERSITY PRESS

Copyright © 1980 by Princeton University Press
Published by Princeton University Press, Princeton, New Jersey
In the United Kingdom: Princeton University Press, Guildford, Surrey

All Rights Reserved
Library of Congress Cataloging in Publication Data will be
found on the last printed page of this book

This book has been composed in VIP Baskerville

Clothbound editions of Princeton University Press books
are printed on acid-free paper, and binding materials are
chosen for strength and durability

Printed in the United States of America by Princeton
University Press, Princeton, New Jersey

To Martin Luther King, Jr.,

WHO HELPED US UNDERSTAND WHAT IT MEANS TO BE A PLANETARY CITI-
ZEN, AND TO ALL THOSE WHO SEEK TO LIVE ACCORDING TO THIS
UNDERSTANDING.

Contents

List of Tables

List of Illustrations

Acknowledgments

THIS book has been influenced by values that took root during my childhood and college years. That early learning was pruned and strengthened as I and our society responded to the experiences of activists in the civil rights, peace, feminist, and environmental movements. All of the persons who have touched my life during those years and shaped this book cannot be acknowledged here. But I am confident that these friends will sense, in the following pages, their influences. This book is partly a product of our agonizing together about the inadequacies of the present and envisioning an alternative future.

Some influences have been so profound and my indebtedness so great as to deserve special mention. My parents' inspiration and continuing support for my work are foremost among these. For knowledge of fundamental values, a sense of responsibility to implement them, and a determination to face even unpleasant truths, I happily acknowledge my parents' compassionate and morally sensitive instruction. For an encompassing understanding of the preciousness and precariousness of life, I thank my brother, whose short but humane life strengthened my own commitment to resist the politics and economics of human fragmentation and their accompanying prejudice and violence.

While I was a student at Manchester College, several wise though not widely known professors nurtured the growth of some ideas contained herein. When I returned there to teach, many courageous students of the late 1960s and early 1970s helped temper these ideas further by expressing their acute sense of planetary citizenship both inside and outside the classroom. During and since those years I have benefited enormously from the intellectual stimulation and ethical affirmation of my teacher, colleague, and friend, Kenneth L. Brown.

My own professional life and the intellectual orientation for this book have been heavily influenced by Richard A. Falk. His insight, his unique ability to combine normative inquiry with empirical, scholarly rigor, his constant encouragement, penetrating criticism, and ground-breaking scholarship have been a strong example and inspiration for me. Without his support, this project would not have borne fruit. This book also has been influenced by the pioneering work of the Institute for World Order, by the talented transnational group of scholars in the World Order Models Project, and especially by the intellectual contributions of its director, Saul H. Mendlovitz.

Cyril E. Black and others at the Center of International Studies provided an ideal setting at Princeton University where I wrote the first draft. While there, it was possible to enjoy the luxury of full-time study because of financial support from the University Consortium for World Order Studies as a James P. Warburg Fellow, from Princeton University as a John Parker Compton Fellow of the Center of International Studies, and from Manchester College as a professor on sabbatical leave.

I am deeply grateful to Catherine Smith for her outstanding secretarial and administrative talents. These plus her cheerfulness helped make a pleasant task out of what otherwise would have been a lengthy burden in preparing an unwieldly manuscript. Her commitment to the values undergirding the project gave its completion a unity of purpose for which all co-workers hope.

No one has contributed more to this effort than my wife, Ruthann. She has shared with me her own ideas about and commitment to building a more just world order. These have been invaluable. I thank her also for her empathy, her eagerness to debate substantive questions, her self-sacrifice in giving me uninterrupted hours to write, and her liberated unwillingness to let the writing dominate both of our lives completely. By their questions, laughter, hopes, and frustrations, our children Erik and Sonia have made it possible—and necessary—to understand more fully the unfathomable human stakes that await all children in future foreign policy choices. They have given concrete meaning to abstract discussions about the human consequences of foreign policy decisions. In addition, more than it is fair to expect, Erik and Sonia have been quick to forgive and to accept a father who has seemed forever seated at the typewriter.

While accepting responsibility for the contents of this book, I happily express gratitude to all of these people.

Abbreviations

ABM	*Antiballistic missile*
AEC	*Atomic Energy Commission*
AID	*Agency for International Development*
CIA	*Central Intelligence Agency*
DAC	*Development Assistance Committee of* OECD
IAEA	*International Atomic Energy Agency*
ICA	*International Cooperation Administration*
ICBM	*Intercontinental ballistic missile*
IDB	*Inter-American Development Bank*
IMCO	*International Maritime Consultative Organization*
ISRA	*International Seabed Resource Authority*
ITT	*International Telephone and Telegraph*
IWC	*International Whaling Commission*
JCS	*Joint Chiefs of Staff*
MaRV	*Maneuverable reentry vehicle*
MIRV	*Multiple independently-targetable reentry vehicle*
MNC	*Multinational corporation*
NIE	*National Intelligence Estimate*
NSC	*National Security Council*
OAS	*Organization of American States*
OECD	*Organization for Economic Cooperation and Development*
OPEC	*Organization of Petroleum Exporting Countries*
PDC	*Christian Democratic Party (of Chile)*
PN	*National Party (of Chile)*
psi	*pounds per square inch*
SALT	*Strategic Arms Limitation Talks*
SALT I	*Interim Agreement and* ABM *Treaty of 1972*
SLBM	*Submarine launched ballistic missile*
UNCTAD	*United Nations Conference on Trade and Development*
V_1	*Peace without national military arsenals*
V_2	*Economic well-being*
V_3	*Universal human rights and social justice*
V_4	*Ecological balance*

Foreword

IN truth, Americans have always been ambivalent about foreign policy. In the foreground is the special view of American innocence that has existed since the beginning of the Republic. The United States, it was then widely believed, could only be kept pure by remaining aloof from the entanglements of the Old World. Such aloofness always competed with a contrary vision of the United States as a country with a special mission to create a better world. In many respects, the sensibility and outlook of Thomas Jefferson gracefully embodied this ambivalence that has by now deeply insinuated itself into national political consciousness. It was Jefferson who eloquently defended the virtues of detachment while simultaneously working to realize visions of empire, most tangibly, perhaps, by negotiating the Louisiana Purchase and giving, late in his life, a hearty endorsement to the Monroe Doctrine.

This dual heritage is still alive, although its forms are new. The perils and imperatives of involvement are mainly discussed these days in relation to the Third World, and the weight of debate has·shifted from goals to tactics. Yet considerable uneasiness persists; witness the tension between the rhetorical respect given by U.S. leaders to nonintervention, self-determination, and sovereign equality as guiding principles of foreign policy and the actualities of an interventionary, even a counterrevolutionary diplomacy. In recent years, really since the late 1960s when the Vietnam failure became apparent, there has been a domestic mood of despair and discontent about the global role of the United States. Indeed, current attitudes of the American public toward foreign policy waver somewhere between apathy and anger, reflecting both feelings of frustration that nothing effective can be done and resentment about the inability of the government to arrest the relative decline of U.S. power and stature in the world system. As matters now stand United States foreign policy is likely to fail both pragmatic and idealistic tests for most citizens, thereby assaulting that aspect of national character preoccupied with success, as well as that concerned with virtue. Besides, the earlier fear of being drawn into foreign wars is being displaced by the insistence that the United States display a greater willingness to use military capabilities to uphold overseas interests.

Lurking in the shadows are formidable issues that compose the novel and largely repressed agenda of world order challenges. Underlying these challenges are doubts about the framework of state sovereignty, especially questions about whether the old order can provide a satisfactory basis for the security and prosperity of the American people in the nuclear age. Most fundamental here is whether the deterrence system, including its costly and nerve-wracking arms race, will prove morally acceptable and practically effective as a peace system over time, and whether, of course, there are attainable alternatives.

Pressing more directly on public awareness is a set of demands emanating from the countries of Asia, Africa, and Latin America, summarized by their insistence upon "a new international economic order." Interacting with this North-South confrontation are concerns about "resource diplomacy," about the status of rich countries using a disproportionate share of the planet's stock of nonrenewable resources and injecting into the environment a disproportionate share of pollution in forms and quantities that do ecological and hygienic damage. This novel agenda greatly complicates the global setting. Its tone is best suggested by the emergent eco-equity struggle to devise development paths for countries at various stages of industrialization, development paths that would combine environmental protection with the fulfillment of essential human needs and basic societal aspirations for a good life. Such a vision of positive world order seems remote from the reality of arms races, mass poverty, widespread warfare, demographic pressures, and repressive governing tactics. Where in this tangle of torments can one find first the transnational understanding and then the national will in the major countries of the world, to build, in the phrase of one impressive movement for change active in America, "a strategy for a living revolution"?

It is hardly surprising that the current language of political discourse for foreign policy matters in the United States seems vague, hypocritical, and irrelevant. The inconsistent requirements of servicing an empire while claiming to be the benefactor of human society at home and abroad are at the root of the difficulty, yet the actualities of declining power and the political need to disguise the trend and its consequences from the American people have added to the strain. Of course, other great powers with liberal traditions have faced a similar challenge. The experiences of England and France provide recent examples; both countries have undergone many difficulties while adjusting psychically and materially to the loss of empire.

Yet a difference of utmost significance pertains. The rationale of imperial policies and the adjustment to increases and reduction of power relative to other states has been carried on for several centuries within a relatively secure geopolitical framework. The game of nations has often been waged for high stakes, and yet the survival of the system never seemed at issue. Even in the seventeenth century when the transition from feudalism to statism culminated in the Thirty Years War the outcomes of international conflict did not imperil the destiny of the human species. In our era the circumstances are different. Threats of nuclear war and ecological catastrophe carry with them apocalyptic dangers of irreversible damage, even of total collapse. People have, of course, long wondered before about whether life on this planet was or should be sustainable; religious imagery, especially in the West, has been filled with prophetic anticipations of death, transfiguration, and last judgment since Biblical times. Yet today, with global communications and interactions so prominent, we have a crisis of confidence among the prosperous peoples of the North, growing doubts about whether the future will seem an improvement on the past, and even deeper fears about whether the secular materialism of a technology-based image of progress can sustain the morale of modern, affluent, and liberal states.

Such a crisis provokes fundamental rethinking. It becomes natural to consider as a matter of urgency whether the values, beliefs, and techniques of the past are adequate for the future. Obvious questions about the viability of the sovereign state are inevitably raised and yet the issues are confused by that other dominant political reality of our time, namely that of surging nationalism. The numerous peoples of the South are struggling with enthusiasm to create genuine full-fledged states. Nationalism is also on the rise in the North as evidenced by the flourishing of separatist movements in the most settled of states. Considering the world as a whole as the ground upon which foreign policy is enacted also reveals an extraordinary unevenness and diversity of aspiration, situation, and heritage.

Occasionally, elements of the new world order agenda break into public consciousness, as briefly during the early 1970s when the Club of Rome's report stimulated "the limits to growth" debate. Such a break in the ice is bound to be temporary at this stage; old patterns of thought quickly reassert themselves, especially if the challenge cannot be handled within orthodox problem-solving frameworks. The leaders of most states are too preoccupied with the short-run management of foreign policy to cast their gaze on longer-term interpretations that are bound to be exceedingly controversial and for some sectors of society, usually those most influential under present arrangements, exceedingly threatening and costly. As a consequence, the more drastic items on an appropriate world order agenda are continually repressed, and the foreign policy process, unless overtaken by war or economic emergency, reverts to short-term managerial maneuvering and blustering self-confidence.

This assessment leads to one further observation. It is a mistake to rely on government for diagnosis or response to the longer-term, underlying, yet very real, world order challenges. It is a mistake easily made as modern governments, and especially ours, claim the allegiance of the citizenry partly because of their supposed omnicompetence. Confusion is increased, also, by the tendency of governments to preempt and harmlessly ritualize much of the rhetoric of global concern, inducing both complacency and cynical disregard of substance. In our culture where the main instruments of this alleged omnicompetence are technology and military prowess, the prognosis is scary. The tension between short-term maneuver and long-term readjustment is illustrated by debates about both the military and civilian aspects of nuclear policy, where the preferences of official elites increasingly collide with the anxieties of the citizenry. Especially in foreign policy, the government feels the growing burdens of omnicompetence at an historical time of apparently diminishing capabilities. Leaders search for ways to provide reassurance and the public grows increasingly restive and narrow-minded as various developments are blamed for erosions of prosperity, security, and serenity. This process of dissolution goes on throughout the trilateral world of North America, Western Europe, and Japan with perhaps its most acute expressions involving recourse to terror as political stratagem and to drugs as private consolation.

Despite the severity of indictment, lines of deeper analysis of our political situation as a nation have so far aroused very little scholarly interest among social scientists. Traditional inquiry into relative economic and political power continues to share the foreign policy scene with an array of modernist methodologies designed to make interpretation less impressionistic. The focus is mainly on a conventional agenda of foreign policy priorities: maintaining reliable access to sufficient overseas oil, keeping the Soviet Union contained without provoking World War III, and holding back Third World demands for major reforms in the international economic order.

The foreign policy literature continues to be dominated by managerial appraisals and proposals, with some revival of the "classical" inquiry into how to achieve equilibrium under conditions of changing global configurations of power and alignment. Little attention is being given to the gaps between words and deeds, between deeds and needs, and between needs and values as these pertain to U.S. foreign policy. It is one thing to discern the gaps and quite another to depict these gaps concretely enough to suggest what might be an alternative foreign policy based on the longer term imperatives of the country.

Against this background, Robert Johansen's book strikes me as a major achievement. Proceeding on a solid foundation of empirical depth, Johansen demonstrates the character of the first gap between declared ends and performance in U.S. foreign policy. Not only do his carefully constructed cases reveal the extent of the gap, but also its quality, especially the consistent interplay between pious rhetoric and expedient activity. As such, the public justification of American foreign policy sets up a distorting filter between the government and the citizenry that inhibits informed discussion and trivializes public discourse on momentous matters.

Johansen's cases lend both concreteness and structural depth to his argument. Each case is inherently significant as an illustration of a specific set of choices by American makers of foreign policy and suggestive of a recurrent theme that can be reexamined in the light of earlier and later "cases." For instance, the CIA role in Allende's Chile can be considered in relation to Arbenz's Guatemala (1954) or the movement that drove the Shah from power in early 1979. Context, as well as structure, matters. We cannot be sure what has been "learned" from the Chilean case and what results from an analysis of American goals and capabilities in the Iranian case. Has American statecraft shifted? If so, does the shift reflect a new willingness to accommodate revolutionary nationalism in Third World countries or merely the provisional acquiescence by a given group of U.S. leaders to a political outcome beyond their capacity to control? American foreign policy toward Iran might revert to an interventionary approach as a consequence of either an electoral mandate in the United States or as a result of a further challenge to American interests in the Gulf region. The response of the United States to internal political developments in a foreign country perceived as adverse to American interests is both a structural feature of American foreign policy and a distinctive "instance." By putting his case studies within an overall framework Johansen illuminates our understanding of both policy and structure.

More impressive, still, Johansen links this revealing critique of American foreign policy to the longer term framework of global reform. In the past decade, "world order" has started to supplant "balance of power" as a focus for the ends of foreign policy, and yet this allegedly new perspective is often deceptive. It often seems to mean no more than finding verbal formulations suitable for the expanded scope of a global system to stabilize relations (including economic relations) among sovereign states. Johansen, in contrast, uses world order to mean the realization of those values which he believes necessary to achieve a humane and secure existence for the peoples of the world. Such a program of global reform implies for Johansen a series of structural changes in the framework of international relations, although it doesn't imply or propose shifting from the state system to world government. At root, Johansen associates the dynamic of change with value shifts in the advanced industrial sectors of world society that will spontaneously erode the legitimacy of the highly coercive structures of the modern state. His image of a different future for American foreign policy places as much emphasis on destructuring the state from within as it does on the growth of external central guidance capabilities to achieve the levels of coordination and regulation required for activity that is of planetary scale and significance. In the end, Johansen insists that a mixed moral and prudential challenge calls for the reorientation of American foreign policy. We must do what we say, seek what we need, and affirm what we want for the future.

It is, of course, too soon for policymakers to heed such wisdom. They are too constrained by their own immediate concerns to confront seriously the argument that their cosmology is outmoded. Instead, as with astronomers throughout the ages, they tinker with old beliefs, long after these have been discredited, devising various ingenious schemes to obscure the realities of their failure, and as with any establishment they will do their best to discredit the new astronomers who propose a different cosmology. Of course, the stakes are higher than achieving a more satisfying apprehension of reality. An inquiry into global reform is, at minimum, a quest for a safer, saner world political system. It involves nothing less than evaluating and influencing the evolutionary destiny of the human race. It also challenges our passivity at a time of danger and turbulence. It is one of the prime opportunities available to scholars in a free society to set forth the unfashionable case for drastic reform, and it is a call to the rest of us to listen and respond as openly as we can. Very few books on American foreign policy have ever set forth so forceful and fundamental a challenge as this one.

Johansen's scholarly inquiry is informed by a citizen's passionate insistence on a foreign policy fit for the American people before it is too late. It is also informed by an understanding that to be a patriotic American late in the twentieth century is indistinguishable from being a loyal citizen of the planet as a whole. In this respect his participation in the World Order Models Project where diverse orientations toward global reform interact gives his outlook a cultural depth that is a happy contrast with the sort of vague globalism that is the sentimental substance of Sunday sermons.

Issuing planetary death warrants is neither novel, nor helpful. At the same time, we require no mysterious or inspired being to warn us that ours is a time of jeopardy for earth and earthlings. The United States, with its awesome capacity to wreck, whether by weapons or its intricate life style, is in an especially responsible position. What we do and don't do in relating to others will seriously, possibly decisively, influence the unfolding of the future.

If Americans are going to stop acting like subjects and start acting like citizens, then they have to become informed and caring about the foreign policy of their nation. Knowledge can be profoundly empowering. Indeed, this conviction underlies Johansen's animating vision of a preferred, alternate world order that is peaceful and just. It can happen, but only if we make it happen, if we move from realms of feeling through realms of thought to realms of actions and activities.

Johansen tells us that by being true to ourselves we will also help forge the still uncreated conscience of the human race, embarking thereby upon what may be the most exciting (and perilous) voyage of discovery ever contemplated. Reality is fundamentally encouraging, but only if we act accordingly, out of a sense of urgency, yet with patience and perseverance (the most revolutionary of virtues).

Richard Falk

The National Interest and the Human Interest
An Analysis of U.S. Foreign Policy

ONE · *The Elusiveness of A Humane World Community*

PURPOSE

WE live on a planet possessing the potential for peace and fulfillment for all, but societies have been distressingly unsuccessful in achieving these conditions for most of the human race. Why? This book begins to answer this fundamental question by examining two others: What has been the United States role in helping to achieve a secure and humane existence for all people? In pursuit of this goal, what should be the content of U.S. foreign policy now and during the remainder of this century?

In addressing these questions, my purpose is to examine recent U.S. foreign policy in order to clarify its impact on insuring the survival and well-being of U.S. citizens and the entire human race. Does the past conduct of U.S. foreign policy justify confidence that it can meet the unprecedented challenges of the 1980s? This analysis assesses the influence of U.S. policies on the prospects for realizing widely shared humanitarian values and for transforming the international system into one with an improved capacity to implement those values.

The present chapter will (1) illustrate the unprecedented foreign policy problems that will confront political leaders in the last quarter of the twentieth century; (2) explain why the complexity and worldwide dimensions of these problems demonstrate a pressing need for different normative standards for policy making than have been used historically; (3) describe the guidelines which seem essential to insure human survival and to facilitate the realization of other important values, such as the promotion of human rights and the abolition of worldwide poverty; and (4) explain the analytic approach employed in this study.

THE CHALLENGE TO HUMANITY'S FUTURE

Global Problems in a National Context

Why should scholars, politicians, and ordinary citizens reassess the goals of U.S. foreign policy at this time? The answer is

3

rooted in considerations of both prudence and morality. First of all, some fundamental policy adjustments will be required to satisfy the basic drive for security and survival in the future. Second, the fulfillment of our most cherished humanitarian values can be greatly facilitated by some modifications in the present national approach to policy decisions.

THE THREAT TO SURVIVAL

In the first instance, unprecedented problems that are global in scope increasingly exceed the capacity of traditional diplomatic practices and institutions to resolve. In general, our perception of foreign policy problems and opportunities has failed to stay abreast of rapidly changing world realities. This has meant that many policies have been growing increasingly unrealistic in the sense that they simply cannot achieve the ends sought. To oversimplify only slightly, the political leadership and attentive public apply essentially nineteenth-century diplomatic ideas[1] to the solution of twenty-first-century problems, the technical and social origins of which are in the present. Nineteenth-century diplomatic ideas encourage (1) the continued emphasis on serving the national interest defined largely in terms of military power and sovereign control over a carefully defined piece of territory and segment of humanity; and (2) the assumption that the present system of competing national sovereignties either cannot or should not be fundamentally changed, and that it both can and will respond adequately to the foreseeable problems of national security, widespread poverty and resource shortages, severe ecological damage, and pervasive denial of human rights. Under the influence of old diplomatic habits and strong vested interests in the political and economic system inherited from the past, officials continue diplomacy as usual to confront newly emerging twenty-first century problems. For example, traditional diplomatic ideas and institutions persist even though their inadequacy is obvious for averting misuse of nuclear technology, the consequences of which cannot be confined to a carefully defined piece of territory, layer of the atmosphere, or segment of humanity. Traditional uses of military power and sovereign control, however sincerely and faithfully practiced, are impotent in the face of irresponsible behavior by a relatively small number of people who could affect millions of

4

others in many countries for decades, centuries, or millennia to come.

A stark reality faces all inhabitants of the earth: through consequences resulting from major war or ecological imbalance, widespread suffering for millions of people and even eventual extinction of the human species are possibilities. Such statements have become commonplace, and thus they have lost their ring of urgency.[2] Yet predicaments mount while time slips away, making remedial action more difficult and perhaps less likely. Even without major war or ecological collapse, existing political institutions prevent a billion of the world's people from having sufficient food, often resulting in permanent mental or physical disability, even though adequate nutrition is technically feasible. In brief, the decentralized structure of world power and authority, distributed among many sovereign states, perpetuates a relatively anarchic international system in which the danger of war, the shortage of food and other resources, and the presence of persistent ecological hazards threaten the survival of many people, if not, in the long run, of all human civilization. The survival question will not be examined in detail here, but a few brief comments about the political impact of nuclear technology and ecological hazards will illustrate the need to consider an alternative approach to the conduct of U.S. foreign policy.[3] Subsequent chapters will substantiate this argument in greater detail.

The existence of nuclear weapons without their use in warfare since 1945 has produced a perhaps unjustified confidence that weapons of mass destruction will never be used. Yet, many dangers remain inherent in a strategy of nuclear deterrence.[4] Although the United States is the most powerful nation on earth, it has no effective defense against a nuclear attack. The government can only hope to *deter* an attack. Yet as nuclear weapons technology spreads to additional countries, the likelihood that such weapons will be used in war increases. A well-known group of strategic experts in a Harvard-M.I.T. Arms Control Seminar have predicted that nuclear weapons will be used in combat before the end of the century—most likely by middle-range powers.[5] Other experts have calculated that the probability of a *general* nuclear war is increasing.[6] The danger of nuclear war will grow further as tactical nuclear weapons become smaller, lighter, "cleaner," and more mobile, because they will be more easily purchased, transported, and viewed as similar to conventional explosives. Although any single national government may believe that its security is increased if it accumulates more and more advanced weapons, for world society as a whole both the likelihood and the potential destructiveness of future wars are increased by the growth of military equipment and the spread of militarism around the world.

With the dispersal of command and control required by submarine-launched missiles and tactical battlefield weapons, an excessively eager team of officers or a miscommunicated signal could initiate the use of nuclear weapons. While the probabilities for accidental war are no doubt low, the impossibility of eliminating the danger of accidents completely is a rather unsatisfactory condition given the awesome consequences of a mistake.[7]

Nuclear war could also begin through miscalculation by some officials about the anticipated actions of another government. Since deterrence is based on the ability of government X to make government Y believe that X will use nuclear weapons in the face of certain provocations, the only way to insure the credibility of one's posture is to use nuclear weapons occasionally. If the threat to use nuclear weapons is only a bluff by X, then Y could rationally proceed to ignore the threat. Thus the leadership in Y could miscalculate the seriousness of X, and precipitate war.

Furthermore, given the absence of dependable screening procedures in selecting government officials, an emotionally unstable person may, in some country, at some time in the future, exercise decisive power in a government equipped with nuclear weapons. Similarly, political leaders who assume office with normal emotional maturity may, when under political pressure, emotional stress, or fatigue, make decisions with some degree of diminished rationality. President John F. Kennedy deliberately raised the risk of nuclear war to odds he estimated as "even,"[8] because he did not like having Soviet missiles ninety miles away in Cuba, even though nuclear missiles could exist legally as close as twelve miles away, in submarines cruising just outside United States territorial waters.

Although there was no apparent security need to risk nuclear war, U.S. officials executed policies that, by their own admission, brought nuclear war frightfully closer: "Not one of us at any

6

time believed that any of the choices before us could bring anything but either prolonged danger or fighting, very possibly
leading to the kind of deepening commitment of prestige and
power from which neither side could withdraw without resort to
nuclear weapons."[9] A key participant in the decisions, Robert
Kennedy, reported that, while they hoped to avoid war, "the *expectation* was a military confrontation."[10] During the discussions,
FBI Director J. Edgar Hoover informed U.S. officials that the
FBI had received information that Soviet personnel in New
York were preparing to destroy all sensitive documents in the
belief that the United States would "probably be taking military
action against Cuba or Soviet ships, and this would mean war."[11]
Robert Kennedy summed up his own and President Kennedy's
feelings: "There was the realization that the Soviet Union and
Cuba apparently were preparing to do battle. And there was the
feeling that the noose was tightening on all of us, on Americans,
on mankind, and that the bridges to escape were crumbling."[12]

The tension and anxiety accompanying such a crisis often lead
to overreactions. Attorney general Kennedy reported that, for a
brief time at least, nearly all advisers favored an air attack: "At
first there was almost unanimous agreement that we had to attack early the next morning with bombers and fighters and destroy the SAM [surface to air missile] sites."[13] During the brief
time that the President was waiting for a Soviet response to the
United States demand for withdrawal of Soviet missiles, Theodore Sorensen reported growing support among Presidential
advisers for a direct air strike and invasion of Cuba: "The pressures for such a move . . . were rapidly and *irresistibly* growing,
strongly supported by a minority in our group and increasingly
necessitated by a deterioration in the situation."[14] During one
day of long, almost continuous discussions in the White House,
the crisis produced rising tempers and irritability among the
small group of decision makers. "Pressure and fatigue, he [the
President] later noted privately, might have broken the group's
steady demeanor in another twenty-four or forty-eight hours."[15]

Great exhilaration followed the "successful" U.S. testing of
Soviet will. Sorensen reported the President "had, as Harold
Macmillan would later say, earned his place in history by this one
act alone. He had been engaged in a personal as well as national
contest for world leadership and he had won."[16] Contesting for
the personal and national leadership of the world (or a region of

7

the world) through military confrontation is a motivation that other leaders may have in the future and that can hardly avoid questions of human survival.

The possibilities for nuclear war or for terrorist use of nuclear technology are increased by the spread of fissionable materials to additional private organizations and governments. In addition to the six nuclear weapons countries, a score of other states have the resources and technical skills to produce nuclear weapons within one or two years. No existing international organization can prevent even a signatory to the nonproliferation treaty from *deliberately* diverting materials to weapons purposes. Moreover, the purchase of nuclear weapons and delivery systems could become a serious possibility. Even without nuclear weapons a determined group could inflict catastrophe on other states. A few pounds of plutonium distributed as a finely ground powder could devastate a city like New York with lethal radiation lasting for centuries. Such an act might even be committed by persons representing no nation-state against which the United States could retaliate. The destruction of civilian nuclear reactors also could cause the loss of thousands of lives. These conditions make deterrence ineffective because no one can genuinely be defended against a determined opponent.

It may bear repeating that major nuclear war would kill most of the urban populations of the antagonists. It would destroy most industry and commerce. Perhaps more than half of the populations in small towns and rural areas would die from fallout, depending on weather conditions, wind direction, and the height of detonations. Living standards and life expectancies would be substantially reduced for any persons remaining. Millions of cancer and leukemia deaths would occur outside the territories of the two antagonists. Untold numbers of genetic problems and birth deformities would await those still living. There would be dangerous effects on the atmosphere, the soil, and the water, as well as consequences presently unanticipated. As Herbert York, former director of defense research and engineering for the Department of Defense, has written:

> If for any political, psychological or technical reasons deterrence should fail, the physical, biological and social consequences would be completely out of line with any reasonable view of the national objectives of the United States or Soviet Union. . . . [T]here would be a substantial chance that the whole civilized world could go up in nuclear smoke. This is

8

simply too frightful and too dangerous a way to live indefinitely; we *must* find some better form of international relationship than the current dependency on a strategy of mutual assured destruction.[17]

Given the dangers of nuclear technology, a prudent foreign policy would convey a sense of urgency about establishing the new values and institutions that could make the prohibition of nuclear weapons a feasible, enforceable, compulsory, universal obligation.

Although less dramatic in its immediacy, pollution of the atmosphere and oceans also illustrates a long-range challenge to survival and to the quality of our lives—a challenge that again demonstrates the interconnection of every life on the planet. Although all earthly plant and animal life depends upon the air and the sea, no one exercises sovereignty over or protects vast expanses of the atmosphere and oceans. Nations now pollute them without much regard for long-range consequences to the planet or even for short-range effects outside their national jurisdiction. Yet all ecosystems are part of a delicate ecological balance; all have limits of deterioration beyond which they cannot recover. In many cases we do not know the planetary limits which, if surpassed, would endanger our species.

The consequences of depleting the amount of ozone in the stratosphere illustrate the problem. Without ozone protection, ultraviolet light would break down molecules on earth that are essential to life. Crops, bacteria, and micro-life in general would be affected. Ultraviolet light also causes skin cancer and genetic damage that can severely endanger both animal and plant life. In addition to protecting life from extraplanetary lethal radiation, ozone, by absorbing ultraviolet light, contributes substantially to heating the upper atmosphere surrounding the planet. The depletion of ozone could radically alter the climate of the earth, as well as eventually expose all forms of life to deadly radiation. Even a small drop in density would increase the incidence of birth defects and skin cancer.

Ozone is threatened by some aerosol sprays, nitrogen fertilizers, exhaust gases of supersonic planes, and atmospheric nuclear explosions. Fred Iklé, Director of the Arms Control and Disarmament Agency, has reported that nitric oxides injected into the stratosphere by nuclear war could seriously damage the ozone layer.[18] The effects of some harmful substances will increase for years after their release because of the time required for them to rise to the stratosphere. All of the threats to the earth's ozone shield produce consequences that obviously transcend national boundaries and exceed the capacity of separate state sovereignties to combat effectively.

A similar conclusion emerges from an examination of marine pollution. The oceans play a vital role in maintaining dependable rainfall, climate, and carbon dioxide levels for the planet. More than a third of the earth's oxygen supply is produced by the process of photosynthesis in plants living in the oceans of the world. Pollutants harmful to these plants could affect the earth's oxygen supply. Even the wastes of landlocked states affect the oceans, because pollutants are transported to the sea through rivers and the atmosphere.

The oceans are a major source of animal protein, the lack of which contributes to malnutrition for one third of the human population. Even though a majority of marine fish remain palatable, nearly all species now contain DDT residues. Pollution diminishes the protein supply by decreasing the reproductive capacity of marine life, killing larvae and untold tons of fish, making some fish unfit for human consumption, and harming marine plant life on which fish feed.[19] Despite more intensive attempts to catch fish, total world harvest has declined since 1970. Overfishing and pollution are the primary causes. Neither is now effectively regulated to produce the maximum sustainable yield.

The preceding discussion of the dangers of unregulated nuclear technology and environmental hazards poses the question whether past foreign policy values, diplomatic habits, and institutions can meet the demands of modern technology and human interaction for global control. We have examined here only two of many possible examples that demonstrate the need for a fundamental reassessment of foreign policy goals and international institutions.

THE THREAT TO PREFERRED VALUES

A reassessment is also useful because present goals and institutions make it increasingly difficult to implement our most cherished values and ethical principles. Indeed, the existing international structure of power in itself violates these principles. For example, the globe is presently divided into nation-states with power unsystematically and inequitably related to population. This means that the simple exercise of sovereignty by a superpower violates the principle of self-determination on a global basis. It is doubtful that any democratic society can long survive with its democratic principles intact if those principles are repeatedly denied in its own conduct. Yet in following the traditional approach to serving the national interest the U.S. government regularly carries out policies that affect millions of people outside its borders who have no control over the making of U.S. policies. When the United States pursues economic policies and consumption patterns that stimulate world inflation, thus decreasing the buying power of non-U.S. citizens, this is a modern, global equivalent of taxation without representation. Similarly, United States citizens are touched directly by the acts of other great powers, although we are unrepresented in their political processes. If other governments put radioactive substances in the atmosphere, American citizens suffer contamination without representation.[20]

Even though he has kept his administration well within the guidelines of traditional diplomacy, President Jimmy Carter seemed to acknowledge part of the representation problem when he delivered a message to the "citizens of the world" immediately after his inaugural address: "I have chosen the occasion of my inauguration . . . to speak not only to my own countrymen—which is traditional—but also to you, citizens of the world who did not participate in our election but who will nevertheless be affected by my decisions."[21]

Rapidly changing technology and patterns of social interaction are making societies inseparable from one another, but the present pattern of international political participation remains relatively unchanged. As long as this system remains constant, it authorizes some people to make decisions that affect other people who are unrepresented in the decision-making process. As this incongruity between political institutions and social needs is allowed to deepen, self-government will be undermined in a national context because it will be unable to respond to citizens' needs. It will fail to take root and flourish in a global context because intra- and inter-societal inequities will not diminish, and severe inequities of wealth and power make it impossible to fulfill the democratic principle in which power must be widely shared. Democracy cannot indefinitely survive within a global political structure that prevents people from participating in decisions that affect their own lives.

Consider the capacity of present political institutions to fulfill

11

a person's most basic need and right—adequate food. The world today faces—for the first time in its history—shortages in each of the four basic agricultural resources: land, water, energy, and fertilizer. No nation can isolate itself from these scarcities or their economic and political consequences. Japan imports more than half of its total cereal supplies. Egypt imports about 40 percent. The farmers of the European Economic Community import 80 percent of their high protein feed for livestock. Nearly all their petroleum is imported. The United States is the supplier of 85 percent of all soybeans on the entire world market, so when in 1973 it ordered an export embargo in order to curb price rises at home, numerous other people, with no opportunity to influence the U.S. decision, were adversely affected. In another example, when Thailand once restricted its rice exports, the action "wreaked havoc with efforts to prevent runaway food prices in other Southeast Asian countries."[22]

Each year approximately one billion people suffer from malnutrition. Fifteen million children die annually before reaching age five because of insufficient food and infections that become lethal due to malnourishment. That is one quarter of all deaths in the world. Almost all children born to poor parents in the less developed countries suffer some degree of malnutrition at one time or another.[23] In the early 1970s, experts estimated that an average of 10,000 people died weekly from lack of food.[24]

Overpopulation is not the only source of this human tragedy. Because of the petroleum-based fertilizer shortages partially resulting from the oil embargo imposed by the Organization of Oil Exporting Countries (OPEC) in 1973-74, the United States suspended its usual fertilizer exports. This action contributed to a 1.5-million-ton fertilizer shortage in the less developed countries, which cost them 15 million tons in lost grain production in 1974. Yet, during the same year, people in the United States used on lawns, cemeteries, and golf courses about 3 million tons of fertilizer—twice the shortage in the poor countries.[25] Obviously, no food grew from this U.S. usage. Moreover, for each pound of fertilizer applied to grain production in the nearly saturated soils of the United States, farmers could increase their yields by an average of only two to three pounds. But in nutrient-starved India, each pound of fertilizer could have yielded an additional production three times as large as the increment derived from U.S. use of the fertilizer.[26] Thus, a slight decrease in U.S. productivity would have yielded a major increase in productivity for fertilizer-poor countries.

Of the total grain produced in the United States, much is fed to cattle, which are inefficient converters of grain into protein. Georg Borgstrom estimates that the world's cattle eat as much food as would be required to feed 8.7 billion people, or twice the world's present population.[27] By including less meat and more grain in their diets, people in the rich countries could enable existing food supplies to extend to far more persons on the globe. In India, where the major source of protein is feed grains, direct and indirect consumption averages about 400 pounds of grain per person per year. In the United States, where much protein is eaten in the form of meat, eggs, or milk, the grain consumed directly or indirectly through production of meat is almost 2000 pounds per person per year.[28] Thus, the average North American consumes five times as many agricultural resources as the average person in India. U.S. average consumption exceeds by two to four times the quantity of protein that the human body can utilize. The remainder is excreted. If Americans were to reduce their meat consumption by only 10 percent, in one year 12 million tons of grain would be freed for human consumption. This amount would feed 60 million people for one year, enough to have prevented famine in parts of India and Bangladesh in 1974.

Sufficient resources exist to feed everyone *if* the resources are shared fairly. Many demographers believe this condition would also cause population growth to decline. However, past policies of food distribution have been governed by traditional diplomatic habits. As the former Secretary of Agriculture, Dr. Earl Butz once explained: "Food is power. Food is a weapon. It is now one of the principal tools in our negotiating kit."[29] A CIA research study, written shortly before the World Food Conference in Rome in 1974, concluded that the world grain shortages in the future "could give the United States a measure of power it had never had before—possibly an economic and political dominance greater than that of the immediate post-World War II years." The report predicted that "in bad years . . . Washington would acquire virtual life-and-death power over the fate of the multitudes of the needy." (Without exaggeration, the hungry might view such a condition as starvation without representation.) The report warned that when societies became desperate the hungry but powerful nations (which possessed nuclear weapons) might engage in nuclear threats or in massive migration backed by force. They might even seek to induce climatic changes, such as "trying to melt the Arctic ice cap."[30] Despite the

13

exaggerated expression of alarm in the image of a rising tide of poor people engulfing the United States, the report accurately described the power of life and death that can be exerted by the world's largest food exporter.

More effectively than existing international organizations, a global food authority could maximize world production, bank grains for periods of drought or famine, ration and allocate fertilizer for optimal increases in production, encourage less consumption of grain by cattle, and decrease the use of food as a diplomatic weapon to gain political influence over other governments. Without increased global coordination of food policies, resentment, repression, and unnecessary human misery are likely to continue throughout the 1980s.

In summary, the decentralized and inequitable distribution of power among states perpetuates an international system in which the most powerful countries maintain privileged positions at the expense of the weak and poor societies. However, even the citizens of the great powers are unable to escape the consequences of other governments' policies that they have no authority to influence. This arrangement of power and authority denies further realization of global justice and basic human rights. Not only is the denial of justice undesirable in itself, it also contributes to the difficulty and detracts from the desirability of maintaining peace. Thus the present distribution of power threatens both the quality of life for a substantial number of coinhabitants of the globe and ultimately the survival of human civilization. Whether one wants to be politically prudent or morally sensitive or both, modern technology has now made it necessary to consider an alternative basis for making foreign policy decisions.

The Westphalian System in a Post-Westphalian Era

The previous discussion of several global problems calls into question the widely held assumption that prevailing political responses are equal to the challenges. If profound problems with historic consequences are not resolved, is this due to unwise foreign policies? If so, then foreign policy could be corrected by getting additional information to officials, improving the policy-making machinery, or selecting new leadership in Washington. Alternatively, one may conclude that global challenges are unmet because the international system is poorly structured to meet present political and economic needs. If that is true,

14

then fundamental structural changes are required to overcome the threats to survival and to preferred values. Finally, the difficulty may be a combination of unwise policies and structural defects, in which case the necessary changes are even more risky to undertake and difficult to bring about.

To increase our understanding of these questions, it is useful to consider the present international system in historical perspective.

THE LIMITS OF DECENTRALIZED, TERRITORIALLY-BASED AUTHORITY

The Peace of Westphalia at the conclusion of the last of the great religious wars of Europe is a convenient benchmark for noting the major shift in European political organization which produced the current international system. Although the selection of any particular date to note systemic changes is somewhat arbitrary, the political changes symbolized by the Peace of Westphalia of 1648 stand in sharp contrast to the political organization of the Middle Ages before the religious wars. In medieval society the Christian commonwealth was hierarchically organized and subject to the authority of the Pope and the Holy Roman Empire. The Roman Catholic Church and its appointed representatives exercised centralized authority across the territorial boundaries of feudalism. Although subunits throughout Europe exercised some power, it was on behalf of and subject to the authority of Pope and Emperor. This continental system gradually changed as authority, power, wealth, and loyalties shifted to a subcontinental or state level. The Peace of Westphalia acknowledged the development of independent, secular, sovereign states, no longer subject to the centralized authority of the Pope or Emperor.[31]

In the Westphalian model, political authority was decentralized on the continent and based on territory, thus making boundaries very important. National governments were all-powerful within their boundaries; no outside authority could legally intrude within each national shell. As the Pope's influence declined and there was no overreaching political authority to regulate conduct between sovereigns, there could be no prohibition of war. Because authority was tied to territory, there was little possibility of establishing sovereignty over the oceans.

The existing international system corresponds to the Westphalian model of a decentralized system of independent states, each exercising dominant authority within its territorial domain.

15

However, mounting evidence of social interpenetration, such as that presented earlier, indicates that we are living during a period pregnant with possibilities for system change. These are similar in significance to the structural transformation registered at Westphalia. This era is marked by rising needs to transform the nation-state or Westphalian system into a new system of order that is in some ways reminiscent of two principal attributes of medieval society. (Of course, one should not assume that the changing world order either should or will develop an authority structure similar to that of the Holy Roman Empire.) First, there is the need to establish a transnational structure of power and authority with increased capacity at the center for coordinating policy and enforcing it on national governments. Second, there is a need for a new structure of authority not limited to a piece of territory for either its sources of legitimacy or the domain of its directives. It must be global in scope and extend its authority even to outer space.

In the emerging system, national boundaries are becoming less important than they were in the nineteenth century. This is illustrated by the growth of multinational corporations and the international regulation of travel, commerce, and communication. The need for additional forms of central guidance is reflected in negotiations about regulating the use of the oceans and the seabed. Incipient supranational institutions are perhaps present in the European economic community. Although governments tenaciously guard their sovereignty, they also advance occasional claims that international organizations may have the right to intervene, such as against apartheid, in areas of traditionally national jurisdiction. In the League of Nations and the United Nations, governments made their first modern effort, although without major success, to control and prohibit aggressive war. The need for international guarantees against war reflects the decline of the invulnerable, impermeable state in the nuclear age.[32]

Yet, the systemic transition now under way reveals a sharp asymmetry. Industrialization and advanced technology have made the earth a post-Westphalian functional unit, but the world remains politically fragmented by Westphalian national divisions of the planet and of human loyalties. Threats posed by the pollution of the atmosphere and oceans, the instability in the supply of food and oil, and the all-encompassing consequences of nuclear war are feebly confronted by a system of sovereign states that recognize no coordinating authority above their national governments.

THE TRAGEDY OF THE COMMONS

The unprecedented scope of the foreign policy problems facing Washington emerges from the incongruity between the *functional unity* and the *political disunity* of the globe. Serving human needs requires cooperative efforts based upon a recognition of the unity of the ecosystem and the universal impact of some political decisions. The Westphalian disunity of political organization encourages self-seeking, competitive efforts. The consequences of this incongruity were illustrated by biologist Garrett Hardin in his well-known discussion of the "tragedy of the commons." He pictured a pasture held in common by a village of cattle herdsmen. As rational beings, the herdsmen seek to maximize their gains from pasturing their animals. Each herdsman asks himself: "What is the utility *to me* of adding one more animal to my herd?" This utility, Garrett explained, has one negative and one positive component. The positive component is nearly $+1$ because of the increment of one animal; the negative component is a function of the additional overgrazing created by one more animal. Excessive overgrazing can lead to severe soil erosion and eventual destruction of the pasture. However, unlike the positive component which accrues entirely to the owner, the negative effect of overgrazing is shared by all the herdsmen. As a result, the negative utility for any particular herdsman is only a small fraction of -1. After adding the utilities of the positive and negative components, the rational herdsman concludes that the most sensible course for him to pursue is to add another animal to the herd. Following the same calculation, a second is added—and then a third, fourth, and so on. The same conclusion is reached by all rational herdsmen sharing the commons. It makes little sense for any one of them to exercise self-restraint and not add to his herd because the pasture will eventually be destroyed anyway due to the overgrazing by others. As Hardin concluded: "Therein is the tragedy. Each man is locked into a system that compels him to increase his herd without limit—in a world that is limited. Ruin is the destination toward which all men rush, each pursuing his own best interest in a society that believes in the freedom of the commons. Freedom in a commons brings ruin to all."[33]

A similar problem was raised much earlier by Jean-Jacques

Rousseau.[34] He described a primitive hunting party in which a small group of hungry men attempted to catch a deer to satisfy their appetites. If, during the hunt, one man noticed a hare which would satisfy the man's hunger, he would pursue it even if his action would provide no food for the rest of the group and would allow the deer to escape because he had left his post. By this simple example, Rousseau demonstrated his belief in a natural inclination to put self-interest above mutual, general interest. Rousseau did not elaborate upon his story, but we might speculate about the alternatives the hunter faced.[35] He might have thought that rational self-interest dictated that he remain faithful to his hunting partners and refuse to pursue the hare. This would be especially true in the long run, because it would establish a precedent for securing future meals. He could have predicted that, by pursuing the hare, his abandonment of the group would enable the deer to escape. He would have regretted that result, but he also knew that if he did not pursue the hare, it would be possible that the second hunter would see the hare, make calculations similar to his own, and then catch the hare for his own meal. In that case also, the deer would escape, leaving many empty stomachs, including that of the first hunter. With these thoughts in mind, the first hunter then left the hunting party to catch the hare.

The story demonstrates that, in the absence of a central administrative system to help coordinate human behavior and make it more dependable, even a sincere, rational actor fails to engage in otherwise desirable cooperation. This is true even though the rational person at first is willing to cooperate to satisfy common needs as basic as food itself. If a central authority existed and required that the captured hare be divided equally among all hunters, then the hunters would ignore the hare as long as there was a reasonable chance of catching the deer.

Today's slow movement toward central, worldwide administration of some aspects of life, such as carried out by multinational corporations and international regulatory organizations controlling transnational air transportation and electronic communication, suggests that the question no longer is: Will there be a worldwide system of order? Instead, the sobering issue has become: What will be its nature? This is true despite the failure of a majority of the world's people to recognize that a global system is in the making. If one acknowledges that, barring nuclear suicide or ecological collapse, the economic and political structures of the world are becoming enmeshed with one another on a global basis, an issue of high importance is to assess whether the incipient system serves the values that one believes are most worthy of support. Given the value orientations of the dominant actors in today's world, it is possible that new forms of inequity or exploitation may be established.

Because the developing system is global in scope, it is especially important that avoidable errors be averted, since there will be no sanctuaries to which to flee should the evolving system prove tyrannical or inhumane. Therefore, it is imperative to construct a normative basis for international transactions to insure that through inadvertence or moral callousness we do not create a system that eventually destroys our highest values.

In summary, citizens in one state or group of states have no way of assuring that actions of other governments will not be harmful to or catastrophic for the lives of all. Means do not exist to insure that various national interests will harmonize with the human interest. The international structures of power and authority and the prevailing criteria for selecting foreign policies are unable (1) to satisfy the security and survival requirements that a prudent foreign policy must, and (2) to implement the preferred values that a just foreign policy should. The apparent need to establish a system of policy coordination commensurate with the global dimensions of modern human behavior poses two remaining questions: First, what are the most useful standards for assessing whether foreign policies are helping to achieve a more secure and humane global community? These standards will be discussed in the remainder of the present chapter. Second, are U.S. foreign policies in fact implementing the values and transforming the structures without which survival will be in question and human dignity indefinitely denied? The answer to this question is pursued in subsequent chapters which contain detailed analyses of four case studies of U.S. foreign policy.

A GLOBAL HUMANIST RESPONSE

In developing a framework around which to build a foreign policy capable of moving safely into the 1990s, it is useful to begin by clarifying the values that one wants to realize. Of course, one's fundamental values are chosen or assumed, not proven. To be sure, students and practitioners of foreign policy frequently justify one particular policy or another by saying that the national interest "requires" it. A certain policy, they say, is "necessary." This language conveys the false impression that the policy is a direct outgrowth or an empirical expression of what *is*, rather than a statement of what someone thinks the policy *ought* to be. A policy is "required" or "necessary" only in the sense that its proponents believe it is necessary for serving certain other values which are usually not stated explicitly. The highly acclaimed concept of the national interest is not scientifically determined. It is a cluster of goals and strategies derived from more fundamental values. Traditionally, foremost among these is the preservation of the security and prosperity of the government and its supporters. This includes maintaining sovereign control over a defined territory and population. The competitive accumulation of military power and, secondarily, of economic resources, are the principal means for pursuing the values of security and prosperity.

If one chooses to depart from traditional definitions of the national interest, one is not less scientific or less empirically oriented than the defenders of traditional definitions. An untraditional orientation may simply mean that one endorses a slightly rearranged hierarchy of values.

An Alternative Framework for Decision Making

The earlier discussion of mounting foreign policy problems called into question the capacity of national societies to provide security and reasonable opportunities for the fulfillment of humanitarian values as long as governments continue acting in accordance with traditional diplomatic precepts. The challenge for policymakers now and in the future will be to bring policies, which in the past have served the national interest as traditionally defined, into harmony with the human interest in abolishing war and poverty and in halting gross denial of human rights and ecological decay. These four problems can also be stated as world order values: peace without national military arsenals (V_1), economic well-being for all inhabitants on the earth (V_2), universal human rights and social justice (V_3), and ecological balance (V_4).[36] It is imperative to make progress in achieving these values if we seek to insure the long-range survival of the species and to improve the quality of human life for all people.

Although these values may appear uncontroversial, they pro-

20

vide a different set of standards for policymaking than are found in traditional understandings of the national interest. Three clarifying principles will establish points of difference between the two approaches. First, the value framework proposed here rests upon the assumption that the human race is the important constituency to consider in policymaking. The world's people should benefit from policy decisions. The traditional approach gives priority to the people of one nation. It also provides more benefits for the governmental elite and its supporters within the nation than for the national population in general. Thus my proposed emphasis on the human interest differs in two ways from traditional diplomacy. First, the scope of human identity extends across national boundaries rather than remains confined to the people within them. Second, human identity expresses bonds of community between those at the top and at the bottom of the class structure. Compared to the traditional foreign policy approach, human community is expanded horizontally to include all nations and vertically to encompass all classes.

A second idea that undergirds the proposed value framework is that the service of human needs should be the guiding principle for major economic and political decisions, rather than the maximization of national power or corporate profit. This does not mean that nationhood or profit are excluded, but only that they should rank lower in the hierarchy of values than service to basic human needs. A corollary of this value orientation is that human transactions based on cooperation and a sense of human solidarity would increase, while transactions that are competitive and based on a denial of community would decrease. Competitiveness among large social groups is less useful when the human race is the subject of concern than when only a national group is the focal point for protection, production, and consumption. If fulfilling human needs is to become the guiding principle for policymaking, then those most in need should be the first to receive attention. A politics of liberation, which the fourfold value framework is designed to advance, is like the practice of medicine at its best: to help first those people who are most in need. It differs sharply from theories of politics that call for triage, the lifeboat ethic, or the trickle-down theory of development.

Third, the *entire* planet, the atmosphere around it, and the high seas are of prime concern. They are to be protected and

21

conserved for both present and unborn generations. In contrast, the exponents of the national interest place the exercise of sovereignty over one *part* of the planet's territory at the top of their hierarchy of values. They are concerned with securing advantages for "their" segment of the planet and of the human race, and they pay little attention to the needs of future generations.

The four preferred world order values and the three clarifying principles provide the value framework that I call *global humanism* in the course of this analysis. The *human interest* is the collection of goals and strategies that are consistent with and will advance the values of global humanism. The term *humane world community* is used to mean a universal human identity or all-inclusive sense of human solidarity combined with social norms and institutions that aim at achieving a life of dignity for all through an equitable sharing of decision-making powers, opportunities, and resources. *Global populism* refers both to (1) the emphasis on a citizens' movement to mobilize and empower the poor and politically weak and (2) the introduction of structural reforms inspired by the preferred values and designed to help the dispossessed.

In the course of this study, U.S. foreign policy is evaluated by the extent to which it implements or is designed to implement the values of global humanism.[37] In earlier discussion, I have argued that a foreign policy informed by such a value framework is necessary to insure human security and is desirable to achieve other values on which there is a high degree of consensus in our own society. To assess the impact of U.S. foreign policy upon the prospects for preferred world order reform, a representative case study has been selected to illustrate U.S. performance in each of the four value areas. This performance cannot be understood merely by comparing officially professed values with the values of global humanism. As in any political system, a wide gap often exists between rhetoric and reality. To account for this possible discrepancy, the analyses below will distinguish *professed values* from *implicit values*. The former are the goal values expressed in official statements about U.S. foreign policy. Implicit values are the unspoken value preferences that are embedded in actual political behavior and revealed in the value impact of the policy.

With these definitions in mind, the effort to explain the global meaning of U.S. foreign policy will proceed as follows: The first section of each case study consists of an empirical description of U.S. policy, with an emphasis on revealing the professed and implicit values of U.S. policy. The analysis clarifies whether the real value impact was consistent with the goals proclaimed in the rhetoric. Next, the implicit values are juxtaposed against the values of global humanism to determine whether U.S. policy was helping to realize a humane world community. Fourth, the global humanist value framework is used to develop specific recommendations for future policy in the area of each case study. Finally, some indicators of world order progress are provided in order to enable scholars or political activists to check on future progress in realizing the preferred values.

One purpose of this analysis is to provide a fresh global framework by which to examine the wisdom and utility of U.S. foreign policies. This framework ideally should transcend both the idiosyncrasies of this historical era and one's own political culture. I doubtless have been unable to accomplish that fully; thus the framework should be viewed as tentative and subject to refinement and modification.

Before examining U.S. policy itself, it will be useful to look at some implications and applications of the value-centered approach proposed here. We turn now to that discussion.

The Utility of a Value-Centered Approach

This study of foreign policy is a value-centered approach. It delineates the values that guide decision makers in their policy choices and that are expressed in official behavior.[38] A value-centered approach to foreign policy analysis is admittedly a break with the prevailing intellectual tradition. Most foreign policy analysis falls into one of two categories. Some authors treat foreign policy as history. They emphasize a chronological description of events. In contrast, behavioral scientists focus on the processes by which policy is made, negotiated, or executed. They discuss the interactions of officials, the effects of policy-making machinery, the politics of bureaucratic bargaining, or occasionally the psychological origins of policy. In both of these approaches, past scholarship has usually focused on the use of power, without giving much attention to the value impact of policy and to who benefits or should benefit from policies. Traditional approaches have impoverished reality and discouraged use of the imagination by excessive emphasis on the way things are and by inattention to the way they ought to be. In contrast,

23

when a value-centered approach incorporates a rigorous empiricism with explicit attention to values embedded in policy, it yields several advantages.

In the first place, one's understanding of political events is enhanced if international politics is viewed as a value-realizing process. The observer's focus shifts away from examining the processes of political interaction by themselves and from viewing policy consequences merely as discrete events. For example, the values of officials as expressed in several policies may be compared to the global humanist values that this analysis suggests are useful guides for political action. The value impacts of specific foreign policies then provide intellectual handles by which one may grasp the normative direction in which a changing system of world order is moving.

Moreover, if observers examine foreign policy as a value-realizing process, they are able to see more clearly the recurring values that apparently idiosyncratic policies often are advancing. If similar values are repeatedly served by political leaders, one can extrapolate from this the structure of interests or the classes that benefit from the ruling group's policies. This is particularly important in attempting to define the nature of a more just world polity and in developing strategies to attain one. By assessing the desirability and consequences of political action in light of a set of explicit norms, a value-centered approach facilitates a structural analysis of social problems and remedies. This in turn helps to identify both the structures that need reform and the people who can be expected to resist or to support such change.

Whenever a state executes foreign policy, some values are advanced and others are negated. Every major policy issue contains within it a moral issue. Practitioners of foreign policy often disguise the moral code that a state follows in order to obscure the real beneficiaries of acts by the state. A value-centered approach directly attacks this problem by clarifying the implicit values of the ruling group. This provides information essential for the practice of self-government. Because many ordinary citizens implement the leadership's political values by paying taxes or sacrificing their own lives in war, they understandably want not to be deceived about the value impact of their own government's policies.

A value-centered approach also is useful for establishing preferred goals for future behavior. It encourages imaginative thinking about the possibility of change in the international system. Because a value-centered approach explicitly emphasizes human preferences, it helps chart action to reform the existing system. If in making foreign policy officials react to crises as they arise, they are unlikely to think about changing the structure of international relations. If instead they ask themselves how to implement preferred values, they would be more likely to develop alternative visions of future world order systems.

Political leaders seldom follow this approach, but when they do the results stand out boldly against the backdrop of routine diplomacy. For example, when Adlai E. Stevenson was U.S. Representative to the United Nations, he once delivered a speech entitled "Working Toward a World Without War." In it he said, "We do not hold the vision of a world without conflict. We do hold the vision of a world without war—and this inevitably requires an alternative system for coping with conflict. We cannot have one without the other."[39]

To emphasize values does not mean that one must proceed with an idealistic or optimistic view of the future. A value-centered approach may lead to a pessimistic assessment of the prospects for world order reform. One might conclude that the prevailing value perspective of officials departs widely from one's own value preferences. In such a case, the tendency of the actors within the system would be to make the future worse than the present in terms of preferred value realization.

Of course, no process of value clarification can eliminate arbitrariness or subjectivity in selecting preferred values. But this approach underscores the need to make deliberate choices and tradeoffs in the interaction of different values. In the short run at least, some preferred values may conflict with others; all cannot be grasped without the right hand knowing what the left hand is doing. To maximize food production, for example, one may need to use chemical fertilizers or pesticides that pollute. An approach that does not emphasize values obscures the choice among conflicting goals.

Moreover, value clarification can diminish unintended consequences of government behavior. The more explicit and accurate a value impact statement is, the more possible it becomes to make behavior implement value preferences. Without a clear statement of the value impact of a given policy, the possible gap between governmental rhetoric and political reality may go un-

25

noticed. Such a condition could lead citizens to support policies that in practice negate a preferred value that officials have embraced only rhetorically. This could produce citizen behavior that in practice resisted rather than encouraged a desirable change.

A value-centered approach also helps overcome the level-of-analysis problem. That is, by adopting a value framework that can be deliberately constructed so as to reflect planetary rather than strictly national concerns, it is easier to avoid the trap of looking at international relations from a parochial nation-state view. Officials can then give adequate attention to both the total world system and the subsystems within it. Sensitivity to double standards is enhanced by this approach because explicit norms can be universally applied.

It is instructive to examine one example of the level-of-analysis problem that is a central issue in this study and that traditional approaches have seldom clarified. From the nation-state vantage point, diplomacy should protect the interests of the state, usually measured in terms of power. But that is a laissez-faire approach to the interests of the *planet*. The nation-state vantage point is the international variant of the "invisible hand" of classical capitalism. Proponents of this doctrine assumed that separate people or businesses each maximizing their private economic advantages would produce desirable results for the entire society. Likewise, proponents of serving national interests assume that separate nations maximizing their national advantages will produce desirable results for world society. Such an approach is sensitive to the needs of the nation but indifferent to the interests of the planet. It oversimplifies reality by assuming that what is good for the nation is good for the world.

The weakness of the laissez-faire approach is evident in both economics and international relations. There is often a fundamental contradiction between the pursuit of private profit and the service of human needs. Some things that are profitable ought not to be done; some things that ought to be done are not profitable. Similarly, there is often a fundamental contradiction between the pursuit of national advantage of separate states and the service of global human needs. For example, taking fertile land out of production in Kansas or Iowa may be good for U.S. farmers who want to sell wheat or corn at a higher price, but not for malnourished south Asians who want to buy grain at low cost. By using preferred world order values for assessing national policies we are sensitized to this possible contradiction.

Finally, a value-centered approach also holds promise for deepening our understanding and improving the quality of decisions made in the context of a presently inescapable lack of knowledge. For example, no one knows the risks of war that are inherent in the strategy of nuclear deterrence. No one knows whether Indians are more or less secure because their government conducted one nuclear explosion in 1974. No one knows the range of values that would be sacrificed or fulfilled by a deliberate U.S. decision to disarm. When there is little knowledge available for calculating the consequences of decisions, value presuppositions become more important in the choice of behavior. In such cases values determine the outcome of decisions at a more primitive stage. The less certain we are about how to achieve our ends, the more we let our values influence the means we select for immediate action. Thus it is extremely important for policy analysts and citizens to know whether national officials value, say, national power or human life more highly.

To clarify this point, consider the following example of a dearth of knowledge. If U.S. citizens knew that the U.S. nuclear arsenal would eventually involve the United States in a nuclear war that would kill 100 million Americans and leave an additional 50 million with radiation sickness or genetic damage, presumably there would be more intense public pressure to disarm. National power or sovereignty might even be restricted in order to protect human lives. But in the absence of dependable knowledge about the risks inherent in using nuclear deterrence as a means to prevent war, the public prefers to protect national power through augmenting the nuclear arsenal. This preference may take priority over other values, including the value of human life. But the nuclear priority does not *appear* to sacrifice the value of human life because uncertain knowledge about negative consequences enables us to hope for indefinite postponement of nuclear war. The lack of knowledge about risks makes this hope plausible, although the probability of avoiding war permanently may in fact be very remote.

In contrast, abundant knowledge clarifies the relationship between means and ends. In such cases, the means chosen to implement policy must conform to the terminal values one professes to serve, or else the inappropriateness of the means can be

27

quickly shown. For example, if a man living in Chicago values a reunion with friends in Long Island, when making travel plans he would not select a flight to San Francisco. If he did, a travel agent could quickly demonstrate the inappropriateness of the action. On the other hand, lack of knowledge lets a decision maker choose *any* means which his or her value system may prefer, because no one can show that the means selected will not lead to the end professed. (Without dependable information, a flight to San Francisco appears as good as a flight to New York for one's trip to Long Island.)

Thus on foreign policy issues where imponderables abound, alarming results can occur. Decision makers are most likely to choose means that serve their vested interests. If the way to peace is seen as uncertain, then policies might as well benefit the leadership's interests while they pursue peace. Yet an elite's vested interests seldom are congruent with the global human interest, either in its domestic or global manifestations. In this example, the policy decisions might be based on a desire to protect power and wealth for national decision makers and their group of supporters within the nation, not to achieve peace or a humane world community. Who benefits most from the worldwide growth of armaments and the accumulation of U.S. power overseas? A political and economic elite? All U.S. citizens? Humanity? A plausible case could be made that the value impact of additional armaments contributes more certain and immediate benefits to the power and wealth of decision makers than to the achievement of security for the human race in the long run. Until the contrasting values—privileges for national security managers or security for ordinary people—are clear, intelligent policy for world order reform is impossible. A value-centered approach helps reveal the occasionally vested nature of the values being realized.

The Application of a Global Humanist
Framework to Alternative Images of World Order

In addition to the benefits of a value-centered approach listed above, both citizens and officials could use the four values of global humanism to construct a range of future world order options, to compare the value-realizing potential of each, and to select the foreign policies most likely to achieve the preferred values. In contrast to the waning Westphalia system, one might envisage at least four types of future world order systems:[40] a concert of great powers, a concert of multinational corporate elites, world government, and global humanism.[41]

CONCERT OF GREAT POWERS

One possible future system of world order is a slightly remodeled version of the existing system, with new emphasis on cooperation among the great powers. This could be thought of as a global, twentieth-century equivalent of Metternich's effort to achieve a concert of European great powers after the Congress of Vienna in 1815. The United States, the Soviet Union, Western Europe, Japan, and China could lower tensions among themselves and together administer many of the economic and political affairs of the rest of the world. Because such a system would be hierarchical and inequitable, it would doubtless be exploitative. It probably would not attack worldwide poverty, political repression, or ecological decay. It would flourish with client states and sphere-of-influence politics. It would also work to repress terrorism, to stabilize the world economy, and to exploit ocean resources.

If United States policy aimed to implement this option for achieving international stability, it would give priority to protecting or enhancing its power position vis-à-vis the other great powers, to seeking consensus among the great powers while ignoring the grievances of smaller powers, to defending the dollar in the world monetary system, and to developing strategies to insure access to vital raw materials from foreign markets. The government would be unconcerned about Third or Fourth World countries except insofar as liberation movements or political instability might jeopardize the opportunities for U.S. corporations to invest, buy, or sell abroad, and insofar as the former's political orientation might bear upon the power of the United States within the concert of great powers. When threats to U.S. power would arise, counterrevolutionary intervention by the United States would be likely after seeking concurrence from, or at least neutralizing the opposition of, the Soviet Union or any other relevant great powers.

CONCERT OF MULTINATIONAL CORPORATE ELITES

A second variant of future world order is global, private government by multinational corporations. In this model, corporate

29

elites act together to maximize profit and economic growth, to secure worldwide markets, and to protect the wealth and privilege of relatively few owners and managers against the protests of the poverty-stricken masses. Multinational corporate elites managing global resources would probably lead toward dampened international political conflict, increased transnational class conflict, rapid but uneven economic growth in the private sector, use of resources to maximize profit rather than the service of human needs, and relative unconcern about environmental and humanitarian issues. The Trilateral Commission, a group of wealthy, influential business people from North America, Japan, and Western Europe, illustrates this possibility. Its purposes include a transnational effort to adapt corporate capitalism to changing economic and political forces to insure capitalism's future in a nonterritorially-oriented economy facing possible conflicts with territorially-based national governments or dispossessed classes.

Multinational corporations may have some advantages over states in the approaching play of social forces leading to a new system of world order. For the first time in history, managerial skills and technology make the management of the globe as an integrated unit a genuine possibility.[42] Multinational corporations, as private agencies, can respond with more flexibility and speed to the functional unity of the globe than many national governments, which are restrained by nationally-oriented ideological and political inertia. Markets and the field for investment, after all, are nonterritorial and include the planet, whereas national governments still operate from a territorial base. The nonterritorial perspective of corporate managers maximizing profits may put them at odds with the national government ruling the territory in which the corporation is primarily based. For example, when the price of crude oil increases, this may be much less objectionable to U.S.-based multinational oil corporations than to the United States government, representing a constituency territorially more limited in scope than the oil companies themselves. Multinational corporations place less emphasis than national governments on the interests of one state in the system or the well-being of its domestic population.

U.S. foreign policy could serve this image of world order by facilitating the movement of capital abroad, by allowing corporations to escape the domain of any national government's effective regulation, by not restricting high profits on the corporate provision of vital resources, and by declining to insure that the major corporations scrupulously respect the environment or serve the general public rather than private interest. If large corporations are able to influence governmental policies sufficiently, either through the placement of members of the business elite in positions of political decision making or through financial support and control of government officials recruited from outside the business elite, the government itself will serve the interests of multinational corporations more directly, meanwhile giving less attention to national interests more traditionally defined as territorially-based security and prosperity.

WORLD GOVERNMENT

The prescriptions favored by most traditional advocates of world government are contained in *World Peace Through World Law* by Grenville Clark and Louis Sohn. They described a greatly strengthened United Nations with modified voting procedures, world disarmament, and world federation on a sufficient scale to prevent future military buildups. This model aims to create "an effective system of *enforceable* world law in the limited field of war prevention."[43] It gives less attention to the other values of global humanism.

If U.S. policy were to aim at achieving this option, policymakers would seek to amend the UN Charter in order to democratize the voting procedures and qualify the veto principle. In addition, after accepting enhanced decision making and enforcement authority for the UN, the United States would need to undertake substantial arms reductions. Until an effective strategy is developed for implementing this vision, its very low political feasibility makes it unrealistic in the foreseeable future. Its implementation rests on agreement among national governments to restrict their sovereignty voluntarily. This is unlikely given present political attitudes and institutions.

GLOBAL HUMANISM

A system based on global humanism can be illustrated by the image of world order developed by the North American team of participants in the World Order Models Project. Richard A. Falk has elaborated this model in *A Study of Future Worlds*.[44] It calls for drastic changes in the existing configuration of power, wealth, and authority during the next thirty years. The transition strategy calls for widespread education, attitudinal changes, and

31

populist mobilization to realize substantial gains in preferred values without recourse to violence and without the traumas that would attend nuclear war, widespread famine, or ecological collapse.

This model, slightly revised by the present author, is described here in greater detail than the other models because it provides a tentative vision of how the world might look if global humanist values were pursued in U.S. foreign policies.

One particularly appealing feature of the model is that it avoids merely a transferal of state power and authority to a unified world government. Instead, authority and power are dispersed in *two* directions from the national level: "downward" toward provincial or local governments as well as "upward" toward a central guidance agency. The happy result is a form of policy coordination that increases the capacity for global administration without increasing the overall bureaucratic presence in human life at various levels of social organization. Two countervailing organizational tendencies would be present: (1) *centralization* of functional control and planning to enable more equitable allocation of scarce resources, to protect endangered values in the "commons," and to enforce provisions for disarmament; and (2) *decentralization* of political structures combined with localization of identification patterns. The focus of human identity, now pinpointed upon national symbols, would be dispersed to include global human solidarity on the one hand, and increased subnational identification and participation in political and economic decisions on the other.

This model avoids the hierarchical centralization implicit in most classical schemes for world government. It seeks to create global policy coordination with wide dispersion of authority and distribution of power among various actors, such as global and regional intergovernmental organizations, national governments, local or provincial governments, and transnational coalitions of people or private organizations acting in the global arena without going through their respective national governments.

In general, this constitutional structure would tolerate less efficiency to achieve diverse, equitable participation and to inhibit the abuse of concentrated powers. Proposed governing machinery might include the following:

1. A world assembly would set general policy respectful of global humanist values. It would be organized to represent

peoples, nongovernmental organizations, states, and regional groups.

2. A smaller council would apply the policy of the assembly and act in its place during emergencies.

3. Supporting administrative agencies would assure that directives of the former bodies are carried out by other actors in the system. It would also provide feedback useful for tailoring policies to fulfill the values of global humanism. Agencies for implementation would be organized around the following four functions.

a. A world security system would include a transnational peace force, a world disarmament service, and a world grievance system. The latter would insure that all states could respond to policy decisions. It would also facilitate peaceful change to avoid the danger that a global system did not merely enforce a peace of the status quo. Individuals and nongovernmental organizations, as well as governments and intergovernmental organizations, could forward complaints to this body.

b. A world economic system would include agencies for economic planning, equity, world monetary policy, taxing authority, and development. This cluster of agencies would facilitate economic development aimed at insuring economic well-being for all, promoting intergroup and intragroup economic equity and achieving balance between human activity and ecological capacities for disposal and resource use. Economic policies would be tailored to curtail wasteful growth and to encourage growth aimed at fulfilling human needs.

c. A human rights commission and court would enhance the prospects for respecting human dignity and human rights. Any person or group could take grievances to these bodies.

d. A global environmental authority would establish procedures to monitor pollutants, to set and enforce waste disposal standards, and to conserve and allocate scarce resources fairly. The authority would seek to implement a humane transition from a growth orientation to an equilibrium orientation respectful both of nature and of human needs. An effort would be made to establish an index of Gross National Quality to highlight the qualitative rewards that may compensate for the quantitative decline in Gross National Product which some wealthy societies may encounter during the effort to equalize world incomes and to avoid injury to the environment.

The benefits from this system, as well as the strategy for

33

ONE · *A Humane World*

Table 1-1
A Summary Comparison of Alternative
World Order Systems, 1980-2000[a]

Leadership	Westphalian nation-state system	Concert of great powers
Basic aspirations	Sovereign independence, unregulated governmental behavior	Geopolitical stability, political and economic inequity
Strategy for fulfillment of aspirations	Competitive power-seeking in decentralized international system	Consensus of dominant governments, stratified inter-governmental system, regional spheres of influence
Performance in implementing global humanist values:		
Peace	Low	Medium
Economic well-being	Low	Low
Social justice	Low	Low
Ecological balance	Low	Medium
Performance in achieving human solidarity:		
Vertical (transclass) identity	Medium	Medium
Horizontal (transnational) identity	Low	Low

[a] Several of the categories in this table are adapted from Richard A. Falk, "A New Paradigm for International Legal Studies," p. 1001.

achieving it, are consistent with populism in a global context. This image of world order seeks to avoid both the multinational corporate elite's tendency to put corporate profit and growth above human needs and conservation, and the national governmental elite's tendency to impose nationalist advantages and values upon major political and economic activity, with little regard for global implications.

In contrast to the world government approach, the populist

34

Table 1-1 (cont.)

Concert of multinational corporations	World government	Humane world community
Unregulated economic growth, profit maximization, capital intensive technology, high consumption	Enforced disarmament, strengthened international institutions	Dependable peace, economic well-being for all, respect for human rights and social justice, ecological balance
Consensus among privileged elites, stratified transnational system	Negotiations among national governments	Global populist movement, major attitudinal and value change
High	High	High
Low	Medium	High
Low	Low	High
Low	Medium	High
Low	Medium	High
High	Medium	High

image places greater emphasis on the likelihood of political conflict with entrenched elites in the process of transforming the existing system, and on the need to mobilize support among dispossessed peoples presently not influential in government processes. The global humanist perspective emphasizes values that transcend the limits of class and national boundaries and that anticipate the emergence of a system of nonterritorial central guidance. This perspective is based on an understanding that the outcome of the present transition period will be determined by the interplay of statist, business, and populist social forces.

This approach reflects a belief that the most beneficial future world order system will be responsive to populist demands for peace, economic equity, social and political dignity, and ecological balance.

The global humanist vision offers a humane alternative to the neo-Darwinian trend in the establishment of a concert of great powers or multinational corporate elites. This trend is encouraged by resource scarcity and political or economic competition, in which both national governmental and corporate elites seek to accumulate more power and prosperity for their respective national or corporate constituencies, neither of which represents humanity at large. The global humanist option seeks to reorient institutions so they will serve the needs of all people rather than the wants of a privileged minority.

Images of the Future and the Content of Foreign Policy

The preceding four images of alternative futures help us understand the present. With an awareness of several alternatives it is easier to appraise the meaning of contrasting foreign policies for the future of humanity. Without some reflection about alternative futures, policymaking is little more than tactical calculation to maintain an unsatisfactory status quo or to gain a short-range advantage in an otherwise aimless drift on the expansive, uncharted waters of the future. Or even worse, some narrowly based but powerful elites may seek to implement an image of the future that the majority of people would oppose if the future world prospects were openly exposed.

The preceding models also enable one to take steps toward the particular future that one desires. Of the four options discussed, world government seems politically unfeasible, and the concerts of great powers or corporate elites are deficient in realizing one or more important values. Therefore, the global humanist image of world order will be used to assess the performance of U.S. policy in the remainder of this study.

The political attractiveness of a vision of world order based on an open, self-correcting understanding of the values of global humanism could be critically important in determining which of several alternative models of the future will in fact become reality. What people implicitly believe about how the world functions and will function in the future contributes to making it function that way in the present as well as in the future. It is commonplace to say that past events influence or determine the

36

present, but growing evidence suggests it is no less accurate to say that one's image of the future determines the present.[45] For example, when a foreign policy bureaucracy views the present international system as continuing indefinitely into the future, that bureaucracy constructs policy in ways that prevent another future from being realized.

In making decisions, an official must extend lines of action into the future and select among alternatives according to his or her expectations about future events.[46] An official's image of the immediate future, even if not explicitly stated, influences current governmental behavior. That behavior opens some doors and closes others for the future. As sociologists Wendell Bell and James A. Mau have correctly warned: "Today's images of the future need elaboration, refinement, and revision; the actual future is rolling over people and whole societies before they are prepared; the possibilities of a better life are not being fulfilled as adequately as they could be."[47]

Taking this advice into account, the chapters that follow seek to clarify (1) the image of world order upon which current U.S. foreign policies are based and (2) the image of a preferred future that could inspire future foreign policies that will be likely to produce a more humane world community.

TWO · *The Strategic Arms Limitation Talks*

THE possibility of nuclear war is an obvious and immediate threat to all human civilization. Permanent peace remains one of the most profound yet unrealized human yearnings. Approximately since the incineration of Hiroshima, technological conditions have existed for both (1) an irreversible disaster for the human race in event of war and (2) a truly worldwide, demilitarized system of public order. Political and social institutions have conditioned human beings more for acceptance of world war than for promotion of world community. Since the Second World War, more than ten million persons have been killed in various wars. Every person on the planet lives under the threat of unfathomable destruction or inescapable radiation hazards posed by the prospect of even distant nuclear conflicts. Since 1945, the worldwide quantity of resources devoted to military purposes has more than tripled. The proportion of world output going to military uses has increased to about 6.5 percent, roughly twice the proportion of output during the years preceding World War I.[1]

Although many persons would deny its attainability, few would dispute the desirability of the first value of global humanism: to minimize collective violence and eventually to establish permanent peace without massive military arsenals. V_1 aims at the elimination of war; disarmament; and the establishment of dependable procedures for peaceful change, adjudication of disputes, and enforcement of disarmament. Advocates of global humanism do not view the minimization of collective violence in isolation from the other world order values. Its realization, for example, is both more desirable and more feasible with the concomitant achievement of worldwide human rights and justice.

It is difficult to assess governmental performance in implementing the first value of global humanism because of our inability to predict the causes, scope, duration, and probability of wars. Nonetheless, some commonsense assessments are possible about the merits of national security policies, the destructive capabilities of states, and, perhaps, even the countries most likely to engage in war.[2] Destructive capability, speed of inflict-

38

ing injury, the indiscriminate character of weaponry, and the vulnerability of human civilizations to extinction by military technology have all increased in this century. At the same time, the weapons of mass destruction have not substantially reduced the perceived likelihood of war. On the contrary, government officials of the superpowers perceive a constant need for continued increments to their arsenals, with the tacit assumption that some day the weapons may be used in lethal conflict. In the meantime, the arsenals are instruments of psychological and diplomatic conflict, confirming a second tacit assumption that the major actors in the international system are unprepared to move away from a system of mutual threat that is ultimately based on massive military firepower.

Progress toward minimizing collective violence could be measured in part by various indexes:

—total battlefield casualties per year;

—total military expenditures, or military expenditures as a percentage of total world output;

—the rate of change in military expenditures compared to expenditures in other fields of social endeavor;

—the size and configuration of arms sales or transfers;

—the spread of knowledge and capability to produce weapons of mass destruction;

—the growth and utilization of nonlethal procedures for settlement of disputes;

—the fluctuation of patterns and objects of loyalty for national and global political or economic structures;

—the growth of international restraints, such as arms control agreements, upon deployment of weapons.

Even these relatively simple indicators present unresolvable controversies and uncertainties. For example, it is widely believed among government officials that the best way to prevent war is to be able to win (or, in the nuclear age, at least, not to allow the opponent to win) any war that may occur. For those who believe that violence is minimized by building the most powerful and efficient instruments of death, a decrease in military expenditures represents regress. For those who believe that present wars must be fought to avoid future wars, even a decline in battlefield casualties for one or several years may be cause for discouragement. Proponents of these and other defense postures are inclined to maintain that a high probability for particular wars may come and go, but the war system is here to stay.

39

Thus, they give their attention to relatively short-run calculations about specific conflicts breaking into war. The analysis that follows is less concerned with the slightly fluctuating odds for war—significant though they are in any particular year—than with assessing the progress toward supplanting the existing militarized international system with a security system that would eventually make possible the elimination of large national military establishments.[3]

Recognizing the controversy that will surround any effort to assess the realization of a demilitarized world system, I have attempted to select an illustrative case study that offers some analytic promise for those who seek peace through the military equality of the superpowers, as well as for those who seek disarmament.[4] This analysis focuses on United States military expenditures, capabilities, and strategic doctrine within the context of efforts for armament limitations. The development of arms control policy represents the most accessible and important effort by the United States to build a more peaceful system of world order. Officials as well as the general public have widely embraced arms control as one of the most promising approaches to halting the arms buildup and setting the stage for disarmament. Perhaps most important, the focus on arms control makes sense because dependable world peace is unlikely without disarmament. The perpetuation of nuclear deterrence encourages a permanent war mentality because a well-armed "enemy" is never more than a few minutes away. Moreover, the technical requirements of deterrence as a mechanism for security will ensure an influential role in policymaking for the military-industrial complex which has a built-in propensity to press for new armaments.

The Vladivostok agreement of November 23, 1974, provides an instructive case study for examining the impact of United States policy on the first value of global humanism. Rooted in the Strategic Arms Limitation Talks (SALT) which began in 1969, it was the result of long planning by senior officials of the United States, and of a major diplomatic initiative spanning two administrations. In addition, the Vladivostok agreement was a product of efforts by both the United States and the Soviet Union to promote an atmosphere of détente. It came at a juncture of technological development (before deployment of multiple independently targetable reentry vehicles [MIRVs] by the Soviet Union) during which a major new step in arms competition was likely, but not yet politically impossible to prevent. If the Vladivostok agreement was not typical of arms control negotiations, then it was an atypically positive experience, insofar as it actually provided the basis for an arms control agreement that may be formally consummated in the Carter administration. The accord and the earlier SALT agreements of 1972 are the most important strategic products of arms control negotiations since 1963. Thus, the Vladivostok agreement presents the prospects for arms control in a favorable context.

U.S. policies on arms control negotiations and strategic military doctrine, the trend of military spending and foreign arms sales, and the extent of international structural change that officials have envisaged were all revealed by SALT. The accord mirrors the accomplishments and failures of previous negotiations, extending back to 1946.[5] By scrutinizing the accord's provisions and omissions in the context of earlier negotiations, the principal recurring interests of the United States—whether defended or ignored—are vividly portrayed.

The process of continually increasing and modernizing U.S. armaments involves far more than merely adding to the number of missiles or submarines in the arsenal. More than half of the undesignated funds in the national budget are spent annually for military purposes; the executive and legislative branches are therefore heavily preoccupied with military power and its possible applications around the world. The governing process itself becomes militarized. With the consideration of force always near the center of foreign policymaking, many civilian officials of the vast defense bureaucracies and chairmen of the influential armed services and appropriations committees in Congress develop a military mind-set not unlike that of career military officials. Military planners, administrators, employees, weapons researchers, arms producers, and labor unions dependent on military production represent a formidable array of talent and sheer numbers. They are well financed, and many are strategically located to influence the policy process in order to encourage lavish military spending and the dominance of military considerations in foreign policy.

The mere availability of military power, as well as the desire to enhance it, often influences the outcome of decision making. For example, the existence of sophisticated counterinsurgency equipment encouraged officials to think first about a military response to events in Indochina in the 1960s, and only secondarily

41

about a political settlement without violence. The application of military power makes officials insensitive to the human consequences of policies where force is never far from the central consideration. Governments with enormous military power at their disposal usually react less compassionately than they would without such power. A continuing arms buildup has led the United States to seek military allies and to arm other governments, thus contributing to the militarization of the political processes in other countries. A refusal to cut back military expenditures generally decreases support for human rights as well as the resources available for the economic development of less developed countries.

This analysis will proceed as follows: first, by describing the fruits of U.S. policy in the SALT I and Vladivostok agreements; second, by explaining the professed values and policy goals of U.S. officials in justifying United States policy; third, by comparing these professed values with the values implicit in governmental behavior itself; and fourth, by comparing the value impacts of United States policy with those sought by advocates of global humanism.

DESCRIPTION OF U.S. ARMS CONTROL POLICIES

Antecedents of the Vladivostok Agreement

The Vladivostok agreement of 1974 grew out of efforts that began in 1969, and that had produced the earlier agreement known as "SALT I," which included two documents signed on May 26, 1972. The first of these limited antiballistic missile systems (ABMS) to no more than two sites. The parties also agreed not to develop, test, or deploy ABM systems that were sea-based, air-based, space-based, or mobile land-based. These obligations were of unlimited duration.[6]

The second document, called the Interim Agreement, limited strategic offensive arms.[7] It prohibited the construction of additional fixed land-based intercontinental ballistic missile launchers for a period of five years. The two governments also agreed not to convert existing land-based launchers for "light" ICBMs into launchers for heavy ICBMs. In practice, this agreement restricted, to a maximum of 313, the deployment of the very large Soviet SS-9 missile, capable of carrying a 25-megaton warhead. In addition, the parties were prohibited from exceeding the numbers of submarine-launched ballistic missiles (SLBMs) then in operation and under construction, except by following special conditions for replacement. These conditions enabled the United States to increase its SLBM launchers from the existing 656 to 710 on a one-for-one replacement basis for ballistic missile launchers deployed on land before 1964, or for older submarine launchers. On the same basis, the Soviet Union could increase its SLBM launchers to 950. In practice, therefore, SALT I limited ABMs to two sites in each country, and ICBMs and SLBMs to levels operational or already under construction.

Because of the technological lead of the United States in developing MIRVs, the Interim Agreement enabled the United States to have more than twice the number of deliverable warheads that the Soviet Union could deploy (5,700 to 2,500 at the time of signing). United States missiles were also generally recognized to be more accurate than Soviet missiles, and those installed on submarines had a longer range than their Soviet counterparts. In addition, because of U.S. submarine-tending bases overseas, it took three Soviet submarines for every two in the U.S. fleet for equivalent numbers "on station." The Soviet Union had larger warheads on many of its launchers than did the United States, but this factor was less important in calculating total destructive capability (in terms of number of targets) than the accuracy and number of independently targetable warheads. In both of these areas, the United States had large advantages.

The United States and Soviet Union also agreed that further negotiations should aim to limit strategic weapons for longer than the five years covered in the Interim Agreement itself. The accord at Vladivostok was the product of those efforts.

The Vladivostok Agreement

At Vladivostok, President Gerald Ford and Party Secretary Leonid Brezhnev agreed to limit strategic offensive weapons to 2,400 launch vehicles, with no more than 1,320 of them containing MIRVs. The ceilings, which were to continue until 1985, included ICBMs, SLBMs, and strategic bombers. The "mix" of the three types of launchers could be determined and changed unilaterally by each party. Construction of new missile silos and enlargement of existing silos beyond 15 percent of existing capacity were prohibited. NATO forces and U.S. vehicles part of the

NATO European force were not counted in the total launch vehicles. Although the terms of the agreement appeared to be simple and apparently equal, the picture became complicated and controversial when assessments were made of the meaning of Vladivostok for future arms competition. Indeed, after more than four years had passed since the Vladivostok ceilings were announced, they had not yet been incorporated into a legally binding treaty. When the Carter administration took office in 1977, it tried to lower the ceilings from the Vladivostok levels, and preliminary reports suggested that they would be reduced by approximately 10 percent. Given the large numbers involved in the original ceilings, plus the range of subjects not covered by either the Ford or Carter proposals, the conclusions drawn from the following analysis of the Vladivostok accord apply also to the SALT II agreement.

From a global perspective, the central question is whether the potential agreement will lay the groundwork for reversing the general arms buildup. To answer that question, we will examine, first of all, official statements explaining U.S. policy and, secondly, that policy's concrete impact on the arms competition.

OFFICIAL RATIONALE COMPARED TO THE VALUES IMPLICIT IN U.S. POLICY

Nearly all officials in both the executive and legislative branches agreed that the most important goals in the conduct of foreign policy were to promote national security and international stability and peace. For most, these three were inseparable. Only a secure United States, the argument went, could help secure the world. And international stability, which perpetuated U.S. preeminence, was seen as the essential condition for peace.

Arms control, among other means, could help achieve stability. The government declared that the Strategic Arms Limitation Talks served the purposes of "enhancement of national security, strategic stability, and détente through dialogue and agreements with the Soviet Union." The negotiations were "aimed at the limitation and reduction of both offensive and defensive strategic arms."[8] Officials maintained that an arms control agreement, such as one based on the Vladivostok accord, would contribute to security because it would (1) slow the arms race; (2) curtail military spending; (3) pave the way for future arms reductions; and (4) reduce international tensions that

44

caused war. Let us examine these instrumental values and then assess whether they were implemented in United States arms control policy.

Professed Value 1: To Slow the Arms Race

Executive officials hailed the Vladivostok agreement as a major step toward stopping the arms competition between the United States and the Soviet Union. President Ford described the agreement as "a real breakthrough [that] puts a cap on the arms race." He announced that "we put a firm ceiling on the strategic arms race which has heretofore eluded us since the nuclear age began. . . . [W]e have . . . set firm and equal limits on the strategic forces of each side, thus preventing an arms race with all its terror, instability, war-breeding tension and economic waste."[9]

Secretary of State Henry Kissinger appeared equally certain of the historic importance of the agreement. He said that the agreement "marks the breakthrough with the strategic arms limitation negotiations that we have sought to achieve in recent years."[10] He promised that when it was formally ratified, it would "be seen as one of the turning points in the history of the post-World War II arms race."[11] The secretary declared that "a cap has been put on the arms race for a period of ten years. . . . The element of insecurity, inherent in an arms race in which both sides are attempting to anticipate not only the actual programs but the capabilities of the other side, will be substantially reduced."[12] Moreover, he stated: "For the first time in the nuclear age . . . the arms race will not be driven by the fear of what the other side might be able to do but only by the agreed ceilings that have been established. That can be justly described as a major breakthrough."[13] The president and the secretary of state even declared that the agreement "actually reduces a part of the buildup at the present time. . . . [W]e actually made some reductions below present programs."[14] Secretary of Defense James Schlesinger echoed these sentiments in describing the agreement as "a very major step forward . . . and a major accomplishment."[15]

NEW CEILINGS COMPARED WITH EXISTING ARMS

The truthfulness of this promising rhetoric can be tested by comparing the missiles deployed before the Vladivostok agreement with those allowed afterwards. Two principal elements of

45

the agreement must be examined: the maximum permissible number of strategic launch vehicles for nuclear weapons and the sublimit established for the maximum number of vehicles that could carry MIRVs. As Table 2-1 indicates, a total of 4,473 strate-

Table 2-1

Comparison of the Vladivostok Ceilings for Strategic Delivery Vehicles with the Total Number of Vehicles Deployed by 1974

	Launch vehicles deployed by 1974	*Launch vehicles allowed by the Vladivostok Agreement*
U.S.		
ICBMs	1,054	
SLBMs	656	
Bombers		
(B-52s)	420[a]	
Subtotal	2,130	2,400
USSR		
ICBMs	1,567	
SLBMs	636	
Bombers		
(Mya-4s and Tu-20s)	140	
Subtotal	2,343	2,400
Total deployed	4,473	Ceiling set 4,800
Increase of 327 launchers or 7.3 percent		

NOTE: [a] The Department of Defense has often considered FB-111s capable of strategic bombing missions. Their range is 3,300 nautical miles. (See, for example, James R. Schlesinger, *Annual Defense Department Report*, FY 1976, p. II-19.) However, FB-111s are not included in this table because they were excluded from the original Vladivostok ceilings. The United States possessed 76 of them.

gic launchers were deployed by the two countries at the time the Vladivostok agreement set a new ceiling of 4,800. The new ceiling represented an increase of 7.3 percent, or a total of 327 launch vehicles, which, if MIRVed, contained far more than enough power to devastate any national society on earth.

The MIRV ceiling most fully revealed the true significance of the agreement. At the time of the Vladivostok meeting, the United States had deployed 832 MIRVed vehicles, 352 on submarines and 480 Minutemen. The Soviet Union had no MIRVs. President Ford's "very major step forward" allowed a total of 2,640 MIRVed vehicles, an increase of 217 percent. The ceilings allowed 1,808 new MIRVed vehicles resulting in a total that was 3.3 times higher than the existing levels. (See Table 2-2.)

Conservatively estimated, a MIRVed missile may carry an average of 4 warheads more than an un-MIRVed missile; on that basis the Vladivostok agreement allowed a total superpower increase

Table 2-2
Comparison of the Total MIRVs Deployed by 1974
with the Vladivostok Ceilings

	MIRVs *deployed by 1974*	MIRVs *allowed by the Vladivostok Agreement*
U.S.	832	1,320
USSR	0	1,320
Total	832	2,640
	Increase of 1,808 MIRVed vehicles, or 217 percent	

of 7,232 warheads, or nearly three times the total existing Soviet arsenal of 1974. The increase was almost equivalent to the existing number of warheads in the total U.S. strategic arsenal. Poseidon nuclear missiles carried a maximum of 14 warheads, and a convention among strategists was to use a figure of 10 warheads per Poseidon to figure their average capacity. (Decreasing the number of warheads allowed the missile to fly further or also to carry penetration aids, such as decoys.) The Trident C-4 missile will carry 20 warheads. If one assumed a less conservative average of 9 extra warheads per missile over the number possible without MIRVs, the destructive potential added by the Vladivostok agreement was nearly equal to twice the combined United States-Soviet ICBM and SLBM capacity of 1974.[16]

Throughout the years before, during, and after the Interim and Vladivostok agreements, the United States set the pace for warhead deployment. The United States had a three-to-one lead over the Soviet Union in 1974. Nonetheless, between mid-1974 and mid-1975, the United States increased its number of warheads by 850. In the same period, the Soviet Union increased its force by 300. During the five years in which the Interim Agreement was in force (1972-77), the number of warheads in the U.S. strategic missile arsenal increased by 100 percent.[17]

The replacement of a single warhead on a launch vehicle by multiple independently targetable warheads generally de-

47

Figure 2-1
Total U.S. and U.S.S.R. Strategic Delivery Vehicles[a]

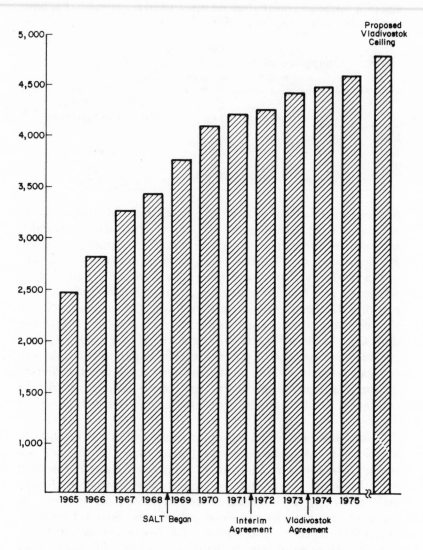

[a]This graph excludes 66 U.S. FB-111's which were not included in the original Vladivostok agreement. See note, Table 2-1.

Figure 2-2
Total U.S. and U.S.S.R. Warheads on Strategic Delivery Vehicles[a]

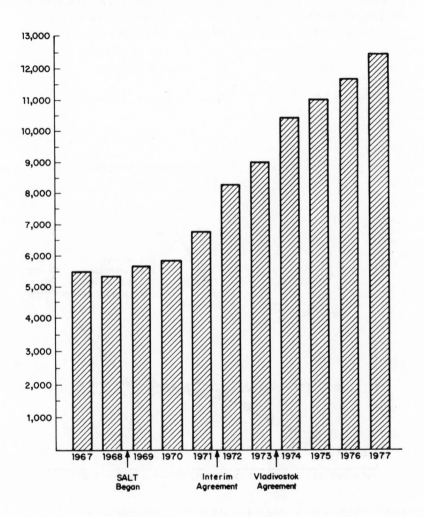

Source: Robert C. Johansen, "A Global Humanist Critique of National Policies for Arms Control," *The Journal of International Affairs*, Vol. 31 (Fall/Winter, 1977), p. 226. Reprinted with permission.

[a] Totals include U.S. FB-111's.

creased the total megatonnage that a given missile could carry, due to added weight of the separate warheads and triggering mechanisms. For example, a single 3-megaton warhead might be replaced with three .7-megaton MIRVs on the same missile. Thus, the MIRVing of launchers usually increased destructive capabil-

Figure 2-3
U.S. and U.S.S.R. Strategic Vehicles and Strategic Warheads[a]

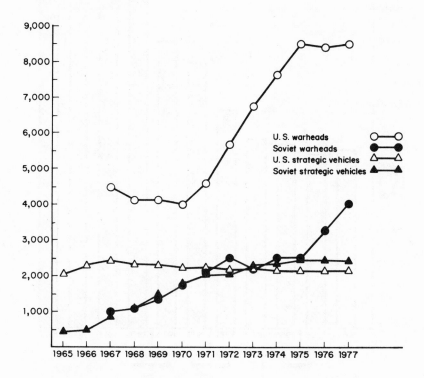

Source: Data taken from Stockholm International Peace Research Institute, *World Armaments and Disarmament: SIPRI Yearbook 1974* (Cambridge: MIT Press, 1974), pp. 106-07, and *SIPRI Yearbook 1977* (Stockholm: Almquist & Wiksell, 1977), pp. 24-25

[a]Totals include U. S. FB-111's.

ity, in terms of the number of targets that could be hit, although it did not increase megatonnage per launcher. Three .7-megaton warheads, if delivered on target, could destroy three cities, whereas one 3-megaton weapon would destroy only one city and some surrounding suburbs.[18]

Compared with the ceilings allowed for launchers in the accord of 1972, with the quantities of vehicles deployed at the time of the Vladivostok meeting, or with the total number of deliverable warheads possessed by both sides in 1974, the new ceilings set by the Vladivostok agreement allowed substantial increases in the size of the forces.

Even the preceding analysis, however, does not fully reveal the extent to which the arms race continued unabated after the Vladivostok agreement. The omissions of the agreement nullified the significance of its prohibitions. A country's destructive capability, one must recall, depended not only on the number of its launchers, but also on the number of its warheads, the yield of the various warheads, and the accuracy of the vehicles in delivering the warheads on target. Of these four factors, the agreement sought only to regulate the first, which was becoming less and less important in the then current stage of weapons development. Given the areas of competition that remained uncontrolled, what was the significance of the agreement?

First of all, even the highly acclaimed limit on the number of strategic launchers was far less significant than officials asserted. The ceiling meant little, since new, more accurate, and more powerful vehicles could replace the old. Existing silos could be loaded with indefinitely "improved" missiles of similar diameters, or the silos themselves could be increased by 15 percent to accommodate even larger missiles. In defending the agreement's "flexibility," Kissinger noted that the United States could, through technical improvements, deploy missiles with larger throw weight, "so there is no effective limit on the increase in our throw weight."[19] Except for retaining the freeze on the deployment of the Soviet SS-9 or other equally "heavy" ICBMs, as established in the Interim Agreement, no limits were set on the throw weight of replacement missiles.

The refusal of the superpowers to limit throw weight to that of existing deployments was significant, because they also chose to set no ceiling on the number of warheads and bombs each side might possess. Neither did the two governments place a maximum upon the total megatonnage each side could deploy.

51

By increasing the throw weight of their missiles, the parties could also increase the number of warheads per missile and the yield per warhead. Since modifications in the capabilities of the launchers were allowed, even the absolute limit on launchers, which was the central "accomplishment" of the accord, meant very little.

The failure to restrict improvements in missiles, increases in the number of warheads, and total deployable megatonnage also undermined the Vladivostok agreement's second major accomplishment—the sublimit on MIRVed vehicles. To begin with, the ceiling of 1,320 MIRVs was well above existing levels. More importantly, since each MIRVed vehicle could carry an unspecified number of warheads, the overall limit of 1,320 had little restrictive significance.

Any constraining quality of the already weak accord was eroded further by Soviet and American unwillingness to ban the testing and development of new missiles, bombers, and guidance systems. Technological competition would continue without limits. With no restraint on testing and development of missiles, totally new weapons—such as strategic cruise missiles launched from mobile platforms on land, sea, or air—could be deployed. U.S. programs to improve the accuracy of missiles and the yield-to-weight ratios of warheads would increase the U.S. capacity to destroy a large portion of the Soviet land-based ICBM force. Although well behind the United States in such technology, the Soviet Union could eventually develop a similar capability. Testing could also proceed on "cold launch" or "pop-up" missile launchers. This technique would facilitate heavier payloads and, when perfected, allow rapid firing of a second or third missile from a single silo. (The missile would be ejected from the silo before the main engines were ignited, thus sparing the silo from the fire damage that normally prevents the silo from being used again immediately.) Should these techniques be successfully developed, the limit on even the number of silos would be insignificant.[20]

Futhermore, the agreement's failure to prohibit underground testing of nuclear weapons allowed both sides to continue the type of testing that would enable them to increase the explosive power per pound of warhead. The result would be to add more independently targetable warheads to each missile. The Atomic Energy Commission's test program was actually *accelerated* after the Vladivostok accord, so a more destructive warhead could be prepared for deployment on the Minuteman.[21]

In addition, the SALT I sublimits on SLBMs were completely abandoned at Vladivostok. This opened the way for military officials to deploy the new Trident submarine, already under development. The previous arms control agreement could be cast aside when it inhibited deployment of a new weapon that officials wanted to manufacture.

There were no limits placed on *any* intermediate-range weapons, including missiles and bombers, any number of which could be stationed within appropriate range for large-scale attack. Thus, technical breakthroughs which occurred during the unrestricted testing and development could be incorporated in unlimited numbers in a country's nuclear arsenal if it were deployed in a "non-strategic" role. This possibility, of course, was facilitated by not establishing a limit in the total megatonnage either side could poise for attack. The possession by the United States of about 7,000 nuclear weapons in Europe that did not come under the strategic limitations demonstrated that this potential was by no means small. Some tactical weapons contained three times the explosive power of the Hiroshima bomb. Paul Nitze, the former deputy secretary of defense and defense department representative on the U.S. SALT delegation, declared that by not including the Soviet "Backfire" and the U.S. FB-111 (medium-range bombers) and by not restricting tankers (which can give long-range capability to medium-range aircraft), "the entire concept of a 2,400 ceiling on ICBMs, SLBMs, and heavy bombers becomes essentially meaningless."[22] Finally, as Secretary Kissinger confirmed, the Vladivostok agreement did not curtail any weapons program then in progress or planned before the agreement.[23] "In fact," said Air Force Secretary John McLucas, "SALT II proposed ceilings generally consistent with our previously planned programs."[24]

In order to slow the arms race, the most important areas to control were those in which the agreement was unrestrictive. The single exception to this was the MIRV ceilings, but these were so high as to constitute little dampening effect during a ten-year period. Well before the Vladivostok agreement, Malcolm R. Currie, the director of defense research and engineering, testified that the most disquieting aspects of the arms competition were "qualitative improvements," such as sophistication of ICBMs

53

and SLBMs, improved accuracy, increased throw weight, and MIRVed warheads.[25] Of all these, only MIRVs were limited by a ceiling; and that became a target toward which each side would *increase* its arsenals.

In trying to refute the criticism that the agreement's ceilings were too high, the Ford administration argued that, in spite of the continued buildup permitted in the agreement, it kept the levels of weaponry lower than they would have been otherwise. It was, of course, impossible to know what might have occurred without the agreement. Nevertheless, some evidence cast doubt on the Ford-Kissinger contention. Secretary Schlesinger offered detailed information supporting his belief that the agreement encouraged larger strategic forces than previously planned. Given the very high MIRV ceilings, defense officials perceived a major "restructuring" of strategic forces as even more necessary than before the accord. The restructuring would place less emphasis on land-based missiles and more emphasis on the relatively invulnerable submarine-based missiles and highly flexible manned bombers. After the Vladivostok agreement was signed, Schlesinger announced the United States would need (1) to build two more Tridents than the ten already planned, at a cost of about $2 billion each; (2) to keep ten Poseidon submarines in service longer than planned; (3) to decide definitely in favor of manufacturing a new strategic bomber; (4) to develop and deploy a new, larger ICBM in existing silos; and (5) to develop larger and more accurate warheads for the existing Minuteman missiles. To be sure, each of these categories of weapons had been under development before the Vladivostok agreement. But Schlesinger believed the agreement confirmed and, in some cases, expanded the need for deployment of these new weapons.[26]

Space does not permit a listing here of the scores of weapons programs that were initiated or pushed forward after the Vladivostok agreement. But some of the most important should be mentioned. Research, development, and in some cases deployment of the following were carried forward after the Vladivostok agreement:

—the Trident submarine with 24 missile tubes;

—the long-range Trident missile;

—a maneuverable reentry vehicle (MaRV) with pinpoint accuracy;

—additional ICBM research, to provide greater yield, accuracy, and throw weight for the Minuteman;

—the Command Data Buffer System, permitting the Minuteman III to be retargeted remotely and rapidly;

—the M-X, an entirely new, larger ICBM;

—alternative basing modes for warheads, such as land-mobile or aircraft-launched missiles;

—the cruise missile, which could maneuver and target itself after being launched from a submarine, ship, aircraft, or mobile land base;

—a new aerial tanker for airborne refueling, to give bombers greater range and carrying capacity;

—various sophisticated guidance and command technologies, such as the Advanced Ballistic Reentry System (ABRES), which would give warheads increased penetrativeness, maneuverability, and terminal guidance;

—a totally new reentry vehicle capable of carrying a higher yield warhead;

—a worldwide communication satellite system, called NAVSTAR Global Positioning System, which was designed to give pinpoint accuracy even to SLBMs.[27]

In summary, the Vladivostok agreement was neither "a firm ceiling on the strategic arms race," nor "a cap . . . on the arms race," as the president and the secretary of state had claimed. It merely registered a recognition that for ten years at least no more than 2,400 strategic launchers should be built, while the arms race shifted to perfecting multiple warheads and guidance systems, and sophisticating underwater launching, cruise missiles, and new bombers. The accord merely emphasized and accelerated a shift toward qualitative improvements of weapons while establishing only a porous quantitative ceiling toward which the governments would build. The agreement allowed the continuation of an unabated arms buildup in areas preferred by military officials, while appearing to regulate arms deployment in directions that were no longer of interest to them. Vast qualitative and substantial quantitative dimensions of the arms race would continue.

Using the Vladivostok agreement to slow the arms race is analogous to attempting to dam a wide stream by dropping one large rock in its middle. No water will pass through the space actually displaced by the rock, but the stream will flow around it without decreasing its volume by increasing its speed on both sides of the rock. If implemented in a treaty, the Vladivostok ceilings would be relatively insignificant limits through which neither side would pass for ten years. But the arms competition would swirl undiminished around those barriers. Official rhetoric lacked even minimal resemblance to reality. Contrary to professed value 1, the behavior of officials as registered in the Vladivostok agreement contained an alternative, operative value: *to allow the arms buildup to continue without significant restriction* (implicit value A).

THE ACCORD AND LEGITIMATION OF COUNTERFORCE STRATEGY

The case for implicit value A—that the Vladivostok agreement allowed the arms race to continue—can be so strongly substantiated that it suggests a further question: did SALT in fact legitimize and accelerate the arms race?

The question cannot be easily answered, but some significant evidence is available on four dimensions of the issue:

a) Were the Vladivostok ceilings serious limits for deployment of launchers or, instead, goals for additional deployment?

b) Did the two ceilings slow down, or stimulate, development in related areas?

c) Did the use of bargaining chips at SALT become, in fact, an easy way for officials to overcome objections to otherwise controversial arms initiatives?

d) Did the Vladivostok agreement undermine political opposition to the procurement of additional weapons?

Ceilings or targets? After the meeting at Vladivostok, the figures of 2,400 launch vehicles and 1,320 MIRVs became accepted almost overnight as targets for planning in the next ten years. Before November 24, 1974, the public had had no inclination to regard those levels as legitimate. After that date, the political forces that earlier would have opposed such major increases did not wage a serious struggle against them. As Fred Iklé, the director of the U.S. Arms Control and Disarmament Agency warned, "one of the dangers of prolonged bargaining in arms control negotiations is that if you do not watch out it could lead to agreements to *augment* arms, arms augmentation agreements instead of arms reduction agreements. . . . You compare all these numbers and before you know it you have to level *up* to what the other side has instead of leveling down."[28]

President Ford clearly expected that the United States would build up to the levels enumerated in the agreement: "We do have an obligation within the limits of 2,400 on delivery systems and 1,320 on MIRVs to keep our forces up to that level." He repeated this view later in the same news conference on the Vladivostok agreement: "We do have an obligation to stay up to that ceiling, and the budget that I will recommend will keep our strategic forces either up to or aimed at that objective."[29]

In the Defense Department's annual report, Secretary Schlesinger rhetorically offered to stay below the ceilings if the Soviet Union did. But rather than exercise self-restraint in an effort to implement such an idea, he declared: "Until we obtain solid evidence of Soviet restraint, we shall plan for deployment of approximately 2,400 strategic delivery vehicles and 1,320 MIRVed missiles." Even though the United States clearly held the technological lead and had deployed far more warheads than the Soviet Union, he advised that "we should plan toward the Vladivostok goals."[30]

After the Vladivostok meeting, most officials assumed that the Soviet Union would build up to the ceilings. Since few people wanted to be accused of advocating that the United States deliberately fall behind Soviet military capability, U.S. deployment which was aimed at the ceilings encountered criticism far less vigorous than would have been likely had there not been a Vladivostok agreement. The latter set a level *below* which advocates of arms control could aim only by opening themselves to the charge that they wanted to make the United States a second-class power. After hearing exhaustive testimony on the Department of Defense requests for post-Vladivostok weapons, Senator Stuart Symington, a member of both the Armed Services Committee and the Arms Control Subcommittee, concluded that the Vladivostok agreement had fixed ceilings that were targets for *increased* deployment of weapons.[31]

The former U.S. chief negotiator at SALT and head of the Arms Control and Disarmament Agency commented, "the MIRVed missile ceiling was apparently chosen to permit the United States to *complete* programs for land- and sea-based MIRVed missiles."[32] Indeed, the U.S. proposal of 1,320 MIRVs reportedly exceeded by 30 percent the number of MIRVs the Soviet Union had been willing to accept in the spring of 1974.[33]

Stimulus in related areas. In addition to setting goals for a continued arms buildup of strategic launchers and MIRVs, the agreement also stimulated new development in related areas, such as guidance systems, throw weight, and yield. It focused energies on the most dangerous, destabilizing, and volatile components of arms competition: technological "advances" to increase the lethal capability of the launchers within the set limit.

57

As Malcolm Currie explained, "Because it limits total numbers of weapons and weapon carriers, the accord on strategic nuclear weapons at Vladivostok re-enforces our need for technological progress." The Vladivostok agreement, therefore, did not merely maintain the past pace of technological "progress" in arms competition; the accord also encouraged officials to pour more energy into the process of technically refining the instruments of destruction: "The Vladivostok agreement . . . inevitably . . . *places a premium* on steady technological progress and on . . . qualitative improvements to maintain deterrence, which new technology can change overnight."[34] The increased attention given to accelerating technological innovation was most often expressed as a need to increase lethal capacity per weapon, since the number of launchers was limited. General David C. Jones, chief of staff of the U.S. Air Force, explained that, "as ceilings are imposed on *quantity* of systems, the *qualitative features of remaining systems assume even more importance*."[35]

This consequence of the Vladivostok agreement, described as the need for "high unit performance," also meant that officials sought to erode the influence of budgetary limits as a restraint on military spending. As Secretary of Defense Schlesinger explained to the Senate Armed Services Committee in discussing his desire to have a new strategic bomber, "given the strict limitation on bomber numbers [due to the Vladivostok accord] . . . *there is much less relevancy to the cost-quantity trade-off that would automatically apply were a procurement decision to be inherently less limited.* Given the limitation on numbers, there is a powerful incentive to achieve high unit performance—associated with the lesser degree of relevance of the cost-quantity trade-off."[36] In other words, the usual need to justify weapons purchases on economic grounds no longer applied when an arms control agreement went into effect. The Vladivostok agreement could subvert its professed purpose and facilitate arms procurement.[37] It undermined budgetary limits which in the past had been the single most effective restraint on the purchase of new weapons.

Bargaining chips. Although there was no outright conspiracy between the military officials of the Soviet Union and the United States to prolong the arms race, the practical consequences of their respective policies were almost the same as if there had been. During informal discussions with Soviet military advisers at the SALT negotiations, the Soviet advisers indicated that an arms control agreement on launchers would merely mean there

would be a race in technology.[38] Each side's actions or anticipated actions were used to justify deployments by the other.

Continuous rounds of arms negotiations enabled advocates of
weapons innovations to initiate research, testing, and development of a wide variety of new weapons under the pretense that a
U.S. lead in weaponry could be used either as a bargaining chip
to be traded off for some Soviet compromise in negotiations or
as a demonstration of such superior U.S. technology that the
Soviet Union would be persuaded to halt the arms race rather
than try to imitate U.S. technological progress.[39]

Since the Soviet Union has sought no less than equality in armaments since World War II, neither the bargaining-chip strategy nor the negotiation-from-strength approach was likely to
work. In the former case, the Soviet Union would be unwilling
to prohibit development of weapons that the United States had
tested but the Soviet Union had not. The latter approach was
unworkable because the United States was reluctant to ban what
it had developed, and the Soviet Union refused to freeze a position of U.S. superiority. As a result, U.S. bargaining chips and
arms advantages were seldom negotiated away; instead, they
launched new stages of arms competition. As a study group of
the Federation of American Scientists concluded: "First
weapons systems are moved toward procurement as bargaining
threats, and then the subsequent negotiations ratify the procurement of everything in the pipeline. [The Vladivostok ac-
cord] did exactly that, approving or leaving room for all
weapons already used as 'chips.' Under such conditions, it would
be preferable not to put discussion of new armaments on the
arms control agenda where negotiations could serve as a pretext
for further development of bargaining chips."[40]

Official arguments for developing MIRVs illustrated how arms
control negotiations could provide a convenient rationale for
weapons that lacked a good military justification on their own
merits. Given the U.S. possession of a deterrent capable of assured destruction, plus overall strategic advantages and technological superiority over the Soviet Union, the MIRV was not an
important addition to United States security.[41] For several years
during its development, the MIRV was justified and funded not as
a weapon necessary for security but as an item useful for arms
control negotiations. In the late 1960s, officials argued that the
MIRV should be developed as a bargaining chip to secure an
agreement on ABM limitation with the Soviet Union or, if no

agreement were possible, as a necessary device to penetrate possible future Soviet antiballistic missile forces. However, when SALT I limited ABMs to a militarily insignificant number, officials justified the continued deployment of MIRVs as a bargaining chip for negotiations to prohibit the deployment of MIRVs.[42] But, as development and deployment proceeded, officials dropped efforts to prohibit MIRVs.

At that time, there were no Soviet MIRVs ready for deployment. It was widely acknowledged, however, that U.S. deployment would, within a few years, stimulate a similar Soviet effort, thus casting doubt on the survivability of a majority of both sides' land-based ICBMs in a first strike.[43] Such a development would also generate new pressures for creation of alternative weapons systems, less vulnerable than Minuteman, as well as for the perfection of precise guidance systems to enable the destruction of hardened silos. The latter technology would be highly destabilizing in a case where one side thought its ICBMs were truly vulnerable. But, rather than slow the unilateral U.S. deployment of the MIRV, installation continued at a steady rate both during and after SALT I, justified substantially by the professed desire to make SALT successful. By the end of 1974, the United States had deployed a total of 7,940 deliverable nuclear warheads (including non-MIRVed warheads) on its strategic vehicles, as opposed to the Soviet Union's 2,600.[44]

Negotiations encouraged weapons proponents to move programs along faster than opponents could prepare to control them, thus providing a stimulus for the arms race that had nothing to do with any external military threat. Such *intra*national arms racing occurred between those who wanted disarmament and those who wanted more arms. As Herbert York, former director of defense research for the Department of Defense and a member of the General Advisory Committee on Arms Control and Disarmament, concluded: "[The MIRV program] has some of the earmarks of being something that the military is trying to get done before the arms control people can stop it."[45] The bargaining-chip ploy strengthened the hand of the arms advocates by speeding the forces for development and slowing those for self-restraint.

Reading the testimony of various defense officials during the years of the SALT negotiations, one gets the clear impression that the arms talks made it harder to cut the defense budget and restrain arms procurement. Officials would tell their critics: "We must build these weapons to make the Soviet Union negotiate seriously at SALT." In the case of the MIRV and ABM, the bargaining-chip argument was used to gain support for weapons systems which would not have been supported on their merits, thus stimulating the arms competition rather than the negotiations. "In retrospect . . . it is clear that on balance the bargaining chip tactic as it has been used has raised the military competition to levels more difficult to bring under control."[46]

Neutralization of opposition. If there had been no arms control negotiations, it would have been clearer to Congress and the public that they were paying for an open-ended arms race, whereas during SALT many people were led to believe that they were supporting limited arms increments for the purpose of facilitating arms control. In addition, arms talks seemed to place the burden for continuing buildups on the "enemy," because the latter failed to come to an agreement. Without such negotiations, the responsibility of one's own country for the buildup would have been at least as visible. Deeper awareness of U.S. responsibility for the arms competition could have nurtured the idea that self-restraint might have produced more restrictive results than SALT. With the prospect of an agreement continuously being raised, people presumed that the United States should build new weapons until an agreement halted the buildup. This presumption for going ahead in the absence of an agreement was so strong that the Joint Chiefs of Staff unhesitatingly rejected a Senate inquiry about conducting a yearly review of the impact of Defense Department programs on arms control: "An annual analysis of the arms control implications of the defense budget would seem to be of little or no value."[47] Finally, in the absence of arms negotiations, the assumption that advanced technology should be exploited for new weapons could have been challenged more directly. The justification for weapons programs, at the least, would then have had to rest on military rather than on arms control needs.[48]

Although it cannot be conclusively demonstrated, it is possible that, in the early 1970s, congressional opposition to MIRVs was bothersome enough to military officials that they decided that an arms control "ceiling" for MIRVs would be a good way to facilitate MIRV deployment and harmlessly vent the pressure for MIRV reductions. To be sure, there would have been pressures to develop the MIRV even without SALT, but the belief was widespread that there was no genuine deterrence *need* for MIRV. The convenient SALT justification for MIRV substantially increased the chances for its initial deployment. This was especially true since the liberal critics of the new weapons were the same persons who supported arms control. Precisely because of the liberals' enthusiasm for arms control, military officials could use the SALT negotiations to entice liberals to support an arms buildup. Although never stated explicitly, an implicit theme of many discussions was that more weapons were needed for arms control than for military security. The arms control negotiations transformed political opposition to arms spending into initial support for new programs.

In terms of public expectations, defense planning, and military appropriations, the Vladivostok agreement actually helped *to legitimize a further arms buildup* (implicit value B). The editors of the *New York Times* commented after the Vladivostok meeting that, if both sides deployed weapons to the limits specified, the arms race would go on "just about as now planned, and possibly a little faster in some areas—*legitimized*, in fact, by international compact."[49] After conducting extensive hearings on arms control and the shifting rationales for weapons innovation, Senator Edmund Muskie correctly observed, "my suspicion is that the SALT talks actually stimulated the arms race rather than stabilized it."[50]

Because of SALT, officials created an atmosphere designed to convince the public that all was being done that could be done to achieve a disarmed world. The arms control talks legitimized existing arms programs as well as justified new ones as bargaining chips. To some extent, the negotiations actually deterred meaningful efforts at disarmament.[51]

THE SIGNIFICANCE OF VLADIVOSTOK-LEGITIMIZED SHIFTS IN STRATEGIC DOCTRINE

What was the significance of the changes in strategic doctrine and arsenal size that occurred during the arms control negotiations? Since the first days of its nuclear monopoly, the United States had pursued a "countercity" or "countervalue" strategy of nuclear deterrence based on the capacity to destroy the cities and industrial centers of the Soviet Union in event of war. After the Soviet Union acquired a formidable nuclear arsenal of its own, the two deterrents produced a balance of terror based on "mutual assured destruction" (MAD). In maintaining this posture, both sides possessed enough nuclear weapons to suffer a first strike from the other side and still be able to inflict assured destruction on the attacker in a retaliatory response. Both governments assumed that such a capability would be sufficient to deter nuclear war.

A second approach, called "counterforce" strategy, had also been a subject of discussion since the mid-1960s. A counterforce strategy selects Soviet military capability, such as ICBM silos or airports, as targets instead of Soviet cities. A "first-strike" or "damage-limiting capability" is one in which the counterforce capacity is so large and effective as to enable one side to disarm the opponent in a massive first strike. An essential condition of a first-strike strategy is to destroy the opponent's ability to retaliate against the attacker.

For many reasons, a genuine first-strike capability, with high promise of disarming the opponent, remains unattainable by either side at the present time.[52] For example, an entire fleet of nuclear submarines cannot be located and destroyed instantaneously. Neither can weapons be launched at precisely the same time in a coordinated attack on SLBMs, ICBMs, and bomber bases. If weapons were launched at different times, the warning period would be sufficient for the potential victim to employ the undestroyed segment of its deterrent in a retaliatory response.[53]

During SALT, U.S. strategy moved markedly from being based primarily—though not entirely—on a countercity and assured destruction approach to one that included an extensive counterforce capability far in excess of the forces needed for assured destruction only. Critics of this shift feared that the enlargement of the counterforce arsenal would be destabilizing because it was likely to stimulate Soviet fears that the United States was moving toward a first-strike strategy. Even if these fears were not fully substantiated, a mere step in that direction could stimulate Soviet planners to take countermeasures in order to avoid leaving part of their deterrent in a vulnerable position. A counterforce capability short of a first-strike potential might conceivably be used to destroy most of the land-based missiles of one side while holding back further missiles to destroy the cities of the victim in order to deter the victim from retaliating with its SLBMs. Although such a scenario, with its assumed precise and restrained responses, seems implausible, it nonetheless influenced defense planners and was used by them to justify deployment of more weapons.[54]

The potential for development of new weapons vastly increased the appeal of counterforce strategy to Pentagon officials because the new weapons they desired (MIRVs, pinpoint accuracy in guidance systems, cruise missiles, Trident, and larger yield reentry vehicles) could be militarily justified by movement toward a counterforce strategy. The new weapons were not needed for deterrence (MAD) in itself. Military officials were possessors of a technology in search of a strategic rationale. Aside from counterforce strategy, the only possible justification for MIRVs was the bargaining-chip argument—to build MIRVs in order to negotiate an agreement for banning them. Counterforce strategy and cynical, bargaining-chip use of the SALT talks professedly to *avert* counterforce deployment were used to provide the needed rationale for which military officials had been searching. And because the Soviet Union would not agree to freeze its own inferiority in an agreement, military planners made sure, by remaining ahead of the Soviet Union in deployment of MIRVs, that the bargaining chips would never serve as the basis for a genuine ban of the new technology.

Deployment of MIRVs was a major technological and strategic innovation of doubtful security value because MIRVs allowed a single missile with multiple warheads to destroy several enemy missiles, thus giving an advantage to the side launching a first strike. For example, one missile with six warheads could destroy three enemy missiles if two warheads were targeted on each missile to insure penetration and nearly certain destruction. In pre-MIRV days, the attacker would have needed to use two missiles (given only one warhead per missile) to destroy each enemy missile, at the same two-to-one ratio. Thus the attacker would always deplete its missile arsenal faster than it would destroy its opponent's missiles. MIRVs reversed the balance of advantages. Since the Vladivostok agreement did not prohibit MIRVs or limit their number to a low level, it facilitated and encouraged movement toward a counterforce strategy. That was doubtless one of its most serious weaknesses.

In the years preceding the Vladivostok meeting, the United States had taken the earliest steps toward deploying a first-strike capability in the arms race with the Soviet Union. The United States had long deployed far more warheads than were required for assured destruction of the Soviet Union and its allies. In addition, the United States began development of the single most crucial technological prerequisite of a counterforce strategy, the MIRV, early in the 1960s.

The United States also outpaced the Soviet Union in the second most important condition for establishing a first-strike capability: vehicle accuracy. Without high accuracy, even the delivery of many warheads would not insure the destruction of an opponent's missiles. The Minuteman III and Poseidon missiles had relatively high accuracy (.25 to .15 of a nautical mile). Soviet ICBMs of the same period were credited with an accuracy of about one mile.[55] In computing the ability of a warhead to destroy a silo, accuracy was far more important than yield, an area in which the Soviet deployment exceeded U.S. weapons.[56] In terms of counterforce capability, the heavier throw weight and larger warheads of the Soviet Union did not compensate for U.S. advantages in accuracy and multiple warheads and did not constitute any *technological* advantage. The United States had in hand the technology to increase both of these factors whenever it sought to imitate Soviet forces. (The United States had unilaterally decided years earlier that it did not need more throw weight or warheads of larger yield.) The Soviet Union, on the other hand, could not match United States forces because it lacked the technology possessed by the United States in accuracy, yield-to-weight ratios, and MIRVs.

Congressman Robert L. Leggett, a California Democrat on the House Armed Services Committee, analyzed the counterforce capability of the United States and Soviet Union, using predictions based on weapons then deployed or in the process of development.[57] As Table 2-3 shows, the Vladivostok agreement legitimized vast increases in counterforce capability, expressed as index K. In 1974, K for both sides totaled 31,243. Leggett predicted it would increase by more than 3½ times by the early 1980s, and could jump by 169 times to 5,277,275 by the late 1980s. Most of those who disputed Leggett's estimates maintained only that the Soviet Union would have a *higher* counterforce capability than his tables showed, thus further confirming the point that the Vladivostok agreement was anything but an arms limitation agreement.

To Soviet observers, United States armament policies also might have seemed designed to attain a partial first-strike capability because all one thousand of the modern ICBM silos, which were hardened with concrete and steel to withstand nuclear blast overpressure of 300 pounds per square inch (psi), were scheduled to be hardened further. The new silos were designed to withstand 900 psi and perhaps as much as 1,200 psi.[58] Ninety of the latest Soviet silos were believed to withstand 600 psi. But

65

Table 2-3
Counterforce Capability of 1974 Compared with Predicted Counterforce Capability after the Vladivostok Agreement

Missile	Yield, megatons (per warhead)	Accuracy nautical miles	Warheads (per missile)	Number of missiles	K^a (per missile)
		PRESENT PROGRAMS			
		U.S.			
Minuteman III	280 (.17)	.2	1,650 (3)	550	12,127 (22.1)
Minuteman II	450 (1)	.3	450 (1)	450	5,000 (11.1)
Titan	270 (5)	.5	54 (1)	54	631 (11.7)
Poseidon	198 (.04)	.3	4,960 (10)	496	6,393 (12.8)
Polaris A-3	96 (.6)	.7	160 (1)	160	240 (1.5)
U.S. total	1,294		7,274	1,710	24,391
		USSR			
SS-9	7,200 (25)	.7	288 (1)	288	5,011 (17.4)
SS-11	1,010 (1)	1.0	1,010 (1)	1,010	1,010 (1.0)
SS-13	60 (1)	.7	60 (1)	60	120 (2.0)
SS-8	545 (5)	1.5	109 (1)	109	142 (1.3)
SS-7	500 (5)	2.0	100 (1)	100	70 (0.7)
SS-N-6	528 (1)	1.5	528 (1)	528	211 (0.4)
SS-N-8	180 (1)	.8	180 (1)	180	288 (1.6)
USSR total	10,023		2,275	2,203	6,852
Combined U.S. and USSR totals			9,549		31,243

Missile	Yield, megatons (per warhead)	Accuracy nautical miles	Warheads (per missile)	Number of missiles	K^a (per missile)
EARLY 1980s					
U.S.					
Minuteman III	(.35) 578	.1	(3) 1,650	550	(148) 81,675
Minuteman II	(1) 450	.3	(1) 450	450	(11.1) 5,000
Titan	(5) 270	.5	(1) 54	54	(11.7) 631
Trident II	(.08) 230	.18	(20) 2,880	144	(114) 16,416
Trident I	(.08) 499	.18	(10) 6,240	624	(57) 35,568
Polaris A-3	(.6) 96	.7	(1) 160	160	(1.5) 240
U.S. total	2,123		11,434	2,095	139,480
USSR					
SS-18	(1) 1,878	.3	(6) 1,878	313	(66) 20,658
SS-19	(.2) 1,208	.3	(6) 6,042	1,007	(23) 22,825
SS-13	(1) 60	.7	(1) 60	60	(2.0) 120
SS-8	(5) 545	1.5	(1) 109	109	(0.4) 142
SS-N-8	(1) 910	.5	(1) 910	910	(4) 3,640
USSR total	4,601		8,999	2,399	47,385
Combined U.S. and USSR totals			20,433		186,865

Table 2-3 (cont.)

LATE 1980s

Missile	Yield, megatons (per warhead)		Accuracy nautical miles	Warheads (per missile)		Number of missiles	K[a] (per missile)	
U.S.								
Minuteman III	(.25)	412	.02	(3)	1,650	550	(2205)	1,212,750
Minuteman II	(1)	450	.3	(1)	450	450	(11.1)	5,000
Titan	(5)	270	.5	(1)	54	54	(11.7)	631
Trident II	(.06)	345	.02	(20)	5,760	288	(6500)	1,822,000
Trident I	(.06)	288	.02	(10)	4,800	480	(3250)	1,560,000
U.S. total		1,765			12,714	1,822		4,650,381
USSR								
SS-18	(2)	3,756	.1	(6)	1,878	313	(948)	296,724
SS-19	(.4)	2,417	.1	(6)	6,042	1,007	(324)	326,268
SS-13	(1)	60	.7	(1)	60	60	(2.0)	120
SS-8	(5)	545	1.5	(1)	109	109	(0.4)	142
SS-N-8	(1)	910	.5	(1)	910	910	(4)	3,640
USSR total		7,678			8,999	2,399		626,894
Combined U.S. and USSR totals					21,713			5,277,275

SOURCE: Robert L. Leggett, "Two Legs Do Not a Centipede Make," *Armed Forces Journal* (February 1975), pp. 30-32. Reprinted by permission.

NOTE: [a] Index "K" measures the capability of one state's nuclear forces to destroy an opponent's unlaunched nuclear weapons. This capability is determined by the number of warheads, their yield, and their accuracy. In figuring K, accuracy is far more important than yield. See note 56.

only two-thirds of the then current Soviet ICBM force was emplaced in silos of the 300 psi grade, with the remainder substantially less hard.[59] Thus Soviet ICBMs were clearly more vulnerable to counterforce attack than United States missiles, and since the Soviet Union's deterrent was proportionately more dependent on ICBMs than the U.S. triad of ICBMs, SLBMs, and bombers, U.S. policy was far more threatening to the Soviet Union than vice versa.

The United States further demonstrated an intention to enhance its counterforce potential by the development of "remote retargeting" of missiles from central launcher control facilities. This procedure provided speed and flexibility in enabling commanders to target *replacement* missiles for first-round missiles that had been observed to fail. Such a capability was unnecessary in countercity strategies, but was useful for a first-strike or damage-limiting capability to insure the destruction of all Soviet retaliatory vehicles.

The United States also sought to improve its SLBMs to give them more counterforce capability. Development was being conducted before and after the Vladivostok agreement to increase the accuracy of the warheads through use of a Global Positioning System to provide "a continuous, worldwide, all-weather positioning capability with an accuracy of tens of feet in three dimensions."[60]

In sum, during the years preceding the Vladivostok agreement, the Soviet Union did far less to increase the counterforce capabilities of its strategic forces than did the United States. The Soviet Union did not even test a MIRV until mid-1973[61]—three years after the first U.S. *deployment*. To be sure, the Soviet Union had laid the groundwork for the subsequent development of a counterforce capability by constructing missiles with large throw weight. It seemed reasonable to conjecture, however, that the original intention of developing such large missiles was to compensate by the use of heavier warheads for inferior Soviet technology in yield-to-weight ratios and accuracy compared to U.S. advanced technology even in the pre-MIRV stage. The United States, on the other hand, had most of the needed counterforce technology available and had begun deploying weapons that were useful primarily as an enlargement of its counterforce capability. In the wake of the Vladivostok accord, both parties—with the United States far in the lead—pursued deployment of counterforce capability even more seriously.

69

Although the Vladivostok accord certainly was not the cause of initial pressures within the United States for shifting to a counterforce posture, it facilitated the process and proved more useful to advocates of arms buildup than of arms control. By legitimizing MIRVs and channeling arms competition into technological innovation, the accord facilitated a doctrinal shift—from emphasis on deterrence of war through assured destruction, to deployment of more sophisticated weapons useful for counterforce targeting. This shift also meant the central strategic premise changed—from traditional deterrence of major nuclear war, toward deploying precise instruments of nuclear war-fighting ability useful for "limited" nuclear war.[62] Bernard T. Feld, a physicist with long experience in weapons research for the United States, concluded that "the main result of SALT has been to initiate a new phase of the nuclear arms competition, in which both sides are moving steadily, from their earlier posture of reliance on nuclear weapons for the sole purpose of deterring a first-strike by the other side, towards postures that can only be interpreted as preparations for use of these weapons in any conflict against any kind of target, regardless of the actions of the other side."[63]

The Vladivostok agreement legitimized MIRVs at the very moment when there remained the last, easy opportunity to prohibit them altogether or to restrict them to very low levels. Once the number 1,320 was included in an international agreement, it meant legitimation of weapons that had been understood, throughout the years of congressional debate about research and development, not to be needed in themselves.

In facilitating the shift to counterforce strategy and limited war-fighting capability, the Vladivostok accord kept open the military's desires for "flexible options." With MIRVs and precise accuracy, officials could attack a few or many specific and small targets. Counterforce strategy required continued arms development in the areas of accuracy, yield, throw weight, and global guidance systems. The Vladivostok accord neatly avoided significant restraints in all these areas. By legitimating MIRVs and "flexible response," it supported a principle in fundamental contradiction with the purpose of arms control, which by definition must *restrict* flexibility and constrain behavior. A chronic desire for increased flexibility meant unlimited weapons development, and could be perceived by the opponent as movement toward a first-strike capability.[64]

70

Schlesinger used the Vladivostok agreement in another way to buttress his argument for additional weapons. The agreement, he argued, enshrined the principle of equality in weaponry for the two superpowers. By projecting the Soviet *potential* for MIRV-ing on heavier Soviet throw weight, U.S. officials justified the procurement of many new weapons in order to maintain equality with the Soviet Union.[65] As Secretary Schlesinger stated, "There is just no possibility that a high confidence disarming first strike is attainable for either side, even against the ICBM components of the strategic forces on both sides."[66] In short, despite higher Soviet throw weight, under *no* foreseeable circumstances could the Soviet Union achieve a first-strike capability. Nonetheless, if Soviet leaders put MIRVs on their ICBMs, and developed more accurate warheads, and deployed more MIRVs than the United States, then the Soviet arsenal could give the Soviet Union "a capability that we ourselves would lack, and it could bring into question the sense of equality that the principles of Vladivostok so explicitly endorse."[67] Additional weapons were necessary not primarily for security but for fulfilling the principle of equality—which was included in an agreement ostensibly intended for reduction of armaments. By using graphs and slides based on cleverly manipulated statistics, the secretary of defense showed congressional committees what the Soviet Union might be able to deploy in the 1980s, given its great throw weight potential.[68] Military officials argued that the United States ought to begin deploying in 1975 what they estimated the Soviet Union might have in the 1980s.[69] The United States had to remain the number one military power in the world.[70]

Officials also announced a new condition for an adequate deterrent: "perceived balance." "Political sufficiency" or "perceived balance" meant that "no major asymmetrics should exist in the basic factors which determine force effectiveness, and that the forces and capability are perceived by everyone, ourselves, our enemies, and third countries, to be in relative balance."[71] Even if there were no security need for additional weapons, the United States should procure them if United States intelligence predicted that the Soviet Union would eventually deploy such forces.

As Senator Thomas McIntyre, chairman of the Armed Services Subcommittee on Research and Development, explained, "The real Pentagon justification for counterforce is, in fact, not military, but political or diplomatic. They primarily justified

71

these programs on the basis of what they call 'political perception.' " Military officials asserted that without such a capability, the political position of the United States might be adversely affected in the world. The enlargement of U.S. counterforce capability "was designed not to perform a military function in the classic sense but to be used as a diplomatic device or tool in world politics."[72]

In sum, the shift in strategic doctrine that was facilitated by the SALT negotiations produced an extraordinarily provocative chain of political and technological events that were likely to stimulate the arms buildup at a substantially higher level than had been occurring during the 1960s.

Although space does not permit a comprehensive treatment of the ways an enlarged counterforce capability can exacerbate the arms race,[73] one aspect of the rationale for counterforce strategy bears examination here because it is related to the Vladivostok agreement. The question that confronted officials was: if the Soviet Union deployed a counterforce capability, should the United States increase its own counterforce, *offensive* arsenal, leading toward a first-strike strategy; or should it pursue *defensive* development programs aimed at nullifying any Soviet effort to acquire a first-strike capability?

In weighing the pros and cons of counterforce strategy, opponents of the shift in strategic doctrine argued that movement toward an enlarged counterforce capability would exacerbate the arms race (since the Soviet Union would probably seek to match U.S. efforts); increase the lethal capacity of both sides without any increase in security; raise the cost of weapons; cause "crisis instability" either by providing an incentive for a preemptive, disarming first strike by a country fearing attack (in order to insure that its missiles would not be destroyed in their silos), or by putting nuclear weapons on a hair trigger (in the sense that the side fearing a first strike by its opponent would aim to launch its missiles on warning of attack, rather than wait for unambiguous evidence of a first strike before retaliating as would occur in the old deterrence doctrine); increase the likelihood that nuclear weapons would be used in war, not so much between the United States and Soviet Union, as against other countries (since the United States was shifting to a doctrine based on limited warfighting capability); and, by perpetuating the further sophistication of weapons in ways that would make them easier to use on

72

limited battlefields, pose a threat to smaller powers, and encourage them to procure nuclear weapons themselves.

Advocates of the new U.S. strategy asserted that it would make the use of nuclear weapons possible at lower thresholds of violence. This possibility, they said, would increase the credibility of the threat to use them, and thus provide a better deterrent.[74] Nevertheless, proponents of the counterforce doctrine were unable to demonstrate that the vast new expenditures and risks would appreciably increase deterring capacity beyond that of the old doctrine, since limited counterforce strategy was possible by simply targeting existing weapons on Soviet military installations instead of on cities. Obviously, something more was required to justify the vast increase in warhead deployment sought by the Pentagon.

Even the prediction that the Soviet Union would deploy a counterforce capability was not a persuasive argument for a U.S. counterforce strategy, because the most economical and militarily least destabilizing response to such a Soviet deployment would have been to decrease the vulnerability of the U.S. deterrent, not to increase U.S. offensive capability. The latter would stimulate an equivalent Soviet response and encourage the further development of Soviet counterforce weapons. In short, the United States could have nullified the effects of Soviet counterforce deployment by hardening its own silos, by putting some ICBMs on mobile platforms, or by deploying more launchers at sea where they could not be found, so that a Soviet first strike could serve no purpose. Serving no purpose, such costly deployments would have been unlikely, as the ABM case has demonstrated. But such a rational response of self-restraint would not have fulfilled the desire of U.S. military officials for vast new weapons deployments. Thus they rejected it.

Military officials intended first to complete research on the technologically most difficult foreseeable innovations (before the arms controllers could restrict them)—innovations such as MIRVs and MARVs, increased accuracy, and better yield-to-weight ratios. Afterwards, the argument of arms controllers that Soviet counterforce efforts should be met by making U.S. forces less vulnerable would still remain valid and could be used for further weapons innovations. Officials sought to avoid the possibility that the defensive path toward less vulnerability be taken first, because then the country might never deploy offensive, counterforce, hard-target weapons. The same bureaucratic strategy had been used when officials decided not to deploy the technologically easy, high throw-weight missile, and instead sought first to develop the technology for more accurate and higher yield-to-weight, multiple warheads. Development of additional throw weight could come later, if desired, as the technology was near at hand. This in fact happened in the development of the new M-X. Thus the arms control negotiations not only accelerated the pace of certain weapons development, they also encouraged military officials to concentrate their efforts on the most advanced and often most destabilizing technology in order to have it perfected before arms controllers could close off their preferred options.

The negotiations thus encouraged a game of technological leapfrog, in which military planners always jumped ahead to the most advanced technology anticipated. Later on, they could favor the deployment of more stabilizing weapons based on an intermediate stage of technology more suitable for defensive than offensive purposes. This kept up a steady flow of new research and weapons, but it also meant that the least provocative measures to provide for defense, based on intermediate technology, were taken only *after* the more provocative steps of arms innovation, based on advanced technology, were well under way and difficult to stop. The military planners emphasized technological progress much more than genuine defense or protection of people.

Thus officials rejected the militarily most sensible and least costly response to the possibility of Soviet MIRV deployment. The discussions leading to the Vladivostok accord aided this rejection by providing the rationale to build counterforce weapons as a pretext for encouraging the Soviet Union to limit counterforce weapons in arms control negotiations. Before congressional committees, military officials frequently expressed reluctance to develop counterforce weapons; they coupled this professed reluctance with arguments of the necessity to do so in order to help the SALT negotiations. Without this cynical approach, the authorization for such needless and provocative weapons would have been far more difficult. The Vladivostok agreement signaled that the bargaining-chip argument had worked to the advantage of the proponents of more arms and that the crucial doctrinal corner of following a war-fighting strategy with significant counterforce capability had been turned. The pressures for increased armaments had been in part sustained and inflated by the very people who professed to favor arms control.

In brief, the consequences of the shifts in strategic doctrine legitimized at Vladivostok further confirm the accuracy of implicit values A and B. Military officials used the arms control negotiations to help justify and marshal support for development of weapons for which there was no clear security necessity.

Professed Value 2: To Curtail Arms Expenditures

The Ford administration maintained that the Vladivostok agreement provided a substantial saving in military expenditures compared to what would have been spent without an agreement—even though officials announced no major cutbacks in previously planned, upcoming programs. The president declared: "I can say this without hesitation or qualification: if we had not had this agreement, it would have required the United States to substantially increase its military expenditures in the strategic areas." The Vladivostok accord limited the strategic forces of both countries, "thus preventing an arms race with all its . . . economic waste."[75] Kissinger supported this view, telling Congress that it would need to appropriate $5 to $10 billion more than currently requested if it did not support the agreement. Intelligence estimates indicated, according to Kissinger, that in the absence of an agreement, Soviet armaments would have been substantially higher than under the agreement.[76]

The actual amount that would have been spent in the absence of an agreement cannot be known with any reasonable degree of certainty. One can, however, note actual spending patterns and compare levels that were foreseen before the agreement with those favored afterwards, in order to gain some rough estimation of the agreement's consequences.

Before making comparisons, it is necessary to acknowledge several difficulties surrounding the use of data on military expenditures. First of all, only limited data are available for estimating the size of Soviet military expenditures. Even after the rouble figure is determined, the exchange rate to be used for comparative purposes is a second difficult estimate, since official exchange rates do not reflect equivalent purchasing values between roubles and dollars.

Moreover, the relationship between expenditures and armaments is not perfect. Inflation aside, it may be true that in some cases destructive capability—which we seek to measure here—does not rise with a commensurate increase in expenditures. Or, possibly, a decrease in expenditures does not result in a decrease in destructive capability; for instance, if a state purchased a nuclear arsenal during a ten-year period and then stopped all further strategic spending for several years, the nuclear arsenal would still represent enormous firepower. Moreover, two countries with similar expenditures in one year may not have equivalent lethal power, especially if one has previously maintained higher expenditures than the other for a period of years.

In spite of these problems, overall expenditures for military purposes remain the most convenient index of destructive capacity.[77] Especially if one examines data for numerous countries over the long run, it is possible to obtain a fairly accurate picture of the trends in weapons procurement. Regardless of the much-debated causal linkage between arms expenditures and the likelihood of war, it is widely acknowledged that high levels of military spending are undesirable, given a world of scarcity, and that they are considered necessary only because of the continued expenditures of one's opponent.

As the experienced authors of the *SIPRI World Armaments and Disarmament Yearbook* have pointed out, expenditure data are useful for several reasons. First, "the growth in the lethal power of the world's armaments results not so much from increases in the number of men under arms or in the stock of weapons, as from the replacement of existing arms by new and more effective ones."[78] Thus it is necessary to examine the deployment of new weapons or improvements in old ones—both of which require new funds—rather than simply count guns or rockets. Second, expenditure data often reveal trends in weapons development, such as the transfer of resources from constructing new ballistic missile silos to developing multiple independently targetable warheads. Such data are crucial to understanding an arms race that may be in process but is obscured by examination of aggregate expenditures alone. Even a constant or slightly declining level of spending, therefore—if it goes for new research or weapons instead of for maintenance, payroll, and overhead costs—is a likely sign of a continuing arms buildup. Finally, for the limited purposes of this analysis, none of the conclusions drawn would be substantially affected by the somewhat varying estimates of expenditures provided by alternative sources.

With these caveats in mind, one must begin by noting that doubt is cast on the claim that the SALT agreements restricted spending (professed value 2) by the evidence already presented (for implicit values A and B), which demonstrates that the agreement curtailed no major U.S. weapons program in the planning or development stage.

Furthermore, the testimony of officials themselves substantiated the idea that future United States expenditures for new, advanced weapons would be equivalent to or somewhat higher than expenditures of the past. For example, the president explained that the Vladivostok agreement meant "we must continue our present strategic research, development, deployment [and] maintenance program. . . . The net result is that costs will probably go up as we phase out some [weapons] and . . . phase in some."[79] The secretary of defense publicly announced that the Vladivostok agreement would require some "upward adjustment" of spending.[80] Tens of billions of dollars were needed, he said, to shift to greater reliance on new bombers and mobile missiles on land, in aircraft, and at sea.[81] The shift was, in his mind, a necessary response to the agreement's legitimation of deploying enough MIRved vehicles to destroy nearly all land-based ICBMs in a first strike.

The SIPRI data in Table 2-4 show that United States and Soviet outlays from 1970 through 1975 declined slightly in constant

Table 2-4
Military Expenditures

	1970	1971	1972	1973	1974	1975	1976
	Billions of Current Dollars						
United States	77.9	74.9	77.6	78.4	85.9	90.9	99.1
Soviet Union	63.0	63.0	63.0	63.0	61.9	61.1	61.1
Total	140.9	137.9	140.6	141.4	147.8	152.0	160.2
	Billions of 1973 Dollars and 1973 Exchange Rates						
United States	89.1	82.1	82.5	78.4	77.4	75.1	77.4
Soviet Union	63.0	63.0	63.0	63.0	61.9	61.1	61.1
U.S. and USSR							
Total	142.1	145.1	145.5	141.4	139.3	138.2	138.5
World total	254.1	252.9	258.4	258.5	263.0	268.2	276.0
U.S. and USSR							
as % of total	56	57	56	54	53	51	50

SOURCE: Tables are compiled from data reported in Stockholm International Peace Research Institute, *World Armaments and Disarmament: 1977*, pp. 222-225.

dollars and increased slightly in current dollars.[82] The decline in U.S. real expenditures during 1970-75 was due more to the eroding effects of inflation than to any scaling down of arms because of the Interim Agreement.[83] In current dollars, the FY 1976 budget climbed 28 percent above the FY 1972 budget that was in effect when the Interim Agreement was signed. But purchasing power had not kept pace with inflation. Inflation "has achieved what the Pentagon's Congressional critics never could do. It has reduced the nation's defense program."[84] Most significantly, the slight decline in real expenditures from 1970-75 was *reversed* during the first complete fiscal year following the Vladivostok accord. (See Table 2-5.) After the Vladivostok

Table 2-5
Total Obligational Authority of United States Military Expenditures

	Billions of Current Dollars	Billions of Constant 1979 Dollars
Fiscal Year		
1970	75.6	144.9
1971	72.9	131.1
1972	76.6	127.1
1973	79.0	121.8
1974	81.8	115.5
1975	86.2	111.6
1976	95.9	116.4[a]
1977	108.3	122.6
1978	116.8	123.7

SOURCE: Department of Defense, "Total Obligational Authority," mimeo., p. 21.
NOTE: [a] First complete fiscal year after the Vladivostok Accord.

agreement was signed, Pentagon requests for expenditures were far above previously authorized levels. Secretary Schlesinger presented what he called a "turnaround defense budget" that, in addition to maintaining the existing military establishment, would purchase new strategic weapons and provide a large initial down payment for future growth in military spending. Officials designed the budget request for fiscal 1976 to reserve an unusually large portion of the appropriation increment for future years, thus providing the basis for a steadily increasing defense budget. Even taking inflation into account, officials requested an $8.2 billion increase over the previous, pre-Vladivostok year.[85] Despite unusually large congressional cuts in the requested defense budget for FY 1976—cuts made primarily to stay within a self-imposed congressional limit on total governmental spending—the increase in the budget over the previous year exceeded the anticipated rate of inflation by more than 1 percent, thus permitting a slight real growth in the defense program.[86]

In its projected budgets after the Vladivostok agreement, the Defense Department sought an increase in its *real* purchasing power of 2 to 4 percent annually between 1976 and 1981.[87] By contrast, in the Defense Department's *Annual Report* for the fiscal year preceding the Vladivostok agreement, the Pentagon had projected a smaller real increase of about 1.5 percent yearly. By 1980, the Pentagon planned to be spending $148 billion annually.[88] Part of the increase was earmarked for the accelerated development of new strategic weapons that were increasingly stressed in the wake of the Vladivostok accord.[89]

Although the Vladivostok agreement covered strategic weapons, Pentagon officials estimated that a 25 percent increase in strategic spending was necessary over the two or three years following the signing of the accord.[90] Defense Department officials said they needed 40 percent more for equipment in fiscal 1976 than in the previous fiscal year (during which the Vladivostok accord was agreed upon), in order to modernize forces and increase weapon inventories. The Air Force asked for $600 million more than in the previous year and made requests for fourteen new programs.[91] Requests for aircraft and missiles in 1976 were higher by 30 percent than amounts spent in 1975.[92]

The size of increases within the budget category of research and development, which influenced the size and direction of future budgets, also revealed that the arms competition was continuing without restraint. The budget increased by eight times from 1950 to 1978, even after discounting the effect of inflation. (See Table 2-6.) Expenditures for research, development, testing, and evaluation fluctuated but generally rose from 1950 to 1964, after which they declined somewhat in real terms until FY 1976. However, during the second budget year following the Vladivostok accord, the Pentagon was able to reverse the decline. Director of Defense Research and Engineering, Malcolm Currie, said that the fiscal year 1976 request of $10.2 billion, compared with $8.6 billion appropriated in 1975, represented a "conscious decision to reverse the downward trend in . . . RDT & E [Research, Development, Testing, and Evaluation] in the last decade . . . and establish an overall RDT & E program for the long haul." New exploratory research and development "have been increased purposefully to enhance and revitalize our base of technology options for the future."[93] The United States goal was "to maintain world leadership in defense-related technology."[94]

According to Currie, increased spending for research and development of new weapons was vital because "Vladivostok limits

Table 2-6
Department of Defense Budget for Research, Development,
Testing, and Evaluation

Fiscal Year	Millions of Current Dollars	Millions of 1978 Dollars
1950	$ 413	$ 1,394
1951	867	2,796
1952	1,490	4,413
1953	1,953	5,612
1954	2,178	6,080
1955	2,400	6,547
1956	3,080	7,970
1957	3,961	9,733
1958	4,270	10,131
1959	4,652	10,783
1960	5,310	11,960
1961	6,131	13,526
1962	6,319	13,734
1963	6,376	13,629
1964	7,021	14,753
1965	6,236	12,867
1966	6,259	12,578
1967	7,160	13,898
1968	7,746	14,505
1969	7,457	13,351
1970	7,166	12,064
1971	7,303	11,629
1972	7,881	11,928
1973	8,157	11,802
1974	8,582	11,491
1975	8,866	10,750
1976	8,923	10,132
1977	9,993	10,604
1978	11,416	11,416

SOURCE: Department of Defense mimeo.

the total [number of launchers]. It obviously places a premium, a growing premium, on technological progress." Currie reported and agreed with a Soviet Communist Party statement that "the scientific technological revolution has become the most important part of the competition between the two opposed world systems."[95] In a prepared statement, Secretary James Schlesinger said: "The stringent limits on bomber numbers under present circumstances and a prospective arms limitation agreement . . . both reduces the relevance of cost-quantity tradeoff calculations and enhances the incentive for higher performance in deployed units."[96] The Vladivostok accord thus failed to slow the most important and potentially destabilizing part of the arms buildup—the race for technology. At the same time that the latter brought with it the likelihood of increasing military expenditures for weapons technology, the secretary of defense said the arms control agreement weakened traditional budgetary restraints.

In sum, military spending did not decrease after the Vladivostok agreement. The eroding effect of inflation curtailed expenditures, as the secretary of defense pointed out, more than the Vladivostok agreement did. New budget requests and appropriations, even in real terms, were higher than had been appropriated or anticipated before the agreement. Similarly, projected budgets increased after the Vladivostok agreement. It would be a mistake to conclude that the Vladivostok accord caused all of these increases but clearly the accord did not dampen spending.

Some evidence demonstrated that spending increased because the accord speeded the shift toward a partial counterforce strategy and away from existing land-based stationary missiles. Equally important, arms spending continued at high levels for the purpose of purchasing weapons that did not substantially increase either side's ability to deter an attack. By increasing their relative lead in military technology over other countries, and by taking no serious steps to diminish the role that military power played in international affairs, the Vladivostok agreement stimulated military expenditures in other countries and encouraged the continued consumption of scarce resources for construction of weapons of mass destruction. Thus, U.S. policy served another unarticulated value: *to maintain*—rather than curtail—*high levels of United States and world military expenditures* (implicit value C).

Professed Value 3: To Lay the Foundation for Future Arms Reductions

Secretary Kissinger stated that the Vladivostok agreement was extremely valuable because, once ceilings were established for launch vehicles, "reductions will become much easier."[97] President Ford similarly declared, "we have . . . created the solid basis from which future arms reductions can be . . . negotiated."[98]

The official view that the Vladivostok agreement would lead to arms reductions was based upon the assumption that past arms races had produced self-generating forces for an arma-

81

ments buildup. Each side aimed to counteract the anticipated potential buildup of the opponent. Once the Vladivostok accord stabilized competition, anticipatory weapons develpment would be nipped in the bud and reductions could be made. As Kissinger explained, "Once a ceiling exists, both military establishments can plan without the fear that the other will drive the race through the ceiling, which is one of these self-fulfilling prophecies which has fueled the arms race." The Ford administration thus portrayed the agreement as "one of the turning points in the history of the post-World War II arms race."[99]

In spite of official pronouncements supporting the professed value, there were many actions that negated it. In the first place, the preceding discussions of implicit values A, B, and C cast doubt on the likelihood of any future reductions. On the basis of Secretary Kissinger's own logic, Vladivostok would lead to arms reductions only if the agreement had, in fact, stopped an open-ended arms race. The earlier analysis has demonstrated that the accord did not accomplish this. The premise upon which Kissinger's conclusion depended was absent and thus the conclusion was faulty.

By their own concrete acts, officials have shown that they accepted and anticipated a continued arms buildup. The ceilings were targets for enlarging lethal capacity and future defense budgets. Official statements and proposed policies for the post-Vladivostok years demonstrated the unlikelihood of any arms reductions. In the president's words, "we must continue our present strategic research, development, deployment, maintenance programs. And we are going to move into the present program some additional new weapons systems." Ford felt an "obligation to stay up to that ceiling" of 2,400 launchers and 1,320 MIRVs. Despite the need to build *up* to those levels, he predicted that "the new agreement . . . will constrain our military competition over the next decade."[100] Even the latter assertion, one should note, contained the assumption that the arms competition would continue, not that reductions would follow in the wake of the Vladivostok meeting. Kissinger's defense of the agreement's virtues also demonstrated the prevailing assumption that disarmament would not occur: "for a 10-year period the arms race will not be driven by the fear of what the other side might be able to do but only by the agreed ceilings that have been established."[101]

The absence of any serious intention to reduce armaments

82

was substantiated by the failure of the original wording of the agreement to call for any reductions before the expiration of the accord in 1985. However, between the signing of the agreement on November 24 and the detailed, public explanation of it by the president on December 2, intense public criticism condemned the ceilings as being far too high. As a result, Kissinger successfully sought to change the language of the aide-mémoire to *allow*, at least, for reductions before 1985, if they could be mutually agreed upon. Kissinger acknowledged that the language had been changed to meet criticism of the accord.[102]

It is equally revealing of the administration's attitude toward disarmament that Kissinger admitted that the ceilings for MIRVed vehicles could possibly have been lower, but that he had made no effort to establish a lower limit:

> . . . the MIRV limits resulted substantially from American proposals and not from Soviet proposals. Basically, the judgment of our Defense Department was that once the MIRVs went beyond the point where, over a period of time, the land-based missiles might become vulnerable, a difference of a *few hundred* was not decisive. And therefore we geared the MIRV limits to a minimum program that we had established as being in the interest of our own security and made the proposed number consistent with that program. *No major attempt was made to see whether a hundred less would have worked.*[103]

This is an astonishing statement when one recognizes that 100 extra MIRVed vehicles for each side might easily represent 1,000 additional nuclear weapons for each country. One should recall that the Soviet Union, for example, has only about 240 cities in excess of 100,000 people. Thus this "negligible" increase to the U.S. arsenal would be far more than enough to constitute a satisfactory deterrent in itself. A prime candidate for transporting some of these additional MIRVs would be the new Trident submarine, which can carry 24 missiles, and which costs about $2 billion. At that rate, even 100 fewer MIRVs on Tridents, for which Kissinger made no effort to negotiate, could have saved $8 billion.

Of course, officials did not ordinarily express so clearly their indifference to reducing weapons. For example, Kissinger later asserted that, "The only way we could plausibly have achieved lower numbers is to begin building up our strategic forces dramatically in order to produce an incentive to reduce numbers on the other side."[104] In spite of Kissinger's earlier admission that he had not even tried to get a lower MIRV level in negotiations with the Soviet Union, he illogically argued that to have gotten a lower ceiling, the United States would have had to build up to higher levels. Without attempting to reduce or even restrict arms to the U.S. deployments then existing, Kissinger advocated building to higher levels to achieve arms control. While negotiations proceeded, of course, both sides would deploy more weapons, making an agreement to reduce armaments even less likely. This was typical of the specious thinking and the familiar bargaining-chip arguments that had stimulated the arms race many times since the end of World War II. Despite Kissinger's own illogic, he chided critics: "It doesn't make any sense to instruct us to get better numbers without at the same time being prepared to pay the price of the arms buildup that will be the *only* possible incentive by which an agreement for lower numbers could be achieved."[105]

The *New York Times* reported that, toward the end of the Nixon Administration, the Soviet Union accepted a ceiling of 1,100 MIRVed vehicles for the United States to 1,000 for the Soviet Union, with the expectation that the five-year ceiling would probably continue after 1980. (In 1978, the Carter administration sought to return the MIRV ceiling to roughly this level.) As Kissinger acknowledged, the 1,320 level was a U.S. proposal. "All this suggests that the impetus for the high MIRV ceiling came from the Pentagon, rather than the Kremlin."[106] According to Alton Frye, "the Air Force and Navy were so committed to MIRV deployment that neither within the Defense Department nor at the committee of principals was there a concerted campaign to include a MIRV ban in the SALT package."[107]

The press also reported that the United States had offered a lower MIRV ceiling only four months earlier. But Kissinger argued that the earlier U.S. proposal was not lower than the November agreement. "The July proposal, first of all, called for a five-year agreement. If you double the number that we proposed for the five-year agreement, you would have a higher number than the one we settled on for 10 years."[108] Kissinger inexplicably assumed that the number of arms by 1985 would be twice the number in 1980, and that the five-year levels would not be extended another five years, a possibility the Soviet Union reportedly was willing to consider. In addition, the statement demonstrated Kissinger's presumption that any arms control agreement would simply ratify the armament procurement plans already in existence, and that the buildup would continue indefinitely. It contradicted his earlier public stance, taken in praise of the Vladivostok agreement, that one arms control treaty would increase the chances for comprehensive reductions in the future. Following the Interim Agreement, the behavior of the United States demonstrated its assumption that the arms race would continue in the face of agreements professedly concluded for the purpose of arms control. SALT I, which limited the deployment of ABMs, had indicated that both sides would adopt a no-damage-limiting posture.[109] That is, each side would accept as a fact that it was vulnerable to destruction by the other side in case of war. No efforts would be undertaken to try to erode the other side's nuclear capability to inflict unacceptable damage on an attacker, because to do so would stimulate the other side to new weapons deployment. By not deploying ABMs in more than one site, both sides seemingly recognized the futility of any arms programs that moved toward a counterforce capability.

However, in the Vladivostok agreement officials completely eliminated that assumption of SALT I. MIRVs meant that damage-limiting capability would be developed, even though sufficient capability could not be developed to make one side or the other really invulnerable to attack.

Since the Interim Agreement already had limited all strategic vehicles except bombers, the existing *pre*-Vladivostok limitation removed any pretext for enlarging offensive forces. If arms reductions would in fact follow the establishment of a ceiling, as claimed, then the Vladivostok accord (SALT II) should have set ceilings lower than the number of weapons allowed in SALT I. At the least, the Vladivostok negotiations should logically have extended the Interim Agreement in slightly modified form and unconditionally banned multiplication of offensive warheads.[110] Instead, negotiators paved the way not simply for adding more sophisticated weapons to existing arsenals, but also for legitimizing the deployment of hundreds of new warheads.

Furthermore, the Vladivostok agreement failed to increase the prospects for general disarmament because it did nothing to decrease incentives for weapons procurement by other countries. Among the most relevant of these incentives was the pace-setting role of the United States and Soviet Union in armaments development. If the superpowers deployed more sophisticated weapons and moved quickly from one weapon generation to another, other countries were bound to feel a need to update their forces also. If the major powers gained prestige, power, wealth, and psychological dominance from their possession of arms, it was hypocritical and discriminatory for them to ask the weaker countries of the world to refrain voluntarily from also seeking to obtain instruments of military power.

For example, the nuclear Non-Proliferation Treaty was an effort at enforcing inequity.[111] Only the countries without nuclear weapons accepted obligations for international inspection of nuclear installations. The countries that had nuclear weapons did not. If honored, such controls would in practice make it impossible for the militarily weaker states to produce nuclear explosions while the superpowers would continue development, increasing their hegemony even more. In Article VI, the superpowers undertook to negotiate "in good faith on effective measures relating to cessation of the nuclear arms race at an early date and to nuclear disarmament, and on a treaty on general and complete disarmament." If implemented, that measure would have begun to decrease the power differential between nuclear and nonnuclear states. However, neither superpower has taken the provision seriously.[112] Similarly, the Limited Test Ban Treaty of 1963 had included a promise of "seeking to achieve the discontinuance of all test explosions of nuclear weapons for all time."[113] After more than fifteen years, that goal has yet to be realized.

The SALT negotiations did not take into account the hopes or fears of the nonnuclear-weapons countries. Limiting ABMs and establishing high ceilings on strategic launchers meant little to the nonnuclear states; even a 50 percent cut in existing launchers would still have left the superpowers in an overwhelmingly superior position in strategic weapons. What the Vladivostok agreement allowed and even encouraged—the qualitative side of the arms race—carried the greatest risks for the small powers. Miniaturization, increased accuracy, and improved yield-to-weight ratios of nuclear explosives make such weapons more appropriate for fighting "limited" wars in the weaker countries. The battlefields for such new weapons, as Alva Myrdal has pointed out, are not likely to be the homelands of the superpowers, protected by strategic weapons, but the homelands of other nations.[114] President Ford's public declaration (even if merely a verbal threat) only seven months after the Vladivostok meeting, that nuclear weapons were a serious option for use in war against North Korea, could not help but increase North Korea's desire for nuclear weapons.[115]

Because the superpowers were unwilling to work toward international equity, the societies that were cast, through no fault of their own, into inferior conditions and status, were likely to seek to redress the imbalance of power and wealth against them by imitating the least desirable features of superpower behavior: in the quest for achieving genuine equity as full members of the planetary family, they would be tempted—encouraged by the militaristic values and actions of the superpowers—to waste resources on expenditures for items such as aircraft and nuclear explosives.

The prospects for disarmament were dimmed further by growing Soviet and U.S. arms exports. The estimated value of worldwide arms exports by all suppliers rose from $4.4 billion in 1963 to $8.7 billion by 1973 (in constant 1972 dollars).[116] During the year of the Vladivostok agreement, the United States government alone sold about $8.3 billion worth of military equipment to seventy different foreign countries. Direct sales by manufacturers, plus aid provided by the U.S. government, brought the 1974 total of arms given or sold by Americans to $12.5 billion,[117] or more than twice the level of the previous year and about ten times the average level of the late 1960s. U.S. arms exports from 1972 through 1974, the years of the SALT I and Vladivostok agreements, exceeded total sales in the previous two decades.[118] On the basis of a growing number of multi-year contracts, Pentagon officials predicted that a high volume of foreign sales would continue for the foreseeable future.[119]

The United States exported more arms in 1973 than all other countries combined.[120] Because of the long U.S. tradition of arms sales, about two-thirds of world armaments outside of the Soviet Union and the United States are U.S.-made and -distributed.[121] If one includes the lesser munitions exported by hundreds of small companies, the value of military equipment the United States either sold, lent, or has given away since World War II totals about $100 billion. Selling munitions to foreign armies has been so lucrative that over 1,000 U.S. corporations produce or export arms. Of the fifty largest industrial companies in the United States, thirty-two make or export munitions. The State Department's Office of Munitions Control has reported in vivid detail the extent to which United States wealth and many working people's livelihoods are intertwined with arms sales. The munitions manufactured by General Motors Corporation, for example, required ten pages simply to list the categories of weapons, ranging from rifles, bayonets, and flame throwers to "biological agents adapted for use in war to produce death or disablement in human beings or animals, or to damage crops and plants." Even smaller companies, long associated with consumer goods, produce an imposing array of equipment. The Bulova Watch Company, for instance, turns out "mechanical and electronic ammunition manufacturing machines, devices for activation and devices for detonation of missiles . . . missile . . . arming devices, [and] missile fusing devices."[122]

In order to increase United States power and profits, officials sought to promote rather than to restrict the sale of armaments.[123] As the Department of Defense and Secretary of Defense James Schlesinger have acknowledged, arms exports have enhanced the political hegemony of the United States. Officials specifically designed the supply of weapons to foreign governments to increase U.S. influence over those governments, and "to maintain the political and economic advantages that accrue from the resultant supplier relationship."[124] When Senator Edward Kennedy proposed slowing arms transfers to the Persian Gulf area, Schlesinger rejected the idea, saying "We are engaged in attempting to maintain influence in these areas."[125] In another instance, he explained, "The degree of influence of the supplier is potentially substantial, and typically, those relationships are enduring."[126]

Military advisers and technicians usually followed military sales. In the year after the Vladivostok agreement, the Defense Department sent out 132 technical assistance and training teams to 34 foreign governments because of foreign military sales contracts.[127] Since 1950 the United States has trained 428,000 foreign military personnel.[128] These missions not only increased United States influence abroad, but also made foreign military establishments more sympathetic toward U.S. strategic interests and more dependent on continued good relations with the United States in order to receive maintenance support, spare parts, technical improvements, and training.

A related objective in providing military assistance and sales has been to continue "an uninterrupted access to bases and facilities important to the worldwide U.S. military posture."[129] To protect its hegemony, the United States has promoted the transfer of arms to other governments to increase their stake in U.S.

predominance and to make them more pliable in allowing this hegemony to continue.

The United States also has sold arms abroad in order to lower the per unit cost of weapons to the Department of Defense. As General Fred C. Weyand, Chief of Staff of the U.S. army, explained: "From the pure economics of it, [the military equipment] the foreign military buy pays for a share of the research, development, and engineering, and the tooling up costs."[130] In addition to subsidizing the production of weapons, selling arms to the Third World also has been a convenient way to enlist the poor of the world to aid an unstable United States economy, to redress shortages in its balance of payments, to recover petrodollars, and to expand the profits of arms manufacturers.[131]

The United States further promoted military assistance and sales in order to maintain political stability—sometimes through repression of reform movements—in the recipients' domestic politics in the hope that that would in turn contribute to stability of the international order in which the United States enjoyed preeminence. The vast arms exports increased the political and economic power of military persons and institutions in all of the recipients' societies. Because military organizations are inherently authoritarian and therefore uncongenial to democratic processes, to augment the power of such organizations with money, weapons, and training programs made it more difficult to build a world in which military power would play a decreased role.

In sum, the superpowers have contributed greatly to the arms competition among smaller nations. This competition is so difficult to dampen that some officials of smaller powers have argued that the problems of regional arms races can be solved only in the context of worldwide disarmament.[132]

Future arms reductions were also unlikely to flow from the Vladivostok agreement because it did not prohibit enough weapons to reduce the number of people in military production who in the long run exerted pressures for more armaments. This was an important deficiency because the arms race since World War II had been fueled by a combination of domestic bureaucratic, corporate, and labor pressures for military spending, as well as by the perceived threat of the Soviet Union. Determining the extent of the various influences is beyond the scope of this study. Nevertheless, there is substantial evidence that domestic pressures for weapons development constituted a significant driving force in the arms buildup—a force often more influential than either the capability or the intention of the Soviet Union.[133]

These pressures included corporate desires for easy profits, labor unions' thirst for more jobs and higher wages, a national political obsession and official psychological need to remain the strongest military power in the world, bureaucratic pressures for continuing or expanding ongoing programs, and the scientific community's inclination to exploit and expand the limits of technology for weapons purposes.[134]

The high profitability of defense contracts to major corporations has been well documented.[135] It would be an exaggeration to suggest that arms producers determined U.S. national security policy; still, the Vladivostok agreement was clearly constructed in such a way that corporate interests were not harmed by the ceilings. Insofar as the agreement legitimized the deployment of weapons at new levels, it aided the future profits of defense industries and at the same time kept the unions happy. Many legislators translated votes on military appropriations into jobs in their respective districts.

The desire to maintain the United States as the most powerful military force in the world also inflated budgets and arsenals beyond actual security needs.[136] Secretary Schlesinger declared: "I am convinced . . . the American public wishes to remain [militarily] second to none. There may be difficulties in any fiscal year or any program year, but over the course of a decade or more . . . the United States will not consent to a position of being second to anyone else."[137] Since not all other countries of the world were happy with the superior position of the United States, this attitude encouraged arms competition. If there were benefits for the United States in being number one, there were costs to some of those who were not number one. In their efforts to diminish the United States lead, rivals deployed more weapons, and the United States in turn sought to meet or exceed these new efforts. Precise equality between the United States and the Soviet Union was hardly possible, given the biased perspectives from which each set of leaders viewed the opponent's arsenals. In any case, each side doubtless preferred superiority to equality. As long as those conditions prevailed, the simple notion that the United States should be second to none made arms reductions impossible.

The widespread belief that additional military capability would contribute to the bargaining power of a country in its international relations has also encouraged the growth of arsenals, even if such growth was unrelated to the enhancement of security. Admiral Moorer, for example, said that if the Soviet Union achieved strategic superiority, "we will pay a very high price in the effectiveness of our diplomacy . . . even were that superiority to have no practical effect on the outcome of an all-out nuclear exchange."[138] Secretary Schlesinger believed that the never-ending drive to stay ahead of the Soviet Union "is also important for symbolic purposes, in large part because the strategic offensive forces have come to be seen by many—however regrettably—as important to the status and stature of a major power."[139]

The desire to remain the biggest military power was buttressed by the familiar argument that the Soviet Union would take arms control seriously only if the United States negotiated from a "position of strength." That statement was an older, more general version of the bargaining-chip argument. As Kissinger told those who wanted lower ceilings, an "arms buildup . . . will be the only possible incentive by which an agreement for lower numbers could be achieved. . . . The only way we could plausibly have achieved lower numbers is to begin building up our strategic forces dramatically."[140] According to Kissingerian logic, in order to hit the target of disarmament, one should aim at armament. Of several weaknesses in this approach, the one relevant here is that such a negotiating strategy encouraged powerful domestic economic and bureaucratic constituencies to coalesce behind new programs and made them difficult to stop in subsequent arms control proceedings.[141]

Malcolm Currie advanced a technological variation of the argument for seeking superiority over other countries: "[Military] technology . . . appears to offer us our place in the sun—the means to insure our security and economic vitality."[142] Currie believed that the best way "to protect our technological lead is to continue to advance and exploit our technological base. In so doing, we can show the Soviets that they will never catch up, that the military balance will be maintained because the technological balance will always be in our favor." Currie warned, "The stakes in this [technological] competition are high. They involve national survival."[143] By seeking military and technological

91

superiority, the United States stimulated the arms race and demonstrated its unwillingness to limit its military programs to a minimum necessary for security.[144]

Furthermore, misleading government statements nullified effective domestic political action by critics of the arms race and thereby facilitated continued military expenditures. For example, officials virtually promised that arms reductions would follow the Vladivostok agreement, but, in fact, they were hardly any more likely than before. Kissinger's skillful manipulation of language either confused or convinced reporters sufficiently that they failed to press him for concrete elaboration of his claim that the Vladivostok agreement reduced armaments.[145] Kissinger said the accord's "significance becomes all the more clear if one compares the numbers not with some hypothetical model that one might have in mind but with what would have happened in the absence of this agreement. . . . [I]t is not a fair comparison to compare these [Vladivostok] figures with some abstract model."[146] In that manner he silenced critics who called for lower ceilings by accusing them of forming judgments based on "hypothetical models" of the future, in contrast to his policies based on "what would have happened in the absence of this agreement." The latter, of course, was merely a prediction, which was also unavoidably hypothetical. Kissinger did not estimate what would have happened if the United States had offered to dismantle its MIRVs before the Soviet Union deployed any at all.

Some critics said that the United States had such a strong deterrent, including sizable overkill, that there was no need for more weapons, even if the Soviet Union developed them. Kissinger said this condition "would be true at almost any foreseeable level, or at any level that has been publicly suggested by any of the protagonists in this debate. This is a problem that is inherent in the nature of nuclear weapons and in the size of existing nuclear stockpiles." Astonishingly, reporters apparently accepted this as a reasonable explanation for why the United States should have more weapons. Kissinger had said that overkill would exist at any of the contemplated strategic ceilings, thus the ceilings might as well be higher (to have more overkill). In other words, since both sides had more than enough weapons to destroy the other several times, a ceiling high enough to deploy several thousand more weapons needed no new justification. Kissinger also commented upon the criticism that the Vladivostok accord did not stop the qualitative arms race: "It is of course extremely difficult to stop qualitative changes in the best of circumstances, because it is very difficult to control what one is not able to describe, which is inherent in the nature of technological change."[147]

Although that explanation seemed reasonable on an abstract level, it was simply untrue in practice. MIRVs, an important part of the qualitative arms race, could have been reduced or prohibited relatively easily. Under the Vladivostok guidelines both sides planned to distinguish, through national means of verification, between MIRVed and non-MIRVed vehicles. If that could be done, there was no technical reason why all MIRVs could not have been banned on all land-based ICBMs and, if desired, even on SLBMs. The rule agreed upon was that any vehicle tested in a MIRV mode would be counted against the MIRV total, so the limit could have been set at any level. Similarly, it would have been easy in 1974 to prevent deployment of the even newer maneuverable reentry vehicles (MARVs) by prohibiting their testing (which could be verified). Once they had been tested, control would become more difficult. Moreover, the Interim Agreement's ban on future deployment of MIRVed or otherwise more sophisticated ABMs demonstrated that weapons yet undeveloped *could* be banned.[148] Kissinger misled reporters and the public by suggesting that control became easier after weapons had been developed and tested, when actually the opposite was true. Because national verification of testing programs was simpler than controlling deployment once the technology was in hand, a ban on each of the following major weapons would have been technically easier to achieve before they were tested than afterwards: the atomic bomb, the hydrogen bomb, ICBM, SLBM, ABM, MIRV, and MARV. The problem was not to control the unknown, as Kissinger described it, but to prevent the testing of the experimental.

The preference of military and State Department officials for developing rather than banning new weapons was clearly revealed in the negotiation over mobile missiles. The United States, in late 1974 or early 1975, proposed that mobile missiles be prohibited. U.S. officials thought the Soviet Union would have several advantages in mobile missiles if they were allowed. First, U.S. citizens and Congress might disapprove of mobile missiles moving around the country on truck or rail launchers. Second, such missiles could be stolen more easily by terrorist groups, if not in the United States, then in other countries that might eventually get them. Third, the Soviet Union had more territory in which to hide mobile missiles than did the United States. As a result, the Air Force began to test an air-launched intercontinental missile in order to use it as a bargaining chip to induce the Soviet Union to give up their land-mobile missiles. But after the Soviet Union agreed to the U.S. position, the United States reversed itself and decided that it was more important to keep new missile options open than to prohibit them.[149] The U.S. later developed the M-X, which avoided most of the problems indicated in the first and second reasons above. In brief, a prohibition on a new weapon was deliberately rejected by the U.S. government at the time when verification of the ban would have been most feasible.

Moreover, Kissinger claimed that the Vladivostok agreement "reduces substantially the incentive of an unlimited arms race. The nightmare in qualitative changes had always been the linkage of qualitative change with quantity."[150] Again, it was deceptive to say that the Vladivostok agreement reduced the incentive for qualitative improvements. As indicated above, the limits on the number of launchers *emphasized* additional sophistication and destructive power per unit. Kissinger's distortions undermined consciousness-raising efforts by those genuinely seeking disarmament. By reporting but failing to probe Kissinger's specious explanations, the press aided the administration in its deception of the public.

The continued and largely uncontested existence of bureaucratic pressures for military procurement also undermined the propects for arms reductions resulting from the Vladivostok meeting. The creation of powerful bureaucratic and economic forces in arms production had changed the face of American politics since World War II. These forces showed a Parkinsonian proclivity to resist any decline in their institutional expressions and to promote their own expansion. Many of the requests for new weapons were buttressed by arguments that the Pentagon should be able to spend a certain percentage of total U.S. output. Military officials sought to convince Congress that the military establishment had a "right" to maintain a given percentage of spending regardless of more narrowly defined security needs. They tried to establish expenditures for military equipment on an economic footing similar to that for education, roads, and environmental protection. In their minds, military spending should be viewed as a value in itself. Yet, none explained why military spending should grow as the total economy or national budget grew, despite an era of détente, a widely acclaimed arms control agreement, and an abundance of nuclear weapons on hand from previous purchases.

Pentagon officials also sought to preserve their status within the government as a whole. Moderate as the effects of the Interim Agreement were, Admiral Moorer testified before the Senate Appropriations Committee that the Joint Chiefs of Staff (JCS) agreed to the Interim Agreement only after receiving "assurances" from the White House that in return they would get "a very extensive research and development program, and . . . aggressive improvement and modernization programs to include the B-1 and the Trident." The Joint Chiefs approved the 1972 five-year accord because it was a temporary, stop-gap measure, not a permanent treaty: "No matter what we did during this 5-year period, there was no way we could add to our force levels. . . . We had made the decision to level off our force levels [even in the absence of any agreement]. . . . Now we never would have accepted this [Interim] agreement as a treaty; we accepted it as an interim agreement for that 5-year period because we felt we knew that we could not add to our forces during that time."[151] It is clear, therefore, that the SALT I agreement was not designed to stop the arms buildup. In 1972, Melvin Laird, then secretary of defense, proposed a cruise missile program as part of a package of "strategic initiatives" designed to win the Joint Chiefs of Staff's approval of the accord. Since such missiles would not be covered by the Interim Agreement, Laird suggested them as a legal way to evade the restrictive impact of the agreement upon defense planners.[152] As indicated below, later U.S.-Soviet arguments over the cruise missile jeopardized the effort to transform the Vladivostok accord into a more formal agreement.

Obviously, the SALT ceilings were determined heavily by what the Pentagon wanted to deploy;[153] they were maintained only for as long as the Defense Department thought they would not be restrictive. In return for accepting the admittedly nonrestrictive provisions of the Interim Agreement, the Pentagon received promises that it could later deploy its new weapons then undergoing research and development. To the extent that an agreement might have meant a serious halt to arms procurement, the Pentagon's enormous bureaucratic forces would have opposed it.

Finally, the desire of some groups of scientists and government bureaucrats to exploit the limits of technology for weapons advances contributed to the drive for new armaments.[154] The intense exploitation of technology for military purposes has been more pronounced since 1945 than ever before. Between the First and Second World Wars, military support for science and technology absorbed less than 1 percent of the military budgets of the major powers. The share of major military budgets devoted to research and development ranged from 10 to 15 percent during the late 1950s, and has remained at that level. U.S. research and development costs rose from about $30 million in 1939 to 330 times that in 1975.[155]

One of the most important features of the technological process that has stimulated the armaments buildup has been the long lead-time required for new weapons. Ten years may pass between the initial stage of development and eventual deployment. This has meant that each side has felt it is necessary to begin immediately the development of weapons that the other side *might* deploy only ten years later. In any case of uncertainty, officials have wanted to go ahead with development to prepare for the worst possible contingency. Each side has therefore built weapons not for current security needs, but to counteract weapons anticipated for some years in the future. Since the range of possibilities for the opponent's arsenal has been almost limitless, a full range of development programs has continued on both sides.

Once various programs have been begun, of course, the energies and money put into them for research have been used as arguments to justify eventual production and deployment. Moreover, as the opposing side has probably developed similar weapon prototypes independently, this development has been used as a "justification" for deployment of the weapons that years earlier were studied only because of a possibility that the other side might seek to gain a qualitative technological advantage. The MIRV was a case in point.

The rapid pace of applying technological innovations to new weapons often has little to do with any external military threat. First the technology is developed—as in the case of the MIRV— and then officials search for a strategic doctrine that will justify

96

the "need" for the technology.[156] The unilaterally determined pace of innovation has, in the long run, no doubt *decreased* U.S. security. Although the United States has been in the vanguard of military power, other states have followed—buying, borrowing, or copying the technology for destructive weapons that the United States invented, and which, when possessed by others, will later come to haunt us.

Once new weapons were off the drawing boards and in production, officials tailored strategic doctrine to justify military "requirements" that were pegged to production capability rather than to objective security needs. Alain C. Enthoven, former assistant secretary of defense for systems analysis, testified that in preparing budget requests for "necessary" weapons, "year after year the *requirement* came out to use all of the available production capability."[157]

The technological emphasis on weapons development has had another self-generating feature. Because development of modern military equipment requires highly skilled people and specialized resources, the laboratories and industries engaged in development are regarded as national assets. Persons employed there cannot be allowed to drift away to other tasks because of fear that new development might be missed in one year, which would have dangerous consequences ten years later. To keep these resources intact means that they must be fully employed at all times, and this in itself creates many new technical possibilities for sophisticating weapons.[158]

As weapons become more complex and expensive, the number of persons involved at the peak of development on any given weapon becomes larger. An ever-growing technological agenda is therefore required to keep those additional research teams employed. The reason that the employment capacity at the peak of a program's development cannot be held constant is that officials consider it impossible to increase the length of time required for the development process. If it took longer, the weapon might become obsolete before it had been deployed. The development process therefore not only required that research and development teams be fully employed at all times, but also meant that the increase in their size was difficult to control.

Although it is beyond the scope of this chapter to explain the reasons for the arms buildup, the preceding discussion offers evidence that the arms race has not been exclusively a pattern of action and reaction in which each side responds to the minimum level necessary to protect its security in the face of incremental changes in the arsenal of the opponent. On the contrary, there is little evidence to suggest that the action-reaction pattern even is the most important influence in the arms race.[159] The rate of increasing armaments has not been noticeably influenced by any improvement in the relations of the two countries. Bureaucratic pressures for weapons development, coupled with a desire to exploit technological opportunities as they arise, have led to a much more rapid sophistication of weaponry than would have resulted from an arms race stimulated merely by the action-reaction pattern.

In assessing the consequences of the arms control negotiations, Senator Edmund Muskie observed: "SALT doesn't mean anything unless it is going to produce some reductions on both sides of capabilities which we both [the United States and Soviet Union] regard as important to our respective strategic policies. If we are giving away nothing, the thing isn't worth anything."[160] By that standard, the Vladivostok accord was worth very little.

As the foregoing discussion suggests, instead of laying the foundation for future arms reductions (professed value 3), the Vladivostok agreement mirrored and conformed to the desires of the forces seeking more armaments. It expressed implicit value D—*to reach an agreement (1) that was tailored to the officially held assumption that the arms competition would continue indefinitely; (2) that maintained political and military incentives for other countries to increase the size and cost of their arsenals; (3) that enjoyed the support of those persons and institutions with vested interests in continuing the arms buildup; and (4) that avoided deflating economic, bureaucratic, and technocratic pressures at home for more arms spending.*

Professed Value 4: To Reduce International Tensions
Exacerbated by the Arms Race

General George J. Brown, the Chairman of the Joint Chiefs of Staff, told the Senate Armed Services Committee that the Vladivostok agreement "is a significant milestone toward improving relations between the U.S. and U.S.S.R., reducing the risk of war, and enhancing the chances of world peace."[161] In explaining the significance of the accord, President Ford said that it would "prevent . . . an arms race with all its terror, instability, [and] war-breeding tension."[162] In his state-of-the-world message to Congress, Ford said that a treaty incorporating the Vla-

98

divostok agreement "would mark a turning point in postwar history and would be a crucial step in lifting from mankind the threat of nuclear war."[163]

The conclusion that the Vladivostok agreement would decrease tensions rested on the assumption that it had stabilized armaments significantly. However, the agreement allowed the deployment of new submarines, bombers, missiles, warheads, cruise missiles, and the development of additional "improvements." It encouraged movement away from a posture of finite deterrence based on assured destruction, toward the less stable posture of attaining a damage-limiting capability against land-based missiles. The legitimization of MIRVs increased the possibility that in time of crisis one side might launch a preemptive strike in an effort forcibly to disarm its opponent, at least in part. "Crisis instability—the penultimate danger of the nuclear era, second only to the ultimate horror of an actual nuclear exchange—clearly has been brought closer by the failure at Vladivostok to limit MIRV missiles to low levels."[164] In assessing the political impact of the Vladivostok conference, the editors of the *New York Times* wrote, "The new agreement seems almost calculated to increase instability. By vastly increasing the number of warheads, it enshrines the doctrine that a nuclear war-fighting capability is needed. Planning to fight a nuclear war, rather than merely to deter one, is certain to reduce the inhibitions against using nuclear arms."[165] Tensions arising among various other countries would also be exacerbated by continuing United States-Soviet buildups, rapid technological innovation, and the export of advanced weapons. Precision-guidance systems increase the prospects for nuclear weapons being used against third parties.

To summarize, the Vladivostok agreement may have increased military instability between the superpowers. It also failed to discourage superpower participation in intrastate violence. Neither did the accord do anything to dampen tensions arising from growing militarism and internal class or ideological conflicts in other countries that often, at least since World War II, precipitated violence involving direct or indirect military participation by the superpowers. Once again, the Vladivostok accord produced a value impact that contrasted sharply with professed values. By enabling the arms race to continue without significant restriction, its practical effect was *to perpetuate an international political process heavily influenced by military power and therefore to*

99

continue both the intranational and international tensions arising from further militarization of the planet (implicit value E). To the extent that tensions were lessening during the 1970s, détente was less a product of restraint in military procurement than of general great-power realignments due to changing political conditions.

Table 2-7
A Comparison of Professed and Implicit Values
in U.S. Policies for Arms Reduction

Professed Values	*Implicit Values*
1. To slow the arms race.	A. To allow the arms buildup to continue without significant restriction.
	B. To legitimize a further arms buildup.
2. To curtail arms expenditures.	C. To maintain high levels of U.S. and world military expenditures.
3. To lay the foundation for future arms reductions.	D. To reach an agreement (1) that was tailored to the officially held assumption that the arms competition would continue indefinitely; (2) that maintained political and military incentives for other countries to increase the size and cost of their arsenals; (3) that enjoyed the support of those persons and institutions with vested interests in continuing the arms buildup; (4) that avoided deflating economic, bureaucratic, and technocratic pressures for more arms spending.
4. To reduce international tensions exacerbated by the arms race.	E. To perpetuate an international political process heavily influenced by military power and, therefore, to continue both the intranational and international tensions arising from further militarization of the planet.

An Opposing View of the Arms Buildup

The present case study demonstrates that the Vladivostok accord did not reverse or even significantly limit the arms buildup. Nor, it seems, did officials really try to take any steps toward a

100

disarming world. Both superpowers were intent upon deploying their newest generation of weapons and keeping their options open for future deployments. To some extent, each side was locked in competition to develop new technology as soon as the other side did. There are of course some who may dispute these findings. It is instructive to examine briefly the views of one of the most respected and informed critics of some of the conclusions reached in this case study. Albert Wohlstetter, in an exchange with other students of arms control,[166] has argued at some length that there has been no arms race between the two superpowers for at least fourteen years. According to Wohlstetter, U.S. intelligence predictions of future Soviet strategic deployments in the 1950s and 1960s underestimated actual Soviet deployments. Because predictions had consistently been too low, the U.S. did not overreact to Soviet deployments, and thus there was no action-reaction pattern between the two states that could have stimulated an arms race. "If we underestimated, then exaggerated fears cannot have driven us in a race."[167] Second, Wohlstetter presented data showing that in recent years Soviet expenditures for strategic deployments were increasing while U.S. strategic expenditures were decreasing.

Because Wohlstetter's analysis typifies so much of official and academic thinking, it is useful to respond briefly to these two points. The fact that Wohlstetter showed U.S. intelligence predictions to have been too low in anticipating Soviet deployments does not refute the notion that U.S. officials may have exaggerated the threat posed by Soviet hardware actually in existence. This possible exaggeration could have produced unwarranted U.S. strategic deployments and an excessively confrontational diplomatic posture that stimulated the arms buildup. Wohlstetter seemed to recognize the possibility of exaggerating the Soviet threat when he criticized the Vladivostok agreement in another context: "Vladivostok also illustrates the absurdity of the exaggerated threat/'worst case' dynamic. Here, overblown estimates of future Russian programs may lend a specious urgency to rapid agreement—another 'miracle' for the Secretary [of State]."[168] But Wohlstetter did not acknowledge that an "overblown estimate" or exaggerated threat based on an intelligence underestimate makes the *under*estimate little different from an overestimate in terms of the practical consequences for deployments and for the action-reaction pattern. Such an acknowledgment would, of course, have negated Wohlstetter's

101

argument that underestimates could not have produced an overreaction.

More importantly, there is another reason why an action-reaction pattern could have come into play in spite of intelligence underestimates by the United States. Arms proponents like Wohlstetter seem to assume that U.S. weapons procurement was somehow linked to intelligence predictions, and that, if predictions were low, then U.S. deployments could not have been too high. However, since 1945 the U.S. government has simply wanted to be first among all nations in military technology and power. (Wohlstetter curiously overlooks frequent official statements and actions embracing this goal.) U.S. officials have deployed weaponry far in excess of security needs in order to perpetuate United States superiority. In doing so, they have encouraged the Soviet government—itself not satisfied with being an inferior power—to deploy a vast arsenal. One need not necessarily believe that the United States overestimated Soviet forces and then overreacted to these predictions, to know that as a matter of historical fact the United States has deployed more weapons than needed for deterrence, and the Soviet Union has spent most of its strategic effort during the 1950s and 1960s trying to catch up to the United States.

In addition, it is at least possible that because of the U.S. lead—and regardless of U.S. intelligence underestimates—the Kremlin may have deployed its weapons at an even faster pace than originally planned. If so, American actions could very well have stimulated Soviet reactions that made potentially accurate U.S. intelligence predictions appear too low with the passage of time.

Moreover, regardless of the extent to which one believes that Wohlstetter has successfully argued that the weapons buildup was not due to an action-reaction pattern, his argument in no way refutes the idea presented in this case study that unilateral U.S. decisions, unrelated to security needs, were an important stimulus to the annual appropriation of billions of dollars for more strategic weapons. Domestic pressures for more arms may produce vast deployments, regardless of whether intelligence predictions are too high or too low. Such pressures also discourage intensive efforts to develop models of a disarming world.

To recapitulate: (1) the presence of U.S. intelligence underestimates fails to prove that an action-reaction pattern of arms competition could not have developed anyway, and (2) the al-

102

leged absence of an action-reaction pattern fails to prove that the United States did not deploy far more weapons than were necessary for security or than were desirable for achieving a disarmed world.

If, for the sake of arguing Wohlstetter's second point, we assume that U.S. expenditures on strategic weapons have recently decreased in real terms, this decline does not constitute convincing evidence that a race for weapons superiority has ended. The United States had a considerable headstart in the arms competition, and has recently been able to remain in the competition even with declining strategic expenditures. Except over a long period, strategic expenditures in themselves may prove little about whether the United States is vigorously competing at the forefront of important strategic innovations. That is especially true for U.S. breakthroughs which have produced more sophisticated weapons at less cost.

In two of the articles in *Foreign Policy*, Wohlstetter insisted that the term "race" should not be used to describe the strategic rivalry between the United States and Soviet Union. To justify the word "race," he argued, the United States government must be "rapidly increasing its strategic budgets and forces."[169] This statement reveals Wohlstetter's assumption—one also held by many officials—that a constant level of annual expenditures for strategic weapons is a norm. If the U.S. government spent less this year than last, Wohlstetter would think of this as a decrease in the amount spent for strategic weapons, even though there is clearly an increase in the accumulated total expenditures for strategic arms. Buying missiles is not like buying groceries, where the food is soon eaten and must be resupplied. Once missiles and submarines are purchased, they remain in the arsenal for years. Wohlstetter ignored that U.S. expenditures annually exceeded the amount that would have been necessary simply to pay for maintenance of old weapons. The government in fact has been upgrading its forces each year, even when less is spent than previously.

Wohlstetter's idea that the word "race" must be reserved for only a "rapidly increasing" rate of expenditure may be contrasted with the view of long-distance runners who consider themselves in a race even though for much of the race they are not increasing their pace at all. Any movement toward a goal can be a race—even without any increase in pace—if in the process one competes with another.

103

Since the United States has decreased its real expenditures for strategic weapons while the Soviet Union had increased that segment of its annual budget, Wohlstetter commented that "it is surely stretching it to talk of a 'race' between parties moving in quite different directions."[170] In a later article, he again declared that the superpowers "have been moving not only at different speeds, but in *opposite directions*. If that doesn't do lethal damage to the arms race metaphor, nothing will."[171]

For Wohlstetter and other strategic analysts to say that the United States was moving in an "opposite direction" to the Soviet Union is the equivalent of telling the front-runner in a marathon race that if he decreased his rate of progress, he would be running in the opposite direction to the runner in last place who is picking up speed. In fact, the front-runner is moving in the same direction, and he will win the race if he does not decrease his pace too far. Similarly, both the Soviet Union and the United States have been expending additional money every year for more sophisticated weapons—even if the United States has spent less per year than in some previous years.[172] The two states are headed in the same direction, but at different speeds, at least insofar as budgetary statistics reflect the pace of "progress." Because Wohlstetter judges arms procurement from the norm of a constant level of expenditure rather than from the norm of a disarming world, he sees a decline in annual strategic expenditures as a "different direction." Even if United States strategic expenditures declined when compared to previous years, annual expenditures for new hardware may still be to the advocates of disarmament an undesirable continuation of the same direction.

In the preceding discussion, I have assumed the validity of Wohlstetter's data in order to point out the contrast in perspective between one who assumes that ongoing arms policies are largely satisfactory and one who believes that policies should aim toward the minimization of collective violence. Without going into detail about the actual data, however, one should note that some of Wohlstetter's critics have disputed his interpretation of recent spending trends in the strategic area.[173]

Wohlstetter also denies that U.S. destructive capability has increased. He comes to this conclusion by emphasizing a decline in the total yield of all deployed strategic weapons. Any decrease in overall strategic megatonnage available for destroying soft

104

targets means little, since both sides have far more capability than required to destroy all soft targets even in a second strike. Hard-target destructive capability, however, has increased enormously because improvements in accuracy and increases in the number of warheads more than offset any decline in total megatonnage deployed in 1975 as compared to pre-MIRV deployments.

Why has Wohlstetter worked so hard to prove that there has been no arms "race?" Perhaps because he believes that, "We may want, in general, to stop or curb a race, but not a competition in arms."[174] By demonstrating that no arms race has occurred, Wohlstetter facilitates continued weapons development and deployment. Therefore, according to Wohlstetter, it is not a race for the United States and the Soviet Union to spend billions and billions of dollars for strategic arms year after year; it is competition that one should not stop. Regardless of whether one uses the word "race" or "competition" to describe the continuing application of massive energies and resources to producing military equipment, it is clear that present policies in Washington and Moscow have failed to make progress in arms reductions.

A GLOBAL HUMANIST APPROACH

Comparison of Professed Values, Implicit Values, and the Minimization of Collective Violence

This analysis began by examining the widely professed value of promoting international peace, stability, and national security through arms control. Officials articulated four instrumental values in their program for realizing the terminal value: to stop the arms race, to curtail military expenditures, to pave the way for future arms reductions, and to lessen tensions caused by arms competition. These values are in harmony with the first value of global humanism, but in contrast to official practice. U.S. policy actually served interests reflecting an alternative set of implicit values. The following were imbedded in United States behavior: (A) to allow the arms buildup to continue without significant restriction; (B) to legitimize and stimulate arms procurement; (C) to maintain high levels of military expenditures; (D) to reach an agreement that enjoyed the support of persons with vested interests in continuing the arms buildup, and that in the domestic area avoided deflating economic, bu-

105

reaucratic, and technocratic pressures for more arms spending; and (E) to perpetuate the tensions arising from a continued military buildup.

No doubt most officials would deny that they preferred any of the preceding consequences of policy as an end in itself. However, they rated the preservation of the U.S. economic-political position higher than other values, and to accomplish their ends they selected militarily oriented instruments. Thus, in practice, officials served values A through E, and often furthered interests that produced value impacts which no one endorsed publicly. Both the executive and legislative branches preferred these five implicit values to the consequences that would attend a scaling down of U.S. military strength.

If these implicit values express the operational code of official behavior, then the professed value itself must be qualified. A more accurate statement of the central value impact of United States arms control policy would be: to harm the long-range security of U.S. citizens and the prospects for world peace. When the values implicit in U.S. behavior—as opposed to rhetoric—are stated explicitly, it becomes clear that they directly contradicted the aim of minimizing collective violence.

Two principal differences separate the values expressed in United States policies at Vladivostok from the first value of global humanism: U.S. policies represent a willingness to maintain and even increase the destructive capacity of the superpowers' nuclear deterrents, whereas advocates of global humanism seek to nurture an *un*willingness to use or to possess nuclear weapons. Global humanists search for ways to undermine the legitimacy of massive national arsenals and to facilitate disarmament by transforming the existing international system into a demilitarized system of world order. In contrast, U.S. officials did not question the legitimacy and utility of the sovereign-state worldview as a guide for policymaking. (The contrasting perspectives are more fully summarized in Table 2-8.)

Because the preceding conclusion—that U.S. policy damaged the long-range prospects for security and peace—may at first appear too severe a judgment, it deserves further elaboration. It rests, of course, primarily upon the delineation of implicit values. In general, the agreement at Vladivostok facilitated a further arms buildup, continued the East-West and North-South tensions resulting from arms competition, and prolonged the poverty of the Third and Fourth Worlds by wasting human and

106

material resources on military technology and hardware. The accord also discouraged effective political activity by opponents of military spending and proponents of disarmament because it appeared to demonstrate serious governmental efforts to stop weapons buildups.

Even if one believes that the preceding statement of implicit values is too harsh an indictment of U.S. policy, two consequences stand out among the various SALT proceedings: neither party demonstrated any intention to disarm or to change the structure of the international system in order to make disarmament more feasible. Regardless of the differences among governmental opponents and proponents of the Vladivostok agreement, the notion that nuclear weapons were a legitimate instrument of foreign policy was never in question.[175] Even if the agreement is viewed in the glowing terms of its most ardent advocates, it unequivocally embraced as legitimate both nuclear deterrence and growing destructive capability. Arms control in its modern Vladivostok variant would not lead to disarmament even if continued indefinitely.

The SALT negotiations also discouraged a reassessment of foreign policy priorities and the development of a strategy for international systemic change as a long-range technique for minimizing violence. Without a fundamental reassessment no new initiatives can replace incremental arms control which at best only slightly adjusts the balance of terror, the particular mode of the arms competition, and the gradual spread of nuclear weapons around the world. Such limited arms control does not substantially increase human security. As Senator Edmund Muskie, chairman of the Subcommittee on Arms Control, concluded after extensive hearings on armaments: "Without control of the arms race, there can be no long-term security. In an arms-race situation, the continuous effort to maintain an ever-changing strategic balance simply dooms us to buying more and more defense with no net increase in our national safety."[176] Officials preoccupied with remaining number one militarily did not think about building a new global system to implement disarmament. Nor did they publicly consider the extent to which current armaments were an inevitable consequence of the existing international system.

Genuine security in the long run can come only through a dismantling of the weapons of mass destruction and the creation of a global system to facilitate peaceful change and prevent fu-

Table 2-8

Selected Values of Global Humanism Compared to U.S. Policies for Arms Reductions

Global Humanism	U.S. Policy
Peace	
1. Major arms reductions are desirable. First steps toward disarmament are presently possible.	1. In the foreseeable future, major arms reductions are neither desirable nor feasible. Despite rhetoric, officials have sought to retain nuclear deterrence as a national security policy.
2. An international norm against the use of nuclear weapons should be strengthened.	2. Officials have sought to increase the preparedness of the United States to use nuclear weapons.
3. The United States should make a unilteral declaration never to be the first to use nuclear weapons.	3. Officials have refused a no-first-use pledge.
4. By showing greater political and military self-restraint, the role of military power in international relations should be diminished.	4. Officials have sought to retain the role of military power in diplomacy because such power helps keep the United States "number one."
5. It is more important to slow nuclear proliferation through self-restraint in weapons deployment than to stay equal in overkill to the Soviet Union.	5. Although officials have been unhappy with nuclear proliferation, they have sacrificed little to prevent it. Officials have shown less interest in discouraging proliferation than in deploying more sophisticated weapons and maintaining massive arsenals with substantial overkill.
6. Profit or other material benefits from foreign arms sales should be discouraged.	6. U.S. officials have favored foreign arms sales in order to increase U.S. influence abroad, recover petrodollars, provide jobs at home, and solve balance-of-payments problems, as well as to increase the profits of U.S. manufacturers.
7. The power and authority of the superpowers should be shared more equitably within a global security system that could make disarmament feasible.	7. Officials have sought to retain and increase the national power of the United States within the world system.
8. Security policy should be guided by a sense of human solidarity that transcends the nation rather	8. The sovereign state system in which states compete for more and more power is the appropriate worldview

than by a desire to maximize national military power.

9. The security of people must be met more by satisfaction of human needs than by accumulation of national power.

10. Pursuit of security for the human race should influence policy at least as much as the drive for security for any national government

Economic Well-being

1. Military spending distracts from the effort to eliminate world poverty and the general achievement of economic and social well-being.

Human Rights and Social Justice

1. Maintaining present levels of military spending by the superpowers undermines global justice by perpetuating inequity of wealth.

2. Because of an overemphasis on military power, corrupt, elitist, and repressive foreign governments are often supported because they will be loyal U.S. allies. Emphasis on these types of military allies should end.

Ecological Balance

1. Present arms buildups exacerbate the problems of wasteful resource depletion, unnecessary pollution, and ecocide.

for guiding national security policy.

9. U.S. officials have emphasized the security of the state by enhancing its military power

10. People's security is less important than the security of the state.

Economic Well-being

1. Military spending is more important than promoting the economic and social well-being of the world's poverty-stricken people.

Human Rights and Social Justice

1. The U.S. should not decrease its military spending in order to eliminate inequity. In fact, the U.S. should keep spending high enough to be able to defend its present position of wealth from threats posed by other nations.

2. Whether a foreign government is pro- or anti-United States is more important than whether the government deals justly with its own people.

Ecological Balance

1. Environmental concern should not be allowed to distract from weapons innovation and production. Conservation of resources has been of no significant influence on military policy.

ture weapons deployments. By discouraging steps for transforming the international system, by exacerbating the arms buildup, and by legitimizing a less stable strategic doctrine, the Vladivostok agreement contributed to a loss of security for Americans.[177]

From a global, humanitarian perspective, the national security policies of the superpowers could with some justification be viewed as a conflict of interests between the national security managers in Moscow and Washington implicitly working together on the one hand, and the security interests and humanitarian needs of the majority of the people of the world on the other. The most important disagreement in the debate about weapons policy was not between the military establishments of the two countries; it was between the officials of both countries on one side, who wanted more arms, and the few people of both countries working for arms reductions and system change on the other. The editors of the *New York Times* correctly observed that the Vladivostok agreement was "an agreement between the military on both sides—achieved through the intermediary of the chiefs of government—to permit the build-ups each desired."[178] One reason for the agreement and its particular timing was the desire of Brezhnev, Ford, and Kissinger to perpetuate the atmosphere of détente and to resist pressures mounted against it by military and civilian hard-liners in both the United States and Soviet Union.[179] To the extent that this appraisal was accurate, there existed two unpromising alternatives: either to accept a Vladivostok-type agreement in order to decrease the influence of militarists, even though they virtually dictated the terms of the agreement anyway; or to achieve no agreement at all and allow the opponents of détente to exercise their influence more openly.

Events since the Vladivostok meeting confirmed the reality of this pessimistic set of alternatives. At the meeting, officials expressed the intention soon to conclude a more formal treaty based on the Vladivostok accord. However, serious disagreement erupted in drafting the formal document. The military officials of both the United States and Soviet Union raised new issues. They pressed their respective governments so intensely that the entire Vladivostok accord was jeopardized and delayed for more than four years. Because of pressures by the Department of Defense, the United States reneged somewhat on its earlier positions and insisted upon restrictions for the new Soviet

110

medium-range "Backfire" bomber.[180] The Soviet Union attempted to restrict development and deployment of the U.S. cruise missile.

The United States strongly resisted limits on the cruise missile.[181] It could evade Soviet radar and, with its terminal guidance, strike within thirty yards of a target after flying thousands of miles.[182] It could carry nuclear warheads and be launched from land, airplanes, or submarines. Secretary Kissinger reported that the United States could potentially deploy 11,000 cruise missiles on existing bombers and transport planes and 10,000 more on nuclear submarines. All would be capable of reaching targets in the Soviet Union.[183] New weapons such as these made the Vladivostok ceilings virtually meaningless in terms of halting the weapons race. When one or the other side insisted that such weapons be included, then even a relatively nonrestrictive agreement like the Vladivostok accord could hardly be consummated—precisely because banning the new weapons would make the agreement too restrictive. The folly of trying to stop the arms race without imposing serious restrictions was clearly exposed.

Without going into detail, it is possible to see that the Carter administration has failed to overcome the gap between professed and implicit values that characterized previous administrations. During his campaign for the presidency and in several important presidential addresses, Carter pledged to reduce armaments and military expenditures.[184] None occurred. In his inaugural address, Carter promised to persevere in efforts "to limit the world's armaments to those necessary for each nation's own domestic safety. We will move this year a step toward our ultimate goal—elimination of all nuclear weapons from this earth."[185] However, Carter increased the United States' destructive capability and deployed more advanced equipment for improved nuclear warheads early in his presidency.[186] These acts increased the U.S. capacity to fight a nuclear war but contributed little to, and possibly detracted from, U.S. "domestic safety." Testing and development proceeded on a wide range of new strategic equipment, such as the M-X missile and the Trident submarine. Only the B-1 bomber was cancelled. But that decision was taken less to halt the arms buildup than to take advantage of the militarily more useful and technologically more sophisticated cruise missile, which had overtaken the B-1 during its long and costly development.

111

Carter at first predicted an early SALT II agreement based on revisions of the Vladivostok principles, but negotiations faltered, in part because the Carter administration would not accept a ban on cruise missiles or the inclusion of them within ceilings for strategic launch vehicles in an eight-year agreement. The cruise missile programs, one should recall, were started in part because the Interim Agreement of 1972 put a five-year limit on ballistic missiles. Thus the cruise missile program, which helped the Pentagon circumvent the spirit of SALT I limitations on ICBMS and SLBMS, became a stumbling block for SALT II. Once cruise missiles were tested and prototypes produced, verification of future ceilings would become so complicated that new SALT efforts to prohibit the missile appeared unpromising.

A SALT II agreement on other matters, however, remained within the realm of possibility. During 1978 the United States and the Soviet Union appeared to be reaching agreement on a treaty incorporating most of these provisions:

(1) A seven-year treaty (in contrast to ten years discussed previously) that would set these restrictions: (a) a top limit of 2,250 strategic launch vehicles, or slightly less than a 10 percent reduction from the Vladivostok limits; (b) a maximum of 1,320 MIRVS (as agreed at Vladivostok), including within this total ICBMS, SLBMS, and bombers equipped with cruise missiles; (c) no more than 1,200 of the 1,320 could be ICBMS and SLBMS, and no more than 800 could be ICBMS; and (d) the large Soviet land-based missile, the SS-18, would be restricted to 308.

(2) A three-year protocol limiting the deployment of the cruise missile. The protocol would place a range restriction of 1,500 miles on cruise missiles launched by bombers and a range limit of 360 miles on the testing and deployment of cruise missiles launched from ships, submarines, or land. It would also ban for a three-year period, the deployment of the M-X.[187]

Although the potential agreement is somewhat more restrictive than the Vladivostok limits, the conclusions drawn from analyzing the Vladivostok accord still largely apply. The most positive new development in the potential treaty is clearly the possibility of achieving some qualitative limits on deployment of new weapons. However, it appears that such limits may continue only for a period of three years, and the limits apply only to weapons that will not be ready to deploy anyway until the protocol has expired. Reminiscent of the first deployment of MIRVS, one must note that this potential treaty will, in fact, reject the opportunity to ban the cruise missiles before they are deployed. Instead it will legitimize their deployment, albeit with restricted ranges at first. Surely the Pentagon knows that later it will be almost impossible to verify range restrictions with only satellite observation. Hence once the Soviet Union matches the limited U.S. cruise missile capability, the door will be open for deployment of cruise missiles of ever greater ranges, justified by the United States' inability to know with certainty what the Soviet Union has deployed. Whether this will occur depends heavily upon whether the restriction can be extended indefinitely, once a three-year ban is achieved. If it cannot be made permanent, then on this point U.S. officials carefully tailored their position to allow the continued development of the cruise missile on a limited basis for three years with the testing and deployment of it coming at approximately the time that technology will have advanced sufficiently to provide an effective cruise missile of greater range.

The slight reduction in overall strategic vehicles, while welcome, is not very significant. The limits will still legitimize vastly greater destructive capability than was deployed when the Vladivostok accord was reached. With the prospect of adding numerous warheads to allowable launch vehicles, even a formalized treaty will yield an extremely porous ceiling. Significantly, in the minds of most officials, the MIRV ceiling was desirable not for the purpose of abolishing nuclear arms, but for maintaining the utility of the land-based ICBM force of the United States. By using an arms control agreement to protect Minuteman missiles from a preemptive Soviet attack, U.S. officials have demonstrated their desire to retain these weapons as ends in themselves, rather than as a means to enhance security. They are no longer an essential part of a credible deterrent. With Soviet satellites pinpointing U.S. land-based missiles as targets, and with the MIRVing of Soviet missiles (stimulated by earlier U.S. deployment of MIRVs), U.S. stationary missiles are becoming obsolete. Thus, even with all of the new enthusiasm generated for arms control by Carter and Paul Warnke, the potential agreement legitimizes the continuation of a nuclear force far in excess of what is required for deterrence. The agreement does much more to protect and increase war-fighting capability than to reduce or abolish it.

Similarly unpromising policies were carried out by the Carter administration on military expenditures and international arms

113

sales. Although in 1976 and early 1977 Carter promised to cut the defense budget, by 1978 he called for a $56 billion increase in military expenditures over a five-year period. The increase, after accounting for inflation, would mean a growth of 2.7 percent a year. The president sought a 3 percent real increase for the 1978-79 fiscal year.[188]

The president also made firm promises to reduce international arms transfers, declaring that the United States could not be "both the world's leading champion of peace and the world's leading supplier of weapons of war."[189] In a statement promising restraint, he said arms sales would be "an exceptional foreign policy implement, to be used only in instances where it can be clearly demonstrated that the transfer contributes to our national security interests." Yet the preliminary figures for FY 1977 and FY 1978 showed a rise in arms sales, with total sales for 1978 likely to reach a record $13 billion.[190] The United States remained by far the world's leading exporter of arms. A lengthy study prepared for the Senate Foreign Relations Committee by the Library of Congress concluded that "rather than being used as an 'exceptional foreign policy implement,' United States arms transfers continue to occur on a rather routine basis."[191] In sum, Carter's rhetoric seemed more enlightened than that of his predecessors. He and his official appointees generated new activity and enthusiasm for arms control. But there was not the slightest evidence that the arms buildup—even the strategic arms buildup—was being reversed.

The record of arms control negotiations since 1945 demonstrated that, at best, the United States has tailored arms control policy to restrict weapons in areas of relative unimportance, while allowing the arms competition to continue earnestly in areas where new research and development lead toward more sophisticated weapons. The United States offered either proposals that were designed to produce such one-sided advantages for the United States that the Soviet Union could not be expected to accept them, or else proposals that covered such limited areas of the weapons buildup as to make a consummated agreement largely inconsequential for the arms race. For example, after World War II, the Baruch proposals to establish international control over nuclear testing would have given the United States a monopoly on the technology to produce nuclear weapons—a result obviously unacceptable to the Soviet Union.

The proposal of the mid-1950s to stop further production of fissionable materials for weapons purposes came only after the U.S. had stockpiled so much material that the plan would have had no significant restrictive effect on the United States nuclear arsenal, but would have handicapped all other potential or actual nuclear powers, which had much smaller stockpiles. Even though an agreement banning atmospheric nuclear testing was concluded in 1963, officials earlier had opposed a test ban until the United States reached the point at which any further testing would probably have contributed little to arms innovation. Moreover, officials agreed to end atmospheric tests only after legalizing the further testing of weapons underground. In any case, the 1963 treaty did not decrease the intensity of testing. During the eighteen years between 1945 and 1963, nuclear powers tested 477 devices (including 98 underground). During the ten years between 1963 and 1973, nuclear powers exploded 456 devices (including 48 French and Chinese tests in the atmosphere).[192] Officials recognized in the 1950s that a ban on the first test-firing of ICBMs was the easiest way to prevent deployment of ICBMs, but serious pursuit of such a plan was delayed until after the missiles had been tested, making control much more difficult. The Threshold Nuclear Test Ban Treaty of 1974 prohibited test explosions exceeding 150 kilotons, but this limit was the size of ten Hiroshima bombs, and test devices exceeding that amount represented no more than 10 percent of the Soviet and American tests during the years immediately preceding the new accord.[193] Similarly, the superpowers discussed ceilings on delivery vehicles only after the number of vehicles had become less important than developing MIRVs and precision guidance systems. A detailed analysis of postwar arms talks would confirm the idea that arms control proposals bore fruit only in areas of weapons development that were peripheral to the principal dimensions of the arms buildup, while new areas for arms competition remained unrestricted.

To conclude: Because of important domestic pressures for an arms buildup, bolstered by United States-Soviet competition, new destructive capability was being added to the arsenals of both sides during every year in which the two superpowers discussed arms control accords. The arms buildup continued despite widely acclaimed arms control agreements and despite evidence that the buildup decreased humanity's overall security. In the absence of radically different policies, there is good reason to expect that the future world will contain even more potential for violent cataclysm than the past.

An Alternative Framework

A policy approach based on the values of global humanism would take initiatives to (1) halt the testing and deployment of new weapons;[194] (2) reduce military budgets by a regular percentage each year; (3) reduce and eventually abolish national military arsenals; (4) prohibit the production of military equipment; (5) establish a global monitoring agency to inspect and verify all agreements limiting and reducing arms; (6) study the use of civilian resistance and nonviolent techniques for defense and social change; (7) establish a transnational peace force to help protect security during the transition to a new peace system; and (8) make plans for converting domestic industries to peaceful purposes.

This approach would shun prolonged arms control negotiations that are used to legitimize armaments and to justify unneeded weapons. Many national initiatives to reverse the arms buildup can be taken by either superpower without jeopardizing its security during the first one or two years, even if there were no immediate reciprocation. Acts of self-restraint or initial arms reductions should probably precede negotiations in order to avoid the following negative consequences that frequently accompany diplomatic efforts:

—Arms control negotiations often focus attention on inequalities in weapons deployed by two sides, so that the inferior side steps up its efforts to become equal, while the superior side tries to move farther ahead in order to be able to negotiate from a position of strength.

—Weapons that might never have been deployed, or that might not have been deployed so soon, are quickly developed to serve as bargaining chips to "negotiate away" during arms control talks. However, weapons developed as bargaining chips often are later deployed in expanded arsenals.

—The domestic vested interests that favor military expenditures are so powerful that often only cosmetic agreements, formalizing what would have been done without any agreement, are possible.

—If an agreement is eventually reached, the Department of Defense often can be moved to accept a treaty only if it is promised something in return, such as the right to develop a more advanced and more destructive weapon.

—Continuing arms control negotiations encourage the public to believe, mistakenly, that the government is doing all that can be done to end the arms buildup.

Because the arms competition is driven mainly by international political conflicts or by domestic pressures for weapons expenditures, it is not likely that arms can be reduced by focusing mainly on negotiations for arms reductions. Substantial reductions will occur only when a sufficient number of people press their governments for decreased expenditures and a transformation of the present international system in which military power plays a key role in settling disputes. Negotiations will not bring this shift in citizens' attitudes and values.

If negotiations for disarmament were preceded by wide public education for planetary citizenship and diplomatic efforts at system transformation, then they would be very useful. But they would then become a process for registering and facilitating a fundamental shift in the priorities of the superpowers, rather than a diplomatic exercise aimed at discovering a rare formula that both sides can agree upon without significantly decreasing their military weapons or abolishing the existing war system.

Reorientation of U.S. policies can be aided by a government decision to devote substantial bureaucratic resources to developing models of a disarming and of a disarmed world. In the long run, of course, global agencies will be required to monitor and enforce disarmament and facilitate peaceful change. The focus of global humanists is therefore on *system* change, not on incremental arms control measures that set high ceilings on equipment and fail to treat the fundamental causes of arms buildups and collective violence.

None of the major forces propelling the world toward more and more arms can be dependably halted or disarmament achieved without some fundamental changes in the existing nation-state structure of political organization. At this stage of history, that structure is both unacceptably dangerous (because war could be suicidal for an entire civilization) and totally unnecessary (because modern communication, technology, and values could, if properly applied, support a system that allowed only peaceful settlement and enforcement of political decisions). The "only" barriers to disarmament and a preferred system of world order are political. Thus a life-sustaining shift in the beliefs and values of U.S. citizens could replace the contemporary neo-Westphalian political leadership with a leadership less alienated from reality and better equipped for the fulfillment of human needs, including security, in the twenty-first century.

For skeptics who doubt that such shifts are possible, it is instructive to note the rapid expansion in the size of the group with whom people identified during the rise of European nationalism in the seventeenth and eighteenth centuries. Dramatic changes are possible in a relatively short time. A growth of global community and modern breakthroughs in information technology permit dependable policy coordination without heavy-handed, hierarchical political structure.[195] Moreover, global economic and technological currents are running so strong that the issue probably is no longer whether a global political tapestry is now being woven. Instead, it is concern that the new creation be artfully conceived, harmoniously constructed, and vividly colored by humane values, instead of being tailored for the benefit of the world's few and erected to cover up the overt and covert violence of global society.

Indicators of World Order Progress

The following questions provide convenient points of departure for assessing the performance of the United States (or another great power) in minimizing collective violence in the subject covered by this case study:

1. Has the government made a firm commitment—in terms of behavior as well as rhetoric—to global system change that will eventually make disarmament feasible?

2. Has the government devoted substantial resources to developing models of a disarming world?

3. Has the government increasingly sought impartial non-military means for dispute settlement, such as accepting without reservation the compulsory jurisdiction of the International Court of Justice?

4. Has the government sought to subject its foreign arms sales to international inspection and regulation?

5. Has the government supported educational efforts aimed at developing citizens' loyalties to reach beyond the nation-state to the global human community?

6. Has the government halted the deployment of new strategic weapons?

7. Is destructive capability in national arsenals decreasing?

8. Is military spending for strategic weapons decreasing, both absolutely and as a percentage of the national budget?

9. Are international arms sales decreasing?

10. Has the government passed legislation that dampens or prohibits the accumulation of profit as a stimulus to the production and sale of military equipment?

11. Are the combined financial, educational, institutional, and communications resources of the domestic proponents of disarmament increasing in comparison to the same resources possessed by the military-industrial-scientific complex that favors arms production?

I. *Interim Agreement Between the United States of America and the Union of Soviet Socialist Republics on Certain Measures With Respect to the Limitation of Strategic Offensive Arms*

The United States of America and the Union of Soviet Socialist Republics, hereinafter referred to as the Parties,

Convinced that the Treaty on the Limitation of Anti-Ballistic Missile Systems and this Interim Agreement on Certain Measures with Respect to the Limitation of Strategic Offensive Arms will contribute to the creation of more favorable conditions for active negotiations and limiting strategic arms as well as the relaxation of international tension and the strengthening of trust between States,

Taking into account the relationship between strategic offensive and defensive arms,

Mindful of their obligations under Article VI of the Treaty on the Non-Proliferation of Nuclear Weapons,

Have agreed as follows:

Article I

The Parties undertake not to start construction of additional fixed land-based intercontinental ballistic missile (ICBM) launchers after July 1, 1972.

Article II

The Parties undertake not to convert land-based launchers for light ICBMs, or for ICBMs of older types deployed prior to 1964, into land-based launchers for heavy ICBMs of types deployed after that time.

Article III

The Parties undertake to limit submarine-launched ballistic missile (SLBM) launchers and modern ballistic missile submarines to the numbers operational and under construction on the date of signature of this Interim Agreement, and in addition to launchers and submarines constructed under procedures established by the Parties as replacements for an equal number of ICBM launchers of older types deployed prior to 1964 or for launchers on older submarines.

Article IV

Subject to the provisions of this Interim Agreement, modernization and replacement of strategic offensive ballistic

120

missiles and launchers covered by this Interim Agreement may be undertaken.

Article v

1. For the purpose of providing assurance of compliance with the provisions of this Interim Agreement, each Party shall use national technical means of verification at its disposal in a manner consistent with generally recognized principles of international law.

2. Each Party undertakes not to interfere with the national technical means of verification of the other Party operating in accordance with paragraph 1 of this Article.

3. Each Party undertakes not to use deliberate concealment measures which impede verification by national technical means of compliance with the provisions of this Interim Agreement. This obligation shall not require changes in current construction, assembly, conversion, or overhaul practices.

Article vi

To promote the objectives and implementation of the provisions of this Interim Agreement, the Parties shall use the Standing Consultative Commission established under Article xiii of the Treaty on the Limitation of Anti-Ballistic Missile Systems in accordance with the provisions of that Article.

Article vii

The Parties undertake to continue active negotiations for limitations on strategic offensive arms. The obligations provided for in this Interim Agreement shall not prejudice the scope or terms of the limitations on strategic offensive arms which may be worked out in the course of further negotiations.

Article viii

1. This Interim Agreement shall enter into force upon exchange of written notices of acceptance by each Party, which exchange shall take place simultaneously with the exchange of instruments of ratification of the Treaty on the Limitation of Anti-Ballistic Missile Systems.

2. This Interim Agreement shall remain in force for a period of five years unless replaced earlier by an agreement on more complete measures limiting strategic offensive arms. It

121

is the objective of the Parties to conduct active follow-on negotiations with the aim of concluding such an agreement as soon as possible.

3. Each Party shall, in exercising its national sovereignty, have the right to withdraw from this Interim Agreement if it decides that extraordinary events related to the subject matter of this Interim Agreement have jeopardized its supreme interests. It shall give notice of its decision to the other Party six months prior to withdrawal from this Interim Agreement. Such notice shall include a statement of the extraordinary events the notifying Party regards as having jeopardized its supreme interests.

Done at Moscow on May 26, 1972, in two copies, each in the English and Russian languages, both texts being equally authentic.

II. *Protocol to the Interim Agreement Between the United States of America and the Union of Soviet Socialist Republics on Certain Measures With Respect to the Limitation of Strategic Offensive Arms*

The United States of America and the Union of Soviet Socialist Republics, hereinafter referred to as the Parties,

Having agreed on certain limitations relating to submarine-launched ballistic missile launchers and modern ballistic missile submarines, and to replacement procedures, in the Interim Agreement,

Have agreed as follows:

The Parties understand that, under Article III of the Interim Agreement, for the period during which that Agreement remains in force:

The U.S. may have no more than 710 ballistic missile launchers on submarines (SLBMs) and no more than 44 modern ballistic missile submarines. The Soviet Union may have no more than 950 ballistic missile launchers on submarines and no more than 62 modern ballistic missile submarines.

Additional ballistic missile launchers on submarines up to the above-mentioned levels, in the U.S.—over 656 ballistic missile launchers on nuclear-powered submarines, and in the U.S.S.R.—over 740 ballistic missile launchers on nuclear-powered submarines, operational and under construction, may become operational as replacements for equal numbers of ballistic missile launchers on older types

122

deployed prior to 1964 or of ballistic missile launchers on older submarines.

The deployment of modern SLBMS on any submarine, regardless of type, will be counted against the total level of SLBMS permitted for the U.S. and the U.S.S.R.

This Protocol shall be considered an integral part of the Interim Agreement.

Done at Moscow this 26th day of May, 1972.

SOURCE: U.S. Arms Control and Disarmament Agency, *Arms Control and Disarmament Agreements* (Washington, D.C.: Government Printing Office, 1975), pp. 139-142.

III. *Joint U.S.-Soviet Statement on Strategic Offensive Arms Issued at Vladivostok*

During their working meeting in the area of Vladivostok on November 23-24, 1974, the President of the U.S.A. Gerald R. Ford and General Secretary of the Central Committee of the CPSU, L. I. Brezhnev discussed in detail the question of further limitations of strategic offensive arms.

They reaffirmed the great significance that both the United States and the U.S.S.R. attach to the limitation of strategic offensive arms. They are convinced that a long-term agreement on this question would be a significant contribution to improving relations between the U.S. and U.S.S.R., to reducing the danger of war and to enhancing world peace. Having noted the value of previous agreements on this question, including the Interim Agreement of May 26, 1972, they reaffirm the intention to conclude a new agreement on the limitation of strategic offensive arms, to last through 1985.

As a result of the exchange of views on the substance of such a new agreement, the President of the United States of America and the General Secretary of the Central Committee of the CPSU concluded that favorable prospects exist for completing the work on this agreement in 1975.

Agreement was reached that further negotiations will be based on the following provisions.

1. The new agreement will incorporate the relevant provisions of the Interim Agreement of May 26, 1972, which will remain in force until October 1977.

2. The new agreement will cover the period from October 1977 through December 31, 1985.

123

3. Based on the principle of equality and equal security, the new agreement will include the following limitations:

a. Both sides will be entitled to have a certain agreed aggregate number of strategic delivery vehicles;

b. Both sides will be entitled to have a certain agreed aggregate number of ICBMs and SLBMs [intercontinental ballistic missiles; submarine-launched ballistic missiles] equipped with multiple independently targetable warheads (MIRVs).

4. The new agreement will include a provision for further negotiations beginning no later than 1980-1981 on the question of further limitations and possible reductions of strategic arms in the period after 1985.

5. Negotiations between the delegations of the U.S. and U.S.S.R. to work out the new agreement incorporating the foregoing points will resume in Geneva in January 1975.

November 24, 1974.

SOURCE: *Department of State Bulletin*, 71 (December 23, 1974), 879.

IV. *Excerpt from President Ford's News Conference of December 2, 1974*

We agreed on the general framework for a new agreement that will last through 1985. We agreed it is realistic to aim at completing this agreement next year. This is possible because we made major breakthroughs on two critical issues:

—Number one, we agreed to put a ceiling of 2,400 each on the total number of intercontinental ballistic missiles, submarine-launched missiles, and heavy bombers.

—Two, we agreed to limit the number of missiles that can be armed with multiple warheads, MIRVs. Of each side's total of 2,400, 1,320 can be so armed.

These ceilings are well below the force levels which would otherwise have been expected over the next 10 years and very substantially below the forces which would result from an all-out arms race over that same period.

What we have done is to set firm and equal limits on the strategic forces of each side, thus preventing an arms race with all its terror, instability, war-breeding tension, and economic waste.

We have, in addition, created the solid basis from which future arms reductions can be made and, hopefully, will be negotiated.

124

It will take more detailed negotiations to convert this agreed framework into a comprehensive accord, but we have made a long step toward peace on a basis of equality, the only basis on which an agreement was possible.

SOURCE: *Department of State Bulletin*, 71 (December 23, 1974), 861.

CHRONIC, pervasive poverty is the most distressing and persistent obstacle to humanizing life for two-thirds of the world's population. Few needs press so urgently or present opportunities so potentially fruitful for advocates of world order reform as maximizing economic well-being for all people. The principal immediate purpose of the second value of global humanism (V_2) is, at the least, to insure that no person lacks the minimal amounts of food, shelter, clothing, medical care, and education necessary to live a healthy life with reasonable fulfillment and dignity. A more complete expression of this second value is the achievement of economic justice on a planetary scale.[1]

Because the United States is the wealthiest nation in the world, it bears the heaviest moral responsibility for assisting in the promotion of universal human welfare. Thus it is instructive to investigate the impact of United States policy upon the realization of V_2 and thereby to assess this second dimension of the U.S. role in achieving general world order reform. To provide focus for this analysis, I have chosen to examine United States development assistance to India.

The selection of the Indian case study is appropriate for several reasons. India is a significant country because of its geographical area, location, and enormous population. Its 600 million people constitute a major segment of the population of Asia and even of the world. India is by far the most important political power in south Asia. During all but two years of the period examined in this study, India enjoyed a democratic, parliamentary system. India's commercial records have been relatively good, and important data for economic planning have been available. The Indian strategy for development has been often contrasted, wisely or unwisely, with the Chinese approach as an instructive example for others to follow. Finally, the economic needs of India have been great. India's enormous population presses heavily upon the available land, food, jobs, housing, and other vital welfare services.

Given India's attributes, United States policy toward that country should be a fair test of United States performance on

126

V_2. India has been too large to be overlooked inadvertently, too important politically to be dismissed as of no concern to the future of Asian or worldwide international relations, too open and communicative to be accidentally misunderstood, too democratic and too close to the British parliamentary tradition to be incomprehensible, and too needy to be cast aside as unworthy of United States help. How, then, have American policies influenced the realization of V_2 in the Indian context? Has aid been designed to fulfill basic human needs, to reduce worldwide economic inequity, and to restructure global commercial relations and political authority in order to increase the influence of the weak and poor in planetary economic decisions that affect their lives? Or have national advantages in U.S. military and economic relations been the major motivation for development assistance?

This chapter will proceed by (1) describing the amount and mode of U.S. development assistance; (2) assessing whether this empirical statement of aid policies confirms or negates the official rationale for the aid; and (3) contrasting the values implicit in U.S. policy with the values of global humanism.

DESCRIPTION OF U.S. AID POLICIES

For several years after the Indians won their independence in 1947, the United States gave no development assistance to India, in part because foreign aid had not yet become an established part of United States foreign policy and in part because the United States' first concern was European postwar recovery. Perhaps a humanitarian motive was present in the U.S. Marshall Plan aid for reconstruction of Europe, but no such humanitarianism aroused the United States to undertake the enormous, obvious opportunities to help India.

The aid program for India and other less developed countries was rooted in President Harry Truman's perception of a world communist movement that threatened U.S. interests. This perception encouraged him in January 1949, to include an item in his inaugural address that was to become the well-known Point Four Program: "We must embark on a bold new program for making the benefits of our scientific advances and industrial progress available for the improvement and growth of underdeveloped areas." The United States should help "peace-loving peoples," he continued, in order "to help them realize their aspirations for a better life."[2] Still, no actual disbursements were

127

forthcoming for India until fiscal year 1951, when a grant of $4.5 million was extended to help India overcome food shortages resulting from poor weather conditions.

Total Assistance

Total development assistance in the form of loans and grants rose in succeeding years to a high in 1962. Commitments that year came to a total of $465.5 million, or the equivalent of $2.49 for every U.S. citizen, as indicated in Table 3-1. For the entire period from 1950 through 1976, the average yearly grant and loan development assistance to India per United States capita was $.74. This amounted to $.30 per Indian per year.[3]

Table 3-1
Total Grant and Loan Commitments[a] to India
for Economic Development from U.S. Agency for International
Development and Predecessor Agencies[b]

Fiscal Year	Total grants and loans in millions of U.S. dollars	Total grants and loans per U.S. capita, in dollars	Total grants and loans per Indian capita, in dollars
1950	0.0	0.00	0.00
1951	4.5	0.03	0.01
1952	52.8	0.34	0.14
1953	44.3	0.28	0.12
1954	87.2	0.53	0.23
1955	85.7	0.52	0.22
1956	60.0	0.36	0.15
1957	65.3	0.38	0.16
1958	89.8	0.51	0.22
1959	137.0	0.77	0.33
1960	194.6	1.08	0.45
1961	200.8	1.09	0.46
1962	465.5	2.49	1.04
1963	397.2	2.10	0.86
1964	336.5	1.75	0.71
1965	264.6	1.36	0.55
1966	308.8	1.57	0.62
1967	202.5	1.02	0.40
1968	241.5	1.20	0.47
1969	167.2	0.82	0.32
1970	159.0	0.78	0.29

Table 3-1 (cont.)

Fiscal Year	Total grants and loans in millions of U.S. dollars	Total grants and loans per U.S. capita, in dollars	Total grants and loans per Indian capita, in dollars
1971	202.1	0.97	0.37
1972	2.5	0.01	0.00
1973	12.0	−.06	−.02
1974	13.6	.06	.02
1975	19.7	.09	.03
1976	−1.5	−.01	.00
Total net obligations	3,789.2		

SOURCES: Up to 1971, U.S. Agency for International Development, Office of Statistics and Reports, *U.S. Economic Assistance Programs Administered by the Agency for International Development and Predecessor Agencies, April 3, 1948 to June 30, 1971.* After 1971, U.S. Agency for International Development, Statistics and Reports Division, Office of Financial Management, *U.S. Overseas Loans and Grants and Assistance from International Organizations, July 1, 1945-June 30, 1973,* and subsequent years. Population figures for computing per capita amounts were taken from United Nations, *Demographic Yearbook.*

NOTES [a] Commitments may be defined as development loans authorized and obligations of other AID funds. Annual commitment data are on a "net" basis, that is, new obligations from funds appropriated for that fiscal year, plus reobligations and minus deobligations of prior years' funds. Negative figures represent deobligations in excess of new commitments during one fiscal year.

[b] Predecessor agencies dealing with economic assistance programs during the Marshall Plan period and the Mutual Security Act period were, successively: The Economic Cooperation Administration (1948-1951); the Mutual Security Agency (1951-1953); the Foreign Operations Administration (1953-1955); the International Cooperation Administration (1955-1971); and the Development Loan Fund (1957-1961).

Although fluctuations have occurred, there was a gradual decline from 1962 until 1971, when the U.S. aid program was cut back sharply because of United States hostility toward Indian military intervention in the war beween West Pakistan and what was to become Bangladesh. These figures should be considered in light of a recognition that in the 1970s the United States GNP per capita exceeded that of India by approximately 57 times.

A loan or grant to India of $.74 per United States citizen may seem low in comparison to India's needs and to United States wealth, but this figure in fact gives an exaggerated picture of aid to India. In the first place, less than 14 percent of the economic assistance was in the form of grants. Loans, representing by far

129

the largest portion, are being repaid with interest. To be sure, if given at below commercial rates, loans themselves contain a "grant element." The extent to which loan aid was genuinely concessional depended on what the capital might have yielded from possible alternative uses, minus the rate of return received from Indian interest payments on the loans. Many economists estimate that the concessional element is from 15 to 30 percent of the nominal value of loans.[4]

The need to repay indebtedness has created new shortages of foreign exchange for India and a sense of resentment about the political leverage wielded by the lending state. India's service payments on external public debt as a percentage of its income from exports of goods and services have been gradually increasing.[5] As of June 30, 1973, India's external debt totalled an estimated $9 billion, excluding debts owed to the Soviet Union. In 1974, the effort to repay former debts cost India over $500 million a year, or nearly one-third of its total income from exports.[6] From 1969 to 1974, India's inflow of new grants and loans from all sources averaged $980 million per year; this amounted to $400 million per year after meeting service charges on outstanding debt. The International Bank for Reconstruction and Development projected a deficit in India's international payments of $12 billion for 1975-80.[7]

The requirements for debt repayment meant that in order to prevent net foreign assistance from declining, assistance to India would have to grow higher each year to offset increased repayments to suppliers of assistance. Decreases in utilizable funds actually resulted if there was a failure to offset the annual back flow of capital to repay previous loans. In recent years, for example, United States net grant and loan assistance averaged less than $5 million annually. At the same time, India sent over a quarter billion dollars to the United States for debt repayment, and thus became a net exporter of capital to the United States.[8]

Second, in addition to the repayment problem, 90 percent of U.S. loans and grants have been tied to purchases in the United States, so that Indians have had no choice but to use the credit to purchase equipment or materials from U.S. corporations, sometimes at inflated prices. When aid has been tied to the United States and also to a proposed project, suppliers sometimes have enjoyed near monopoly conditions. The excess cost of goods imported from the United States over the cost from alternative sources represented an export subsidy which India paid to U.S.

exporters to secure the aid-financed contracts. Aid-tying amounted roughly to a 20-25 percent savings for the United States (and cost to India) over the nominal value of the aid.[9] In effect, tied loans have been a type of "foreign aid" that created jobs for Americans, stimulated demand for products of United States corporations, and provided a United States-financed, Indian subsidy for the corporations benefiting from aid allocations.

The Agency for International Development (AID) has not, as a general rule, spent money overseas to assist in Indian development. As William S. Gaud, former administrator of AID has reported, "The biggest single misconception about the foreign aid program is that we send money abroad. We don't."[10]

Jagdish N. Bhagwati has attempted to estimate the real cost of total aid programs by using data including grants, loans, and commodity assistance. After adjusting these combined aid flows for aid-tying, loan repayment, and the lower opportunity costs of commodity assistance, he concluded that the *real* cost "may well be somewhere between 55 and 70 percent *below* their nominal values."[11] Where in that range the cost of aid might fall, of course, would depend heavily on the percentage of the aid which was extended in the form of grants.

One final caveat must be noted. The costs of aid for the United States and the benefits of aid to India were not necessarily symmetrical. A costless U.S. disposal of agricultural surplus may have been valuable to India. Likewise, an expensive capital transfer for the United States may have had little value to India. A study conducted by the Secretariat of the United Nations Conference on Trade and Development (UNCTAD) for 1964 and 1965 suggested that the real worth of aid may have been 30 to 35 percent of the nominal aid values (grants and loans combined).[12] Thus the overall real worth of aid may not be far out of line with the real cost of aid, but both are far below the nominal figures for aid.

Grants

A somewhat oversimplified but nonetheless useful picture of the burden of aid-giving on the American taxpayer comes from examination of the grant portion of the aid program.[13] Like loans, grants have not been payments of cash to India. They have been donations of goods and services to India, valued at prevailing U.S. prices, with the Federal government paying U.S.

131

producers. The highwater mark for grant commitments to India came long ago, in 1954, at the conclusion of the Korean War, as shown in Table 3-2. The quantity of grants has generally declined ever since, in spite of the fact that India's needs, ability to utilize aid, and United States wealth have all increased. Since 1950, the average yearly grant commitment to India per United States capita has been $.10. On an Indian per capita basis, it has been $.04.[14] In the last decade, U.S. citizens each spent an average of three pennies a year for Indian development grants at a time when the average per capita income of United States citizens was forty-five times greater than the per capita income of Indians.[15]

Before attempting to assess the impact of this level of assistance upon the realization of economic well-being for all, it is necessary to clarify both the professed and implicit values of U.S. aid policy.

OFFICIAL RATIONALE COMPARED TO THE VALUES IMPLICIT IN U.S. POLICY

The values explicitly professed as motivations for granting foreign assistance to India have been expressed in various rationales for foreign aid over the years since the Point Four Program began in 1949. U.S. officials have publicly advocated foreign aid (1) to enhance United States security, (2) to promote United States economic growth and prosperity, and (3) to express humanitarian concern for others. Although these three objectives have been expressed in different ways by various officials, they have been remarkably constant since 1949, as the following elaboration demonstrates.

Professed Value 1: To Serve U.S. Security Interests

In surveying policy statements, whether originating from the legislative or the executive branch, five themes constantly recur, although with different emphasis, as explanations of how foreign assistance contributes to United States security. Officials said that foreign aid could help: (1) to dampen conflict anywhere on the globe and to discourage threats to stability in the international system;[16] (2) to create and strengthen allies among the nonindustrialized states in the U.S. struggle against communism; (3) to prevent nonallies from becoming communist or friendly toward communist states; (4) to discourage internal instability in nonindustrialized countries and thereby to avert

132

Table 3-2
Total Grant Commitments[a] to India for Economic Development from
U.S. Agency for International Development and Predecessor Agencies

Fiscal year	Grants in millions of U.S. dollars	Grants per U.S. capita in U.S. dollars	Grants per Indian capita in U.S. dollars	Ratio of U.S. GNP per capita to Indian GNP per capita
1950	0.0	0.00	0.00	50
1951	4.5	0.03	0.01	52
1952	52.8	0.34	0.14	51
1953	44.3	0.28	0.12	50
1954	87.2	0.53	0.23	48
1955	40.7	0.25	0.11	50
1956	22.5	0.13	0.06	49
1957	17.8	0.10	0.04	49
1958	14.8	0.08	0.04	46
1959	17.0	0.10	0.04	48
1960	23.3	0.13	0.05	45
1961	20.7	0.11	0.05	45
1962	19.6	0.10	0.04	47
1963	4.9	0.03	0.01	47
1964	5.9	0.03	0.01	46
1965	8.8	0.05	0.02	51
1966	9.5	0.05	0.02	54
1967	7.7	0.04	0.02	52
1968	12.8	0.06	0.02	53
1969	8.6	0.04	0.02	52
1970	27.6	0.13	0.05	51
1971	9.5	0.05	0.02	52
1972	4.2	0.02	0.01	56
1973	−3.2	−.02	−.01	57
1974	3.2	.02	.01	b
1975	.1	.00	.00	b
1976	−.1	.00	.00	b

Total net obligations, 464.5

SOURCES: Up to 1971, U.S. Agency for International Development, Office of Statistics and Reports, *U.S. Economic Assistance Programs Administered by the Agency for International Development and Predecessor Agencies, April 3, 1948 to June 30, 1971.* After 1971, U.S. Agency for International Development, Statistics and Reports Division, Office of Financial Management, *U.S. Overseas Loans and Grants and Assistance from International Organizations, July 1, 1945-June 30, 1973,* and subsequent years. GNP data are from United Nations Department of Economic and Social Affairs, Statistical Office, *Yearbook of National Accounts Statistics.*
NOTES: [a] Commitments are defined in Table 3-1. All aid figures are net.
[b] Not available.

133

spreading instability to the international system; (5) to encourage a "demonstration effect" in order to prove that economic growth, capitalism, and democratic, or at least anticommunist, political institutions go hand in hand. Let us examine these in turn.

TO DAMPEN INTERNATIONAL CONFLICT AND DISCOURAGE THREATS TO STABILITY

Defending the international status quo meant protecting United States hegemony and prosperity and moderating the harsher conditions of foreign poverty in order to decrease threats to the international status quo. President Nixon's rationale for U.S. policy was typical:

> . . . as long as millions of people lack food, housing, and jobs; starvation, social unrest and economic turmoil will threaten our common future. . . . Peace and poverty cannot easily endure side by side. All that we have worked, and fought, and sacrificed to achieve will be in jeopardy as long as hunger, illiteracy, disease, and poverty are the permanent condition of forty percent of the populace in developing nations of the world.[17]

> We must respond to the needs of those [less developed] countries if our own country and its values are to remain secure. . . . No more abroad than at home can peace be achieved and maintained without vigorous efforts to meet the needs of the less fortunate. . . . Political stability is unlikely to occur without sound economic development.[18]

The hallmark of aid policy was the use of U.S. money to promote political stability in less developed countries in order to enhance U.S. security. In a candid statement of United States foreign assistance objectives, John Hannah, a former director of AID, explained:

> It is unrealistic to think that thirty years from now 300 million Americans can live comfortably here while across the continents of Asia, Africa, and Latin America in the LDCs [less developed countries] more than twice the present population, some seven billions of people, struggle to eke out an existence. There can be no assured peace for Americans unless we join the other developed nations of the world in a continuing effort to develop a stable world order.[19]

134

Earlier, President Johnson had spoken of a similar goal: "The foreign aid program . . . is designed to foster our fundamental American purpose: to help root out the causes of conflict and thus ensure our own security."[20] Dollars spent for foreign assistance, the argument went, decreased the likelihood of conflict and social upheaval, thus increasing United States security. "Dollar for dollar," said President Johnson, "no United States expenditures contributed more to United States security and world peace than dollars spent in foreign aid."[21]

The use of aid to promote stability in the international environment also meant, of course, discouraging any increase in the influence of United States rivals overseas. President Nixon warned that "the unmet needs of South Asia, and its unresolved enmities, could make the area vulnerable to an undesirable level of foreign influence."[22]

As an intended guarantor of national security, aid was based on the idea that peace was indivisible, that worldwide stability was a virtue, and that a threat to peace and stability anywhere in the world was a threat to world peace and U.S. interests. In justifying aid requests to less developed countries in 1964, President Johnson had explained: "Our own security rests on the security of others."[23] Secretary of State Dean Rusk later said that both United States safety and economic well-being "require a safe world environment; for America cannot find security apart from the rest of the world. And we can be neither prosperous nor safe in the long run if most other people live in squalor or if violence consumes the world around us."[24] In reflecting upon the many years of American foreign assistance, Undersecretary of State Nicholas Katzenbach commented that "our policy toward the less developed world has been based on the assumption that these countries are, on the whole, important to United States national security."[25] Secretary of State Henry Kissinger declared that foreign assistance requests "are the resources required to carry America's role in building a more secure and stable world."[26]

During 1974 and 1975, Kissinger began to express the desire for stability in a somewhat new form by stressing the management of global interdependence.[27] Earlier, officials had emphasized a threat to United States security that was one step removed from the present. The United States would be threatened by newly independent states only if they became communist or friendly toward the Soviet Union and China. By

135

1974, the threat was perceived as more immediate, simple, and direct: if the world order were disrupted, regardless of whether communists were behind it, it was a threat to the privileged position of the United States. Kissinger explained, "Economics, technology, and the sweep of human values impose a recognition of global interdependence and the necessity of American participaton in its management."[28] Furthermore, "If we fail to manage the growing pains of an interdependent world, we risk a return to the autarkic policies of the thirties—policies which led to a collapse of world order." Thus, Kissinger said, aid programs should be seen "not as 'do good' programs, but as the vital tools through which we help build an international climate conducive to American interests."[29]

When India failed to support Kissinger's definition of U.S. interests, the impact on aid expenditures was sometimes swift. India's support for Bangladesh in seeking independence from Pakistan so angered Kissinger that U.S. aid programs were, for all practical purposes, suspended. Eighty-seven million dollars of previously promised aid was withheld after the Indian-Pakistan war in December 1971.[30]

A list of the twenty states (Table 3-3) receiving the largest quantities of grants for economic development from 1949 to 1974 confirms the security-dominated design of even "economic" development assistance. Among the largest recipients almost all were important military allies or military client states. India, which refused to become an ally, ranked eighteenth, even though its needs and population vastly exceeded those of every state that was accorded higher United States priority. Thailand, for example, with one-sixteenth the population of India, received $54 million more in grants. Spain received more grants than did India. Tiny Laos, with 1/200 the population of India, and relatively wealthy Austria, both preceded India on the list.[31]

TO CREATE AND TO STRENGTHEN ALLIES IN THE STRUGGLE AGAINST COMMUNISM

Since the Mutual Security Act of 1953, officials often have expressed a direct relationship between foreign assistance and a perceived communist threat. In AID's first annual report summarizing past mutual security activities and explaining future "working concepts" for AID, the agency clarified the basis for assistance: "Aid programs will be tailored to the capacity of a

Table 3-3
The Twenty Largest Recipients of Grant Assistance from the United
States Agency for International Development and Predecessor
Agencies, 1949-1974

	Millions of dollars
1. South Vietnam	$4930.1
2. United Kingdom	3450.1
3. France	2964.7
4. South Korea	2556.6
5. Italy	1554.7
6. Fed. Rep. of Germany	1255.5
7. Republic of China	1154.8
8. Turkey	984.9
9. Greece	962.3
10. Netherlands	839.1
11. Laos	827.1
12. Austria	726.0
13. Pakistan	685.4
14. Jordan	585.2
15. Thailand	517.4
16. Belgium-Luxembourg	492.0
17. Spain	480.6
18. India	461.3
19. Cambodia	426.0
20. Yugoslavia	386.3

SOURCE: Data are taken from U.S. Agency for International Development, Statistics and Reports Division, *U.S. Overseas Loans and Grants and Assistance from International Organizations July 1, 1945-June 30, 1973* and subsequent years.

country to use assistance effectively, as well as to the varied needs of different countries with respect to the threat of Communism."[32]

Three principal United States objectives in Asia were typically articulated by the House Committee on Foreign Affairs:

(a) To develop sufficient military power where needed to maintain internal security and discourage Communist military aggression.

(b) To assure, in cooperation with the present free governments, that the forces of nationalism are associated with the rest of the free world instead of with Communism.

(c) To assist in the creation of social and economic conditions that will permit the growth and survival of non-communist

137

political institutions under which the people can feel that the fulfillment of their basic needs and aspirations is being effectively sought by their own free governments.[33]

In a report on foreign aid to India, Pakistan, Thailand, and Indochina, a subcommittee of the House Foreign Affairs Committee explained:

(a) That it is in our interest to help the free nations of Asia in resisting Soviet dominance;

(b) That United States military aid is required to enable certain countries in the area to maintain internal security and discourage Communist encroachment from without;

(c) That economic and political stability are interdependent and together increase the capacity and the will to resist internal and external Communist aggression.[34]

In noting the crucial relationship between foreign aid and the struggle against a perceived communist threat, Secretary of State John Foster Dulles warned: "The present world situation demands, as a first priority, the maintenance of unity and cooperation among the non-communist nations. None of us alone could face with assurance an all-out struggle with the Communist empire." The safety of the United States, he said, "no longer depends merely upon our own Armed Forces . . . but upon the combined military power and political and economic stability of the free world as a whole. For this reason, I . . . say with complete assurance that every dollar in this mutual security program is designed to protect and advance the security and well-being of the United States."[35] Dulles' successor, Christian Herter, reaffirmed the anticommunist security motivation for foreign economic assistance. The foreign economic aid program, he said, was "essential" in the U.S. effort to construct a barrier of strength against "the threat of communist expansion."[36] In 1964, Secretary of Defense Robert McNamara declared: "This [military assistance] program, and the foreign aid program generally, has now become the most critical element of our overall national security effort."[37]

TO DISCOURAGE NONALLIES FROM ESTABLISHING FRIENDLY
RELATIONS WITH COMMUNIST GOVERNMENTS

If the cold war with communism and the creation of allies were prime motivating forces behind foreign assistance, Washington officials were willing to settle for half a loaf, merely to create friends unwilling to become allies, if alliances could not be established. The purpose was simply to avert the building of friendly relations between newly independent states and the Soviet Union, a distinct possibility given the serious grievances of recent colonies against the former imperial powers. In addition, the United States feared the effects of the flexible diplomacy of Nikita Khrushchev, begun in the mid-1950s. Therefore, the militant anticommunism of U.S. foreign policy expressed in Dulles' earlier condemnation of Indian neutralism required some modification.[38] Although nonalignment was not appreciated, it was still a preferable alternative to communism.

Congressional reluctance to accept nonalignment was expressed in a House report on a special study mission to India: "Many Indians aspire to have their country play the sort of role in Asia that Sweden plays in Europe. Others, more realistic, recognize that India's geography and economy and hope of retaining her independence inevitably place her in the Western World. In the opinion of the study mission such a position of neutrality is neither tenable nor desirable."[39] The report also explained that many influential Indians agreed that neutrality was not desirable and that India should be more closely associated with the United States. The House study then suggested a foreign assistance strategy to strengthen the political influence of those Indians who were sympathetic to a pro-American position.

Secretary of State Christian Herter pointedly discussed the reason for United States interest in the development of societies that were nonaligned: "Ignoring their problems and their needs would inevitably leave them no alternative but recourse to the Communists. It is true that their absorption into the Communist fold would confront us with a grim if not hopeless security position." The secretary of state explained aid policy as a quasi-military holding action, to retain United States influence around the world. Although the military defense of the United States was the first preoccupation, "it is very dangerous to assume merely because we have military security that we are going to be able to hold these large areas of the world that are in ferment and wanting a higher standard of living on our side of the free world, unless we continue with the economic program." Herter concluded, "We have a tremendous selfish stake in having the

139

uncommitted . . . nations of the world . . . not succumb to the Soviet bloc."[40]

Washington's fear of and opposition to threats to the political stability of the international system were matched by opposition to internal political instability in most of the less developed countries, including India. Officials assumed that internal stability would contribute to maintaining the status quo in the international system. Foreign assistance, therefore, was useful insofar as it dampened the expression of internal grievances that might break out into open rejection of existing governments by domestic reformers. The latter claimed that the Congress party in India, for example, was too much an agent of the status quo, defending the residues of colonialism and privilege for a few within India. U.S. officials assumed that dissatisfied Indians would become agitators for change, if not outright communists. Aid was designed to decrease the level of domestic economic dissatisfaction.

The intention to use economic aid as an instrument of political influence in the internal affairs of other states was usually expressed as an effort at peacekeeping. For example, AID administrator Daniel Parker explained: "The central theme of our request is that U.S. foreign assistance programs are essential components of our foreign policy strategy for strengthening world peace and for expanding international economic cooperation in a rapidly changing world environment."[41] The utility of aid for enhancing international stability depended upon insuring definite internal political consequences. The United States discouraged structural reforms demanded by political radicals in less developed countries.[42] Former White House National Security Adviser and M.I.T. economist, Walt Rostow, wrote that

> We alone in all the world have the resources to make steady and substantial economic growth an active possibility for the underdeveloped nations of the Free World. *But our basic objectives are political rather than economic.* They are political in the sense that our most pressing interest is to help the societies of the world develop in ways that will not menace our security— either as a result of their own internal dynamics or because they are weak enough to be used as tools by others. But our ability to influence political development by direct argument

140

or intervention is very slight. Indeed, direct political intervention is almost certain to set up resentments and resistances
which will produce the exact reverse of the result we seek.
Economic programs . . . can be effective instruments of political influence.[43]

Thus foreign aid programs, in his judgment, were perhaps the
only way "around the impasse which confronts us when we try to
use our political influence directly. . . . [E]conomic programs are
one of our few potentially effective levers of influence upon
political developments in the underdeveloped areas."[44]

Like most U.S. officials, Rostow sought to circumvent rather
than respect the desire of foreign governments to exclude
foreign interference:

There is no point in evading the fact that these [U.S. policy
goals in the Third World] . . . involve an attempt to interfere
in the evolution of other societies. . . . The task of American
policy is not to delude yourself that we are, in fact, respecting
other people's sovereignty. In a world as intimately interacting
as ours you cannot respect sovereignty in the old purist sense,
notably if you are the major power.[45]

In short, the use of economic assistance to influence political
events in recipient nations was "the key relation which underlies
American foreign aid programs. Since the end of the Second
World War, almost without exception, the ultimate objective of
these programs, from UNRRA to the Indian surplus food deal,
has not been economic but political."[46]

Harold E. Stassen, as director of the United States aid program in 1954, explained that it was necessary to extend economic assistance to India so "that it not fall into the chaotic
conditions that could lead to Communist domination of that
country."[47] Secretary Dulles declared many times in similar language: "The Communists move into every situation in the world
where there is some ingredient of injustice." Dulles frankly admitted that "India's foreign policy . . . is not one which measures
up to what we think are the best standards." Nevertheless, he favored foreign aid to India because "Nehru is conducting a very
strong campaign against communism within India; the Communists are his bitter enemies domestically."[48]

President Johnson declared that, in order to ease domestic
unrest in the less industrialized countries, the foreign assistance
programs were "as important and as essential to the security of

this nation as our military defenses. . . . If most men can look forward to nothing more than a lifetime of backbreaking toil which only preserves their misery, violence will always beckon, freedom will ever be under siege."[49] President Nixon also commented that "the prospects for a peaceful world will be greatly enhanced if the two-thirds of humanity who live in [poor] countries see hope for adequate food, shelter, education and employment in peaceful progress rather than in revolution."[50]

TO ENCOURAGE A POSITIVE DEMONSTRATION EFFECT
FOR NONCOMMUNIST SYSTEMS

In the background of most discussions of aid to India was the desire of officials to prove that India would not be outdone by the communist government of China, with which it so frequently has been compared because of some obvious similarities in development needs. As the Foreign Assistance Act establishing AID and an early AID report explained, the purpose of United States foreign aid was "to help make a historic demonstration that economic growth and political democracy can go hand in hand."[51] Secretary Dulles expressed the notion more pointedly: "There is no doubt in my mind that the people of Asia will be much influenced by their comparison of the economic progress made under the democratic system of India and the Communist dictatorship system in China."[52] Dulles' summation was typical of other official statements: "[United States aid] . . . does contribute quite an essential element in helping India to win this particular contest with communism which, from our standpoint, it is very important that India should win."[53]

In summary, an important part of the foreign aid strategy was to insure stability in the international system. Stability meant preserving an economic and political structure in which the United States enjoyed a per capita income more than forty times that of many less developed countries, and an unequaled worldwide political influence that protected its preeminence. It also meant the United States had the freedom to improve its position if possible. For the poor states, stability meant the perpetuation of a grossly unjust structure of wealth that kept them in poverty.

In the quest for protecting the existing global structure of power and wealth, the United States used aid to create allies, to promote internal stability, to discourage domestic dissatisfaction in less developed countries and the resulting reform movements

142

that might be unfavorable to U.S. interests, to promote anticommunist political and economic institutions, and to demonstrate that pro-Western governments held more promise for economic development than anti-Western governments or socialist institutions.

Professed Value 2: To Protect or Improve Economic Benefits from International Trade and Investment

Since 1950 officials have repeatedly used three principal, interrelated arguments in their economic rationale for foreign assistance: (1) to increase foreign demand for U.S. goods and services; (2) to maintain open commercial relations with countries supplying raw materials to the United States; and (3) to expand United States overseas commercial influence and benefits by encouraging private enterprise both as an economic system and as an ideology. Each of these ideas deserves elaboration.

TO INCREASE FOREIGN SALES OF UNITED STATES GOODS AND SERVICES

President Kennedy was one of many officials who noted that foreign aid gave U.S. business access to otherwise closed markets, encouraged foreign consumers to develop lasting preferences for U.S. exports: "Too little attention . . . has been paid to the part which an early exposure to American goods, American skills, and the American way of doing things can play in forming the tastes and desires and customs of these newly emerging nations which must be our markets for the future."[54] Without U.S. foreign assistance to less developed countries, "their traditional ties are in Europe and Europe will be the beneficiary." With aid-inspired exports from the United States, Kennedy explained, business and industry in these countries would become acquainted with United States goods, and a tradition would be laid for growing future markets for U.S. products long after the developing economies no longer required foreign aid.

Soon after World War II ended, many U.S. officials believed that the United States would need foreign outlets to absorb the surplus of U.S. postwar production. They recognized that a regulated United States economy would not need to induce foreign purchases of excess U.S. goods resulting from economic expansion, but they did not consider such an economy to be a desirable alternative.[55] As John Hannah, former administrator of AID, explained: "The United States cannot achieve our aspira-

143

tions for . . . an expanding economy in isolation from the [less developed countries]."[56] He noted that developing countries that experienced a substantial measure of economic growth also substantially increased their imports of U.S. products.[57]

Officials frequently used empirical data to make their point. In 1972, the less industrialized countries provided a $14.6 billion market for United States goods and services, a market larger than U.S. exports to the European community. These countries bought about a third of all United States exports. As a group, they have purchased more from the United States than the United States has from them.[58] William J. Casey, under secretary of state for economic affairs, noted the importance of promoting exports to developing countries: "The United States needs the foreign exchange from expanded exports and from investment earnings to pay for our growing raw material requirements."[59] In recent years, "the less developed part of the world was the only area in which we had any kind of a significant trade surplus."[60] Another former administrator of AID, William Gaud, pointed out that in the late 1960s, for example, more than 4,000 United States firms in all fifty states received well over a billion dollars a year in AID funds for products supplied as part of the foreign aid program.[61] As George D. Woods, the president of the World Bank Group, told the UN Conference on Trade and Development in New Delhi in 1968: "Bilateral programs of assistance have had as one of their primary objectives helping the high-income countries themselves; they have looked toward financing export sales."[62]

TO MAINTAIN OPEN COMMERCIAL RELATIONS WITH COUNTRIES PROVIDING RAW MATERIALS

Secretary Kissinger believed that foreign aid was an important device to "place us in a better position to enlist the developing nations' cooperation in sustaining an open global economy."[63] In using foreign aid to establish commercial relations with aid recipients, trade is also encouraged in both directions. Aid-inspired personal contacts among bankers and business people across national boundaries facilitate business outside the realm of foreign aid programs. It is good business to be a customer for one's own customer whenever possible.

Foreign assistance programs have helped maintain access to raw materials imported from the less developed countries, which have accounted for over one-third of United States raw material imports.[64] As the dependency of the United States on foreign raw materials has increased, a higher percentage of foreign goods has come from these developing countries. For example, of essential industrial raw materials purchased abroad, the United States imported approximately 65 percent from the developing countries and only 35 percent from the developed countries.[65]

Although the United States historically has had only limited interest in direct purchase of raw materials from India itself,[66] the United States has had an intense interest in access to raw materials from the less developed countries in general. Since Indian development strategy might influence other societies, the United States sought to pull India, and thereby India's Asian neighbors, toward the private enterprise system in order to keep the global as well as the Indian economy more open to U.S. investment and trade.[67]

Douglas Dillon, under secretary of state in the 1950s, once candidly remarked: "I am an investment banker by trade, and I speak as an investment banker when I say that today's less developed nations are tomorrow's richest economic and political asset."[68] Secretary of State William Rogers noted that, with only 6 percent of the world's population, the United States consumed 40 percent of the world's annual output of raw materials and energy. "Increasingly, we depend on the developing countries for these supplies."[69]

William Casey, the under secretary of economic affairs, explained how the need for foreign resources was matched by a need for earnings from foreign investments in order to purchase materials, and how both of these needs were served by aiding developing nations: "Our increasing dependence on foreign sources of energy and raw materials brings with it a need for greater access to foreign markets and a need for investment income to pay for the larger volume of imports. . . . We invest more when the investment climate is best, and this normally is in stable countries."[70]

TO ENCOURAGE PRIVATE ENTERPRISE IN OTHER COUNTRIES AND TO EXPAND U.S. COMMERCIAL INFLUENCE OVERSEAS

A recurring theme during the policy discussions about economic assistance was that it should be used to foster private enterprise. It is difficult to separate the diverse sources of support for private enterprise as a matter of American ideology, as an

145

intentional effort to encourage U.S. economic and political expansion abroad, as an expression of the vested interests of financiers with capital to invest abroad at high rates of profit, and as a genuine belief that economic development proceeded most efficiently when left to private enterprise. These various motivations, of course, were mutually reinforcing. Washington officials assumed that development of a private enterprise system in India, as opposed to a socialist system, would encourage commercial intercourse with the United States instead of, say, the Soviet Union. Sales and investments abroad by United States nationals would enhance the economic power of the United States in southern Asia.

This did not mean that the United States government made a major effort to encourage the economic penetration of India in order to gain political influence there, but instead that the foreign assistance program was intended to tilt the Indian economic structure in favor of a private enterprise system that would be open to United States investors, that would facilitate the sale of American goods in India, and that would produce secondary effects throughout Asia. U.S. Ambassador to India, Daniel P. Moynihan, explained that the United States effort to remove some of the Indian irritation caused by the food assistance program of the 1960s, which produced enormous rupee credits for the United States, was based on the hope that the debt settlement would create "an improving investment climate for U.S. firms seeking opportunities to manufacture in India and search for and develop oil deposits off its coast."[71]

The mutually reinforcing dimensions of the preference for promoting private enterprise were ubiquitous and sometimes surprisingly straightforward in official rationales for aid policy. A typical position was expressed in a Senate Foreign Relations Committee Report: "Development achieved under State direction . . . cements fewer strong ties with the United States than development achieved largely by way of the activation of latent private resources in the less developed countries."[72] Harold Stassen, as administrator of the Foreign Operations Administration, explained, "We encourage private enterprise, private investment, strengthened stability, and anti-Communist development."[73] The AID statement of goals typically declared: "It is a major objective of AID to encourage increased United States private investment in the developing countries and to strengthen the growth of strong, vigorous private sectors in these economies."

146

Under Secretary Casey reported that in 1972 the United States had offset a $6 billion trade deficit with a $7 billion net inflow in dividends and interest from United States investment abroad. "As a country which faces increasing needs for resources of energy and raw materials from abroad, we will have to invest abroad and increase the inflow of investment earnings to justify that investment."[74] Secretary Rogers pointed out that whereas United States foreign investment is concentrated in industrial countries, 50 percent of the U.S. income from foreign investment has come from the less developed countries.[75]

The preference for promoting private enterprise was not simply a product of Soviet-American rivalry. With the waning of the cold war in the 1960s and 1970s, loans and grants have been continuously channeled to encourage private enterprise abroad.[76] This has been done by often loaning money to private investors instead of to public corporations, by having the United States government guarantee the foreign investments of U.S. investors, and by providing credit for private foreign purchases from United States corporations.

As might be expected, the strongest political support in the United States has been for programs that would bring potential profits for United States corporations. The development of foreign industries which might compete with U.S. corporations has not been encouraged. Instead, U.S. corporations have supported the construction of infrastructure, such as roads and electric power, which the corporations need to market their goods but do not want to construct themselves. They also have favored "concentrating aid in priority problem areas, such as rural development, food production, population and disease control, and education."[77] They have expressed a decided preference for assistance measures that will encourage Indians to become consumers of U.S. manufactured goods. As the president of the National Association of Manufacturers explained, his organization "supports the concept of helping low-income countries in the development process, since it reduces human suffering and raises the world standard of living which, in the long run, means new and expanded markets for American products."[78] David Rockefeller, president of Chase Manhattan and founder of the Trilateral Commission, once noted that United States exports to the lowest income countries were "doing poorly." This was, he explained, because of foreign exchange problems and financing on terms that made U.S. exports uncompetitive. Thus he urged extending credit to the less developed countries as "a necessary and useful instrument for American exports to become competitive in this neglected market."[79]

In 1973 Edward Hood, vice-president of General Electric, assessed future markets in the developing countries of the Far East and Africa with a GNP per capita of $200 or less, and projected a market there in the next five years of $4.1 billion for electrical equipment. He told the House Committee on Foreign Affairs that this was a potential of about 16,000 additional jobs on an average annual basis. This estimate was on the conservative side since it did not include the potential increase in demand for allied equipment in related fields.[80]

In summary, from the early 1950s until the present, one of the objectives uppermost in the minds of officials was that private enterprise should be encouraged by foreign aid. Concrete aid programs were tailored to increase foreign demand for U.S. goods; to insure profits—through the tying of aid—for U.S. corporations; to protect opportunities for United States investment abroad; to facilitate continued access to foreign raw materials; and to promote the establishment of capitalist enterprises in the less developed countries in order to protect and expand the rewards of the United States economic system for Americans.

Professed Value 3: To Express Humanitarian
Concern for Helping People in Need

In the public rationales for foreign aid to India, most advocates expressed a humanitarian motive. Officials occasionally spoke simply about a moral obligation to people in need. For example, Undersecretary of State Nicholas Katzenbach explained: "Our people want to help their less fortunate fellow man. They want this because it is right. To do otherwise would be to deny an essential part of our national heritage."[81] A director of AID put it bluntly: "We . . . seek to help the poor two-thirds of the world because it is right. Hunger is wrong. Ignorance, disease, and hopelessness are wrong. . . . Indifference to poverty and despair is wrong."[82] Henry Kissinger once declared, "The economic assistance program of the United States is a faithful expression of our moral values." For Cyrus Vance, "Foreign assistance efforts demonstrate America's humanitarian compassion for the world's poor."[83]

Yet for most officials the humanitarian motive was almost inseparable from the security motive. From their perspective, the world would be more humane if it were secured behind a benevolent U.S. military shield. Such a secure world system would avoid the suffering of revolutions and social dislocation concomitant with rapid changes in the structures of power and wealth, whether on the domestic or global level.

In 1964 President Johnson typically expressed the convenient marriage of practical concern for security with principled expression of compassion: "There is no conflict between 'humanitarian' goals and 'national' goals. Our own security rests on the security of others. Their good health is our good health. As they prosper we prosper. Our concern must—and does—transcend national borders."[84] Several years later he continued to repeat the familiar theme of convergence between prudence and ethical prescription: "Foreign aid serves our national interest. It expresses our basic humanity. It may not always be popular but it is right. Foreign aid . . . is a commitment to conscience as well as to country."[85] Johnson said that "the pages of history can be searched in vain for another power whose pursuit of that self-interest was so infused with grandeur of spirit and morality of purpose."[86]

Beginning in the 1970s, the humanitarian-security motif occasionally was expressed as a global, rather than strictly national, bilateral concern: "Our economic assistance is designed to reinforce developing nations' efforts to bring a better life to their citizens, increasing their stake in a cooperative global economy at a time when events threaten to divide the world anew—between North and South, developed and developing, consumer and producer."[87] The most dramatic rhetorical expression of a new global perspective came from Secretary of State Cyrus Vance at the Conference on International Economic Cooperation and Development. He sought to counter the idea "that we, as a rich and powerful nation, can only be addressed as though we were an adversary." He declared: "I want the policy of the U.S. to be understood. There should be a new international economic system. In that system, there must be equity; there must be growth; but above all, there must be justice. We are prepared to help build that new system."[88]

Despite this rhetoric, the Carter administration has not made any substantial departure in practice from the implicit values of previous Republican and Democratic administrations. The percent of U.S. GNP going into development assistance failed to in-

149

crease. Less than half of bilateral development assistance went to countries with per capita incomes of less than $200 per year. On the one hand, the president promised before the UN that the United States was ready to "promote a new system of international economic progress and cooperation."[89] On the other hand, the Department of State directly rebuffed the desire of the less developed countries for a restructuring of the global economy in a new international economic order: "The United States believes that the best way for LDC's [less developed countries] to attain development objectives is within the existing international economic system."[90] U.S. officials, in effect, would continue to seek first their own political and economic advantages in the face of an overwhelming need for a new structure of commercial relations and global economic decision making that would place more emphasis on serving human needs and less on producing unessential consumer items.

Comparison of Professed Values, Implicit Values, and the Maximization of Economic Well-Being

We turn now from a discussion of the rationale for aid that was articulated by political leaders to a delineation of the values implicit in the aid policy itself. The implicit values, which were actually expressed in concrete governmental behavior, can then be compared with the values expressed in official rhetoric. Such a comparison will clarify the extent to which rhetoric has been an accurate indicator of the normative basis for United States policy. In the final portion of this chapter, the values that have guided United States aid policy will be compared to the guidelines for foreign assistance that are derived from the values of global humanism.

The discussion of values to this point has focused primarily on what officials said, which may of course have been different from what they believed. Regardless of individual beliefs, however, widespread agreement among official policy statements does provide an indication of the prevailing norms guiding foreign aid policy. We may assume that it has been politically useful for officials to discuss foreign aid in terms of its contributions to United States security, prosperity, and humanitarian concern. In contrast, officials have not customarily spoken in favor of redistributing the world's wealth, nor proclaimed that the United States should equitably share the power to decide how the world's resources should be used. Nothing has been said about

establishing a minimum standard of living for all persons on the
globe. When these generally ignored values are juxtaposed
against the recurring public statements of policymakers, it is
possible to discern the rough outlines of official consciousness
and intentions.

AID AS AN INSTRUMENT OF SECURITY

The mode and amount of U.S. aid given to India leave little
doubt that *enhancing U.S. power and strategic advantages was a
major reason for U.S. economic assistance* (implicit value A). Aid
began after the United States took a new interest in helping
Asian countries during the Korean War. The largest amount of
grants came in 1954, at the conclusion of the war, and at the
height of Dulles' efforts to encircle the Soviet Union and China
with military alliances. At that time, the United States attempted
unsuccessfully to enroll India as a member of SEATO. During
the 1960s, as the cold war diminished, United States grant and
loan economic assistance to India (as to most other countries)
gradually declined. Pakistan, a staunch Asian ally in the sense of
being willing to join SEATO and CENTO, received larger
amounts of aid after SEATO was formed than did India, in spite
of India's vastly greater population and needs. Indeed, grants to
Pakistan from 1948 to 1976 exceeded those to India by $732 to
$464 million. This was in spite of an additional $712 million in
military aid going to Pakistan during these years as opposed to
$144 for India, given largely because of India's border war with
China. In short, India received limited amounts of aid to encourage internal stability, discourage communism, and insure
some degree of progress in its competition with China. But its
nonaligned status and professed intention to build a socialist society served as constraints upon the amount of aid the United
States was willing to extend. The most compelling and consistent
explanation for aid was its usefulness as a tool to produce military and political benefits for U.S. security policies.

AID AS AN INSTRUMENT FOR U.S. ECONOMIC BENEFIT

There is no significant evidence to suggest that the values implicit in United States aid policy were inconsistent with the professed value of bringing economic rewards to the United States.
U.S. dollars channeled through the foreign assistance program
ended up in U.S. pockets. Hundreds of thousands of jobs in the
United States resulted from the aid programs.[91]

151

Perhaps the best example of United States efforts to use aid specifically for United States benefit has been the requirement that aid be used to purchase goods from the United States. Between 1960 and 1964, when tying was begun in earnest, a number of aid-financed exports were affected: sale of United States fertilizers quadrupled; chemical products more than doubled; textiles and industrial machinery increased five times over. As AID reported in 1964: "One result of these increased exports is that new markets are being opened up for American products in parts of the world where they have never before been seen."[92]

When some officials once proposed discontinuing tied aid,[93] they faced corporate protest that to do so would "undermine American opportunities to develop long-range trade relationships with these nations. Experience shows that as emerging nations grow into a viable economy, they tend to do business with the commercial ties developed under AID programs."[94] Those ties also encouraged investment. By 1975 about 60 percent of all new U.S. investment went to developing countries.[95]

The percentage of tied aid has generally increased since 1950. By the late 1960s, 93 percent of AID funds were spent directly in the United States. Ninety-eight percent of AID's commodity requirements were procured in the United States.[96] All grants were normally spent in the United States. The shipment of U.S. goods abroad was restricted to American ships, and no AID funds could be paid to foreign flag vessels.[97] Even replenishment capital that the United States gave to the Asian Development Bank for concessional loans was tied to procurement of United States goods and services.[98]

The 1968 AID report proudly announced the creation of an "Additionality Working Group" whose purpose was to insure that United States commercial exports were not adversely affected by AID-financed exports. In short, this group required that a country like India continue importing goods from the United States at a level constant with past purchases before AID credits could be used to finance similar goods, thus insuring that any AID purchases would be in addition to what might have been bought without any aid.[99]

As a result of these policies, aid has stimulated the exports and profits of developed countries. Meanwhile, the share of world total exports for the less developed countries has dropped from 30 percent in 1948 to 23 percent in 1958 to 18 percent in 1969.[100] Exports from developed countries increased 156 percent during the decade of largest assistance from 1959 to 1969, while exports from the less developed countries rose only 87 percent.[101] By 1976, 27 percent of U.S. exports—more than the amount going to the members of the European communities, Eastern Europe, and the Soviet Union combined—went to non-OPEC developing countries. Altogether, the less developed countries bought 40 percent of total U.S. exports. If the United States retains with developing countries the same trade patterns established by foreign aid during the decade of the 1960s, by 1985 U.S. exports to developing countries would account for two million additional jobs in U.S. export industries.[102]

Implicit value B is synonymous with professed value 2: Aid was valued as an instrument *to promote economic benefits for the United States derived from international trade and investment.*

AID AS HUMANITARIAN CONCERN

In assessing the impact of humanitarianism upon American foreign aid policy, the professed humanitarian value is contradicted by several values implicit in the aid policies themselves. To be sure, if one views various AID projects as isolated cases, they often produced local humanitarian benefits. But if one examines the cumulative effects of the overall aid policy in the context of world geopolitics, the policy looks far different. The important questions in this examination are: To what extent did U.S. policy contribute to genuine internal or global structural change that helped decrease economic injustice and eliminate poverty? Did officials aim at structural change, or simply at moderating some of the worst economic conditions enough to perpetuate a roughly similar planetary distribution of wealth?[103] Did aid—insofar as it had a humanitarian element at all—express a charity mentality that offered relief to the poverty-stricken, or instead a concern with economic justice that promised eradication of poverty for millions of inhabitants of the globe? For aid to be considered humanitarian, it would need to be extended as a matter of right to persons, regardless of their race, ideology, or strategic importance, who lacked minimal requirements for physical existence and a life of dignity. Humanitarian assistance also would decrease the recipient's dependency on the donor and promote structural change empowering the weak to achieve greater equity in global decision making on economic affairs.

The values implicit in U.S. behavior contradicted the pro-

153

fessed value of humanitarianism. Officials consistently negated humanitarianism by shaping aid to promote military and political advantages for their own government. Official statements themselves frequently revealed U.S. priorities. The United States should give humanitarian aid to developing countries, most officials argued, because (1) aid would bind recipients to the service of U.S. economic and security needs and (2) without aid, the entire existing structure of world order, upon which U.S. wealth and power depended, would collapse in disorder, violence, and revolution. Officials feared that if the United States did not help the developing countries, their governments or reformers within their societies, would try to upset the prevailing allocation of power and wealth in the world, to the great disadvantage of the United States. In a typical speech entitled "Reform of the U.S. Foreign Assistance Program," President Nixon noted that the United States had built a "world order which insures peace and prosperity for ourselves and for other nations. . . . This world order cannot be sustained if . . . two-thirds of the world's people see the richer third as indifferent to their needs and insensitive to their aspirations." The purpose of aid was to enable the two-thirds of humanity who live in poor countries to "see hope . . . in peaceful progress rather than in revolution."[104] Kissinger believed that "economic assistance programs are essential instruments as we seek to shape a cooperative international order that reflects our interests." Vance warned that failure to undertake substantial aid obligations would mean the United States could not protect its security interests "in a hungry, angry, and bitter world."[105] Similarly, President Johnson on one occasion explained: "The forces of human need still stalk this globe. Ten thousand people a day . . . die from malnutrition. Diseases long conquered by science cut down life in villages still trapped in the past. In many vast areas, four out of every five persons cannot write their names." With understandable concern, he continued, "These are tragedies which summon our compassion." But, somewhat surprisingly, "More urgently, they threaten our security. They create the conditions of despair in which the fires of violence smoulder."[106] The president's conviction that mass starvation or widespread illiteracy were conditions that "more urgently" threaten United States security than call forth compassion demonstrated the secondary importance of U.S. compassion.

There was, perhaps, one possible exception to the generalization that humanitarianism failed to guide U.S. aid policy. When

154

India faced severe food shortages, the United States did sell large quantities of grain to India, financed from credit extended by the United States under P.L. 480. The program known as "Food for Peace" or "Food for Freedom" enabled the United States to make foreign concessionary sales of its unwanted agricultural surpluses. The government had these on hand as a result of its vast purchases from American farmers in its domestic farm price-support program.

There is considerable disagreement about the costs of P.L. 480 aid to the United States and its benefits to India. India received more feed grain through the program than any other country in the postwar period, as indicated in Table 3-4. The commodities

Table 3-4
The Twenty Largest Recipients of Total P.L. 480 Assistance

	Millions of Dollars
India	$4718
Pakistan	1714
South Korea	1677
South Vietnam	1281
Yugoslavia	1133
Indonesia	888
Brazil	844
Egypt	700
Israel	635
Turkey	553
Italy	465
Morocco	444
Spain	438
Tunisia	398
Taiwan	338
Colombia	269
Philippines	265
Greece	247
Chile	246
Algeria	177

SOURCE: Data are taken from U.S. Agency for International Development, Statistics and Reports Division, *U.S. Overseas Loans and Grants and Assistance from International Organizations, July 1, 1945-June 30, 1973.*

obviously benefited thousands of Indians who suffered from malnutrition. On the other hand, the program has been the object of several serious criticisms. First, it often provided insufficient assistance, arriving too late to prevent physical and mental impairments that result from malnutrition, especially among children. Second, some Indians feared that the aid—and the threat to withhold it—gave the United States political leverage in Indian affairs. AID officials have privately acknowledged that occasionally the United States delayed food shipments until the Indian government shifted some of its economic policies, such as to deflate its currency or raise its agricultural prices, in directions the United States favored. Third, the provision of aid may have enabled the Indian government to postpone painful but apparently necessary economic and agricultural reforms, thus actually slowing the movement toward economic autonomy and self-sufficiency in agriculture.[107] Finally, the particular arrangements in which most of the grain was sold rather than given to India produced a separate set of new problems. These were caused by the "blocked rupees" which the United States accumulated as India repaid the loans extended for the purchase of the grain. The loans were to be repaid in rupees that could not be converted to dollars or taken out of the country. Thus new rupees were deposited on U.S. accounts in India with each additional grain shipment. The United States used a portion of the money (roughly 15 percent) for paying the cost of running its embassy in India and similar overhead expenses. In addition, approximately 5 percent of the money went into so-called "Cooley loans," which were made to U.S. businesses for expenses in India, as a strategy for encouraging private investment there.[108] The remainder of the funds were to be granted or loaned to the Indian government for purposes that both governments agreed upon. Of this portion, 50 to 80 percent was usually restricted to loans.

Blocked rupee sales caused several problems.[109] The United States-owned rupees promised to grow indefinitely, since the United States was unable to spend them all or to take them out of India. U.S. agreements also restricted interest on loans to making future loans to India. By 1974, 3.3 billion dollars' worth of rupees were credited to the U.S. account for repayment of loans to finance the purchase of U.S. farm surpluses. The United States technically possessed about 20 percent of all Indian currency. Interest alone amounted to over $100 million per year,[110] a figure that exceeded by $80 million the average annual total U.S. grants to India for economic development.

U.S. Ambassador to India, Daniel P. Moynihan, said "We could never spend this amount of money. Twice as much is now coming in as going out. There is no possible escape from indebtedness for India. It could go on into the twenty-second century." Even without further grain purchases, the interest would have accrued to produce a total of $6 billion by the end of the century.[111]

U.S. ownership of so much Indian currency became an embarrassment for both governments and, in Moynihan's judgment, poisoned relations between the two societies.[112] Indian political resentment about the accumulation of these funds grew, even though the United States could not use most of the funds without the approval of the Indian government. Some Indians feared United States manipulation of the Indian economy, where the United States could, through reloaning of rupees, create money, aggravate inflation, or otherwise distort the economy.[113] The large rupee balance led the United States to build up an aid and diplomatic establishment twice as big as any other country, in part just to spend the money. Canada, in contrast, had provided large-scale food aid in the form of grants.[114] Some believed the United States should have erased all of the rupee indebtedness acquired as a result of United States disposal of its surpluses. However, the United States refused.

Instead, Moynihan succeeded in making a less sweeping arrangement in which rupees worth $2.03 billion were forgiven. The one third of indebtedness not forgiven would continue to be used by the United States for operating its embassy and for other educational and cultural programs. In addition, India agreed to pay $64 million to the United States in dollars over a ten-year period.[115] Fifty-one million dollars over a forty-year period had been due before the new agreement.[116]

Assessing the costs of the aid program to the United States is no easier than comprehending its political and economic impact upon India. Since the United States had to pay the costs of storing new U.S. grain if it remained unsold, some have argued that P.L. 480 disposal of agricultural surplus actually incurred savings.[117] The United States also augmented its economic benefit from P.L. 480 aid by occasionally imposing the requirement that the recipient buy a certain quantity of grain at commercial rates as part of the agreement to receive the P.L. 480 grains at a concessionary price.[118]

The element of humanitarianism in P.L. 480 aid must be viewed in the light of these qualifications:

157

(1) Although the gross figures in Table 3-4 show that India was the beneficiary of enormous food aid, it is not clear that the aid program was aimed solely or even mainly at serving human needs. Among the countries needing and receiving food assistance, on a per capita basis Indians ranked *forty-fifth*. Seldom was the aid swift or massive enough to avert starvation or malnutrition for many persons. A majority of the states that received more food assistance than India (shown in Table 3-5) also had significantly higher average per capita incomes. P.L. 480 programs in general were not focused on the poorest of the poor. Of the twenty top recipients, only two—South Vietnam and Burundi—were among the forty poorest states in the world (listed in Table 3-9).

Table 3-5
Largest Per Capita Recipients of P.L. 480 Aid

1.	Israel	$212	24. Jamaica	$17
2.	Iceland	110	25. Pakistan and Bangladesh	16
3.	South Vietnam	80	26. Lesotho	16
4.	Tunisia	80	27. Colombia	15
5.	Jordan	64	28. Sri Lanka	15
6.	South Korea	60	29. Botswana	15
7.	Yugoslavia	60	30. Guinea	15
8.	Ryukyu	56	31. Spain	14
9.	Burundi	46	32. Panama	14
10.	Cyprus	44	33. Ecuador	12
11.	Dominican Republic	38	34. Hong Kong	12
12.	Morocco	34	35. Portugal	12
13.	Chile	31	36. Austria	12
14.	Malta	30	37. Ghana	11
15.	Bolivia	28	38. Nepal	11
16.	Taiwan	28	39. Syria	11
17.	Greece	27	40. Gambia	11
18.	Lebanon	26	41. Liberia	11
19.	Egypt	23	42. Peru	11
20.	Uruguay	22	43. Afghanistan	11
21.	Libya	22	44. Brazil	10
22.	Paraguay	18	45. India	10
23.	Turkey	18		

SOURCE: Data were taken from U.S. Agency for International Development, Office of Statistics and Reports, *U.S. Economic Assistance Programs Administered by the Agency for International Development and Predecessor Agencies, April 3, 1948 to June 30, 1971*; U.S. Agency for International Development, Statistics and Reports Division, *U.S. Overseas Loans and Grants and Assistance from International Organizations, July 1, 1945-June 30, 1973*; United Nations, *Demographic Yearbook*.

(2) The original intention of the Title I P.L. 480 aid was not to make the grain an outright gift, but to enable food importers to buy U.S. farm surplus. Although this preference for loans rather than grants no doubt owed more to U.S. domestic political reasons than to economic selfishness, it nonetheless demonstrates that the prevailing values did not sanction an act so "generous" as giving away wheat and corn held by the U.S. government in such quantity that officials paid U.S. farmers to remove fertile land from production. Moreover, once commodity surpluses began to decline in 1966, the United States required a transition from sales in Indian currency to sales in U.S. dollars.[119] Food aid dwindled when wheat could be sold for a sizable profit to nations less needy but richer than India. P.L. 480 aid did not increase Indian agricultural self-sufficiency nor decrease dependency on U.S. commodities nearly as much as would have grant assistance to upgrade Indian agricultural and fertilizer production.

(3) The relatively late decision to forgive two-thirds of the loans stopped short of completely abolishing Indian indebtedness under P.L. 480. Of the remaining one-third, Moynihan said, "we would retain control over our use of these rupees for the full ranges of purposes and programs we previously funded with rupees." Thus, "what we have granted India costs us very little."[120]

(4) The rupee agreement was intended not merely to end "a period of massive U.S. assistance and involvement in Indian economic policy decision-making." The United States also sought, according to Ambassador Moynihan, to improve sales opportunities for U.S. manufacturers in the country with the tenth largest GNP in the world. Moreover, officials hoped, as noted above, that the agreement would lead to a more receptive climate for U.S. investors in India and for corporations interested in exploring for oil off India's coast.[121]

(5) The most compelling arguments—hardly humanitarian—for the Moynihan arrangement were that the United States could never use the Indian currency it possessed, and that to continue the soft currency indebtedness would exacerbate India's difficult economic position so much as to make repayment of $3.4 billion in U.S. hard currency loans almost impossible.[122] Moreover, the World Bank's estimate that India would have a shortfall of foreign exchange of $12 billion from 1974-80 also impressed U.S. officials as having such serious economic implications for India's poor that it would produce political unrest and

159

instability within India, which the United States sought to prevent.

Therefore, in the framework of this analysis, the decision to eliminate two-thirds of the P.L. 480 debt was done more in the service of the first and second professed values—to serve the strategic and economic interests of the United States—than to achieve structural reform of the global economy, and thereby eliminate the gap between rich and poor. Upon close examination, even programs as apparently humanitarian as food aid fail to be a serious or unequivocal expression of the second value of global humanism.

To the extent that aid *was* humanitarian, it was rooted in a charity mentality, and not in a sense of global justice or a belief that no society had the right to withhold the "excess" fruit of its soil while others on the planet starved. Emergency food aid kept the Indians and Americans in their accustomed relative positions in the geopolitical structure. Apparently United States officials believed that the Indians were worthy of charity in moments of desperation, but the same officials did little to facilitate Indian equality in terms of standard of living or participation in decisions about allocating the world's wealth. The United States sent emergency food aid when it was easy to give in the form of loans to Indians so they could purchase U.S. surplus. But at the same time, the United States opposed structural change for a more equitable distribution of wealth and an increase, even to the level of one percent of GNP, in the burden of United States assistance to all countries.

Returning to our wider assessment of the humanitarian element in United States aid policy, the pattern of assistance shows that aid was, to a significant extent, a function of anticommunism. During the late 1950s, United States officials began to understand that what they perceived as a communist threat could not be handled exclusively by military equipment and alliances. Thus Secretary of State Dulles' harsh criticism of India's neutralism was moderated as Washington officials began to see nonaligned countries as potential outposts of stability in a world of flux. The subsequently increased aid program for India reflected the American change of mood, but the motivation remained tied to national security.

The United States shifted tactics to counter new Soviet diplomatic flexibility toward the less developed countries during the mid and late 1950s. As James H. Smith, the director of the

160

THREE · *Values Implicit in Policy*

International Cooperation Administration (ICA) explained before the House Committee on Foreign Affairs: "The Soviet economic program . . . must be given due weight in the formulation of our policies. The Soviets have revealed a large and apparently highly effective apparatus. The administration of Soviet aid is of particular significance to the operations of ICA."[123]

The strategy of using aid as an instrument for buying influence was publicly denied. As Nicholas Katzenbach reported, "faithful conformity to our foreign policy views has not been, and should not be, the criterion for eligibility."[124] In practice United States aid carried political strings insofar as it was aimed at resisting socialism. With the exception of Yugoslavia, a "deviant" from the Warsaw Pact, aid was limited to noncommunist states. For a nation as rich as the United States, simply the power to withhold aid from the poor constituted significant political influence. Even the well-known liberal administrator of the Foreign Operations Administration, Harold Stassen, said: "We should, and we do take a more generous attitude toward Pakistan, particularly . . . as they join with us in the defense arrangements, than we do toward India."[125] Because of the linkage between economic aid and building military alliances, from 1950 through 1973 Pakistan received three times as much economic aid per inhabitant as did India. Countries neither allied to nor sympathetic with U.S. strategic interests were unlikely to receive substantial economic assistance.[126] In surveying the pattern of U.S. aid on a per capita basis for all countries (with populations in excess of two million) from 1946 through 1973, of the twelve states receiving the most grant assistance for *economic* development, eleven were also among the largest recipients of *military* aid.[127]

Furthermore, the professed value of humanitarian concern is negated by the glaring inequities between the aid levels extended to India and to relatively more wealthy countries. Other things being equal, if humanitarian values had been paramount, a country with a smaller population and higher standard of living would not have received more assistance than India. As Table 3-6 shows, aid followed a radically different pattern. Relatively wealthy Iran, for example, received six times as much grant and loan assistance per capita as did India. Laos received almost four hundred times as much per capita grant aid as did India. The Laotian aid was high, of course, because of U.S. military involvement there, not because of an enormous effort to

161

fulfill human needs. Similarly, military activity or alliance-building was responsible for the higher levels of aid in all the other cases in Table 3-6.

If one examines per capita grant and loan economic assistance to other U.S. aid recipients worldwide (Table 3-7), India ranks sixtieth. The top two dozen states in the U.S. aid program received eight to forty times as much per capita assistance as Indians. The Indian case was not atypical of many poor states. Of the forty largest per capita recipients of U.S. economic assistance from 1946 to 1974, only three states—Cambodia, Laos, and South Vietnam—were among the forty poorest countries of the world.[128]

Table 3-6

Economic Assistance to Selected Asian Countries:
Average Annual Per Capita Grant and Loan Net Commitments
from AID and Predecessor Agencies, in Dollars

Country	Years Covered	Loan and Grant Assistance	Grant Assistance
Laos	1955-73	$19.74	$19.74
South Vietnam	1955-73	16.83	16.52
Taiwan	1949-63	10.67	9.19
South Korea	1952-73	5.61	4.91
Cambodia	1955-73	4.05	4.05
Turkey	1949-73	3.10	1.53
Iran	1952-66	2.08	1.34
Pakistan	1952-73	1.19	.35
Thailand	1951-73	.93	.82
India	1951-73	.35	.05

SOURCES: Data were taken from U.S. Agency for International Development, Office of Statistics and Reports, *U.S. Economic Assistance Programs Administered by the Agency for International Development and Predecessor Agencies, April 3, 1948 to June 30, 1971*; U.S. Agency for International Development, Statistics and Reports Division, *U.S. Overseas Loans and Grants and Assistance from International Organizations, July 1, 1945- June 30, 1973*; United Nations, *Demographic Yearbook*.

If loans are separated from total assistance, the remaining figures for grant assistance substantiate the conclusion that U.S. aid was not designed to help those most in need. (See Table 3-8.) Among per capita grants for all U.S. aid recipients in the world, India ranks ninety-third. Of the thirty-five states receiving the largest per capita grant assistance, again only three were among the forty poorest countries of the world—the same three in

162

Table 3-7
Total Loan and Grant Commitments from U.S. AID and Predecessor
Agencies to 60 Largest Recipients on a Per Capita Basis, 1946-1973

1.	South Vietnam	$314	31.	Honduras	$49
2.	Jordan	304	32.	Ireland	49
3.	Iceland	301	33.	Paraguay	47
4.	Laos	276	34.	Trinidad-Tobago	39
5.	Israel	204	35.	Ecuador	34
6.	Panama	191	36.	Italy	32
7.	Liberia	169	37.	Yugoslavia	30
8.	Guyana	123	38.	El Salvador	30
9.	Greece	118	39.	Lebanon	29
10.	Taiwan	114	40.	Morocco	27
11.	South Korea	107	41.	Ghana	26
12.	Bolivia	105	42.	Venezuela	26
13.	Austria	104	43.	Fed. Rep. of Germany	25
14.	Dominican Republic	91	44.	Iran	24
15.	Nicaragua	90	45.	Pakistan-Bangladesh	24
16.	Libya	86	46.	Uruguay	22
17.	Netherlands	83	47.	Somalia	21
18.	Malta	80	48.	Haiti	20
19.	Chile	77	49.	Thailand	19
20.	United Kingdom	71	50.	Afghanistan	19
21.	Cambodia	71	51.	Spain	18
22.	Costa Rica	70	52.	Peru	18
23.	Norway	69	53.	Brazil	18
24.	Turkey	69	54.	Zaire	16
25.	Tunisia	66	55.	Philippines	14
26.	France	65	56.	Sweden	13
27.	Denmark	56	57.	Guinea	13
28.	Belgium-Luxembourg	56	58.	Ethiopia	10
29.	Colombia	52	59.	Venezuela	8
30.	Guatemala	50	60.	India	8

SOURCES: Data are taken from U.S. Agency for International Development, Statistics and Reports Divisions, *U.S. Overseas Loans and Grants and Assistance from International Organizations, July 1, 1945-June 30, 1973*; United Nations, *Demographic Yearbook*.

which the U.S. had been pressing military objectives for years: South Vietnam, Laos, and Cambodia. The total assistance to India also has been below that which went to richer states many years ago. Countries that received forty to three hundred times as much aid per capita as India included, among others: Denmark, Norway, France, United Kingdom, Netherlands, Israel, Greece, Austria, Taiwan, Cambodia, and South Vietnam.

163

Table 3-8

Total Grant Commitments from U.S. AID and Predecessor Agencies on a Per Capita Basis, 1946-1973

1.	South Vietnam	$308	34.	Costa Rica	$21	67.	Dahomey	$3
2.	Jordan	293	35.	Yugoslavia	20	68.	Togo	3
3.	Laos	276	36.	Haiti	18	69.	Central African Rep.	3
4.	Iceland	178	37.	Thailand	17	70.	Senegal	3
5.	Israel	126	38.	Somalia	15	71.	Cyprus	3
6.	Greece	107	39.	Iran	15	72.	Malawi	3
7.	Austria	104	40.	Spain	15	73.	Indonesia	2
8.	Taiwan	96	41.	Afghanistan	14	74.	Brazil	2
9.	Liberia	93	42.	Ecuador	13	75.	Iraq	2
10.	Korea	91	43.	El Salvador	12	76.	Morocco	2
11.	Libya	81	44.	Zaire	11	77.	Mali	2
12.	Cambodia	71	45.	Sweden	11	78.	Egypt	2
13.	Netherlands	70	46.	Guinea	10	79.	Cameroon	2
14.	United Kingdom	64	47.	Philippines	10	80.	Tanzania	2
15.	Malta	63	48.	Chile	10	81.	Niger	2
16.	France	61	49.	Pakistan	9	82.	Congo (Brazzaville)	2
17.	Bolivia	60	50.	Peru	7	83.	Venezuela	2
18.	Norway	59	51.	Gabon	7	84.	Gambia	2

19.	Panama	59	52.	Yemen Arab Republic	7
20.	Denmark	50	53.	Jamaica	7
21.	Belgium-Luxembourg	49	54.	Ireland	6
22.	Dominican Republic	41	55.	Nepal	6
23.	Trinidad, Tobago	39	56.	Sierra Leone	6
24.	Guyana	33	57.	Bangladesh	5
25.	Turkey	32	58.	Uruguay	5
26.	Italy	30	59.	Ethiopia	5
27.	Guatemala	28	60.	Nigeria	4
28.	Tunisia	27	61.	Sudan	4
29.	Lebanon	26	62.	Saudi Arabia	4
30.	Nicaragua	22	63.	Colombia	4
31.	Honduras	22	64.	Ghana	4
32.	Paraguay	22	65.	Kenya	3
33.	Fed. Rep. of Germany	21	66.	Uganda	3

85.	Portugal	2
86.	Chad	2
87.	Ivory Coast	2
88.	Sri Lanka	1
89.	Zambia	1
90.	Upper Volta	1
91.	Burma	1
92.	Rwanda	1
93.	India	1
94.	Argentina	1
95.	Malagasy Republic	1
96.	Botswana	1
97.	Lesotho	1
98.	Mauritania	1

SOURCES: Data are taken from U.S. Agency for International Development, Statistics and Reports Division, *U.S. Overseas Loans and Grants and Assistance from International Organizations, July 1, 1945-June 30, 1973*; United Nations, *Demographic Yearbook*.

Table 3-9
The Forty Countries with Lowest Gross Domestic Product Per Capita

Afghanistan	60
Botswana	150
Burma	97
Burundi	55
Cambodia	124
Cameroon	188
Central African Republic	127
Chad	67
Dahomey	81
Ethiopia	66
Gambia	123
Guinea	80
Haiti	88
India	94
Indonesia	92
Kenya	134
Laos	65
Lesotho	64
Madagascar	131
Malawi	68
Mali	54
Mauritania	170
Nepal	78
Niger	97
Nigeria	99
Pakistan	128
Rwanda	53
Sierra Leone	176
Somalia	65
South Vietnam	194
Sri Lanka	162
Sudan	110
Tanzania	93
Thailand	178
Togo	148
Uganda	123
Upper Volta	67
Yemen, Dem. Rep. of	56
Yemen, Dem.	97
Zaire	85

SOURCES: Data are taken from *UN Yearbook of National Accounts Statistics* (New York: United Nations, various years), and *Statesman's Yearbook* (New York: St. Martin's Press, 1978). Data are estimated in U.S. dollars for fiscal or calendar year 1969, a representative year for the period covered in this study.

Table 3-10
U.S. Loans and Grants for Military Assistance on a Per Capita Basis,
1946-1973

1.	South Vietnam	$914
2.	Israel	477
3.	Laos	437
4.	Taiwan	284
5.	Greece	260
6.	Norway	229
7.	South Korea	216
8.	Belgium-Luxembourg	126
9.	Denmark	125
10.	Turkey	120
11.	Jordan	119
12.	Netherlands	105
13.	Cambodia	101
14.	France	89
15.	Iran	55
16.	Italy	46
17.	Saudi Arabia	42
18.	Thailand	38
19.	Portugal	38
20.	Yugoslavia	37
21.	Spain	26
22.	Chile	23
23.	Philippines	22
24.	Uruguay	20
25.	United Kingdom	20
26.	Lebanon	17
27.	Austria	17
28.	Fed. Rep. of Germany	16
29.	Venezuela	15
30.	Ecuador	13

SOURCES: Data are taken from U.S. Agency for International Development, Statistics and Reports Division, *U.S. Overseas Loans and Grants and Assistance from International Organizations, July 1, 1945-June 30, 1973*; United Nations, *Demographic Yearbook*.

These trends were also evident in a simple country-by-country analysis, on a *non*-per capita basis. Of the states receiving the most bilateral development grants from AID and predecessor agencies from 1949 to 1974, India ranked eighteenth, even though India's needs exceeded those of each of the states receiving higher United States priority.[129] Why should the national governments of Thailand, Spain, Austria, the United Kingdom,

167

or Laos, for example, have received more grant aid than India?

These data also demonstrate no correspondence between the ability of a country to repay aid and the inclination of United States officials to extend grants as opposed to loans. The fact that the United Kingdom received nearly seven and a half times as much grant assistance as India demonstrated the racial, national, and cultural limits of United States generosity.[130] In sharp contrast, total development loans to India ($3,296 million) by 1974 were roughly comparable in amount to grants to the United Kingdom ($3,450 million), whereas grants to India ($461 million) were somewhat similar in amount to loans to Britain ($385 million).[131]

Many other European countries, which were better able than India to repay loans, received grants greatly in excess of those going to India. To be sure, much of the aid for European countries helped reconstruction after World War II. (None of the figures in this analysis include postwar relief, in contrast to reconstruction.) Yet the needs of India following its struggle for independence and the civil strife and partition with Pakistan were not less than those of postwar Europe. Any determination of aid policy that was based on ability to repay loans—ignoring, for the moment, humanitarian concern—would never have resulted in the allocation of more grants to the rich than the poor.

Clearly, those countries receiving more aid than India—even on a non-per capita basis—represented client states of the United States, such as Taiwan, Thailand, South Korea, and South Vietnam, or military allies, such as the Federal Republic of Germany, France, the United Kingdom, Pakistan, Turkey, and Greece (Table 3-3). The one exception was neutral Austria, which received its assistance during the Marshall Plan and while Austria was still a bone of contention between the United States and the Soviet Union.

The high levels of economic aid received by South Vietnam, South Korea, and other client states casts doubt on the extent to which most economic aid is categorically different from military aid, even though it is spent on nonmilitary items.[132] From 1954 to 1958, South Korea received more economic aid (in addition to enormous military aid) than all of India, Pakistan, the Philippines, Burma, and Ceylon combined.[133] During the same period, even before the more direct United States military involvement in Laos and the southern segment of Vietnam, those governments received grants and loans almost equal in sum to those received by India and Pakistan, which had populations exceeding Laos and South Vietnam by over 450 million, or more than twice the total population of the United States. In 1966 alone, Vietnam received almost twice as much AID assistance as any other country of the world.[134] In the first two years following the January 1973 ceasefire in Vietnam, U.S. aid in all forms (military and economic) to Indochina was $8.2 billion,[135] or more than twice the total loan and grant commitments to India from AID and predecessor agencies for the entire period from 1949 to 1974.

Just as building military power dominated the humanitarian motive for aid, when a conflict arose between serving humanitarian interests and U.S. economic interests, the humanitarian concern again had lower priority. Despite U.S. wealth, the amount of development aid supplied by the United States has fallen short of the capital flows asked by the United Nations,[136] and compares unfavorably with the aid records of other industrialized states in the Organization for Economic Cooperation and Development (OECD).[137] Of sixteen members of OECD, the United States ranked twelfth. On the basis of aid commitments as percentage of GNP, only Japan, Switzerland, Italy, and Austria performed more poorly than the United States.[138]

In contrast, the newly rich grantors of aid, members of OPEC (Organization of Petroleum Exporting Countries), did much better than the United States. Aid-giving oil exporters contributed 1.8 percent of their gross national product in 1974. In 1975, the major OPEC donors were giving 2 percent of their GNP, and Kuwait, the oldest Arab donor, contributed 6 percent of its GNP. The United States was among only four Western countries that rejected, as too high, an international aid target of 0.7 percent of their GNP for official development assistance.[139] Moreover, nearly 40 percent of OPEC aid went to what the United Nations called "the most seriously affected countries," the poorest of the poor. Only 28 percent of Western aid went to that group.[140]

When United States official development assistance of all kinds to all countries is added together, the amount in constant dollars has declined by 50 percent over the last 15 years. During this period, U.S. GNP climbed by more than 20 percent. In 1977, for each dollar of GNP, the United States committed itself to spend .24 percent, or about one-fourth of one cent to help all the developing countries.[141] Even this tiny figure exaggerates

169

Table 3-11
Official Development Assistance in Relation to Gross National Product, 1962-1975

Countries	1962	1963	1964	1965	1966	1967	1968	1969	1970	1971	1972	1973	1974	1975
Australia	0.43	0.51	0.48	0.53	0.53	0.60	0.57	0.56	0.59	0.53	0.61	0.44	0.55	0.61
Austria	0.03	0.05	0.08	0.11	0.12	0.14	0.14	0.11	0.07	0.07	0.09	0.14	0.18	0.17
Belgium	0.54	0.57	0.46	0.60	0.42	0.45	0.42	0.50	0.46	0.50	0.55	0.51	0.51	0.59
Canada	0.09	0.15	0.17	0.19	0.33	0.32	0.26	0.33	0.42	0.42	0.47	0.43	0.50	0.58
Denmark	0.10	0.11	0.11	0.13	0.19	0.21	0.23	0.38	0.38	0.43	0.45	0.47	0.55	0.58
France	1.27	0.98	0.90	0.76	0.69	0.71	0.67	0.67	0.66	0.66	0.67	0.58	0.59	0.62
Germany	0.45	0.41	0.44	0.40	0.34	0.41	0.41	0.38	0.32	0.34	0.31	0.32	0.37	0.40
Italy	0.18	0.14	0.09	0.10	0.12	0.22	0.19	0.16	0.16	0.18	0.08	0.14	0.14	0.11
Japan	0.14	0.20	0.14	0.27	0.28	0.31	0.25	0.26	0.23	0.23	0.21	0.25	0.25	0.24
Netherlands	0.49	0.26	0.29	0.36	0.45	0.49	0.49	0.50	0.61	0.58	0.67	0.54	0.63	0.75
Norway	0.14	0.17	0.15	0.16	0.18	0.17	0.29	0.30	0.32	0.33	0.41	0.46	0.57	0.66
Portugal	1.26	1.46	1.48	0.59	0.54	0.54	0.54	1.29	0.67	1.42	1.91	0.59	a	a
Sweden	0.12	0.14	0.18	0.19	0.25	0.25	0.28	0.43	0.38	0.44	0.48	0.56	0.72	0.82
Switzerland	0.05	0.05	0.07	0.09	0.09	0.08	0.14	0.16	0.15	0.12	0.22	0.16	0.15	0.18
United Kingdom	0.52	0.48	0.53	0.47	0.45	0.44	0.40	0.39	0.37	0.41	0.40	0.35	0.38	0.37
United States	0.56	0.59	0.56	0.49	0.44	0.43	0.37	0.33	0.31	0.32	0.29	0.23	0.24	0.26
Total DAC Countries	0.52	0.51	0.48	0.44	0.41	0.42	0.37	0.36	0.34	0.35	0.34	0.30		

SOURCE: OECD, *Development Assistance Efforts and Policies, 1973 Review*, p. 189; *1974 Review*, p. 116; *1976 Review*, p. 206.
NOTE: [a] Not available.

American generosity. As noted earlier, when aid is properly adjusted for factors such as the repayment of loans and the tying of aid by source, the real cost of aid to the United States is reduced by 55 to 70 percent of the nominal figures. With or without the adjustment that economists suggest,[142] the amount of aid is so small a portion of the GNP that it can hardly be called a "burden" at all.

The United States contributed aid in a more generous and genuinely humanitarian spirit (2 percent of GNP) during the Marshall Plan when the sharing of wealth was among the relatively rich, than after the Marshall Plan when the sharing (.2 percent of GNP) was with the poor, who were also nonwhite and culturally different from U.S. officials. For example, in 1949, when United States gross national product was $257 billion, the United States committed $5.5 billion to foreign assistance for the Marshall Plan. After twenty-five years, the gross national product had quintupled, but foreign aid, then going to the relatively poor, had shrunk by more than one-third.

An accurate picture of the relationship between United States wealth and its effort to help the poor is portrayed by constructing an aid burden index in which yearly total grant and loan commitments for development assistance are divided by the gross national product per capita, as shown in Table 3-12. The aid burden index in 1974 was only one-twelfth of its level in 1949, even though during that same period the gross national product increased by five times. (See Figure 3-1.) These data include, one should recall, AID economic assistance to military client states, such as South Vietnam, South Korea, Laos, and Cambodia. If the index were to account only for aid going into economic development more narrowly defined, it would be substantially lower.

When sharing more than 2 percent of its GNP with Europe, the United States asked European states to decide their own plans for development and the United States pledged to support them. When sharing .24 of 1 percent of its GNP with less developed countries, the United States hedged its support with self-serving restrictions. After World War II, the United States government permitted Europe to discriminate against its exports, overcoming strong business pressures at home to avoid excessive profit-taking on European problems.[143] In India, the United States government has insisted that aid serve the profit motive of U.S. exporters.[144] The United States has refused to forego even

171

Table 3-12
Aid Burden Index[a] for Total Commitments to All Countries
By AID and Predecessor Agencies

Fiscal Year	Aid Burden Index[a]	U.S. GNP	Loans	Grants
			millions of dollars	
1949	3.22	256500	1165	4352
1950	1.93	284800	163	3451
1951	1.24	328400	45	2577
1952	0.91	345500	201	1784
1953	0.86	364600	26	1934
1954	1.00	364800	114	2114
1955	0.76	398000	197	1624
1956	0.61	419200	208	1298
1957	0.63	441100	322	1305
1958	0.63	447300	417	1202
1959	0.70	483700	626	1291
1960	0.67	503700	564	1302
1961	0.71	520100	707	1315
1962	0.84	560300	1330	1180
1963	0.74	590500	1346	954
1964	0.65	632400	1333	808
1965	0.58	684900	1129	904
1966	0.67	749900	1228	1326
1967	0.56	793900	1091	1162
1968	0.44	864200	929	963
1969	0.32	930300	570	879
1970	0.35	977100	680	988
1971	0.33	1055500	608	1091
1972	0.37	1155200	625	1446
1973	0.33	1294900	664	1338
1974	0.27	1397400	519	1290
1975	0.35	1516000	809	1710
1976	0.30	1692000	857	1476

SOURCES: GNP data were taken from *Economic Report of the President* (Washington, D.C.: Government Printing Office, 1974, 1976). Population data are from United Nations, *Demographic Yearbook*, various years. Data for total loan and grant commitments for development assistance were taken from U.S. Agency for International Development, *U.S. Economic Assistance Programs Administered by the Agency for International Development and Predecessor Agencies, April 3, 1948-June 30, 1971*; after 1971, U.S. Agency for International Development, *U.S. Overseas Loans and Grants and Assistance from International Organizations*, various years.
NOTES: [a] Aid Burden Index = (total annual commitments for grants and loans to all countries from AID and predecessor agencies)/(U.S. GNP per capita).

relatively minor trade advantages in commercial intercourse with India, even though this stance doubtless harms Indian economic planning and development. Two-thirds of the aid to Europe was in outright grants; less than one-seventh of development aid to India was in grants. During the aid program to Europe, U.S. officials were inclined to ask: what do recipients need? For aid to less developed countries, officials have tended to ask: what return will the United States receive? When the United States was most generous in giving aid, its programs were also less selfish in their techniques of execution.

Perhaps a Senate study on technical assistance best sums up the normative foundation upon which United States development aid has been based:

> . . . the sole test of technical assistance is the national interest of the United States. Technical assistance is not something to be done, as a Government enterprise, for its own sake or for the sake of others. The United States Government is not a charitable institution, nor is it an appropriate outlet for the charitable spirit of the American people. . . . the cost of any foreign activity of the United States becomes significant only when it is related to the benefits which the United States receives from that activity.[145]

Were it not for U.S. military activity, fear of political instability, or a perceived threat of a disliked ideology, there would have been little, if any, reallocation of wealth to the developing countries at all. The amount of aid has been determined more by assumed military needs and economic self-interest than by a humanitarian desire to reform the global economic and political structures that perpetuate poverty.[146]

While the average per capita income in the United States has been more than 40 times that of India, while the annual increase in the goods and services produced in the United States during some years equalled *all* the goods and services produced annually in India,[147] while the number of Indians living below the rock-bottom Indian poverty line of $60 per year has exceeded the total population of the United States, while the United States annually has absorbed 40 percent of the world's annual energy output and nonrenewable resources,[148] and while a substantial portion of this wealth has originated from the less developed countries, the United States in the last decade has granted to India about three cents a year for each U.S. citizen. Surely it

173

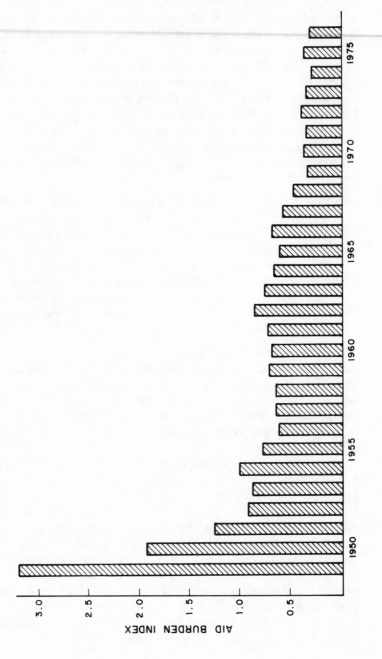

Figure 3-1
Total U.S. Grant and Loan Commitments to All Countries as Ratio of U.S.
GNP per Capita

Figure 3-2
Comparison of U.S. and Indian GNP per Capita in Constant 1972 Dollars

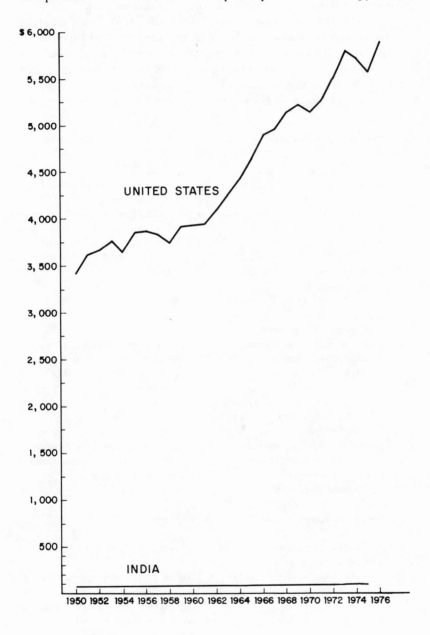

stretches the bounds of credibility to suggest that such a level of assistance represents tangible humanitarian concern.[149]

The preceding evidence demonstrates that humanitarian rhetoric has been used to disguise the fundamental purpose of economic aid: namely, *to maximize power, strategic advantages, and economic benefits for those in charge of United States foreign policy and for the privileged minority that effectively supports them, even at the expense of economic well-being and equity for other societies* (implicit

Table 3-13

A Comparison of Professed and Implicit Values in U.S. Aid Policies

Professed Values	*Implicit Values*
1. To serve U.S. security interests.	A. To enhance U.S. power and strategic advantages.
a. To discourage threats to the stability of the international system.	a. To discourage social reformers who would be less sympathetic than existing governments to U.S. interests in world politics.
b. To strengthen allies against communism.	b. Same.
c. To discourage nonallies from developing friendly relations with communist governments.	c. Same.
d. To encourage internal political stability in developing countries.	d. To encourage internal stability in developing countries that were sympathetic to U.S. interests.
e. To encourage a demonstration effect showing the superiority of noncommunist systems.	e. Same.
2. To provide economic benefits for the U.S. from international trade and investment.	B. To promote economic benefits for the U.S. from international trade and investment.
a. To increase exports of U.S. goods and services.	a. Same.
b. To insure access to raw materials.	b. Same.
c. To encourage private enterprise overseas.	c. Same.
3. To express humanitarian concern.	C. To maximize strategic advantages and economic gains for the U.S. even at the expense of economic well-being, equity, and compassion for other societies.

176

value C). To be sure, some sincere persons had humanitarian motives in favoring foreign assistance. But there can be no doubt that the values cumulatively expressed in actual aid programs failed to include both a sense of urgency about structural change and a meaningful concern by the relatively rich, U.S. segment of the world's population for meeting the basic human needs of the world's poor.

A GLOBAL HUMANIST APPROACH

The final portion of this chapter will compare the values implicitly expressed in United States foreign assistance policy with the second value of global humanism, namely the maximization of economic well-being for all persons on the planet. If one assumes this value position, it is evident that substantial redistribution of wealth throughout the globe is imperative. Regardless of how one figures personal incomes and basic costs for a decent livelihood, there is no persuasive normative justification for the vast income and consumption differentials that exist between the people of the United States and the people of India.

Universal Minimum Standard of Living

All human beings deserve an equitable opportunity to acquire the basic essentials for physical existence. These include sufficient food, shelter, clothing, medical care, and educational opportunities to achieve some degree of human fulfillment without chronic anxiety about continuing existence. Until all persons of the globe are fed, there can be no compelling justification for color television sets, conspicuous consumption, or other luxuries that absorb scarce energies and resources which, from a global standpoint, are in short supply. Although controversy may surround the debate about whether one person's luxury is another's necessity, there need be little debate about the glaring inequity of enormous expenditures by the wealthy minority of the world's population that lives in the United States and other industrialized nations and the inability of a majority of people on earth to buy the minimum requirements for a healthy physical existence. Such requirements can, to a satisfactory degree, be objectively defined.

Attention also should be given to the more difficult issue of what constitutes an equitable sharing of resources globally, over and above a minimum for existence, but that troublesome ques-

177

tion need not detain us much at present. Current efforts should be aimed at the less controversial goal of insuring that every person on the globe has a minimum standard of living to meet the necessities for survival. During the second stage of transition toward realizing the values of global humanism, the emphasis should shift from building an income floor for overcoming poverty and establishing minimal human decency, toward constructing greater economic equity and human justice.

Critics of the relatively modest proposal presented here for a universal minimum standard of living will argue with some justification that resources should not be sent abroad while some Americans still suffer from malnutrition. The strength of this argument and the presence of widespread poverty in the United States reveal further, of course, the extent to which humanitarianism is absent from the United States political process even domestically. For millions of Americans to be living in poverty—not as a temporary phenomenon, but as a permanent subculture—is morally outrageous in a society as rich and wasteful as the United States.

The opponents of a universal minimum standard of living are likely to be the same people who oppose elimination of poverty and income equalization within the United States. The importance of this understanding is to illustrate the genuine, common interests between advocates in this country of the universal minimum standard of living and people in the less developed countries who together can work against the political forces that seek to perpetuate the political and economic status quo. There is, in short, a potentially strong moral and practical bond between advocates of global humanism, regardless of nationality, and the dispossessed people of the world, whether in the United States or India. It is this commonality which could provide the basis for a genuinely multinational movement for world order reform.

Empowering the Dispossessed

The values of global humanism suggest another major departure from past aid programs. It is important not merely to share wealth equitably enough to achieve a universal minimum standard of living, but also to share participation in decision making about how the resources of the world should be utilized. On the one hand, it is economically intolerable for 6 percent of the world's population living in the United States to consume 40

178

percent of the world's raw materials and energy resources, because such disproportionate consumption deprives others of reaching the universal minimum standard of living; on the other hand, it is politically intolerable to allow a small number of the world's people to make the decisive determination of how to use the resources that belong to many more. The existing political structure of the world is unjust in failing to allow all persons to participate fairly in the decisions that affect the use of the resources of the planet. That structure is presently tipped far in the direction of giving the United States more influence on decisions than equity dictates.

A second reason for sharing decision-making authority more widely is that wealth redistribution is politically infeasible without wide sharing of power. Historically, whether in the nineteenth century extension of the franchise in Britain or in the recent civil rights movement in the United States, poor people have sought greater participation in the political process as a means for achieving more economic egalitarianism. The dispossessed could not achieve redistribution of wealth without extension of the franchise. To equalize the distribution of wealth in the world, it is necessary to equalize the distribution of power. Conversely, when wealth is to some extent redistributed, as it was after the oil-exporting states raised the price of oil, power begins to shift as well. In short, substantial foreign aid is unlikely to come merely by cajoling the American electorate to "give" more to others. Equalization of wealth will come when the "others" become a part of the decision-making process for allocating wealth.

The above changes, of course, cannot occur without the spread in the United States of a political consciousness that emphasizes the solidarity of all human beings, not just of United States citizens; that seeks to promote the well-being of all humans, not just the security and wealth of the privileged in the United States; that aims at the service of human needs, not the maximizing of profit through production of goods that fail to contribute to human health, safety, or welfare.

Contrasting Value Orientations

IMPLICIT VALUES AND FUTURE TRENDS

By rejecting policies aimed at realization of global socioeconomic welfare, U.S. officials have also impeded the implementa-

179

tion of the other three world order values. If past U.S. policies continue, one can expect these consequences in the various value areas:

(V_1) Social unrest and both repressive and revolutionary uses of violence will doubtless accompany the conflict between rich and poor societies, as well as between rich and poor classes within a given society. Terrorism will increase. Military power will be used to protect the nonsharing wealthy from change and to keep the poor powerless.

(V_2) Structural changes leading to the elimination of poverty will not occur. The gap between rich and poor will grow.

(V_3) Economic inequities defended through repression will perpetuate injustice and unequal opportunity for human fulfillment. Many persons will starve; many others will live without dignity and without being able to use their creative abilities.

(V_4) Overconsumption and wasting of nonrenewable resources by wealthy, overdeveloped, and misdeveloped countries will prevent the reasoned diminishing of pollution, the conservation of resources, and the concentration of productive capacity upon necessities (such as food) for human survival. In short, there are striking contrasts between the values expressed in United States foreign aid policy and the four values of global humanism. (See Table 3-14.)

WORLD ORDER RHETORIC

One difficulty in reforming U.S. aid policies is that occasionally official rhetoric, unlike official practice, closely resembles the values of global humanism. Governmental and corporate spokesmen have used enough language of global concern to convince some constituencies that the United States acts with unusual magnanimity in its development assistance. This inaccurate perception undermines efforts to bring about fundamental change in aid programs. Meanwhile, officials engage in little follow-through to implement their lofty rhetoric.

In recent years, officials of both the Nixon-Ford and Carter administrations have occasionally spoken of the need to take account of a global interest. Secretary Kissinger stressed the need for global cooperation to prevent the breakdown of the international order. Jimmy Carter declared that "we must replace balance-of-power politics with world-order politics." Secretary Vance said that the United States was ready to help build a new economic system that was, above all, just.[150]

180

Table 3-14
Selected Values of Global Humanism Compared to U.S. Policy
for Development Assistance to India

Global Humanism	*U.S. Policy*

Peace

1. Substantial redistribution of wealth should occur in order to alleviate poverty and promote equality, thereby decreasing the likelihood of both civil and international wars.

1. Small transfers of wealth should occur in order to gain influence or cement alliances useful for U.S. military and political advantages. Aid should also help decrease overseas domestic dissatisfaction that is the breeding ground for anti-U.S. or anticapitalist movements.

Economic Well-being

2. Current patterns of income and consumption are inequitable and unfair. The wealth of rich societies has to a significant degree been achieved at the expense of the poor.

2. Current patterns of income and consumption are uneven, but that does not mean they are unjust. The U.S. has wealth because its people worked hard and developed a good economic system. They deserve the wealth they have.

3. Current economic patterns should be altered radically by establishing a universal minimum standard of living.

3. Current economic patterns should not be altered radically. To establish a universal minimum standard of living would bring excessive governmental, and possibly intergovernmental, involvement in the economy. Sufficient economic development in poor countries should occur to maintain stability.

4. The guiding purpose of foreign aid, as well as more general use of natural resources and human energies, should be to serve universal human needs.

4. The guiding purpose of foreign aid, as well as the more general use of natural resources and human energies, should be to serve the security and economic interests of the U.S. These interests are defined in terms of maximizing power and wealth.

5. Reallocation of wealth should involve yearly transfers of from 1 to 5 percent of GNP from the industrialized countries to the less developed countries in official development assistance.

5. There is little intention to redistribute wealth from rich to poor. Instead there is a vague hope that a global form of the "trickle down theory" will work. The rich countries may retain a wide gap with the poor countries in terms of income per capita, but eventually the poor will be better off because the rich will be so much better off than at present.

181

Table 3-14 (cont.)

Global Humanism	*U.S. Policy*
6. Amount of aid should not be contingent upon the "threat" of ideologies. In this respect, ideologies are almost irrelevant, as the goal is to serve human needs.	6. Aid has been linked with the threat of communism or movements perceived to be hostile to U.S. influence. Poverty is incidentally undesirable because it provides fertile ground for alien ideologies. Rather than using aid in the general service of human needs, it has been designed to discriminate against human beings with disliked ideologies.

Human Rights and Social Justice

1. Present economic and trade policies deny human rights by preventing (1) fair participation in global economic decision making and (2) the achievement of a standard of living sufficient for mere physical survival, without which other human rights are meaningless.	1. The present distribution of wealth and power for economic decision making is seldom discussed by U.S. officials as an issue of justice; the international economic status quo is assumed to be fair in general. Although human suffering is unfortunate, the existing allocation of wealth and decision-making power is not perceived as a fundamental violation of human rights and social justice.
2. Equality of opportunity is a basic human right.	2. Equality of opportunity is not, in a global context, a human right.
3. All people in the world should share as equitably as possible in the decisions about how to use the resources of the world.	3. Decisions about using the world's resources should be left in the hands of officials from national governments or corporations, thus in practice enabling the U.S. to utilize an enormously disproportionate share of the world's resources. The U.S. seeks multilateral cooperation to protect its position, but not on an equitable or democratic basis.
4. A bond of solidarity among all human beings should guide policies.	4. A bond of solidarity between U.S. citizens and their allies should guide policies. People outside this group are in practice used as objects to serve U.S. interests. The selection of policy means is dictated by U.S. interests, not planetary needs.

Table 3-14 (cont.)

Global Humanism	*U.S. Policy*

Ecological Balance

1. Past and present policies have produced ecologically dangerous world priorities. Industrial states are overdeveloped or misdeveloped. Continued unplanned economic growth poses threats to survival from unnecessary pollution and resource depletion. Continued poverty and illiteracy in the less developed countries make population planning difficult.

1. Global economic priorities are not viewed as a major contributor to environmental problems. While growing attention is paid to environmental questions, there is a reluctance to take international action based on the assumption that the industrial nations are consuming too much, or endangering human life by failing to regulate their economic growth in the interest of serving first the human needs of all.

Yet, regardless of rhetoric, the United States has not gone far toward helping create a more just and economically rational economic order. Officials have made no statement that the amount of resources consumed by the United States has been disproportionate, unfair, or has contributed to human misery in other parts of the world. Also, proposals for fairer pricing and decision making in global economic relations have been repeatedly rejected. The United States has shown no embarrassment in its desire to take resources from both the less developed countries and the high seas—once declared the "common heritage" of humankind—to enhance its own wealth.

After examining United States aid to India for a quarter of a century, one must also be skeptical about government intentions to engage in any genuine redistribution of the world's wealth. Public opinion about foreign assistance over the long run has been roughly balanced between favorable and unfavorable attitudes toward aid among the general public. One recent survey showed that 79 percent of U.S. citizens favored development assistance when they believed that the aid actually reached the people for whom it is intended.[151] Thus, the leadership could have provided much more aid, presumably, if it had chosen to do so.

Finally, the expression of concern for global, as distinct from strictly national well-being, usually has rested upon an implicit assumption that what is good for the United States is good for the world. The United States government is concerned about

183

maintaining a system of global order and stability in order to protect its own presently privileged position.[152] As a result, "despite high-minded rhetoric," says Senator Mark Hatfield, "our Government has sat on its bureaucratic hands while millions eke out a malnourished existence or starve."[153] In fact, past aid programs and the official rhetoric of global concern mask a policy that seeks to enlist the rest of the globe in the service of United States special privilege.

Since the maintenance of a privileged share of the world's wealth and decision-making power by the United States is a major obstacle to the realization of V_2, one must consider the possibility that continuing past aid policies may be less progressive than abolishing the aid program altogether. Full consideration of that possibility is beyond the scope of this study, and such a conclusion is likely to be more accurate for some aid recipients than others. Nonetheless, it is instructive to examine several arguments against foreign aid in general.

RADICAL PERSPECTIVES

First, radical critics point out that aid may encourage economic and political stability when the imperative is for change. Aid has on occasion fortified elitist governments in the underdeveloped countries against the mobilizing lower classes intent upon major reform.

Aid to some countries has made them dependent upon continued U.S. assistance and subjected them to U.S. political influence. This dependency has enabled the United States to influence internal politics sufficiently to serve U.S. interests and prevent the radical socioeconomic change necessary for realization of V_2. To be sure, in subtle and complicated ways, the United States has sought to influence Indian affairs. AID officials point out that their efforts usually were designed to encourage Indian development, but their vision of development always encompassed a largely United States-dominated world of capitalist enterprises. Even when U.S. AID officials' suggestions may have been economically rational from the Indian point of view, they were irritating to Indians because of Indian self-consciousness about being economically vulnerable to pressures by capital exporting nations.[154] The net result of this relationship among unequals has not encouraged generous assistance nor greater economic equity. Paternalism, even when well-intentioned and well-received, leads to results that are qualitatively different from the results that arise from equal participation in decisions about how to use the world's wealth.

In the mid-1960s, for example, the United States directly, as well as through the World Bank and International Monetary Fund (IMF), pressed the Indian government to devalue the rupee. U.S. AID officials believed that devaluation plus increased aid would help solve India's economic difficulties. However, after Indian compliance with U.S. requests, U.S. aid decreased, in part because so much money was spent for the war in Vietnam.[155] As former AID official John Lewis commented, U.S. aid to India seemed inversely correlated with the worthiness of the recipient.[156] Devaluing the rupee, of course, lowered the price of Indian goods for U.S. purchasers, and it provided a more profitable field for U.S. investment.

The United States has, through multilateral financial institutions and bilateral aid negotiations, persuaded many less developed countries at various times to devalue their currencies to combat inflation and to facilitate foreign private investment. By improving the climate for U.S. investment and increasing the dollar's buying power abroad, such policies have effectively foreclosed some alternatives for autonomous national development, thus slowing the achievement of economic independence in the long run. And, some critics point out, economic dependency has contributed to the perpetuation of an international economic system featuring U.S. wealth and the poverty of the less developed nations.[157]

Furthermore, aid opponents argue that as long as U.S. capital goes primarily to nonsocialist economic structures, it will inevitably be used for the production of goods that maximize profits. That means producing goods for which there is a demand generated by those with money to buy goods. Other persons too poor to create demand will continue, under such an economic system, to have many of their most fundamental needs ignored. As Herbert Feldman has observed, in some poverty-ridden cities on the Asian subcontinent, more time, money, and effort have been expended in providing popular (and profitable) brands of fizzy drinks than in providing a hygienic milk supply.[158] The wealthy can buy Coke, but the poor lack means to generate demand for milk. In short, if maximizing profits determines what will be produced, then even with the influx of new foreign capi-

185

tal, the poor will doubtless remain poor. Historically, the aid program has demonstrated a fundamental contradiction between maximizing private profit and serving human needs.[159]

The U.S. desire for profitability has slowed autonomous economic development in India to some degree. In the early years of foreign aid, the United States resisted the idea that Indians should manufacture items such as machinery or chemicals because that would have deprived U.S. producers of markets in India and brought new competition in other world markets.[160] U.S. aid also skewed some economic decisions in the direction of capital intensive industries[161] when labor intensive projects might have been wiser. The latter form of Indian self-sufficiency, however, would have been less profitable for U.S. producers.

It was, perhaps, a sign of the arrogance of wealth to assume without any question that the less developed countries were better off with U.S. aid than without it. The Chinese model provides a unique but instructive exception to aid recipients, insofar as it has had no substantial outside assistance, and thus is not burdened with heavy loan repayments. Yet, the Chinese government has done far better than many less developed countries in serving human needs of food, clothing, housing, and medical care. Radical political economists note that instead of investing where the rate of return was greatest, as occurs in capitalist development, the Chinese sought to eradicate poverty. They focused on what to produce and for whom, not on how quickly they could produce goods to earn foreign exchange.[162]

To the extent that U.S. foreign assistance has discouraged internal and global structural change, influenced Indian politics toward serving U.S. present and future economic interests at the expense of domestic equity, inhibited the growth of either genuine economic self-sufficiency or interdependency among equals, to that degree it has been imperialistic. So many difficulties attend the bilateral transfer of capital from rich societies to economically less powerful societies that some critics believe that the process is often damaging to the recipient.[163] If humanity is one, then any unilaterally determined, disproportionate use of the world's resources by one society can be viewed as imperialistic. In a world of scarcity, for some to consume more than they need while others have less than they need means one society enjoys privilege at the other's expense, sacrifice, and misery.

Elements of an imperialistic mentality have been present even among some well-intentioned liberal advocates of foreign assistance. They have often overlooked structural origins of poverty. For example, the Pearson Commission concluded that "the major external constraint [for economic development] may be summed up as the availability of foreign exchange."[164] Yet, the reason Indians need foreign exchange is that the prices paid for their exports are too low in comparison to the prices paid for their imports, chiefly manufactured goods and food. There is nothing inherently virtuous about the setting of those prices. They are a product of the configuration of political and economic power in the world, not of any conception of justice. If global political self-determination could suddenly be realized, no doubt the world's people would change the pricing structure. But the United States, as the largest producer of manufactured goods and food for export, has refused to alter those prices in the interest of the poor at the same time that it has used its military strength and covert CIA activities to inhibit a more influential exercise of power by the world's poor.[165]

The imperialistic element in aid policies springs from the assumption that what Americans have is in fact their possession. Yet the sources of wealth (or poverty) are somewhat arbitrary, and historical accidents often determine whether one society is richer than another. To the extent that economic affairs are not arbitrary and are under human control, the wealth of rich societies often has been—whether intentionally or unintentionally—deprived from the poor because the poor were less powerful.

This idea was illustrated by U.S. officials' response to the explosion of an Indian nuclear device. They expressed dismay, and accused the Indians of wasting their scarce resources.[166] Some officials urged a reevaluation of U.S. aid to India as an expression of displeasure, but aid was at the time almost nonexistent, so that potential political lever was absent. Meanwhile, the U.S. government saw nothing wrong with continued United States explosion of nuclear devices. However, if a sense of human solidarity had motivated U.S. officials, they would have understood that the scarcity of Indian resources should impinge as much on the conscience of U.S. officials as they argued it should have on Indian officials. From a planetary perspective, the wasting of global resources on United States nuclear development hurt the Indian poor as much as a similar Indian use of resources.

One might even argue that the Indian effort, unlike U.S. nuclear development, could possibly give India more political power through which to achieve greater global economic equity. Insofar as the acquisition of power by the weak has been a key to more equitable distribution of wealth, the Indian nuclear explosion—deplorable though it was in terms of V_1—seemed a symbolic statement that V_1 could hardly be realized if V_2 were ignored. Significantly, the United States has objected to other states acquiring equality in nuclear power as much as it has refused to share its wealth globally as a matter of human right. By opposing economic justice and nuclear proliferation, U.S. officials have sought to perpetuate both their economic and military advantages. In pursuing this policy, however, officials have actually encouraged nuclear proliferation. The governments of the less developed countries can recognize that U.S. political and economic preeminence have been mutually reinforcing. Thus, in the effort to overturn U.S.-sponsored global economic inequities, poor states will be inclined to erode, through partial imitation of U.S. military might, the expensive military capabilities by which the United States retains its economic position, wasteful though such expenditures might otherwise be.

In short, radical critiques of U.S. foreign aid policies alert us to the counterproductive consequences of many past aid programs. One need not fully agree with these critiques to understand that, in the Indian case, even if the aid program had been allowed to develop according to the direction featured in its best years, it would have had little redistributive content meaningful for world order reform. Aid tended to be limited philanthropy, largely irrelevant to structural economic transformation.

The well-known liberal Under Secretary of State, George Ball, accurately reported that the goal of U.S. foreign aid policies was neither to remove nor even to narrow the gap between the rich "North" of the planet and the poor "South." "[I]n spite of the hyperbole of political speeches, we are not going to reduce the disparity in wealth between North and South. In the face of all our foreign efforts, that disparity has been growing and it will continue to grow. . . . With luck the poor will get richer, but the rich will, in absolute terms, get richer much faster."[167]

Redistribution of Wealth

A foreign policy truly aimed at achieving V_2 should consider discontinuing all programs designed to serve short-range national security and economic interests of the United States as these have been traditionally defined. These interests are worthy of support only if they are redefined to give priority to long-term considerations of human security and global economic needs. Such redefinition would free policymakers from the past chronic tension between national security and human compassion; it would allow political prudence to converge with moral principle.

Policymakers should consider replacing all existing aid programs with an alternative program based upon the frank assumption that a universal minimum standard of living is a human right. In the absence of its achievement, existing income inequities of forty or fifty to one are morally and politically wrong. If a universal minimum standard of living is a matter of right, aid should not be considered a gift. Income redistribution is required because the resources of the world belong to the people of the world.

If one proceeds from this assumption, income redistribution should not be curtailed or halted if India criticizes United States foreign policy, if India refuses to be a military ally, or if Indian ideologies are dissimilar to American. What matters is that Indians are human beings every bit as much as Americans. When, in a world of scarcity, there is insufficient food to nourish everyone, then all nationalities should bear equally the burden of insufficiency and any requisite decrease in life expectancy.

From this vantage point, aid should not be tailored to buy friends, to stimulate demand for United States goods, nor to alleviate a United States balance of payments problem. Income redistribution aimed at global equity can be justified both for friend and "enemy" simply to achieve minimal essentials of life for all human beings. If aid were justified on these grounds, debate would not focus on "who are our friends?" but instead on "what are the minimum requirements for life which are a matter of responsibility for all members of the world community?"

Larger amounts of aid might be forthcoming if the government refused to justify aid in terms of contributing to United States security and instead made a frank, humanitarian appeal for global justice. Past programs have been intellectually deceptive and politically self-defeating in their claim to aid development and at the same time serve the strategic interests of the United States. If a program failed to produce strategic dividends, then aid was curtailed.[168]

189

To grasp the philosophical underpinnings of the approach proposed here, it is useful to distinguish three general orientations toward aid. U.S. policy has been a combination of the first two. The advocate of a conservative policy generally has opposed foreign aid on the grounds that the rich deserve their wealth and the poor deserve their poverty. From this perspective, the main U.S. interest in assistance for India was strategic, and since aid failed to produce dividends, it should be terminated. The liberal view has favored limited aid to help persons less fortunate. Desiring "change within the system," liberals have sought to remodel it enough to perpetuate it and retain economic and political control largely in the same national hands. This has been a "charity mentality" based upon the trickle down theory of assistance, in which it was assumed that as the rich nations got richer, the poor would also improve their lot, but little attention was given to diminishing the gap between the two as an end in itself. In a world of scarcity and finite growth, however, the liberal vision is seriously challenged, because the rich can maintain their pace of material accumulation only if they refuse to divert needed resources to eliminating poverty.

A third perspective, represented by V_2, calls for a strategy in which the purpose of political and economic activity should be to help first those people in the worst conditions. This view bases the argument for aid not only on a sense of moral obligation to help the poor survive, but more firmly on a concept of justice that affirms a humane existence based upon equal opportunity as a matter of right. Adherents advocate structural change, not only to eliminate economic inequities, but also to share power widely so that the presently dispossessed may participate in decisions about allocation of planetary resources.

The difference between what I have called the liberal, charity mentality and the idea of structural reform can perhaps be best understood by drawing an analogy from the United States civil rights movement in the 1960s. Liberals espoused civil rights as long as the goal was congenial-sounding "integration," which often meant in practice that blacks would join white society. Some of the same liberals experienced deep, negative, emotional reactions when the goal of civil rights groups became "black power." Already we have forgotten how serious were the debates among liberals about the extent to which black power was tinged with tones of black supremacy and intimidation of whites. Whites were threatened when blacks asked for power because

190

then blacks asked not merely to join white society, but to exercise power in determining what that society would be and how it should be structured.

Similarly, liberal advocates of foreign aid have been willing to share a relatively small amount of surplus wealth with the poor states who were willing to "join," in effect, the U.S. model of international society and capitalist values. But many liberals have resisted the idea that Indians (and others) actually have a right to determine what to do with that part of "United States wealth" that exceeds the rightful share of the people who happen to live in the United States. Like liberals uneasy about black power in the 1960s, foreign aid liberals react to the idea of equal Indian power with emotional arguments of incredulity. For Indians to ask for an equal share of the world's pie, when the pie is finite, is viewed as dangerously destabilizing.

Given the dominance of the conservative and liberal perspectives in U.S. politics, is realization of economic well-being for all really feasible? It is not feasible given the prevailing attitudes and political forces in the United States today. Nevertheless, this alternative image is useful in the urgent effort to change attitudes and realign political forces so that its implementation may become feasible in the near future. Compared with past programs, the alternative suggested above certainly is no less "realistic" or effective even in serving some of the traditionally defined national interests; it is much more promising than current programs in serving the values of global humanism.

For example, past efforts to use aid to buy friendship and strategic advantage have worked poorly because these programs have not maximized development potential. Moreover, in retrospect it is clear that strategic goals have been shortsighted and counterproductive in some cases, due to the unpredictability of political forces. Often the United States has put its money on the wrong political horses. Much aid has contributed to dictatorships and military takeovers instead of to the service of human needs.[169]

In contrast, the aid approach suggested here would free policymakers from any necessity to make uncertain assessments about which potential pro-American political leaders might be the best future bets. Aid severed from the desire for strategic advantage makes it unnecesary to support domestic repression even in the short run in return for alliances. Aid would be designed to alleviate human suffering universally, instead of to

191

create political fortunes for clients of the United States. The United States could thus avoid making enemies or offending potential, yet-to-emerge foreign leaders by a discriminatory aid policy that can never fully predict nor control events.

Aid would not insult the governments of less developed countries by seeming to compromise their independence or their possible preference for non-American systems and ideologies. Such an aid perspective need not view all radical reformers as hostile to the United States, because the overriding goal would be to serve human needs instead of maintaining alliances or existing economic arrangements. Aid would not need to serve as a quasi-military holding action against social change, as it so often has in the past. Under this proposed approach, assistance could go much further in producing development, since investments could be spent for purchases from the economically most rational sources instead of from only the donating country's corporations. This approach, in addition, would decrease the likelihood of violent conflicts between rich and poor nations that may occur if the present distribution of wealth is perpetuated indefinitely. Thus, this alternative program holds substantial promise even in terms of contributing to global security.

Furthermore, the global humanist approach would, in the long run, enhance global prosperity insofar as it would greatly increase the productivity of human societies and eliminate the drag upon economic and social services of millions of persons living in poverty with resulting physical, educational, and mental impairments. It would help rich nations, such as the United States, (1) correct present misperceptions of the poor as undeserving of an equal share of wealth and power and (2) decrease the self-serving exploitation of the poor. Both of these problems, however unintentional, seem to be almost inevitable whenever wealth is seriously maldistributed in human societies.

An alternative aid program underscores the need for more policy coordination at the global level. The rich would be more willing to help implement income redistribution if in turn a central guidance network would facilitate meaningful efforts to relate population size to scarce resources. In addition, it is necessary to insure that wealth redistribution would be used to serve human needs rather than the repressive inclinations of some totalitarian systems. It seems reasonable that a degree of measurable performance in serving human needs should be a condition of income redistribution. In this sense, strings would be attached to aid, but the strings would be community-established, and would not be tied to serving the economic or strategic interests of the United States, as in current aid programs. The norms governing both income redistribution and population planning would be a product of global political processes.

Despite many warnings during the 1960s that the longer development problems were put off the more difficult would be their solution, the United States did not transform its assistance programs. They were "falling short at the very time when some of the most important, most promising, and hardest pressed of the developing nations are doing what they most need to do and when they can use far more aid than they are getting."[170] The decade of the 1960s was a crucial period in India's development plan because of the particular convergence of economic conditions, potential for unwanted population growth, and political moderation. One of the most knowledgeable aid officials in India, John P. Lewis, wrote in the early 1960s: "The massive expansion program to which India now is deeply committed is one whose momentum cannot be slowed much below its designed pace without grievously disrupting the economy."[171] Failure to achieve a minimal level of growth would place protracted and debilitating drains on India's foreign exchange, as well as waste psychological resources built during the first decade of independence.

Moreover, Lewis argued, political instability after the sixties and early seventies would doubtless be a growing problem if development did not progress at a pace that exceeded population growth. In the absence of rapid economic development during the sixties, Lewis warned, traditional subnational divisions would be increasingly expressed, disappointment and frustration might result in irreparable political breakdown. "India's still-novel constitutional habit would be broken, and there would be no assurance that she would find her way back to it from whatever pattern of authoritarianism intervened."[172] In little more than a decade after Lewis wrote, events confirmed his fears. By mid-1975, Indira Gandhi suspended civil liberties, silenced the press, and jailed the political opposition. The trickle of U.S. aid and Indian economic policies had failed to satisfy the internal demands for fairness and decency. Thus the Indian government—in a manner not unlike British responses to Mohandas Gandhi's call for civil disobedience—suppressed advocates of structural change in order to preserve stability.

193

The return to constitutional government in 1977 demonstrated the miscalculations of an authoritarian government as well as the resiliency of Indian democracy. But new elections did not solve any of India's economic problems nor change the uncongeniality of the present global economic and political structure to their solution.

Despite the warning signs, the United States has not made any real sacrifices in shouldering obligations for achieving economic equity and a life of decency throughout the world. Nor has the United States been willing to take substantial steps "to counteract the market forces that in the field of trade and capital movements have continuously been holding the underdeveloped countries down in poverty since colonial times."[173] The sharing with Indians by U.S. citizens of an average of less than ten cents per person per year over a twenty-seven year period reveals the need for a radical reversal of current policies.[174]

Indicators of World Order Progress

How can citizens assess progress or regress by their own government in constructing policies for redistribution of wealth? From our examination of United States foreign assistance to India and our discussion of an alternative approach, it is possible to suggest some indicators of the extent to which a rich country's aid policy is conducive to implementing the values of global humanism.

1. How firm are officials' commitments to establishing and implementing a universal minimum standard of living? What concrete steps have been taken in this direction?

2. How firm are officials' commitments to increasing participation of other societies in decisions about how to use the world's resources?

3. How firm are officials' commitments to decreasing a globally disproportionate share of resource usage by the rich nations? What concrete steps have been taken to decrease overconsumption, for example, of food and energy by the rich nations?

4. Is aid officially justified on grounds of, and in fact designed to serve, national security? Or to serve universal human needs?

    a. Are political strings attached to recipients of aid in order to encourage them to become military allies? Or, is aid given as a matter of right to those below a minimum standard of living, regardless of their strategic alignment?

194

b. Does the commitment to a universal minimum standard of living include reasonable precautions to insure that aid in fact reaches the needy, instead of the rich elite in the less developed countries?

5. Is aid justified on grounds of, and designed to serve, the national economic benefit of the donor? Or to serve universal human needs?

a. Is aid tied to purchases from the donating country or instead freed for use where it is economically most rational?

b. To what extent is aid concessional?

c. Is aid designed to encourage inequitable economic systems that will allow further economic advantage for the foreign donor and possible exploitation of the less developed country? Or, is it designed to encourage the economically most rational division of labor globally?

6. To what extent does the level of aid represent a fair share of the global burden of wealth redistribution?[175]

a. Is official development assistance at least one percent of GNP?

b. Is aid per dollar of GNP increasing every year?

7. Are aid programs viewed as charity for helpless, somewhat less worthy people, or are they aimed at structural reform of the socioeconomic order and designed to realize the human right of equality of opportunity?

FOUR · *The United States and Human Rights in Chile*

THE value of laws and political institutions, as of society itself, may be judged largely by the extent to which they protect and facilitate the fulfillment of human rights and dignity. Most people in the United States are proud of what they perceive as the unusual degree to which human rights are practiced within their society and honored in their external relations with other countries. A long-standing, positive human rights image has been tarnished recently by a growing awareness of past violations of human rights. These have been illustrated at home by mistreatment of American Indians, women, blacks, and political dissidents; and overseas by brutality in Vietnam, support for repressive military governments, and a plethora of secret interventions by the CIA in less wealthy and powerful societies.

The purpose of this chapter is to clarify the overseas performance of the United States in implementing the human rights and principles of social justice that are represented by the third value of global humanism.[1] The main objective of this value is to assure conditions that will facilitate the realization of individual and group dignity.[2] Its principal dimensions include the prevention of genocide; the elimination of colonial regimes or imperialistic policies; the drastic modification of racist regimes; the elimination of torture and cruelty; progress toward equality of treatment for different races, sexes, ages, religions, tribes, and political groups; and realization of the rights of self-expression and equitable political participation, both globally and domestically.

In particular, the present chapter will examine U.S. respect for procedural and normative restraints against arbitrary governmental interference in people's lives and in the exercise of their rightful decision-making authority. In foreign relations, the question of respect for this kind of right most frequently arises in the context of supporting or resisting the exercise of self-determination by other societies. Self-determination is defined as the right of a nation to make political decisions and to choose its form of government without illegal or unjust inter-

196

vention by outside governments and powerful private organizations.[3] For our purposes, self-determination can be viewed in conjunction with the principle of nonintervention by one state in another state's domestic affairs. The principal focus will be upon the legally binding obligation not to intervene, especially in a subversive way, in another state's internal exercise of self-determination. In addition, the impact of U.S. policies upon other human rights, such as the conduct of open elections and the exercise of a free press will be discussed where relevant. Special attention will be paid to the attitude of U.S. officials toward the protection of human rights in the conduct of their foreign policies.[4]

Self-determination will be treated as an important illustrative component of a more comprehensive cluster of human rights. To be sure, self-determination does not touch all other rights, but it offers a reasonable focal point for assessing official attitudes toward human rights in general. Although firm U.S. support for self-determination might not mean similarly strong support for other human rights (such as elimination of racism or sexism), the failure to respect self-determination is likely to be accompanied by similar indifference to most other human rights. This indifference is not unlike the callousness that historically has characterized imperialism, the classic violation of the right of self-determination.

The modern drive for self-determination is one of the most powerful political forces in contemporary societies. To be free of unwarranted external interference, whether in the form of imperial control or less visible external manipulation, is widely recognized as an important human right in our era. One of the purposes of the United Nations, stated in Article 1 of the Charter, is to "develop friendly relations among nations based on respect for the principle of equal rights and self-determination of peoples." Even before the influx into the UN of newly-independent states that led the struggle against colonialism, the General Assembly formally recognized self-determination as a fundamental human right and asked the Economic and Social Council and the Commission of Human Rights to suggest means to "ensure the right of peoples and nations to self-determination."[5] The UN Covenant on Human Rights declares: "All peoples have the right of self-determination. By virtue of that right they freely determine their political status and freely pursue their economic, social, and cultural development." Parties to the covenant are required to "promote the realization of the right of self-determination."[6]

In the "Declaration on the Granting of Independence to Colonial Countries and Peoples," the Assembly adopted—with the United States abstaining—the proclamation that "subjection to alien . . . domination and exploitation constitutes a denial of fundamental human rights, [and] is contrary to the Charter of the United Nations." It asked all governments to respect the principle of "noninterference in the internal affairs of all states."[7] U.S. officials have endorsed the "inherent and inalienable right of self-determination"[8] and the "duty" of states "to respect the principle of self-determination."[9] In short, governments generally endorse the right of self-determination defined as freedom from external intervention.[10] No states explicitly claim a right to intervene in the domestic affairs of other states.

Yet the world's most powerful national governments and multinational corporations frequently yield to the temptation to violate self-determination. As people in the developing countries exercise greater influence over decisions that affect their lives, the influence of major external governments diminishes in areas where these governments have served their own strategic and economic interests at the expense of the less developed countries. The prospect of an unwanted relative decline in the globally disproportionate privileges of the United States, especially if accompanied by the growth of radical movements overseas, will probably tempt U.S. officials to violate self-determination through covert interventions or to condone repression by reactionary governments. Thus self-determination and other human rights issues are likely to be of central importance for U.S. policies in coming decades. Insofar as the fuller expression of self-determination contributes to a more equitable distribution of power among nations, it aids the achievement of V_3. Any effort to impede this shifting of power and authority prevents the achievement of the third global humanist value. Because self-determination is a necessary (though not sufficient) condition to satisfy the aspiration for human liberation and yet is frequently under attack in the political arena, self-determination provides an instructive focus for studying the realization of worldwide human rights and justice.

Self-determination is also a useful focus because it lies at the center of foreign policy debates that profoundly affect the prospects for world order reform. Present and future generations must address the question: What political units shall decide what range of issues? What degree and kind of influence in other societies' political processes constitute a violation of human rights? When does such action amount to "manipulation without representation," a twentieth-century equivalent of King George's eighteenth-century taxation without representation?

U.S. performance on the self-determination question will be examined in the context of U.S. policy toward Chile from 1970 to 1974. This case has been selected for these reasons:

1. The often-noted problem of deciding who deserves the right of determination does not arise in this case. Chile clearly constituted a nation deserving self-determination.

2. The human rights issue of self-determination was clearly tested. A government existed which was democratically elected but not favored by the United States.

3. Chile was small and distant enough to constitute no security threat to the United States, thus enabling the investigator to avoid entangling the human rights question in a security issue.

4. The political process in Chilean politics was sufficiently similar to other European and Latin American political systems to be easily understood by United States officials.

5. The Chilean example presented a case where the economic interests of large corporations were present. Thus it is possible to examine the idea, anticipated in Chapter One, that multinational corporations will play a salient role in the future of foreign policy decision making.

6. Issues posed within Chile, especially for a radical internal alteration of the distribution of wealth, are likely to be repeated in coming decades in other contexts.

7. Policy toward Chile was typical of U.S. policy elsewhere insofar as it was not an aberration or a fluke based on faulty information or official actions lacking in proper authority. United States behavior resulted from deliberate, repeated, informed discussion by officials at the highest level of the government.

8. A focus on U.S. policy towards a Latin American country provides a case study in the geographic area where the United States has had the greatest historical experience and the most conscious, long-standing discussion of self-determination. In Latin America, one could most reasonably expect a seasoned, well-informed sensitivity on the part of U.S. officials to the right of self-determination.

United States interest in self-determination for Latin Ameri-

199

can countries goes back, at the least, to the early nineteenth-century recognition of independent Latin American governments and the Monroe Doctrine of 1823, in which the United States warned European states against seeking to impose control over any states in the Western Hemisphere. Of course, the principle of prohibiting extrahemispheric intervention was later transformed, with the help of the Roosevelt Corollary, the Platt Amendment, and similar actions, into a self-proclaimed right for the United States to intervene and establish virtual de facto control over the governments of some Latin American societies. That is a familiar story to students of history.

At the same time, there has been a fairly constant repetition, sometimes voiced by only a few, of a genuine intention to restrain the United States from violating the political independence of Latin American countries. This voice of restraint often has been honored in the rhetoric of officials, if not always in their practice. Nonetheless, the point remains that the principle has been frequently discussed, and the United States has had numerous opportunities to learn from its mistakes and hone its policy to a sharper recognition of self-determination during the many years of foreign relations with Latin America.

Precisely because of the greater power and interventionist policies exercised by the United States in inter-American relations, Latin American states have been particularly sensitive to the prohibition of outside intervention. In the Charter of the Organization of American States (OAS), the principle of self-determination is given prominent attention: "No state . . . has the right to intervene, directly or indirectly, for any reason whatever, in the internal or external affairs of any other state. The foregoing principle prohibits not only armed force but also any other form of interference."[11]

The governments of Chile and the United States, among others, in the Puente del Este Declaration, declared their adherence to "the principles of self-determination and non-intervention as guiding standards of coexistence among the American nations." They pledged support for "the principle of non-intervention and the right of peoples to organize their way of life freely in the political, economic, and cultural spheres expressing their will through free elections, without foreign interference."[12]

The relevant treaties, such as the OAS Charter, were duly ratified by the United States Senate, and thus their provisions carry the constitutionally-defined status of "the supreme law of the land."[13] The principles of self-determination and noninterference are firmly and unequivocally established as legal obligations for the United States and its officials.

DESCRIPTION OF U.S. POLICY TOWARD CHILE

The Problem of Secrecy

A question of whether to respect the right of self-determination in Chile arose in U.S. policy because of the strong opposition of U.S. officials and the executives of several multinational corporations to the political success of Salvador Allende Gossens, a physician and leader of a socialist party in Chile. In a three-way race for president on September 4, 1970, Allende won a national popular election by a narrow margin, receiving 36.3 percent of the total vote. In cases where the highest candidate had a plurality but not a majority of the votes, the Chilean Constitution required that the selection of a president from among the two highest candidates be decided by the Congress. This was normally a formality: Congress had always elected the front-runner in the popular vote. On October 24, following their constitutional tradition, the Congress did overwhelmingly elect Allende president of Chile.

From the moment that Allende won the popular election for the presidency of Chile, Washington officials showed their displeasure. They publicly promised, however, not to interfere in the affairs of another people who had expressed themselves freely at the ballot box. Three years later, in September 1973, Allende died during a violent military takeover of his government. U.S. officials, denying any United States complicity in supporting anti-Allende forces, showed their pleasure that the Allende administration had collapsed by quickly extending recognition and financial assistance to a new military dictatorship.

Between the election and the death of Allende, rumors flourished about United States intervention in Chile. All rumors were officially denied. In truth—or as much truth as investigators have with difficulty ferreted out—the CIA and Department of Defense played a substantial role in creating conditions designed to achieve a speedy overthrow of the elected government. For example, when in October 1970, the Chilean Congress ratified Allende's electoral victory, the Department of State solemnly told the American people that the United States had "firmly rejected" any attempt to block his inauguration. But already $350,000 had been secretly authorized for an unsuccessful effort to bribe members of the Chilean Congress to prevent Allende's inauguration.[14]

In attempting to reconstruct the actions of the United States government in this case, we must assume that the story remains partially hidden. What is known has been revealed in successive waves, after each of which government officials have claimed that the "whole story" was then known. Syndicated columnist Jack Anderson first reported intervention involving the effort of International Telephone and Telegraph (ITT), which had substantial holdings in Chile, to urge the CIA to prevent an Allende victory. Lengthy congressional hearings were conducted on that incident, and investigations were closed. Months later, a largely new story developed about separate CIA authorization of money supposedly to help save a free press in Chile. Later still, it was disclosed that the money went not merely to help threatened news media but also to disrupt Chilean society in order to make it impossible for the Allende administration to govern. After the CIA came under criticism for illegal activities within the United States, yet another series of investigations revealed that the United States had been involved in planning the abduction of a high Chilean military official (who was eventually assassinated) in order to pave the way for a military coup d'état that would have prevented Allende from taking the oath of office in 1970.[15]

At every stage of investigations, the executive branch refused to provide the evidence in its hands that was sought by legitimate investigators. In the final report of the Senate Subcommittee on Multinational Corporations,[16] which examined the role of ITT, the committee expressly criticized "the refusal of the State Department to cooperate" in making available documentary evidence that would have established more clearly the substance of United States policy during the time of the Chilean elections.[17] After the second wave of revelations, several senators on the subcommittee said they earlier had been deceived.[18] The committee staff reported that several high-level officials testifying before the subcommittee were possibly in contempt of Congress.[19]

Despite the reluctance of officials to divulge information that might subject them to criticism, substantial evidence is available that reveals the behavior of United States officials in the Chilean case.

202

U.S. Policy Toward Self-Determination

PREINAUGURAL CLANDESTINE INTERVENTION

According to the staff report of the Senate Select Committee to Study Governmental Operations with Respect to Intelligence Activities, covert U.S. involvement in Chile between 1963 and 1973 was "extensive and continuous."[20] Secret U.S. efforts influenced "almost every major election in Chile in the decade between 1963 and 1973. In several instances the United States intervention was massive."[21] In the 1964 presidential election, for example, the CIA spent three million dollars to manipulate the Chilean electoral process and prevent Allende from winning the presidental election. The United States secretly financed more than half the total cost of his opponent's campaign, carried out under the banner of the Christian Democratic party. According to the Senate Select Committee, the propaganda campaign in the 1964 election was "enormous." During the first week of intensive propaganda activity, a CIA-sponsored propaganda group produced twenty radio spots per day in Santiago and on 44 provincial stations; twelve-minute news broadcasts five times daily on 27 radio stations throughout Chile; thousands of cartoons; and numerous paid advertisements in newspapers and magazines. Later the CIA group produced 24 daily newscasts in Santiago and the provinces, all colored by an "anti-communist scare campaign."[22]

The United States also intervened in Chilean congressional elections, and according to CIA internal memoranda, the U.S. manipulation of the electoral process had substantial impact, including the defeat of a number of leftist reform candidates who might otherwise have won congressional seats. The CIA also spent money for bribery and supported and helped organize student, women's, professional, and peasant groups for political activity.[23]

One year before the election in which Allende finally won the presidency despite U.S. efforts, the CIA spent $500,000 to mobilize anti-Allende forces.[24] This money was authorized by the then top secret 40 Committee in the White House, which included the secretary of state, chairman of the Joint Chiefs of Staff, deputy secretary of defense, under secretary of state for political affairs, and director of the CIA. President Ford later reported that the 40 Committee "reviews every covert operation undertaken by our Government."[25]

Beginning in May 1970, discussions about the elections oc-

curred between officials of International Telephone and Telegraph and the U.S. government. John McCone, an ITT director, held several meetings with Richard Helms, then CIA director. McCone was a former director of the CIA and he remained a consultant to the CIA after joining ITT. (Helms had
been McCone's former subordinate.) At least two conversations
between Helms and McCone took place in CIA headquarters in
Langley, Virginia. At least one was at McCone's home in
California. In these conversations McCone told Helms that ITT
expected Allende to win the election and that Allende was running on a platform calling for expropriation of foreign businesses, including ITT's properties. McCone said that the United
States national interest, as well as business interests, were at
stake. McCone asked if the CIA needed funds to intervene in
the election to encourage the support of "one of the candidates
who stood for the principles that are basic in this country."
Helms said that the 40 Committee had considered intervention
and that a decision had been made that "nothing of consequence
should be done." Helms did indicate that "some minimal effort
was authorized" which "could be managed within the flexibility
of their [the CIA's] own budget."[26]

More than two months before the general elections, the 40
Committee authorized the CIA to spend $400,000 to $500,000
secretly in Chile in opposition to the Allende candidacy.[27] In
July, the National Security Council Staff was also at work on its
top secret Study Memorandum 97, which outlined policy options toward Chile.[28]

On July 16, 1970, as a result of directives from McCone and
Helms, a meeting occurred between William V. Broe, the chief
of the CIA's Clandestine Services Western Hemisphere Division
(also known as the Directorate of Plans) and Harold Geneen,
ITT's chief executive officer and chairman of the board, at
ITT's Sheraton-Carlton Hotel in Washington. Geneen offered
to provide an election fund for Jorge Alessandri Rodriguez, the
conservative candidate running against Allende. Geneen said
the fund would be "substantial" and that he wanted the fund
controlled and channeled through the CIA. The amount discussed was reportedly "up to seven figures." Broe reported that
he refused the offer.[29]

The CIA did, however, offer advice about "reliable" individuals who might serve as a conduit for ITT funds to the Alessandri campaign. The CIA also advised ITT about a secure funding

mechanism for making secret payments to the National party, which opposed Allende. This procedure utilized two CIA contacts in Chile who were also channeling United States government money to the CIA operation to defeat Allende. ITT and other U.S. private corporations secretly paid at least $700,000 to anti-Allende efforts during the electoral campaign.[30]

After Allende's victory in the national election but before the congressional confirmation vote making the results final, there was a flurry of activity in Washington. McCone met with Henry Kissinger and Richard Helms and offered to give a million dollars "in support of any plan that was adopted by the government for the purpose of bringing about a coalition of the opposition to Allende [in the Chilean Congress] so that when confirmation was up . . . this coalition would be united and deprive Allende of his position." Mr. Geneen testified that "even if the plan did not block Allende's election, he hoped it would create a situation in which Allende would go slowly on the nationalization of American property in Chile.[31] Significantly, ITT offered these large-scale financial inducements to officials to encourage a more widespread effort of CIA subversion, even though ITT's chief executive knew Helms had already told McCone that CIA plans could be handled within the existing CIA budget.

At the same time, the 40 Committee, in response to Kissinger's request, authorized the expenditure of $250,000 to $350,000 to overturn the results of the popular election by bribing Chilean congressmen to vote for Allende's campaign opponent, Alessandri Rodriguez.[32] He was the candidate of the right-wing National party, a fusion of the Conservative and Liberal parties. According to those involved, the money was not used because United States operatives in Chile feared such a plan would not work. Not enough Chilean congressmen could be bribed to swing the elections. Also, some CIA officials feared that a strategy of bribes could not be kept secret. The reason for failing to use the authorized money for bribes did not include official restraint based on a belief that bribery would be wrong.[33] Restraint was based on fear of ineffectiveness and exposure.

During the interval between the general and congressional elections, ITT officials kept in close touch with the CIA. On one occasion, William R. Merriam, vice-president and head of the Washington office of ITT, showed some suggestions from ITT operatives in Chile to William Broe. The recommendations, which Broe said were good, included the following:

1. We and other U.S. firms in Chile pump some advertising into *Mercurio* [the leading conservative newspaper]. (This has been started.)
2. We help with getting some propagandists working again on radio and television.
3. Assist in support of a "family relocation" center in Mendoza or Baires [Buenos Aires] for wives and children of key persons involved in the fight. This will involve about 50 families for a period of a month to six weeks, maybe two months.
4. Bring what pressure we can on USIS [United States Information Service] in Washington to instruct the Santiago USIS to start moving the *Mercurio* editorials around Latin America and into Europe.
5. Urge the key European press, through our contacts there, to get the story of what disaster could fall on Chile if Allende & Co. win this country.

These are immediate suggestions and there will be others between now and October 24 as pressure mounts on [President] Frei and the Christian Democrats [to help in averting a congressional confirmation of the general election].[34]

On September 29, 1970, Broe met with E. J. Gerrity, ITT senior vice-president. Under instructions from Helms, Broe proposed a plan "to accelerate economic chaos in Chile as a means of putting pressure on Christian Democratic Congressmen to vote against Dr. Allende or in any event to weaken Dr. Allende's position in case he was elected." Broe's suggestions were based upon ideas that originated from ITT operatives in Chile. These suggestions included the following:

1. Banks should not renew credits or should delay in doing so.
2. Companies should drag their feet in sending money, in making deliveries, in shipping spare parts, etc.
3. Savings and loan companies there are in trouble. If pressures were applied they would have to shut their doors, thereby creating stronger pressure.
4. We should withdraw all technical help and should not promise any technical assistance in the future. Companies in a position to do so should close their doors.
5. A list of companies was provided [to contact and enlist their support].[35]

Broe said the plan to create economic chaos had been developed after determining the points of vulnerability in Chilean society. Since some middle-class Chileans were uneasy about the future of the economy and were withdrawing their money from banks, the CIA thought that if additional pressure were placed on the Chilean economy, "the deterioration would be accelerated and Christian Democratic Congressmen who were planning to vote for Allende would be shocked into changing their minds and [voting for] Alessandri."[36]

In short, the Senate Subcommittee on Multinational Corporations reported "the CIA suggestion to ITT was that they work to create economic chaos in Chile by causing a run on financial institutions." ITT rejected the plan, company officials said, because ITT concluded that it was unworkable in the limited time before the congressional vote, but not because they thought it was wrong.[37]

At the same time, ITT asked its employee in Santiago, Bob Berrellez, to contact Alessandri's brother-in-law, Dr. Arturo Matte, and offer support, financial or otherwise, if that would help implement what was known as the "Alessandri formula."[38] This was a maneuver in which Alessandri promised that, if the Congress would elect him president on October 24, 1970, he would immediately resign, thus paving the way for a new general election in which Frei (the then current president) would be eligible to run against Allende. Frei had been unable to run against Allende in the September election because the Chilean Constitution forbade any president to succeed himself. ITT and the CIA hoped that in a two-man race, Frei would beat Allende. The U.S. ambassador to Chile, Edward Korry, told the Senate subcommittee that the United States "obviously" was against Allende and that Frei, his associates, the Chilean military, and all political observers in Chile knew that the United States sympathized with the Alessandri formula.[39]

On September 17, 1970, Hal Hendrix (another ITT reporter in Chile) and Berrellez cabled Gerrity: "We know that the Chilean army has been assured full material and financial assistance by the U.S. military establishment." However, they also reported that the military was unwilling to move unilaterally to prevent Allende from taking office as this would be a clear violation of the Constitution.[40] Hendrix also reported that at this time Korry was maneuvering with the Christian Democrats and the Radical and National parties to implement the Alessandri formula. Korry denied all such activity,[41] but later hearings confirmed that it did take place.

In spite of these plans and surreptitious activities, sufficient

Christian Democratic votes could not be turned against Allende (even to give their own leader, Frei, a chance to run again), the Alessandri formula could not be implemented, and on October 24, Allende won the congressional election by a vote of 153 to 42.

During the interval between the general and congressional elections, ITT reporters in Chile informed their company's headquarters that on September 15, Edward Korry "finally received a message from [the] State Department giving him the green light . . . to do all possible—short of a Dominican Republic-type action—to keep Allende from taking power."[42]

Significantly, Korry, who received the cable from the State Department, refused to divulge what his instructions were. Assistant Secretary of State for Inter-American Affairs, Charles Meyer, who sent the message, also refused to testify about the contents of cables at that time. Both denied requests to testify before the Senate Foreign Relations Committee even in executive session. The State Department refused to furnish copies of the cable in question. Later hearings in 1975 confirmed the general accuracy of the report by Hendrix about the "green light" cable.[43] Korry cabled Washington immediately after Allende's victory in the popular election saying that an Allende presidency would not be in the best interests of the United States.[44] Korry was immensely displeased with the results of the general election.[45]

In a background briefing to a group of newspaper editors in Chicago on September 16, 1970, Kissinger said an Allende presidency would cause substantial problems for the United States as well as for Latin American countries bordering on Chile. Kissinger suggested that the Congress of Chile should break with tradition, refuse to ratify the winner of the popular vote, and instead install the runner-up, the conservative candidate for president. Kissinger expressed certainty that Allende had little respect for constitutional processes: "I have yet to meet somebody who firmly believes that if Allende wins there is likely to be another free election in Chile. . . . So I don't think we should delude ourselves that an Allende takeover in Chile would not present massive problems for us, and for democratic forces and for pro-U.S. forces in Latin America, and indeed to the whole Western Hemisphere."[46]

In June 1970, Kissinger chaired the 40 Committee that authorized the CIA to use $400,000 secretly to oppose Allende's candidacy. And in July, the National Security Council prepared plans for U.S. intervention. Two days after the off-the-record briefing for reporters, Kissinger reportedly advocated allocating $350,000 in the effort to bribe Chilean congressmen.[47] In October, Kissinger supported a military coup. There can be no doubt, concluded the Senate Subcommittee on Multinational Corporations in its final report, "that both the U.S. Embassy in Santiago and high levels of the U.S. Government in Washington viewed with hostility the prospect of an Allende Government."[48]

When it seemed apparent that economic pressure and bribery would not work to stop Allende's election, "President Nixon informed CIA Director Richard Helms that an Allende regime in Chile would not be acceptable to the United States and instructed the CIA to play a direct role in organizing a military coup d'état in Chile to prevent Allende's accession to the Presidency."[49] The CIA then attempted, directly, to foment a military coup.[50] During October the CIA made more than twenty contacts with key military and police officials in Chile. The United States threatened to cut off U.S. military aid and sales if Chilean officers refused to carry out a coup before the October 24 congressional vote. The United States also promised those plotting a coup that they would receive U.S. support, both before and after a coup, with all means possible short of direct U.S. military intervention.[51] Washington cabled Ambassador Korry in Santiago: "If any steps the [Chilean] military should take should result in civil disorder, we would also be prepared to deliver support and material that might be immediately required."[52]

One of the main obstacles to a coup was the firm, constitutionalist stance of the Chilean Army Commander-in-Chief, René Schneider. At the request of the CIA, pro-United States Chilean officers attempted to persuade Schneider to go along with a coup, but he flatly refused to move illegally against the Allende election. Thus Schneider himself became a target for the CIA. If he were removed, it was assumed that Allende's inauguration could be more easily prevented. The CIA's mission was to overcome "the apolitical, constitutional-oriented inertia of the Chilean military."[53]

A group of Chilean military officers, whom the CIA actively supported, unsuccessfully attempted to abduct Schneider on October 19, 1970. A second unsuccessful attempt was made the following day. Two days later the CIA gave nontraceable machine guns and ammunition to the group that had failed in the

209

first abduction. Later that day General Schneider was mortally wounded in a third kidnapping attempt. The Senate report concluded that the shooting was "apparently conducted by conspirators other than those to whom the CIA had provided weapons earlier in the day." The report acknowledged, however, that the Senate committee "has not been able to determine whether or not the machine gun at the scene of the Schneider killing was one . . . supplied by the CIA."[54]

There is really no point in debating whether Schneider's death was at the muzzle of a particular CIA-supplied gun. The United States government attempted to foment a coup,[55] it discussed coup plans with the Chileans later convicted of Schneider's abduction, it advocated his removal as a step toward overturning the results of a free election, it offered payment of $50,000 for Schneider's kidnapping, and it supplied weapons for this strategy—acts that clearly signaled disrespect for human rights and involved significant probability of his death.[56]

In short, the United States government did not merely hope for a coup; the White House applied "intense pressure" to get CIA operatives to execute one. Thomas Karamessines, the CIA deputy director for plans, said that Kissinger "left no doubt in my mind that he was under the heaviest pressure to get this accomplished, and he in turn was placing us under the heaviest pressures to get it accomplished." The deputy chief of the Western Hemisphere Division of the CIA testified that the pressure was "as tough as I ever saw it in my time there, extreme." William Broe testified that "I have never gone through a period as we did on the Chilean thing. I mean it was just constant, constant . . . just continual pressure . . . from the White House."[57]

POSTINAUGURAL POLICY

After Allende took office, U.S. pressure against him intensified. The contacts between U.S. intelligence agents and Chilean military officers were maintained and, where possible, tightened. The Department of Defense played a less well-known but in the end no less decisive role than the CIA in overthrowing Allende. Significantly, the Senate Select Committee on Intelligence concentrated on CIA activities, not the role of the Pentagon's Defense Intelligence Agency. Armando Uribe, counselor to the Chilean embassy in Washington from 1968 to 1970 and later a consultant to the Allende administration on U.S.-Chilean military relations, reports that the Department of Defense played the central role in developing plans for a coup d'état in 1970 and again in communicating support to Chilean military officers for the 1973 implementation of parts of the original plan.[58]

After CIA efforts at destabilization caused internal dissatisfaction and economic panic, the Pentagon was surprised when the Allende coalition of parties gained strength in the congressional elections of 1973. At that time, according to Uribe, the Defense Intelligence Agency decided upon resurrecting the 1970 plans for a coup by dissident officers.[59] The plan called for working mainly through Naval Intelligence because the Chilean Navy was more conservative than the rest of the armed forces. Also, the plan was to be carried out in conjunction with Chile-U.S. naval maneuvers that were scheduled for September of each year.

Among the many Chilean officers who had been trained and indoctrinated by U.S. military personnel, some had maintained close contact with U.S. officers over many years. Chilean armed forces were equipped and, to some extent, dependent upon the United States for replacement parts, maintenance, and technological innovations. Some Chilean officers doubtless felt more comfortable collaborating with longtime friends in the U.S. military than with a Chilean Marxist president, even if democratically elected.

According to Gabriel Garcia Marquez, in several meetings in Washington and Santiago before Allende's election, U.S. military officials had discussed and agreed upon contingency plans in which "those Chilean military men who were bound most closely, heart and soul, to United States interests would seize power in the event of Allende's Popular Unity Party victory in the election."[60]

Chilean officers in those discussions included General Ernesto Baeze, who led the attack on the presidential palace, gave the order to burn it, and became director of national security in Chile. Two of his subordinates at the time of the meetings with Pentagon officials were General Augusto Pinochet, who became president of the military government, and General Javier Palacios. Also present at some meetings were Air Force Brigadier General Sergio Figueroa Gutierrez, who became minister of public works and was an intimate friend of another member of the military junta, Air Force General Gustavo Leigh, who ordered the rocket bombing of the presidential palace. Another participant was Admiral Arturo Troncoso, later named naval

211

governor of Valparaiso; he was instrumental in carrying out the bloody purge of progressive naval officers.[61]

U.S. congressional hearings established that, from 1970 until the coup, the CIA instructed its agents to develop additional contacts with Chilean military officials plotting a coup against Allende. CIA officials acknowledged the difficulty of drawing a firm line between monitoring coup plotting and becoming involved in it. They also realized that their desire to be in clandestine contact with those plotting a violent takeover could easily be interpreted as U.S. support for a coup. The CIA subsidized an antigovernment news pamphlet aimed at the armed services, compiled arrest lists and other data useful in a coup, and engaged in at least one "deception operation" which included a fabricated letter designed to turn the military against Allende.

U.S. agents had frequent communication with the group that carried out the successful coup against Allende on September 11, 1973.[62] In addition to the promotion of an outright, violent overthrow of the Chilean government, after Allende's election the 40 Committee authorized the CIA to spend at least seven million dollars to "destabilize" Chilean society.[63] The CIA exchanged U.S. currency on the black market, thus magnifying its purchasing power in Chile by as much as 500 to 800 percent.[64] The purpose of this program was both to discredit a socialist government and to encourage domestic discontent useful for making the population receptive to a coup d'état. Those persons authorizing the money sought to make it impossible for elected Chilean officials to govern.[65]

In seeking to "destabilize" Chile and to create "economic chaos," as officials described it, the CIA secretly financed opposition groups from before Allende's inauguration until after his violent removal from office. The CIA gave money to the Christian Democratic party, the National party, and several splinter groups. These funds strengthened antigovernment activity and enabled the Christian Democratic party and the National party to purchase their own radio stations and newspapers. Additional CIA money and intrigue were aimed at breaking up Allende's Popular Unity coalition. Although United States officials professed a desire to distinguish between support for opposition parties and support for groups trying to bring about a military coup, this distinction was impossible to make in practice. There were many connections among CIA-supported political parties, the militant trade associations, and paramilitary groups prone to

212

terrorism and violent overthrow of the government. The 40 Committee was aware of these links. The *Patria y Libertad* (Fatherland and Liberty) was a prominent right-wing paramilitary group which formed before Allende's inauguration during the period the CIA was attempting to organize a coup. The CIA helped finance this group's efforts in order to create tension and to provoke intervention by the Chilean military. The group received some additional funding in 1971, and it is possible that it received still further CIA money which was channeled through political parties with close ties to *Patria y Libertad*. Two months before the successful coup against Allende, the *Patria y Libertad* claimed responsibility for an abortive coup (June 29), and later announced its intention to unleash a total armed offensive to overthrow the government.[66]

Considerable controversy has arisen about whether the CIA directly helped a truck owners' strike that led to disorders and eventually precipitated the final coup. William Colby denied the CIA was *directly* involved in the last prolonged strike by Chilean truckers that preceded the coup. Nevertheless, the United States passed money to private sector groups which supported various strikes during the Allende administration. Some intelligence officials reported substantial funds went directly to various unions and strikers.[67] The money provided strike benefits and other means of support for strikers, thus prolonging work stoppages by truckers, middle-class shopkeepers and taxi drivers who together disrupted the capital city of Santiago immediately before Allende was overthrown.

The staff report of the Senate Select Committee noted: "All observers agree that the two lengthy strikes (the second lasted from July 13, 1973 until the September 11 *coup*) could not have been maintained on the basis of union funds. . . . It is clear that anti-government strikers were actively supported by several of the private sector groups which received CIA funds." The CIA continued to pass money to at least one group that it knew gave money directly to strikers.[68] Thus the 40 Committee's claim that it did not approve money for direct support of the truck strike may be technically accurate but politically misleading in view of indirect U.S. support.

Because of Chile's peculiar geography and general transportation network, trucking was absolutely necessary to maintain an adequate supply of food and other materials for a healthy economy. The country depended far more heavily on trucks than on

213

the state-owned railways for movement of goods. Thus the truck strikes seriously crippled Chile's economy, stimulated inflation and black marketeering, and provoked a chain reaction of discontent. Shortly before the military moved against Allende, strikes involved a total of 250,000 truck and taxi drivers, shopkeepers, and professionals, making a violent overthrow of the government more likely. The CIA's support of strikes was only one part of a "broad effort to infiltrate all areas of Chile's governmental and political life." One official with direct knowledge of the decision making on Chile explained, "What we really were doing was supporting a civilian resistance movement against an arbitrary Government. Our target was the middle-class groups who were working against Allende."[69]

It is difficult to know precisely the effect of Chilean public opinion on the level of United States involvement, but some evidence shows that Allende's continuing popularity surprised the CIA and worried the Pentagon. U.S. intervention increased after Allende's party coalition continued to enjoy popular support and showed electoral strength. Allende retained a substantial base of support throughout his tenure—though not a majority—in spite of the economic dislocation caused by his economic policies and the United States credit squeeze. Although the results of the municipal elections of 1971 were doubtless influenced by local issues, they were also viewed by many as a test of Allende's popularity. Thus the CIA secretly helped fund all opposition parties in those elections. Nonetheless, Allende's Popular Unity coalition received 50 percent of the votes.[70]

Following this disappointment for Kissinger's interventionist policy, the CIA poured more money into strengthening the National party, the Christian Democratic party, and splinter groups. U.S. funds also aimed at manipulating four congressional by-elections in 1971 and 1972. The money passed to political parties not only supported opposition candidates in various elections, but also encouraged the parties to maintain strong antigovernment campaigns throughout the Allende years, including demonstrations of opposition to the government.[71] During the legislative elections of March 1973, which came almost at midpoint of the presidential term, the CIA contributed at least $1.5 million to opposition candidates who hoped to gain a two-thirds congressional majority that would have enabled them to impeach Allende. Surprisingly, despite all U.S. efforts, the Marxist Popular Unity coalition received 43.4 percent of the

214

popular vote, compared with the 36.3 percent that Allende had received in the presidential race in 1970. Thus Allende supporters picked up two Senate seats and six seats in the Chamber of Deputies.[72]

Soon after these elections, money in new amounts suddenly began to arrive from businesses in neighboring countries for the purpose of helping to finance the Chilean strikes that, along with intervention by Chilean military forces, eventually brought down the Allende government. The funds for strikers came from companies based in Mexico, Venezuela, and Peru. Businessmen there said they had personally channeled funds to strikers amounting to $200,000 in the weeks preceding the fall of Allende.[73] It is probable, although not certain, that much of this money originated from CIA funds. In discussing the August 1973 truck strike, one intelligence official reported: "If we give it [money] to A, and then A gives it to B and C and D, in a sense it's true that D got it but the question is—did we give it to A knowing that D would get it?"[74]

In addition to funding political opposition groups, the 40 Committee spent enormous amounts to buy or influence media in order to launch what the Senate report called a "hard-hitting propaganda campaign." Chile's largest newspaper, *El Mercurio*, alone received $1.5 million. CIA-inspired editorials were published "almost daily" in *El Mercurio*, and after 1968 the CIA exerted substantial control over the content of the paper's international news section.[75] The CIA intervention included producing several magazines with national circulations; publishing a large number of antigovernment books and special "studies"; placing its own material in the *El Mercurio* chain, which amounted to a total daily circulation of over 300,000; financing opposition party newspapers; and getting anti-Allende propaganda played on all radio stations controlled by opposition parties and on several regular television shows on three different channels. The CIA also funded over 75 percent of an opposition "research" organization. A constant stream of economic and technical material—all slanted against Allende—flowed from this organization to opposition parties and other private groups. Many of the bills introduced in the legislature by opposition politicians were in fact drafted by CIA personnel working in the CIA's own Chilean research organization.[76]

Within two weeks of Allende's electoral victory, the CIA brought journalists, who were CIA agents, to Chile from at least

215

ten different foreign countries. These journalist-agents and other foreign correspondents were directed by high-level CIA agents who held managerial posts in the media field.[77] The journalist-agents wrote slanted reports which were published in foreign newspapers as genuine on-the-scene reporting. The published articles were then circulated to President Frei, military and political leaders, and the Chilean domestic press in order to create the impression that unbiased foreign press comment was highly unfavorable to Allende.

The CIA also gave special intelligence and "inside" briefings to U.S. journalists. Although the impact of these efforts at influencing the press can hardly be assessed, one example illustrates the possibilities. According to CIA documents, a *Time* correspondent in Chile was writing what later became a cover story about Allende. This correspondent reported that Allende intended to uphold the Chilean Constitution. Briefings by the CIA for *Time* in Washington changed the basic thrust of the *Time* story on Allende.[78]

By spreading "black" propaganda—material falsely purporting to be the product of a particular individual or group—the CIA attempted to sow discord among the parties in Allende's Popular Unity coalition. Moreover, the CIA paid teams of Chileans to erect signs and paint posters that depicted Allende as a Stalinist dictator, complete with firing squads for innocent people. The scare campaign used large photographs of Soviet tanks in Prague alongside of tanks in Santiago. Some CIA posters warned that an Allende victory would "mean the end of religion and family life in Chile."[79]

While no statistics are available for the size of the propaganda activity during Allende's administration, during the six-week period between his election and inauguration the scope of the activity was revealed by Senate investigators. According to CIA records, which admittedly were only partly reported, 726 articles, broadcasts, and editorials in the Latin American and European media directly resulted from agency activity. The CIA concluded that this work produced "substantial and significant" impact.[80] According to internal CIA documents, the propaganda efforts "played a significant role in setting the stage for the military coup of September 11, 1973."[81]

In addition to support for opposition groups and propaganda activity, U.S. officials deliberately designed both overt and covert U.S. economic policies to wreck the Chilean economy. Economic

216

hardship, U.S. officials calculated, would insure Allende's demise and discredit socialism as well. Although the precise effect of U.S. actions remains controversial, there is little doubt that in general U.S. policies succeeded in encouraging economic panic among many Chileans. The Chilean economy was vulnerable to abuse by U.S. governmental and private economic pressures because it was so dependent upon commercial intercourse with the United States. The Chilean economy depended on the uninterrupted importation of 30 percent of its goods, including food, machinery, and machine parts which could not be produced in Chile. About 40 percent of these came from the United States.

More importantly, Chile had a record of dependency on U.S. credit to finance its day-to-day life. Chile had been the largest per capita recipient of U.S. aid in Latin America. This dependency had been encouraged by past United States efforts to increase exports of U.S. goods and to maintain a buoyant Chilean economy to prevent the growth of electoral support for left-wing parties. Because previous Chilean administrations had made large-scale credit purchases from the United States, the Allende administration inherited the second highest per capita foreign debt in the world when it took office.[82] This debt presented no insurmountable problem if the United States continued to offer generous credit to finance the importation of United States goods and to ease the repayment of previous loans. On the other hand, a restriction of credit would cause severe hardship, exacerbated by falling prices on the world markets for copper, Chile's single basic export. The latter event, of course, curtailed scarce foreign exchange earnings necessary to finance imports.

Like the United States government, many private corporations publicly assumed a correct posture toward Santiago while secretly attempting to overthrow the Chilean government. Following Allende's inauguration, ITT sought to protect its assets in Chile by simultaneously pursuing two different strategies. First, ITT tried to insure the overthrow of Allende by pressing the United States government, through Kissinger's office, to oust the new president. Second, ITT wanted to secure, through guarantees from Allende, the payment of full book value for any ITT property that might eventually be nationalized.

In January 1971, ITT sought help from other companies with investments in Chile to persuade Kissinger to block loans to Chile by institutions such as the World Bank and the Inter-

217

American Development Bank. By confronting the Chilean government with economic collapse, William Merriam, head of ITT's Washington office, said ITT would more easily gain concessions from Allende.[83] Allende had not, at that time, taken any expropriatory action against any United States company.

At the same time that it secretly promoted economic chaos, ITT prepared for negotiations with Allende on its primary investment in Chile, the ownership of 70 percent of the Chilean telephone company, Chiltelco. ITT's holdings in Chile, including Chiltelco, totaled approximately $160 million. During the first negotiations, Allende personally told ITT representatives that he had not decided what course of action to follow with Chiltelco. He had, however, mentioned the possibility of nationalizing Chiltelco in a campaign speech of September 2, 1970. On May 26, 1971, Allende informed ITT that Chiltelco would be nationalized. ITT asked for compensation at the full book value of $153 million. The Chilean government offered $24 million for ITT's interest. Allende then proposed valuation by international arbitration, with the government managing the company pending the arbitration. ITT opposed this arrangement allegedly because of fears that the value of the property would deteriorate under Chilean management.[84] Thus they reached no agreement.

During the negotiations, ITT attempted to convince Allende that by making a satisfactory deal with ITT, he could then confiscate with impunity other U.S. companies without creating an image of being totally hostile to foreign investments. ITT used this negotiating technique successfully in Peru, when faced with expropriation there.[85]

Through Nixon's White House confidant, John Ehrlichman, Merriam arranged for a meeting with Kissinger's deputy, General Alexander Haig, and Peter Peterson, assistant to the president for international economic affairs. Following the meeting, under instructions from ITT Chairman Geneen, Merriam forwarded an 18-point action plan to the White House to insure that Allende would not "make it through the next six months."[86] The plan included these suggestions:

> Continue loan restrictions in the international banks such as those the Export/Import Bank has already exhibited.
> Quietly have large U.S. private banks do the same.
> Confer with foreign banking sources with the same thing in mind.

218

Delay buying from Chile over the next six months. Use U.S. copper stockpile instead of buying from Chile.

Bring about a scarcity of U.S. dollars in Chile.

Discuss with CIA how it can assist the six-month squeeze.

Get to reliable sources within the Chilean Military. Delay fuel delivery to Navy and gasoline to Air Force. . . . A false delay could build up their planned discontent against Allende, thus bring about necessity of his removal.

Help disrupt Allende's UNCTAD plans.

As many U.S. markets as possible should be closed to Chile.[87]

Thus, one year after the CIA proposed a plan to accelerate economic chaos in Chile, ITT was proposing to the president's assistant for international economic policy a more comprehensive plan to exacerbate the economic situation. Peterson denied that government action was taken to implement the plan.[88] But, as Colby later revealed, by that time the CIA had a twelve-month start in implementing its own seven million dollar plan to destabilize Chilean society. And Peterson's testimony to the contrary notwithstanding, ample evidence demonstrates that many parts of the plan were implemented and caused a serious shortage of credit in Chile.

Negotiations between ITT and the Allende government resumed in December 1971, through Chile's ambassador in Washington, Orlando Letelier. Until March 20, 1972, Letelier focused discussions on arranging for international appraisal of the company's assets, an approach that Chile favored. On that date Jack Anderson published his first column explaining ITT's secret efforts in September and October 1970 to avert congressional ratification of the Chilean national election. A previously scheduled meeting with ITT was canceled by the Chilean embassy after Anderson's revelations. Negotiations were never resumed.[89]

As indicated earlier, both governmental and corporate officials hoped that either the Alessandri formula or a military coup would prevent Allende from taking office, and that if inaugurated, he would be ousted. These officials initiated plans to destabilize Chile even before Allende took office, and long before anyone could know the extent to which nationalization of United States companies would include adequate compensation. Five weeks before Allende was sworn in as president, Richard Helms met with President Nixon and recorded his instructions:

219

"Make the economy scream." A week after that meeting Ambassador Korry reported telling the Frei administration that "not a nut or a bolt would be allowed to reach Chile under Allende."[90]

The later inability of U.S. companies to reach agreement with Chile on compensation for expropriated copper interests served as a convenient rationale for a restrictive United States economic policy already underway. Thus it is inappropriate to focus exclusively on the expropriation issue, or to see United States economic policy as a response to expropriation without compensation. Nevertheless, the hostility toward Allende was based to a significant degree on a widely held belief that private investors would not fare well with a socialist president. The point is that United States policies to destabilize Chilean society were at first based on general dislike for socialism and fear of future expropriation, not on a specific or empirical finding that U.S. investors were being mistreated by Allende's government. But in the arena of public debate, officials reversed the chronology: They sought to document their presuppositions against Allende on the basis of later expropriations of United States corporations by Chile.

Nurtured by statements from Washington, the idea also spread in the United States that the U.S. copper corporations enjoyed substantial support in Chile, except for the Allende coalition. That was not true. By the end of the Frei administration there was little or no domestic support within Chile for the large copper companies. Support had dwindled to such an extent that, when the Frei administration asked for a joint ownership arrangement between the Chilean government and Anaconda, the company preferred to get out completely and asked for nationalization rather than accept joint ownership. Thus some copper interests were nationalized during the Frei term of office, even before Allende assumed the presidency.

The deep feeling against the copper companies was due to the extent to which Chile had been affected by these giant foreign interests. All the *Fortune* 500 companies combined do not play a role in the economy of the United States equivalent to the role of Anaconda and Kennecott in Chile. U.S. corporations controlled the production of 80 percent of Chile's copper, which accounted for four-fifths of Chile's foreign exchange earnings. Compared to the strength and past profits of the companies, the Chilean response was muted and cautious.[91]

Chilean support for nationalizing the foreign copper com-

220

panies was overwhelming. Ten months after Allende's electoral victory, the Chilean Congress, although controlled by the non-Marxist opposition Christian Democrat and National parties, unanimously passed a constitutional amendment nationalizing the copper mines. Even the head of Chile's Roman Catholic bishops, Raúl Cardinal Silva Henríquez, said that the nationalization was right and that "the process . . . had been constitutionally impeccable."[92] The congressional vote "reflected widespread popular sentiment that the country had been plundered" by U.S. copper corporations over the previous sixty years.[93] These companies included among their largest stockholders the Rockefeller and Morgan financial groups. The nationalization legislation called for compensating the companies at full book value, less excess profits.

The determination of "excess profits," which became an extremely controversial doctrine, was carried out by the comptroller general's office, the members of which had been appointed before Allende took office. This autonomous body weighed the facts of each corporation in light of the 10 percent annual return considered normal in Chile. The comptroller's office determined that compensation should be for full book value for two new mines, but found that in the other mines, the excess profits of Kennecott and Anaconda already exceeded the total book values. In the eyes of United States investors and officials, who denied the legitimacy of the excess profits doctrine, this was tantamount to expropriation without compensation. The excess profits doctrine looked much more reasonable, of course, in the eyes of people whose wealth had been extracted for many years by foreign corporations without concern for economic justice.

The Chilean action, based upon the excess profits doctrine, intensified the determination of Washington officials already intent upon Allende's ouster. This doctrine was reasonable and likely to spread to other countries if not opposed by the United States. Any reservations about U.S. policy among lower echelons in the State Department were ignored as the initiative for policy making moved to the Treasury Department and White House.[94] This occurred in large part because the curtailment of United States commercial benefits in Chile was an economic issue and a central irritant in White House and corporate hostility to Allende.

Faced with the prospect of further expropriations of United States companies in Chile or elsewhere, plagued by growing

221

economic difficulties within the United States, and spurred by the secretary of the treasury's extreme hostility toward socialism and the decline in United States overseas commercial influence, the Treasury Department, under the direction of Secretary John Connally, set the tone for U.S. policy and coordinated economic sanctions against Chile. The goal was to protect over $1 billion of U.S. private investment in Chile, as well as to insure no default on the additional $1 billion of indebtedness to the U.S. government which was incurred by Allende's predecessors.[95] "Once policy had been defined through Connally's initiative, the State Department moved toward the more extreme position, shedding its reservations."[96]

Connally, Nixon, and Kissinger shaped an extremely hard, vengeful policy line against the Chilean government. Connally acted on behalf of the vested interests of the United States business community. He was angry over nationalizations of private holdings in countries such as Chile, Peru, and Bolivia. He said it was time to "get tough" with Latin American countries that expropriated U.S. property.[97] *Business Week* reported that "Connally is forcing the reopening of debate at top levels on what U.S. policy should be. He is particularly bitter about Latin American hostility toward U.S. investment."[98]

Treasury officials, most of whom were drawn from the business world, reflected the attitudes and interests of large business and financial institutions. As Collins concluded after his extensive study of U.S. economic policy toward Chile: "When Chile dared to try to gain a modicum of freedom from foreign financial domination, it came up against . . . financial giants working out of the Executive branch and dictating U.S. foreign policy."[99] Some key officials designing U.S. economic policy toward Chile were: Assistant Secretary of the Treasury for International Affairs, John M. Hennessey, formerly general manager of the First National City Bank in Lima and La Paz; Assistant Treasury Secretary John R. Petty, formerly a vice-president of Chase Manhattan Bank and later a partner of Lehman Brothers; Under Secretary of the Treasury for Monetary Affairs, Paul A. Volcker, a vice-president and director of planning for the Chase Manhattan Bank and on the board of directors of the Overseas Private Investment Corporation; Deputy Secretary of the Treasury, Charles E. Walker, formerly special assistant to the president of the Republic National Bank of Dallas and former executive vice-president and chief lobbyist of the American Bankers Association; and the Assistant to the President for International Economic Policy, Peter Peterson, a director of the First National Bank of Chicago and former chairman of Bell and Howell.

Just as governmental officials making policy toward Chile were dominated by businessmen, U.S. businesses utilized people from government to work for their interests in Chile. For example, prior to becoming secretary of the treasury, John Connally had been hired as legal counsel by ITT.[100] And for thirty-five years before he became ITT's International Relations Director, Jack Neal had been an influential official at the Department of State. McCone, of course, was former director of the CIA; later he was a consultant to the CIA and simultaneously a director of ITT.

These officials harbored professional hatred for the excess profits doctrine because its spread would mean that other countries might expropriate companies and deduct past excess profits of a corporation from payment for nationalization. Assistant Secretary of the Treasury for International Affairs, John M. Hennessey, termed the effort to establish an excess profits doctrine "a very dangerous precedent."[101]

In order to avert future expropriations, the White House and Treasury Department undertook several studies and set forth, in an executive statement of January 19, 1972, the following guidelines: "When a country expropriates a significant U.S. interest without making reasonable provision for . . . compensation to U.S. citizens, we will presume that the U.S. will not extend new bilateral economic benefits to the expropriating country. . . . We will presume that the United States government will withhold its support from loans under consideration in multilateral development banks."[102] Assistant Treasury Secretary John Petty indicated that in the future "you'll find the U.S. less prepared to turn the other cheek. It's a new ball game with new rules."[103] The "new rules" were a more explicit intention to strangle the economy of any country that expropriated United States business without compensation satisfactory to the United States.

The response to the Chilean case was thus part of a general policy to prevent the decline of United States commercial—and political—influence in countries where a quasi-colonial relationship has existed for years. It was not really a new policy; it had been used in Cuba, Bolivia, Peru, and elsewhere in Latin America. Benjamin Welles reported that Connally's strategy was

223

"a business version of a military domino theory. . . . Mr. Connally is said to believe that his policy of deterrence—cracking down on Chile—may frighten off other possible expropriating countries."[104]

The above attitudes and policies produced these concrete results:

1. The Treasury Department's Export-Import Bank denied all the Allende administration's requests for credit, which normally had been generously extended to Chile for purchases from the United States. (The Export-Import Bank gives short-term credit to facilitate sales of United States goods to foreign purchasers.) Chile traditionally had purchased about 40 percent of its total imports from the United States, and in the 25 years preceding Allende's election, Chile received $600 million worth of direct credits from the bank.[105] Its credits dropped to zero after Allende entered office.[106]

The first Chilean request for credit came early in 1971, before the nationalization of copper mines. It was from the Chilean airline, which had a flawless repayment record. At that time, United States officials acknowledged that Chile had been scrupulous in paying debts, and the Commerce Department admitted that Chile's "credit worthiness" was not the central issue.[107] The decision to block loans to Chile was political, made on the White House level and under pressure from corporation executives.

2. The Export-Import Bank also terminated its long-standing policy of guaranteeing and insuring commercial transactions of United States banks and other companies with Chile. This insurance program, carried out through the Foreign Credit Insurance Association, normally made it possible for U.S. commercial interests to engage in foreign transactions with the United States government undertaking most of the extra risks involved in foreign trade. This cutoff not only directly discouraged private commercial relations with Chile, but also signaled private banks and suppliers to follow the Treasury Department's example of general economic hostility. At the same time that the Export-Import Bank denied Chile new loans, it extended new loans to economically unstable countries such as Haiti and Bangladesh. This communicated a message of importance to other governments and private banks. As Henry Kearns, former president of the Export-Import Bank explained, "Eximbank credit ratings have an enormous influence on other bankers. If we are not willing to loan to a country, few others will."[108]

For a dozen years before Allende's administration, Chile normally had available about $300 million in short-term private commercial credits, mainly from United States banks. Such loans from U.S. banks dropped to about $30 million by 1972. The drop "seriously affected the Allende government's ability to purchase replacement parts and machinery for the most critical sectors of the economy: copper, steel, electricity, petroleum, and transport."[109]

3. Economic assistance to Chile from the Agency for International Development was dramatically reversed in 1970 because of United States hostility toward the Chilean government. Table 4-1 shows the annual net quantities of aid Chile received from the Agency for International Development and its predecessor agencies.

Three major discontinuities in United States assistance reveal the political use of aid. During the first new U.S. fiscal year (1960) following the 1958 Chilean election—the point at which the United States became seriously concerned with the growing electoral strength of Allende's party—United States assistance to Chile suddenly increased. The increase was designed to dampen popular support for left-wing parties. Aid rose more than sixfold over previous years, the single earlier exception being the year before the election itself. During this period of generally rising AID budgets, the assistance to Chile by 1961 climbed tenfold over 1959, and by 1962 jumped to forty-seven times the 1959 level. [110]

Aid was also curtailed after the electoral success of the Popular Unity coalition. Although $5.5 million had been authorized to go to Chile in 1971 and 1972 under previously negotiated AID programs, no new assistance agreements were made with the Allende government.[111] During the entire nineteen-year period (1952-70) of economic assistance to Chile prior to Allende's election, aid amounted to an average of $33.7 million per year. During the three U.S. fiscal years that overlapped Allende's administration (1971-73), United States net aid, due to cancellation of previous obligations, amounted to a *negative* figure of $26.7 million.

The third reversal in AID policies coincided with the overthrow of Allende and the installation of the military dictatorship. As Table 4-1 shows, as soon as the antisocialist generals were in power, aid was quickly resumed.

4. The Nixon administration also used its enormous economic power to prevent the extension of credit to Chile by multilateral

225

Table 4-1
Loan and Grant Commitments[a] to Chile from the United States
Agency for International Development and Predecessor Agencies

Fiscal Year	Net Obligations, Millions of Dollars
1952	1.1
1953	1.3
1954	1.4
1955	2.0
1956	2.1
1957	3.0
1958	12.8
1959	3.1
1960	18.3
1961	31.1
1962	142.4
1963	40.4
1964	78.5
1965	99.0
1966	85.6
1967	12.0
1968	53.9
1969	34.6
1970	17.2
1971	−25.1
1972	.4
1973	−2.0
1974	5.1
1975	25.5
1976	20.5

SOURCES: U.S. Agency for International Development, *U.S. Economic Assistance Programs Administered by the Agency for International Development and Predecessor Agencies, April 3, 1948-June 30, 1971* (Washington, D.C.: U.S. Agency for International Development, 1972); U.S. Agency for International Development, Statistics and Reports Division, *U.S. Overseas Loans and Grants and Assistance from International Organizations.*
NOTE: [a] Commitments are given in net terms. That is, the figures include total new obligations entered into during each year, less deobligations of prior years' funds. Negative figures mean that canceled obligations exceed new obligations.

lending institutions. The Inter-American Development Bank (IDB), in which the United States held what amounted to a veto, had extended 59 loans to Chile since 1959, totaling over $310 million. But with two very limited exceptions, the IDB denied all new loans to Chile during the Allende administration. The exceptions were two small loans of $7 and $4.6 million for private universities. These had been tentatively promised to the previous Chilean government.[112]

The first requests by the Allende government were for development of electric power, natural gas, and a petrochemical complex. These had already undergone favorable preliminary examination by the IDB before Allende's election. They were denied, however, after Allende took office. Similarly, the IDB even refused relief to victims of the earthquake of 1971. Chile faithfully repaid its pre-Allende obligations to the bank, and thus it became an exporter of capital to a multilateral development bank that would not even lend it aid for emergency humanitarian needs.

The United States pursued a similar policy in the World Bank. Before Allende's election, Chile had received loans of $234,650,000 from the bank. After the election, the bank refused to act upon all Chilean loan requests. No new loans went to Chile between 1970 and 1973. Among other projects, the bank refused to finance the second stage of a cattle breeding program, even though the first stage was begun with bank assistance. A request for continued support for an ongoing electrification program was rejected, although for the previous twenty years the bank had provided similar assistance.[113]

The International Monetary Fund (IMF), where the United States had less decisive influence, provided a sharp contrast. The Allende government continued normal drawing rights there and received $148 million in partial compensation for falling copper prices. The action of IMF suggests that the reason given by the United States for denying credit, namely that Chile was a poor credit risk, was largely a ploy to deceive the public.[114] To be sure, Chile's exchange position was weakened by declining copper prices and internal economic difficulties, but a major influence upon Chile's credit scarcity was the United States' concerted effort to deny Chile the credit upon which it had grown dependent over the years before Allende's election. During previous economic crises, as well as after the Allende government fell, both the United States and the IDB did not hesitate to provide generous assistance.

U.S. economic policies had a devastating effect upon Chile. Washington policymakers had correctly calculated that denying Chile credit would encourage economic chaos. In the absence of additional credit from the United States, the Chilean government needed to reschedule its previous timetable for debt re-

227

tirement and institute an internal program of austerity to cut imports and curtail the need for foreign currency. But the United States resisted efforts to reschedule debt repayment.[115] Moreover, lacking the strong support of the middle class, and faced with a mobilizing right wing and a military prejudiced against socialism, an austerity program was a political impossibility for Allende. This was especially true because of his intention to avoid repressive measures. The politically sensitive and influential middle class was accustomed to imported U.S. goods, and thus would be irritated by any cutoff of those goods.

Within two years, Chile's imports from the United States declined from 40 to 15 percent of total imports. In addition, total imports declined. While the large lower class improved its access to basic goods as a result of Allende's economic reforms, the middle class suffered dislocation of their usual consumption patterns. Many goods were simply unavailable. Perhaps most important politically, a severe shortage of replacement parts developed for all machinery previously purchased from the United States. Production suffered as a result of machines left idle. Since a large percentage of all buses and trucks were of U.S. origin, by 1972, 30 percent of privately owned city buses, 21 percent of taxibuses, 33 percent of state-owned buses, and about 33 percent of the diesel trucks at Chuquicamata Copper Mine were immobilized because of lack of parts.[116] Private owners of vehicles, who participated in the prolonged strike that led to the military takeover, often gave lack of replacement parts as a reason for their striking. On the one hand, United States government and businesses withheld credit and slowed shipment of goods in order to stimulate parts shortages that encouraged potential strikers to halt work. On the other hand, the United States secretly spent money to sustain strikers and increase the economic agony. The U.S. Treasury Department worked hand in hand with the CIA to promote conditions that would mean the ruin of Chile's constitutional government.

Two more points will complete this description of United States policy toward the Allende government: the first includes some events that were omitted from policymakers' considerations; the second shows the reversal of United States policy after the violent end to Allende's government.

The severe policies of United States officials gave no deference whatever to the Chilean Congress, controlled by opposition parties, which passed expropriation legislation unanimously. U.S. officials spoke disparagingly of Allende as a "minority" president, but contemptuously sought to reverse the sweeping mandate for nationalization expressed by Chilean voters who freely elected a Congress two-thirds of which had campaigned for expropriation. U.S. officials failed to acknowledge that some United States businesses received satisfactory compensation. Additional corporations might have received payment if the United States had showed willingness to terminate its credit squeeze. The Bank of America, for example, received in compensation "precisely the amount that we originally invested."[117] Other companies, such as Bethlehem Steel and North Indiana Brass Company, also negotiated satisfactory settlements.[118]

As indicated earlier, negotiations with ITT were in progress until the Jack Anderson columns showed that ITT was trying to stimulate an illegal overthrow of Allende at the same time that it was demanding full book value compensation for its properties.[119] According to ITT officials, Allende said that "he did not want to expropriate or nationalize fully, emphasizing he would prefer a partnership arrangement of some sort."[120] Despite this, ITT enlisted the support of other corporations, Kissinger's office, and the CIA to force Allende's hand. Even ITT's legal department expressed concern about the surreptitious activities of ITT in Chile, fearing that they might make null and void the U.S. government-sponsored insurance to pay companies expropriated without compensation. But ITT officials were convinced that the potential benefits of promoting economic chaos would outweigh any negative repercussions that might result should their secret activities be discovered. Significantly, the first ITT discussions with government officials to prevent Allende from governing were made over a year before the Chilean government's decision to administer the telephone company.[121]

The nature and intention of United States policy were starkly revealed when U.S. officials terminated the economic squeeze. Immediately upon seizing power from Allende, the Chilean military dictatorship promised to wash away any vestige of socialism, to compensate U.S. copper interests, and to return to private hands "the vast majority" of the foreign and domestic concerns that were nationalized by the Allende government.[122] In turn, the United States reversed all economic policies carried out against the previous constitutional government. Post-Allende

United States efforts aimed at assisting the economy and helping the new dictatorship remain in power. As the United States increased aid, Britain, Sweden, and other states ended assistance to the new regime because of its ruthlessness.

The United States had maintained contact with the Chilean military during the Allende administration. At the same time that the United States denied Allende credit for hydroelectric projects and even for 300,000 tons of wheat during a foreign currency shortage, the United States had ample funds to give to the professional military in Chile. The United States sought to perpetuate its influence with the Chilean military through authorizations of $45.5 million in military aid from 1970 to 1974.[123] The single largest disbursement was $10 million during 1972.[124]

In contrast to the AID *de*obligations that produced a net loss of $25 million in assistance during the Allende years, AID programs quickly resumed after the coup.[125] During fiscal 1974, United States aid to Chile was $21 million, of which $16.5 million was for the armed forces. In 1975, the United States gave $85 million in aid, including $22 million for the armed forces.[126] U.S. officials underscored the point of their policy only a few weeks after rejecting Allende's request for credit to buy wheat: as soon as the generals seized power, the United States granted $24.5 million for wheat purchases.[127]

Soon the Export-Import Bank reopened its program for Chile. Private banks began lending again, and by mid-1974, Chile's short-term credits were nearly at pre-Allende levels. The IDB granted Chile several very large loans for hydroelectric and agricultural projects similar to those that went unfunded under Allende. The United States renegotiated Chile's debt repayments. The World Bank announced a $5.25 million loan for "preinvestment studies."[128]

The National Foreign Trade Council estimated in March 1974 that the credit granted the new Chilean regime from the United States, Brazil, Argentina, the IMF, the World Bank, the IDB, and the Andean Development Corporation amounted to $468.8 million. Private banks had given credit worth another $250 million. As Elizabeth Farnsworth has concluded: "The loans granted since the coup represented phase two of the U.S. counterinsurgency program in Chile—they prop up a brutal dictatorship which rules through terror but promises good investment opportunities for American businesses. Questions of credit worthiness are not even raised. As Secretary of Agriculture Earl L. Butz said in justifying the Department of Agriculture [wheat] credits, 'they were made in the interest of national security.' The Allende government 'was not friendly. It was essentially a diplomatic decision.' "[129] .

In summary, United States officials from the White House, Treasury Department, State Department, and CIA developed policies in cooperation with United States investors in Chile. At the same time, the Department of Defense maintained close ties with friendly military officers in the Chilean armed forces. Together, U.S. officials implemented a policy to cut off Chile's customary sources of private and public financing from the United States and other nations at the same time they fed money and support to Allende's internal opponents and the Chilean military. The staff report of the Senate Select Committee concluded that, as a result of the 40 Committee's actions, "a major financial panic ensued."[130] To be sure, the decline of the Chilean economy should not be attributed exclusively to U.S. harassment. Some responsibility for the economic dislocation must be placed upon Allende's policies and the response from powerful internal economic forces resisting Allende's initiatives. However, even though Allende's nationalization and income redistribution policies may be subject to criticism, the shortages that were so irritating to middle-class Chileans would have been much less severe if Allende had not been prevented by the United States from receiving normal credit and purchases from the United States. U.S. policy reinforced the polarization of Chilean society, as well as directly contributed to economic hardship.

When considered in both economic and psychological terms, U.S. economic policies had a devastating effect upon Chile. According to Laurence Birns, a former economist for the United Nations Economic Commission for Latin America in Santiago: "The U.S. bears major responsibility for what happened in Chile. Its systematic policy of economic strangulation created a momentum which led to the death of constitutional democracy. This policy reflected the demands of the American corporations that had been nationalized or controlled in Chile."[131] In the context of strikes, political disruption, and economic distress, the stage was set for the intervention of dissatisfied Chilean military officers whom the U.S. had urged to intervene in 1970, and with whom the U.S. had maintained close ties during Allende's tenure in office.

OFFICIAL RATIONALE COMPARED TO THE VALUES
IMPLICIT IN U.S. POLICY

The foregoing survey of United States behavior toward Chile
raises several questions: To what extent did U.S. officials violate
the right of self-determination and the treaties that constituted
part of the supreme law of the land? What justification have officials given for their policy? Were the values they professed to
serve consistent with the values implicit in actual governmental
behavior?

The principal official justification for U.S. intervention was to
protect democracy in Chile. In a nationwide televised statement,
President Ford elaborated upon this central purpose by adding
these other broad dimensions: "I think this [policy of interven-
tion] is in the best interest of the people in Chile." The activity
was designed "to help implement [U.S.] foreign policy and protect national security." The CIA policy of intervention "is . . .
certainly in our best interest."[132] These explicit public justifications of United States policy should be examined in light of the
values implicit in the means used to implement policy.

*Professed Value 1: To Sustain Democratic Parties and Maintain
Political Pluralism in Chile*

Before United States intervention was publicly acknowledged,
President Nixon assured the American people that the United
States was willing to live happily with a "community of diversity"
among Latin American governments. "Our relations depend
not on their internal structures or social systems, but on actions
which affect us in the inter-American system."[133] In another
speech commenting on Latin America, the president said, "We
therefore deal with governments as they are—right and left . . .
we respect the hemispheric principle of non-intervention."[134] In
affirming support for this principle, the president proclaimed,
"Our relations with Chile are an example. . . . Our relations will
hinge not on their ideology but on their conduct toward the outside world. As I have said many times, we are prepared to have
the kind of relationship with the Chilean Government that it is
prepared to have with us."[135]

In September 1974, after a *New York Times* story by Seymour
Hersh made it impossible for officials to maintain the lie that the
United States had undertaken no clandestine political activity in
Chile, Secretary Kissinger and President Ford justified the CIA
involvement by saying its purpose was solely to keep alive sup-

posedly threatened opposition political parties and news media. Kissinger said that the "very minor" role of the CIA was aimed at strengthening the "democratic political parties."[136]

In an effort professedly to clear the political air and tell the "whole story," Kissinger gave separate briefings to congressional leaders and the Ford Cabinet at the White House. In both meetings persons present reported that, according to Kissinger, "All we did was support newspapers and political opponents of Allende who were under siege."[137] Kissinger repeated this to the Senate Foreign Relations Committee, meeting in secret session. According to sources present during the briefing, at no time did Kissinger mention the financing of labor unions or trade groups. He denied that any efforts were aimed at subverting the Chilean government.[138]

A similarly misleading description of the U.S. role was given by Ford on nationwide TV. He said that U.S. intervention was a response to attacks by Allende on a free press and opposition parties: "There was an effort being made by the Allende Government to destroy opposition news media, both the writing press as well as the electronic press. And to destroy opposition political parties. And the [CIA] effort that was made in this case was to help and assist the preservation of opposition newspapers and electronic media and to preserve opposition political parties."[139]

This principal justification of United States policy becomes unbelievable after consideration of available evidence. First of all, both United States purposes and policies directly violated—rather than protected—the democratic process itself. The United States sent secret money and agents into Chile over a period of at least ten years to prevent the Popular Unity parties from receiving the support at the polls that they would have received in the absence of a United States covert effort against them. The United States sought to use illegal means to prevent Allende from being elected by Congress after he won the national election. The United States infiltrated the Chilean government and created civil strife and economic chaos to discredit the Allende government and to encourage a coup by the U.S.-trained and supplied Chilean military officers. The United States, through the CIA, penetrated labor unions, trade groups, and all areas of Chile's government. The CIA had agents in every major party making up Allende's Popular Unity coalition.[140]

Second, United States policies could not have been, as officials

233

publicly claimed, primarily a response to alleged offenses of the Allende administration. Three U.S. presidents and their close advisers authorized secretly spending millions of dollars to manipulate Chilean elections before Allende came to power. The United States promoted a coup d'état to abort the results of a free election. Former CIA Director Richard Helms reported that "the Nixon administration would like to have had President Allende overthrown," and made an effort to determine whether it could be done, even before the Allende government had taken office.[141] Surely those actions could not have been inspired as a result of the policies of an Allende administration which had not then taken office.

Some persons might justify United States policy as "anticipatory intervention," based on a calculation (mistaken, as it turned out) about Allende's attitude toward civil liberties. Yet, to argue that officials acted before Allende was inaugurated in anticipation that, if elected, Allende would be antidemocratic, even if true, in no way negates the conclusion that the United States purpose was to prevent Chileans from freely expressing at the polls their right of self-determination.

Moreover, the argument that some officials genuinely feared that Allende would establish a one-party government insensitive to civil liberties is uncompelling, given U.S. intelligence reports confirming Allende's commitment to democratic freedom and the willingness of U.S. officials to acquiesce in gross violations of civil liberties in countries such as Brazil and post-Allende Chile. The real meaning of the decisions by the 40 Committee, as well as the constancy and unambiguous intention of both Republican and Democrat administrations, becomes clear when viewed in the context of earlier policy.

U.S. efforts had been designed to prevent the electoral success of the coalition of Chilean socialist parties ever since the 1958 election in which Allende's coalition lost to Jorge Alessandri by only 35,000 votes. Thereafter, the United States gave Chile more economic assistance per capita than any other country in Latin America.[142] In the months just before the 1964 election, the United States Agency for International Development gave Chile a grant of $40 million to buoy up the economy and lower unemployment in order to decrease popular support for the parties of the Left.[143] For at least a dozen years, Chile had been regarded as a pivotal country in Latin America. Allende and the forces supporting him, according to Latin American specialist

234

Richard R. Fagen, "had been considered the chief threats to American interests. Directly and indirectly, perhaps a billion dollars in public funds had been committed by the United States during this period to the 'battle to preserve democracy in Chile,' largely defined as a battle to prevent the Left from coming to power."[144]

When Allende ran against Eduardo Frei in 1964, according to William Colby, at least three million dollars of CIA funds went into covert efforts to prevent an Allende victory.[145] *Washington Post* reporter Laurence Stern, on the basis of interviews with intelligence officers at the time, estimated as much as $29 million in funds were involved. As one strategically placed intelligence officer told Stern: "U.S. Government intervention in Chile in 1964 was blatant and almost obscene. We were shipping off people right and left, mainly State Department but also CIA with all sorts of covers."[146]

Immediately after the socialist government of Chile was overthrown by the pro-U.S. military dictatorship, the United States made no serious efforts to protect democratic pluralism or a free press. When the new regime shut down the legislature, banned political parties, and shackled the free press, the United States used its secret agents "to assist the junta in gaining a more positive image, both at home and abroad, and to maintain access to command levels of the Chilean government." The CIA retained its penetration of Chilean media outlets in order "to help build Chilean public support for the new government." The CIA efforts aimed "to present the junta in the most positive light for the Chilean public." The CIA also helped the new military government organize and implement policy. CIA collaborators helped prepare an initial overall economic plan that served as the basis for the junta's most important economic decisions, decisions which have proved as disastrous for the lower classes as they were rewarding for U.S. investments in Chile.[147] Two CIA collaborators assisted the junta in writing the *White Book of the Change of Government in Chile*. This book, widely distributed in Washington and other foreign capitals, was written to justify the overthrow of Allende. The CIA also developed new contacts with Chilean police and internal security forces.[148]

The nature, duration, and timing of U.S. covert actions in Chile clearly demonstrate that U.S. policy was not aimed primarily at rescuing newspapers or political parties from a repressive Chilean government. On the contrary, when many civil liberties

235

were vigorously practiced by diverse groups during the Allende period, the United States sought to overthrow the democratically elected government. When the same civil liberties were extinguished by a military dictatorship, the United States assisted the military officials in securing power. The United States helped organize and support those who wrote and distributed propaganda to improve the dictatorship's image at home and abroad. By violating the Chilean electoral process, the United States helped destroy—rather than protect—political pluralism and self-government in Chile. For more than a decade, Washington officials opposed the expression of self-determination and then actively worked to overturn the results of a legal election after it had occurred. Thus the United States violated self-determination in both of its conventional usages, whether defined as freedom from external interference or as internal democratic government. In direct conflict with the U.S. officials' professed value of protecting Chilean democracy, an alternative value was embedded in United States behavior: *to undermine and prevent the exercise of the right of self-determination* (implicit value A).

In order to implement this value, the United States violated its pledge, solemnly given in duly ratified treaties, to refrain from intervening or encouraging conditions likely to produce violence in other Latin American countries. The United States directly promoted a coup in 1970. The staff report of the Select Committee on Intelligence Activities concluded that the CIA's propaganda " 'scare campaign' contributed to the political polarization and financial panic of the period."[149] In 1973 the United States nurtured conditions designed to provoke a coup. The second U.S.-encouraged coup brought widespread, arbitrary arrests, imprisonments, torture, and executions. The new, harsh dictatorship extinguished the free press, prohibited activity by political parties, forced the Chilean Congress to close, and deliberately violated civil liberties.[150]

In spite of public statements by Kissinger and Ford to the contrary, the majority of secret money sent into Chile by the CIA during Allende's administration went to finance clandestine, disruptive activity in Chile—not to protect civil liberties. "Broadly speaking, U.S. policy sought to maximize pressures on the Allende government."[151] To the extent that money did go to friendly media, one high official explained that this support was necessary not because the United States wanted opposition media in themselves—the CIA usually has not encouraged opposition media in pro-United States authoritarian governments—but because "it wouldn't have been good to have strikes if nobody knows about it."[152] Moreover, money that appeared as if it was designed to help a beleagured press was designed in fact to play "an important role in setting the stage for the . . . military coup which overthrew Allende."[153]

The CIA willingly supported specific parties, movements, and policies that were unequivocally antagonistic to legal and democratic political processes. This support went in some cases to those promoting violence and an end to civilian politics altogether. As late as July 25, 1973, the CIA sought authorization to spend $200,000 for clandestine support of the National party, which had urged Chileans to reject the Allende administration by violence if necessary. During the twelve months before Allende's overthrow, it had close ties with the *Patria y Libertad*, which openly boasted of its involvement in military efforts to overthrow the Allende government.[154] The CIA's "rule of thumb apparently was to throw its weight behind the strongest source of opposition to the Allende Government."[155]

The tone of United States policy was vividly captured by one United States diplomat who served in Chile. He said that officials at the U.S. embassy in Santiago felt that "they were engaged in a kind of warfare. People either were with you or against you when it came to Allende. There were a lot of people in Santiago on the far right who were essentially dedicating their lives to the overthrow of Allende—it was like a holy war. These people were increasingly seen at the Embassy in 1972 and 1973. Just putting some resources at their disposal alone would be enough."[156] In sum, U.S. behavior *encouraged conditions likely to produce civil strife and violence* (implicit value B).

The accuracy of the analysis underlying implicit values A and B is confirmed by a series of National Intelligence Estimates (NIEs). These were joint assessments by all U.S. intelligence agencies. An NIE issued on Chile in August 1971, nine months after Allende came to power, suggested that Allende was not the threat to democracy that some officials had originally expected. The NIE said that the consolidation of a Marxist political leadership was *not* inevitable. The report acknowledged that Allende preferred to adhere to constitutional means, although it also speculated that he might be impelled to circumvent the Constitution to stay in power. It noted that Allende had taken great

237

care to observe all constitutional requirements, and that he enjoyed substantial popularity in Chile. An NIE of June 1972 stated that the democratic political system of Chile possessed remarkable resiliency and that the prospects for the continuation of democracy in Chile were higher than at any time since Allende's inauguration. Legislative, student, and trade union elections continued to take place in normal democratic fashion. Pro-Allende forces willingly accepted election results when they were adverse. The NIE stressed that the Christian Democratic party and the National party were using their control of both houses of Congress to stall government legislation and to pass their own legislation designed to curtail Allende's powers. The news media continued to criticize the government. This NIE concluded that Allende would probably slow the pace of his program for change in the next year in order to accommodate the opposition and to preserve the gains he had made.

U.S. intelligence agencies issued another NIE shortly before Allende's overthrow in September 1973. This one stated clearly that Allende was unlikely to establish an Eastern European style Marxist regime. The NIE reported that the majority of low-income Chileans knew that Allende had improved their conditions and represented their interests. The NIE noted that support for the Popular Unity coalition had grown because of Allende's political ability and the popularity of his measures. The NIE also warned that growing polarization of Chilean society was harming the Chilean predilection for political compromise.[157]

These NIEs initially carried a predictable governmental hostility toward Allende and the expectation that he would impose a heavy-handed dictatorship of the Eastern European variety. But as Allende proved himself to be serious about protecting both civil liberties and the Chilean Constitution, the NIEs reported that dictatorship was unlikely and that Allende was indeed popular among the segments of the electorate most in need of governmental action to promote their personal, economic, and political liberty. Despite these reports, the United States opposition to Allende became more intense as he succeeded in upholding democratic practices. At the same time as the NIEs became more certain that Allende would not impose a dictatorship, the 40 Committee authorized more and more money for covert operations to promote his downfall.[158]

Professed Value 2: To Protect the Interests of the Chilean People

Whose interests were served by U.S. policy? Economically, the Chileans who benefited most from United States intervention were those who needed help the least. Upper-class people, who collaborated with United States corporate interests in Chile, could, after 1973, once again control a disproportionate share of Chilean income. The military, who were trained and equipped by the United States, were in complete control. And middle-class people, who clung to a moderately satisfactory yet somewhat precarious social position, could, by acquiescing in the repression of the poor, once again enjoy the importation of goods from the United States. The large lower class, whose interests were historically ignored and whom Allende sought to raise above second-class citizenship, were hurt most by United States intervention.

Politically, the beneficiaries of U.S. policy that President Ford apparently had in mind were anti-Allende political parties and newspapers. However, even in the alleged effort to protect political pluralism, once again those who needed help the most—the dispossessed people lacking political resources—were harmed by United States intervention. Far from benefiting most Chileans, the military government that replaced Allende's administration executed profoundly vengeful and inhumane policies. Upon taking power, the junta controlled the people by military force. The military government seized the universities, abolished labor organizations, and suspended political parties.[159] Ten to fifteen thousand persons were killed. Over a million were ejected from their jobs and blacklisted so they could not obtain employment elsewhere. Over twenty thousand were driven into exile.[160] Tens of thousands were imprisoned, often without specific charges against them, and many of the imprisoned were tortured. According to the International Commission of Jurists, torture was widely practiced and included "electric shock, burning with acid or cigarettes, extraction of nails, crushing of testicles, sexual assault, and hanging."[161] Approximately one million Chileans moved outside their homeland in order to escape the repressive government.

In contrast, Laurence Birns, a former UN employee for the Economic Commission for Latin America in Santiago, reported that there was "far less intentional police brutality under Al-

239

lende than existed under the previous Christian Democratic regime. There were hardly any cases of imprisonment on political grounds. The universities were entirely free although some faculties became heavily politicized. Political life was almost entirely free of secret police surveillance."[162] According to Birns, "Not a single newspaper was censored by the civilian authorities, and opposition political parties could rage at will against the government. . . . Allende was scrupulously correct in maintaining unimpaired, under unrelieved internal and external pressure, all the nation's institutions."[163] Paul Sigmund, a U.S. critic of the Allende government, admitted that until the junta took power away from Allende in September 1973, Chile "had a more open political structure than our own."[164]

Kissinger's disregard for the Chileans' right of self-determination was paralleled by his lack of concern for the loss of individual human rights within Chile after the pro-United States military government deposed Allende. Richard Holbrooke, editor of *Foreign Policy*, reported that Kissinger was "wholly free of any constraint based on a set of moral beliefs [and] without feeling for human suffering." He did not let "human beings interfere with policy."[165] When the United Nations General Assembly passed a resolution urging Chile to restore human rights and free political prisoners, the United States abstained. Only seven other Latin American countries voted with Chile against the resolution.[166]

Kissinger also reportedly rebuked David H. Popper, the new United States ambassador to Chile, after Popper had attempted to discuss torture and other human rights issues with Chilean officials in the context of negotiations about military aid to Chile. As a result of a Kissinger directive, a formally drafted State Department letter of complaint went to Popper. Some State Department officials indicated that Popper's rebuke was a demonstration of the administration's unwillingness to press human rights issues with the junta. Kissinger's aides defended the action by arguing that Kissinger's objection was based on Popper's efforts to link "unrelated" issues such as human rights with United States military aid to the junta.[167]

This Kissinger action took place in spite of legislation passed by Congress in 1973 calling on the Nixon administration to request that the Chilean government "protect the human rights of all individuals." Congress also declared that any military or economic assistance should be conditional upon Chilean guarantees

240

of safe conduct for refugees, humane treatment of prisoners, and no imprisonment of people for political purposes.[168]

One might attempt to defend United States interventionist policy by arguing that United States officials may not have wanted such a vengeful regime to take the place of Allende's. Nevertheless, United States policies did promote civil strife. Assistance was not limited to democratic opponents of Allende. It was widely assumed in the United States government that any political alternative in Chile was preferable to a Marxist government. For example, even after the brutality of the military government was convincingly documented, Ray S. Cline, director of the State Department's Bureau of Intelligence and participant in the 40 Committee's deliberations from 1970-73, said that the Chilean people were better off under the military government than when governed by Allende.[169] Throughout the Allende administration, the United States maintained separate, direct contact with the Chilean military, and discussed plans for a coup d'état. Therefore, even if United States officials preferred a less vengeful regime, the nature of their intervention makes it clear that the United States never seriously sought to avoid promoting conditions likely to bring a brutal regime into power.

In addition, the United States government and at least some corporation officials made a concerted effort to encourage the corruption of Chilean political leaders through the use of money for bribery of candidates or members of Congress and the Chilean executive branch. Although bribery is a constitutionally defined cause for impeachment in the United States, officials of the United States and of U.S. corporations developed a policy in Chile to bribe political leaders and then to enthrone those successfully bribed.

Finally, U.S. intervention lent support to the notion, of significance to reformers around the world, that a program of fundamental change could succeed only if accompanied by widespread force and repression. By helping eliminate a democratic road to reform in Chile, U.S. officials mocked moderate reformers who genuinely believed that the United States would not subvert their legal processes. As a result of the destruction of the Allende government by U.S.-supported Chilean militarists, Allende was more likely to be viewed by observers either as a naive social democrat or as a revolutionary failure because he tried to make changes without a Leninist hold on the apparatus

241

of state power. U.S. policy vindicated the proponents of more authoritarian models of change. Within Chile, the United States encouraged the polarization of citizens toward two irreconcilable camps: those of the authoritarian right, who believed that their government should repress social reformers and cooperate with United States economic and strategic interests, and those of the authoritarian left, who believed that achieving economic equity would be possible only through a violent, centrally-directed movement to oust the United States and its indigenous collaborators.

In sum, U.S. policy served those Chileans most willing to collaborate with the perpetuation of U.S. interests in Chile, rather than the wider Chilean public. William Colby stated U.S. intentions more accurately than President Ford when he explained that covert operations were taken in Chile to serve "the best interests of our country, and friendly elements in another one."[170] For several U.S. administrations to help violent, militaristic, and antidemocratic groups meant that officials preferred the retention of economic inequities and the promotion of authoritarian government to the acceptance of an elected government committed to radical socioeconomic change aimed at greater equity in Chile. U.S. actions meant Washington officials believed they knew what was good for Chileans even better than Chileans expressing themselves at the polls. U.S. policies meant a Latin American country would not be allowed to choose a different economic system, less subject to United States investment, profit-taking, and commercial and political influence, without suffering United States reprisals. In its policies of overt economic pressure and covert support of Allende's opponents, the United States helped set in motion and sustain forces that led to the eventual death of the Allende government.

Thus, rather than protecting the interests of the Chilean people, as officials professed, United States behavior expressed an alternative value cluster: *to encourage disrespect for individual human rights and the rule of law, to promote the corruption of Chilean officials, and to discourage nonviolent, humane processes of social change* (implicit value C).

In support of the implicit values noted above, United States policy carried other implications which were generally applicable to many less developed countries. U.S. policy tended *to discourage overseas elites from solving their real domestic problems of injustice and human suffering* (implicit value D). United States policy invited foreign officials, such as the Chilean dictatorship, to focus on developing pro-United States relations and at the same time to enrich a small Chilean group of collaborators with U.S. economic interests, to cater to middle-class consumers of U.S. exports, and to ignore the grievances of the lower classes. For an elite to stay in power in Chile, after all, depended as much on retaining friendly relations with the United States as with meeting the needs of their own dispossessed people.

U.S. policy also served *to discourage overseas elites from dealing with underlying international dimensions of their internal problems* (implicit value E). U.S. officials induced foreign political leaders to overlook the extent to which the poverty of their suppressed classes was due to the wealth-extracting role of capital-exporting states and of indigenous collaborators with the latter. The preoccupation of many Latin American governments with bilateral relations with the United States has deterred them from recognizing the need to transform the international economic structure for greater fulfillment of human needs. They have failed to press for global systemic change that would facilitate political self-determination, redistribute the world's wealth more equitably, and yield a greater degree of economic justice internally. They have remained happy with their privileged positions within their national structures, often propped up by United States-based multinational corporations, overt U.S. aid, and covert CIA activity.

Professed Value 3: To Protect United States National Security

Objectively, the existence of the Allende government in itself could hardly have threatened United States security. Chile was thousands of miles away, with 5 percent of the population and one half of one percent of the GNP of the United States. Allende made no plans to attack the United States nor to harm any neighboring states. Why, then, did the United States fear Allende enough to violate self-determination and to spend millions of dollars for his demise?

The security rationale for United States intervention contained two dimensions, one ideological and the other economic, neither of which constituted a direct strategic threat. First of all, many officials continued to view the spread of socialism, especially to the Western Hemisphere, as a threat to United States security. This was an ideologically determined assumption, not an empirically rooted conclusion. These ideological beliefs, al-

243

though unfounded, guided policy just as surely as if they were rooted in reality.

The earlier cold war belief that the spread of communism threatened United States security continued to influence officials. In mentioning security as a rationale for United States policy, Ford fell back upon the standard cold war strategy that CIA operations were a necessary part of a policy of opposing communism. Since the United States was anticommunist, the argument went, any Marxist government must be part of an anti-United States communist coalition. But this line of argument was unpersuasive for at least two reasons. In the first place, Allende was in no sense an agent of the Soviet Union or China or even of the Communist party of Chile, with which he had occasionally been at odds during his career as leader of Chilean socialists. Second, if the United States could normalize relations with the communist giants—China and the Soviet Union—it made little sense, from a strategic viewpoint, to disrupt relations with a small power like Chile. As the cold war had waned, officials learned to accept existing communist governments, but still retained the belief that the spread of Marxism was a danger. Thus United States officials promoted détente with the Soviet Union and China at the same time they sought to overturn the relatively weak Chilean government's more moderate Marxism.

The hold of cold war rhetoric upon the minds of officials was echoed by the president himself in condoning the superpowers' practice of maintaining client states. In justifying the United States clandestine intervention, Ford revealed how much even in his own mind the guiding principle—if not the dollar amount—of United States foreign policy was similar to Soviet policy: "Communist nations spend vastly more money than we do for the same kind of purposes."[171] The common purpose, apparently, was to maintain in power foreign elites more sympathetic to a superpower's interests than would have existed without clandestine superpower intervention.[172]

United States officials were angry about Allende because his government represented the expansion of socialism in the Western Hemisphere, but more importantly because he represented something that the ideologically molded worldviews of officials could not tolerate: a Marxist who was elected through a fair, democratic process. In this sense, a constitutional Marxism, respecting many civil liberties, was more of a threat to U.S. officials than Fidel Castro's more authoritarian version of communism.

244

As a Marxist and a democrat, Allende existed in two mutually exclusive categories. To make Allende fit their presuppositions, U.S. officials constantly distorted his position on civil liberties, and discussed him in nearly Stalinist terms. Rather than bring their ideology into conformity with reality, they sought to change reality to fit their ideology. Thus the longer Allende continued in office without abolishing civil liberties, the more money Washingtonians spent to hasten his demise.[173] The long tradition of anticommunist thinking and the constraints of personal ideology upon policymaking prevented a realistic foundation upon which to build policy.

The Allende government was feared and hated because it represented radical economic change and could stimulate a chain of events—falling economic dominoes—that would be disorderly and costly for the U.S. Allende's vision of radical change encouraged a fundamental altering of the status quo in which the United States enjoyed vastly disproportionate wealth and power. In spite of the economic difficulties of Allende's government, we should recall that he "attempted to undo a system in which 5 percent of the families controlled some 35 percent of the agricultural land, in which the banks worked only for the established rich and industries underproduced products that were overpriced. He attempted, and with significant success, to bring health, housing, a better diet, and education to the poor, and a sense of dignity and of national participation to those for whom Chile's constitutional system had previously been unreal and fraudulent."[174]

The main objection of U.S. officials to democratic socialism was that it meant less opportunity for foreign investment of U.S. capital, less opportunity for profit for U.S. corporations, and less influence by the United States over the affairs of other countries. Thus the fear of corporation executives and U.S. government officials that private enterprise would be nationalized without compensation was only one part of a much larger fear that future investment and profit opportunities in Chile would be foreclosed. (They had, in previous years, been steadily growing.)

U.S. policymakers would not have been happy to have accepted expropriation even if it were carried out with fair compensation. The United States declined Allende's request to submit the disputed offers for compensation to international arbitration. Since 1916 a treaty had been in force between Chile and the United States which established a commission of five

245

persons to solve disputes between the two countries. Chile proposed that its interpretation of the nationalization proceedings be studied by the international commission according to the provisions of the treaty. The United States recognized that the treaty was valid, but refused.[175]

The fear of diminished profits for investors explains why officials were promoting more credit and trade with the Soviet Union at the same time they curtailed them with Chile: in the Soviet case, where there were no large U.S. private investments, détente promised new economic benefits for U.S. businesses; in the Chilean case, where profitable investments had long paid dividends, the advent of socialism promised loss of profits. With Allende in power, U.S. corporations, which had not benefited the lower classes in Chile, would be required to participate in distributing wealth more equitably. Thus officials opposed Chilean economic nationalism and control of U.S. corporations more than they opposed Marxism itself in China or the Soviet Union.

Thus the ideological rigidity toward Chile was buttressed by a larger design in world politics. As indicated above, Ambassador Korry and others feared that a successful Allende government would aid the rising electoral strength of communist parties in Italy and France.[176] When Kissinger briefed congressional leaders about Chile, he also said that CIA activity was necessary in other contexts, such as to prevent the Italian government from becoming communist.[177] Within the hemisphere, the demonstration-effect or domino theory had a different variation. Rather than expect other socialist parties to win election, United States officials worried—as Connally openly admitted—about the likelihood that simply having a Chilean government strongly opposed to continued United States profit-taking in Latin America would encourage reformist tendencies in Bolivia, Peru, and elsewhere. As Fagen has reported, Washington officials feared that the Popular Unity government "would profoundly affect the correlation of political forces on the landmass of South America, link economic nationalism more directly to socialist forms and solutions, and give a new and difficult-to-counter legitimacy to anti-Americanism and the nationalization of banks, large industries, and subsoil resources."[178]

Ideological hostility toward radical Latin Americans, who were skeptical about the utility of the profit motive of United States corporations for serving the human needs of their lower

246

classes, reinforced the desire to protect the present and potential profits of U.S. investors, who were often important architects of U.S. policy in Washington. By helping discredit Allende, U.S. leaders could in a single act, reestablish their ideology overseas, reduce the cognitive dissonance caused by the incompatibility of their ideology with reality, promote their own personal and institutional wealth, and protect their national power.

It would be erroneous to suggest that there were no differences among United States policymakers about the specific policies to pursue toward Chile. There were differences of opinion within the Department of State, as well as between members of the State and Treasury Departments, between ITT and the State Department, between the CIA and the State Department. Kissinger reportedly took over the direction of the covert action of Chile because he felt that Charles Meyer, assistant secretary of state for Latin America, might be unenthusiastic about a hardline policy. Nevertheless, these disagreements seldom reflected significant differences in policy goals. In general, the entire bureaucratic apparatus was cooperating in the implementation of policies designed to make it impossible for the Popular Unity coalition to govern.[179]

After examining the security considerations in United States policy, it is clear that the professed value of serving national security was hardly reflected in actual practice. U.S. behavior would be more accurately characterized by implicit value F: *to maintain United States overseas economic and political influence in the face of a radical movement to realize greater self-determination and economic equity.*

In several ways, United States policy negatively affected national security. In the first place, the intervention contributed to a United States image throughout the world of a manipulative, unfair, dishonest, ruthless giant resisting the rights of the weak and poor. At the time of the Chilean revelations, Ambassador Daniel P. Moynihan noted this effect in India.[180] Washington's posture meant the United States exposed itself to blame even for some subversion of which it was innocent. In the long run this image could hardly serve the legitimate security needs of any United States citizen.

The policy of secret intervention also violated United States security interests because it encouraged other states to employ "dirty tricks" more widely. Such policies victimize small societies, subject them to great power machinations, and make orderly, humane change less likely. Reformers in the less developed countries are taught to accept the status quo or else become violent revolutionaries.

Thirdly, the policy of secret intervention violated United States security interests because it lowered the expectations in the international community for legal behavior. It would be foolish, of course, to believe that if the CIA avoided interventions that the Soviet KGB would immediately stop them also, but it would be equally foolish to ignore that norms for behavior do influence decision makers to some extent, and that the norms themselves are strengthened or weakened by United States behavior. When Ford justified U.S. intervention on the grounds that the USSR engaged in similar action, he encouraged a worldview which, if generalized, would result in a gradually deteriorating expectation about what constituted conventional, legitimate international behavior. That jeopardized the security not simply of all U.S. citizens, but of all citizens on the planet.

Moreover, interventionism violated United States security interests because, when repeated, it distracted U.S. decision makers from constructing foreign policies to deal with root causes of social conflict throughout the world. The CIA intervention in Chile was only one of a long list of examples that showed the United States opposed to self-determination if it brought radical reallocation of wealth and power. Other examples of United States intervention included: the overthrow of the reform government of President Jacobo Arbenz Guzman of Guatemala (1954); the engineering of economic and political agitation against Cheddi Jagen, the socialist premier of British Guiana (1961-62); the training, transport and air support for the invasion of Cuba to overthrow Fidel Castro (1961); intervention in the Dominican Republic by 18,000 U.S. marines to oppose the return to power of reform-minded President Juan Bosch, who was earlier deposed by a military takeover; infiltration and establishment of political and economic control of the Ecuadorian labor movement in the early 1960s leading to the overthrow of the civilian government by a military dictatorship; the use for more than two years of a Bolivian cabinet official as a CIA operative; and the overthrow of Iranian Premier Mohammed Mossadegh (1953) who had nationalized the Iranian oil industry. According to the findings of the Senate Select Committee, the United States instigated assassination plots against at least two foreign leaders and became embroiled in plotting that led to the deaths of three others. CIA officials gave orders to assassinate Patrice Lumumba in 1960 although his death may not have been due to CIA activity. Eight unsuccessful schemes were planned against Fidel Castro's life between 1961 and 1965. Three other high officials who were targets for removal, kidnapping, or assassination were Rafael Trujillo of the Dominican Republic, Ngo Dinh Diem of South Vietnam, and General René Schneider of Chile, all of whom eventually were killed, although apparently not directly by the CIA. The CIA also supplied arms to dissidents planning the overthrow of President Sukarno of Indonesia.[181]

In addition, many less dramatic interventions have occurred in recruiting and paying money to foreign officials willing to collaborate with the CIA. For example, Jose Figueres, the former president of Costa Rica, admitted he had worked for the CIA in "twenty thousand ways" since it was founded. He said other Latin American presidents had done the same.[182] Philip Agee asserted that Mexican President Luis Echeverria worked as a "collaborator" with the CIA while he was Minister of the Interior.[183]

In the hope that secret financing of strikers, bribing officials, stuffing ballot boxes, or assassinating politicians would produce pro-U.S. governments, U.S. officials have ignored more basic issues. of self-determination and social justice in developing societies, as well as issues of human survival on the planet. Addressing these basic issues could have done far more, in the long run, to serve United States security. Thus, surprising though it might have seemed to the leadership, it was true that insensitivity to human rights actually harmed efforts to achieve genuine security for United States citizens.

Finally, a policy of intervention discouraged a long-run approach to transform the present nation-state structure to a more fully global structure of world order. The CIA provided a crutch for a limping international political system, and sought to prolong the system's life through more crafty use of national sovereignty, when in fact without the covert, interventionist crutch officials would have seen more clearly that competitive sovereignty and excessive unregulated power at the national level were part of the infirmity. In sum, the cumulative impact of U.S. policy in Chile directly contradicted professed value 3. Rather than safeguard U.S. citizens, Washington's policies served *to undermine U.S. security in the long run* (implicit value G).

249

Professed Value 4: To Protect the Interests of U.S. Citizens

Kissinger, Nixon, Ford, and others claimed that U.S. policy served the interests of the people of the United States. Although these officials never specified precisely whose interests they had in mind, the most obvious beneficiaries were the owners of United States corporations in Chile. Companies such as ITT, Anaconda, and Kennecott were promised compensation by Allende's successors.

Although some United States corporations did benefit economically from the collapse of constitutional government in Chile, this did not mean that intervention benefited the U.S. public in general. Not even all businesses agreed that U.S. intervention served their interests.[184] Except for the average citizen's predilection for private enterprise systems, there is little evidence of any benefits to the U.S. public from the subversion of self-determination. At the same time, citizens' interests in protection of constitutional government and human rights, and elimination of poverty in Chile all were damaged by United States policy.

As revealed in the foregoing examination of professed values, the best explanation for U.S. policy was the desire on the part of U.S. officials *to oppose the political and economic success of a newly established socialist government as a strategy to advance economic benefits for large U.S. investors* (implicit value H).[185]

By rhetorically wedding the economic interests of some United States-based multinational corporations with the public interest, the U.S. government—intentionally or unintentionally—encouraged the public to believe that overseas reformers, especially socialists, pursued policies that were contrary to the interests of the U.S. public because they were contrary to the profit maximizing desires of multinational corporations. In many cases, of course, this was untrue. Because these corporations decided what to produce on the basis of profitability, they frequently reduced productive capacity for less profitable goods that could have fulfilled the human needs of large sections of the public in the United States as well as in Chile. But because the poor lacked money to generate demand for such products, multinational corporations had no interest in producing them. By using patriotic appeals to induce public support for United States foreign policy, by drawing upon the traditional preference of the public for private enterprise, by combining antiradical inclinations and dislike for foreign "disorder" with the assumption that what was good for big corporations was good for all United States citizens and all Chileans as well, the U.S. government has slowed the growth of public support for overseas social reform movements.

In the Chilean case, the U.S. government's actions misled the public about the nature of social problems and political activity in Chile. United States leaders encouraged their constituents to believe that Allende's goals were alien to the people of Chile and to the Western Hemisphere. Yet, however strongly one may accuse Allende of economic misjudgment in his conduct of public affairs, many of his goals enjoyed the support of a majority of Chilean citizens, as the unanimous passage of expropriation legislation indicated. Tomic, the presidential candidate of the centrist Christian Democrat party, ran on a platform that resembled Allende's in many respects, and which included nationalization of the major industries. Thus in the long run, only indefinite United States manipulation of Chilean politics or a right-wing Chilean dictatorship could have prevented growing Chilean control over United States corporations, regardless of what happened to Allende. The new military government was an oligarchic force, representing the coalition of big business and big landowners that had opposed the reforms of President Frei as well.[186] Both Republican and Democratic administrations discouraged the U.S. public from understanding these political realities. Officials sought *to prevent the growth of public support in the United States for overseas radical movements aiming at more equitable distribution of economic and political resources globally and within their own societies* (implicit value I).

U.S. officials justified their policies in terms of widely held humanitarian values, but perverted those values in executing specific policies. In the words of the Senate Select Committee on Intelligence, official deceptiveness sustained covert actions that were "inconsistent with our basic traditions and values."[187] The inconsistencies were demonstrated in several ways.

In the first place, for more than three years U.S. leaders continually denied taking either overt or covert action to harm the Allende administration. They did this because they feared that their policies would not be supported by the general public if the truth were known. After the *New York Times* story first reported major CIA involvement, officials continued to cover up as much of the activity as possible, rather than give a full accounting.[188] The further those in power moved beyond the publicly-defined limits of generally acceptable behavior, the more they hid their acts under a blanket of secrecy.

Second, rather than tolerate a diversity of views on issues of overseas social reform, the United States government harrassed even U.S. citizens, living in Santiago, who were neutral or pro-Allende. The U.S. embassy in Santiago spied on the activities of U.S. citizens and perhaps even communicated their findings to Chilean military officials.[189]

Finally, even if by some disjointed logic one might argue that the CIA intervention served the interests of the United States public, that would not have justified overthrowing the constitutional government chosen by the Chilean public. Surely most U.S. citizens would have agreed that no errors of political judgment and no peculiarities of ideology on the part of an elected U.S. president would justify intervention by a foreign power in the affairs of the United States.

In sum, U.S. officials designed policies *to utilize the public preference for private enterprise systems in a strategy that, on a concrete level, contradicted the public's humanitarian sympathies, ideas of political rectitude, and sense of fair play* (implicit value J).

Secret CIA activity abroad spilled over into illegal governmental behavior at home. The *Pentagon Papers*, the Watergate scandals, and a twenty-year record of illegal CIA domestic activities[190] provide ample evidence that decision makers who develop strategies to subvert self-determination abroad are irresistibly tempted to subvert it at home. As Daniel Ellsberg said after the first Watergate revelations, the logic of Watergate was the same as the logic of Vietnamese policy documented in the *Pentagon Papers*: for United States officials, the law stopped at the White House fence. In making policy for Chile, the members of the 40 Committee saw themselves as above the law. Some of the same people who covered up Watergate misdeeds similarly claimed that they were circumscribing investigations in order to protect national security and CIA secrets. Typically, when some of Kissinger's covert policies began to be discussed in public, he approved the wiretapping of his own advisers and staff in order to prevent public scrutiny of United States policies.[191] Rather than confine their conduct to the legally-defined limits, officials in several administrations preferred *to risk undermining the legitimacy of the United States government within U.S. society* (implicit value K).

CIA operations like the Chilean intervention lowered the expectations of citizens that their government would be honest and open. After all, if "dirty tricks" were performed, officials could be expected to lie about them. They would publicly deny what they privately did. In Henry Kissinger's own words, the CIA was used for covert actions "because it was less accountable."[192] When accurate information about public affairs is no longer available or highly valued in a society, the practice of democracy becomes impossible. When U.S. leaders insisted upon the widespread need for secrecy, they indicated that they did not welcome participation in decisions. They did not favor self-government. In this sense, Washington national security managers made themselves enemies of the people.

Executive officials deliberately deceived members of Congress, who were duty-bound to carry the preferences of the people into the policymaking process. During the Allende campaign, the State Department maintained a public facade of nonintervention and proclaimed it repeatedly. Long after the United States had spent millions of dollars to create economic chaos, manipulate elections, and foment a coup, the president told Congress: "We respect the hemispheric principle of nonintervention. . . . We recognize that [Chile's leaders] . . . are serious men whose ideological principles are, to some extent, frankly in conflict with ours. Nevertheless, our relations will hinge not on their ideology but on their conduct toward the outside world."[193]

After the coup in 1973, the State Department formally denied any financial involvement in opposition protests and strikes, declaring "such suggestions are absurd."[194] Edward Korry, former ambassador to Chile, testified under oath to a subcommittee of the Senate Foreign Relations Committee that it was true and "obvious from the historical record that . . . the United States gave no support to any electoral candidate; that the United States had maintained the most total hands-off the military policy from 1969 to 1971 conceivable; that the United States did not get involved in the so-called Alessandri formula; that the United States did not seek to pressure, subvert, influence a single member of the Congress at any time in the entire 4 years of my stay."[195] Again and again, Charles A. Meyer, former assistant secretary of state for Latin American affairs, assured senators:

The policy of the Government . . . was that there would be no intervention in the political affairs of Chile. . . . We financed

253

no candidates, no political parties. . . . The policy of the United States was that Chile's problem was a Chilean problem to be settled by Chile. As the President stated in October of 1969, "We deal with governments as they are."

The policy of the U.S. government . . . remained non-interventionist. We neither financed candidates nor financed parties nor financed Alessandri gambits. Nor tried to precipitate economic chaos, and promoted neither civil nor military nor any other coup. The policy of Chile's future was Chile's.

We bought no votes, we funded no candidates, we promoted no coups. . . . We were religiously and scrupulously adhering to the policy of the Government of the United States . . . of nonintervention.[196]

Assistant Secretary of State Jack Kubisch told the House Subcommittee for Inter-American Affairs on September 20, 1973:

The United States had no desire to provoke a confrontation with the Allende Government. On the contrary, strong efforts were repeatedly made to seek ways to resolve our differences. . . . The position of the United States was quite correct. . . . We were not involved in the coup in any way. . . . It is untrue to say that the United States government was responsible—either directly or indirectly—for the overthrow of the Allende regime. We were not responsible for the difficulties in which Chile found itself, and it is not for us to judge what would have been best or will now be best for the Chilean people. That is for the Chileans themselves to decide, and we respect their right to do this.[197]

Corporate officials were equally blind or deceptive in describing their own role. For example, ITT senior vice-president E. J. Gerrity testified, "We did everything possible to build good faith with Mr. Allende."[198]

CIA Director William Colby's later testimony demonstrated that officials from the Department of State, the Treasury Department, the CIA, and the White House repeatedly, intentionally misled the public and Congress. Jerome Levinson, chief counsel for the subcommittee investigating the ITT role in Chile, reportedly said the subcommittee had been "deliberately deceived."[199] The White House described what later was revealed to have been a highly misleading briefing by Kissinger as a "full and frank discussion of the full range of CIA activities."[200]

Because of executive deception and congressional inaction, the public was deprived of any effective role in policymaking during the years of the Allende government. For example, a confidential staff report of the Senate Foreign Relations Subcommittee on Multinational Corporations reportedly charged that misleading testimony under oath had been given by Henry Kissinger; Charles Meyer, assistant secretary of state for Latin America; Edward M. Korry, ambassador to Chile from 1967 to 1971; Nathaniel Davis, Korry's successor as ambassador; Richard Helms, CIA head; William Broe, director of CIA clandestine activities for Latin America; and John Hennessy, assistant secretary of the treasury for international affairs. The staff memorandum reportedly urged contempt of Congress charges for at least some of the officials, and said that Helms, Meyer, and Hennessy might have committed perjury.[201] Senators Church, Symington, Muskie, Case, and Percy, the members of the subcommittee, failed to implement the staff report. As Laurence Birns correctly concluded, the available evidence about United States policymaking reveals "the staggering immorality of the policy's architects and the ineffectuality and irrelevance of most scholars, journalists and Congressional leaders, whose professional obligation it was to oversee executive policies toward Chile."[202]

Instead of promoting public participation, based on truthful information about U.S. behavior, Washington officials preferred *to undermine the conditions essential for democracy in the United States* (implicit value L). As Table 4-2 shows, the values implicit in U.S. policy differed widely from the professed values of the Washington leadership.

A GLOBAL HUMANIST APPROACH

Comparison of Professed Values, Implicit Values, and the Promotion of Human Rights

The preceding appraisal of United States policy toward Chile has revealed a cluster of implicit values expressed in official behavior. They represent U.S. performance on the particular issue of self-determination and will be compared, in this concluding section of the chapter, with the third value of global humanism:

255

Table 4-2
A Comparison of Professed and Implicit Values
in U.S. Policy on Self-determination

Professed Values	Implicit Values
1. To sustain democratic parties and maintain political pluralism in Chile.	A. To undermine and prevent the exercise of the right of self-determination and democratic government.
	B. To encourage conditions likely to produce political polarization, civil strife, and violence.
2. To protect the interests of the Chilean people.	C. To encourage disrespect for individual human rights and the rule of law within Chile, to promote the corruption of Chilean officials, and to discourage nonviolent, humane processes of social change.
	D. To discourage overseas elites from solving their real domestic problems of injustice and human suffering.
	E. To discourage overseas elites from dealing with underlying international dimensions of their internal problems.
	F. To maintain U.S. overseas economic and political influence in the face of a radical movement to realize greater self-determination and economic equity.
3. To protect U.S. national security.	G. To undermine U.S. security in the long run.
4. To protect the interests of U.S. citizens.	H. To oppose a newly established socialist government as a strategy to advance economic benefits for U.S. investors with property in Chile.
	I. To prevent the growth of public support in the U.S. for overseas radical movements aiming at more equitable distribution of economic and political resources globally and within their own societies.

256

Table 4-2 (cont.)

Professed Values	Implicit Values
	J. To utilize the U.S. public's preference for private enterprise systems in a strategy that, on a concrete level, contradicted the public's humanitarian sympathies, ideas of political rectitude, and sense of fair play.
	K. To risk undermining the legitimacy of the U.S. government within U.S. society.
	L. To undermine the conditions essential for democracy in the U.S.

the promotion of universal human rights and justice (V_3).

The articulated goals of United States policy were frequently in harmony with V_3. To support democratic constitutional government in Chile, and to serve the common interests of Chileans and U.S. citizens were goals obviously compatible with V_3. However, if one moves from the abstract level of policy goals as expressed in official rhetoric to the concrete level of government behavior, United States policy directly violated fundamental human rights.

In particular, U.S. policy aimed at preventing the exercise of self-determination by a people who had, in a constitutional election, favored substantial socioeconomic change. The covert intervention of officials in itself violated the solemn commitment, given in several duly ratified treaties, to respect the principles of self-determination and noninterference in the affairs of other states. Moreover, subverting self-determination was not an incidental or accidental consequence of official behavior; it was a deliberate intention. Officials aimed at perpetuating the disproportionate power of the United States in Chile through covert manipulations, rather than expanding the perimeters of participation in decision making to include Chileans affected by United States government and corporate actions. In defense of United States policy, many have argued that Allende would have fallen somewhat later, due to internal opposition, even without United States intervention. That may perhaps have been true, although

257

if Allende had been actively assisted by the United States in the way that pre- and post-Allende governments were, the conclusion would hardly have followed. Nevertheless, this argument is largely irrelevant to the main point here. Regardless of what would have happened to Allende if left on his own, the fact remains that the United States deliberately intervened numerous times at decisive moments, and for more than a decade, to subvert the practice of self-determination.

Moreover, even if indigenous right-wing forces could have ousted the Allende government, these forces expressed the same elitist, profit-motivated political interests and hostility to human rights and needs that were expressed by U.S. officials. Regardless of the array of internal forces against Allende, an important conclusion is that, in practice, the United States threw its weight against the forces of political and economic reform.

The issue of human rights had a very low priority in policy-making, ranking below capitalist ideological sympathies; human rights were unimportant to strategic advantages and irrelevant to the protection of investment and profit advantages for U.S. corporations. The United States weakened the movement for human rights both internationally and internally in Chile.

The Chilean case study also shows that the ideologically-skewed perception of U.S. officials made them ill-equipped to understand the value impact of U.S. policy and to promote human rights. U.S. leaders operated with a false consciousness[203] from which they made decisions that served their apparent interests, but which overlooked the general public's long-range interests—interests that were partially expressed in the professed values of those in power.

The gap between professed values and behavior suggests the existence of a bureaucratic version of truth that includes a deeply entrenched distortion of reality. Those in power confirmed one another's distortions of reality as policy was set in motion. Bureaucratic disagreements, which might have given opportunity for reality-testing, were confined to the best tactics to follow. Instead, there should have been a debate about whether United States goals were wrong.

Several examples illustrate this faulty comprehension of the real world. Kissinger believed that Allende lacked legitimacy because he had not won a clear majority of the popular vote in the national election. Yet only once in this century had a Chilean president won a majority in a popular election. The Constitution fully anticipated this possibility and defined the procedures, which were followed, for a congressional election of the president. Moreover, Kissinger never questioned the legitimacy of United States presidents, including Nixon in his first term, who were elected by a minority of those voting. The former director of the CIA also misperceived the meaning of the Chilean elections: "I have a difficult time feeling that the Chileans, who are very superior people . . . really wanted that [socialist] type of a government imposed on them, and it was only through the unfortunate division of the opposition that the situation turned out the way it did. Without such a division the results would have been as they were in 1964."[204] In fact, no government was "imposed" on Chile until the U.S.-supported military junta came to power. Allende did not take office primarily because of a split in the opposition. Many Christian Democrats were closer ideologically to the Popular Unity coalition than to Alessandri. Every member of the Christian Democratic party, which McCone described as part of the "opposition" and which won the 1964 election to which McCone referred, freely voted in the Congress to elect Allende to the presidency. They voted for him precisely because the national mandate expressed in the combined vote for the Christian Democrats and the Popular Unity coalition—well over a simple majority—had been in support of major social reform, rather than the reactionary policies of the right-wing candidate.

This faulty hold on reality extended to the corporate world as well. The chief executive officer and chairman of the board of ITT, Harold Geneen, said that the United States would naturally oppose Allende because the United States supported democratic regimes.[205] Ignoring the naiveté of the belief that the United States had guided its policies by opposition to dictatorships and by support for democracies, Geneen failed to comprehend that a socialist system was also democratic if it was chosen as a result of democratic processes and continued to respect those processes. Likewise, ITT's Director of Public Relations for Latin America, Hal Hendrix, reported from Santiago with certainty: "There is no doubt among trained professional observers with experience in the United States, Europe and Latin America that if Allende and the UP [Popular Unity coalition] take power, Chile will be transformed quickly into a harsh and tightly-controlled Communist state, like Cuba or Czechoslovakia today. The transition would be much more rapid than Cuba's.[206] This prediction ignored Allende's lifetime of support for democracy, his opposition to Marxist totalitarianism and to a violent road to socialism, and the assessments of many "trained professional observers."

Government officials also justified United States violation of self-determination because Allende expropriated United States property without compensation. Yet, intervention began long before any expropriation occurred. Officials implied that Allende's government was behaving unconstitutionally in expropriating United States property. Yet, in the general election, the population overwhelmingly voted for candidates espousing policies of nationalization.

Another justification for United States action came from a high intelligence official: "As long as you don't make it sound like we were trying to start a coup, it [intervention] will be all right. You've got to understand that he [Allende] was taxing them [the middle-class] to death."[207] Yet surely Chile's tax laws could not justify United States interference with Chilean self-determination.

United States officials continuously distorted Allende's position on civil liberties and elections. In fact, free elections were held as scheduled. Allende's Christian Democratic opponent, Radmiro Tomic, attested to Allende's faithful adherence to democratic principles until he paid with his life for honoring them.[208]

The ideological blindness of United States officials was summed up well in Kissinger's reported comment: "I don't see why we need to stand by and watch a country go Communist due to the irresponsibility of its own people."[209] If Kissinger had possessed an accurate grasp of reality, he would have understood that the expression of people at the polls was the essence of "responsible" government, and that to overturn the mandate of the people was the true irresponsibility. Officials ignored both the right of Chileans to self-determination, and the legal prohibitions that, if applied, doubtless would have shown U.S. officials to be in violation of the law.

U.S. leaders reinforced one another's comforting deception that, from a moral and legal standpoint, as long as their activity was covert, it did not occur. Thus Korry and Meyer could say that it was the policy of the United States not to intervene, because they did not consider the work of the CIA as part of the policy of the United States. Those in power felt a deep need for secrecy to protect their operative ideology from open scrutiny and to manipulate the public more effectively. That United States interference with self-determination could go unchecked for a decade demonstrated the pervasive acceptance of secrecy among Washington officials and their willingness to collaborate in self-justifying deceptions. This widespread code of behavior not only prevented democratic policymaking, it also made the realization of human rights impossible.

The Chilean case shows that the most highly respected U.S. officials of both political parties consistently deceived their constituents about their own human rights policies. They lied not to protect U.S. security, as they eventually claimed, but to disguise the true intent and value impact of their actions. U.S. leaders continued the coverup even after the alleged security threat had been killed and his government overthrown.

The main constraint upon policymakers was the fear of public exposure. Breach of the curtain of secrecy would have revealed the subordination of human rights to corporate-government desires for profit and power. Investigative reporters, such as Seymour Hersh and Jack Anderson, did as much to penetrate government secrecy and to enable the public to comprehend the gap between reality and the bureaucratic version of it as did the internal governmental system of checks and balances. Some CIA and ITT plans were aborted because of fear of publicity or the knowledge that the plans would be counterproductive if discovered. Fear of public reaction forced the government to rule out gunboat diplomacy and substitute two techniques, consistent with a "low profile": (1) covert intervention and (2) overt, politically unsensational but economically damaging credit curtailment. In brief, respect for human rights was inversely related to the degree of government secrecy.

The substance of policy and the process of policymaking were heavily influenced by multinational corporations like ITT, Anaconda, and Kennecott. Profit took priority over human rights. In examining the enormous, detailed hearings and studies on the policymaking process, one of the most striking features is the frequency with which corporate officials, advocating Allende's overthrow, had meetings with government officials. At least weekly contact occurred between ITT officials and William Broe, the CIA's chief of clandestine activity for Latin America. Daily reports were dispatched between the two offices. Occasionally, ITT officials would talk with Kissinger or his chief aides Alexander Haig and Viron Vakey. Other private meetings were arranged with White House advisers John Ehrlichman and Charles Colson; Assistant to the President for International Economic Policy, Peter Peterson; Secretary of State William Rogers; Secretary of the Treasury John Connally; Attorney General John Mitchell; Secretary of Commerce Maurice Stans. Frequently, ITT Director John McCone met or talked with CIA Director Richard Helms.

The policy process was tilted radically against any balanced consideration of viewpoints. There was no opportunity for those sympathetic to Allende to have similar meetings with high-level officials. No spokespersons were invited to argue for defense of humanitarian values. Not only were advocates of an alternative view unable to gain frequent access to key officials, they were also continuously deceived about the content of policy by those officials denying them access.

Even in the post-Vietnam era of "new awareness," Congress failed to exercise an effective human rights check on United States policy. In analyzing U.S. performance on the self-determination issue, it is instructive to examine the impact upon policy of those who opposed intervention in Chile.[210] The most apparently influential opposition came from members of Congress, especially from some members of the Senate Foreign Relations Committee and the Subcommittee on Civilian and Refugee Problems, plus the individual work of Representative Michael Harrington. Legislators' public speeches were useful in informing the public on some issues, usually long after the policy in question had been implemented. Congressional hearings collected evidence that otherwise may not have become known. However, there was little effective follow-through to insure that United States policy would be any different on human rights issues in the future.

Members of Congress generally lacked sufficient time, dedication, energy, persistence, and imagination to redirect U.S. human rights policy. In the first place, Congress was relatively slow and inactive. The rise and fall of the Allende government had occurred before Congress began to conduct rigorous investigations to learn the real nature of U.S. policy. The House and Senate subcommittees charged with CIA oversight were inactive. For example, the Senate Armed Services Subcommittee met a total of only 26 times between January 1966 and December 1975 to watch over, among other things, all CIA activities. During the years of the most intense pressures on Allende, the subcommittee met not at all in 1971 and only once each year in 1972 and 1973.[211]

Full disclosure hardly ever occurred even when the subcommittees did meet. Of the 33 covert action projects which the 40 Committee approved to undermine the electoral process in Chile, Congress was briefed in some fashion on only eight. Often briefings were after the fact. Among the projects on which Congress was not briefed at all were authorizations to purchase Chilean radio stations and newspapers, to support candidates in anti-Allende parties, and to support opposition parties themselves. Moreover, Congress was not consulted or informed about projects which were not reviewed by the full 40 Committee. One of these was the attempt by the CIA, at the instruction of the president, to prevent Allende from taking office in 1970 by instigating a coup d'état.[212]

Second, to the extent that the ITT hearings conducted before the 1973 coup did expose the tip of the iceberg, leads were not persistently pursued. After the more complete story was known, the Subcommittee on Multinational Corporations could have acted to improve the reliability of its information in future cases, but it did not. In spite of misleading testimony by officials, Congress did almost nothing to call the officials to account or to reaffirm and specify the norms that should insure that accurate information would be forthcoming to Congress in the future. In the legislation passed by the Senate in response to investigations of the ITT role,[213] U.S. citizens were prohibited from contributing to a U.S. governmental agency in an effort to influence the outcome of a foreign election. Also, United States officials were prohibited from soliciting or accepting contributions from any United States citizen for the purpose of influencing foreign elections. But these matters were not central to the Chilean intervention. In contrast, there was no legislative effort by the Subcommittee on Multinational Corporations to restrict direct foreign efforts by United States corporations to influence the outcome of foreign elections so long as they did not attempt to work through the U.S. government. Nor was interest shown in effectively preventing the United States government itself from directly intervening or hiring local agents to influence foreign elections. Yet these possibilities were the most likely future strategies for preventing self-determination abroad.[214]

Finally, like the executive participants who disagreed somewhat with Kissinger-Nixon-Connally tactics, up to 1974 Congress failed to raise questions about policy goals. Throughout

263

the hearings by the Subcommittee on Multinational Corporations, Senators paid enormous deference to the interests of U.S. corporations in Chile, and only suggested that corporate officials may have gone too far in using questionable tactics to protect their interests. There was no expression of general support for the Chileans seeking economic and political self-determination.[215] During the ITT hearings, no Senator pressed the idea that the United States should respect self-determination, even at the cost of diminishing the profits of some multinational corporations. Corporate values, not humane values, dominated the practice of Congress as much as of executive participants.

Specifically, a striking omission from the final report of the Subcommittee on Multinational Corporations was its failure flatly to condemn the then known interventions of ITT and the CIA as violations of the right of self-determination and the principle of noninterference in the internal affairs of another state. Instead, the committee report based its criticism on the argument that such tactless policy might jeopardize the future investments of other corporations.

> What is not to be condoned is that the highest officials of the ITT sought to engage the CIA in a plan covertly to manipulate the outcome of the Chilean presidential election. In so doing the company overstepped the line of acceptable corporate behavior. If ITT's actions in seeking to enlist the CIA for its purposes with respect to Chile were to be sanctioned as normal and acceptable, no country would welcome the presence of multinational corporations. Over every dispute or potential dispute between a company and a host government in connection with a corporation's investment interests, there would hang the spectre of foreign intervention. No sovereign nation would be willing to accept that possibility as the price of permitting foreign corporations to invest in its territory. The pressures which the company sought to bring to bear on the United States Government for CIA intervention are thus incompatible with the long-term existence of multinational corporations; they are also incompatible with the formulation of U.S. foreign policy in accordance with U.S. national, rather than private interests.[216]

The final report did not conclude that the ITT role constituted a violation of human rights in Chile.

In assessing the significance of the then known United States

264

governmental intervention in Chilean affairs, there was even less inclination to assess the illegality or immorality of United States manipulation of Chilean politics. Instead, CIA policy, like ITT activity, was primarily assessed in terms of its impact on United States corporate interests: "It is clear from this case that there were significant adverse consequences for U.S. corporations which arose out of the decision to use ITT in the way it was used—willing as ITT may have been—and that it was not in the best interests of the U.S. business community for the CIA to attempt to use a U.S. corporation to influence the political situation in Chile."[217]

The emphasis of the main Senate staff study on covert action in Chile stressed the self-defeating nature of clandestine activity. CIA support for overseas politicians could become the kiss of death if the support became known. For example, the report concluded that "it would be the final irony of a decade of covert action in Chile if that action destroyed the credibility of the Chilean Christian Democrats."[218]

The shallowness of the report was partially revealed in its own closing paragraphs: "This report does not attempt to offer a final judgment on the political propriety, the morality, or even the effectiveness of American covert activity in Chile." The report stopped short of saying that U.S. intervention violated the obligation of nonintervention. It concluded by explaining: "Given the costs of covert action, it should be resorted to only to counter severe threats to the national security of the United States. It is far from clear that that was the case in Chile."[219]

Yet the point that needed to be made was not merely that the costs involved may have been too great for the benefits desired, but that the benefits sought were themselves wrong. The United States had no right—and it had said so in legally binding documents—to intervene to overthrow a democratically elected Chilean government in order to secure political, economic, or even security benefits for the United States.

Congress became more forthright in its criticism of the CIA's overseas operations only after being confronted by undeniable evidence of illegal CIA actions within the United States. A desire to examine the CIA's domestic role, more than concern for universal human rights, prompted new congressional investigations.

The final report of the Senate Select Committee to Study Governmental Operations with Respect to Intelligence Activities

265

was clearly unique in calling attention to the undesirability of overthrowing democratically-elected governments: "It is the Committee's view that the standards to acceptable covert activity should . . . exclude covert operations in an attempt to subvert democratic governments or provide support for police or other internal security forces which engage in the systematic violation of human rights."[220] Legislation strictly to prohibit such activity, however, seemed unlikely. If the committee had sought to end the subversion of human rights by the CIA, it could have supported legislation to terminate covert activity. However, it left the door open by saying that covert action should "be undertaken only when the national security requires it and when overt means will not suffice."[221]

The loopholes provided by such language were illustrated in an action unrelated to the work of the Senate Select Committee. Congress in 1974 passed a provision, known as the Hughes-Ryan Amendment, to the Foreign Assistance Act. This amendment prohibited CIA use of funds for operations not intended solely for obtaining intelligence, unless "the President finds that each such operation is important to the national security of the United States." As a result of this legislation, the CIA took the position that the amendment "clearly implies that the CIA is authorized to plan and conduct covert action."[222] The Senate Select Committee concluded that as a result of the passage of the amendment and subsequent developments, "there is little doubt that Congress is now on notice that the CIA claims to have the authority to conduct, and does engage in, covert action. Given that knowledge, congressional failure to prohibit covert action in the future can be interpreted as congressional authorization for it."[223]

Throughout the ten-year period studied by the Select Committee, Congress displayed a notable "hesitancy . . . to use its powers to oversee covert action by the CIA." Part of the hesitancy "flowed from the fact that congressional oversight committees are almost totally dependent on the Executive for information on covert operations. The secrecy needed for these operations allows the Executive to justify the limited provision of information to the Congress."[224] In addition, many members of Congress were reluctant to learn about "dirty tricks" that would bother their consciences if they knew about them and were unable or unwilling to prevent them. Given this congressional atmosphere, to sanction further covert action in the interest of national security was not an effective barrier to further violation of the right of self-determination. Finally, even in the unlikely event that the CIA would be prohibited from covert activity, coups and similar action could continue to be promoted without any legal restrictions if the operations were carried out by contacts between U.S. military officials—rather than CIA personnel—and foreign military or civilian leaders. In this area, the Select Committee sought no limits at all.

As the preceding analysis shows, to realize human rights more fully, the most critical need was not for better control and oversight of the CIA, but for a fundamental revision of officials' values and objectives.[225] The bureaucracy was not acting without deliberation or instructions from the highest authorities. The leadership was not tactically foolish. It pursued goals antagonistic to human rights.

This conclusion takes on deeper importance when one understands that the Chilean case, while unusually dramatic in its reportage to the public, is typical of much U.S. foreign policy. Soon after the Central Intelligence Agency was established, covert action became "a routine program of influencing governments and covertly exercising power." This effort involved literally hundreds of projects each year. By 1953 there were major covert operations underway in forty-eight countries. Several thousand individual covert action projects have been undertaken since 1961.[226] As the staff report of the Senate Select Committee on Intelligence concluded: "The pattern of United States covert action in Chile is striking but not unique. It arose in the context not only of American foreign policy, but also of covert U.S. involvement in other countries within and outside Latin America. The scale of CIA involvement in Chile was unusual but by no means unprecedented."[227]

The Carter Administration

This analysis has focused on a distinct case study that preceded the Carter presidency and its highly visible emphasis on human rights. Although at the time of this writing it is too early to assess Carter policies conclusively, it is instructive to examine the first evidence of Carter's human rights policies. On the positive side, the Carter administration

—gave strong rhetorical support to human rights in several presidential news conferences and major speeches;

—indicated its intention to sign the UN covenants on human rights and to ratify the Genocide Convention;

—took the unprecedented step of ending military aid to

Uruguay and of cutting it to Argentina and Ethiopia on human rights grounds;

—halted military aid to Chile, as required by congressional action barring military aid to countries that consistently violated human rights;

—published, as required by the 1976 military aid law, a critique of human rights practices in aid-receiving countries; as a result of this, Brazil, Guatemala, Uruguay, Argentina, El Salvador, and Chile all took offense and withdrew from the U.S. military aid program; and

—supported a UN embargo on arms for South Africa.

On the negative side, the administration

—contributed to multilateral aid (through World Bank loans) to Argentina, Chile, Uruguay, and Ethiopia, even though Congress sought to ban bilateral military aid to these states because of rights violations;

—requested increases in military aid to several repressive governments for fiscal year 1978: for example, a 77 percent increment for South Korea ($280 million total) and a 40 percent increment for Indonesia ($58 million total);

—opposed congressional legislation requesting the United States to vote in multilateral lending agencies against extending loans to countries violating human rights; the administration's counter proposal, favored by the White House and Treasury and State Departments, would have allowed U.S. representatives to vote for loans to governments grossly violating human rights, including even loans for purposes unrelated to direct meeting of human needs;

—opposed a UN resolution for comprehensive economic sanctions against South Africa;

—opposed congressional efforts to terminate military training programs for Argentina;

—continued high levels of aid to Thailand, the Philippines, Brazil, Nicaragua, and other countries with poor records on human rights;

—continued major arms sales to countries, such as Iran, with a record of serious violations of human rights;

—made public statements in support of secret CIA payments to overseas officials;

—supported restrictive executive branch procedures to insure greater secrecy in execution of U.S. covert policies; and

—justified CIA covert political intervention on national security grounds.

This evidence presents a decidedly mixed, and at first glance, confusing picture. The Carter administration has used human rights advocacy to recapture the spirit of a highly moral foreign policy—a spirit lost during the long years of the Vietnamese war and Watergate. Especially the treatment of the human rights issue with the Soviet Union seems colored by a desire to show the superiority of the United States in this area. To threaten to withhold aid from less developed countries for human rights violations is a step forward, even if not a giant step. Aid recipients either may comply with the Carter request for respect for human rights, or they may—as some did—get angry and tell the United States to keep its aid. Either way, self-determination is likely to benefit, at least slightly.

On the other hand, Carter has not moved far enough to make substantial or comprehensive policy changes. Consistent with the posture of his predecessors, Carter has frequently subordinated the promotion of human rights to economic and strategic advantages for the United States.

The public support for human rights, especially as evidenced in congressional action to compel the president to curtail aid to brutal regimes, is a sign of a more enlightened world order struggling to be born. Resisting this new potential is a deep governmental reluctance to apply its lofty rhetoric in cases where U.S. security benefits are jeopardized. Government refusal to establish a global political order more congenial to human rights is a frank admission by officials that when it matters most human rights will be sacrificed for national advantage.

This does not mean that Carter's intentions are fundamentally hostile to human rights, but that powerful vested interests and the apparent requirements for functioning effectively within the international system force human rights into a subordinate position. Structural impediments—such as discrimination against others because of territorial location—and the traditional attitude toward human rights were evident early in the policies of President Carter, even though he prided himself on a willingness to break from the past and respect moral values. Only one month after taking office, for example, Carter, Vance, and CIA Director Stansfield Turner all publicly argued that it was proper for the CIA to pass money secretly to officials of other governments. After reviewing some newly revealed CIA payments to various heads of governments over the past twenty years, Carter concluded, "I have not found anything illegal or improper."[228] Turner euphemistically called clandestine CIA payments "foreign aid, in secrecy," and described such aid as "a very common and a very legitimate tool of foreign policy."[229]

The Carter administration behaved on this issue similarly to the 40 Committee in its earlier dismissal of the self-determination question. The Carter administration said that violation of the noninterventionist principle was legitimate if the purpose would benefit the United States. As Turner explained, the propriety of secret payments "depends on the purpose of that money." If the government thinks the money should be sent, then it "does not involve things that are improper."[230]

Time and again during his campaign the president said he wanted a government as decent as the American people. Such decency surely includes respect for the U.S. Constitution. Yet bribery is explicitly mentioned there as grounds for impeachment of a U.S. president. How can Carter publicly endorse undercover payments, which could easily be construed as bribes, to other presidents and prime ministers? He can do that only by traveling down the road of secrecy, by invoking national security justifications, by discouraging wide disclosure of such acts in Congress, and by preaching a double standard of human rights to the world's publics.

Consistent with the preceding argument, Carter expressed, as did Nixon, Ford, and Kissinger before him, deep concern about the secret payments being revealed to the public. It could be "extremely damaging" to national security, he said, "for these kinds of operations which are legitimate and proper to be revealed." To prevent disclosures in the future, he initiated measures to reduce the number of persons in the executive branch and Congress who would know about such actions. He said also that knowledge of these policies "makes it hard for us to lay a groundwork" for meeting future threats to national security, when similar payments might be used in future policy.[231]

The Carter administration's attitude was also similar to that of preceding administrations in protecting official secrecy rather than the public's right to know. For example, when Richard Helms was finally brought under investigation for dishonesty during hearings on his confirmation as ambassador to Iran, Carter authorized the Attorney General to arrange a plea bargain with Helms.[232] Helms pleaded *nolo contendere* (no contest) and in return escaped a trial. The Carter administration justified this failure to pursue fully a case of prosecutable perjury on familiar national security grounds. It seemed apparent that the administration's policy was designed to protect the system of secrecy and the reputations of officials more than the security of the U.S. people.

Like preceding administrations, the Carter leadership also invoked the national security justification for continuing foreign aid to South Korea and the Philippines even while reducing it to Argentina, Uruguay, and Ethiopia because of the latter's repressive policies. In using the security argument to justify U.S. aid to repressive governments, Carter seemed to endorse human rights violations, because all regimes rationalize their repression on national security grounds. If national security is a good reason to overlook human rights violations, then human rights are no longer inviolable rights but mere privileges that governments may extend or deny at their pleasure. In the absence of any global authority to render impartial assessments of such national security claims, every government of the world defines its own security needs. Carter himself therefore has provided a rationale for rights violations. For example, if Carter argues that the world's security is so precarious that the South Korean ally of the United States must have U.S. aid despite Seoul's brutality, then the South Korean government might similarly argue that its security is precarious enough to justify its own ruthlessness.

Secretary Vance also made it clear that where "the strategic situation is of critical importance," the U.S. would not allow human rights questions to curtail arms transfers.[233] Although there were no obvious security interests at stake, Carter used this argument to continue selling sophisticated arms to the Shah of Iran at an unprecedented rate, despite Amnesty International's report that Iran had the highest rate of death penalties in the world, no valid system of civilian courts, and a long history of torture. Moreover, "freedom of speech and association are non-existent."[234] When the Shah visited Washington in November 1977, Carter praised the Shah for his leadership in maintaining a "strong, stable and progressive Iran."[235]

In brief, it appears that Carter policies have not gone as far to bolster some repressive regimes, like the one in Chile, as those of his predecessors. Carter draws the line at a different point in answering the question: "How many human rights violations must we accept in order to maintain friendship with repressive regimes?" However, on a more fundamental level, the Carter administration is not substantially different from its predecessors:

officials still in principle condone violating self-determination and other rights in the name of U.S. security; they view covert activity as legitimate; they protect pervasive secrecy for intelligence operations. Carter's rhetoric and his withholding of aid for rights violations may be viewed as a slight change toward global humanist values. But the domination of these progressive policy elements by the traditional policies is correctly seen as the resistance of the present system to necessary change. The Carterian human rights ambivalence—if not schizophrenia—indicates an inherent inability to fulfill human rights within the present structure of interests and institutions. The pursuit of advantages for national governments continues to overwhelm the achievement of universal human rights.

An Alternative Framework

If United States policies toward human rights were to become responsive to the values of global humanism, these policies would depart sharply from past governmental behavior as illustrated in the Chilean case. The global humanist approach would seriously seek to move toward the following goals.

1. Terminate all covert intervention.[236] Because such intervention inherently violates self-determination, respect for legal processes, and the fulfillment of democracy in the United States and abroad, it should be prohibited as an instrument of policy. Critics of this view postulate that in a few cases, at least, covert intervention is necessary. However, if a certain foreign policy is of such vital and overriding importance that some form of intervention is generally recognized as legitimate, then it can be carried out publicly. Clandestine intervention is not consistent with the values of global humanism.

2. Terminate all covert intelligence gathering. Many persons who have acknowledged the need to end all secret CIA political operations still have insisted that the CIA needs to gather intelligence through secret means. But one must ask: Can not any information required by the United States be learned openly? Newspaper reporters, business people, scholars, and the United States embassy all supply information about a country. U.S. citizens are likely to justify the open gathering of any necessary information. It is not easy to find legitimate reasons for secret intelligence work in Chile.

The implementation of 1 and 2, of course, would eliminate

most of the need for the CIA. If CIA work had been terminated before 1970, this would have vitally served the cause of human rights in Chile.[237] There would have been far less temptation to violate self-determination, no concern about oversight to control CIA foreign or domestic activities, a substantial economic saving, and an enhanced reputation for the United States that would have made its conventional, legitimate diplomacy no less effective.

Additional benefits might accrue from the absence of secret intelligence. The president might actually develop a more accurate picture of reality. Without the availability of what he believes are "inside" or "secret" reports, the president would not so easily assume that his view was singularly correct. Nicholas Katzenbach, who has worked closely with two administrations, described the effect of secret intelligence on the policy process: "Unfortunately, Presidents are inclined to think . . . [that] blind trust in their wisdom is wholly justified. . . . Having almost sole access to the full range of classified information and expert opinion, Presidents are tempted to think that the opinions of Congressmen, academics, journalists and the public at large are, almost unavoidably, inadequately informed."[238]

More openness would increase the accuracy of information available to the outsider. It would also encourage wider utilization of existing information by scholars, journalists, and the public and enable them to render more autonomous judgments, which would serve as checks on official perceptions of reality. Outsiders would be less intimidated by the usual official response to policy suggestions: "If only you knew what I know but cannot say because it is classified." Finally, more openness would encourage the president to consider the advice of persons outside the White House, whose views would be of enhanced value because of their exposure to all available information. Not only would this approach produce greater wisdom and generate opportunities for social unity based on discussions among people using the same information pool, it is also far more consistent with democratic principles than is current practice.

Moreover, less dependency on secret information would at last open the door to understanding that value questions are more important in major decisions than technical details contained in intelligence reports. The latter encourage presidents erroneously to assume that the irrelevancy of outsider's views on

273

technical questions is matched by the irrelevancy of the out-sider's discussion of value questions. In the Chilean case, for example, officials considered technical issues such as: How many Christian Democrats could be bribed to vote for Alessandri, or how much economic chaos would result from credit curtail-ment? They gave almost no attention to the much more impor-tant value question: Who will do more to fulfill human needs and serve humanitarian values in Chile—Allende or the leaders of a military coup? To answer the latter question, one had no need for secret intelligence. The very availability of secret intel-ligence narrowed official vision on human rights questions.

3. Extend credit and aid on the basis of objective determina-tion of human needs, not according to the extent to which the ideology of the recipient's government is sympathetic to the in-terests of multinational corporations. In order to discourage the tendency to serve the profit and power of a few at the expense of universal human rights, financial assistance should be restricted to nonmilitary purposes and channeled through multilateral or-ganizations that include equitable representation of the poor.

4. Prohibit United States-based multinational corporations from undertaking clandestine political activities. These activities usually are aimed at securing advantages for corporations in preference to securing human rights for the most needy and vic-timized members of societies. Indeed, even public activities, such as making campaign contributions, should be strictly regulated. Toward this end, where multinational corporations are not ex-propriated, consideration should be given to establishing su-pranational regulatory agencies, with heavy representation on the part of less developed countries, to govern the multinational corporations. Such agencies could restrict the political activity of these corporations, and prevent their economic activity from ex-ceeding a mutually agreed upon amount of return on invest-ment. Even more important, such regulatory agencies could in-sure the production of goods for meeting human needs, rather than for returning a profit regardless of the usefulness of the goods.

If relatively poor and militarily weak societies were brought into the decision-making process of large multinational corpora-tions, which often possess more economic power than their host governments, these underdeveloped societies would be more likely to appreciate the positive contributions that such corpora-tions can make. This would encourage the less developed coun-

274

tries to deal fairly with multinational corporations. Likewise, an increase of citizen control would make these corporations more responsive to human needs.

5. Use the influence of political leadership positions in the United States to educate the public to accept and even support rapid socioeconomic change abroad where an indigenous demand is expressed for it. Radical change may help achieve the values of human dignity even though such change may seem contrary to the short-run interests of U.S. investment and political influence.

6. Agree in advance to submit any disputes over nationalization to an existing judicial tribunal or to an ad hoc board of arbitration selected by both parties. An impartial judicial procedure would defuse the compensation issue. The United States business-government elite could not so easily use the issue to justify intervention. On the other hand, radical governments of developing countries could agree to provide some compensation, impartially determined, without feeling embarrassed by their more radical critics who may want to avoid any compensation that appears to submit directly to United States pressure.

7. Use principles of human rights to restrict policy means as well as to guide policy ends. Officials should first clarify policy goals by giving explicit attention to value questions such as these:

—Should the United States accept self-determination when it is expressed as support for socialism, or use covert means to maintain U.S. economic and political benefits in other societies at the expense of the politically weak and poor?

—Should the United States seek to distribute global wealth more equitably in order to help the poor achieve dignity, or continue to protect the current U.S. income advantage compared to other societies?

—Should U.S. corporations refuse to conduct business in, say, South Africa until they can implement racial equality in corporate life?

The Chilean case demonstrates the insufficiency of merely comparing policy ends with professed, terminal values without also scrutinizing policy means. Too often, rhetoric about goals in Chile sounded sympathetic to human rights. At the same time, the means used, as expressed in the preceding discussion of implicit values, clearly violated almost all human rights related to the rhetorical goals. Many who accept the need to select policy goals in light of human rights often reject the selection of means

275

on the same basis. They ask: Is not some violation of self-determination justifiable in the present in order to achieve greater fulfillment of human rights in the future? Is it not appropriate to use covert means to speed the demise of an unwanted government?

In the Chilean case, even if covert intervention would have produced more moderate results, it would have still carried with it some serious obstacles to realizing V_3. Suppose, for example, that as a result of United States-supported internal unrest, President Allende had resigned and the Christian Democrats were victorious in a special election. Still, covert intervention would have encouraged disrespect for due legal process in Chile; eroded international norms against intervention by other nations; instilled an unhealthy dependency in the new government on the CIA and its potential for future intervention; postponed social reforms that served the needs of the lower class of Chile; reinforced the attitude of United States officials that they may, with impunity, violate reciprocity in international relations, thus encouraging repetition of covert activity and perhaps precipitating a major conflict in a context where reciprocity was expected by another great power; signaled United States corporations that the government would protect their investments and profits with little regard for the overseas domestic implications of their investments; disenfranchised Chileans who in the future might be, as a result of past United States intervention, more violent and authoritarian; and encouraged officials to depend in the future on unilateral manipulation of foreign governments in order to salvage threatened United States interests, thus postponing the realization of systemic changes in the global political structure. If intervention is justified to advance human rights, it should be undertaken openly, as a result of multilateral decision making, and only on behalf of the world community.

Even granting that the global humanist approach would facilitate the realization of human rights, some critics still reject such policies because of fear that they would jeopardize United States security. However, in spite of short-run detriment to some investments and to United States overseas political control, honoring self-determination could, in the long run, enhance prospects for world peace. The traditional effort to throw United States weight against radical social reform movements probably postpones present "disorder" by making likely the more violent expression of discontent at some point in the future. Counter-

276

revolutionary policies that deny equity will doubtless encourage some dispossessed nations to acquire nuclear weapons and some dispossessed people dominated by their own repressive government to seek outside help for sustaining a revolutionary movement. By opposing the right of self-determination in the short run, the United States dehumanizes the process of change in the long run. An alternative approach could help realize V_1 by reducing the violence that results from the postponement of demands for equity and from the prospect of frequent U.S. covert actions that might precipitate counterintervention.

This approach is based on the notion that the best way to avoid violent upheavals is to invite those parties with grievances to share in decision making instead of repressing them and denying them a legitimate role in the political processes. It is also rooted in the assumption that, in general, governments more responsive to human needs will be created in Third World societies as a result of the unimpeded interplay of indigenous forces than as a result of United States intervention and military assistance. This is a policy of political and military noninterference, not a policy of isolationism. It promises substantial international assistance for redistribution of wealth and the inclusion of all societies in decision making.

Such an alternative approach finds the traditional arguments for CIA action uncompelling. The most common justification is that the United States must have and use a secret intelligence agency because the Soviet Union or some other political rival has one. To be sure, it would be unrealistic to conclude that other governments would refrain from foreign interventions simply because the United States did. However, an awareness of the United States' absolute rejection of covert intervention, coupled with support for self-determination, would have some healthy effects in the less powerful countries. First of all, it would encourage governments to develop more equitable domestic programs and popular support or else to face the prospect of falling from power. Thus, being more responsive governments, they would not be such easy prey for covert intervention by U.S. rivals. Moreover, this policy would encourage other states to aid in establishing regional or global processes for protecting self-determination and averting outside intervention against self-determination. The success of such efforts would promote human rights by complicating the task of other great powers who sought to retain quasi-colonial relationships of their own.

277

Although the approach I propose is far from a panacea and contains many explicit risks, it promises a future that is at least as secure for humanity as the present approach. In addition, it contains much greater potential for realizing human rights and the other values of global humanism. If 1 and 2 above were implemented, they would remove the most important political instruments that operated against human rights in the context of the present case study. The third and fourth suggestions would eliminate the economic instrumentalities and incentives for opposing human rights. Building public support for global reform, which will be painful for some U.S. citizens, would be facilitated by 5 and 6. And 7 would provide a general normative guideline for the formulation of future policy. The extent to which policy makers implement these suggestions can be used as a measure of U.S. performance on V_3.

In sum, United States officials ignored human rights in formulating the goals and means of United States foreign policy whenever human rights came into sharp conflict with the vested economic and hegemonic interests of government and corporate officials. As Table 4-3 indicates, stark contrasts separate the picture of the world painted by U.S. officials from the picture envisaged by advocates of global humanism.

Indicators of World Order Progress

The following questions can be used to assess the extent to which governmental behavior helps realize V_3 in the areas examined in this case study:

1. Has the government terminated all clandestine political operations in foreign countries? Has it dismantled institutions designed for such operations?

2. Has the government supported legislation prohibiting U.S. corporations from making secret contributions to political parties, candidates, or other persons seeking to influence political activity in other countries?

3. Has Congress terminated all revenue for covert political activity abroad? Has Congress passed legislation making it a criminal act to use public revenues for such purposes?

4. Has Congress declared and enforced the principle that any occupant of public office must be barred from holding further office if it is determined, after due process, that the official lied during congressional testimony?

5. Has the government demonstrated its respect for human

278

rights by curtailing overseas programs that deliver weapons and training more useful for repressive police or military operations than for exercising self-determination?

6. Has the government consistently supported multilateral aid programs that promote self-determination and other human rights? Or, has the government instead curtailed aid as a political reprisal against governments seeking greater autonomy from U.S. economic and military influence?

7. Has the government applied equal human rights standards in its relations with allies and opponents alike—for example in Iran or South Africa, as well as the Soviet Union—and thereby demonstrated that human rights will not be subordinated to advancing the special interests of U.S. economic and political leadership?

8. Has the government supported the presence and investigatory work of respected private or UN agencies whose purpose is to expose violations of human rights?

9. Has the political leadership made reasonable efforts to inform the U.S. public of the need in many less developed countries for internal, radical (structural) change to eliminate poverty and political repression?

Table 4-3

Selected Values of Global Humanism Compared to U.S. Policy Toward the Exercise of Self-Determination by the Chilean Electorate and Congress in 1970

Global Humanism	U.S. Policy
Peace	
1. Although in the short run the exercise of self-determination may lead to civil strife in some cases, in the long run self-determination is valued because it increases the likelihood for peace by facilitating the participation of all groups in the determination of their own affairs. Opposing self-determination will prolong and increase the suffering that may accompany radical change.	1. Self-determination in less developed countries is valued as conducive to peace where its exercise serves the strategic and economic interests of the United States; it is viewed as dangerously destabilizing where its exercise would not benefit U.S. investors or increase the influence of U.S. national security managers.
2. Covert intervention should not be used to inhibit self-determination, even if the latter affects U.S. property or overseas influence.	2. Covert intervention to prevent severe economic or hegemonic losses to the U.S. is preferable to allowing the exercise of self-determination.
Economic Well-Being	
1. By increasing the effective participation of politically and militarily weaker societies in planetary decision making, self-determination facilitates a more equitable sharing of the economic resources of the globe.	1. Insofar as respect for self-determination and other human rights might bring more equitable sharing of global economic and political resources of which the U.S. now enjoys a privileged portion, these rights are commonly opposed.
2. Economic and political self-determination should apply internally to all people within a society as well as externally between societies.	2. There is a tendency to favor control by the middle and upper classes within nonsocialist foreign societies, rather than extend internal self-determination to the poor. A similar attitude applies between rich and poor nations.
3. Collective responsibility and human equality are emphasized more than the privilege of wealthy individuals to pursue unregulated profits.	3. The liberty of those with capital to an unhindered right to accumulate more capital is emphasized rather than the right of the poor to an equal share in decision making or an equal opportunity to accumulate wealth.

Human Rights and Social Justice

1. Human rights are profoundly important guidelines for policymaking.

2. Self-determination is a fundamental human right that should be universally nurtured. It is valued because it facilitates a more just participation in planetary decision making and contributes to spiritual and psychological well-being.

3. The exercise of self-determination is desirable because in the long run it encourages the achievement not only of V_3, but also V_1, V_2, and even to some extent, V_4.

1. Human rights for citizens of the less developed countries are insignificant considerations as ends in themselves. Their rights should be subordinated to U.S. strategic and economic interests. Rhetorical support for human rights is useful primarily to disguise an interventionist strategy for opposing the decline of the privileged position of the U.S.

2. Self-determination is useful primarily as a means to achieve other ends. It is favored for developing countries only insofar as its exercise does not impinge upon the wealth and influence of the U.S.

3. The exercise of self-determination in many less developed countries, while honored in rhetoric, is in fact feared as a stimulus to instability and to the alteration of existing global structures of wealth and power.

Ecological Balance

1. By respecting the rights of other societies and encouraging their participation in global decision making, productivity in the long run will conform more closely to meeting universal human needs, rather than to serving the military hegemony of a superpower and the profitability and growth of multinational corporations. More widespread participation in global decision making will encourage the conversion of existing productive capacity from the provision of unessential goods into production of food and other essential items. This in turn will increase the feasibility of more enlightened disposal of pollutants and conservation of resources.

1. Respecting the rights of other societies and encouraging their participation in decision making are not favored as techniques for shifting productive capacities away from careless resource depletion and unnecessary consumption. Little weight is given to the idea that popular local control or global coordination of U.S.-based multinational corporations would establish a more rational response to ecological limits and basic human needs than occurs under present systems of entrepreneurship and decision making.

FIVE · *U.S. Policy for International Control of Marine Pollution*

No problem better demonstrates the need and potential for global cooperation than the improvement of ecological quality, where "everything is related to everything else." Atmospheric nuclear tests in China may, depending on where the winds blow, affect unborn babies in the United States. The use of DDT to protect dairy cattle from flies in Wisconsin a decade ago will increase the quantity of DDT in a tuna fish sandwich in Copenhagen today. Radioactive emissions from nuclear reactors in the Federal Republic of Germany affect residents in Switzerland and France. The sewage dumped into New York Bight adds to the decay of the oceans that affects vacationers in the Bahamas. In many parts of the world, humanity fails to conserve scarce living and nonliving resources of the planet; disposes harmful quantities of toxic chemicals and other wastes into the soil, oceans, and atmosphere; and refuses to relate global resource usage and productive capacity to fulfillment of basic human needs. Separate national groups, each maximizing its own immediate gains, violate the common good and decrease the global commons' productivity.

Environmental protection requires global cooperation on a variety of problems: ecological disasters of a sudden character (e.g., oil tanker collision); gradual deterioration of environmental quality through cumulative processes (e.g., ozone depletion); the disposal of ultrahazardous materials (e.g., radioactive wastes); destruction of endangered species or historically, archeologically, or scientifically valuable sites; depletion of resources required for a life of dignity; consumption of resources for unproductive or wasteful purposes (e.g., luxury items or military spending); and employment of environmental warfare (e.g., inducement of floods or poisoning of rice crops).[1]

In promoting ecological balance, global humanists seek to contain pollution, to control population, and to use resources for the most rational service of human needs, for both present and future generations. Furthermore, the fourth world order value encourages aesthetic appreciation of nature and the protection of diverse forms of plant and animal life. Both qualitative (e.g., the preservation of endangered species) and quantitative (e.g., the promotion of agricultural production and family planning to provide food for all people) considerations are part of V_4. Pollution control in the oceans, for example, contributes quantitatively to the protection of marine food resources and qualitatively to the aesthetic appreciation of beaches, both now and in the future.

The promotion of environmental quality is complicated by the delicacy of ecological balances, the inadequacy of knowledge about tolerable pollution limits, and the shortsightedness and selfishness of political actors. Many environmental problems at present are politically unmanageable because they defy national boundaries and literally encompass the globe. Environmental action also poses difficult choices among conflicting values. A society may seek to maximize food production by using chemical fertilizers and pesticides, but residues of these chemicals impede the effort to avoid pollution.

Recent international discussions regarding the use and protection of the marine ecosystem have touched upon many areas of concern within V_4. First of all, no issue holds more serious long-range consequences for the human race than the problem of maintaining a healthy marine ecosystem. Climate, rainfall, ultraviolet radiation, cloud cover, the oxygen-carbon dioxide balance essential to life, and the movements of winds and tides are all affected by the seas. They could be unpredictably disrupted if careless human activity changes the marine ecosystem.[2] If the oceans die, so will humanity. As Russell Train, administrator of the U.S. Environmental Protection Agency commented, "Not only are resources and nourishment essential to billions of human beings increasingly threatened by pollution of the seas, but our very survival on this planet is dependent upon the healthy functioning of the natural systems of the seas."[3] Former UN Secretary-General U Thant similarly reported: "For the first time in the history of mankind there is arising a crisis of worldwide proportions involving developed and developing countries alike—the crisis of the human environment. . . . If current trends continue, the future of life on earth could be endangered."[4] While there is disagreement among marine biologists on the precise extent of the harm in present patterns of pollution, most agree that the seas are in decline.[5]

Second, the marine environment provides a unique arena in

283

which to observe the rise or fall of the modern age's tide of
national prerogatives. The seas represent the two-thirds of the
planet's surface over which national sovereignty has not been
exercised in the past. This global commons has presented an
extraordinary, historic opportunity to establish a new regime
based on global policy coordination. The oceans cannot be protected or rationally exploited by nations acting separately. Yet
the traditional demands of the global system of national
sovereignty keep transnational collaboration in a state of
anemic, chronic infancy.

In preparing U.S. positions for international negotiations on
marine pollution, policymakers have debated a variety of political arrangements to govern future uses of the oceans. They have
clearly understood, for example, that in a decentralized, international legal system the rational maximization of self-interest,
such as increasing one's harvest of "free" fish on the high seas,
will lead, like the demise of the English commons, to the destruction of the resource for all concerned.

Third, the United States has long diplomatic, commercial, and
military experience as a great sea power. For more than twenty
years the United States has participated in various international
negotiations to prevent pollution of the oceans. As citizens of a
scientifically advanced nation, U.S. officials have had opportunity to inform themselves about the dangers of pollution. As a
wealthy country, the U.S. has possessed ample resources for pollution control. As an industrialized nation, the United States has
been a major polluter. As a geographically large country with
the most coastal waters of any state in the world and as a great
trading nation, harvester of fish, and sea power, much is at stake
for the United States. U.S. ocean policy provides a fair test of
U.S. performance in implementing V_4.

This chapter will examine U.S. policies to control marine pollution within the three major contexts where the issue has been
addressed: the International Maritime Consultative Organization (IMCO) to control discharges from vessels at sea; in negotiations to control ocean dumping; and in the effort to control
marine pollution at the Third UN Law of the Sea Conference.
Although marine pollution was not a central issue at the Law of
the Sea Conference, it was an explicit agenda item and its treatment within that conference is instructive. Because the negotiations covered many difficult issues, there was a constant need to
consider trading off one value against another in order to reach

a compromise agreement with approximately 150 other nations. As a result, value preferences became clear as officials set policy priorities.

DESCRIPTION OF U.S. POLICIES TO CONTROL MARINE POLLUTION

In the past two decades, humanity has revolutionized the uses of the ocean by building giant oil tankers, harvesting more fish, submerging nuclear submarines beneath the waves, extracting oil from the continental shelf, mining valuable metals from the deep seabed, and depositing millions of tons of wastes annually in the oceans. Traditional international law has failed to protect the marine environment. No state or international organization acts on behalf of the global community to protect environmental quality in the unowned, high seas. No organization manages marine activity to maximize the often competing benefits of mining, fishing, oil recovery, recreation, and navigation.

Before considering the impact of U.S. pollution control policies, we must examine briefly the main ocean pollutants in order to assess the need for environmental action. We are here concerned with the introduction by human activity of substances on a scale which threatens the marine environment, "resulting in such deleterious effects as harm to living resources, hazards to human health, hindrance to marine activities including fishing, impairment of quality for use of sea water and reduction of amenities."[6] This task is complicated by the variety of pollutants, their different sources and pathways to the ocean, the nature and extent of their effects, and the degree to which they pose a threat in the future. Some pollutants persist for centuries, others become harmless in hours or days. Some threaten the environment and human health immediately, others do so only because of long-term cumulative effects. The full danger of most pollutants, and the point at which damage may reach a self-generating, rapid deterioration is still unknown.[7]

Pollutants

PETROLEUM

Of all the serious known pollutants in the sea, oil is present in the largest quantities. Scientists disagree on the exact amount that enters the oceans directly from various human activities, but most estimates range from 6 to 11 million tons per year.[8] If one includes all land-based vaporization of petroleum which moves eventually to the seas, the annual rate of petroleum products entering the ocean may be nearer 100 million tons annually.[9] Most petroleum pollutants enter the oceans from land-based activity. Of these, approximately 90 percent come from vaporization of petroleum products used on land, transmitted through the atmosphere, and dropped into the ocean by rain and wind.[10] Additional land-based pollution enters the oceans through rivers and coastal waste disposal. Pouring dirty motor oil into municipal sewers is one example.

Seagoing vessels and offshore wells discharge roughly 1.5 to 2 million tons yearly.[11] Captains of oil tankers deliberately pump oil into the oceans as part of the process of flushing tanks and draining ballast water. Ocean water is pumped into empty tankers on return voyages to increase seaworthiness. During the voyage, the seawater mixes with the oil sticking to the inside walls of the "empty" tanker, forming an oily emulsion that vessels discharge into the sea before reloading.

The lightest fractions of petroleum hydrocarbons on the sea surface evaporate quickly when exposed to the atmosphere. The remainder form slicks which float on the ocean surface until absorbed by solid particles which may sink. Oil remaining on the surface undergoes a process of oxidation which consumes dissolved oxygen from the water. This means that oil-polluted waters suffer serious decreases in oxygen which is vital to all high-order marine life. In areas of the oceans where temperatures remain below ten degrees centigrade, the oxidation process is inhibited, and Arctic oil spills may remain as long as fifty years.[12] Similarly, in deep waters, bacterial degradation may be very slow because of less light and oxygen.[13] Oil that remains on the sea forms balls of tar. These have been found throughout the Atlantic, affecting hundreds of thousands of square miles of surface water.[14]

The effects of pollution vary greatly depending on the nature of the petroleum and the conditions of the area where it is present.[15] Especially in coastal waters where most marine life is concentrated oil is present in seriously harmful amounts. Some marine life retains hydrocarbons, which then become protein-bound and concentrated in organisms that feed upon previously contaminated lower forms of life in the food chain.[16] Thus low-level contamination may have long-range consequences caused by the concentration of hydrocarbons moving up the food chain. Fish that do not themselves receive lethal doses of crude oil may nevertheless contain too much oil to be palatable.[17]

Petroleum also injures plant life such as the tiny phyto-plankton, which is the basic material in the ocean's food chain and an important source of oxygen. This plant life is heavily affected by oil pollution throughout the Atlantic.[18] A chronic film of oil on the ocean surface interrupts cellular division of phyto-plankton, retards the photosynthetic cycle that maintains oxygen-carbon dioxide balance, and could lead to other secondary effects.[19]

Recovery of coastal areas suffering from oil spills can be very slow, and chronically polluted areas comprehensively destroy marine life. When the oxidation process causes the dissolved oxygen supply to fall too low, marine animals suffocate. The growth of phytoplankton, necessary to replenish the oxygen supply, is inhibited. Some coastal areas are presently threatened with ecological collapse,[20] and a few have passed beyond the point of recovery without drastic and monumental international efforts.

Virtually nothing is known about the long-range consequences of widespread low-level oil pollution.[21] Yet the subtle effects of such pollution on marine life are likely to be the most serious in the long run.[22] No one knows, for example, the long-term effects of oil which has sunk to the deep ocean floor where the supply of dissolved oxygen is very limited. Nearer the surface of the sea, an increase in the incidence of cancerous lesions, leukemia, skin ulcerations, tail deformities, and genetic changes among marine animals indicates serious long-term problems.[23] An international group of ecologists, collaborating in a study sponsored by the Food and Agricultural Organization (FAO) concluded, "There is inadequate information on the . . . effects of oil discharges. . . . There is no doubt, however, that the quantities of oil discharged to the oceans must be markedly reduced."[24]

Because of increased drilling, transportation, and consumption of oil, the amount discharged into the seas will probably increase several times during the next decade.[25] The percentage of oil production coming from offshore wells will also rise rapidly, thus increasing the probability of accidents per million tons produced. Drilling will occur in deeper waters, making blowouts harder to plug and accidents more likely. Moreover, the number and size of supertankers will increase. The largest ones are extremely difficult to navigate. With emergency "crash stop" procedures and engines in full reverse, a 200,000 ton tanker cannot stop in less than approximately two and a half miles. During engine reversal, steering is impossible.[26] The largest tankers ride so deeply in the water that they are in "shallows" when they move over the continental shelf. Between 1960 and 1973 the transport of oil by sea tripled. Between 1973 and 1980 it will double, making a sixfold increase in twenty years.[27] Giving additional attention to vessel and drilling safety is unlikely to compensate for the increased probability of accidents and deliberate discharges of oil at sea. In any case, because of rising consumption and consequent vaporization of oil in land-based activities, even if deliberate and accidental vessel-source pollution and drilling risks could be magically and completely eliminated by 1980, the oceans would still receive a larger volume of petroleum pollutants than in 1970.[28]

CHLORINATED HYDROCARBONS

Chlorinated hydrocarbons that are known to be harmful to the marine environment include the insecticides DDT, dieldrin and endrin; polychlorinated byphenyls (PCBs); and polyvinyl chloride by-products. No one knows precisely how much DDT is in the oceans, but by 1970 there were approximately one billion pounds of DDT in the biosphere.[29] Insecticides are sprayed into the atmosphere for agricultural and public health purposes, and thus the atmosphere contributes a majority of the chlorinated hydrocarbons in the oceans. Since DDT persists for many years, probably 40 to 60 percent of the total amount produced will eventually enter the oceans from the atmosphere or as runoff from the land.[30] DDT is widely distributed through the world's oceans and is even found in penguins in Antarctica. In one research study, twenty whales born and bred in the East Greenland current coming from the North Pole were found to contain six identifiable pesticides, including DDT.[31] The global distribution is roughly what might be expected if the sprays were spread by prevailing winds.[32]

DDT affects the growth, reproduction, and mortality of marine animals at levels currently existing in coastal ocean waters.[33] DDT is dangerous even in concentrations of only a few parts per trillion, because it, too, accumulates in the food chain. Phytoplankton at the base of the food chain acts as a concentrator of DDT. Oysters alone have amplified small concentrations of DDT 70,000 times in a month.[34] Concentrations as low as three parts per trillion have been lethal to shrimp.[35] DDT prevents the hatching of fish larvae and oyster and mussel

288

eggs.[36] It causes death of some fish in concentrations of five parts per trillion. Rain water falling on the ocean often contains eighty parts per trillion.[37] DDT currently in some marine fish approaches levels associated with the collapse of fisheries in fresh-water areas. Thus many experts believe some species of fish life in the oceans will be destroyed.[38]

DDT has caused deaths of bald eagles, common loons, peregrine falcons, and other birds which eat fish. In the Channel Islands Wilderness area, the bald eagle and peregrine falcon have completely disappeared because of DDT.[39]

DDT harms plant life also. Algae reproduction is altered by minor doses of DDT, dieldrin, or endrin.[40] At concentrations of four parts per billion, it inhibits photosynthetic activity in phytoplankton, which supply nearly one third of the world's oxygen. Most scientists do not expect the atmospheric oxygen supply to be adversely affected in the foreseeable future, but since plankton are at the base of many marine food chains, any change in the rate of primary photosynthesis is certainly critical to humanity's food resources.[41]

There are over 45,000 registered pesticidal formulations in the United States alone. These highly toxic and carcinogenic substances have been released in such large quantities and so broadly that they are among the most widely distributed chemicals on this planet. Scientists at a recent FAO technical conference agreed that pesticides "have the ability to exert biological effects on all living organisms." Thus international regulation "must be devised" to curtail the use of persistent pesticides.[42]

The DDT that in the past has been released into the atmosphere will continue to enter the seas in the years to come; thus the polluting effects of DDT will, for some time, become more severe even if it were completely banned now on a worldwide scale.[43] The amount of DDT compounds in marine life is estimated to be less than 0.1 percent of total production, yet this amount has produced a demonstrable negative impact upon the marine environment. Perhaps as much as 25 percent of the DDT compounds produced to date have been transferred to the sea.[44] Further concentration of DDT in marine life will continue to occur from both the DDT already present in the sea as well as from DDT yet to enter the water.

The rate at which DDT degrades to harmless products is unknown, but the National Academy of Sciences report on chlorinated hydrocarbons estimated that the half-lives of some of the more persistent materials "are certainly of the order of years, and perhaps even of decades or centuries." The report continued: "If these compounds degrade with half-lives of decades or longer, there will be no opportunity to redress the consequences. The more the problems are studied, the more unexpected effects are identified. In view of the findings of the past decade, our prediction of the potential hazards . . . may be vastly underestimated."[45]

Other chlorinated hydrocarbons, such as PCBs, have been available since 1929, but they were not identified in the ocean until 1966. They are used in the plastics, electronics, paint, and rubber industries. Like DDT, they have been disbursed all over the world. PCBs enter the oceans through sewage effluents, runoff, and atmospheric transport following incineration. Their properties are similar to DDT but even more toxic and persistent.[46]

The long-term effects of these materials are not fully known, nor are the quantities being introduced annually to the sea. Some corporations, such as Monsanto Chemical Company, have refused to release production figures for PCBs although requested to do so by many scientists and government officials.[47] Sufficient evidence is available, however, to demonstrate that the anticipated industrial growth and continued production of hazardous chlorinated hydrocarbons will decrease the marine protein supply and affect the total ecosystem; it already constitutes "a serious hazard to human health."[48]

HEAVY METALS

At least 4,000 to 5,000 tons of mercury per year enter the oceans from the mercury compounds that humans release to the rivers and atmosphere.[49] Industrial wastes are the largest source of this pollutant, but mercury has also been used as a fungicide in dressing seeds for agricultural purposes.[50] In the early 1970s, people in the Northern Hemisphere alone injected 350,000 tons of lead, a second heavy metal, annually into the atmosphere by burning antiknock automobile fuels.[51] These metals are widely dispersed and fall in the oceans remote from the areas of their origin and use. More of these metals enter the oceans through the atmosphere than through any other source.[52]

Mercury's toxicity is permanent. Like the pollutants previously discussed, marine organisms concentrate mercury in the food chain. The amount of mercury in fish may be 10,000 times

290

that found in seawater itself.[53] Mercury has toxic and genetic effects on marine life and upon those who feed on that life. As a result, extensive shellfish grounds have been closed in Canada, the United States, Spain, France, Germany, Japan, and elsewhere because of metal pollution. Additional shellfish grounds will be closed if the present rate of pollution continues. Mercury killed the swordfish industry in the United States and temporarily forced mackerel and tuna off the market.[54] The toxicity of mercury to human beings is well-documented.[55] In Minimata and Niigata, Japan, 168 people suffered mercury poisoning and 52 people died from mercury-contaminated fish and shellfish. Because there is no means of treatment, prenatal poisoning causes permanent disability.[56] Mercurialism, a chronic form of poisoning, affects the nervous system in a way in which the patient may exhibit no well-defined symptoms for months or years after exposure.

Because the industrial uses of mercury and other metals are likely to increase in the future, in the absence of international pollution control, their levels in the oceans will continue to rise.[57] In the United States alone, the quantity of industrial wastes is expected to increase sevenfold within a decade.[58] UN experts concluded that measures "must be devised" for international control of mercury.[59] In brief, mercury is highly toxic to most forms of life, a nearly permanent poison once introduced into the environment, biologically accumulated in organisms including human beings, and utilized in increasing quantities throughout the world. It "threatens to become critical in the world environment."[60] Moreover, although mercury and lead are generally considered to be the most threatening inorganic pollutants, approximately two dozen additional metals are highly toxic to plants and animals.

NATURAL ORGANIC WASTES AND INORGANIC NUTRIENTS

Natural organic pollutants (such as human fecal matter from municipal sewage) and inorganic nutrients (such as nitrogen fertilizer runoff) are a mixed blessing, because they can enrich the marine environment if they are diluted in proper degree. In this sense, they are unlike the pesticides and heavy metals, which are poisonous to living organisms. Natural organic pollutants, even though biodegradable, are harmful when they are so concentrated that bacteria, which help decompose the pollutants, use up much of the oxygen dissolved in the water, thus leading to eutrophication. This process decreases the capacity of the marine ecosystem to sustain and renew life in the sea. When eutrophication progresses to extreme stages, all useful marine species die. Even if not all oxygen in the water is exhausted at first, extreme enrichment may lead to "blooms" of plants which cut down the water's productivity because dense phytoplankton at the surface decrease the penetration of light and hence the total amount of oxygen-producing photosynthesis in the water column. In Europe, for example, the oxygen content of the Baltic has fallen severely since 1900, to a point where it is almost exhausted in a substantial area.[61]

Eutrophication of estuaries and adjacent coastal areas has occurred in some areas through overfertilization of waters by phosphorus and nitrogen. Approximately 60 percent of phosphorus in North American coastal waters comes from disposal of municipal waste. The remaining portion comes from urban and agricultural runoff.[62]

Even slight eutrophication in estuaries is extremely costly, because estuaries are the permanent residence, passage zone, or nursery area for about 90 percent of commercially important fish. Over 20 percent of the world's minimal protein needs could come from the sea by the year 2000, if estuaries remained healthy.[63] Precise figures on the decline of fish populations in coastal areas are unavailable, but there are many instances of estuarine harvesting being terminated because of pollution. Most of the world's large urban centers are located on estuaries and discharge wastes into coastal waters. Industrialization, urbanization, and population are all increasing. Agricultural uses of nitrogen fertilizer can also be expected to increase. Thus without major efforts to cut down nutrient pollutants, coastal pollution will become more serious.

RADIOACTIVE WASTES

Radioactive wastes released by humans to the marine environment probably amount to less than 3 percent of the background radiation from natural sources. Nevertheless, human activity has injected sufficient radionuclides in all of the oceans to present a potential health hazard as well as a disruption of the marine environment.[64] The principal sources of contamination are: fallout from atmospheric nuclear weapons tests, direct or indirect wastes from nuclear power reactors and fuel processing plants, wastes from medical, scientific, and industrial uses, and

292

accidents involving reactor malfunctions, the transport of nuclear materials, or mobile power units in nuclear submarines or artificial earth satellites.

"Transuranics"—elements with atomic numbers greater than that of uranium—are highly dangerous materials some of which must be isolated from the environment as long as a *half-million years*.[65] A National Academy of Sciences panel studying ocean pollutants estimated that by 1970, the release of over 20,000,000 kilocuries[66] of alpha-emitting plutonium into the oceans as fallout had resulted in plutonium contamination of marine organisms throughout the world. Of this total, 200,000 curies were plutonium 239.[67] It has a half-life[68] of 24,000 years. (See Table 5-1.) It cannot be retrieved once dispersed, and thus it will continue to affect the environment for more than 100,000 years.

Table 5-1
Half-Lives of Plutonium Isotopes

Plutonium Isotope	Half-life in years
236	3
238	88
239	24,400
240	6,540
241	15
242	387,000

SOURCE: National Research Council, Study Panel on Assessing Potential Ocean Pollutants, *Assessing Potential Ocean Pollutants*, p. 31.

Fallout from nuclear weapons tests has been the largest source of marine contamination in the past. However, since the United States and Soviet Union have banned atmospheric nuclear tests, and because the demand for nuclear power plants is increasing, the wastes from nuclear power reactors and the fuel processing plants that prepare nuclear materials are likely to become the greatest radioactive pollutants in the future.[69] This picture could change suddenly if several nonnuclear countries or nonsignatories of the test ban treaty, such as China and France, should undertake major testing programs. Use of any weapons in war would also completely change all predictions of modest pollution from fallout.

Radioactive wastes are generated in nearly all stages of the nuclear fuel cycle, including the process of uranium enrichment, the use of fissionable material in a reactor for generating electricity, and the reprocessing of the spent fuel from reactors. Wastes may accumulate as liquids, solids, or gases, and at enormously varying radiation levels. High-level wastes, characterized by extremely hazardous and persistent radioactivity, are produced in greatest quantities during the purification stage of a reprocessing plant. Low-level wastes have shorter half-lives and are generated at nuclear power plants and by industrial operations. Liquid wastes are held or released under controlled conditions; solids are packaged and shipped to regulated burial sites.[70] The United States Atomic Energy Commission (AEC) predicted sizable increases in the future quantities of low-level solid wastes from U.S. commercial activity alone:[71]

Year	Cubic feet
1968	666,570
1970	1,000,000
1975	3,000,000
1980	6,000,000

The AEC expected that high-level wastes would increase as follows:

Year	Gallons
1970	17,000
1980	4,400,000
2000	46,000,000

As far back as 1946, the United States dumped hazardous radioactive wastes into the Atlantic in steel drums. Before this practice was terminated, the United States had deposited 86,758 containers on the ocean floor.[72] Later, Europeans followed the same practice. In 1967-68, the European Nuclear Energy Agency sank approximately 60,000 containers with approximately 30,000 curies of beta/gamma radiation into the North Atlantic.[73] Japan has also dumped wastes into the oceans off its coast. In 1976, traces of plutonium and cesium contaminating the ocean floor were discovered off the east and west coasts of the United States. The radioactive materials appeared to have leaked from the drums of low-level wastes dumped there between 1946 and 1970. In the Pacific dumping site, the level of plutonium contamination ranged from two to twenty-five times higher than the maximum expected concentration that would have resulted from weapons testing fallout. In the Atlantic site,

294

plutonium contamination was up to seventy times higher than weapons testing fallout.[74] Throughout the world, hundreds of millions of gallons of high-level wastes are now in storage. They will remain highly active for hundreds of years, but the tanks will last only decades.[75]

Because nuclear power reactors generate enormous amounts of heat in the process of making electricity, they are usually constructed close to rivers or oceans so that water may be used as a coolant. Tritium is emitted as tritiated water, has a half-life of about twelve years, and thus has potential for affecting other countries.[76] Most reactor owners, such as the United Kingdom, France, Italy, and India discharge low-level radioactive wastes directly or indirectly into the oceans.[77] Standards defining tolerable limits are not universal. British policy permits greater release of radioactivity in the oceans than U.S. policy, and Soviet policy is more restrictive than the United States.[78] Reactors also release gaseous wastes to the atmosphere, including xenon, tritium, krypton 85, iodine 129, and carbon 14. These have half-lives sufficiently long to affect populations outside the country of release.[79] Nuclear-powered ships, and submarines also discharge contaminated wastes into the sea.[80]

Accidents contribute sporadic but significant amounts of radioactivity to the environment. Some scientists estimate that the accidental release of plutonium 238 had almost tripled the global deposit of this isotope by 1970. An accident at the Windscale (United Kingdom) plant in 1957 released more radioactivity into the atmosphere than fell on Hiroshima in 1945.[81] In 1964, the disintegration of a United States earth satellite spread plutonium 238, which was aboard for power generation, into the atmosphere. It behaved much as fallout from weapons tests.[82] Nuclear bombs may cause local contamination as a result of accidents even though the bombs do not explode. Similarly, the loss of nuclear submarines at sea may present danger to the ocean environment, both from their reactors and nuclear warheads.[83]

Small doses of radioactivity probably harm, even if imperceptibly, nearly all forms of plant and animal life. Although low levels of radioactivity may produce no obviously harmful effects in the short run, any increase in the amount of radiation absorbed by a population will increase the incidence of cancer or genetic damage in the population.[84]

The most serious threat to human life and health from transuranic elements in the sea comes from their extreme toxicity, their persistence, their potentially harmful effects to marine plants and animals, and their subsequent danger to humans through ingestion of seafood.[85] Like chemical toxins, marine organisms may concentrate radioactive elements throughout the food chain. Thus oysters 250 miles from any nuclear source have contained 200,000 times more radioactive zinc than the surrounding ocean. River plankton of the Columbia River downstream from U.S. nuclear production facilities in Washington have had concentrations of radioactivity 2,000 times higher than the water. Fish and ducks feeding on plankton had concentrations 15,000 and 40,000 times greater, and radioactivity in egg yolks of water birds was more than a million times greater.[86] Strontium 90 in the oceans already may have accumulated in some fish to levels which contribute to high mortality rates.[87] The presence of small amounts of radioactivity in algae that are often used to fertilize potato fields in coastal areas also constitute a hazard for human beings.[88]

Experiments have shown that continuous discharge of low-level wastes can cause damage to hereditary material of all kinds of organisms and cause abnormal growth and fatalities.[89] Radio-activity causes cancer, liver and kidney failure, and genetic defects in marine life, but often defects are unnoticeable at low dosages. Radioactivity also affects the life-sustaining photosynthetic process, although the precise consequences and long-term effects are unknown.[90]

Despite the relatively low levels of radioactive pollution of the marine environment and the absence of scientific knowledge about some of the potentially most dangerous long-term hazards, the National Academy of Sciences study of ocean pollutants cautioned that all releases of transuranic elements to the environment should be carefully regulated. Both accidental and planned releases "should be kept to an absolute minimum." The experts warned: "The rapidly increasing production of transuranic elements, combined with the present and potential leakages to the environment, could lead to concentrations in the environment that, because of the toxicity of these elements, would jeopardize the health of man and the integrity of ecosystems."[91] The Federal Radiation Council, the National Council on Radiation Protection and Measurements, and the International Commission on Radiological Protection have all recommended restricting exposure to the lowest practicable level.[92] Because radiation hazards are cumulative and irreversible, the International Atomic Emergency Agency (IAEA) warned that even small increments could spell disaster for future generations.[93]

Despite the gravity of increasing levels of radioactive pollution, more transuranic elements will inevitably enter the ocean. Some of the radioactivity released into the atmosphere by weapons tests has yet to fall into the lower atmosphere and into the oceans. The leaching activity of fresh water to propel land-based contamination to the oceans also takes time. Perhaps, as one study speculated, radioactive materials from underground nuclear tests, such as on Amchitka Island in 1970, may reach the ocean years after a test.[94] The containers dumped by the United States and European nations into the oceans may begin to disintegrate with age or become damaged by fishing trawlers or earthquakes. Some nations may conduct atmospheric tests of nuclear weapons.

Demand for more nuclear power reactors is likely to rise. Some experts have predicted that commercial nuclear reactors are "bound to multiply three- or four-fold even over the next 10 to 15 years."[95] A 1,000 megawatt nuclear power reactor has an annual output of radioactive materials equal to a 23 megaton bomb.[96] There may be 400 large nuclear plants around the world by 1985, perhaps 2,000 by the year 2000.[97] Because of the growth of nuclear power, the storage of liquid wastes and fission materials could be multiplied more than a hundredfold by 2000.[98] While such an increase of fissionable materials is being mined, enriched, transported, stored, used, and reprocessed, the risks of leakage or accident will increase enormously, in spite of the closest attention to safety. Reactors malfunction, transportation vehicles have accidents, storage tanks leak.[99] The intentional discharge of radioactive waste products will also increase.

It is possible that a discontented party may engage in environmental war using highly toxic materials. Even a few grams of plutonium dispersed in a city or a major river as a finely divided powder would produce lethal consequences for millions of people. Contamination could last for thousands of years.

The future thus promises increased risks of radioactive pollution. One must add to this ominous trend the possibility that some pollutants already discharged may cause damage presently unanticipated. Automobiles were driven for fifty years before

297

the injurious qualities of exhaust fumes were recognized. It took a quarter century of spraying DDT before scientists understood DDT's most dangerous characteristics.

SYNERGISTIC EFFECTS

We are largely ignorant of the synergistic effects pollutants may produce when several are present in the same ocean space.[100] Nonetheless, "it is a serious oversimplification to consider the effects of materials separately."[101] Some substances produce unforeseen combinations which may have a wholly unanticipated and more powerful effect than the sum of the substances taken separately. Smog, for example, is a familiar example of the combination of smoke, exhaust fumes, and atmospheric conditions.

In the marine environment, one serious synergistic consequence of oil pollution could arise from the property of chlorinated hydrocarbons, such as DDT and dieldrin, to be highly soluble in oil films floating on the ocean's surface. Some measurements in a slick in Biscayne Bay, Florida, showed that the concentration of dieldrin in the top one millimeter of water was over ten thousand times higher than in the underlying water. Since the small larval stages of fishes and both plant and animal plankton tend to spend some of the night hours near the surface, it is highly probable that they will extract, and concentrate further, the pesticides present in the surface layer. This could have "seriously detrimental effects on these organisms,"[102] which form the basis for the food chains of most marine life.

Oil, DDT, plastics, heavy metals, radioactive wastes, and concentrated sewage from growing coastal cities are likely to have synergistic effects. Roughly a thousand new and untested materials are added each year to modern chemical manufacturing. Most are not biodegradable. In all of the general categories of pollutants discussed here, the quantities in the oceans are increasing.[103]

Even if all synergistic effects were understood, we would still be ignorant of the permissible threshold of pollutants that the ocean can accommodate before irreversible, snowballing consequences occur.[104] The sea obviously has enormous capacity for renewal and regeneration, but as an organic system, it is vulnerable to death at some point. It is not known when the dangerous threshold for some marine plants and animals may be crossed, thereby causing imbalances elsewhere in the ocean ecosystem. The dissolved oxygen levels of the Caspian, Baltic, and Mediterranean seas, for example, are extremely low in many parts. To be sure, these are enclosed waters but so, ultimately, are all the oceans.

Moreover, the bulk of plankton and other marine life dependent on photosynthesis is concentrated in an upper layer of ocean water no deeper than the Great Lakes. The surface waters do not mix rapidly with deep waters. About 80 percent of the world's fish catch is derived from waters less than 200 meters deep, which is half the depth of Lake Superior. About 90 percent of all marine animal life is concentrated above the continental shelves in coastal waters which are the most polluted.[105] The Great Lakes are vulnerable to ecological collapse, even though located between two—only two—wealthy and scientifically advanced nations of the world. If these governments have found it impossible to prevent acute ecological decay in the Great Lakes, where they "own" the marine environment, how much more difficult it will be to prevent ecological disaster in the oceans, where jurisdiction belongs to no one and where political rivalries and ideological rigidities will make cooperation less likely. Yet, if one conclusion is clear from the preceding discussion of pollutants, it is that the oceans cannot be protected by national action alone. Standards for tolerable pollution must encompass the globe.

International Efforts to Control Marine Pollution

Most ocean pollutants originate within the national jurisdiction of states, but the pollutants affect distant populations and the global environment. Thus, serious efforts to reduce pollution naturally require some international cooperation. This requirement was recognized in the 1958 Geneva Convention on the High Seas, which asked all parties to "draw up regulations to prevent pollution of the seas by the discharge of oil from ships . . . or resulting from the exploitation . . . of the sea-bed and its subsoil."[106] In addition, states agreed "to prevent pollution of the seas from the dumping of radioactive waste."[107] Similarly, the 1958 Continental Shelf Convention specified that all coastal states were obliged to take "all appropriate measures for the protection of the living resources of the sea from harmful agents."[108] These vague obligations have been neither specifi-

299

cally defined nor effectively enforced. Although legally binding upon parties to the treaties, in practice they have been statements of intention rather than standards for behavior.

In three areas, however, the United States and other countries have discussed more concrete environmental standards: to regulate petroleum discharges by ships at sea; to control the dumping of wastes into the seas; and to define international standards for environmental protection. We will examine these in turn.

POLLUTION BY SHIPS AT SEA

The United States and other nations slowly have established more exact standards for marine protection in several conventions negotiated within the Inter-Governmental Maritime Consultative Organization (IMCO). Through this specialized agency of the United Nations, U.S. officials have aimed at reducing the discharge of oil and other hazardous substances from ships at sea. A brief survey of the important treaties will clarify the results of IMCO negotiations.

The first IMCO action regulated the discharge of oil, primarily from tankers. The International Convention for the Prevention of Pollution of the Sea by Oil was completed in 1954 but not ratified by the United States until 1961. It specified that tankers could not discharge any waste or ballast with more than one hundred parts of oil per million and closer than fifty miles from the nearest land. This measure helped protect coastlines but not the oceans in general. Dirty ballast of any amount could be discharged beyond the fifty-mile limit. Nontankers had even less stringent standards for oily discharges. The seven-year delay for United States ratification reflected official indifference to protecting the environment. Moreover, the United States refused to ratify two provisions of the treaty: the requirement that signatories provide adequate port reception facilities for receiving waste materials that should not be dumped in the prohibited zones; and the obligation for ships to carry oily-water separation equipment for bilge discharges.[109]

During negotiations in 1962, the 1954 agreement was modified to expand the prohibited discharge zones to one hundred miles in some cases. In 1969 it was amended to institute modest standards for all discharges even outside the prohibited zones. In 1971 limits were established on compartment size within tankers. The 1969 amendments took effect in 1978, but the 1971 amendments have yet to come into force.

300

Table 5-2
IMCO Treaties to Control Oil Pollution from Ships

	Text Completed	Date in Force	U.S. Ratification
1. International Convention for the Prevention of Pollution of the Sea by Oil			
London	1954	1958	1961
2. Amendment to #1 (expands zones to 100 miles)			
London	1962	1967	1966
3. Amendment to #1 (sets standards *outside* zones)			
London	1969	1978	1973
4. Amendment to #1 (sets compartment size in tankers)			
London	1971		
5. International Convention Relating to Intervention on the High Seas in Cases of Oil Pollution Casualties			
Brussels	1969	1975	1974
6. International Convention on Civil Liability for Oil Pollution Damage			
Brussels	1969	1975	
7. International Convention on the Establishment of an International Fund for Compensation for Oil Pollution Damage			
Brussels	1971		
8. International Convention for the Prevention of Pollution from Ships			
London	1973		

In 1973, important negotiations performed a major overhaul of the 1954 treaty[110] and resulted in the International Convention for the Prevention of Pollution from Ships. If ratified by enough states, the new treaty will replace the 1954 agreement. The new convention expands coverage to include discharges of refined petroleum products.[111] In addition to repeating previous restrictions on oily wastes close to shore, the 1973 treaty prohibits all discharges in five special areas—the Red, Black, Baltic, and Mediterranean seas, and the Persian Gulf. "Clean ballast," however, is not regulated. It is defined as containing no more than fifteen parts of oil per million. Total discharges in one voyage must not exceed one fifteen-thousandth of the vessel's cargo-carrying capacity. Existing ships will have to be fitted with "load on top" equipment which enables ballast water to be drained out from the bottom of tanks after oil residue has separated on top. The new load is then added on top, thus making it unnecessary to discharge oily ballast into the sea. Finally, for new tankers which are over 70,000 deadweight tons and placed under contract after December 31, 1975, the convention requires segregated ballast tanks. Total discharges for new ships may not exceed 1/30,000 of the vessels cargo capacity.

The treaty requires that port facilities be provided to receive oil residues from ships, the provision rejected by the United States in 1961. Moreover, new regulations were introduced to set international standards for size limitation and arrangement of cargo tanks, tank subdivision, and ship stability. In a major improvement over the 1954 convention, the negotiators expanded the scope of the treaty to include the bulk transport of noxious liquid substances other than oil.

In three areas, the United States advocated environmentally more progressive positions than were accepted by other governments. First, the United States and the Soviet Union sought to require double bottoms in ships over 70,000 deadweight tons. U.S. officials believed that such bottoms would decrease oil spills in case of grounding. Second, the United States wanted to make visible discharges in a ship's wake presumptive evidence of violation. The burden of proof would then have been imposed on the suspect ship to show that it was adhering to the regulations. Third, the United States and Canada wanted to give port states the right to punish owners of ships coming into their ports if the ships violated regulations when outside territorial waters.[112] This provision, if included, would have closed some of the loopholes in previous treaties, which allowed flag states to regulate their own delinquent ships. Similar port state prerogatives have been used successfully to enforce regulations against slave trading and skyjacking. In these cases a government has jurisdiction beyond its territory, thus making enforcement possible even if an offense is not committed in its territory and the ship is not owned by its nationals.

Three more international treaties, if ratified by a sufficient number of states, will regulate the transport of oil at sea. The International Convention Relating to Intervention on the High

Seas in Cases of Oil Pollution Casualties specifies that parties may take action on the high seas to protect their coastlines after a maritime casualty has occurred.[113] The International Convention on Civil Liability for Oil Pollution requires shipowners to compensate persons, up to a ceiling of $14 million, for damage from a maritime casualty involving petroleum-carrying ships.[114] The International Convention for the Establishment of an International Fund for Compensation for Oil Pollution Damage[115] insures that injured parties will receive compensation for pollution damage even if they are unable to obtain it from the owner of the ship concerned. It also attempts to give relief to shipowners for the additional financial burden imposed on them by the Liability Convention. The Fund will receive contributions from persons that transport more than 150,000 tons of crude oil annually.

The regulations established in these conventions to control the discharge of oil and other substances from vessels at sea are significant departures from past practice. The United States favored most of the provisions strengthening the original 1954 agreement.[116] Still, when the conventions are compared with the threats to the marine environment, they are little more than a drop of prevention in an ocean of need.

First of all, except for the 1954 oil pollution convention as amended in 1962 and 1969, none of the standard-setting IMCO conventions was in force by the end of 1978. The slow record of ratification reveals governments' unresponsiveness to the need for environmental protection. Even if all the conventions eventually come into force, they will provide inadequate protection of the environment. Some states may choose not to join in order to avoid the restrictions that the more conscientious states implement. In addition, most tankers are not "new" according to the treaty's definition. They can escape the stricter standards, such as the segregated ballast requirement.[117] All military ships and other government-owned vessels employed in noncommercial service escape international regulation. Seeking to avoid any international intrusion into military affairs, the United States favored allowing military vessels to discharge toxic wastes without any international control whatsoever. Parties will, however, accept the vague obligation that such ships behave in a manner consistent with the treaty "so far as is reasonable and practicable."[118]

For the regulated vessels, the legal discharges—"clean

ballast"—may prove ecologically disastrous to the ocean because the limits are high and are defined as a percentage of the total tonnage transported.[119] As tonnage increases each year, the absolute amount of legal pollution increases. To protect the oceans, maximum acceptable levels must decrease to prevent total pollution from growing, even assuming that all conventions will be widely implemented and honored.

Although the strengthened IMCO treaty allows the discharge of only a small percentage of the cargo hauled, for a 200,000 ton tanker 13 metric tons of oil could be discharged legally during each voyage. In 1974, tankers carried 1,800,000,000 metric tons of oil.[120] Given that total tonnage, the new treaty, if in force, would have allowed legal discharge of 120,000 metric tons. These amounts will probably double by 1985. Yet in practice, the quantity of oil pollution is likely to be much higher than these legally allowed deballasting ceilings. If tanker spills increase at rates proportional to those projected for world petroleum production and for tanker transport, Robert Citron, director of the Smithsonian Institution's Center for Short-Lived Phenomena, estimates that by 1985, 4 to 5 million tons of oil will enter the oceans annually from tanker operations and accidents.[121] Moreover, additional oil is discharged each year by nontankers from bilge-pumping operations, which account for a substantial portion of ship-generated oil pollution.[122] The IMCO treaties lack strong measures to prevent oil discharges before they occur.[123] For example, provisions emphasize compensating victims of damages after spills occur, rather than establishing international inspection to prevent damage in the first place. Furthermore, international cooperation is arranged to ease the payment of casualties by owners of tankers, but no international procedures were established for citizens to sue for damages to the high seas.

Most importantly, enforcement of the treaties depends mainly on the goodwill and conscientiousness of a contracting government to apply the provisions to ships flying its flag. Yet states like Panama and Liberia, which offer flags of convenience to substandard vessels, are interested in the fees paid by shipowners, not in necessary safety improvements in construction and navigational procedure. Should their registration requirements be as strict as other states, these flag-of-convenience states would lose many of their ships (and fees) to other countries. Tankers fly flags of convenience precisely because they seek to evade rigorous standards for safety. The ill-fated *Argo Merchant* and *Torrey Canyon* for example, were Liberian tankers. Flag-of-convenience vessels comprise 23 percent of the world's merchant fleet, but account for more than half of all tonnage lost.[124] Since the effectiveness of the IMCO treaties depends largely upon the voluntary cooperation of governments in imposing standards on their citizens or customers, the temptation is to cut corners and costs in order to gain advantage. Safer ships, higher insurance, and sophisticated navigational aids all cost more money. The results are clear: After a twenty-year effort to regulate oil emissions, two million tons of oil are still poured into the sea each year.[125]

Protection of the oceans can hardly depend upon the willingness of governmental collaborators with profit-motivated shippers to replace cheap waste disposal with more expensive discharge of wastes. Even assuming more conscientious attitudes by flag-of-convenience states, most lack the necessary equipment for effective policing. Many of their vessels never rest in their own ports. A major difficulty is simply identifying the source of pollution at sea. To enforce IMCO treaties, states would need inspection forces all over the globe. In the absence of these on the high seas, self-policing by shippers is the only enforcement.[126] When asked by a Senate committee whether the discharge standards of the potential IMCO treaty could be enforced, U.S. Coast Guard officials reported that "there is no known means of determining the oil content of a discharge once it has entered the sea."[127] Except in cases of blatant violations, enforcing agents would be unable to know whether the rules had been honored.

One of the most serious deficiencies of the oil conventions is that they ignore the hydrocarbons that enter the ocean from non-vessel sources. A study by the National Academy of Sciences estimates that more than 95 percent of the petroleum polluting the oceans each year comes not from tanker breakups on deballasting, but from using petroleum products ashore.[128] By themselves the IMCO treaties will not protect the sea. They even allow a state to receive oily ballast from a tanker in an onshore reception point and then pump it directly into the sea from a land-based source. Although the state would be polluting the ocean close to its own shores, the past record of coastal pollution suggests that such an event is within the realm of possibility.

In general, during negotiations for the 1973 IMCO treaty

305

(still not in force) the United States favored almost all of the provisions specifying standards for vessel-source pollution. In addition, the United States sought to implement some construction standards and port state enforcement which other states would not accept. These represented desirable steps toward recognizing an international obligation to protect the oceans. Yet, the IMCO treaties are a bit like closing the chicken house door after the fox has walked inside. The IMCO treaties give the appearance of protection, and do protect against a few problems, but the treaties do not offer a response at all proportional to the dimensions of the threat.

IMCO, like some national regulatory agencies, has been a club of maritime nations, and it has served rather than regulated the interests of shippers. Many provisions of the conventions have done little more than codify existing commercial practices among the major maritime nations.[129] The willingness to establish slightly more stringent standards in the 1973 conference was encouraged by a fear that continued IMCO delinquency might prod coastal states like Canada to act unilaterally or nonseapowers to press for action at the Law of the Sea Conference where the maritime nations had proportionately less influence.[130] According to a representative of the U.S. Environmental Protection Agency at the 1973 IMCO conference, none of the new treaty provisions were due to the participants' concern for the global environment.[131] Instead, states pressed for stricter controls to protect their own shippers from cut-rate competitors and their own territory from foreign polluters. That falls far short of a policy aimed at protecting the commons.

United States policy was determined less by ecological concern than by a desire to protect navigational freedom for its warships and merchant marine, the commercial value of its own coasts, and economic benefits for oil companies and shippers. During the late 1960s and early 1970s, domestic environmentalists had pressed Congress and the executive branch to take national pollution control measures.[132] Domestic pressures and the costs of heavy coastal pollution, plus the comparatively wealthy position of the United States, encouraged the United States to enact domestic environmental legislation before most other countries. Since environmental protection costs money, domestic legislation placed U.S. shippers, oil companies, and consumers of oil at a competitive disadvantage unless the United States could extend its domestic control regulations to the rest of the world.[133]

Thus, the domestic U.S. legislation of 1970 and 1972 led directly to the international treaty of 1973.

Trying to eliminate competitive disadvantage, Congress directed the president, in the Water Pollution Control Act, to reach agreements with other nations to upgrade international standards. Members of Congress had noted that if foreign vessels were not forced to comply with the domestic standards imposed on U.S. flag ships, the foreign shippers "obviously . . . have a subsidy."[134] Spokesmen for the executive branch viewed the 1973 convention as "an agreement which fulfills that Congressional mandate to a substantial degree."[135] Russell Train, the director of the Environmental Protection Agency, reported that avoiding competitive disadvantages for U.S. commercial interests was "one of the reasons for the U.S. interest in a convention of this sort. . . . We have been concerned over the competitive problem. It is our desire or interest in achieving . . . uniformity of standards and operating rules around the world that has led us to push for this convention."[136] Similarly, Admiral Chester R. Bender, commandant of the Coast Guard, which was charged with enforcing environmental protection legislation on the ocean, warned: "If standards are imposed on only U.S.-flag vessels stricter than those standards adopted internationally, serious inequities could arise when U.S. vessels call in U.S. ports alongside foreign vessels engaged in the same trade but not subject to the same regulatory constraints."[137]

Because of concern for competitive disadvantage rather than for global environmental protection, Coast Guard officials cautioned Congress against requiring stricter standards or more vigorous enforcement of standards for U.S. ships than for foreign vessels, even if such action was suggested in the Ports and Waterways Safety Act of 1972: "In adjudging the sufficiency of the Convention in respect to the Ports and Waterways Safety Act, it must be recognized that unilateral action presents intrinsic dangers. We should avoid unilateral action which would result unnecessarily in economic disadvantage to the U.S. Merchant Marine."[138]

If the United States established standards more strict than IMCO's, other states might similarly introduce requirements that U.S. shippers would not want to meet in, say, Canadian ports or territorial seas. Thus the United States opposed any treaty provision that would allow states to set standards above the lowest common denominator established at the IMCO conference. Interest in relatively unrestricted navigation thus took priority over restrictive measures for environmental protection.[139]

If the United States genuinely sought to implement rigorous standards and still avoid competitive disadvantage, Washington could have advocated strong international enforcement. However, the United States did not favor international regulation of private commercial affairs. Thus U.S. policy stopped far short of supporting international inspection and enforcement of standards for the offshore extraction or transport of oil. Neither did the United States favor a global regime to prevent unlimited extraction, refinement, and shipping of oil from threatening the environment.

In sum, U.S. officials gave highest priority to maintaining navigational freedom and to gaining international sanction for the minimum vessel discharge and construction standards necessary to avoid competitive disadvantages for U.S. commercial interests.

POLLUTION FROM DUMPING

In the second major field of international activity for protecting the seas, eighty governments in 1972 negotiated the Convention on the Prevention of Marine Pollution by Dumping of Wastes and Other Matter. It took effect in 1975 and regulates the deliberate disposal of most materials at sea. It does not cover the discharges of ships from their operations, such as oily ballast, nor pollution caused by fishing, deep sea mining, oil drilling, or other exploitation of oceanic resources.[140]

The treaty prohibits dumping of extremely hazardous materials including mercury, cadmium, high-level radioactive wastes (the definition of which was left to the International Atomic Energy Agency), and organohalogen compounds (such as DDT and PCBs), persistent plastics, petroleum, and agents of biological and chemical warfare. Second, it allows the licensed dumping of arsenic, lead, zinc, fluorides, certain pesticides, and non-high-level radioactive wastes, if permitted by a designated national authority. Each contracting party governs the disposal of all waste material loaded in its ports for the purpose of ocean dumping, regardless of the ship's flag. In addition, each government is required to regulate the activity of its own flag ships anywhere in the world if they load waste material in the port of a state not a party to the treaty.[141] This treaty to establish international controls for dumping many hazardous substances is a departure from previous practice, and should slow the anticipated increases of these materials in the sea. Yet, when examined carefully, the treaty falls far short of providing effective guarantees against further environmental deterioration.

In the first place, although the treaty was opened for ratification in 1972, many states had not yet ratified it by 1979, including the industrial countries of Japan, West Germany, Italy, and Belgium. The states that do not ratify the treaty are free to ignore its provisions.

Even with the treaty in force for the ratifying parties, many loopholes remain. For example, United States officials insisted on exempting military ships and aircraft from all international regulations.[142] In addition, the convention does not apply to all ships and aircraft entitled to "sovereign immunity," which means all state-owned vessels. In an age when an increasing proportion of the world's ships and aircraft are owned by states, to exempt such vessels—even if used for commercial ends—is a significant omission. Moreover, the prohibition against dumping biological and chemical agents of warfare could be a somewhat meaningless provision, since parties would be free to assign such dumping to military vessels. States are, however, expected to require their own vessels to operate in a manner consistent with the convention. Yet, as one critic observed, "the restrictive effect of this watered-down version of the provision is virtually nil."[143] The treaty will do little to compel states to behave any more responsibly than they would have without it.

Another loophole in the dumping convention is the "emergency clause." This allows dumping of prohibited substances "in emergencies, posing unacceptable risk relating to human health and admitting no other feasible solution." On this particular provision, the United States said that "emergencies" included situations "requiring action with a marked degree of urgency, but . . . not limited in its application to circumstances requiring immediate action."[144]

In addition to these problems, universal adherence to treaty provisions will be difficult to insure. There will be at least three general problems. First of all, noncontracting parties are unaffected. Even a state ratifying the treaty may terminate the limited restrictions of the treaty by withdrawing whenever convenient. Second, the familiar weaknesses of flag-state enforcement are present. A government that ratifies the treaty may fail to enforce the provisions if dumping occurs far from the flag state's shores. Competitive advantages, after all, would accrue to the states and corporations that violate the treaty if other states honor it. Some governments may want to violate the convention to dispose of hazardous chemicals, such as nerve gas.[145] Not even well-intentioned governments will know if their ships have loaded materials in distant foreign ports for dumping beyond territorial waters. Jurisdiction on the high seas is limited to the flag states, so a nonflag state or an international organization cannot seek to enforce the treaty on another state's ships.[146]

Third, the prospect that states will leniently grant licenses to their own ships for dumping designated substances provides an easy way to circumvent treaty guidelines. Given the economic savings derived from ocean dumping, to give states the right to license their own dumping is hardly an effective restraint. If nations pollute their own rivers and lakes, they will not refrain from contaminating the high seas far from their own coasts. As the U.S. Council on Environmental Quality concluded, the treaty has no protection against nonimplementation.[147]

Furthermore, approximately 90 percent of all the pollutants in the ocean come from polluted rivers or atmospheric fallout.[148] Thus even an extremely restrictive dumping treaty would not affect most ocean pollution. States and corporations seeking to avoid the treaty prohibitions could simply allow disposal of wastes in rivers where many of the substances would eventually flow to the ocean anyway.

In examining the interests served by U.S. policy on ocean dumping, one finds many parallels with the IMCO treaties. The United States supported a treaty on ocean dumping primarily to encourage other nations to pass national environmental legislation similar to the domestic regulations established for United States industries. If foreign governments would not establish standards similar to those contained in U.S. domestic law, their industries could gain a competitive edge, because the price of their products would not reflect the costs of pollution abatement.[149]

In the late 1960s, the U.S. Environmental Protection Agency became concerned about environmental danger caused by U.S. dumping in coastal areas such as the New York Bight. As a result, in 1970 the Council on Environmental Quality published a lengthy study containing strong recommendations to curtail ocean dumping.[150] The president proposed and Congress passed the Marine Protection, Research and Sanctuaries Act of 1972, which prohibited dumping material in territorial and contiguous waters without a permit. The act laid the basis for most of the provisions later included in the international treaty. Thus domestic legislative activity encouraged U.S. officials to negotiate an international convention that would, in effect, solicit other national governments to help implement similar regulations worldwide.[151]

During the international negotiations, the United States strongly resisted attempts by some nations to establish state responsibility for extraterritorial environmental damage caused by dumping. This resistance demonstrated that officials were less concerned about enhancing global ecological quality than about avoiding competitive disadvantage for U.S. corporations that were prohibited by domestic legislation from dumping in U.S. coastal areas. The United States did not want to assume responsibility for damage to the environment committed by its nationals. U.S. official rhetoric endorsed the Stockholm Declaration of Principles which said in Article 21: "States have . . . the responsibility to ensure that activities within their jurisdiction or control do not cause damage to the environment of other states or of areas beyond the limits of national jurisdiction."[152] U.S. official behavior entailed advocating an amendment to prevent Principle 21 from being included in the treaty on dumping. A U.S. substitute proposal (Article 10) took the place of Principle 21 in the treaty. The contrast was clear: Principle 21 said states were responsible for damage to the environment; Article 10 merely said states should consult about establishing procedures for settling disputes over dumping.[153]

In summary, as in the IMCO case, officials gave global environmental protection low priority in the dumping convention. The treaty provided no international enforcement. Nor did it offer international inspection, which should have been less objectionable than enforcement to states jealous of sovereignty. The United States also refused to place state-owned vessels under any international obligation even though the United States government would be the only enforcement agent overseeing U.S. ships under the treaty.[154] To be sure, the United States did support some environmental measures to avoid competitive disadvantages. But rather than bring about more effective implementation of standards—even for the sake of prohibiting competitive disadvantage more fully—by advocating a

311

strong central authority, U.S. officials preferred to have no international interference with U.S. ships and aircraft. Officials were unwilling to pay even a small price in restricting their sovereignty in order to protect the marine environment.

THE THIRD UN LAW OF THE SEA CONFERENCE

A third field of international activity to protect the marine environment existed within the Third UN Law of the Sea Conference. This conference, spanning several years, grew out of a 1967 proposal by Malta's ambassador, Arvid Pardo. He said that the UN should establish international control over the vast mineral wealth of the seabed and ocean floor in order to avoid conflicts arising from competing national claims to those resources. In addition, ocean resources should be regarded as the "common heritage of mankind" and should serve global human needs. His proposal provided an opportunity to implement a new, genuinely international regime with broad powers to administer the more than two-thirds of the earth's surface covered with oceans. The new international agency should, in Pardo's view, use the financial benefits derived from the exploitation of seabed resources for promoting the development of the poor countries.[155]

In response to the Maltese proposal, the General Assembly created a seabed committee to discuss issues raised by Pardo. By 1970, the Assembly decided to convene a Third UN Law of the Sea Conference to consider not only seabed resources but also the width of the territorial sea, freedom of movement through international straits, management of fishing on the high seas, regulation of marine scientific research, and protection of the marine environment.[156]

The first substantive session of the Third Law of the Sea Conference, upon which this analysis focuses, was held in Caracas, Venezuela in 1974. It was followed by a second in Geneva in 1975, the original target year for concluding an agreement. None was achieved, and three more series of sessions were held in New York during 1976 and 1977. Clearly, the global sweep of discussions and the nearly universal governmental participation made the Law of the Sea Conference an appropriate arena for United States action to guarantee international protection of the ocean ecosystem.

Pollution abatement, however, was not a major concern of the United States at Caracas or at subsequent conferences.[157] In-

stead, officials worked hard to establish international guarantees
(1) for unimpeded passage of military (and commercial) vessels
through international straits falling within other states' territorial waters; (2) for maximum freedom of the seas to allow
movement as close as possible to the land masses of all countries;
and (3) for maximum national access, through U.S. corporations, to hard minerals on the ocean floor and to the oil and natural gas resources in the U.S. continental shelf. The pollution
issue was pushed far down the ladder of priorities. Because U.S.
officials pressed other delegates hard on the strategic and mineral issues, they thereby constricted the range of feasible political compromise on the pollution question. To understand U.S.
priorities, we must begin by examining briefly the competing national claims on the strategic and economic issues.

From the beginning, U.S. ocean policy gave highest priority to
strategic interests.[158] The Department of Defense held the
strongest hand during bureaucratic infighting over ocean policy,
and it aimed to achieve unimpeded transit by U.S. military vessels over as large an area of the oceans as possible. This goal required limiting the territorial seas to the widely agreed upon
12-mile limit. Such a limit, if generally accepted in a treaty,
would roll back the 200-mile limit that some states claimed. The
Department of Defense preferred a territorial sea even narrower than 12 miles, but in order to gain international consensus
on a limit that clearly would prevent the wider claims from becoming law, the 12-mile limit was accepted with one condition.
There must be "unimpeded transit" through straits used for
international shipping, including the more than 100 straits that
would fall within territorial waters if the territorial limit were increased from the traditional 3 to the proposed 12 miles.

Without unimpeded transit, United States military vessels
would have been subject to the right of "innocent passage,"
which provided that vessels had the right of transit if their passage was innocent. That is, passage must not be "prejudicial to
the peace, good order and security" of the coastal country
through whose territorial sea the ships are transiting. Under this
doctrine, submarines would be required to surface and show
their flags when passing through a strait that forms part of a
foreign nation's territorial sea.

U.S. negotiators attempted, with considerable success, to build
support for a "free transit" rule to replace "innocent passage"
through straits. The U.S. proposal, supported by the USSR,

313

would enable all kinds of surface ships, submarines, and aircraft to travel in the air, on the surface of the sea, or under water through international straits without coastal state control. "The failure of a vessel to act 'innocently,' that is, in a manner which complies with the long recognized doctrine of innocent passage, would not be a bar to . . . [the vessel's] right to transit straits under the U.S. proposal." In short, U.S. military vessels would enjoy even broader legal protection for navigational freedom through straits than they had in the past under innocent passage.[159]

Some states argued that large petroleum tankers and all nuclear-powered vessels "are inherently non-innocent."[160] The United States, however, maintained that free transit, even for the most dangerous vessels afloat, was of vital strategic and economic importance.[161] In Senate hearings, John R. Stevenson, chief of the U.S. delegation and special representative of the president for the Law of the Sea Conference, was asked why the U.S. delegation devoted so much of their energy and political leverage at Caracas to gain even freer navigation than existed under innocent passage. He replied: "Mobility . . . in one word is the most important single factor, the ability of our Navy and our Air Force to navigate the seas without interference." He cautioned that the need for U.S. submarines "to navigate without surfacing is very, very critical. . . . The ability to get through important straits such as the Strait of Gibraltar has been very critical. . . . The whole question of being able to transport oil without interference is very critical for [national security]. I think these are critical U.S. interests and our whole effort has been to advance the whole complex of U.S. interests."[162] Stevenson flatly told the international conference that the United States could accept no treaty that did not insure unrestricted transit of ships up to the 12-mile limit and within that limit through international straits.[163]

Defense officials, in short, sought to minimize other states' national jurisdiction over the oceans in order to retain maximum opportunity for themselves, as operators of the largest military force in the world, to send ships, submarines, and aircraft where they chose. The weak and poor states, in contrast, wanted to circumscribe the behavior of the maritime powers by claiming sovereignty over straits and wider areas of the oceans. Claims by smaller states for a 200-mile territorial sea aimed at insuring national control over fisheries and offshore oil, as well as keeping foreign military vessels farther from shore.

314

U.S. officials at first (1970) based their negotiating strategy upon gaining international support for narrow territorial waters by generously offering other coastal states control over minerals and fish in their coastal waters and continental shelves. The control would be exclusively national to a distance from shore where the water reached a depth of 200 meters. Beyond that depth, coastal states would exercise jurisdiction over exploitation of living and nonliving resources up to 200 miles or to the edge of the continental margin, but only as "trustees" for the international community. Revenues from minerals beyond the 200-meter isobath would go to an international agency to be used for economic development of poor states.[164] The Pentagon wanted the coastal waters beyond the 200-meter depth to be formally part

Figure 5-1
Profile of the Continental Terrace (vertical scale exaggerated)

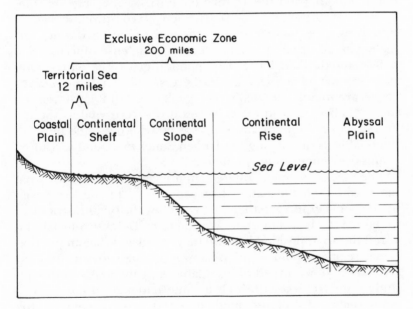

of an international regime because defense officials feared "creeping jurisdiction" in an expanding exclusive *national* resource or economic zone. The Nixon administration asked that all nations adopt as soon as possible a treaty renouncing national claims over seabed resources beyond the 200-meter isobath and agree to regard those resources as the common heritage of humanity. Thus some offshore oil would be placed under the authority of an international regime.

U.S. oil companies bitterly opposed the 1970 proposals advanced by the Department of Defense. Their political power, expressed through the National Petroleum Council and the Department of the Interior, soon proved irresistible.[165] U.S. officials shifted their position toward support of a broader economic zone 200 miles in width.[166] This assured the oil companies exclusive access to oil under the U.S. continental shelf. The shift was possible only with the assurance to the Pentagon that navigation must be unimpeded throughout the coastal economic zone beyond the 12-mile territorial sea.[167] The oil companies forced the Defense Department to compromise slightly insofar as the economic zone in the new proposals was not formally part of an international regime as defense officials originally wanted. To achieve their political goals, the oil corporations "combined an ingenious early version of a national 'energy crisis' argument with elaborate geological and legal reasoning."[168] They claimed offshore resources were vital to the nation's security. The oil industry was clearly the single most influential force in moving the United States to extend territorial claims over minerals to 200 miles.

The U.S. government offered a more generous and somewhat more powerful international seabed regime to the less developed countries in 1970 than in 1974, after the oil industries had mobilized their strength in Washington. Defense officials favored the 1970 position because they calculated that an international regime would never be strong enough to restrict their navigation. They urged oil companies to gain access to foreign underwater reserves through an international authority. The Department of Defense pointed out that 92 percent of the world's continental margins were off foreign, not United States, shores. The Pentagon was willing to risk oil resource interests in U.S. coastal areas in return for internationally agreed rights of transit.[169]

Oil companies, on the other hand, were willing to risk the unlikely encroachment of "creeping jurisdiction" upon navigation in order to secure national control of the U.S. continental shelf. In addition to wanting assured access to U.S. coastal waters, oil companies assumed that they could achieve better access to and higher profits from oil deposits in foreign coastal waters by dealing bilaterally with other national governments than by operating through an international regime. In addition, if an international authority were established in an intermediate zone between the 200-meter isobath and the end of the shelf, the less developed countries in such an authority might have power to extract large royalties. The oil companies were calculating from past experience that national governments, handled separately, were more amenable to allowing corporate profits and could be more easily influenced by oil companies than an unfamiliar international regime.[170]

Although defense officials favored and oil executives opposed an international regime over the coastal and deep seabed beyond 200 meters' depth, both groups had the same goal of minimizing interference by other governments or international organizations in their own affairs. Neither side sought to create a genuinely transnational regime to govern navigation, pollution, and resource usage of the oceans. The defense officials' position appeared more generous, but their generosity was the assumed necessary price to gain internationally-sanctioned freedom of transit for military craft. Officials hoped to sail nuclear submarines secretly, to implant submarine listening posts, and to gather intelligence with ships and aircraft close to the shores of other nations. In the final U.S. proposals for the Caracas conference, strategic considerations were accorded priority over resource interests, but resource interests received priority over environmental protection.[171]

Mining corporations also eventually exerted enormous impact upon the U.S. negotiating position, but their influence developed more slowly than that of the Pentagon and National Petroleum Council. Whereas the Defense Department promoted its interests throughout all the sea, and the oil companies sought access to hydrocarbon reserves under the continental shelves, the mining companies were concerned instead with scooping up potato-shaped "manganese" nodules that lay on the ocean floor in the deepest parts of the sea. In addition to manganese, the nodules contained copper, nickel, cobalt, and iron. No politically feasible extension of the territorial seas or of a wide economic

317

zone for resources could bring the nodules within the mining corporations' control. Thus the mining companies had a simple goal: to establish a modest international authority that would register companies' claims to mine in designated areas of their choice and protect them against claim jumping by other companies. Beyond this, the less international control of mining and the less onerous the royalties or profit-sharing requirements, the better the corporation officials liked it. Most advocated making the international regime only a registration agency.[172] The debate between the National Petroleum Council and the Defense Department was not central to the concerns of miners, but the latter did not view favorably any international regime that promised significant revenue for the less developed countries or international regulation of mining activities.[173]

Mining officials faced formidable opposition to their goals, however, from the less developed nations who wanted to maximize their own economic benefits from the common heritage on the ocean floor. At first the mining companies believed that the executive branch pressed their corporate position with insufficient vigor during international negotiations.[174] Although the Interior Department was sympathetic to the miners' interests, its personnel seemed occupied with forwarding the position of the oil industries on the issue of the 200-mile zone.

Fearful that the Nixon administration's proposals of 1970 were too generous in offering the common heritage to other countries, the mining corporations turned to congressional allies to influence the United States position. One of the most receptive groups was the Senate Committee on Interior and Insular Affairs, chaired by Senator Henry Jackson. Senator Lee Metcalf presided over this committee's Special Subcommittee on the Outer Continental Shelf and spoke boldly in behalf of mining interests. The Senate Committee on Commerce was also sympathetic to the mining corporations.[175]

Senator Jackson sent staff members to attend the 1971 sessions of the UN Seabed Committee and to report their findings. Their report expressed a belief that the U.S. delegation placed too much emphasis on military objectives and too little on securing seabed resources: "We fear that the Defense Department might urge the administration to abandon its deep seabed mining objectives and support the creation of an international seabed mining monopoly controlled by less developed nations as a trade-off for the votes of such less developed nations in favor of the Defense Department-sponsored free transit proposal."[176] Through congressional pressure and increasing effort by the Interior Department, the Administration did, at the least, honor the mining corporations' demand that national access to the nodules be internationally guaranteed. From the beginning the Nixon proposals called for nothing less.

The less developed nations wanted to create an international authority with exclusive right to exploit minerals of the seabed beyond the economic zones of coastal states. The authority would either directly or through contracts explore the seabed, and mine and market the nodules. The international machinery should have broad, general powers, including the right to set prices and production levels for the nodules. The developing nations argued that the poorest countries should be the principal recipients of the benefits derived from the exploitation of the deep sea minerals.[177]

In sharp contrast, the United States and other industrial states, which were leading in deep sea mining technology, wanted an international authority that would merely issue licenses to national or private companies and receive small royalties. The industrial countries, led by the United States, sought an international guarantee to right of access to the materials. Guaranteed access included a requirement that mining rights be granted automatically to any qualified applicant.[178] The United States also opposed any international controls on profit or production.[179]

The debate between the United States and the less developed countries on the seabed regime helps explain various national positions on pollution abatement. Thus this debate deserves some elaboration here. Insisting upon national access to the minerals, U.S. officials at Caracas and Geneva astonishingly denied that the international community could "own" the "common heritage of mankind." Leigh S. Ratiner, the U.S. representative, said the idea of international ownership "is completely unacceptable to us." The proposed authority should not "have title in a legal sense to the Common Heritage of Mankind." The common heritage should be kept out of any international hands. "This [authority] is not a sovereign State but a regulatory body for the Common Heritage of Mankind."[180] According to U.S. officials, national governments and private mining corporations possessed the right to exploit the common heritage. The international community lacked the right to own and control it. U.S.

319

officials clung tenaciously to this view, because if the international community owned the resources of the high seas, then it would have the right to exploit the minerals on its own behalf if it so decided. Such a decision could have decreased potential profits for U.S. corporations from the vast ocean wealth.

The U.S. delegation devoted enormous energy at the Caracas conference to promoting the idea that an international authority should not be allowed directly to exploit the resources of the common heritage. This promotional effort described the issue as one of "non-discrimination." U.S. officials said that for an international authority to mine nodules would be "discrimination" against the "right" of states with advanced mining technology to take the nodules. Less developed countries wanted to build an international authority to prevent industrial states from discriminating against nonindustrial states by mining the choicest areas before the poor countries developed the necessary technology.

With consistency inspired by selfish interest, the United States insisted that, if the nonindustrial states agreed to an international licensing agency, the treaty establishing it must prohibit the agency from choosing among applicants for mining rights. The United States demanded that the international authority be required to grant licenses to all applicants satisfying one condition: they must begin mining within a reasonable number of months after the license was granted. Since the less developed countries lacked the technical skills and capital required for exploitation, the United States in effect was proposing a "non-discriminatory" system that discriminated against the technically less advanced. Lacking the capability to mine, the less developed states could not even secure licenses to mine in the distant future.[181]

The United States also insisted that no limit could be set on the number of claims it could request and be granted. Stevenson declared: "If the authority has the power to restrict the number of areas available for commercial development and to select among applicants, my government would not be satisfied that our access was secure and free of potential discrimination."[182] Ratiner warned: "It is not reasonable or proper to impose restrictions on the area available for exploitation or the number of such areas which a particular country or company may be permitted to mine."[183] Thus United States officials asked for conditions in which corporations would be guaranteed the right to exploit as many areas as they were able to mine at once. There would be no limits on their production or profits. The United States informed the other delegates that without such arrangements the United States would not ratify any law of the sea treaty.[184]

Stevenson emphasized that the right that "most critically" must be guaranteed was the "right to nondiscriminatory access . . . to the seabed's resources."[185] Ratiner explained: "Industrialized countries . . . cannot be expected to agree that . . . they will surrender rights or access to the abundant raw materials of the seabed by agreeing to a system in which an international Authority could limit or exclude their access."[186]

Because the United States also feared that an international authority might provide subsidies to poor countries for exploiting the nodules, U.S. officials insisted that detailed provisions be included in the treaty to govern conditions of exploitation. Ratiner told the conference that agreement on "fundamental conditions of exploitation is essential if we are to have a successful treaty on the Law of the Sea. . . . For my delegation it is essential that fundamental conditions of exploitation be included in the treaty." Ratiner said that "the principal United States interest in that part of the treaty which Committee I is responsible for is to guarantee to ourselves and to all other countries a right to a secure supply of the minerals which the United Nations said were the Common Heritage of Mankind."[187]

The United States proposals for a seabed regime were largely determined by a desire to maximize U.S. national economic benefits and corporate profits from ocean wealth. Officials sought to recover previous U.S. corporate investment in deep-sea mining technology by securing international recognition of the claims of U.S. companies to mine specific seabed areas and to reap unregulated profits.[188] "Non-discriminatory access" facilitated the opportunity for the states and corporations leading in mining technology to accumulate the largest economic benefits. The American Mining Congress stressed in congressional testimony that any delay in seabed mining would erode the existing U.S. technical lead and competitive advantages.[189] The United States wanted to define the conditions for exploitation in the treaty to insure that "the private enterprise system will produce nodules from the sea [and] . . . will have an opportunity to make profits."[190]

Except for maximizing U.S. profits, there was no reason why

the nodules could not be exploited by an international authority, if the majority in the world community preferred that approach. The authority would no doubt arrange contracts with some U.S. companies to do the mining, since these companies had the most advanced technology to do it. No company could be forced to sign a contract against its will. If companies from Japan, the Soviet Union, or other countries could offer better terms to the international authority for exploitation, that would not harm the international community, nor would it deprive the world of the use of the minerals. But the U.S. refused such an arrangement precisely because an international authority might not guarantee U.S. companies all the minerals they wanted. As Stevenson explained, the United States "has sought in the deep seabed negotiation to protect its principal national interest in access to these mineral resources."[191] The economic conditions for exploitation were, according to Ratiner, "the most important subject in this part of the Law of the Sea negotiation."[192]

The United States opposed socializing the distribution of ore taken from the sea, even though this practice might stabilize the price of raw materials, and greatly benefit less developed countries. Ratiner informed the other delegates that, even though the nodules were part of the common heritage, "My delegation is not prepared to see the Authority control processing and marketing."[193] Moreover, U.S. advantages might be compromised if the world community had knowledge about where the richest source of nodules in the common heritage was located. Thus, even though the nodules supposedly were part of a common heritage, U.S. companies, with the backing of the U.S. government, would not divulge their knowledge about where the richest ore deposits lay: "A blanket provision that the exploiter turn over to the authority all data is a death warrant to manganese nodule production and to the realization of benefits for mankind. Companies will not do it. We know they do it in sovereign States, but the Authority is not a sovereign State." Until the international authority had been tested, Ratiner said "no company will be willing to give the Authority its most basic and valuable information."[194] Of course, if an international authority owned, mined, processed, and marketed the nodules, and distributed the proceeds equally to all people, there would have been no need for keeping knowledge secret about the richest sites.

The United States also wanted national access to the nodules in order to insure an increasing abundance of copper, nickel, manganese, and cobalt for the U.S. at lower prices. The U.S. trade deficit from imports of these minerals totaled over $1.1 billion in 1972 and was steadily increasing. T. S. Ary, representing the American Mining Congress, claimed that without the nodules the balance of payments deficit for primary minerals would reach $64 billion by the year 2000, assuming only 1970 prices.[195] Moreover, the United States wanted to eliminate the possibility of any future OPEC-like actions by producer cartels in metals such as copper. This desire buttressed the mining companies position, despite a State Department study which concluded that price-raising metal cartels were unlikely and hardly feasible, regardless of the nature of a new seabed regime and U.S. access to ocean floor minerals.[196]

Officials felt a general responsibility to make the United States less dependent upon foreign sources of materials.[197] Rather than seek to conserve minerals and arrange a dependable supply of metals at stable prices through an international agreement for resource allocation keyed to meeting human needs, the United States chose unilateral action that would not constrain U.S. consumption. Because a majority of the governments at Caracas seemed intent on establishing international control over the nodules, congressional sentiment grew for allowing U.S. mining operations to begin without any international agreement on the subject.[198] Many members of Congress, reflecting the position of the mining corporations, preferred risking investment capital without international protection for their claims rather than allowing the international community to regulate the mining operation and limit their profits.

To protect future access to resources and profits for U.S. corporations, the United States refused to support a UN resolution declaring a moratorium on all exploitation of the seabed resources pending the establishment of an international seabed regime.[199] The Department of State wanted to protect the right of U.S. corporations to proceed with unilateral action in the absence of a treaty.[200]

The year after the Caracas session, the Law of the Sea Conference at Geneva produced a single negotiating text for future consideration. It was written by chairmen of the committees and reflected the discussions of the delegates, but it was not a negotiated document. Because it did not fulfill U.S. goals, it was widely denounced in Congress. Senator Lee Metcalf said the

323

part of the single negotiating text which described the mining regime was "an unmitigated disaster."[201] "It would appear that we're in bad trouble. As I read it [the single negotiating text], the international community owns, and runs, everything beyond 200 miles. . . . The international agency is going to adopt budgets, make rules, decide on benefit sharing, determine compensation, borrow money, and be exempt from taxes and customs. . . . It may itself conduct research. It regulates fixed installations. It may do its own developing, processing, transportation and marketing."[202]

The chairman of the Oceanography Committee in the House of Representatives expressed similar fears that the international community would take control of the common heritage. He said that "of highest priority before my Oceanography Committee is legislation dealing with how Americans can gather a part of the three trillion dollars worth of nickel, manganese, copper, and cobalt concentrated in tomato-sized nodules on the deep ocean floor." He concluded that "the interests of the American people will best be served by speedy Congressional action in the above areas on a unilateral basis."[203]

Both the legislative and executive branches opposed an international authority that could allocate seabed minerals among competing purposes and potential recipients. U.S. officials wanted to allow the United States to continue using the most resources per capita of any country in the world. An international decision-making process might favor moving toward equity. Such a process, in the words of the U.S. spokesman, "breeds discrimination. Sovereign States have the right to discriminate, the Authority does not. A Sovereign State does not administer the Common Heritage of Mankind, the Authority does."[204] U.S. officials favored discrimination once the materials were in national hands—since United States hands were fullest—but not when the materials were in the hands of the world community.[205] The United States preferred the discrimination of unregulated inequity to the discrimination of regulated equity.

Because the United States wanted a treaty to protect its interests, during 1976 and 1977 it shifted its negotiating position in important respects to accommodate the less industrialized nations. In brief, the new U.S. posture favored (1) establishing an International Seabed Resource Authority (ISRA) that would be allowed to conduct its own mining in addition to that of private or government corporations; (2) diverting some revenues from

324

the ISRA to assist less developed countries, especially those affected by seabed mining; (3) reserving some mining sites for exclusive exploitation by the ISRA; (4) sharing mineral revenues, derived from a system of royalties or profit-sharing, with the international community; (5) providing some technical assistance to the less industrialized nations to upgrade their capabilities in deep-sea mining; (6) creating a permanent seabed tribunal with compulsory jurisdiction to adjudicate disputes; and (7) accepting a temporary limitation, for a fixed period of time, on production of seabed minerals so that total seabed extraction would not exceed the growth in the world demand for nickel, anticipated to be about 6 percent a year.

These concessions, although significant, were designed to sweeten the bargain so that developing countries would accept an international regime that still fell far short of furthering a genuinely new economic order. "Sweeteners" were offered, because, as Kissinger explained, "no one recognizes more clearly than American industry that investment, access and profit can best be protected in an established and predictable environment"[206] which only a treaty could provide. Modest concessions by the United States to achieve international legitimacy for long-range U.S. access to rich minerals were a good bargain. Because the United States sought stability within a favorable legal framework, it also supported compulsory adjudication of disputes.

Kissinger stressed the importance of reaching a binding agreement: "There is no alternative to chaos but a new global regime defining an agreed set of rules and procedures. The problem of the oceans is inherently international. No unilateral or national solution is likely to prevail without continual conflict." He argued that "a cooperative international regime to govern the use of the oceans and their resources is . . . an urgent necessity. . . . Only rarely does mankind comprehend the significance of change in the world as we so clearly do today." The Law of the Sea meetings were "an unprecedented opportunity for the nations of the world to devise the first truly global solution to a global problem."[207]

U.S. policies hardly matched these words of realism and promise. Despite Kissinger's self-proclaimed comprehension of the unique opportunities for global community-building, many of the old U.S. reservations about a treaty remained. Even though he said that the alternative to agreement was chaos, he insisted that the United States "cannot delay in its efforts to develop an assured supply of critical resources through our [national] deep seabed mining projects." Unilateral action, he argued on the one hand, would lead to "continual conflict"; yet "if agreement is not reached this year [1976] it will be increasingly difficult to resist pressure to proceed unilaterally." Indeed, "the United States can and will proceed to explore and mine on its own."[208]

Would the United States concede that the common heritage of humanity should be reserved for common usage in order to achieve a "truly global solution to a global problem"? Once again, national greed dominated global humanitarianism. The United States threatened not to sign any treaty that contained "restrictive limitations on the number of mine sites which any nation might exploit." Kissinger declared: "What the United States *cannot* accept is that the right of access to seabed minerals be given exclusively to an international authority."[209] As Robert Vastine of the Treasury Department put it, U.S. officials "are inalterably opposed to attempts to impose any system which would arbitrarily limit the number of sites that firms of any one signatory can exploit."[210]

The apparent concession to limit seabed production to about 6 percent a year of the existing nickel market for a fixed period was inconsequential. The chief U.S. negotiator in 1976, Ambassador T. Vincent Learson, said that that provision would not affect the anticipated level of operation by U.S. private industry anyway. The reason for including it, he explained, was that such a provision "was essential to bring the developing world along to agree to access by nations and States and their contractors."[211]

The voting procedure in the council of the ISRA was a matter of severe dispute. U.S. officials favored weighted voting as in the World Bank, whereas the less developed countries favored an equal vote for each member. Technologically advanced countries were already given weighted membership within the 36-member body.[212] The Ford Administration also sought to exercise future influence on the proposed ISRA through direct governmental control of revenue going to it. Less industrialized nations and some U.S. companies favored revenue collection for the ISRA through a system of company payments that could be taken as a foreign tax credit. Since such monies would not require the ISRA funds from U.S. corporations to go through Washington, the United States opposed this approach.[213] In sum, despite the admitted profound importance of the Law of the Sea deliberations for the future of humanity, the Nixon and Ford administrations objected to placing the seabed under the general control of a global authority.

The Carter administration, represented by Elliot Richardson as head of the U.S. delegation, seemed much more enthusiastic about achieving progress at the conference. During informal negotiations in 1977, many of the developing countries moved closer to accepting U.S. positions, so that for the first time an agreement seemed a serious possibility. According to Richardson, the compromise proposals "were by no means acceptable from our standpoint," but they provided the basis for further negotiation.[214]

Then at the last minute in the 1977 session, the chairman of Committee I, Paul Barnela Engo of Cameroon, changed some articles to reflect once again a regime more favorable to the less developed countries.[215] Richardson reacted strongly, recommending publicly that "the United States undertake a most serious and searching review of both the substance and procedures of the conference." He denounced the provisions on exploiting seabed minerals as "fundamentally unacceptable." He even said the United States should consider withdrawing from the conference, despite good progress in all subject areas except mining.

His complaints about the negotiating text included the following points:

—mining companies might not have automatic access to seabed minerals;

—a condition for access by such companies might be the transfer of mining technology to the international enterprise conducting mining for the ISRA;

—the international community might set unwanted limits on the quantities of minerals to be exploited;

—the industrialized states, being a minority in the international organs to govern the seabed, might be unable to defend their interests in its deliberations;

—the provision calling for an international review conference after twenty years might mean that parallel exploitation by both private companies and the ISRA might be terminated, with exploitation thereafter being exclusively in the hands of an international enterprise.[216]

The U.S. position, as reflected in Richardson's press conference, represented a strong bias, characteristic of previous

327

administrations, in favor of exploiting the common heritage through national means. Although the Carter administration offered concessions that were slightly more favorable to the less developed countries, officials still tailored their proposals to fit familiar national and corporate economic interests. Without substantial progress in achieving a more equitable economic order, there probably was little prospect of achieving a new international environmental order. We turn now to an examination of environmental issues at the conference.

Despite the growing public appeal of ecological protection, marine pollution did not even appear as a subject of United States policy in the first two years of preliminary meetings. The United States preferred to handle pollution questions on a piecemeal basis in IMCO and other organizations. Even after the item became part of the Law of the Sea Conference, United States activity on the issue was minimal. The environmental subcommittee of the U.S. advisory committee on the Law of the Sea contained only two members until 1973, and it remained one of the smallest subcommittees. The Environmental Protection Agency and the Council on Environmental Quality did not even participate in the law of the sea negotiations from 1970 until the summer of 1973.[217]

Although the Caracas conference possessed the authority to negotiate specific measures for pollution control in all of ocean space, the United States sought to avoid setting standards in that forum. As Ambassador Stevenson explained, in the area of environmental protection, "detailed rule making may best be left to the future."[218] The United States saw little purpose in Subcommittee III (which was charged with pollution control) other than general discussion of issues. Despite United States support for general statements obliging national governments to prevent pollution, both the decision to omit specific provisions that would give meaning to the generalities and the desire to transfer issues to a not-yet-established international authority demonstrated the modest extent of U.S. concern with marine pollution. Ratiner explained: "We take this [environmental protection] matter seriously, but we are not in a position at this time to recommend conditions on preservation of the environment—too little is known. So this task must be done by the Authority, and done well. . . . We are sure that we have a good idea of what will encourage investment [for exploiting nodules] but on this [environmental] one we are not so sure what the rules should be."[219] Thus, the United States asked for no specific standards for environmental protection, while it demanded that guarantees be entrenched in the treaty for free navigation and the opportunity to extract profits from mining nodules.

Although the UN Conference on the Law of the Sea was responsible for considering all forms of marine pollution, the United States limited its modest negotiating activities in this area mainly to pollution produced (1) by seabed activities, such as recovery of oil and nodules, and (2) by vessels at sea.[220] In the first area, the United States favored an International Seabed Resource Authority that could prescribe rules limited to guarding against pollution arising from activity on the seabeds.[221] The Authority would have the duty to grant licenses for mineral exploitation, to set pollution standards related to mineral extraction, to monitor the results, and to impose penalties for noncompliance. Yet the Authority was also vested with an exploitation mandate. It would suffer from a conflict of interest. Furthermore, the provisions were vague about the scope of the Authority's standard-setting and enforcement functions.

Within the entire subject area of pollution control, U.S. officials devoted by far their most attention at Caracas to vessel-source pollution. But here their purpose was not to enforce stricter international standards. Instead, it was to prevent the proposed international authority from taking control of this source of pollution. Officials reserved the exclusive right for IMCO to set such standards. They opposed the setting and enforcing of restrictions either by a unified international environmental protection agency or by national governments seeking to regulate commerce passing through their own coastal waters. If non-flag-state inspection and enforcement were allowed, it might interfere with U.S. vessels.[222]

In a seven-page special report entitled, "U.N. Law of the Sea Conference 1975," the State Department summarized U.S. positions on all issues during the Caracas and Geneva sessions. The complete summary of the "U.S. Position" on marine environmental protection was a single sentence: "We have strongly urged that standards for vessel-source pollution should only be set internationally through IMCO, by flag states for their own vessels, or by port states for vessels using their ports."[223] This report accurately summarized U.S. activity. The central environmental thrust was to retain most of the inadequate standards and enforcement procedures that had not protected the oceans in the past, rather than to launch a bold, new protection program.

Some environmentalists concluded that a coastal state authority to enforce stricter standards in the economic zone would provide "the most effective means for controlling vessel-source pollution and protecting vulnerable coastal zones."[224] Thus in continuing to resist the requests of coastal states to set non-emergency pollution standards, U.S. officials opposed the single most promising measure for upgrading standards against vessel-source pollution. In effect, the effort of coastal states to get stronger pollution standards was "the principal problem" for the United States in the committee discussing pollution in the economic zone.[225] According to Stevenson, "the most troublesome problem in the pollution area is the extent of coastal state control of vessel source pollution in the economic zone."[226]

As a leading specialist on U.S. ocean policies concluded after her study of the Law of the Sea Conference, "The overriding concern was to accommodate coastal state concerns while avoiding pollution [control] zones and other potential restrictions on maritime transit."[227] The Senators on the U.S. delegation at Caracas reported that "the basic goal of the U.S. pollution articles is to protect U.S. navigational interests by preventing coastal nations from asserting and enforcing vessel pollution standards in their economic zones."[228] Thus, the small amount of official U.S. activity devoted to marine pollution was largely aimed against coastal state protection of the environment in order to maintain a greater navigational freedom. Since the United States required the exemption of all military vessels from such provisions anyway,[229] the U.S. opposition seemed particularly aimed at protecting vested oil and shipping interests at the expense of the environment.

Within the 200-mile economic zone, the United States did support the principle that international standards should be set for pollution arising from seabed activity, such as extracting oil and natural gas.[230] In addition, the United States favored the idea that states were obliged to conserve fish that lived or spawned in the various national economic zones.[231] Yet no specific standards were proposed. The most serious problems were left to the future. States were not obliged to establish international regulations within any specific length of time. No provisions explained how the international obligations would be defined and enforced. Although the United States supported international inspection to insure that coastal states followed international pollution guidelines for seabed activities in their own economic zones,[232] there was no procedure for enforcing the requirement that national standards at least equal the internationally prescribed guidelines. Without an enforcement procedure, coastal states would be tempted to ignore international standards in order to give their own oil corporations a competitive advantage or to finance development at lowest cost.

In another departure from past practice, the United States asked for compulsory settlement of disputes arising under the proposed treaty.[233] This was desirable from an environmental point of view. Yet until there were compulsory standards to enforce, compulsory judicial settlement would be of limited value. Nonetheless, the widespread agreement at the conference that compulsory judicial settlement should be a part of the treaty did appear to be a significant step toward a preferred global system.

With regard to land-based pollution of the oceans, U.S. negotiators argued that an international convention suggesting guidelines for national pollution legislation would be "universally beneficial in preserving the marine environment, especially in the inshore regions of the world where excessive pollution is beginning to have an adverse effect upon the marine environment."[234] Despite such a promising statement, U.S. officials made no effort to establish international restrictions on marine pollution originating from territorial waters, the atmosphere, or land-based sources. "Control of such pollution must come largely from national legislation and local action."[235] The proposals for a new international authority were restricted to pollution caused by seabed exploration and exploitation.[236] Thus even if all U.S. draft articles had been accepted and fully successful in stopping ocean pollution from ships at sea, from mining and extracting oil from the seabed, and from dumping, the largest sources of damage to the ocean environment, which are land-based, would remain unregulated.

As is clear from the preceding survey, U.S. policies were neither overtly hostile to nor vigorously supportive of environmental protection. Strategic and economic self-interest in the short run clearly dominated the development of U.S. policies. Pursuing short-range self-interest prevented the United States from responding sensitively to the requests of the less developed

331

countries for greater economic equity. For several reasons, this posture virtually foreclosed progress in environmental protection.

First of all, many developing countries were unenthusiastic about pollution control. The industrialized countries had partially financed their industrialization during the past century by contaminating the environment. Only after becoming relatively affluent did the rich consider environmental quality. Some poor nations also were willing to finance their development in the cheapest way possible. Restrictions upon industrial growth and diversion of capital to environmental protection would slow the development of the poorer nations.[237] Among private enterprise systems, capital moves to regions where profits may be maximized. Thus capital could be encouraged to move from rich to poor societies by creating pollution havens in the less developed countries.

Furthermore, many less industrialized nations were concerned that costs for sea transportation, energy, fertilizer, herbicides, and insecticides would rise if high safety standards were imposed upon tankers and drilling operations, and if the cheapest chemical substances, such as DDT, were banned. Some countries exporting raw materials feared that export earnings would decline because of pollution abatement measures. Products from the poorer nations might even be discriminated against on environmental grounds, with consequences similar to protectionist tariff walls erected against them. Retrieval of deep-sea nodules would affect the cobalt exports of Zaire, Morocco, and Zambia; the nickel exports of Indonesia and Cuba; the manganese exports of Ghana and Gabon; and the copper exports of Chile and Zambia.[238]

Brazil and India both pressed the idea that a lower standard should be allowed for pollution by developing countries in the 200-mile economic zone. Brazil argued that all seabed activities within the economic zone should be under exclusive national jurisdiction, thus enabling Brazilians to extract minerals more cheaply from their seabed if they were willing to pollute more freely. India opposed a binding obligation to accept international standards for dumping in its zone, reserving the right to apply less stringent standards.[239] Many of the developing countries supported the provision that in considering whether a country has discharged its obligations under the treaty "due regard must be paid to . . . the economic and financial ability of a

332

State to provide the resources necessary for the discharge of such obligations and the stage of economic development of the State."[240] Most less industrialized countries wanted the industrialized states to pay for cleaning up the environment and to provide assistance equivalent to any financial costs that developing countries might incur from environmental action,[241] including declines in export earnings that resulted from ecological concern.[242]

U.S. negotiators said that the level of economic development was irrelevant to the performance of obligations by developing countries.[243] Equal standards must be applied to industrialized and developing nations alike. Going beyond this, the United States opposed resolutions asking for foreign aid to soften any decrease in earnings from export of raw materials as a result of environmental protection. "As a matter of principle, [the United States government] opposes compensating countries for declines in their export earnings for whatever cause and believes that a commitment to pay such compensation would serve as a disincentive to environmental controls."[244] The United States also opposed an effort on the part of the less developed countries to increase assistance to meet the additional environmental requirements of developed countries. U.S. officials argued that there was no rationale for singling out environmental protection costs from among other costs for special accounting in giving aid.[245] The United States refusal to grant a double standard for performing pollution control obligations was environmentally sound. But the reluctance of the United States to help the poor states perform their responsibilities was politically self-defeating and environmentally dangerous.

The debate over who should pay for clean oceans was merely one issue of the broader question: What is a just distribution of global resources? No one denied that there could be better protection of the marine environment. But almost all improvements required more capital, more skills, and more reasonable allocation of resources among competing needs. If, for example, tighter regulation of oil discharges and strengthened safety standards increased the price of petroleum products, who should pay for the increase? The rich nations answered "the consumer should pay." But many poor nations argued that the cost of environmental cleanup should be borne by the users of unnecessary consumer goods and luxury items. The point here is not that all virtue lies on one side of the question, but that legitimate issues of pollution abatement bear directly upon global resource allocation and use.

U.S. officials ignored the environmentally crucial issue of economic equity. Equity could not be achieved by stressing the freedom of states to have unrestricted access to seabed resources. That produced a decided advantage for those with technology and capital. Equity could be achieved only by allowing nations fair participation in a global political process that would preside over the exploitation and marketing of the minerals. United States resistance to that option doomed the cause of environmental protection. If the governments of the less industrialized states had to choose between allowing people to starve or rivers to be polluted, pollution would be the preferable alternative. When people worry about their next meal, they can hardly be expected to be concerned about amenities for the next generation of vacationers at a distant beach.

U.S. proposals contributed to environmentally-threatening, economic inequity. The United States opposed efforts to link world strategies for marine protection with strategies to adjust resource allocation. No development assistance was offered for raising environmental standards. Officials made no effort to enable the developing countries to pay for the increased costs of pollution abatement without increasing the gap between rich and poor.[246] In assessing the accomplishments of the Law of the Sea conference, Ann Hollick concluded: "From the perspective of international equity the likely outcome is a worsening of the already monumental gap between the poorest nations and the rest of the world."[247] F. H. Knelman commented: "A minority of people controls the majority of the world's resources from calories to capital. This fact is perhaps the most urgent threat to global survival."[248]

At present the industrial nations are by far the greatest polluters of the oceans. The rich also most rapidly deplete scarce resources. Some critics have labeled industrial countries like the United States "pollution imperialists" because the global burden of pollution that they impose on others is roughly equal to the proportion of their consumption. Thus the rich now bear the major responsibility for the stresses on the global ecosphere.[249] But as the rich gain environmental sensitivity—if they do—and as the developing countries industrialize and increase the size of their urban populations, pollution will no longer be a product primarily of the presently rich countries.

334

Rather than build upon the common heritage idea, nations at the Third Law of the Sea Conference scrambled for more resources and for extending national control over ocean space. The United States began this process after World War II with the first Truman Proclamation. In this statement, the president informed the world that the United States would unilaterally extend national control over its continental shelf beyond the limits of the territorial seas.[250] The purpose was to extract offshore oil. Within a few years, one coastal state after another made similar claims for various reasons.

Three decades after the United States exploitation of minerals outside its territorial jurisdiction, the less developed countries made a concerted effort to improve their own economic well-being and prevent further extension of the economic advantages of the rich. They imitated but went beyond the Truman Proclamation by claiming a 200-mile economic zone. This was a means of countering the advantages of the maritime powers in a regime based on freedom of the seas.[251] Less developed countries sought to overcome their powerlessness through extension of national sovereignty over more ocean territory, formerly a part of the commons. Given the legacy of colonialism and territorial expansion, this reaction was not surprising. Poorer nations did not want to compete with large factory fishing ships of the great powers; nor did they want supertankers spilling oil close to their shores since they lacked technology to clean up spills. The history of colonialism, economic exploitation, and CIA interventions also conditioned many of these countries to be suspicious of what the United States favored; hence, the early support for the Pardo proposals, which maximized the dimensions of the common heritage, evaporated in part because the less developed countries later learned that the United States—especially the Pentagon—favored a narrow continental shelf as Pardo recommended.[252]

The less wealthy countries could support a narrow shelf approach only with apprehensiveness about the intentions of the industrial states. If the latter continued to oppose a strong international agency, then the narrow shelf thesis would work greatly toward economic vulnerability of the poorer countries. A maximum area of the high seas would be open to exploitation by the technically advanced states without any obligations being incurred to the developing world. The less advanced states reasoned that if they could not jointly gain a distributable income

335

from the exploitation of the high seas, then they should individually maximize their opportunities for sharing in the wealth of the ocean by extending their claims as far seaward as possible.[253]

The poorer countries may, however, have pursued a strategy that violated their own best interests. Only a small percentage of them will benefit from the 200-mile resource zone. The biggest losers will be the landlocked, shelflocked, short coastal states, and states with comparatively few resources off their coasts, a group of nations which includes among its numbers some of the poorest countries of the world. By letting the offshore oil and natural gas reserves come under coastal state control, over 90 percent of those minerals were transferred outside the common heritage. If the smallest islands of mid-ocean are given a 200-mile economic zone or if their colonial parents may declare them archipelagoes with base lines drawn to their outermost points, and if coastal states with major bights can connect them within their zones, then as much as half of the world's mine-grade nodules could also fall under national jurisdiction.[254] The United States would gain more square miles of exclusive economic zone than any other country in the world. The proposed treaty provisions, if ratified, will produce consequences opposite to the proclaimed intentions of those favoring a new international economic order.

Because the less developed countries sought to overcome their disadvantages by staying within a territorial system of national sovereignty, they could not achieve their objectives. Pardo's original idea was a collective global regime for the benefit of all. This was rejected as states sought to maximize individual gain through the sovereign territorial state. A more equitable division of resources would have been ensured by enlarging, not narrowing, the domain of the common heritage. By increasing the dimensions of the common heritage and asserting the right to an equitable portion of the petroleum, fish, and nodules within the 200-mile economic zones of the industrialized nations, the poorer countries could more fully have redressed the imbalance of resource allocation. However, the political difficulties of accomplishing this goal and the fear that the rich states would control any new global regime encouraged the poor states to fall back upon the more familiar territorial principle and anti-imperialist strategy of maximizing their sovereign control wherever they could.

The more pronounced and persistent the gap between rich

336

and poor nations, the more impossible it will be to protect the marine environment. Poor nations will feel justified in passing weak environmental legislation. The absence of international consensus on pollution standards will encourage the industrialized nations to be satisfied with inadequate safeguards in order to avoid competitive disadvantages for their industries.

The failure of the United States to exercise farsighted leadership for pollution control at Caracas and Geneva portends a grim future for the ocean. The United States could have agreed that costs of environmental protection reasonably should be charged to states according to their ability to pay. The United States could have advocated rules prohibiting the transfer of capital to pollution havens. The United States could have proposed that benefits from deep-sea mining should be granted to poor countries on a scale proportional with the pollution standards achieved in the recipient nation. The United States could have insisted upon an international commitment to transfer annually one percent of the GNP of the richest nations to international efforts to protect the environment in poorer nations only now acquiring industries. Such measures would be easier to institute when industries were developing than after they acquired vested interests in polluting the environment. But the United States rejected all these ideas for environmental protection.

OFFICIAL RATIONALE COMPARED TO THE VALUES IMPLICIT IN U.S. POLICY

By describing the environmental policies of the United States in the three principal international proceedings for marine protection, the basis is laid for comparing the values expressed in official behavior with the values expressed in the rhetoric of U.S. officials. In public statements and at international conferences U.S. officials articulated a deep concern about ocean pollution and spoke with pride about United States actions for environmental protection. Most statements contained professions of one or more of the following three values.

Professed Value 1: To Undertake All Measures Necessary to Protect the Marine Environment

The United States government publicly committed itself to "take all possible steps to prevent pollution of the seas by substances that are liable to create hazards to human health, to

337

harm living resources and marine life, to damage amenities or to interfere with other legitimate uses of the sea."[255] Moreover, officials formally assumed the responsibility "to ensure that activities within their jurisdiction or control do not cause damage to the environment of other states or of areas beyond the limits of national jurisdiction."[256] A further U.S. profession of intent is contained in Article I of the convention on dumping: "Contracting parties shall individually and collectively promote the effective control of all sources of pollution of the marine environment."[257] In President Nixon's 1972 State of the Union Message on Natural Resources and the Environment, he informed Congress that the United States attacked the pollution problem "with all the power at our command. There is encouraging evidence that the United States has moved away from the environmental crisis that could have been and toward a new era of restoration and renewal."[258]

The preceding examination of the U.S. role at the conferences on the Law of the Sea, ocean dumping, and vessel discharges calls professed value 1 into serious question. Surely the optimism that the United States "has moved away from the environmental crisis" was unwarranted. In the proceedings for the dumping and IMCO conventions, as well as at the Law of the Sea Conference, the protection of the environment was consistently subordinated both to the Defense Department's insistence upon sweeping navigational freedom and to the oil, mining, and shipping industries' requests for protection of their economic interests. To be sure, the United States did favor minimum international standards for pollution in the exclusive economic zones. This posture reflected the interests of U.S. oil companies, which were subject to U.S. domestic legislation governing their operations in U.S. coastal waters. U.S. officials wanted similar restrictions applied to other nations. Thus the United States favored modest international standards that would help protect the environment while, as the U.S. representative said, "assuring coastal states that they will not suffer competitive economic disadvantage by applying such standards."[259] As a result of the general desire to enhance U.S. prosperity, Edward Wenk, the former presidential adviser and executive secretary of the U.S. National Council on Marine Resources and Engineering Development, reported that environmental issues were "grasped as chips in the international poker game without regard for long-term implications."[260]

U.S. policies expressed laxity in establishing pollution standards and enforcement measures in each of the three areas examined. Officials made no effort to set any international standards for by far the largest source of marine pollution, namely land-based activity. In brief, these analyses of U.S. ocean policies suggest that U.S. behavior reflected implicit values quite different from professed value 1. The United States sought *to subordinate environmental protection to U.S. military, navigational, and economic interests* (implicit value A).

On a more concrete level, the most obvious failure to attack pollution vigorously was the U.S. opposition to establishing an international regime that could effectively implement even modest international standards. The United States favored a fragmentary, haphazard approach to environmental protection. Guidelines for use of the seabed would be set by a proposed seabed authority, for vessels by IMCO, for radioactive materials by a third agency; for pollution originating from other sources, there would be no international control at all. The United States never sought to establish a general environmental protection authority that could coordinate pollution abatement measures, set universal standards, reduce unfair competitive advantages, and take account of synergistic effects throughout all the sea.

Enforcement procedures were even weaker than pollution standards. In the three general areas of pollution control examined above, with the exception of the limited area of seabed mining, the United States did not even attempt to establish an organization for global enforcement of environmental standards.[261] The United States advocated non-flag state enforcement—far different from enforcement by an international organization—only in a few narrowly limited cases where such enforcement protected U.S. companies against competitive disadvantages, but not in other cases where it "merely" could have protected the environment. At Caracas and Geneva the United States moved to port state enforcement only under some pressure, and never accepted coastal state enforcement except in emergency situations. In sum, the United States chose *to avoid creating effective international enforcement procedures for protection of marine ecology* (implicit value B).

Professed Value 2: To Protect and Share Equitably the Common Heritage for All Humanity

At various times in the late 1960s and early 1970s the United States renounced national claims to the common heritage. In 1966 President Lyndon Johnson promised that throughout the

339

oceans: "Under no circumstances . . . must we ever allow the prospects of rich harvests and mineral wealth to create a new form of colonial competition among the maritime nations. We must be careful to avoid a race to grab and to hold the lands under the high seas. We must ensure that the deep seas and the ocean bottoms are, and remain, the legacy of all human beings."[262] In 1970 the United States supported a General Assembly resolution, entitled "Declaration of Legal Principles," which stated: "The seabed and ocean floor, and the subsoil thereof, beyond the limits of national jurisdiction . . . as well as the resources of the area, are the common heritage of mankind."[263] In the proposals developed by the United States for the Law of the Sea Conference, the government declared in Article 1: "The international Seabed Area shall be the common heritage of all mankind."[264] The Nixon administration proposed that "all nations adopt as soon as possible a treaty under which they would renounce all national claims over the natural resources of the seabed beyond the point where the high seas reach a depth of 200 meters and would agree to regard these resources as the common heritage of mankind."[265]

In addition U.S. officials professed a desire to share the benefits of the oceans equally with all people. In the first report to Congress under the Marine Resources and Engineering Development Act of 1967, President Johnson promised: "We shall bring to the challenge of the ocean depths . . . a determination to work with all nations to develop the seas for the benefit of mankind." He pledged that "the wealth of the ocean floor must be freed for the benefit of all people."[266] Three years later President Nixon said that the central issue of ocean policy was whether the seas would be used "rationally and equitably and for the benefit of mankind or whether they will become an arena of unrestrained exploitation." He assured Congress and the public that the U.S. proposals for the Law of the Sea Conference would utilize the sea "for the benefit of all."[267]

Among the very first principles U.S. officials introduced for negotiation at the United Nations Conference on the Law of the Sea was the idea that "there should be no discrimination in the availability of the area for exploration, scientific research [and] . . . the exploitation of resources." The U.S. representative said the Law of the Sea negotiations were "the first clear opportunity to begin to manage in common resources of great value, to create situations of equality with respect to resources which have

340

not previously existed but should exist in the future."[268] In contrast to this rhetoric, the United States in practice transformed steps toward "equality" into a strategy for maximizing U.S. access to the richest supplies of minerals. Equal opportunity to exploit meant those countries best able to exploit in the near future could exploit the most. "Equality" did not mean establishing global coordination for the exploitation and sale of the nodules.

The same set of priorities determined the evolution of U.S. policy on the continental shelf. The U.S. position in 1970 placed more shelf resources in the common heritage than the 1973 position, which bore the imprint of oil interests within Washington.[269] The extension of national jurisdiction from the 200-meter isobath to the 200-mile limit contributed to national wealth at the expense of universal environmental protection and resource conservation. Undersecretary of State Russell Train had argued that by extending the national claim over marine resources to 200 miles, oil companies would reap greater profits. The president later appointed him chairman of the Council on Environmental Quality. Congress, the Interior Department, and the State Department all opposed an expansion of the common heritage, even though it could have aided the poor states as well as provided a more universal context for pollution abatement.[270] As time passed, U.S. negotiators spoke less and less about ocean resources belonging to the people of the world.

Thus, rather than implement the second professed value, the United States sought *to maximize national access to the common heritage* (implicit value C).

Furthermore, U.S. officials worked vigorously to insure U.S. opportunities for profit from the common heritage. At Caracas, officials rejected all controls on profits, refused limits on the number of claims the United States would be granted, opposed high royalties, favored guarantees against loss of capital investment, and made no proposals for specific environmental standards related to mining. At the same time, the United States sought to avoid any general international financial commitments to help poor states implement international standards, or to transfer mineral consumption from luxury use in rich countries to, say, food production in poor countries. Similarly, global equalization of wealth was never a goal of U.S. policy. Royalties from mining or "transfer payments" to the less developed countries were acceptable primarily as political lubricants to move the UN machinery toward sanctioning the right of unrestricted

341

navigation and national access to the ocean wealth. Knowledgeable U.S. observers calculated that if U.S. proposals were implemented, the gap between the rich and poor states would widen. The second professed value was subordinated to an alternative preference: *to maximize U.S. economic benefits from mining, with little regard for international equity* (implicit value D).

In addition to securing national economic advantages, U.S. officials opposed international coordination of resource usage. This policy exacerbated two serious environmental problems. First, increased urbanization and industrialization clearly endangered the ocean environment if pollution abatement measures did not accompany socioeconomic changes. Thus one measure for slowing the pace of pollution would have been for the industrialized nations to restrict their economic growth to production for serving basic human needs, especially of the poorest nations. Such a cooperative effort would also have helped minimize the desire of the less developed countries, nurtured by an international variation of keeping up with the Joneses, for some forms of industrialization that might harm the environment yet remain a relatively inefficient means for serving human health and welfare.

Second, in a world where states sought national competitive advantage, environmental deterioration was inevitable. As long as the industrialized states consumed an inequitable share of the world's output, the developing states hesitated to slacken their development in order to pay for environmental protection. Yet the rich states were reluctant to limit their prosperity for environmental protection of areas beyond their national jurisdiction. The United States refused to limit its consumption of minerals and energy, to tailor its consumption and profits to help serve non-U.S. needs, or to consider environmental protection equal in importance to rapid national access to seabed resources.

The U.S. president had warned in 1970: "The stark fact is that the law of the sea is inadequate to meet the needs of modern technology and the concerns of the international community. If it is not modernized multilaterally, unilateral action and international conflict are inevitable."[271] Despite this warning, U.S. corporate and military interests mobilized and exerted enormous pressure upon the executive branch and Congress. They shaped U.S. policy so that modernizing the law multilaterally, according to U.S. guidelines, meant enlisting the rest of the world in the

342

service of U.S. interests. Official behavior expressed implicit value E: *to refuse global coordination of resources for the purpose of maximizing environmental protection and the service of global human needs.*

In failing to support some global coordination of resource usage and in refusing to charge pollution abatement to those with the most ability to pay, the United States subordinated environmental protection to increasing its already high standard of living. Never did United States officials acknowledge a need to decrease the U.S. share of the global consumption of resources. This omission occurred in the face of statements by environmentalists that the planet was literally incapable of supporting the world's existing population at the level of U.S. consumption.[272]

Global guidelines for resource usage and pollution control were even more objectionable to U.S. officials than competitive disadvantages for U.S. companies. In many instances, protection against competitive disadvantage could have been increased by replacing flag-state or national enforcement with enforcement by an international authority. Yet if an international authority were created to set pollution ceilings and conservation standards for various nations, the consequences would be serious for the United States as the biggest industrial economy with high per capita consumption and as one of the worst polluters of the world. (The United States, for example, injected into the sea one-third to one-half of the waste products resulting from the burning of fossil fuels.)[273] Thus a further qualification to the second professed value is required: U.S. officials sought *to protect the U.S. position as a disproportionately large consumer of resources and energy, despite the negative ecological consequences* (implicit value F).

Professed Value 3: To Provide Environmental Leadership Among Other Nations

The U.S. president informed the citizenry that the United States has attacked the environmental problem "with all the power at our command." The environmental crisis, the president reassured Congress in 1973, was diminishing in the face of a "new era of restoration and renewal. . . . We are well on the way to winning the war against environmental degradation— well on the way to making our peace with nature."[274] The president said that international concern for the environment "is encouraging. Many significant international actions have been taken in recent years, and the United States can be proud of its leadership."[275]

U.S. Ambassador John Stevenson often stressed the importance of international cooperation that transcended narrow national interests. The Law of the Sea Conference, he said, "may well determine whether we have the will and the institutional structure to achieve cooperative solutions for important global problems."[276] Stevenson warned that if the international community "cannot deal effectively with the problems of lawmaking in this area, in which a large measure of mutual accommodation appears feasible and in which there is a very broad common interest in minimum rules of order on which all can rely, thus giving negotiation a dimension going beyond the mere maximization of particular national interests, the prospects for dealing with other more intensely political disputes is bleak indeed."[277] Congressional legislation also acknowledged that a U.S. program for ocean space could not be effective unless it worked "for the benefit of mankind."[278] All parties in Washington seemed aware that unbridled nationalism would destroy the marine environment.

Thus it was an ominous sign when, in all the proceedings examined, the United States government did not exercise creative leadership for environmental protection. The main trade-off among policymakers within Washington between 1970 and 1977 was between strategic and economic interests.[279] Environmental protection was not even an important stake in the bargaining process. At the Law of the Sea Conference, officials used their important political capital to win enlarged freedom of transit for aircraft and seagoing vessels and insured access to nodules and petroleum for U.S. corporations. Except for limited provisions in the IMCO and dumping conventions, U.S. officials did not work for preventive measures against pollution. Instead, arrangements were suggested to recover damages after injury. In contrast, when it came to protecting the mining companies against loss of profit, the United States insisted that the international authority for dispute settlement must be empowered "to give interlocutory decrees, and injunctive relief. In an operation where the Authority's orders can cause losses that amount to thousands of dollars per day, the exploiter can't wait to learn whether he must comply. That is no way to run a business." For mineral exploitation, "it is essential that fundamental conditions

344

of exploitation be included in the treaty."[280] For the environment, "detailed rule making may best be left to the future."[281] Thus the optimistic 1967 observation of the U.S. Commission on Marine Science proved untrue: "In these vast areas of untold riches few, if any, national economic interests have been vested, nor have the nations of the world as yet any fixed political positions. . . . There is opportunity, therefore, to design a framework that will eliminate international conflict from this area of human endeavor."[282] Vested interests of U.S. corporations and the power of Pentagon officials made 1970 already too late to respond rationally to the common heritage idea. Strategic and economic interests violated environmental needs. After the Geneva session of the Law of the Sea Conference, the environmental provisions in the Single Negotiating Text, which were not greatly dissimilar from United States preferences, promised sufficient future damage to the oceans that many environmental groups opposed the treaty. The Environmental Defense Fund, the Friends of the Earth, the National Audubon Society, the Natural Resources Defense Council, and the Sierra Club informed the Senate Commerce Committee that if a treaty including such provisions came before the Senate for advice and consent to ratification, they would recommend that the Senate *reject* the treaty.[283]

United States officials doubtlessly would have preferred to increase U.S. strategic strength and economic prosperity and at the same time to encourage the rest of the world to participate in modest environmental protection. But if that were not possible, officials sought material prosperity—even inequitable prosperity—at the price of marine deterioration.

As indicated above, U.S. officials opposed limits on national sovereignty even more than loss of potential national wealth. This was most evident in the failure to press for enforcement by a global environmental authority. Officials feared the latter might somehow encroach upon U.S. military activity. National security led the list of considerations on ocean policy, followed closely by oil and mining interests.[284] If, as argued in implicit value F, officials preferred to protect national advantages through self-help rather than to achieve greater equity through international organizations representing more of a planetary interest, then Washington required a military presence around the world. Characteristically, official behavior expressed a desire *to be more responsive to military and corporate interests than to the needs of*

345

the international community for environmental leadership (implicit value G).

To gain a few billion dollars more in mineral wealth, to retain a degree of unregulated navigational freedom more appropriate for the nineteenth century, and to guard its vast military power located in and above the sea, the United States risked the deterioration of the marine ecosystem. Policies of the United States and most other nations were narrowly nationalistic and of fleeting insignificance in terms of humanity's existence on the globe. It is impossible to know whether the Law of the Sea Con-

Table 5-3
A Comparison of Professed and Implicit Values
in U.S. Policy for Reducing Marine Pollution

Professed Values	*Implicit Values*
1. To undertake all measures necessary to protect the marine environment.	A. To subordinate environmental protection to U.S. military, navigational, and economic interests.
	B. To avoid creating effective international enforcement procedures for protection of marine ecology.
2. To protect and share equitably the common heritage for all humanity.	C. To maximize U.S. access to the common heritage.
	D. To maximize U.S. economic benefits from deep-sea mining, with little regard for international equity.
	E. To refuse global coordination of resources for the purpose of maximizing both environmental protection and the service of global human needs.
	F. To protect the U.S. position as a disproportionately large consumer of resources and energy, despite the negative ecological consequences.
3. To provide environmental leadership among other nations.	G. To be more responsive to military and corporate interests than to the needs of the international community for environmental leadership.

ference was the last, best hope for securing environmental protection, or whether another opportunity may appear before the oceans reach a stage of irreparable harm. However, the health of the oceans will decline as long as U.S. officials continue each year to give highest priority to acquiring, through shrewdly-waged competition with other states, a little more national wealth and power.

A GLOBAL HUMANIST APPROACH

Implicit Values and Environmental Protection

Compared to other states, the various U.S. positions on marine pollution were among neither the most nor the least enlightened in the three contexts examined here. If behavior had conformed with official rhetoric, the implementation of ecological balance would have been an integral part of U.S. foreign policy. However, the values implicit in U.S. policy differed significantly from professed values.

Predictable interests determined the various U.S. positions during complex negotiations to control pollutants. To gain the right for a nuclear submarine to remain submerged in straits or to prevent non-United States jurisdiction over U.S. ships at sea, the United States sacrificed international regulation of hazardous vessels. To gain national access to oil under the U.S. continental shelf and minerals on the deep seabed, the United States eroded the common heritage and undermined economic incentives for developing countries to join the effort for environmental protection. To protect U.S. companies from competitive disadvantage, the United States sought to apply universally the standards established in its domestic legislation, but without helping to achieve the worldwide equity that made equal environmental standards politically feasible and morally justifiable.

Inadequacies of Past International Action

Understanding the following inadequacies of the U.S. approach to pollution abatement helps define a contrasting, global humanist perspective for harmonizing humanity's relationship to nature.

THE PIECEMEAL PROBLEM

In the absence of a global environmental authority,[285] various international organizations might set modest pollution control standards in isolated areas, but wide gaps would probably remain between areas. For all of the most toxic substances, such as heavy metals, PCBs, pesticides, oil, and radioactive wastes, there remain absolutely no international ceilings for the total amounts that can be transferred to the oceans each year. Haphazard regulations apply to dumping or discharging these substances from ships—but here enforcement usually is to be carried out by governments now allowing pollution of the seas. Even this restriction applies only to ships of states voluntarily agreeing to sign the various conventions. All substances may be disposed freely, in any quantities, from within territorial waters if they do not directly harm a neighboring state. Moreover, the piecemeal approach has failed to prevent cumulative and synergistic effects of pollution. These cannot be managed successfully with a collection of uncoordinated international organizations such as IMCO, IAEA, and others. International organizations can hardly be blamed for the haphazard approach to pollution control. They accomplish what national governments expect of them. The absence of coordination and effective follow-through reveal "the lack of political will and the inability of the sovereign nation-state system to adapt to today's needs."[286]

THE COMMON POOL PROBLEM AND THE TERRITORIAL PRINCIPLE

The most serious criticism of the probable Law of the Sea treaty is its shortsighted response to population increases, industrial growth, and resource scarcity. At Caracas, national governments sought to manage the consequences of these forces by extending the principle of territorial control to coastal waters and parts of the deep seabed. However, even if the extension of national sovereignty may work for the management of fixed mineral resources, it cannot successfully regulate marine pollution or nurture certain forms of marine life.[287] The past record of destroying habitats for fish within territorial seas where individual nations have had control for decades makes this clear. As a result, the potential world fish harvest will probably fall to a level far below the maximum possible sustainable yield.

Moreover, expanding the territorial principle of national control over ocean resources will exacerbate existing international inequities and probably generate more conflicts than it resolves.[288] At points where the line between two states' coastal waters meet above a subterranean oil field, there will no doubt be rapid efforts by each party to pump oil before the other can. Not only are many competing wells along a given boundary inefficient, they are environmentally harmful because each well has attendant risks of leaks, blowouts, or other accidents. Rivalry will encourage cutting corners on safety. Oil slicks may appear with each state blaming the other, and neither accepting responsibility for damages or expensive cleanup. A similar set of problems arises for protecting fish that live in waters covering two or more states' jurisdictions. Each state may seek to harvest the fish before the other side does. Fear that the stocks are in decline motivates states seeking national advantage to maximize the harvest before it is gone.

Judging by the results of the Caracas, Geneva, and New York meetings, the Law of the Sea Conference will accentuate the state system. The territorial principle will be extended, not transcended. The global environmental interest will not be protected by officials who view the central issue as one of resolving conflicts between those who want to maximize territorial prerogatives over the sea's bounty and those who want to maximize national prerogatives for unregulated navigation. The negotiations seem headed toward an outcome that will render humanity's future ability to protect the sea as ineffectual as its past inability to protect against irresponsible national activities that injured lakes, streams, and territorial waters.[289]

Particularly discouraging for advocates of both equity and ecological protection was the failure of the most natural governmental allies of a new economic order to support a strong common heritage position at the Law of the Sea Conference. The small and poor countries, who presumably would have had the most to gain from maximizing the common heritage, feared that any new global regime would be controlled by the major powers. Thus many disadvantaged states sought to protect their interests through following the traditional habit of the major powers, i.e., by expanding their sovereign claims rather than by implementing a vision of a cooperative world order.

This stance illustrates how difficult it is to move into a new political framework while still operating within the intellectual and attitudinal parameters of the old order. The nonindustrialized powers seemed frozen in their response to the common heritage idea. Understandably, they reacted as if trying to gain control of their own land, still held by an imperialist power. Just

349

as the imperialist legacy made it unlikely that formerly exploited governments would opt for a new, untried vision of global cooperation, so the legacy of competing sovereignties among both the former imperial powers and the newly independent states make movement into an ecologically secure age extremely difficult. Such an age cannot be founded upon the existing system's attributes of unregulated growth, wasteful competition, and the pursuit of national advantages over rivals. Operating within the patterns of the present system, neither the rich nor the poor favored an ecologically sound global framework.

Indeed, the gap of wealth and power between the most and the least privileged nations will continue to be an obstacle to wise environmental policies. The side inferior in wealth and technology refuses to accept an environmental treaty that might lengthen its period of economic inferiority because of environmental standards that are difficult to implement. On the other hand, the side that is superior in wealth refuses to accept an environmental treaty that seems to require it to pay for the pollution of others, to restrict its consumption for the benefit of competing societies, or in general to concede more than its opponents in negotiations.

The aforementioned dilemma is so profound that it is difficult to believe that ecological decay can be halted before greater economic equity is achieved.

THE NONSIGNATORY PROBLEM

Enlightened national efforts by themselves—like separate acts of self-restraint on the English commons—can hardly be effective.[290] The U.S. ban on the use of DDT could be offset by increased spraying of it elsewhere. Even international control efforts could not succeed if states were allowed to exclude themselves from the standards. As persistent poisons pile up, one or two offending states could contaminate a major region of the oceans, and unalterably affect the environment. A handful of nuclear powers have already done this by increasing radioactivity in every corner of the globe. As our earlier discussions showed, even the positive examples of environmental progress—the IMCO and dumping conventions—apply only to those agreeing to the conditions. With many economic incentives for desperately poor or selfishly acquisitive societies to create pollution havens, such an approach cannot provide assurance of achieving ecological balance.

350

ENFORCEMENT

As long as sovereign states oppose worldwide enforcement measures, many environmental goals will remain impossible to achieve. Weak enforcement of regulations that do exist produces a practical effect no different from the absence of regulations. Flags of convenience must some day disappear from the sea. Probably a single global regime will need to register all vessels of large size, of hazardous nature, or of questionable purpose. Because of ineffective enforcement, for example, the International Whaling Commission has been unable to save the blue whale from near extinction because of overhunting by only two countries: the Soviet Union and Japan. Protecting this whale encroaches very little upon any state's sovereignty and threatens no state economically. Moreover, the national governments of the world have voted overwhelmingly for a moritorium on hunting this whale. Yet enforcement has been ineffective.[291] Similarly, the bilateral International Joint Commission for regulating United States and Canadian fresh waters reportedly has enforcement problems and lacks powers to compel obedience to its decisions.[292] Global regulation will be far more difficult to achieve than enforcement between two friendly, wealthy states. Nowhere is the inadequacy of enforcement better illustrated than in the handling of radioactive materials. Even obligatory standards for waste disposal would hardly be sufficient, since discovery of a violation after it occurred could not avert irretrievable damage to the environment. No procedure would be adequate for after-the-fact enforcement, once materials with a contamination life of centuries or millennia have entered the ocean. Effective regulation within the existing decentralized legal order is simply not possible.[293]

LAND-BASED POLLUTION

Because more than three-fourths of the contaminants in the oceans come from land-based sources,[294] an environmentally healthy ocean must eventually be protected by world regulation of land-based polluting activity. Without a global regime, pollutants will probably accumulate in the high seas for one of two reasons: (1) states will pollute the commons to save their own land and territorial waters from contamination, or (2) states will contaminate their own land, waters, and atmosphere with pollutants, many of which eventually will find their way to the oceans, because of intersocietal economic competition.

351

FINANCING POLLUTION ABATEMENT

Just as the absence of a global environmental authority will enable nonsignatories or delinquent signatories to escape environmental obligations, so it also will allow industrial states to escape their financial responsibilities to protect marine ecology. Few states on the planet possess sufficient expertise or resources to prevent and clean up major environmental problems, like oil spills or blowouts. Indeed, it would be wasteful if all oil-producing states individually acquired the capacity to take comprehensive measures against pollution. Continued IMCO efforts to place the burden of environmental responsibility on separate states are economically inefficient, politically divisive, and environmentally hazardous. Moreover, outright bans on persistent herbicides and pesticides without internationally subsidized substitutes could, some developing countries claim, bring disaster to their peoples from disease and famine.[295] Only some variation of global authority would be capable of systematically subsidizing nonpolluting alternatives to hazardous substances and expensive measures for enforcement and cleanup.

COORDINATING POLLUTION CONTROL

Global coordination of pollution does not require an absolute ban on waste discharges. Nature can provide for some waste treatment of substances such as oil and municipal sewage. The problem is one of overloading. The solution is to insure that permissible levels are not exceeded and that the tolerable quantity of pollution results from producing the goods most useful to enhancing the quality of human life, as opposed to enhancing profit or national power as ends in themselves. The need is to coordinate pollution abatement in one area with "acceptable pollution" in another area. For example, if the oceans can withstand only a severely limited quantity of a given pesticide, then a global decision-making process is required to insure that the allowable amount is used to protect humans against malaria, not to serve another less life-preserving function.[296] Global coordination is also needed to insure that waste disposal prohibited in one area is not simply transferred to another. In the long run, it is environmentally useless to prohibit oil discharges in coastal waters if the oil is simply discharged from land-based reception tanks into internal or territorial waters; to prohibit dumping plastics if they are then incinerated on land and the hazardous substances are later transferred through the atmosphere to the sea; or to ban nuclear tests in one state if others continue them.

352

COORDINATING RESOURCE USAGE

If tolerable pollution must be globally coordinated, the use of certain resources cannot be left uncoordinated. In the cases examined, the question of equity was never far removed from ecological issues. Global environmental control without a redistribution of power and resources was unacceptable to many have-not nations because they viewed such control as likely to freeze fundamental inequalities.[297] In addition, if restrictions are imposed on use of hazardous substances, the determination of allowable national quotas would be extremely controversial. For example, if the environment can withstand only 5,000 tons of mercury per year, some authority must resolve how much may be used as a fungicide for dressing seeds to increase agricultural productivity and how much may be used for industrial processes to manufacture military equipment. Often one state might prefer to accomplish the former goal and a different state the latter. If production of any substance is limited either to advance conservation or avert environmental overload, choices will inevitably need to be made among competing national claims for diverse purposes. Only a system global in its reach can rationally accomplish these tasks.

There would, of course, be ecological benefits resulting from planetary resource coordination. For example, arrangements guaranteeing purchases from a developing country for a ten-year period at designated prices could help poor states plan for the recovery of some costs of pollution abatement measures. In order to insure that stable commodity prices on trade "concessions" be used to avert the potential pollution attending industrialization, some agency would need to link such arrangements directly to environmental protection measures. Because of the need to set global standards for waste disposal and to avoid competitive disadvantages within industries, this linkage could most conveniently be established through a global organization with compulsory jurisdiction.

THE COMMONS IN A DECENTRALIZED COMPETITIVE
INTERNATIONAL SYSTEM

The problem of the English commons could have been solved by distributing the land to the herdsmen using it. Each herdsman might have enclosed his or her share of the commons and increased the herd size up to but not beyond the limit the enclosed pasture would bear. Regulating marine pollution is more difficult. Distributing ownership of all the oceans to various coast-

353

al "herdsmen" will not suffice. One country's use of its waters would influence adjoining sections of "enclosed" oceans belonging to other states. Eventually all the oceans are affected by such things as the use of DDT or the atmospheric explosion of nuclear devices. National control over segments of the oceans divides the planet, while ecological protection requires managing the planet as a single entity. Governments serving traditional national interests, even if expressed and mediated in an international organization, will not protect the environment. Under such conditions, no powerful actor speaks for the general (ecological) interest; all speak for separate, particularized interests.

On a concrete level, it is neither rational nor likely that one state will spend its resources to protect the high seas—which it does not own—if other states fail to assume a fair share of the burden of restrictions on national behavior. Even worse, as long as the goods are "free" and the oceans held in common, each state will gladly harvest nodules or fish without even assuming the responsibility for the pollution generated by its own harvesting. Within the existing, competitive international system, governments seek to increase the relative share of wealth enjoyed by their national subjects. Each state seeks to maximize its gross national product and to expand its share of the gross world product. Uncoordinated economic growth and unrestrained national economic competition are the rule. Both forms of self-assertion are contrary to ecological rationality and to the collective good.[298]

Planetary welfare can only be pursued through transnational cooperation. Yet the present structures for restraint and coordination are inadequate both at the national and international levels. This case study suggests that states may use positive rhetoric for protecting the oceans, but they will not produce the structures of regulation and control that are necessary for fulfilling their professed goals. Richard Falk notes that even among developed nations, where "interests . . . are convergent in relation to environmental quality, the prospect of an implementing (as distinct from a pious) consensus on action remains poor. Just as with disarmament . . . the dynamics of competition lead to an endless search for relative advantage, to distrust of rival proposals, and to a self-interested set of perceptions that induce contradictory assessments of what constitutes a reasonable adjustment [of interests]."[299] Events at the Caracas, Geneva, and New York Sessions of the Law of the Sea Conference confirm this view. The intense conflicts between industrial and poor states diverted the attention of many observers from the failure of the industrial powers to agree upon international standards for pollution or to establish concrete measures for international enforcement.

POLITICAL FEASIBILITY

The extent to which environmental policy changes are probable depends greatly on how the environmental question is perceived by those persons able to influence the vested interests resisting change. These interests have established a strong hold upon our institutions and behavior because previous generations living in the industrialized countries thought little about future inhabitants when they promoted their own prosperity at the expense of the environment and nonindustrialized societies. The legacy of uneven global development has produced severe political problems today in terms of ecological and egalitarian imperatives which call for industrial states to pay to clean up their own wastes, and in addition, to subsidize the cost of environmental protection in the poor states. Most citizens in the rich states are not prepared to do this now. Certainly governments will not do this in the absence of citizen pressure.

The resistance of those with vested economic interests was voiced quite honestly by the Kennecott Copper Company's Director of Ocean Resources, in commenting on the seabed negotiations: "As long as we face the rhetoric and aspirations of the new economic order, real progress is not possible." Rather than trying to build the best possible international regime to serve human needs, Kennecott Copper's executives concluded: "The time has come for all to face these facts [that progress is impossible] and to take the necessary alternative [unilateral] steps to foster the needs and well-being of the United States."[300] Similarly, Exxon Corporation opposed any agreement that treated the richest states differently from the poorest states. Despite the enormous inequality in income levels and per capita resource usage between the industrial states and less developed countries, to give the latter a bigger share of revenues from oil under the high seas "is surely unjustified."[301]

When—if ever—the United States and other industrial states will be willing to make economic sacrifices for environmental protection of the commons remains uncertain. But it is quite clear that they will not assume the responsibility to pay for international efforts unless there are some reciprocal guarantees of

355

Table 5-4

Selected Values of Global Humanism Compared to U.S. Policy for Reducing Marine Pollution

Global Humanism	U.S. Policy
Peace	
1. Protecting the future of the global ecosystem is more important than preserving the military superiority of one state over another.	1. Protecting U.S. strategic advantages is more important than long-range problems of environmental deterioration.
2. Uneven global economic development is undesirable because it (1) perpetuates disharmony within and among nations, and (2) wastes resources in military production and unnecessary consumption.	2. Officials have not seen uneven global economic development as a significant cause of the strains placed on the environment, whether in the form of ecocide in warfare, environmental overload, depletion of scarce resources, or population pressure upon resources. In any case, ecologically sound cooperation among nations is less important than perpetuating U.S. strategic and economic advantages.
3. The desire of maritime states for unregulated navigation and the interest of their military officials in unimpeded transit should be restrained in order to achieve world environmental protection.	3. The desire of U.S. officials for sweeping navigational freedom, including unimpeded transit for military and intelligence work, takes priority over measures for world environmental protection.
Economic Well-being	
1. Maldistribution of the world's resources, both intra- and internationally, is undesirable because it produces ecologically damaging relationships between the world's population and resources. If all people followed the consumption and pollution patterns of the rich, the earth's eco-system would be overloaded. Resources should be reallocated to reflect concern for ecology and equity.	1. Official behavior has denied that unequal distribution of the world's resources is a cause of damage to the environment. The poverty of the less developed countries and the overconsumption of the industrial states are not central concerns for U.S. officials.

2. Evironmental protection should be financed by those most able to pay.

3. Per capita consumption of the rich states should not be increased until the gap between rich and poor is substantially narrowed and protection of the world's ecosystem is more nearly secured.

4. Economic growth is not desirable as an end in itself; it should be tailored to maximize fulfillment of human needs and minimize environmental overload. Conservation of resources and endangered species is highly valued.

Human Rights and Social Justice

1. Respect for human rights and elemental justice requires that the benefits of the common heritage be used for overcoming poverty in the poorest societies.

2. The poor states should pay the costs they incur for environmental protection, without substantial aid from the U.S.

3. Increasing per capita consumption and corporate growth are primary goals, even if these goals widen the gap between rich and poor societies.

4. Economic growth is desirable in itself because it promises greater prosperity for U.S. citizens. U.S. officials have resisted establishing international guidelines to focus resource use on maximizing fulfillment of human needs, because this focus could constrain U.S. consumption. The impulse to exploit has taken precedence over the need to conserve and to avoid environmental overload.

Human Rights and Social Justice

1. "Nondiscriminatory access" to the common heritage means that the international community should allow nearly unlimited access to ocean wealth by those corporations presently best able to extract it.

Table 5-4 (cont.)

Global Humanism	U.S. Policy
2. The right of the poor to have basic needs satisfied should influence decisively the allocation of world resources when a balance must be struck between exploitation of resources and conservation of the environment.	2. The right of the rich to invest, exploit, profit, and consume need not be compromised in order to alleviate their effect on poor societies. U.S. officials did not tailor resource use to the need for environmental balance, conservation, or equity.

Ecological Balance

Global Humanism	U.S. Policy
1. Many industrial states are "misdeveloped" and should reorient priorities so they no longer unnecessarily deplete scarce resources by using them for wasteful forms of consumerism and for the prosperity of a small minority of the world's population.	1. Policy is based on the unexamined assumption that the United States is not "misdeveloped." U.S. citizens do not waste or consume too many resources.
2. Securing long-range survival of the species and harmonizing the relationship between humanity and nature (e.g., relating food to population) are more important than achieving national competitive advantages.	2. Securing the survival of the species in the long run and improving the quality of life for non-U.S. people are less important goals than the short-range enhancement of U.S. strategic and economic interests.
3. Some qualification of national sovereignty should occur to facilitate global coordination of resource policies and environmental standards.	3. International environmental regulation is undesirable if it encroaches on U.S national sovereignty or decreases U.S. political advantages. Officials envisage a world with largely voluntary standards and without supranational universal enforcement.

support from the poor nations.[302] That cannot be achieved unless the developing nations participate in major planetary decisions about resource usage—decisions which are now made in
the capitals of industrial states and the boardrooms of multinational corporations. The less developed countries will not want
and should not agree to become part of a strengthened global
political and commercial system without having genuinely equitable participation in its decision making. Anything less would
be a new variety of imperialism. In short, to insure the health of
the marine ecosystem and the human species, a reasonable portion of the existing structures of authority, power, and wealth
must be placed in the hands of developing countries.

An Alternative Framework

The preceding analysis suggests that following past national
priorities holds little promise for environmental protection. A
planetary—not national or class—focus is necessary for environmental protection. Despite the inadequacies of U.S.
policies when compared to the need for fundamental change,
these policies do contain some indications of the direction in
which future policy must move to become more effective. The
following are examples:

1. Construction standards for tankers, regulations for dumping, and international guidelines for seabed mining and mineral
extraction on the continental shelf lead toward the idea that universal standards must eventually be used to protect the oceans.

2. U.S. acceptance of port state enforcement of pollution and
construction standards for non-U.S. ships entering U.S. harbors
illustrates the need to establish enforcement that will penetrate
the exclusive jurisdiction of sovereign states over their own nationals and flag ships. This is a small recognition that eventually
there must be nonterritorial jurisdiction applying to all actors,
regardless of geographic location or nationality.

3. The U.S. concession to allow some transfer of revenues
from seabed minerals to the less developed countries, as well as
its acceptance in principle that new mineral exploitation should
not exceed the growth of demand in key mineral markets, is a
small recognition of the idea that greater economic equity will be
required to achieve even minimal international cooperation, to
say nothing of a new global regime.

4. Allowing the International Seabed Resource Authority, if
created, to set some standards for pollution control during the
mining of hard minerals represents a tacit admission that a

359

global agency must handle the setting of some standards for environmental protection. Insofar as the members, especially the industrialized states, seek what will in effect amount to a collective veto in the Authority, it would be a mistake to characterize the ISRA as a supranational organization. Instead, it will operate more as familiar UN organizations, acting on behalf of a collection of national interests, rather than on behalf of the global interest. It would, however, move beyond the UN General Assembly in being able to take decisions that are legally binding, and beyond the UN Security Council in allowing no single nation a veto. In these regards, it could be one institutional step closer to the necessary global authority.

5. Finally, the U.S. acceptance of compulsory judicial settlement in disputes arising out of the obligations of the treaty is a more genuine step toward a supranational organization.

Although some of these innovations were taken to enable the traditional sovereign state system to better serve national interests rather than to advance global coordination, they illustrate the extent to which technological progress and the fledgling environmental movement have moved even national policies toward a planetary orientation. Strengthening these trends would be the most productive activity for advocates of a new policy based on global humanism. A genuinely global environmental authority would be even less restricted by commercial, navigational, and national economic interests than the authority contemplated in the Law of the Sea Conference. Its potential utility can be illustrated by considering the possibilities for controlling a common pollutant, such as petroleum.

A global authority could assume a commitment to insure ecological quality of all the oceans, instead of merely enabling states to act for recovery of damages suffered within the seas under their national jurisdiction. The proposed approach would attempt to establish state, corporate, and individual responsibility for injuries to the marine environment anywhere on the seas. A new authority could set an annual global maximum of permissible oil pollution from all vessels, and then allocate specific allowable maximums for every state or shipper. It could also establish international safety inspection of tankers as a prerequisite to annual international licensing for all ocean transport.

A global environmental authority could base enforcement upon the idea that the right to use any part of the sea depended upon honoring the obligation not to abuse it. The authority could dispatch aircraft with sophisticated photographic equip-

360

ment to detect even at night the sheen of ship discharges on the surface waters below. Such an enforcement agency could have authority to obtain other kinds of evidence, to board and inspect ships at any point on their voyages, and to initiate prosecution, regardless of the location of the discharge and the registry of the vessel. A universal public authority to regulate oil transport could initiate plans to move oil from tankers to internationally organized and maintained pipelines in some parts of the world, especially across isthmuses or through shallow and narrow waters.

Moreover, a global authority could institutionalize cooperative efforts for cleanup of spills on the high seas. In the past, such spills were not cared for because they would involve expense by one state for the common good. Furthermore, a universal antipollution organization could help to clean up spills adjacent to countries which lack the necessary technology or finances to protect their own coasts.

Finally, many complex political issues could be better handled in a global system for environmental protection. For example, at some point in history it may become necessary to set an annual world maximum for pesticide or petroleum consumption to prevent the oceans from deteriorating. If an average of 0.2 percent of the oil transported enters the oceans through accidents or intentional discharge, and if another given percentage of oil consumed enters the oceans through the atmosphere and rivers, then the world's people may be forced to conclude that in the interest of environmental protection, only a certain maximum of petroleum can be carried by ships and consumed each year. How will that difficult decision be made? Will the rich decide that they need more oil to drive heavy cars or travel frequently by jetliner while the poor have inadequate petroleum for fertilizer? Until a transnational environmental movement and a global authority are established, such decisions will continue to be made with no effective voice for the planetary interest in protecting the commons.

In general a global humanist approach to the control of marine pollution would aim to fulfill these needs:

(1) to create a global environmental authority whose principal task would be to protect the planetary environment;

(2) to create and enforce community-established standards for total annual permissible marine pollution of the most hazardous substances; in addition, to set national, regional, or per capita quotas as components of the general maximum allowed;

361

(3) to provide incentives for compliance with standards and to establish sanctions for violators, including such measures as deprivation of navigational rights and the privilege to use marine resources;

(4) to place the economic burden for environmental protection upon those most able to pay the costs;

(5) to establish global guidelines for national consumption of nonrenewable resources;

(6) to establish global guidelines for long-range national economic policies in order to encourage economic growth that serves human needs, meanwhile discouraging economic expansion for other purposes.[303]

Efforts to strengthen environmental legislation domestically may be the most potent political lever to encourage a more progressive posture internationally. On the basis of the cases examined here, a reliable rule of thumb would seem to be that any success in strengthening domestic legislation will both benefit the environment and increase the likelihood for establishing improved global standards. National governments will be likely to support international environmental action in order to avoid competitive disadvantages, for shippers or manufacturers, imposed by domestic legislation. Some corporations may not be concerned about uneven enforcement of environmental standards if they are free to move operations to pollution havens. Global enforcement, of course, should discourage such possibilities.[304] A global authority could be useful to support and stiffen efforts of governments to prevail against antiecological vested interests within their own societies.

The proposed approach would seek to overturn the prevailing idea that marine pollution is acceptable until widespread damage has occurred. Large segments of the oceans have already been endangered and only one-third of humanity has entered the industrial era. Extrapolations of comparable industrial output and waste disposal to match rising world industrial activity show massive increases of toxic substances in the oceans by 2000.[305]

Most importantly, an alternative approach could yield many presently unrealized fruits. For example, some scientists believe that appropriate pollution abatement, fertilization, and conservation practices could provide ten times the already bountiful harvest of protein obtained from the sea.[306] This food, as well as the windfall hard minerals of the common heritage, could provide enormous assistance in eliminating poverty. The industrial states could avoid costly duplication of efforts to test, monitor, and clean up the hundreds of new substances being introduced into the environment each year. This might partially compensate them for their "losses" in sharing resources with the developing countries. Finally, the aesthetic and recreational uses of the sea—hardly mentioned in this study—are an unmeasurable treasure that can be retained with more enlightened policies.

Indicators of World Order Progress

The following questions can be used to assess the extent to which a major industrial power, such as the United States, is helping to realize a more harmonious balance between humanity and nature within the range of issues covered by this case study:

1. Has the government favored a mode of exploiting the common heritage that leads to global equity and protection of the marine environment?

2. Has the government committed at least 1 percent of its annual GNP to international efforts for subsidizing pollution abatement in the developing countries?

3. Has the government established guidelines for curtailment of its own excessive economic growth in areas unsuitable to fulfilling human needs or contrary to conservation of scarce resources and endangered species?

4. Has the government committed itself to strong domestic environmental legislation?

5. Has the government given all useful data to international agencies monitoring known pollutants, including information about disposal of toxic substances such as chemical warfare agents and radioactive wastes produced in the course of weapons procurement?

6. Is the disposal of hazardous substances decreasing, whether measured on a per capita or total basis?

7. Has the government extended invitations to international agencies, such as the IAEA, to inspect all (not just nonmilitary) production and waste disposal facilities of extremely hazardous materials, such as nuclear fuel processing plants, to encourage institutional and attitudinal movement toward eventual regulation by a global environmental authority?

8. In concrete cases, has the government given higher priority to protecting the planetary environment or to advancing national economic and strategic benefits?

SIX · *Building a Just World Order*

ASSESSING PROGRESS TOWARD A JUST WORLD ORDER

EACH of the four case studies illustrates a different value of global humanism and provides the basis for assessing the impact of U.S. foreign policy on the prospects for achieving a more humane and secure system of world order. In each case, the values implicit in U.S. political behavior differed sharply from the values of global humanism. The juxtaposition of professed values and implicit values defined the policy gap between rhetoric and reality. A realistic understanding of the values served by U.S. policy leads inescapably to pessimistic conclusions about the prospects of that policy for transforming the present international system into one better able to provide a secure and humane life for all people. The conflicts between the values implicit in U.S. policy and the values of global humanism will not be repeated here because summaries of these differences have already been presented in separate chapters on the case studies. It will be useful for readers to refer to the summaries again while considering this concluding chapter.[1]

The remaining pages will describe the value foundation for U.S. policy, the domestic constraints on policy innovation, and the world view that undergirded official thinking. The discussion then turns to the impact of the existing international system upon efforts for world order reform. The chapter closes with an analysis of the implications of this study for political action by persons interested in promoting system change.

The Normative Orientation of U.S. Policy

As the previous analysis has shown, behavior was a more reliable guide than rhetoric to the normative content of U.S. policy. In the following description of the value foundation for U.S. policy, generalizations about the values of officials will, like all generalizations, simplify reality. The nuances of some positions cannot be included in a brief summary. At the same time, U.S. policies contained sufficient consistency to make possible a description of a composite official perspective encompassing the four value areas examined above.[2]

364

PEACE

Three decades of arms control negotiations have produced nine major bilateral treaties between the United States and the Soviet Union and seven multilateral agreements among many states. But these have not significantly reduced the nuclear threat to humanity.[3] Throughout the long years of negotiations, officials have believed that accepting the risks of the arms build-up and the proliferation of nuclear weapons was wiser than undertaking minimal risks for arms reductions. Policymakers sought neither to decrease the capacity of the superpowers for inflicting violence nor to change the international system to one less violence-prone. By perpetuating the existing international system and the attitudinal base upon which this system rested, officials made disarmament virtually impossible. In general, they did not seek to decrease the role of military power in human affairs. Neither Republican nor Democratic leadership used bureaucratic resources to devleop models of a disarming world.

ECONOMIC WELL-BEING

Just as officials sought in the first value area to protect the U.S. power position through deploying advanced military technology rather than halting the arms competition, so within the scope of the second value they shaped economic relations with other states to enhance U.S. prosperity and to nurture strategic collaboration rather than to contribute generously to the fulfillment of human needs beyond U.S. territory. The single most influential determinant of aid policy was the desire to maximize U.S. strategic advantages. Within the policy boundaries of U.S. strategic desires, officials further shaped aid programs to enhance the interests of U.S. investors and producers. One of the least significant determinants of aid policy was the unmet human needs of other societies.

Officials intended no substantial redistribution of global wealth. Only once in the thirty years studied did the United States contribute as much as 1 percent of its GNP to foreign assistance. That was when aid went to Europe after World War II. Never did the United States extend such generosity toward the poorer, darker-skinned peoples of the world. At the very best, officials saw aid as charity, not as an instrument of systemic change in which the poor would eventually be on an equal footing with the rich.

Among the serious shortcomings of U.S. aid policies, one

365

stands out. The aid "burden" of the U.S. has declined sharply during the last decade, while U.S. per capita wealth has grown. Recently the United States has contributed less than a third of a penny for each dollar of its GNP to the fulfillment of non-U.S. human needs. For the richest and most powerful national society on earth to do so little to relieve human misery provides a bleak portent for achieving a life of decency for much of the world's population. In brief, the United States gave low priority both to abolishing the suffering of poverty-stricken people and to creating a new economic order that would distribute wealth more equitably and concentrate productive capacity on serving human needs.

HUMAN RIGHTS AND SOCIAL JUSTICE

The tradition of respect for civil liberties within the United States and the revolutionary, anticolonial origins of the U.S. government have provided a long-standing foundation for widespread support of self-determination and other human rights elsewhere in the world. But this foundation has been undermined by policies subordinating human rights to what officials perceived or professed as national security needs.

Despite rhetoric to the contrary, United States violation of Chilean self-determination did not enhance human dignity. Instead, officials intervened to satisfy ideological hostility toward socialism in the Western Hemisphere, to protect U.S. private investments in Chile and other countries potentially influenced by the Chilean example, and to maintain U.S. political influence in Latin America. U.S. leaders in fact feared self-determination as a stimulus to instability in the existing international structure of wealth and power. Rhetorical support for human rights justified and disguised intervention against human rights. This was part of a political strategy, which included the denial of human rights when their exercise came into conflict with U.S. policies, to manipulate Chilean political groups that aimed at decreasing U.S. economic or political control of and benefits from Chile.

ECOLOGICAL BALANCE

On ecological questions, officials served the same value priorities as in the three areas already discussed. The government gave environmental protection only slight weight compared to that given military, navigational, and economic interests. U.S. officials placed highest value upon enhancing the opportunities for U.S. military aircraft, ships, and submarines to navigate without restriction. Preserving economic opportunities for corporate interests, such as expressed by shipping, oil, and mining companies, received slightly less emphasis, but still ranked well above environmental protection in priority.

The United States more fully recognized the need for global collaboration in the environmental area than in the other value areas. This was due to the obvious impossibility of administering environmental standards through national action alone or even through multilateral action that permitted a few major actors to remain outside of environmental norms that others followed. However, the awareness of the need for global coordination was not matched by a willingness to organize the relationship between humanity and nature in a way to provide equal benefits for all people, to respect the needs of future generations, or to protect important natural resources. Environmental collaboration was aimed at protecting the interests of what might be called the global upper class—the industrialized as opposed to the poor societies, and the owners and managers of private corporations and public bureaucracies as opposed to the less powerful.

Domestic Constraints on U.S. Policy

It is easy but in itself not very useful to criticize officials for failing to implement preferred world order values. Decisions were the result of politics, not logic about world order imperatives. In addition to international constraints, domestic political forces heavily influenced the government's decisions. Table 6-1 shows that powerful domestic interests in each case study expressed themselves against global humanism in all four value areas. (The various domestic influences included in the table were not, of course, of equal intensity or effect.) For example, large military expenditures not only inhibited realization of V_1, but also discouraged implementation of V_2 because money spent for arms could not help fertilize rice fields in India; of V_3 because reinforcing the role of military power in human affairs made political repression more likely; and of V_4 because unproductive use of resources for weapons caused pollution and resource depletion that exceeded what was necessary if productive capacity were rationally focused upon meeting human needs.

The domestic constituency for each of the global humanist values was weak and uncoordinated. Military and industrial forces pressed for a further military buildup. The Vladivostok

Table 6-1

Illustrative U.S. Domestic Pressures Against the Realization of Preferred World Order Values

Value area	Vladivostok Accord	Aid to India	Self-determination in Chile	Marine Pollution
Peace	The military-industrial complex pressed for deployment of more weapons.	The drive for U.S. security and economic benefits—not human needs—determined most aid programs.	Corporate and governmental leadership wanted a pro-U.S. government in power to secure U.S. influence, even if establishing a pro-U.S. government produced violence and repression	The desire for unimpeded military transit and the jealous protection of sovereignty made international pollution control unfeasible.
Economic Well-being	Money for military equipment detracted from resources available for increasing food production.	Money allocated to buy influence with allies and to open opportunities for U.S. investors did not maximize the service of human needs.	Corporate and governmental leadership opposed a Chilean government that advocated radical change, even though it was designed to help abolish poverty for the lower classes.	Giving the United States greater national access to oil and nodules did not serve the needs of the planet's poor. U.S. proposals if implemented, would widen the gap between rich and poor.

Human Rights	Perpetuating the role of military power in world affairs encouraged the militarization of the entire planet and the denial of human rights by military governments.	The right of the rich to invest and to make profit was stressed, while the right of equity was rejected.	Corporate and governmental leadership opposed radical socioeconomic change aimed at achieving human rights for the dispossessed.	Governmental and corporate leadership gave higher priority to the right of unregulated transit and of access to nodules than to the right of poor people to economic equity.
Ecological Balance	The Vladivostok Accord demonstrated no concern for ecocide in event of nuclear war or for environmental hazards of nuclear proliferation. The ecological strains caused by continued production and operation of military equipment were ignored.	The "trickle-down" approach to development meant that pollution and resource depletion would exceed the minimum necessary to achieve a standard of decency for all. Without official objection, the rich continued to overconsume while the poor had inadequate resources for a life of dignity.	Corporate greed focused resources and productive capacity upon maximizing profit rather than fulfilling human needs. Unnecessary pollution and resource depletion continued without official objection.	The corporate and government impulse to exploit resources for private profit and lavish national consumption took precedence over the need to conserve or to share resources with the world's population. This exacerbated the imbalance between humanity and nature.

case corroborated many other observers' conclusions that domestic pressures, rather than security needs arising from competition with the Soviet Union, often stimulated U.S. weapons innovations.[4] Development assistance also had no substantial domestic constituency, unless the aid was designed to benefit U.S. producers or alliance policy. But under those conditions U.S. policy could not lead toward V_2. Similarly ITT, Kennecott, and the CIA cared far more about protecting their investments and influence than about human rights. The environment issue seemed, on the surface, to be the least highly politicized of the four value areas. Yet the development of the U.S. position for the Law of the Sea Conference illustrated the regressive power of military and corporate influences on decision makers. To be sure, officials at first constructed a policy that seemed to grow out of some genuine desire to avoid destruction of the oceans (with the exception of seeking unreasonable navigational freedom for military planes and ships). But as the political and economic costs of a generous common heritage and strong environmental program became clear, and as oil and mining interests mobilized, officials retreated from their relatively enlightened 1970 position. Even ignoring the direct expression of corporate and military hostility to V_4, few U.S. citizens wanted to decrease their consumption or raise tax revenues to aid developing countries in curtailing global pollution.

In sum, bureacratic, economic, military, and ideological forces reinforced the inclination of those in power to give low priority to the values of global humanism. The presence of these forces meant that officials would hesitate to implement global humanist values, even if they privately favored them, because such efforts would cost them political support essential for preventing their being displaced by political opponents who were even more opposed to preferred world order values. A progressive official thus often was forced to choose between two unpleasant alternatives. The official could do little to advance global humanism against hostile domestic forces and thereby advance his or her own political career. Or, he or she could embrace global values vigorously and soon be replaced by a member of Congress or another bureaucrat more sympathetic to nationalistic, military, oil, and mining interests. As a result of such a dilemma, even those leaders with private sympathies for the values of global humanism would often implement values consistent with the generally accepted, less humanitarian operational code.

370

The Operational Code of Officials

The political leadership's fundamental assumptions about the nature of international relations, the motivation for human behavior, and the possibility of human influence on history provided the background against which the decisions analyzed in the case studies were made. These fundamental beliefs constituted an "operational code"[5] which provided the guidelines that influenced the weighing of alternative courses of action and the choice of strategy and tactics for action. The values implicit in U.S. policy and delineated in each case study give shape to the U.S. operational code that was the spring from which policies flowed.

THE PERVASIVE POWER GAME

Washington officials seemed heavily influenced by a bureaucratic model of reality—a model which often did not correspond to reality more objectively perceived. Adopting the bureaucratic model of truth seemed the key to prestige and influence in Washington. The basic premise of this model was that international politics was a game, the object of which was to avoid losing influence and if possible to gain more. Power was measured in terms of the capacity to dominate or exercise influence over the decision of other governments. Toughness was a positive attribute. For officials exhilarated by the game of nations, "the whole field of international relations is a confrontation."[6] As we have seen, the desire to maintain power heavily influenced U.S. policies at the Vladivostok and Caracas meetings, and determined the stance taken toward the governments in New Delhi and Santiago.

Officials pictured Western civilization as threatened by the demands of the developing countries, perhaps backed by major industrialized rivals of the United States, for a redistribution of the world's wealth, power, and authority. Despite recognition of a new global interdependency and rhetorical support for equity, U.S. officials expected other states to continue allowing the United States to maintain a preeminent position in global economic and political structures. Instead of shouldering responsibilities commensurate with its resources in order to realize a humane structure of interdependency, the United States developed policies to maintain the U.S. global position. Officials assumed that what was good for the United States would also benefit the rest of the world. As Henry Kissinger explained in a

371

reflective interview with James Reston: "When we talk interdependence, we are not just talking [about] an American desire to exploit the resources of other nations. What we are saying is for our own benefit, of course. But it is also for the benefit of everybody else." Kissinger warned nations pressing for change that if they ignored U.S. interests "the Western civilization that we now have is almost certain to disintegrate because it will first lead to a series of rivalries in which each region will try to maximize its own special advantages. That inevitably will lead to tests of strength of one sort or another. These will magnify domestic crises in many countries, and they will then move more and more to authoritarian models. I would expect then that we will certainly have crises which no leadership is able to deal with."[7] In spite of these dire warnings, Kissinger himself demonstrated little inclination—as the case studies showed—to implement policy that put global interests above national advantages.

HUMAN MOTIVATION

A second tenet of the bureaucratic model of reality was that the international system functioned best as a threat system. The premium placed on toughness dictated that negative reinforcements and deprivations were used more often than positive inducements to influence behavior. To offer positive inducements in the form of concessions meant losing points in the competition for power.

The officials in the above case studies viewed intergroup human relations as basically conflictual rather than cooperative. For example, in the Vladivostok case study, U.S. political leaders thought self-restraint in weapon deployments was tantamount to diplomatic or military retreat. They assumed that the only way of encouraging the Soviet Union to negotiate seriously was to amass superior weaponry in order to force Soviet officials to the bargaining table. Even in environmental affairs, U.S. policies were based upon the assumption that national conflict rather than transnational cooperation would be the bedrock for future human transactions. That assumption made compromise on the nodule issue—relatively unrelated to the sensitive security area—so difficult.

To the extent that the struggle for power was waged through psychological means, symbolic actions became important. Thus officials destabilized Chilean society not only to save their influence in Chile, but also to demonstrate that socialism and pro-

372

grams for nationalization of U.S. capital could not work elsewhere. This would be a lesson to any countries contemplating Chilean-like expropriation. To respect self-determination as a human right was alien to the prevailing diplomatic approach of punishing those countries that pursued unwanted policies. Thus such respect was unimportant in policymaking. Consistent with a carrot-stick diplomacy, enough aid might be sent to India to retain some influence there, but aid programs were never designed to produce structural change in India or in the international system. The United States curtailed aid when it failed to buy political support.

If officials used tough, shock tactics in the psychological competition for power and wealth, they largely ignored world opinion that supported the preferred world order values. An unusually blunt but typical expression of this approach came from John McCloy, a frequent White House consultant. When once recommending that the United States resume nuclear testing, he told President Kennedy: "World opinion? I don't believe in world opinion. The only thing that matters is power."[8] As the arms control case study revealed, it mattered little that many nations had explicitly called, through various resolutions at the UN, for disarmament. It mattered little that the nuclear powers had formally bound themselves to negotiate arrangements for nuclear disarmament. In the case of foreign aid, it mattered little that world opinion favored transferring a minimum of .7 percent of GNP from the rich to the poor each year. In the Chilean case, it mattered little that the United States had legally committed itself not to intervene in any Latin American state for any reason. Officials assumed they could win few points by acting generously, graciously, or even legally.[9]

INEFFECTIVENESS OF LEGAL AND MORAL RESTRAINTS

The four case studies showed that legal restraints and global humanist values were not an important determinant of official behavior. The United States' violation of human rights in Chile concerned officials only because they feared public disclosure of their acts. They were unmoved by legally binding treaties which had been duly approved by the Senate and were thus part of "the supreme law of the land." Similarly, oil and nodules for U.S. citizens were sought without much regard for equity or ecology. Those in power pursued the national advantages of unregulated navigation even if this helped kill the prospects for

373

international enforcement of pollution control. Within this bureaucratic understanding of human motivation, the U.S. leadership judged humanitarian arguments to be irresponsible as a guide to policy, although excellent for rhetorical purposes.

VIEW OF HISTORY

Just as U.S. leaders advanced the interests of only a small segment—rather than all—of humanity, they also designed policies for only a short span—rather than a long term—of history. A short-range view of history meant that marine resources could be exploited or a pro-United States government could be kept in Chile. Pollution or longer-range structural change in Chile could be dealt with by some later administration. However, a continuous series of administrations thinking in four-year spans would never consider how to make long-range structural changes in international society.

As long as officials were unconcerned about the more distant future, a policy influenced heavily by global equity and compassion seemed to contradict a policy determined by self-interest. Yet in the long run, moral principles and pragmatic imperatives are not contradictory. Respect for nature may seem a desirable moral principle but an impractical restraint on profits and prosperity in the immediate future. However, in the more distant future, environmental protection is prudent as well as moral. Similarly, many people in the 1970s might believe that war would be prudent to stop communist advances and that the political conflict between U.S. capitalism and Soviet communism justified nuclear deterrence. But by 2080, someone looking back might well think that the differences between United States and Soviet societies in the 1970s, while significant, were small compared to the imprudence of risking nuclear war. Thus governmental preoccupation with maximizing power and wealth in the present and immediate future turned policy away from realizing global humanist values in the long run.

U.S. officials displayed a curiously ambivalent set of assumptions about their own ability to influence history. On the one hand, they were optimistic that they could avoid eventual ecological catastrophe, even though there was little empirical basis in past performance for this notion. Likewise, they thought they could partially control Chilean society, or avert nuclear destruction during moments of crisis. This reflected a strong belief that

374

they could influence the direction of historical events. On the other hand, they assumed that they were powerless to change the structure of the international system in order to increase human cooperation and global equity. This ambivalence once again grew out of their own vested interests. Both their optimism about averting crises and manipulating political events and their pessimism about system change to curb Darwinian national appetites justified the acquisition of further power and wealth by the United States.

NATIONAL PARTISANSHIP

Rather than recognize the positive links among all human beings, officials practiced national partisanship. The government rewarded friends and punished enemies. Thus it was "natural" to give much more aid to authoritarian Pakistan, an ally, than to more populous and democratic India, a nonally. A radical Chilean government should be punished, but a pro-U.S. Chilean dictatorship which abolished civil liberties while compensating U.S. corporate owners should receive aid. The equity-seeking countries at the Caracas conference were viewed as ideological, rigid, and unreasonable. Equity-denying proposals for harvesting nodules were nonideological and reasonable.

The U.S. government failed to practice reciprocity. "Equal access" to the common heritage for U.S. officials meant those states with the most technology got the most nodules. It did not mean equal benefits for all. The United States insisted on unlimited nuclear capability for itself, but it sought to discourage other nations from acquiring equal power. Within their distorted model of reality, U.S. officials could condone deployment of thousands of nuclear warheads by the United States and simultaneously condemn India for one test explosion. U.S. corporations and the CIA could intervene in Chile, but reciprocal intervention by foreign powers in the United States would outrage the governmental elite. Because the United States had excess capital to export to India, the United States could influence Indian economic decisions, but because India had "excess population" it gained no opportunity to influence U.S. economic affairs.

Because those in power lacked both a sense of human solidarity extending beyond national territory and a long-range view of history, their worldview excluded two dimensions that were crucial to human survival. Without these, policies failed to tran-

375

scend the parochialism and narrow selfishness of the leadership's own vested interests, ethnicity, and historical era. National partisanship flourished in such a congenial environment.

COMPREHENSION OF REALITY

The leadership resisted the examination of opposing views.[10] To entertain perspectives that differed substantially from the official version of reality would open one to the charge of sympathizing with the adversary. Kissinger and Helms did not listen to those who believed that Allende's reforms were desirable, but they repeatedly heard those who saw Allende as the embodiment of evil. To take a second example, advocates of sharing the common heritage on the basis of population and need were unheard among senior officials in Washington. It did not matter that such resource allocation would have advanced equity, been reasonable, and reflected the highest ideals in the United States own value tradition. Such allocation would have been a softhearted giveaway.

Because they refused to consider alternative views seriously, those in high office lacked objectivity. They characteristically expressed support for a lofty world order principle, and then carried out a policy that denied the principle in practice. What in reality were targets for new deployments of more advanced weapons, officials called ceilings for arms control. Strategically motivated foreign aid was labeled "humanitarian." Several administrations described intervention to undermine self-government as protection of democracy. Weak pollution standards with no international enforcement became environmental protection.

Officials lacked objectivity also because they derived their self-identity and prestige from the organizations they served. Loss of national power eroded self-importance. Enhancing national power was exhilarating. Similarly, within the nation, such officials fought against decreased budgets for their governmental department or corporation because that signalled a demise of their own importance. If they thought about the global interest at all, they equated it with the national interest, and the national interest with their organization's or department's interest.[11] Defense officials wanted to build redundant weapons, which they justified as being vital to U.S. security, in order to maintain a powerful self-image for themselves and their own department. ITT officials fought to protect their investments in

Chile by arguing that Allende posed a threat to the security of the United States. The National Petroleum Council and American Mining Congress advanced their interests in the Law of the Sea debate by saying that undersea soft and hard minerals were essential to the strategic position of the United States. The Pentagon advanced the same justification for its pleas to let nuclear submarines sail through narrow waters without surfacing.

The need to serve vested economic and political interests distorted the perceptions of the most astute officials. For example, Secretary Kissinger several times explained why the U.S. government had been so slow to understand the world food problem. "Until 1972," he said, "we thought we had inexhaustible food surpluses, and the fact that we have to shape our policy deliberately to relate ourselves to the rest of the world did not really arise until 1973."[12] Of course, starvation had been a problem for many years in some parts of the world, and for more than a decade well-known demographers had specifically predicted a world food shortage in the 1970s.[13] That a person as intelligent as Henry Kissinger could believe up until 1972 that the world had "inexhaustible food surpluses" and that the United States did not need to shape its policies "deliberately to relate . . . to the rest of the world" demonstrated the resistance of official minds to unpleasant truths.

This bureaucratically-reinforced, nationalist version of reality produced psychological and material incentives to seek further U.S. advantages through competition with other nations. These incentives drowned out any inclination toward recognizing a global human interest. Unable to look beyond the statist, Westphalian image of the world, U.S. leaders were ill-equipped to guide the international system toward the twenty-first century.[14]

The official operational code violated both reason[15] and preferred moral values. In their actions on behalf of the United States, officials developed new weapons of mass destruction aimed at extinguishing life in scores of cities, trampled the rights of Chilean social reformers, squandered vital opportunities to advance international environmental protection, and designed aid policies that caused untold persons to starve who might have lived and others to suffer needlessly. Yet these same officials did not see themselves as insensitive, self-serving, or shortsighted. Instead, they saw themselves as responsive to the call of duty as they perceived its demands within the nation-state system.

377

Some simple defense mechanisms enabled those in power to profess one value while implementing a contrary one. Reason and consciousness were isolated from action to escape the potential pain attending unreasonable and unconscionable acts. There were several modes of absolution. The unconscious lie was a belief that one should know to be false but has come to believe is true.[16] Many examples exist in the four case studies. Officials at the Caracas conference believed that their proposals for equal access to the common heritage would produce a fair share of the harvest. Some CIA officials believed that clandestine intervention to overturn the results of a free election would protect democracy. Aid officials believed that assistance in behalf of strategic advantage or against socialism was genuinely humanitarian.

The "need not to know" also freed officials of responsibility that they should have taken seriously. Congress for months deliberately avoided ferreting out the facts about the Chilean intervention. Once investigations were begun, members of Congress failed to press most witnesses on crucial issues. When evidence of perjury arose, Congress quickly closed the issue and chose not to investigate further in order to avoid ruining the reputations of some longtime friends and acquaintances in the executive branch.

By taking a narrow view of issues and by denying information that did not fit their limited image of reality, officials decreased the scope of their felt responsibilities. In each of the case studies, they refused to analyze their policy preferences within a larger value context that might reveal the moral bankruptcy of their actions. They chose not to articulate the concrete consequences of their behavior viewed as a process of value realization. At the Law of the Sea Conference, U.S. leaders chose not to tailor policy to a calculation of what would maximize benefits for humanity and the environment. Instead, they began by articulating the goals of oil, mining, and naval interests. From there they moved to an explanation of what concessions the rest of the world must make to accommodate U.S. interests. Similar criticisms could be made of the Vladivostok-legitimized deployment of MIRVs as a measure of arms control, the use of foreign aid to bolster strategic interests instead of serve human needs, and the secret intervention to oppose self-determination. In each case, global humanist values, which would have served universal human needs instead of national advantages, were turned on their heads by isolating and narrowing the context for analysis.

378

Thus more weapons for war became "an historic step forward" in arms control; aid to buy friends for strategic advantages became humanitarian assistance; reversal of self-determination became protection of democracy; and self-serving exploitation of marine resources by the already resource-wasteful United States became respect for the common heritage. Only when seen in the wider value context were official claims visibly untrue.

Those in power lacked empathy for the poor. They seemed to fear that policy based on identity with the poor would make the United States less prosperous or a weak participant in the power-seeking international arena. Clearly, U.S. officials would have advocated different behavior if they had been born in sub-Saharan Africa or a peasant village of southern Asia. They avoided the psychologically troublesome consequences of information that did not dovetail with personally and nationally self-seeking behavior. By believing that they did not need to understand the views of those with whom they differed, they could overlook the advice of those sympathetic to disarmament, global equity, Allende reforms, or radical measures for environmental protection. Through the processes of unconscious, selective perception and deliberate decision about what they needed to know and understand, it was possible for highly respected officials who were good parents and neighbors to commit acts with profoundly inhumane consequences. Their reasonable behavior in some areas of life was not matched by reasonable behavior in other areas.

As we have seen, the manipulation of language was one of the most effective means of deception. Although official behavior had a generally negative or regressive impact on the prospects for world order reform, official rhetoric often supported the four preferred world order values. This disarmed governmental critics and blurred the distinction in the public's minds between the genuine reformer and the rhetorically progressive but politically reactionary leader. For example, to support the "management of global interdependence" may have meant structural reform in conformity with global humanism, or—as it did for U.S. officials—enlistment of the rest of the world's cooperation to protect existing trade, energy, consumption, political, and military arrangements in which the United States enjoyed preeminence.

On the other hand, to embrace global humanist values, even if only rhetorically, was probably a favorable portent. During the

379

last three decades rhetoric seemed increasingly supportive of some global humanist values. This reflects a changing mythology that eventually may provide the basis for system change. A fundamental gap between behavior and rhetoric is an attribute of a transition period between different systems of social order.[17] Rhetoric may begin to take into account present realities, even though policy substance remains patterned on past habits rather than present needs. Rhetoric in support of preferred values is better than no support at all, because it provides a new standard by which to judge behavior. Milton Rokeach, the well-known student of human values, has reported that humans possess a psychic need to believe that their behavior conforms with their professed values.[18] Thus by noting the gap between rhetoric and behavior, eventually officials may be encouraged to move behavior toward rhetoric.

Perhaps more importantly, frequent repetition of preferred values encourages the public to believe that the values should be honored. This may in the long run have a political impact. Historic repetition of the idea that all people are created equal eventually eased social acceptance of belated changes for sexual and racial equality. The decades of inequality, however, suggest that favorable rhetoric means little without accompanying political struggle to stimulate behavioral change.

Many of the ideas that U.S. officials advanced did indeed disguise reality for the public and inhibit and deflect genuine efforts to reform the international system. Government spokespersons told the public that the United States was making all possible efforts to disarm, to help the poor, to encourage human rights, and to protect the environment. The preceding case studies show that this picture was false. Because many persons erroneously believed government reports were true, they failed to support genuine change. They vented their indignation for the arms race primarily upon the Soviet Union. They viewed poverty as a hopeless tragedy rather than as an unnecessary condition resulting from unfair economic structures. They blamed denial of human rights on military dictatorships instead of recognizing United States complicity in the militarization of the planet. They tempered their disappointment about polluted oceans with the wistful hope that some day a UN agency might do more. Posturing and professions by members of Congress facilitated the executive branch's obfuscation of issues. When questionable executive policies were first reported by the press, chairmen of congressional committees frequently announced they would hold hearings on relevant issues. But usually the congressional action died without producing substantial change. Congressional committees made only weak recommendations after the Chilean intervention. Congress allowed those officials responsible for human rights violations to continue in public office. Useful hearings by Senator Edmund Muskie and Thomas McIntyre on armaments later proved to little avail as the military buildup continued. In the area of marine pollution many of the hearings advanced the interests of oil, mining, and shipping companies rather than environmental protection. And most hearings on foreign aid were relatively unconcerned about achieving a minimum standard of living for all. Thus congressional checks on the executive branch's shortsightedness or abuse of power were so limited that they often simply nurtured the process of misinforming the public. Congressional activity was sufficiently visible to give an air of rationality and legitimacy to policy, but insufficiently penetrating and purposeful to justify the rationality and legitimacy widely attributed to U.S. policy. Congressional efforts were useful for making incremental policy changes within the existing international system, but not for generating support to change the system itself.

The failure of Congress to open debate on a global humanist platform suggests that, while the constitutionally prescribed sharing of powers in the U.S. federal system may work satisfactorily for writing domestic legislation, it does not work well for serving global needs. Too many interests within the United States executive branch, Congress, and the judicial system are all on the same (national) side of the global issues. Instead of the threefold separation of powers extant on domestic questions, there is a threefold concentration of mutually reinforcing powers on global issues.[19] The president, Congress, and even the Supreme Court often agree on policies that are· antagonistic to universal human and environmental needs. Although the authors of the U.S. Constitution successfully averted the abuse of power that might have resulted from monolithic U.S. national government, there is no similar system of global checks and balances against excessive national power abusing the global commonweal.[20]

The work of official mythmakers is well-received by citizens who understandably want or psychologically need to believe in the righteousness of their own government. To favor the preferred structural changes, after all, means recognizing that the existing global structure is neither fair nor life-enhancing. When one is at the top of the existing structure, that conclusion does not come easily or pleasantly. It requires a tacit admission, at least to a limited degree, of one's own past involvement in perpetuating and reaping rewards from the obsolescent system.

HIERARCHY OF VALUES

The four case studies demonstrate that officials gave highest priority to two values: maintenance of the U.S. power position in world affairs, and promotion of economic benefits for U.S. corporations. All other values were subordinated to these two. Officials in practice gave very low priority to the human interest as expressed in the world order values. (See Table 6-2.) The government aimed policies toward preservation of the international status quo in which the United States enjoyed preeminence, whereas the preferred world of global humanism required restructuring the international system. The U.S. government actively resisted progressive steps in each value area.

Table 6-2
Official Priorities on Selected Issues

World Order Value	Issue	Value Priority		
		High	Medium	Low
Peace (V₁)	Strategic arms reductions			X
Economic Well-being (V₂)	Redistribution of wealth to serve human needs			X
Human Rights and Social Justice (V₃)	Respect for self-determination			X
Ecological Balance (V₄)	International control of marine pollution			X

To be sure, peace, economic well-being, human rights, and environmental protection were rhetorically supported. It is possible, as Table 6-3 shows, to formulate isolated value statements in which officials *appeared* to support world order values. But where officials gave a high or medium level of priority to a certain isolated value, their support carried conditions that were disallowable if one genuinely wanted to implement all four preferred values. The positions in lines 1 and 2, 4 and 5, 7 and 8, and 10 and 11 (Table 6-3) sacrifice other values and fall short of a worldview consistent with global humanism. In line 1, for example, peace without diminishing U.S. power would retain national nuclear arsenals (V_1-denying), perpetuate inequity of wealth (V_2-denying), maintain disproportionate U.S. influence over global political and economic issues (V_3-denying), and preserve ecologically hazardous military weapons and patterns of consumption and resource depletion (V_4-denying). A similar set of criticisms could be made about each of the other seven areas in which officials might appear to be giving high or medium support to preferred world order values. In fact, the statements in lines 3, 6, 9, and 12 were more fully compatible with global humanism. Officials shunned those value positions.

The accuracy of this appraisal is borne out by the low priority given to systemic change, regardless of how intensely an official might support a value like peace or human rights. Officials did not endorse positions 3, 6, 9, and 12 because they did not welcome structural change.[21] The general opposition to structural change meant leaders often gave high priority to one of the four world order values while opposing progress in one or more of the other three areas. In effect, this nullified the apparent support for the rhetorically embraced value. For example, self-determination or peace would be supported only if there were no danger of decreasing U.S. power or wealth. Likewise, elimination of poverty would be supported only if its elimination did not unfavorably alter the U.S. position in the overall geopolitical structure.

The introduction or omission of crucial but hidden assumptions during policy debates made many people perceptually confused and politically ineffective. By taking a narrow view of different value questions and by deemphasizing implicit assumptions such as contained in statements 1, 4, 7, and 10, one could plausibly argue that the United States favored peace, universal human welfare, social justice, or environmental protection. But by examining policy on a less abstract level and by emphasizing implicit values, one began to understand that the United States favored these goals under conditions that simultaneously negated one or more world order values. This normative approach reveals the hidden value compensations that officials sought in adopting a posture that appeared to favor the four values of global humanism.

383

Table 6-3
U.S. Value Priorities Viewed in the Context of Implicit Value Assumptions

Value Area	Illustrative value statements with implicit assumptions made explicit	Official value priority		
		Strongly favor	Modestly favor	Strongly oppose
Peace V₁	1. Pursue peace without erosion of present U.S. power and prosperity	X		
	2. Pursue peace with slightly more equitable global distribution of political power and economic advantages		X	
	3. Pursue peace by taking steps toward abolition of the war system and creation of effective central guidance in a world security agency			X
Economic Well-being V₂	4. Fulfill human needs at no political or economic cost to the U.S.	X		
	5. Fulfill human needs by transferring some U.S. wealth to other societies in return for potential pro-U.S. sentiment		X	
	6. Fulfill human needs through redistribution of wealth aimed at global equity and by creation of a world tax and development agency based upon balanced representation of weak and poor			X
Human Rights and Social Justice V₃	7. Implement human rights by demanding self-determination in states not presently pro-U.S.	X		
	8. Implement human rights even if supporting self-determination meant a few pro-U.S. states may move toward less deferential relations with the U.S.		X	
	9. Implement human rights by supporting international			

Table 6-3 (cont.)

Value Area	Illustrative value statements with implicit assumptions made explicit	Official value priority		
		Strongly favor	*Modestly favor*	*Strongly oppose*
	structural changes that encourage internal and international justice and provide transnational monitoring of violations of rights, thus penetrating traditional sovereignty			X
Ecological Balance V_4	10. Achieve environmental protection without additional costs to U.S.	X		
	11. Achieve environmental protection without suffering major competitive disadvantages, but with some alteration of global consumption patterns and the use of U.S revenue to help less developed countries in environmental protection		X	
	12. Achieve environmental pro-.tection through creation of a world environmental authority with power to create and enforce guidelines to protect against worldwide environmental hazards			X

MUTUALLY REINFORCING VALUE POSITIONS

Officials carried out a remarkably consistent foreign policy. They did not serve a particular value in one context and an opposing value in another. On the contrary, their positions in the four value areas were mutually reinforcing. For example, restrictive foreign aid policies (V_2-denying) in Chile dovetailed with covert intervention to undermine self-determination (V_3-denying). These in turn perpetuated the international status quo which augmented United States political and military influence in Latin America (V_3- and V_1-denying). Maintenance of the status quo in the first three value areas enabled the United States to use scarce resources for its own excessive consumption, thus producing an inefficient global relationship between population and resources (V_4-denying).

The reinforcing quality of U.S. positions can be stated more generally. Large military budgets (1) enabled the United States to resist reformist challenges to an inequitable international system; (2) decreased the funds available for realizing V_2; (3) encouraged the militarization of many societies and thereby discouraged respect for V_3; and (4) made implementation of V_4 less feasible because the United States military, corporate elites, and the less developed countries would resist universal standards and supranational enforcement as uncongenial, respectively, to their hegemonial and developmental interests. In addition, these policies would not respect nature or allocate resources for optimum fulfillment of the necessities of life for all people.

In general, officials designed V_1 policies to prevent major rivals or guerrilla movements from modifying the status quo through use of force. U.S. policies in the areas of V_2 and V_3 aimed at aborting nonviolent reform movements for radical change. For example, the government tailored V_2 policies to create Third World allies that would buttress U.S. V_1 policies, to shore up unpopular but pro-U.S. regimes, and to defuse or to repress potential "disorder" from internal social reformers. In the V_3 area, policies were developed which utilized the CIA for manipulation of foreign polities to protect U.S. strategic and economic advantages. Finally, the regressive stance on V_4 to maximize U.S. navigational freedom and access to resources was conditioned by and contributed to U.S. strategic (V_1-denying), economic (V_2-denying), and manipulatory or managerial (V_3-denying) preferences.

The Normative Deficiency of U.S. Policy

The global meaning of U.S. policy was clear: the United States stood firmly and sometimes ruthlessly as a major impediment to the fulfillment of the values of global humanism in a new world order. Officials served a state-centered version of vested interests rather than a new image of order aimed at meeting global human needs. Where global humanist goals only modestly threatened the status quo, as in short-range steps for pollution abatement, U.S. policies protected national interests and at the same time accommodated some imperatives for international cooperation. Where a proponent of global humanism would seek fundamental shifts in the planetary distribution of wealth, power, and authority in order to facilitate disarmament, equitable distribution of wealth, self-determination, and environmental protection, U.S. officials launched counterhumanitarian attacks. Their purpose was to maintain the privileged U.S. geopolitical position in world society. Never, one is forced to conclude, did the United States government vigorously pursue implementation of any of the four world order values in the cases examined here.

The seriousness of this conclusion raises the question: have the selected case studies fairly represented the normative content of U.S. policy? To be sure, some differences inevitably existed among different policies. Nonetheless, by focusing on the fundamental values and structural impact of U.S. policies rather than the idiosyncratic nature of specific issues or the policymaking processes, typical behavior patterns serving a recurrent structure of interests have become clear. An investigation of any phase of arms control policy since World War II would reveal essentially the same value patterns evinced in the Vladivostok accord. Similarly, the findings about implicit values embedded in the aid policy to India could be duplicated by studies of numerous other recipients. The brief discussion of U.S. economic aid to all countries in comparison to the Indian case has confirmed this notion. The study of foreign aid covered all administrations over a twenty-five year period. Likewise, a student of human rights would doubtless find a structure of interests being served similar to the Chilean case, whether one studied U.S. policies toward South Africa, Brazil, the Dominican Republic, Portugal, Indonesia, Iran, South Korea, or South Vietnam. Where the United States more genuinely supported self-determination, the exercise of it frequently meant the demise of another colonial power or a U.S. strategic rival, thus providing potential advantages to U.S. strategic and economic interests. As noted earlier, the Senate Select Committee called the U.S. role in Chile "typical" of other U.S. interventions around the world from the Truman years to the present. Finally, U.S. officials have treated land-based and atmospheric pollution in general in the same manner as marine deterioration. On the related question of resource usage, U.S. food and energy policies also have shown no sense of urgency to abolish hunger.

In short, among the various cases one might select, the instrumentalities for carrying out U.S. policy may differ some-

387

what, but the hierarchy of values and the interests served were conspicuously constant. The constancy applies both to issues and to the two major political parties. The studies show no significant differences among various administrations from 1945 to the present on the issue of structural transformation. Variations are inconsequential when measured against overriding world order issues and the need for system change.

THE CONSTRAINTS OF THE PRESENT INTERNATIONAL SYSTEM

Protecting the preeminent position of the United States was, of course, precisely what officials were expected to do, if one accepted the dynamics of present international relations. The prevailing operational code assumed the perpetuation of a system of sovereign states competing for national advantages. According to the widely accepted "realist" paradigm—whether one preferred the nuances of Niccolo Machiavelli, Otto von Bismarck, Hans Morgenthau, or Henry Kissinger—governments do and should seek to enhance their power positions. The United States, one might argue, constructed a deceptively congenial international structure for implementing Machiavellianism of a most selfish nature. The United States pursued narrow, short-range interests at the expense of others, as many great powers have done in the past. Officials were hypocritical when they claimed that their policies adhered to preferred values more closely than did comparable policies of other states, especially when their respective resources and opportunities are taken into account.

Since other major powers were not vigorously pursuing the values of global humanism, can it fairly be argued that U.S. leaders should have adopted a global humanist operational code in the absence of any global authority? Would that not have been foolish? As the parable of the commons illustrates, it is not rational for one actor to behave as if an overarching authority administers the commons when in fact none exists. The greed of other actors will nullify the self-restraint of the morally most scrupulous. My point here is *not* that U.S. officials should have based their policies on the faulty assumption that a system of global policy coordination already existed. On the contrary, the point is that they should have stopped basing their policies on quite different but similarly faulty assumptions. These were the ideas that (1) a more equitable global system of policy coordination was impossible to create, or (2) if such a system were possible, steps toward its creation should be actively resisted. More positively, officials should have recognized the compatability of the global human interest with their own professed values and then have taken preliminary steps toward the establishment of a just and nonviolent system. These steps might have included, for example, a public announcement that the United States would not be the first country to test or deploy any new generations of weapons, like the maneuvering reentry vehicle, a mobile ICBM, or the cruise missile. Other steps, such as annually transferring 1 or 2 percent of GNP to poor societies, could have been taken to move toward economic equity, probably a prerequisite for establishing global cooperation for a new international economic order, enforcement of international norms for human rights, for war prevention, and for ecological protection. These and similar innovations could have improved the prospects for global policy coordination and structural change without sacrificing any of the professed values of the leadership.

The innovations were not taken because the material interests and psychological orientation of those in power made their worldview or operational code extremely resistant to change. The rigidity of the official outlook was illustrated throughout the case studies and revealed again in a reflective assessment by Henry Kissinger of his own achievements as the president's national security advisor and the secretary of state: "What will probably give me satisfaction in the longer term are structural achievements: the attempt to create a foreign policy based on permanent values and interests."[22] "Structural achievements" were aimed at preserving "permanent" U.S. interests. Kissinger did not favor a new international structure. Nor did he, during his service to two administrations, reassess U.S. interests. For him, they were unchanging. Implicit assumptions about the permanency of U.S. interests and of the state system made Kissinger and his colleagues ineffective and inefficient servants of even traditional U.S. interests, as evidenced in Kissinger's Vietnamese policies, because they did not take into account changing global realities.

U.S. policies produced disastrous consequences aside from the unnecessary human suffering that directly resulted from the policies themselves. Many potential supporters of a movement for a just world order have become disillusioned because they have erroneously believed that humanity's last, best hope (the

389

United States) has been unable to bring a better system into being. The failure to usher in the new age has forced many people back into a self-defeating political posture shaped by the belief that the world is such a hard and cruel place that the way things are now is the way they have to be. Such people acquiesce in an unsatisfactory status quo because they have been discouraged from rising above national parochialism to build institutions capable of furthering a sense of human solidarity.

In practice, the U.S. policy approach has ignored the certainty that when self-seeking national behavior is added up on a planetary scale, the aggregate of many separate pursuits for national advantage will work to the disadvantage of all. The U.S. government designed policies that served its separate (national) interests and took a laissez-faire approach to fulfilling planetary interests. In a system devoid of central guidance, when states compete with one another to achieve national economic and political advantages, officials will not disarm, wealth will not be used rationally to maximize fulfillment of human needs, the drive for overseas political influence and economic exploitation will ride roughshod over respect for human rights, and nationally selfish exploitation of resources plus environmentally hazardous (though economically cheap) waste disposal will occur. A competitive situation encourages those governments with the most economic and political resources to protect and increase their advantages without much regard for the plight of those with fewer resources. Only a planetary political process which opens itself to the politically effective expression of grievances by the have-nots can prevent the imbalances in wealth and power from remaining intolerably unjust. Only by constructing a global umbrella of central guidance to protect humanity's common interest in averting nuclear war and in decreasing poverty, injustice, and ecological imbalance will it become rational for separate actors to cooperate and exercise self-restraint for the good of all.

Justice cannot be achieved without empowering the people who presently lack political and economic resources in order to enable them to express their needs in the political process. This principle U.S. officials flatly rejected in the global area, even though it was precisely the same principle upon which Jeffersonian democracy was based: fair representation is the key to avoiding tyranny, whether by a king, by a distant Parliament imposing an unwanted tax on tea, or by an economic superpower taking advantage of its leverage in the marketplace. Because the human species faces threats that extend beyond national boundaries in their scope, the political process in which these threats can be successfully challenged must necessarily be global.

In examining the complexities of controlling marine pollution, for example, it became clear that the concept of sovereignty and the idea that governments should exercise exclusive control over "their" land or sea divided the planet in a way that made environmental protection hopeless. Separate governments ruling separate territories violated the ecological imperative of planetary unity. Similarly, disarmament will not occur until national arsenals are superfluous for protecting security, and this result will not occur within the existing nation-state system. Wealth will not be redistributed and productive capacity sharply focused on helping the world's poorest people without empowering the weak to influence the allocation of the world's resources. Concomitantly, the rich and strong will be most likely to support reallocation of wealth only when they receive guarantees that the poor are behaving "responsibly," and this cannot be politically and psychologically assured within the existing international system, short of imposing some modern variety of imperialism. Human rights can better be advanced and dependably respected with a transnational authority to arbitrate disputes, to detect violations reliably, and to discourage rights-denying mutual counterinterventions by groups like the CIA and the KGB. Each of the four case studies revealed strong arguments for supplementing sovereign states as prime centers of international decision making with supra- and sub-national centers of new strength and vitality. Some kind of world authority eventually must monitor planetary pollution, ration scarce resources and the right to pollute, enforce pollution standards, and react quickly to disasters in the commons. Other world agencies would be useful to enforce disarmament, to create a tax authority for redistribution of wealth, and to realize human rights.

Therefore, either the national interest, which fashionably clothes even the most unfashionable implicit values and modes of conduct, must be stripped of its prevailing virtuous disguise, or else redefined to make it consistent with the global human interest. If, as I have argued above, there is a growing planetary unity to the functions vital to meeting human needs, then the national interest begins to converge with the global interest, insofar as any threat to the species as a whole threatens every part

391

of it. During periods of growing scarcity, however, the temptation will be to secure resources and power for one national or regional segment of the species, while letting other segments of the species suffer or die. (This is, to a large extent, the operational definition given to the national interest by the superpowers.) Thus the global human interest differs radically from traditional national interests insofar as the former protects the resources of the world for the people of the world, whereas the latter seeks to serve the people of one nation. The contrast between the two interests is as clear as the difference between species solidarity and subspecies solidarity.

We have come to the point in history when even the wisest practitioners of statecraft operating with traditional operational codes based on Westphalian logic are themselves a serious threat to the human species. They frustrate opportunities for improving the quality of our lives. No political leader, however enlightened, who rationally pursues the traditionally defined national interest of his or her own state can realize the preferred world order values. Policymakers serving traditional national interests are agents of the past and subverters of a more humane future.

It is time to discard the idea that an enlightened pursuit of competitive national interests is consistent with the global or human interest. As we have seen, in the world of competing sovereignties it did not seem rational or in the national self-interest for industrial states to give up the deep-sea nodules. Only if acts were inspired by some notion of human solidarity would the use of deep-sea minerals fulfill the most pressing human and environmental needs. It is possible, of course, to argue that the long-range national interest takes into account the good of all. But that is true only if one chooses to take into account the human misery and suffering in the weak and poor societies of the earth. Such extranational concern is frequently resisted by dominant national institutions. Increased understanding may be gained by stating frankly the obsolescence of the national worldview. I have little doubt that current expressions of great power nationalism and the self-seeking policies of sovereign states will eventually be understood to be as morally outrageous as racism is viewed today. None of us, after all, chose the race or the nation into which he or she was born. Privileges that automatically accrue to one's nationality (or race) because of economic and political structures cannot be justified either by reason or the most widely professed moral philosophies of the world.

In summary, the preceding case studies point toward two general conclusions. United States policies were normatively defective because they either failed to advance or actively resisted realization of the four world values. Second, the existing international system severely inhibited the implementation of the same values. One can rightly criticize U.S. officials for shortsightedness and for hypocritical indifference to pressing human needs and aspirations. There was no leadership offered on world order questions and often progressive initiatives by others were opposed. At the same time, the structure of both the domestic and international economic-political orders pressed and to some extent seduced officials to serve the implicit values delineated in preceding chapters. In other words, domestic and international political environments determined policy sufficiently that global concerns were subordinated to narrower, self-serving goals. The political leadership failed to point out to the citizenry that the international system itself inhibited the realization of the values everyone professed to be serving. The dysfunctional nature of the international system and the implicit values of U.S. policy together offered little promise that the future would hold substantially more peace, economic equity, social justice, or environmental harmony than the past.

THE IMPLEMENTATION OF WORLD ORDER VALUES

Organizing for System Change

What can be done to implement the preferred world order values? First, it is wise to acknowledge the obstacles to change. Left to its own pursuits, the U.S. government probably will not lead the way toward a system characterized by more equal distribution of wealth and power. U.S. officials are privileged persons within a national society that is, in global terms, also highly privileged. Unless vigorously pressed, officials are unlikely to favor structural change that would to some extent decrease their preeminent positions. The world's strongest military state is unlikely to be enthusiastic about building a world system in which military power would play no role. The world's richest society is reluctant to promote genuine redistribution of wealth. To wait for the United States government, which enjoys so many advantages in the existing system, to initiate steps toward a new, demilitarized, more equitable system is almost as unreasonable as centuries ago to expect a divine-right king to lead a democratic revolution to abolish his throne and establish majority rule. One of the most important conclusions to draw from this analysis is that citizens who favor the four preferred values should not wait for the governments of the major powers to take the first measures to implement the values. Citizen action will have to precede progressive government policies.

Although the small states benefit far less than the great powers from the present international system, even the elites in the less powerful states enjoy their seats of national power. Thus they are frequently indifferent or hostile to creating more humane global governance. The four case studies show that political change is most needed precisely at the points where power is most concentrated in the existing political order. That is why incremental shifts of policy, not aimed at fundamental systemic change, will do little to realize global humanism.

Existing international organizations, at least for the present, provide only slightly more hope for world order reform because they are designed to serve the interests of the member states. An organization such as the United Nations, however, does contribute symbolic importance and some institutional innovations useful for bringing about systemic change. It symbolizes the idea of universal human solidarity so vital to world order reforms. In addition, some international organizations are doubtless likely to create an authority-accumulating momentum that will increase the degree of global policy coordination, even though it may be unwanted by member states who unsuccessfully resist the historical trend.

A third group of international actors, the multinational corporations, offer less certain results. Although they are more interested than nation-states in peace and functional reorganization of the planet on a nonterritorial basis, they seek a new order to enlarge their markets and profits. Realization of their preferred world might encourage peace between national governments, but it also would concentrate capital and maximize profit for a few instead of promote human rights, protect the environment, or guide productive capacity to focus first on eliminating poverty. In such a world, war between states might be replaced by conflict between transnational classes of poor and rich. Repression of the poor would be likely. One may hope that at some point the U.S. national government and multinational corporations will become allies in the movement toward the preferred world of global humanism, but it would be foolish to expect widespread governmental and corporate sympathy before substantial attitudinal changes have occurred in the United States electorate.

As in the antimonarchical movements of years ago, the large majority of citizens have a long-range interest in developing a global system better able to realize the values of global humanism. Yet U.S. officials have not advanced a system based on those values. Thus in this regard the political leadership has not represented or served the long-range interests of most citizens. Insofar as Washington policymakers violate the interests of U.S. citizens and of humanity as a whole, to that degree the government lacks moral legitimacy, even though it may continue to enjoy political legitimacy which people, acting out of habit or misunderstanding, give to it.

Citizens commonly look to their government for leadership, especially on foreign policy issues. Most people allow the government with its complicated military strategies and intelligence networks to carry out the policy it chooses. This posture flows partly from choice and partly from a feeling of resignation that citizens cannot affect policy even if they try. In any case, most people have been politically and psychologically conditioned to accept a generally passive role toward determining governmental policy that affects their own destiny. They are obedient to a national authority that is now becoming obsolete, and they are socialized to violate their own and the species' long-range interests. No matter how sensible such a citizen response may have been in the past, to continue it will have disastrous results because we live now in an era when *systems*, not simply policies, must be changed. The existing political system and its prime actors lack the flexibility, imagination, and freedom from vested interests to generate the imperative transformation to a new, more humane order. The drive to change the prevailing operational code and thereby the international system will require energy from outside the existing political institutions. Whether one describes the process of transformation as consciousness-raising, fundamental attitudinal change, spiritual rebirth, or revolution, the passive relationship of citizens to authority must be broken in order to implement the preferred values.

A remodeled international system might be engineered without the mobilization of citizens working on behalf of global humanist values. However, such a system would probably be an intergovernmental global hierarchy dominated by a concert of great powers and regional hegemonies that served many of the same people and values as the present system. Such a system would serve, with greater efficiency than ever before, the implicit values that were revealed in the case studies. In short, it would deny the values of global humanism.

The desired change to a preferred world will occur probably only after a globally minded minority educates and organizes an increasingly larger group of citizens to exert pressure for structural change. As Richard Falk once commented: "The renewal of America and more generally the reform of world society will depend on a kind of populism arising among people who lose faith in the capacity of their governments to be the repository of legitimacy and to serve as the valid expression and agency of national interests."[23] Like Ulysses who ordered himself tied to the mast when his ship passed the island of the sirens, citizens must bind themselves to their view of a preferred world future and develop a consensus-building yet nondoctrinaire global belief system, lest they be seduced by governmental rhetoric, the attractiveness of power, or the lure of wealth in the existing order to adopt a posture of subspecific solidarity and to defer to a species-endangering, national authority.[24] Guided by global humanist values and strengthened by a transnational network of local support groups, citizens would detect the deceptiveness of officials who speak of humanitarian concern while they protect a 45 to 1 superiority in national per capita income, or who speak of disarmament while tailoring agreements to legitimize arms deployment in new areas. Without skepticism of the old order, citizens will be misled by officials seeking to pacify and co-opt advocates of change. As each case study showed, officials produced enough policy results to give the appearance of serious efforts to implement rhetorical support for world order values, even though there was no intent to implement structural change.

Even small-scale efforts at local education and political organization for structural change is probably of greater usefulness than more glamorous lobbying in Washington for incremental improvements in current pieces of legislation. It is more important to educate citizens about the fundamental threat the arms buildup poses to humanity than to work to decrease the defense budget by, say, one billion dollars in any given year. (Of course, working at the latter issue may advance the former idea if the issue is posed in structural terms.) Similarly, it is of dubious utility to lobby strenuously for Senate support of an agreement based on revised Vladivostok ceilings, even though it may have some desirable elements, when one instead could emphasize that retaining 1,320 MIRVs or 2,250 launch vehicles is an illegitimate enterprise in the sense that no foreseeable political objective could justify using such weapons in combat. Intellectuals should probably spend less time in cynical complaints about governmental mistakes or in status-seeking cultivation of contacts with current decision makers as a professed technique for change, and more time in developing strategies and organizations to encourage new value consensus and to nurture a world social movement that would eventually bring irresistible pressure to bear on existing structures to move them toward the values of human dignity.

The aim of political activity should be to make fundamental alterations in both the domestic and world geopolitical orders. Disarmament most likely cannot occur without a world security system of some sort, but effective strides toward it depend upon first curtailing the excessive influence of the military-industrial complex within our own national decision-making processes. The creation of a world environmental authority will be needed to save the oceans, but it cannot be established until the National Petroleum Council and American Mining Congress have been bridled and their headlong rush to maximize profit is redirected toward fulfillment of human needs.

One technique for stimulating Washington officials to act more in the global interest is to pass domestic legislation that places the United States at a competitive economic or political disadvantage unless the government negotiates with other states to implement universally the principles that U.S. legislation established nationally. Especially in the area of environmental protection, relatively progressive standards for U.S. producers and shippers in coastal waters encouraged action on both the IMCO and dumping conventions in order to avoid competitive disadvantages. Thus to get international environmental action, one might first pass protective environmental legislation domestically. To stimulate action for disarmament, the U.S. military budget might be cut. To advance the right of self-determination, one might pass restrictive legislation for the CIA and U.S. corporations with foreign investments. To move the United States toward using its diplomatic leverage in OECD to encourage all industrial states to give 1 percent of their GNP to less developed countries, citizens could press for congressional action to set the same target immediately for the United States.

The main drawback in the approach of the preceding paragraph is that the same domestic forces oppose national legislation as obstruct more progressive international action. Pressing for such legislation, however, does give concerned citizens a focus for mobilization and an immediate opportunity to attempt to advance national institutions toward respect for preferred values.

International politics is a value-realizing process. The advocate of global humanism stresses the need for value clarification in the selection of U.S. foreign policy goals. Officials could be required to demonstrate that their arms control proposals will lead to disarmament rather than to a further buildup, that foreign aid will lead to a new structure of economic relationships, that human rights are honored in deed as well as word, that environmental protection will not be sacrificed to military and shipping interests. Rather than uncritically accepting the statement that the government will do what is "required" to serve the national interest, one might ask: Who benefits from this policy? Does it increase the likelihood of peace, equity, justice, and ecological protection?

A movement for global humanism may at times create coalitions of unlikely allies. For example, multinational corporations may eventually provide a powerful restraint on national ambitions that threaten to violate the peace. Thus they could help to realize V_1. In the quest for V_2 and V_3, groups in the less developed countries should forge an alliance with world order activists in the industrial states to help restrain both the power-seeking desires of the superpowers and the profit-maximizing motives of multinational corporations. If domestic environmentalists gain sufficient influence in Washington, then the national government can become an ally in persuading multinational corporations and reluctant foreign governments to respect the environment.

The Selection of Means

Consensus on the values and goals of global humanism is imperative among those seeking to develop a successful transnational social movement. On the selection of means, however, wisdom requires one to remain experimental. Knowledge about political effectiveness is presently too limited to select any single approach to system change. A counterculture life-style in an intentional community may in certain contexts be as useful in transforming society as an academician's scholarship or a candidate's campaign on a global platform.

The values of global humanism do define certain limits for means that may be considered acceptable. For example, if global humanists were able to gain influence in a national government somewhere, it would be inappropriate for them to threaten nuclear war in order to compel disarmament. Because the preferred world is a humane world, respectful of life and nature, and based on human solidarity of all on the planet, the means for change should be nonviolent. Nonviolent action underscores the basic humaneness of the ends sought. It is a powerful force, yet at the same time less threatening to the elites that must relinquish some of their unfair control over power and wealth. Nonviolence facilitates a degree of psychological openness to considering alternative images of world order.[25] Nonviolent means also take into account the allies of global humanism who are within the national bureaucracy, even though reticent and politically outnumbered. Their support will be valuable in the movement for fundamental change.

The consistency between ends and means of global humanists will sharpen the contrast between themselves and governmental spokespersons for the obsolete social order. Many of the contradictions between the present leadership's implicit and professed values in the four case studies could be viewed as the use of means that were inconsistent with the ends professed. Officials said they wanted peace, but they sought to achieve it through threats and the buildup of more weapons of war. The president and secretary of state claimed to want civil liberties for Chileans but they used means that denied human rights and were consistent with authoritarian dictatorships. By requiring that means be more consistent with ends, the movement for change can avoid the kinds of hierarchical command structures, organizations, and actions that so frequently corrupt the existing actors in international politics.

To advocate nonviolent change does not mean that the process will occur without great personal sacrifice by many people. When the world order movement becomes more successful, it

399

will become more threatening to those who resist it.[26] As in the U.S. civil rights movement, people may have to risk their jobs and even their lives to correct past prejudices. Deep political conflict may accompany the decision about whether policies will serve the old interests or the movement toward a new, more humane system of governance. These decisions will not, of course, come all at once. Except in retrospect, it may not even be evident when the tide was turning. The pain of systemic change will be serious. But that pain doubtless will be less severe than the agony of nuclear war, the death of the sea, or the continuation of poverty for one billion people. The pain of change can be no greater than the suffering of the 10,000 persons who died each week as these chapters were written. Those were the people who succumbed from lack of adequate nutrition even though other humans had more food than they needed but did not share it with their poorer coinhabitants of the planet because the latter happened to live on the other side of an economic or political boundary.[27]

Many persons argue that the fundamental changes described above can be brought about only through violent revolution. There are strong historical arguments to support the view that people in positions of political and economic privilege will not relinquish their preeminence voluntarily. Yet the loss of life and the political and military obstacles to such a revolution in the United States would yield an unacceptable cost and uncertain results. Precisely because the political debate and conflict may be attended by bitterness and hostility, it is especially important to make explicit the nonviolent character of the movement for change.

Of course, it is a mistake to focus only upon the negative, conflictual side of social change. More important is the attractiveness of the unifying and mobilizing potential of a vision of human liberation and positive innovation. This vision will become politically more powerful as people from religious organizations, environmental groups, labor unions, the peace movement and many other professional and interest groups build coalitions to abolish war and poverty and to create new institutions for security, social justice, and ecological health.[28]

Indicators of World Order Progress

The indicators of world order progress, which are included at the end of each case study, suggest landmarks which can be used

400

to survey the position of the United States within the world order landscape. These indicators are not the only dimensions of performance that should be examined in appraising U.S. positions on world order values, but they are a starting point. The political activist can use them as criteria for assessing U.S. policies and for questioning candidates running for office.

Most of the indicators also can be used to assess the performance of other great powers. The percentages of GNP devoted to foreign aid or military spending, for example, suggest fairly clear directions when examined over several years. Such figures may be summed for regions or for the entire world to indicate rough movement toward or away from the preferred world order system.

The Transition Process

There is probably an inverse relationship between the interval of time available for system transformation and the likelihood of violence and coercion accompanying the process of change.[29] Moreover, the later that the consciousness-raising process begins, the lower the odds that the emerging global system—if and when it comes into existence—will nurture preferred humanist values instead of new institutional expressions of the old values that now undergird hegemonic structures based upon class and nationality. The longer people wait to act for system change, the more desperate will be the conditions under which change must occur. Ecological problems mount, armaments expand, the gap between rich and poor widens. From the vantage point of global humanism, the years since World War II have largely been lost opportunities. Rather than set long-range goals and plan a strategy for implementing fundamental changes based on a rational appraisal of human needs and respect for nature, U.S. policies have been deliberately designed to maintain and strengthen the structural status quo.

From at least the inception of the Truman Doctrine, U.S. policy was set on an anticommunist course that eventually resisted many radical movements, rather than on a course aimed at eliminating human suffering and injustice. No one can know with certainty whether opportunities like those symbolized by meetings at Vladivostok and Caracas, by AID policy in India, and by Allende reforms will reappear in future policy decisions. But many opportunities that arose since 1945 cannot be repeated. Some opportunities that were missed have already

401

caused untold misery for many people. The coming generation faces unnecessary malnutrition, injustice, and violence because U.S. and other national officials served the values of statism rather than the needs of humanity. For many people, change is already too late. For others it will not come in time to save their desperate lives. For the human species, we can only hope that sufficient time remains to change the course upon which national governments and economic enterprises are now headed.

Our fate is uncertain because irreversible political or ecological trends may be set in motion before their seriousness is recognized. As reported above, for example, we have yet to discover the ecological effects of some hazardous chemicals already set loose in the planet's environment. We will probably have no last chance to vote against nuclear war if a crisis takes us to the brink of violence. The desires of many national governments and corporations for prestige, profit, and energy are so strong that the increase of nuclear power plants and the spread of nuclear fuels around the world pose threats both to the environment and to the effort to avoid proliferation of nuclear weapons. The frightening consequences of human and ecological damage from the use of nuclear weapons in war, in terrorist acts, or from nuclear accidents will produce consequences that will last hundreds of years. It is highly probable that, during the years in which the superpowers discussed the decision to allow 2,400 strategic launchers, they squandered the last relatively easy opportunity to limit and dismantle nuclear arms in time to prevent additional nations from acquiring plutonium and enriched uranium.

U.S. policymakers failed to take seriously the possibility that the United States might some day find itself no longer the most wealthy and powerful society on earth—regardless of what officials now do. Historical experience suggests that a relative decline of United States preeminence, as of Roman grandeur and the British Empire, eventually is likely. A wise diplomacy would create global institutions now to protect humane values long after the United States will lack the power to protect itself by itself. One might expect officials to establish global guidance procedures for peaceful change, for assuring equitable sharing of resources, for respecting human rights and nature so that the descendents of Washingtonians will not suffer a plight similar to the one that the West inflicted on the rest of the world when imperialism flourished and industrial prosperity turned its back on overseas poverty.

402

It is unclear whether the opportunities for establishing those humane and just institutions for future generations will increase in the future. Our children will doubtless long regret the more than three decades wasted since 1945, during which so many energies were needlessly devoted to building massive armaments, to waging ideological warfare, and to isolating admittedly imperfect but nonetheless understandable revolutions in China, Indochina, Cuba, Chile, and elsewhere. Those were years in which the United States could have advanced global equity and human rights without jeopardizing its own security. The United States could have avoided reaping the whirlwind of justifiable resentment that the poor may increasingly focus on the industrial states. From the standpoint of structural change, those were the years of opportunity to achieve great progress without great cost.

Citizens should no longer retain in public office persons who act as if it is certain that the United States should and always will be the greatest military power in the world, the consumer of the most resources per capita, and the owner of the most advanced technology. To say this is not to wish failure upon the United States, but simply to recognize that the tides of wealth, power, science, and organizational skills ebb and flow. We cannot now foresee when U.S. advantages may recede or in what areas of endeavor the lead may pass to other hands. But to assume that the United States will remain number one in so many fields for the indefinite future will prove a regretable form of self-indulgent presumptuousness. Yet the foundation upon which United States foreign policies are based is precisely this erroneous, ethnocentric presumption.

If one contemplates the future with a mind less bound by national culture and historical era than the official mind, one sees more clearly that the United States should now move generously to establish new world and local agencies designed to implement the values of global humanism. To try to preserve such values only within the shell of the United States and its allies will be self-defeating and ultimately impossible. The time may come— indeed is at hand—when the United States will need unprecedented help and cooperation from other parts of the world. Such cooperation cannot be secured and is actively discouraged within the existing international system.

Is there any likelihood that officials will really implement the values of global humanism if they seem to conflict with acquiring

403

further power and wealth? Judging from the investigation of policies that showed the destruction of democracy in Chile, the deployment of additional nuclear weapons that did not increase human security, the lack of enthusiasm for a universal minimum standard of living, and the opposition to international control for environmental protection, it may already be too late to reconstruct the self-serving models of reality that flourish in government offices.

If officials base decisions on a system of values that deny the primacy of global human needs, then it is likely that the future will include more violence, inequity, repression, and ecological damage than the past. Poverty and the debilitating consequences of malnutrition often encourage a high birthrate. Consumerism and materialism of the industrialized states deplete resources and pollute the environment. Therefore, the postponement of economic well-being and equity will continue to increase the pressures upon available resources and systems of waste disposal. If industrialization proceeds with growing populations, the prospects for environmental overload will also increase. The continuation of gross inequalities of wealth is likely to polarize political forces within and between societies as well as encourage the creation of a world system designed for the benefit of the rich and maintained by repressing the poor through psychological, political, and military means. Proliferation of nuclear materials makes it more difficult to avert nuclear war or serious environmental damage.

Realism demands that we note the negative trends evinced in the case studies. Awareness of such trends will help citizens understand that the implicit values served by those presently in power and reflected in the general public are values that threaten the well-being of the species. Thus morally sensitive citizens should take their political future into their own hands. Happily, people are capable of extraordinary attitudinal change and social adjustment when they feel that all persons will share the necessary sacrifices equally, when they are convinced that change is imperative because of external circumstances (such as a diminishing supply of oil), and when the need for change is related directly to the pursuit of higher values. U.S. citizens could, with graciousness and even good spirits, make the sacrifices necessary to implement the values of global humanism if they knew that the purpose was to create a more just global order, to relieve human misery, and to build the foundation for transnational cooperation on other issues.

404

Milton Rokeach has persuasively argued that the political implications of our existing knowledge about value change has not been taken seriously by most social scientists. His studies show that major changes in values, attitudes, and behavior are possible when a person becomes aware of contradictions that exist among his or her fundamental values.[30] Change could be rapid when people eventually become conscious of the contradiction between ranking compassion and peace highly in their system of values, on the one hand, and ranking loyalty and unreflective obedience to the nation-state highly, on the other. Political values represent basic ideological predispositions that are related to many different kinds of attitudes and behaviors. A value change would affect one's positions on specific political issues and one's willingness to take political action.[31]

The values of global humanism provide the foundation for developing a positive vision which can help to mobilize people for establishing more humane governance on a planetary scale. This vision includes dependable nonviolent means to settle disputes, a prohibition against the deployment of nuclear weapons, and the reduction of national military arsenals because they will be superfluous for providing security. It is a world where careful planning and fair distribution can eliminate starvation. By increasing economic coordination and cooperation, poverty and unemployment can be abolished. Human rights might be transnationally monitored and encouraged. The common heritage could be shared equitably according to a formula that recognized the needs of all societies.

Peace, economic well-being, justice, and ecological balance will not be permanently guaranteed by any system, but they can become the goals for action to establish a new system in which their realization would be a reasonable possibility. Economic and political decisions *can* be based upon a genuine feeling of human solidarity. Conflicts will remain in any transformed system, but it is possible to build a wide consensus that decisions ought to serve universal human needs rather than to maximize the power or profit of institutions seeking competitive advantages without regard for human or environmental consequences.

Such a backdrop for political decisions would produce significantly different political results. The bonds that unite humanity need not be envisaged as a sentimental feeling of the people of Chicago for the people of Shanghai. The necessary sort of identity is the far more limited and possible sense of solidarity felt by the people in Florida for those in California. It

405

should not be impossible for the people in Florida to care about the people in Cuba as much as they care about those in California.[32]

Critics will perhaps argue that I have been ungenerous in evaluating governmental actions. Have U.S. officials not done their best to implement the values of world order, but been rebuffed by a hostile world? To be sure, most officials would like to see world peace, food for all, respect for certain human rights, and a clean ocean. However, their behavior reveals that they usually wanted to achieve these global goals only under conditions that did not erode their vested interests or special privileges that attended their leadership position in the world's most privileged society. These narrower interests, especially in the short run, often conflicted with global interests, which remained unrealized because they were not given a high priority. The government and its citizenry have spent more money for achieving a killing capacity that exceeds Hitler's most extreme military hope than for initiating a disarmament process. We have curtailed U.S. food production to keep food prices high rather than feed malnourished children. We have violated self-determination and destabilized another society rather than allow the changes that would be brought about by democratic socialism. We have satisfied a self-indulgent appetite for minerals, profits, and unimpeded military navigation rather than safeguard the marine ecosystem. This painful assessment of U.S. priorities is not mine alone. It is not the result of some ingenious interpretation of events. It is evident from any careful analysis of the impact of U.S. political behavior, as opposed to the rhetoric of U.S. officials. Were it not so, the Vladivostok agreement would not have been called an "historic breakthrough"; children in southern Asia would have been fed; Latin Americans would not suffer today, after years of the Good Neighbor policy, from pervasive, structurally perpetuated injustice and poverty; and at least a few effective measures for global enforcement of pollution abatement would have been initiated.

For U.S. citizens and public officials to want peace only if we can be number one is not to want peace. To want universal economic well-being only if we can continue a wasteful materialism is not to want an end to poverty. To want human rights only if we can protect our dominant power position is not to want justice. To want pollution abatement only if we can have unregulated navigation and continue to consume a disproportionate

406

share of the world's resources is not to want genuine harmony between humanity and nature.

In summary, U.S. behavior failed to support the values of global humanism. Although officials could have helped realize the preferred values, which they often supported rhetorically, the structure of both the domestic and international economic-political systems made supportive behavior unlikely. It will remain unlikely until political values, attitudes, and institutions begin to reflect a genuine sense of human—as opposed to national—solidarity. Pending fundamental changes, the existing array of governmental and internal forces against global humanism will probably either perpetuate the nation-state system until a major trauma occurs, or, in a severely limited way, adjust present institutions to the need for some global organization of economic and political power. Such minor adjustment, however, will not substantially reduce the unfair privileges of the presently well-off, abolish the war system and the weapons of mass destruction, liberate the poor and oppressed, or respect environmental limits.

In a world where system change is desirable and necessary but where dominant institutions resist change, an extraordinary responsibility falls upon the individual citizen, religious communities, and other nongovernmental agencies to bring about the required changes. These groups should make themselves more genuinely transnational and then provide the bridge between the present and the future systems, while pressing institutions with a vested interest in the prevailing structures of power and wealth to join the forces for a humane transformation. Realizing the four values of global humanism will indeed be difficult. But failing to realize them will be disastrous for millions of coinhabitants of our planet, if not eventually for all of human civilization. The road leading to destruction is easy because it is familiar. The road toward achieving peace, economic well-being, justice, and ecological balance is difficult and unfamiliar but promises some hope. Traveling down that road during the remainder of the twentieth century depends upon a popular movement fueled by our own imagination and willingness to act.

407

Notes

ONE. THE ELUSIVENESS OF A HUMANE WORLD COMMUNITY

1. These ideas both support and are reinforced by the present international system. Its roots extend back to the fundamental political changes that accompanied the transformation from feudalism to modern nationalism more than four centuries ago.
2. See, for example, Louis Beres and Harry Targ, *Reordering the Planet*; Barry Commoner, *The Closing Circle*; Richard A. Falk, *A Study of Future Worlds* and *This Endangered Planet*; Garrett Hardin, *Exploring New Ethics for Survival*; Robert L. Heilbroner, *An Inquiry into the Human Prospect*; Ervin Laszlo, *A Strategy for the Future*; Mihajlo D. Mesarovic and Eduard Pestel, *Mankind at the Turning Point*; Dennis C. Pirages and Paul R. Ehrlich, *Ark II*; Jan Tinbergen, *Reshaping the International Order*; Van Rensellaer Potter, *Bioethics*; Warren Wagar, *Building the City of Man*.
3. Exhaustive treatments of the contemporary challenges to the human race are available elsewhere. The reader seeking further substantiation of the assertion that there is a planetary crisis should consult the sources cited in note 2.
4. The discussion that follows is not a critique of the theory of deterrence itself but a statement of several of the instabilities inherent within such a strategy. For a somewhat dated but still useful examination of deterrence, see Philip Green, *Deadly Logic*. Falk has discussed the dangers of the war system itself, and has included a brief critique of deterrence in *This Endangered Planet*, pp. 105-132. For some frequently overlooked criticisms of deterrence logic, see Jonathan Knight, "Risks of War and Deterrence Logic," *Canadian Journal of Political Science*, 6 (1973), 22-36.
5. Paul Doty, Richard Garwin, George Kistiakowsky, George Rathjens, and Thomas Schelling, "Nuclear War by 1999?," pp. 19-25; reprinted in *Current*, January 1976, pp. 32-43.
6. Frank Barnaby, "The Mounting Prospects of Nuclear War," p. 11, and "The Technological Explosion in Armaments," *Bulletin of Peace Proposals*, 8 (1977), 347.
7. The illegal, deep penetration of Soviet airspace by a U.S. spy plane during the height of the tension over the United States "quarantine" of Cuba in 1962 is an example of how easily dangerous mistakes can occur. On this occasion, a number of Soviet fighters quickly took off in response to the U.S. plane. President Kennedy "wondered if Khrushchev would speculate that we were surveying targets for a preemptive nuclear strike." Theodore Sorensen, *Kennedy*, p. 804

409

8. Ibid., p. 795.
9. Ibid., p. 767.
10. Robert Kennedy, *Thirteen Days*, p. 109. Emphasis added.
11. Ibid., p. 93.
12. Ibid., p. 97.
13. Ibid., p. 98.
14. Sorensen, *Kennedy*, p. 807. Emphasis added. The "deterioration" mentioned here was the shooting down of a United States U-2 plane illegally overflying Cuban airspace to photograph the construction of missile sites.
15. Ibid.
16. Ibid., p. 808.
17. Herbert F. York, "Deterrence Gone M.A.D.," pp. 5, 7.
18. For Iklé's statement, see the *New York Times*, September 6, 1974; Fred Iklé, "Nuclear Disarmament without Secrecy," speech before the Council on Foreign Relations, Chicago, September 5, 1974 (Washington, D.C.: United States Arms Control and Disarmament Agency, n.d., mimeo.), p. 5. For other discussions of atmospheric pollution and the ozone problem, see Steven C. Wofsy and Michael McElroy, "HO_x, NO_x, and C_{10x}: Their Role in Atmospheric Photochemistry," *Canadian Journal of Chemistry*, 52 (April 15, 1974), 1582-1591; Richard S. Stolarski and Ralph J. Cicerone, "Stratospheric Chlorine," ibid., pp. 1610-1615; and Paul Crutzen, "A Review of Upper Atmospheric Photochemistry," ibid., pp. 1569-1581; Ralph Cicerone, Richard Stolarski, and Stacy Walters, "Stratospheric Ozone Destruction by Man-Made Chlorofluoromethanes," *Science*, 185 (September 27, 1974), 1165-1166; *New York Times*, September 26, 1974, and November 23, 1975.
19. Study of Critical Environmental Problems, *Man's Impact on the Global Environment*, pp. 127-136; Bostwick Ketchum, "Biological Implications of Global Marine Pollution," in Fred Singer, ed., *Global Effects of Environmental Pollution*, pp. 190-194; Frank Graham, *Since Silent Spring*, p. 113; Georg Borgstrom, *The Hungry Planet* (New York: Macmillan, 1965), pp. 352, 382-383, Commoner, *The Closing Circle*, p. 227; C. F. Wurster, "DDT Reduces Photosynthesis by Marine Phytoplankton," pp. 1474-1475; D. W. Menzel, J. Anderson, and A. Randtke, "Marine Phytoplankton Vary in their Response to Chlorinated Hydro-carbons," *Science*, 1970, p. 167.
20. Of course, U.S. citizens usually are better represented than citizens of smaller nations whose governments lack the economic and diplomatic power to express their views forcefully in other capitals.
21. Jimmy Carter, "Remarks by President Jimmy Carter Videotaped for Delivery to People of Other Nations," p. 1.
22. Lester R. Brown, *By Bread Alone*, pp. 4-7.
23. Harold M. Schmeck, *New York Times*, October 7, 1974.

410

24. Bernard Weinraub, *New York Times*, February 2, 1975; see also Catherine Lerza and Michael Jacobson, eds., *Food for People—Not for Profit*, p. 3.

25. James P. Grant, "U.S. Policy and the Food Parley," *New York Times*, November 3, 1974; Jean Mayer, "By Bread Alone," *New York Times Book Review*, December 15, 1974, p. 19.

26. *New York Times*, November 5, 1974.

27. Ibid.

28. Martin M. McLaughlin, "Feeding the Unfed," *Commonweal*, July 12, 1974, p. 376. Average American consumption was about twice that of Western Europe. See also Brown, *By Bread Alone*; *New York Times*, October 25, 1974.

29. *New York Times*, March 17, 1975; Lerza and Jacobson, *Food for People*, p. 1.

30. *New York Times*, March 17, 1975. The CIA report was based in part on speculation about climatic changes. Although most climatologists doubt that the assumption of climatic changes is presently warranted, the political consequences of food shortages, regardless of cause, could be similar to those described in the CIA report.

31. For a more comprehensive treatment of these themes, see Richard A. Falk, "The Interplay of Westphalia and Charter Conceptions of the International Legal Order," in Richard A. Falk and Cyril E. Black, eds., *The Future of the International Legal Order*, 1, 32-70. See also Richard A. Falk, "A New Paradigm for International Legal Studies," 978-987.

32. John Herz discussed the demise of the territorial state in *International Politics in the Atomic Age*. He revised his assessment of the end of territoriality in "The Territorial State Revisited," pp. 11-34.

33. Garrett Hardin, *Exploring New Ethics for Survival*, p. 254.

34. "On the Origin and Foundation of the Inequality of Mankind," translated by G.D.H. Cole, *The Social Contract and Discourses* (London: J. M. Dent, 1913), p. 194. Kenneth Waltz discusses this passage in *Man, the State and War* (New York: Columbia University Press, 1954), pp. 167-168.

35. Waltz in part suggests this reasoning, *Man, the State and War*, p. 169.

36. This fourfold value framework was first suggested by a transnational group of scholars representing all major regions of the world and participating in the World Order Models Project. Their purpose has been to develop models of a preferred world order for the 1990s. In the early stages of their efforts, they agreed to focus upon these four value areas to provide a basis for studying strategies of world order reform. For an early statement of the objectives of this project, see Ian Baldwin, "Thinking About a New World Order for the Decade 1990," *War/Peace Report*, 2 (January 1970), 3-7. For a more recent statement, see Saul H. Mendlovitz and Thomas G. Weiss, "Towards Consensus: The World Order Models Project of

the Institute for World Order," in Grenville Clark and Louis B. Sohn, eds., *Introduction to World Peace Through World Law*, pp. 74-97. The important products of this project to date are a series of books on "Preferred Worlds for the 1990s." See Falk, *A Study of Future Worlds*; Johan Galtung, *The True Worlds*; Rajni Kothari, *Footsteps Into the Future*; Gustavo Lagos and Horacio H. Godoy, *Revolution of Being*; Ali A. Mazrui, *A World Federation of Cultures*; Saul H. Mendlovitz, *On the Creation of a Just World Order*.

37. The values of global humanism could, of course, be used as yardsticks to measure the foreign policy behavior of any government at various points in time. Such indicators could also be used to judge the relative merit of differing policies advocated by competing sets of leadership within a single country at the same time.

38. For the role of values as guides for decision making, see Milton Rokeach, *The Nature of Human Values*, p. 12.

39. The text of this speech of November 15, 1961 was reprinted in United States Arms Control and Disarmament Agency, *Disarmament*, p. 18.

40. The typology and following analysis of alternative models of world order are drawn in part from the ground-breaking scholarship of Richard A. Falk, especially "A New Paradigm," pp. 999-1017.

41. The political structures of each type of system could vary somewhat. A range of normative orientations is also possible in the first three models, although their structures limit the extent to which they could realize the preferred values. The prospects are most severely limited in the first two examples. The models are described in what the author calculates are their most likely manifestations.

42. See Richard Barnet and Ronald Mueller, *Global Reach*.

43. Clark and Sohn, *World Peace Through World Law*, p. xv. (Italics in original.)

44. Falk, *A Study of Future Worlds*, pp. 224-276.

45. In some cases, development of socially destructive values has correlated more closely with a person's expectation for future conflicts than with the subject's background and experience. For example, Arthur L. Stinchombe found that different images of the future in part determined whether young people rebelled: "the future, not the past, explains adolescent rebellion, contrary to the hypothesis that deviant attitudes are the result of distinctly rebel biographies." *Rebellion in High School* (Chicago: Quadrangle Books, 1964), p. 6, noted in Wendell Bell and James A. Mau, eds., *The Sociology of the Future*, p. 33.

46. Bell and Mau, *Sociology of the Future*, p. 18; Harold Lasswell, *The Analysis of Political Behavior: An Empirical Approach* (London: Routledge and Kegan Paul, 1948), and "The Changing Image of Human Nature: The Socio-cultural Aspect, Future-oriented Man," *American Journal of Psycho-Analysis*, 26 (1966), 157-166; Heinz

Eulau, "H. D. Laswell's Developmental Analysis," *Western Political Quarterly*, 2 (1958), 229-242.

47. Bell and Mau, *Sociology of the Future*, p. 14.

Two. The Vladivostok Accord

1. Stockholm International Peace Research Institute, *World Armaments and Disarmament: SIPRI Yearbook 1974*, p. 123. Hereafter cited as *SIPRI Yearbook*, various years.
2. See Alan Newcombe, Gernot Koehler, and Maire A. Dugan, "The Inter-Nation Tensiometer for the Prediction of War," paper presented at the International Studies Association Annual Meeting, Washington, D.C., February 21, 1975.
3. This approach assumes that nuclear deterrence does not satisfy minimum long-range essentials for security. The failure of deterrence would produce irreversible disaster for perhaps the entire human race, or at least large segments of it. Even the secondary consequences of radioactive fallout, such as the weakening of the ozone shield, could inflict severe suffering upon humanity. A quarter-century of deterrence has not substantially increased human security; instead, it has increased destructive capacity far beyond the minimum necessary even for deterrence.

   Problems posed by deterrence as a guarantor of security are discussed in Richard A. Falk, *A Study of Future Worlds*, pp. 13-17. For a criticism of the war system, see ibid., pp. 96-103 and Richard A. Falk, *This Endangered Planet*, pp. 105-132. An early but still useful criticism of deterrence is Philip Green, *Deadly Logic*. For comments on counterforce strategy, see G. W. Rathjens, "Flexible Response Options," pp. 677-688 and Robert C. Johansen, "Countercombatant Strategy: A New Balance of Terror?," pp. 47-53.
4. "Equality" is used here to mean rough equivalence in military power rather than an identical matching of capabilities at every point along the force spectrum.

   "Disarmament" refers to measures aimed at major arms reductions and the eventual abolition of nuclear and conventional forces used for war. Usually disarmament measures mean large reductions, but they may also refer to small reductions if they are part of a process leading toward general and complete disarmament. Disarmament, as used here, does not include the abolition of equipment used by police for maintaining domestic tranquility.

   "Arms control" is used to refer to policies aimed at stabilizing levels of armaments. Such policies may specify that arms be modestly reduced, increased, or maintained at existing levels.
5. The representative nature of the Vladivostok accord and its appropriateness for assessing U.S. performance on the minimization of collective violence are amplified in the concluding section.

413

6. In a later agreement, the two parties restricted ABMS to one site, since neither country had shown interest in deploying ABMS at more than one site. The agreement entered into force on October 3, 1972. The text for the ABM agreement may be found in *SIPRI Yearbook 1973*.

7. For an analysis of this agreement, see *SIPRI Yearbook 1973*, pp. 1-28. The text for the Interim Agreement is reprinted in Appendix 1.

8. U.S. Arms Control and Disarmament Agency, *SALT Lexicon*, No. 71 (Washington, D.C.: Government Printing Office, 1974), p. 1.

9. The text is in the *New York Times*, December 3, 1974. Hereafter, all direct quotations from officials' speeches or news conferences which are cited from the *New York Times* refer to the texts of official statements.

10. *New York Times*, November 25, 1974; see also Kissinger's statement in *New York Times*, December 1, 1974.

11. "Interview for 'Bill Moyers' Journal.' " *Department of State Bulletin*, 72 (February 10, 1975), 176.

12. *New York Times*, November 25, 1974; for corroborating statements, see *New York Times*, December 1, 1974, and *Department of State Bulletin*, 71 (December 23, 1974), 899.

13. "Secretary Kissinger's News Conference of December 7," *Department of State Bulletin*, 71 (December 30, 1974), 910.

14. *New York Times*, December 3, 1974; see also "Secretary Kissinger's News Conference of December 7," p. 910.

15. *New York Times*, December 7, 1974. Malcolm Currie, director of defense research and engineering, called it a "major breakthrough." See also U.S. Congress, Senate, Committee on Armed Services, *Fiscal Year 1976 and July-September 1976 Transition Period Authorization for Military Procurement, Research and Development, and Active Duty, Selected Reserve, and Civilian Personnel Strengths, Hearings*, p. 2693. Hereafter cited as *FY 1976 Authorizations*.

16. The Soviet Union had 2,031 warheads on missiles and a total of 2,500 warheads on bombers and missiles combined. The United States possessed 7,086 and 7,650 warheads, respectively. Stockholm International Peace Research Institute, *Armaments and Disarmament in the Nuclear Age*, p. 49.

17. Ibid.

18. A .7-megaton warhead is fifty times the size of the Hiroshima bomb.

19. *Department of State Bulletin*, 71 (December 30, 1974), 911. See also Ford, *Department of State Bulletin*, 71 (December 23, 1974), 863-864.

20. E. C. Aldridge, deputy assistant secretary of defense for strategic programs, noted that the Vladivostok agreement had no effect on reloading but only on the number of silos. See *FY 1976 Authorizations*, p. 1741.

21. James R. Schlesinger, *Annual Defense Department Report FY 1976 and FY 197T* (Washington, D.C.: Government Printing Office, 1975), p. II-21. Hereafter cited as *Defense Department Report FY 1976*.

22. Paul H. Nitze, "The Vladivostok Accord and SALT II," p. 160.

23. *New York Times*, November 26, 1974, p. 6.

24. *FY 1976 Authorizations*, p. 469.

25. U.S. Congress, Senate, Committee on Appropriations, *Department of Defense Appropriations, Fiscal Year 1975*, p. 487. Hereafter cited as *Appropriations Hearings FY 1975*. Kissinger's advocacy of a high MIRV ceiling would allow the Joint Chiefs of Staff to complete their existing modernization programs. Leslie Gelb, *New York Times*, December 3, 1974; December 10, 1974.

26. *New York Times*, December 7, 1974; December 10, 1974; February 12, 1975.

27. See Secretary Schlesinger's advocacy of advanced research in all of these areas, *Defense Department Report FY 1976*, pp. II-10, 11, 20-54; Currie, *FY 1976 Authorizations*, pp. 2644, 2694-2709; George J. Brown, chairman of the Joint Chiefs of Staff, ibid., p. 212.

28. U.S. Congress, Senate, Committee on Foreign Relations, *ACDA* [Arms Control and Disarmament Agency] *Authorization*, p. 20. Hereafter cited as *ACDA Authorization*.

29. *Department of State Bulletin*, 71 (December 23, 1974), 862-863.

30. *Defense Department Report FY 1976*, pp. I-9, II-8.

31. *FY 1976 Authorizations*, p. 502.

32. Gerard C. Smith, "SALT After Vladivostok" p. 8. Emphasis added.

33. *New York Times*, November 29, 1974.

34. *FY 1976 Authorizations*, pp. 2640, 2644, 3998. Emphasis added.

35. Ibid., p. 489. Emphasis added.

36. Ibid., p. 2154. Emphasis added. See also statement by John L. McLucas, ibid., p. 468.

37. This point was confirmed by frequent references to the Vladivostok agreement in justifying the need to develop a new M-X missile to replace the Minuteman, and to develop the Trident missile to supplement the Polaris and Poseidon. In each case, officials sought to replace existing weapons with weapons of higher performance per unit. They argued that these should not be subject to the normal fiscal constraints, since new weapons could not readily meet past standards, in terms of increased firepower per dollar spent, if only a limited number of each weapon would be deployed. See statements, ibid., by David C. Jones, p. 489; John L. McLucas, p. 468; Malcolm Currie, p. 2644; James R. Schlesinger, p. 2154.

38. E. C. Aldridge, ibid., p. 2141.

39. In the secretary of defense's classified statement on the FY 1975

defense budget, he said: "Strategic programs . . . affect the prospects for arms control. And specific weapons systems are the coin of this particular realm. Not only are such systems the mediums of exchange; they are also the basis for expanding or contracting the forces. As a consequence, arms control objectives must have a major impact on our planning." For differing interpretations of this statement, see the brief exchange between Senator Symington and Secretary Schlesinger, *Appropriations Hearings FY 1975*, pp. 35-36.

40. Federation of American Scientists, "Scientists Comment on SALT Agreement" (press release of December 12, 1974).

41. Carl Kaysen, former deputy special assistant to the president for national security affairs and consultant to the weapons systems evaluation group of the Department of Defense, told the Senate Arms Control Subcommittee that "if there is no substantial ABM, the only excuse for MIRV then is a counterforce or first strike weapon." United States Congress, Senate, Committee on Foreign Relations, Subcommittee on Arms Control, International Law and Organization, *Arms Control Implications of Current Defense Budget*, p. 75. Hereafter cited as *Arms Control Implications*.

42. See the statement by David Packard, deputy secretary of defense, ibid., pp. 181-183.

43. For example, Senator Edmund Muskie, chairman of the Arms Control Subcommittee, argued that by developing and deploying MIRV "we reduce the possibility of a MIRV limitation." Ibid., p. 183.

44. *SIPRI Yearbook 1974*, pp. 105, 107.

45. *Arms Control Implications*, p. 100. The Limited Nuclear Test Ban Treaty of 1963 was another example of arms control efforts' increasing the pace and extent of military innovation. The United States conducted more tests than it would likely have carried out if the treaty had not been negotiated. See George W. Rathjens, "Future Limitations of Strategic Arms," in Mason Willrich and John Rhinelander, eds., *SALT: The Moscow Agreements and Beyond*, p. 236.

46. Marshall D. Shulman, "SALT and the Soviet Union," in Willrich and Rhinelander, *SALT*, p. 120.

47. Written response from the Joint Chiefs, reprinted in *Arms Control Implications*, p. 43.

48. For discussion of a view contrary to the ideas expressed in this paragraph, see Smith, "SALT After Vladivostok," p. 13. He argued that the prolonged SALT negotiations produced some benefits even if no agreements were reached in the end.

49. *New York Times*, December 1, 1974. Emphasis added.

50. *Arms Control Implications*, p. 25.

51. In assessing the consequences of SALT I, the authors of the *SIPRI Yearbook 1973* came to the conclusion that "the technological arms

race is encouraged and even legitimized" (p. 17). George Rathjens concluded, "I believe that efforts to negotiate a treaty based on the Vladivostok Agreement are more likely to facilitate than to inhibit the acquisition of superfluous strategic arms. The effects on Soviet-American relations are likely therefore to be adverse in the medium and long term if not immediately. . . . Perhaps most serious of all, these efforts are likely to be a stimulus to nuclear proliferation." "Scientists Comment on SALT Agreement," p. 6.

52. See statement by James Schlesinger, United States Congress, Senate, Committee on Foreign Relations, Subcommittee on Arms Control, International Law and Organization, *U.S.-U.S.S.R. Strategic Policies*, p. 18. Hereafter cited as *Strategic Policies Hearings*. See also *Defense Department Report FY 1976*, pp. I-15, 16; II-9, 10; *FY 1976 Authorizations*, p. 2101.
53. *Defense Department Report FY 1976*, p. II-18.
54. See, for example, *Strategic Policies Hearings*, p. 18; *Defense Department Report FY 1976*, p. II-90; *FY 1976 Authorizations*, p. 19.
55. *SIPRI Yearbook 1974*, p. 110.
56. Counterforce capability for hard targets was proportional to the square of the accuracy of the warhead (doubling accuracy increased capability fourfold), whereas it was proportional to the 2/3 power of the yield of the warhead (increasing megatonnage by a factor of eight would increase counterforce capability only four times). See Robert L. Leggett, "Two Legs Do Not a Centipede Make," p. 30.
57. Ibid., pp. 30-32.
58. *SIPRI Yearbook 1974*, pp. 110-111; *New York Times*, March 21, 1971; A. B. Martin, "The Land-Based ICBM," paper presented at the American Institute of Aeronautics and Astronautics, 10th Annual Meeting, Washington, D.C., 1974.
59. *SIPRI Yearbook 1974*, p. 111.
60. *SIPRI Yearbook 1974*, p. 117.
61. Herbert Scoville, "A Leap Forward in Verification," in Willrich and Rhinelander, *SALT*, p. 176.
62. Senator Thomas McIntyre called it a "radical revision of our strategic policy from one of mutual deterrence to one of nuclear warfighting." "Security Through Détente: Limits and Possibilities," speech before the International Studies Council, University of New Hampshire, May 5, 1975.
63. Bernard Feld, "Doves of the World Unite," *New Scientist*, December 26, 1974, p. 912.
64. J. P. Ruina, "U.S. and Soviet Strategic Arsenals," in Willrich and Rhinelander, *SALT*, p. 41. For an appraisal of objections to flexible options see Rathjens, "Flexible Response Options," pp. 677-688.
65. See the secretary of defense's vague justifications for more U.S. weapons, based on the assumed need to equal potential Soviet de-

417

ployments, *Defense Department Report FY 1976*, p. 1-13; *FY 1976 Authorizations*, p. 19; *Strategic Policies Hearings*, p. 18; *Appropriations Hearings Fiscal 1975*, p. 97. See also the statement of Paul C. Warnke, former assistant secretary of defense, in the United States Congress, Senate, Committee on Foreign Relations, Subcommittee on United States Security Agreements and Commitments Abroad and Subcommittee on Arms Control, International Law and Organization, *Nuclear Weapons and Foreign Policy*, p. 55. Hereafter cited as *Nuclear Weapons Hearings*. See also Schlesinger's statement in *Strategic Policies Hearings*, pp. 2, 7, 29, that sufficient targeting flexibility could be achieved with existing weapons and guidance systems.

As early as 1964, Secretary of the Navy Paul Nitze testified that eight on-station Polaris submarines could destroy 25-35 million Soviet people and most of the industrial war-making potential of the Soviet Union; *Arms Control Implications*, p. 42. That was a tiny fraction of the total U.S. force by 1974. Even one-tenth of the U.S. bomber force could inflict damage equivalent to about a thousand Hiroshima bombs; Ruina, "U.S. and Soviet Strategic Arsenals," p. 58. Senator Symington reported that "we have the capacity to destroy the Soviets hundreds if not thousands of times." *Arms Control Implications*, p. 40. Many knowledgeable, independent observers believed that SLBMs alone (which even a new Soviet counterforce strategy could not destroy), were "sufficient to meet our overall needs." See the statement by Carl Kaysen, *Arms Control Implications*, p. 59. If, out of the entire U.S. arsenal, only several Poseidons were to escape a Soviet first strike, they could inflict destruction on the Soviet Union sufficient to make a first-strike strategy unworkable. Thus any alleged threat posed to land-based ICBMs by increased Soviet throw weight could not in itself justify an enlarged buildup of U.S. counterforce. On the absence of need for the new weapons sought, see Rathjens, "Flexible Response Options," p. 681; Kaysen, *Arms Control Implications*, p. 62. On Soviet inability to launch a successful first-strike attack against the United States, either in 1974 or by 1985, see Schlesinger's statements in *Defense Report FY 1976*, p. 1-15; *Nuclear Weapons Hearings*, p. 193; and United States Congress, Senate, Committee on Foreign Relations, Subcommittee on Arms Control, International Law and Organization, *Briefing on Counterforce Attacks*, p. 9. Hereafter cited as *Counterforce Hearings*.

66. *Strategic Policies Hearings*, p. 38. See also p. 19.
67. *Defense Department Report FY 1976*, pp. 1-15, 16.
68. See, for example, *Nuclear Weapons Hearings*, pp. 161-192.
69. Military planners were far ahead of the arms controllers in planning for the future. Even before the Vladivostok accord became a treaty, new weapons were being prepared for deployment after

the potential treaty was scheduled to expire. See, for example, the statement of E. C. Aldridge, *FY 1976 Authorizations*, p. 2119.

70. Schlesinger, *Defense Department Report FY 1976*, p. 1-14. *Appropriations Hearings FY 1975*, p. 89.
71. *FY 1976 Authorizations*, pp. 2079, 2089-2095. See also Schlesinger's statement in *Counterforce Hearings*, p. 8; McIntyre, "Security Through Détente," p. 8; Admiral Thomas Moorer, *Arms Control Implications*, p. 19.
72. McIntyre, "Security Through Détente," p. 8.
73. For a discussion of this point, see Rathjens, "Flexible Response Options"; Johansen, "Countercombatant Strategy," pp. 47-53; McIntyre, "Security Through Détente"; Warnke, *Nuclear Weapons Hearings*, pp. 55, 139; and Muskie, *Arms Control Implications*, p. 145.
74. See Schlesinger, *Strategic Policies Hearings*, p. 35; *Defense Department Report FY 1976*, p. 1-11.
75. *New York Times*, December 3, 1974.
76. Kissinger, "*Newsweek* Interview," *Department of State Bulletin*, 72 (January 21, 1975), 58.
77. *SIPRI Yearbook 1974*, p. 123.
78. Ibid., pp. 159-160.
79. *New York Times*, December 3, 1974.
80. *New York Times*, December 8, 1974.
81. *New York Times*, December 18, 1974.
82. Outlays are funds actually spent, whether authorized in the current or previous years. Budget authority suggests the trend of future outlays.
83. *Defense Department Report FY 1976*, Appendices A, B, and C.
84. John W. Finney, *New York Times*, February 9, 1975. Pentagon calculations showed that 1974 defense spending was 18 percent below the level of 1964, before the Vietnam buildup. In taking account of inflation to arrive at this figure, however, officials not only compensated for price increases because of inflation but also for military pay increases. This questionable accounting procedure ignored that most of the pay increases were made not to offset inflation, but because of a political decision in 1968 that the military should receive higher pay, comparable to that of civilians.
85. *New York Times*, February 4, 1975; *Defense Department Report FY 1976*, Table 2, Appendix B.
86. *New York Times*, November 19, 1975.
87. *FY 1976 Authorizations*, p. 28; Donald H. Rumsfeld, *Annual Defense Department Report FY 1977*, pp. 28-30.
88. *Defense Department Report FY 1976*, p. 1-26, Appendix A, p. A-1.
89. *New York Times*, February 7, 1975.
90. *New York Times*, December 4, 1974.
91. *FY 1976 Authorizations*, pp. 2001-2003.

92. U.S. Congress, House, Committee on Armed Services, *Hearings on Military Posture and H.R. 3689, Department of Defense Authorization for Appropriations for Fiscal Year 1976 and 197T*, p. 985. Hereafter cited as *Military Posture Hearings*.

93. *FY 1976 Authorizations*, pp. 2773, 2789, 3995; *Military Posture Hearings*, p. 237.

94. *Appropriations Hearings Fiscal 1975*, pp. 483-484.

95. *FY 1976 Authorizations*, p. 2775.

96. "Remarks by Hon. James R. Schlesinger, Secretary of Defense, at Rollout Ceremony for B-1 Bomber," ibid., p. 2115.

97. " 'Bill Moyers' Journal,' " p. 176.

98. *New York Times*, December 3, 1974.

99. " 'Bill Moyers' Journal,' " p. 176.

100. *Department of State Bulletin*, 71 (December 23, 1974), 863, 865; *New York Times*, November 25, 1974.

101. *Department of State Bulletin*, 71 (December 30, 1974), 910. See also " 'Bill Moyers' Journal,' " p. 176.

102. *New York Times*, December 23, 1974.

103. *Department of State Bulletin*, 71 (December 30, 1974), 912. Emphasis added.

104. Ibid., p. 913.

105. Ibid. Emphasis added.

106. Editorial, *New York Times*, December 26, 1974; see also the editorial of November 29, 1974.

107. Frye, "U.S. Decision Making for SALT," in Willrich and Rhinelander, *SALT*, p. 76; see also Donald R. Westervelt, "The Essence of Armed Futility," p. 703.

108. Kissinger, "*Newsweek* Interview," p. 58.

109. "In essence, both sides have agreed not to challenge the effectiveness of each other's deterrent missile forces." "Current Negotiations on Arms Limitations," *U.S. Arms Control and Disarmament Agency*, No. 72 (April 1974), p. 1.

110. See *SIPRI Yearbook 1973*, p. 18.

111. For the text of the treaty, see U.S. Arms Control and Disarmament Agency, *International Negotiations on the Treaty on the Nonproliferation of Nuclear Weapons* (Washington, D.C., 1969).

112. See Alva Myrdal, "The High Price of Nuclear Arms Monopoly," p. 30.

113. The text is in U.S. Arms Control and Disarmament Agency, *Arms Control and Disarmament Agreements* (Washington, D.C.: Government Printing Office, 1975), pp. 40-42. For comprehensive and penetrating analysis of the failure of the superpowers to work seriously for arms reductions, see William Epstein, *The Last Chance*, and Alva Myrdal, *The Game of Disarmament*.

114. Myrdal, "High Price," p. 36.

115. *New York Times*, June 26, 1975.

116. U.S. Arms Control and Disarmament Agency, *World Military Expenditures and Arms Trade 1963-1973*, p. 72. Hereafter cited as *World Military Expenditures*.

117. U.S. Congress, Senate, Committee on Foreign Relations, *Foreign Assistance Authorization 1974*, p. 245.

118. U.S. Congress, House, Committee on Foreign Affairs, *Fiscal Year 1975 Foreign Assistance Request*, p. 74. Hereafter cited as *FY 1975 Foreign Assistance Request*.

119. *New York Times*, April 14, 1975.

120. Ibid. The United States' share of total world exports was 54.5 percent; the Soviet share was 27.5 percent.

121. *Foreign Assistance Authorization 1974*, p. 69.

122. An analysis of the State Department study is in the *New York Times*, October 21, 1975.

123. The secretary of defense has used financial and political inducements to expand U.S. arms sales abroad. For example, see inducements to Belgium in 1975 to purchase F-16s, *New York Times*, June 5, 1975.

124. *Foreign Assistance Authorization 1974*, p. 248. This statement was the written response of the Department of Defense to questions raised in the Senate Foreign Relations Committee.

125. *The Baltimore Sun*, February 26, 1975. The Arabian American Oil Company (owned 60 percent by Saudi Arabia and 40 percent by Exxon), as well as Texaco, Standard Oil of California, and Mobil Oil have exported from the United States "firearms, ammunitions, explosives, aircraft and related articles, military electronics, auxiliary military equipment and miscellaneous articles." From the report of the State Department's Office of Munitions Control, quoted in the *New York Times*, October 21, 1975.

126. *FY 1975 Foreign Assistance Request*, p. 80. Schlesinger also said the export of arms was used to continue "an uninterrupted access to [foreign] bases." Ibid., p. 44.

127. *New York Times*, April 14, 1975.

128. *New York Times*, February 20, 1975.

129. Schlesinger, *FY 1975 Foreign Assistance Request*, p. 44.

130. *FY 1976 Authorizations*, p. 433.

131. Charles R. Gellner, senior specialist in international relations, Foreign Affairs Division, Congressional Research Service, in U.S. Arms Control and Disarmament Agency, *The International Transfer of Conventional Arms: Report to Congress*, p. CRS-11. Hereafter cited as *Transfer of Arms*. This point is confirmed by Vice Admiral Ray Peet, director of Defense Security Assistance Agency, in *FY 1975 Foreign Assistance Request*, pp. 321-322, and by ACDA in *Transfer of Arms*, p. 94.

132. *Transfer of Arms*, p. 88.

133. Cf. Herbert York, who served on the president's Scientific Advi-

421

sory Committee during two administrations: "Over the last 30 years we have repeatedly taken unilateral actions that have unnecessarily accelerated the race. Our unilateral decisions have set the rate and scale for most of the individual steps in the strategic-arms race." *Race to Oblivion*, p. 230. See also Richard J. Barnet, *The Economy of Death*, especially chap. 11, and *Who Wants Disarmament?*; Jerome H. Spingarn, "The Cosmetics of Disarmament," *War/Peace Report*, 13 (June 1974), 11-13; Robert C. Johansen, "Arms Control Chicanery," *War/Peace Report*, 13 (June 1974), 16-19.

134. Rathjens, "Future Limitations of Strategic Arms," p. 231.

135. See Barnet, *The Economy of Death*; York, *Race to Oblivion*; Ralph E. Lapp, *The Weapons Culture*; John M. Swomley, *The Military Establishment*; Clark Mollenhoff, *The Pentagon*; Seymour Melman, *Pentagon Capitalism*; Fred J. Cook, *The Warfare State*; Tristram Coffin, *The Armed Society*; George Thayer, *The War Business*.

136. For comment on the need to remain number one, see the statements by Nixon, quoted in *Arms Control Implications*, p. 44; in Chalmers Roberts, "The Road to Moscow," Willrich and Rhinelander, *SALT*, p. 32; Schlesinger, *Defense Department Report FY 1976*, p. II-1; *Appropriations Hearings FY 1975*, p. 65; *Military Posture Hearings*, pp. 92, 238; *Nuclear Weapons Hearings*, p. 173; Malcolm Currie, in *FY 1976 Authorizations*, p. 2639.

137. Press conference of December 6, 1974, Department of Defense, mimeo.

138. *Arms Control Implications*, p. 8.

139. *Defense Department Report FY 1976*, p. II-7.

140. *Department of State Bulletin*, 71 (December 30, 1974), 913.

141. Ted Greenwood and Michael L. Nacht, "New Nuclear Debate," p. 778.

142. *FY 1976 Authorizations*, p. 2639.

143. *Military Posture Hearings*, pp. 238, 246.

144. See Rathjens, "Future Limitations of Strategic Arms," p. 230; Herbert York, *Arms Control Implications*, p. 99.

145. He made this claim in *Department of State Bulletin*, 71 (December 30, 1974), 910.

146. Ibid.

147. Ibid.

148. Gerard Smith, former director of the Arms Control and Disarmament Agency, has noted that the 1972 ABM Treaty "bans deployment of a defensive system not based on the type of ABM existing in 1972, thus banning exotic future systems. . . . The ABM Treaty proved that qualitative restrictions can be negotiated." See Gerard C. Smith, "SALT After Vladivostok," p. 11.

149. Leslie H. Gelb, "Our Arms Offer Rejected by U.S.," *New York Times*, January 18, 1976.

150. *Department of State Bulletin*, 71 (December 30, 1974), 910.

151. *Appropriations Hearings FY 1975*, p. 293.
152. *New York Times*, June 16, 1975.
153. *New York Times*, December 6, 1974.
154. The following brief discussion of technocratic pressures for weapons innovation is based in part on *SIPRI Yearbook 1974*, pp. 125-128.
155. Ibid., p. 127.
156. Herbert York, in *Arms Control Implications*, pp. 83, 99; Rathjens, "Future Limitations of Strategic Arms," p. 228; Alton Frye, in Willrich and Rhinelander, *SALT*, p. 97.
157. *Nuclear Weapons Hearings*, p. 140. Emphasis added. Schlesinger confirmed this description, ibid., p. 197.
158. General William J. Evans, deputy chief of staff for research and development, for example, argued that the United States needed to build additional B-1 prototypes to keep Rockwell plants operating. *Fiscal Year 1976 Authorizations*, p. 1962.
159. See *SIPRI Yearbook 1974*, p. 126.
160. *Nuclear Weapons Hearings*, p. 190.
161. *FY 1976 Authorizations*, p. 205.
162. *New York Times*, December 3, 1974.
163. *New York Times*, April 11, 1975.
164. *New York Times*, December 18, 1974.
165. *New York Times*, December 4, 1974.
166. This debate included the following articles in *Foreign Policy*: Albert Wohlstetter, "Is There a Strategic Arms Race?" pp. 3-20 and "Rivals, But No 'Race,' " pp. 48-81; Philip Odeen, "In Defense of the Defense Budget," pp. 93-108; Paul H. Nitze, Joseph Alsop, Morton H. Halperin, and Jeremy Stone, "Comments," No. 16, pp. 82-92; Paul H. Nitze, "The Strategic Balance Between Hope and Skepticism," pp. 136-156; David Aaron, "SALT: A New Concept," pp. 157-165; Paul C. Warnke, "Apes on a Treadmill," pp. 12-29; Johan Jorgen Holst, "A Strategic Arms Race? What is Really Going On?", pp. 152-162; Michael L. Nacht, "The Delicate Balance of Error," pp. 163-177; Albert Wohlstetter, "How to Confuse Ourselves," pp. 170-198.
167. Wohlstetter, "How to Confuse Ourselves," p. 179.
168. Ibid., p. 198.
169. Wohlstetter, "Rivals, But No 'Race,' " p. 57. The same point is made in Wohlstetter, "How to Confuse Ourselves," p. 176.
170. Wohlstetter, "Rivals, But No 'Race,' " pp. 79-80.
171. Wohlstetter, "How to Confuse Ourselves," p. 178. Emphasis added.
172. Of course, if spending decreased every year until it was less than required for weapons maintenance, then a genuine change in direction—toward disarmament—would occur through the decay of existing weapons.

423

173. See the discussion of the data in Nacht, "The Delicate Balance of Error," p. 172; also, Alton H. Quanbeck and Barry M. Blechman, *Strategic Forces*, pp. 91-94.

174. Wohlstetter, "How to Confuse Ourselves," pp. 176-177.

175. For example, see the statement of Senator Clifford Case in *Arms Control Implications*, p. 179.

176. Ibid., p. 167.

177. For discussion of the idea that recent innovations have impaired security, see Schlesinger, *Nuclear Weapons Hearings*, pp. 167-168; Edmund Muskie, *Arms Control Implications*, p. 23; Paul Warnke, *Nuclear Weapons Hearings*, pp. 206-207; Carl Kaysen, *Arms Control Implications*, pp. 66-67.

There was no widespread public debate about the real possibility that the citizens of both the Soviet Union and the United States, to say nothing of the rest of the world, would all have been better off if only one side had such a substantial counterforce capability, regardless of whether it was Soviet or American. Even if a partial first-strike capability could not have been altogether prohibited, the security of the people of the United States could probably have been enhanced by letting the Soviet Union go ahead with such a capacity but preventing the U.S. government from matching it. If only one side had such a capability, "crisis instability" could have been avoided.

178. *New York Times*, December 4, 1974.

179. *New York Times*, December 1, 1974.

180. Immediately after the Vladivostok meeting, Secretary Kissinger said that the "Backfire" and the FB-111 were not considered strategic weapons and therefore did not come within the overall ceilings. Since the Soviet Union had deployed only 25 planes within a year after the Vladivostok meeting, their impact on the Soviet strategic force was not large. The dispute, however, posed a threat to the consummation of the entire agreement. For an analysis of the shifting Kissinger and Schlesinger positions, see John W. Finney's article in the *New York Times*, October 10, 1975. See also *New York Times*, October 14, 1975, and October 15, 1975.

181. At Vladivostok, the participants specified that airplane-launched missiles with a range of more than 360 miles were to be considered as strategic delivery vehicles. Later, the United States maintained that this understanding included only ballistic missiles which follow a high trajectory after being launched. The Soviet Union contended that the agreement also covered airbreathing missiles which follow a low trajectory and may be guided constantly during their flights. See John W. Finney, "The Soviet Backfire Bomber and the U.S. Cruise Missile," *New York Times*, December 3, 1975.

182. *New York Times*, June 16, 1975; October 15, 1975.

183. *New York Times*, December 3, 1975.

184. Address at the United Nations, March 17, 1977, text in *New York Times*, March 18, 1977; commencement address at Notre Dame University, text in *New York Times*, May 23, 1977.

185. Text in *New York Times*, January 21, 1977.

186. The Carter administration approved the first stage of development for a more accurate and powerful warhead, the Mark 12 A, which would sharply increase the ability of the United States to attack Soviet missiles in their silos. Improved guidance systems were to be installed on Minutemen in 1977, with the new warhead itself planned for completion in 1979. *New York Times*, June 1, 1977.

187. *New York Times*, October 23, 1977.

188. *New York Times*, February 13, 1978.

189. *New York Times*, January 30, 1977. See also his comments in *New York Times*, October 11, 1977; address at Notre Dame University, *New York Times*, May 23, 1977.

190. *New York Times*, February 13, 1978.

191. *New York Times*, October 11, 1977.

192. *SIPRI Yearbook 1974*, pp. 508-509. The data for 1973 are preliminary.

193. Marek Thee, "The Nuclear Momentum: Arms Race and Disarmament," *Internasjonal Politikk* (Oslo), No. 1 (1975), reprinted in part in *Bulletin of Peace Proposals*, 6, No. 2 (1975), 133.

194. Many advocates of nuclear deterrence have informed Congress that deployment of additional weapons was wasteful and unnecessary for protecting security. Carl Kaysen, a former consultant to the Defense Department's Weapons Systems Evaluation Group, and deputy assistant to the president for national security affairs, testified: "It is my judgment that we would be making no compromise with our security and sustaining no deterioration of the effectiveness of our deterrent posture if we forewent all new developments and deployments of land-based ICBMs and long-range aircraft. . . . [T]here are no reasons that can justify planning the deployment of new systems." *Arms Control Implications*, p. 62.

195. For discussion of this point, see Falk, *A Study of Future Worlds*, pp. 50-52, 224-276, and "Arms Control, Foreign Policy, and Global Reform," p. 52, n. 36; W. Michael Reisman, "Sanctions and Enforcements," in Cyril E. Black and Richard A. Falk, eds., *The Future of the International Legal Order*, III, 273-335.

THREE. UNITED STATES FOREIGN AID TO INDIA

1. The justness of the current distribution of wealth is considered here, as well as the provision of necessities for physical existence, although the distributive issue could as well be viewed as part of worldwide human rights (V_3).

2. *New York Times*, January 21, 1949.

425

3. Data for these computations are taken from U.S. Agency for International Development, Office of Statistics and Reports, *U.S. Economic Assistance Programs Administered by the Agency for International Development and Predecessor Agencies, April 3, 1948 to June 30, 1971*; after 1971, U.S. Agency for International Development, Statistics and Reports Division, Office of Financial Management, *U.S. Overseas Loans and Grants and Assistance from International Organizations: Obligations and Loan Authorizations, 1945-73, 1945-74, 1945-75, 1945-76.*

4. See Jagdish N. Bhagwati, *Amount and Sharing of Aid*, pp. 14-15. Some Marxist writers, in contrast, assume that the aid is "excess capital" and that the various returns derived from loans to India could be interpreted as producing net returns for the donating country. This would be true if the opportunity cost were zero.

5. United States Congress, Senate, Committee on Foreign Relations, *United States Participation in ADB* [Asian Development Bank] *and IDA* [International Development Association], p. 45. Hereafter cited as *ADB Hearings*.

6. See Willard L. Thorp, *The Reality of Foreign Aid*, p. 210; *The Economist*, March 30, 1974, p. 127.

7. *The Economist*, March 30, 1974, p. 127.

8. U.S. Congress, House of Representatives, Committee on Foreign Affairs, Subcommittee on the Near East and South Asia, *Indian Rupee Settlement Agreement*, p. 2. Hereafter cited as *Rupee Settlement Hearings*. See also, *New York Times*, April 27, 1974.

9. Bhagwati, *Amount and Sharing*, p. 17.

10. William S. Gaud, "Foreign Aid: What It Is; How It Works; Why We Provide It," p. 603.

11. Bhagwati, *Amount and Sharing*, p. 18. Emphasis added. Swedish economist Gunnar Myrdal estimates that "considerably less than half of the appropriations and disbursements . . . would remain as genuine aid" after making necessary adjustments to nominal values. Gunnar Myrdal, *The Challenge of World Poverty*, p. 352.

12. Bhagwati, *Amount and Sharing*, p. 18. See also UNCTAD Conference, New Delhi, Second Session, *Problems and Policies of Financing*, IV (New York: United Nations, 1968), 45-110; John Pincus, "The Cost of Foreign Aid," *The Review of Economics and Statistics*, 45 (November 1963), 360-367.

13. In order to satisfy its own desire to avoid "charity" and to demonstrate its self-reliance, the Indian government itself has, on occasion, preferred loans to grants. Nevertheless, the point remains that loans constitute a substantially lighter form of wealth redistribution than do grants.

14. The data for these computations are taken from sources cited in note 3.

15. See the national income figures in United Nations Department of Economic and Social Affairs, Statistical Office, *Yearbook of National Accounts Statistics*.
16. "Stability" in fact meant preserving an international structure that enabled the United States to protect or increase its preeminence in the global distribution of power and wealth.
17. Richard Nixon, "President's Message Transmitting Draft of Proposed Legislation to Amend the Foreign Assistance Act of 1961," U.S. Congress, House of Representatives, Committee on Foreign Affairs, *Fiscal Year 1975 Foreign Assistance Request*, pp. 717, 720. Hereafter cited as *FY 1975 Hearings*.
18. Richard Nixon, "Foreign Assistance for the 'Seventies,' " pp. 372-378.
19. John A. Hannah, "Institutional Problems in the Developing Countries," p. 301. See also William J. Casey, "A Comprehensive Development Policy for the United States," p. 692.
20. Lyndon Johnson, "To Build the Peace—The Foreign Aid Program for Fiscal 1969," p. 322.
21. Lyndon Johnson, "The Importance of Foreign Aid to U.S. Security and World Peace," p. 178.
22. Richard Nixon, "U.S. Foreign Policy for the 1970's: Building for Peace," p. 385.
23. Lyndon Johnson, "Letter of Transmittal," U.S. Agency for International Development, *The Foreign Assistance Program: Annual Report to the Congress, 1964*, p. iii. Hereafter cited as *AID Report*, various years.
24. Dean Rusk, "Testimony Before the Senate Committee on Appropriations," *Department of State Bulletin*, 59 (October 21, 1968), 419. See also U.S. Agency for International Development, *Principles of Foreign Economic Assistance*, p. 1.
25. Nicholas Katzenbach, "United States Policy Toward the Developing World," p. 209. See also the statement of G. Lewis Jones, assistant secretary of state for Near Eastern and South Asian affairs, United States Congress, Senate, Committee on Foreign Relations, *Mutual Security Act of 1960*, p. 266. Hereafter cited as *Mutual Security Act of 1960*.

    For other examples of the theme that peace is indivisible and stability in the newly independent countries is essential for American security, see the following statements: John Foster Dulles, United States Congress, Senate, Committee on Foreign Relations, *Mutual Security Act of 1954*, pp. 8-9; Harold E. Stassen, director of Foreign Operations Administration, ibid., p. 42; G. Lewis Jones, *Mutual Security Act of 1960*, p. 273; Secretary of State Christian Herter, ibid., pp. 5-11; Cyrus Vance, "Secretary Testifies on Administration's Approach to Foreign Assistance," p. 237.

427

26. Henry Kissinger, "The Foreign Assistance Program and Global Stability," p. 290. Hereafter cited as "The Foreign Assistance Program."

27. See, for example, Kissinger's emphasis on stability in *FY 1975 Hearings*, p. 2.

28. Kissinger, "The Foreign Assistance Program," p. 290.

29. Henry Kissinger, "The Foreign Assistance Program: A Vital Tool in Building a More Cooperative World," p. 50. Hereafter cited as "A Vital Tool."

30. *New York Times*, July 17, 1973.

31. Although much of the aid to European governments was given for the purpose of rebuilding Europe after World War II, it should be noted that these figures from 1949 through 1973 do not include postwar relief to Europe, which began in 1945.

32. *AID Report*, 1962, p. 4.

33. United States Congress, House, Committee on Foreign Affairs, *Report of Special Study Mission to Pakistan, India, Thailand, and Indochina*, p. 21. Hereafter cited as *Study Mission Report*.

34. Ibid., p. 1.

35. *Mutual Security Act of 1954*, pp. 8-9.

36. *Mutual Security Act of 1960*, p. 7.

37. U.S. Congress, House of Representatives, Committee on Foreign Affairs, *Foreign Assistance Act of 1964*, pp. 83-85. Also quoted in Michael Hudson, *Super Imperialism*, pp. 156-157.

38. Dulles had denounced neutralism several times during his career. He once explained that in a world where there are aggressors "neutrality is no protection, rather it encourages aggression. [A] . . . policy of neutrality means in fact 'conniving at aggression.' " See Dulles, "Peace Without Fear," p. 729. On another occasion, Dulles said that "neutrality . . . except under exceptional circumstances . . . is an immoral conception." Quoted by Emmet John Hughes, *America the Vincible* (Harmondsworth, Middlesex: Penguin, 1960), p. 241; also, E. I. Brodkin, "United States Aid to India and Pakistan," p. 665.

39. *Study Mission Report*, p. 21. The curious sentence referring to the Western world must have meant to the authors that allies of the United States were part of the Western world. In conventional usage, of course, Sweden could not leave the Western world by being a nonally, nor India become part of the Western world by becoming an ally. This demonstrates the extent to which human affairs were viewed through the distorting lenses of military alliances.

40. *Mutual Security Act of 1960*, pp. 8, 10-11.

41. Daniel Parker, *FY 1975 Hearings*, p. 92.

42. The long-range consequences, of course, may be socially explosive. After two decades of development in India, the problems of

428

the very poor had not decreased. "There is a consensus that the discontent of the disadvantaged is nearing some kind of ignition point." John P. Lewis, *Wanted in India*, p. 27.

43. Max F. Millikan and Walt W. Rostow, *A Proposal*, p. 39. Emphasis added.

44. Ibid., p. 33.

45. W. W. Rostow, *The Relation Between Political and Economic Development*, speech before the Foreign Service Institute, October 31, 1956, Massachusetts Institute of Technology, Center for International Studies, Economic Development Program, General Project Pamphlets, 1, 10; see also Walt W. Rostow, *The United States in the World Arena*, p. 252.

46. Rostow, *Relation Between Political and Economic Development*, p. 1.

47. *Mutual Security Act of 1954*, p. 67.

48. Ibid., pp. 14-15, 20.

49. Johnson, "To Build the Peace," p. 322. Rusk believed that insufficient aid would result in violent revolutions, "Testimony," pp. 421-422. See also Thorp, *Reality of Foreign Aid*, p. 30; John P. Lewis, *Wanted in India*, p. 27.

50. Richard Nixon, "Reform of the U.S. Foreign Assistance Program," p. 614. Zbigniew Brzezinski argued in 1956 that rapid industrialization might encourage totalitarian regimes in the less developed countries. But, in his view, the great tragedy was that "any effort to slow down the development of these areas will immediately play into the hands of the extremists, particularly the Communists, who are waiting on the sidelines." "The Politics of Underdevelopment," p. 73.

51. *Foreign Assistance Act of 1961*, p. 424; *AID Report, 1962*, p. 2.

52. *Mutual Security Act of 1954*, p. 5. The sentiment regarding competition with China was echoed by Henry Byroade, assistant secretary of state for Near Eastern, South Asian and African affairs, ibid., p. 282, as well as by Senators J. W. Fulbright, ibid., p. 72 and Alexander Smith, ibid., p. 14. See also the statement of Vice-President Richard Nixon in *India and the United States*, ed. Selig S. Harrison, p. 144; Henry Kissinger's press conference of December 27, 1973, quoted by Daniel Moynihan in *Rupee Settlement Hearings*, p. 7; Katzenbach, "United States Policy," p. 210.

53. *Mutual Security Act of 1954*, p. 15.

54. John Kennedy, address before the White House Conference on Export Expansion, *Department of State Bulletin*, 49 (October 14, 1960), 597-598.

55. Bruce Nissen, "Building the World Bank," in Steve Weissman, ed., *The Trojan Horse*, p. 39.

56. United States Congress, House, Committee on Foreign Affairs, *Mutual Development and Cooperation Act of 1973*, pp. 47-48. Hereafter cited as *Mutual Development and Cooperation Act of 1973*.

57. Hannah, "Institutional Problems," p. 300.
58. Secretary of the Treasury, George P. Shultz, *ADB Hearings*, p. 11. Also, Hannah, *Mutual Development and Cooperation Act of 1973*, p. 51.
59. William J. Casey, "A Comprehensive Development Policy," pp. 692-693. See also Cyrus Vance, "Secretary Vance Emphasizes Importance of Foreign Assistance Programs," p. 336.
60. Casey, *ADB Hearings*, pp. 55-56.
61. Gaud, "Foreign Aid," p. 603. See also, Myrdal, *Challenge of World Poverty*, p. 355.
62. Quoted from a speech by George D. Woods of February 9, 1968, in Myrdal, *Challenge of World Poverty*, p. 359. See also William J. Casey, "A Comprehensive Development Policy," pp. 692-693.
63. Kissinger, *FY 1975 Hearings*, p. 4.
64. Rusk, "Testimony," p. 419. See also, Casey, "A Comprehensive Development Policy," p. 692.
65. Charles O. Sethness, U.S. Congress, House, Committee on Appropriations, Subcommittee on Foreign Operations and Related Agencies, *Foreign Assistance and Related Agencies Appropriations for 1975*, p. 844. The source of the study quoted in testimony is: *Mining and Minerals 1973*, Second Annual Report of the Secretary of the Interior Under the Mining and Minerals Policy Act of 1970 (Washington, D.C.: Government Printing Office, 1974).
66. India's main exports are jute products, tea, and cotton textiles. The United States is one of India's principal trading partners, but imports from India are a small part of total U.S. imports. In 1972, the United States exported goods worth $349.9 million and imported goods valued at $426.5 million. *ADB Hearings*, p. 58. India is a major supplier of sheet mica, the U.S. supply of which is 100 percent imported. *FY 1975 Hearings*, p. 734. In 1974, Ambassador Moynihan noted U.S. interest in offshore oil.
67. The desire for United States investment and sales in India, noted earlier, was probably a stronger motive for determining the mode of assistance to India than India's raw materials.
68. Douglas Dillon, "The Contribution of Trade to the Cause of Peace," p. 881.
69. *Mutual Development and Cooperation Act of 1973*, p. 255.
70. *ADB Hearings*, pp. 55-56.
71. *Rupee Settlement Hearings*, p. 7.
72. United States Congress, Senate, Committee on Foreign Relations, *American Private Enterprise, Foreign Economic Development and the AID Program* (Washington, D.C.: Government Printing Office, 1957), p. xiii. Emphasis added. Quoted in Leo Tansky, *U.S. and U.S.S.R. Aid to Developing Countries*, p. 6.
73. *Mutual Security Act of 1954*, p. 50.
74. William J. Casey, "The Rule of Law in International Economic Affairs," p. 326.

75. *Mutual Development and Cooperation Act of 1973*, p. 255; Casey, "The Rule of Law," p. 326.
76. See Richard Nixon, *AID Report, 1969*, p. iii.
77. Letter from E. D. Kenna, president of the National Association of Manufacturers, to Thomas E. Morgan, chairman of the House Committee on Foreign Affairs, *Mutual Development and Cooperation Act of 1973*, p. 647.

    David Rockefeller, president of Chase Manhattan Bank, expressed a similar hope that development aid would concentrate "particularly on those problems so basic to the broad modernization of the developing countries, including food production, rural development, education, health, and family planning." Ibid., p. 497.
78. Kenna, ibid., p. 647.
79. Ibid., p. 497.
80. Ibid., p. 495.
81. Katzenbach, "United States Policy," p. 210. See also Herter, *Mutual Security Act of 1960*, p. 8.
82. Gaud, "Foreign Aid," p. 605.
83. See Kissinger, *FY 1975 Hearings*, p. 10; Cyrus Vance, "Secretary Vance Gives Overview of Foreign Assistance Programs" (statement made before the Subcommittee on Foreign Operations of the House Committee on Appropriations on March 2, 1977), p. 284.
84. *AID Report, 1964*, p. iii.
85. Johnson, "To Build the Peace," p. 322.
86. Quoted by Lloyd Black, *The Strategy of Foreign Aid*, p. 20.
87. Kissinger, "A Vital Tool," p. 50. An earlier expression of the global dimension was made by William Rogers: "The world remains divided politically, but it is being drawn together functionally. U.S. foreign relations increasingly reflect the need to deal with issues—many of them new ones—which are global, not bilateral, in nature." William Rogers, "United States Foreign Policy 1969-70," p. 474.
88. Cyrus Vance, "Secretary Vance Attends Ministerial Meeting of the Conference on International Economic Cooperation," p. 645.
89. Jimmy Carter, "Peace, Arms Control, World Economic Progress, Human Rights," p. 333.
90. U.S. Department of State, "North-South Dialogue," pp. 235-236. Confirmation of the intention not to restructure the global economy is found in the March 22, 1977 statement of the Deputy Assistant Secretary for Near East and South Asia, Adolph Dubs, before the House Committee on International Relations, "Department Discusses South Asia and U.S. Assistance Programs," pp. 344-346.
91. Douglas Dillon, *Mutual Security Act of 1960*, p. 51.
92. *AID Report, 1964*, p. 19.
93. Such a proposal was made because tied aid was (1) economically

costly to the recipient; (2) politically irritating to U.S. relations with the less developed countries; and (3) not so important for growing U.S.-based multinational corporations, which could often sell goods at a profit from one of their foreign subsidiaries.

94. "Fertilizer Group Raps AID Program Change as Harmful to Industry," *Journal of Commerce*, November 9, 1970. Quoted in Michael Hudson, *Super Imperialism*, p. 147.

95. U.S. Agency for International Development, *AID's Challenge in an Interdependent World* (Washington, D.C.: AID, 1977), p. 6. Hereafter cited as *AID's Challenge*.

96. Gaud, "Foreign Aid," p. 603. Secretary Dulles testified that all dollars of the Mutual Security program directly or indirectly go into the payroll of American workers. *Mutual Security Act of 1954*, p. 14.

97. *AID Report, 1965*, p. 8.

98. George P. Shultz, "Administration Stresses Importance of U.S. Action on Funding for IDA and ADB Replenishment," p. 735.

99. *AID Report, 1968*, p. 2.

100. Thorp, *Reality of Foreign Aid*, p. 273.

101. Another indication of the self-serving nature of foreign aid is found in the return on investment that often is a companion of foreign assistance and a result of perpetuating stability in the less developed countries. Senator Charles Mathias noted in 1969 that "capital flows from Latin America and into the United States are now over four times as great as the flow south. The countries of Latin America, in a way, are actually giving foreign aid to the United States, the wealthiest country in the world." Quoted by Myrdal, *Challenge of World Poverty*, pp. 322-323, from a mimeographed speech delivered at the University of Maryland, July 22, 1969.

102. John W. Sewell, *The United States and World Development*, p. 2.

103. The extent to which U.S. aid may have prevented internal economic structural change in India is beyond the scope of this essay. There was, however, no doubt that some U.S. officials hoped aid would prevent radical change.

104. Nixon, "Reform of the U.S. Foreign Assistance Program," pp. 614, 624. According to W. W. Rostow, "In the Administration's initial strategic dispositions economic aid had only one clear purpose—to assist the nation's Eurasian allies to maintain deterrent forces on a scale sufficient for the United States to cut down its own ground forces and concentrate on weapons of mass destruction, their means of delivery, and the means of defense against them." See *The United States in the World Arena*, p. 364.

105. Kissinger, *FY 1975 Hearings*, p. 7; Cyrus Vance, "Secretary Testifies on Administration's Approach to Foreign Assistance."

106. *AID Report, 1967*, p. 1.

107. *New York Times*, April 27, 1974; Baldev Raj Nayar, "Treat India Seriously," p. 142.

108. Indian rupee payments for U.S. surpluses in effect helped finance U.S. private enterprise in India to the extent of 1,250,701,337 rupees from 1960 to 1972. *Rupee Settlement Hearings*, pp. 111-113.

109. For a more complete treatment, see John P. Lewis, *Quiet Crisis in India*, pp. 315-332; *Rupee Settlement Hearings*.

110. *New York Times*, June 18, 1974; January 30, 1975.

111. *New York Times*, June 18, 1974; February 19, 1975.

112. *New York Times*, June 18, 1974; *Rupee Settlement Hearings*, p. 3.

113. *Rupee Settlement Hearings*, p. 7.

114. *New York Times*, June 18, 1974; April 27, 1974.

115. *New York Times*, January 20, 1975; February 19, 1975.

116. *Rupee Settlement Hearings*, pp. 26-27.

117. Bhagwati, *Amount and Sharing*, p. 17.

118. Hudson, *Super Imperialism*, p. 145.

119. Thorp, *Reality of Foreign Aid*, p. 55.

120. These purposes included: "All USG expenditures in India, including Congressional travel, payment of official and personal obligations, international transportation, procurement for overseas use, payments to USG annuitants, contributions to international organizations." In addition, the Cooley loan portfolio for U.S. businesses was not transferred to the Indian government. *Rupee Settlement Hearings*, pp. 5-6, 15.

121. Ibid., pp. 7, 12.

122. According to the General Accounting Office and Ambassador Moynihan, "we could expect to spend only a small portion of these claims." The chairman of the subcommittee, Lee Hamilton, wrote that "rupees were coming into the account twice as quickly as we were able to spend them. . . . We would never be able to spend all the rupees we had." Ibid., pp. v, 2-6.

123. United States Congress, House, Committee on Foreign Affairs, *Mutual Security Act of 1958*, p. 388. Also cited in Tansky, *U.S. and U.S.S.R. Aid*, p. 5.

124. Katzenbach, "United States Policy," p. 211.

125. U.S. Congress, House, Committee on Foreign Affairs, *Mutual Security Act of 1955*, p. 99. Hereafter cited as *Mutual Security Act of 1955*.

126. See Lewis, *Quiet Crisis in India*, p. 253.

127. The single exception was Austria, unable to receive military aid because of its internationally guaranteed neutral status. The largest recipients of grant aid are listed in Table 3-8. For this comparison Iceland, Liberia, Libya, and Malta were omitted as their populations were each less than two million. The largest recipients of military aid are listed in Table 3-10.

128. In making comparisons of this sort, the specific rankings should not be given undue weight, as possible adjustments of data or differing approximations for missing data might make a difference of several places in rank. However, the enormous variations in the

amounts of aid between the top and the bottom of the list are profoundly significant.

129. See Table 3-3 above.

130. The differences have nothing to do with "ability to absorb aid." India could have easily utilized much more assistance. See Jagdish N. Bhagwati, ed., *Economics and World Order*, pp. 11-12.

131. In addition, these figures do not account for the inflationary trend of the dollar since 1949. Because the UK received the bulk of its aid earlier in time than India, and because the figures are given in current dollars, the UK received even more, compared to India, in actual purchasing power than the figures indicate. I have made these comparisons using data from the U.S. Agency for International Development, Statistics and Reports Division, *U.S. Overseas Loans and Grants*.

132. AID administrator Parker explained that economic assistance could have a military function. It served this end in Cambodia, for example, "by enabling the Cambodian Republic to remain in place and to resist the attacks of the Khmer Communists." Some AID funds also went to such "private" agencies as Air America, which carried out military functions for the CIA and Department of Defense. See *FY 1975 Hearings*, pp. 102, 122.

133. Myrdal, *Challenge of World Poverty*, p. 343.

134. *AID Report, 1967*, p. 5.

135. *New York Times*, January 9, 1975.

136. The General Assembly of the United Nations established a goal for capital transfers of one percent of national income for industrialized nations as early as 1960 [Resolution 1522 (xv)]. Before then, this figure was widely accepted among liberal writers and political parties, such as the British Labor party, which included it in its party platform in the 1950s. The original conception of one percent of national income referred only to official aid [Jagdish Bhagwati, *Amount and Sharing*, p. 45], but the UN discussions referred to both official capital flows and to private capital transfers. This goal was restated in 1961 in Assembly Resolution 1711 (xvi), at the beginning of the First United Nations Development Decade. It was later adopted at numerous other forums, including the UNCTAD Conferences in 1962 and 1968, and by the DAC. The inclusion of private capital flows, which are transferred at commercial rates and with the intent of profit-taking, makes the goal in effect lower than it should be, as well as misleading insofar as aid is viewed as a concessional flow of capital. Consequently, there is increasing awareness of the need to define a goal in terms of official flows alone. In 1968, at the New Delhi UNCTAD Conference, the less developed countries attempted to formulate a subsidiary target of .75 percent of GNP for official flows, but several donor countries opposed this move. The Pearson Commission

Report stated a target for official aid transfers at the level of .70 percent of GNP. See Bhagwati, *Amount and Sharing*, pp. 45, 47.

137. The Development Assistance Committee of the OECD includes major noncommunist industrial countries: Australia, Austria, Belgium, Canada, Denmark, France, Germany, Italy, Japan, Netherlands, Norway, Portugal, Sweden, Switzerland, United Kingdom, United States.

138. Organization for Economic Co-operation and Development, *Development Co-operation Efforts and Policies of the Members of the Development Assistance Committee*, 1973, p. 188. Hereafter cited as OECD *Development Co-operation*, various years.

139. *New York Times*, April 19, 1975. The others were Austria, Italy, and Switzerland.

140. Jonathan Power, "Cranking Up Oil Producers' Aid-Giving Machines," *New York Times*, April 15, 1975.

141. See Sewell, *United States and World Development*, p. 127.

142. See Bhagwati, *Amount and Sharing*, p. 117; David Wall, *The Charity of Nations*, p. 21.

143. Myrdal, *Challenge of World Poverty*, p. 337.

144. In addition, during some recent years the United States has extended less aid than it received in payment from earlier aid programs. Michael Hudson reported that in 1970, the United States earned $1.3 billion on its foreign aid programs, the amount by which its hard currency interest and principal repayments exceeded the balance of payments cost of its new aid extensions (*Super Imperialism*, p. 166).

145. United States Congress, Senate, Committee on Foreign Relations, *Technical Assistance*, 1957, pp. 18-19. Also cited in Hudson, *Super Imperialism*, p. 131.

146. If aid sprang more from strategic than humanitarian interests, one must ask: why was not more assistance given? Why was the program almost phased out in the early 1970s? There are many explanations for this, but only two need be mentioned here. First of all, Washington officials began to doubt that aid produced sufficient strategic dividends in countries like India—which refused to become client states—to justify it. India, as members of Congress never tired of pointing out, had refused to become a U.S. ally and in fact had improved relations with the Soviet Union (long before détente was fashionable in the United States). The absence of any important humanitarian concern for India in the extension of aid facilitated its decline after the strategic argument had been discredited.

Second, there was growing congressional dislike for bilateral aid that might result in new military involvements like Vietnam. Thus liberal critics joined the traditional conservative opponents of aid, who had seldom pretended that aid should be humanitarian.

The per capita data also show that officials' state-centric view of reality leads them to ignore the number of people living inside the legal shell of the state; aid is given to state entities instead of to people. Thus states with small populations, sometimes by legislative "accident," may receive higher aid per capita than larger, more populous societies. This state-centric perception of the world, therefore, adds to the propensity to deny the realization of V_2.

147. Leonard Woodcock, *Mutual Development and Cooperation Act of 1973*, p. 652.

148. William Rogers, "United States Foreign Policy," p. 724.

149. Although conclusions about U.S. aid policies to all countries can only be tentatively advanced from this limited study, the evidence collected here is typical of the entire aid program and is corroborated by the work of several other students of aid policies. See, for example, John G. Sommer, *Beyond Charity*; Bhagwati, *Amount and Sharing*; Bhagwati, ed., *Economics and World Order*, pp. 1-15; Myrdal, *Challenge of World Poverty*, pp. 3-29, 275-385; Thorp, *Reality of Foreign Aid*, pp. 128-148, 215-216, 234-244, 266-267, 324; Wall, *Charity of Nations*, pp. 32-49; Hudson, *Super Imperialism*; Denis Goulet and Michael Hudson, *The Myth of Aid*; Weissman, *The Trojan Horse*.

150. The text of Henry Kissinger's revealing interview with James Reston is in the *New York Times*, October 13, 1974. The new Carter perspective was discussed in the *New York Times*, July 7, 1976; see also Carter, "Basic Priorities"; Vance, "Secretary Vance Attends Ministerial Meeting," pp. 645-648.

151. *AID's Challenge*, p. 4; see also Michael Kent O'Leary, *The Politics of American Foreign Aid*, pp. 77, 112.

152. See Henry Kissinger, "A Vital Tool," p. 49.

153. Senator Mark Hatfield, *New York Times*, December 19, 1974.

154. Lewis reported that Indians were most vulnerable to foreign influence when suffering shortages of foreign exchange, *Wanted in India*, pp. 18-19.

155. William J. Barnds, "India and America at Odds," pp. 379-380.

156. Lewis, *Wanted in India*, pp. 20-21.

157. Cheryl Payer, "The IMF and the Third World," in Weissman, *The Trojan Horse*, p. 68; Nissen, "Building the World Bank," ibid., p. 55.

158. Herbert Feldman, "Aid as Imperialism?," p. 229.

159. One example is the aid-tying which insured U.S. corporate profits but gave lower priority to serving human needs in India.

160. Harrison, *India and the United States*, p. 143.

161. Speech by John Lewis at Princeton University, Woodrow Wilson School of Public and International Affairs, April 23, 1975.

162. Steve Weissman, "Inside the Trojan Horse," in *The Trojan Horse*, p. 13.
163. Ibid.
164. Lester Pearson, *The Crisis of Development*, p. 69; Goulet and Hudson, *Myth of Aid*, p. 18.
165. Henry Kissinger's opposition to a new global economic order in which prices offered for raw materials would be adjusted according to prices charged for manufactured goods was explicitly expressed in his speech on raw materials reported in *New York Times*, May 14, 1975.
166. *New York Times*, June 15, 1974.
167. George Ball, *The Discipline of Power*, pp. 222-223.
168. See Myrdal, *Challenge of World Poverty*, p. 347. Sweden perhaps provides the best evidence up to the present for realistic assessment of prospects for implementing some features of this approach. In Sweden, Myrdal reports, the only reason given for aid to the less developed countries "is the moral one of solidarity with people in distress." That is the same principle upon which Swedes have built their domestic welfare state (*Challenge of World Poverty*, p. 363). Sweden has rapidly increased its assistance, aid is not tied to purchases from Sweden, and about half of its aid is given through international organizations.
169. See Richard Barnet, *Intervention and Revolution* (New York: World Publishing Company, 1968).
170. William S. Gaud, "Development—A Balance Sheet," p. 705. See also Hannah, "Institutional Problems," p. 297, and John N. Irwin, "A Strengthened and Revitalized Foreign Aid Program," p. 659.
    In India in 1975, 65 percent of all deaths were under age five. Malnutrition was a direct or associated cause for at least 57 percent of all these deaths. See Parker's statement about the effects of poverty in *FY 1975 Hearings*, p. 161.
171. Lewis, *Quiet Crisis in India*, p. 11.
172. Ibid., p. 19.
173. Myrdal, *Challenge of World Poverty*, p. 313. See also Roger D. Hansen, "The Political Economy of North-South Relations," p. 927.
174. The annual spending of Americans on tobacco and alcohol is several times larger than the total foreign economic assistance program to all countries.
175. A useful guide is an aid burden index where burden index = total aid in millions of dollars/GNP per capita.

FOUR. THE UNITED STATES AND HUMAN RIGHTS IN CHILE

1. In the realm of international relations, human rights might be separated into individual and collective rights. The European

437

Convention of Human Rights contains some of the best examples of individual rights that are given an international status. Signatories to this agreement recognize an international legal obligation to respect the right to life; the right to liberty and security of person; the right to a fair trial; the right to an effective remedy if one's rights are violated; freedom from torture and from inhuman treatment; freedom of thought, conscience, and religion; freedom of expression and freedom of assembly and association. In these examples, individuals are treated as subjects of international law with specifically guaranteed rights. Other, historically older examples of individual rights under international law include the prohibition of slavery, the protection of innocents during war, and the obligation to insure humane treatment of prisoners of war.

On the other hand, collective human rights might include the following: the international protection of minority rights, such as required of the successor states of the Austro-Hungarian Empire after World War I; the prohibition of racial discrimination, such as expressed in frequent UN resolutions condemning apartheid; the prohibition of genocide; the obligation of colonial governments to protect the rights of non-self-governing peoples; and the right of all nations to self-determination.

Although the international community has recognized both individual and collective human rights, individual human rights have not played as important a part in foreign policy as have collective rights.

2. For discussion of this value, see Richard A. Falk, *A Study of Future Worlds*, pp. 23-26.

3. This chapter will not seek to resolve the debate over the degree of economic self-determination that must occur to achieve meaningful political self-determination. The analysis will focus on the exercise of political self-determination and U.S. policies—whether political or economic—relevant to that exercise.

4. One particular virtue of a normative approach to foreign policy analysis is illustrated here. The "level of analysis problem" is overcome insofar as a normative framework transcends the more traditional nation-state focus of inquiry. The Chilean case reveals official attitudes toward human rights in at least these three loci of human transactions: within Chile, between Chile and the United States, and within the United States.

5. General Assembly Resolution 420 (v), December 4, 1950. The United States and Britain cast votes against the resolution. See Louis K. Hyde, *The United States and the United Nations: Promoting the Public Welfare* (New York: Manhattan Publishing Company, 1960), p. 176.

6. In the crucial vote in 1955 on including the first article in the Cov-

enants, the United States, United Kingdom, and France voted "no." See Vernon Van Dyke, *Human Rights, the United States, and World Community*, p. 78; Arthur Henry Robertson, *Human Rights in the World*, p. 95.

7. United Nations General Assembly, Resolution 1514 (xv), December 14, 1960.

8. Harlan Cleveland, "Reflections on the Pacific Community," *Department of State Bulletin*, 48 (August 19, 1963), 286; Van Dyke, *Human Rights*, p. 79.

9. General Assembly *Official Records*, xxi, 1966. Annexes, Vol. iii, Agenda item 87, p. 91, quoted in Van Dyke, *Human Rights*, p. 79. A survey of UN practice led Rosalyn Higgins to the "inescapable" conclusion that self-determination "has developed into an international legal right." *The Development of International Law Through the Political Organs of the United Nations* (New York: Oxford University Press, 1963), p. 103.

10. Van Dyke, *Human Rights*, p. 80.

11. Article 15. Text is in Inter-American Institute of International Legal Studies, *The Inter-American System*, p. 133.

12. "Punta del Este Declaration," *American Journal of International Law* (December 1962), pp. 605, 607.

13. Article 6 of the U.S. Constitution.

14. United States Congress, Senate, Committee on Foreign Relations, *CIA Foreign and Domestic Activities*, pp. 13, 24. Hereafter cited as *CIA Hearings*. See also *New York Times*, September 8, 1974. Officials have reported that although the money was authorized it was not used because United States operatives in Chile thought the plan would backfire. The point remains that United States officials did authorize the use of money to reverse the results of an election.

15. *New York Times*, November 21, 1975.

16. This committee, headed by Senator Frank Church, was a subcommittee of the Senate Foreign Relations Committee. Other members included Stuart Symington, Edmund Muskie, Clifford Case, and Charles Percy. Chief counsel was Jerome Levinson.

17. United States Congress, Senate, Committee on Foreign Relations, Subcommittee on Multinational Corporations, *The International Telephone and Telegraph Company and Chile, 1970-71*, pp. 1, 7. Hereafter cited as *ITT and Chile*.

18. *New York Times*, September 8, 1974.

19. Richard R. Fagen, "The United States and Chile," pp. 309-310. None of these witnesses was recalled before the subcommittee, nor charged with contempt of Congress. Helms was later asked about CIA activity in Chile by the full Senate Foreign Relations Committee (*CIA Hearings*), but many of the questions raised were never fully answered.

20. U.S. Congress, Senate, Select Committee to Study Governmental

Operations with Respect to Intelligence Activities, *Covert Action in Chile 1963-73*, p. 1. Hereafter cited as *Covert Action in Chile*.

21. Ibid., p. 9.
22. Ibid., pp. 15-16.
23. Ibid., pp. 1, 9.
24. *CIA Hearings*, p. 8.
25. *New York Times*, January 19, 1975.
26. United States Congress, Senate, Committee on Foreign Relations, Subcommittee on Multinational Corporations, *Multinational Corporations and United States Foreign Policy*, Part I, p. 96. Hereafter cited as *MNC Hearings*, with designation of whether source is Part I or Part II. See also *ITT and Chile*, p. 3.
27. *CIA Hearings*, p. 8.
28. Fagen, "United States and Chile," p. 298.
29. *ITT and Chile*, p. 4.
30. *Covert Action in Chile*, pp. 12-13.
31. *ITT and Chile*, p. 5.
32. *New York Times*, September 8, 1974; *CIA Hearings*, p. 8; *Covert Action in Chile*, p. 24. The latter sets the figure at $250,000.
33. *Covert Action in Chile*, p. 24; *CIA Hearings*, p. 8.
34. *ITT and Chile*, p. 7.
35. Ibid., p. 10.
36. Ibid.
37. Ibid., pp. 10-11.
38. Ibid., pp. 8, 16; *MNC Hearings*, Pt. II, p. 610. The Hendrix cable read: "The anti-Allende effort more than likely will require some outside financial support. The degree of this assistance will be known better around October 1. We have pledged our support, if needed." Hendrix denied in the hearings that he meant financial support (*MNC Hearings*, Pt. I, p. 136); text of message to Gerrity is in ibid., Pt. II, p. 610. In addition, ITT sought to support *El Mercurio*, the leading conservative paper in Chile (ibid., Pt. I, pp. 2-30).
39. Ibid., Pt. I, pp. 282, 313, 315.
40. Ibid., Pt. II, p. 610.
41. Ibid., Pt. I, p. 134.
42. *ITT and Chile*, pp. 6, 7; *MNC Hearings*, Pt. II, p. 608.
43. See *Covert Action in Chile*, pp. 1-40.
44. *ITT and Chile*, p. 9.
45. For example, see the Hendrix report to Gerrity (*MNC Hearings*, Pt. II, p. 610) about Korry's brusque, cold treatment of Allende's emissary sent to the U.S. embassy to pay respects and to say that the "Allende government wanted to have good relations with the Ambassador and the United States."
46. *MNC Hearings*, Pt. II, pp. 452-453; *ITT and Chile*, p. 9.

440

47. Fagen, "United States and Chile," p. 289; *New York Times*, September 8, 1974.
48. *ITT and Chile*, p. 9.
49. *Covert Action in Chile*, p. 23.
50. Ibid., p. 2.
51. The chief of the CIA operation in Chile told a high-ranking Chilean police official that "The U.S. Government favors a military solution and is willing to support it in any manner short of outright military intervention." U.S. Congress, Senate, Select Committee to Study Governmental Operations with Respect to Intelligence Activities, *Alleged Assassination Plots Involving Foreign Leaders*, p. 240. Hereafter cited as *Assassination Plots*. See also p. 232 and *Covert Action in Chile*, p. 26. In fact, military assistance was not cut off after Allende became president. Ibid., p. 37.
52. *Assassination Plots*, p. 232.
53. Ibid., p. 240.
54. Ibid., pp. 225-226.
55. After a meeting at the White House on October 15, 1970, the CIA headquarters cabled the results of the meeting to its mission in Santiago: "It is firm and continuing policy that Allende be overthrown by a *coup*. . . . We are to continue to generate maximum pressure toward this end utilizing every appropriate resource." Ibid., p. 243.
56. Ibid., pp. 239-246.
57. Ibid., p. 235.
58. Armando Uribe, *The Black Book of American Intervention in Chile*, pp. 43, 125-150.
59. Ibid., p. 125. Uribe provides a detailed description of the Pentagon plan for a takeover by Chilean armed forces (pp. 126-133).
60. Gabriel Garcia Marquez, "Why Allende Had to Die," *New Statesman*, 87 (March 15, 1974), 356.
61. Ibid.
62. *Covert Action in Chile*, pp. 38-39.
63. *CIA Hearings*, pp. 23-24; *Covert Action in Chile*, p. 27.
64. *New York Times*, September 20, 1974, and October 16, 1974. Fagen estimated the purchasing power of the 8 million was about 40 or 50 million ("United States and Chile," p. 298).
65. *New York Times*, September 8, 1974. This article by Seymour Hersh was based on the secret testimony of CIA Director William Colby.
66. Ibid., pp. 28, 31.
67. *New York Times*, September 20 and October 16, 1974; *Covert Action in Chile*, p. 2; Tad Szulc, "The CIA and Chile," *Washington Post*, October 21, 1973, reprinted in Laurence Birns, ed., *The End of Chilean Democracy*, p. 157. Many of the direct strike subsidies were

441

initiated in 1972 after Nathaniel Davis, a specialist on Eastern Europe, was assigned as ambassador to Chile.

68. *Covert Action in Chile*, p. 31.

69. *New York Times*, September 20, 1974.

70. Paul E. Sigmund, "Chile: What Was the U.S. Role? Less Than Charged," p. 148; *Covert Action in Chile*, p. 28. Two observers suggest that the abortive rightist coup leading to the assassination of the commander in chief of the Chilean army, General Schneider, may have contributed to the increase of leftist support from 36 to 50 percent in 1971. James F. Petras and Robert LaPorte, "Can We Do Business with Radical Nationalists? Chile: No," p. 132.

71. *Covert Action in Chile*, pp. 28-29.

72. *New York Times*, October 16, 1974.

73. Ibid.

74. *New York Times*, September 20, 1974.

75. *Covert Action in Chile*, p. 19.

76. Ibid., pp. 8, 29-30.

77. Ibid., p. 24.

78. Ibid., p. 25.

79. Ibid., pp. 7, 22.

80. Ibid., p. 25.

81. Ibid., p. 29.

82. Only Israel had a larger per capita debt. Pierre Kalfon, *Le Monde*, June 20 and 21, 1973, reprinted in Birns, *End of Chilean Democracy*, p. 11.

83. *ITT and Chile*, p. 13.

84. Ibid., pp. 13-14.

85. Ibid.

86. Ibid., p. 15.

87. Ibid.; also *MNC Hearings*, Pt. II, Appendix III.

88. *ITT and Chile*, p. 15.

89. Ibid., p. 16.

90. *Covert Action in Chile*, p. 33.

91. The discussion of the copper expropriation is based largely on Theodore Moran, *Multinational Corporations and the Politics of Dependence*, pp. 7, 120, 146, 150, 213-215; *Covert Action in Chile*, p. 33.

92. *New York Times*, Oct. 24, 1971.

93. Joseph Collins, "Tightening the Financial Knot," in Birns, *End of Chilean Democracy*, p. 179.

94. *New York Times*, August 15, 1971; Fagen, "United States and Chile," p. 305.

95. *MNC Hearings*, Pt. I, p. 334.

96. Petras and LaPorte, "Can We Do Business," pp. 141-142. After conducting extensive interviews with State Department officials, Petras and LaPorte concluded that the State Department had not

been frequently consulted about events after the copper nationalization crisis.

97. *New York Times*, August 15, 1971.

98. *Business Week*, July 10, 1971; quoted in Collins, "Tightening the Financial Knot," p. 183.

99. Collins, "Tightening the Financial Knot," p. 182.

100. *MNC Hearings*, Pt. I, p. 40.

101. Ibid., Pt. I, p. 332.

102. Collins, "Tightening the Financial Knot," p. 183.

103. Mark L. Chadwin, "Foreign Policy Report: Nixon Administration Debates New Position Paper on Latin America," *National Journal* (January 15, 1972), p. 97, quoted in Collins, "Tightening the Financial Knot," p. 180.

104. *New York Times*, August 15, 1971.

105. Collins, "Tightening the Financial Knot," p. 184.

106. *Covert Action in Chile*, p. 33.

107. *Wall Street Journal,* June 4, 1971; Collins, "Tightening the Financial Knot," p. 189.

108. Elizabeth Farnsworth, "Chile: What Was the U.S. Role? More Than Admitted," p. 131. This is part of an important exchange with Sigmund, "Chile."

109. *Covert Action in Chile*, p. 32; Jonathan Kandell, "Private U.S. Loan in Chile Up Sharply," *New York Times*, November 12, 1973, reprinted in Birns, *End of Chilean Democracy*, p. 194. For slightly different comparisons, see Farnsworth, "Chile," p. 132 and Sigmund, "Chile," p. 146.

110. Assistance in 1958 was higher than the average for 1952-59 because of the election that year. Thus 1959 is most useful as a base from which to measure.

111. Sigmund, "Chile," p. 144.

112. *MNC Hearings*, Pt. I, pp. 327, 335.

113. Collins, "Tightening the Financial Knot," p. 187; *Covert Action in Chile*, p. 33.

114. The Staff Report of the Senate Select Committee on Intelligence declared: "It seems clear from the pattern of U.S. economic actions and from the nature of debates within the Executive Branch that American economic policy was driven more by political opposition to an Allende regime than by purely technical judgments about Chile's finances." *Covert Action in Chile*, p. 35.

115. In the negotiations with Chile's principal foreign creditor nations, the United States alone refused to consider rescheduling Chile's foreign debt payments. Ibid., p. 35.

116. Collins, "Tightening the Financial Knot," p. 185; *Covert Action in Chile*, p. 33.

117. *MNC Hearings*, Pt. I, p. 389. William Bolin, senior vice-president, testified before the subcommittee.

118. *New York Times*, August 15, 1971.

119. *MNC Hearings*, Pt. I, pp. 48-49.

120. Ibid., Pt. I, p. 48.

121. Ibid., Pt. I, pp. 37, 75-76.

122. Kandell, "Private U.S. Loan," p. 195.

123. Farnsworth, "Chile," p. 139.

124. *MNC Hearings*, Pt. I, p. 338.

125. In resuming the assistance program, AID reported: "Given the willingness of outstanding bilateral problems of debt and compensation, the efforts underway to regularize Chile's international financial obligations, and the serious Chilean stabilization effort, reactivation of the AID loan program is proposed." See "U.S. Response to the Chilean Coup," *Inter-American Economic Affairs*, 28 (Summer 1974), 89.

126. Gary MacEoin, "The U.S. Government and Chile," p. 222.

127. Szulc, "CIA and Chile," p. 156.

128. Farnsworth, "Chile," p. 140.

129. Ibid., p. 141. Butz was quoted by the *Miami Herald*, November 26, 1973.

130. *Covert Action in Chile*, p. 25.

131. Laurence Birns, "The Demise of a Constitutional Society," in Birns, *End of Chilean Democracy*, p. 26.

132. *New York Times*, September 17, 1974.

133. "Second Annual Report to the Congress on United States Foreign Policy," February 25, 1971, in Richard Nixon, *Public Papers of the Presidents of the United States* (Washington, D.C.: Government Printing Office, 1972), pp. 246-247; *ITT and Chile*, p. 19.

134. "Message From the President of the United States Transmitting His Annual Report on the State of U.S. Foreign Policy," February 1972. Text is reprinted in U.S. Congress, House, Committee on Foreign Affairs, Subcommittee on Inter-American Affairs, *United States and Chile During the Allende Years, 1970-1973* (Washington, D.C.: Government Printing Office, 1975), p. 453. Hereafter cited as *United States and Chile*.

135. Ibid. Identical wording was used in Nixon's "Second Annual Report," pp. 246-247. Charles Meyer, assistant secretary of state for inter-American affairs attested to the accuracy of the president's assertion that U.S. policy in fact followed the principle of nonintervention and was based on the president's statement, which he quoted, that " 'We will deal with governments as they are.' The policy of the United States was that Chile's problem was a Chilean problem, to be settled by Chile." *MNC Hearings*, Pt. I, p. 402.

136. Kissinger's statements are in *New York Times*, September 20 and 21, 1974; for Ford's statement, see ibid., September 17, 1974.

137. *New York Times*, September 21, 1974.

138. *New York Times*, September 20 and 21, 1974.

139. *New York Times*, September 17, 1974. House Speaker Carl Albert said that the Kissinger-Ford private briefing for congressional leaders at the White House contained the same information as the president gave in his TV appearance. *New York Times*, September 21, 1974.

140. *New York Times*, September 20, 1974.

141. *CIA Hearings*, pp. 6, 24.

142. Fagen, p. 303.

143. *Washington Post*, April 6, 1973.

144. Fagen, "United States and Chile," p. 304.

145. *CIA Hearings*, p. 3; Fagen, "United States and Chile," p. 303.

146. *Washington Post*, April 6, 1973.

147. *Covert Action in Chile*, p. 40.

148. Ibid.

149. Ibid., p. 23.

150. *New York Times*, September 13 and 23, 1974.

151. *Covert Action in Chile*, p. 29.

152. *New York Times*, September 20, 1974.

153. *Covert Action in Chile*, p. 8.

154. *New York Times*, October 21, 1974.

155. *New York Times*, October 16, 1974.

156. *New York Times*, September 20, 1974.

157. *Covert Action in Chile*, p. 45.

158. Ibid., p. 48.

159. Ramsey Clark, "The Law and Human Rights in Chile," p. 164.

160. MacEoin, "U.S. Government and Chile," p. 221.

161. Ibid., p. 222; Clark, "Law and Human Rights," p. 163; *New York Times*, September 23, 1974. Covey Oliver, former assistant secretary of state for Latin America, was a member of the fact-finding mission. A special five-nation investigating team of the Organization of American States and an independent study by Amnesty International confirmed the reports of widespread torture and repression. The findings of the OAS's Inter-American Committee on Human Rights were described in the *New York Times*, December 10, 1974. Studies by Amnesty International were reported in the *New York Times*, January 20, May 30, and September 11, 1974.

162. Birns, *End of Chilean Democracy*, p. 24.

163. Laurence Birns, "Allende's Fall, Washington's Push," *New York Times*, September 15, 1974.

164. Paul Sigmund, "Correspondence," *Foreign Affairs*, 53 (January 1975), 376.

165. *The Boston Globe Magazine*, September 15, 1974; also MacEoin, "U.S. Government and Chile," p. 223.

166. *New York Times*, January 10, 1975.

167. Ibid., September 27, 1974.

168. Ibid.; MacEoin, "U.S. Government and Chile," p. 222.

445

169. Statement in panel discussion, Princeton University, October 21, 1974.

170. "Interview with William E. Colby, Director of Central Intelligence," *U.S. News and World Report*, 77 (December 2, 1974), 29.

171. The text of President Ford's statement about national security is in *New York Times*, September 17, 1974.

172. The similarity of United States policies to Soviet interventionist policies was ironically highlighted in the 1962 statement of foreign ministers at Punta del Este. At the urging of the United States, the foreign ministers adopted a statement warning governments against the deceptiveness and spread of communism in Latin America: "With the pretext of defending popular interests, freedom is suppressed, democratic institutions are destroyed, human rights are violated." "Punta Del Este Declaration," *American Journal of International Law*, 56 (April 1962), 604. One could accurately use the same language to describe U.S. intervention in Chile.

173. *Covert Action in Chile*, pp. 43-49. A similarly distorted perception afflicted officials before the Bay of Pigs invasion to overthrow Castro in 1961. Then officials held the mistaken belief that a large popular uprising would occur in Cuba if only the CIA would help set it in motion. In both cases, U.S. officials seemed reluctant to believe that a Marxist could have a substantial degree of popular support.

174. Birns, "Demise of a Constitutional Society," in Birns, *End of Chilean Democracy*, p. 25.

175. See Project for Awareness and Action, "Chile's Foreign Debt," Birns, *End of Chilean Democracy*, p. 192; Uribe, *Black Book*, p. 107.

176. *MNC Hearings*, Pt. 1, p. 298; Fagen, "United States and Chile," p. 301.

177. *New York Times*, September 27, 1974.

178. Fagen, "United States and Chile," p. 303.

179. Ibid., p. 305.

180. *New York Times*, September 13, 1974.

181. For discussion of various assassination plots, see U.S. Congress, Senate, Select Committee to Study Governmental Operations With Respect to Intelligence Activities, *Alleged Assassination Plots Involving Foreign Leaders, An Interim Report*, pp. 4-5; *New York Times*, November 21, 1975 and March 12, 1976; Richard Barnet, *Intervention and Revolution*.

182. *New York Times*, March 10, 1975.

183. See *New York Times*, March 18, 1975.

184. Although many banking institutions did cut off credit to Allende's government [*New York Times*, November 12, 1973], they seemed less enthusiastic than ITT about covert intervention. Many United States banks pursued a strategy of keeping their capital at home until the political climate stabilized in Chile. If the resulting government was socialist, they believed there would still be future op-

portunities to do business in Chile. The Allende government, after all, continued to need credit. One U.S. business in Chile, Ralston Purina, refused to take part in the ITT-sponsored meetings to press Kissinger to intervene in Chilean affairs.

185. Petras and LaPorte, "Can We Do Business," p. 135. After a detailed study of U.S. policy in Chile, James Petras and Robert LaPorte came to a similar conclusion: "Policy tends to follow the line favored by a single interest—the U.S. investor community. U.S. economic interests appear to be the only concrete, specific, and visible reference point to which policy-makers refer."

186. Birns, "Demise of a Constitutional Society," *End of Chilean Democracy*, p. 22.

187. U.S. Congress, Senate, Select Committee to Study Governmental Operations with Respect to Intelligence Activities, *Foreign and Military Intelligence, Final Report*, Book 1, p. 445. Hereafter cited as *Select Committee Final Report*.

188. Even the Select Senate Committee to investigate the CIA failed to get good cooperation from the executive branch. *New York Times*, March 6, 1975.

189. Fagen detailed the evidence in a lengthy letter to J. W. Fulbright, reprinted in Birns, *End of Chilean Democracy*, pp. 166-167. A career foreign service officer told Fagen that Frederick Purdy, chief consul of the embassy, was a CIA agent. Charges against Purdy were corroborated by the *New York Times*, November 20, 1973. In one case, it appears as if embassy officials were inactive in protecting a young U.S. citizen working in Santiago, and may even have condoned his arbitrary arrest, detention, and killing by the newly-formed junta.

190. See the *New York Times*, March 6, 1975.

191. After examining U.S. policy in Chile, Gary MacEoin concluded: "What is now overwhelmingly clear is that government by deceit, treachery, and perjury is firmly entrenched in Washington and that the liquidation of Watergate has been strictly cosmetic." See MacEoin, "U.S. Government and Chile," p. 223.

192. *Select Committee Final Report*, p. 157.

193. "President's Annual Report on Foreign Policy," p. 453.

194. *New York Times*, September 20, 1974; *Washington Post*, April 6, 1973.

195. *MNC Hearings*, Pt. 1, pp. 281, 301.

196. Ibid., p. 402; pp. 414, 426; p. 406.

197. Jack Kubisch, "The United States is Innocent of Complicity," statement of September 20, 1973, before House Subcommittee for Inter-American Affairs, in Birns, *End of Chilean Democracy*, pp. 151-153.

198. *MNC Hearings*, Pt. 1, p. 189.

199. *New York Times*, September 8, 1974.

200. *New York Times*, September 21, 1974.

201. MacEoin, "U.S. Government and Chile," p. 221; Fagen, "United States and Chile," pp. 309-310.
202. Birns, "Allende's Fall, Washington's Push."
203. "False consciousness" is discussed in Richard A. Falk, *This Endangered Planet*, pp. 84-85. According to Falk, "Alienation involves false consciousness, an estrangement so extreme that a person loses the ability to discern his own interests, the conditions of his own fulfillment, or the actuality of his role as a victim or perpetrator of exploitation."
204. *MNC Hearings*, Pt. I, p. 121.
205. Ibid., p. 478.
206. Memo of September 17, 1970, ibid., Pt. II, p. 611.
207. *New York Times*, September 20, 1974.
208. Address at Princeton University, March 11, 1975. Professor Laurence Birns, a former UN economic affairs officer in Santiago, has written: "Allende was scrupulously correct in maintaining unimpaired, under unrelieved internal and external pressure, all the nation's institutions. . . . Not a single newspaper was censored by the civilian authorities and opposition political parties could rage at will against the Government." See Birns, "Allende's Fall, Washington's Push." Sigmund confirmed the openness of Chilean society in "Correspondence," p. 376.
209. MacEoin, "U.S. Government and Chile," pp. 220-221; Fagen, "United States and Chile," p. 304; *New York Times*, September 26, 1974.
210. As Petras and LaPorte, "Can We Do Business," have concluded: "Congress serves as a forum for airing dissident and critical opinions, but has been of little importance except where the position of Congress coincides with that of the executive branch and the business community," p. 136.
211. *Select Committee Final Report*, p. 150.
212. Ibid., pp. 150-151.
213. See S. 2239, 93rd Cong., 1st Sess.
214. Subsequent legislation attached to foreign assistance appropriations did ask that foreign CIA covert political activity be limited to national security questions and that Congress be informed of covert activities. However, provisions for implementation of this idea were weak, and the legislation itself fell far short of prohibiting covert intervention, even intervention undertaken for the purpose of overturning free elections.
215. The report said: "We hold no brief for President Allende's decision, in effect, to expropriate the property of U.S. owned corporations without adequate compensation. On the contrary, we condemn it." *ITT and Chile*, p. 18.
216. Ibid.
217. Ibid., p. 20.
218. *Covert Action in Chile*, p. 55.

448

219. Ibid., p. 56.
220. *Select Committee Final Report*, pp. 159, 160, 448.
221. Ibid., pp. 160, 446.
222. Ibid., p. 507. The act is quoted on p. 506.
223. Ibid.
224. Ibid., p. 157.
225. On this point, see Stephen D. Krasner, "Are Bureaucracies Important? (Or Allison Wonderland)," p. 178.
226. *Select Committee Final Report*, pp. 153, 445.
227. *Covert Action in Chile*, p. 2.
228. Text in *New York Times*, February 24, 1977.
229. Printed transcript of interview on "Face the Nation," CBS Television, March 20, 1977, mimeographed, p. 3.
230. Ibid., p. 4.
231. Text in *New York Times*, February 24, 1977.
232. *New York Times*, November 4, 1977.
233. Press conference text, *Department of State Bulletin*, 76 (February 28, 1977), 164.
234. Amnesty International, "Iran," *Amnesty International Briefing*, November 1976, p. 10.
235. *New York Times*, November 16, 1977.
236. Former Attorney General and Under Secretary of State Nicholas Katzenbach has come to a similar conclusion: "We should abandon publicly all covert operations designed to influence political results in foreign countries. Specifically, there should be no secret subsidies of police or counterinsurgency forces, no efforts to influence elections, no secret monetary subsidies of groups sympathetic to the United States, whether governmental, nongovernmental, or revolutionary." See Nicholas deB. Katzenbach, "Foreign Policy, Public Opinion, and Secrecy," p. 15.
237. In contemplating the abolition of the CIA, one immediately thinks of the effort to learn the size of the Soviet missile arsenal as a more troublesome problem. However, artificial earth satellites currently gather such information regularly, and this work can be done openly. Likewise, the effort to detect any possible Soviet violations of future arms control agreements, such as a comprehensive test ban, can best be carried out through open, public means.
238. Katzenbach, "Foreign Policy, Public Opinion, and Secrecy," p. 8.

FIVE. U.S. POLICY FOR INTERNATIONAL
CONTROL OF MARINE POLLUTION

1. For a discussion of these environmental problems as world order issues, see Richard A. Falk, *A Study of Future Worlds*, pp. 27-28.
2. Robert M. Hallman, *Towards an Environmentally Sound Law of the Sea*, p. 6.
3. "Statement of the Honorable Russell E. Train, Chairman, (U.S.)

Council on Environmental Quality, Executive Office of the President of the United States, Before the Council of the Inter-Governmental Maritime Consultative Organization," London, June 5, 1973, mimeographed, p. 3. See also Robert A. Shinn, *The International Politics of Marine Pollution Control*, p. 183; Colin Moorecraft, *Must the Seas Die?*, p. 2.

4. Quoted in George Kennan, "To Prevent a World Wasteland," p. 401.

5. Moorecraft, *Must the Seas Die?*, p. 3.

6. This most widely used definition of marine pollution was developed by the United Nations Group of Experts on the Scientific Aspects of Marine Pollution (GESAMP), a group of experts drawn from the Inter-Governmental Maritime Consultative Organization (IMCO), the Food and Agricultural Organization (FAO), the United Nations Educational, Scientific and Cultural Organization (UNESCO), the World Meteorological Organization (WMO), the World Health Organization (WHO), and the International Atomic Energy Agency (IAEA). See "Comprehensive Outline of the Scope of the Long-Term and Expanded Programme of Oceanic Exploration and Research," UN Doc. A/7750 (November 1969), Annex I, section 3.

7. Shinn, *International Politics*, p. 1.

8. National Academy of Sciences, *Petroleum in the Marine Environment* (Washington, D.C.: National Academy of Sciences, 1975), p. 6; Swadesh S. Kalsi, "Oil in Neptune's Kingdom," p. 79; National Academy of Sciences, Ocean Science Committee of the NAS (National Academy of Sciences)-NRC (National Research Council) Ocean Affairs Board, *Marine Environmental Quality*, p. 7 (hereafter cited as *NAS Study on Marine Environmental Quality*); Oscar Schachter and Daniel Serwer, "Marine Pollution Problems and Remedies," p. 89; Workshop on Global Ecological Problems, *Man in the Living Environment*, p. 256.

9. See *NAS Study on Marine Environmental Quality*, pp. 7-8; Hallman, *Towards an Environmentally Sound Law*, p. 5; E. W. Seabrook Hull and Albert W. Koers, "A Regime for World Ocean Pollution Control," *International Relations and the Future of Ocean Space,* Symposium on International Relations and the Future of Ocean Space, University of South Carolina, 1972, ed. Robert G. Wirsing (Columbia, South Carolina: University of South Carolina Press, 1974), p. 93.

10. Study of Critical Environmental Problems, *Man's Impact on the Global Environment*, pp. 139-141; Kalsi, "Oil in Neptune's Kingdom," p. 81; U.S. Council on Environmental Quality, *Environmental Quality, Annual Report*, 1972, p. 86. Hereafter cited as *Environmental Quality, Annual Report*. The *NAS Study on Marine Environmental Quality* estimated that "over 95 percent . . . [of the pollutants from petroleum products] is air-borne." See pp. 7-8.

11. FAO Technical Conference on Marine Pollution and Its Effect on Living Resources and Fishing (Rome, 1970), *Marine Pollution and Sea Life* (London: Fishing News Books, 1972), p. 451 (hereafter cited as *FAO Technical Conference*); see also Schachter and Serwer, "Marine Pollution Problems," p. 89; Shinn, *International Politics*, p. 8.

12. Schachter and Serwer, "Marine Pollution Problems," p. 89.

13. *FAO Technical Conference*, p. 114.

14. Richard Bernstein, "Poisoning the Seas," p. 15.

15. M. Blumer, for example, has stated categorically that "all crude oils and all oil fractions except highly purified and pure materials are poisonous to all marine organisms." Workshop on Global Ecological Problems, *Man in the Living Environment*, p. 256.

16. *FAO Technical Conference*, p. 534.

17. Schachter and Serwer, "Marine Pollution Problems," p. 92; *FAO Technical Conference*, p. 534.

18. Bernstein, "Poisoning the Seas," p. 15.

19. *FAO Technical Conference*, pp. 2, 192.

20. Barbara Ward Jackson and René Dubos, *Only One Earth*, p. 201. *FAO Technical Conference*, p. 534.

21. Richard Sandbrook and Anita Yurchyshyn, "Marine Pollution from Vessels," in *Critical Environmental Issues on the Law of the Sea*, ed. Robert E. Stein, p. 19.

22. Schachter and Serwer, "Marine Pollution Problems," p. 90.

23. Bruce Halstead, "Toxicological Aspects of Marine Pollution," mimeographed, quoted by Shinn, *International Politics*, p. 10.

24. *FAO Technical Conference*, pp. 452-453. The UN Secretary-General drew a similar conclusion in "Marine Pollution and Other Hazardous and Harmful Effects Which Might Arise From the Exploration and Exploitation of the Seabed and the Ocean Floor, and the Subsoil Thereof, Beyond the Limits of National Jurisdiction," *Report of the Secretary-General*, UN Doc. A/7924 (June 11, 1970), p. 4. Hereafter cited by document number only.

25. Kalsi, "Oil in Neptune's Kingdom," pp. 79-80; Study of Critical Environment Problems, *Man's Impact*, p. 139; Schachter and Serwer, "Marine Pollution Problems," p. 91; Robert W. Holcomb, "Oil in the Ecosystem," *Science*, No. 166 (October 10, 1969), p. 204; The Study of Critical Environmental Problems estimated that production will roughly double during the 1970s (*Man's Impact*, p. 266).

26. Kalsi, "Oil in Neptune's Kingdom," p. 93; E. Gold, "Pollution of the Sea and International Law," *Journal of Marine Law Command*, 3 (1970), 42.

27. "Statement of the Honorable Russell E. Train," p. 2. See also Robert J. McManus, "New Treaty on Vessel Pollution," p. 59; J. Porricelli et al., "Tankers and the Ecology," *Transactions of the Society of Naval Architects and Marine Engineers*, 79 (1971), 169-170.

451

28. Michael Hardy, "International Control of Marine Pollution," *International Organization*, ed. James E.S. Fawcett and Rosalyn Higgins, p. 162.

29. Wallace S. Broecker, "Man's Oxygen Reserve," *Science*, 168 (June 26, 1970), 1538.

30. IMCO/FAO/WMO/WHO/IAEA/UN Joint Group of Experts on the Scientific Aspects of Marine Pollution, "Report of the Third Session" (Rome: FAO, 1971), UN Doc. GESAMP III/19, Annex IV, p. 6. Hereafter cited by document number only.

31. Jackson and Dubos, *Only One Earth*, p. 199.

32. UN Doc. GESAMP III/19, Annex IV; Schachter and Serwer, "Marine Pollution Problems," p. 96; Bernstein, "Poisoning the Seas," p. 16.

33. Study of Critical Environmental Problems, *Man's Impact*, p. 127.

34. Tony J. Peterle, "Pyramiding Damage," *Environment*, 11 (July-August 1969), 34.

35. Shinn, *International Politics*, p. 33.

36. *FAO Technical Conference*, p. 193.

37. Study of Critical Environment Problems, *Man's Impact*, p. 128.

38. See Schachter and Serwer, "Marine Pollution Problems," p. 97.

39. Study of Critical Environmental Problems, *Man's Impact*, p. 129.

40. *FAO Technical Conference*, pp. 191-192.

41. Broecker, "Man's Oxygen Reserve," p. 1538; quoted in Schachter and Serwer, "Marine Pollution Problems," p. 96.

42. *FAO Technical Conference*, pp. 534, 602.

43. Workshop on Global Ecological Problems, *Man in the Living Environment*, p. 253.

44. National Research Council, Panel on Monitoring Persistent Pesticides in the Marine Environment, Committee on Oceanography, *Chlorinated Hydrocarbons in the Marine Environment*, pp. 1-2.

45. National Research Council, ibid., pp. 1-2. See the identical conclusion of the MIT Study of Critical Environmental Problems, *Man's Impact*, p. 136.

46. Workshop on Global Ecological Problems, *Man in the Living Environment*, p. 254.

47. National Research Council, *Chlorinated Hydrocarbons in the Marine Environment*, p. 17.

48. IMCO/FAO/UNESCO/WMO/WHO/IAEA/UN Joint Group of Experts on the Scientific Aspects of Marine Pollution, "Report of the Fourth Session" (Geneva, September 1972), text reprinted in United States Congress, Senate, Committee on Commerce, *1973 IMCO Conference on Marine Pollution from Ships, Hearings*, p. 66. Hereafter cited as *1973 IMCO Hearings*.

49. Edward D. Goldberg, "Chemical Invasion of Ocean by Man," *Man's Impact on Terrestrial and Ocean Ecosystems*, ed. William H. Matthews, Frederick E. Smith, and Edward D. Goldberg, p. 262.

50. Workshop on Global Ecological Problems, *Man in the Living Environment*, p. 257.
51. Goldberg, "Chemical Invasion," p. 264.
52. Coastal Zone Workshop, *The Water's Edge*, ed. Bostwich H. Ketchum, p. 152.
53. Workshop on Global Ecological Problems, *Man in the Living Environment*, p. 257.
54. Douglas M. Johnston, "Marine Pollution Control," p. 72.
55. See Workshop on Global Ecological Problems, *Man in the Living Environment*, p. 257.
56. Study of Critical Environmental Problems, *Man's Impact*, p. 137. Two major incidents occurred in 1953 and 1964. See also T. Nitta, "Marine Pollution in Japan," *FAO Technical Conference*, pp. 77-81.
57. Organization for Economic Cooperation and Development, *Mercury and the Environment*, p. 30. One exception to the general increase anticipated is the substitution of unleaded gasoline for leaded gasoline, thus eliminating one major source of lead pollution.
58. Schachter and Serwer, "Marine Pollution Problems," p. 102.
59. *FAO Technical Conference*, p. 602.
60. Study of Critical Environmental Problems, *Man's Impact*, p. 138.
61. Jackson and Dubos, *Only One Earth*, p. 66. Sharp declines were measured at Landsort Deep.
62. Study of Critical Environmental Problems, *Man's Impact*, p. 146; Johnston, "Marine Pollution Control," p. 71.
63. Study of Critical Environmental Problems, *Man's Impact*, p. 148.
64. A. H. Seymour, "Introduction," in National Research Council, *Radioactivity in the Marine Environment*, p. 1.
65. *Environmental Quality, Annual Report*, 1974, p. 166.
66. A curie is a unit of radioactivity equal to 3.7×10^{10} disintegrations per second.
67. National Research Council, Study Panel on Assessing Potential Ocean Pollutants, *Assessing Potential Ocean Pollutants*, pp. 27, 35. Hereafter cited as *Assessing Ocean Pollutants*.
68. Half-life is a measure of the time it takes for half of the radioactivity to dissipate from a given source. This should not be misunderstood as half of the amount of time the material is dangerous. Plutonium 239, for example, has a half-life of 24,400 years, which means that its radioactivity will be decreased by half after the first period of 24,400 years, but only half of the remaining emissions will be dissipated after the second period of 24,400 years. Thus one-fourth of the original radioactivity would still remain after 48,800 years, one-eighth after 73,200 years, and so on.
69. Seymour, "Introduction," *Radioactivity in the Marine Environment*, p. 2; Herbert Volchok, Chemist for the Environmental Studies Division, Atomic Energy Commission, in U.S. Congress, Senate,

Committee on Commerce, Subcommittee on Oceans and Atmosphere, *Ocean Pollution*, p. 56. Hereafter cited as *Ocean Pollution*.

70. U.S. Atomic Energy Commission, *The Nuclear Industry, 1973*, pp. 57, 59, text reprinted in U.S. Congress, Joint Committee on Atomic Energy, *Development, Growth, and State of the Nuclear Industry*, pp. 328, 330.

71. Ibid., p. 330; Harold P. Green, "Radioactive Waste and the Environment," p. 284.

72. Jack W. Hodges, "International Law and Radioactive Pollution By Ocean Dumping: 'With All Their Genius and With All Their Skill . . . ,' " *San Diego Law Review*, 2 (May 1974), 760; U.S. Congress, House, Committee on Merchant Marine and Fisheries, Subcommittee on Fisheries and Wildlife Conservation and Subcommittee on Oceanography, *Hearings on H.R. 285*, 92nd Cong., 1st Sess. (Washington, D.C.: Government Printing Office, 1971), p. 235.

73. The European Nuclear Energy Organization for Economic Cooperation and Development, *Radioactive Waste Disposal Operations in the Atlantic, 1967* (Paris: OECD, 1968), quoted in Shinn, *International Politics*, p. 30.

74. *New York Times*, May 21, 1976.

75. Richard H. Wagner, *Environment and Man*, pp. 194-195.

76. Study of Critical Environmental Problems, *Man's Impact*, p. 76.

77. *Assessing Ocean Pollutants*, pp. 42-43.

78. Shinn, *International Politics*, p. 28.

79. International Atomic Energy Agency, *Nuclear Power and the Environment*, p. 76.

80. Shinn, *International Politics*, p. 44; Edward Wenk, *The Politics of the Ocean*, p. 185.

81. Moorecraft, *Must the Seas Die?*, p. 107.

82. *Assessing Ocean Pollutants*, p. 44.

83. Two United States nuclear submarines, the Thresher and Scorpion, and at least one Soviet submarine carrying nuclear warheads have sunk.

84. Jackson and Dubos, *Only One Earth*, p. 133. In 1963, the Atomic Energy Commission asked John W. Gofman and Arthur R. Tamplin to conduct a study of the effects of contamination due to the release of radioactivity. They concluded that if the radiation dosage "acceptable" under AEC standards were in fact received by the total United States population, the result would be 32,000 deaths each year from cancer and leukemia. The expected expansion of the nuclear power industry might move radiation exposures beyond even the present permissible standard by the year 2000. See Barry Commoner, *The Closing Circle*, p. 58.

85. *Assessing Ocean Pollutants*, p. 27.

86. Moorecraft, *Must the Seas Die?*, p. 109.

87. J. W. Hedgpeth, "The Oceans: World Sump," *Environment*, 12 (April 1970), 44.
88. *Assessing Ocean Pollutants*, p. 51.
89. Moorecraft, *Must the Seas Die?*, p. 109.
90. *Assessing Ocean Pollutants*, pp. 37-38, 51.
91. Ibid., pp. 10, 12, 53.
92. R. F. Foster, I. L. Ophel, and A. Preston, "Evaluation of Human Radiation Exposure," in National Research Council, *Radioactivity in the Marine Environment*, p. 258; International Atomic Energy Agency, *Nuclear Power and the Environment*, p. 76.
93. International Atomic Energy Agency, *Nuclear Power and the Environment*, p. 76.
94. Moorecraft, *Must the Seas Die?*, pp. 104, 108.
95. William O. Doub and Joseph M. Dukert, "Making Nuclear Energy Safe and Secure," p. 756.
96. See Hallman, *Towards an Environmentally Sound Law*, p. 7.
97. *New York Times*, September 11, 1975.
98. Jackson and Dubos, *Only One Earth*, p. 133.
99. Even low-level storage facilities in Kentucky leaked plutonium into the surrounding soil. Although no humans were directly harmed by the leakage, the radioactive results will be in the Kentucky soil for thousands of years. *New York Times*, September 8, 1977.
100. The group of UN experts concluded: "There is an almost complete lack of data on the synergistic effects of these poisons on both marine organisms and man." *FAO Technical Conference*, p. 535.
101. *Assessing Ocean Pollutants*, p. 9; Workshop on Global Ecological Problems, *Man in the Living Environment*, pp. 257-259; *FAO Technical Conference*, p. 114.
102. Study of Critical Environmental Problems, *Man's Impact*, pp. 142-143.
103. Hallman, *Towards an Environmentally Sound Law*, pp. 5, 7. See also, *Identification and Control of Pollutants of Broad International Significance*, report prepared for Stockholm Conference, UN Doc. A/CONF. 48/8 (January 7, 1972); *The Sea: Prevention and Control of Marine Pollution*, Report of the Secretary-General, UN Doc. E/5003 (May 7, 1971).
104. *FAO Technical Conference*, p. 113; Kalsi, "Oil in Neptune's Kingdom," p. 79.
105. See Jackson and Dubos, *Only One Earth*, pp. 197-198.
106. Article 24.
107. Article 25.
108. Article 5 (7).
109. McManus, "New Treaty," p. 59. The text of the 1954 treaty as amended in 1969 is in *International Legal Materials*, 9 (1970), 1-24.

110. For a brief comparison of the 1973 and 1954 treaties, see the *1973 IMCO Hearings*, pp. 20-21. The text of the treaty is in ibid., pp. 101-177.
111. McManus, "New Treaty," p. 61.
112. Statement of Russell Train, *1973 IMCO Hearings*, pp. 5, 13, 18.
113. Text in *International Legal Materials*, 9 (1970), 22-44.
114. Text in ibid., 9 (1970), 45-67.
115. Text in ibid., 11 (1972), 284-302.
116. *Environmental Quality, Annual Report*, 1973, p. 333.
117. Ibid., p. 61. The definition of new ships is contained in Annex I.
118. Article 3.
119. Kalsi, "Oil in Neptune's Kingdom," p. 86.
120. Statement by Robert Citron in U.S. Congress, Senate, Committee on Commerce, National Ocean Policy Study, *Tankers and the Marine Environment, Hearings*, p. 39. Hereafter cited as *Tankers and Marine Environment Hearings*. McManus reported that in 1970 tankers hauled about 1,300,000,000 metric tons of oil. Of this amount shippers lost roughly 2,500,000 or about 0.2 percent of their cargo. McManus, "New Treaty," p. 59; Porricelli, "Tankers and the Ecology," pp. 169-170. John M. Hunt, vice chairman of the National Academy of Sciences Workshop on Inputs, Fates, and Effects of Petroleum in the Marine Environment, reported that 0.4 percent of the cargo is, on the average, retained on the inside wall of the "empty" tanker. *Tankers and Marine Environment Hearings*, p. 36.
121. Robert Citron in *Tankers and Marine Environment Hearings*, p. 39.
122. McManus, "New Treaty," has reported that only about 40 percent of the ship-generated oil pollution is attributable to tank washing and deballasting operations (p. 59). Six percent is due to accidents.
123. *Environmental Quality, Annual Report*, 1973, pp. 332-333.
124. *Marine Week*, September 13, 1974, reprinted in *Tankers and Marine Environment Hearings*, p. 142.
125. Jackson and Dubos, *Only One Earth*, p. 204.
126. Kalsi, "Oil in Neptune's Kingdom," pp. 86, 98.
127. *Ocean Pollution*, p. 190.
128. *NAS Study of Marine Environmental Quality*, pp. 7-8. See also *Environmental Quality, Annual Report*, 1972, p. 86.
129. A spokesman testifying before the Senate Commerce Committee for five well-known environmental groups commented upon the IMCO proceedings that preceded negotiation of the treaty: "As presently proposed . . . the Convention appears to do little more than codify existing commercial standards among the major maritime nations, provides no incentive to *improve* such standards, and offers insufficient environmental protection." Eldon Greenberg on behalf of the Environmental Defense Fund, Friends of

the Earth, Natural Resources Defense Council, National Parks and Conservation Association, and Sierra Club. *Ocean Pollution*, p. 201.

130. McManus, "New Treaty," p. 60; Russell Train, *Ocean Pollution*, p. 171.

131. McManus, "New Treaty," p. 64.

132. For example, the Water Quality Improvement Act of 1970; the Marine Protection, Research and Sanctuaries Act of 1972; the Water Pollution Control Act Amendments of 1972; the Ports and Waterways Safety Act of 1972.

133. See *Environmental Quality, Annual Report*, 1973, p. 334.

134. Senator Ted Stevens (Alaska), *1973 IMCO Hearings*, p. 12.

135. Statement of Admiral Chester R. Bender, commandant, U.S. Coast Guard, ibid., p. 22.

136. Ibid., p. 12. See also statements by Russell Train, Senator Ted Stevens, and James Reynolds of the American Institute of Merchant Shipping, *Ocean Pollution*, pp. 169-186.

137. *1973 IMCO Hearings*, p. 23.

138. Bender, ibid., p. 23.

139. Said Bender: "We should avoid any unilateral action which would encourage the proliferation of differing regulatory schemes imposed by individual nations." Ibid.

140. Article III. Text in *International Legal Materials*, 11 (1972), 1291.

141. Article VI.

142. Article VII (4). Robert J. McManus, "The New Law on Ocean Dumping," p. 31.

143. Johnston, "Marine Pollution Control," p. 92.

144. McManus, "New Law," p. 31.

145. Two years before the treaty was signed, the U.S. sank nerve gas in the Atlantic. Some experts have judged that this action violated international law. See the discussion by E. D. Brown, "International Law and Marine Pollution," pp. 249-255.

146. The single exception is where the foreign flag ship has loaded material for dumping from a port of the state seeking to enforce the law on the high seas. Such loading requires a license from the port state.

147. *Environmental Quality, Annual Report*, 1973, p. 335.

148. McManus, "New Law," p. 26; *Clean Air and Water News*, 5 (January 25, 1973), 1.

149. See McManus, "New Law," p. 26.

150. U.S. Council on Environmental Quality, *Ocean Dumping*.

151. *Environmental Quality, Annual Report*, 1973, p. 335.

152. *Stockholm Declaration on the Human Environment*, adopted by consensus at the United Nations Conference on the Human Environment held at Stockholm in June 1972, text in James Barros

457

and Douglas M. Johnston, *The International Law of Pollution*, p. 301. See also United Nations Conference on the Human Environment, Report of the UN Conference on the Human Environment, UN Doc. A/CONF.48/14/Rev.1.

153. On this point, see also Johnston, "Marine Pollution Control," p. 96.

154. The only exception was that foreign states would need to grant a license for U.S. ships in foreign ports to load waste material for ocean dumping.

155. United Nations, General Assembly, *Declaration and Treaty Concerning the Reservation Exclusively for Peaceful Purposes of the Sea-Bed and of the Ocean Floor Underlying the Seas Beyond the Limits of Present National Jurisdiction, and the Use of Their Resources in the Interests of Mankind*, A/6695, August 18, 1967 (XXII). See also U.S. Congress, House, Committee on Foreign Affairs, Subcommittee on International Organizations and Movements, *The United Nations and the Issue of Deep Ocean Resources*, 90th Cong., 1st Sess. (Washington, D.C.: Government Printing Office, 1967), pp. 267-286; U.S. Congress, Senate, Committee on Commerce, *The Third UN Law of the Sea Conference*, p. 9. Hereafter cited as *Third UN Law of the Sea Conference*, p. 9.

156. United Nations, General Assembly, Resolution 2750 (XXV).

157. Ann L. Hollick, "Bureaucrats at Sea," in Ann L. Hollick and Robert E. Osgood, *New Era of Ocean Politics*; Ann L. Hollick, "What to Expect from a Sea Treaty," pp. 68-78; *Third UN Law of the Sea Conference*; U.S. Congress, Senate, Committee on Foreign Relations, *The Third UN Law of the Sea Conference, Report to the Senate*, 94th Cong., 1st Sess. (Washington, D.C.: Government Printing Office, 1975). Hereafter cited as *Senate Report on the Caracas Conference*. The texts of all important statements by Ratiner and Stevenson before the Caracas Conference are reprinted in this report.

158. U.S. Congress, Senate, Committee on Interior and Insular Affairs, *Ocean Manganese Nodules*, p. 90. Hereafter cited as *Senate Report on Ocean Nodules*.

159. U.S. Congress, Senate, Committee on Interior and Insular Affairs, *The Law of the Sea Crisis*, pp. 9-10. Hereafter cited as *Law of the Sea Crisis*.

160. John Norton Moore, "U.S. Position on Law of the Sea Reviewed," p. 398.

161. *Third UN Law of the Sea Conference*, p. 28.

162. U.S. Congress, House, Committee on Merchant Marine and Fisheries, Subcommittee on Oceanography, *Oceanography Miscellaneous*, p. 55. Hereafter cited as *Oceanography Hearings*.

163. *Third UN Law of the Sea Conference*, pp. 25, 28, 29. See also the ad-

dress of John Stevenson to the conference on July 11, 1974, reprinted in *Senate Report on the Caracas Conference*, pp. 8-9.

164. United Nations, General Assembly, *Draft United Nations Convention on the International Seabed Area.* UN Doc. A/AC.138/25 (1970); United Nations, ECOSOC, *Uses of the Sea*, UN Doc. E/5120 (1972), p. 5; Hollick, "Bureaucrats at Sea," p. 3 and "What to Expect," p. 76.

165. Wenk, *Politics of the Ocean*, describes the conflict between the Department of Defense and the National Petroleum Council, pp. 268-278.

166. *Third UN Law of the Sea Conference*, p. 26. See also United Nations, Third Conference on the Law of the Sea, *United States of America: Draft Articles for a Chapter on the Economic Zone and the Continental Shelf*, UN Doc. A/CONF.62/L.47 (1974).

167. Stevenson address of July 11, 1974 in *Senate Report on the Caracas Conference*, p. 8.

168. Hollick, "Bureaucrats at Sea," pp. 18, 57-58. The first publication of the oil industry's argument was July 1968 in *Petroleum Resources Under the Ocean Floor*.

169. Hollick, "Bureaucrats at Sea," p. 20.

170. Ibid., pp. 19, 32.

171. Ibid., pp. 40-41.

172. See the statement of T. S. Ary, speaking on behalf of the American Mining Congress, *Senate Report on Ocean Nodules*, p. 62.

173. Hollick, "Bureaucrats at Sea," p. 25.

174. Ibid., pp. 57-58.

175. Other committees that held hearings on law of the sea issues included: Senate Committee on Interior and Insular Affairs, Subcommittee on Minerals, Materials, and Fuels; Senate Committee on Foreign Relations, Subcommittee on Ocean Space; Senate Committee on Commerce, Subcommittee on Oceans and Atmosphere; House Committee on Foreign Affairs, Subcommittee on International Organizations and Movements; House Committee on Merchant Marine and Fisheries, Subcommittee on Oceanography.

176. *Law of the Sea Crisis*, p. 10; *Senate Report on Ocean Nodules*, pp. 63-64.

177. See *Senate Report on the Caracas Conference*, p. 5; Stevenson's statement in *Oceanography Hearings*, p. 15; *New York Times*, May 9, 1975.

178. *Senate Report on Ocean Nodules*, p. 93.

179. Stevenson, *Oceanography Hearings*, p. 15.

180. Leigh Ratiner address of August 9, 1974 in *Senate Report on the Caracas Conference*, pp. 34, 44-45.

181. By 1975, sustained, vigorous pressure from the less developed countries encouraged the United States to shift its position. The

United States agreed to set aside, or to "bank," areas for later exploration if the less developed countries would agree to let U.S. companies begin mining immediately.

182. Stevenson address of July 17, 1974 in *Senate Report on the Caracas Convention*, p. 17.

183. Ratiner address of August 9, 1974, ibid., p. 54.

184. Ratiner address of August 9, 1974, ibid., pp. 30, 39. Under strong international pressure, the United States in 1975 agreed to allow some joint ventures and profit-sharing, but retained the demand that no limits be set on number of claims, total production, or overall profits. See the statement by Moore in U.S. Congress, Senate, Committee on Commerce, *Geneva Session of the Third United Nations Law of the Sea Conference*, p. 5. Hereafter cited as *Geneva Session Hearings*. See also *Senate Report on Ocean Nodules*, p. 96.

185. Stevenson address of July 11, 1974 in *Senate Report on the Caracas Convention*, p. 10.

186. Ratiner address of June 4, 1975, text reprinted in U.S. Congress, Senate, Committee on Interior and Insular Affairs, Subcommittee on Minerals, Materials, and Fuels, *Status Report on the Law of the Sea Conference*, pp. 1198-1199. Hereafter cited as *Senate Status Report on the Law of the Sea Conference*.

187. Ratiner address of August 9, 1974 in *Senate Report on the Caracas Convention*, pp. 30-31. Committee I discussed all matters related to the deep seabed.

188. See *Senate Report on Ocean Nodules*, p. 97.

189. Statement of T. S. Ary, ibid., p. 72. Several U.S. companies had already begun exploring for the richest mining sites. Howard Hughes' Summa Corporation reportedly possessed the most advanced deep-sea mining technology, possibly aided by CIA funds to build the Glomar Explorer, which attempted secretly to lift a sunken Soviet submarine from the Pacific ocean floor. Kennecott Copper and Deep Sea Ventures, a subsidiary of Tenneco Corporation, also had plans underway to exploit deep-sea hard mineral resources. (See Brian Johnson, "Environmental Controls in the Deep Seabed Under International Jurisdiction," in Robert E. Stein, ed., *Critical Environmental Issues*, p. 33.) The latter two corporations formed international consortia, which included other Japanese, Canadian, British, and Belgian companies. A third international consortium, the "CLB Group," was based upon more than twenty-five major companies from six countries. *Senate Report on Ocean Nodules*, pp. 35-36. Consortia not only shared the capital requirements, but also diminished the risks that a claim staked by a corporation from one nation would be jumped by a competing firm from another country. Claim jumping, of course, was a serious problem in an area owned by no one or everyone. Finally, consortia decreased the number of individual producers,

thus laying the groundwork for possible manipulation of metal prices.

190. Ratiner address of August 9, 1974 in *Senate Report on the Caracas Convention*, pp. 32, 38; Moore, "U.S. Position," p. 400. The U.S. also insisted that expropriation of foreign investment in the 200-mile economic zones be expressly prohibited. Hollick, "Bureaucrats at Sea," pp. 53-54.

191. Stevenson statement, *Senate Status Report on the Law of the Sea Conference*, pp. 853-854; *Senate Report on Ocean Nodules*, p. 94.

192. Ratiner's address of August 9, 1974 in *Senate Report on the Caracas Convention*, pp. 31-32.

193. Ibid., p. 41.

194. Ibid., p. 38.

195. *Senate Report on Ocean Nodules*, pp. 72, 85.

196. Ibid., pp. 85, 97.

197. See the statements of the secretary and assistant secretary of the interior, quoted by Senator Lee Metcalf, *Congressional Record*, February 26, 1975, p. S 2711; *Senate Report on Ocean Nodules*, pp. 82-83.

198. Prominent spokesmen for unilateral action were also active in the House Committee on Merchant Marine and Fisheries, the House Committee on Oceanography, the Senate Commerce Committee, and the Senate Committee on Interior and Insular Affairs.

199. General Assembly Resolution 2574 (XXIV); *Senate Report on Ocean Nodules*, p. 89.

200. U.S. Congress, Senate, Committee on Interior and Insular Affairs, Special Subcommittee on Outer Continental Shelf, *Outer Continental Shelf* (Washington, D.C.: Government Printing Office, 1970), p. 23; *Senate Report on Ocean Nodules*, pp. 63-98.

201. *Congressional Record*, June 23, 1975. Much of Metcalf's language was similar to that of Marne A. Dubs, director of the Ocean Resource Department, Kennecott Copper Corporation. Dubs said the negotiating text was good for the less developed countries, but was "an unmitigated disaster" for the United States. *Geneva Session Hearings*, pp. 37-49.

202. *Senate Status Report on the Law of the Sea Conference*, p. 1162.

203. Text of statement by John M. Murphy, April 15, 1975, reprinted in ibid., pp. 1168-1169. A somewhat more extreme position was taken by Congressman Paul Rogers, who said "the United States should have the right to occupy the ocean floor to the Mid-Atlantic Ridge and assume the responsibility to defend it." Quoted in U.S. Congress, House, Committee on Foreign Affairs, *Exploiting the Resources of the Seabed*, 92nd Cong., 1st Sess. (Washington, D.C.: Government Printing Office, 1971), p. 24.

204. Ratiner, address of August 9, 1974 in *Senate Report on the Caracas Convention*, p. 36.

461

205. In contrast, advocates of global humanism argue that scarce resources even in national jurisdiction should be seen as part of the common heritage, and a global guidance system should help allocate certain vital resources regardless of their point of origin. In this view, there should not be discrimination by oil producers, for example, against states lacking petroleum resources of their own.

206. Henry Kissinger, "The Law of the Sea: A Test of International Cooperation," address of April 8, 1976 (Washington, D.C.: Bureau of Public Affairs, U.S. Department of State, 1976), p. 5.

207. Ibid., pp. 2, 3, 8.

208. Ibid., pp. 5, 7.

209. Ibid., p. 6.

210. U.S. Congress, Senate, Committee on Interior and Insular Affairs, Subcommittee on Minerals, Materials and Fuels, *Status Report on Law of the Sea Conference*, p. 1662.

211. Ibid., pp. 1639, 1651.

212. U.S. Delegation, "The Third United Nations Conference on the Law of the Sea," New York (March 15-May 7, 1976), p. 7. Text reprinted, ibid., p. 1624.

213. Ibid., p. 1665.

214. Elliot L. Richardson, "Review of the Law of the Sea Conference and Deep Seabed Mining Legislation," p. 751.

215. There was speculation about the possibility that Engo's revisions may have been influenced by conversations with Ratiner, the former U.S. negotiator. Ratiner became an employee of Kennecott the day after resigning his government position. He met socially with Engo and may have cynically encouraged Engo to take a more pro-Third World stance, which would alienate the United States and thereby scuttle the negotiations. This would both enable Kennecott to proceed with mining unilaterally and increase the prospects that the U.S. Congress would pass legislation providing public guarantees for private investment in order to eliminate much of the private corporate risk in deep-sea mining ventures. See "Poker Over Seabed Mining: Tale of the Ubiquitous Lobbyist," *Washington Post*, August 14, 1977.

216. Elliot L. Richardson, "Law of the Sea Conference," p. 390.

217. Hollick, "Bureaucrats at Sea," p. 66.

218. John R. Stevenson, "Lawmaking for the Seas," p. 190.

219. Ratiner address of August 9, 1974 in *Senate Report on the Caracas Convention*, pp. 42-43.

220. See "United States Draft Articles—Protection of the Marine Environment and the Prevention of Marine Pollution," UN Doc. A/AC.138/SC.III/L.40 (1973). The text is reprinted in *Senate Report on the Caracas Conference*, pp. 74-79.

221. Article III (1). See also the statement of Donald L. McKernan, alternate U.S. representative to the Committee on Peaceful Uses of

the Seabed and the Ocean Floor Beyond the Limits of National Jurisdiction, August 17, 1971, reprinted in *Law of the Sea Crisis*, p. 47. See also Moore address of July 20, 1973, UN Doc. A/AC.138/SC.III/SR.41 (1973).

222. See *Third UN Law of the Sea Conference*, pp. 30-31. Flag states, of course, each could set higher standards for their own flag ships, but that was unlikely, as it would put their ships at a competitive disadvantage.

223. U.S. Department of State, "U.N. Law of the Sea Conference 1975," p. 6.

224. Sandbrook and Yurchyshyn, "Marine Pollution from Vessels" in Stein, *Critical Environmental Issues*, p. 26.

225. Stevenson, *Oceanography Hearings*, p. 59.

226. Stevenson, *Senate Status Report on the Law of the Sea Conference*, pp. 5, 38. See also Thomas A. Clingan, deputy assistant secretary of state for Oceans and Fisheries Affairs, ibid., p. 44.

227. Hollick, "Bureaucracies at Sea," p. 67.

228. *Senate Report on the Caracas Conference*, p. 4.

229. Moore, address of July 22, 1974, ibid., p. 23; Article XXIII. The United States did, however, include a provision that military vessels should "act in a manner consistent" with the purposes of the treaty even though they were legally exempt (Article XXIII).

230. Moore, "U.S. Position," p. 400; Robert M. Hallman, "Environmental Regulation of Marine Based Activities in Areas of National Jurisdiction," in Stein, *Critical Environmental Issues*, p. 12.

231. Stevenson, address of July 11, 1974 in *Senate Report on the Caracas Convention*, p. 9.

232. UN Doc. A/AC.138/SC.III/SR.41, p. 3.

233. Article XXIV, text reprinted in *Senate Report on the Caracas Conference*, p. 79. Stevenson, address of July 11, 1974 in *Senate Report on the Caracas Conference*, p. 11.

234. Donald McKernan address of August 17, 1971, *Law of the Sea Crisis*, p. 49.

235. Ibid.

236. Stevenson, address of July 17, 1974 in *Senate Report on the Caracas Conference*, p. 14; UN Doc. A/CONF.62/WP.8/Part I, p. 5. The address is reprinted in *Senate Status Report on the Law of the Sea Conference*, p. 1283.

237. *Third UN Law of the Sea Conference*, p. 31.

238. Johnson, "Environmental Controls" in Stein, *Critical Environmental Issues*, p. 36.

239. "The Third United Nations Conference on the Law of the Sea," Geneva (March 17-May 9, 1975); *Senate Status Report on the Law of the Sea Conference*, p. 1241; "The Third United Nations Conference on the Law of the Sea," Caracas (June 20-August 29, 1974) in U.S. Congress, *Oceanography Miscellaneous*, p. 98.

240. UN Doc. A/CONF.62/C.3/L.15.

241. *Third UN Law of the Sea Conference*, p. 31. See also the statement of Kenya in UN Doc. A/AC.138/SC.III.SR.41, p. 6.

242. *Environmental Quality, Annual Report*, 1972, pp. 80, 93.

243. *Third UN Law of the Sea Conference*, p. 32.

244. *Environmental Quality, Annual Report*, 1972, pp. 80, 93.

245. Ibid., p. 93.

246. Jackson and Dubos, *Only One Earth*, p. 208.

247. Hollick, "What to Expect," p. 68.

248. F. H. Knelman, "What Happened at Stockholm," p. 43.

249. Ibid.

250. *Third UN Law of the Sea Conference*, p. 4. The text of the Truman Proclamation (September 28, 1945) is contained in Shigeru Oda, *The International Law of the Ocean Development* (Leiden: Sijthoff International Publishing Company, 1972), p. 341.

251. Hollick, "What to Expect," p. 71.

252. Hollick, "Bureaucrats at Sea," pp. 52-53; L. F. E. Goldie, "The Management of Ocean Resources: Regimes for Structuring the Maritime Environment," *The Future of the International Legal Order: The Structure of the International Environment*, ed. Cyril E. Black and Richard A. Falk, 4 (Princeton: Princeton University Press, 1972), 210-211; Wenk, *Politics of the Ocean*, p. 280.

253. Goldie, "Management of Ocean Resources" in Black and Falk, *Future of the International Legal Order*, p. 211.

254. Johnson, "Environmental Controls" in Stein, *Critical Environmental Issues*, p. 35.

255. This statement, quoting from Principle 7 of the Declaration of the Stockholm Conference on the Human Environment, is contained in "Statement of the Honorable Russell E. Train," p. 3.

256. *Stockholm Declaration*, Principle 21.

257. Text in Barros and Johnston, *International Law*, p. 251.

258. *Environmental Quality, Annual Report*, 1973, p. 440.

259. John Stevenson, "Department Discusses Progress Towards 1973 Conference on the Law of the Sea," p. 672.

260. Wenk, *Politics of the Ocean*, p. 287.

261. The U.S. delegation even objected to other delegations' use of language depicting an "ocean space" regime, saying that such a sweeping authority was outside the competence of the conference. See Johnson, "Environmental Controls" in Stein, *Critical Environmental Issues*, p. 34; UN Doc. A/CONF.62/C.1/SR.7; R. C. Ogley, "Caracas and the Common Heritage," *International Relations*, 4 (November 1974), 620.

262. Lyndon Johnson, "Remarks at the Commissioning of the Research Ship *Oceanographer*," July 13, 1966, text, Wenk, *Politics of the Ocean*, p. 476.

263. UN Doc. A/6628, Res. 2749 (xxv); *Senate Report on Ocean Nodules*, p. 89.

464

264. United Nations, General Assembly, *Draft United Nations Convention on the International Seabed Area*, UN Doc. A/AC.138/25 (1970), p. 1.

265. Nixon, "United States Oceans Policy," *Public Papers*, p. 455.

266. Lyndon Johnson, "Report of the President to the Congress on Marine Resources and Engineering Development, Marine Science Affairs—A Year of Transition," U.S. President, National Council on Marine Resources and Engineering Development, *Marine Science Affairs*, 1st Report (Washington, D.C.: Government Printing Office, 1967), pp. v, iii.

267. Nixon, "United States Oceans Policy," *Public Papers*, p. 456.

268. Ratiner, address of August 9, 1974 in *Senate Report on the Caracas Convention*, p. 35.

269. Wenk, *Politics of the Ocean*, p. 262. *Marine Science Affairs*, 1st Report, p. v; Hollick, "Bureaucrats at Sea," pp. 3, 53-54, 70-71.

270. Wenk, *Politics of the Ocean*, pp. 266-267, 274.

271. Nixon, "United States Ocean Policy," *Public Papers*, p. 455.

272. Lynton K. Caldwell, *In Defense of Earth*, p. 237.

273. Goldberg, "Chemical Invasion" in Matthews, Smith, and Goldberg, *Man's Impact*, p. 268.

274. Nixon, "State of the Union Message," in *Environmental Quality, Annual Report*, 1973, p. 440.

275. Nixon, "State of the Union Message," January 30, 1974, *Environmental Quality, Annual Report*, 1974, p. 542.

276. Stevenson, "U.S. Urges Early Conclusion of Law of the Sea Treaty," p. 153.

277. Stevenson, "Lawmaking for the Seas," p. 190.

278. See the Marine Resources and Engineering Development Act of 1966, P. L. 89-454, *U.S. Statutes*, 80 (June 17, 1966); U.S. Commission on Marine Science, Engineering and Resources, *Marine Resources and Legal-Political Arrangements for Their Development* (Washington, D.C.: Government Printing Office, 1969), p. VIII-2.

279. Hollick, "Bureaucrats at Sea," p. 70.

280. Ratiner, address of August 9, 1974 in *Senate Report on the Caracas Convention*, pp. 30, 36-37.

281. Stevenson, "Lawmaking for the Seas," p. 190.

282. U.S. Commission on Marine Science, Engineering, and Resources, *Marine Resources and Legal-Political Arrangements for Their Development*, p. VIII-3.

283. Frank, *Geneva Session Hearings*, p. 58. In order to gain domestic support for a treaty, the United States needed to take a stance less objectionable to U.S. environmental groups. This was accomplished in 1977, as the negotiating text was modified so that it became consistent with U.S. national legislation imposing standards on ships using U.S. ports. However, the other previously noted deficiencies in the treaty remained.

284. Wenk, *Politics of the Ocean*, p. 263; Hollick, "Bureaucrats at Sea," pp. 2, 70-71.

285. For one view of such an agency, see Falk, *Study of Future Worlds*, pp. 268-274.

286. Shinn, *International Politics*, p. 125. Shinn concludes: "The first sign of serious cooperative efforts will be massive consolidation of old organizations or the establishment of new forums with comprehensive capability. Without one or the other, international environmental efforts are reducible to empty rhetoric and meaningless verbiage."

287. See Hollick, "What to Expect," p. 77.

288. On this point, see Hollick, ibid.

289. See John Lawrence Hargrove, *Ocean Pollution*, pp. 127-128.

290. To be sure, the United States has such a large impact on both the political climate and the quantity of pollutants introduced in the seas that strong national legislation would alleviate, although not arrest, the decline of the oceans.

291. Gerald Elliott, "Fishing Control—National Or International," *World Today*, 28 (March 1972), 134-135.

292. O. P. Dwivedi, "The Canadian Government Response to Environmental Concern," p. 15.

293. Controlling radioactive pollution is nearly as difficult as preventing the proliferation of nuclear weapons. William O. Doub and Joseph M. Dukert comment: "If a nation is determined, as India was, to demonstrate the ability to build its own nuclear weapons, probably no international framework can prevent it from doing so; the raw materials and the technology exist, to the point where no amount of international policing consistent with present concepts of national sovereignty . . . can prevent nations from developing and exploding 'devices' " ("Making Nuclear Energy Safe," p. 756).

294. Johnston, "Marine Pollution Control," p. 70; Hardy, "International Control" in Fawcett and Higgins, *International Organization*, p. 110.

295. Shinn, *International Politics*, p. 181.

296. Malarial spraying reportedly accounted for only 15 percent of the general use of DDT in the early 1970s. Quoted in Clyde Sanger, "Environment and Development," p. 118.

297. On this point, see Knelman, "What Happened at Stockholm," pp. 33-34.

298. As Knelman, ibid., has explained: "Economic power thrives on competition. Ecology is based on mutuality and indivisibility. Power is based on zero-sum games. Ecology is based on non-zero-sum games" (pp. 34-35).

299. Richard A. Falk, "Environmental Policy as a World Order Problem," in Albert E. Utton and Daniel H. Henning, eds., *Environmental Policy*, pp. 146, 151.

300. See the statement of Marne Dubs, *Geneva Session Hearings*, p. 45.

466

301. Gordon L. Becker, Counsel, Law Department, Exxon Corporation, *Geneva Session Hearings*, p. 35.
302. These might include, for example, family planning, control of inflation, and improvement of agricultural production.
303. Ambassador Pardo advocated an international regime with three categories of membership for states over 100,000 population: (1) states over 100 million or which meet other criteria, such as length of coastline, catch of fish, and volume of merchant shipping; (2) all other coastal states, and (3) landlocked countries. Decisions would require a majority vote in two of the three categories. All members would have one vote, but could express it only in their own category.

   Hallman, *Towards an Environmentally Sound Law*, offers a brief but relatively comprehensive treatment of the environmental protection that could be satisfied with only a minimum of structural change. Other proposals for an international regime are contained in the following: The Commission to Study the Organization of Peace, *New Dimensions for the United Nations* (New York: UN Plaza, 1968), 17th Report, pp. 44-46; "Malta: Draft Articles on the Preservation of the Marine Environment," pp. 583-590; Borgese, *Pacem in Maribus*; U.S. Congress, Senate, Foreign Relations Committee, *The United Nations at Twenty-One*, Report by Senator Frank Church, 90th Cong., 1st Sess. (Washington, D.C.: Government Printing Office, 1967), p. 25.
304. Jack Davis, Canada's minister of the environment, said that nations will have to agree on international pollution standards for specific industries before the issue of environmental quality versus economic development is resolved. Otherwise, capital will flow to pollution havens. See Sanger, "Environment and Development," p. 104.
305. Jackson and Dubos, *Only One Earth*, p. 201. In the United States alone, dumping of wastes in the oceans multiplied five times during the 1950s and 1960s. According to monitoring surveys of the United States National Oceanographic and Atmospheric Administration, this practice fouled more than one million square miles of the Atlantic and extended into the Caribbean as far as the Yucatan Peninsula. See Hallman, *Towards an Environmentally Sound Law*, p. 6; *MARMAP* Report, NOAA, United States Department of Commerce, January 1974.
306. Jacques Cousteau, "The Perils and Potentials of a Watery Planet," p. 42.

SIX. BUILDING A JUST WORLD ORDER

1. Two sets of tables are relevant here. The first compares professed and implicit values (Tables 2-7, 3-13, 4-2, and 5-3). The second

compares the values implicit in U.S. policy with the values of global humanism (Tables 2-8, 3-14, 4-3, 5-4).

2. There are, of course, additional dimensions that make up a more complete worldview.

3. For a summary of these agreements, see Stockholm International Peace Research Institute, *World Armaments and Disarmament, SIPRI Yearbook, 1977*, pp. 368-380. For an assessment of the impact of these agreements on the arms buildup, see Stockholm International Peace Research Institute, *Armaments and Disarmament in the Nuclear Age*, pp. 217-223; Bernhard G. Bechhoefer, *Postwar Negotiations for Arms Control*; Robert C. Johansen, *Toward a Dependable Peace*.

4. For example, Herbert York, who served as scientific advisor to presidents during three administrations has concluded: "Over the last 30 years we have repeatedly taken unilateral actions that have unnecessarily accelerated the arms race. Our unilateral decisions have set the rate and scale for most of the individual steps in the strategic-arms race." *Race to Oblivion*, p. 230.

5. This concept was developed by Nathan Leites in *A Study of Bolshevism* (Glencoe, Ill.: The Free Press, 1953). Alexander L. George refined it in "The 'Operational Code,' " pp. 190-222. Richard J. Barnet used the concept in *The Roots of War*. Although his study was limited to national security affairs and published before the present studies occurred, the implicit values delineated in the case studies here substantiate many of his findings.

6. These ideas are more fully elaborated in Barnet, *Roots of War*, pp. 95-96, 98.

7. Text, *New York Times*, October 13, 1974.

8. Quoted in Arthur Schlesinger, *A Thousand Days*, p. 481; cited in Barnet, *Roots of War*, p. 106.

9. See Barnet's similar conclusion, *Roots of War*, pp. 93-98; 109-114; 120-129.

10. For elaboration of this point, see ibid., pp. 120-121.

11. For elaboration of this point and general discussion of bureaucratic politics, see ibid., p. 122; Graham Allison, *Essence of Decision*; Graham Allison and Morton Halperin, "Bureaucratic Politics," pp. 40-79.

12. Interview with James Reston, text, *New York Times*, October 13, 1974.

13. One example is the book, *Famine—1975!* (Boston: Little, Brown and Company, 1967). It was written by William and Paul Paddock, two brothers with pertinent experience: one was an agronomist and plant pathologist who headed a tropical research station and also a school of agriculture in Central America; the other was a retired foreign service officer with experience in the developing

countries of Asia and Africa. Part I of the book is entitled "Inevitability of Famine in the Hungry Nations."

14. Richard A. Falk has described similar forms of human estrangement as "false consciousness." Such a person "loses the ability to discern his own interests, the conditions of his own fulfillment, or the actuality of his role as a victim or perpetrator of exploitation." See *This Endangered Planet*, pp. 84-85.

15. Many observers would argue that the actions of U.S. officials did not violate reason. To be sure, because their policies were rooted in priorities that differed sharply from those of global humanism did not in itself make their behavior unreasonable. However, to the extent that they were motivated by ideological and material interests which increased selective perception, made them blind to important dimensions of reality, and stimulated unreflective policy responses, to that extent one could say that their behavior "violated reason." The case studies demonstrate that official behavior contained a high degree of such behavior. For both psychological and material reasons, officials resisted modification of their operational code that would bring it into closer harmony with a rapidly changing reality.

16. Barnet, *Roots of War*, p. 126.

17. Of course, the changes may not always be positive. Also, some gaps between rhetoric and behavior may indefinitely disguise normatively deficient policies.

18. Milton Rokeach, *The Nature of Human Values*, pp. 328-330.

19. Although the role of the court system has not been discussed in this study, an example of the judicial branch's national partisanship is the refusal of the federal courts to consider the legality of the war in Vietnam and the legal defense of deserters who claimed to be following the Nuremburg precedent and international treaties prohibiting war crimes.

20. The "balance of power system" does not serve this function. In such a system, one nation may seek to offset another state's potential abuse of power, but usually none of the competing nation-states genuinely promotes the global interest. They pursue different national interests. In contrast to the international system, within most domestic political systems there are many incentives for competing political actors to express different versions of the society's common interest, rather than simply to advance particular vested interests. To be sure, often special interests are disguised as the public interest, but in democratic societies their expression is usually muted and the prospect of their fulfillment less absolute than is the case of superpowers pursuing special interests within the international system.

21. For a discussion of some central guidance possibilities, such as sug-

gested in numbers 3, 6, 9, and 12, see Richard A. Falk, *A Study of Future Worlds*, pp. 224-276.

22. Quoted in Leslie H. Gelb, "The Kissinger Legacy," p. 85.

23. Quoted in Donald McDonald, "American Guilt," p. 30. Commenting upon the influence of the military-industrial complex on national policy, Richard Barnet concluded that "the only force capable of bringing about the conversion of the society is a nationwide movement of Americans who see the militarism of America as our number-one security problem and are prepared to fight for a generation if necessary to free the nation from its grip" (*The Economy of Death*, p. 135).

24. More often than not, on foreign policy issues national governmental rhetoric has been deceptive. This does not mean that all government officials are dishonest, but simply that there is frequently a fundamental contradiction between what they say and what they do. In some instances they *are* dishonest; in others they have faulty perceptions of reality and their own behavior.

25. For a discussion of the possibilities for using nonviolence effectively, see Gene Sharp, *The Politics of Nonviolent Action* and George Lakey, *Strategy for a Living Revolution*.

26. For example, to establish merely a world authority for environmental protection will raise enormous political opposition. Commenting upon the prospects for such an authority, George Kennan concluded: "If the present process of [environmental] deterioration is to be halted, things are going to have to be done which will encounter formidable resistance from individual governments and powerful interests within individual countries." But Kennan did not seem to take his own analysis seriously enough to draw the conclusion that change would need to begin in opposition to present centers of power. In spite of the anticipated governmental and corporate resistance, Kennan offered no plan of action for the creation of a new authority other than to hope that precisely the privileged forces that now resist change will soon implement it. "Only an entity that has great prestige, great authority and active support from centers of influence within the world's most powerful industrial and maritime nations will be able to make headway against such recalcitrance." George F. Kennan, "To Prevent a World Wasteland," p. 409.

27. *New York Times*, February 2, 1975.

28. Although it is impossible to describe precisely how a grass roots popular movement can transform the present institutional structures of the international system, it is useful to outline plausible strategies with feasible steps leading from the present to a preferred system. For discussion of one possible transition strategy aimed at abolishing the war system, see Johansen, *Toward a Dependable Peace*.

470

29. See Falk's "first law of ecological politics," *This Endangered Planet*, p. 353.
30. Rokeach, *Nature of Human Values*, p. 331.
31. As Rokeach commented, the idea that "enduring value changes can be induced by a single experimental session takes on rather awesome . . . political implications." Ibid., p. 324.

   The possibilities for value change, of course, will not automatically serve the values of global humanism, consistent though they are with many psychologists' and religious leaders' understandings of human health, sanity, and spiritual enrichment. Because of an effective socialization process, most people in practice give national loyalty and prevailing subspecific political values priority over the principle of universal compassion which is prescribed by the dominant religious faiths in the United States. In practice, peoples' highest loyalties are to national symbols, even though universal brotherliness and sisterliness are the hallmarks of both Christianity and Judaism.
32. Many critics scoff at the suggestion that foreign policy can, even if it should, reflect extranational humanitarianism. The pervasiveness of self-interest, they say, precludes the transfer of as much as 1 or 2 or 5 percent of GNP to poor states "merely" out of a sense of solidarity with other humans. In the past, the argument goes, national societies have more often than not pursued their own advantages without much regard for, or even at the expense of, other nations. They are likely to continue doing so in the future.

   Such statements are similar to the arguments raised by slave owners in the 1850s who said that some groups, possessing superior skills and racial qualities, had dominated other groups in the past and therefore should continue to do so in the future. The idea of human solidarity between blacks and whites was as unthinkable to such people before the Civil War as is the idea today of human solidarity among all nations of the globe. The past failure to achieve human solidarity transcending either races or nations is not a convincing argument that human solidarity is unachievable. During the last three centuries subnational loyalties in many parts of the world were rapidly replaced with intense feelings of national solidarity. In several noteworthy instances—including the growth of United States nationalism—these new national solidarities transcended previous linguistic, racial, religious, and cultural differences.

Bibliography

Aaron, David. "SALT: A New Concept." *Foreign Policy*, No. 17 (Winter 1974-1975), pp. 157-165.

Adede, A. O. "System for Exploitation of the Common Heritage of Mankind at the Caracas Conference." *American Journal of International Law*, 69 (January 1975), 31-49.

Agee, Philip. *Inside the Company: CIA Diary*. London: Penguin, 1975.

Allison, Graham. *Essence of Decision: Explaining the Cuban Missile Crisis*. Boston: Little, Brown and Company, 1971.

Allison, Graham and Halperin, Morton. "Bureaucratic Politics: A Paradigm and some Policy Implications." *World Politics*, 24 (Spring 1972), 40-79.

Artin, Tom. *Earth Talk*. New York: Grossman, 1973.

Baldwin, David A. *Foreign Aid and American Foreign Policy*. New York: Praeger, 1966.

Ball, George. *The Discipline of Power*. Boston: Little, Brown and Company, 1968.

Barnaby, Frank. "The Mounting Prospects of Nuclear War." *Bulletin of the Atomic Scientists*, 33 (June 1977), 11-21.

Barnds, William J. "India and America at Odds." *International Affairs*, 49 (July 1973), 317-384.

Barnet, Richard J. "Dirty Tricks and the Intelligence Underworld." *Society* 12 (March/April 1975), 52-57.

———. *The Economy of Death*. New York: Atheneum, 1970.

———. *Intervention and Revolution*. New York: The World Publishing Company, 1968.

———. *Roots of War*. New York: Atheneum, 1972.

———. *Who Wants Disarmament?* Boston: Beacon Press, 1960.

———, and Mueller, Ronald. *Global Reach: The Power of the Multinational Corporation*. New York: Simon and Schuster, 1974.

Barros, James and Johnston, Douglas M. *The International Law of Pollution*. New York: Free Press, 1974.

Bechhoefer, Bernhard G. *Postwar Negotiations for Arms Control*. Washington, D.C.: The Brookings Institution, 1961.

Bell, Wendell and Mau, James A., eds. *The Sociology of the Future*. New York: Sage, 1971.

Beres, Louis and Targ, Harry. *Reordering the Planet: Constructing Alternative World Futures*. Boston: Allyn and Bacon, 1974.

473

Bernstein, Richard. "Poisoning the Seas." *Saturday Review/World*, 1 (November 20, 1973), 14-16.

Bhagwati, Jagdish N. *Amount and Sharing of Aid*. Washington, D.C.: Overseas Development Council, 1970.

———, ed. *Economics and World Order: From the 1970's to the 1990's*. New York: Macmillan 1972.

Birns, Laurence R. "Allende's Fall, Washington's Push." *New York Times*, September 15, 1974.

———, ed. *The End of Chilean Democracy*. New York: Seabury Press, 1973.

Black, Lloyd. *The Strategy of Foreign Aid*. Princeton: Van Nostrand, 1968.

Blackstock, Paul. *The Strategy of Subversion*. Chicago: Quadrangle, 1964.

Bleicher, Samuel A. "An Overview of International Environmental Regulation." *Ecology Law Quarterly*, 2 (Winter 1972), 1-90.

Bloomfield, Lincoln P. "Nuclear Spread and World Order." *Foreign Affairs*, 53 (July 1975), 743-755.

Borgese, Elisabeth Mann, ed. *Pacem in Maribus*. New York: Dodd, Mead and Company, 1972.

Borgstrom, Georg. *The Hungry Planet*. New York: Macmillan, 1965.

Bowen, V. T. and Sugihara, T. T. "Oceanographic Implications of Radioactive Fallout Distributions in the Atlantic Ocean." *Journal of Marine Research*, 23 (April 1965), 123-146.

Brodkin, E. I. "United States Aid to India and Pakistan." *International Affairs*, 43 (October 1967), 664-677.

Brown, E. D. "International Law and Marine Pollution: Radioactive Waste and Other Hazardous Substances." *Natural Resources Journal*, 11 (April 1971), 221-255.

———. "The Conventional Law of the Environment." *Natural Resources Journal*, 13 (April 1973), 203-234.

Brown, Lester R. *By Bread Alone*. New York: Praeger, 1974.

Brown, Norman W. *The United States and India, Pakistan, Bangladesh*. Cambridge: Harvard University Press, 1972.

Brownlie, Ian. *Basic Documents on Human Rights*. Oxford: Clarendon Press, 1971.

Brynes, Asher. *We Give to Conquer*. New York: Norton, 1966.

Brzezinski, Zbigniew. "The Politics of Underdevelopment." *World Politics*, 9 (October 1956), 55-75.

Caldwell, Lynton K. *In Defense of Earth: International Protection of the Biosphere*. Bloomington: Indiana University Press, 1972.

Carter, Jimmy. "Peace, Arms Control, World Economic Progress, Human Rights: Basic Priorities of United States Foreign Policy." *Department of State Bulletin*, 76 (April 11, 1977), 329-333.

———. "Remarks by President Jimmy Carter Videotaped for Delivery to People of Other Nations." White House Press Release, January 20, 1977, mimeo.

Casey, William J. "A Comprehensive Development Policy for the United States." *Department of State Bulletin*, 69 (December 3, 1973), 688-694.

———. "The Rule of Law in International Economic Affairs." *Department of State Bulletin*, 69 (September 3, 1973), 321-326.

Clark, Grenville and Sohn, Louis B., eds. *Introduction to World Peace Through World Law*. Chicago: World Without War Publications, 1973.

———. *World Peace Through World Law*. Cambridge: Harvard University Press, 1960.

Clark, Ramsey. "The Law and Human Rights in Chile." *Christianity and Crisis*, 34 (July 22, 1974), 161-164.

Clarkson, Kenneth W. "International Law, U.S. Seabeds Policy and Ocean Resource Development." *Journal of Law and Economics*, 17 (April 1974), 117-142.

Clemens, Walter C. "Ecology and International Relations." *International Journal*, 28 (Winter 1972-73), 1-27.

———. "Nicholas II to SALT II: Continuity and Change in East-West Diplomacy." *International Affairs*, 49 (June 1973), 385-401.

Coastal Zone Workshop, Woods Hole, Massachusetts, 1972. *The Water's Edge*. Ed. Bostwich, H. Ketchum. Cambridge, Massachusetts: MIT Press, 1972.

Coffin, Tristan. *The Armed Society*. Baltimore: Penguin Books, 1964.

Commoner, Barry. *The Closing Circle*. New York: Bantam, 1971.

Connor, Walker. "Self-Determination: The New Phase." *World Politics*, 20 (October 1967), 30-53.

Cook, Fred J. *The Warfare State*. New York: Macmillan, 1962.

Cooper, Chester. "The CIA and Decision Making." *Foreign Affairs*, 50 (January 1972), 223-236.

Cousteau, Jacques. "The Perils and Potentials of a Watery Planet." *Saturday Review/World*, 1 (August 24, 1974), 41 ff.

Dillon, Douglas. "The Contribution of Trade to the Cause of Peace." *Department of State Bulletin*, 38 (May 26, 1958), 881-882.

Dornan, James E. "Maybe No Agreement Would be Better." *Armed Forces Journal*, January 1975, pp. 28-32.

Doty, Paul; Garwin, Richard; Kistiakowsky, George; Rathjens, George; Schelling, Thomas. "Nuclear War by 1999?" *Harvard Magazine*, 78 (November 1975), 19-25.

Doub, William O. and Dukert, Joseph M. "Making Nuclear Energy Safe and Secure." *Foreign Affairs*, 53 (July 1975), 756-772.

Dubs, Adolph. "Department Discusses South Asia and U.S. Assistance Programs." *Department of State Bulletin*, 76 (April 19, 1977), 344-346.

Dulles, John Foster. "Peace Without Fear." *Department of State Bulletin*, 24 (May 7, 1951), 726-731.

Dwivedi, O. P. "The Canadian Government Response to Environmental Concern." *International Journal*, 28 (Winter 1972-1973), 134-152.

Eckert, Ross D. "Exploitation of Deep Ocean Minerals: Regulatory Mechanisms and U.S. Policy." *Journal of Law and Economics*, 17 (April 1974), 143-177.

Ehrlich, Paul and Ehrlich, Anne H. *Population, Resources, and Environment*. San Francisco: W. H. Freeman, 1972.

Epstein, William. "Inexorable Rise of Military Expenditures." *Bulletin of the Atomic Scientists*, 31 (January 1975), 17-19.

———. *The Last Chance: Nuclear Proliferation and Arms Control*. New York: Free Press, 1976.

Fagen, Richard R. "The United States and Chile: Roots and Branches." *Foreign Affairs*, 53 (January 1975), 263-313.

Falk, Richard A. "Arms Control, Foreign Policy, and Global Reform." *Daedalus*, 104 (Summer 1975), 35-52.

———. "A New Paradigm for International Legal Studies: Prospects and Proposals." *The Yale Law Journal*, 84 (April 1975), 969-1021.

———. *A Study of Future Worlds*. New York: Free Press, 1975.

———. *This Endangered Planet: Prospects and Proposals for Human Survival*. New York: Vintage, 1971.

———. "Towards a World Order Respectful of the Global Ecological System." *Environmental Affairs*, 1 (June 1971), 25-65.

———, and Black, Cyril E., eds. *The Future of the International Legal Order: Trends and Patterns*. 4 vols. Princeton: Princeton University Press, 1969-75.

———, and Mendlovitz, Saul H. *Regional Politics and World Order*. San Francisco: W. H. Freeman, 1973.

476

Farnsworth, Elizabeth. "Chile: What Was the U.S. Role? More Than Admitted." *Foreign Policy*, No. 16 (Fall 1974), pp. 127-141.

Fawcett, James E. S. and Higgins, Rosalyn, eds. *International Organization: Law in Movement*. London: Oxford University Press, 1974.

Feldman, Herbert. "Aid as Imperialism?" *International Affairs*, 43 (April 1967), 219-235.

Fisher, David W. "Some Social and Economic Aspects of Marine Resource Development." *American Journal of Economics and Sociology*, 32 (April 1973), 113-127.

FAO Technical Conference on Marine Pollution and Its Effect on Living Resources and Fishing, Rome, 1970. *Marine Pollution and Sea Life*. London: Fishing News Books, 1972.

Frank, Richard A. "The Law at Sea." *New York Times Magazine*, May 18, 1975, pp. 14 ff.

Friedheim, R. L. "Quantitative Content Analysis of the U.N. Seabed Debate." *International Organization*, 24 (Summer 1970), 479-502.

Galtung, Johan. *The True Worlds*. New York: The Free Press, forthcoming.

Garcia-Amador, F. V., ed. *The Inter-American System*. Dobbs Ferry, New York: Oceana, 1966.

Garcia Marquez, Gabriel. "Why Allende Had To Die." *New Statesman*, 87 (March 15, 1974), 356-358.

Gaud, William S. "Development—A Balance Sheet." *Department of State Bulletin*, 59 (December 30, 1968), 703-706.

———. "Foreign Aid: What It Is; How It Works, Why We Provide It." *Department of State Bulletin*, 59 (December 9, 1968), 603-606.

Gelb, Leslie H. "The Kissinger Legacy." *New York Times Magazine*, October 31, 1976, pp. 13 ff.

Gelba, Harry M. "Technical Innovation and Arms Control." *World Politics*, 26 (July 1974), 509-541.

George, Alexander L. "The 'Operational Code': A Neglected Approach to the Study of Political Leaders and Decision-Making." *International Studies Quarterly*, 13 (June 1969), 190-222.

Gillette, Robert. "Radiation Spill at Hanford: The Anatomy of an Accident." *Science*, 181 (August 24, 1973), 728-730.

Gilligan, John J. "United States Seeks Improved U.N. Programs to Meet Basic Needs of World's Poor." *Department of State Bulletin*, 77 (August 15, 1977), 204-207.

Goldsmith, Edward et al. *Blueprint for Survival*. Boston: Houghton Mifflin, 1972.

Goldwin, Robert A. *Why Foreign Aid?* Chicago: Rand McNally, 1963.

Goulet, Denis. *The Cruel Choice: A Normative Theory of Development*. New York: Atheneum, 1971.

————, and Hudson, Michael. *The Myth of Aid*. New York: IDOC North America, 1971.

Graham, Frank. *Since Silent Spring*. Boston: Houghton Mifflin, 1970.

Green, Harold P. "Radioactive Waste and The Environment." *Natural Resources Journal*, 11 (April 1971), 281-295.

Green, Philip. *Deadly Logic: The Theory of Nuclear Deterrence*. Columbus, Ohio: Ohio State University Press, 1966.

Greenwood, Ted and Nacht, Michael. "New Nuclear Debate: Sense or Nonsense?" *Foreign Affairs*, 52 (June 1974), 761-780.

Hallman, Robert M. *Towards an Environmentally Sound Law of the Sea*. Washington, D.C.: International Institute for Environment and Development, 1974.

Halperin, Morton H. "Decision-Making for Covert Operations." *Society*, 12 (March/April 1975), 45-51.

Halpern, Manfred. *The Morality and Politics of Intervention*. New York: The Council on Religion and International Affairs, 1963.

Hannah, John A. "Institutional Problems in the Developing Countries." *Department of State Bulletin*, 64 (March 8, 1971), 297-301.

Hansen, Roger D. "The Political Economy of North-South Relations: How Much Change?" *International Organization*, 29 (Fall 1975), 921-947.

Hardin, Garrett. *Exploring New Ethics for Survival*. Baltimore: Penguin, 1972.

Hardy, E. P., Keey, P. W. and Volchok, H. L. "Global Inventory and Distribution of Fallout Plutonium." *Nature*, 241 (February 16, 1973), 444-445.

Hardy, Michael. "International Control of Marine Pollution." *Natural Resources Journal*, 11 (April 1971), 296-348.

Hargrove, John L., ed. "Conference on Legal and Institutional Response to Problems of the Global Environment." *Law, In-*

478

stitutions, and the Global Environment. Dobbs Ferry: Oceana Publications, 1973.

——, ed. *Who Protects the Ocean?* St. Paul: West Publishing Co., 1975.

Harrison, Selig S., ed. *India and the United States*. New York: Macmillan, 1961.

Heilbroner, Robert L. "Growth and Survival." *Foreign Affairs*, 51 (October 1972), 139-153.

——. *An Inquiry into the Human Prospect*. New York: Norton, 1975.

Herz, John. *International Politics in the Atomic Age*. New York: Columbia University Press, 1959.

——. "The Territorial State Revisited," *Polity*, 1 (September 1968), 11-34.

Hollick, Ann L. "What to Expect From a Sea Treaty." *Foreign Policy*, No. 18 (Spring 1975), pp. 68-78.

——, and Osgood, Robert E. *New Era of Ocean Politics*. Baltimore: Johns Hopkins Press, 1975.

Hollings, Ernest F. "National Ocean Policy Study." *Oceans*, 8 (January/February 1975), 6-7.

Holst, Johan Jorgen. "A Strategic Arms Race: What is Really Going On?" *Foreign Policy*, No. 19 (Summer 1975), pp. 152-162.

Hudson, Michael. *Super Imperialism: The Economic Strategy of American Enterprise*. New York: Holt, Rinehart, and Winston, 1972.

Ingersoll, Robert S. "Economic Interdependence and Common Defense." *Department of State Bulletin*, 71 (October 7, 1974), 473-476.

Inter-American Institute of International Legal Studies. *The Inter-American System: Its Development and Strengthening*. Dobbs Ferry, New York: Oceana Publications, 1966.

International Atomic Energy Agency. *Nuclear Power and the Environment*. Vienna: International Atomic Energy Agency, 1973.

International Colloquium on the European Convention on Human Rights. *Human Rights in National and International Law*. Manchester: Manchester University Press, 1968.

International Institute for Strategic Studies. *The 1974-75 Military Balance*. London: International Institute for Strategic Studies, 1976.

479

"Interview with William E. Colby." *U.S. News and World Report*, 77 (December 2, 1974), 29-32.

Irwin, John N. "A Strengthened and Revitalized Foreign Aid Program." *Department of State Bulletin*, 64 (May 24, 1971), 657-664.

Jackson, Barbara Ward and Dubos, René. *Only One Earth: The Care and Maintenance of a Small Planet*. New York: Norton, 1972.

Jacobson, Jon. "Caracas 1974: A No-Progress Report on the Law of the Sea." *Oceana*, 7 (November-December, 1974), 66-68.

Johansen, Robert C. "Countercombatant Strategy: A New Balance of Terror?" *Worldview*, 17 (July 1974), 47-53.

————. "A Global Humanist Critique of National Policies for Arms Control." *Journal of International Affairs*, 31 (Fall/Winter 1977), 215-241.

————. *Toward a Dependable Peace: A Proposal for an Appropriate Security System*. New York: Institute for World Order, 1978.

Johnson, Lyndon. "To Build the Peace—The Foreign Aid Program for Fiscal 1969." *Department of State Bulletin*, 58 (March 4, 1968), 322-329.

————. "The Importance of Foreign Aid to U.S. Security and World Peace." *Department of State Bulletin*, 59 (August 21, 1968), 178.

Johnston, Douglas M. "Marine Pollution Control: Law, Science and Politics." *International Journal*, 28 (Winter 1972-73), 69-102.

Kalsi, Swadesh S. "Oil in Neptune's Kingdom: Problems and Responses to Contain Environmental Degradation of the Oceans by Oil Pollution." *Environmental Affairs*, 3, No. 1 (1974), pp. 79-108.

Katzenbach, Nicholas deB. "Foreign Policy, Public Opinion and Secrecy." *Foreign Affairs*, 52 (October 1973), 1-19.

————. "United States Policy Toward the Developing World." *Department of State Bulletin*, 59 (August 26, 1968), 209-213.

Kay, David and Skolinikoff, Eugene B. *World Eco-Crisis*. Madison: University of Wisconsin Press, 1972.

Kennan, George F. "To Prevent a World Wasteland: A Proposal." *Foreign Affairs*, 48 (April 1970), 401-413.

Kennedy, John F. "Message of the President to the Congress." *Department of State Bulletin*, 44 (April 10, 1961), 507-514.

————. "New Opportunities in the Search for Peace." *Department of State Bulletin*, 49 (October 7, 1963), 530-535.

————. "White House Holds Conference on Export Expansion: Address by President Kennedy." *Department of State Bulletin*, 44 (October 14, 1963), 595-599.

Kennedy, Robert, *Thirteen Days*. New York: Norton, 1969.

Kissinger, Henry. "The Foreign Assistance Program and Global Stability." *Department of State Bulletin*, 71 (August 19, 1974), 286-290.

————. "The Foreign Assistance Program: A Vital Tool in the Building of a More Cooperative World." *Department of State Bulletin*, 71 (July 8, 1974), 45-55.

————. "A Just Consensus, a Stable Order, a Durable Peace." *Department of State Bulletin*, 69 (October 15, 1973), 469-473.

————. "Moral Purposes and Policy Choices." *Department of State Bulletin*, 61 (October 29, 1973), 525-531.

————. "Towards a Global Community: The Common Cause of India and America." *Department of State Bulletin*, 71 (November 25, 1975), 740-746.

Klare, Michael T. "The Political Economy of Arms Sales." *Society*, 11 (September-October 1974), 41-49.

Knelman, F. H. "What Happened at Stockholm." *International Journal*, 28 (Winter 1972-1973), 28-49.

Kothari, Rajni. *Footsteps Into the Future: Diagnosis of the Present World and a Design for an Alternative*. New York: Free Press, 1974.

Krasner, Stephen D. "Are Bureaucracies Important? (Or Allison Wonderland)." *Foreign Policy*, No. 7 (Summer 1972), pp. 159-179.

Lagos, Gustavo and Godoy, Horacio H. *Revolution of Being: A Latin American View of the Future*. New York: Free Press, 1977.

Lakey, George. *Strategy for a Living Revolution*. San Francisco: W. H. Freeman, 1973.

Land, Thomas. "Dividing Up the Deep." *The Progressive*, 38 (June 1974), 35-37.

Lapp, Ralph E. *The Weapons Culture*. New York: Norton, 1968.

Laszlo, Ervin. *A Strategy for the Future*. New York: Braziller, 1974.

Laudicina, Paul. *World Poverty and Development: A Survey of American Opinion*. Washington, D.C.: Overseas Development Council, 1973.

Legault, L.J.H. "The Freedom of the Seas: A Licence to Pollute." *University of Toronto Law Journal*, 21 (April 1971), 39-49.

Leggett, Robert L. "Two Legs Do Not a Centipede Make." *Armed Forces Journal*, February 1975, pp. 30-32.

Lerza, Catherine and Jacobson, Michael, eds. *Food for People—Not for Profit*. New York: Ballantine, 1975.

Lewis, John P. *Wanted in India: A Relevant Radicalism*. Center of International Studies, Policy Memorandum No. 36. Princeton, N.J.: Princeton University, 1969.

———. *Quiet Crisis in India: Economic Development and American Policy*. Washington: Brookings, 1962.

McDonald, Donald. "American Guilt," an interview with Richard A. Falk, *Center Magazine*, 7 (January-February 1974), 26-32.

MacEoin, Gary. "The U.S. Government and Chile: An Exercise in Deception." *Christianity and Crisis*, 34 (October 14, 1974), 219-223.

McGarvey, Patrick J. *CIA: the Myth and the Madness*. New York: Saturday Review Press, 1972.

McIntyre, Thomas J. "Security through Détente: Limits and Possibilities," speech before the International Studies Council, University of New Hampshire, May 5, 1975.

McManus, Robert J. "The New Law on Ocean Dumping." *Oceans*, 6 (September-October 1973), 25-32.

———. "New Treaty on Vessel Pollution." *Oceans*, 7 (June 1974), 59-65.

"Malta: Draft Articles on the Preservation of the Marine Environment." A/Ac. 138/SC.III/L.33. *International Legal Materials*, 12 (1973), 583-590.

Marchetti, Victor and Marks, John D. *The CIA and the Cult of Intelligence*. New York: Dell, 1974.

Marx, Wesley. *The Frail Ocean*. New York: Ballantine, 1969.

Matthews, William H.; Smith, Frederick E.; and Goldberg, Edward D. *Man's Impact on Terrestial and Ocean Ecostystems*. Cambridge: MIT Press, 1971.

Mazrui, Ali A. *A World Federation of Cultures: An African Perspective*. New York: Free Press, 1976.

Melman, Seymour. *Pentagon Capitalism: The Political Economy of War*. New York: McGraw-Hill, 1970.

Mendlovitz, Saul H. *On the Creation of a Just World Order: Preferred Worlds for the 1990's*. New York: Free Press, 1975.

Mesarovic, Mihajlo D. and Pestel, Eduard. *Mankind at the Turning Point*. New York: Dutton, 1974.

Millikan, Max F. and Rostow, Walt W. *A Proposal: Key to an Effective Foreign Policy*. New York: Harper and Brothers, 1957.

482

Mollenhoff, Clark. *The Pentagon: Politics, Profits and Plunder*. New York: Putnam, 1967.

Montagu, Ashley. *The Endangered Environment*. New York: Mason and Lipcomb, 1974.

Moore, John Norton. "U.S. Position on Law of the Sea Reviewed." *Department of State Bulletin*, 70 (April 15, 1974), 397-402.

Moorecraft, Colin. *Must the Seas Die?* Boston: Gambit, 1973.

Moran, Theodore. *Multinational Corporations and the Politics of Dependence: Copper and Chile*. Princeton, N.J.: Princeton University Press, 1974.

Morgenthau, Hans. "A Political Theory of Foreign Aid." *American Political Science Review*, 56 (March 1962), 301-309.

Mostert, Noel. *Supership*. New York: Alfred A. Knopf, 1974.

Moyer, Bill. "Interview for 'Bill Moyer's Journal.' " *Department of State Bulletin*, 72 (February 10, 1975), 165-180.

Myrdal, Alva. *The Game of Disarmament: How the United States and Russia Run the Arms Race*. New York: Pantheon Books, 1976.

———. "The High Price of Nuclear Arms Monopoly." *Foreign Policy*, No. 18 (Spring 1975), pp. 30-43.

———. "International Control of Disarmament." *Scientific American*, 231 (October 1974), 21-33.

Myrdal, Gunnar. *The Challenge of World Poverty*. New York: Pantheon, 1970.

Nacht, Michael L. "The Delicate Balance of Error." *Foreign Policy*, No. 19 (Summer 1975) pp. 163-177.

National Academy of Sciences. Ocean Science Committee of the NAS-NRC Ocean Affairs Board. *Marine Environmental Quality*. Washington, D.C.: National Academy of Sciences, 1971.

National Research Council. Panel on Monitoring Persistent Pesticides in the Marine Environment. *Chlorinated Hydrocarbons in the Marine Environment*. Washington, D.C.: National Academy of Sciences, 1971.

———. Panel on Radioactivity in the Marine Environment. *Radioactivity in the Marine Environment*. Washington, D.C.: National Academy of Sciences, 1971.

———. Study Panel on Assessing Potential Ocean Pollutants. Ocean Affairs Board, Commission on Natural Resources. *Assessing Potential Ocean Pollutants*. Washington, D.C.: National Academy of Sciences, 1975.

Nayar, Baldev Raj. "Political Mainsprings of Economic Planning in the New Nations: The Modernization Imperative Versus Social Mobilization." *Comparative Politics*, 6 (April 1974), 341-366.

———. "Treat India Seriously." *Foreign Policy*, No. 18 (Spring 1975), pp. 133-154.

Newhouse, John. *Cold Dawn: The Story of SALT*. New York: Holt, Rinehart and Winston, 1973.

Nitze, Paul. "The Strategic Balance Between Hope and Skepticism." *Foreign Policy*, No. 17 (Winter 1974-1975), pp. 136-156.

———. "The Vladivostok Accord and SALT II." *Review of Politics*, 37 (April 1975), 147-160.

Nixon, Richard. "Foreign Assistance for the Seventies." *Department of State Bulletin*, 63 (October 5, 1970), 369-378.

———. "Pragmatism and Moral Force in American Foreign Policy." *Department of State Bulletin*, 71 (July 1, 1974), 1-5.

———. "President Nixon Interviewed for CBS Television." *Department of State Bulletin*, 63 (September 21, 1970), 327-330.

———. "Reform of the U.S. Foreign Assistance Program." *Department of State Bulletin*, 64 (May 10, 1971), 614-625.

———. "Special Message to the Congress on Marine Pollution From Oil Spills," May 20, 1970. *Public Papers of the Presidents of the United States*. Washington, D.C.: Government Printing Office, 1971.

———. "U.S. Foreign Policy for the 1970's: Building for Peace." Report to Congress of February 25, 1971. *Department of State Bulletin*, 64 (March 22, 1971), 341-432.

———. "United States Policy for the Seabed." *Department of State Bulletin*, 62 (June 15, 1970), 737-738.

Odeen, Philip. "In Defense of the Defense Budget." *Foreign Policy*, No. 16 (Fall 1974), pp. 93-108.

Ohlin, Goran. *Foreign Aid Policies Reconsidered*. Paris: Development Center of the Organization for Economic Cooperation and Development, 1966.

O'Leary, Michael Kent. *The Politics of American Foreign Aid*. New York: Atherton Press, 1967.

Organization for Economic Co-operation and Development. *Development Assistance Efforts and Policies of the Members of the Development Assistance Committee*. Paris: OECD, annual reviews.

———. *Mercury and the Environment*. Paris: OECD, 1974.

———. *Resources for the Developing World: Flow of Financial Resources to Less-Developed Countries, 1962-68*. Paris: OECD, 1970.

Packenham, Robert A. "Political Development Doctrines in the

American Foreign Aid Program." *World Politics*, 18 (January, 1966), 194-234.

Pearson, Lester. *The Crisis of Development*. New York: Praeger, 1970.

Petaccio, Victor. "Water Pollution and the Future Law of the Sea." *International and Comparative Law Quarterly*, 21 (January 1972), 15-42.

Petras, James F. and LaPorte, Robert. "Can We Do Business with Radical Nationalists? Chile: No." *Foreign Policy*, No. 7 (Summer 1972), pp. 132-158.

Pirages, Dennis C. and Ehrlich, Paul R. *Ark II*. San Francisco: W. H. Freeman, 1974.

Potter, Van Rensellaer. *Bioethics: Bridge to the Future*. Englewood Cliffs, N.J.: Prentice-Hall, 1971.

Quanbeck, Alton H. and Blechman, Barry M. *Strategic Forces: Issues for the Mid-Seventies*. Washington, D.C.: Brookings Institution, 1973.

Ransom, Harry Howe. "Secret Intelligence Agencies and Congress." *Society*, 12 (March/April 1975), 33-38.

Rathjens, George W. "Flexible Response Options." *Orbis*, 18 (Fall 1974), 677-688.

——. "The Dynamics of the Arms Race." *Scientific American*, (April 1969), pp. 15-25.

Richardson, Elliot. "Law of the Sea Conference: Problems and Progress." *Department of State Bulletin*, 77 (September 19, 1977), 389-391.

——. "Review of the Law of the Sea Conference and Deep Seabed Mining Legislation." *Department of State Bulletin*, 77 (November 21, 1977), 751-756.

Robertson, Arthur Henry. *Human Rights in the World*. Manchester: Manchester University Press, 1972.

Rogers, William. "United States Foreign Policy 1969-70: A Report of the Secretary of State." *Department of State Bulletin*, 64 (April 5, 1971), 465-477.

Rokeach, Milton. *The Nature of Human Values*. New York: Free Press, 1973.

Rosa, Nicholas. "What is Leviation's Future?" *Oceans*, 7 (May 1974), 45-53.

Rostow, Walt W. *The United States in the World Arena*. New York: Simon and Schuster, 1969.

Rotkirch, Holger. "Claims to the Ocean." *Environment*, 16 (June 1974), 34-41.

Russett, Bruce M. "Assured Destruction of What? A Counter-combatant Alternative to Nuclear Madness." *Public Policy*, 22 (Spring 1974), 121-138.

Sanger, Clyde. "Environment and Development." *International Journal*, 28 (Winter 1972-1973), 103-120.

Schachter, Oscar. "Just Prices in World Markets: Proposals *De Sege Ferenda.*" *American Journal of International Law*, 69 (January 1975), 101-109.

————, and Serwer, Daniel. "Marine Pollution Problems and Remedies." *American Journal of International Law*, 65 (January 1971), 84-111.

Schertz, Lyle P. "World Food: Prices and the Poor." *Foreign Affairs*, 52 (April 1974), 511-537.

Schlesinger, Arthur. *A Thousand Days*. Boston: Houghton Mifflin, 1965.

Schlesinger, James R. *Annual Defense Department Report FY 1976*, and *FY 1977*. Washington, D.C.: Government Printing Office, 1975, 1976

Schultze, Charles T. "The Economic Content of National Security Policy." *Foreign Affairs*, 51 (April 1973), 522-540.

Schwelb, Egor. *Human Rights and the International Community*. Chicago: Quadrangle, 1964.

Sewell, John W. *The United States and World Development*. New York: Praeger, 1977.

Sharp, Gene. *The Politics of Nonviolent Action*. Boston: Porter Sargent Publisher, 1973.

Shields, Linda P. and Ott, Marvin C. "Environmental Decay and International Politics: The Uses of Sovereignty." *Environmental Affairs*, 3, No. 4 (1974), 743-767.

Shinn, Robert. *The International Politics of Marine Pollution Control*. New York: Praeger, 1974.

Shultz, George P. "Administration Stresses Importance of U.S. Action on Funding for IDA and ADB Replenishment." *Department of State Bulletin*, 69 (December 17, 1973), 731-736.

Sigmund, Paul E. "Chile: What was the U.S. Role? Less than Charged." *Foreign Policy*, No. 16 (Fall 1974), pp. 142-156.

Singer, Fred, ed. *Global Effects of Environmental Pollution*. New York: Springer-Verlag, 1970.

Sivard, Ruth Leger. *World Military and Social Expenditures, 1974, 1975, 1976, 1977*. Leesburg, Virginia: WMSE Publications, 1974-1977.

Smith, Gerard C. "SALT After Vladivostok," *Journal of International Affairs*," 29 (Spring 1975), 7-18.

Sohn, Louis B. and Buergenthal, Thomas. *International Protection of Human Rights*. New York: Bobbs-Merrill, 1973.

Sommer, John G. *Beyond Charity*. Washington, D.C.: Overseas Development Council, 1977.

Sorensen, Theodore. *Kennedy*. New York: Bantam, 1965.

Stein, Eric. "Legal Restraints in Modern Arms Control Agreements." *American Journal of International Law*, 66 (April 1979), 255-289.

Stein, Robert E., ed. *Critical Environmental Issues on the Law of the Sea*. Washington, D.C.: International Institute for Environment and Development, 1975.

Stevenson, Adlai E. "Working Toward a World Without War." In U.S. Arms Control and Disarmament Agency, *Disarmament: The New U.S. Initiative*. Washington, D.C.: Government Printing Office, 1962, pp. 13-28.

Stevenson, John R. "Conflicting Approaches to the Control and Exploitation of the Ocean." *American Journal of International Law Proceedings*, 65 (Summer 1971), 107-143.

———. "Department Discusses Progress Towards 1973 Conference on the Law of the Sea." *Department of State Bulletin*, 66 (May 8, 1972), 672-679.

———. "Lawmaking for the Seas." *American Bar Association Journal*, 61 (February 1975), 185-190.

———. "U.S. Urges Early Conclusion of Law of the Sea Treaty." *Department of State Bulletin*, 72 (February 3, 1975), 153-154.

———, and Oxman, Bernard H. "The Preparations for the Law of the Sea Conference." *American Journal of International Law*, 68 (January 1974), 1-32.

———. "The Third United Nations Conference on the Law of the Sea: The 1974 Caracas Session." *American Journal of International Law*, 69 (January 1975), 1-30.

Stockholm International Peace Research Institute. *Armaments and Disarmament in the Nuclear Age*. Stockholm: Almqvist and Wiksell International, 1976.

———. *World Armaments and Disarmament, S.I.P.R.I. Yearbook*. Cambridge: MIT Press, various years.

———. *World Armaments: The Nuclear Threat*. Stockholm: SIPRI, 1977.

Stone, Jeremy O. "When and How to Use SALT." *Foreign Affairs*, 48 (January 1970), 262-273.

Strong, Maurice F. "One Year After Stockholm: An Ecological Approach." *Foreign Affairs*, 51 (1973), 690-707.

———, ed. *Who Speaks for Earth?* New York: Norton, 1973.

Study of Critical Environmental Problems. *Man's Impact on the Global Environment*. Cambridge: MIT Press, 1970.

Swing, John Temple. "Law of the Sea at the Brink." *Oceans* (September 1977), pp. 4-5.

Swomley, John M. *The Military Establishment*. Boston: Beacon, 1964.

Symposium on International Relations and the Future of Ocean Space, 1972. *International Relations and the Future of Ocean Space*. Columbia, S.C.: University of South Carolina Press, 1974.

Tansky, Leo. *U.S. and U.S.S.R. Aid to Developing Countries*. New York: Praeger, 1967.

Teclaff, Ludwik A. "International Law and the Protection of Oceans from Pollution." *Fordham Law Review*, 40 (March 1972), 529-564.

Thayer, George. *The War Business: The International Trade in Armaments*. New York: Simon and Schuster, 1969.

Thorp, Willard L. *The Reality of Foreign Aid*. New York: Praeger, 1971.

Tinbergen, Jan. *Reshaping the International Order*. New York: Dutton, 1976.

Train, Russell E. "Statement of the Honorable Russell E. Train Before the Council of the Inter-Governmental Maritime Consultative Organization." Mimeographed. London, June 5, 1973.

United Nations. *Demographic Yearbook of the United Nations*. New York: United Nations, various years.

————. "Draft UN Convention on the Seabed Area." UN Document A/AC. 138/25. *International Legal Materials*, 9 (1970).

————. Department of Economist and Social Affairs, Statistical Office. *Yearbook of National Accounts Statistics*. New York: United Nations, various years.

————. General Assembly. "U.S. Draft Articles on the Protection of the Marine Environment and the Prevention of Marine Pollution." UN Document A/AC. 138/SC.III/2.40, July 13, 1973.

U. S. Agency for International Development. *The Foreign Assistance Program: Annual Report to Congress*. Washington, D.C.: Government Printing Office, various years

————. *Report to Congress: Foreign Assistance Program Fiscal Years 1962-1971*. Washington, D.C.: Government Printing Office, various years.

————. Program Coordination Staff. *Principles of Foreign Eco-*

nomic Assistance. Washington, D.C.: Government Printing Office, 1963.

———. Statistics and Reports Division. *U.S. Economic Assistance Programs April 3, 1948-June 30, 1963*. Washington, D.C.: Government Printing Office, various years.

———. Statistics and Reports Division. *U.S. Economic Assistance Programs Administered by the Agency for International Development and Predecessor Agencies, April 13, 1948-June 30, 1971*. Washington, D.C.: Government Printing Office, 1972.

———. Statistics and Reports Division. *U.S. Overseas Loans and Grants and Assistance from International Organizations: Obligations and Loan Authorizations, 1945-73, 1945-74, 1945-75, 1945-76*. Washington, D.C.: Government Printing Office, 1974, 1975, 1976, 1977.

U.S. Arms Control and Disarmament Agency. *Arms Control and Disarmament Agreements*. Washington, D.C.: Government Printing Office, 1975.

———. *Disarmament: The New U.S. Initiative*. Washington, D.C.: Government Printing Office, 1962.

———. *The International Transfer of Conventional Arms: Report to the Congress*. Printed for the use of the House Committee on Foreign Affairs, House of Representatives, 93rd Congress, 2nd Session. Washington, D.C.: Government Printing Office, 1974.

———. *World Military Expenditures and Arms Trade, 1963-1973, and 1966-1975*. Washington, D.C.: Government Printing Office, 1975 and 1976.

U.S. Commission on Marine Science, Engineering, and Resources. *Marine Resources and Legal-Political Arrangements for Their Development*. Washington, D.C.: Government Printing Office, 1969.

U.S. Congress. House. Committee on Appropriations, Subcommittee on Foreign Operations and Related Agencies. *Foreign Assistance and Related Agencies Appropriations for 1975*. 93rd Congress, 2nd Session. Washington, D.C.: Government Printing Office, 1974.

U.S. Congress. House. Committee on Armed Services. *Hearings on Military Posture and H.R. 3689 Department of Defense Authorization for Appropriations for Fiscal Year 1976 and 197T*. 94th Congress, 1st Session. Washington, D.C.: Government Printing Office, 1975.

U.S. Congress. House. Committee on Foreign Affairs. *Fiscal Year*

489

1975 Foreign Assistance Request. 93rd Congress, 2nd Session. Washington, D.C.: Government Printing Office, 1974.

———. *Foreign Assistance Act of 1964*. 88th Congress, 2nd Session. Washington, D.C.: Government Printing Office, 1964.

———. *Mutual Development and Cooperation Act of 1973*. 93rd Congress, 1st Session. Washington, D.C.: Government Printing Office, 1973.

———. *Mutual Security Act of 1955*. 84th Congress, 1st Session. Washington, D.C.: Government Printing Office, 1955.

———. *Mutual Security Act of 1958*. 85th Congress, 2nd Session. Washington, D.C.: Government Printing Office, 1958.

———. *Report of Special Study Mission to Pakistan, India, Thailand, and Indochina*. Report No. 412. 83rd Congress, 1st Session. Washington, D.C.: Government Printing Office, 1953.

———. *Status of the U.N. Law of the Sea Conference*. 93rd Congress, 2nd Session. Washington, D.C.: Government Printing Office, 1975.

———. Subcommittee on International Organizations and Movements. *Human Rights in the World Community*. 93rd Congress, 2nd Session. Washington, D.C.: Government Printing Office, 1974.

———. Subcommittee on the Near East and South Asia. *Indian Rupee Settlement Agreement*. 93rd Congress, 2nd Session. Washington, D.C.: Government Printing Office, 1974.

U.S. Congress. House. Committee on Merchant Marine and Fisheries. Subcommittee on Oceanography. *Oceanography Miscellaneous*. 93rd Congress, 2nd Session. Washington, D.C.: Government Printing Office, 1975.

———. Subcommittee on Fisheries and Wildlife Conservation and the Environment. *Ocean Dumping*. 93rd Congress, 1st Session. Washington, D.C.: Government Printing Office, 1973.

U.S. Congress. Senate. Committee on Appropriations. *Department of Defense Appropriations Fiscal Year 1975*. 93rd Congress, 2nd Session. Washington, D.C.: Government Printing Office, 1974.

U.S. Congress. Senate. Committee on Armed Services. *Fiscal Year 1976 and July-September 1976 Transition Period Authorization for Military Procurement, Research and Development, and Active Duty, Selective Reserve, and Civilian Personnel Strengths*. 94th Congress, 1st Session. Washington, D.C.: Government Printing Office, 1975.

U.S. Congress. Senate. Committee on Commerce. *Geneva Session of the Third United Nations Law of the Sea Conference*. 94th Congress, 1st Session. Washington, D.C.: Government Printing Office, 1975.

———. *International Maritime Consultative Organization: 1973 Conference on Marine Pollution*. 93rd Congress, 1st Session. Washington, D.C.: Government Printing Office, 1974.

———. *Offshore Marine Environment Protection Act of 1973*. 93rd Congress, 1st Session. Washington, D.C.: Government Printing Office, 1973.

———. *1972 Survey of Environmental Activities of International Organizations*. 92nd Congress, 2nd Session. Washington, D.C.: Government Printing Office, 1972.

———. *Tankers and the Marine Environment*. 94th Congress, 1st Session. Washington, D.C.: Government Printing Office, 1975.

———. *The Third U.N. Law of the Sea Conference*. 94th Congress, 1st Session. Washington, D.C.: Government Printing Office, 1975.

———. Subcommittee on Oceans and Atmosphere. *Ocean Pollution*. 93rd Congress, 1st Session. Washington, D.C.: Government Printing Office, 1974.

U.S. Congress. Senate. Committee on Foreign Relations. *ACDA Authorization*. 93rd Congress, 2nd Session. Washington, D.C.: Government Printing Office, 1974.

———. *CIA Foreign and Domestic Activities*. 94th Congress, 1st Session. Washington, D.C.: Government Printing Office, 1975.

———. *Foreign Assistance Authorization 1974*. 93rd Congress, 2nd Session. Washington, D.C.: Government Printing Office, 1974.

———. *Mutual Security Act of 1954*. 83rd Congress, 2nd Session. Washington, D.C.: Government Printing Office, 1954.

———. *Mutual Security Act of 1960*. 86th Congress, 2nd Session. Washington, D.C.: Government Printing Office, 1960.

———. *Technical Assistance: Final Report of the Committee on Foreign Relations*. 87th Congress, 1st Session. Washington, D.C.: Government Printing Office, various years.

———. *The Third United Nations Law of the Sea Conference. Report to the Senate*. 94th Congress, 1st Session. Washington, D.C.: Government Printing Office, 1975.

———. *U.S. Participation in ADB and IDA*. 93rd Congress, 1st Session. Washington, D.C.: Government Printing Office, 1974.

491

U.S. Congress. Senate. Committee on Foreign Relations. Subcommittee on Arms Control, International Law and Organization. *Arms Control Implications of Current Defense Budget*. 92nd Congress, 1st Session. Washington, D.C.: Government Printing Office, 1971.

———. Subcommittee on Arms Control, International Law and Organization. *Briefing on Counterforce Attacks*. 93rd Congress, 2nd Session. Washington, D.C.: Government Printing Office, 1975.

———. Subcommittee on Arms Control, International Law and Organization. *U.S.-U.S.S.R. Strategic Policies*. 93rd Congress, 2nd Session. Washington, D.C.: Government Printing Office, 1974.

———. Subcommittee on Multinational Corporations. *The International Telephone and Telegraph Company and Chile, 1970-1971*. 93rd Congress, 1st Session. Washington, D.C.: Government Printing Office, 1973.

———. Subcommittee on Multinational Corporations. *Multinational Corporations and United States Foreign Policy*. 93rd Congress, 1st Session. Washington, D.C.: Government Printing Office, 1973.

———. Subcommittee on U.S. Security Agreements and Commitments Abroad and Subcommittee on Arms Control, International Law and Organization. *Nuclear Weapons and Foreign Policy*. 93rd Congress, 2nd Session. Washington, D.C.: Government Printing Office, 1974.

U.S. Congress. Senate. Committee on Interior and Insular Affairs. *The Law of the Sea Crisis: A Staff Report on the UN Seabed Committee*. 92nd Congress, 1st Session. Washington, D.C.: Government Printing Office, 1972.

U.S. Congress. Senate. Committee on Interior and Insular Affairs. *Ocean Manganese Nodules*. Committee Print prepared by James E. Mielke of the Congressional Research Service. 94th Congress, 1st Session. Washington, D.C.: Government Printing Office, 1975.

———. Subcommittee on Minerals, Materials, and Fuels. *Status Report on the Law of the Sea Conference*. 94th Congress, 1st Session. Washington, D.C.: Government Printing Office, 1975.

U.S. Congress. Senate. Committee on Judiciary. *Refugee and Humanitarian Problems in Chile*. 92nd Congress. 1st Session. Washington, D.C.: Government Printing Office, 1973.

U.S. Congress. Senate. Joint Committee on Atomic Energy. *Development, Growth, and State of the Nuclear Industry*. 93rd Congress, 2nd Session. Washington, D.C.: Government Printing Office, 1974.

U.S. Congress. Senate. Select Committee to Study Governmental Operations with Respect to Intelligence Activities. *Alleged Assassination Plots Involving Foreign Leaders*. 94th Congress, 1st Session. Washington, D.C.: Government Printing Office, 1975.

———. *Covert Action in Chile 1963-73*. 94th Congress, 1st Session. Washington, D.C.: Government Printing Office, 1975.

———. *Foreign and Military Intelligence, Final Report*. 94th Congress, 2nd Session. Washington, D.C.: Government Printing Office, 1976.

U.S. Council on Environmental Quality. *Environmental Quality, Annual Report*. Washington, D.C.: Government Printing Office, various years.

U.S. Council on Environmental Quality. *Ocean Dumping: A National Policy, A Report to the President*. Washington, D.C.: Government Printing Office, 1970.

U.S. Department of Defense. *Annual Report of the Secretary of Defense*. Washington, D.C.: Government Printing Office, various years.

U.S. Department of State. "North-South Dialogue." *Department of State Bulletin*, 77 (March 14, 1977), 235-236.

———. "U.N. Law of the Sea Conference 1975." *Special Report*, Publication 8764, February 1975.

———. Bureau of International and Scientific and Technological Affairs. *United States National Report on the Human Environment*. Washington, D.C.: Government Printing Office, 1971.

———. Bureau of Public Affairs. "Status Report on Law of the Sea Negotiations After Geneva." *Special Report*, May 22, 1975. Washington, D.C.: Government Printing Office, 1975.

"United States Draft of the U.N. Convention on International Seabed Areas." August 3, 1970. *International Legal Materials*, 9 (1970), 1046-1080.

U.S. Secretary of State's Advisory Committee on the 1972 UN Conference on the Human Environment. *Stockholm and Beyond*. Washington, D.C.: Government Printing Office, 1972.

Uribe, Armando. *The Black Book of American Intervention in Chile*. Boston: Beacon Press, 1974.

Utton, Albert E. and Henning, Daniel H., eds. *Environmental Policy: Concepts and International Implications*. New York: Praeger, 1973.

Vance, Cyrus. "Secretary Testifies on Administration's Approach to Foreign Assistance." *Department of State Bulletin*, 76 (March 14, 1977), 236-241.

———. "Secretary Vance Attends Ministerial Meeting of the Conference on International Economic Cooperation." *Department of State Bulletin*, 76 (June 20, 1977), 645-648.

———. "Secretary Vance Emphasizes Importance of Foreign Assistance Programs." *Department of State Bulletin*, 76 (April 11, 1977), 336-340.

———. "Secretary Vance Gives Overview of Foreign Assistance Programs." *Department of State Bulletin*, 76 (March 28, 1977), 284-289.

Van Cleave, William R. and Barnett, Roger W. "Strategic Adaptability." *Orbis*, 18 (Fall 1974), 655-676.

Van Dyke, Vernon. *Human Rights, the United States and the World Community*. New York: Oxford University Press, 1970.

Wagar, Warren. *Building the City of Man: Outlines of a World Civilization*. San Francisco: W. H. Freeman, 1971.

Wagner, Richard H. *Environment and Man*. New York: Norton, 1974.

Wall, David. *The Charity of Nations: The Political Economy of Foreign Aid*. New York: Basic Books, 1973.

Warnke, Paul C. "Apes on a Treadmill." *Foreign Policy*, 18 (Spring 1975), 12-29.

Weissman, Steve R., ed. *The Trojan Horse*. San Francisco: Ramparts Press, 1974.

Wenk, Edward. *The Politics of the Ocean*. Seattle: University of Washington Press, 1972.

Westervelt, Donald R. "The Essence of Armed Futility." *Orbis*, 18 (Fall 1974), 689-705.

Willrich, Mason and Rhinelander, John, eds. *SALT: The Moscow Agreements and Beyond*. New York: Free Press, 1974.

Wilson, Thomas W. *International Environment Action: A Global Survey*. Cambridge, Mass.: Dunellen, 1971.

Wohlstetter, Albert. "How to Confuse Ourselves." *Foreign Policy*, No. 20 (Fall 1975), pp. 170-198.

———. "Is There a Strategic Arms Race?" *Foreign Policy*, No. 15 (Summer 1974), pp. 3-20.

———. "Rivals, But no 'Race.' " *Foreign Policy*, No. 16 (Fall 1974), pp. 48-81.

Workshop on Global Ecological Problems. *Man in the Living Environment*. Madison: University of Wisconsin Press, 1972.

Wurster, C. F. "DDT Reduces Photosynthesis by Marine Phytoplankton." *Science*, 159 (1968), 1474-1475.

York, Herbert F. *Race to Oblivion: A Participant's View of the Arms Race*. New York: Simon and Schuster, 1970.

———. "Deterrence Gone M.A.D." *Bulletin of the Atomic Scientists*, 30 (March 1974), 5-8.

Young, Andrew. "Framework for a Dynamic North-South Dialogue." *Department of State Bulletin*, 77 (September 19, 1977), 383-389.

Zener, Robert V. "Environment and the Law of the Sea." *Marine Technology Society Journal*, 11 (May 1977), 27-30.

Index

500

504

Books Written Under the Auspices of the
CENTER OF INTERNATIONAL STUDIES
PRINCETON UNIVERSITY
1952-79

Gabriel A. Almond, *The Appeals of Communism* (Princeton University Press 1954)

William W. Kaufmann, ed., *Military Policy and National Security* (Princeton University Press 1956)

Klaus Knorr, *The War Potential of Nations* (Princeton University Press 1956)

Lucian W. Pye, *Guerrilla Communism in Malaya* (Princeton University Press 1956)

Charles De Visscher, *Theory and Reality in Public International Law*, trans. by P. E. Corbett (Princeton University Press 1957; rev. ed. 1968)

Bernard C. Cohen, *The Political Process and Foreign Policy: The Making of the Japanese Peace Settlement* (Princeton University Press 1957)

Myron Weiner, *Party Politics in India: The Development of a Multi-Party System* (Princeton University Press 1957)

Percy E. Corbett, *Law in Diplomacy* (Princeton University Press 1959)

Rolf Sannwald and Jacques Stohler, *Economic Integration: Theoretical Assumptions and Consequences of European Unification*, trans. by Herman Karreman (Princeton University Press 1959)

Klaus Knorr, ed., *NATO and American Security* (Princeton University Press 1959)

Gabriel A. Almond and James S. Coleman, eds., *The Politics of the Developing Areas* (Princeton University Press 1960)

Herman Kahn, *On Thermonuclear War* (Princeton University Press 1960)

Sidney Verba, *Small Groups and Political Behavior: A Study of Leadership* (Princeton University Press 1961)

Robert J. C. Butow, *Tojo and the Coming of the War* (Princeton University Press 1961)

Glenn H. Snyder, *Deterrence and Defense: Toward a Theory of National Security* (Princeton University Press 1961)

Klaus Knorr and Sidney Verba, eds., *The International System: Theoretical Essays* (Princeton University Press 1961)

Peter Paret and John W. Shy, *Guerrillas in the 1960's* (Praeger 1962)

George Modelski, *A Theory of Foreign Policy* (Praeger 1962)

Klaus Knorr and Thornton Read, eds., *Limited Strategic War* (Praeger 1963)

Frederick S. Dunn, *Peace-Making and the Settlement with Japan* (Princeton University Press 1963)

Arthur L. Burns and Nina Heathcote, *Peace-Keeping by United Nations Forces* (Praeger 1963)

Richard A. Falk, *Law, Morality, and War in the Contemporary World* (Praeger 1963)

James N. Rosenau, *National Leadership and Foreign Policy: A Case Study in the Mobilization of Public Support* (Princeton University Press 1963)

Gabriel A. Almond and Sidney Verba, *The Civic Culture: Political Attitudes and Democracy in Five Nations* (Princeton University Press 1963)

Bernard C. Cohen, *The Press and Foreign Policy* (Princeton University Press 1963)

Richard L. Sklar, *Nigerian Political Parties: Power in an Emergent African Nation* (Princeton University Press 1963)

Peter Paret, *French Revolutionary Warfare from Indochina to Algeria: The Analysis of a Political and Military Doctrine* (Praeger 1964)

Harry Eckstein, ed., *Internal War: Problems and Approaches* (Free Press 1964)

Cyril E. Black and Thomas P. Thornton, eds., *Communism and Revolution: The Strategic Uses of Political Violence* (Princeton University Press 1964)

Miriam Camps, *Britain and the European Community 1955-1963* (Princeton University Press 1964)

Thomas P. Thornton, ed., *The Third World in Soviet Perspective: Studies by Soviet Writers on the Developing Areas* (Princeton University Press 1964)

James N. Rosenau, ed., *International Aspects of Civil Strife* (Princeton University Press 1964)

Sidney I. Ploss, *Conflict and Decision-Making in Soviet Russia: A Case Study of Agricultural Policy, 1953-1963* (Princeton University Press 1965)

Richard A. Falk and Richard J. Barnet, eds., *Security in Disarmament* (Princeton University Press 1965)

Karl von Vorys, *Political Development in Pakistan* (Princeton University Press 1965)

Harold and Margaret Sprout, *The Ecological Perspective on Human Affairs, With Special Reference to International Politics* (Princeton University Press 1965)

Klaus Knorr, *On the Uses of Military Power in the Nuclear Age* (Princeton University Press 1966)

Harry Eckstein, *Division and Cohesion in Democracy: A Study of Norway* (Princeton University Press 1966)

Cyril E. Black, *The Dynamics of Modernization: A Study in Comparative History* (Harper and Row 1966)

Peter Kunstadter, ed., *Southeast Asian Tribes, Minorities, and Nations* (Princeton University Press 1967)

E. Victor Wolfenstein, *The Revolutionary Personality: Lenin, Trotsky, Gandhi* (Princeton University Press 1967)

Leon Gordenker, *The UN Secretary-General and the Maintenance of Peace* (Columbia University Press 1967)

Oran R. Young, *The Intermediaries: Third Parties in International Crises* (Princeton University Press 1967)

514

James N. Rosenau, ed., *Domestic Sources of Foreign Policy* (Free Press 1967)

Richard F. Hamilton, *Affluence and the French Worker in the Fourth Republic* (Princeton University Press 1967)

Linda B. Miller, *World Order and Local Disorder: The United Nations and Internal Conflicts* (Princeton University Press 1967)

Henry Bienen, *Tanzania: Party Transformation and Economic Development* (Princeton University Press 1967)

Wolfram F. Hanrieder, *West German Foreign Policy, 1949-1963: International Pressures and Domestic Response* (Stanford University Press 1967)

Richard H. Ullman, *Britain and the Russian Civil War: November 1918-February 1920* (Princeton University Press 1968)

Robert Gilpin, *France in the Age of the Scientific State* (Princeton University Press 1968)

William B. Bader, *The United States and the Spread of Nuclear Weapons* (Pegasus 1968)

Richard A. Falk, *Legal Order in a Violent World* (Princeton University Press 1968)

Cyril E. Black, Richard A. Falk, Klaus Knorr and Oran R. Young, *Neutralization and World Politics* (Princeton University Press 1968)

Oran R. Young, *The Politics of Force: Bargaining During International Crises* (Princeton University Press 1969)

Klaus Knorr and James N. Rosenau, eds., *Contending Approaches to International Politics* (Princeton University Press 1969)

James N. Rosenau, ed., *Linkage Politics: Essays on the Convergence of National and International Systems* (Free Press 1969)

John T. McAlister, Jr., *Viet Nam: The Origins of Revolution* (Knopf 1969)

Jean Edward Smith, *Germany Beyond the Wall: People, Politics and Prosperity* (Little, Brown 1969)

James Barros, *Betrayal from Within: Joseph Avenol, Secretary-General of the League of Nations, 1933-1940* (Yale University Press 1969)

Charles Hermann, *Crises in Foreign Policy: A Simulation Analysis* (Bobbs-Merrill 1969)

Robert C. Tucker, *The Marxian Revolutionary Idea: Essays on Marxist Thought and Its Impact on Radical Movements* (W. W. Norton 1969)

Harvey Waterman, *Political Change in Contemporary France: The Politics of an Industrial Democracy* (Charles E. Merrill 1969)

Cyril E. Black and Richard A. Falk, eds., *The Future of the International Legal Order*. Vol. I: *Trends and Patterns* (Princeton University Press 1969)

Ted Robert Gurr, *Why Men Rebel* (Princeton University Press 1969)

C. Sylvester Whitaker, *The Politics of Tradition: Continuity and Change in Northern Nigeria 1946-1966* (Princeton University Press 1970)

Richard A. Falk, *The Status of Law in International Society* (Princeton University Press 1970)

515

John T. McAlister, Jr. and Paul Mus, *The Vietnamese and Their Revolution* (Harper & Row 1970)

Klaus Knorr, *Military Power and Potential* (D. C. Heath 1970)

Cyril E. Black and Richard A. Falk, eds., *The Future of the International Legal Order*. Vol. II: *Wealth and Resources* (Princeton University Press 1970)

Leon Gordenker, ed., *The United Nations in International Politics* (Princeton University Press 1971)

Cyril E. Black and Richard A. Falk, eds., *The Future of the International Legal Order*. Vol. III: *Conflict Management* (Princeton University Press 1971)

Francine R. Frankel, *India's Green Revolution: Economic Gains and Political Costs* (Princeton University Press 1971)

Harold and Margaret Sprout, *Toward a Politics of the Planet Earth* (Van Nostrand Reinhold Co. 1971)

Cyril E. Black and Richard A. Falk, eds., *The Future of the International Legal Order*. Vol. IV: *The Structure of the International Environment* (Princeton University Press 1972)

Gerald Garvey, *Energy, Ecology, Economy* (W. W. Norton 1972)

Richard H. Ullman, *The Anglo-Soviet Accord* (Princeton University Press 1973)

Klaus Knorr, *Power and Wealth: The Political Economy of International Power* (Basic Books 1973)

Anton Bebler, *Military Rule in Africa: Dahomey, Ghana, Sierra Leone, and Mali* (Praeger Publishers 1973)

Robert C. Tucker, *Stalin as Revolutionary 1879-1929: A Study in History and Personality* (W. W. Norton 1973)

Edward L. Morse, *Foreign Policy and Interdependence in Gaullist France* (Princeton University Press 1973)

Henry Bienen, *Kenya: The Politics of Participation and Control* (Princeton University Press 1974)

Gregory J. Massell, *The Surrogate Proletariat: Moslem Women and Revolutionary Strategies in Soviet Central Asia, 1919-1929* (Princeton University Press 1974)

James N. Rosenau, *Citizenship Between Elections: An Inquiry Into The Mobilizable American* (Free Press 1974)

Ervin Laszlo, *A Strategy for the Future: The Systems Approach to World Order* (George Braziller 1974)

R. J. Vincent, *Nonintervention and International Order* (Princeton University Press 1974)

Jan H. Kalicki, *The Pattern of Sino-American Crises: Political-Military Interactions in the 1950s* (Cambridge University Press 1975)

Klaus Knorr, *The Power of Nations: The Political Economy of International Relations* (Basic Books, Inc. 1975)

James P. Sewell, *UNESCO and World Politics: Engaging in International Relations* (Princeton University Press 1975)

516

Richard A. Falk, *A Global Approach to National Policy* (Harvard University Press 1975)

Harry Eckstein and Ted Robert Gurr, *Patterns of Authority: A Structural Basis for Political Inquiry* (John Wiley & Sons 1975)

Cyril E. Black, Marius B. Jansen, Herbert S. Levine, Marion J. Levy, Jr., Henry Rosovsky, Gilbert Rozman, Henry D. Smith, II, and S. Frederick Starr, *The Modernization of Japan and Russia* (Free Press 1975)

Leon Gordenker, *International Aid and National Decisions: Development Programs in Malawi, Tanzania, and Zambia* (Princeton University Press 1976)

Carl von Clausewitz, *On War*, edited and translated by Michael Howard and Peter Paret (Princeton University Press 1976)

Gerald Garvey and Lou Ann Garvey, *International Resource Flows* (D. C. Heath 1977)

Walter F. Murphy and Joseph Tanenhaus, *Comparative Constitutional Law: Cases and Commentaries* (St. Martin's Press 1977)

Gerald Garvey, *Nuclear Power and Social Planning: The City of the Second Sun* (D. C. Heath 1977)

Richard E. Bissell, *Apartheid and International Organizations* (Westview Press 1977)

David P. Forsythe, *Humanitarian Politics: The International Committee of the Red Cross* (Johns Hopkins University Press 1977)

Paul E. Sigmund, *The Overthrow of Allende and the Politics of Chile, 1964-1976* (University of Pittsburgh Press 1977)

Henry S. Bienen, *Armies and Parties in Africa* (Holmes and Meier 1978)

Harold and Margaret Sprout, *The Context of Environmental Politics: Unfinished Business for America's Third Century* (University Press of Kentucky 1978)

Samuel S. Kim, *China, The United Nations, and World Order* (Princeton University Press 1979)

S. Basheer Ahmed, *Nuclear Fuel and Energy* (D. C. Heath 1979)

517

Library of Congress Cataloging in Publication Data

Johansen, Robert C
    The national interest and the human interest.

    Bibliography: p.
    Includes index.
        1.   United States—Foreign relations—1945-
2.   International organization.   I.   Title.
JX1417.J63   327.73   79-83994
ISBN 0-691-07618-9
ISBN 0-691-02196-1 pbk.

Social Media Marketing

ALL-IN-ONE

FOR DUMMIES®

2ND EDITION

by Jan Zimmerman
and
Deborah Ng

WILEY

John Wiley & Sons, Inc.

Social Media Marketing All-in-One For Dummies®, 2nd Edition

Published by
John Wiley & Sons, Inc.
111 River Street
Hoboken, NJ 07030-5774

`www.wiley.com`

WILEY

About the Author

Jan Zimmerman has found marketing to be the most creative challenge of owning a business for the more than 30 years she has spent as an entrepreneur. Since 1994, she has owned Sandia Consulting Group and Watermelon Mountain Web Marketing (www.watermelonweb.com) in Albuquerque, New Mexico. (*Sandia* is Spanish for *watermelon*.) Her previous companies provided a range of services including video production, grant writing, and linguistic engineering R&D.

Jan's web marketing clients at Watermelon Mountain are a living laboratory for experimenting with the best social media, search engine optimization, and other online marketing techniques for web success. Ranging from hospitality and tourism to retail stores, B2B suppliers, trade associations, colleges, and service companies, her clients have unique marketing needs but share similar business concerns and online challenges. Her consulting practice, which keeps Jan aware of the real-world issues facing business owners and marketers, provides the basis for her pragmatic marketing advice.

Throughout her business career, Jan has been a prolific writer. She has written three editions of *Web Marketing For Dummies*, four editions of another book about marketing on the Internet, as well as the books *Doing Business with Government Using EDI* and *Mainstreaming Sustainable Architecture*. Her concern about the impact of technological development on women's needs led to her book *One Upon the Future* and the anthology *The Technological Woman*.

The writer of numerous articles and a frequent speaker on Web marketing and social media, Jan has long been fascinated by the intersection of business, technology, and human beings. In her spare time, she crews for the hot air balloon named *Levity* to get her feet off the ground and her head in the clouds.

Jan can be reached at books@watermelonweb.com or 505-344-4230. Your comments, corrections, and suggestions are welcome.

Deborah Ng is a former freelance writer who used her gift of gab to grow a successful blog into the number one online community for freelance writers before selling in 2010. Deb's the former community manager for several online brands and can currently be found enjoying her role as Director of Community for New Media Expo. When she's not oversharing on the social networks, Deb blogs at Kommein.com and enjoys her time with her extremely handsome husband and brilliant son.

Dedication

Jan Zimmerman:

For All the Survivors

Deborah Ng:

To Arline Dederick: Educator, mother of six, and breast cancer survivor. I'm so grateful.

Author's Acknowledgments

Jan Zimmerman:

No nonfiction writer works alone, and this book is no exception. The more books I write, the more I realize how much I depend on others. In particular, this edition couldn't have been written without my wonderful researchers Esmeralda Sanchez and Patricia Jephson.

Both conducted background research, compiled sites for the numerous tables in this book, created graphics, and rooted out arcane online facts. Working on my truly crazy schedule, they checked thousands of links and reviewed hundreds of sites for screen shots. (Not many people are asked to search for a good marketing tweet!) Finding exemplary companies for case studies — and clearing hundreds of copyrights — required endless calls and e-mails, for which these two people deserve all the credit.

Shawna Araiza, senior web marketing associate at Watermelon Mountain Web Marketing, supplemented their efforts, drawing on her extensive knowledge of the Internet to suggest sites, experiment with new techniques, and help with Photoshop. I owe my staff a great debt for giving me the time to write by working overtime with our clients — not to mention their patience and computer support.

As always, my family, friends, and cats earn extra hugs for their constant encouragement. I'm lucky to have friends who accept that I cannot be there for them as much as they are there for me. The garden, the house, the car, and the cats, alas, are not so forgiving. Special thanks to my clients, who teach me so much and give me the opportunity to practice what I preach.

I'd also like to thank Brian Walls, project editor at Wiley, for his flexibility and patience, and copy editors, Virginia Sanders, Teresa Artman, and Debbye Butler, and technical editor, Claudia Snell, for their knowledgeable assistance. Together, they made this book much better than it started out. My thanks to all the other staff at Wiley — from the art department to legal — who have provided support. If errors remain, they are indubitably mine.

My appreciation also to my agent, Margot Hutchison of Waterside Productions. Margot and her extraordinary family continue to teach us, at `http://teamsam.com`, lessons about what's truly important in life. If you profit from reading this book, please join me in donating to The Magic Water Project in memory of Sam Hutchison at `www.magicwater.org`. Thank you in advance, dear readers, for making a contribution "because of Sam."

Deborah Ng:

Thank you to my family, friends, and co-workers. Your support and encouragement mean more to me than you'll ever know.

Publisher's Acknowledgments

We're proud of this book; please send us your comments at http://dummies.custhelp.com. For other comments, please contact our Customer Care Department within the U.S. at 877-762-2974, outside the U.S. at 317-572-3993, or fax 317-572-4002.

Some of the people who helped bring this book to market include the following:

Acquisitions, Editorial, and Vertical Websites

Project Editor: Brian Walls, Kelly Ewing

Acquisitions Editor: Amy Fandrei

Copy Editor: Virginia Sanders, Teresa Artman, Debbye Butler

Technical Editor: Claudia Snell

Editorial Manager: Kevin Kirschner

Vertical Websites Project Manager: Laura Moss-Hollister

Vertical Websites Project Manager: Jenny Swisher

Supervising Producer: Rich Graves

Vertical Websites Associate Producers: Josh Frank, Marilyn Hummel, Douglas Kuhn, Shawn Patrick

Editorial Assistant: Leslie Saxman

Sr. Editorial Assistant: Cherie Case

Cover Photo: ©Joshua Hodge Photography/ iStockphoto and ©mediaphotos/iStockphoto

Cartoons: Rich Tennant (www.the5thwave.com)

Special Help

Nicole Sholly, Michelle Krasniak, Melanie Nelson

Composition Services

Project Coordinator: Sheree Montgomery

Layout and Graphics: Carl Byers, Jennifer Creasey

Proofreaders: Lindsay Amones, Christine Sabooni

Indexer: BIM Indexing & Proofreading Services

Publishing and Editorial for Technology Dummies

Richard Swadley, Vice President and Executive Group Publisher

Andy Cummings, Vice President and Publisher

Mary Bednarek, Executive Acquisitions Director

Mary C. Corder, Editorial Director

Publishing for Consumer Dummies

Kathleen Nebenhaus, Vice President and Executive Publisher

Composition Services

Debbie Stailey, Director of Composition Services

Contents at a Glance

Table of Contents

Book II: Cybersocial Tools 107

Introduction

You sat back, sighing with relief that your website was running faultlessly, optimized for search engines, and producing traffic, leads, and sales. Maybe you ventured into e-mail marketing or pay-per-click advertising to generate new customers. Then you thought with satisfaction, "I'll just let the money roll in."

Instead, you were inundated with stories about Facebook and fan pages, Twitter and tweets, blogs and podcasts, Pinterest, Google+ and all other manner of social media buzz. Perhaps you tried one of these social media channels and didn't see much in the way of results, or perhaps you played ostrich.

Much as you might wish, you cannot ignore social media any longer — not when 80 percent of Internet users visit blogs and social media; not when your position in search engine results may depend on the recency and frequency of social media updates. Since the first edition of this book, social media marketing has indeed come of age.

The statistics are astounding: Facebook topping 900 million active users; more than 120 million blogs on the Internet; more than 250 million tweets sent per day on average; 4 billion video views streamed daily on YouTube. New company names and bewildering new vocabulary terms continue to flood the online world: Groupon, Pinterest, pinning, community building, image-sharing, and sentiment monitoring, for example.

Should your business get involved in social media marketing? Is it all more trouble than it's worth? Will you be left hopelessly behind if you don't participate? If you jump in, how do you keep it all under control and who does the work? This book helps you answer both sets of questions: Should or shouldn't your business undertake social media marketing? If so, how? (Quick answer: If your customers use a social media service, you should consider it. If not, skip it.)

About This Book

The philosophy behind this book is simple: Social media marketing is a means, not an end in itself. Social media services are new tools, not new worlds. In the best of all worlds, you see results that improve customer acquisition, retention, and buying behavior — in other words, your bottom line. If this sounds familiar, that's because everything you already know about marketing is correct.

Having the most Likes on Facebook or more retweets of your posts than your competitors doesn't mean much if these achievements don't have a positive impact on your business. Throughout this book, you'll find concrete suggestions for applying social media tactics to achieve those goals.

If you undertake a social marketing campaign, we urge you to keep your plans simple, take things slowly, and always stay focused on your customers. Most of all, we urge you to follow the precepts of guerrilla marketing: Target one niche market at a time; grow that market; reinvest your profits in the next niche.

What You Don't Have to Read

You don't have to read anything that seems overwhelming or insanely complicated, deals with a particular social marketing service that you dislike or disdain, or doesn't apply to your business. Content following a Technical Stuff icon is intended for developers or particularly tech-savvy readers.

Reading the case studies in sidebars isn't critical, though you might enjoy reading about honest-to-goodness business owners who successfully use the social marketing techniques we discuss. Often, they share a helpful tip that will make your social media life easier.

If you have a limited budget, focus your explorations on the free or low-cost tools and resources that appear in various tables, instead of enterprise-level options, which are designed for large companies with large marketing budgets. Sometimes, however, a tool with a moderate price tag can save you lots of time or expensive labor.

You can skip any of the Books III, IV, V, VI, or VII on individual social media services (blogs, image-sharing, and podcasts; Twitter; Facebook; Google+; and Pinterest) if you don't include them in your social media marketing plan. If you decide to add one or more of them later, simply return to that book for freestanding information. Of course, if you're looking for a thorough understanding of the social media whirl, read the book straight through, from cover to cover. You'll find out all about social media — at least until a totally new service launches tomorrow.

Foolish Assumptions

In our heads, we visualize our readers as savvy small-business owners, marketers in companies of any size, and people who work in any of the multiple services that support social media efforts, such as advertising agencies, web developers, graphic design firms, copywriting, or public relations. We assume that you

✦ Already have or will soon have a website or blog that can serve as the hub for your online marketing program

✦ Are curious about ubiquitous social media

✦ Are comfortable using keywords on search engines to find information online

✦ Know the realities of your industry, though you may not have a clue whether your competitors use social media

✦ Can describe your target markets, though you may not be sure whether your audience is using social media

✦ Are trying to decide whether using social media makes sense for your company (or your boss has asked you to find out)

✦ May already use social media personally and are interested in applying your knowledge and experience to business

✦ May already have tried using social media for your company but want to improve results or measure return on your investment

✦ Have a passion for your business, appreciate your customers, and enjoy finding new ways to improve your bottom line

If our assumptions are correct, this book will help you organize a social marketing presence without going crazy or spending all your waking hours online. It will help you figure out whether a particular technique makes sense, how to get the most out of it, and how to measure your results.

How This Book Is Organized

We've built this book like a sandwich: The first two and last two books are overviews of marketing or business issues, or of social media tools and techniques. The five books in the middle are how-to manuals for incorporating blogs, podcasts or image-sharing services, Twitter, Facebook, Google+, or Pinterest into your social media marketing campaign.

Like most For Dummies books, this one enables you to get as much (or as little) information as you need at any particular moment on a specific topic. You can return to it as a reference guide at any time. However, unless you're certain that you're interested only in a specific social marketing service covered in Books III through VII, we recommend that you read Book I first to establish your goals, objectives, and schedule for social media marketing.

For information on a specific topic, check the headings in the table of contents or look at the index.

Book I: The Social Media Mix

Book I gets you off on the right foot. Chapter 1 explains what social media services are, individually and collectively, categorizes the overwhelming number of social media options by type, and explores how social media are the same and different from other forms of online and offline marketing. In the next two chapters, you define your own marketing goals, objectives, and methods for social media, with a particular emphasis on return on investment (ROI) and learn how to research where your target audiences "hang out." The final chapter in this book offers some practical tips on how to manage your social media effort in terms of precious resources: time, money, and people.

This book includes three key planning forms: the Social Media Marketing Goals form, to establish the purpose of your campaign; the Social Media Marketing Plan, to select and document your tactics; and the Social Media Activity Calendar, to assign and schedule tasks.

Book II: Cybersocial Tools

Implementing and tracking social media marketing campaigns across multiple services is a daunting task. In the first chapter of Book II, we offer a variety of productivity tools to help you post content in multiple locations, notify search engines, and monitor your growing social notoriety. The second chapter deals in depth with integrating social media into a coordinated search engine optimization strategy, and the third deals with social bookmarking, social news, and social sharing as new methods of viral marketing.

Book III: Blogs, Podcasts, and Video

Your content is your most important online asset. It's through your content that you catch the attention of the search engines, raise brand awareness and establish your expertise. In the first chapter of Book III, we delve into the importance of content, what goals you hope to achieve with your content marketing strategy, and explore the different types of content available to you online. In Chapter 2, we cover blogs and why they're such an important marketing tool. Chapter 3 touches on podcasts and videos for those of you who hope to expand beyond print to reach your online communities and Chapter 4 discusses sharing images and the legalities involved.

Book IV: Twitter

Twitter is an essential marketing tool for brands wishing to grow their online presence. Brevity is key and though some find it challenging to communicate in 140 characters, most agree that it's a great way to learn more about the people using a product or service, and grow a community of supporters. In Book IV we cover the basics of Twitter marketing and even some not so basic areas like hosting a Twitter chat, uploading a Twitter background and using Twitter to search for brands, jobs and clients.

Book V: Facebook

Facebook is where the people are, and you owe it to yourself and your brand to be a part of the action. In Book V, we'll take you through setting up a Facebook account and Timeline as well as marketing to your community through conversation, photos and other content.

Book VI: Google+

Google+ may be the new kid on the block, but that doesn't mean you shouldn't look into it. With some unique features, such as video hangouts, Google+ offers some perks other social networks don't. In Book VI, we'll explore using Google+ as a marketing tool. We'll also take you through setting up a brand page, uploading photos and hosting your own video chat.

Book VII: Pinterest

Book VII covers Pinterest, a social networking force to be reckoned with. With Pinterest a picture really does say a thousand words and we're going to show you how to find the photos that best tell your brand's story. But don't worry; we won't just toss you into the water without teaching you to swim first. We'll take you through creating an account, uploading photos, creating boards and even some unique uses for your Pinterest account.

Book VIII: Other Social Media Marketing Sites

In addition to the "big guys" covered in the Books III through VII, there are hundreds of social media services with smaller audiences. Some of them are networks specific to a demographically-segmented audience, and some focus on narrowly targeted vertical markets. Book VIII, which analyzes the value of working with smaller services and surveys many options, also includes chapters on LinkedIn for business-to-business companies; geosocial marketing with sites like foursquare; group coupons, social gaming; and social mobile sites.

Book IX: Measuring Results; Building on Success

Book IX returns to business principles with a chapter on the importance of measuring your results. The first chapter offers details on Google Analytics for your website in general, and on Google Social Analytics to assess the performance of your social media campaigns. We do a deep dive into the metric sea with details on internal performance measurements for content-sharing services, Twitter, Facebook, Google Plus, LinkedIn, Pinterest, and social mobile sites. Book IX concludes with chapters covering discussing how to compare social media metrics with other forms of marketing and suggestions for using data to guide your marketing decisions.

Icons Used in This Book

To make your experience easier, we use various icons in the margins to identify special categories of information.

These hints help you save time, energy, or aggravation. Sharing them is our way of sharing what we've figured out the hard way — so that you don't have to. Of course, if you prefer to get your education through the school of hard knocks, be our guest.

This book has more details in it than any normal person can remember. This icon reminds you of points made elsewhere in the book or perhaps helps you recall business best practices that you know from your own experience.

Heed these warnings to avoid potential pitfalls. Nothing we suggest will crash your computer beyond repair or send your marketing campaign into oblivion. But we tell you about business and legal pitfalls to avoid, plus a few traps that catch the unprepared during the process of configuring social media services. Not all those services create perfect user interfaces with clear directions!

The geeky-looking Dummies Man marks information to share with your developer or programmer — unless you are one. In that case, have at it. On the other hand, you can skip any of the technical-oriented information without damaging your marketing plans or harming a living being.

Conventions Used in This Book

Doing something the same way over and over again may be boring, but consistency makes information easier to understand. In this book, those consistent elements are *conventions*. We use only a few:

✦ When URLs (Web addresses) appear within a paragraph or table, they look like this: www.dummies.com.

✦ New terms appear in *italics* the first time they're used, thanks to the copy editor.

✦ Navigation on Web sites appears as tab or option names in sequence, to indicate the order in which you should make selections, such as choose Tab Name⇨Choice One⇨Choice Two.

✦ Any text that you have to type is in **bold**.

Where to Go from Here

You can find helpful information on the companion Web site for this book at www.dummies.com/go/socialmediamarketing2e. From the site, you can download copies of the Social Media Goals and Social Media Marketing Plan forms, which you can use to develop your own marketing plans. You can also find an online Cheat Sheet to print and keep handy near your computer at www.dummies.com/go/socialmediamarketing2e. If you find errors in this book, or have suggestions for future editions, please e-mail us at books@watermelonweb.com. We wish you a fun and profitable experience going social!

Book I

The Social Media Mix

The 5th Wave   By Rich Tennant

"Here's an idea. Why don't you start a social network for doofuses who think they know how to set a broken leg, but don't."

Contents at a Glance

Chapter 1: Making the Business Case for Social Media

In This Chapter

✔ Defining social media

✔ Accentuating the positives

✔ Eliminating the negatives

✔ Latching on to the affirmatives

✔ Integrating social media into your overall marketing plan

✔ Evaluating the worth of social media

*I*n the best of all worlds, *social media* — a suite of online services that facilitates two-way communication and content sharing — can become a productive component of your overall marketing strategy. These services can enhance your company's online visibility, strengthen relationships with your clients, and expand word-of-mouth advertising, which is the best type.

Given its rapid rise in popularity and its hundreds of millions of worldwide users, social media marketing sounds quite tempting. These tools require minimal upfront cash and, theoretically, you'll find customers flooding through your cyberdoors, ready to buy. It sounds like a no-brainer — but it isn't.

Has someone finally invented a perfect marketing method that puts you directly in touch with your customers and prospects, costs nothing, and generates profits faster than a perpetual motion machine produces energy? The hype says "yes"; the real answer, unfortunately, is "no." Marketing nirvana is not yet at hand.

This chapter provides an overview of the pros and cons of social media to help you decide whether to join the social whirl and gives a framework for approaching a strategic choice of which media to use.

Making Your Social Debut

Like any form of marketing, social media takes some thought. It can become an enormous siphon of your time, and short-term profits are rare. Social media marketing is a long-term commitment.

So, should you or shouldn't you invest time and effort in this new marketing avenue? If you answer in the affirmative, you immediately confront another decision: What form should that investment take? The number of options is overwhelming; you can never use every technique and certainly can't do them all at once.

Figure 1-1, which compares the percentages of small businesses using various social media to attract new customers, shows that most use Facebook and/or LinkedIn. Although some U.S. small businesses have taken a wait-and-see attitude, more and more are trying social media. According to a January 2011 survey (`www.networksolutions.com/smallbusiness/wp-content/files/State_of_Small_Business_Report_Wave_5.pdf`), about 33 percent of small businesses used some form of social media marketing for some purpose, up from 24 percent the preceding year. Most businesses on the sidelines give the best reason in the world for not participating — their customers aren't there yet.

Figure 1-1: Of small businesses using social media, the greatest number use Facebook and/or LinkedIn.

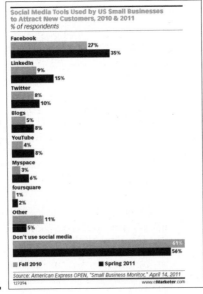

Social Media Tools Used by US Small Businesses to Attract New Customers, 2010 & 2011
% of respondents

Facebook — 27% / 35%
LinkedIn — 9% / 15%
Twitter — 8% / 10%
Blogs — 5% / 8%
YouTube — 4% / 8%
Myspace — 3% / 6%
foursquare — 1% / 2%
Other — 11% / 5%
Don't use social media — 61% / 56%

■ Fall 2010   ■ Spring 2011

Source: American Express OPEN, "Small Business Monitor," April 14, 2011
127094   www.eMarketer.com

Courtesy eMarketer

Defining Social Media Marketing

The bewildering array of social media (which seem to breed new services faster than rabbits) makes it hard to discern what they have in common: shared information, often on a peer-to-peer basis. Although many social media messages look like traditional broadcasts from one business to many consumers, their interactive component offers an enticing illusion of one-to-one communication that invites individual readers to respond.

The phrase *social media marketing* generally refers to using these online services for relationship selling — selling based on developing rapport with customers. *Social media services* make innovative use of new online technologies to accomplish the familiar communication and marketing goals of this form of selling.

 The tried-and-true strategies of marketing (such as solving customers' problems and answering the question, "What's in it for me?") are still valid. Social media marketing is a new technique, not a new world.

This book covers a variety of *social media services* (sometimes called social media *channels*). You may hear social media services referred to as *Web 2.0* (interactive) techniques. At least one prominent marketing company distinguishes between the two, constraining the term *Web 2.0* to enabling technologies and reserving *social media* for relationship-building activities.

For the purpose of this book, this distinction is somewhat academic. Instead of using that distinction, we group tools that improve the performance or effectiveness of social media into one category, regardless of the underlying technology. We use the phrase *social media site* to refer to a specific, named online service or product.

You can categorize social media services, but they have fuzzy boundaries that can overlap. Some social media sites fall into multiple categories. For instance, some social networks and online communities allow participants to share photos and include a blog.

Here are the different types of social media services:

✦ **Social-content sharing services:** These services facilitate posting and commenting on text, videos, photos, and podcasts (audio).

- *Blogs:* Websites designed to let you easily update or change content and allow readers to post their own opinions or reactions. Figure 1-2 shows an example of a blog with verve at `www.easylunchboxes.com/blog`.

 Examples of blog software are WordPress, TypePad, Blogger (formerly Blogspot), and Tumblr. Blogs can be hosted on third-party sites or integrated into your own website.

Figure 1-2:
The blog for
EasyLunch
boxes uses
punchy
graphics.

Courtesy Kelly Lester/EasyLunchboxes.com

- *Video:* Examples are YouTube, Vimeo, or Ustream. Figure 1-3 shows a YETI Coolers video on its YouTube channel at `www.youtube.com/ user/YetiVideos`.

- *Photos:* Flickr, Photobucket, or Picasa.

- *Audio:* Podcast Alley or BlogTalkRadio.

✦ **Social networking services:** Originally developed to facilitate the exchange of personal information (messages, photos, video, and audio) to groups of friends and family, these full-featured services offer multiple functions. From a business point of view, many social networking services support subgroups that offer the potential for more targeted marketing. Common types of social networking services include

- *Full networks,* such as Facebook, Google+, or myYearbook.

  Figure 1-4 shows the Facebook timeline of fab'rik Atlanta (`www. facebook.com/pages/fabrik-Atlanta/109417261393`), which also sells directly on Facebook at `http://apps.facebook.com/ fabrikstore`. After adding items to a cart and clicking Checkout, the user is linked to a third-party cart to make payment (`https:// secure1.spidercart.com/secure/checkout.asp`).

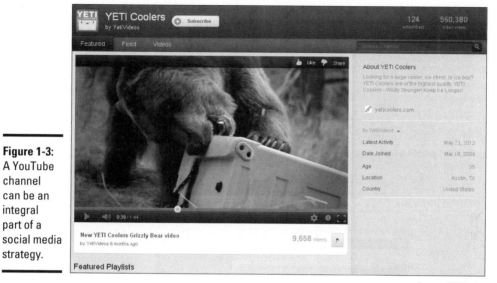

Figure 1-3:
A YouTube channel can be an integral part of a social media strategy.

Courtesy YETI Coolers

Figure 1-4:
Clicking the Shop fab'rik link on fab'rik Atlanta's Timeline brings customers to a store catalog that resides on Facebook.

Courtesy fab'rik boutique; www.fabrikstyle.com

- *Microblogging (short message) networks,* such as Twitter or Plurk, which are often used for sharing announcements, events, sales notices, and promotions.

  Figure 1-5 shows how ecycler.com (a recycling company trying to reduce landfill waste) creatively uses its Twitter account at `http://twitter.com/ecycler` to enable a dialog between people discarding items and those who want them. By connecting discarders and collectors online, Twitter reduces the need for ecycler staff to make cold-calls.

- *Professional networks,* such as LinkedIn and Plaxo.

- *Specialty networks* (which target specific groups, rather than the general public) within a vertical industry, demographic, or activity segment.

✦ **Social bookmarking services:** Similar to private bookmarks for your favorite sites on your computer, social bookmarks are publicly viewable lists of sites that others have recommended. Some are

- *Recommendation services,* such as StumbleUpon and Delicious

- *Social shopping services,* such as Kaboodle and ThisNext

- *Other bookmarking services organized by topic or application,* such as sites where readers recommend books to others using bookmarking techniques

Figure 1-5: Twitter can be used to share announcements, events, sales notices, and promotions, and enable dialog with and between customers.

Courtesy ecycler

✦ **Social news services:** On these peer-based lists of recommended articles from news sites, blogs, or web pages, users often vote on the value of the postings. Social news services include

- Digg

- Reddit

- Other news sites

✦ **Social geolocation and meeting services:** These services bring people together in real space rather than in cyberspace:

- Foursquare

- Loopt

- Other GPS (Global Positioning System) applications, many of which operate on mobile phones

- Other sites for organizing meetups and tweetups (using Twitter to organize a gathering)

✦ **Community-building services:** Many comment- and content-sharing sites have been around for a long time, such as forums, message boards, and Yahoo! and Google groups. Other examples are

- *Community-building sites* with multiple sharing features, such as Ning

- *Wikis,* such as Wikipedia, for group-sourced content

- *Review sites,* such as TripAdvisor and Epinions, to solicit consumer views

As you surf the web, you can find dozens, if not hundreds, of social tools, apps (freestanding online applications), and widgets (small applications placed on other sites, services, or desktops). These features monitor, distribute, search, analyze, and rank content. Many are specific to a particular social network, especially Twitter. Others are designed to aggregate information across the social media landscape, including such monitoring tools as Google Alerts or Social Mention or such distribution tools as RSS or Ping.fm. Book II offers a survey of many more of these tools; specific social media services are covered in their respective books.

Understanding the Benefits of Social Media

Social media marketing carries many benefits. One of the most important is that you don't have to front any cash for most social media services. Of course, there's a downside: Most services require a significant investment of time to initiate and maintain a social media marketing campaign.

As you read the following sections, think about whether each benefit applies to your needs. How important is it to your business? How much time are you willing to allocate to it? What kind of a payoff would you expect? Figure 1-6 shows how other small businesses rate the relative effectiveness of social media in meeting their goals.

Figure 1-6:
The effectiveness of social media marketing (column 2) to other marketing tactics small businesses use.

Reasons that US SMBs Use Select Marketing Tactics, April 2011 % of respondents						
① Email ④ Advertising						
② Social media ⑤ QR codes						
③ Direct mail ⑥ Mobile marketing						
	①	②	③	④	⑤	⑥
Ease of use	60%	53%	40%	39%	34%	32%
It is cost-effective	59%	54%	31%	30%	19%	27%
Comfort and knowledge in this area	40%	39%	35%	38%	24%	18%
Proven effectiveness with response rate, sales, etc.	38%	30%	36%	43%	17%	18%
My competitors are using this channel	20%	30%	22%	28%	29%	25%
None of these	4%	3%	9%	7%	11%	16%
Source: Pitney Bowes, "Small and Medium Business Owners Summary Report," May 20, 2011						
128122					www.e**Marketer**.com	

Courtesy eMarketer

Casting a wide net to catch your target market

The audience for social media is huge. In early 2012, Facebook claimed almost 800 million active users, half of which log in on any given day. (In the same time period, weekly traffic on Google exceeded that of Facebook.)

Twitter claims more than 100 million registered users and claims that 230 million *tweets* (short messages) are posted daily. A relatively small number of power users — those who post 10 or more times per day — drive a huge number of tweets. About 40 percent of users read tweets only, without posting. More people read tweets than are accounted for, however, because tweets can be read on other websites.

Even narrowly focused networking sites claim hundreds of thousands of visitors. Surely, some of the people using these sites must be your customers or prospects. In fact, one popular use of social media is to cast a wide net to capture more potential visitors to your website. Figure 1-7 shows a classic *conversion funnel,* which demonstrates the value of bringing new traffic to the top of the funnel to produce more *conversions* (actions taken) at the bottom.

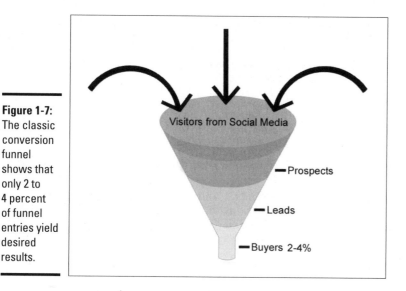

Figure 1-7:
The classic
conversion
funnel
shows that
only 2 to
4 percent
of funnel
entries yield
desired
results.

The conversion funnel works like this: If more people arrive at the top of the funnel, theoretically more will progress through the steps of prospect and qualified lead to become a customer. Only 2 to 4 percent, on average, make it through a funnel regardless of what action the funnel conversion depicts.

In Book I, Chapter 3, we discuss how you can assess traffic on social media sites using tools such as Quantcast or Alexa and match their visitors to the profiles of your customers.

Branding

Basic marketing focuses on the need for branding, name recognition, visibility, presence, or top-of-mind awareness. Call it what you will — you want people to remember your company name when they're in need of your product or service. Social media services, of almost every type, are excellent ways to build your brand.

Social media works for branding as long as you get your name in front of the right people. Plan to segment the audience on the large social media services. You can look for more targeted groups within them or search for specialty services that may reach fewer people overall but more of the ones who are right for your business.

Building relationships

You will hear repeatedly that social media marketing takes time to produce sales results. If you're focused on short-term benefits, you'd better shake that thought loose and get your head into the long-term game. To build effective relationships in social media, you're expected to

✦ Establish your expertise

✦ Participate regularly as a "good citizen" of whichever social media world you inhabit; follow site rules and abide by whatever conventions have been established

✦ Avoid overt self-promotion

✦ Don't use "hard sell" pressure techniques

✦ Provide value with links, resources, and unbiased information

Watch for steady growth in the number of your followers on a particular service; the number of people who recommend your site to others; increased downloads of *white papers* (articles that provide detailed information on a topic); or repeat visits to your site. All these signs indicate you're building relationships that may later lead, if not to a direct sale, then to a word-of-web recommendation to someone who does buy.

In the world of social media, the term *engagement* refers to the length of time and quality of interaction between your company and your followers.

Social media is a long-term commitment. Other than little experiments or pilot projects, don't bother starting a social media commitment if you don't plan to keep it going. Any short-term benefits you see aren't worth the effort you have to make.

Improving business processes

Already, many clever businesses have found ways to use social media to improve business processes. Though individual applications depend on the nature of your business, consider leveraging social media to

✦ Promptly detect and correct customer problems or complaints

✦ Obtain customer feedback and input on new product designs or changes

✦ Provide tech support to many people at one time; if one person has a question, chances are good that others do, too

✦ Improve service delivery, such as cafés that accept to-go orders on Twitter or Facebook or food carts that notify customers where and when their carts will arrive

✦ Locate qualified new vendors, service providers, and employees by using professional networks such as LinkedIn

✦ Collect critical market intelligence on your industry and competitors by watching content on appropriate social media

✦ Use new geolocation services to drive neighborhood traffic to brick-and-mortar stores during slow times and to acquire new customers

Marketing is only part of your company, but all of your company is marketing. Social media is a ripe environment for this hypothesis, where every part of a company, from human resources to tech support, and from engineering to sales, can be involved.

Improving search engine rankings

Just as you optimize your website, you should optimize your social media outlets for search engine ranking. Now that search engines are cataloging Twitter and Facebook and other appearances on social media, you can gain additional front page real estate for your company on Google and Yahoo! and Bing (whose search functions have merged).

Search engines recognize some, but not all, appearances on social media as inbound links, which also improve the page rank of your site.

Use a core set of search terms and keywords across as many sites as possible. Book II, Chapter 2 deals with search optimization, including tactics to avoid that could get you in trouble for spamming.

Optimization pays off in other ways: in results on real-time searches, which are now available on primary search engines; on external search engines that focus on blogs or other social media services; and on internal, site-specific search engines.

Selling when opportunity arises

Conventional thinking says that social media is designed for long-term engagement, for marketing and branding rather than for sales. However, a few obvious selling opportunities exist, particularly for business-to-consumer (B2C) companies, that won't offend followers.

✦ **Sell CDs and event tickets.** SoundCloud and CD Baby, which cater to music and entertainment, are appropriate social media sites for these products.

✦ **Include a link to your online store on social shopping services.** Recommend products — particularly apparel, jewelry, beauty, and decor — as Stylehive does.

✦ **Offer promotional codes or special deals to followers.** Offering codes or deals on particular networks encourages your followers to visit your site to make a purchase. You can also announce sales or events.

✦ **Place links to online or third-party stores like Etsy.com (see Book II, Chapter 1) on your profile pages on various services.** You can rarely sell directly from a social media service, but some permit you to place widgets that visually showcase your products and link to your online store, PayPal, or the equivalent to conclude a transaction.

✦ **Include a sign-up option for your e-newsletter.** It offers a bridge to sales.

The chart in Figure 1-8 shows a 2011 HubSpot survey of the percentage of companies that succeeded in acquiring a customer by way of a specific social media service. The survey encompassed both B2B (business-to-business) companies on the left of each pairing and B2C companies on the right. It shows that many businesses succeed in closing sales initiated through a social media service.

Figure 1-8:
B2B
and B2C
companies
are
successfully
finding
customers
through
social
media.

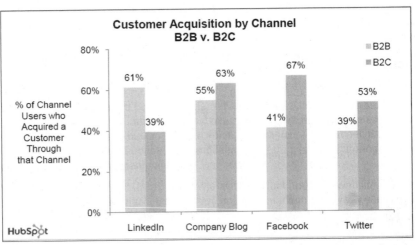

Courtesy HubSpot; www.hubspot.com

Include sales offers within a stream of information and news to avoid turning your social media site into a series of never-ending advertisements.

Saving money on advertising

Although time is money, the magic word is *free*. If you're a start-up company, "free" social media is likely the only advertising you can afford. If you decide to approach social media for this purpose, construct your master campaign just as carefully as you would a paid one:

✦ Create a plan that outlines target markets, ad offers, publishing venues, and schedules for different ad campaigns.

✦ If necessary, conduct comparative testing of messages, graphics, and offers.

✦ Monitor results and focus on the outlets that work best at driving qualified visits that lead to conversions.

✦ Supplement your free advertising with search optimization, press releases, and other forms of free promotion.

Advertising is only one part of marketing!

As you see traffic and conversions building from your social media marketing campaigns, you may want to reduce existing paid advertising campaigns. Just don't stop your paid advertising until you're confident that you have an equally profitable stream of customers from social media. Of course, if your ad campaign isn't working, there's no point continuing it.

Understanding the Cons of Social Media

For all its upsides, social media has its downsides. As social media has gained in popularity, it has also become increasingly difficult to gain visibility among its hundreds of millions of users.

In fact, sometimes you have to craft a campaign just to build an audience on a particular social media site. It's quite similar to conducting optimization and inbound link campaigns so that your site is found in natural search results.

Don't participate in social media for its own sake or just because "everyone else is."

By far, the biggest downside in social media is the amount of time you need to invest to see results. You need to make an ongoing commitment to review and respond to comments and to provide an ongoing stream of new material. An initial commitment to set up a profile is just the tip of the iceberg.

Keep in mind that you need to watch out for the addictiveness of social media. Individually and collectively, social media is the biggest-ever time sink. Don't believe us? Ask yourself whether you became addicted to news alerts during the 2012 presidential campaign or couldn't take your eyes off live coverage of the Mars landing. Or maybe you play FarmVille or other video games with a passion, continuously run instant messaging, check e-mail every ten seconds . . . you get the idea. Without self-discipline and a strong time schedule, you can easily become so socially overbooked that other tasks go undone.

As you consider each of the social media options in this book, also consider the level of human resources that are needed. Do you have the time and talents yourself? If not, do other people within your organization have the time and talent? Which other efforts will you need to give up while making room for social media? Will you have to hire new employees or contract out services, leading to hard costs for this supposedly "free" media?

Integrating Social Media into Your Overall Marketing Effort

Social media is only part of your online marketing. Online marketing is only part of your overall marketing. Don't mistake the part for the whole.

Consider each foray into social marketing as a strategic choice to supplement your other online marketing activities, which may include

+ **Creating and managing a marketing-effective website:** Use content updates, search engine optimization (SEO), inbound link campaigns, and event calendar postings to your advantage.

+ **Displaying your product or service's value:** Create online press releases, and e-mail newsletters. Share testimonials and reviews with your users and offer affiliate or loyalty programs, online events, or promotions.

+ **Advertising:** Take advantage of pay-per-click ads, banners, and sponsorships.

Social media is neither necessary nor sufficient to meet all your online marketing needs.

Use social media strategically to

✦ Meet an otherwise unmet marketing need

✦ Increase access to your target market

✦ Open the door to a new niche market

✦ Move prospects through the conversion funnel

✦ Improve the experience for existing customers

For example, The Pioneer Woman site (`http://thepioneerwoman.com`) links to Twitter and Facebook sites, as well as its blog (`http://tasty kitchen.com/blog`), to attract its audience. For more information on overall online marketing, see Jan's book, *Web Marketing For Dummies,* 3rd Edition.

To get the maximum benefit from social media, you must have a *hub site,* the site to which web traffic will be directed, as shown in Figure 1-9 (`http://personaltrainercommunity.com/246/what-is-the-first-website-you-should-build`). It can be a full website or a blog, as long as the site has its own domain name. It doesn't matter where the site is hosted — only that you own its name, which appears as `yourcompany.com`, or `blog.yourcompany.com`. Though you can link to `yourcompany.wordpress.com`, you cannot effectively optimize or search for it. Besides, it doesn't look professional.

Figure 1-9:
A blog hubsite, connecting social media and pages on the website.

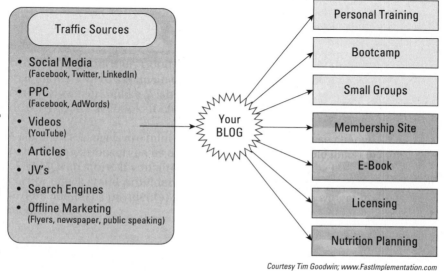

Courtesy Tim Goodwin; www.FastImplementation.com

Consider doing some sketching for your own campaign: Create a block diagram that shows the relationship between components, the flow of content between outlets, and perhaps even the criteria for success and how they will be measured.

Developing a Strategic Social Media Marketing Plan

Surely you wrote an overall marketing plan when you last updated your business plan and an online marketing plan when you first created your website. If not, it's never too late! For business planning resources, see the Starting a Business page at `www.sba.gov/category/navigation-structure/starting-managing-business/starting-business` or read *Business Plans For Dummies*, 2nd Edition, by Paul Tiffany and Steven D. Peterson.

You can further refine a marketing plan for social media marketing purposes. As with any other marketing plan, you start with strategy. A Social Media Marketing Goals statement (Figure 1-10 shows an example) would incorporate sections on strategic goals, objectives, target markets, methods, costs, and return on investment (ROI).

You can download the form on this book's website (`www.dummies.com/go/socialmediamarketing2e`), and read more about ROI in Book I, Chapter 2.

Here are some points to keep in mind when putting together your strategic marketing overview:

✦ The most important function of the form isn't for you to follow it slavishly, but rather to force you to consider the various facets of social media marketing before you invest too much effort or money.

✦ The form also helps you communicate decisions to your board of advisors or your boss, in case you need to make the business case for getting involved in social media.

✦ The form provides a coherent framework for explaining to everyone involved in your social media effort — employees, volunteers, or contractors — the task you're trying to accomplish and why.

Social Media Marketing Goals

Related to Hub Site (URL): _____

Prepared by: _____ **Date:** _____

Business Profile

Is the social media plan for a new or established company?
◯ New company   ◯ Existing company, years in business:

Does the company have an existing brick-and-mortar operation?
◯ Yes   ◯ No

Does the company have an existing website or web presence?
◯ Yes   ◯ No

Does the company have an existing blog or social media presence?
◯ Yes   ◯ No
If yes, list all current URLs for social media.

Will your site serve:
◯ Business   ◯ Consumers

What type of business is the website for?
◯ Manufacturer   ◯ Service provider   ◯ Retailer
◯ Distributor   ◯ Professional

What does the company sell?
◯ Goods   ◯ Services

Describe your goods or services:

What geographical range does the social media campaign address?
◯ Local (specify)   ◯ Regional (specify)
◯ National (specify if not US)   ◯ International (specify)

Social Media Campaign Goals

Rank the applicable goals of your social media campaign from 1-7 with 1
your top goal

_____ Increasing traffic/visits to hub site

_____ Branding

_____ Building relationships

_____ Improving business process (e.g. customer service, tech support)

_____ Improving visibility in natural search

_____ Increasing sales revenue

_____ Saving money on paid advertising

Figure 1-10:
Establish
your social
marketing
goals,
objectives,
and target
market
definition on
this form.

Financial Profile

Social Media Campaign Budget for First Year

Outside development, contractors, includes writing, design, technical $ _____

Special content production (e.g. video, podcasts, photography): $ _____

Marketing/paid ads on social media $ _____

Inhouse labor (burdened rate) $ _____

Other costs, e.g. tools, equipment $ _____

TOTAL: $ _____

Break-even point: $ _____   Within: _____ ○ mo ○ yr

Return on investment: _____ %   Within: _____ ○ mo ○ yr

Objectives

Repeat for appropriate objectives for each goal within timeframe specified (for instance, 1 year).

Traffic objective (# visitors per month): _____   Within: _____

Conversion objective: _____ %   Within: _____

Sales objectives (# sales per month): $ _____   Within: _____

Average $ per sale: $ _____   Within: _____

$ revenue per month: $ _____   Within: _____

Other objectives specific to your site, e.g. for branding, relationships, search ranking   _____   Within: _____

_____   Within: _____

_____   Within: _____

Marketing Profile

Describe your target markets. Give specific demographic or other segmentation information. For B2B, segment by industry and/or job title.

What is your marketing tag?

Value proposition: Why should someone buy from your company rather than another?

Name at least six competitors and list their websites, blogs, and social media pages.

© 2012 Watermelon Mountain Web Marketing www.watermelonweb.com

© 2012 Watermelon Mountain Web Marketing; www.watermelonweb.com

Book I, Chapter 3 includes a Social Media Marketing Plan, which helps you develop a detailed tactical approach — including timelines — for specific social media services, sites, and tools.

In the following sections, we talk about the information you should include on this form.

Establishing goals

The Goals section prioritizes the overall reasons you're implementing a social media campaign. You can prioritize your goals from the list of seven benefits of social media, described in the earlier section "Understanding the Benefits of Social Media," or you can add your own goals. Most businesses have multiple goals, which you can specify on the form.

Consult Table 1-1 to see how CMO.com ranks various social media services in terms of helping you reach some of your goals.

Table 1-1	Matching Social Media Services to Goals			
	Customer Communication	*Brand Exposure*	*Traffic to Your Site*	*SEO*
Digg	Okay	Good	Good	Good
Facebook	Good	Good	Okay	Poor
Flickr	Okay	Okay	Poor	Good
*Google+	Poor	Good	Okay	Good
LinkedIn	Okay	Good	Poor	Okay
*Pinterest	Okay	Good	Good	Poor
Reddit	Okay	Poor	Okay	Okay
StumbleUpon	Poor	Okay	Good	Good
Tumblr	Good	Good	Poor	Good
Twitter	Good	Good	Okay	Okay
YouTube	Good	Good	Okay	Good

Adapted from CMO.com; www.cmo.com/sites/default/files/CMOcom-SocialMediaLandscape2011.pdf. Starred rows added by the author.

Setting quantifiable objectives

For each goal, set at least one quantifiable, measurable objective. "More customers" isn't a quantifiable objective. A quantifiable objective is "Increase number of visits to website by 10 percent," or "add 30 new customers within three months," or "obtain 100 new followers for Twitter account within one month of launch." Enter this information on the form.

Identifying your target markets

Specify one or more target markets on the form, not by what they consume, but rather by who they are. "Everyone who eats dinner out" isn't a sub-market you can identify online. However, you can find "high-income couples within 20 miles of your destination who visit wine and classical music sites."

You may want to reach more than one target market by way of social media or other methods. Specify each of them. Then, as you read about different methods in this book, write down next to each one which social media services or sites appear best suited to reach that market. Prioritize the order in which you plan to reach them.

Book I, Chapter 3 suggests online market research techniques to help you define your markets, match them to social media services, and find them online.

Think niche! Carefully define your audiences for various forms of social media and target your messages appropriately for each audience.

Estimating costs

Estimating costs from the bottom up is tricky, and this approach rarely includes a cap. Consequently, costs often wildly exceed your budget. Instead, establish first how much money you're willing to invest in the overall effort, including in-house labor, outside contractors, and miscellaneous hard costs such as purchasing software or equipment. Enter those amounts in the Cost section.

Then prioritize your social marketing efforts based on what you can afford, allocating or reallocating funds within your budget as needed. This approach not only keeps your total social marketing costs under control but also lets you assess the results against expenses.

To make cost-tracking easier, ask your bookkeeper or CPA to set up an activity or a job within your accounting system for social media marketing. Then you can easily track and report all related costs and labor.

Valuing social media ROI

Return on investment (ROI) is your single most important measure of success for social media marketing. In simple terms, *ROI* is the ratio of revenue divided by costs for your business or, in this case, for your social media marketing effort.

You also need to set a realistic term in which you will recover your investment. Are you willing to wait ten weeks? Ten months? Ten years? Some forms of social media are unlikely to produce a fast fix for drooping sales, so consider what you're trying to accomplish.

Figure 1-11 presents a brief glimpse of how HubSpot clients assessed the average cost of *lead generation* (identifying prospective customers) for B2B companies in February 2011, comparing social marketing to other forms of marketing. It's just a guide. Keep in mind that the only ROI or cost of acquisition that truly matters is your own.

Figure 1-11:
The cost of B2B lead generation for social media and blogs compared to pay-per-click ads and natural search.

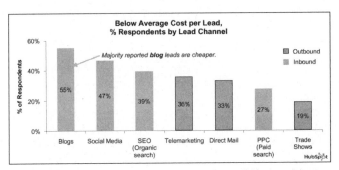

Courtesy HubSpot; www.hubspot.com

Costs usually turn out to be simpler to track than revenues that are traceable explicitly to social media. The next chapter discusses techniques for figuring ROI and other financial metrics in detail.

Whatever you plan online will cost twice as much and take twice as long as anticipated.

A social media service is likely to produce results only when your customers or prospects are already using it or are willing to try. Pushing people toward a service they don't want is quite difficult. If in doubt, first expand other online and offline efforts to drive traffic toward your hub site.

Saddling up with social media

Toll Booth Saddle Shop, a second-generation, family-owned business run by Patricia Janssen, started as a brick-and-mortar store in New Jersey in 1974 by Janssen's mother, Rose Hunter. Toll Booth established its website around 2006 to show customers what products were available in the store. The website has since evolved into a full-blown e-commerce site with links to Facebook, Twitter, and other social media services.

Courtesy Harold Hero Horse

"My daughter, Andrea, got us started in social media while she was in college, and I learned from her," says Janssen proudly. "She still helps out by running our Facebook contests and overall strategy." Andrea got Toll Booth on Facebook in early 2010, followed by a blog. Later that year, she added LinkedIn and Twitter. In 2011, the team began building a YouTube presence with a series of humorous animations about a crime-fighting steed called "Harold Hero Horse."

Janssen thinks social media quickly became a natural and integral part of their marketing strategy because they relied almost solely on word of mouth advertising for many years. She uses Facebook, with its mix of both new and loyal customers, for building brand awareness and customer loyalty. "We do share products from our website from time to time," she explains, "but we try to create a good balance between content creation, content *curation* (re-publishing others' content), and asking for the sale."

(continued)

(continued)

She views Twitter as an extension of their Facebook presence. "Our target market has not yet embraced Twitter enough to warrant having its own content," Janssen observes, although she does plan on giving Twitter its own content in the future. In contrast, YouTube is used primarily as a way to have fun with the brand and create fun content for the audience, and LinkedIn is used to connect with other vendors and to find valuable industry information.

Janssen schedules most content distribution through HootSuite, but she checks pages daily (multiple times a day when possible!) to answer customer questions and respond to customer comments. "HootSuite is nice for distributing content," she notes, "but it doesn't replace good-old human interaction."

Toll Booth uses social media buttons and widgets as much as possible to cross-promote its presence, as well as the social bookmarking sites Digg and StumbleUpon to promote its blog.

Toll Booth supplements social media with SEO, e-mail newsletters, and links from free horse-related directories online to drive non-social traffic to the website, plus it uses offline advertising in some horse show prize lists and local horse newspapers.

Toll Booth has found that contests with branded merchandise as prizes help keep its brand top-of-mind. "Our contests do a great job sharing our message across Facebook, and tend to get us a decent amount of new fans each time. We have run two photo contests so far, and plan on launching another 'You Know You're a Horse Person When…' contest." The Facebook business page for Toll Booth Saddle displays both the contest option and a link to the YouTube site featuring Harold. "We're hoping to generate excitement around shopping online and ultimately increase our web sales," says Janssen with an eye on the bottom line.

Courtesy Harold Hero Horse

Based on statistics from Google Analytics and Facebook Insight, Janssen notes, "Facebook seems to drive the most web traffic of any of our social pages. While we do not get as many direct sales as we'd like through our website, we have noticed a significant increase in foot traffic in our store."

Janssen is candid about Toll Booth's social media experience. "At first, we used our Facebook page like you would use any other online directory. We put our information up, and figured, 'if you build it, they will come.' We quickly learned that is not at all the case. You have to have some sort of strategy behind your social media presence, just like you would for any of your traditional marketing efforts."

"If you're going to use social media, you have to be willing to go all in. It's nice that it's free to use, but it takes a lot of your time. You need to devote time each and every day to managing each of your social communities. After all, social media is on 24/7! Another lesson we've learned is that you don't have to be a content machine to have a successful social media presence. Posting relevant content is as easy as being in tune with what's going on in your industry."

Finally, Janssen reminds other business owners that "customers are your best resource. Not sure what you should post? Just ask! The nice thing about being a small business is that you are able to develop personal relationships with many of your customers. Use that to your advantage!"

Toll Booth Saddle Shop's web presence

www.tollboothsaddle.com

www.tollboothsaddle.com/Blog/Blog.html

http://tollboothsaddle.equiteampro.com

http://digg.com/tollboothsaddle

www.facebook.com/tollboothsaddle

www.youtube.com/user/TBSSPJ

http://twitter.com/tollboothsaddle

www.linkedin.com/in/tollboothsaddle

http://pinterest.com/tollboothsaddle

Chapter 2: Tallying the Bottom Line

In This Chapter

✔ Estimating the cost of customer acquisition

✔ Figuring sales metrics and revenue

✔ Managing and converting leads

✔ Breaking even

✔ Calculating return on investment (ROI)

*I*n this chapter, we deal with business metrics to determine whether you see a return on investment (ROI) in your social media marketing services. In other words, you get to the bottom line! For details on performance metrics for various types of social media as parameters for campaign success, see Book VIII.

By definition, the business metric ROI involves revenues. Alas, becoming famous online isn't a traditional part of ROI; it might have a public relations value and affect business results, but fame doesn't necessarily make you rich. This chapter examines the cost of acquiring new customers, tracking sales, and managing leads. After you reach the break-even point on your investment, you can (in the best of all worlds) start totaling up the profits and then calculate your ROI.

To get the most from this chapter, review your business plan and financial projections. You may find that you need to adjust some of your data collection efforts to ensure that you have the information for these analyses.

 If numbers make your head spin, ask your bookkeeper or accountant for assistance in tracking important business metrics from your financial statements. That person can ensure that you acquire the right data, set up spreadsheets to calculate key metrics, and provide regular reports — and then he or she can teach you how to interpret them.

You don't want to participate in social media marketing for its own sake or because everyone else is doing it. The following sections help you make the business case for yourself.

Preparing to Calculate Return on Investment

To calculate ROI, you have to recognize both costs and revenue related to your social media activities; neither is transparent, even without distinguishing marketing channels.

Surprisingly, the key determinant in tracking cost of sales, and therefore ROI, is most likely to be your sales process, which matters more than whether you sell to other businesses (B2B) or consumers (B2C) or whether you offer products or services.

The *sales cycle* (the length of time from prospect identification to customer sale) affects the timeline for calculating ROI. If a B2B sale for an expensive, long-term contract or product takes two years, expecting a return on your investment within a month is pointless.

For a pure-play (e-commerce only) enterprise selling products from an online store, the ROI calculation detailed in this chapter is fairly standard. However, ROI becomes more complicated if your website generates leads that you must follow up with offline, if you must pull customers from a web presence into a brick-and-mortar storefront (that method is sometimes called *bricks-and-clicks*), or if you sell different products or services in different channels. Table 2-1 provides resource sites that relate to these issues and other business metrics.

Table 2-1		Resources for Business Metrics
Site Name	*URL*	*What You Can Do*
ClickZ	www.clickz.com/clickz/column/2140755/under standing-importance-social-media-roi	Measure social media success
Frogloop.com	www.frogloop.com/social-network-calculator	Download or calculate online your social media ROI
Harvard Business School Toolkit	http://hbswk.hbs.edu/archive/1262.html	Use the break-even analysis tool
	http://hbswk.hbs.edu/archive/1436.html	Calculate lifetime customer value

Site Name	URL	What You Can Do
Interactive Insights Group	www.interactive insightsgroup.com/ blog1/social-media-metrics-superlist-measurement-roi-key-statistics-resources	Scan annotated super-list of dozens of articles on social media ROI and measurement
Olivier Blanchard Basics of Social Media ROI	www.slideshare.net/ thebrandbuilder/ olivier-blanchard-basics-of-social-media-roi	View an entertaining slideshow introduction to ROI
Panalysis	www.panalysis.com/ resources/sales-target-calculator.aspx	Calculate online sales
	www.panalysis.com/ resources/customer-acquisition-cost.aspx	Calculate customer acquisition costs
Search Engine Watch	http://searchengine watch.com/article/ 2079336/4-Steps-to-Measure-Social-Media-ROI-with-Google-Analytics	Set up Google Analytics to measure social media ROI
Search CRM.com	http://searchcrm. techtarget.com	Find information about customer relationship management (CRM)
Shop.org	www.shop.org/web/ guest/researchand industryinfo	Peruse reports about research, consumer data, and the state of retailing online (SORO)
WhatIs.com	http://whatis. techtarget.com	Search a dictionary and an encyclopedia of business terms

Include the business metrics you intend to monitor in the Business Goals section of your Social Media Marketing Plan, found in Book I, Chapter 3, and the frequency of review on your Social Media Activity Calendar discussed in Book I, Chapter 4.

Accounting for Customers Acquired Online

The *cost of customer acquisition* (CCA) refers to the marketing, advertising, support, and other types of expenses required to convert a prospect into a customer. CCA usually excludes the cost of a sales force (the salary and commissions) or payments to affiliates. Some companies carefully segregate promotional expenses, such as loyalty programs, that relate to branding or customer retention. As long as you apply your definition consistently, you're okay.

If your goal in social media marketing is branding or improving relationships with existing customers, CCA may be a bit misleading, but it's still worth tracking for comparison purposes.

The definition of your customers and the cost of acquiring them depends on the nature of your business. For instance, if you have a purely advertising-supported, web-only business, visitors to your site may not even purchase anything. They simply show up, or perhaps they register to download some information online. Your real customers are advertisers. However, a similar business that's not supported by advertising may need to treat those same registrants as leads who might later purchase services or pay for subscriptions.

The easiest way to define your customers is to figure out who pays you money.

Comparing the costs of customer acquisition

You may want to delineate CCA for several different revenue streams or marketing channels: consumers versus businesses; products versus services (for example, software and support contracts); online sales versus offline sales; consumers versus advertisers. Compare each one against the average CCA for your company overall. The formula is simple:

```
cost of customer acquisition = marketing cost ÷ number of leads
```

Be careful! This formula can be misleading if you calculate it over too short a time frame. The CCA may be too high during quarters that you undertake a new activity or special promotion (such as early Christmas sales or the introduction of a new product or service) and too low during quarters when actual spending is down but you reap benefits from an earlier investment in social media.

Calculate your CCA over six months to a year to smooth out unique events. Alternatively, compute rolling averages (taking an average over several months at a time adjusting the start date each month — January through March, February through April, March through May, and so on) to create a better picture of what's going on.

In Figure 2-1, Rapport Online ranks the return on investment, defined as cost-effectiveness in generating leads, for a variety of online marketing tactics. The lowest ROI appears at the bottom of the cube, and the highest appears at the top.

Figure 2-1:
Social media would fit near the top of the ROI scale for Internet marketing tactics.

Courtesy Rapport Online Inc., ROI-web.com

Social media marketing runs the gamut of "rapport building" options because it involves some or all of these techniques. On this scale, most social media services would probably fall between customer referral and SEO or between SEO and PR/link building, depending on the type and aggressiveness of your effort in a particular marketing channel. Traditional offline media, by contrast, would have a lower ROI than banner advertising.

As with performance metrics, business metrics such as CCA and ROI aren't perfect. If you track everything consistently, however, you can at least compare results by marketing channel, which can help you make informed business decisions.

If you garner leads online but close your sales and collect payments offline, you can frame CCA as the cost of lead acquisition, recognizing that you may need to add costs for staff, collateral, demos, travel, and other items to convert a lead.

For a rough idea of your cost of customer acquisition, fill out the spreadsheet (adapted from the spreadsheet at `www.forentrepreneurs.com`) shown in Figure 2-2 with your own data. For start-up costs, include the labor expense, contractors for content development, and any other hard costs related to your social media activities. Or, try the CCA calculator at `www.panalysis.com/resources/customer-acquisition-cost.aspx`, substituting social media costs for web expenses.

Figure 2-2: Compare CCA for social media marketing with the average CCA across your entire business.

Cost of Customer Acquisition			Save As Excel	Exit Full Screen View
40R x 1C				
	A	B	C	D	E
1	Simple Cost of Customer Acquisition Calculation				
2					
3	Input Variables for 6 months				
4	Total SMM Visiors	10,000			
5	Start-up SMM costs for content, programmer, contractors	$1,000.00			
6	CTR to site %	7%			
7	Conversion to customer %	4%			
8	No of Sales & Marketing Staff	1			
9	Ave 6 month labor cost for staff & contractors for SMM time app. 15 hr/mo @ $20	$1,800			
10					
11					
12	Flow	City	Conversion %		
13	Total SMM Visits	10,000			
14	Site Visits	700	7%		
15	Customers	28	4%		
16					
17	SMM Marketing Spending (non-recurring)	$1,000			
18	Total Recurring Staff Costs	$1,800			
19					
20	Cost of Customer Acquisition				
21	Recurring staff costs only	$64.29			
22	Start-up costs only	$35.71			
23	Total costs	$100.00			
24					
25					
26					
27					
28					
29					
	Sheet1				

Courtesy For Entrepreneurs; www.forentrepreneurs.com

To put things in perspective, remember that the traditional business school model for offline marketing teaches that the CCA is roughly equivalent to the profit on the amount a customer spends during the first year.

Because you generally see most of your profits from future sales to that customer, you must also understand the *lifetime customer value* (how much and how often a customer will buy), not just the revenue from an initial sale. The better the customers, the more it's worth spending to acquire them. Harvard Business School offers an online calculator for determining lifetime customer value at `http://hbswk.hbs.edu/archive/1436.html`.

Be sure that the cost of customer acquisition (CCA) doesn't exceed the lifetime customer value.

In its *State of Retailing Online 2009* report for Shop.org, Forrester Research estimated that the cost of acquiring an online customer was about half the cost of acquiring an offline customer. However, as shown in the calculations in Figure 2-2, even *half* doesn't mean *cheap*. Since then, the cost of acquiring new customers through online advertising has crept up, making social media an attractive alternative.

Try to keep the total cost of marketing by any method at 6 to 11 percent of your revenues; you can spend less after you have an established business with word-of-mouth referrals and loyal, repeat customers. Remember, customer acquisition is only part of your total marketing budget; allow for customer retention and branding expenses as well.

Small businesses (under 100 employees), new companies, and new products usually need to spend toward the high end of the scale on marketing initially — perhaps even more than 11 percent. By comparison, mature, well-branded product lines and companies with a large revenue stream can spend a lower percentage on marketing.

Obviously, anything that can reduce marketing costs offers a benefit. See whether your calculation bears out that cost level for your investment in social media.

One is silver and the other gold

You might remember the words to that old Girl Scout song: "Make new friends but keep the old; one is silver and the other gold." To retain customers, apply that philosophy to your policy of customer satisfaction. That may mean anything from sending holiday greetings to establishing a loyalty program with discounts for repeat buyers; from entering repeat customers into a special sweepstakes to offering a coupon on their next purchase when they sign up for a newsletter.

According to DealSavant.com (www.dealsavant.com/tag/customer-loyalty), it costs four to six times more to acquire a new customer than to retain an existing one. In case you needed it, DealSavant's statement gives you a significant financial reason to listen to customers' concerns, complaints, product ideas, and desires.

While you lavish time and attention on social marketing to fill the top of your funnel with new prospects, don't forget its value for improving relationships with current customers and nurturing their engagement with your brand.

Establishing Key Performance Indicators for Sales

If you track ROI, at some point you must track revenue and profits as business metrics. Otherwise, there's no ROI to compute.

If you sell online, your storefront should provide ways for you to slice and dice sales to obtain crucial data. However, if your sales come from services, from a brick-and-mortar store, or from large contractual purchases, you probably need to obtain revenue statistics from financial or other external records to plug into your ROI calculation.

 If you manage a bricks-and-clicks operation, you may want to integrate your online and offline operations by selecting e-commerce software from the vendor who provides the *point-of-sales* (POS) package for your cash registers. That software may already be integrated with your inventory control and accounting packages.

Just as with performance metrics, you should be able to acquire certain key performance indicators (KPI) for sales by using storefront statistics. Confirm that you can access this data before purchasing your e-commerce package:

✦ You should be able to determine how often customers buy (number of transactions per month), how many new customers you acquire (reach), and how much they spend per transaction (yield).

✦ Look for sales reports by average dollar amount as well as by number of sales. Plugging average numbers into an ROI calculation is easier, and the results are close enough as long as the inputs are consistent.

✦ You should be able to find order totals for any specified time frame so that you can track sales tied to promotions, marketing activities, and sale announcements.

✦ Look for the capability to sort sales by new and repeat customers; to allow for future, personalized offers; and to distinguish numbers for CCA.

✦ Your sales statistics should include a conversion funnel (as described in Chapter 1 of this minibook). Try to trace the path upstream so that you can identify sales initiated from social media.

✦ Check that data can be exported to a spreadsheet.

✦ Make sure that you can collect statistics on the use of promotion codes by number and dollar value so that you can decide which promotions are the most successful.

✦ Having store reports that break down sales by product is helpful. Sometimes called a *product tree,* this report shows which products are selling by SKU (Stock-Keeping Unit) and category.

Table 2-2 lists some storefront options that integrate with social media and offer sales analytics. Unfortunately, not all third-party storefront solutions offer ideal tracking. Many storefront solutions use Google Analytics, shown in Figure 2-3, to track transactions.

Table 2-2	Social Media Store Solutions Offering Sales Statistics	
Name	*URL*	*Type of Sales Stats Available*
Google E-Commerce Tracking	`http://code.google.com/ apis/analytics/docs/ tracking/gaTracking Ecommerce.html`	Google Analytics or e-commerce
ProductCart	`www.earlyimpact.com`	Google Analytics integration; can track social media widgets as affiliates
Mercantec	`www.mercantec.com`	Google Analytics e-commerce tracking and statistics
Payvment	`www.payvment.com`	Built-in sales analytics; track data on social media sales by product
Venpop	`http://venpop.com`	Analytics for Facebook shopping solution

If you created alternative SKUs for products sold by way of social media for tracking purposes, be sure to merge them into the same category of your product tree. Using multiple SKUs isn't recommended if your storefront solution includes inventory control.

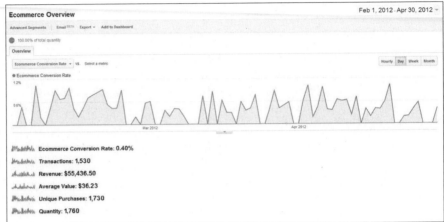

Figure 2-3:
E-commerce
statistics
from Google
Analytics.

Courtesy Early Impact/ProductCart

You can input the numbers from your social media sales metrics into a sales calculator to forecast unit sales needed to meet your goals. Figure 2-4 shows a calculator from Panalysis at www.panalysis.com/resources/ sales-target-calculator.aspx.

Figure 2-4:
Sales
forecasting
calculator
from
Panalysis.

Courtesy Panalysis.com

Tracking leads

Often, your social media or web presence generates leads instead of, or in addition to, sales. If your sales process dictates that some or all sales are closed offline, you need a way to track leads from initiation to conversion. Marketing Sherpa, a marketing research firm, tracks the process of tracking leads from the initial acquisition of customers' names or e-mail addresses from sales. Percentages given are for each step compared to the original number of visitors. See Figure 2-5.

Customer relationship management (CRM) software helps you track prospects, qualified leads, and customers in an organized way. A simple database might allow different managers, salespeople, and support personnel to share a client's concerns or track the client's steps within the selling cycle.

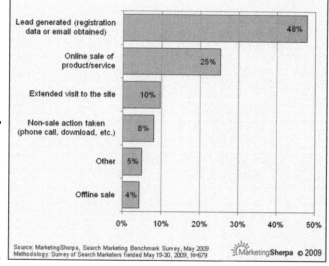

Figure 2-5:
A typical progression from generating leads to converting a buyer.

Source: MarketingSherpa.com

The process of CRM and lead management may also include qualifying and nurturing leads, managing marketing campaigns, building relationships, and providing service, all while helping to maximize profits. Table 2-3 lists some lead monitoring and CRM software options.

Table 2-3	Lead Monitoring and CRM Software		
Name	*URL*	*What You Can Do*	*Cost*
Batchbook	www.batchblue.com	Integrate social media with CRM	Free 30-day trial with unlimited contacts; starts at $14.95 per month
HubSpot	www.hubspot.com	All-in-one software; manage inbound leads, lead generation, and more	Free 30-day trial; starts at $200 per month
LEADS Explorer	www.leads explorer.com	See who's visiting your website	Free 30-day trial; starts at $41.67 per month
Splendid CRM	www.splendid crm.com/Products/ SplendidCRM Community/tabid/ 71/Default.aspx	Install open source CRM software	Free core version; fee starts at $10 per user per month
Zoho CRM	www.zoho.com/crm/ index.html	Implement customer relationship management software	Free for 3 users; starts at $12 per user per month

Though often thought of as the province of B2B companies offering high-ticket items with a long sales cycle, lead-tracking tools can help you segment existing and prospective customers, improve the percentage of leads that turn into clients, and build brand loyalty.

Figure 2-6 shows the distribution of leads and sales, respectively, with analytical tools provided by HubSpot. Note how the distribution of leads by marketing channels differs from the ultimate distribution of sales.

You can export your Google Analytics results to a spreadsheet and create a similar graphical display.

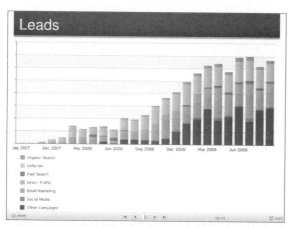

Figure 2-6:
HubSpot
offers lead
monitoring
software
that
displays the
distribution
of leads and
sales by
originating
marketing
channel.

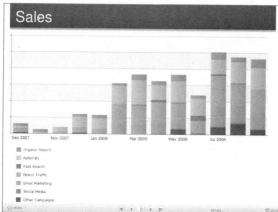

Courtesy HubSpot®; www.HubSpot.com

Understanding Other Common Business Metrics

Your bookkeeper or accountant can help you compute and track other
business measurements to ensure that your business turns a profit. You may
want to pay particular attention to estimating your break-even point and
your profit margin.

Break-even point

Computing the *break-even point* (the number of sales needed for revenues
received to equal total costs) helps determine when a product or product
line will become profitable. After a product reaches break-even, sales start
to contribute to profits.

To calculate the break-even point, first you need to figure out the *cost of goods* or *average variable costs* (costs such as materials, shipping, or commission that vary with the number of units sold) and your *fixed costs* (charges such as rent or insurance that are the same each month regardless of how much business you do). Then plug the amounts into these two formulas:

```
revenues - cost of goods (variable) = gross margin

fixed costs ÷ gross margin = break-even point (in unit sales)
```

Figure 2-7 shows this relationship. This graph of the break-even point shows fixed costs (the dashed horizontal line) to variable costs (the solid diagonal line) to plot total costs. After revenues surpass the break-even point, each sale contributes to profits (the shaded area on the right).

Figure 2-7: The break-even point plots fixed plus variable costs. Each sale made after reaching the break-even point contributes to profits.

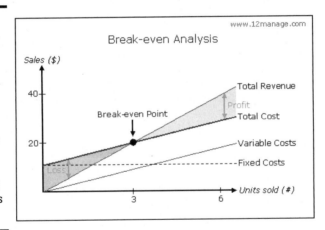

The break-even analysis tool from the Harvard Business School Toolkit (http://hbswk.hbs.edu/archive/1262.html) can also help you calculate your break-even point.

Profit margin

Net profit margin is defined as earnings (profits) divided by revenues. If you have $10,000 in revenues and $1,500 in profits, your profit margin is 15 percent.

Revenue versus profit

One of the most common errors in marketing is to stop analyzing results when you count the cash in the drawer. You can easily be seduced by growing revenues, but it's profit that matters. Profit determines your return on investment, replenishes your resources for growth, and rewards you for taking risks.

Determining Return on Investment

Return on investment (ROI) is a commonly used business metric that evaluates the profitability of an investment or effort compared with its original cost. This versatile metric is usually presented as a ratio or percentage (multiply the following equation by 100). The formula itself is deceptively simple:

```
ROI = (Gain from Investment - Cost of Investment) ÷ Cost of
    Investment
```

The devil is, as usual, in the details. The cost of an investment means more than cold, hard cash. Depending on the type of effort for which you're computing ROI, you may need to include the cost of labor (including your own!), subcontractors, fees, and advertising for an accurate picture. When calculating ROI for your entire business, be sure to include overhead, cost of goods, and cost of sales.

You can affect ROI positively by either increasing the return (revenues) or reducing costs. That's business in a nutshell.

Because the formula is flexible, be sure that you know what other people mean when they talk about ROI.

You can calculate ROI for a particular marketing campaign or product or an entire year's worth of marketing expenses. Or, compare ROI among various forms of marketing, comparing the net revenue returned from an investment in social media to returns from SEO or paid advertising.

Run ROI calculations monthly, quarterly, or yearly, depending on the parameter you're trying to measure.

Try the interactive ROI calculator at `www.clickz.com/website-optimization-roi-calculator`, also shown in Figure 2-8. You can modify this model for social media by treating Monthly Site Visits as social media visits, Success Events as click-throughs to your main site, and Value of Success Events as the value of a sale. See what happens when you improve the business metric (the value of a sale) instead of, or in addition to, improving performance (site traffic or conversion rate).

ROI may be expressed as a *rate of return* (how long it takes to earn back an investment). An annual ROI of 25 percent means that it takes four years to recover what you put in. Obviously, if an investment takes too long to earn out, your product — or your business — is at risk of failing in the meantime.

If your analysis predicts a negative ROI, or even a very low rate of return over an extended period, stop and think! Unless you have a specific tactical plan (such as using a product as a loss leader to draw traffic), look for an alternative effort with a better likelihood of success.

Technically speaking, ROI is a business metric, involving the achievement of business goals, such as more clicks from social media that become sales, higher average value per sale, more repeat sales from existing customers, or reduced cost of customer acquisition.

Figure 2-8: Play around with variables like the value of a sale, as well as performance criteria.

Calculating ROI: Website Optimization   ZAAZ

There is value in optimizing your website. How much value? Depending on your desired outcomes, the ZAAZ Calculator is designed to estimate the return on investment. Plug in the numbers and see how it changes the present and future value of your business.

Current Site Behavior

Total Average Monthly Site Visits — 5,000

Average Monthly Success Events — 250
Identify specific targeted behavior (lead conversion, sales conversion, etc.)

Success Event Conversion Rate — 5.00 %
Shows success event conversion from total site visits.

Enter Average Value of a Success Event Visit — $ 25
Please refer to blogs.zaaz.com or here for more information on calculating this value.

Potential Improvement

Increase Site Traffic by X% — 10 %
Enter a value (percentage) of the potential increase in site traffic (example 10%).

Increase Conversion by X% — 10 %
Enter a value (percentage) of the potential increase in site conversion (example 10%).

Estimated Cost to Improve Performance — $ 3,000
Enter estimated costs to optimize identified behaviors (e.g., agency fees, marketing and/or operational costs).

Enter the average value associated with a single Average Monthly Success Event Visit. Example: each visit is worth $25 on average.

Estimated Impact of Site Optimization

■ Monthly   ■ Annually

Current Value — $6,250 | $75,000

Estimated Future Value — $7,563 | $90,750

Courtesy of Clickz.com and Zaaz/Possible Worldwide

Many people try to calculate ROI for social media based on performance metrics such as increases in

✦ The amount of traffic to website or social media pages

✦ The number of online conversations that include a positive mention of your company

✦ References to your company versus references to your competitors

✦ The number of people who join your social networks or bookmark your sites

✦ The number of people who post to your blog, comment on your Facebook wall, or retweet your comments

These measurements may be worth monitoring, but they're only intermediate steps in the ROI process, as shown in Figure 2-9.

Figure 2-9:
This figure illustrates the relationship between performance metrics and business metrics for ROI.

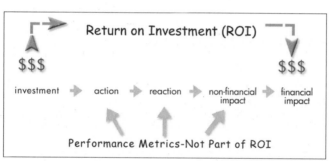

Source: BrandBuilder, "Olivier Blanchard Basics of Social Media ROI"
www.slideshare.net/thebrandbuilder/olivier-blanchard-basics-of-social-media-roi (#35)

Here's how to calculate your return on investment:

1. **Establish baselines for what you want to measure before and after your effort.**

   For example, you may want to measure year-over-year growth.

2. **Create activity timelines that display when specific social media marketing activities take place.**

   For example, mark an event on an activity timeline when you start a blog or Twitter campaign.

3. **Plot business metrics over time, particularly sales revenues, number of transactions, and net new customers.**

4. **Measure transactional precursors, such as positive versus negative mentions online, retail store traffic, or performance metrics.**

   For example, keep a tally of comments on a blog post or of site visits.

5. **Line up the timelines for the various relevant activities and transactional (business) results.**

6. **Look for patterns in the data that suggest a relationship between business metrics and transactional precursors.**

7. **Prove those relationships.**

Improvement in performance metrics doesn't necessarily produce better business results. The only two metrics that count toward ROI are whether your techniques reduce costs or improve revenue.

Neenah Paper stacks up social media

Neenah Paper, the premium paper division of Neenah Paper, Inc., a large, publicly traded company (NYSE: NP), generates leads via Twitter and other social media. Neenah Paper's website (www.neenahpaper.com), the hub of its web presence, offers useful ideas for B2B companies of any size.

Neenah Cabinet™ and Personal Proof® are registered trademarks and trademarks of Neenah Paper, Inc. Neenahpaper.com and neenahpaperblog.com (Against the Grain) are ©Neenah Paper, Inc. All rights reserved.

Neenah Paper created its website in 2001 and updated it in August 2010, about the time it decided to move forward with social media marketing in light of a changing customer base. Instead of setting up meetings at large agencies or print houses, Neenah found that it needed to reach small businesses, particularly designers and printers, who often have employees working from home. After starting with an iPhone app, Neenah followed up quickly with Facebook, Twitter, and a blog. In 2011, they added more apps, listed at the end of this sidebar.

Neenah had been using the Twitter handle @NeenahPaper for about a year, says Jamie Saunders, Marketing Communications Manager, when they read about companies who were using Twitter for lead generation. Although Neenah sales reps already relied on LinkedIn for client contact, the marketing department suggested testing Twitter with a group of reps willing to tweet from their phones (`https://twitter.com/PaperTwit`). The following figure shows how Neenah sales rep, Kim Shannon, uses Twitter to communicate with leads and prospects.

Neenah Cabinet™ and Personal Proof® are registered trademarks and trademarks of Neenah Paper, Inc. Neenahpaper.com and neenahpaperblog.com (Against the Grain) are ©Neenah Paper, Inc. All rights reserved.

With a tight focus on the graphic arts and print communities, Twitter works best for passing along articles or information of interest, discount codes for web purchases, and keeping Neenah top-of-mind for paper choice. "Our group of Twitter users has grown in size, and we've developed ongoing training/development for the entire team so they stay up-to-date on how to best use Twitter to meet new clients, stay in touch with current clients, and increase their paper sales," notes Saunders.

(continued)

(continued)

Although Neenah has tried various automated methods to manage its social media, Saunders prefers old-fashioned, manual posting to "ensure that we are communicating directly with our customers as a live person." The company tries to post at least once a day. "There's no magic formula to the number of times we share, as you never know when a great conversation will just take off!" she adds.

For monitoring, Neenah uses Google Analytics plus TwitterCounter for detail on Twitter traffic. "Interestingly, much of our website traffic is generated by Twitter. We reward our followers often by providing exclusive discount codes for ordering on our site, or giving away exclusive promotional materials. We see the benefits to this tactic in traffic to our site, purchases through e-commerce, and in the general value of communicating directly with our customers."

Success in social media can't always be defined in sales volume, cautions Saunders. Neenah includes internal performance measures to measure social media success: customer engagement and customer service, including resolution of customer service issues, helping customers pick the right paper for their projects, reporting an insider's view from conferences and events, and providing the latest news and information.

With so many team members participating, Neenah created an extensive, but flexible, social media policy. "We want to keep our internal social media users up-to-date on the latest uses for this type of media, dangers to watch out for, and how to handle themselves in any situation."

Efforts to promote its social presence have grown in the past year, as Neenah began putting its Twitter and Facebook addresses on business cards. "We also have our social media pages interconnected on our website, blog, certain promotions, advertising, conference materials, press releases, everywhere! Every type of technology we use is meant to drive the user back to Neenah Paper."

"In the beginning, we struggled with how to use social media. We began by talking at our customers instead of talking with them," acknowledges Saunders. "The moment we realized that it was a two-way conversation, the magic happened." She advises first figuring out your goals for social media. Is it to create a more meaningful connection with your customers? Or is it to sell more products?

"We've found that our customers can react negatively to hard selling on Twitter and Facebook, so be careful how much you push your product versus conversing with your followers. Once you figure out why you are there, you will find it much easier to maintain a balance between promoting and conversing."

Neenah Paper's web presence

www.neenahpaper.com

www.facebook.com/NeenahFinePaper

www.neenahpaperblog.com

https://twitter.com/#!/NEENAHPAPER

http://feeds.feedburner.com/neenahpaperblog/HZDS **(RSS)**

https://plus.google.com/u/0/116195680569593332909/posts

www.pinterest.com/neenahpaper

Apps

www.neenahpaper.com/cabinet

www.neenahpaper.com/personalproof

www.neenahpaper.com/Home/Resources/Calculators/PaperCalculator

www.neenahpaper.com/Home/Resources/Applications/BlackBerryApps

www.neenahpaper.com/Home/Resources/Calculators/ECalculator

www.neenahpaper.com/Home/Resources/Applications/iPhoneApplications

Newsletter

www.neenahpaper.com/AboutNeenah/ReplyCards/SpecAndConnect

Chapter 3: Plotting Your Social Media Marketing Strategy

In This Chapter

✔ **Finding your audience online**

✔ **Segmenting B2C markets**

✔ **Conducting B2B research online**

✔ **Planning your strategy**

*I*n Book I, Chapter 1, we talk about making the business case for social media marketing, looking at the question of whether you should or shouldn't get involved. That chapter is about strategy, goals, and objectives — this one is about tactics. It helps you decide which social media services best fit your marketing objectives and your target market. Let your customers and prospects drive your selection of social media alternatives. To see the best return on your investment in social media, you need to try to use the same social media as they do. This principle is exactly the same one you apply to all your other marketing and advertising efforts. Social media is a new tactic, not a new world.

Fish where your fish are. If your potential customers aren't on a particular social media outlet, don't start a campaign on that media.

In this chapter, we show how to use online market research to assess the match between your target markets and various social media outlets. After you do that, you're ready to start filling out your own Social Media Marketing Plan, which appears at the end of this chapter.

Locating Your Target Market Online

Nothing is more important in marketing than identifying and understanding your target audience (or audiences). After you can describe your customers' and prospects' demographic characteristics, where they live, and what social media they use, you're in a position to focus your social marketing efforts on those people most likely to buy your products or services. (Be sure to include the description of your target market on your Social Media Marketing Goals statement in Book I, Chapter 1.)

Because social media techniques focus on inexpensive ways to reach niche markets with specific messages, they're tailor-made for a guerrilla marketing approach. As with all guerrilla marketing activities, target one market at a time.

Don't dilute your marketing budget or labor by trying to reach too many audiences at a time. People still need to see your message or brand name at least seven times to remember it. Trying to boost yourself to the forefront of everyone's mind all at once is expensive.

Focus your resources on one niche at a time. After you succeed, invest your profits in the next niche. It may seem counterintuitive, but it works.

Don't let setting priorities among niches paralyze you. Your choice of niches usually doesn't matter. If you aren't sure, go for what seems to be the biggest market first, or the easiest one to reach.

Segmenting Your B2C Market

If you have a business-to-consumer (B2C) company, you can adapt the standard tools of *market segmentation,* which is a technique to define various niche audiences by where they live and how they spend their time and money. The most common types of segmentation are

+ Demographics
+ Geographics
+ Life stages
+ Psychographics or lifestyle
+ Affinity or interest groups

These categories affect not only your social media tactics but also your graphics, message, content, offers, and every other aspect of your marketing.

Your messages need to be specific enough to satisfy the needs and wants of the distinct subgroups you're trying to reach.

Suppose that you want to sell a line of organic, herbal hair care products using social media. If you described your target market as "everyone who uses shampoo" on your Social Media Marketing Goals statement (see Book I, Chapter 1), segment that market into different subgroups before you select appropriate social marketing techniques.

When you're creating subgroups, keep these concepts in mind:

✦ **Simple demographics affect your market definition.** The use of fragrances, descriptive terms, and even packaging may vary by gender. How many shampoo commercials for men talk about silky hair? For that matter, what's the ratio of shampoo commercials addressed to women versus men?

✦ **Consider geography.** Geography may not seem obvious, but people who live in dry climates may be more receptive to a message about moisturizers than people who live in humid climates. Or, perhaps your production capacity constrains your initial product launch to a local or regional area.

✦ **Think about life stages.** For instance, people who dye their hair look for different hair care products than those who don't, but the reason they color their hair affects your selling message. (Teenagers and young adults may dye their hair unusual colors in an effort to belong to a group of their peers; older men may hide the gray with Grecian Formula; women with kids may be interested in fashion or color their hair as a pick-me-up.)

✦ **Even lifestyles (psychographics) affect decisions.** People with limited resources who are unlikely to try new products may respond to messages about value and satisfaction guarantees; people with more resources or a higher status may be affected by messages related to social grouping and self-esteem.

✦ **Affinity or interest groups are an obvious segmentation parameter.** People who participate in environmental organizations or who recycle goods may be more likely to be swayed by a "green shampoo" appeal or shop in specific online venues.

Different niche markets are drawn to different social media activities in general and to specific social media service providers in particular. In the following several sections, we look in detail at different online tools you can use to explore the parameters that seem the most appropriate for segmenting your audience and selecting specific social media sites.

For more information on market segmentation and research, see *Small Business Marketing For Dummies,* by Barbara Findlay Schenck.

The most successful marketing campaigns are driven by your target markets, not by techniques.

Demographics

Demographic segmentation, the most common type of market differentiation, covers such standard categories as gender, age, ethnicity, marital status, family size, household income, occupation, social class, and education.

Sites such as Quantcast (`www.quantcast.com`) and Alexa (`www.alexa.com`) provide basic demographic information compared to the overall Internet population, as shown in Figure 3-1. Quantcast also displays the distribution by subcategory within the site. As you can see, the sites don't always share the same subcategory breakdowns or completely agree on the data. However, either one is close enough for your social marketing purposes.

Use these tools to check out the demographic profile of users on various social media services, as well as your own users and those of your competitors. For instance, by comparing the demographics on Quantcast, you can see that LinkedIn appeals to an audience that is older, male-dominated, and better educated than visitors to Facebook.

Look for a general match between your target audience and that of the social media service you're considering.

Always check for current demographic information before launching your social media campaign.

Geographics

Marketing by country, region, state, city, zip code, or even neighborhood is the key for location-based social media outlets, such as foursquare, or any other form of online marketing that involves local search.

Geographic segmentation also makes sense if your business draws its primary target audience from within a certain distance from your brick-and-mortar storefront — for example, it makes sense for grocery stores, barber shops, gas stations, restaurants, movie theaters, and many other service providers, whether or not your social media service itself is location-based.

Many social media services offer a location search function to assess the number of users within your geographical target area:

+ **Twitter users within a certain radius:** Enter the city, state, and radius at `http://twitter.com/#!/search-advanced`.

+ **LinkedIn users within a certain radius:** Enter the zip code or city, state, and radius at `www.linkedin.com/search`.

+ **Facebook users near a certain location:** Enter a search term (for example, **consultants**) in the search box and select All Results from the drop-down list. Select People in the left navigation. In the Filter by Location Box, type a city name, state, or region.

Figure 3-1:
Quantcast
(top) and
Alexa
(bottom)
provide
demographic
profiles
comparing
users of
a site (in
this case,
LinkedIn)
with the
general
Internet
population.

(Top) Courtesy Quantcast.com.
*(Bottom) "Alexa the Web Information Company," "Alexa Top Sites," "Alexa Site Thumbnail," the Alexa® logo
and name are trademarks of Amazon.com, Inc. or its affiliates in the United States and/or other countries.*

If you can't determine the number of potential users of a service within
your specific geographic location, use the Help function, check the blog, or
contact the company.

Several companies combine geographical information with demographics and behavioral characteristics to segment the market more finely. For example, the Nielsen Claritas PRIZM, available from Tetrad (`www.tetrad.com/demographics/usa/claritas/prizmneappend.html`), offers demo-geographic data organized into 66 distinct sub-segments, some of which are described in Table 3-1. You can download the entire list at `www.tetrad.com/pub/prices/PRIZMNE_Clusters.pdf`.

Again, you're looking for a fit between the profile of your target audience and that of the social media service.

Table 3-1	Top-Level Demo-Geographic Social Groups from Nielsen PRIZM
Name	*Description*
Urban Uptown	Wealthiest urban (highest-density) consumers (five sub-segments)
Midtown Mix	Midscale, ethnically diverse, urban population (three sub-segments)
Urban Cores	Modest income, affordable housing, urban living (four sub-segments)
Elite Suburbs	Affluent, suburban elite (four sub-segments)
The Affluentials	Comfortable suburban lifestyle (six sub-segments)
Middleburbs	Middle-class suburbs (five sub-segments)
Inner Suburbs	Downscale inner suburbs of metropolitan areas (four sub-segments)
Second City Society	Wealthy families in smaller cities on fringes of metro areas (three sub-segments)
City Centers	Middle-class, satellite cities with mixed demographics (five sub-segments)
Micro-City Blues	Downscale residents in second cities (five sub-segments)
Landed Gentry	Wealthy Americans in small towns (five sub-segments)
Country Comfort	Upper-middle-class homeowners in bedroom communities (five sub-segments)
Middle America	Middle-class homeowners in small towns and exurbs (six sub-segments)
Rustic Living	Most isolated towns and rural areas (six sub-segments)

Courtesy The Nielsen Company; Source: Nielsen Claritas

Life stages

Rather than look at a target market solely in terms of demographics, *life stage analysis* considers what people are doing with their lives, recognizing that it may affect media behavior and spending patterns.

Figure 3-2 shows the percentage of Internet users who access social media frequently sorted by age, according to Pingdom's analysis of 19 social media sites (http://royal.pingdom.com/2010/02/16/study-ages-of-social-network-users). Usage may also differ by life stages, as shown in Table 3-2. Note that the set of life stages described in the table may not accurately reflect the wider range of today's lifestyles.

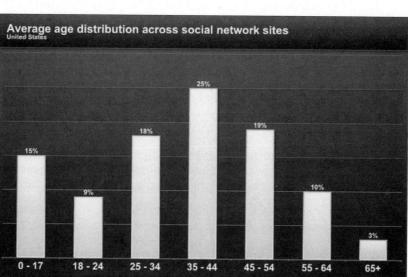

Figure 3-2: Recent research indicates that the use of social media varies by age.

Courtesy Pingdom

Table 3-2	Life Stage Segmentation
Life Stage	*Products They Buy*
Single, no children	Fashion items, vacations, recreation
Married, no children	Vacations, cars, clothing, entertainment
New nesters, children under 6	Baby food and toys; furniture and new homes

(continued)

Table 3-2 (continued)

Life Stage	Products They Buy
Full nest, youngest over 6	Children's items, activities, and education
Full nest, children over 16	College; possibly travel and furniture
Empty nest, children gone	Travel, cruises, vacations
Retired couples	Moves to warmer climates, housing downsizing
Solitary working retiree	Travel, vacations, medical expenses
Retired solitary survivor	Medical expenses

Source: Adapted from http://academic.brooklyn.cuny.edu/economic/friedman/mmmarket segmentation.htm#C1

With more flexible timing for going through life passages, demographic analysis isn't enough for many types of products and services. Women may have children later in life; many older, nontraditional students go back to college; some retirees re-enter the workforce to supplement Social Security earnings. What your prospective customers do each day may influence what they buy and which media outlets they use more than their age or location.

For instance, the Pew Research Center's Internet and American Life Project found in 2011 that parents are more likely than non-parents to use social media to connect with old friends, whereas middle-aged and older adults use social media as a tool to connect around a hobby or interest. (`http://pewinternet.org/Reports/2011/Why-Americans-Use-Social-Media/Main-report.aspx`).

Psychographics or lifestyle

Psychographic segmentation divides a market by social class, lifestyle, or the shared activities, interests, and opinions of prospective customers. It helps identify groups within a social networking service or other, smaller, social networks that attract users meeting your desired profile.

Behavioral segmentation, which is closely related, divides potential buyers based on their uses, responses, or attitudes toward a product or service. To obtain this information about your customers, consider including a quick poll as part of your e-newsletter, website, or blog. Although the results from those who reply may not be exactly representative of your total customer base — or that of prospective customers — a survey gives you some starter data.

Don't confuse the psychographic profile of a group with personality traits specific to an individual.

Psychographic segmentation helps you identify not only where to promote your company but also how to craft your message. For instance, understanding your specific target group, its mindset, and its lifestyle might help you appeal to customers such as the Innovators shown in Figure 3-3, who might be interested in your high-end line of fashion, home decor, or vacation destinations. Or you might target Experiencers for an amazing new cosmetics line, a wild new restaurant, or an energy drink.

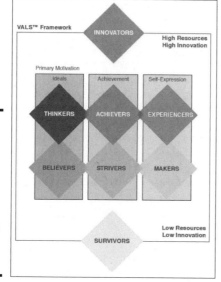

Figure 3-3:
Psycho-
graphic
segment-
ation is
shown on
the VALS
(Values and
Life Styles)
chart.

*Courtesy Strategic Business Insights (SBI);
www.strategicbusinessinsights.com/VALS*

To develop a better understanding of psychographic profiling, take the quick VALS (Values and Life Styles) survey yourself at www.strategicbusiness insights.com/vals/presurvey.shtml.

Affinity groups

Segmenting by *affinity group* (a group of people sharing similar interests or participating in similar activities) fills in the blank at the end of the "People who like this interest or activity also like . . ." statement. Because psychographic segmentation uses "activity" as a subsection, that approach is somewhat similar.

For example, Figure 3-4 estimates other interests of Facebook users under the Audience Also Likes option at the Quantcast site. On Alexa, check the Related tab and the Clickstream tab for lists of other websites viewed by visitors to a particular site. For more on *clickstream analysis* (where visitors come from and where they go), see Book VIII, Chapter 2.

The warning icon in the upper right of Figure 3-4 indicates that Quantcast data are estimated, rather than directly measured.

Warning icon

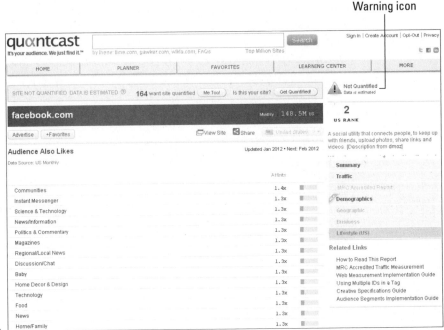

Figure 3-4: Quantcast estimates of topics that interest Facebook users.

Courtesy Quantcast.com

By using Quantcast and Alexa in this way, you can obtain public information on visits to specific social media services or to your competitors or other related businesses. You can also use these services to profile your own business, although your website might be too small to provide more than rough estimates. If your business is too small, estimate the interest profile for your target market by running Alexa for a large corporation that offers a similar product or service.

Request a free profile of your site at `www.quantcast.com/user/signup`.

Interest categories for your site, based on the types of other websites your visitors frequent, are also available from a Yahoo! Web Analytics account under Visitor Behavioral Reports (`http://web.analytics.yahoo.com/features`). Yahoo! Web Analytics free enterprise-level solution is the Yahoo! answer to Google Analytics. Otherwise, consider polling your customers to find out more about their specific interests.

Google Analytics doesn't offer a similar capability, but you can use Google Insights (`www.google.com/insights/search/#`), which sorts Google searches by interest category, as shown in Table 3-3. Because searches are organized by search term trend, not by source site, you gain a different form of market intelligence.

Table 3-3	Main Categories Available on Google Insights	
Arts & Entertainment	Autos & Vehicles	Beauty & Fitness
Books & Literature	Business & Industrial	Computers & Electronics
Finance	Food & Drink	Games
Health	Home & Garden	Hobbies & Leisure
Internet & Telecom	Jobs & Education	Law & Government
News	Online Communities	People & Society
Pets & Animals	Real Estate	Reference
Science	Shopping	Sports
Travel		

Researching B2B Markets

Market research and social media choices for business-to-business (B2B) markets are somewhat different from business-to-consumer (B2C) markets because the sales cycle is different. Usually, B2B companies have a longer sales cycle, high-ticket purchases, and multiple people who play a role in closing a sale; consequently, B2B marketing requires a different social media presence.

In terms of social media, more B2B marketing efforts focus on branding, top-of-mind visibility, customer support, customer loyalty, and problem-solving compared to more sales-focused messages from B2C companies.

You can treat the interest groups in the earlier section "Affinity groups" as vertical market segments and take advantage of Google Insights to discern trends over time. You might also want to assess competitor presence on different forms of social media.

One key step in B2B marketing is to identify people who make the buying decision. Professional social networks such as LinkedIn and Plaxo may help you research people on your B2B customer or prospect lists.

According to research by *BtoB* magazine, 93 percent of all B2B marketers use some form of social media (`http://socialmediab2b.com/2011/04/`

93-of-b2b-marketers-use-social-media-marketing). As shown in Figure 3-5, business-to-business firms may emphasize different forms of social media than businesses in general. In many cases, the choice of social media varies by company size, industry type, experience with social media, and the availability of budgetary and human resources.

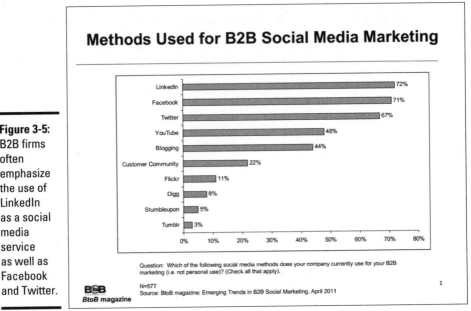

Figure 3-5: B2B firms often emphasize the use of LinkedIn as a social media service as well as Facebook and Twitter.

Courtesy BtoB Magazine/BtoBonline.com Intelligence Center: Emerging Trends in B2B Social Marketing, April 2011

For more information on using social media for B2B marketing, visit www.meclabs.com/training/misc/EXCERPT-PLAIN-BMR-2011-Social-Marketing.pdf or www.btobonline.com/section/research reports5. HubSpot (www.hubspot.com) also offers a range of B2B market research tools and webinars.

As always, the key is ensuring that your customers are using the type of social media you're considering. Use the search feature and group options on major social networking sites to test your list of existing customers. Chances are good that if a large number of your existing customers are using that service, it will be a good source for future customers as well.

In addition to participating in general market research, you might want to try SimilarSites.com (www.similarsites.com), which not only assists with research on social media alternatives that reach your target market but also helps you find companies that compete with yours.

Check competing sites for inbound links from other sites, as well as their outbound links, to see how they reach their customers.

Conducting Other Types of Market Research Online

The amount of research available online can be paralyzing. A well-crafted search yields most, if not all, of the social marketing research you need. You aren't writing an academic paper; you're running a business with limited time and resources. Set aside a week or two for research and then start laying out your approach.

Don't be afraid to experiment on a small scale. In the end, what matters is what happens with your business as you integrate social media into your marketing plan, not what happens to businesses on average.

Despite these statements, you might want to touch on two other research points:

+ **The most influential sites, posters, or pages on your preferred social media:** You can learn from them.

+ **Understanding what motivates people to use certain types of social media:** Make the content you provide meet their expectations and desires.

Identifying influencers

Whether you have a B2B or B2C company, you gain valuable insight by reviewing the comments of *influencers* (companies or individuals that drive the conversation within your industry sector). To see the most popular posters on Twitter, use services such as Klout, at `http://klout.com` (by topic), or Twitaholic, at `http://twitaholic.com` (by followers or number of posts), as shown in Figure 3-6.

You may be surprised to find that the most frequent posters aren't necessarily the ones with the most followers, and vice versa.

Updates

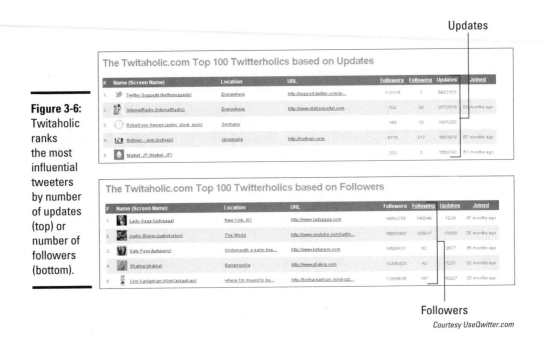

Figure 3-6:
Twitaholic
ranks
the most
influential
tweeters
by number
of updates
(top) or
number of
followers
(bottom).

Followers

Courtesy UseQwitter.com

These sites can help you identify people you might want to follow for research purposes. You can find more information about tools for identifying influencers for each of the major services in their respective minibooks.

Understanding why people use social media services

The expectation that people gravitate toward different types of social media to meet different needs seems reasonable. The challenge, of course, is to match what people seek with particular social sites. The advertising network, Chitika, surveyed its own clients, reviewing downstream visits from social networks and sorting them by type, as shown in Figure 3-7. Ask yourself whether these patterns match your expectations and whether they match what you see on these sites.

A review of successful social media models may spark creative ideas for your own campaign. Take a look at Ana White's blog in Figure 3-8 (and check out the nearby sidebar "Social media is a DIY project for Ana White") to see how her commitment to good content on her blog brought her success.

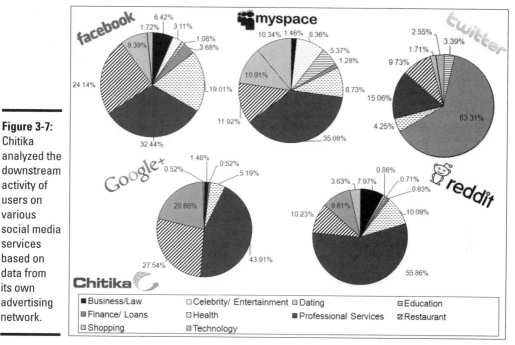

Figure 3-7:
Chitika
analyzed the
downstream
activity of
users on
various
social media
services
based on
data from
its own
advertising
network.

Courtesy Chitika Insights

Figure 3-8:
Ana White's
blog was
the jumping-
off point
for what
has grown
into an
expansive
social media
presence.

Courtesy Ana White

Social media is a DIY project for Ana White

"I know it sounds crazy, but I really was — and still am — a stay-at-home mom with an incredible passion for building furniture with no experience in blogging or social media. I never had a grand plan or strategy. I just did my best to share how I saved money by building my own furniture," explains Ana White.

In October 2009, she began blogging about do-it-yourself (DIY) furniture, offering free, easy, step-by-step plans. "My blog, though a woodworking blog, is written primarily for women just like me," she says, modestly proposing that difficult economic times have had much to do with the success of Ana-White.com (`http://ana-white.com`).

"I do not think it was so much my posts that made the difference, although I relentlessly posted new free plans, often staying up until three in the morning. It was posts from readers saying, '*yes, this can be done, and I did it!*' that sparked confidence in new readers."

White runs a do-it-yourself site in more ways than one. "It's just me. My husband has stepped up to help and I am so thankful to be assisted by many readers who answer questions, help other builders, and build projects to test new plans."

She started on Facebook in January 2010. By January 2012, it had garnered more than 57,000 fans. "The growth was purely organic," she says, "and the page is as Plain Jane as they come." Facebook soon became an open forum for her to share new posts, answer questions, and read comments. "Unlike a comment on a blog post, a Facebook comment is seen by the social graph of the commenter," expanding awareness of her blog site.

White isn't opposed to promotions to reward new fans or to direct traffic to a "Like" page on Facebook, but she cautions that you may end up with fans who join just for a promotion, not because they want to be part of your community. She also cautions to be careful about over-posting on Facebook, which could result in lost fans.

She tried auto-posting to Facebook with dashboard tools, but found it "too impersonal and dry." While she uses an online tool called Tweetdeck to schedule tweets, she handwrites each one herself. White is adamant about updating each of her social media accounts separately, customizing and personalizing each post or response to fit the outlet.

"My social media strategy has always been to let the social media complement the blog, not take center stage." She uses her Twitter account less often but is working on creating more YouTube videos. She also takes advantage of the increasingly popular Pinterest, which she sees as the forefront of an image-based Internet. Although she does little to share her own content on Pinterest, she optimizes images so that they're more appealing and shareable.

"If I can say anything, it's this: Focus on providing extremely valuable, truly free content, and lots of it. Be a servant to your readers, be thankful for each and every click, bend over backwards to help someone you don't even know, selflessly care about your readers, and you will be rewarded with loyalty and traffic. Oh, and don't forget the pretty picture."

As White puts it, "Social media has never been just another chore — it's a time to visit with friends." She'll often spend an hour answering posts while sitting on the couch with her family, As a result, her smile comes through in her posts on every medium.

Courtesy Ana White

She segments her social media by purpose. The blog is for building her brand and offering content. Everything else serves to bring visitors to the blog or communicate with readers. She finds that Facebook is the best place to announce new posts, get instant feedback, serve as an open forum for general questions, and share readers' photos and tips.

For her, "Twitter is all about pushing as much valuable content as possible out to new readers," with value gained from multiple posts in a day. She uses Twitter to promote other bloggers, tweet about upcoming blog posts, share tips, and link to inspiring photos. However, "I never waste my follower's time, and always focus on delivering high-value tweets."

Because she's betting on content and adding value to readers, White spends little time on SEO and instead prepares her site for what she foresees as the mainstream adoption of image-based, user-rated search and discovery engines like Pinterest.

For the amount of work involved, she hasn't found traditional media to be as effective as social media — a few thousand leads from a magazine article (though it's wonderful for credibility) compared to hundreds of thousands of new leads from one photo on Pinterest.

(continued)

(continued)

White watches her Google Analytics daily to check traffic coming from various social media and determine how to spend her time. Google search, Pinterest, and direct entry each account for 25 to 30 percent of her site traffic. Facebook brings in about 10 percent, followed by RSS feeds and other referring sites.

Her site is now supported by advertising. "Understanding the heart of blogging is authenticity and trust. I work with maybe just one or two out of 100 advertisers that approach me. I'd never try to sell [my readers] something I wouldn't myself buy!" Advertising success demands a solid stream of readers, so she stays attuned to efforts that bring new visitors.

"If there's one rule I've learned the hard way, it's always to stay positive. Even if your audience is forgiving and friendly, any negativity will override months of positivity. Let your readers see you in your best light, not in your occasional down moment. When you receive bad comments, answer positively, addressing the issue with kindness and consideration.

"For new businesses starting out on social media, do not feel like you need to be on every social media channel all the time. Do not try to do everything, stretching yourself thin. Instead, consistently focus on the social media outlets that work for you and your readers, providing high value, personal engagement to your fans and followers.

"And finally, do not bet your business on social media. You do not own Facebook, Twitter, or Pinterest. They could close down tomorrow, ban your account, or be overtaken by a new player, and there's little you could do to prevent it. Social media outlets are simply a means of connecting your audience to your main product — be that a blog like mine, or a product for resale, or even a giant brand."

Ana White's web presence

```
http://ana-white.com
```

```
http://pinterest.com/knockoffwood
```

```
www.facebook.com/knockoffwood
```

```
http://twitter.com/#!/anawhite
```

```
www.youtube.com/knockoffwood
```

```
www.flickr.com/groups/knockoffwood
```

Setting Up Your Social Media Marketing Plan

You can dive into social media marketing headfirst and see what happens. Or, you can take the time to research, plan, execute, and evaluate your approach. The Social Media Marketing Plan, shown in Figure 3-9, is for people taking the latter approach. (You can download the form at `www.dummies.com/go/socialmediamarketingaio2e`.)

Social Media Marketing Plan

Company Name _____ Date _____

Hub Site (URL of website or blog with domain name traffic will be driven to)

_____

Standard Social Media Identification Name/Handle _____

Social Media Project Director   _____

Social Media Team Members & Tasks   _____   _____

                                          _____   _____

Programming/Technical Team   _____   _____

Social Media Policy URL   _____

Check all applications used. Items noted by ☒ are strongly recommended.

SOCIAL MEDIA PLANNING

❑ **Dashboard** (Select one: Enter URL & login info)
  - ○ Netvibes
  - ○ HootSuite
  - ○ Other – Name:
  - ○ Custom

❑ **Calendar** (Select one: Enter URL & login info)
  - ○ Google Calendar
  - ○ Yahoo! Calendar
  - ○ Microsoft Office Calendar
  - ○ Other – Name:

❑ **Social Sharing Service** (Select one: Enter URL & login info)
  - ○ AddThis
  - ○ ShareThis
  - ○ Shareaholic
  - ○ Other – Name:

❑ **Social Media Resources** (Insert one resource site or blog to follow)
  - ○

SOCIAL MEDIA TOOL KIT

❑ **Monitoring** (Select at least one: Enter name, URL, & login info for all used)
  - ○ Brand Reputation/Sentiment Tool with fee (e.g., BrandsEye)
  - ○ Topic Monitoring Tool (e.g., Google Trends, Addict-o-matic)
  - ○ HowSociable
  - ○ MonitorThis
  - ○ Social Mention
  - ○ Trackur
  - ○ WhosTalkin
  - ○ Blog Monitoring Tool
  - ○ Twitter Monitoring Tool
  - ○ Social News, Forums, RSS Monitoring Tool
  - ○ Google Alerts
  - ○ Other – Name:

Figure 3-9:
Build a
social media
marketing
plan for your
company.

❑ **Distribution Tools** (Select at least one: Enter name, URL & login info for all used)
- ○ RSS/Atom Feeds
- ○ Seesmic Ping
- ○ Hellotxt
- ○ HootSuite
- ○ OnlyWire
- ○ TweetDeck
- ○ Other – Name:

❑ **Update Notification Tools** (Select at least one: Enter Name, URL & login Info for all used)
- ○ Pingdom
- ○ Feed Shark
- ○ GooglePing
- ○ King Ping
- ○ Other – Name:

❑ **URL Clipping Tool** (Select one: Enter URL & login info)
- ○ Bitly
- ○ Snipurl
- ○ TinyURL
- ○ Other – Name:

❑ **E-commerce Tool or Widget** (Select one: Enter URL & login info)
- ○ Netcarnation
- ○ Payvment
- ○ TabJuice
- ○ ProductCart
- ○ Etsy Widget
- ○ Amazon Widget
- ○ PayPal Widget
- ○ Other – Name:
- ○ Custom Widget

❑ **Search Engine Tools** (If needed, enter URL & login info; include submission dates)
- ○ Search Engine Ranking Tool (Select One)
- ○ Google Search Engine Submission
- ○ Bing/Yahoo! Search Engine Submission
- ○ Automated XML Feed
- ○ Specialty Search Submission Sites
- ○ Other – Name:

STANDARD SET PRIMARY KEYWORDS/TAGS

- ❑
- ❑
- ❑
- ❑
- ❑
- ❑
- ❑
- ❑

STANDARD PAGE DESCRIPTION TAG
(Enter 150-character description: Include at least four of the keywords above)

SOCIAL MEDIA SERVICES

☐ **Social Bookmarking Sites** (Select at least one: Enter name, URL, & login info for all used)
- ○ Delicious
- ○ StumbleUpon
- ○ Y! Bookmarks
- ○ Other

☐ **Social News Sites** (Select at least one: Enter name, URL, & login info for all used)
- ○ Digg
- ○ Reddit
- ○ Newsvine
- ○ Slashdot
- ○ Other

☐ **Social Shopping & Specialty Bookmark Sites** (Enter name, URL, & login info for all used)
- ○ Kaboodle
- ○ This Next
- ○ StyleHive
- ○ Other

☐ **Blogging Site** (Enter name, URL, & login info for all used)
- ○ Primary Blog
- ○ Blog directory submission site
- ○ Blog monitoring site
- ○ Blog measuring tool sites
- ○ Other

☐ **Primary Social Networking Services** (Select at least one: Enter name, URL, & login info for all used)

Facebook
- ○ Groups
- ○ Events
- ○ Metrics
- ○ Follow Us On/Like Us

Twitter
- ○ Hashtags/Lists
- ○ Tools
- ○ Metrics
- ○ Follow Us On

LinkedIn
- ○ Groups
- ○ Events/Answers
- ○ Metrics
- ○ Follow Us On

Google+
- ○ Circles
- ○ +1 (Ratings)
- ○ Metrics
- ○ Follow Us On

Pinterest
- ○   Metrics
- ○   Follow Us On

- ○ Specialty Networks
- ○ Other Professional Networks (e.g., Ryze)
- ○ Other Vertical Industry Networks (e.g., DeviantArt)
- ○ Other Demographic Networks (e.g., Grandparents.com)

❑ **Social Media Sharing Sites** (Enter name, URL, & login info for all used)
- ○ YouTube
- ○ UStream
- ○ Vimeo
- ○ FlickR
- ○ Instagram
- ○ Picasa
- ○ Podcasts
- ○ Other

❑ **Social Community Sites** (Enter name, URL, & login info for all used)
- ○ Ning
- ○ Forums
- ○ Message Boards
- ○ Other

❑ **Other Social Media Services** (Enter name, URL, & login info for all used)
- ○ Geolocation (e.g., foursquare, Google Latitude, Facebook Location)
- ○ Collective Shopping (e.g., Groupon, Living Social)
- ○ Social Gaming
- ○ Social Mobile
- ○ Other

SOCIAL MEDIA METRICS

Key Performance Indicators (Enter eight; e.g., Traffic, CPM, CPC, Conversion Rate, ROI)

❑	❑
❑	❑
❑	❑
❑	❑

❑ **Analytical/Statistical Tool** (Select at least one: Enter name, URL, & login info for all used)
- ○ Google Analytics
- ○ Yahoo! Analytics
- ○ AWstats
- ○ StatCounter
- ○ SiteTrail.com
- ○ Other

SOCIAL MEDIA ADVERTISING

❑ Facebook
❑ LinkedIn
❑ Twitter
❑ Other

❑ **Advertising Metrics** (for reports on impressions, clicks, CTR, CPC, CPM, etc.)
(Enter the following information for each social media advertising service, e.g. Facebook Ads, used.)
- ○ Name/Account Log-in URL/User Name/Password
- ○ Name/Account Log-in URL/User Name/Password

Plan your work; work your plan.

Depending on its complexity and availability of support, think in terms of a timeline of 3 to 12 months to allow time to complete the following steps. Estimate spending half your time in the planning phase, one-quarter in execution, and one-quarter in evaluation and modification:

1. Market research and online observation

2. Draft marketing goals, objectives, and plan

3. In-house preparation

   • Hiring, outsourcing, or selecting in-house staff

   • Training

   • Team-building

   • Writing social media policy document

4. Preparatory development tasks

   • Design

   • Content

   • Measurement plan and metric implementation

   • Social media tool selection and dashboard development

   • Set up your social media activity calendar (see Book I, Chapter 4)

   • Programming and content modifications to existing website(s) as needed

5. Create accounts and pilot social media program

6. Evaluate pilot program, debug, and modify as needed

7. Launch and promote your social media campaign one service at a time

8. Measure and modify social media in a process of constant feedback and reiteration

Don't be afraid to build a pilot program — or several — into your plan to see what works.

Chapter 4: Managing Your Cybersocial Campaign

In This Chapter

✔ Scheduling social media activities

✔ Building a team

✔ Writing a social media policy

✔ Keeping it legal

✔ Protecting your brand reputation

After you create a social media marketing plan, one major task you face is managing the effort. If you're the only one doing the work, the simplest — and likely the hardest — task is making time for it. Though social media need not carry a lot of up-front development costs, it carries a significant cost in labor.

In this chapter, we discuss how to set up a schedule to keep your social media from draining all your available time. If you have employees, both you and your company may benefit if you delegate some of the social media tasking to them. You can also supplement your in-house staff with limited assistance from outside professionals.

 For small businesses, it's your money or your life. If you can't afford to hire help to work on social media, you carve it out of the time you've allocated to other marketing activities — unless, of course, you want to add another two hours to your workday.

Finally, this chapter carries a word of caution. Make sure that everyone posting to a social media outlet knows your policy about what is and isn't acceptable, as well as how to protect the company's reputation and confidential material. As you launch your marketing boat onto the churning waters of social media, you should ensure that everyone is wearing a legal life preserver.

Managing Your Social Media Schedule

As you know from the rest of your business experience, if something isn't important enough to schedule, it never gets done. Social media, like the rest of your marketing efforts, can easily be swallowed up by day-to-day demands. You must set aside time for it and assign tasks to specific people.

Allocate a minimum of two hours per week if you're going to participate in social media, rather than set up pages and abandon them. Otherwise, you simply don't see a return from your initial investment in setup. If you don't have much time, stick with the marketing you're already doing.

Bounding the time commitment

Social media can become addictive. If you truly like what you're doing, the time problem might reverse. Rather than spend too little time, you spend too much. You might find it difficult to avoid the temptation of continually reading what others have to say about your business or spending all your time tweeting, streaming, and posting.

Just as you stick to your initial dollar budget, keep to your initial time budget, at least for the first month until you see what works. After you determine which techniques have the greatest promise, you can rearrange your own efforts as well as your team's.

Social media marketing is only part of your online marketing effort, and online marketing is only part of your overall marketing.

Selecting "activity" days

One way to control the time you spend on social media is to select specific days and times for it. Many business people set aside regularly recurring blocks of time, such as on a quiet Friday afternoon, for marketing-related tasks, whether they're conducting competitor research, writing press releases or newsletters for the following week, obtaining inbound links, or handling their social marketing tasks.

Other people prefer to allocate their time early in the morning, at lunchtime, or just before leaving work each evening. The time slot you choose usually doesn't matter, unless you're offering a time-dependent service, such as accepting to-go orders for breakfast burritos via Twitter.

Whatever the case, allot time for every task on your social media activity calendar, followed by the initials of the person responsible for executing the task.

Allowing for ramp-up time

Even if you're the only person involved, allow time for learning before your official social media launch date. Everyone needs time to observe, master new tools, practice posting and responding, experiment, and decide what works before you can roll out your plan.

Bring your new social media venues online one at a time. This strategy not only helps you evaluate which social media venue works but also reduces stress on you and your staff.

Developing your social date book

There are as many ways to schedule social media activities as there are companies. Whatever you decide, don't leave your schedule to chance.

Larger companies may use elaborate project management software, either proprietary solutions or open source programs such as Endeavour Software Project Management (http://endeavour-mgmt.sourceforge.net), GanttProject (www.ganttproject.biz), or OpenProj (http://source forge.net/projects/openproj). Alternatively, you can schedule tasks using spreadsheet software.

However, the simplest solution may be the best: Calendar software, much of which is free, may be all you need. Paid options may merge schedules for more people and allow customized report formats. Several options are listed in Table 4-1. Look for a solution that lets you

✦ Choose a display by day, week, or month or longer

✦ Lists events or tasks in chronological format

✦ Select different time frames easily

✦ Easily schedule repeat activities without requiring duplicate data entry

Table 4-1	Calendaring Software	
Name	*URL*	*Free or Paid*
Calendar & Time Management Software Reviews	`http://download.cnet.com/windows/calendar-and-time-management-software`	Free, shareware, and paid
Connect Daily	`www.mhsoftware.com/connectdaily.htm`	Paid, free trial
EventsLink Network	`www.eventslink.net`	Paid, free trial
Google Calendar	`www.google.com/intl/en/googlecalendar/about.html`	Free
Mozilla Lightning	`www.mozilla.org/projects/calendar`	Free, open source
Trumba	`www.trumba.com/connect/default.aspx`	Paid, free trial
Yahoo! Calendar	`http://calendar.yahoo.com`	Free

If several people are involved in a substantial social media effort, select calendar software that lets you synchronize individual calendars, such as Google, Yahoo!, Mozilla Sunbird, and others. Figure 4-1 shows a sample of a simple social marketing calendar using Yahoo! The calendar shows the initials of the person responsible. Clicking an event or a task reveals item details, including the time allotted to the task, the sharing level, and whether a reminder is sent and to whom. Figure 4-2 offers an example of an event detail listing in a Google calendar.

Note: Google and Yahoo! will require you to set up an account before using their calendars.

Throughout this book, we refer to this calendar as your *Social Media Activity Calendar,* and we add frequent recommendations of tasks to include on your schedule.

Set your calendar to private but give access to everyone who needs to be aware of your social media schedule. Depending on the design of your social media program, some outside subcontractors may need access to your calendar to schedule their own production deadlines.

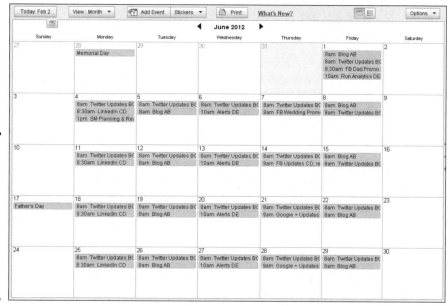

Figure 4-1:
Using
Yahoo!
Calendar,
you can
easily
schedule
your social
media
activities.

*Reproduced with permission of Yahoo! Inc. ©2012 Yahoo! Inc. YAHOO!, the YAHOO! logo, FLICKR,
and the FLICKR logo are registered trademarks of Yahoo! Inc.*

Figure 4-2:
On the
Google
Calendar,
you can
provide
specifics for
a marketing
task by
modifying
an event
detail
window.

Screenshot © Google Inc. Used with permission.

Creating a social media dashboard

Your social media marketing efforts may ultimately involve many tasks: post to multiple venues; use tools to distribute content to multiple locations; monitor visibility for your company on social media outlets; and measure results by using several analytical tools. Rather than jump back and forth among all these resources, you can save time by using a graphical dashboard or control panel.

Like the dashboard of a car, a social media dashboard puts the various required functions at your fingertips in (you hope) an easy-to-understand and easy-to-use visual layout. When you use this approach, the customized dashboard provides easy access in one location to all your social media accounts, tools, and metrics. Figures 4-3 and 4-4 show several tabs of a customized Netvibes dashboard — one for social media postings and another for tools.

The items on your primary dashboard may link to other, application-specific dashboards, especially for analytical tools and high-end enterprise solutions; those application dashboards are designed primarily to compare the results of multiple social media campaigns.

Table 4-2 provides a list of dashboard resources, some of which are generic (such as iGoogle and My Yahoo!) and others of which, such as Netvibes and HootSuite (see Figure 4-5), are specific to social media.

Figure 4-3:
This mock-up of a social media dashboard from Netvibes gathers the user's various social media services on the Social Media Choices tab.

Courtesy Netvibes

Figure 4-4:
The Tools
& Stats
tab of this
mock-up
Netvibes
dashboard
displays
tools for
distributing,
monitoring,
searching,
and
analyzing
data.

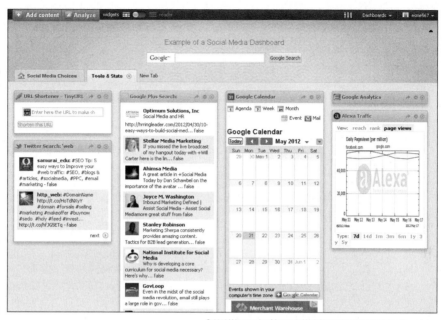

© 2012 Watermelon Mountain Web Marketing; www.watermelonweb.com

Table 4-2	Social Media Dashboard Resources	
Name	*URL*	*Description*
Goojet	www.goojet.com	Free mobile short-message dashboard client
HootSuite	www.hootsuite.com	Free short-message dashboard that focuses on Twitter
iGoogle	www.google.com/ig	Free, customizable Google home page
Marketing Profs	www.marketingprofs.com/articles/2010/3454/how-to-create-your-marketing-dashboard-in-five-easy-steps	Instructions for customizing a dashboard (sign up for the free trial to view)
My Yahoo!	http://my.yahoo.com	Free, customizable Yahoo! home page
Netvibes	http://netvibes.com	Free, customizable dashboard for social media

(continued)

Table 4-2 (continued)

Name	URL	Description
Search Engine Land	`http://searchengine land.com/b2b-social-media-dashboard-a-powerful-tool-to-uncover-key-customer-insights-17839`	Tips on how to use a social media dashboard for B2B
uberVU	`www.ubervu.com`	Paid social media dashboard client
Unilyzer	`http://unilyzer.com`	Paid social media dashboard client

Figure 4-5:
The social media dashboard from HootSuite allows you to monitor and update multiple social network services.

Courtesy HootSuite Media, Inc. 2012

Before you try to build a dashboard, list all the social media sources, services, and reports you want to display, along with their associated URLs, usernames, and passwords. It will help if you indicate whether services are interconnected (for example, note whether you're using a syndication service to update multiple social media at once) and how often statistical reports should be updated for each service (hourly, daily, weekly, or monthly).

The more complex the social media campaign, the more functionality the dashboard needs.

Dashboards sound simple to use, but they can be a bit of a challenge to set up. In some cases, your programmer needs to create or customize *widgets* (mini applications). Plan to create and test several versions of the dashboard until everyone is satisfied with the results.

Consider implementing password access for approved users to various functions within the dashboard. Some users might be constrained to viewing reports, whereas others might be allowed to change the dashboard configuration.

Building Your Social Media Marketing Dream Team

Just for the moment, assume that you have employees who can — and are willing to — share the burden of social media. If you live a rich fantasy life, assume that you might even hire someone to take the lead.

In a larger company, the nexus for control of social media varies: In some cases, it's the marketing department; in others, corporate communications, public relations, sales, or customer support takes the lead.

Some companies disperse responsibilities throughout the company and have tens to dozens of people blogging and tweeting.

If your plan requires multiple employees to leverage LinkedIn profiles for B2B reasons, as well as post on multiple blogs in their individual areas of expertise and tweet current events in their departments, your need for coordination will increase.

Be cautious about asking employees to coordinate links and comments with their personal social media accounts. This task should be voluntary. Alternatively, on company time and on an account that "belongs" to your company (using a business e-mail address), ask employees to develop a hybrid personal-and-business account where their personalities can shine. Now, individual privacy and First Amendment rights are respected on their separate personal accounts, and you have no liability for the content they post there.

No matter who does the bulk of the work — your staff members, contractors, or a combination of the two — always monitor your program randomly but regularly. In addition to getting routine reports on the results, log in to your accounts for a few minutes at various times of the day and week to see what's going on.

Seeking a skilled social media director

A good social media director should have an extroverted personality, at least in writing. This person should truly enjoy interacting with others and take intrinsic pleasure in conversation and communication. You might want to look, based on your chosen tactics, for someone who can

+ Write quickly and well, with the right tone for your market

+ Listen well, with an "ear" for your target audiences and their concerns

+ Post without using defamatory language or making libelous statements about competitors

+ Communicate knowledgeably about your company and products or services

+ Recognize opportunities and develop creative responses or campaigns

+ Work tactfully with others, alerting them when problems or complaints surface

+ Articulate the goals of social media well enough to take a leadership role in encouraging others to explore its potential

+ Analyze situations to draw conclusions from data

+ Adapt to new social media and mobile technologies as they arise

+ Learn quickly (because this field is extremely fluid)

This combination of skills, experience, and personality may be hard to find. Add to it the need to reach different submarkets for different reasons. Now you have several reasons to build a team with a leader, rather than rely on a single individual to handle all your social media needs.

You usually can't just add social media to someone's task list; be prepared to reassign some tasks to other people.

Depending on the size and nature of your social media effort, your dream team may also need someone with production skills for podcasting or videocasting, or at least for producing and directing the development of those components. Though this person may not need extensive graphical, photographic, presentation, or data-crunching skills, having some skills in each of those areas is helpful.

Hiring twenty-somethings (or younger) because they're familiar with social media may sound like a good idea, but people in this age group aren't as likely to be familiar with business protocol or sensitive to business relationships, as someone older and more experienced might be. You might need to allow extra time for training, review, and revision.

Looking inside

Before implementing a social media plan, speak with your employees to invite their input, assess their level of interest in this effort, evaluate existing skill sets, and ascertain social media experience. Consider all these factors before you move forward; by rearranging task assignments or priorities, you may be able to select in-house personnel to handle this new project.

Leave time for communication, education, and training both at the beginning and on an ongoing basis.

Hiring experts

Think about using professionals for the tech-heavy tasks, such as podcasts, videocasts, or design, unless you're going for the just-us-folks tone. Professionals can get you started by establishing a model for your staff to follow, or you may want to hire them for long-term tasks such as writing or editing your blogs for consistency.

Many advertising agencies, PR firms, search engine optimizers, marketing companies, and copywriters now take on social media contracts. If you've already worked with someone you like, you can start there. If not, select social media professionals the same way you would select any other professional service provider:

- ✦ Ask your local business colleagues for referrals.
- ✦ Check sources such as LinkedIn and Plaxo. If appropriate, post your search criteria on your site, blog, social media outlets, and topic-related sites.
- ✦ Request several price quotes. If your job is large enough, write and distribute a formal Request for Proposal (RFP).
- ✦ Review previous work completed by the contractors.
- ✦ Check references.

Creating a Social Media Marketing Policy

Even if you're the only person involved in social media marketing at the beginning, write up a few general guidelines for yourself that you can expand later. In Figure 4-6, the ITBusinessEdge site shows a simple social media policy; download this example and others from `www.itbusinessedge.com/search/?q=social+media+policy&filter=ITDownload`.

Figure 4-6:
A basic
social media
policy may
be enough
to get you
started.

NarrowCast Group, LLC ●●● 10400 Linn Station Road, Suite 100 ●●● Louisville, KY 40223

Sample Social Networking Policy

The following is the company's social media and social networking policy. The absence of, or lack of explicit reference to a specific site does not limit the extent of the application of this policy. Where no policy or guideline exists, employees should use their professional judgment and take the most prudent action possible. Consult with your manager or supervisor if you are uncertain.

1. Personal blogs should have clear disclaimers that the views expressed by the author in the blog is the author's alone and do not represent the views of the company. Be clear and write in first person. Make your writing clear that you are speaking for yourself and not on behalf of the company.
2. Information published on your blog(s) should comply with the company's confidentiality and disclosure of proprietary data policies. This also applies to comments posted on other blogs, forums, and social networking sites.
3. Be respectful to the company, other employees, customers, partners, and competitors.
4. Social media activities should not interfere with work commitments. Refer to IT resource usage policies.
5. Your online presence reflects the company. Be aware that your actions captured via images, posts, or comments can reflect that of our company.
6. Do not reference or site company clients, partners, or customers without their

Courtesy QuinStreet, Inc.

Most policies address the social media issue both in terms of what employees are allowed to do on behalf of the company and on what they aren't allowed to do. For example:

✦ Employees may not be allowed to use personal social accounts on company time.

✦ Some trained employees may be allowed to post customer support replies on behalf of the company, whereas others are responsible for new product information.

For additional information and examples, see the resources listed in Table 4-3.

Table 4-3	Social Media Policy Resource Sites	
Name	*URL*	*Description*
Daniel Hoang	`www.danielhoang.com/ 2009/02/21/social- media-policies-and- procedures`	Social media policy article
Digital Brand Expressions	`www.digitalbrand expressions.com/ services/company- social-media- policy.asp`	Free checklist
emTRAiN	`www.emtrain. com/site/page. php?p=resources`	Free articles and guidelines
Inc.com	`www.inc.com/ articles/2010/01/ need-a-social- media-policy.html`	Article titled "Do You Need a Social Media Policy?"
ITBusinessEdge	`www.itbusinessedge. com/search/?q=socia l+media+policy&filt er=ITDownload`	Social media guidelines, templates, and examples
Mashable	`http://mashable. com/2009/04/27/ social-media-policy`	Article titled "Should Your Company Have a Social Media Policy?"
Mashable	`http://mashable. com/2009/06/02/ social-media- policy-musts`	Article titled "10 Must-Haves for Your Social Media Policy"
PolicyTool for Social Media	`http://socialmedia. policytool.net`	Free social media policy generator
Social Media Governance	`http://social mediagovernance. com/policies.php`	Free database of policies for review
Toolkit Cafe	`http://toolkitcafe. com/social_media_ policies.php`	Policies toolkit ($149)

To increase compliance, keep your policy short and easy to read. Try to focus on what people *can do* rather than on what they cannot do.

A typical policy addresses risk management, intellectual property protection, individual privacy protection, and the respect of your audience, company, and fellow employees. Given the rapidly changing world of social media, you'll have to keep your policy flexible and update it often.

Try to incorporate the following suggested concepts, adapted from Mashable (`http://mashable.com/2009/06/02/social-media-policy-musts`):

✦ Hold individuals responsible for what they write.

✦ Disclose who you are, including your company name and title.

✦ Recognize that clients, prospects, competitors, and potential future employees are part of your audience.

✦ Be respectful of everyone.

✦ Understand the tenor of each social media community and follow its precepts.

✦ Respect copyright and trademarks.

✦ Protect your company's confidential trade secret and proprietary i nformation in addition to client data, especially trade secret information under nondisclosure agreements.

✦ Do *not* allow personal social media activity to interfere with work.

The complexity of your social media policy depends on the extent of your social media marketing effort and the number of people and departments involved. Generally, the larger the company, the longer the policy.

Staying on the Right Side of the Law

Just about everything in social media pushes the limits of existing intellectual property law. So much information is now repeated online that ownership lines are becoming blurred, much to some people's dismay and damage.

When in doubt, don't copy. Instead, use citations, quote marks, and links to the original source. Always go back to the original to ensure that the information is accurate.

Watch blogs such as Mashable and TechCrunch for information about legal wrangling. New case law, regulations, and conflicts bubble up continually.

Obtaining permission to avoid infringement

You can't (legally) use extended content from someone else's website, blog, or social media page on your own site, even if you can save it or download it. Nope, not even if you include a credit line saying where it came from. Not even if you use only a portion of the content and link to the rest. Not text, not graphics, not compiled data, not photos. Nothing. Nada. Nil. Zilch.

Though small text extracts with attribution are permitted under fair use doctrine, the copyright concept is intended for individuals and educational institutions, not for profit-making companies. If you don't obtain permission, you and your company can be sued for copyright infringement. In the best-case scenario, you can be asked to cease and desist. In the worst case, your site can be shut down, and you might face other damages.

The way around this situation is simple: Send a permission request such as the one in the nearby sidebar "Sample copyright permission."

Sample copyright permission

Dear _____:

Watermelon Mountain Web Marketing wants permission to use your *(information, article, screen shot, art, data, photograph)* on our *(website/blog/social media page)* at *[this URL: WatermelonWeb. com]* and in other media not yet specified. We have attached a copy of the information we want to use. If it meets with your approval, please sign the following release and indicate the credit line you want. You can return the signed form as an e-mail message, a PDF file, a digitally signed document, a fax, or a first class mail message. Thank you for your prompt response.

The undersigned authorizes Watermelon Mountain Web Marketing to use the attached material without limit for no charge.

Signature:

Printed name:

Title:

Company name:

Company address:

Telephone/fax/e-mail:

Company domain name:

Credit line:

Be especially careful with photographs, which are usually copyrighted. Here are a few places to find free or low-cost images legally:

+ Select from the wealth of material offered under a Creative Commons license (`http://creativecommons.org`) or copyright-free images from the federal government.

+ The Commons on Flickr (`www.flickr.com/commons`) has thousands of free photographs.

+ Search `http://images.google.com` and read the copyright information at the top of each image.

+ Look for stock images from inexpensive sources such as iStockphoto (`www.istockphoto.com`), Stock.XCHNG Exchange (`www.sxc.hu`), or Freerange Stock (`http://freerangestock.com`).

Trademarks and logos also usually require permission to use, though the logos (icons) that social media companies provide for Share This or Follow Us On functionality are fine to use without permission. If you find an image in the Press or Media section of a company's website, you can assume that you have permission to reproduce it without further permission. Generally, a disclaimer that "all other logos and trademarks are the property of their respective owners" will suffice.

If it's illegal offline, it's illegal online.

Respecting privacy

Providing a disclaimer about keeping user information private is even more critical now that people sign up willy-nilly online. Individual privacy, already under threat, has become quite slippery with the newly released plans for making a Facebook Connect sign-in available on all sorts of third-party sites. Facebook Connect may make sign-ins simpler for a user, but it gives Facebook access to user behavior on the web while giving third parties access to users' Facebook profiles for demographic analysis.

Photographs of identifiable individuals, not taken in a public space, historically have required a waiver to use for commercial purposes. When individuals post their images on Facebook, LinkedIn, MySpace, or elsewhere, they may not intend to give permission for that image to appear elsewhere.

Respect a person's space; do not post publicly viewable images of people's faces on any of your social media pages unless you have permission. For a simple photo waiver, see `www.nyip.com/ezine/techtips/model-release.html`.

Revealing product endorsement relationships

Taking aim at companies that were arranging paid recommendations from bloggers, the Federal Trade Commission (FTC) issued regulations in October 2009 that gave the blogosphere conniptions. The rule requires bloggers to disclose whether they've received any type of payment or free products in exchange for a positive review.

The rule doesn't appear to apply to individuals who post a review on public review sites (such as Epinions.com, TripAdvisor, or Yelp), but it applies if you review other companies' products on your blog or send products to other bloggers to request a review.

You can find out more about this requirement from the disclosure resources listed in Table 4-4. Some bloggers, offended by the rules, have found humorous or sarcastic ways to comply; others, such as Katy Widrick, whose blog appears in Figure 4-7 (`http://katywidrick.com/about/disclosure-policy`), are simply matter-of-fact about it.

Table 4-4	Legal Resource Sites	
Name	*URL*	*Description*
American Bar Association	`www.abanet.org/intelprop/home.html`	Intellectual property resource lists
CasesBlog	`http://casesblog.blogspot.com/2010/04/guidance-on-blogger-disclosure-and-ftc.html`	Blog disclosure summary
Disclosure Policy.org	`http://disclosurepolicy.org/`	Generate free disclosure policies
Edelman Digital	`http://edelmandigital.com/2010/03/18/sxsw-essentials-practical-guidance-on-blogger-disclosure-and-ftc-guidelines`	Blog disclosure article
Electronic Frontier Foundation	`www.eff.org`	Not-for-profit focused on free speech, privacy, and consumer rights

(continued)

Table 4-4 *(continued)*

Name	URL	Description
Federal Trade Commission	`www.ftc.gov/opa/2009/10/endortest.shtml`	Blog disclosure law
FindLaw	`http://smallbusiness.findlaw.com/business-operations/small-business-internet`	Online legal issues
International Technology Law Association	`www.itechlaw.org`	Online legal issues
Internet Legal Research Group	`www.ilrg.com`	Index of legal sites, free forms, and documents
Nolo	`www.nolo.com/legal-encyclopedia/ecommerce-website-development`	Online legal issues
U.S. Copyright Office	`www.copyright.gov`	Copyright information and submission
United States Patent and Trademark Office	`www.uspto.gov`	Patent and trademark information, databases, and submission
Word of Mouth Marketing Association	`http://womma.org/ethics/disclosure`	Blog disclosure article

Regardless of what you think of the policy, reveal any payments or free promotional products you've received. You can, of course, be as clever, funny, cynical, or straightforward as you want. Feeling lazy? Auto-generate a policy at `http://disclosurepolicy.org`.

Figure 4-7:
This blogger
sets out
a clear
acknowledg-
ment policy
on product
endorsement.

Courtesy KatyWidrick.com

Protecting Your Brand

The three important aspects to protecting your brand online are copyright protection, trademark protection, and brand reputation.

Copyrighting your material

Copyright protects creative work in any medium — text, photos, graphics, audio, video, multimedia, software — from being used by others without permission or payment. Your work becomes your intellectual property as soon as you've created it in a fixed form. The rules for copyright are simple: Protect your own work and don't use other people's work without permission.

Whenever you sign an agreement with a subcontractor, especially a photographer, to create original work for your website, social media pages, or other advertising venue, read the contract to determine who will own the copyright on the work they create. In most cases, you can stipulate that their efforts constitute a work-for-hire arrangement, so the copyright belongs to you. (Photographers may give you only a limited license to use their creative work in one application.)

Your employee agreement should clearly state that your company retains ownership of any intellectual property that employees create for you. This area gets interesting if employees post things about your company on their personal social media accounts. It's another reason, if you needed one, for creating a hybrid personal/business account.

Put a copyright notice on your website. The standard format includes the word *copyright* or *copr* or the symbol © followed by the year, name of copyright holder, and, usually, the phrase "All rights reserved." The easiest way to do this is in the footer so that it appears on every page. Here's an example you can incorporate into your website, blog, or other uniquely created material:

© 2012 Watermelon Mountain Web Marketing All rights reserved.

This common law copyright notice informs other people that the material is copyrighted and gives you basic protections. For more protection, file officially at www.copyright.gov. Basic online submissions start at only $35. Copyright is usually easy enough to file yourself, but call the copyright office or your attorney if you have questions.

You cannot copyright ideas or titles.

Trademarking your brand names

Trademarks (for goods) or *service marks* (for services) give you the exclusive right to use a particular name or logotype within specific commercial categories. You can trademark your own name, if you want, and you must acknowledge the trademarks and service marks of others. The first time you use a trademarked name (including your own) in text on your site, follow it with the superscript ® for a registered mark or ™ for a pending mark that hasn't yet been issued. Provide a notice of trademark ownership somewhere on your sites.

Trademark rights apply online. For instance, only the trademark owner has the legal right to register a domain name with that trademark. The same constraint applies to celebrity names. If you think a competitor is infringing one of your trademarks, see your intellectual property (IP) or business attorney.

Fees for online filing start at $275 depending on which form you must file. Filing a trademark is a bit more complicated than filing a copyright application. For directions, see the trademark section of the United States Patent and Trademark Office site (`www.uspto.gov/trademarks/index.jsp`). Check the trademark database (`http://tess2.uspto.gov`) for availability of the trademark within your class of goods or services, and then follow the prompts. Though you can legally submit a trademark application yourself, you might want to call an IP attorney for help.

Filing a patent is much more difficult, and much more expensive, than filing a trademark. Be sure to consult an IP attorney for patent filings.

Protecting your brand reputation

Start protecting your brand now by registering your name for social media accounts. To avoid *brandjacking* (others using your company or product brand name on social media for their own purposes or to write misleading or negative things about your company), try to choose the most popular, available "handle" that will work across multiple sites. Use your company or product name and keep it short.

Even if you don't plan to do anything else in social media for a year or more, register your name now on Facebook, Twitter, LinkedIn, and Google Plus and on any other sites you might want in the future, such as Pinterest, or YouTube. You can do this on every site as you read this book or reserve them all now.

A number of companies now offer tools that claim to assess the "quality" of what people are saying about your company, products, or staff. In addition to counting how many times your name appears, they try to assess the "sentiment" of postings — whether statements are negative or positive. Some also offer an assessment of the degree of engagement — how enthusiastic or hostile a statement might be.

Some people then take this information, along with frequency of posting, and use their own, proprietary formulas to assign a quantitative value to your online reputation, as shown in the example from Trackur (`www.trackur.com`) in Figure 4-8.

Be cautious about assigning too much weight to these brand reputation tools, some of which are described in Table 4-5. They may produce widely varying results, and most rely on software that cannot understand complex sentences or shortened phrases with words omitted. If you think your dense sibling doesn't understand irony, don't try sarcasm with a computer!

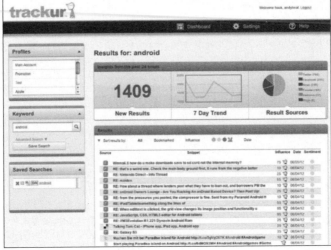

Figure 4-8:
Trackur
offers an
inexpensive
reputation
management
tool that
scales up
for large
companies.

Courtesy Trackur

Table 4-5	Brand Sentiment Resources	
Name	*URL*	*Description*
Alterian SM2	www.alterian.com/socialmedia	Social media sentiment tool; paid
Attentio	http://attentio.com	Social media dashboard to track sentiment and more; paid
Biz360	www.biz360.com/products/community insights.aspx	Blog and message board sentiment analysis; paid
BrandsEye	www.brandseye.com	Online reputation tool; starts at $150 per month
Collective Intellect	www.collective intellect.com	Consumer perception tool based on semantic analysis
HubSpot Blog	http://blog.hubspot.com/blog/tabid/6307/bid/30525/How-You-and-Rick-Santorum-Can-Fix-a-Damaged-Search-Reputation.aspx	Article with examples of what not to do to monitor and manage your online reputation

Name	*URL*	*Description*
Lithium Social Media Monitoring	`www.lithium.com/what-we-do/social-customer-suite/social-media-monitoring`	Social media sentiment tool; paid, free trial
Mashable	`http://mashable.com/2011/10/15/protect-small-business-reputation-online/`	Article about small businesses protecting their reputations online
Naymz	`www.naymz.com`	Personal reputation on social media
Net-Savvy Executive	`http://net-savvy.com/executive/tools/monitoring-social-media-before-you-have-a-bud.html`	List of sentiment tools
NM Incite (formerly BlogPulse from Nielsen)	`http://www.nm incite.com/?page_id=537`	Customizable dashboard, track customer engagement; high-end solution
Reputation.com	`www.reputation.com/for-business`	Reputation monitoring tool; starts at $99/month; free personal scan
TentBlogger	`http://tent blogger.com/brand-tools`	List of ten free reputation tools
Trackur	`www.trackur.com/free-brand-monitoring-tools`	Reputation protection tool; freemium model
Trendrr	`www.trendrr.com`	Qualitative, influence, sentiment, and other trends across multiple social media; paid
TweetFeel	`www.tweetfeel.com`	Twitter sentiment tool; free
Twitrratr	`http://twitrratr.com`	Twitter sentiment tool; free
Twitter Sentiment	`http://twitter sentiment.appspot.com`	Twitter sentiment tool; free
WE twendz pro	`http://twendz.waggeneredstrom.com`	Twitter sentiment tool; paid, free trial

Notwithstanding the warnings, experiment with one of the free or freemium sentiment-measuring tools in Table 4-5 to see what, if anything, people are saying. (*Freemium* tools offer a free version with limited features; more extensive feature sets carry a charge.) Those results, such as they are, will become one of many baselines for your social media effort. Unless you already have a significant web presence, you may not find much.

Of course, many of these tools are designed for use by multinational corporations worried about their reputations after negative events, such as a Toyota auto recall or the British Petroleum oil spill in the Gulf of Mexico.

For you, the sentiment results might be good for a laugh or make excellent party chatter at your next tweetup (your real-world meeting arranged with tweets).

Book II

Cybersocial Tools

The 5th Wave   By Rich Tennant

Serch Injin
Optamazashun

Kee Werd
Stratageez

1. Top

"How long has he been programming our META tags?"

Contents at a Glance

Chapter 1: Discovering Helpful Tech Tools

In This Chapter

✔ Keeping current with social media

✔ Distributing content efficiently

✔ Keeping search engines in the loop

✔ Giving long URLs a haircut

✔ Selecting shopping tools that work with social media

✔ Monitoring the buzz

*I*n Book I, you discover that the key to social media success is planning. This minibook reviews useful tools and resources to make your plan easier to execute. Before you start, you may also want to skim Chapters 1 and 2 in Book VIII, which focus on measurement tools for traffic, costs, and campaign performance.

As you select tools and schedule tasks from suggestions in this chapter, remember to enter them on your Social Media Marketing Plan (Book I, Chapter 3) and Social Media Activity Calendar (Book I, Chapter 4). You can also download blank copies of these forms at

www.dummies.com/go/socialmediamarketingaio2e

Try to select at least one tool from each category:

✦ Resource, news, and blog sites that cover online marketing and social media

✦ Content-distribution tools

✦ Tools for notifying search engines and directories of updates

✦ URL-clipping tools

✦ Shopping widgets for social media, if appropriate

✦ Buzz-tracking tools to monitor mentions of your business

You can always jump right into the social media scene and figure out these things later, but your efforts will be more productive if you build the right framework first.

Keeping Track of the Social Media Scene

Unless you take advantage of online resources, you'll never be able to stay current with the changes in social media. Here's a quick look at how much the landscape changed in the course of just one year:

✦ LinkedIn, Zynga, and Facebook went public.

✦ Google deployed its new social networking site, Google+.

✦ Pinterest took visual social media by storm.

✦ Facebook bought Instagram (which it kept going as an independent company) and bought Gowalla (which it absorbed and closed).

✦ Twitter bought Tweetdeck and Posterous (now Posterous Spaces).

✦ Multiple social media services went belly-up.

To keep current on the changing tides, subscribe to feeds about social marketing from social marketing blogs or news services; check at least one source weekly. Too, review traffic trends on social media services weekly; they're amazingly volatile. Table 1-1 lists some helpful resource sites.

Table 1-1	Social Media Marketing Resources	
Name	*URL*	*Description*
AddThis	`www.addthis.com/services`	Traffic trends on social media
BIG Marketing for Small Business	`www.bigmarketing smallbusiness.com`	Social media, online, and offline marketing tips
HubSpot	`blog.hubspot.com`	Inbound marketing blog
Marketing Land	`http://marketing land.com`	Internet marketing news and forums
MarketingProfs	`www.marketingprofs. com/marketing/ library/100/social- media`	Social media marketing tips, including business-to-business (B2B)
MarketingSherpa	`www.marketingsherpa. com/social-networking- evangelism-community- category.html`	Social networking research with B2B focus
Mashable	`mashable.com`	Premier social media guide

Name	URL	Description
Online Marketing Blog	`www.toprankblog.com`	Blog about online and social marketing
Practical eCommerce	`www.practical ecommerce.com/blogs/ 5-The-Social-Retailer`	Blog about social marketing for retailers
Slashdot	`slashdot.org`	Social news service about technology
Social Media Marketing Blog	`www.scottmonty.com`	Perspectives on social media data from the head of social media for Ford
Social Media Marketing Group on LinkedIn	`www.linkedin.com/ groups?gid=66325`	Professional, nonpromotional discussion group; approval required
Social Media Today Blog	`www.socialmedia today.com`	Social media blog
Social Networking Business Blog	`http://social-networking- business.blogspot.com`	Social networking blog for business
TechCrunch	`http://techcrunch.com`	Technology industry blog
Techmeme	`http://techmeme.com`	Top technology news site

Saving Time with Content-Distribution Tools

Social media marketing obviously can quickly consume all your waking hours — and then some. Just the thought of needing to post information quickly to Facebook, Twitter, Google+, social bookmarks, blogs, Pinterest, or social news services might make any social marketer cringe.

Time to work smarter, not harder, with content-distribution tools to post your content to many places at once for tasks like the following:

✦ **Routine maintenance:** Use a content-distribution tool whenever you make updates according to your Social Media Activity Calendar. What a time-saver!

✦ **Quick event postings:** Share information from a conference, trade show, meeting, or training session from your phone to send short text updates to Twitter and LinkedIn. Or, take a picture with your cellphone and send it to Flickr, Twitter, and Facebook. To send something longer, use a distribution tool to e-mail your post to your blog and Facebook.

✦ **Daily updates:** Group all social media services that you might want to update with rapidly changing information, such as a daily sale or the location of your traveling cupcake cart by the hour.

If you have more than three social media outlets or frequently update your content, choosing at least one distribution tool is a must-have way to save time.

Some businesses prefer to craft custom postings for Facebook, Twitter, and other services based on the specific audience and content needs of each channel, while others find this too time-consuming. Do what seems right for your business: automate cross-postings (set up a service so that postings on one social media service automatically appear on others to save time), customize by channel, or mix and match.

In addition to Seesmic Ping, OnlyWire, and other tools described in the next few sections, you can use really simple syndication (RSS) to feed content to users and to your various social media profiles.

Alternative content distribution services

You can select from several content-distribution services to syndicate (copy) your content from one social media service to another. All work roughly the same, but each has its own peculiarities. Choose the one that's the best fit for you.

Reconfigure your settings on content distribution tools whenever you decide to add or drop a social media service, or create a new, special purpose group for marketing purposes.

HelloTxt

According to the HelloTxt dashboard (`http://hellotxt.com/dashboard`), HelloTxt updates 50 services, although you can't create groups for different types of content. However, you can add a hash tag (#) to mark keywords or topics in a Tweet to help your postings end up in the right categories on the destination services. You can update by IM, e-mail, and text messaging.

HootSuite

Self-described as "the leading social media dashboard," HootSuite (`http://hootsuite.com`) has expanded from its origins as a way to manage only the Twitter experience. From scheduling to stats, HootSuite now integrates Twitter, Facebook, LinkedIn, foursquare, WordPress, Myspace, Mixi, and Ping.fm accounts for multiservice postings with one submission.

OnlyWire

OnlyWire (`http://onlywire.com`) updates as many as 33 services simultaneously, and it's the only tool we talk about here that passes updates to your own website or blog via a content management system (CMS). You'll need to implement the OnlyWire API (application programming interface), or ask your programmer to do it for you.

OnlyWire also offers five handy bookmarklets (convenient mini-apps that add one-click functionality to a browser toolbar or web page) at `http://onlywire.com/tools`:

✦ A toolbar add-in to submit to OnlyWire with one click from your own browser.

✦ A customizable Bookmark & Share button that lets users share your site with all their own accounts at one time. OnlyWire offers the choice of an ad-supported free version or a paid service for $3 per month or $25 per year.

✦ The OnlyWire Submitter, which allows you to automate submissions from your PC, Mac, or Linux computer.

✦ A WordPress plug-in that automatically submits your WordPress posts to OnlyWire services.

✦ RSS feeds to submit any RSS feed automatically to OnlyWire services.

Posterous Spaces

Posterous Spaces (`http://posterous.com`) has a unique approach: First, you create one or several spaces; then you can e-mail your text, photo, video, or audio files to Spacename@posterous.com, and it automatically posts to your page or appends your material and autoposts your content to as many as 12 social media and video services. You can specify posting to only a subset by e-mailing to a different address (`http://posterous.com/manage/#autopost`) or specify an e-mail address for a service that it doesn't ordinarily support. Posterous also handles RSS subscriptions and integrates with Google Analytics for statistical tracking.

Postling

Like HootSuite, Postling lets you cross-post to all major social networking services and blogging platforms: Facebook, Twitter, LinkedIn, WordPress, Tumblr, and Flickr. You can post immediately or schedule posts to go out at a later time. When people respond to your posts, Postling organizes them all in one place and allows you to answer them from the Postling site. Postling e-mails a daily recap of the most recent activity on your social network sites, Yelp and Citysearch reviews, and tracking results. You can also add other users for specific social media channels to help you respond to posts.

Seesmic Ping (formerly Ping.fm)

Seesmic Ping replaced Ping.fm in June 2012. The new service allows you to distribute content with Twitter, Facebook, LinkedIn, and Tumbler. Instead of a strictly web-based application, Seesmic Ping offers dashboard applications for the desktop, iPhone, Android, and BlackBerry.

TweetDeck

This content-distribution tool, owned by Twitter, offers a reduced suite of features compared with the older version. It now offers control of only Twitter and Facebook campaigns, allowing you to update your status, post comments, upload photos or videos, and follow friends' activities from the TweetDeck control panel.

UberSocial

If you're on your smartphone all the time, UberSocial may be perfect for you. This Twitter app, available for Android, BlackBerry, and iPhone, allows users to post and read tweets from a smartphone. Features vary slightly between the three formats but all integrate LivePreview, which enables users to view embedded links next to tweets without closing the app and opening a new browser, making it an efficient way to use Twitter on your smartphone. Other features include cross-posting to Facebook, managing multiple accounts, and what UberSocial calls "Uberchannels" (categories like sports, entertainment, or news) that help you track incoming data by topic.

Putting RSS to work

It almost sounds quaint, but RSS technology, which has been around for a decade, is still a viable way to distribute (syndicate) information for publication in multiple locations. The familiar orange-and-white icon shown in Figure 1-1 gained prominence years ago as a way to notify others automatically about often-updated content such as headlines, blogs, news, or music: an RSS feed.

Figure 1-1:
The RSS
icon.

The published content — *feed* — is provided for free in a standardized format that can be viewed in many different programs. RSS feeds are read on the receiving end in an RSS reader, a feed reader, or an aggregator. Readers come in three species:

✦ Standalone, such as FeedDemon

✦ Add-ons that are compatible with specific applications, such as an RSS plug-in for a WordPress blog

✦ Web-based, like Mozilla Firefox's Live Bookmarks, which adds RSS feeds to a user's Favorites folder

Feeds may be delivered to an individual subscriber's desktop, e-mail program, or browser Favorites folder, or they can be reproduced on another website, blog page, or social media page.

You can offer an RSS feed from your site, blog, or social media pages — or display your own or others' RSS feeds on your pages. This feature requires some technical skills; if you're not technically inclined, ask your programmer to handle the implementation.

Subscribing is easy: Users simply click the RSS icon and follow directions. After that, the RSS reader regularly checks the list of subscribed feeds and downloads any updates. Users can receive automatic alerts or view their updates on demand. The provided material is usually a linkable abstract or headline, along with the publisher's name and date of publication. The link opens the full article or media clip.

Subscribers not only receive timely updates from their favorite sites but also can use RSS to collect feeds from many sites in one convenient place. Rather than check multiple websites every day, for instance, political junkies can have RSS feeds about Congress delivered automatically from The Huffington Post, *The Nation, The Washington Post,* and *The New York Times.*

Unless you're targeting a market that's highly proficient technically, be cautious about using RSS as your only option for sharing content. Recent studies have found that more than 12 times the number of people will subscribe to an e-mail newsletter than to an RSS feed — except in technology fields, that is. The general public sees RSS as too technical or complicated.

Be sure to enter your choices for content distribution on your Social Media Marketing Plan, and create a schedule for distributing updates (daily? weekly? monthly?) on your Social Media Activity Calendar.

If you're interested in RSS, you'll find the resources in Table 1-2 helpful.

Table 1-2	RSS Resources	
Name	*URL*	*Function*
Atom	`www.xml.com/lpt/a/1619`	Atom feed details
Feedage.com	`www.feedage.com`	Directory of RSS feeds
FeedDemon	`www.feeddemon.com`	Free-standing RSS reader for Windows
FeedForAll	`www.feedforall.com`	RSS feed creation tool
FeedBurner	`https://accounts.google.com/ServiceLogin?service=feedburner`	Create, manage, and monitor RSS feeds
Netvibes	`www.netvibes.com/en`	Combination personal aggregator and social network
NewsFire	`www.newsfirerss.com`	RSS reader for Macs
NewsGator	`www.newsgator.com/rss-readers.aspx`	Offers RSS readers for multiple applications
RSS: News You Choose	`http://reviews.cnet.com/4520-10088_7-5143460-1.html`	About RSS feeds
RSS Toolbox	`http://mashable.com/2007/06/11/rss-toolbox`	Annotated list of more than 120 RSS tools

RSS offers a distinct advantage for sharing site content with readers: one-time-and-forget-about-it installation. After RSS is installed on your site or blog, you don't have to do anything except update your master site. You don't even have to type an entry like you do with the other content distribution tools. Everyone who subscribes gets your feed automatically, and you know that they're prequalified prospects because they've opted in.

From a user's point of view, RSS means that after requesting a feed, the user doesn't have to go anywhere or do anything to receive updates because updates arrive at their fingertips.

Unfortunately, RSS coordinates with social media distribution services only if you (or your programmer) enable your other social media pages to accept and display your RSS feed. Alternatively, your programmer might be able to use a tool like the OnlyWire API to configure your RSS feed to accept updates for distribution to social media.

You may see an icon or a link for an Atom feed. A newer format for syndication, an Atom operates similarly to RSS but uses different technical parameters. Although many blogs use Atom feeds, the older RSS format remains more popular overall. Some sites offer or accept only one or the other, so your choice of source and destination services partly drives your selection of syndication format. For more information, see www.atomenabled.org or www.intertwingly.net/wiki/pie/Rss20AndAtom10Compared.

Notifying Search Engines about Updates

Some people think that search engines, especially Google, know everything about everybody's websites all the time. Not so. Even the Google grandmaster needs a tip now and again. Even though all search engines routinely *crawl* or *spider* (visit and scan) websites to keep their own results current and relevant, your cycle for updates won't necessarily match their cycles for crawling.

Keeping search engines updated is valuable: Your site is not only more likely to appear in relevant search results, but its ranking will also improve from frequent updates.

The solution — *pinging* — is a simple way to get the attention of search engines and directories whenever you update your blog or website. Pinging has several other uses online: confirmation that a site or server is operating, as a diagnostic tool for connectivity problems, or confirming that a particular IP address exists.

Don't confuse the type of pinging that notifies search engines of changes to your site or blog with Ping.fm, the tool for distributing content to multiple social media services.

Pinging can be done on demand with a third-party service, or you can configure your blog, RSS feed, and some other sites to do it automatically. Generally, you simply enter the name of your blog or post, enter your URL, select your destination(s), and click the Submit button. The service then broadcasts a message that your site contains a new post or other content.

Select only one pinging service at a time. Search engines don't take kindly to "double pinging."

WordPress, TypePad, Blogger, and most other blog services offer built-in, automatic pinging every time you post. On some smaller blog hosts, you may have to set up pinging (or submit to search engines) in a control panel. Table 1-3 summarizes some of the most popular pinging options.

Table 1-3	Pinging Resources	
Name	*URL*	*Description*
Feed Shark	`feedshark.brain bliss.com`	Free ping service for blogs, RSS feeds, and podcasts; offers tracking
GooglePing	`googleping.com`	Ping Google blog search
King Ping	`www.kping.com`	Paid, automated pinging for blogs, tweets, online publishers; free manual version
Pingdom	`www.pingdom.com/about`	Uptime monitoring service, free for one site; paid service for multiple sites
Pingates	`www.pingates.com`	Ping service for blog search engines and directories
Pingler	`www.pingler.com`	Free and paid services for pinging multiple sites on a regular schedule; useful for developers and hosts
Ping-O-Matic!	`pingomatic.com`	Ping service for blogs, RSS, and podcasts
Weblogs	`weblogs.com`	Original, free pinging service on the web for blogs, news, and other sources
What is Pinging	`ezinearticles.com/?What-is-Pinging-and-Why-Do-You-Need-to-Ping-Your-Blog?&id=1584692`	Pinging information
WordPress Pinging	`en.blog.wordpress.com/2010/02/11/reach-out-and-ping-someone`	WordPress pinging service (owns Ping-O-Matic!)

Be sure to enter your choices for a pinging service on your Social Media Marketing Plan. If pinging isn't automatic, enter a task item for pinging below each update on your Social Media Activity Calendar.

Snipping Ugly URLs

The last thing you need when microblogging (on sites like Twitter) is a URL that takes up half your 140-character limit! Long, descriptive URLs that are useful for search engines are also messy in e-mail, text messages, text versions of e-newsletters, and blogs, not to mention making it difficult to re-tweet within the limit. The solution is to snip, clip, nip, trim, shave, or otherwise shorten ungainly URLs with a truncating service. Take your choice of those in Table 1-4 or search for others.

Book II
Chapter 1

Discovering Helpful
Tech Tools

Table 1-4	URL Snipping Services	
Service Name	*URL*	*Notes*
2 Create a Website	`http://blog.2createa website.com/2012/01/09/ popular-url-shorteners- for-redirecting-tracking- affiliate-links`	Comparison review article
bitly	`https://bitly.com`	Popular for Twitter; free versions with history, stats, and preferences
is.gd	`www.is.gd`	Users can find out where a short URL points
Ow.ly	`http://ow.ly/url/ shorten-url`	HootSuite's URL shortener
Snipurl	`http://snipurl.com`	Stores, manages, and tracks traffic on short URLs
TinyURL	`http://tinyurl.com`	One of the oldest and best-known truncators
Twitter	`http://t.co`	Twitter's own link-shortening service; can still use third-party providers

The downside is that the true owner of shortened URLs may be a mystery, so it doesn't do much for your branding. Figure 1-2 shows a typical URL truncating service and the result.

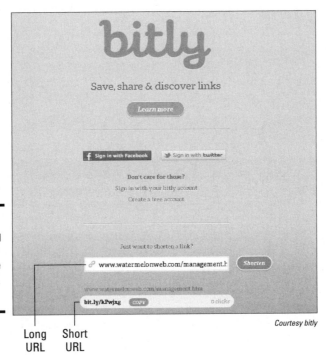

Figure 1-2:
Enter a long URL at bitly and receive a short URL in return.

Long Short
URL URL

Courtesy bitly

As always, enter the name of your URL snipping service on your Social Media Marketing Plan. To make it easier to track URLs and their snipped versions, select just one service.

Using E-Commerce Tools for Social Sites

If money makes the world go 'round, e-commerce takes the cybersocial world for a dizzying spin. There have been many different options for promoting or linking to your online store from blogs and social networks, but several applications now let you sell directly (or indirectly) from social media pages.

Always check the terms of service on social media sites to be sure you aren't violating their rules. Some services may prohibit selling directly from their site.

Selling through links

The easiest way to sell from social networks and blogs is simply to post a banner or a text link to your own website or to other sites (Etsy, for example) that sell your products. Additionally, you can post images on a site like Facebook with links to your website or other sites.

The British Corner Shop does this in a sophisticated manner, as shown in Figure 1-3. Clicking an item in their Facebook storefront

```
www.facebook.com/britishcornershop?sk=app_189977524185
```

takes shoppers to the British Corner Shop's primary site (`www.british cornershop.co.uk`) to fill their carts and check out.

Powell's Books does something similar, as shown in Figure 1-4, using shortened links in its Twitter stream (`www.twitter.com/#!/Powells`) to take visitors directly to pages on its website.

Displaying products on social media services

If you're looking for a more seamless experience, consider e-commerce tools that display items on your blog or social profile (the portion of a social media service on which you describe your company) and then link to a third-party application or a web store to complete the transaction.

For example, Wishpond (`www.wishpond.com`) integrates your Facebook presence with your e-commerce site. Users select their items on Facebook, but finish their checkout from your online store.

Other apps go further. Goodsie (`goodsie.com`) is a shopping cart app that allows you to set up an online store on Facebook or as a standalone entity. However, unlike Wishpond, Goodsie can accept credit card payments directly from Facebook. It charges as little as $15 per month,

E-commerce widgets are mini-displays of products; these changeable badges (which appear onscreen as a large button with multiple links) link to an existing web store. If you already have an online store, check your shopping cart or check stand provider (the section of your online store that totals orders and takes payments) to see whether it offers a widget for social media, too.

Figure 1-3:
Product offerings can begin on Facebook (top) and then link to a primary website (bottom).

Image courtesy www.britishcornership.co.uk

Book II
Chapter 1

Discovering Helpful
Tech Tools

Figure 1-4:
Powell's
Books links
visitors from
its Twitter
feed to
individual
listings on
its online
store.

Shortened URL

Courtesy Powell's Books

Many vendors of online stores offer widgets with functionality equivalent to third-party shopping apps for use on some compatible social media services. For instance, Zazzle.com offers both a Merch Store application for Facebook and a separate Merchbook widget for Myspace; PayPal offers widgets for TypePad blogs, Facebook, and Myspace.

Combining a virtual storefront with a payment service

By comparison, a *virtual storefront* on a social media service either imports products from an online store already in place on your own website or allows products to be uploaded directly from a freestanding, online store like Etsy. At the check stand stage, these storefronts link to your regular web store or to a third-party site to process the transactions. Although virtual storefront strategies may be a useful way to cast a wider net for customers, they may complicate your recordkeeping when used in addition to a web store.

E-commerce tools described in this chapter, which let you promote and sell only your own products, are quite different from social shopping services, which aggregate products from multiple sources, often suggested by consumers themselves and linking viewers back to your website. We discuss social shopping services — essentially, social bookmarks for products — in Book II, Chapter 3.

Third-party e-commerce tools that link to PayPal or other payment services generally don't integrate with inventory and accounting packages as a full-featured, shopping cart on your website might. If your business inventory system doesn't link to the shopping cart on your website, you may need to adjust those records manually.

If you use a virtual storefront in addition to an existing store on your own website, but don't track inventory automatically, here's another way to track the source of sales. For tracking purposes, you could create separate SKUs for products that will be listed on different online store locations or set a different price: for example, discounting items specifically for your Twitter audience. However, this approach wouldn't work with automated inventory controls.

Exercising social media options

Designer and entrepreneur Cassey Ho founded oGorgeous (`www.oGorgeous.com`), an online retailer of custom-designed fitness accessories and apparel, in 2009 when she was still a college senior. "I designed my own yoga bag when I couldn't find one that was fashionable and functional enough for my needs as a Pilates instructor." The now-profitable company has four employees, an online store, a vibrant blog, and multiple social media outlets.

"There was definitely no master plan," she says somewhat ruefully, acknowledging an unexpected branding challenge. Ho started giving free Pilates lessons on YouTube as a marketing tool, placing one of her yoga bags in the background. Initially, she linked her YouTube fans to an oGorgeous Facebook Page to buy the bags.

To her surprise, instead of selling yoga bags, she developed a fan base as an online trainer under the name Blogilates (`blogilates.com`). "I ended up becoming a popular YouTube fitness personality for my POP Pilates workouts and then I became a widely read health and fitness blogger on Tumblr. So, naturally, I got a new Facebook Page, which [thrived] as an active community for my students."

When Ho realized that her target markets for oGorgeous products differed from her YouTube Blogilates fans, she did more than simply putting her yoga bags in her videos. She developed a deliberate strategic relationship between her two online identities, using Blogilates channels to drive traffic to her online store.

Although both operations target women interested in fitness and fashion, her YouTube videos mainly target younger customers who like to buy Blogilates fan gear and apparel. "It also helps [to wear] my own merchandise when I work out!" She uses oGorgeous.com as a sponsor for Blogilates videos and links from YouTube to the oGorgeous site for purchases.

Courtesy oGorgeous

Her slightly older customers at oGorgeous.com come from multiple sources, but she credits exposure on different fitness blogs as a big factor in branding that name, generating leads for new customers, and boosting sales.

She uses oGorgeous's Facebook page as a customer service tool for sizing. "That works really well," Ho enthuses, "because everyone gets to see the question and answer, and gets excited about it. My fans also love posting pictures of themselves on Facebook and Twitter when they get their stuff! It is such a perfect way to build community and brand at the same time!" She eventually decided to duplicate stock from the oGorgeous.com site to a separate web store on Facebook using an easy storefront tool from Highwire (www.highwire.com).

(continued)

(continued)

"I decided to open a Facebook Shop because the feature became available, and I was like, why not?" Actually, the Facebook Shop doesn't produce direct revenue. "All my sales are on my oGorgeous.com site, and I get leads from my Facebook Pages when I post about a sale or new product," she explains.

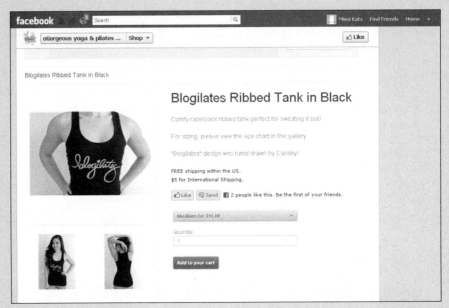

Courtesy oGorgeous

Blogilates has the stronger social media presence, including Tumblr, YouTube, Facebook, Twitter, and Pinterest. Ho tries to blog every day, upload one to two videos on YouTube per week, update her Facebook status as much as possible, and tweet real-time. Her Facebook posts connect to Twitter. "I used to use HootSuite but felt too detached from my community, so I stopped." A true entrepreneur, Ho does all her own social media, using Google analytics and store statistics from Highwire to track results based on source.

Pinterest drives a lot of traffic to Blogilates.com, "but it all comes down to making great content. Content that people want to reblog or repin," she emphasizes. She also includes the call-to-action widgets *tweet this, like this,* and *comment via Facebook* on oGorgeous.com. "[That's] fabulous because when someone leaves a comment, it also shows on their Facebook page and feed." Ho uses Google alerts to see when someone is talking about her or her business, but "a lot of the time my fans will tell me when they see me featured somewhere."

She offers an important reminder. "Social media is constant. You cannot stop if you want to grow. And you must be genuine and authentic — you must be YOU. Social media is a way for fans to get to know their gurus or favorite companies on a more intimate level, so you need to be accessible and not too out of reach. You must engage in your fans' conversations."

oGorgeous's web presence

```
www.oGorgeous.com
```

```
www.blogilates.com
```
(blog)

```
www.facebook.com/ogorgeous
```

```
http://blogilates.tumblr.com
```

```
www.facebook.com/ogorgeous?sk=app_137036186323012
```
(Facebook Shop)

```
www.facebook.com/blogilates
```

```
http://pinterest.com/blogilates/cute-workout-gear
```

```
http://pinterest.com/blogilates
```

```
https://twitter.com/#!/ogorgeous
```

```
https://twitter.com/#!/blogilates
```

```
www.youtube.com/blogilates
```

```
www.youtube.com/blogilatestv
```

Reviewing sample products for selling on social media

The following sections discuss some of the many specific tools and products available for selling products through social media. Consider these items examples in the range of products available. You should research and evaluate products to meet your own needs.

Netcarnation

Netcarnation Marketplace (`netcarnation.com`), a virtual storefront, supports customizable displays on Facebook, Ning, and Twitter. A mini-version of the display can appear on your profile page as well. It imports product information from many platforms, including Zazzle, Etsy, and eBay.

Netcarnation comes in free or pro versions. The free version, which is ad-supported and can display as many as ten products, is perfect if you're just dipping a toe into e-commerce or you want to feature a subset of your products for a particular audience. Premium Netcarnation storefronts can be managed from any sites on which they appear.

Payvment

Payvment (www.payvment.com) is a social e-commerce widget that allows you to set up a Facebook storefront and augment it with social sharing on Facebook, Google+, Twitter, Pinterest, and e-mail to reach more customers. (See Figure 1-5 for an example of the Payvment widget.) You can easily add Like discounts to increase your fan base. Customers pay using credit cards or PayPal. Free and fee versions are available.

Figure 1-5:
The McMullin Design Group sells directly from Facebook using Payvment.

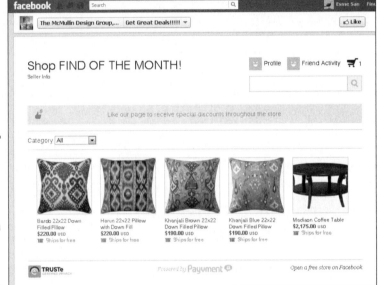

Courtesy The McMullin Design Group, Haddonfield, NJ

ProductCart

Early Impact's (www.earlyimpact.com) ProductCart widget is one of many popular shopping cart software systems that help businesses run and manage their online storefronts. Their free ECommerce Widget for Blogs, a tool that allows existing ProductCart users to redisplay products taken from the existing store on their website on a blog, a social networking page, or another website. For example, the Euphoria Blog (www.euphoriababy.com/blog), shown in Figure 1-6, uses the ECommerce Widget to drive traffic to its Euphoria Baby web store (www.euphoriababy.com).

 When selecting a storefront solution for your website, you might want to investigate which ones offer a solution like this for social media compatibility. If you already have a storefront on your website, check with your vendor to see if they offer a similar widget; many more companies are now adding this feature in response to demand.

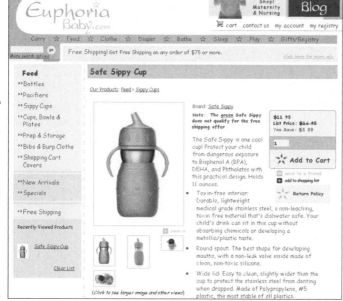

Courtesy EuphoriaBaby.com and EuphoriaMaternity.com

Figure 1-6: The Euphoria Blog uses the e-commerce widget from ProductCart (top) to drive traffic to its web store (bottom).

Generated by a click from the ProductCart control panel, operation is straightforward. The web store manager designates specific items in the web store's catalog as "portable." The widget dynamically loads the selected product information from the web store's database and displays it on the page where the widget is placed.

When viewers click items displayed by ProductCart's ECommerce Widget, they link to the ProductCart store on your site. The advantage of this approach is that it keeps inventory and reporting functions centralized. Of course, all this functionality comes at a price; ProductCart licenses start at $695.

TabJuice

TabJuice (`www.tabjuice.com`) is a virtual storefront designed specifically for Facebook. You create and customize your storefront on a Facebook account. There are no startup fees, and you're not charged commission on what you sell. You don't even need to have a store on your website or on another third-party site because transactions run through PayPal. TabJuice offers business and social analytics that show who is shopping at your storefront and track your business.

Other resources for selling on social media

Table 1-5 lists other e-commerce widgets, storefronts, and resources you may want to check out.

Table 1-5	Social E-Commerce Widgets, Storefronts, and Resources	
Name	*URL*	*Notes*
Amazon	`https://affiliate-program.amazon.com/gp/associates/network/store/widget/main.html`	E-commerce widget for your Amazon store
BigCartel	`http://bigcartel.com`	Hosted e-commerce website geared toward artists, clothing designers, and bands; capability to set up freestanding e-commerce sites and add to a Facebook site
BigCommerce	`http://big commerce.com`	E-commerce platform that allows you to design a web store and add a widget to Facebook

Name	URL	Notes
eBay	`http://developer.ebay.com/business benefits/money`	E-commerce widget for your eBay store
E-junkie	`www.e-junkie.com`	Cart or Buy Now buttons for Myspace; fee based on size and volume; handles downloads
Etsy	`www.etsy.com/ storque/etsy-news/ tech-updates-etsy- mini-679`	Directions for using e-commerce widget for your Etsy store
Highwire	`www.highwire.com`	Free, 100-item Facebook storefront; integrates with fee-based e-commerce website solution
Mercantec	`www.mercantec.com/ google/index.html`	Snippet generator that adds shopping cart to sites, blogs, Myspace, or Facebook; has analytics
PayPal	`http://storefront. paypallabs.com/ authenticate/review`	E-commerce widget for TypePad blogs, Myspace
Practical eCommerce	`www.practicale commerce.com/search? q=social+media+ecomm erce+widgets`	Articles about using e-commerce widgets with social media
StoreFrontSocial	`http://storefront social.com/`	Allows you to create a Facebook shop in minutes
ToldYa	`www.toldya.com`	Sell on Facebook, Myspace, other social networks and blogs; transaction-based fees
Zazzle	`www.zazzle.com/sell/ promotion/promotion basic#flashPanel Widget`	E-commerce Facebook app and Myspace widget

Keeping Your Ear to the Social Ground

The onslaught of data from social media sites can be overwhelming. To garner some value from all the noise, you can take advantage of certain tools to monitor what's being said about your company.

Social media *monitoring* is about who's saying what. It's about your brand, your products, and your reputation. It's not the same as social media *measurement,* which deals with traffic statistics, conversion rates, and return on investment (ROI). Measurement is covered in Book IX, including chapters about measurement tools specific to particular social networks.

Bring user feedback directly to you. Place a free feedback widget on your site from `http://feedback.widget.me`, `http://getbarometer.com`, or `www.snapengage.com`. More elaborate versions are available for a fee from `www.makeuseof.com/dir/snapabug-visual-feedback` or `GetSatisfaction.com`. This feature takes some programming knowledge; if you're not up to the task, ask your programmer.

You can find some monitoring tools for specific types of services in the sections that follow.

Deciding what to monitor and why

If you didn't have anything else to do, you could monitor everything. That situation isn't realistic, so you need to set some constraints. Start with your goal and ask yourself what you want to accomplish. For example, you may want to

+ Track what's being said about your company and products, both positive and negative

+ Conduct competitor or market research

+ Stay up-to-date on what's happening in your industry

+ Watch trends in terms of mentions, topics of interest, or volume of comments

+ Gain a competitive advantage

+ Monitor the success of a specific press release, media campaign, or product promotion

+ Monitor infringement of trademark or other intellectual property

+ Obtain customer feedback so you can improve your products and services

After you decide your goal, it should be obvious what search terms or keywords to monitor. Your list might include

✦ Your company name

✦ Your domain name

✦ Names of executives and staff who speak with the public

✦ Product names and URLs

✦ Competitors' names

✦ Keywords

✦ Topic tags

Deciding which tools to use

The number of monitoring tools is almost as great as the amount of data they sift through. Research your options and choose at least one tool that monitors across multiple types of social media. Depending on the social media services you're using, you might want to select one from each appropriate service category as well.

The frequency with which you check results from these tools will depend on the overall visibility of your company, the schedule for your submissions to different services, and the overall intensity of your social media presence. For some companies, it might be a daily task. For others, once weekly or even per month will be enough.

If you're not sure where to start, begin with weekly Google Alerts to monitor the web and daily Social Mention alerts to monitor social media. Add one tool each for blogs and Twitter, if you use them actively or think people may be talking about your business on their own. Adjust as needed.

Using free or inexpensive social monitoring tools

Pick one or more of the tools in this section to monitor across multiple types of social media.

Mark your choices on your Social Media Marketing Plan. If the tool doesn't offer automated reporting, you'll need to enter the submission task, as well as the review task, on your Social Media Activity Calendar.

Addictomatic: Inhale the Web

Addictomatic (`http://addictomatic.com/about`) lets you "instantly create a custom page with the current buzz on any topic." It searches hundreds of live sites, including news, blog posts, videos, and images and offers a bookmarkable personalized dashboard for making updates.

Alterian SM2

Alterian (`alterianSM2.com`, formerly Techrigy) monitors and measures social media, stores the results, and allows in-depth analysis. A high-end solution for larger companies, Alterian's Social Media console allows companies to respond, track, and audit social media interaction from one dashboard.

Google Alerts

One of the easiest and most popular of free monitoring services, Google Alerts (`www.google.com/alerts`) are notifications of new results on up to 1,000 search terms. Alerts can be delivered via e-mail, your iGoogle page, or RSS feed.

You can receive results for news articles, websites, blogs, video, and Google groups or a comprehensive version, which comprises news, web, and blog results.

You set the frequency with which Google checks for results and other features on a Manage Your Alerts page. Think of Alerts as an online version of a "clipping" service. Yahoo! (`alerts.yahoo.com`) offers something similar.

Google Trends

Google Trends (`www.google.com/trends`) compares how frequently searches have been made on up to five topics over time, how frequently those terms have appeared in Google News, and the geographic location that generated the searches.

HowSociable?

Type any brand name at `www.howsociable.com`, as shown in Figure 1-7, to see how visible it is in social media. The free version checks a limited number of social channels and a limited number of brands. Click any element for additional detail, as shown on the report for the Department of Homeland Security in Figure 1-7.

Klout

Klout (`www.klout.com`) claims to measure the influence and impact of your content across social media. The Klout score encompasses information about how many people you reach, how much you influence them, and the impact of your network. You can sign up for free, but Klout offers custom packages for owners of major brands.

Figure 1-7:
How Sociable displays social media visibility for the Department of Homeland Security.

monitorThis

A free aggregator for up to 25 search engine feeds covering websites, blogs, microblogs, articles, news, photos, video, and tags, monitorThis (`http://monitorthis.77elements.com`) is a manual search on a single term. Results can be sorted by publication date or search engine.

Moreover Technologies

Moreover (`www.moreover.com/index.html`) offers free RSS feeds from thousands of news and social media sources, enabling you to track your company, your competitors, and a nearly endless list of keywords and topics. For in-depth business intelligence, its Social Media Metabase located at

`www.moreover.com/products/metabase/social-media-metabase.html`

searches and monitors hundreds of thousands of blogs, podcasts, video-sharing sites, photo-sharing sites, microblogs, wikis, reviews, and forums on a paid basis.

Social Mention

Social Mention (`http://socialmention.com`) tracks and measures what's being said about a specific topic in real time across more than 100 social media services. It provides a social ranking score based on its own definition of "popularity" — which includes self-defined criteria of strength, sentiment, passion, and reach — for every search. Figure 1-8 shows the results for the term *Pinterest.* For more information on measuring sentiment, see the section on "protecting your brand reputation" in Book I, Chapter 4.

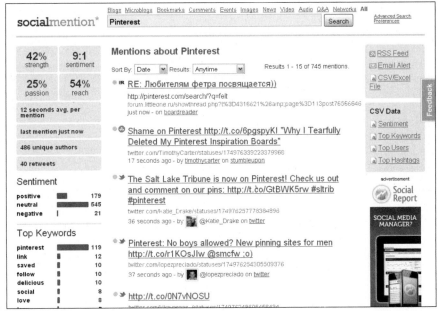

Figure 1-8:
Social
Mention
provides
a social
ranking
score
based on its
definition of
"popularity."

Courtesy Social Mention

You can select to monitor only specific services and choose among service categories of bookmarks, blogs, microblogs, comments, news, networks, video, audio, images, Q&A, or all. Although you can input only one term at a time, if you set up social alerts (`http://socialmention.com/alerts`), you can receive daily reports — much like Google Alerts — for multiple terms compiled into a spreadsheet.

In addition, Social Mention aggregates trends (`www.socialmention.com/trends`) in near–real time about social media discourse — which is handy for doing market research.

Social Mention also offers real-time widgets (`http://socialmention.com/tools`) to place on your site or in your browser bar. The browser is a simple plug-in, but your programmer will need to copy and paste the widget code onto your site.

Trackur

Trackur (www.trackur.com) tracks all forms of social media including blogs, news, networks, RSS feeds, tweets, images, and video. In addition to displaying conversational content, it presents trends and analyzes any website mentioning a term being monitored. You can get a free account with one saved search and unlimited results. Monthly plans with updates twice per hour start at $18 per month.

WhosTalkin.com

WhosTalkin.com (www.whostalkin.com) is another free, real-time search tool. It surveys 60 social media services for current conversations in the categories of blogs, news, networks, videos, images, forums, and tags. It lacks the reporting capabilities of Social Mention, but it does include actual comments. WhosTalkin.com provides results for only one term at a time but offers a browser search plug-in and an iGoogle gadget.

Measuring the Buzz by Type of Service

The number of monitoring tools competing for market share is astonishing. The following tables are not intended to be comprehensive lists but simply to provide some idea of what's out there.

Table 1-6 lists tools for monitoring blogs and forums; Table 1-7 tools for news, RSS, and geolocation sites; Table 1-8 tools for Twitter; and Table 1-9, some high-end tools at the enterprise level. You can always search for free tools in each category to get more options.

To ensure that your blog appears in a timely fashion in blog-monitoring tools, submit your blog to each one and set up pinging (which you can read about earlier in this chapter).

Table 1-6	Blog- and Forum-Monitoring Tools	
Name	*URL*	*Description*
Attencio	http://attentio.com	Multilingual social media monitoring; fee

(continued)

Table 1-6 *(continued)*

Name	URL	Description
BoardTracker	www.boardtracker.com	Searches forums and message boards; free and premium accounts
Blogdigger	www.blogdigger.com	Delivers blog search content in an RSS feed
Bloglines	www.bloglines.com	Delivers blog search content in an RSS feed
Google Blog Search	http://blogsearch.google.com	Master search engine for all blogs with an RSS or Atom feed, not just Google's own blogger.com; can segment by topic; displays by popularity
IceRocket	http://trend.icerocket.com	Blog-trend and buzz monitor for blogs, images, Twitter, and Facebook
Lijit	www.lijit.com	Geared toward advertisers and publishers; free dashboard and audience analytics to improve performance
Technorati	http://technorati.com	The first real-time blog search engine; ranks authority and influence of blogs and has more comprehensive index of blog popularity

Table 1-7	Social News and RSS Tools	
Name	URL	Description
Find Articles	www.findarticles.com	Monitor traditional media channels for keyword mentions
Google News	http://news.google.com	Keyword search of Google News saved into RSS for automated updates
Google Reader	http://reader.google.com	Aggregates your news services and blogs in one place

Name	URL	Description
PubSub	`www.pubsub.com`	Keyword searches saved to RSS feed; allows alerts for posts constrained to specific areas, such as press releases, filings with the Security & Exchange Commission, news groups, or blogs
Yahoo! News	`http://news.yahoo.com`	Keyword search of Yahoo! News saved into RSS for automated updates

Table 1-8	Twitter Monitoring Tools	
Name	**URL**	**Description**
SocialOomph	`www.socialoomph.com`	Formerly TweetLater.com, one-stop shop to monitor and manage Twitter; paid version includes Facebook
Twalala	`http://twalala.com`	Twitter client that filters your twitter stream by keywords; has a mute button
TweetBeep	`http://tweetbeep.com`	Like Google Alerts for Twitter
TweetDeck	`www.tweetdeck.com/features/follow-topics-in-real-time-with-saved-searches/index.html`	Auto-update search results from Twitter on multiple search terms; one of many tools available
TweetMeme	`http://tweetmeme.com`	Aggregates popular links on Twitter for popularity reporting
Twellow	`http://twellow.com`	Analyzes public tweets by categories to narrow search and identify influential tweeters in your categories
Twitter Search	`http://search.twitter.com`	Twitter's own search filter with advanced queries

Figure 1-9 shows the results of a typical Twitter search.

Figure 1-9: Results page from search. twitter. com for *Portland + Restaurants.*

Table 1-9	Fee-Based, Enterprise-Level Monitoring Tools	
Name	*URL*	*What It Does*
BrandsEye	www.brandseye.com	Tracks every online mention of a brand name, starting at $199/month
Cymfony	www.cymfony.com	Identifies people, issues, and trends in social and traditional media; for marketing and PR pros
eCairn Conversation	www.ecairn.com	Integrates and analyzes multiple social media sources for marketing and PR pros

Name	URL	What It Does
Gigya	www.gigya.com/public/ platform/Analyze.aspx	Social optimization tools for online businesses, including monitoring and analysis
Jive Fathom	www.jivesoftware.com/ social-business/social- media-monitoring	Engagement and sentiment analysis for social media
Lithium	www.lithium.com/ what-we-do/social- customer-suite/social- media-monitoring	Web-based application to monitor customer response
Nielsen's BuzzMetrics	www.nielsen-online. com/products_buzz. jsp?section=pro_buzz	Deep web analysis of consumer-generated content in online communities, message boards, groups, blogs, opinion sites, and social networks
Radian6	www.radian6.com	Monitors real-time conversations in all forms of social media, including boards, forums, networks, blogs, video, images, opinion sites, and mainstream media; designed for marketing and PR pros
Spiral16's Spark	www.spiral16.com/spark	Advanced software tools for monitoring social media and sentiment with sophisticated reporting
Sysomos' Heartbeat	www.sysomos.com/ products/overview/ heartbeat	Real-time monitoring and measurement tool for buzz and sentiment

Chapter 2: Leveraging Search Engine Optimization (SEO) for Social Media

In This Chapter

✔ Learning why SEO still matters

✔ Focusing on the SEO basics of keywords and metatags

✔ Optimizing content and sites for search engines

✔ Implementing local search campaigns

✔ Ensuring search success in mobile formats

✔ Conducting inbound link campaigns

✔ Implementing SEO on social media

✔ Gaining visibility in real-time search

No matter how popular social media may be, search engine optimization (SEO) must still be a part of your toolkit for a successful, broad-spectrum web presence. The goal of SEO is to get various components of your web presence to appear near the top of search results — preferably in the top ten — on general search engines or in search results for specific social media services.

You accomplish this by selecting appropriate search terms or keywords and then optimizing content, navigation, and structure to create a web page or profile that's search-friendly for your selected terms. At the same time, you maximize cross-links from social media to increase the number of inbound links to your primary website.

Fortunately, you can optimize social media, from blogs to Facebook, very much the same way that you optimize a website. Some people call this social media optimization (SMO), referring to the application of SEO techniques to social media. SMO has become even more critical with search engines such as Google moving toward personalization and semantic analysis, which skews users' results on the basis of location and past searches.

If you do a good job optimizing multiple components of your web presence — your website, blog, Facebook page, Twitter profile, and more — they may all appear near the top of Search Engine Result Pages (SERP) on selected terms, increasing your company's share of that premium screen real estate.

As mentioned in Book I, Chapter 1, improving search engine ranking is one strategic justification for implementing a social media campaign in the first place.

Making the Statistical Case for SEO

News of the growth of social media usage sometimes overshadows the actual numbers. For instance, The Nielsen Company shows that by December 2011, Facebook, with its exponential growth, rose to second place in unique U.S. monthly visitors (153.4 million), beating out Yahoo! (144.2 million) but lagging behind Google, which still topped the charts with 173.3 million.

And just because more than 800 million people worldwide (80 percent outside North America) are called active Facebook users doesn't mean they're all using it to search for information that might lead them to your company.

In fact, a study in January 2011 by the Local Search Association (published by eMarketer) showed that the vast majority of Internet users of all ages in the United States still opt for search engines rather than social media networks to find information about local businesses, as shown in Figure 2-1. To reach that majority, SEO remains the technique of choice.

Sobering reminder: Older audiences still gravitate toward print.

Sources Used Most Often to Find Local Business Information by US Consumers, by Age, 2010
% of respondents in each group

	18-24	25-34	35-54	55-64	65+
Search engine	54%	51%	36%	27%	15%
Yellow pages*	21%	25%	33%	36%	39%
Internet yellow pages	12%	15%	11%	7%	5%
Print yellow pages	9%	10%	22%	28%	34%
Newspaper	5%	4%	6%	10%	14%
Store circular/email promotion/coupon	7%	8%	10%	13%	16%
Magazine	2%	2%	2%	1%	1%
Internet social network	10%	6%	4%	2%	1%

Figure 2-1: In 2011, U.S. Internet users still favored search engines and directories over social media for info about local businesses.

Note: *print and internet
Source: Local Search Association, "Local Media Tracking Study" conducted by Burke, June 13, 2011

Courtesy eMarketer

Though Internet users in the United States spent more than four times as many hours per month on Facebook as they did on Google in September 2011, they weren't using Facebook to search for business information, but to communicate with friends and family.

At the moment, no social media alternative covers as wide a base of web pages or as commanding an algorithm for assessing relevance as search engines. What will happen in the future? Get out your crystal ball or watch eMarketer and other sites for more data. One thing about the web is for sure — like the world, it always turns.

Given these statistics, do you still need to bother with search engine optimization techniques for your hub website as we discuss in Book I, Chapter 1? Absolutely. Here's why:

✦ Not all members of your target audience are active users of social media, especially if you have a business-to-business (B2B) company or target an older consumer audience.

✦ After you optimize your hub website or blog, registered under your own domain name, you can quickly transfer the techniques, tools, and results to social media, especially to blogs and tweets.

✦ Inbound links to a hub website remain key to high ranking in search results, especially on Google. Your social media pages are a rich source of these links.

✦ You can optimize social media pages all you want, but they're always of secondary importance, except in real-time search.

✦ Social media services still aren't as well equipped to handle e-commerce, database applications, forms, or many of the other myriad features as a full-fledged website. For your website or blog to be found other than by links from social media, it must perform well on search engines.

✦ SEO remains an essential, though not sufficient, method of ensuring site visibility based on a method other than the number of friends, fans, or followers you have. You're chasing profits, not popularity.

SEO isn't an end in itself. The goal is to draw qualified visitors to your website so that you can turn them into customers and clients. A strong SEO foundation helps direct traffic to your full-featured hub from your social media presence.

For more information about search engine optimization, see *Search Engine Optimization All-in-One For Dummies,* 2nd Edition, by Bruce Clay and Susan Esparza.

Thinking Tactically and Practically

The best results for SEO sprout from the best content — and so does the largest stream of qualified prospects. Though we talk about many SEO techniques in this chapter, none of them will work unless you offer appealing content that draws and holds the attention of your audience.

Two schools of thought drive SEO tactics for social media:

✦ Optimize your website and all your social media for the same search terms, occupying the first page of results with one or more pages of your web presence.

✦ Use your social media pages to grab a good position for some relatively rare search terms that your website doesn't use.

Get greedy. Go for the best of both worlds. Use your standard search terms on social media profiles and the more rarely used terms on individual posts, photo captions, or updates.

Use a free trial at sites such as http://seosuite.com or the low-cost trial at www.zoomrank.com to see how your site ranks on different search terms. Your tactical decisions about keyword selection may depend on those results, as well as on the goals and objectives of your social media campaign.

Search engine jargon

Help yourself by mastering the terminology you see on search engine resource sites or in articles:

✔ **Natural or organic search** refers to the type of search results produced by a search engine's *algorithm* (set of rules) when indexing unpaid submissions.

✔ **Paid search results** are those for which a submission fee or bid has been paid to appear in sponsorship banners at the top of a page, in pay-per-click (PPC) ads in the right margin, or in some cases at the top of the list of search results.

✔ **Search engine marketing (SEM)** combines both natural and paid search activities.

✔ **Search engine optimization (SEO)** is the process of adjusting websites and pages to gain higher placement in search engine results.

✔ **Social media optimization (SMO)** is the process of adjusting social media profiles and posting to gain higher placement in search engine results.

✔ **Spiders, crawlers, or robots (bots)** are automated programs used by search engines to visit websites and index their content.

In the later section, "Choosing the right keywords," you discover how to select terms that people are likely to use and ones that give you a chance of breaking through to the first page of search results.

Focusing on the Right Search Engines

Ignore all those e-mails about submitting your site to 3,000 search engines. You need to submit only to the top three: Google, Yahoo! and Bing. Remember though that Yahoo! and Bing share the same algorithm. Although you submit your site at separate URLs, the results may be the same.

Table 2-1 tells where to submit your sites to those search engines.

Table 2-1	Submission URLs for Key Search Engines		
Name	*URL*	*Search Percentage in January 2012*	*Feeds*
Google	`www.google.com/webmasters/tools`	66.2	AOL, iWon, Netscape
Yahoo!	`www.search.yahoo.com/info/submit.html`	16	AltaVista, AlltheWeb, Lycos
Bing	`https://ssl.bing.com/webmaster/SubmitSitePage.aspx`	13.8	Standalone

According to comScore, these three accounted for 96 percent of all searches in January 2012, with Google executing more than four times as many searches as Yahoo!, its closest competitor. All remaining search engines together accounted for the remaining 4 percent of searches. Together, the three primary search engines feed results to all the significant secondary search engines. (Refer to Table 2-1.)

You can also check out `www.bruceclay.com/searchenginerelationshipchart.htm`.

These primary search engines now send out spiders to crawl the web incessantly. You don't need to resubmit your site routinely. But you should resubmit your site to trigger a visit from the arachnids if you add new content or products, expand to a new location, or update your search terms.

Fortunately, you can ping search engines to notify them of changes automatically, as discussed in Book II, Chapter 1. After receiving a ping, search engines crawl your site again.

Different search engines use different *algorithms* (sets of rules) to display search results, which may vary rapidly over time. To complicate matters further, they tend to attract different audiences. Optimize your site for the search engine that best attracts your audience. Here are some facts about the top search engines and their audiences:

✦ Google has about a 77 percent market share for B2B purchasing.

✦ According to Alexa, Google's 2012 audience tends to be younger than Yahoo! or Bing users and slightly more affluent than the overall Internet population. Also, more of Google's audience members have a graduate school education.

✦ Alexa data show that users are somewhat more likely to use Yahoo! or Bing at home and Google at work.

✦ Yahoo! and Bing attract older users than Google does, with Yahoo! drawing the most users over 65, and Bing's users are more likely to be female. Bing draws the largest share of African-American users.

✦ Bing, while having a much smaller share of users, attracts those who are 55–64, the demographic with the most buying power. As a result, TechSling cites Microsoft analysts who claim that, "Bing users are 11 percent more likely to buy than Google users and 31 percent more likely to purchase than the web's general user." Bing has a reputation for searchers who are more apt to convert to buyers.

Knowing the Importance of Keywords

Users enter search terms into the query box on a search engine, website, or social media service to locate the information they seek. The trick to success is to identify the search terms that your prospective customers are likely to use.

For good visibility on a search term, your site or social media profile needs to appear within the top ten positions on the first page of search results for that term. Only academic researchers and obsessive-compulsives are likely to search beyond the first page.

Fortunately or unfortunately, everyone's brain is wired a little differently, leading to different choices of words and different ways of organizing information. Some differences are simple matters of dialect: Someone in the southern United States may look for *bucket,* whereas someone in the north looks for a *pail.* Someone in the United Kingdom may enter *cheap petrol,* whereas someone in the United States types *cheap gas.*

Other differences have to do with industry-specific jargon. *Rag* has one meaning to someone looking for a job in the garment industry and another meaning to someone wanting to buy a chamois to polish a car.

Other variations have to do with spelling simplicity. Users will invariably spell *hotels* rather than *accommodations,* or *army clothes* instead of *camouflage* or *khaki.* And users rarely type a phrase that's longer than five words.

The average length of a search query has been increasing. As of January 2012, it was between four and five words per search, but this number varies by search engine. Longer search queries are more likely to lead to conversions.

Choosing the right keywords

Try to come up with a list of at least 30 search terms that can be distributed among different pages of your website. You must juggle the terms people are likely to use to find your product or service with the likelihood that you can show up on the first page of search results.

Book II
Chapter 2

Here are some tips for building a list of potential keywords:

✦ Brainstorm all possible terms that you think your target audience might use. Ask your customers, friends, and employees for ideas.

✦ Be sure your list includes the names of all your products and service packages and your company name. Someone who has heard of you must absolutely be able to find you online.

✦ Incorporate all the industry-specific search terms and jargon you can think of.

✦ If you sell to a local or regional territory, incorporate location into your terms: for example, *Lancaster bakery* or *Columbus OH chiropractor.* It's very difficult to appear on the first page of results for a single word such as *bakery* or *chiropractor.*

✦ For additional ideas, go to Google, enter a search term, and click the Search button. Then click the Related Searches option in the left margin. You may be surprised by the other search phrases that users try.

✦ If you already have a website, look at your analytics results to see which search phrases people are already using to find your site.

✦ Use one or more of the free search tools listed in Table 2-2 to get ideas for other keywords, how often they're used, and how many competing sites use the same term. Figure 2-2 displays results and synonyms from the Google Keyword Search tool for the phrase *dog grooming.* (Intended to help buyers of Google AdWords, this tool is also useful when you're brainstorming search terms.)

Table 2-2   **Keyword Selection Resources**

Name	*URL*	*Description*

Digital Point	`www.digitalpoint.com/tools/keywords`
	
	`http://tools.digitalpoint.com/tracker`
		Free keyword tracker and keyword ranking tool

EzineArticles.com	`http://ezinearticles.com/?Keyword-Selection-For-Your-Website-Marketing---Top-Tips-to-Think-About-For-Your-Website&id=3487516`	Keyword selection tips
Google Insights	`www.google.com/insights/search`	Research trends in search terms
Google Keyword Tool	`https://adwords.google.com/select/KeywordToolExternal`	Free keyword generator and statistics
KGen	`https://addons.mozilla.org/en-US/firefox/addon/4788`	Shareware add-on for Firefox toolbar showing which keywords are strong on visited web pages
SEMRush.com	`http://semrush.com`	Competitor keyword research for Google organic search and AdWords
Wordpot	`www.wordpot.com`	Keyword suggestion tool; free basic version
WordStream	`www.wordstream.com/keyword-generator`	Free basic keyword tools
Wordtracker	`www.wordtracker.com`	Keyword suggestion tool; free trial

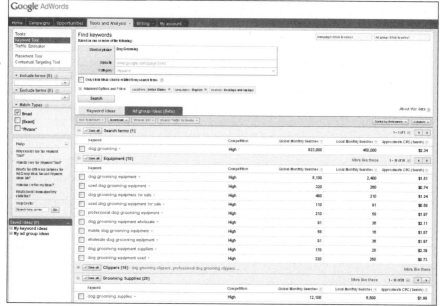

Figure 2-2:
The Google Keyword Tool displays the frequency of requests for related search terms and estimates the advertising competition for a term.

Book II
Chapter 2

Leveraging Search Engine Optimization for Social Media

✦ Check your competitors' search terms for ideas. Visit your competitors' sites and right-click to view page source, or look in the browser toolbar for something like View⇨Source. The keywords are usually listed near the top of the source code for a page. If you don't see them, try using the Find command (Ctrl+F) to search for *keyword*.

✦ Not sure who your competitors are? Enter one of your search terms to identify similar companies appearing on the first page of search results. Then you can go look at their other keywords, too.

✦ Look at the *tag clouds* for topics on social news services or blog search engines such as Technorati (`http://technorati.com`) to assess the relative popularity of different search terms. Tag clouds visualize how often keywords appear in specific content or how often they're used by searchers, with the most popular terms usually appearing in larger type. (You can find more on tag clouds in the following section.)

✦ Avoid using single words except in technical fields where the word is a term specific to a particular industry, such as *seismometer* or *angiogram,* with only hundreds of thousands, instead of millions, of competing pages. Not only will you have too much competition on generalized single words, but results for single words also produce too wide a range of options. People simply give up.

Crafting a page, blog posting, or social media profile for more than four or five search terms is difficult. Break up your list of terms into sets that you think you can work into a single paragraph of text while still making sense.

Optimizing for search terms that real people rarely use doesn't make sense. Sure, you can be number one because you have no competition, but why bother? The exceptions are your company and product names and terms highly specific to your business.

Always test your selected search terms to be sure that sites like yours show up in the results for that term. For instance, entering *artificial trees* as a search term yields inexpensive artificial Christmas trees, especially at the holiday season, and perhaps some silk palm trees. However, that term doesn't produce appropriate results if your company offers $30,000 tree sculptures designed for shopping malls, zoos, or museums.

Understanding tags and tag clouds

We want to dispense with one major source of confusion. *Tags* are the social media equivalent of search terms (several keywords together, such as *New Mexico artists*). Tags are commonly used on blogs, social media, and content-heavy sites other than search engines to categorize content and help users find material.

Tag clouds are simply a way to visualize either how often keywords appear in specific content or how often they are used by searchers.

Keywords in a tag cloud are often arranged alphabetically or with common terms grouped and displayed as a paragraph. The more frequently used terms (minus common elements such as articles and prepositions) appear in the largest font, as shown in Figure 2-3.

Tag clouds can help you quickly grasp the popularity of particular topics, the terms that people most often use to find a topic, or the relative size or frequency of something, such as city population or usage of different browser versions.

When you submit your site to social bookmarking or social news services (as we describe in Book II, Chapter 3), you're often asked to enter a list of helpful tags so that other people can search for your content. The first rule is to use tags that match your primary search terms and ensure that those terms appear within your text.

Figure 2-3:
This tag cloud from wordle.net shows the frequency (popularity) of words used on sba.gov.

You can quickly generate a tag cloud for content by using a tool such as the Tag Cloud Generator at `www.tagcloud-generator.com` or `www.wordle.net`. Simply paste in text or enter a URL. You can then enter the most frequently appearing words as the tags when you submit content to a social media service.

Some social media services display tag clouds created on a running basis to identify trending topics. Use these tag clouds on social media to help determine the popularity of various topics as you decide which content to post. You can also modify the tags you use to categorize your postings. Include or default to commonly used tags when you make your submission, to increase the likelihood that your posting shows up in search results.

Maximizing Metatag Muscle

Search engines, especially Yahoo!/Bing, use *metatags* to help rank the relevance of a website, blog, or social media page to a search query. Historically, engines needed many types of *metadata* (data that describes a web page overall) to categorize a website, but now only the page title and page description metatags are required; the keywords metatag is now more helpful to human beings than to search engines. Search engines can automatically detect the rest of the information they need, and too many metatags just slow them down.

Don't confuse the term *metatags,* which appear in page source code, with the term *tags*, the label used to refer to assigned keywords in social media.

To view metatags for any website, choose View⇨Source in Internet Explorer; look for a similar command in other browsers. (On a PC, you can also right-click a web page and choose View Source.) You see a display like the one shown in Figure 2-4, which shows the primary metatags for Pennington Builders (`http://penningtonbuilders.com`).

Metatags in the page source

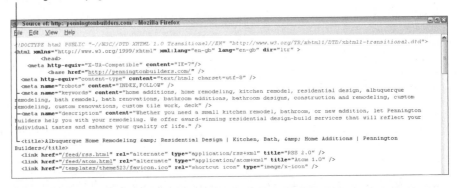

Figure 2-4: The page source (top) for the home page of Pennington Builders (bottom) shows the keywords, description, and page title metatags.

Courtesy Pennington Builders

Keywords on the website

The first paragraph of the page shown in Figure 2-4 (bottom) is optimized for some of the same search terms that appear in the keyword list. Note the page title above the browser toolbar, which also includes three of the search terms. We talk more about this metatag in a later section of this chapter.

If you see no metatags in the page source for your own site, you may be in trouble. That could partially account for poor results in search engines.

You can usually insert metatags and `<alt>` tags for photos quite easily if you use a content management system (CMS) to maintain your website or if you use blog software. If you don't, you may need to ask your programmer or web developer for assistance.

Keeping up with the keywords metatag

Though the keywords metatag, which lists your chosen search terms for a page, isn't essential for search engines, it helps you track keywords manually. This metatag isn't visible to others while they're viewing pages; however, it's visible in the source code. Because different search engines truncate the keywords metatag at different lengths, try to vary the position of search terms within the tag on different pages.

You have as many different ways to list search terms as there are search engine optimizers. Try these helpful guidelines:

✦ Make an alphabetical list of all your search terms in lowercase.

✦ Search engines ignore prepositions, conjunctions, articles, and punctuation; you can include them, but engines see the terms without them.

✦ Because simple plurals include singulars (*comets/comet*), use only the plurals. However, if the spelling of a plural changes its root, include both versions in your list (for example, *scarf/scarves* or *salary/salaries*).

✦ If your list is too long, stick with root words; for example, *photograph* covers *photographs, photography, photographer, photographers, photographed,* and *photographing.*

✦ Separate phrases with commas; commas don't matter to search engines, but they make reading easier for you.

✦ If words within a term must be kept together, put them between quotes — for example, "north dakota." Otherwise, search engines index words in any order. The term *red sneakers* is indexed in results even if someone enters the search term *sneakers red.*

✦ Put your unique words, such as your company or product name, at the end of the list. It doesn't matter as much if they're trimmed off because search engines will find your unique terms anyway. Those terms are likely to appear so often on your site that you don't have to optimize for them.

✦ Pull out the four or five terms that will comprise the primary "set" of keywords for a particular page and put them at the beginning of the list.

Refer to Figure 2-4 to see how Pennington Builders handles the keywords metatag on one page of its website.

Assign four to five search terms per page for optimization. Plan to reuse the set of terms you assign to your home page on multiple social media pages.

Tipping the scales with the page title metatag

Perhaps the most important metatag, the page title, appears above the browser toolbar when users are on a website. (Refer to Figure 2-4, bottom, to see where the title tag's output appears on the screen.) A good page title metatag includes one or more keywords followed by your company name. Select one or more search terms from the set of keywords you've assigned to that particular page.

Because browsers may truncate the title display, place the search term first. Limit the `<title>` tag to seven to ten words and fewer than 70 characters. A long, long time ago, way back in the dinosaur age of the Internet, page names were used to index a website. That method is now unnecessary; it's an absolute waste of time to use a phrase such as *home page* rather than a search term in a page title. It's almost as big a waste of time as having no `<title>` tag. The `<title>` tag (Albuquerque Home Remodeling & Residential Design | Kitchen, Bath, & Home Additions) that appears in Figure 2-4 (top) is a good example.

Google and other search engines dislike multiple pages with identical metatags. Changing the `<title>` tag on each page is one of the easiest ways to handle this preference. Simply pull another relevant search term from your list of keywords and insert it in front of the company name in the `<title>` tag.

Pumping up page description metatags

The page description metatag appears as several sentences below the link to each site in natural search results. Search engines display the first line of text when a page description metatag isn't available. Some search engines truncate description metatags after 150 to 250 characters. Just in case, front-load the description with all the search terms from the set you've assigned to that page.

Why pass up a marketing opportunity? Just because your site appears near the top of search results, you have no guarantee that someone will click through to your site. Write your page description metatag as though it were ad copy, including a benefits statement and a call to action.

Figure 2-5 displays natural search results on Google with the page description for the homepage of Pennington Builders. Note the inclusion of search terms (for example, *kitchen remodel, residential design*) from the keywords metatag in Figure 2-4 (top), the benefits statement (*reflect your individual tastes and enhance your quality of life*), and the call to action (*let Pennington Builders help you with your remodeling*).

Figure 2-5:
The page description metatag for pages on the Pennington Builders site appears in the natural search results for *Albuquerque residential design*.

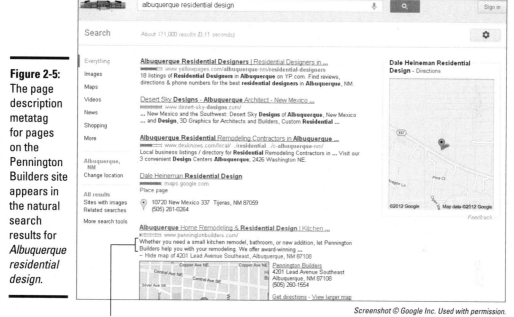

Page description

Optimizing Your Site and Content for Search Engines

Optimization is the process of adjusting your site, blog, or social media profiles to play well with search algorithms. You do so primarily by having plenty of relevant content, updating it often, and making sure that your web presence is easy for general and on-site search engines to discover with their spiders. I cover a few of the most important tricks of the trade in the following sections. For additional information on search engines and site optimization, check out some of the resources listed in Table 2-3.

Table 2-3	Search Engine and Optimization Resources	
Name	*URL*	*Description*
Google Webmaster	`https://support.google.com/webmasters/bin/answer.py?hl=en&answer=35769`	Guidelines and suggestions for site optimization and helpful blog with SEO information for webmasters
Linkvendor	`www.linkvendor.com`	Suite of SEO tools
MarketingSherpa	`http://www.marketingsherpa.com/freestuff.html`	Search Marketing Benchmark Report 2012 (free excerpt)
Pandia Search Central	`www.pandia.com`	Search engine news
Search Engine Guide	`www.searchengineguide.com/marketing.html`	Search engine articles, blog, marketing
Search Engine Journal	`www.searchenginejournal.com/seo-101-resources-learn-with-guides-tutorials-and-more/35740`	Best practices for URLs
Search Engine Watch (ClickZ)	`www.searchenginewatch.com`	Articles, tutorials, forums, blogs, SEO articles, and tips
SEOmoz	`www.seomoz.org`	SEO resources, toolbar, blog, spam detector, membership
UrlTrends	`www.urltrends.com`	Suite of SEO tools and reports

Google is in the midst of another algorithm dance, which is expected to upset page rankings for 10–20 percent of websites. Google plans to supplement its current keyword-search system with something called *semantic search*. This approach will enable the search engine to supply the actual response to queries from a database or associate words with one another, such as a brand (Nike) with its product (athletic shoes). According to CNET News, Google is targeting sites that appear to be "overly optimized" compared to sites with solid content.

Because these changes will unfold over time, your best option is to watch your search engine results weekly and take action as needed. You can also monitor any of the sources in Table 2-3 for news.

Writing an optimized first paragraph

First and foremost, use the four or five search terms from each assigned set in the first paragraph of text on a page or the first paragraph of a blog posting. (See Figure 2-6.) Basically, most search engines don't check entire websites or blogs, so the engines continue until they reach a hard return or 200 words. That's too many words for a paragraph on the web, so get those search terms in early.

There's nothing like on-site social media, such as a blog or forum, to generate keyword-rich content for search engines to munch on. Best of all, other folks are helping you feed the beast!

Figure 2-6 shows a well-optimized posting and its source code from the Changing Aging blog. Ecumen, a nonprofit organization specializing in senior housing and services, owns the blog. This entry at www.changingaging blog.org/posts/view/1272-boston-college-analysis-projects-seniors_27-long-term-care-costs includes the phrase *long term care* in its URL, post title, tags, categories, and text. The source code uses the same term in the page title and keywords metatags, and it indicates that the Ecumen Changing Aging blog has both an XML site map and an RSS feed.

Don't try to force more than one set of terms into the paragraph. If another phrase or two from the keywords metatag fit naturally, that's fine. Trying to cram more words into your text may render it unintelligible or jargon-loaded to human readers.

No matter where the first paragraph of text appears on the page, place the text near the top of the source code. The text should appear above any tags for images, video, or Flash.

Updating often

Search engines, especially Google, love to see updated content. Regular updates are a sign that a website is loved and cared for, and easily updated content is one of many reasons for having a blog or content management system on your site. If changing content is simple and free, you're more likely to do it.

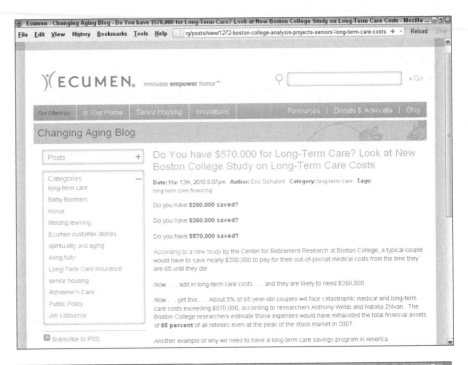

Figure 2-6:
This blog post uses several keywords in its title, tags, categories, and text and includes an XML site map and RSS feed.

Courtesy Ecumen

At least once a month, change a paragraph of content on your site. Include this task on your Social Media Activity Calendar. (See Book I, Chapter 3.) If you can't commit to this task, at least ask your programmer to incorporate some kind of automatically updated material, whether it's a date-and-time stamp, a quote, or an RSS feed, for example.

If you follow no other search optimization tips in this chapter, make sure that you follow at least these two: Update often and optimize the first paragraph of text on every page.

Using search terms elsewhere on pages

Guess what? You score extra jelly beans in the relevance jar if your search terms appear in particular places on your website. Follow these tips to optimize your web page or blog for your selected set of search terms. However, if they don't work naturally, don't force them.

+ **Links:** Use the words from your priority set of search terms as *text links* or *anchor text* (words that form an active link to another internal page or external site). Don't waste valuable real estate on meaningless phrases such as *Learn more* or *Click here.* They don't do a darn thing for your search ranking.

  If a clickable image opens another page, such as a product detail page, add a clickable caption that includes a search term or the product name. Score some points!

+ **Headings:** Headlines and subheads help organize text and assist readers who are skimming your copy for the information they want. Headings that include your search terms can also improve your search engine ranking.

  Onscreen, these words usually appear in bold and in a larger font size or different color (or both) from the body copy.

  Headings must carry the <h1> to <h6> tags that define HTML headings, rather than appear as graphics. Search engines can't "read" words embedded in a picture.

+ **Navigation:** Search terms that appear as navigational items, whether for main or secondary pages, also earn extra relevance "jelly beans." As with headings, navigation must be in text form, not in graphic form.

Sometimes you have to weigh the design considerations or limitations of your CMS or blog against search engine optimization needs. Some designers prefer the greater control and flexibility of font styles available in a graphic. Ultimately, only you can decide what matters more to you.

Under no circumstances should you implement *black hat* techniques, which are scams promoted as the search engine equivalent of a get-rich-quick scheme. For instance, don't even think about stuffing a page with keywords, hiding search terms in the same color as the background, installing "magic pixels," or any other shifty tricks. These techniques might get you blacklisted from search engines.

Making your site search engine friendly

In addition to trying the techniques in the previous section, which apply at the page level, you can take specific actions to make your site, as a whole, friendly to search engines.

Avoiding elements that search engines hate

If you expect a search engine to rank your site or blog favorably, you have to give it something to work with. Computers may be getting smarter all the time, but they cannot yet "read" pictures, videos, or soundtracks, let alone minds. They need to be fed a rich diet of words. The list of search engine "detestable content" is short, but they can all be avoided without harming your message.

✦ **Pictures without descriptions:** As much as artists and photographers love pages without words, search engines hate them. Simple solutions can make your pictures search engine friendly: Provide an `<alt>` tag and/or caption; have text appear below the fold (as long as the text appears near the top of the code); or include a descriptive paragraph near the image. For an extra boost, include keywords in the filenames for photos.

✦ **Flash animations:** Whether developers provide Flash animation because it's lucrative or because their clients demand it, search engines (not to mention Macs and mobile phones) detest it. A search engine has nothing to "grab on to" at an all-Flash site. Though there are now some ways around this problem, your best bet is to incorporate Flash much as you would incorporate a video — as an element on a page, not as an entire page.

✦ **Frames:** This old-fashioned way (anything ten years old on the Internet is practically an antique) of controlling the appearance of pages lets you modify content within a box. Unfortunately, search engines can't see anything inside a frame. Many alternatives now exist, from tables to cascading style sheets. If your developer insists on using frames, find a new developer.

✦ **Duplicate content:** Be sure to delete old versions of pages that have been replaced. Even if they sit in archives, search engines may try to index them and reduce your page rank for duplicate information.

✦ **Splash pages:** This misguided attempt to design a website as though it were a book with a cover does real harm to site traffic. Generally, a site loses half its audience every time a click is required. Why cut your prospect list in half before you even have a chance to explain your benefits? Splash pages often consist of beautiful images or animations that make a statement about a company but carry no content or navigation.

Often found on sites of companies specializing in entertainment, web development, architecture, arts and crafts, or graphic design, splash pages usually offer viewers an option to skip the introduction and an arrow cuing them to click to enter the "real" site.

The simple solution is to not include a splash page on your site. If you must, have an entry page with a nice graphical element that includes one paragraph of text (preferably filled with benefits) and primary navigation.

If you insist on having a splash or entry page, at least don't annoy your visitors. Direct the navigational link for *Home* to the main page of real content, not to the splash page. With a bit of clever naming, you may be able to get search engine spiders to crawl over the first page of content and ignore the splash page.

Configuring URLs

The best URLs are readable and might include one of your search terms or a descriptive title: www.*yourdomain*.com/social-media-small-businesses. Using a search term from your set of keywords for your web or blog page earns you another point for relevance. At least try to keep the URLs as readable text, as in www.*yourdomain*.com/pages/socialmedia/article1234.htm.

If the content in this entire section makes your eyes glaze over, just hand this chapter to your developer!

Problems with page URLs tend to occur when they're automatically assigned by a content management system or when the pages are created dynamically. Those URLs tend to look like gobbledygook: www.*yourdomain*.com/shop/AS-djfa-16734-QETR. Though search engines can review these URLs, they do nothing for your search engine ranking and aren't helpful to users.

Even worse are database-generated URLs or pages created on the fly that include multiple nonalphanumeric characters: www.*yourdomain*.com/cgi-bin/shop.pl?shop=view_category=ASDFJ%20&subcategory=XYZ%6734. Search engines are becoming less fussy than they used to be, but many still have problems indexing URLs that have more than four nonalphanumeric characters. (Hyphens and underscores are okay.) Some still have problems with only three such characters.

Be careful when redesigning a blog or website, especially if you're changing developers or platforms. If the existing site is already doing well in search engines, try to preserve its URLs. Not all transitions to a new platform accommodate this strategy. Ask your programmer before you begin.

A badly configured URL is simply not indexed. This problem can become significant with product databases on e-commerce sites, especially when you want every individual product detail page to appear in search engines.

If your site is hosted on an Apache server, a technical fix exists. You (or your programmer) can implement the Apache Mod Rewrite Module, which converts URLs on the fly to a format that's search engine friendly. See `http://httpd.apache.org/docs/current/mod/mod_rewrite.html` for more information.

Indexing a site

You can easily create a virtual path to ensure that search engines crawl your entire site. A virtual path of links is especially important in two cases:

✦ When the top and left navigational elements are graphics, making it impossible for search engines to know which pages are really on the site

✦ When you have a large, deep, database-driven site without links to all pages easily available in the navigation

For a small site with graphical navigation, you have a simple fix: Create a parallel series of linkable main pages in the footer of your site, as shown in Figure 2-7. The linkable footer on each page of `www.elcdc.com` highlights important site pages and acts as a partial site index for search engines. Alternatively, create a navigational *breadcrumb trail* at the top of the page to help both search engines and human beings know where they are within your site structure.

A breadcrumb trail (think Hansel and Gretel) helps users track where they are on a complex website. It typically consists of a series of page links that extend horizontally across each page, just above the content. Breadcrumb trails, which may either display the site structure or the actual navigation path a user has followed, usually look something like this:

`Home page > Main section page > Internal page > Detail page`

Put these links in a server-side include (SSI) within the footer to ensure that links are displayed consistently on all pages. You then make future changes in only one place (other than in the site itself, of course).

For a site with a significant number of pages, especially on several tiers, the best solution is to include a linkable site map or site index, shown in Figure 2-8. It may look a lot like a junior high school outline, which is a perfectly fine solution for both search engine friendliness and site usability.

Figure 2-7:
Footer links
on this
website
highlight
pages and
act as a
partial site
index.

Footer links

Courtesy Enchantment Land CDC

Figure 2-8:
Site index
page links
provide
easy access
to all pages
on the site.

Courtesy Webb Design, Inc.

Another solution exists for very large database-driven sites and large stores. Sitemap (XML) feeds that connect directly to Google, Yahoo!, and Bing provide current content to all your pages. Direct your programmer to www. xml-sitemaps.com, http://antezeta.com/yahoo/site-map-feed. html, or www.google.com/support/webmasters/bin/topic. py?topic=8476 for more information. If nothing changes often, these feeds can be updated manually every month. If you have continually changing inventory and other content, have your programmer upload these feeds automatically, at least once a day, using RSS.

If you want to index your site to see what pages you have, try one of these free tools:

+ **Yahoo! Site Explorer:** Sign in at www.bing.com/toolbox/webmaster, enter your domain name, click Status, and then click the Explore button.

+ **Xenu's Link Sleuth** (http://home.snafu.de/tilman/xenulink. html)**:** Download and run this link-verification program. In the results, click the link labeled Site Map of Valid HTML Pages with a Title.

Minimizing download time

Google now includes download time in its methods for ranking websites in search results. Companies continue to post pages that take too long to download, testing viewers' patience and occasionally overloading their Internet service provider's (ISP's) facilities. Perhaps it's a case of content expanding to fit the bandwidth available.

Try to keep sites to less than 70KB to 80KB per page, even though many users now have high-speed connections such as DSL and cable. High-resolution photos are usually the main culprits when a page is too large. It isn't the number of photos, but rather the total size of files on a page that counts. A couple of tips can help reduce the size of your page:

+ When saving photos to use online, choose the Save for Web option, found in most graphics programs. Stick to JPEG or GIF files, which work well online, and avoid TIFF and BMP files, which are intended for print.

+ Post a thumbnail with a click-to-view action for the larger version in a pop-up window. Be sure to save the larger image for the web. (Refer to the first bullet.)

Check the download size and time for your home page for free at sites such as www.websiteoptimization.com/services/analyze or www. gomez.com/instant-test-pro. Call your developer if changes are needed.

Optimizing for local search campaigns

Local search has obvious value for brick-and-mortar retail businesses using the web and social media to drive traffic to their stores. However, it's just as valuable for local service businesses such as plumbers, or even for non-local businesses seeking online customers from a particular region.

Local optimization is needed for your site to appear near the top of results in spite of geolocation devices on smartphones (not always turned on), geographic tagging of images on Flickr and other photo-sharing sites, or the localization settings on Google results.

Chances are good that your business is not the only one of a particular type in your city or neighborhood. Localization is absolutely critical for restaurants, tourism, hospitality, and entertainment businesses.

The concepts used for local optimization on websites apply equally well to social media:

✦ **Optimize search terms by city, region, neighborhood, or even zip code.** Rather than use a locality as a separate keyword, use it in a search term phrase with your product or service.

✦ **Include location in any pay-per-click ads.** This is equally true whether your ads appear on a search engine, Facebook, or other social media.

✦ **Post your business on search maps such as Yahoo! Local, Google+ for Business, Google+ Local, Bing Business Portal, and MapQuest.** As site link extensions (when possible), consider using one or more of your social media pages. Appearing on search maps is absolutely critical for mobile search, as discussed in the upcoming "Optimizing for mobile search" section.

✦ **Take advantage of local business directories, events calendars, and review sites to spread the word about your company and its social media pages.** In some cases, you might want to use one of your social media pages instead of your primary website as the destination link. Most directories are also excellent sources of high-value inbound links.

✦ **Use specialized local social media with a geographic component.** These options include social channels such as foursquare, Loopt, and Meetup. You can find more on these social media services in Book VIII, Chapter 4.

Optimizing for mobile search

The rapid adoption of smartphones and tablets is stunning: PewInternet.org estimates that nearly half of all U.S. adults owned web-enabled smartphones as of February 2012.

Combined with rapid technological advancements in location-based and integrated real-time search, this trend in smartphone adoption pushes business owners to ensure that their sites appear just as high in mobile search results and on mobile social media as they do on desktops.

Users see even fewer results on mobile search than they do on a larger screen. With all that competition, you need to take every possible step to improve your rankings in results, including the local optimization techniques mentioned in the preceding section.

Here are a few techniques to incorporate:

+ **Mobile site ranking is much more susceptible to technical performance characteristics than desktop site ranking.** According to Mashable (`http://mashable.com/2011/06/03/mobile-seo`), your mobile site needs to be friendly for mobile search browsers based on such characteristics as usability, download speed, and screen rendering. Broken links or poor navigation will reduce your rank in results. Extended functionality similar to your full website will lead to higher rankings.

+ **Your mobile site must work on all brands of smartphones.** It should use standard HTML coding. Better yet, incorporate next-generation languages such as HTML5 to enhance the performance of your mobile site, leading to higher rankings.

+ **Apply SEO optimization and localization techniques from earlier in this chapter to your mobile site.** Use appropriate keywords in headlines and text. It's critical to use keyword-loaded page titles and accurate page description metatags. That's all the content that may be scanned to produce mobile search results.

+ **Incorporate outbound links to relevant sources and other elements of your social media presence.** Mobile users consume social media constantly, especially Facebook and Twitter. If your prospects are using mobile media, you might want to pay particular attention to incorporating and optimizing these channels in your social media strategic plan.

+ **Include links to your mobile site in e-newsletters and social media.** More than 20 percent of e-mail marketing is read from smartphones, and mobile users can share links quickly with their friends.

Search behavior on mobile sites is somewhat different from search behavior on a desktop in the home or office. Mobile searchers are highly focused on the task at hand and want results — often local ones — quickly. They may not have the time or patience to search beyond the first two or three results.

Well-optimized mobile sites can increase traffic, enhance brand loyalty, and improve revenue. It's worth the investment of your time. For more on mobile social media, see Book VIII, Chapter 7.

Building Effective Inbound Links

An *inbound link* from another site to your website, blog, or social media page acts as a recommendation. Its presence implicitly suggests that visitors to the original site might find useful content on yours. Testimonial links are particularly important for social media, where they are measured in rating stars, number of views, retweets, "likes," and "favorites." These recommendations enhance credibility and build traffic, as they encourage other viewers to visit your original post.

Conversely, an *external link* goes from your page to someone else's, providing the same referral function. All these links form a web of connections in cyberspace. A site may require a *reciprocal link* back to its site before it will post one to yours.

It sounds simple. However, identifying places that will link to yours and getting them to post the link can be quite time-consuming.

Why bother? Although all search engines track the number of sites that link to yours, Google (and only Google) uses the number and quality of these inbound links to determine your position on search engine results pages. In essence, Google runs the world's largest popularity contest, putting to shame every high school's search for a prom king and queen.

Sometimes companies link to `http://yourdomain.com` and sometimes to `http://www.yourdomain.com`. Search engines consider them separate pages and may not give full credit for your inbound links. Do a permanent 301 redirect from one to the other. (Google likes www domains better.) Alternatively, you can accomplish this task from Google Webmaster Central, but it applies to only Google.

Google PageRank

A popularity contest is truly an apt metaphor for Page Rank because not all inbound links are equal in the eyes of Google. Links from `.edu` and `.org` domains carry extra credit, as do links you receive from other sites that Google ranks as having good content and good traffic. Think of them as votes from the in crowd. Google factors these parameters, and others, into its proprietary PageRank algorithm. For more information, see `www.google.com/about/company/tech.html`.

The algorithm ranks pages on an earthquake-style scale from 0 to 10. (Google Search and *The New York Times* both have a page rank of 9.) Empirically speaking, a Google PageRank of 5 is usually enough to place your site on the first page of search results — with no guarantees, of course. Figure 2-9 shows the Google PageRank tool in action. You can download the Google Toolbar with the PageRank display from `www.google.com/toolbar/ie/index.html`. (The toolbar doesn't work with all versions of all browsers.)

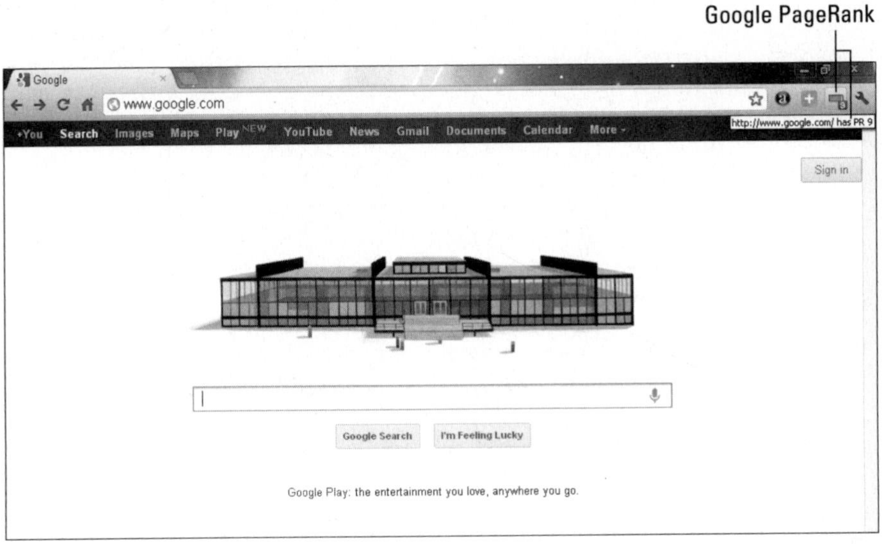

Google PageRank

Figure 2-9: Google has a PageRank of 9.

If you're serious about SEO, install the Google PageRank tool on your browser so that you can quickly check the PageRank of your site or blog and that of your competitors. Follow these steps:

1. **Download the Google Toolbar at** `www.google.com/toolbar/ie/index.html` **and install it.**

   The PageRank tool doesn't automatically appear on the toolbar, so you must enable it.

2. **On most browsers, choose View⇨Toolbars⇨Google Toolbar. If that option is not already checked, do so.**

   The Google toolbar should now be visible.

3. **If you're using Chrome, click the wrench icon to open the Toolbar Options dialog box instead of following Step 2.**

   If you don't see the wrench icon on the Google Toolbar, right-click any option on the toolbar.

4. **From the Tools tab, select the PageRank check box and click Save.**

   You now see the PageRank tool on the Google toolbar. (Refer to Figure 2-9.) Its specific location and size depend on how you have personalized your toolbar.

To see the page rank for a website, enter its domain name into the address box on your browser and wait for the page to load. Hover your mouse pointer on the PageRank tool until the box with page rank results appears below the toolbar.

To check page rank for multiple competitors' sites at once, try the free tool at `www.cascandra.com/web-tools/multiple-pagerank-checker`.

Knowing what makes a good inbound link

In a nutshell, good inbound links (sometimes called backlinks) come from sites that have these characteristics:

+ **Relevance:** The quickest way to determine relevance is to see whether the other site shares a search term or tag with your site.

+ **A decent amount of traffic:** Check `www.alexa.com` or `www.quantcast.com` to estimate traffic on other sites.

+ **Your target market:** Whether or not a link helps with PageRank, links from other appropriate sites help with branding and deliver qualified traffic to your site.

+ **A good Google PageRank:** Look for a score of 5 or higher in the PageRank tool. Higher-ranking sites, which often have high traffic volume and good content value, are considered more credible references; they pass along link juice (share page ranking) from their site to yours.

Lists of inbound links differ on different search engines. Because Google counts only sites with a high PageRank, the list on Google is always the shortest.

To see your own or others' inbound links on a particular engine, enter `link:http://yourdomainname.com` (where *yourdomainname*.com is replaced by your own domain name) in the search box for Yahoo! or Google.

Hunting for inbound links

No matter how hard you try, it's hard to find good sites from which you can request an inbound link to your own website or blog. Try link-checking tools such as `webmaster-toolkit.com/link-popularity-checker.shtml` or Alexa (`www.alexa.com`), shown in Figure 2-10, and the other tools listed in Table 2-4.

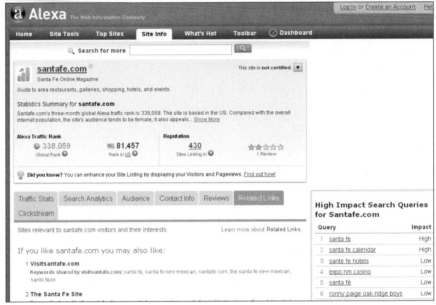

Figure 2-10:
For each
site it
indexes,
Alexa
displays
a list of
not only
inbound
links but
also related
links, such
as these for
SantaFe.com.

"Alexa the Web Information Company," "Alexa Top Sites," "Alexa Site Thumbnail," the Alexa® logo and name are trademarks of Amazon.com, Inc. or its affiliates in the United States and/or other countries.

Table 2-4	Free Inbound Link Resources	
Name	*URL*	*Description*
Alexa	www.alexa.com	Link checker, related links, clickstream, and more
ClickZ	www.clickz.com/search?per_page=20&date=this_year&query=linking www.clickz.com/search?per_page=20&date=this_year&query=link+building	Articles on link campaigns
Get Elastic	www.getelastic.com/social-link-building-the-latest-fashion-in-SEO	Link-building article on e-commerce blog
Internet Public Library	www.ipl2.org/IPL/Finding?Key=search+engine+directories&button.x=49&button.y=12	Directory of search engines

Name	*URL*	*Description*
LinkPopularity. com	`http://linkpopularity. com`	Link checker for Google, Bing, and Yahoo!
Majestic SEO	`www.majesticseo.com`	Check backlinks and history on other sites in bulk
Page Inlink Analyzer	`http://ericmiraglia. com/inlink`	Check backlinks plus tags and bookmarks on Delicious
Quantcast	`www.quantcast.com`	"Audience also likes" function
Search Engine Colossus	`www.searchengine colossus.com`	Directory of international search engines
Search Engine Guide	`www.searchengineguide. com/searchengines.html`	Meta-index of topical search engines
Webmaster Toolkit	`http://webmaster-toolkit. com/link-popularity- checker.shtml`	Link checker for multiple engines
WebWorkshop	`www.webworkshop.net/ inbound-links.html`	Tips and forum on link campaigns
WhoLinksToMe	`http://wholinkstome.com`	Backlink analysis and link building tools
Yext	`www.yext.com`	Check which directories link to your website

You can hunt for potential links with a few tried-and-true techniques. Try looking at:

✦ Inbound links to other sites that rank highly in Google on your search terms

Be sure that your company truly has something in common with the other site. Shared terms may not be enough — there's a big difference between companies that run a fish restaurant and those that sell lead-free weights for catching fish.

✦ Inbound links to your competitors' sites

✦ "Related link" sites at `www.alexa.com` for your competitors or highly ranked sites that share your share terms

+ The resource lists of outbound links found on competitors' sites or other highly ranked sites

+ Industry-based business directories

+ Yellow Pages and map sites

+ Local business directories

+ Blog-specific directories

+ Trade associations and other organizations you belong to or sponsor

+ Inbound links to suppliers' websites, including your web development and hosting company

+ Inbound links to sites owned by distributors, clients, customers, or affiliates

+ *Meta-indices* (sites with master lists of directories), some of which appear in Table 2-4

+ The implementation of cross-links with all your social media sites, even though some of these do not help with PageRank

+ Blogs you recommend in your *blogroll* from which you could request a link back

+ Inbound links to related but not directly competing businesses that your target audience might also visit

Prequalify every potential link. Visit every link site to ensure that it accepts links and is truly relevant and that it has a Google PageRank of 5 or higher and represents the quality and audience you want.

Stay away from *link farms* (sites that exist only to sell links), *web rings* (a closed loop of companies that agree to link to each other), and *gray-market link sites* (sites that sell links at exorbitant prices and guarantee a certain result). Your site can be exiled from search engines for using them. Besides, they don't raise your PageRank!

Implementing your link campaign

You will need to e-mail requests for a link to each of the potential sites you identify. Try for at least 50 links and hope that 30 of them come through. There's no upper limit — the more, the better.

You might want to create a spreadsheet to track your link requests. Create columns for these elements:

+ Domain name

+ Appearance URL

✦ Submission URL or e-mail address

✦ Submission date

✦ URL of the landing page you asked others to link to

✦ Reciprocal link requirement

✦ Date you checked to see whether a link was posted

Don't be afraid to group spreadsheet rows by target market. For instance, if you sell products for toddlers, you might have a group of links for sites used by single parents and another group for sites used by daycare centers.

Break this task into bite-size pieces so that it doesn't become overwhelming. On your Social Marketing Activity Calendar (found in Book I, Chapter 4), limit the search-and-submission task to only five to ten links per week.

After you qualify prospective links and add them to your spreadsheet, follow the directions on each site to submit your URL or e-mail your request to the site owner.

Getting inbound links from social sharing, social bookmarks, and social news services

Leverage your social marketing activities to increase the number of inbound links to your site. If it's permissible, post your site to some of the social sharing, bookmarking, shopping, and news services described in Book II, Chapter 1 and Chapter 3. (Not all social bookmarks allow you to submit your own site, so you may need to ask a friend to help.) You're generally required to include either your domain name or a specific page URL with your submission.

These links encourage both inbound links and traffic. Some of these sites pass link juice, especially if you have multiple links from social news sites back to different news stories or content on your main site. For more information, see Book II, Chapter 3.

Not all link shorteners are equal. Choose ones that will pass link juice with a 301 redirect. The bitly, Ow.ly, goo.gl, and cli.gs shorteners are safe bets. Of course, surround your links with relevant keywords. Just as with inbound link campaigns for search engines, don't link everything from social bookmarking, news, or shopping services to your home page. For example, multiple product recommendations on social shopping sites should link to the appropriate product detail pages in your store.

Cross-link by submitting especially good blog entries to several social news services or by linking from one product recommendation to another on social shopping sites or from one review site to another.

Reaping other links from social media

Another easy way to build inbound links is by distributing (syndicating) content as described in the previous chapter. By repurposing content on multiple social media sites, you not only increase your audience but also increase the number of inbound links.

Taking advantage of the many places to post links on social media pages will not only drive traffic to multiple elements of your web presence but also improve your search engine rankings in the process.

Somewhere on your website or blog — at least on the About Us or Contact page — display a list of links to all your profiles on social media services, along with buttons for ShareThis and Google's Plus One. This form of passive link-building can pay off big-time with improved ranking in search results.

The more places these links appear, the better. You can also repeat text links to your social media pages in your linkable footer.

Don't be shy! Include calls to action to share your web page in the body copy of ads or e-newsletters. These links don't always have to hide their charms in the header or footer.

Here are a few other ideas for laying down a link:

+ Every profile on a social network has a place to enter at least your web address and blog address, if you have one. If possible, link to both. The links in profiles usually provide link juice, although the ones in status updates usually do not.

+ Include your web address when you make comments on other people's blogs, post reviews on recommendation sites, or submit someone else's news story. You may have to work it into the content. Use at least *yourcompanyemailaddress@yourdomain*.com for branding reasons!

+ Include your company name for branding and your web address for linking when you post to groups on any social networking site, as long as it's appropriate, relevant, and not too self-promotional.

Read the Terms of Service on each site to be sure that you comply with requirements for use of e-mail addresses, submissions, and links.

+ Post events on LinkedIn, MySpace, Facebook, and elsewhere with a link to your site for more information.

+ Include a share button, described in Book II, Chapter 3, to encourage additional distribution. People who receive content they like often pass it along or link to it from their own pages or blogs.

+ Be sure to post cross-links on newsletters and on all your social media profiles to all your other web pages, including to your primary site and your blog.

Now that social media are included in ordinary search results, using search terms consistently can help you occupy more than one slot in search engine results pages.

This strategy works well for the Brooklyn Kitchen Store, shown in Figure 2-11. Their local listings and Yelp reviews, as well as its website, blog, and store links, help the Brooklyn Kitchen Store occupy four of the top six results for *"brooklyn kitchen stores."* Bing search results are shown at the top, and the website is shown at the bottom.

Creating a resource page for outbound links

One item to include when optimizing your site for search engines is a Link Resources page, by that name or any other, for external or outbound links.

You need this page in order to post reciprocal links to other sites but also to help viewers find useful, neutral information on `.edu`, `.gov`, and `.org` domains. Nestling reciprocal links within an annotated list of informational sites makes reciprocal links less noticeable and less self-serving. Good ideas about places for neutral links to appear are described in this list:

Book II
Chapter 2

Leveraging Search Engine Optimization for Social Media

✦ Sites with information about materials used in your products or how to care for them

✦ Educational sites discussing the services you provide, such as *feng shui* for offices, the benefits of massage, or tips on tax deductions

✦ Sites for trade associations and other business organizations to which you belong

✦ Local, state, and federal government sites whose regulations or procedures may affect your business or customers

✦ Nonprofit sites that share your values; for example, sites talking about recycling electronics or supporting entrepreneurs in developing countries

✦ Sites that talk about the history of your business or industry or the local history of your brick-and-mortar storefront

✦ Other sites that may interest visitors to your site; for example, a hotel site that links to a local dining guide or events calendar

Quid Interactive, for example, links to helpful sites at `www.quid-interactive.com/relevant-links`. (See Figure 2-12.)

A good starting place for neutral outbound links is to see related links for a high-ranked competitor. Enter its domain name into the search field on Alexa; then click the Get Details button on the results. On the ensuing page, click the Related Links tab. Also look under the Resources by Subject link on the home page for the Internet Public Library (`www.ipl2.org/div/subject`).

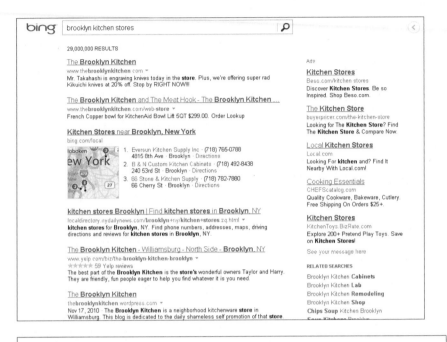

Figure 2-11:
Yelp reviews and blogs are included in Bing search results for *"brooklyn kitchen stores."*

Courtesy Quid Interactive, Inc.; www.Quid-Interactive.com

Figure 2-12:
Quid
Interactive
offers
visitors
helpful links
to other
sites.

Risking the personalized search

All bets are off with personalized search on Google. Google now defaults to a customized list of search results based on an individual's past searches, location, and the results she clicked. In theory, these search results, derived either from a browser cookie or web search history, are continuously refined to become more relevant to users' needs.

In practice, that relevance is debatable; users tend to see results that are "more of the same," distorting the reality of what's out there and reducing the likelihood of receiving new information.

Users must take a distinct action to turn off personalized search by clicking the Web History link in the upper-right corner of any Google search results page and then toggling the Disable Customizations Based on Search Activity option. Most users don't even know that personalized search exists, let alone how to turn it off or how to delete repeatedly occurring, undesirable sites from results to make room for new ones. (The latter option requires logging into your Google account to personalize settings for your Web History.)

Unfortunately, the algorithm for personalized search tends to produce results reflecting a philosophy of "Them that has, gets." Your website may have more difficulty breaking through to new prospects or achieving a presence on the first page of some individuals' search results. Sadly, you can do nothing about it. Whether users who see your site are more qualified as prospects and more likely to buy remains to be seen.

Optimizing Social Media for Search Engines

Here's the good news: Everything we've covered in this chapter about using SEO for your website or blog applies to other social media too. Whew! You still have to implement the techniques, but you can save time by reusing search terms, metatags, inbound links, and optimized text.

Every search engine has its own rules. You may need to tweak your terms for not only general search engines but also internal search engines on specific social media services.

Placing your search terms on social media

Start by reviewing your research for keywords and phrases. Decide on a primary set of four to six terms that best describe your company. Because your search terms must still relate to your content, you may want to reuse other sets for individual posts from your SEO research, mix them up, or include additional terms not optimized on your primary site.

You can place these terms in many locations:

✦ **Tags:** Tags, which are the social media equivalents of keywords, are assigned to specific content. Because many social media services place a limit on the number of tags that can be assigned to a given piece of content, pick a few from your primary set of search terms and select others (for example, brands, products, market, or competition) from your secondary list or elsewhere that are specific to your content.

If you're pulling tags out of thin air, remember to confirm which synonyms are most popular with the users of that service. For example, do people search for *Barack* or *Obama* or *president?* Use a keyword selection tool for websites listed earlier in this chapter (refer to Table 2-2) or check a tag cloud, discussed earlier in this chapter, if it exists on the service you're using for the latest trends in tag usage.

✦ **Profiles:** Just about every form of social media asks you to establish an account. Most profiles ask for a brief description of your company and location as well as the URLs for your website and blog. Work your primary set of keywords and brands into your profile and any other place you can comfortably integrate them, including featured products, department names, the marketing tagline, and staff bios.

Occasionally, a service requests only your e-mail address. Of course, you use the one with your domain name in it.

If you haven't already set up e-mail to forward from `you@yourdomain.com` to whatever e-mail address you have from your ISP, do so now. Most hosting packages include at least five free e-mail addresses. E-mail from `@yourdomain.com` not only makes you look more professional but also adds to brand value.

✦ **Page content, status updates, and comments:** Obviously, you should include search terms in the first paragraph of text for each blog post. They don't need to be part of your primary set of terms, so you have some creative flexibility. Incorporate search terms in updates and comments, too, to increase the likelihood of being found in on-site search results.

✦ **Metatags, titles, and headlines:** Use search terms from your list in the title of your blog or page name; in the title of your post; in <alt> tags, captions, or descriptions for images; and within metatags. Each service handles these elements a little differently, as we discuss in the later sections on individual services.

Duplicate content can reduce rankings on search engines. If you use a service such as Ping.fm to update everything at one time, you may pay a bit of a penalty. Because SEO is only one of the online marketing arrows in your quiver, you might not want to worry about duplicate content until your social media campaigns take off. Only you can weigh the pros and cons based on your available time, staffing levels, and campaign objectives.

Optimizing blogs

Because blogs (discussed in Book III, Chapter 2) are basically websites in a different format, the same principles of site optimization and configuration apply, including the need for inbound links and cross-promotion on social media services. Hard-learned lessons and best practices truly pay off because search engines crawl frequently updated blogs at least daily.

Integrate your domain name with your blog URL (*yourblog.yourdomain. com*) or buy a separate, related domain name (*yourcompanyblog*.com), even if a third-party server hosts your blogs. For SEO purposes, you must own your own blog domain name. A blog at www.*MyCompanyBlog*. blogspot.com or www.typepad.com/*MyCompanyBlog* isn't acceptable.

Blogs are primo link bait. The casual sharing of relevant, text-based links within posts, the use of *blogrolls* (bloggers' linkable recommendations of other blogs), and related thematic material attract inbound links like black jackets attract white cat fur. With all that link juice, plus rapidly updated content, many blogs quickly zoom to page one in search engine results.

Review all requests for inclusion on your blog roll or reciprocal link offers. Make sure that the requesting site is relevant, has a decent page rank, and is one that you feel good about recommending.

Different blog platforms operate somewhat differently, leading to some confusion on the part of bloggers trying to optimize sites for search engines. Whatever your platform, the same methods you follow for websites still apply, with a multitude of additions.

◆ Include keywords from your primary list in your blog name, such as *YourCompany*.com/social_media_blog. The blog name should appear with an HTML <h1> tag on only the front page. On other pages of your blog, the heading level can be as low as <h3>.

◆ Include keywords in individual titles for each post. Use these keywords in the <title> tag in the source code for that entry, as well as in the page URL. Put those titles at the HTML <h1> level.

◆ Include primary keywords in the first sentence of content, which becomes the page description metatag by default, unless you write one manually. Use your secondary keywords in the body of your post.

◆ Fill out the tag box with your keywords.

◆ Incorporate search terms in anchor text for links on your blog.

◆ Use <alt> tags, captions, and descriptions with search terms for any images or media you upload to your blog.

◆ Post rich, appealing content with search terms regularly and often.

◆ Make sure the search engine spiders can crawl your blog easily by including a side navigation column on all pages and by offering access to archives and previous posts from all pages of your blog.

◆ Include a linkable, keyword-loaded breadcrumb trail.

◆ Provide internal text links to your own related posts.

◆ Submit your blog to blog directories and RSS submission sites. An excellent list is at http://web-marketing.masternewmedia.org/rsstop55-best-blog-directory-and-rss-submission-sites.

◆ Use your blogroll as a resource — just having a blogroll is not enough. Contact other bloggers to request a backlink or offer a reciprocal appearance on your blogroll in exchange for a backlink.

◆ Get backlinks to your blog with *trackbacks* (an automated way of notifying other bloggers that you've referenced their blog) or by posting comments on other blogs. Not all blogging hosts support trackbacks. For more on trackbacks, check out Book III, Chapter 2.

◆ Create an XML site map and submit it to search engines, just as you would for your website.

◆ Use *permalinks* (permanent links) to maintain blog URLs permanently.

◆ Use analytics tools to monitor traffic and user behavior.

If you need quick suggestions for good blog keywords, install the free tool at http://labs.wordtracker.com/seo-blogger. It sits next to your blog editor on the screen so that you can consider keyword suggestions as you write.

Long blog pages with lots of responses, including those from spammers, may end up with too many outbound links. Placing an HTML `nofollow` attribute in the code just before links from comments will discourage people from leaving "fake" comments with links to their own sites in hopes of increasing their own search rankings.

Optimizing WordPress

Although WordPress automatically optimizes titles for search engines and generates metatags, you may want to tweak the automated SEO results for important posts. Autogeneration is fine for mundane posts or when you're short on time. For more information on selecting plug-ins, see Book III, Chapter 2.

For more flexibility and additional optimization features, try the All in One SEO Pack at `http://wordpress.org/extend/plugins/all-in-one-seo-pack`.

Make your overall WordPress life easier by reviewing the entire list of plug-ins at `http://wordpress.org/extend/plugins`.

Here are a few things you can do to optimize your WordPress blog posts:

✦ **Swap elements of the blog post title.** Reverse the WordPress default arrangement by putting the post title first, which contains keywords, followed by the name of your blog.

✦ **Use a consistent format for keyword-rich page titles on all pages.** You can set up the format once in your template and apply it everywhere by using the All in One SEO Pack plug-in.

✦ **Insert a longer title description, with more search terms, into the image title field.** WordPress automatically uses the title you give an image as its `<alt>` tag. Insert a longer title description with more search terms into the image title field.

When you write a post and add tags, WordPress automatically adds your tags to its global tag system. The global system determines the WordPress list of hot topics in real time. Users can click any word in the real-time tag cloud to view the most recent posts for that tag.

WordPress, like other blogs, often duplicates content by showing the same posts on archive, author, category, index, and tag pages. To remove duplicate content, which can have a negative effect on SEO, create a `robots.txt` file. See `http://sixrevisions.com/wordpress/optimizing-wordpress-for-search-engines`.

Optimizing Blogger

Contrary to myth, Google doesn't necessarily give preference to blogs hosted on its own service, Blogger. However, Blogger poses some unique advantages and challenges:

+ Blogger templates place `<h1>` through `<h6>` tags into the source code automatically, thereby helping with SEO. You can easily adjust page titles and blog names for the correct heading level in page templates.

+ Blogger lacks theme-related categories, which makes it a little more difficult for you and for theme-based SEO. To overcome that problem, create permalinks that include your categories or directory names. We discuss permalinks in the next section.

+ Because Blogger doesn't provide a related-links feature, create that list of related text links within or at the bottom of each post. These links should lead to your other postings on the same topic. Or, take advantage of unlimited sidebar space to create a separate section for related links above your blogroll.

+ Blogger defaults to weekly archiving, but the time frames for archiving are malleable. Adjust the time frame based on your volume of posts and comments to maintain good keyword density. If you post only weekly, it might make more sense to archive monthly. For an extremely active blog, you might want to archive daily.

+ Creating text links is easy, so use your keywords in links whenever possible.

Assigning permalinks

Because most blogs are created on dynamic, database-driven platforms, their posts don't have fixed web addresses. Links to individual posts disappear after the posting is archived and no longer available on a page. Obviously, that's bad news for inbound links and SEO.

Permalinks (short for *permanent links*) solve that problem by assigning a specific web address to each post. Then individual posts can be bookmarked or linked to from elsewhere, forever.

Most blog software programs, such as WordPress, already offer this option; you just have to use it. If your blog doesn't offer it, you can generate permalinks at `www.generateit.net/mod-rewrite`, though you may need help from your programmer to install them. Try to avoid links that look like this: `www.`*yourblog*`.com/?p=123`. Instead, choose an option to use one or more keywords, such as `www.`*yourblog*`.com/contests/summer-travel-sweepstakes`.

To generate WordPress permalinks, open the Settings option in the Admin panel. From there, select the Permalinks panel and choose a common option or enter your own. (For example, you might want to insert a category.) For new blogs, that's it; for existing blogs, you may need to use the Redirection plug-in as well. For more information, see `http://codex.wordpress.org/Using_Permalinks`. Permalinks on Blogger are a little more complicated. Go to `www.google.com/support/blogger/bin/answer.py?hl=en&answer=41436` for directions.

Optimizing images, video, and podcasts

Because search engines can't directly parse the contents of multimedia, you must take advantage of all opportunities to use your relevant search terms in every metatag, descriptive field, or `<alt>` tag. You can find more about podcasts and video in Book III, Chapter 3.

Make these fields as keyword- and content-rich as you can. In these elements, you can often use existing keyword research, metatags from your website or blog, or optimized text that you've already created:

+ **Title and `<title>` metatag for your content:** This catchy name should include a search term.

+ **Filenames:** Using names such as `image1234.jpg` or `podcast1.mp3` doesn't help with SEO; names such as `PlushBrownTeddyBear.jpg` or `tabbycats-sing-jingle-bells.mp3` are much more helpful. Use terms also in category or directory names.

+ **Tags:** Use relevant keywords, just as you would with other social media.

+ **`<alt>` tags:** Use these tags for a short description with a search term; for example, *Used cat tree for sale.*

+ **Long description metatags:** Follow this example: `longdesc=for sale-gently used, gray, carpeted 6 foot cat tree with 4 platforms.`

+ **Content:** Surround multimedia elements with keyword-rich, descriptive content.

+ **Transcriptions:** Transcribe and post a short excerpt from a keyword-loaded portion of your video or podcast.

+ **Anchor text:** Use keywords in the text link that opens your multimedia file.

+ **Large images:** Upload large versions as well as the thumbnails that are visible on your blog or website.

+ **RSS and XML:** Expand your reach with media RSS and site maps.

For more information on indexing multimedia, see `www.google.com/support/webmasters/bin/answer.py?hl=en&answer=114016`.

TIP

Even though search engines can't read watermarks, you may want to mark both videos and large images with your domain name and logo to encourage visits and for branding purposes.

Optimizing Twitter

In addition to adhering to the standard admonishments about providing good content and using well-researched keywords, you can follow a few extra guidelines to improve your ranking in search results on both internal Twitter searches and on external searches:

✦ **Your name on Twitter acts like a `<title>` tag.** If you want to benefit from branding and to rank on your own or your company name, you have to use it! If you haven't already done this, log in to your Twitter account and click the Settings link. Then change your name.

✦ **Your username, or Twitter *handle*, should relate to your brand, company name, or campaign and be easy to remember.** It can include a keyword or topic area. Change it in the Settings area.

✦ **Pack your one-line bio with keywords.** Your Twitter bio serves as the page description metatag and is limited to 160 characters. Use résumé-style language and include some of your primary search terms. Talk about yourself or your company in the third person. From the drop-down menu on the top right of the page select Settings. Then click the Profile tab in the navigation on the left side of the page and complete the Bio box.

✦ **On the same Profile page, use your business address as your location.** (Or select the Settings option in the drop-down menu and then the Profile tab to modify.) Doing so helps with local searches. Remember to save your changes.

✦ **Collect Twitter followers.** Each follower is essentially an internal, inbound link on Twitter. They carry special value if your followers have a large number of their own followers. As the Twitter variant of link popularity, a good follower count may improve your Google PageRank.

✦ **Include keywords in your tweets and retweets whenever possible so you have more to offer search engines than a time stamp.** With the 140-character limit, Twitter might be a good place to use those single-word terms. Use keywords in your Twitter #hashtags, too.

✦ **Remember the importance of the initial 42 characters of a tweet.** They serve as the `<title>` tag for that post. Your account name will be part of that count. Search engines will index the full tweet, however.

✦ **Format your retweets.** Keep them under 120 characters so there's room for someone to add his or her retweet information at the front. When you retweet, avoid sending duplicate content by changing the message a bit.

✦ **Maximize retweets as a measure of popularity.** Write interesting content or share good articles, especially when the direct link to detailed content goes to your own site.

✦ **Increase your visibility.** When linking to your Twitter profile from other sites, use your name or company name rather than your Twitter handle as the anchor text for the link. (The @ in a Twitter handle for example, @watermelonweb, isn't handled well by search engines.)

Because Twitter adds a `nofollow` attribute to links placed by users, linking to your site doesn't help with PageRank. Truncated URLs (such as the TinyURLs described in Book II, Chapter 1) behave just like their longer-version cousins because they're permanent redirects.

However, links from Twitter still boost branding and drive traffic to your site. More traffic to your site improves your ranking at Alexa (`www.alexa.com`), which in turn improves one of the quality factors Google uses for setting PageRank. It's all one giant loop.

For more information on Twitter, see Book IV.

Optimizing Facebook

Take advantage of myriad opportunities to gain traffic from your Facebook pages by applying optimization techniques. Next to blogs, Facebook pages offer the highest number of opportunities to use SEO on social media to reach people who don't already know you. Fortunately, Facebook search engines can index all shared content on Facebook.

Every social network has different rules for its account names and profiles. Though consistency is preferable for branding purposes, follow the rules carefully. Try these techniques when you first create a Facebook page for your business:

✦ On the initial login page at `www.facebook.com`, click the link labeled Create a Page for a Celebrity, Band, or Business. If you already have a personal account, scroll down any of your pages all the way to the bottom and click the Create a Page for My Business link. Either link takes you to `www.facebook.com/pages/create.php`. (If you create your business page from your personal page, you're automatically listed as the administrator for the page.)

✦ Use an easy-to-remember version of your business name alone or combined with a search term as your Facebook business page name. If possible, use the same username on both Twitter and Facebook for branding reasons. Facebook doesn't like generic names.

When you have at least 25 people connected to your page, you can claim a username as your own at `www.facebook.com/username`, instead of seeing a long string of numbers in your Facebook URL. After you select a name, you cannot change it.

✦ After you create your business page, click the About tab just above the timeline, and then click the pencil icon next to Edit Information. You find several content fields to fill in, which expand when you begin to enter all the essential information.

✦ Under Websites, list all your relevant domain names, including your blog and other social media pages. Later, you can also place links to your website or blog or another type of social media within your page stream. Generally, it's easier to use the actual URL.

✦ Place keyword-loaded content in the first paragraph of each of the remaining boxes, all of which help with on-site product searches. Include your address and contact information in the Company Overview box; address information also helps with local searches. Your page description metatag may work well in the Mission box since it is already optimized for search terms. Be sure to include all your brand names and all the products or services that you offer in the Products box.

✦ As with Twitter, popularity matters. The more Facebook fans you have, the more internal links you have to your own page. Even better, when fans comment on or recommend your content, Google sees reciprocal links between your page and your fans' pages, which may increase your Google PageRank.

✦ More search term opportunities abound if you use iFrame-based solutions to create HTML boxes and tabs. These additional iFrame boxes or tabs can display text, images, and more links. Be sure to use a good search term in your box name (which is limited to ten characters) and include text links in your content. It's a bit of a pain, but you can do this on your own. (Facebook no longer supports or displays content written in Static FBML — Facebook Markup Language.) If you're a page administrator, you can use the apps at `www.hyperarts.com/social-media/tabpress-facebook-app.html` or `https://apps.facebook.com/static_html_plus/?ref=ts`, or find a list at `https://www.facebook.com/search/results.php?q=static%20html&init=quick&tas=0.6347709277179092`. For more information about one of the most popular iFrame apps, see `www.wildfireapp.com`.

For more information on creating a Facebook account and business pages, see Book V.

Optimizing Google+

Not surprisingly, the rules for optimizing Google+ track well with the principles for optimizing websites for Google. To maximize your search engine visibility on Google+, SEO Hacker recommends the following:

✦ Include one of your essential keywords and company name in the title of your Google+ page, just as you would for a `<title>` tag.

+ Copy the page description metatag for your website into the Meta Description field on your Google+ page. You already optimized that tag for several of your important keywords.

+ Because the Introduction section is the body of your Google+ page, you can use the same keyword-optimized content that appears as the first paragraph on your homepage or on other essential pages of your site.

+ Use search terms in the descriptive filenames for the five main photos that appear on your Google+ page.

+ In the Recommended Links section, first link to your website and blog to increase the number of inbound links to those sites. Of course, include links for all your other social media pages, as well.

+ As with your main website, update your Google+ page every two to seven days to indicate activity. When appropriate, you'll find that linking to your Google+ page can help boost your search rankings. It's just another example of Google's self-love!

For more information on creating a Google+ page, see Book VI.

Optimizing Pinterest

With its visual content, Pinterest is perhaps the most challenging social media to optimize for search engines. Take advantage of several tried-and-true techniques to give your Pinterest site some search oomph:

+ Use your four most important search terms and your page description metatag in the About section of your company profile (under Settings).

+ Optimize for local search by including your city, state, and zip code in the Location field of the profile. Of course, include the URL for your website and blog in the website field.

+ Set the Visibility option to OFF in your Profile; you *don't* want to "Hide your Pinterest profile from search engines." Be sure to select the cross-link options to Twitter and Facebook and upload your logo graphic.

+ Use a descriptive filename that includes a keyword for each of the images you pin from your website or blog. The source link for each image will go back to your website or blog to increase your inbound links and drive traffic to specific pages. If you have optimized images on Flickr or other photo-sharing sites, you can use your Flickr URL as the image source for a pin.

At the moment, Pinterest passes link juice only for an image description. Unfortunately, Pinterest has added the `nofollow` attribute to images themselves, thus diminishing the value of those links as repins.

✦ Include keywords in the title *and* description for each board and pin, whether the boards are employee headshots, photos of your company at tradeshows, or images also used on your blog. For local optimization, include your city. You might want to structure boards by customer type, product, service, or brand name to maximize the search terms you use.

✦ If you create data charts or infographics (try one of the tools listed at `http://socialnetworkinglibrarian.com/2011/09/22/10-tools-for-creating-great-info-graphics`), be sure to include keywords in your headline.

✦ Remember to add the linkable Pinterest *icon* and link to your suite of social media buttons on your website, blogs, and other social media pages.

Use only images you own or have permission to use on Pinterest. You're liable for any copyright infringement. Respect the use of any credit lines required by Creative Commons or the owner of the image.

As with other social media, Pinterest is a "back-scratching" site. You "like" me, and I'll "like" you. To increase traffic to your Pinterest posts (and eventually to your website), follow other Pinterest users and boards related to your company, re-pin relevant images, and click their Like buttons.

For more information on creating and using Pinterest for marketing purposes, see Book VII.

Optimizing LinkedIn

LinkedIn (discussed in Book VIII, Chapter 2) doesn't offer quite as many options for SEO as other forms of social media do. Start by including search terms within your profile text, in the descriptions of any LinkedIn groups you start, and within postings to a group. Just keep it gentle and unobtrusive. Follow these steps to optimize your profile and to pass along some SEO credibility:

✦ Use your name or company name in your LinkedIn URL (for example, `www.linkedin.com/in/watermelonweb` or `www.linkedin.com/in/socialmarketing`). Because search engines look at keywords in URLs, this technique makes your company easier to find.

✦ Use content similar to your page description metatag within the first paragraph of your LinkedIn profile. It should already contain some of your primary search terms.

✦ Unlike Twitter, links from LinkedIn to other sites carry link juice. You can have as many as three links on your profile. Set one to your website and another to your blog. Use keyword-based link text on a third link to drive traffic to another page on your site or to another of your social media pages. Nothing says that all links have to lead to different domains.

Gaining Visibility in Real-Time Search

Needless to say, all the emphasis on social media has forced search algorithms to adjust accordingly. Search engines vary in how they handle social media services within natural search results. Google and Yahoo! note your social media presence but don't include individual tweets or posts in results because they're private. However, if you go to www.bing.com/social, you can search for public posts on Twitter, Facebook, or both, by either most recent or best match. (See Figure 2-13.)

Bing also offers a Social option under its More tab (www.bing.com/explore/social) to ask friends for their ideas about your search, for instance when you're looking for a good movie or restaurant.

Book II
Chapter 2

Leveraging Search
Engine Optimization
for Social Media

Search filters

Figure 2-13:
Real-time
search
results
for the
term *small
business* on
Twitter and
Facebook
are easily
visible
within
Bing's
Social
search
results.

Dedicated real-time search engines are available for different services, such as Facebook, Twitter, RSS feeds, and blogs. These engines, some of which are listed in Table 2-5, may also index comments and other elements found only on a particular social media service.

You can't benefit from real-time search unless you're active on Facebook, Twitter, and other services. Looking for something to say? Add your twist on the latest trends in your market sector. For ideas on current topics, use Google Trends (http://google.com/trends) or the hot-topic searches on most social media services.

Table 2-5	Real-Time and Specialty Search Engines for Social Media	
Name	*URL*	*Description*
48ers	www.48ers.com	Real-time search of news and social media across the web; includes Twitter and Facebook
Bing Social Search	www.bing.com/social	Real-time search includes Facebook and Twitter posts
Facebook	www.facebook.com/#!/home.php?sk=lf	Real-time (most recent) search of Facebook for postings and public stories from friends
Google Plus	https://plus.google.com	Most recent posts on Google+ only
Icerocket	www.icerocket.com	Limited real-time search of Twitter, Facebook, images, video or blogs, or search all under Big Buzz
LinkedIn	www.linkedin.com/search	Real-time search built-in for people, jobs, answers, groups
Search Engine Land	http://search engineland.com/the-social-search-revolution-8-social-seo-strategies-to-start-using-right-now-113911	Resource article on real-time and social search
Sency	http://sency.com	Real-rime search engine that searches microblogs and can search certain U.S. and international cities
Stinky Teddy	http://stinky teddy.com	Real-time search that allows you to choose what type (web, news, video, real time, and images) of results you get
Topsy	http://topsy.com	Real-time search for the social web (primarily Twitter, blogs, images, video
Twitter Search	http://search.twitter.com	Real-time Twitter search
Yahoo!	http://search.yahoo.com	Real-time search from Yahoo! (includes Twitter, Yahoo! Blogs, news, Yahoo! Shopping, and videos)

Gaining Traction on Google's New Social Search

Sigh. Nothing ever stands still in the social whirl — or maybe social tornado is a better description.

Regular Google search results for the past hour no longer include Twitter or real-time results from social media channels other than blogs, press release sites, or Google Plus.

Instead, Google has revised its Social Search function to incorporate a belief that social links or mentions from your personal or frequent contacts mean more than others (`http://googleblog.blogspot.com/2012/01/search-plus-your-world.html`). To utilize this option, you must set up a Google+ account. The search results you see depend on the content you and your friends have on your Google+ pages. Whether or not this approach will stick is anybody's guess. Watch the search engine resources in Table 2-4 for news.

In Google's world view, this approach gives small companies a chance to jump over others in search results, leveling a playing field that's impossibly tilted by experienced keyword optimizers. If you want to take advantage of Google's new algorithm, try these steps recommended by Search Engine Land:

✦ **Enhance your Google+ listing with frequent posts, shares, and participation in Google+ Circles.** Google+ results show up in both social search and standard, natural search. For more information on Google+, see Book VI.

✦ **Google is back to popularity contests.** Just as it favors sites with lots of inbound links, Google favors social media pages with many followers. You may need to run a campaign or contest just to gain followers. In the worst case, shameless self-promotion and giveaways may do the trick.

✦ **Post early, post often.** Real-time search creates pressure to update frequently on social media so that you can stay near the top of the results stream. Like voting in Chicago, multiple, recent posts can tip the scale. Schedule times on your Social Media Activity Calendar (found in Book I, Chapter 4) to post to your blog, add to your Facebook timeline, or send tweets at least twice a day. Use management tools like those in Book I, Chapter 4 to make this easier.

✦ **Share and share-alike.** Post lots of keyword-rich content that you're willing to share and explicitly invite others to share it.

✦ **+1 +1 = 3, or maybe 30.** Put Google +1 buttons, as we describe in Book VI, Chapter 3, anywhere and everywhere — on your social media, your website, your newsletters, your forehead. . . .

✦ **Pin your hopes to Pinterest.** The Google spider now crawls pins and boards, looking for relevant keywords. Use hashtag keywords for each pin for extra SEO-om-pa-pa.

✦ **Add Pin It and StumbleUpon buttons to your content.** For referral traffic, these two sites offer special value. Get the boost now, while these sites are highly popular.

To view real-time results in Google+, enter your search term in the search box. When you see results, click the option for Most Recent at the top of the results list. From then on, relevant posts will appear in real time.

Think about which messages are truly time-critical and save your real-time efforts for them. On your Social Media Activity Calendar, enter the times that you expect your target market might be searching, such as first thing in the morning or right before lunch. Make sure to ping all search engines with your updates.

Get some sleep! There's no point tweeting in the middle of the night when your customers are in bed (unless you're selling to insomniacs or international customers halfway around the world). Your tweets may be long buried by tweets from dozens — if not hundreds — of others by the time the sun rises.

Monitoring Your Search Engine Ranking

As always, if you're serious about SEO, you'll want to monitor how well you're doing. Table 2-6 lists some search engine ranking software that shows where your site appears on search engines by keyword or page. Most ranking software carries a charge, but some either offer a free trial or will rank a limited number of pages, keywords, or engines for free.

Table 2-6	Search Engine Ranking Services	
Name	*URL*	*Starting Price*
Google rankings.com	`www.googlerankings.com/ index.php`	Free, need free API key
Rank Tracker	`www.link-assistant.com/ rank-tracker/buy.html`	Free trial; then $99.75
Search Engine Rankings	`www.mikes-marketing-tools.com/ranking-reports`	Free

Name	URL	Starting Price
SERank	www.ragesw.com/products/search-engine-rank.html	$99.95
SiteReportCard	www.sitereportcard.com/checkranking	Free
WebPosition	http://webposition.com	Free 30-day trial; then starts at $29 per month
ZoomRank	www.zoomrank.com	Trial period $4.95; then starts at $7 per month

SEO is a long-term strategy to deliver solid traffic over time to your hub website or blog. It takes time for your investment in SEO to pay off, and results can vary unpredictably from one week or month to the next. Generally, after you have everything set up and running smoothly, monitoring once per quarter should be enough except for exceptionally large and constantly growing sites.

Enter your preferred SEO tools in your Social Media Marketing Plan and insert the tasks into your Social Marketing Activity Calendar.

Chapter 3: Using Social Bookmarks, News, and Share Buttons

In This Chapter

✔ Differentiating between social bookmarks and social news

✔ Gaining marketing benefits from bookmarks

✔ Submitting to social bookmarking sites

✔ Submitting to social news sites

✔ Motivating people to bookmark and rate your site or content

✔ Using social share buttons

Social bookmarks and social news services are essentially peer-to-peer referral networks. Each one is an expansion of the former "tell-a-friend" call to action. Rather than e-mail a link to a site or some content to one or two people, users can notify many people at a time. Advocates of these recommendation services often argue that they filter the avalanche of websites that appear in standard search engines. Because social bookmarks and social news services rely on popular input from "real people" rather than from algorithms, some Internet users place a greater value on these search results.

Hundreds of these services exist, which you can see on the All Services tab at http://addthis.com/services/all. In this chapter, we discuss the benefits of using these services; including higher search engine ranking, more traffic, and free visibility for minimal effort. We also emphasize using share buttons to encourage viral sharing of social media and website content.

 Search engines recognize inbound links from many (but not all) of these services, so appearing on them can improve your search engine ranking. See Book II, Chapter 2 for more information on search engine optimization.

Bookmarking Your Way to Traffic

You most likely already know how to bookmark sites in a browser. Social bookmarking services work in much the same way, but you save bookmarks to a *public* website rather than to an individual computer. Then, users of bookmarking services can easily share links to their favorite sites or content with friends or colleagues (or with the world) while enjoying convenient access to their own bookmarks from any browser, anywhere.

Social bookmarks act as testimonials from one amorphous group of web users to many others. Bookmarking services, such as StumbleUpon and Delicious (shown in Figure 3-1), recommend websites, blogs, videos, products, or content. At StumbleUpon, among other things, users can view bookmarks from their own list of favorites, friends' favorites, or everyone in the StumbleUpon database of submitters. Several subsets of bookmarking services are specific to certain applications (blogs only, for example) or activities (shopping only, for example).

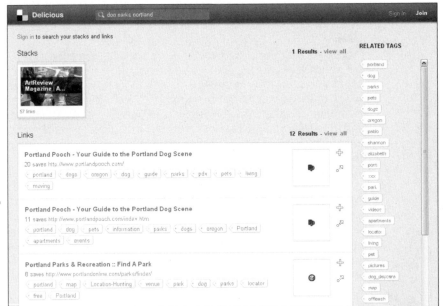

Figure 3-1: Use bookmarking services to recommend websites.

Courtesy AVOS Systems, Inc.

Participating in social bookmarking is a no-brainer. Even if you do no other social media marketing, you should submit your site to several social bookmarking services, if they permit it, as part of your search engine optimization (SEO) efforts. Note that some services may not permit direct submission but will allow you to include a badge on your site to encourage your viewers to submit the site (for example, `http://su.pr`). (Read more about badges in Book II, Chapter 1.)

Users generally search for listings by tag (keyword), category, most recent, most popular, or individual submitter. Bookmarking services rank items by the number of people who have cited them.

Table 3-1 lists some of the dozens of popular social bookmarking services and shows whether you're allowed to submit your own site. The Passes "Link Juice" column indicates whether search engines recognize a link from that service, as discussed in Book II, Chapter 2.

The visibility of your website on search engines improves when you have inbound links from a site that already has a high ranking in search results, but only if it passes "link juice." Search the source code for a site to see whether it contains a `<nofollow>` tag. Sites with a `<nofollow>` tag do not pass "link juice." Without that tag, links "follow" by default.

Table 3-1	Popular Social Bookmarking Services		
Name	*URL*	*Allows Self-Submission*	*Passes "Link Juice"*
BlinkList	`www.blinklist.com`	No	No
Delicious	`http://delicious.com`	No	No
Diigo	`www.diigo.com`	Yes	No
Google Bookmarks	`www.google.com/ bookmarks`	Yes	Yes
Linkroll	`www.linkroll.com`	Yes	No
Mister Wong	`www.mister-wong.com`	No	No
Pinterest	`www.pinterest.com`	Yes	No for images; yes for description
StumbleUpon	`www.stumbleupon.com`	No	Yes
Y! Bookmarks	`http://bookmarks. yahoo.com`	No	Yes

You can find more specialty bookmarks on the eBusiness Knowledgebase list of the top 15 social bookmarking sites:

`www.ebizmba.com/articles/social-bookmarking-websites`

The three largest search engines (Google, Yahoo!, and Bing) also have bookmarking services.

Later in this chapter, we discuss how to research bookmarking services, decide which ones to use, and then submit a site.

Bookmarking with Pinterest

One type of bookmarking site deserves particular attention, especially if you have significant visual content. Pinterest, the online scrapbooking site, is attracting huge audiences and driving traffic to commercial websites, especially in the areas of weddings, home décor, and shopping. ModCloth, a retailer of independently designed fashion and decor, is an example of a company using Pinterest (see Figure 3-2).

Figure 3-2: At Pinterest, companies can use different boards (categories) of images (pins) based on product lines and users' interests.

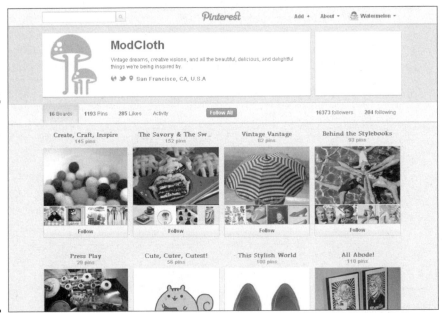

Courtesy ModCloth Headquarters San Francisco, CA 94117

By March 2012, Pinterest had already surpassed 18.7 million unique visitors per month, with "pinners" spending more time on the site than on Twitter, LinkedIn, or Google+ — although far less time than they spend on Tumblr or Facebook. According to ComScore, the demographics are a retailer's dream: 54–70 percent of users are women age 24–35 with incomes of $30,000–$100,000.

For more on Pinterest, see Book VII.

Traffic has skyrocketed for vendors specializing in home, lifestyle, apparel, food, and weddings as users follow pins back to their source. If these are your target markets, start pinning!

Sharing the News

In comparison with social bookmarking services, social news services such as reddit and Digg (shown in Figure 3-3) point to time-sensitive individual postings and articles. Whereas bookmarking services look at sites without reference to timeliness, social *news* services focus on "what's news now."

Users can recommend dozens of different content pages on a particular website to a social news service, quickly driving significant amounts of traffic to the originating site. Many social news services rely on users to "vote" on submissions, with more popular results appearing on the service's front page. Unlike bookmarks, social news services aren't designed to share a list of recommendations with friends.

Figure 3-3 shows recently posted popular articles in the Business News category on Digg. Although most entries link to standard news sources, business press releases and even special offers may appear.

**Book II
Chapter 3**

Using Social
Bookmarks, News,
and Share Buttons

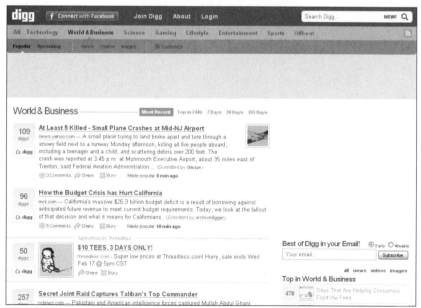

Figure 3-3:
Digg shows links to individual articles submitted by hundreds of thousands of Internet readers.

Courtesy Digg.com

Peer-based recommendations aren't always golden. Because they reflect whoever randomly happens to have posted, these posts may be volatile, biased, and nonrepresentative. They certainly don't reflect scientific results. In fact, you may find some recommended articles shocking or disgusting. Watch the articles that appear for a few days to be sure you feel comfortable with the quality of what people recommend.

Table 3-2 lists some popular social news sites and whether you can submit your own site or press releases. The Passes "Link Juice" column indicates whether search engines recognize a link from that service.

Table 3-2	**Popular Social News Services**				
Name	*URL*	*Uses Popularity Voting*	*Allows Self-Submission*	*Allows Press Releases*	*Passes "Link Juice"*
Buzzup	`http://buzzup.com/us`	Yes	Yes	Yes	Yes
Digg	`http://digg.com`	Yes	Yes	Yes	Yes
Dropjack	`www.dropjack.com`	No	Yes	Yes	No
Fark	`www.fark.com`	No	Yes	Yes	No
I am bored	`www.i-am-bored.com`	Yes	Yes	Yes	No
Metafilter	`www.metafilter.com`	Yes	Yes	Yes	Yes
Newsvine	`www.newsvine.com`	Yes	No	Yes	Yes
reddit	`www.reddit.com`	Yes	Yes, but not often	Yes	No
Slashdot	`http://slashdot.org`	No	Yes	Yes	No

Benefiting from Social Bookmarks and News Services

Social bookmarks and news services offer multiple benefits. To start with, they're free — always a positive factor for online guerrilla marketers. In addition, you may benefit in many other ways by using these services:

✦ **Improved search engine ranking:** By using your primary search terms in tags and other elements of your submissions, you may improve your overall web presence in general search engines. The appearance of your content on these services supplements your own site in general search results.

✦ **Inbound links:** Inbound links from social bookmarking and news services may dramatically improve your position in search engine results and your Google PageRank as well as deliver visitors directly to your site.

✦ **Increased brand visibility and traffic:** The more people who see your website or content listed on one of these services, the more people will remember your name and visit your site. Like many other social marketing techniques, bookmarks and news services help fill the conversion funnel.

✦ **Increased readership and membership:** If you're a writer, pundit, professional speaker, or consultant, these services can be extraordinarily valuable. After you establish a reputation on a service, you may find that you have loyal followers as well as many new readers, subscribers, clients, and speaking gigs.

✦ **Increased earnings:** You can consider people who visit your URL from social bookmarking and news services as prequalified prospects, pushing them farther down the funnel toward "likely buyer" status. Be sure that your site validates the ratings it has earned, though.

✦ **Triggering the influentials:** Many online "influentials" watch social bookmarking and news services to spot trends and decide whether to mention a site or an article in their own blogs or tweets. Of course, submissions by these influential people carry additional value in the eyes of their followers.

Monitor comments about your site to confirm that recommended pages, content, or products continue to appear and that links still work. Visitors shouldn't see 404 File Not Found messages.

Your task is to ensure that your business is listed in the appropriate services and shows up near the top of results. Always review a potential social news service to make sure it's not just a spam aggregator; that postings are recent; what is permitted in its Terms of Use; and how it ranks on Google. Sounds a lot like the process of finding inbound links in the prior chapter, doesn't it?

In the following sections, we talk about researching social news services, selecting the right ones for your business, and submitting to them.

Book II
Chapter 3

Using Social Bookmarks, News, and Share Buttons

For more social news sites, check out

```
http://addthis.com/services/all?c=social_news
http://newinternetorder.com/get-backlinks-social-news-site
www.seodiscovery.org/top-44-niche-social-news-bookmarking-sites-list
```

Researching a Social Bookmark and Social News Campaign

Listing your website, blog, or content initially is easy. You, or others, can post your site on as many services as you want. Being listed high in the rankings is a more difficult task, though.

Check the Terms of Use on these services; in some cases, you cannot submit your own site or content. Many news services have more constraints on the voting process than on submissions.

Here's how to do it:

1. **Research appropriate social bookmarking and news services.**

   For an overview, try Quantcast or Alexa to review the user base, demographics, and traffic statistics for each prospective service. A handy chart on the Trends tab at `http://addthis.com/services` shows traffic trends on the top 50 social media services, or you can select only bookmarking or social news subsets. Generally, you're looking for services that

   - *Receive a lot of traffic*
   - *Specialize in your market niche*
   - *Attract your target market*

2. **Visit each site to confirm that it fits your needs and attracts your audience.**

   To understand more about the kinds of people who use a particular service, look at other top sites bookmarked in your category or at the content rated most favorably. Are the businesses and articles complementary to yours? To your competitors? Are the users of each service likely to try the products or services you offer?

   You can sometimes tell whether an audience might be receptive to your offerings by looking at who's paying for ads on particular pages.

3. **Sort by the names who submitted postings to see which individuals or companies are responsible for most of the public listings.**

   Don't be surprised if the results follow the 80/20 rule: 80 percent of posts will come from 20 percent of users. The top ten submitters are likely to be the influentials on that service.

Executing your plan

Because a distinct effort is involved in recruiting other people to submit your site, select just a few services from your research to begin. Start with the popular ones listed in Tables 3-1 or 3-2 to see whether readers will vote for your content or repost your links on smaller services, saving you the effort.

Some groupthink takes place on these services. If you have a popular post on Digg, for instance, someone may copy it to reddit or StumbleUpon for you. Some services, such as Dropjack, display a list of icons above every story for readers to share elsewhere.

Most users select only one social bookmarking service because they want only one place for their own favorites. That behavior complicates your task because you may need to submit to multiple services to obtain broad coverage. Strive for a realistic balance between coverage and the level of effort you can commit. If you're short of time, don't worry. Start small — you can always do another campaign later.

After you select your list of appropriate services, write them into your Social Media Marketing plan (found in Book I, Chapter 2) with a schedule for regular postings and review. Then create an account and a profile, if appropriate, for each selected service. Finally, submit the URLs for your site (or sites) or content as appropriate. Your schedule will probably reflect

✦ An initial mix of multiple one-time submissions to social bookmarking services

✦ Regular, repeat submissions to one or two social news services, within the constraints of their Terms of Use

✦ Occasional additions to your social bookmarks

✦ Regular monitoring of links to your site and mentions in the cybersocial whirl

WARNING!

Watch for scam services offering hundreds of automated social bookmark submissions. You don't need hundreds, any more than you need hundreds of search engines. Besides, you could end up blacklisted for using them.

Many services offer a toolbar add-in to help users easily submit sites or content whenever they find something they like. You might find it handy to install toolbar add-ins for the specific services you expect to use regularly. Better yet, install a share button (see the section "Using Social Media Buttons" later in this chapter) on your site and use the button to access your suite of accounts.

Monitoring results

As we discuss in Book IX, you always need to monitor the results of all your marketing techniques. Watch traffic statistics to identify which services produce the most referrals and when you see spikes in traffic. Stick with the services that become good referrers, of course, especially if they eventually lead to qualified prospects and sales. Replace the ones that don't work.

Consider trying a tool specifically designed for monitoring appearances on social bookmarking and social news sites, including when others have recommended or rated you. You can use these monitoring tools to assess these elements:

✦ The success of your social bookmarking and social news campaign

✦ The efficacy of one posting compared with another

✦ The unauthorized use of trademarks

✦ The effectiveness of a specific press release or sales promotion

✦ The appearances of your competitors on social bookmarks and news services

Book II, Chapter 1 discusses multiple tools for monitoring mentions of your business or website on social networks and blogs. Many of those tools also monitor bookmarking and news services. You might also want to try

✦ **Alltop.com:** Collects current headlines and lead paragraphs from websites and blogs and sorts by topic

✦ **BuzzFeed.com:** Monitors "hot" stuff online to share

✦ **popurls.com:** Aggregates current headlines from the most popular sites on the Internet

✦ **Social Media for Firefox:** Status bar add-on that displays how many votes content has at Digg, StumbleUpon, Delicious, and reddit

✦ **Trackur:** A fee-based topic search

✦ **WhosTalkin.com:** A free topic search for multiple social media sites

Submitting to Bookmarking Services

Consider submitting URLs to bookmarking services from a personal, rather than business, address or have friends or employees use their personal e-mail addresses as the submission source. Use neutral, nonpromotional language in any comment or review. Figure 3-4 shows how to submit a site to Delicious.com, a popular social bookmarking service. Submitting to social bookmarking services is usually very simple: Create an account and submit a URL with a brief description.

Courtesy AVOS Systems, Inc.

Figure 3-4:
A submission to Delicious.com social bookmarking service.

Try to use appropriate search terms in category names, tags, text, or titles when you submit your site. Select terms that searchers are particularly likely to use. Generally, you can find those terms in traffic statistics for your website or in tag clouds (a graphic display of search terms that appear in an article, with the most frequently used terms appearing in a large font) from the target service. (Read about tag clouds in Book II, Chapter 2.) Enter your site in as many categories as possible.

If you have separate domain names or subdomains for your blog or community site, submit a few of them as bookmarks, along with your primary website, as long as the number is reasonable (say, less than 6). You can also post social bookmarks to where links are permitted on Facebook or LinkedIn or other social networking pages to further enhance your visibility. Just don't personally submit too many of your own pages to one bookmarking site lest you become marked as a spammer.

Be discreet. Do not spam social bookmarking or news services with multiple frequent submissions. Although you can organize a few submissions from others to get the ball rolling, don't set up multiple accounts per user on a social news service to vote for yourself or use automated submitters, which not only might have malware but also might be prohibited. Like regular search engines, these social services act aggressively to detect and blacklist spammers. Read the Terms of Use on every site if you have questions.

Submitting to Social News Services

Think of social news services as peer-reviewed indexes to short-term, contemporary articles, whereas social bookmarks are more useful for longer-term content. Submitting frequently to social news services is not only acceptable but also practically obligatory, particularly if your site generates news within a particular industry or geographical region or if your livelihood is content dependent. Generally, with most social news services, you must create an account first and then submit content.

Because users are in and out of these services often, you always need new content to catch their attention. These users prefer peer-recommended stories versus ones selected by staff editors or that appear in an unfiltered RSS feed from other sources.

People who view your content are asked to "vote" stories up or down and are often given an opportunity to comment as well. You generally need to create an account to post, vote, or comment on stories, but anyone can read the listings.

Always select appropriate categories for your material, such as Technology, World News, Politics, Business, Entertainment, Life Style, or Environment. Avoid vague categories such as General, Other, or Miscellaneous — they're deep, dark pits from which your content may never escape!

Selecting content for social news services

Content choice is critical. Not every item on your blog or website will entice readers to submit or rate an article. Generally, the ones that drive the most traffic to your site will have timely content, such as breaking news; or entertainment, humor, or quality resource information not found elsewhere.

Keep the following in mind when deciding what to post on social news services:

✦ **Social news services are culturally dependent.** If you are trying to reach an international market, you may need to submit your content in languages other than English. Note that other countries and languages might have their own localized social bookmarking and news services. Visit `http://addthis.com/services/compare-countries` or international search engines to identify them.

✦ **Avoid out-of-date material:** If you must submit older stories, look for such items as features, interviews, how-to's, and essays that have longer-lasting interest. Those items are good for social bookmarking sites, too.

✦ **Match your content submissions to sites where readers like the types of stories you want to recommend:** Look at the tag cloud for frequency of use on tags similar to yours over the past 6 to 12 months.

✦ **Select the services with features that best match the content you have to offer and the audience you're trying to reach:** Some social news services allow links to images, video, and audio; others accept only links to text.

✦ **Think tactically:** Initiate posts for specific pages, posts, or articles that have the potential to lead to traffic, prospects, or sales, not for your everyday internal "company news" update.

If you get a reputation for posting meaningless items or using the comment space for hard-sell language, you might find it hard to gain traction on these sites; you might even be banned for posting junk.

Preparing social news stories for success

Although you might be tempted to splatter social news services with your stories, just give them a little thought. Set up tags, titles, and lead lines carefully. Follow these online journalistic steps for improved results:

✦ **Write a catchy headline, not an academic title.** Keep headlines short and memorable. Try to use "vivid" verbs (not just nouns) and active voice. Instead of "New social media app created by local company" for your star-gazing app, try "AstroWare's New App Rockets to the Stars."

✦ **Write a good lede.** The headline and first line of a story (the *lede*) are often the only elements that viewers see. Set a "hook" to catch readers and make them want to link back to your original content. Tell people what's in it for them or how they will benefit by reading the story.

✦ **Write a good description, comment, or summary.** Keep it short (20 to 25 words!) and focus on benefits.

**Book II
Chapter 3**

Using Social
Bookmarks, News,
and Share Buttons

✦ **Check your facts, spelling, and links.** If you make errors, someone is likely to post a negative comment. If your links don't work, you lose potential traffic — a primary reason you're using social bookmarking and news services in the first place.

✦ **Prepare your site for success.** Just in case, be sure to structure your site to take advantage of new traffic. Links to related articles on your site or blog give interested readers more than one story to explore, thus increasing the number of page views per visit. To increase conversion rates, use calls to action and visual reminders to sign up for RSS feeds and newsletters, subscribe to a paid publication, or make a purchase.

✦ **Serving up your site.** Be sure that your hosting package allows for increased traffic. Traffic from social bookmarks tends to build slowly, but an appearance on the front page of a social news site can flood your server with more traffic than it's set up to handle. A quick call to your host or IT department should confirm your preparations.

These writing tactics not only help attract the kind of viewers who are more likely to click-through but also help increase the time users spend on your blog or website.

Using Application-Specific Bookmarks

Some bookmarking and social news services are constrained to specific types of content, such as blogs or video, and others are specific to topic, or activity, such as shopping or product reviews. Table 3-3 provides some examples.

Table 3-3	Bookmarks for Specific Applications
Name	*URL*
Blogs	
BlogCatalog	www.blogcatalog.com
Bloglines	www.bloglines.com
Product, Software, and Travel Reviews	
Epinions	www.epinions.com
SnapFiles	www.snapfiles.com/userreviews/latest.html
TripAdvisor	http://tripadvisor.com

Name	URL
Shopping	
Kaboodle	www.kaboodle.com
Stylehive	www.stylehive.com
ThisNext	www.thisnext.com
Sports	
FanNation	www.fannation.com
Video	
myVidster	www.myvidster.com
Simfany	www.simfany.com

You can find more shopping bookmark sites at

www.pcmag.com/slideshow/story/293956/the-rapid-ascension-of-pinterest-
   and-social-shopping-sites/1

and more sports sites at

www.seoprimary.com/social-bookmarking-websites-sport.html

Search for *topic area + bookmarking site* on any search engine to find more specialty bookmarking services.

Timing Your Submissions

As with search engines, getting yourself on the first page of bookmarking and social news services can be difficult. You generally have only a 24-hour window on social news services to attract enough attention for either lasting value or timeliness. Remember that you may need to coordinate submissions by others to get things started.

There's no point in posting in the middle of the night, when many people are asleep on one side of the country or both. Generally, posting between 10 a.m. and 4 p.m. U.S. Central time works well, with an anecdotal peak of best results around 3 p.m. Workdays are generally better for generating traffic, although weekends see less competition. Of course, you need to adjust submission times if "getting a scoop" is critical or if you seek visibility on an international site.

On the other hand, if you're posting to specific bookmarking services, such as a social shopping or sports bookmarking site, that isn't time-dependent, weekends may find more of your audience available. It's a lot like scheduling an e-newsletter delivery or press release, both of which are audience dependent.

Your best bet is to experiment for yourself. Try submitting the same post to different services at different times of the day, or try submitting different posts to the same service at different times. Monitor traffic to your site by the hour and day, and adjust your plans accordingly.

Generally, social bookmarks drive traffic to your site slowly as people find your URL, but you can generate a spike in traffic by pushing your site on social news services (if they permit it). You can ask several people to submit your site, but leave it to others to vote it up or down.

Try to get 15 to 25 people to submit your posting within the first few hours of its publication. That's usually enough to get attention from others and build momentum for votes. Receiving 25 recommendations within a few hours means a lot more than receiving 25 recommendations within a week!

As your visibility on the service rises, so, too, does traffic to your site.

For all the value these services may have as "recommendation" search engines, the traffic on them is nothing compared with traffic on major search engines, such as Google, Yahoo!, or Bing. Optimization for general search engines is still absolutely necessary, as discussed in Book II, Chapter 2, and forms the basis for your success.

Pinning success on social media

ModCloth (www.modcloth.com) is an innovative online retailer of independently designed fashion and decor. Social Media Manager Natasha Khan sees the company's mission as "nurturing a fun and engaging community and bringing indie designer products to market with customer feedback." Through ModCloth's Be the Buyer program, customers actually "vote" items from emerging designers into production.

Started as an online, vintage clothing shop from a college dorm room by co-founder Susan Gregg Koger, ModCloth has grown into a thriving business with more than 275 employees. With its college origins, social media channels were an obvious marketing fit. Khan says the company selects social channels based demographic match, number of active users, and its ability to participate authentically.

Bookmarking sites like Stumbleupon, Kaboodle, and Polyvore were originally at the forefront for visual discovery. The amount of traffic they drove to the website was proof that ModCloth's products and aesthetic resonated with their audiences.

"Kaboodle and Polyvore are great tools for styling outfits and sharing the final product with peers or consumers," explains Khan. "ModCloth's team of stylists 'clips' products onto Kaboodle and Polyvore to create 'styleboards' for our community and in response to individual customer requests, on a daily basis. However, she emphasizes, "The majority of the bookmarked ModCloth product on these sites is still customer-generated."

ModCloth was an early adopter of Pinterest, launching its brand account in Fall, 2011. With its audience of 18–34-year-old women, it's a perfect demographic match for ModCloth. "Our customer values creativity, wants to be unique, enjoys expressing herself through style, and she tends to like certain authors [like Jane Austen], books, or movies," Khan notes.

The most shared content on Pinterest also matches the type of editorial content that ModCloth generates, such as do-it-yourself crafts, fashion, and food. Following Pinterest etiquette, ModCloth pins a diverse range of topics beyond its product selection. Some of the individual "pins" on its Pinterest boards link back to ModCloth's website or blog.

Courtesy ModCloth Headquarters San Francisco, CA 94117

(continued)

**Book II
Chapter 3**

**Using Social
Bookmarks, News,
and Share Buttons**

(continued)

"We also saw [Pinterest] creeping up within our referral sources, heading toward number one. Since we launched our brand presence, we've seen our traffic from Pinterest grow by 1000%," Khan enthuses. "[One] customer said that [she] loved seeing ModCloth get so much attention on Pinterest, but was disappointed those products were now quickly selling out. Yes, social book-marking sites are generating sales!"

Modcloth also participates actively on Facebook and Twitter, which host the full spectrum of its demographic, on Tumblr and Youtube, which skew younger (13–18), and on specific interest communities like GoodReads. Khan supplements free social media with paid advertising on Facebook and Twitter to target niche marketing segments. For ModCloth, the ads have also been a successful tool for customer acquisition and revenue.

Social media mean more than sales, Khan adds. Customer service and happiness are objectives on all their social channels. ModCloth usesTwitter and Facebook to respond to customer concerns, and it takes advantage of SproutSocial, a third-party monitoring and scheduling tool for Facebook and Twitter, to oversee customer engagement.

For a company this size and with such an extensive social presence, social media has to be a team effort. "Content creators in the writing, blog, video, styling, PR, and recruiting teams are internal brand advocates producing engaging content," Khan says. "Our social team is responsible for the strategy and ROI of each channel. . . . We build schedules for each channel, taking into account the best times to post and messaging needs. We also take care not to over-message our audience as it leads to un-follows."

Early on, Modcloth decided to respond to customers in the first person and remind them that there is a person behind each response. Thus, they sign Twitter/Facebook posts with initials and created a flock of "Social Butterflies" to engage with customers.

For all their success, Khan has some cautions. "The difficulty with social media is that unlike other marketing areas, there is not a lot of research, especially industry-specific research. The field is also at the whim of the social giants (Facebook, Twitter, YouTube). Facebook will release an update, and social media folks around the world have to scramble to adjust their strategy and tactics."

She speaks with the rueful voice of experience. "Social media is a new frontier, and there are a lot of experts who claim to have the magic formula. What makes sense for one company might not make sense for another." ModCloth tries to hold to a set of strong internal values: empowering teams to leverage social media; building a clear voice; creating content that delights viewers and earns clicks; treating customer service as an engagement strategy; and monitoring the social atmosphere for company buzz and sentiment.

Succeeding on Pinterest, Khan concludes, starts with your product and your website. "To motivate users to share your content on visual discovery and bookmarking platforms, your content has to be visually appealing and easy to share as image files. Building a Pinterest brand page and adding Pinterest buttons to your site will encourage your community to pin your site images and also keep you top-of-mind when they are participating on the platform."

ModCloth's web presence

www.modcloth.com

http://pinterest.com/modcloth/pins

http://blog.modcloth.com

www.kaboodle.com/modcloth

www.facebook.com/ModCloth

http://modcloth.polyvore.com

http://modcloth.tumblr.com

http://web.stagram.com/n/modcloth

https://twitter.com/#!/modCloth

www.youtube.com/modcloth

http://www.modcloth.com/storefront/products/be_the_buyer

www.flickr.com/groups/modclothstyleexchange

www.modcloth.com/storefront/ products/product_feed (RSS)

www.modcloth.com/sms-signup

Encouraging Others to Bookmark or Rate Your Site

Like most political campaigns, the "popularity" contest on services that rely on votes or frequency of submission can be managed to your advantage. It just takes a little preplanning. Although illegal vote-rigging and outright manipulation are forms of cyberfraud, these techniques are valid ways to encourage others to submit or rate your site.

✦ **We all get by with a little help from our friends.** Always have other people submit your material; on some services, submission by others is required. One easy way is to e-mail a circle of employees, colleagues, and friends to help when you post a new page or content, or help them set up RSS feeds from your selected services. Ask them to submit or comment on your posting within a few hours after being notified.

✦ **Scratch backs.** In addition to posting your own stories, recommending material on other sites that complement yours (as long as you don't drive traffic to your competition) is good practice. If you help others increase the ratings on their stories through your repostings and votes, they're more likely to return the favor. These practices establish your reputation as a fair-minded individual who's interested in the topic, not just in sales.

+ **Be a courteous responder.** You make friends and influence people by responding to comments on your stories and commenting on others. Again, one good turn deserves another. Consider it as building your cyberkarma.

+ **Become known as the "go-to" poster.** If you frequently post interesting material on one service, you may develop a reputation and a following, with readers watching for new items from you. They will happily rate or rank items you suggest.

+ **Ask.** People who visit your site might be willing to let others know about it, but you need to remind them. Put a call to action or share button at the end of a story or post, reminding them to tell a friend or share your content publicly. If you've decided to focus on a particular service, display its icon with a link (see the later section "Using Social Media Buttons"). You might even include a call to action to install a toolbar.

Don't confuse *popularity* — a subjective and manipulated quantity — with the *quality* of leads that a bookmark or social news mention may generate. Popularity is a means, not an end. Ultimately, you're better off with fewer, but higher-quality, visitors arriving at your site.

Swapping bookmarks

Like exchanging reciprocal links to improve search engine ranking, exchanging bookmarks has become common practice. Like linking, bookmark swapping can be done honestly, but it has a darker side.

Follow the same principles as you do with links:

+ Don't exchange bookmarks with spam-like junk sites — only with ones that offer value.

+ Be suspicious of people who offer to sell bookmarks or votes.

+ Look for relevance, including shared tags or search terms, as well as traffic rankings on the exchanging site.

Because submitting too many of your own pages to a bookmarking service can tag you as a spammer, you can participate in a service in which members bookmark each other. These are similar to some of the old link exchanges, banner exchanges, and web rings. Be cautious. Avoid anything that looks illegitimate.

If you have no friends or colleagues to help you out, you might examine the options of piqqus (www.piqqus.com) for exchanges among Digg and StumbleUpon; http://bookmarkinghub.com or www.lavalinx.com/social-bookmarking.lava offer more comprehensive exchange services.

Avoid automated submission services or scripts. The safest way to participate in social bookmarking is the old-fashioned way: individually, by hand.

Using Social Media Buttons

Social media buttons have two functions: Follow Us buttons crosslink visitors to multiple elements of your web presence; Share buttons enable visitors easily to share your content or website with others. Place buttons consistently near the top of a page or article, where you place key information.

When you repeat smaller versions of the buttons at the end of each post on your blog, users can share a specific item instead of the entire blog. Social media buttons can also be placed on e-newsletters and on multiple social media networks. Anecdotal evidence from some companies that tried organized campaigns shows dramatic increases in traffic on their social media sites.

Follow Us buttons

Follow Us buttons, shown in Figure 3-5 — sometimes called *chicklets* — link visitors to other elements of your web presence, such as to your Facebook profile, Twitter page, or blog. In Figure 3-5, the chicklets in the left navigation on every page of Mountain Springs Lake Resort & Lodge website encourage users to link the user to the Resort's pages on Facebook, YouTube, and LinkedIn. Some services, such as the photo-sharing site Flickr and the community-building site Ning, provide large, customizable graphical badges to promote a link to your alternative presence.

Figure 3-5: On every page of its website, Mountain Springs Lake Resort & Lodge includes chicklet links to its social media pages.

Courtesy Mountain Springs Lake; www.MSLresort.com

Follow Us buttons

Almost all services offer free standard icons along with code to insert them. Alternatively, you can search for creative icons online at sites like

www.evohosting.co.uk/blog/web-development/design/more-free-social-media-icons

www.1stwebdesigner.com/freebies/amazing-free-social-media-icon-packs

and create your own link, or use a social bookmark links generator, such as Keotag (www.keotag.com/sociable.php).

Share buttons

Social share buttons from services like AddThis.com offer a drop-down box with sharing options, as shown in Figure 3-6. This approach lets visitors easily share content by linking them to the sign-in page for their own accounts on other social sharing services. In an interesting variation, www.shareaholic.com/publishers/get_share_button offers buttons that rise up as a user hovers on them (shown on NMSBDC.org in Figure 3-6). Several sources for other social share buttons are listed in Table 3-4.

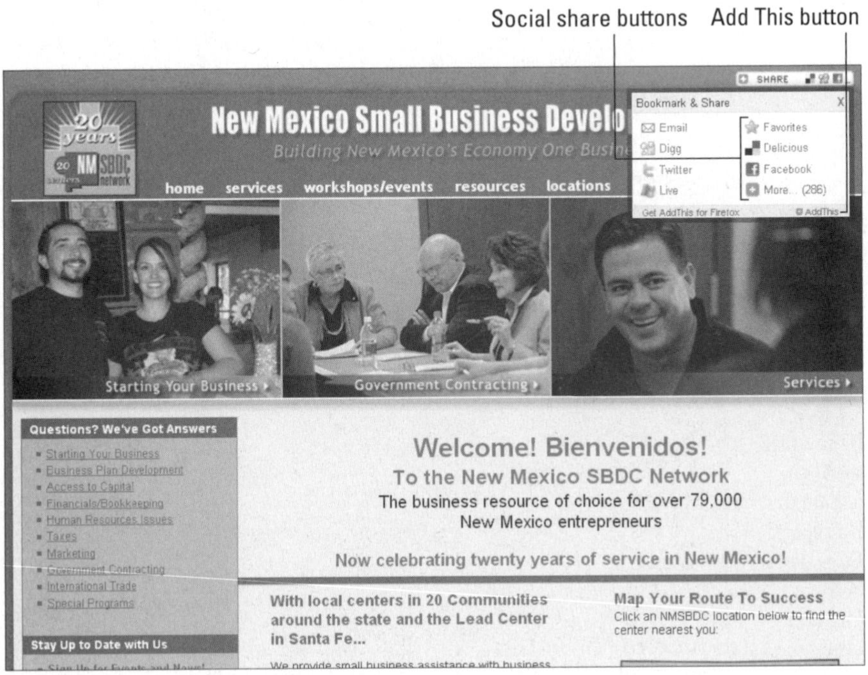

Social share buttons   Add This button

Figure 3-6:
Social share buttons encourage visitors to pass along your site or content through their own accounts.

Courtesy New Mexico SBDC

Table 3-4	Sources for Social Share Buttons
Name	*URL*
AddThis	http://addthis.com
Shareaholic	www.shareaholic.com
ShareThis	http://sharethis.com
Smart Addon	www.smartaddon.com
Social Notes Widget for Products	www.strongmail.com/products/ social-media-marketing/ socialnotes

These free, easy-to-install buttons allow users to transfer content quickly to their own profiles, blogs, preferred social bookmarking service, instant messages, e-mail, or text messages. You can even use a special Social Notes widget from www.strongmail.com/products/social-media-marketing/ socialnotes that facilitates sharing of products from your e-commerce site, as shown in Figure 3-7. This is viral marketing at an epidemic level!

Register for free analytics on sharing services that offer it to see how and where users elected to share your material or site. You can often find a tool-bar add-on for each service on the site. You may want to install the ones you need in your browser and offer that option to your users in a call to action.

Figure 3-7: Widgets, like Social Notes from StrongMail, enable users to recommend products directly from your online store.

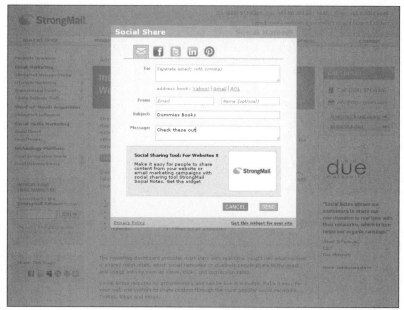

Always include Print, E-mail, and Favorites (for personal bookmarks) in your set of social share buttons. Some people like the convenience of the "old stuff."

If you aren't comfortable inserting code on your site, ask your web developer or programmer to do it for you. Sometimes even your hosting company can help. Specify which Follow Us or share buttons you want to have visible and ask to have the buttons appear on every page of your site.

If all these tasks seem overwhelming, plenty of providers are willing to help you for a fee. Most SEO firms, press and public relations firms, online marketing companies, specialized social marketing ad agencies, and copywriters who specialize in online content now offer assistance with social bookmarking, social news, and other forms of social media marketing. Try searching for *social media services, social media agencies, digital media marketing,* or s*ocial media marketing.*

We discuss more advanced methods for integrating social media into your overall marketing plans in Book VIII, Chapter 8.

Book III

Blogs, Podcasts, and Video

Contents at a Glance

Chapter 1: Growing Your Brand

In This Chapter

✔ Discovering the world of content marketing

✔ Considering your choices

✔ Creating a content marketing plan

✔ Working with social media tools

*E*verything you see online is content — the written word, images, podcasts, radio, video, and so on. Content can amuse or teach, but it's also a powerful tool for catching the attention of the search engines and the people who are looking for whatever it is you do. Many businesses are discovering how to use the different types of content to reach customers and raise brand awareness with positive results.

In this chapter, we go over the different types of online content so that you can determine whether some or all content platforms suit your needs. While you need to consider many points, remember you don't have to do it all. You can use any one or some of these platforms to market your business.

Exploring Online Content

Today is a wonderful time to be in business. Thanks to the web, you can use endless tools to promote your business or brand, and many of them are free. If you have a way with words or a flair for the dramatic, you can sell your product or service online. All you need to do is tap into your creativity. Using online content to promote your personal or business brand can mean the difference between "local" and "global."

Not all content is created equal. For example, blogs are usually text or image heavy, while podcasting and video require recording equipment and a little more technical knowledge. However, all are doable and easy to maintain, and all have the ability to drive traffic and sales and raise awareness for your brand product or service.

Blogging about your brand

Blogs, such as the one shown in Figure 1-1, are no longer link-heavy, personal journals used to describe one's day or give a daily rant. Businesses now use blogs as marketing tools to share updates and industry-related news and offer tips, recipes, or ideas for using products and services.

The good news is that even if your background isn't in writing or web design, you can easily maintain a regular blog. All you need is a way with words and the ability to write in a conversational tone; it's the conversational aspect that sets blogs apart from more newsy and antiseptic articles.

Figure 1-1: You can use blogs to share news or expertise.

The reason people enjoy reading blogs so much is because of the simple language and the ability to add their own comments. At the other end of the spectrum, blogs allow businesses to engage with their customers or community in a new way.

Additionally:

✦ **Blogging catches the attention of the search engines.** If you're looking for a heavier Internet presence, you most likely want people to be able to find you when they're searching Google, Yahoo!, or other search engines. Blogging is perfect for this purpose. With the right content and daily updates to your blog, there's no reason why you shouldn't land in the top results for any number of search terms. (For more content tips, see the section "Introducing Your Content to the Online World," later in this chapter.)

✦ **Blogging catches the attention of the people using the search engines.** With the right headlines, *keywords* (the words and terms people use when using the search engines), and images, web searchers are intrigued enough to land on one of your pages. If your blog is informative, they may even be intrigued enough to explore several different pages.

✦ **Blogging is shareable.** When people find something they like online, they share it via e-mail or on one of the social networks. When a blog post touches on an interesting or sensitive topic, your readers will likely want to pass it on.

✦ **Blogging allows everyone to join the conversation.** Most blogs allow for comments at the bottom of each blog post. Readers love to comment because it gives them the opportunity to add their own thoughts and opinions and share experiences.

✦ **Blogging allows you to manage your reputation.** Sometimes people say something about a business or brand that isn't nice. Sometimes rumors fly. Sometimes you just need to set the record straight. Blogging allows you to speak to your community at a time when you need them most.

✦ **Blogging builds expertise.** When you share tips on a regular basis, you're seen as someone who is knowledgeable in your field. You may even get a reputation as someone who really knows his stuff.

✦ **Blogging can make you the go-to person for the subject matter.** With regular blogging, journalists, authors, conferences, and even other bloggers are likely to contact you for interviews and speaking engagements and to write articles or guest blog posts so that you can share your knowledge with their communities.

✦ **Blogging enables you to grow your community.** When you have regular readers who comment on your blog and share your blog posts, they become your online community. Your community advocates for you and helps spread the word about your brand, product, or service. (We talk more about building an online community in Book III, Chapter 2.)

✦ **Blogging is inexpensive.** Most blog platforms don't cost anything to use. Your biggest expense will be hosting and possibly hiring someone to create a custom design or handle your blogging, if you decide not to do it yourself. However, blogging is one of the least expensive marketing tools you can use.

✦ **Blogging allows you to update thousands of people at one time.** As your community grows and more people read your blog each day, it will become a place where you can update your customers on promotions, news, updates, and new product information.

✦ **Blogging allows you to connect with other businesses, brands, and experts.** Blogs are wonderful networking tools. They allow you to link to people you respect and receive link backs in return. You may even discover that influential people in your niche are following your blog and participating in your conversations.

✦ **Blogging allows you to add personality to your business.** The beauty of blogging is the conversational tone. Because the writing is more casual than news articles, you can add humor and personality to your blog posts. Readers appreciate this lighthearted approach because they don't feel as if they're being talked down to.

✦ **Blogging builds trust.** When you keep your community updated and use your blog as a two-way communication tool, you build trust among your customers and community. People won't feel you have something to hide if you're open and honest on your blog, which gives them a good feeling about using your product or service.

✦ **Blogging is easy.** After you set up your blog and it's ready to roll, maintaining it is easy. In most cases, all you need to do is type the day's blog post and add the necessary links, images, or other bells and whistles.

What types of businesses can benefit from blogs? Truthfully, anyone with a story to tell or a product can benefit from having a blog, but some brands benefit more from this form of content than others. For example, blogs are perfect for product-oriented brands.

Some items that product-oriented brands can blog about are

✦ **Ingredients:** If you take pride in using wholesome ingredients, you should talk about it often. It's an important message and strong selling point. In fact, each individual ingredient can be turned into at least one blog post — probably more.

✦ **Recipes:** If you add two parts water to your household cleaning product, can it be used to clean stains off a rug? Can your brand of peanut butter be used as the base for a number of different dishes? Blog about it!

✦ **Uses for the products:** Vinegar has at least 100 different uses; how about your product? If your product can do a variety of different things, talk about it.

✦ **Launches and product news:** Do you have a new product on the horizon? Are you opening up shop in a new location? These items are worthy of a blog post.

✦ **A behind-the-scenes peek:** Your customers and community would love to know that you and the other people who work for your brand are real. Announce promotions. Take photos around the office. Show your employees hard at work or goofing off, er, team-building. Make your community feel as if they're in on a secret.

A common mistake brands make when blogging is to assume every update has to be a sales pitch or product-oriented content. The best blogs barely sell. Instead, they focus on the benefits of the product. Go beyond the obvious, and you'll have a blog people want to buy.

Here are a few ways to determine whether a blog is right for you:

✦ **You want to save money:** Like most social media, blogs don't have to be expensive to maintain. If you're the do-it-yourself type, you can install and maintain the blog on your own. However, most brands hire professionals to design and write for the blog. The cost is still minimal compared to heavy marketing and advertising campaigns.

✦ **You want to rank higher in the search engines:** The more content you create, the more opportunities you have for people to find your content on the search engines.

✦ **You want feedback from your community:** Blogs are a terrific way to gather feedback. When you post a topic, your community responds, especially if you ask questions throughout your post. Your blog content is a terrific way to gauge your community's wants and needs.

✦ **You want to sell:** Make no mistake. If you turn your blog posts into sales pages, you're going to lose readers. However, all the content you create around your product or service makes it more attractive. The more people know about your brand, and the more transparent you are with your community, the more likely they are to buy.

✦ **You want to share news:** Blogs are a good way to share news and updates with your customers and potential customers. In the past, you had to do so via expensive snail mail newsletters or by placing ads. Nowadays, blog posts keep your customers informed with little cost to you.

✦ **You want others to share your news:** The potential for word of mouth marketing is greater with blogs. If your news is interesting and important, and if you have your blog set up with the proper share buttons, your community will help you to promote.

Just about any business or business person can benefit from regular blogging. If you have something to say, or something to sell, blogs are a simple, cost-effective solution to reach many people at once.

Building a blog takes time. You have to update it often and monitor it several times a day for comments. You also have to promote it on the social networks so your community can learn when you share new blog posts. And don't expect to see massive traffic when you're just starting out. The best blogs have a slow, steady growth rate.

We discuss the finer points of blogging as a marketing tool in Book III, Chapter 2.

Book III
Chapter 1

Growing Your Brand

Podcasting to your audience

The written word and accompanying images are all well and good, but maybe your target customers have no time to read blog posts (see preceding section) and prefer to watch or listen to content while doing other things. Or maybe your target market is highly mobile and prefers to receive its daily enlightenment from a portable device, such as a smartphone or MP3 player.

A *podcast* is similar to Internet TV or a radio broadcast in that you can record your thoughts and allow others to listen, either on your own website or blog or by an iTunes download. Podcasts can be video, but many are audio only. Like a blog post, the podcast is filled with information of interest to your customers or the people who use your product or service. What's also fun about podcasts is how you can bring in special guests or add music or sound effects, if you're so inclined.

However, podcasts are different from Internet TV or a radio broadcast in that programming is not always regular, and you can't necessarily click a button and instantly listen live. Though there are live podcasts, most are recorded ahead of time and shared with a community.

Podcasting is a natural fit if you (or a team member) are entertaining, have a pleasing voice, and the gift of gab.

Here are some podcasting guidelines:

+ **Remember that getting started is simple.** All you need is a good microphone and software program to record the podcast, and you're in business. (Well, it's almost that simple.)

  If you want to show viewers how to use a piece of software, show how a product works, or manage a task, consider a video podcast.

+ **Capture the excitement of live events.** Many podcasters now host their shows live from conferences, meetups, award shows, and more.

+ **Podcast wherever you are.** You can record a podcast almost anywhere. If you're creating a podcast at a live event, you can use a small handheld recorder — a professional-quality recorder, of course — or even your smartphone. If you're recording a podcast at home, all you need is a laptop computer, a good microphone, web cam for video podcasts, and a quiet room.

We talk more about podcasting and why it makes a terrific marketing tool in Book III, Chapter 3.

Video blogging: Marketing with video

Podcasting and blogging are fun and productive ways to promote your business. But what do you do when you need to create a series of videos to promote a product or, for that matter, yourself? In this case, try *video blogging* — the process of creating a series of videos about a product, service, or concept. You can use a video hosting service, such as YouTube (see Figure 1-2), to host your videos and then embed them in your blog or website.

Figure 1-2: Use video when you want to create a more personal touch.

Book III
Chapter 1

Growing Your Brand

Video blogging, which bears a striking resemblance to a video podcast, is podcasting's little brother. The difference is how the content is delivered. Video podcasts stand alone and are delivered to the consumer via RSS 2.0 — a form of content syndication.

You produce video as needed rather than on a schedule. Though video blogging can be similar to podcast production, the frequency of delivering content is a big difference.

Video blogging has many uses. For example:

✦ **Educational videos for customers or employees:** You can use video to let existing customers or potential clients take a behind-the-scenes look at your business. For example, if your company manufactures a product, a series of videos of this type is a helpful way to show clients and potential customers the quality and craftsmanship that go into your product.

✦ **Slice-of-life videos, such as a wedding photographer working with a bride:** A few still images sprinkled in a video give a prospective bride an idea of how the photographer interacts with her clients as well as a sample of the finished product.

✦ **Emotional appeals, such as for a charitable or political campaign:** Your tone and facial expressions often convey what text-heavy content can't. Use video for when you need to tug at heartstrings or make a personal plea.

Many brands are also experimenting with humorous videos in hopes of going viral on YouTube and the social networks. This approach doesn't always lead to sales, but it does lead to brand recognition and a very good vibe.

When you create videos to promote your company, you need to put your best foot forward — no garbled sound or pixilation allowed. Many digital cameras are capable of capturing stunning high-definition video and stereo sound. For much better results, use the best video and audio equipment you can afford.

Before jumping into video blogging, consider the bandwidth available for your website. (Ask your web host, if you aren't sure.) If lots of people access your videos, you can exceed the allowable bandwidth for your Web hosting package and incur extra charges that may be quite hefty.

To bypass these charges, look at free video sharing services that can host your videos, such as YouTube (www.youtube.com). YouTube saves server space, keeps costs down, and allows for easy sharing and captioning.

We discuss video blogging in Book III, Chapter 4.

Determining Content Goals

Before you determine what type of content works best for you, you need to sit down and list your content marketing goals. Not everyone's marketing campaign is created equal, and not everyone needs to use the same methods in their campaigns.

Consider these goals:

✦ **To drive traffic:** If your goal is to drive traffic to your website, blogs are a terrific way to do so. With the right keywords, headlines, and phrases, you'll catch the attention of the search engines, and the people who are searching for your type of business may land on your pages. Text-heavy content is the best way to drive search engine traffic. Book II, Chapter 2 delves into using SEO as part of your content strategy.

✦ **To drive sales:** You can use many different types of content to drive sales. For example, video is a terrific way to show off a product's effectiveness, while an audio podcast enables you to offer expert interviews, and blogs cover it all. In fact, you can even embed your podcast and videos in a blog post.

✦ **To build community:** If you're hoping to effectively communicate with your customers and build community, blogs are your platform. Because readers can comment on blogs, it's an excellent community-building tool.

✦ **To raise awareness:** Though all platforms can help to raise awareness, videos are excellent for visual impact and tugging at heartstrings, while blogs allow for more descriptive phrasing.

✦ **To reach a broad range of people:** All platforms have the ability to reach a broad range of people as long as the content is intriguing and you properly promote it.

✦ **To introduce experts, products, and services to your customers**: Because videos are more visual, they're perfect for product introduction, but all platforms work well for any of these areas.

In addition to setting goals, consider the following when choosing a content platform:

✦ **Time:** How much time do you have to devote to content creation each day? Blogging and podcasting aren't a one-off, set-it-and-forget-it type of deal. In order to build up traffic and interest, you need to set aside regular time each week for your campaigns.

✦ **Skill:** Blogging requires writing skills, while the technically challenged may have issues with video and podcasting. You may find it best to stick within your comfort zone before branching out to a more technical platform.

✦ **Man power:** Will you be handling content creation, or are you hiring a freelancer or delegating to a full-time member of your team? Money and the skill set of the person handling content campaigns are important considerations.

✦ **Tools:** Blogging only requires a computer and an Internet connection. Podcasting and video require microphones and video cameras. Don't invest in any equipment or gadgetry until you're sure that you're ready to make an investment. If you're unsure of which platform you're most comfortable with, start out slowly with a blog and add podcasting and/ or video when you're ready.

You can mix and match any of these goals, and you don't have to choose one content platform if you want to try them all.

After you have a good idea of your goals and objectives with your content, you can move on to hashing out a plan for content creation and distribution.

Putting the Wheels in Motion

After you decide to invest your time in a blog, podcast, or video blog, you have to get your ducks in a row. Before you jump into writing your first blog post, recording your first podcast, or creating the first video, you need to do your homework.

Here are a few guidelines to get you started:

✦ **Study your competition.** If your competitors blog or create a weekly podcast, determine what type of information they offer for potential clients. For example, your competitors may present offerings that are beneficial to potential clients or are just blatant advertisements. If their messages consist of the latter, you have a leg up on your competition. However, chances are good that at least some of them offer valuable content about a similar product or service that you offer. Study the best contributions offered by your competition and then figure out how you can do better by providing more timely or pertinent information. Or perhaps your offering can fill an unfilled niche.

✦ **Read the blogs of the leaders in your industry.** To determine what type of information is considered the norm for your industry, read the blogs of industry leaders. Find out what type of information they're dispensing, how frequently they post to their blogs, and whether they have guest contributors, for example. Popular blogs have large audiences that read every post. That's because the information is timely, pertinent, and relevant. Study the topics that industry leaders blog about, and you'll form a good idea of what you can write about on your blog to build a large and loyal following. After you study popular blogs, put on your thinking cap and come up with a way to put your own spin on similar topics.

✦ **Study the podcasts of leaders in your industry.** Industry podcasts generally have a similar format. After all, they're all vying for the same target audience. Develop a feel for the format and then use your own creativity to create a podcast that's similar to others in your industry, but with your company's personality and flair.

- ✦ **Create an editorial calendar.** Many podcasts and blogs run out of steam after a few weeks because the authors have difficulty staying on track and thinking of good content. You can alleviate this problem if you create an editorial calendar. (Book I, Chapter 3 provides a social media calendar that helps you schedule time and topics.)

   Be sure to keep your calendar filled a few weeks ahead of your current post or episode. Also, schedule a weekly time for brainstorming and add the new content to your calendar.

- ✦ **Practice.** Before you create your first podcast or blog post, pick a topic from your outline and write about it. Or, if your chosen media is podcasting, go ahead and create a podcast. After your practice session is complete, solicit some feedback: Contact friends or colleagues and tell them you want a critique of the session.

Introducing Your Content to the Online World

After you decide which content platform to use, it's time to put the rubber to the road. You may think that creating content is as simple as writing your first blog post, creating your first podcast, or recording your first video and then uploading it to the appropriate server. But creating content involves more than you'd think.

Don't just slap content together. From the beginning, your blog post or podcast is a reflection on your company. Think of the old adage, "You never get a second chance to make a good first impression."

Creating your first blog post

Before launching your blog, consider these suggestions:

- ✦ **Plan for five to ten blog posts.** Create several blog posts to get the feel of working with the software. It's always a good idea to have several — five to ten — blog posts in the can before going live. Starting with several blog posts enables anyone coming to your blog to poke around for a while rather than read a single post and leave. You also have a better chance of gaining subscribers, fans, or customers if you offer more than one piece of content. Plus, multiple blog posts helps you rank better in the search engines.

- ✦ **Leave room for discussion.** The beauty of blogs is that they're a discussion platform. Readers can use the comment box on the bottom of the blog to ask questions and leave comments, and you can respond to them in kind. Make sure that your blog posts are open-ended and allow for comments from your community. Ask questions or invite other opinions.

+ **Set up a regular blogging time.** Choose a time when you're most focused and less likely to have interruptions from the phone, e-mail, or fellow team members.

+ **Use photos and video to break up text and draw in the eye.** You can either take your own images or use a stock photo agency.

+ **Ask for feedback.** Don't be afraid to solicit feedback from trusted peers. You want to know whether your blog is easy to read, easy to navigate, and aesthetically pleasing.

We show you a lot more about blogging in Book III, Chapter 2 and discuss the legalities of sharing images in Book III, Chapter 4.

Creating your first podcast

Before starting your first podcast, follow these suggestions:

+ **Make sure that you have all the equipment you need, but don't buy anything yet.** You may be inclined to purchase expenses equipment at first. Save your purchase until you're sure podcasting is for you. For video podcasts, your webcam or Flip Cam (lightweight, inexpensive video camera) work just fine. Ditto for expensive audio equipment. Though the sound may not be of the best quality for the first couple of recordings, be sure you have the art of recording, mixing, editing, and uploading a podcast down before you go for all the bells and whistles. You may find after a couple of tries that this platform isn't for you.

+ **Find a place to record your podcast.** Many podcasts are created in the comfort of a home or work office space. You need peace and quiet to create a podcast, not only for you but also your intended audience. Try recording your podcasts at a time when the kids are asleep. If you live on a busy road, find a place that doesn't pick up traffic noise. If you often have planes flying overhead, close your windows. After you're ready to really get into podcasting, you'll discover more ways to eliminate background noise.

+ **Be prepared for several takes.** Don't worry about having to stop or start over at first. Even the most seasoned podcasters require several takes to get things right. In time, your confidence will grow. It's only natural to have moments where you have a pause in conversation or you forget what you're going to say.

+ **Prepare a script.** Know what you want to say in advance. Create a script or list of bullet points, but be careful not to read word for word. Practice so that you sound natural.

✦ **Set a schedule.** If you get into podcasting and do it well, your customers and community will expect regular episodes. Work out the best day and time for you to record your podcast and do your best to release it to the public around the same date and time each week or month.

✦ **Solicit feedback.** Before releasing your first few podcasts to the public, get some feedback from trusted peers. They may hear or see some things you didn't notice.

After you create your first podcast episodes, it's time to upload Episode 1 to your web hosting service. After you upload the content, you have to create a way for people to find your podcast. The easiest way is to register your podcast with iTunes. You can then use other social media sites to publicize it. You also need to create some kind of physical presence on the Web where people who don't subscribe to iTunes can view and download your content.

Creating a video blog

Video blogs are usually embedded into a blog post as a way to illustrate the blogger's point.

Here are a couple more video blogging suggestions:

✦ **Test the waters.** As with podcasting, don't run out and buy expensive equipment until you're sure video blogging is for you. Many video bloggers use webcams, Flip cameras, digital cameras, and even smartphones. Over time, if you decide you love video blogging and your community is reacting in a favorable manner, you can go ahead and invest in the heavy artillery.

✦ **Practice using your equipment until you're comfortable with it.** Create a couple of test videos and show them to people in your industry whose opinions you value. Use their feedback to perfect the final result. You may have to rerecord your first attempts. When you're confident that you got it right, you're ready to upload your content to a video sharing service, such as YouTube or Viddy. At that point, you can embed the video in your blog or company website.

You can find out more about video blogging in Book III, Chapter 3

Getting Your Content Noticed

A common mistake made among novice content creators is to expect traffic simply because your content is there. Just because you post content online doesn't mean folks will find it. You're going to have to create a marketing strategy to bring in and grow a community of readers, listeners, and customers. This ongoing process gets easier over time.

Here are some things you can do to get noticed:

✦ **Use keywords in your posts.** This strategy helps with search engine optimization (see Book II, Chapter 2).

✦ **Get involved in the social networks.** Twitter, Facebook, Google+, Pinterest, and other social networks enable you to carry on a conversation with your customers or community and promote your content and brand to the world. (Books IV–VII talk about these social networks and how to effectively use them as marketing tools.)

✦ **Get by with a little help from your friends.** Don't be afraid to ask your friends in the social media space to help you promote their content. Offer to write guest blog posts, give interviews, and find other forms of cross promotion.

✦ **Encourage community participation.** When you allow readers or customers to comment on your content, you're inviting them to be part of the brand. An active community gives off a good vibe and makes your readers more likely to come back for further discussion and recommend your content and brand to others.

✦ **Take advantage of share buttons.** If you spend any time online, you no doubt have noticed *share buttons* on blog posts, news articles, videos, and podcasts. These buttons, featuring the logos of the various social networks, enable your readers and listeners to click a button to share your content with their own communities on the different social networks. Many of your readers and viewers count on seeing announcements on the days you create content via the social networks. To not take the time to share your content can mean out of sight, out of mind.

We discuss putting together a blog content strategy in Book III, Chapter 2.

Mixing and matching your content with other social media

Your content doesn't include only blog posts or videos. Use the social networks to create content as well. Set up a Facebook page and have daily discussions with your community. Use polls, quizzes, and contests to break the serious stuff.

Also explore Twitter, Google+, Pinterest, and other social networks. Monitor the conversations on these social networks to see who is talking about you or your brand and answer questions or address comments and concerns.

A regular online presence is essential to a good marketing strategy nowadays. Customers and community appreciate knowing that you're accessible and forthcoming with news and updates.

The beautiful thing about using the different social media tools is that most of them are free and simple to use. Anyone not using these platforms is missing out on a potentially huge customer base.

Maintaining your enthusiasm

You may believe that maintaining an online presence is a lot of work — and you're right. Investing time each week on blogging, podcasting, videos, and promoting via the different social media tools takes time, but it's time well spent.

At times, you may not feel like socializing, but if you're not showing yourself online on a regular basis, people will forget about you.

Create a schedule and work social media into your daily regime. After a while, it will seem less like something you have to do and more like second nature and something you want to do.

The more content you post online, the more likely search engines and potential customers are to find you. But if you avoid a content marketing strategy, you're missing out on a huge opportunity.

Book III
Chapter 1

Growing Your Brand

Chapter 2: Building Your Blog

In This Chapter

✔ **Deciding on a platform**

✔ **Determining content for your blog**

✔ **Sharing your blog with others**

✔ **Analyzing your readership**

✔ **Building a community of customers and advocates**

*O*riginally, blogs were personal journals where the authors offered their thoughts on anything from parenting to politics. While this vision still holds true today, many brands and businesses are also jumping on the blogging bandwagon because it's an easy, inexpensive way to market a business. A blog offers a way to share expertise, promote products, and services and update customers.

In this chapter, we explore the benefits of blogs as marketing tools and talk about the extra things you can do to your blog in order to make it readable, shareable, and discussable.

Choosing a Blog Platform

A blog *platform* is the service you use to host your blog. WordPress and Blogger are the two most popular blog platforms, but you'll want to read up on all the options available to choose the one that works best for you.

While we're not going to get into step-by-step instructions as to how to set up your blog, we do discuss some considerations when choosing a blog platform. Not all platforms are the same, and you want to be sure to choose the one that works best for you.

What follows are a few things to think about.

Hosting your own blog — or not

Before choosing a blog platform, decide whether you want to host the blog on your own domain or on the blog platform's subdomain. While a hosted blog such as WordPress.com or Blogger.com is free, most bloggers and business owners agree it's more beneficial to put out the money and purchase your own domain and hosting.

Self-hosting

While subdomain blogs are fine for the hobbyist brands, businesses and business people are well advised to choose to host their own blogs, for a variety of reasons:

✦ **Brand recognition:** Say that your brand is BrandX and someone is searching for your website or blog online. He will intuitively look for *brandx.com* — not *brandx.subdomain.com*. You want to have a domain folks will easily remember, which isn't as easy when you use a subdomain.

✦ **A concise URL:** The smaller a URL name and the fewer dots or other characters used, the more intuitive it is to type. It's much easier for someone to remember *brandx.com* than *brandx.blogsubdomain.com*.

✦ **Search engine recognition:** *BrandX.com* is more likely to get a page 1 search engine result than a subdomain, thus making it easier for folks to find you on the search engines.

✦ **Customization:** When you allow the blog platform to host your blog for you, you have to live by a variety of rules. You may not be able to customize your blog the way you want, and you may not be able to use plug-ins and custom themes, host ads, or sell products. (*Plug-ins* help your blog function properly and offer special features to your readers. Plug-ins help the search engines find you and let your readers find older content.)

✦ **The real estate factor:** Blogs are like real estate, and if you sell your business, you'll probably include your blog as part of the transaction. Blogs hosted on their own domain are more desirable and worth more money than blogs hosted on a subdomain.

When researching subdomains, do take some time to read all the fine print to find out what is allowed on your blog and what isn't. Some hosted platforms won't allow you to make design changes or place ads on your blog.

Going with a blog platform

If you're technically challenged (and even if you aren't), you may want to choose a blog platform that's easy to set up and maintain. The two most popular blog platforms, Wordpress.org and Blogger.com, are both. If you're not comfortable making design changes or upgrades, you can always hire someone to do these things for you, but for the most part, the platforms are intuitive and second nature. The important thing is to stick within your comfort level. Once set up, most blog platforms enable you to type and go. Explore the possibilities and make sure that it's simple for you to post text and upload photos, videos, plug-ins, and more. Blogging should be fun and enjoyable. If it becomes a chore, you're not going to want to update your blog as often as you should.

Something else to consider is hosting. With WordPress, you have two options: Wordpress.com hosted by WordPress, which means you'll use the Wordpress.com subdomain, and Wordpress.org that enables you to set up WordPress using your own host and a URL of your choosing.

Blogger is hosted by Blogger, but you have the option of paying for your own domain name instead of using the .blogspot subdomain.

All platforms have tutorials available on their websites, and you can find answers to just about all your questions online.

Choose a platform that allows you to have total control over your blog's theme and plug-in options. Some hosted platforms won't allow you to make too many changes, design wise, nor will they let you use a lot of the available plug-ins. As we explore in the "Using share buttons and plug-ins" section, plug-ins are extremely important for the functionality of your blog.

Customizing your blog

The purpose for creating your blog is to market your brand, product, or service. Choose add-ons, plug-ins, and other items with this goal in mind.

Book III
Chapter 2

Building Your Blog

For example, you want to be sure to offer share buttons below each blog post as well as include social networking buttons in your sidebar. (*Share buttons* are the icons with links you see in a blog's sidebar or at the bottom of a news article inviting you to share the article or blog post with your friends on Facebook, Twitter, Stumble Upon, or a number of social networking, voting, or bookmarking sites.) These buttons encourage your community to not only share your content but also follow you on the social networks.

Other things to consider when customizing your blog is an About page, such as the one shown in Figure 2-1. This page tells everyone who lands on your blog everything they need to know about you and/or your business. Also include tabs for a contact page that lists your e-mail address and physical address (if you wish to share it) and a place to link any press mentions and accolades.

Your blog is not only designed to update and entice potential customers, but it's a place to showcase your achievements and allow people to find out more about your business.

Figure 2-1:
An About
page gives
readers a
place to
find out
more about
you or your
business.

Planning a Blog Content Strategy

It's not enough to have a blog; you need to have a plan as well. Without a plan, your blog will be unfocused and confusing. After your blog is set up, take some time to plan out a content strategy.

Consider the following:

✦ **How often you want to post:** The more content you post, the better you'll be able to catch the attention of the search engines. Once a week should be the absolute least you should post, but do consider three to five posts each week, as more pages mean more search engine results. Plus, you want your blog to be a searchable resource. So by installing a search plug-in on your blog's sidebar, you'll have an important, searchable resource. The more content you have, the more likely folks are to stick around for a while.

✦ **How you will promote each post:** It's not enough to post to your blog; you can't just "set it and forget it." While technically you're able to eventually catch the attention of the search engines, it isn't enough. You're also going to have to promote your content each time you write it. This aspect is where the social networks come in handy. When you share your content on Twitter, Facebook, or other networks, it will not only bring in some readers, but if the content is good, those readers are going to share it with their own communities as well. (We talk more about the various social networks and how you can best use them in Books IV–VII.)

✦ **The use of images:** Images are important for blogs as they catch the eye and break up the text. We talk more about the right ways to find, share, and attribute images in Book III, Chapter 4.

✦ **The use of video:** You may want to you use videos in your blog posts. This video can either be something already created that you found on a video sharing site, such as YouTube, or it can be a video you created.

You don't necessarily have to star in all the videos posted to your blog. If you find a relevant tutorial or humorous infographic on a video sharing network such as YouTube and you're allowed to share it, by all means, embed it on your blog.

✦ **What you will blog about:** When you make the decision to start blogging, you may think you have a good idea of what to blog about. After you actually start blogging, you may run out of things to talk about. Take some time to list all the things you'd like to write about. Make sure that your content is a mixture of news, company updates, relevant informative content, and evergreen content. (*Evergreen content* is the timeless content people will always search for online.) For example, if your brand is a cereal manufacturer, some of the things you can talk about are facts relating to cereals, demographics relating to cereals, nutritional information, recipes, and the benefits of using the healthy ingredients found in your cereals. (We talk more about evergreen versus current content in Book III, Chapter 3.)

✦ **Whether you'll allow comments:** It used to be that comments are what set blogs apart from web news articles, but not anymore. Now every outlet likes to make sure that readers have a place to participate — and why not? When you allow readers to be part of the conversation, they feel better about the brand and are more likely to use it when it's time to buy or make a recommendation. Conversation builds trust. Moreover, many times your comments give you fodder for your blog posts.

✦ **What you want visitors to do at your blog:** Is the purpose of your blog to have people read and discuss your content, or is it to drive sales or establish expertise? If it's to drive sales, be sure to have links to sales pages without it looking like an obvious sales tactic. If you're looking to establish yourself as an expert in your field, continue creating the type of content that shows people you know your stuff and sets you apart from the rest. If your goal is to have readers read and discuss your content, content should be front and center.

✦ **The length of each post:** People read items on the web differently than they read newspapers, books, and magazines. On the web, folks have a shorter attention span. They scan articles rather than read them. To keep folks from getting bored and moving on, make sure your posts are succinct and scannable. Most good blog posts are less than a thousand words long. Optimally, they contain 300 to 500 words.

✦ **Text presentation:** How you present text goes back to that scannable-content thing. Use subheads, images, video, bullet points, and numbered lists to break up text (see Figure 2-2). This type of presentation makes for easier reading. Your readers are more likely to read your post when various points and images jump out at them than if your blog post is an endless block of text.

Figure 2-2: Break up your text with sub-headings, images, video, and lists.

Determining the focus of your blog

It's not enough to know what you want to write about or to have a marketing strategy for your content. You also want to think about your blog's focus. Coming up with a focus goes along with having a plan. Blogs without a specific focus confuse people, and you want them to want to come back again and again.

If your blog is a vehicle for sales, your focus should be product-related. Consider posting news about new products, frequently asked questions about your product or service, and the benefits of using your product.

Content market expert Marcus Sheridan from TheSalesLion.com recommends taking the top 50 questions people are asking about your brand and turning each question into a blog post.

If you want to highlight your achievements and establish yourself as an expert, an informative blog discussing your specialty is the perfect vehicle. Expertise blogs are good showcases for how-to content, news analysis, and evergreen content.

If your blog is a way to attract attention to your service — for example, you're a freelance web designer — use it to showcase some of your custom designs as well as offer design tips to your readers.

With a blog, the possibilities are endless.

Customizing your blog's theme

In addition to outstanding content, a standout design will set your blog apart from the rest. There's a reason most serious bloggers pay extra money for a custom theme: branding.

Mind you, there's nothing wrong with a stock theme layout. In fact, many are free or inexpensive. However, if you go that route, realize that many other bloggers may have that same theme. You want to stand out in a good way, and that won't necessarily happen if your blog is confused with other similarly designed blogs because you all share the same template.

Custom theme must-haves

In the long run, it pays to have someone else implement a custom theme because important components are on the line:

+ **Logo:** Your logo should be original and reflective of you, the type of business you run, and your brand. You want people to look at your blog and think of you. Not all stock themes allow you to easily change your logo.

+ **Design:** An original design says that you're unique and are willing to invest in your business.

+ **Personality:** When you customize your own theme, you're able to inject a little of your personality into it, which you can't always do with a stock theme.

+ **Reliability:** Most blogs with a custom theme are more reliable and have a faster loading time.

+ **Better search engine optimization:** The framework behind many of today's custom themes allows for better search engine optimization.

Must-have's on both stock and custom themes

Whether you decide to have a stock theme or a custom theme, all blogs should have certain components, especially if you want people to find out more about you and your brand, and you want them to share your content.

Don't overlook the following items when choosing a theme and design for your blog:

+ **Share buttons:** Allow others to share your content. These buttons are so important that we discuss them in the upcoming "Using share buttons and plug-ins" section.

+ **Follow Me buttons:** If you have a presence on the different social net-working platforms, be sure to include buttons in your blog's sidebar so that your readers can also follow you on Twitter, LinkedIn, Google+, and Facebook.

+ **About Me page:** Your About Me page tells everyone about your back-ground or information about the brand.

+ **Contact details:** How will people get in touch with you if you don't leave them your contact information? At the very least, provide an e-mail address. Bigger brands also post addresses and a customer service line for the corporate office.

+ **Product or service details:** What good is bringing people to your blog or website if they're not going to be directed to a sales page at some point? If you're an author, have a tab on your blog featuring your books and where to buy them. If you sell jewelry, post images of your best pieces. If you sell gourmet food, make sure that people can go somewhere to view your wares and pricing info.

+ **Subscribe buttons:** If you want folks to keep coming back, be sure to have subscribe buttons at eye level or *above the fold.* Offer several options, such as RSS, Facebook, or e-mail subscriptions. Many times, when people land on blogs, it's a one-off gig because they don't always know how to find you again. If you offer ways to subscribe, you'll find many people returning on a regular basis.

Using share buttons and plug-ins

You have content and a design, but before you go live with your blog, you need to think about share buttons and plug-ins.

You may be inclined to not clutter up your sidebar with such frivolity, but the truth is, you need these buttons, especially if you're writing or producing some killer content.

Adding share buttons

When people consume content that resonates with them in some way, whether it's to laugh, cry, or get angry, they want to share it with others who may share the same point of view. In fact, many online communities use such content as discussion fodder. The problem is they don't want to spend their time cutting and pasting links. Share buttons enable them to bring your content to their friends, family, and followers with one click.

There's nothing more frustrating to people who consume content on a regular basis than to want to share an article and have no way of doing so. In fact, most readers simply won't share information if they can't find a button that makes it easy to do so.

Working with plug-ins

You can use a variety of plug-ins on your blog. Many help you promote your product, service, or personal brand. These plug-ins are as simple as uploading or inserting some code. In addition, the result is almost instant. Upload the plug-in, activate the plug-in, and now you have share buttons!

What follows is a list of recommended plug-ins for those wishing to use a blog as a marketing tool. As WordPress is the most popular and adaptable blog platform at this time, this list of plug-ins is for WordPress blogs.

You can find and download these plug-ins by accessing the plug-in function of your WordPress dashboard and searching for each plug-in. From there you can download the plug-in directly to your blog.

✦ **All in One SEO:** Helps to optimize your blog for search engines.

✦ **Scribe:** Involves a cost, but Scribe is sort of like a checklist of things you have to do before you publish your blog post in order to best catch the attention of the search engines. It also helps with keywords and links so that you're using them to their maximum potential.

✦ **Yet Another Related Posts Plugin:** Offers a list of links to related posts at the bottom of a blog post so that readers can move on to more information.

✦ **Digg Digg/Share This/Sociable:** Once installed, any of these three plug-ins enables share buttons in your sidebar or below each post so that your readers can share your content.

✦ **Broken Link Checker:** Checks content to make sure that all links are in working order.

✦ **FeedBurner:** Integrates your blog with FeedBurner as it redirects your main RSS feed for your content and your comments. (See the section "Using trackbacks" later in this chapter, for more on this trackbacks.)

✦ **Popular Posts:** Shows your most popular content in your sidebar so that your readers can read more, giving you more *page views* (the amount of pages one person views after landing on your page) and a *higher bounce rate* (the amount of time one person stays after landing on your page. High bounce rate means folks leave quickly. Low bounce rate means they're sticking around.)

✦ **Disqus or Livefyre:** Both Disqus and Livefyre are excellent additions to any blog. Though bloggers argue over which one is more beneficial, both help keep out spam and nasty anonymous comments because everyone who uses either one of these plug-ins has to log in at a central location. Their information is stored and follows them whenever they comment at a blog using one of these plug-ins. These plug-ins also enable the blogger to better moderate and analyze comments and commenters.

Take some time now and then to research the different plug-ins and discover what they do as new ones are born each day.

Adding links

Not only do you want to link to your own content within your blog posts, but you should also link to other relevant content around the web and the blogosphere. Linking helps index your pages on the search engines. (See the upcoming section "Catching the Attention of Search Engines.") Links also help others find out about you and encourage them to add reciprocal links back to your blog.

To add links to your content:

1. **Highlight the text you want to add a hyperlink for.**

   For SEO purposes, anchor the link to a specific keyword. Do this by highlighting the keyword and selecting the hyperlink function.

2. **Click the linking tool shown in Figure 2-3.**

   The Insert/Edit link dialog box appears.

3. **Enter the URL you want to link to, as shown in Figure 2-4.**

4. **Click Add Link.**

Links are what make the search engines notice you. Thus, you want to link to as many pages within your content as possible. You also want to use linking as a reference for your readers. Linking allows you to refer back to a previously written blog post, without having to commit to paragraphs of unnecessary description text.

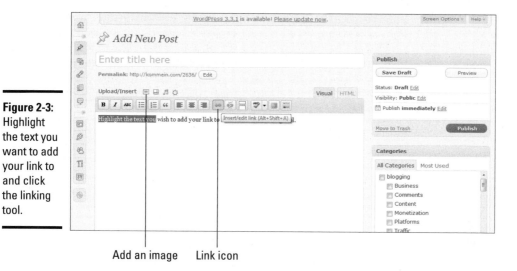

Figure 2-3:
Highlight
the text you
want to add
your link to
and click
the linking
tool.

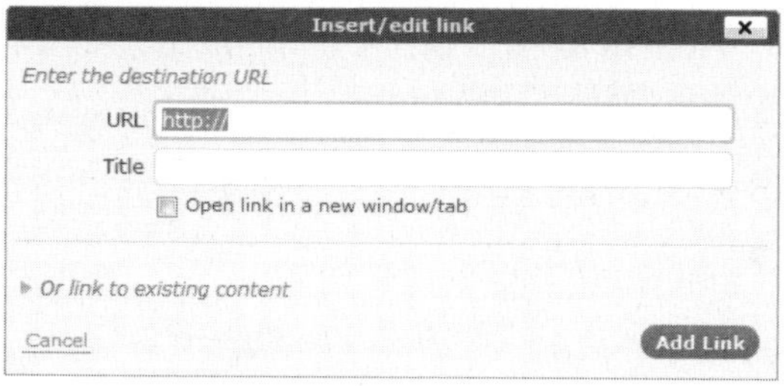

Add an image   Link icon

Figure 2-4:
Enter the
pertinent
information.

Linking to other peoples' content also helps you get noticed. When you link to someone else, you not only catch the attention of the blogger who will appreciate your sending traffic her way, but because most content creators allow trackbacks, a link to your post will either appear in the bottom of the other blogger's post or in the comments section.

Using trackbacks

Trackbacks are the breadcrumbs of the Internet. Whenever another blog or website creates a link to one of your blog posts, the visibility of the post increases. Your post is seen not only by visitors to the site that created the trackback but also search engines, which gives your post a higher priority over a similar one with fewer or no trackbacks.

How do you serve up a heaping helping of these powerful trackbacks? One way is by using your other social media outlets. If you announce a new post to your Twitter followers and one or more of them creates a link to the post, you have trackbacks. Your Facebook page can serve the same function. If you use the option to automatically show new posts on the wall of your Facebook page, your fans will notice. If they add the link on their websites, you have another trackback.

You can create trackbacks the old-fashioned way, of course, by sending a message to a website owner requesting a reciprocal link. However, one of the easiest and quickest ways to publicize your blog and create trackbacks is by using the plug-in FeedBurner. FeedBurner makes it possible for you to publicize your feed, which in essence gets your blog out to the masses.

Including images in your blog

When at all possible, add images to your blog posts. Images break up the text and help to illustrate a point. They also help to catch the eye of readers rather than scanners.

Of course, you can't just use any old image you find. For information on using images legally, see Book III, Chapter 4.

It's equally as simple to upload images to embed in your blog post:

1. **Save the image you want to use.**

2. **Click the image uploading tool. (Refer to Figure 2-3.)**

   The image uploading tool is usually located at the top of your blog's dashboard.

3. **Click Select Files and choose the image from your own files.**

4. **Choose your alignment and size, as shown in Figure 2-5.**

   Most bloggers prefer a right alignment for their images, as it's more eye catching. Don't size your image too big because it will take too long to load and will take away from the text. A thumbnail-sized photo is only good when you want readers to click to a bigger image. Choose a size that people can see at a glance but isn't too big or too small.

5. **Write a caption for your image.**

   Describe the image as it relates to your blog post and use SEO if it sounds natural.

6. **Click Insert into Post.**

   Your image now appears in your blog post.

Figure 2-5:
Choose the size and align the image for your blog post.

When you save your image to your own computer, use keywords. Keywords catch the attention of the search engines, and you can receive some good traffic from Google Images from folks looking for the same type of illustration. For more on using keywords and search terms, see Book II, Chapter 2.

Catching the Attention of Search Engines

In Book II, Chapter 2, we offer tips for search engine optimization (SEO). Using certain techniques to catch the attention of search engines is a necessary part of your content marketing strategy, but there's more to getting in a search engine's good graces than a few keywords. (In fact, an entire book, *Search Engine Optimization For Dummies,* 5th Edition, by Peter Kent, is out on the topic.)

For example, did you know search engines like it when you embed a link — either to your own content or someone else's — in the very first line of your written content? Also, posting keywords, headlines, and subheadlines go a long way in boosting your search engine presence. In fact, many of the things catching a person's eye also catch the attention of the search engines.

Regular readers attract search engines. Some SEO has nothing to do with technicalities, though. If you write good, solid content, you'll attract people who will in return attract the search engines. In short, don't write for search engines; write for people, and the search engines will follow.

There's more to gaining traffic than keywords. You also have to provide a valuable service with your content. People regularly reading and commenting can be just as good as peppering your blog posts with keywords and links.

Also, when you write good content, others will link to you. This inbound linking is extremely important for high search engine rankings. The more folks link, the more attractive you are to Google, Yahoo!, and Bing.

Frequency also matters. If you blog sporadically, the search engines will treat you in kind. You see, every page on your blog is indexed by the search engines. The more you write, the more you're indexed. Fewer pages mean fewer indexed pages. Write constantly and consistently, and the search engines will rank you well.

Not all content is created equal

When you write news analysis, do a product review, launch a product or service, or discuss an industry trend, this content gets more or less dated as time passes. It may bring in some eyeballs when the news first breaks, but after a while, searches for these news items or product news will trickle to a stop.

On the other hand, evergreen content has the potential to be searchable indefinitely. "How to change a tire" is a good example of evergreen content.

Some examples of evergreen content are

- ✦ How to's
- ✦ Histories (even if it's the history of a certain product or service)
- ✦ Biographies
- ✦ Informational posts (for example, "The Health Benefits of Bananas")
- ✦ Etiquette (for example "The Etiquette of Commenting on Blogs")
- ✦ Rules (for example "Rules of Grammar")

Getting the right mix

Achieving a good balance with your content is important. You want both trendy and evergreen content. If not, you'll receive spikes in traffic here and there and not a steady rise, which is what you really want.

Many bloggers go for shocking headlines and controversial content in hopes of snagging the retweet crowd. This approach is good sometimes, but, again, your content and pages will strike and drop off. To keep traffic numbers high all the time, the content has to be consistent and appeal to searchers and readers for months, if not years, in the future.

Evergreen content is highly linkable, as well. With the right kind of content, you'll always have something to link to internally. Plus, other content creators can use your content as a reference for their own blog posts. Something else to consider is how evergreen content works for all platforms: text, video, and audio.

If you write three blog posts per week, try writing one evergreen post once during that week. Soon, you'll see regular, steady streams of traffic rather than one-off spikes such as you would get with scandalous news or controversy.

Recognizing the Importance of Community

Many businesses and brands are now discovering the importance of cultivating an *online community*. Everyone who comments on your content, follows your brand on Twitter and belongs to your Facebook or Google+ groups is part of your online community. How you decide to leverage your community is up to you.

There's a difference, however, between customers and community. Customers are people who use your service or buy your product. On the other hand, community members rally around your brand. They feel good about you because they're spending time with you online, which can lead to some terrific brand advocacy and word-of-mouth marketing.

Online communities are important because they create trust. When a brand is interacting on a regular basis with the people who use their products or services, the people feel as if they're privy to something special — as if they're part of the brand. Plus, interaction and conversation don't feel or look like selling. Because your members are enjoying their time with you, they have a good feeling about buying your product or hiring your service.

Business is no longer local. Thanks to the Internet, you're global and your online communities can help spread the word even farther. Your members are your staunchest allies and advocates.

Your online relationships can lead to partnerships, collaborations, and fame. Even more important, online communities enable you to find out about the people who use your product or service and how you can improve. In fact, online communities are so important, one of your authors wrote an entire book devoted to their intricacies. Check out *Online Community Management For Dummies,* by Deborah Ng.

Creating a community

Though online communities are important for anyone wishing to grow a business online, creating one from your content is easier said than done.

You can't just put up a blog post or send a tweet and wait for everyone to show up. Just like offline communities need encouragement and management, so do the online versions.

Keep in mind that an online community doesn't have to be a huge, elaborate forum or membership site. Your online community can also be made up of the people who follow you on Twitter, engage on your brand's Facebook page, and have you in their Circles on Google+. In short, community is everywhere you have online presence. It's how you engage that determines how active members are in their participation. Find out where the people are and join them.

The most important thing to consider before planning a community-building strategy is to have a reason why people should join your community or communities. Will they receive updates? Will they receive discounts? Will they receive perks the general public aren't privy to? Will you have special expert guest participation? If so, market your online communities so that folks know they'll receive value by following you and your networks.

Something else to consider is that if you're going to have a presence on the different social networks, the conversation has to be different for each one. If you're saying the same thing on every single channel, there's no reason for anyone to join more than one. Try and find a focus for each online community.

For example, you could focus each social network as follows to avoid becoming redundant:

✦ Use your blog for informative articles and discussions related to the day's topic.

✦ Use Facebook for news, updates, polls, quizzes, photos, and videos.

✦ Use Twitter to engage in light conversation and reach out to customers.

✦ Use LinkedIn for career-related discussions.

✦ Use Google+ to discuss current events.

You can't set and forget community. To encourage participation, make sure that your content is open-ended. Ask questions or leave room for discussion, but make sure that everyone has a voice. Use the social networks to discover what people are saying about you and reach out to everyone who mentions your brand, whether it's to say hi or thank you or offer to help with a problem.

To get started with community building, become part of a community yourself. Comment on blogs; join in Twitter conversations; follow like-minded people, products, or services on Facebook; and so on. Don't spam the other community members with links back to your own stuff. Instead, become a positive, productive part of the conversation, and you'll find folks are following you back to your own haunts.

Handling comments and spam and other delights

Many bloggers use their comments section as a gauge of their success of the blog or community. (For more on gauging how well you're doing, see the upcoming section "Measuring Your Success with Analytics.") Lots of comments and thoughtful discussion occurring is a good sign that folks are reading and reacting, and you have a nice community of advocates and customers growing there.

On the other hand, spam can be a problem. Many spammers try to use a blog's comment section as a way of dropping links to all sorts of seedy products and services. Spam used to be obvious, but now spammers are trying to become a part of the conversation so that you don't notice they're really dropping links.

One way to identify spammers is that they don't use real names. In fact, they don't use traditional names at all. Instead, their names are SEO keywords, such as *Cheap Refrigerator* or *New Curtain Patterns*.

A plug-in such as Disqus or Livefyre can help eliminate this problem because all commenters have to be members of this service first or log in as a guest. Anything suspicious looking is held in moderation. Using one of these plug-ins will significantly knock out your spam issue, as will using the Askimet plug-in to detect and capture spam. (For more on plug-ins, see the earlier section "Using share buttons and plug-ins.")

You may be inclined to hold every comment in moderation before allowing them to go public in order to eliminate spam, but we don't recommend it. When all comments go into moderation first, people lose interest in commenting. They come for the conversation; if it's not happening live, they won't be into it. Make sure that you have a spam filter in place and a good commenting plug-in. If someone does post a rude comment, you can come back and deal with it, but you'll definitely lose community and the good vibe if you hold all your comments in moderation for more than a couple of minutes.

You may also be tempted to install a *CAPTCHA* plug-in. These plug-ins require the user to input a code in order to prove he's not a spammer. However, most people are discouraged from commenting when they see CAPTCHA. Many times, the code is difficult to read, and it requires several attempts before commenters gain access. It's not worth the frustration, and they'd rather move on than attempt to crack the code.

Spam doesn't have to be an issue if you deal with it swiftly and effectively. Use a good commenting plug-in and a spam filter and keep a regular eye on comments to make sure that no one is being abusive.

Measuring Your Success with Analytics

An *analytics* program tells you how and why people are coming to your blog. Without it, you know very little about your customers, community, or the content they're consuming.

The type of analytics program you use depends on your needs, but most bloggers are comfortable with the free, tried and true Google Analytics. This free program is available at `www.google.com/analytics` to anyone with a Google account. Use it to see how many visitors are coming to your pages, and what they're doing after they arrive.

Take some time to explore the different programs available. Read the reviews and determine which one is best for you.

Analytics programs are easy to install and come with detailed, easy-to-use instructions. Either it's a matter of uploading a plug-in or placing some code on your blog.

Here is what you can discover from your analytics program:

✦ **How many people visit your blog each day, week, and month:** Your analytics program lists how many people visit on a given day, week, month, or even hour. This information is important because it enables you to pinpoint traffic trends. Knowing the most popular times of the day or week for readers can help you plan content and sales campaigns.

✦ **Your most popular content:** Your analytics program offers a rundown of how many people read your pages, letting you know which content went over well and what people weren't interested in reading.

✦ **Bounce rate:** The amount of time people spend on a page. A high bounce rate means people leave your site quickly. A low bounce rate means folks are staying for a while and reading your content. If you have a high bounce rate, you want to work on having the kind of blog and content people want to read.

✦ **Keywords and search terms:** It's important to know who is visiting your blog and why. Your analytics program will show you exactly which keywords folks are keying into the search engines before landing on your site. These keywords are important because they enable you to use these search terms and keywords in your content in order to attract even more readers.

✦ **Response to advertisements and sales pages:** Many analytics have *heat maps* that allow you to see specifically where most people are spending their time on each page. As a result, you can place ads in the right spot and see whether folks are reading and reacting to your sales pages.

✦ **Top traffic referrers:** Your analytics program shows you if your Twitter or Facebook campaigns are working. In fact, if anyone is sharing or talking about your content at all, you'll be able to follow the trail.

✦ **Page views:** You can discover how many people read a page and move on to read more pages, or if they leave after reading one page only. Page views are different from bounce rate in that page views tell how many individual pages each person reads on your blog.

✦ **Is your content driving sales?:** Your analytics program shows you whether your content is leading folks to sales pages and how many people are taking action.

All this information is important for your marketing strategy because it gives you deeper knowledge about customers and customers. It's like you're spying on their habits, in a noninvasive way. When you know how, when, and why people are consuming your content, you're better able to tweak it for maximum potential. This knowledge can lead to more sales and visibility.

Chapter 3: Using Podcasts or Video in Your Content

In This Chapter

⮕ Deciding whether podcasting is the best option

⮕ Finding focus

⮕ Using podcasting or video as a marketing tool

⮕ Bringing in new traffic

⮕ Sharing your content through video

Text isn't the only game in content marketing. Many brands are now taking advantage of creating podcasts and video blog posts to add a little variety to their written content. In this chapter, we explore the benefits of creating podcasts and video and how you can add them into your marketing plan.

Is Podcasting Right for You?

You don't have to podcast. With social media, you don't have to join every network or pontificate from every platform. Some people love podcasting but others would rather type than talk. Is podcasting right for you?

Podcasting doesn't necessarily have to entail the use of a lot of expensive equipment. Many hardcore podcasters do have their own studios, while others get by with a simple microphone. Sound quality is important, however, and if you host hard-to-listen-to podcasts full of static and feedback, folks are going to stay away.

You don't want to spend lots of money on expensive bells and whistles if you're not into podcasting. Definitely try podcasting a few times to be sure there's interest, not only from you but from your community.

Looking at the downsides

You also have to consider editing. All those perfect podcasts you watch or listen to aren't necessarily first takes, especially if you're just starting out. You're bound to have some fits and starts and even a few "ums." Your options are to leave them in or edit them out — and editing out can be time consuming.

We don't mean to discourage you from podcasting in any way. However, we don't want you to enter into it blind. Here are a few things to consider before launching your first podcast:

✦ **Is podcasting something you want to do on a regular basis?** Will you want to record a podcast once a week and then edit and upload the podcast? For some, this process can take several hours, for newbies.

✦ **Will you be able to handle the technical aspects?** Blog platforms are mostly intuitive, and most people can figure them out without much effort. Editing a podcast isn't difficult, per se, but it's not as easy as pressing a Send button.

✦ **Will you have listeners? Do you know people will tune in?** Will podcasting be worth the effort? Some communities aren't into a regular podcasts. Also, the success of your podcast depends on the brand. For example, if you're a laundry detergent manufacturer, do you think you can come up with enough interesting material to bring in listeners each time you upload a podcast?

✦ **Will you be able to bring in listeners?** Though you're using podcasting as a marketing tool, you'll have to do a fair amount of marketing yourself in order to bring in listeners. Where will you find them, and how will you get them to listen?

✦ **What do you hope to achieve by podcasting?** Determine your reason for podcasting before you begin so that you can tailor your podcast to the right people. For example, if you're raising awareness for a cause, you wouldn't talk about the same thing as if you were selling a product.

✦ **Where will you host your podcast?** Will you post your podcast to your blog, website, or another area? If you host the podcast on your blog or website, your site will receive more traffic. If you host through iTunes, you may have more listeners. And there's nothing wrong with using a combination of both.

If you're beginning to think that podcasting isn't for you, you may want to consider hosting an Internet radio show. Check out the section "Podcasting versus Internet radio," later in this chapter.

Reaping the benefits of podcasts

Not everyone has the time or even patience to read long, lengthy articles and blog posts. Having content people can listen to at their convenience is another great option for spreading your message and can open you up to a whole new audience. Many people enjoy downloading podcasts to their iPods and listening to them in the car or gym. Podcasting can be more convenient than text or video because you can listen much in the way you listen to music while you're going about your day. There's nothing to print, and you're not chained to your laptop.

Because your listeners hear your voice in a podcast, you build a different type of relationship. When they can hear your voice and your emotion and passion as you talk about your favorite topics, you add another element of trust to your message. They laugh with you at jokes and know when you're dead serious. In text, your audience can easily misread tones and inflections. The content of a podcast is more engaging because it's more emotional.

Unlike written content, podcasts aren't scannable. Though people can fast forward as needed, most people are more focused when they're listening than when they're scanning a blog post.

Podcasts also allow you to expand upon your expertise. When you write a blog post, brevity is important. You have to say what you have to say in 500 to 1000 words, or you run the risk of losing your reader. On the other hand, podcasts allow you to talk until the talking is done. Many podcasts run 30 to 60 minutes. Another beautiful thing about podcasts is how you can interview another person of interest and ask as many questions as you'd like.

For more information on podcasting, check out *Podcasting For Dummies,* by Tee Morris, Chuck Tomasi, and Evo Terra.

Determining Your Podcast's Focus

You can't just say you want to host a podcast and leave it at that. Your podcast has to have a focus. That isn't to say that you have to talk about the same thing every day, but you should at least talk about the same types of thing. Without focus, your podcast will be hard to classify, and that means you have the potential to lose out on a big audience who will pass over your content because they don't know what it's about. (If you're not sure who your audience is, see the upcoming section "Determining your target audience," later in this chapter.)

You most likely want to have a podcast featured around your area of expertise. You have to have a passion for a subject to talk about it all the time, right? This topic should also be relevant to your brand. For example, if your brand is an automotive manufacturer, you'll want to keep your podcast car focused. To get even deeper into that subject, do you want your podcast to appeal to car buyers, auto enthusiasts, or the people who also make cars? When you know who your audience is, you can then narrow down into content. For example:

If you're appealing to car buyers, you should focus on

 ✦ Best cars to drive in specific situations

 ✦ Pros and cons of driving specific cars

 ✦ Best-selling automobiles

- Recalls
- Ratings (best and worst cars of the year)
- Interviews with other automotive manufacturers and enthusiasts

If you're appealing to car enthusiasts, you should focus on

- Automotive news
- New releases
- Classic and antique cars
- Auction news, such as which restored classics are fetching the best prices at auction
- Best and worst cars of the year
- Automotive safety
- How different cars react in specific situations
- Interviews with other automotive enthusiasts

If you're appealing to other automotive manufacturers, you should focus on

- Industry news
- New releases
- New regulations
- Product recalls
- Interviews with others in the field

Every niche, genre, and brand has the ability to reach people. Having focus helps you reach the right types of people. Take the time to plan your content well in advance. Use an editorial calendar to keep track of topics and book guests. Post a calendar on your blog or website as well so that your community knows your schedule ahead of time and work on the types of topic that appeal to the people you want to market to.

Using Podcasts to Drive Traffic and Land Sales

When you think about traditional marketing tactics, very few brands considered broadcasting regularly to appeal to more people. Perhaps they'd advertise on a popular program, but they didn't really want to commit staff or cover the cost for 30 minutes or an entire hour of programming. It's different today, though. Many brands are discovering how podcasting appeals to a whole different group of people. As long as your podcast isn't a long sales pitch, you definitely have the ability to drive sales.

How does podcasting drive traffic and sales for your brand?

✦ **Your host page always leads to an action page.** Whether you host your podcast on a blog or website, it should always be embedded on a page offering listeners an opportunity to take further action. It's not enough to embed your podcast. List bullets of the podcast's main points to draw in readers and offer a link to a "more information" page for listeners who want to find out more.

✦ **If you host a good podcast, others will recommend it.** If you have informative, actionable, engaging content, not only will new listeners come back, but they'll also tell others about it.

✦ **The search engines pick it up.** Podcasting pages also catch the attention of the search engines. Use your search terms on your podcast's host page; folks looking for both podcasts in your topic or to find out more about your topic will stop by for a listen.

✦ **Choose buzzworthy content, which always brings in more listeners.** When you podcast an interesting discussion, with notable guests, you'll bring in regular listeners. Regular listeners also bring in new listeners either with share buttons or word-of-mouth recommendation. This traffic, in turn, can lead to action, whether it's sales, awareness, or another goal.

✦ **Get it on iTunes.** When you get your podcast on iTunes, you're opening yourself up to a whole new listener base. So many people browse iTunes each day to find new podcasts to listen to on their morning drive or while working out.

Finding Listeners for Your Podcast

The number one rule in finding people to consume your content is to create the type of content people want to consume. A good, informative, engaging podcast that trumps all the SEO and networking stuff will always keep folks coming back or recommending your podcast to others. However, people can't find podcasts they don't know about, so you still have to bring in listeners.

Finding listeners for your podcast isn't much different than finding readers from your blog. What follows is a list of some ways you can bring in the ears:

✦ **Embed your podcast in a blog post.** When your podcast is attached to the blog post, you get the extra SEO benefits from the post and any optimized images.

✦ **Spend some time in other podcasting communities.** One of the best ways to raise awareness on the web is to become involved in like-minded communities. Find the podcasting forums and discussion groups and join to not only learn but also to receive critiques. If the other podcasters like what you do, not only will they stop by for a listen, but they'll recommend your podcast to their listeners.

+ **Upload your podcast to iTunes.** Podcasts on iTunes have the ability to reach millions. Not all do, but you do bring in a whole new group of listeners when you allow iTunes to host your podcast.

+ **Promote your podcast on the social networks.** Share your podcast with your community. If your podcast is especially good, you'll receive retweets and shares from others.

+ **Use share buttons.** When you use share buttons on your content, others are prompted to help promote your stuff. This impromptu sharing is how really good content goes viral.

+ **Interview people.** Interview important, prominent, or famous people in your niche. Well-respected guests always bring in new listeners, and some may even stick around to become regulars.

+ **Be a guest on other podcasts.** See whether other podcasters are interested in interviewing you. You may gain some new listeners as a result.

+ **Link to other sites, blog posts, and podcasts.** When you link to others, they'll receive a pingback and come to your content to see why you're linking to them. Sharing other people's content can lead to a public thank you or recommendation for others to listen to your podcast. Plus, if the pingback appears on the blog post itself, members of the other community might come by for a listen.

+ **Broadcast live from events.** Many podcasters set up at conferences, concerts, red carpet events, and grand openings. Your listeners will enjoy living vicariously through you, and you'll also generate interest from people who are at the event and see you doing your live show.

Don't be disappointed if the turnout is low for your first few broadcasts. If you keep at it and work hard to share your podcasts, folks will listen. There's nothing wrong with a slow, steady, growth. Sometimes you end up with a more loyal community of listeners than if you had one giant spike in traffic.

Determining your target audience

Who are you trying to reach with your podcasts? You can't just say "people who want to buy my product" or "people who I want to learn about me as an expert in my field" because that's too general. Before you start podcasting, you have to figure out who your core listeners are.

Say that you manage a health food brand. Your podcast will most likely be of interest to people who are into healthy living and perhaps people who are looking to implement a healthier regime into their daily activities. No doubt plenty of people are into discovering the benefits of certain food products or hearing from nutritionists and other experts.

Your target audience is the people who you want to become your community. They're the core group of listeners who will listen as often as they can and interact with others in your community. They're not a general group of listeners or people who come around once in a while.

You determine your target audience by

✦ **Your customer base:** Your customers and clients are your target audience. They're the ones who keep you in business and use your product or service. It's from them that you determine you're on the right track with your business, and they can teach you the same thing with your online content.

✦ **The keywords they're using to land on your website:** Your analytics tell you why and how people come to your website. (For more about analytics, see Book IX.)You'll find out the search terms used to land on your site, as well as the most popular keywords and search terms used by the majority of your community. Knowing what others are searching for can help you determine the content appealing to the bulk of your community.

✦ **Your most popular content:** Your analytics also tell you the most popular content. Knowing what people best respond to helps you provide similar content for the future. This isn't to say you have to talk about the same things all the time, but it does tell you why people are listening.

✦ **Their comments and feedback:** Comments are so telling. You can discover which topics are controversial and which invoke the most passion among your community. You'll also hear from your community about how they feel about the things they talk about.

✦ **Surveys and polls:** Before you start podcasting, offer a poll to find out what people will respond best to. Continue with the surveys and polls every now and then to be sure you're on the right track.

Some of these things don't happen right away, but they'll help you find out about your core group of listeners as your progress.

Finding interview subjects

A terrific way to attract listeners and add credibility to your podcast and brand is to bring in people to interview. Interviews also help provide subject matter and are good SEO because if you think the person is of interest to your community, others will feel the same and will be searching for that person's name.

You can easily find people to interview for your podcast. There's always someone with something to promote, whether it's a product, service, book, or blog. By interviewing them, you help spread their name around. You may find some of these people in your own circles, but if you have a regular podcast, you may eventually run out of friends to interview.

Here are a few suggestions for finding interview subjects:

✦ **Books:** Don't be afraid to reach out to authors. Many are happy to grant interviews, and most have contact info online, usually through a blog or website. If you can't locate their information, you can reach authors through their publishers.

✦ **Blogs:** Many bloggers, podcasters, and other content creators are experts at what they do. Many are happy to grant interviews to help drive traffic to their blogs and build their brands.

✦ **Colleges:** Schools provide an endless assortment of experts who you can reach out to for interviews.

✦ **H.A.R.O:** Also known as "Help a Reporter Out" (`http://helpareporter. com`) enables you to fill out an interview request, which in turn is blasted to experts and professionals who are looking for interview opportunities in exchange for traffic or a boost in credibility.

✦ **Profnet:** Similar to H.A.R.O., Profnet (`https://profnet.prnewswire. com`) also allows you to fill out an interview request, which will reach public relations professionals who in turn will contact you to tell you about their clients.

✦ **LinkedIn:** Some people with very impressive credentials are using LinkedIn. Do a search for your topic and see who you find.

✦ **Local networking groups:** Most areas have clubs that play host to networking groups. See what kind of professional events are happening near you. You may find some interesting people.

✦ **Conferences:** Your search should take you offline as well. Conferences are a wonderful place to network, promote your brand and your business, and, yes, meet intriguing people.

 When you reach out to people for an interview, don't forget to tell them what's in it for them. Giving them an idea of how many people listen to your podcast now and in the future can help sweeten the deal.

Podcasting versus Internet Radio

If you're thinking that podcasting isn't for you, you may be tempted to try having an Internet radio show as opposed to a regular podcast. Surely, a radio show is easier, and you'd have the support of the host community, right? Though some purists may disagree, there's certainly nothing wrong with going this route, especially for the technically challenged. With Internet radio, you don't necessarily have to invest in a lot of heavy equipment, though many hardcore radio hosts do set up a studio to make sure that they're putting out a good quality show.

Internet radio is hosted by a larger website or brand such as BlogTalkRadio. com. Instead of relying on your computer equipment and having to edit and upload sound files, radio hosts and their guests call in to a designated phone number. Listeners can also call in with questions as well. The show is recorded and kept on the host website so that folks can listen in the future. You also have the ability to embed some code on your blog or website so that you can keep the traffic on your own site while your community enjoys listening to the streaming service.

Internet radio sites also offer each show host the ability to have a live chat stream going throughout the original live broadcast. A live chat can be a fun way to interact with your community. You may want to have someone watch the stream and report comments, while you interview your guests so that you don't miss anyone's questions or comments.

The big difference here is that you're not downloading the audio files to your own computer to host on a spot of your choosing. With Internet radio, the website hosts your content and, in some cases, may even own it. Always read all the fine print before agreeing to host a show on an Internet radio website.

**Book III
Chapter 3**

Also, with Internet radio, you may have an opportunity to edit your show, especially if you're doing a live broadcast. With podcasting, you can go back and clean up any "ums" or background noise before uploading, but with a live Internet radio broadcast, you can't always edit before you air.

As with most user-generated content sites, Internet radio sites come with their own Terms of Service (TOS) listing rules and guidelines. If you say something that goes against their TOS, they can yank your show.

Both methods have their pros and cons, but podcasting does allow more freedom to say what you'd like, keep your own content, and edit as needed.

Using Video in Your Blogs

To take your blog to a whole new level, try creating videos to embed in your blog posts. The benefits abound.

*Using Podcasts
or Video in Your
Content*

For starters, video offers a more human element to your blogging. Viewers hear the passion in your voice and see it in your eyes. Most people like video because they feel as if they're talking to a blogger one on one. They trust you because video tells them you have nothing to hide.

Many bloggers prefer video because they can expand upon a point better than they can in a blog post. In addition, bloggers can benefit from video in the following ways:

✦ Your viewers connect better when they see your face and hear the emotional appeal of your voice.

✦ You can create product demonstrations, showing how something works, instead of telling.

✦ You can upload your video to YouTube and other video sharing services, giving you more opportunities to reach people.

✦ You can show your logo on the video, leading to more brand recognition.

✦ You can show off a fun, humorous, or playful side.

✦ People will listen, instead of scanning the text of a blog post.

✦ Seeing your personality and style on a video can lead to speaking engagements.

✦ In addition to optimizing your video and attracting the search engines, you can also drive traffic from YouTube or another video hosting service.

✦ According to Forrester Research, videos can improve your blog's search engine visibility by up to 50 percent.

✦ Using product placement in videos can entice others to use your product or service.

Creating viral videos

Sometimes videos go *viral* — that is, they're shared and viewed thousands (and sometimes millions!) of times on the web. Videos go viral for different reasons, and it's not always an accident. Some brands create videos in hopes that they'll catch the attention of the masses and the press.

 Just about every viral video has one thing in common: It's entertaining. Your video blog about "Top 10 Reasons to Buy Organic" isn't going to go viral because that's just not exciting or interesting to most people. Viral videos are funny or heartwarming, but more importantly, the people who view viral videos look at them and immediately want to share them afterwards.

Here are some more things that help to turn videos into viral sensations:

♦ **They're parodies.** People like to see brands or celebrities poke fun at something, and self-deprecating humor always goes over well. When you poke fun at yourself, your brand, or your genre, people appreciate your ability to keep it real. Just be careful not to be mean and insult the people you're trying to reach,

♦ **People can relate to them.** When people see a video that resonates with them, they're likely to share. Common household mishaps, children being children, bad acting or singing, and a humorous look at the things people go through during their regular routines are especially appealing.

♦ **They appeal to our emotions.** Charitable or campaigns to raise awareness often use unfortunate but real situations to tug at heartstrings and get people talking.

♦ **They're not too deep.** When people have to think about what they're watching or if they just don't get what they're watching, they're not going to stick around. If you have to touch on a deep or intellectual topic, try doing so with humor so that you don't lose your audience.

♦ **They're unique.** You know what makes a video not go viral? When it copies other viral videos. Come up with some ideas no one else is doing and you'll have more viewers.

♦ **They show something remarkable.** Many viral videos show talented people. Singers, athletes, musicians, and others have gone viral.

♦ **They're not staged.** Videos that are staged to look spontaneous usually don't look anything close to spontaneous.

Though some brands or individuals create videos with the intention of them going viral, the truth is most viral videos weren't intended to be that way. They had a real quality to them that people appreciated and shared. What can you create that people will want to share?

Sharing your video with others

In order to send a video on the road to virality or, at the very least, bring in people to watch your video, you're going to have to get your social sharing on. You use some of the same sharing methods as you would with blog posts and podcasts, but you also try a few other methods.

Try these on for size:

♦ **Use your embed code.** When you upload a video to a video sharing website, you'll receive a unique embed code. Use this code in blog posts and your website and make sure that it's made available for others to use in their blog posts as well.

Book III
Chapter 3

Using Podcasts
or Video in Your
Content

+ **Use the social networks.** Share your videos on Facebook, Twitter, Google+, and even Pinterest. With the exception of Twitter, all let viewers play the video in their social media platform so that they don't have to change websites to view it.

+ **Use YouTube.** When you use YouTube, you have the potential to expose your video to millions of people.

Don't forget to use your SEO for videos, too. Use keywords and phrases so that folks can find your video on the search engines and also on the website that is hosting your video. Videos have the ability to catch more search engine attention than text, so it would be unwise not to optimize your videos for search.

Interviewing on camera

People love video interviews. They make more of an impact than text and even audio because viewers can see the faces of both the interviewer and interviewee and see reactions to questions. It's that trust thing again. Videos can show sincerity or catch someone in the middle of a lie. Plus, it's just nice to places faces with names and voices.

Because you're interviewing on camera, your flaws, imperfections, and mannerisms are open for scrutiny. If you're always smoothing your hair or rubbing your nose, it may be the source of embarrassment if you're not mindful of your quirks during the interview. Also, if you're not prepared for your interview, it's more difficult to wing it.

The following tips help you host an awesome video interview:

+ **Do your research.** Know as much about your interview subject as possible so that when you're live on camera, you can get more personal, if needed.

+ **Don't get too personal.** The last thing you want is to make the person with you feel uncomfortable. Not only will it lead to a bad interview, but your viewers may also be uncomfortable, and you may have problems finding future interview subjects.

+ **If you're reading from notes, don't make it obvious.** Place bullet points off camera where you can sneak a glance, but don't spend your interview time reading. It looks unprofessional.

+ **Be mindful of your "uhms."** Sometimes people don't notice their own little habits, but boy, do they show up on camera! It takes some practice, but do pay attention to throat clearings, "ums," and other habits that don't show well on camera.

✦ **Make eye contact.** If you're not looking at the person you're interviewing, look at the camera. Looking off to the side or down at your lap makes you look distracted and not really interested in what's going on around you.

✦ **Talk into the camera.** If you're talking to viewers, look at the camera so that they feel as if you're talking to them.

✦ **Create your list of questions ahead of time and share it with your interview subject.** Always know what you're going to talk about ahead of time. Winging sometimes leads to a lapse in the conversation and sometimes looks unprofessional. Also, if your interview subject knows what questions he'll be asked, he can provide some good information, statistics, and other facts to help back up his point of view.

✦ **Don't let your interview subject take control.** If you're not careful, the person whom you're interviewing will take the lead and talk about only what she wants to talk about or start selling her latest book or blog post. Once you lose control of an interview, it's hard to get back on the right track. Take the lead and keep the lead.

✦ **Ask to expand upon one-word answers.** Nothing turns off viewers more than a boring interview. You'll find most people enjoy talking about themselves or what they do. However, now and then, you'll come across someone who is shy or unpolished. They may even feel "yes" or "no" is an adequate response. It's up to the interviewer to bring out the best in the guests by asking open-ended questions and directing the conversation.

Chapter 4: Sharing Images

In This Chapter

✓ **Finding the right images for your content**

✓ **Following the law**

✓ **Breaking up your content with images**

*I*mages are an important part of content creation. They help illustrate a point, break up text, and add more to the conversation. But using an image in your content isn't as simple as pilfering a photo from Google images and adding it to your blog post. In addition to choosing a photo that helps to enhance your content, you also have legal and copyright considerations. In this chapter, we explore how to add great images without breaking the law.

Using Images for Your Online Content

A picture doesn't always say a thousand words, but it often gives your content a little extra something-something. People like images; their eyes are drawn to them. If it's not the headline that makes them take notice, your image can be the one-two punch. Because online content works best when it's scannable, images give the reader another area to focus on as well.

Images are also good search engine optimization. When you take the time to add keywords to your image when using your blog's upload tool and caption the photo, the search engines will pick up the search terms. Your images then show up in image searches, such as Google Images.

You can also use images for other reasons. For example, you can invite your community to "Caption This" on your Facebook Page or create a Twitter discussion by sharing a photo and inviting discussion. Images are a whole other way to provide content and bring in readers, build community, and, hopefully, drive sales.

Legalities: What You Need to Know about Sharing Images

Adding a photo to your blog isn't as simple as downloading an image, however. People who take photos own the copyright to them. Just because you see a photo online doesn't mean that you have permission to use it. Also, just because you don't see a copyright symbol doesn't mean that the image isn't copyright protected.

Some people feel that because something is posted on the web, it's in the public domain. This assumption isn't true, either. It's always important to check each and every image for the available rights and usage.

You can tell whether you can use a photo by reading all the details around it. If the license says "All rights reserved," it means it's not available for use unless you contact the author for permission (Figure 4-1).

Figure 4-1:
Always check for image rights and ask permission before using a photo.

License

© All Rights Reserved

Privacy

☐ This photo is visible to everyone

After you receive permission to use the image, you may embed it into your blog post as long as you provide attribution. The photographer may also require a link back to the original content. Please note that this requirement usually means that you're only granted one-time usage for that specific blog post or content. You don't have permission to use the photo as often as you'd like.

In addition, most images require a fee to use; if you want to use an image more than once, you'll have to pay extra. Make sure that any agreement between you and the photographer is clear and that you have a good understanding of how many times you can use the image and what other requirements she may have for its use.

Some photos also have a "Some rights reserved" label. This label means that the agreement between you and the photographer isn't as strict, but it also means you should read all the fine print to find out exactly what rights you have when using the image. You may have unlimited use but have to attribute to the photographer each time. It also may mean that you can use the image on a personal blog but not for commercial use.

If you come upon a photo that says "No derivative works," it means you're not allowed to take the photo and alter it in any way and publically post it as your own. You can't add anything to the photo, nor can you change colors or retouch it using Photoshop.

Many online photographers share under the *Creative Commons*. Creative Commons means you're welcome to use the photo, if you follow the listed guidelines. While in many cases Creative Commons photographers allow others to share their photo, usually royalty-free, it doesn't mean that the images are free to use any way you like. Read all the fine print. The photographer may require specific credits, limited usage, and/or a link back to his original content.

Even if no specific requests are made, the right thing to do is to offer attribution to the photographer. Using a photo is the same as quoting another blogger on your blog or sharing someone else's text on your blog. If you post someone else's photo and pass it off as your own, even if that's not your intention, you're not only violating copyright laws, but you're sharing unethically.

A good general rule for anyone looking to use a photo found online (or offline!) is "When in doubt, ask." In some cases, photographers discovered years later that bloggers had used their images and successfully sued for back royalties.

**Book III
Chapter 4**

Sharing Images

Finding Images Online

Don't let all this talk about rights and usage discourage you from finding photos to use for your content. Finding photos to use isn't difficult, and the rights are usually laid out for you under each photo (see Figure 4-2).

Instead of punching keywords into your favorite search engine's image search, which can lead to confusion about rights, it's a better idea to become a member of photo sharing sites. Some sites allow you to use photos for free as long as you follow certain guidelines, such as notifying the photographer and giving attribution. Notifying the photographer, though, isn't the same as asking permission. If the site requires you to notify the photographer, it simply means the photographer has given permission already; he just wants to know where it's going to be used.

Figure 4-2:
Using stock. xchng may save you from a legal headache.

Also, some photographers won't allow their images to be used on certain sites — for example, pornography, political, religious or any other sites where the image may be taken out of context or use of it will reflect poorly on the photographer. However, the photo sharing site explains these limitations for each photo.

Something important to note is that many of the photos shared for free online, even on image sharing sites, aren't shot by professional photographers and can sometimes look a little rough or amateurish. However, you can still find plenty of professional-quality photos.

Most stock image sites require you to pay a fee. It can either be a monthly fee where you're granted permission to use a set amount of photos or a per photo fee. You may also be required to attribute the photo to the photo sharing site so that everyone knows where the image came from.

Table 4-1 lists popular photo sharing sites. Some are free, and some require a monthly or per photo fee.

Table 4-1	Popular Photo Sharing Sites
Site	*Description*
123rf (www.123rf.com)	Offers both free and paying options.
Bigstock (www.bigstockphoto.com)	Requires a subscription fee.
Creative Commons (http://creativecommons.org)	Allows for the posting and sharing of creative commons works.
Dreamstime (www.dreamstime.com)	Offers both free and paying options.
Flickr (www.flickr.com)	Images often fall under the Creative Commons but check the right sidebar of each image page to view rights for each photo as this isn't the case for all.
iStockphoto (www.istockphoto.com)	Requires a subscription fee.
Morgue File (www.morguefile.com)	Offers free photos that are mostly taken by amateur photographers and aren't always professional quality.
Pinterest (www.pinterest.com)	The new kid on the social media block. Pinterest allows members to create their own bulletin boards using photos. Not a site where you can buy images, but you can search out images and contact the original photographer to find out whether you can buy a copy of the photo.
Shutterstock (www.shutterstock.com)	Subscription-based service.
stock.xchng (www.sxc.hu)	Offers a mixture of free and pay-per-use photos.
Wikimedia Commons (http://commons.wikimedia.org)	Offers royalty-free and free photos.
Wylio (www.wylio.com)	A search engine featuring free images for bloggers. A nifty feature for this service is that you can format your image right on the website to cut and paste into your blog post.

**Book III
Chapter 4**

Sharing Images

Using Photo Sharing Sites for Your Own Images

Images aren't only useful for illustrating your content. They're also handy as a marketing tool. When you share and upload your own images, you can reach a whole new audience. For example, if you like to photograph local architecture, you can post your images to a photo sharing site, such as Flickr, and catch the eye of people who are also into architecture (see Figure 4-3). They may end up following you on Twitter or Google+ because they enjoy your take. In the process, they can also become aware of your business, should the need arise.

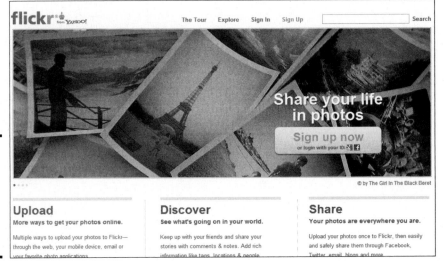

Figure 4-3:
Use a photo sharing site, such as Flickr, to help market your brand.

When you allow others to use your images, you also create an opportunity for backlinks. When users attribute a photograph to you and link to your website, they're alerting the search engines, which is always a very good thing. Moreover, others will follow the attribution to your blog or website, and some may even become members of your community.

Sharing photos is also a way to establish expertise. For example, foodies often share images of their latest culinary creations or a wonderful dinner out. If your business is an auto dealership, sharing images based on the cars you sell can help bring in new business. If you sell cosmetics, sharing before and after makeover pictures can lead to sales.

If you share images of people on your Facebook business page and tag them, your tags can show up in their friends' status updates, if their settings allow, which can also lead to new customers and community members.

Often times, when you post an image on a social network devoted to image sharing, others will comment. Those comments lead to a whole new way to grow your community.

Smartphone users enjoy using the Instagram photo sharing app to upload images to share on the social networks. When you take a photo with Instagram, you have the option to post a few words in the caption and share the photo on Facebook and Twitter.

When you share an image on these sites, make sure to leave contact information, just in case someone wants to share the image or find out more about you.

Book IV

Twitter

"I'd respond to this person's comment on Twitter, but I'm a former Marine, Bernard, and a Marine never retweets."

Contents at a Glance

Chapter 1: Using Twitter as a Marketing Tool

In This Chapter

✔ Understanding the benefits of Twitter for your brand

✔ Embracing brevity

✔ Avoiding a reputation as a spammer

✔ Checking out other brands using Twitter

✔ Making every word count

*T*witter took the world by storm in 2007. At first, the social media and blogging communities mostly embraced Twitter, but soon brands began appreciating its value. Today, Twitter is mainstream.

At first glance, Twitter looks like a lot of people dropping links and talking about nothing important. But before you write this microblogging site off as a lot of noise, consider the benefits of Twitter and how you can use it as valuable marketing tool — because, make no mistake, Twitter can totally make a brand.

In this chapter, we discuss the benefits of Twitter and how you can use it to raise brand awareness and drive traffic and sales.

For more information, check out *Twitter For Dummies,* by Laura Fitton, Michael Gruen, and Leslie Poston, or *Twitter Marketing For Dummies,* by Kyle Lacy.

Deciding Whether Twitter Is Right for You

Even if you've never used Twitter (see Figure 1-1), you've probably heard about this online social networking service. The Twitter icon, with its famous blue bird, is everywhere from cable news broadcasts to your local supermarket. Everyone wants you to follow them on Twitter.

Before you post the Twitter icon on your blog or website or add your Twitter handle to your business cards, you need to know what exactly Twitter is and whether or not it's the right marketing platform for you.

Figure 1-1:
Twitter
allows you
to com-
municate
with your
community
in only 140
characters.

Twitter is a microblogging social network. We're going to get into the micro-blogging aspect more in the next section of this chapter, but suffice it to say that everything you post has to be short and simple. Believe me; communicating in the short form isn't as easy as it sounds, especially if you want to get a message out. Still, millions of people are using Twitter and many brands are finding success.

Different people use Twitter to

✦ **Build a community:** The best reason to join any social network is to grow a community of friends and advocates. Your community consists of the people who you build trust and relationships with because they view you as being accessible. These people are the ones who will have your back.

✦ **Find new customers:** Thanks to the Internet, you now have the ability to reach a whole new global market. With Twitter, you have the ability to reach millions of new people. Each person you interact with has the ability to reach people as well. You can leverage all that reachability into sales.

✦ **Have a conversation:** The best part of Twitter and other social networks is the ability to sell without sounding like you're selling. It's called *conversational marketing*, and it's exactly what it sounds like. When you have a conversation with your friends and followers, people get to know who you are and what you do. When they have a need for someone who does what you do, they're more likely to call on you. They may even like you so much that they decide to buy what you're selling just to support a friend.

✦ **Ask questions:** The best way to learn about your customers and potential customers is to ask questions. We're not saying that you need to have a Twitter poll (unless you want to), but there's nothing wrong with dropping a question now and then to find out about a demographic or habit (see Figure 1-2).

✦ **Get customer support:** Many people like to reach out to their favorite brands on Twitter to ask questions about a product or service or ask for direction or technical support. Twitter is another way to be accessible to your customers.

Figure 1-2:
Use Twitter
to ask
questions
and learn
about your
customers,
community,
and
followers.

◆ **Discover what people are saying about you:** It's important to receive feedback, especially unsolicited feedback. Sometimes folks are talking about your brand online, and you definitely want to know about it.

◆ **Promote your content:** Did you just write up a killer blog post? Are you releasing a new video? Do you want to let folks know about a new product launch? Twitter is an awesome tool for promoting new items.

◆ **Host Twitter chats:** Twitter chats allow you to discuss topics at length or bring in special guests. They're another way to interact with your community. See Book IV, Chapter 5 for an in-depth look at Twitter chats.

◆ **Promote brand visibility:** When people see your logo on Twitter and they see you communicating with customers and other Twitter friends, they feel confident in the brand. They like the human element and especially know that when they reach out to you on the social networks, you'll be there to respond.

◆ **Give out perks:** Some brands share Twitter-only discounts and freebies as a way to reward their followers. Lucky recipients will no doubt share these perks with their own followers.

Twitter is a commitment. Networking on Twitter isn't as simple as sending a tweet and expecting to bring in the masses; it's also a matter of building relationships, getting to know people, and holding a conversation.

Communicating in 140 Characters

Possibly the most challenging part of Twitter is the 140-character limit. This amount may seem like a lot at first — until you try to post something pithy or clever and realize you can't fit everything you want to say. Once you start deleting characters, your sentence can lose all meaning.

Don't fret, and, whatever you do, don't break out the text speak (see Figure 1-3). Brevity is easier than you think.

**Book IV
Chapter 1**

Using Twitter as a
Marketing Tool

Figure 1-3:
Using text
speak hurts
the eyes
and looks
unprofes-
sional.

You may notice that a lot of people use shortened words, such as "u" instead of "you" or "2" instead of "too" or "to." The problem is that using acronyms or abbreviations is unprofessional and hurts people's eyes. Ditto running words together to fit them in the space. A good general rule is that if people can't read your sentence at first glance, you'll lose them.

Here are a few tips for getting the most out of your 140 characters:

✦ **Make every word count.** Use words that show an action or make an impact. Avoid filler words, such as "that."

✦ **Use short words when at all possible.** Try short, eye-catching words over larger words. Just about every "big" word has a shorter counterpart.

✦ **Punctuation matters.** You may be tempted to skip your periods and commas in order to fit in more characters. Run-on sentences don't look very pretty, and they're hard to read. Do your best to use proper grammar and punctuation.

✦ **Use humor.** Do you know what gets lots of retweets and responses? A funny tweet. That isn't to say every post needs to be slapstick, but don't be afraid to say something funny now and again. Your community will enjoy it.

✦ **Get to the point.** Don't take the scenic route; get right to the point. You have only 140 characters to work with, so say what you have to say without mincing words.

✦ **Grammar counts.** Don't use poor grammar because it fits the tweet better. Grammatical errors turn people off from wanting to do business with you because they feel you're unprofessional.

✦ **Use both upper- and lowercase.** All uppercase letters make people feel as if you're yelling at them, and all lowercase letters looks as if you're too lazy to hit the Shift key. Make a good impression by rocking the upper- and lowercases.

✦ **Give value.** Being silly and fun on Twitter is okay, and it's fine to say something frivolous as well. Just be sure to add value into the mix. If you're using Twitter to promote your business, share your expertise as well.

✦ **Don't always make it about you.** Don't make every tweet about you or your business. Visit with your community. Participate in other conversations, ask questions, and share links to other people's stuff.

✦ **Don't break up your tweets.** Be careful dividing up tweets to continue a thought. So many people will see only the first or second half of the tweet and have absolutely no idea what you're talking about.

✦ **It's okay to use characters.** Even though we discourage text speak, feel free to replace the word "and" with an ampersand. Replacing a word with an accepted character isn't considered unprofessional.

Before you get started with tweets, research other brands that are having success using Twitter and observe how they're interacting with their communities. You may come away from the experience with some good ideas for interacting with your own communities. (See the upcoming "Researching Other Brands on Twitter" section.)

Promoting without Seeming You're Promoting

On the social networks, there's a delicate balance between promoting and spamming. If everything you do is calling attention to you or your business, you'll find yourself losing followers faster than you can bat an eye. The beautiful thing about conversational marketing is that you can talk to your friends and followers about anything in the world, and it still has the potential to drive business.

Your first cause of action is to follow the right people (see Book IV, Chapter 2). After all, why be on Twitter if you're not reaching people? Don't worry about starting out slow at first; your numbers will grow if your tweets offer value, and you gain a reputation for being interactive and engaging. The tricky part is to get people to dig what you do without turning them off with spam or over-the-top sales tactics.

You can easily be overly promotional on Twitter, especially when you see others do nothing but drop links. Because of the 140-character limit, many people feel it's more important to fit a link in than some interesting text. The problem is, many of the people who drop too many links either lose their followers, don't gain new follows, or their existing followers begin to ignore them.

**Book IV
Chapter 1**

**Using Twitter as a
Marketing Tool**

What follows is a list of do's and don'ts for promoting your brand on Twitter without looking like you're promoting your brand on Twitter:

- **Do follow the people who will receive the most value from your tweets and your brand.** You may be tempted to follow everyone you can simply to receive a follow-back in return, but this approach only leads to a cluttered, hard-to-follow Twitter stream with people who don't really care about you or your brand. Be selective with your follows for the best level of engagement.

- **Don't auto-follow everyone who follows you.** You may be considering paying for an *auto-follow program* — that is, an app that automatically follows everyone who follows you or who follows a specific Twitter account or keyword. An auto-follow program isn't a good idea because not only don't you know everyone in your Twitter stream, but people who auto-follow are very easy to spot because they have a high ratio of people they follow versus people who follow them. This ratio imbalance is usually the sign of a spammer, and it drives followers away.

- **Do search for specific keywords and topics.** By all means, use your search function to find the people who follow a specific keyword or talk about a particular topic.

- **Don't spam everyone who is talking about those topics and keywords.** Do you know what people who use Twitter regularly hate? They can't stand it when they mention a word, and then all these spammers come out of the woodwork. For example, mentioning "iPad" on Twitter leads to a flurry of hopeful sales people bombarding the unsuspecting tweeter with links to discounts on tablets. You'll find yourself reported as a spammer if you spam.

- **Do ask questions.** Get some interaction going with your Twitter community by asking questions. Keep in mind that you won't get a response every time, but sometimes some great conversations ensue. Also, don't be afraid to use question time to solicit feedback — both positive and negative.

- **Don't respond to each question with a link.** If people reach out to your brand on Twitter, you may at times respond with links and at other times avoid them. For example, if they can't find a sign-up page for your newsletter, by all means respond with a link. If they ask a general information question falling within your area of expertise, don't respond with your latest blog post. That'll get old and spammy after a while.

- **Do be sure to inject your personality into your tweets.** Don't be afraid to use humor, slang (that isn't vulgar or offensive), or any other words that show off your personality. You want to show your human, endearing side. The people who are most successful on Twitter aren't afraid to show their personality and fun, playful side.

✦ **Don't rely solely on the scheduled tweet.** Scheduling your tweets, usually through an app such as HootSuite, helps to make sure that you post announcements throughout your day. However, when all you post are announcements, what you're doing is broadcasting and not interacting. If it helps, go ahead and schedule those announcements, but do stick around in case someone has questions.

✦ **Do answer questions and respond to comments.** If folks are reaching out to you on Twitter, it's a good thing. It means they're putting their faith in you and find you accessible. Make sure to check Twitter throughout the day for questions and comments so that you can be sure to address everything in a timely manner.

✦ **Don't ignore a tweet because you don't want to draw light to negativity.** All feedback is good feedback, even the bad stuff. Answer questions even if they relate to a negative experience, especially because people are watching. If you'd rather not talk about such things with so many people in attendance, invite the tweeter to take it offline with a phone call or e-mail.

✦ **Do share links to your stuff.** Have a great promotion? Share the link! Did you write a great blog post? Share the link! Does someone else have something cool to promote? Share the link! After all, if you're using Twitter as a promotional tool, you're looking for an end result for your ultimate goal, a goal which you can't meet without the link. Don't be afraid to share.

✦ **Don't only drop links.** If your Twitter stream is nothing but links and self-promotional spamminess, no one will care. You'll drive everyone away. Make sure that links are only a small percentage of what you're sharing on Twitter.

✦ **Do share links to other people's stuff.** The social networks aren't only about you. Highlight other people's achievements, and they'll be more likely to highlight yours. Remember, though, a "you scratch my back and I'll scratch yours" mentality gets a bit old.

✦ **Don't share or retweet a link unless you know exactly what it's about.** Have you ever seen a popular tweeter share a link and instantaneously receive hundreds of retweets in return. It's a good bet many of those retweeters didn't even click the link to read what it's all about. Blind faith is cool and all, but what if the tweeter was linking to a post that is a lie or something offensive or inappropriate? A retweet is an endorsement, and it's in the best interests of your brand to know exactly what you're putting out there.

✦ **Do tweet every day.** Consistency is key to social media success. Put yourself out there every day so that you're a visible presence. When folks know when to expect your tweet, it's a good thing.

**Book IV
Chapter 1**

**Using Twitter as a
Marketing Tool**

✦ **Don't let your Twitter account become a ghost town.** People feel better knowing that their favorite brands are socially engaged because it makes them feel as if they're really into what people think or want. When they look up a brand on Twitter and there haven't been any tweets since 2008, it tells folks the brand isn't interested in what their community thinks.

✦ **Do take conversations private.** Not everything has to be out in the open. There's nothing wrong with offering to take an in-depth conversation offline or private. Sometimes, a one-on-on conversation is the best case because you don't want to exclude everyone else in your stream. Also, if you're dealing with a negative situation, there's only so much you can resolve in 140 characters, so taking the conversation private is the way to go.

✦ **Don't auto-DM.** Avoid sending auto private or direct messages (DMs), as shown in Figure 1-4. Some apps instantaneously send "thank you" or "follow this link" private messages as soon as someone follows you. Auto and spam DMs are a sure way to receive an immediate unfollow. DMs are considered a private area, and most tweeters don't want their privacy invaded.

Figure 1-4:
Avoid sending spammy auto-DMs to your new followers. This type of message will cause most of them to immediately unfollow you.

✦ **Do talk about yourself and your brand.** You're going to hear and read a lot about how the social networks aren't for self-promotion and how it's all about the conversation, and that's true. However, it's silly to think you're spending all your time on Twitter or Facebook and can't even promote your brand.

✦ **Don't talk only about yourself and your brand.** It's all about balance. Go ahead and promote your stuff, but make sure that you have a good ratio of conversational tweets versus promotional tweets. Different experts have a good idea of what that ratio should be, but usually trial and error determine what works best for you. Try tweeting one to two promotional tweets out of every ten tweets.

✦ **Do find topics of interest.** Try introducing a different discussion topic or question to your community each day. See whether you find any news that will interest to your niche or talk about the latest tools and technique. Find something discussion-worthy and go for it.

✦ **Don't be corporate and boring.** People don't always want to discuss the brand. While they do enjoy some transparency from time to time, you'll lose people if your tweets are all about the corporate shareholder meeting or yesterday's board meeting. Do share some company business, but all work and no play will make you a very dull tweeter.

✦ **Do talk to everyone.** If your Twitter account has 2,500 followers, 2,500 people are interested in learning about you or your brand. Of course, you can't reach out to everyone by name every day, but ensuring that many of your daily tweets apply to everyone is almost as good as reaching out to everyone. While at times you'll want to reach out to individuals, if your Twitter account is a hotbed of exclusivity, you'll lose followers.

✦ **Don't just reach out to the big names.** Many people feel that if they reach out to the big names on Twitter, they'll receive more attention. When someone with hundreds of thousands of followers retweets your link or mentions you on the social networks, you're bound to get more followers and interest in your brand. However, if you're only reaching out to the big names, it won't be long before you gain a reputation for pandering to the famous people. Your biggest advocates aren't the people with a huge following; they're the people who use your brand and interact with you every day. Collectively, they can have a bigger reach.

Many items on this laundry list of action items and things to avoid may not look like you're promoting at all, and that's the point. On the social networks, people don't want to be pitched to, unless they invite it. They want to enjoy a conversation and share interesting items they find online. If you turn it from a heavy sales pitch to a conversation between friends, you may find that you land more sales than if you did nothing but drop links.

Researching Other Brands on Twitter

Finding out more about how other brands are using Twitter can help you formulate your own Twitter marketing plan. Many brands are achieving success on the social networks because they're interesting and engaging, and there's nothing wrong with scoping them out and learning by their example.

First, get off Twitter and get on Google. Search Google to find the brands that have been successful on Twitter. So many case studies online talk about brands that are doing Twitter right. Read the case studies and follow the brands to see them in action. Note the following:

+ How often are they tweeting each day?
+ What are they tweeting about?
+ How are they handling customer comments, inquiries, and complaints online?
+ How often are they dropping links?
+ Are they offering discounts, freebies, or other perks to their followers?
+ What is setting their Twitter apart from the rest?

The next thing you want to do is determine how brands that are similar to yours are using Twitter. Also, observe them to see how they do things. You may love certain aspects of their community outreach and not agree with others. This contrast is good because it means you won't be tempted to flat out copy their approach.

Finally, you want to research cases of companies that made mistakes — and you can find plenty of these case studies and stories online. For example, some brands haven't reacted well to negative feedback, or a community manager dropped a personal tweet from the company account.

When you learn about the way others are using Twitter and learn by their mistakes, you'll become a positive case study yourself.

Knowing Quality Is More Important Than Quantity

Too many people on Twitter worry more about numbers when they should really be thinking about other things. For example, sometimes brands don't feel as if they're successful unless they have tens of thousands of followers. True, it's great to have such a large reach, but the truth is, there's no way a brand can interact with all those people. By all means, strive for the big numbers, but don't obsess over them. Instead, worry about building up quality followers: the customers and members of your community who truly believe in the brand and will advocate for you online. Build a core follower base, and the rest will fall into place.

You may also be tempted to follow thousands of people right off the bat so that they'll follow you in return. Before you do so, keep in mind that all these people are going to show up in their Twitter stream. Adding thousands of people is much easier than removing them.

While there's nothing wrong with following so many people, sometimes seeing what people are saying in your Twitter stream is hard because so many people are talking at once. Following so many friends can make it very difficult to find the quality, conversational tweets through all the links and spam.

By all means, continue to add new followers, but do so slowly so that you know who you're following and are better able to have a conversation.

You may also be wondering how many tweets you should send out on any given day. While it's true no one wants to see nothing but you in their twitter streams, it's also true that we can't give you a set-in-stone rule regarding the amount of tweets you should be sending out. Spontaneity is what leads to success and if you're counting, planning, and scheduling tweets, you're going to lose a lot of the element of fun and surprise many brand successful accounts have. Do what feels right. If you're deep in conversation with others, you're going to be sending out more tweets than you would on a slow day. Also, if you're launching a new product, you're probably going to spend more time on the social networks than you would on a normal day.

Finally, many brands and individuals are concerned about the number of links they share on a given day. Of course, you don't want to spam links all day, but, again, it depends on the day and what you're sharing. Always do your best to add balance and have more conversational tweets than link tweets because you don't want to be known only for dropping links.

Don't obsess over numbers. Succeeding on Twitter is more about tweeting out quality information to quality people than going overboard with followers or worrying about whether or not you tweeted enough in one day. Good, organic growth trumps big numbers every time.

Chapter 2: Using Twitter as a Networking Tool

In This Chapter

✔ Following people on Twitter

✔ Reaching out to others on Twitter

✔ Finding the right words

✔ Behaving properly on Twitter

✔ Tweeting up

*T*he people who do nothing but drop links on Twitter are missing out on some amazing opportunities. That's because Twitter isn't just a useful promotional tool, but it's also an important networking tool.

Before the Internet, most people had to join professional organizations and attend networking events on a regular basis. While that's still the case now, the truth is, all that in-person networking can be expensive, too. Many people who are just starting out in their fields can't afford to put out the money to attend a lot of events or join many professional groups.

The beauty of Twitter and other social networks is the ability to reach so many people without spending a lot of money. With millions of people on Twitter at any given time, you have ample opportunity to reach out and be reached out to. Make no mistake, Twitter may force you into brevity, but the opportunity to grow your professional network is absolutely there.

In this chapter, we take a look at how to use Twitter as a networking tool and a few best practices for making the most of your experience.

Finding the Right People to Follow

The first step in your Twitter marketing journey is to spend time with the people who make up your community and enjoy their company. To do that, you have to build up a follower base.

The best way to find followers on Twitter is search Twitter for the people who are mostly likely to support your brand. Here are some ideas for getting started:

+ **See how many of your existing customers are online.** If you're already in business, you probably have a list of people who you do business with. They may also be on the social networks. Use your mailing lists to find people to follow on Twitter. Most business people now have their Twitter accounts on their business cards and e-mail signatures. You can also use the search function.

+ **Find your friends and followers from other social networks.** If you already have a Facebook, Google+, or brand page set up on one of the other social networks, see whether those same friends are on Twitter and give them a follow.

+ **Follow other professionals you know from your respective space.** If you share tips or interact online with other professionals, follow them on Twitter as well.

+ **Use Twitter search to find people with similar jobs/brands to yours.** Use the search function located at the top of your Twitter page or Twitter app, or go to `http://twitter.com/#!/search-home`. Search for similar brands and interests.

+ **See who follows similar brands to yours.** When you find brands that do the same or close to what you do, also follow their followers.

+ **Use your keywords in Twitter search.** Take those keywords you use to optimize your pages and use them.

Starting a Twitter follower base is as easy as following someone first. Once you start following people, most will follow you in return.

Finding Out Who Is Talking about You on Twitter

There's nothing voyeuristic or wrong about observing conversations on Twitter. Most people who tweet are hoping others will notice and join the conversation. If they didn't want a public conversation, they'd create a direct message (DM). They also wouldn't mention or `@reply` you unless they wanted you to know what they're saying. So if you see a complaint or `@reply` (see Figure 2-1), it's in your best interest to respond, even if it's just to say "thank you."

As a brand (personal or professional), you always want to keep your ear to the ground. With Twitter, you can easily monitor the conversation and respond to comments and queries.

Figure 2-1:
To get someone's attention on Twitter, use an @reply.

Many times, if someone is talking about or to you, he will `@reply` you. This means that person is putting an @ in front of your Twitter screen name in order to get your attention. Without the @, there's a chance you won't see the tweet. Also, if you're reaching out to someone, you have to also put an @ in front of his screen name, or the tweet will get lost among the thousands of other tweets.

It's good customer service to find out what people are saying about you on Twitter. It gives you an opportunity to learn about problems or concerns and shows your customers and community you're accessible.

If it isn't on your daily schedule already, make time each day to explore Twitter and see who is talking and what they're saying. Don't shy away from criticism or critique. Instead, thank the other party and take it as valuable feedback.

Responding to Tweets

In order to monitor the conversation to find out whether folks are tweeting about you or your brand, keep a Twitter app, such as HootSuite, Seesmic, or Tweetdeck, open on your computer's desktop. You can set up these apps to ping you every time someone `@replies` your name or a posts a specific search term, including your name or that of your brand. (We cover apps in the next chapter.)

You need to set up these searches in order to reach out or respond to the people who are talking about or to you. For example, if you work for a restaurant chain and someone tweets out a picture of one of your dishes and talks about how much he enjoyed his meal, you want to acknowledge the tweet by thanking the other party and encouraging him to visit again. If someone tweets that a meal was subpar, you want to respond with an apology and perhaps even offer a discount or coupon for another meal in order to make things right.

You may be inclined to reach out to people who tweet about you via DM or other private method, and while there's nothing wrong with it, keep in mind that people like to see brands engaging online, even if it's not 100 percent positive. When others see a tweet from you (preferably on the brand account), it tells them the brand is accessible and transparent. When they see you reach out to say "thank you" or "I'm sorry," it tells them you're human. Even if you don't want to publicly address a situation, it's good practice to ask the other party if you can take it private and ask her to DM her e-mail address or phone number. When someone publicly addresses a brand and the brand responds privately, it looks as if they're not responding at all. Always offer some sort of public comment, just in case anyone is watching.

When you `@reply` someone, the comment doesn't show up for the masses, only people you're both friends with. It's not a private conversation — anyone who is searching can find it — but it's not mainstream, either.

If you want everyone to see comments you make when you `@reply` people, put a . in front of it; now everyone can see it. For example, if you wanted everyone to see an `@reply` to me, it would read . `@debng` (see Figure 2-2).

Figure 2-2:
Put a period
in front of
an @reply
if you want
everyone
who follows
you to see it.

Deborah Ng
View my profile page

| 32,843 TWEETS | 561 FOLLOWING | 10,674 FOLLOWERS |

Hey |@blogworldexpo - How are you today?

100   Tweet

Searching on Twitter

Twitter is an excellent search tool. Not only can you use it to discover who is talking about you or your brand, you can use it as an awesome search engine to find people to follow or reach out to, to find similar brands, and to see what's going on with specific keywords, search terms, hashtags, and news items.

Twitter isn't a search engine, but that doesn't mean you can't treat it like a search engine. If you're looking for something, anything, there's a very good chance you'll find it on Twitter.

What follows are some of the ways to use Twitter's search function or the search engine at `http://twitter.com/#!/search-home` as a search tool. You can find

✦ **People:** Search specific names, Twitter handles, professions, or hobbies. Don't forget to give them a follow, so you can connect.

✦ **Brands:** Use Twitter to search out similar brands to see how they're using the platform.

✦ **Clients:** Search terms will help you find potential clients. Also, consider the types of people you seek out offline in order to drum up business and search out the same types of people online.

✦ **Jobs:** You can use a search engine, such as twitterjobsearch.com, to find work or follow one of the many accounts that tweet out jobs. You can also use these search engines to find clients.

✦ **Hashtags:** The Twitter search engines help you follow your favorite hashtags.

✦ **Search terms:** When you use a Twitter search for particular search terms and keywords, you'll find everyone who is talking about those words and phrases.

✦ **Your brand:** Discover what others are saying about your brand.

✦ **Your passion:** Search your favorite subjects.

✦ **News:** Whether you want to go local, international, or very niche-oriented, you can search out the latest news on Twitter.

Tweeting Like a Pro

There's a difference in the way someone wanting to do business uses Twitter as opposed to a teen who only wants to tweet out to her friends. Just as you conduct yourself in a professional manner at offline networking events, you'll also want to conduct yourself as a professional on the social networks. People really do pay attention.

Articulating in 140 characters

Text speak, using abbreviations and shortened words in order to shorten a cellphone text message, is difficult to read and unprofessional when used when representing your brand on any platform. Because Twitter only allows for 140 characters, you may be tempted to use abbreviations or shortened words to fit in everything you want to say, but we don't recommend it.

✦ **Spell out every word.** The last thing you want is for people to mistake your message or get the wrong impression. When you're not spelling out entire words, some people may not understand what words you're trying to use. Also, some people may think you're lazy because you can't be bothered to spell. Keep in mind that every brand abbreviates words on their tweets, and while abbreviating is acceptable now and then, it's not recommended for everyday use.

+ **Use punctuation.** Periods and commas make sentences neat and tidy and help others understand your intended message. Besides, it's more professional to post a real sentence. Run-on sentences or lack of punctuation can change the emphasis, inflection, and meaning of a sentence.

+ **Practice the art of brevity.** There are always short words to use in place of big words. By choosing short words, you're adding the ability to create a longer sentence where the intended meaning comes through.

+ **Let your personality shine through.** Don't get so caught up in professionalism that it takes your personality out of the equation. Quirkiness, humor, and even respectful sarcasm add personality to tweets and make you seem more human.

Using the social networks isn't a reason to forget you're a professional. When you're using your brand account, conduct yourself in the same manner in which you'd conduct yourself at an offline business event.

Using the hashtag

When you put a pound sign (#) in front of a keyword, you're using a *hashtag*. The hashtag makes it easy to follow a conversation centered on a keyword or topic. For example, if yours is a sausage brand and you want to create a recipe contest around your world famous kielbasa, you might use `#kielbasa recipes` as your hashtag. The benefits to using a hashtag over an `@reply` abound:

+ **Hashtags catch the attention of others.** Sometimes people aren't necessarily part of a conversation but join in after espying a catchy hashtag in their Twitter streams.

+ **Hashtags add longevity to a conversation.** An `@reply` can die in a busy Twitter stream, but following the hashtag will allow you to view all tweets in a conversation at one time.

+ **Hashtags allow tweets to appear in a stream even if the other party doesn't @reply you.** Often during Twitter chats or hashtag campaigns, folks in the conversation don't use an `@reply` to catch your attention but instead rely solely on the hashtag. When you view a hashtag chat using an app such as HootSuite or TweetChat, you can better view the entire conversation at one time.

+ **You can measure the results of a hashtag.** Several apps and services, such as Radian6 or Hashtracking, not only have the ability to offer a transcript of a hashtag but also offer data from all the people who use the hashtag — for example, how many people viewed the hashtag (who didn't necessarily participate in the conversation), how many people clicked links, and who are the most influential people using the platform.

When you use hashtags, you can take your Twitter conversations to a whole new level. Hashtags allow you to have, keep track of, and measure a conversation, something very important to anyone marketing a brand.

Please see Book IV, Chapter 3 to discover the benefits and best practices of hosting a hashtag chat.

Sharing on Twitter

The beauty of Twitter is how awesome a tool it is for sharing. The people who use Twitter love to discover new articles, videos, and people. They're quick to offer a recommendation or review and especially enjoy when you ask for their opinions. If they like what you say, they'll even give you a retweet.

Knowing when to @reply and direct message

For the most part, your responses to other tweeters will be public unless someone specifically reaches out to you via direct message (DM). Sometimes, though, you want to take public messages private because you don't want to expose some things to the entire Twittersphere:

✦ **Long conversations between you and someone else:** Yes, Twitter is all about public conversations, but you also don't want to clutter up your friends' Twitter streams with a long conversation with someone else. For something expansive, you may want to offer to take it private.

✦ **Complaints:** If someone has a complaint about your brand or is reaching out in a negative manner, let him know you're sorry for the inconvenience and offer to take it to phone call, e-mail, or DM so that you can better handle the situation. You don't want to sweep the complaint under the rug, nor do you want to ignore it. However, you don't necessarily want to air all your brand's negativity to the masses, either.

✦ **Personal details:** It should go without saying that private e-mail addresses, phone numbers, addresses, and other personal details shouldn't be available to the public. If you need to share this information or need to request that others share it with you, it's best to take it private.

✦ **Information that isn't meant for public consumption:** Sometimes there are details you'd like to share with people but can't put it out to the public yet. By all means, use a Twitter DM.

✦ **Something that may embarrass someone:** Perhaps a negative situation is the result of customer or client error. The last thing you want to do is shame that person on the social networks. If you need to talk to someone because of a potentially embarrassing error, take it private.

For the most part, your Twitter updates are public. However, use your best judgment. Every now and then, you may need to take things private.

Retweeting and being retweeted

For many people on Twitter, getting retweeted is part of their marketing plan. It may not seem like much, but a retweet can go a long way. For example, if you tweet out a link to your latest blog post, and someone else retweets it, more people are likely to view your blog post. The more retweets you get, the further your reach.

If you're on Twitter for any length of time, you may notice that certain "famous" tweeters and those with the most followers get retweets every time they post something. What follows are some tips for retweeting other people's tweets and also for writing the types of things people will want to retweet:

- ✦ **Say something people want to share.** If you're tweeting links to your food or talking about the weather, your content isn't very shareable. The type of content people share is usually funny, unique, profound, or interesting.

- ✦ **Share something others want to share.** Don't share for the sake of sharing; share because you think an item has interest or value. Before tweeting a quote or link, ask "Will this interest my community enough that they want to share it with others?" Think about why you felt compelled to share it and whether your community will feel the same way.

- ✦ **Don't write for the retweet.** Usually people who try hard to think of something clever or pithy to tweet fall flat for trying too hard. Retweetable tweets are usually organic and spontaneous, not forced or flat.

- ✦ **Don't just retweet because someone famous said something.** Many people retweet well-known people in hopes of catching their attention. If you retweet celebrities all the time, it tells your community you don't really care about them as much as you do famous people. If Ashton Kutcher has nothing to do with you, and your community and isn't saying anything all that great, maybe save your retweet for someone more deserving.

- ✦ **Say "thank you" for retweets.** When people retweet something you said or share links to your blog posts, be sure to say "thank you." It shows them you appreciate the community effort.

Avoid the *vanity retweet* — when someone tweets something nice about you and you retweet it. For example, if someone tweeted "@debng is the most brilliant blogger in the world" and I retweeted it, I'd look like a fool. Most people think a vanity retweet looks like bragging and roll their eyes at those who do it.

Blocking people

It's going to happen. There are going to be people on Twitter who are so abusive or spammy that you have no recourse but to ban them. First, don't feel guilty. We all have a list of blocked tweeters, even if we don't talk about them. Second, understand that no one has to put up with abuse.

What does it mean to *block* your tweets? Simply, it means the person you block shouldn't be able to see or respond to your tweets.

Why would you want to block people from viewing your tweets or participating in your conversation?

✦ Because every time they respond to a question or comment, it's with a link to a sales page.

✦ Because every time you post, they respond with something snarky.

✦ Because someone uses vulgarity and profanity on a regular basis, and that's not your thing.

✦ Because someone is abusive to you and your followers.

If someone isn't being very nice on Twitter or if someone is using your conversations as an excuse to sell stuff or drive traffic to his site, go ahead and block that person. Your community will probably applaud you.

Creating a successful Twitter campaign

Your twitter campaign takes careful planning. It's not enough to shoot out a tweet every now and then. You also want to put a strategy in place. If you don't go into it with a specific plan and goal, your tweets may be sporadic and haphazard, and you won't achieve the success you hoped for.

Here are some tips for creating a successful Twitter campaign:

✦ **Plan a follower strategy.** Determine the types of people you want to follow and have follow you in return. Consider a mix of people who are customers, have the potential to be customers, who work in similar jobs, and also brand accounts that may have a tie in with your community. (For more on this topic, see the section "Finding the Right People to Follow," earlier in this chapter.)

✦ **Plan a content strategy.** Think about the types of tweets you want to post each day. Consider a mix of humor, news, questions, retweets, and a few promotional tweets with or without links.

✦ **Plan a hashtag strategy.** Hashtags can be a lot of fun. You can have a regular hashtag chat (see Book IV, Chapter 3 to learn more about hashtag chats) or use it in contests, news, and updates about your brand and more. Plan for at least a couple hashtag updates per day. (See the earlier "Using the hashtag" section.)

✦ **Don't make every tweet a sale.** Plan a balanced content strategy so that your tweets feature more than selling. Perhaps publish two links or sales for every ten tweets.

✦ **Don't make every tweet about your brand.** Share non–brand-related thoughts and ideas so as not to make everything about you.

✦ **Ask questions.** Ask questions not only about your products and services but also about news items, trending topics, and topics geared toward individual members of your community.

✦ **Share other people's stuff.** Share links to blog posts, images, news articles, and videos by a variety of people.

✦ **With all that said, don't be afraid to share your own stuff.** There's no shame in sharing your own blog posts, news, and even links to sales and discounts. Again, it's all about balance.

✦ **Think outside of the box.** Think about ways to reach your community on Twitter that are different from the same old, same old. Plan content or campaigns no one or very few people are doing. Research some unique ways brands are using Twitter and then put your own spin on them. (For more on researching brands, see Chapter 1 of this minibook.)

✦ **Use Twitter in conjunction with other platforms.** Plan content and campaigns that span the platforms. Use teaser tweets to draw attention to blog posts or Facebook content, for example. (For more on marketing with Facebook, see Book V.)

✦ **Call out your community.** If someone in your community has a milestone, offer public congratulations. Wish happy birthdays and anniversaries and offer condolences or congratulations. Don't forget to use the @reply so that the other party knows you're offering good wishes.

✦ **Seek assistance.** If you have any technical questions or would like recommendations on the latest gadgets and gear, reach out to your community. Try to have at least one question per week because your community appreciates seeing your human side.

✦ **Create discount codes for your community.** While you don't want to be spammy, offering perks to your community is a nice gesture. Why not create discount codes for your Twitter members only to thank them for their support? Try for at least one discount per month.

✦ **Be transparent.** Be honest with your community. If you're asked questions, don't tap dance around an issue or fudge numbers because it's sure to backfire on you later.

Using keywords in your tweets

With 140 characters, you need to choose your words wisely, so we don't always recommend that you use keywords in your tweets. However, you can make your Twitter content more searchable by using keywords in some of your tweets. Don't use the types of words and phrases that don't make any sense or don't work in a sentence, but do use words that you know others are searching for online. Try writing your keyword tweets ahead of time, playing with the words so that they make sense. If you're using keywords to make announcements, perhaps take an hour or two to write up a list of tweets that are appropriate. When you try to tweet keywords off the cuff, it often doesn't come out as intended.

To make your tweets even more searchable, use your keywords as hashtags. Using hashtags makes it easy to refer back to them later to see who else is using them. A hashtag is different from a keyword; a hashtag is used to hold a conversation rather than make your tweet visible in a search.

Don't use keywords for every tweet. If folks feel you're only using Twitter to drive traffic or sell something, you're sure to lose followers.

Following the Twitter Rules of Etiquette

Like everything else online, there are certain unwritten rules of behavior on Twitter.

What follows is a list of accepted Twitter practices. Most of these items are common courtesy, and some are things that aren't so intuitive to the new Twitter users. While most of these items won't get you booted off Twitter, not following certain rules of etiquette can cost you some followers.

✦ **Don't spam.** If a potential follower takes a peek at your Twitter stream and it's nothing but preprogrammed links, she's going to turn tail and run. If you post sales or traffic driving links all day, you're going to lose community. If you only talk about yourself, your brand, or your product, you'll never enjoy a good conversation. Balance your promotional tweets with conversational tweets.

✦ **Be positive.** There's a time and place for negativity, and Twitter usually isn't it. Avoid rants, profanity, and depressing "woe is me"-type topics. If you're bringing down the mood of the community, they won't feel the love anymore and will unfollow.

✦ **Don't use all caps.** TYPING IN ALL CAPS IS CONSIDERED YELLING. It hurts the eyes, too. Avoid it at all costs.

- **Leave space for retweets.** Try to make all your tweets retweetable. Because you're only allowed 140 characters, try typing no more than 120 characters so that others have room to retweet your tweets. If it's too much work for them to edit your tweet to add their own commentary, they won't do it.

- **Don't swear unless you're sure that your community isn't easily offended by profanity.** Though some people don't mind a little cursing, most people do. If you're going to go the edgy route, make sure that your community is comfortable with it.

- **If you're joining a Twitter chat, let your community know.** When you participate in a Twitter chat, you generally have more tweets in your stream than usual. Give a tweet before beginning to let everyone know that you're joining a chat and will tweet more than normal for the next hour or so.

- **Don't feel you need to follow everyone who follows you.** Not everyone who follows you is a good fit for you. Don't feel compelled to follow everyone who follows you first.

- **Give credit where it's due.** If you're sharing a tip, quote, or link you saw someone else share, give that person credit. You don't want a reputation as someone who steals everyone's thunder.

- **Don't hijack someone else's hashtag.** Don't use someone else's hashtag to promote your stuff. It's wrong and will turn off both old and new followers.

- **Don't respond to a tweet with a sales push.** If someone is reaching out to the community for assistance, don't respond with a link to something promotional. It makes you look insincere. Instead, reach out with genuine, helpful information.

- **Avoid private jokes.** If you can't share with everyone, don't share at all.

When using Twitter, follow your best practices for business in the offline world. Sure, it's a more casual form of communication, but you're still looking to make a good impression.

Hosting a Tweetup

Enjoying Twitter? Feel like taking your show on the road? Why not grow your community offline with a Tweetup?

Tweetups are Twitter community get-togethers. You see them at many blogging, business, and social media conferences, though they're also held often in cities as well. They don't take much effort to plan, they don't have to cost much money, and promoting them is as simple as getting everyone you know to tweet.

Many brands host tweetups in order to meet their community offline. They invite the people who follow them on Twitter to join them at a pub or restaurant to meet them face to face. Sometimes the brand buys a round of drinks or provides food, and other times it's up to each individual in attendance to provide their own refreshments. It's usually more about the people than what's being served.

Tweetups are easy to set up:

1. **Plan a time and place for your tweetup.**

2. **Contact the venue in advance to make sure that it can accommodate a small gathering.**

3. **Start tweeting out the details of the tweetup at least two weeks in advance.**

4. **Invite your community to share the details with their friends.**

5. **Show up at the designated date and time and meet and greet your community.**

Tweetups can be low-maintenance gatherings, or you can invest money in putting on a full-fledged spread. Either way, your community will be happy to spend time with you.

Chapter 3: Finding the Right Twitter Tools

Sure, you can do all your tweeting from your page at Twitter.com, but you're limited as to what you can do there. Tools and applications, or apps, enhance your experience and take your page from ho-hum to something that's intriguing, eye-catching, and unique.

In this chapter, we discuss the tools that will not only help make your Twitter experience even better, but we also suggest ways to take your Twitter profile page to a whole new level.

Customizing Your Twitter Page

Don't overlook customizing your Twitter page, or else it's just a page with no personality, giving others no reason to follow you. You see, unless potential followers know you, they don't have much to go on. So they want to click your profile page and know immediately whether or not you're worthy of a follow.

On your website, you take the time to create an About page that's best representative of you and your brand (see Book III, Chapter 2). Your Twitter profile page, shown in Figure 3-1, should be no different.

Figure 3-1:
Your Twitter
profile page
offers little
space to
make a big
impression.

Deborah Ng
@debng FOLLOWS YOU
Social media enthusiast, oversharer & Director of Community for
BlogWorld. Author of Online Community Management for Dummies.
Laugh hard at my own jokes.
Central NJ   http://kommein.com

Following

32,219 TWEETS
511 FOLLOWING
10,412 FOLLOWERS

The following elements make up your Twitter profile page:

✦ **Avatar:** A photo or logo you feel best represents your brand

✦ **Bio:** A few lines telling who you are and what you do

✦ **URL:** A link to your blog or website

✦ **Location:** Where you're based

Your profile page also lists the number of people you follow and how many people follow you. These numbers tell people how popular your Twitter account is and whether or not you're a spammer.

As we mention in Book IV, Chapter 2, following more people than you have followers is usually an indication that you're spammy or heavy into the sales because it's a sign of someone who uses auto-follow software. People tend to stay away from those who don't organically grow their followers.

Your most recent tweets are also listed on your profile page. The number of recent tweets is important because it shows potential followers your account is still active.

Creating a custom Twitter background

Generic Twitter pages are boring. By creating a custom background (see Figure 3-2), you're offering a better opportunity for potential followers, customers, and members of your community to find out more about you. A picture is worth 1,000 words, right? You're also proving you're a real human being and not some spammy bot. People who make up accounts for the purpose of selling or spamming don't take the time to create a custom background because they know they'll probably be banned soon. Your background not only represents you as a brand, but it also tells folks you're legit.

Figure 3-2:
This Twitter background page incorporates the community into the profile.

Use the space in your Twitter background page to define your brand and entice people into wanting to learn more about you.

Before you create your background, take a look around. Visit other people and brands to see how they're customizing their Twitter pages and get some ideas. If you're technically challenged and not sure that you can create the right type of background image, you can also hire someone to put together something representative of you or your brand.

Knowing what to include

Consider putting these elements into your background image:

✦ **Name, URL, and contact details:** Place this information in the image so that they appear to the right. Keep in mind that because it's an image, you won't have active links in your background.

✦ **An image representative of your brand:** For example, if you work for a beer company, consider a frosty mug of one of your premium beers as a background.

✦ **A collage:** Some brands and individuals create a collage of images that represent many different facets of what you do or who you are.

Because your Twitter stream will appear down the middle of your customer background page, pay the most attention to what is on the left and right sides of your background. Use these spaces for your most important messages or information.

Uploading a background image

After you create a background image, you're ready to upload to your Twitter page:

1. **Click the Edit Your Profile button in the top-right corner of your profile page (refer to Figure 3-2) to access the different editing options.**

2. **Click the Design option from the left menu that appears to upload your background image.**

3. **Choose File Function to upload your background image.**

   Although you can choose one of the background images provided by Twitter, we don't recommend them because they are rather generic and don't say a thing about your brand or what you do.

4. **Click Save Changes.**

   You now have a custom Twitter background set up that lists all your pertinent information and gives at least a little hint of your brand's message.

Creating a custom Twitter avatar

Your Twitter *avatar* is the small image next to your @name that folks see every time you tweet. If yours is a personal brand, you may want to use an image showing your likeness. If you're managing a professional brand, consider using a logo for your avatar.

Uploading an avatar is simple:

1. **Click the Edit Your Profile button in the top-right corner of your profile page (refer to Figure 3-2) to access the different editing options.**

2. **Choose Profile from the left menu that appears.**

3. **Click Choose File to access the file you wish to upload.**

4. **Select the image you want to use as your avatar.**

5. **Click Save Changes.**

Feel free to change your avatar to reflect the seasons or holidays, but you want your logo to remain familiar to your community. If you change your avatar more than people change shoes, your brand isn't going to be very recognizable on Twitter.

Using a Twitter Application

Twitter apps or applications help enhance your experience. They allow you to manage multiple accounts or see several different search terms at a glance. They can also tell you whether you're using Twitter effectively and help you upload images to your account.

If you're looking to spend any amount of time on Twitter to market your brand and interact with your customers and community, a Twitter app is essential.

Exploring Twitter desktop applications

Twitter applications are programs and websites that allow you to do more things with your Twitter account. For example, an app like HootSuite, TweetDeck, or Seesmic not only allows you to see all your followers' tweets and the messages you tweet, but you can also see direct messages and any search terms or hashtags you follow all at the same glance.

Here are some Twitter apps to consider:

✦ **TweetChat** (http://tweetchat.com): Allows you to keep up with busy hashtag chats.

✦ **HootSuite** (http://hootsuite.com), **TweetDeck** (www.tweetdeck.com), and **Seesmic** (https://seesmic.com): Enable you to see all your followers as well as search terms and hashtags. You can also manage several different Twitter accounts at a time, follow and update your Facebook accounts, and even schedule your tweets. HootSuite also offers a premium (paying version) where you can access reports and statistics.

✦ **TwitterFeed** (http://twitterfeed.com): Allows you to attach your blog's feed to your Twitter account so that the URL for your latest posts are automatically fed to the masses every time you update.

✦ **Timely** (http://timely.is/#): Publishes your tweets at the time when they'll reach the most people.

**Book IV
Chapter 3**

**Finding the Right
Twitter Tools**

✦ **Twitpic** (`http://twitpic.com`): Allows you to post and share images with your followers.

✦ **TweetBeep** (`http://tweetbeep.com`): Sends you e-mail alerts when people talk about you or your brand on Twitter.

Literally thousands of Twitter apps are available. To find out more about Twitter apps, do a web search, as you can find plenty of roundups of the available tools. Just be sure to check the date on the reviews as some of the tools from, say, 2009 aren't available today, and many new ones have been added to the mix. Also, ask your friends and followers for recommendations. Everyone has favorites.

Tweeting from your Phone, iPad, or iPod Touch

Thankfully, we don't have to stay chained to our desks anymore. We can still market our brand online from the beach, grocery store, or coffee shop using our favorite gadgets. In fact, you can use some of the same apps for tweeting online to tweet from your devices.

You can download HootSuite or Seesmic for your iPhone or Android app, enabling you to manage several accounts at once and still follow keywords and hashtags.

Instagram, the popular photo-sharing app for Apple devices, now allows for sharing on Android phones as well, leading to more visual engagement with your community.

What's important to remember is that thumb typing isn't an excuse for poor business practices. Some people feel that because they're not typing on a full-sized keyboard, they have carte blanche to misspell words or use text speak, which isn't the case. These things are considered unprofessional no matter where you're tweeting from.

If you're marketing your brand, treat your mobile tweeting seriously, just as if you were working from your home or office computer. Don't just broadcast; engage. Because sending links from a full-sized keyboard is easier, schedule these types of tweets if you'll be away from your desk for an extended period of time and use your mobile devices to have conversations with your followers.

Here are a few tips for tweeting from a mobile device or tablet:

✦ **Proofread.** People tend to make more typos from gadgets.

✦ **Set up notifications.** If you're away from your desk, your notifications will let you know whether folks are engaging, and you can respond in kind. You can set them up to make noise or just to send an e-mail.

✦ **Install an app for easy tweeting.** Try using a Twitter management app, such as HootSuite, for your mobile tweeting. You can use this app in conjunction with your regular Twitter account and pull all your stats together.

✦ **Use an app that allows you to manage several different accounts at once.** If you have more than one Twitter account (for example, business and professional), find an app that will manage both accounts. This way, you don't have to do a lot of logging on and off.

✦ **Check back as often as you can.** We're not saying that you should tweet from a wedding or funeral, but if you're not in the middle of an important obligation, do check your mobile Twitter app several times a day to be sure you're not missing out on an engagement.

Book IV
Chapter 3

Finding the Right
Twitter Tools

Chapter 4: Supplementing Online Marketing Tools with Twitter

In This Chapter

✔ Using Twitter to gain traffic

✔ Sharing your content on Twitter

✔ Linking Twitter to Facebook

*I*f you're on Twitter for more than just fun and entertainment, you most likely use other social media. You might have a website, a blog, and a presence on Facebook, and these social media channels are possibly feeding content to each other. In this same way, you can use Twitter to draw attention to your Facebook Page, your blog, and your website.

In this chapter, we show you how to seamlessly dovetail Twitter into your other forms of social media.

Blogs and Twitter make a formidable tag team because each can bring new readership to the other. You can drive traffic to your blog using Twitter and also send new followers to your Twitter account using your blog for a double whammy. That's the beauty of using content to market your brand — you can use one platform or a combination of all.

Using Twitter to Drive Traffic

It's not a good idea to do nothing but drop links to your blog posts or sales pages on Twitter. To market properly, you also need to create engaging conversation, ask questions, and field customer service inquiries. The links and traffic are the gravy on the proverbial potatoes. If you do the rest of it right, people have no problem following your links, which will help you to reach your end goal.

Here are some tips for driving traffic to your blog:

✦ **Create a discussion topic around your blog posts.** Instead of simply tweeting a link and leaving it at that, start a discussion around your blog topic. Ask questions and respond to responses. Not only are you engaging with your community, but people in their streams may become intrigued enough to want to see what you're talking about.

+ **Analyze your most productive Twitter times.** Take some time to analyze your Twitter traffic (or use an app such as Timely that does it for you) to find out when your community is most engaged.

+ **Create the type of content people want to share.** If you tweet only to talk about your brand or to sell something, you're going to drive people away rather than to your blog. Create content that teaches, inspires, or engages. Take a look around on Twitter to see what kind of tweets people are sharing or retweeting. These are probably some good examples of engaging tweets.

+ **Thank everyone who shares your content.** People appreciate appreciation. Taking time to say "thank you" encourages your loyal followers to continue recommending your content to others. You can do this publicly or via a direct message; either way is appropriate.

+ **Offer perks.** Make discounts, freebies, or other perks available on your blog so readers are getting a little extra value for sharing.

+ **Use a logo as your profile image.** A recognizable logo and regular presence can inspire trust, which can in turn encourage others to visit your blog and also share your content.

+ **Be friendly.** Your online attitude is everything. If you have a reputation for being friendly and helpful, you'll grow a wonderful community of supporters.

+ **Be consistent.** Have a regular presence on Twitter. There are many people who won't subscribe to your blog's RSS feed but instead will wait to see you tweet the links. If you're not sharing, they're not visiting.

Schedule your blog posts for the same time every day, as shown in Figure 4-1, and use your Twitter feed to broadcast the links to your followers. Your regulars will appreciate seeing and expecting updated content at the same time each day.

Figure 4-1:
Schedule your blog posts for the same time each day for consistency and familiarity.

Sharing with Buttons

To make sharing more intuitive for your followers, you can add share buttons.

Several different types of share buttons are available for Twitter. For example, you can place icons in your blog's sidebar that encourage readers to follow you on Twitter. The sidebar buttons won't enable readers to share links, but they will help you to build your follower base.

To install Twitter share buttons on WordPress, go to `https://twitter.com/about/resources/buttons` and grab the code. When you locate the code, simply copy and paste it into your sidebar. If you have someone designing your blog, you can also have that person create a Twitter share button unique to your blog. Figure 4-2 shows a set of custom share buttons in a blog sidebar.

You can also install plug-ins that appear at each individual post so readers can share the links to that post with their Twitter followers. When readers click the button to share on Twitter, it will automatically tweet the blog post's title and a shortened link.

Figure 4-2: Creating a custom Twitter share button adds a cohesive and professional look to your blog.

Custom share buttons

The most popular WordPress plug-ins for sharing blog posts on Twitter are

✦ TweetMeme

✦ Digg Digg

✦ Share This

✦ Sharebar

To install the TweetMeme button, head to your WordPress dashboard:

1. **Click the Plugins icon (it looks like a little plug) in the left sidebar and choose Add New from the pop-up menu, as shown in Figure 4-3.**

   The Install Plugins Search page appears.

Figure 4-3:
The Plugins
function
allows you
to search
for any
plug-in you
need.

2. **Type** tweetmeme **in the Search text box, as shown in Figure 4-4, and then click the Search Plugins button.**

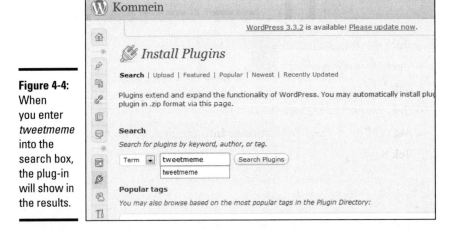

Figure 4-4:
When
you enter
tweetmeme
into the
search box,
the plug-in
will show in
the results.

The Install Plugins Search Results page provides a list of results with the name, version, user rating, and description of each plug-in.

3. **Find the TweetMeme plug-in in the list of results and then click its Install Now link, as shown in Figure 4-5.**

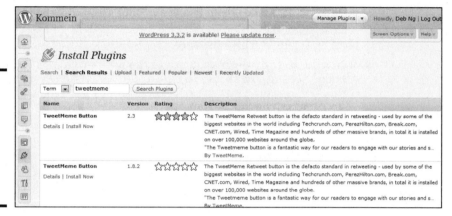

Figure 4-5:
When you select the desired plug-in, it installs automatically.

After your plug-in is installed, you need to return to your WordPress Dashboard's Plugins page (click the Plugins icon in the left sidebar and then choose Plugins; refer to Figure 4-3), select the TweetMeme plug-in, and configure it. You'll need to enter your desired Twitter handle in order to receive retweets. You also want to determine where to place the button, such as at the top, bottom, or side of your posts. Most people find success having the Retweet button at the top of their blog posts or floating along the left sidebar.

If you own a Blogger blog, TweetMeme isn't available as a plug-in. However, Blogger's template editor has several drag-and-drop options for Twitter share buttons. To install a Twitter share button on your Blogger blog:

1. **Sign in to your blog's dashboard.**
2. **Select the Design function.**
3. **Select Page Elements.**
4. **Click Edit.**
5. **Select Show Share Buttons.**
6. **Drag and drop the share buttons into the desired location.**
7. **Click Save.**

   You're all set. After you click Save, the share button is saved to your blog and ready to use.

Linking Twitter to Your Facebook Page

If you have fans on Facebook who aren't Twitter users, you can post your tweets on your Facebook Wall for your fans to see. After you do this, every public tweet you send on Twitter shows up on your Facebook Wall.

Here's how to add your Twitter feed to your Facebook brand Page:

1. **Log in to your Twitter account.**

2. **Click the user drop-down menu in the upper-right corner and then choose Settings, as shown in Figure 4-6.**

The default Account Settings page appears.

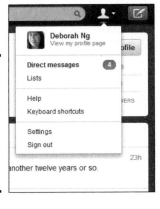

Figure 4-6: Your drop-down menu at the top of the page houses the Settings option.

3. **Click the Profile button on the left and then click the Post your Tweets to Facebook button, as shown in Figure 4-7.**

You might have to scroll down to see the Facebook section.

4. **Click the Sign in to Facebook and Connect Your Accounts button, as shown in Figure 4-8.**

You'll need to enter your Facebook information in order to sync the two accounts.

5. **Select the My Facebook Page option to post your tweets on your Facebook Page as opposed to your personal profile.**

You'll be taken to a menu listing all your Facebook Pages. Select the one you wish to add your feed to.

6. **Click Save Changes.**

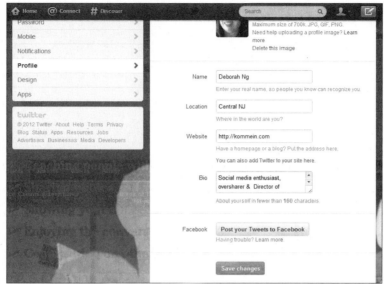

Figure 4-7:
The Post Your Tweets to Facebook button is located near the bottom of the page.

Figure 4-8:
You can't add your Twitter feed to your Page unless you first enter your Facebook login details.

If you're a heavy Tweeter, your Facebook fans may not appreciate every single Tweet appearing in their Facebook News Feeds, and they might Unlike you if you're too prolific. Think very carefully about whether this is appropriate for you, given the way you tweet.

Book IV
Chapter 4

Supplementing
Online Marketing
Tools with Twitter

Chapter 5: Hosting Twitter Chats

In This Chapter

✓ **Reaping the benefits of Twitter chats**

✓ **Creating a hashtag**

✓ **Using Twitter chat tools**

✓ **Promoting and hosting a Twitter chat**

Twitter chats are a way for people with similar interests to come together and discuss relevant information regularly. Generally, one-off events, Twitter chats happen at regular intervals (usually weekly). Twitter chats, when done well, are an excellent way to build and maintain community.

This chapter helps you determine whether a Twitter chat matches your business goals and needs, explains how to choose the best hashtag for your chat, and introduces you to tools to help you manage your chats effectively. If you're concerned that no one will show up to the chat, don't worry, we share some ideas on where to find guests and how to promote your chat so more people will come (and tell their friends). Finally, we give you a complete step-by-step run-through of how to host a Twitter chat.

Benefitting from Twitter Chats

Many brands are hosting Twitter chats as a way to connect with their communities. Hosted regularly, usually once per week, Twitter chats allow for a brand to discuss issues everyone in the community has to deal with or share tips and ideas.

Twitter chats have many benefits. Twitter chats

✦ **Create brand awareness:** When you have an engaging presence on Twitter, people remember you.

✦ **Get folks talking about you:** Not only will your hashtag get people noticing what you're talking about, but if your community has a good time at your regular chat, they'll share with others.

+ **Help others learn about your community:** Twitter chats enable you to interview guests or pose questions to your community. This way, you find out about their likes, dislikes, and needs, even if you aren't directly surveying them about a product or service.

+ **Allow a conversation among like-minded people:** If you're a real estate professional and host a Twitter chat to share tips and ideas and discuss issues pertaining to real estate professionals, you're not only establishing your name and expertise, but you're also allowing those in your profession to rally around a specific topic.

+ **Grow your follower base:** When people participate in a Twitter chat, the hashtag shows up in their Twitter streams, which attracts the attention of others who might also follow your brand and participate.

+ **Let you meet others:** Through your Twitter chats, you can meet other professionals, customer, clients, collaborators, and friends.

Hosting a regular Twitter chat is a commitment because you have to provide value every week at a designated date and time, so don't enter into them lightly. First, try having a Twitter party, a one-off hashtag chat to see whether there's interest on both ends. If you enjoy the experience and you have a decent turnout, you can then determine whether it's worth it to continue the effort.

Coming Up with a Hashtag for Your Chat

The hashtag, the most important part of the Twitter chat, appears next to each and every post and on all promotional tweets, blog posts, and Facebook updates. Everyone who participates in the chat will use the hashtag, which means it has the opportunity to be viewed by millions. Take your time and determine the best hashtag chat for you.

Don't go overboard trying to figure out something pithy and hip. If you overthink your hashtag, you'll fall short. The most popular Twitter chats use obvious hashtags. For example, #blogchat is a chat about bloggers and #speakchat is a chat for public speakers.

Something important to keep in mind is the 140-character limit on Twitter. The last thing you want is for your hashtag to take up so many characters that you can't have a conversation. If you want to represent your brand, do so with brevity. For example, BlogWorld & New Media Expo, the conference for content creators, uses #BWEChat for their weekly Twitter chat as using their full name wouldn't leave any room for the matter at hand.

You also want your hashtag to be more reflective of your niche or your brand. For example, if yours is a soap manufacturer, do you want your hashtag to be soapchat or sudschat or would you rather it was #JoesSoapChat? Be careful, though. While it's a good thing to throw branding in there, a long hashtag takes up precious character space.

By the way, in case you haven't already noticed, make sure the word "chat" is attached to the end of your hashtag so that folks on Twitter know a chat is in session (see Figure 5-1).

Figure 5-1: Attach *chat* to the end of your hashtag word.

Keeping Track of Who Says What

If a lot of people are participating, your Twitter chat will go by fast. You see, you won't just be interviewing a guest; everyone who participates will be talking at once. All this conversation can be a lot to keep up with, and your usual Twitter app won't do.

Some tools can help make your Twitter chat experience work a little better. For example, TweetChat.com is a platform that allows you to view only the tweets for one particular hashtag at a time so that all the other conversations on Twitter don't get caught up in a confusing stream. TweetChat also allows you to respond and retweet to everyone who is taking part.

A platform such as TweetChat, shown in Figure 5-2, is much more manageable than using HootSuite or Seesmic because it updates quicker and shares every tweet by everyone using the hashtag. You can also set it to refresh every five seconds or slow it down so that the tweets aren't coming at you so fast.

Figure 5-2:
A Twitter chat management platform, such as TweetChat.com, will help you follow a busy chat.

Another important Twitter chat tool is hashtracking.com, shown in Figure 5-3. With hashtracking, you can generate a transcript of the chat to share with others, plus you'll receive statistics for each chat so that you know how many people participated, who the most influential people were on the chat, and how many people you reached through the chat.

Figure 5-3:
Use a transcript tool to share the chat with those members of your community who can't make the chat.

Before hosting your Twitter chat, take some time to research the best tools for your needs. They'll make a world of difference.

Finding Guests for Your Twitter Chat

Twitter chats can take on a couple of different formats. You can host a town-hall type format where it's just you and your community, or you can invite special guests to participate. We get in to how to host both types of chats in the section "Hosting Your Twitter Chat," later in this chapter. For now, we focus on how to find guests for your chat.

The beautiful thing about the online social media world is how many people fancy themselves experts and have something to promote. Authors, bloggers, independent musicians, online talk show hosts, podcasters, and a variety of professionals are interested in sharing their knowledge online. What follows are some ways to find these people:

✦ **Social networks:** The people who you follow on the social networks, or who follow you, have interest in your topic. How many of them are experts or have something to share or promote to your community? Many times, you don't have to look farther than the friends, followers, customers, and brands who are sharing with you online.

✦ **Publishing companies:** Book publishers want their authors to succeed. See who has anyone of interest. Many times, if you follow publishers on Twitter or Facebook, you'll see they're promoting their authors. See who is a good fit.

✦ **Brand pages:** Similar brands also have experts who like to share. Don't be afraid to reach out, as it can be the start of a beautiful collaboration.

✦ **Colleges:** Teachers and professors are a gold mine of information and enjoy sharing with others. Invite them to take part in your Twitter chats.

✦ **Web search:** Search Google or Yahoo! to see who the movers and shakers in your world are and invite them to chat.

✦ **Crowd sourcing:** Ask your community members who they'd like to see as a #chat guest.

Now, whenever you interview anyone for anything or invite them to participate in a community project, it's always a good idea to let them know what's in it for them. If you can present your chat as something of value, they're less likely to say no.

Here are some of the ways to sell a Twitter chat:

✦ **Visibility:** Let your guests know your community has great reach. Each person who participates in your chat has the ability to reach hundreds of people, depending on their amount of followers. Estimate all your participants by the amount of people who follow each, and the amount of people who view the hashtag can number in the thousands — the bigger chats average millions of views.

✦ **Stats:** If you use a service such as hashtracking.com to put together your Twitter chat stats, share some of these stats with potential guests so that they can see the value. Let them know the average number of participants, the reach, and how many new followers you gain after each track.

✦ **Influential participants:** Every niche has their influential members. If you have influential regular participants, do share this information with your guest. But don't look like you're name-dropping, as that can be a turnoff.

If you can't find a guest for a particular week's chat don't sweat it. You can find plenty of things to talk about with your community. Sometimes the community-driven chats are livelier than those involving guests.

Promoting Your Twitter Chat

Twitter chats are easy to market and promote. If you have a network and a platform, you have the ability to tell people about your chat.

✦ **Blog:** Use your blog to announce each Twitter chat. Touch on the discussion topic and announce any special guests. Be sure to link to your guest, which will catch her attention and encourage her to share the link with her own community.

✦ **Twitter:** Announce your chat at least once or twice per day. Though you're limited in characters, try and name the topic and guest and don't forget the hashtag, as shown in Figure 5-4.

Figure 5-4: Don't forget to promote your chat on the social networks.

Blog World & New Media Expo
19 hours ago

Join us at 2:00 EST for #BWEChat. Our guest, Tamsen McMahon will tell you how to sell social to skeptics.

Like · Comment · Share

- ✦ **Facebook:** Try announcing the time, hashtag, and date at least once per day.

- ✦ **Google+:** Share with everyone in your circles.

- ✦ **LinkedIn:** Career-oriented chats are especially of interest to the folks on LinkedIn.

- ✦ **Your community:** Ask your community to help spread the word. Don't spam them, but do say "Please share" when tweeting, blogging, or putting it out on the other social networks.

- ✦ **Your guests:** Ask your guests to help promote the event to their communities.

- ✦ **A community calendar:** Create a shareable calendar listing all the #BWEChat dates, topics, and guests. Plan at least a month in advance.

You want to promote your Twitter chat in the same way you promote your business. Share it with your community without being pushy, smarmy, or spammy. Invite them to participate and share with their communities.

You're not going to get the same interest in every topic every week, but you'll find you do have at least a couple of loyal community members who show up each time.

Hosting Your Twitter Chat

Most Twitter chats follow the same format. The host asks questions, the guest and community respond, and conversation ensues. However, put forth in that manner, chaos will also ensue. That's why Twitter chat hosts follow a numbered format for questions and answers. Twitter chats can be fast and busy. If they're not organized, no one will be able to follow the chat, and you won't gain a very strong community of participants.

Try following this format for hour-long Twitter chats:

1. **Welcome community members to your chat and invite them all to share a little about themselves.**

   Allow about three to five minutes for this.

2. **Introduce the format.**

   For most Twitter chats, each question will be prefaced with a Q1 for Question 1 (see Figure 5-5). Those who answer the question will respond A1 for Answer 1. This way, there's no mistake about which questions are being answered because some people come late but start at the beginning.

Figure 5-5:
Following a numbered format will help keep your chat more organized.

When questioning your guest, always `@reply` their name — for example, "@debng, Q1. What is your favorite ice cream flavor?" If you have no guests, don't worry about the `@reply` unless you reach out to a specific person. (Refer to Figure 5-5.)

3. **Retweet your questions as well as the guest's answers.**

4. **See what responses your community is sharing and retweet the best of those, too.**

5. **After about 10 or 15 minutes, ask the next question.**

   Most hosts share four to six questions. Just time them accordingly so that you have enough space for responding.

6. **(Optional) Save the last ten minutes for the community to ask questions to the guests.**

7. **Three minutes before the hour is up, thank your guest and ask him whether he has anything to plug or promote.**

8. **End the chat with any announcement you need to make, including the next week's guests.**

Don't be afraid to ask questions of your community as you see opportunity during the discussion. If you'd like for people to expand upon their answers or to keep the chat flowing between numbered questions, it's fine to throw out some non-numbered questions for your participants.

Here's a bonus tip for you. If you're intrigued by the idea of starting your own Twitter chat, check out some of these popular chats to see how they're handled:

✦ **#BlogChat:** Hosted every Sunday night at 8 p.m. EST

✦ **#SpeakChat:** Hosted every Monday night at 9 p.m. EST

✦ **#CmgrChat:** Hosted every Wednesday afternoon at 2 p.m. EST

✦ **#BWEChat:** Hosted every Thursday afternoon at 2 p.m. EST

Book V

Facebook

The 5th Wave   By Rich Tennant

"Jim and I do a lot of business together on Facebook. By the way, Jim, did you get the sales spreadsheet and little blue pony I sent you?"

Contents at a Glance

Chapter 1: Using Facebook as a Marketing Tool

In This Chapter

✔ Using Facebook Pages

✔ Setting up your Facebook Timeline

✔ Bringing in Likes

✔ Using Facebook Events

*B*y now you have at least heard about Facebook, even if you're not using it. Facebook is the world's most popular social network, where people of all ages, professions, and backgrounds gather to stay in touch with friends and family.

Having millions of people gathered in one place is the perfect opportunity for any brand to raise awareness and grow a community of customers and advocates. If you're not on Facebook already, you're missing out on a huge opportunity. Simply put, Facebook is where the people are, and to succeed in business, you also have to be where the people are.

In this chapter, we explore how Facebook Pages work and how you can make them work for your brand.

For more in-depth coverage, find a copy of *Facebook Marketing All-in-One For Dummies,* by Amy Porterfield, Phyllis Khare, and Andrea Vahl.

Understanding the Appeal of Brands on Facebook

People who *like,* or give a thumbs-up to, a brand on Facebook more likely to buy from said brands. *But they're not liking you to buy from you.* They're liking you to find out more about you and to receive updates and news regarding products and services. Or they had a positive experience with the brand and want to engage more.

We all know plenty of people who like brands on Facebook. They come to Facebook each day to enjoy the company of others not necessarily to engage in a lot of deep reading or thinking. So why are people following brands on Facebook?

+ **Seeking a discount:** The majority of people liking your brand's Page are hoping to receive some sort of benefit. This doesn't mean you have to give discounts and freebies every day, but, if people know at some point they'll receive coupons, codes, or other perks, they're more likely to sign up and remain active members of your Facebook community.

+ **Following a recommendation:** When people feel good about a brand, they leave positive comments on their Timeline and tell their friends, hoping that the friends then enjoy the same positive experience. If their friends also enjoy the experience, they in turn invite their friends and family, and so on.

+ **Expressing their loyalty:** Customers who enjoy the brand offline often seek out the brand to enjoy online. In addition to receiving freebies or updates, they're mostly interested in showing support to a name they believe in.

+ **Wanting entertainment:** If your content is stale with only the occasional business-like updates, you're not going to keep your Facebook fans. However, if they're entertaining, fun, and keep folks coming back to see what you're going to talk about each day, your community will continue to grow.

+ **Needing a question answered:** Your community has many questions, but they may not want to call a customer service line and wait on hold. Being able to reach out via Facebook gives people a way to connect without having to invest a lot of time.

Note: Many people who like your Facebook Page won't interact further on it. That is, they'll read your updates on their News Feeds and may even take advantage of discount codes or calls to action, but they won't comment or communicate. That's fine; marketing to the silent members of your community is still important.

If your Facebook Page is engaging and the person running your brand Page is funny, knowledgeable, and patient, your Facebook community will evolve into something wonderful. Some will comment on posts, others will vote in polls and, yes, a number of folks will buy when you have sales or offer discounts.

Branding with Facebook Pages

You may think you know Facebook pretty well because you have a personal account, but Facebook Pages, formerly *fan pages,* and your Facebook profile have major differences. Facebook Pages, have to follow specific rules so as not to come across as overly spammy. For example, you have to follow specific guidelines for selling or running contests. (For more on these guidelines, see Book V, Chapter 2.)

The purpose of the Facebook Page is simple: to promote a brand. The goal of most brands is to have as many individuals like them as possible in order to best get their message to the masses. Some brands, such as Coca-Cola with over 30 million followers, can reach more people with one Facebook update than with a television commercial — and it's cheaper, too. So those brands' goal is to make their Facebook Page as interactive as possible to get those Likes.

After your brand has fans and followers, a variety of interactions can occur. A representative of the brand posts an update in hopes of getting as many Likes and Shares on that comment as possible. When an individual likes a comment or shares a status update or image, that content appears in that person's status updates as well, which means it's exposed to even more people.

If a brand's update gets liked and/or shared by hundreds of thousands of people, it has the potential to be seen by millions of people. This visibility leads to higher brand recognition, even if the folks who viewed the update didn't share it in return. You want as many people as possible to at least know about your brand on Facebook.

If your Page is truly interactive and offers some cool perks, your community will be inspired to invite others to like the brand as well. So another purpose of the Facebook Page is to create a community of brand advocates and word-of-mouth marketers.

Facebook Pages are a way to humanize your brand and make you seem more real to your customers or community. If you take the time to answer inquiries, post updates, and make them feel as if they're part of the brand, too, your fans will put their faith and trust into you and are more likely to support your efforts.

In 2012, Facebook introduced Timeline for brand Pages. Through Timeline, brands can now share their history and share their story. Knowing a brand's history also tends to make a brand more human, and people have a soft spot for a brand with a good story. We talk about Timeline further in the section "Creating a Facebook Timeline," later in this chapter.

Brands are taking advantage of Facebook Pages because they're a way to reach people honestly and effectively. The most successful brands on Facebook aren't shouting out, "BUY ME!" or posting only product updates. They're having conversations with their communities, and it's working.

Figuring Out a Facebook Page

A Facebook Page has several components (see Figure 1-1), which you'll want to be familiar with before launching your own Page.

Figure 1-1:
Use your
brand's
logo for
the profile
photo.

Profile photo

✦ **Profile photo:** Most brands use this space to post their logo or some-thing that is regularly associated with the brand. Your profile photo isn't the biggest photo on your Timeline, but it's visible at eye level for who-ever visits your Page. (Refer to Figure 1-1.)

Make sure you properly prepare your graphic so it doesn't end up dis-torted when Facebook places the image into its pre-sized box. Facebook recommends the image be at least 180 pixels wide.

✦ **Cover photo:** The biggest photo on your Timeline, this cover photo can be a touching, amusing, or scenic photo that best represents your brand and what it stands for.

✦ **About:** Includes your company's message, mission statement, or a brief bio of who you are and what you do. Your About page should be com-pelling and written in an engaging style. For more on your About page, see the section "Filling Out What Your About" later in this chapter.

✦ **Contact info:** This section should list all the ways people can get in touch with you. At the very least, it should include e-mail addresses where your community can offer feedback. You should also include your Twitter handle, blog, or website.

✦ **Admin Panel:** Your Admin Panel, shown in Figure 1-2, is where you dis-cover how many new Likes you have each week, how many people are sharing on your Wall, what countries people are visiting from, and more. From your Admin Panel, you can learn about your community, and you can also update the content and design of your Facebook Timeline.

Figure 1-2:
Your Admin
Panel
is your
Facebook
toolbox.

✦ **Wall:** Your Facebook Wall, shown in Figure 1-3, is where you and your friends post content.

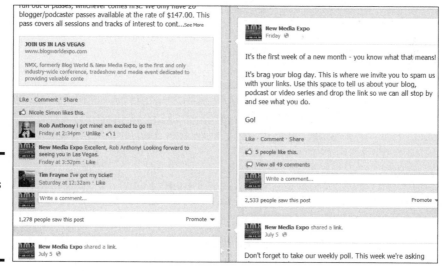

Figure 1-3:
Your Wall is
where you
and your
community
interact.

✦ **Friends:** A list of all the people who like your brand on Facebook.

✦ **Recent Posts by Others:** When people tag your Page in their discussions, it will show up on your Timeline under "Who's Talking About This?"

✦ **Pinned Posts:** Posts you want to keep front and center on your Timeline are pinned posts.

✦ **Tabs:** Extras your community can click to engage with the brand. Polls, quizzes, photos, and other fun items are accessed through tabs.

Creating a Facebook Timeline

Facebook's Timeline feature is no longer optional for Pages. As of March 30, 2012, all Pages must use Timeline as the platform for community engagement. Setting up Timeline is simple and can take as little or as much time as you want, depending on how many bells and whistles you add to your profile.

Because Timeline is so visual, it's the perfect opportunity for you to share your company's story. In fact, with Timeline, you can go back in time to your brand's beginning and share milestones, articles, photographs, videos, and more, all in chronological order.

Some interesting features of the Timeline include

✦ **Private messaging:** Allows your community to reach out and ask questions privately and then receive a personal response in return. Please note, some brands turn off the messaging feature because they'd rather not receive private messages. You can turn off the private messaging feature, but you'll miss valuable community feedback because not everyone wants to publicly post to your Wall.

✦ **Notifications:** A number on the Admin Panel tab, shown in Figure 1-4, shows all your new notifications so that you can welcome new members by name, see who is messaging you, know who is posting to your Wall, and find out who is talking about you on their own Walls.

✦ **The ability to highlight key events and photos:** You can make certain content "sticky" to highlight key dates, milestones, and events.

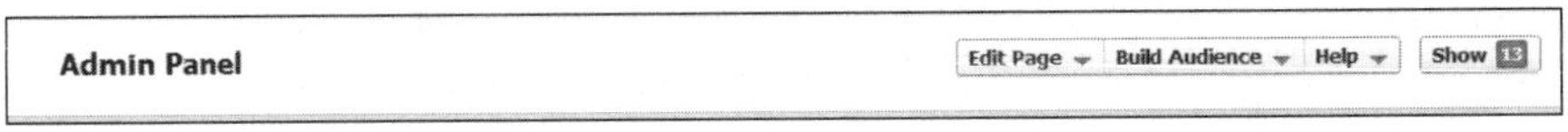

Figure 1-4:
A number
on your
Admin Panel
signifies
new
interactions
and updates.

Admin Panel		Edit Page ▾ Build Audience ▾ Help ▾	Show 13

Adding a profile picture

To set up your Timeline, the first step is to upload a profile picture. Your profile picture is the smaller photo on the left, usually a brand logo. To upload your profile photo:

1. **Hover on the profile image area and click the Edit Profile Picture function that appears.**

A drop-down menu appears, enabling you to choose from a variety of options.

2. **Choose the Upload a New Image option.**

Alternatively, you can choose a photo that's already been uploaded to Facebook or take an image using Facebook's camera function.

3. **Assuming that you're going to upload your brand's logo, choose Upload Photo and choose the file you want to upload.**

4. **Save your profile photo.**

Adding a cover photo

Your next step is to choose your cover photo. This is the large background photo appearing at the top of your Timeline (refer to Figure 1-1) and the first thing people will see when landing on your brand's Page. Your cover photo is more than just a picture; it's a representation of your brand. You have a wonderful opportunity to illustrate your brand, product, or service in any way you want and you want to make a lasting impression. Many top brands, such as Ben & Jerry's, Ford, and Coca-Cola, take great care in designing their Timeline images.

Before you get started, take time to research other brands on Facebook to see how they're using their Timelines. This may give you some good ideas.

To add a cover photo to your Timeline:

1. **Hover on the Cover Photo area and click Add a Cover.**

2. **Choose whether you want to upload a new photo or a photo from an existing photo album.**

- *Choose from Photos:* If you want to use a photo that already resides in your Page's Photo Albums, choose this option.

- *Upload Photo:* If you want to upload an image from your computer, choose this option.

After you choose a photo, you can reposition it by clicking the image and dragging it up or down.

3. Click Save Changes.

A helpful link with information for working with the cover photo is www.facebook.com/help/timeline/cover.

Keep in mind that your Timeline cover image doesn't have to be a permanent thing. You can change it as often as you see fit. Change with the seasons or to coincide with product launches.

To change your Timeline cover image:

1. Hover your mouse on your Timeline cover photo's bottom-right corner and click Change Cover when it appears, as shown in Figure 1-5.

Figure 1-5: Click Change Cover to change your Timeline cover photo.

2. On the Change Cover drop-down menu, choose where you want to upload your image from.

You have these choices:

- *Choose from Photos:* If you want to use a photo that already resides in your Page's Photo Albums, choose this option.

- *Upload Photo:* If you want to upload an image from your computer, choose this option.

- *Reposition:* You can keep your current cover photo and simply reposition it by clicking and holding the cover photo, then dragging it to its new position.

- *Remove:* You can remove the cover photo completely with this option. You don't have to remove the current cover photo in order to change it. Instead, you can just choose one of the first two options.

3. Click Save Changes.

Adding finishing touches

At this point, your Facebook Timeline is pretty much set up except for a little tweaking. From here, you can

✦ **Pin content:** Make certain posts or images *sticky,* meaning they'll stay in the same location until you unpin them. Pinning content is a good way to highlight sales events, announcements, and promotional campaigns. The pins only last for a week, unless you unpin or pin another item before the seven days are up. Please note, Facebook only allows you to pin one item at a time.

✦ **Share your brand's story:** Because Facebook's Timeline allows you to upload content in chronological order, you can now go back to the day your brand launched, even if it's 100 years ago. Scan old newspaper articles, advertisements, photos, and more. Give your community a transparent look into your brand's past.

✦ **Explore apps:** Make your brand's Page even more interactive with apps that allow you to poll your community, share videos, share slides from presentations, post testimonials from customers, connect your Twitter account, share your blog posts, and so much more.

Don't go overboard with the bells and whistles. When you have too many items pinned to your Timeline or if your Page is nothing but Twitter updates and blog feeds, it will become too cluttered and confusing. Take the time to research the best apps for your community and use them in a way so that they don't assault the senses.

Understanding Your Facebook Admin Panel

Your Admin Panel, located at the top right of your Timeline, is where you get a detailed look at the people who are using your Page. If you have new notifications, a red box appears, showing you the number of new interactions. To access these interactions, click the Admin Panel button.

Here are some of the things you can discover when you access your Admin Panel:

✦ **New Likes:** The names of all the people who liked your Page. You can even thank them publicly or privately for their support, if you'd like.

✦ **Who tagged your Page:** You can see what they're saying and interact in kind.

✦ **Who commented on your Page:** You can find out what they're responding to.

✦ **Private messages:** Sometimes your Facebook fans reach out privately with questions or comments. Check your private messages often so no one is left hanging.

✦ **Activity log:** Displays all the activity on your brand's Page. This log is especially helpful if more than one person acts as an administrator. You can look at the activity so that you're kept up to speed and don't duplicate someone else's effort. You can also see who tagged your Page or whether a new item was posted via networked blogs.

✦ **Banned users:** If users are banned for spamming or not playing nice, you can access a list of them via your Admin Panel. This list is especially helpful if you're not *lifetime banning* — for example, if someone wasn't being nice to others in your Facebook community, and you issue a ban for only a specific time period. This feature gives you the ability to unban, if you see fit.

Filling Out What You're About

Your About page, the spot where you share a brief story or description about your brand, is essentially your business profile. You should be able to tell people what your brand is about while not overwhelming them with details.

Your Facebook Page is a vehicle in which to drive traffic to your website or sales page. Keep your profile information brief but intriguing so that they seek out more information from your home page.

Some important details to include in your brand's business profile:

✦ A brief explanation of what your company does, and perhaps your mission statement. This information shouldn't be a sales pitch; focus more on what you believe and what your brand can offer the community.

✦ A link to your blog and/or website

✦ Links to other social media profiles — for example, Twitter and Google+

✦ Contact information

The focus of your brand's Facebook Page is to engage with your community and share your brand's story. Therefore, it's not a good idea to make the About section of your profile a long, historical, manifesto. Instead, keep it brief so that you don't lose anyone before they get to a link where they can learn more.

Using a Custom URL

You have the option to have a custom URL for your brand's Page. A recognizable URL means better search engine optimization, and people are more likely to remember this address over an address featuring lots of random numbers and letters.

Be sure you have at least 25 fans. Only those with 25 fans or more can create a custom URL for their Page.

To create your custom URL:

1. **Go to** `http://facebook.com/username`.

2. **From the drop-down menu, select the Page you want to create a username for.**

3. **Type your desired username.**

4. **Click Check Availability.**

   If that name is available, you're all set (see Figure 1-6). If the name is taken, you'll have to choose another name.

Custom URL

Figure 1-6:
Choose your brand's name for your custom URL.

Category:	Companies & Organizations ▾ Media/News/Publishing ▾
Official Page:	Pick a topic
Username:	You can now direct people to www.facebook.com/NewMediaExpo. Learn more.
Name:	New Media Expo · Request Change
Start Date:	2007 ▾ + Add month
Start Type:	Select Start Type: ▾
Address:	Address
City/Town:	
Postal Code:	
	Note: If you add a valid address, users will be able to see and check in to your page using Facebook Pl hours for our system to process the address.
About:	The Future of Content, Community and Commerce: Bloggers, podcasters, and web

New Media Expo

Your Settings
Manage Permissions
Basic Information
Profile Picture
Featured
Resources
Admin Roles
Apps
Mobile
Insights
Help

It should go without saying it's a good idea to choose your brand name as your username. However, if your brand name is rather common, someone may have already beaten you to the punch. See whether you can add another word to your brand name so that you still have that recognizability.

Don't choose a name having nothing at all to do with your brand. This gets too confusing and doesn't make your Page easy to remember or find.

Inviting a Community

The most important aspect of having a Facebook Page isn't compelling About information or the perfect Timeline cover photo. Instead, it's the community of people who will become your biggest advocates. If you're like most brands, you want to have as many people interacting on your Wall as possible.

Before you begin inviting folks to join your community, keep in mind a couple of things. The first is that you can only invite people you're friends with. (We discuss how to attract people who aren't your friends in the following section.) The second is Facebook frowns upon blatant attempts to get Likes on specific posts.

Inviting people and finding ways to grow your community is okay, but offering prizes and perks to people who like specific posts or comments on your brand's Page isn't a good idea. You can lose your account if you do that.

Inviting friends to like your Page

When choosing friends to invite to like your Page and participate, take care to choose those who will really appreciate being part of that community. When you randomly and regular invite people who don't care to be a part of the brand, it gets annoying and can cost you a Facebook friendship.

To invite friends to like your Facebook Page:

1. **Access your Admin Panel.**

2. **Click the Build Audience drop-down menu, shown in Figure 1-7, and choose Invite Friends.**

   A list of all your friends appears.

3. **Choose the Search All Friends option.**

4. **Click the photos of all friends you want to invite and then click Submit.**

   Your friends will now receive an invitation to like your brand's Page. Not all will accept your invitation, so please don't take it personally. Some people simply don't want to follow brands on Facebook.

Figure 1-7:
Use the
Build
Audience
menu
to invite
friends to
join your
community.

Admin Panel	Edit Page ▼	Build Audience ▼	Help ▼	Show 13
		Invite Friends...		
		Share Page...		
		Create An Ad		

Getting Likes from others

In addition to inviting friends to like your brand on Facebook, you can also try some of these methods for raising brand awareness and getting Likes:

✦ **Use your brand's Twitter, Google+, and Pinterest accounts to bring in new community members.** Without spamming, invite people to join your Facebook Page from time to time. If space permits, also share the benefits of becoming a member of your Facebook community.

✦ **Invite your community to share.** While Facebook frowns upon contests and events where people have to like a Page to participate, there's nothing wrong with inviting your community to share content they like.

✦ **Create the type of content your community will share.** Have you ever logged on to your personal Facebook Page to find that your friends are sharing a funny video, provocative image, or informative article? This is the type of content people enjoy sharing on their Walls. If your Facebook Wall is nothing but brand updates, that's not very compelling. Instead, share informative or fun items with your community, and not only will they share in return, but they may also inspire others to like your brand.

✦ **Place share buttons on your blog and website.** If you want people to share your content, you have to give them a way to share. Having a Facebook share button, included in those shown in Figure 1-8, on your blog or website will encourage readers to like your Page.

✦ **Be consistent.** If you post engaging or compelling content every day, folks are more likely to like your brand. If you're sporadic and haphazard with your content, you won't receive many Likes in return.

✦ **Place share information in offline content.** If you have offline content — for example, if yours is a supermarket brand with a weekly flyer or a retail shop with posters on the windows — be sure to let shoppers know how they can follow your brand on the social networks. If you're a restaurant, add the URL for your social networking channels on the back of your menus or have postcards handy for customers.

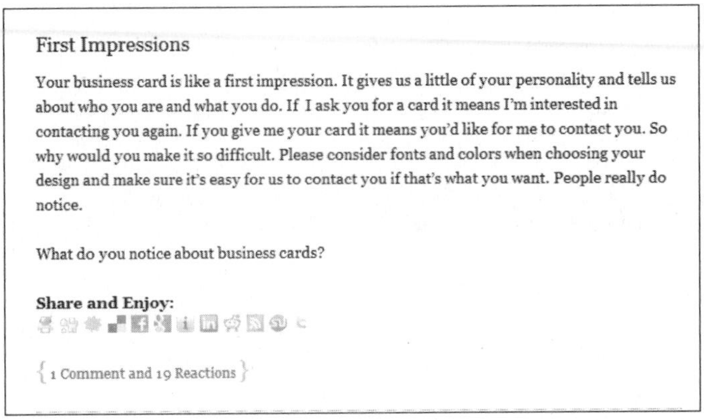

First Impressions

Your business card is like a first impression. It gives us a little of your personality and tells us about who you are and what you do. If I ask you for a card it means I'm interested in contacting you again. If you give me your card it means you'd like for me to contact you. So why would you make it so difficult. Please consider fonts and colors when choosing your design and make sure it's easy for us to contact you if that's what you want. People really do notice.

What do you notice about business cards?

Share and Enjoy:

{ 1 Comment and 19 Reactions }

Figure 1-8:
Use share buttons on your content.

Unlike the popular movie tagline, if you build it, they may not necessarily come. You have to give everyone a reason to want to show up each day. Everyone has a favorite brand of detergent or applesauce, but very few people love these brands so much that they want to receive updates from them every day. It's not enough to have a presence; give everyone a reason to like you.

Liking Other Brands

One step you shouldn't overlook in your Facebook marketing campaign is to like other brands, even competing brands. Many people are afraid to like competitors because they feel they'll lose community to someone else. This fear isn't true at all. People who like brands on Facebook like many different brands, even if some are similar.

Here are some of the benefits for liking brands on Facebook:

✦ **Using your brand account, you can participate in discussions happening on other Pages.** Your comments may inspire others to check out your brand's Page and like you.

✦ **It puts you on the other brand's radar, which may be a good thing.** They may want to use and recommend your product or service one day or collaborate on a promotion.

✦ **It creates brand awareness.** The more people who see your logo, the better. When people see your logo on the social networks, it instills faith. They feel you're more accessible.

✦ **It helps to establish your expertise.** When you participate in discussions and respond to comments and inquiries in a knowledgeable manner, people see you as an authority and are inspired to follow you on the various social media channels.

Be sure to follow the rules of social media etiquette and avoid dropping links on another brand's Pages unless invited to do so. The last thing you want is to have a reputation as a spammer. Also, if Facebook feels you've been spammy, you could lose your account.

Creating Events

The power of community is a wonderful thing. A tight-knit community will rally around the brand for all occasions. They'll comment on blog posts and social networking updates, they'll respond to promotions and discounts, and they'll attend events. In fact, a good way to gauge community interest is to create an event.

What is an event?

+ A sale

+ A party

+ A tweetup, that is a real-world meet up organized on Twitter

+ A conference

Events can also be online affairs, such as

+ Webinars

+ Contests

+ Twitter chats

When you create an event using Facebook, you have the opportunity to invite everyone who likes your brand's Page to attend.

Creating events don't take much time at all and are simple to set up.

1. **Click the Events tab located under your cover photo.**

2. **Click the Create Event button.**

3. **Enter in important information, such as event name, date, time, location, and a few words about the event.**

4. **Select guests who you would like to invite to attend.**

5. **Click Create Event.**

You also have the option to select whether you want your invitation page to show who has been invited to the event. Most people like to see who they know will be attending events, so it's a good idea to check this function.

Folks will also be able to see who has declined and who is a maybe. As you don't want to have an invitation page filled with no thank you's, it's a good idea not to create events for every move your brand makes. Instead, send invites to events you know won't go over well.

Don't use events as invitations to spam. If you send out invitations every other day to drive traffic and sales, you're going to lose your community.

Chapter 2: Creating and Sharing Content on Facebook

In This Chapter

✔ Planning content

✔ Coming up with shareable content

✔ Creating a community

✔ Taking Groups private

*Y*our Facebook brand Page, just like everything else you do for your brand both online and off, requires a strategy as well as a set of goals. Knowing what you hope to achieve with Facebook, as well as how you hope to achieve it, should be planned out before you make your first post or upload your Timeline cover photo. Just as you would take time to plan a marketing or advertising campaign, so should you also think through your Facebook campaign.

Facebook may look like a random bunch of comments and images, but it's much more than that. For the brand Page it's a way to create the type of content people want to both digest and share. Moreover, digesting and sharing isn't your most important objective if you're on Facebook to sell or raise brand awareness.

In this chapter, we discuss how to create the type of content that inspires your Facebook community to share and react.

Creating a Facebook Content Strategy

A common mistake made by many brands is to set up a Facebook account without any idea of what to do with it. Just like with a blog, website, or even a Twitter account, you have to have a plan. To just randomly post topics and hope they stick will lead to inconsistency and confusion. Instead, take some time to create a plan before you get started. If you already have a Facebook account for your brand and need an overhaul, pretend you're starting from scratch and plan a strategy anyway.

The first item to check off your list is your goal. What do you hope to achieve with your Facebook account? You won't be able to plan the right types of content without listing your goals first. For most brands, the goal is to build a community of advocates, which will lead to traffic to the main company website and, hopefully, sales.

Once you know your brand's goal, you want to plan the type of content that will help lead to that goal. Now, this doesn't mean if you're looking for sales, every Facebook post should be selling something. However, that doesn't mean you shouldn't post with sales and the people who help you achieve your ultimate goal in mind. (For more on creating content, see the section "Creating Content That Sings," later in this chapter.)

What follows are some ideas for the types of goals you might want to achieve with your Facebook Page as well as the content to help you best achieve each goal:

✦ **Drive sales:** If sales is your goal, your content should inspire a sale but not necessarily be a sales pitch. For example, has one of your customers been in the news as a result of using your product? If so, share that story. Do the ingredients in your products have health benefits? If so, talk about them and share other healthy living tips. Do you offer a business-oriented coaching service? If so, use your Facebook Page to share tips and best practices. In this manner, you're not exactly selling, but you are putting the idea of the sale in people's minds.

✦ **Grow your community:** If your goal is to grow a community of customers and fans, your content should be more conversational. The people who join your Facebook Page will do so because of the engaging content, which will help to establish trust. This leads to community growth and sales through customer loyalty and word-of-mouth marketing.

✦ **Grow your mailing list:** Do you want more people to sign up for your newsletter? If so, offer sneak peeks of what they will receive if they sign up.

✦ **Create brand awareness:** When you share news and updates regarding your brand, it shows up in News Feeds belonging to the people in your brand. Depending on how their settings are set up, when they Like or comment on your posts, those actions can show up on their friends' and family's News Feeds as well. When people share your content it helps to turn your brand into a household name.

✦ **Establish expertise:** If your goal is to teach and make a name for yourself as an expert, use Facebook to share facts and drop tips. This is especially useful in selling books, providing informational products and services, or promoting blogs.

 ✦ **Receive feedback:** If your goal is to receive customer feedback, use Facebook to create pools, ask questions, and pick the brains of the people who use your product or service. Just be sure you're ready to receive some brutally honest answers.

 ✦ **Drive traffic:** If your goal is to drive traffic, link to your blog posts and web articles and create discussions around the day's topics.

 ✦ **Multiple goals:** Most brands have multiple goals for their Facebook brand Pages. Mixing and matching content to serve many different purposes is okay. As long as you're not spamming your community with links, you'll be fine.

You may not necessarily see your Timeline cover photo as a sales tool, but as the first thing people see when they land on your Facebook Page, that's exactly what it is. The photo may not be of your product or service, but it should inspire the sale. You're not allowed to use your Timeline cover photo as a call to action, but that doesn't mean it can't inspire action. (For more on setting up your Timeline cover photo, see Book V, Chapter 1.)

Take time to understand your community. Watch them interact on the various social networks and watch how they interact on Facebook with you. Observe the types of content they react best to and what they shy away from. When you know your community, you can plan the most successful types of content.

Sharing Your Brand's Story

The new Facebook Timeline is created so that a brand can share its story from the very beginning. This chronological approach is a beautiful opportunity for your customers to find out more about all your milestones and feel connected to your history. When your community members feel as if they're part of the brand, they're more likely to not only buy but share with their friends and family. (For more on sharing, see the upcoming section "Sharing and Being Shared.")

Some items you may want to include on your Timeline are:

 ✦ **A brand logo:** Use your logo as the profile photo, as it helps to promote brand awareness.

 ✦ **A cover photo representative of your brand:** Your Timeline cover photo is designed to catch the eye of anyone landing on your Page.

 ✦ **A blurb describing your brand:** You have the opportunity to grab the attention of potential customers with a couple of impactful sentences under your profile photo.

✦ **A longer brand description in the About section:** Use your Timeline's About section to tell potential customers what you do and how your product or service will benefit them. For more on penning descriptive text for your About page, see Book V, Chapter 1.

✦ **Links to your website and social media pages:** Your Facebook community isn't network exclusive. Many of your customers enjoy interacting at your blog, or on Twitter too. Be sure to include links to all the different places folks can follow you.

✦ **Contact information:** Include your e-mail address in your Timeline's "About" section. Also consider including other important contact details, including a customer service phone line and address.

✦ **Tabs:** You can create a variety of tabs for your Facebook Timeline, including events, polls, FAQs, and so much more. To learn more about tabs, please see the sections "Creating polls, quizzes, and contests" and "Looking at must-have apps for a brand Page" in this chapter.

Creating Content That Sings

Content is king. If you've created a Facebook content strategy, then you should have at least some idea of what to talk about with your Facebook community.

It's not about the sale but rather the conversation and engagement that may lead to the sale. Make sure that your content is a mix of fun questions, photographs, videos, and informative articles and blog posts.

What follows are some tips for creating good content for your Facebook Page:

✦ Don't make everything serious and deep. People like to keep brand interaction light. While thought-provoking questions and discussions are part of a good content strategy, don't forget to add humor to the mix.

✦ Brevity counts. Though you can be wordier than, say, twitter, Facebook isn't your blog. Keep updates brief. Too many words and you begin to lose people.

✦ Stay on topic. When you write about a mishmash of different things having nothing to do with your niche, people get confused. If yours is a cereal brand, your community expects topics centered around cereal, for example, nutrition and recipes. If you start talking about cross-country skiing or barbecue grills, people are going to wonder what any of that has to do with your brand.

✦ Try to create content that's open-ended. Give your community opportunity to respond. Ask questions or talk about the sorts of things that provoke a discussion. Make sure everything you post is inviting a response.

✦ Let your comments be your guide. What kinds of questions does your community ask on your page? What posts do they respond most to? When they do respond, what do they say? Look to your community for topics.

✦ Proofread everything you post. When you don't take the time to read over everything and eliminate errors and typos, it tells your community you don't care enough about them to communicate error free.

✦ Look to your blog or website traffic for ideas. If people are using search terms, phrases, and certain topics to land on your content, use these same topics when creating content for your Facebook community.

✦ Don't be afraid to court controversy. You don't want to always have negativity and squabbles on your Facebook Page, but the occasional controversial topic does wonders to create a discussion.

Sharing and Being Shared

I'm going to let you in on a little secret. Most social media professionals will tell you the interaction with the community and customers is the most important reason to set up your brand on the social networks. They'll tell you it's not important to be big or famous or have viral content, and they'd be just as satisfied interacting with a small community as a big one — and that's true to a certain extent. Though they may not want to admit it, for many, it's equally as important that their community is sharing their content. Figure 2-1 shows content that has been shared several times by fans.

Figure 2-1:
Create the
content
people like
to share.

If you don't allow sharing or create the type of content people want to share, you're going to be stuck with a small clique instead of a community filled with customers and advocates.

When someone clicks the share button under something you posted, it means your content is going to show up in the status of that person's friends as well. If a dozen fans with 200 friends each share your content, your post has the potential to be seen by 2,400 people. Out of all those people, it would be terrific if ten new fans liked your Page as a result. However, even if they don't, sharing is creating brand recognition.

If you're recognized for putting out shareable content, not only will more people follow and use your brand, but your brand will be seen as a respected authority in your field.

So what types of content do people want to share?

+ **Photos:** People share more photos than anything else. Make sure that your photos are relevant, thought-provoking, discussion-worthy, and even amusing, but please don't make them offensive.

+ **Funny or amusing content:** People like to share content that makes them laugh. There's nothing wrong with posting tasteful but amusing photographs, blog posts, or videos.

+ **Heartwarming stories:** People love a good success or comeback story. They enjoy hearing tales of folks who beat the odds. People share inspiration.

+ **Discounts:** Most people who follow brands do so in hopes of receiving special perks that they can share with their friends and family.

+ **Viral videos:** Admit it; you love to share a funny video. That's how videos go viral. Post relevant, fun videos on your Page for more shares.

+ **Lists, tips, and how to's:** People enjoy sharing learning experiences. Share tips or steps to success.

Say thank you to the people who share your content. When they're called out in a positive manner, they're more inclined to continue with the support.

Don't sit around waiting to be shared, however. Do some sharing of your own. Take some time each day to visit other Facebook accounts and find content relevant to your community to share. This goodwill toward other brands puts you on their radar, and they may want to reciprocate. In addition, your community will appreciate you finding discussion topics or images to share with them. This especially works if you switch your Facebook identity to that of your brand Page and not your personal account.

You don't have to limit shared content to Facebook posts or your own content creation. Sharing blog posts, images, videos, and podcasts by others will help create goodwill among different communities and will bring in more awareness of your brand Page.

Using NetworkedBlogs to promote sharing

NetworkedBlogs is a Facebook app that gives you the ability to host your blog's RSS feed on your Facebook Timeline. Every time you post to your blog, a link to the post, thumbnail image, and description will automatically appear on your Timeline or within an app on your Page. This link helps drive more traffic to your content and leads to more sharing.

If your blog is updated more than once or twice per day, people may not want to subscribe because they don't want brand updates appearing in their News Feed all day. NetworkedBlogs works best for blogs updated no more than a couple of times per day. Less is best for this app.

To install the NetworkedBlogs app:

1. **Navigate to** www.facebook.com/networkedblogs.

2. **Click the Go to App button beneath your cover photo.**

   The NetworkedBlogs app page appears.

3. **Click the Log In button to connect your Facebook account with NetworkedBlogs.**

   A permissions page appears.

4. **Choose who can see your activity on NetworkedBlogs (this "activity" includes your subscribing to and reading of other blogs).**

5. **Click the Log In with Facebook button at the top of the page.**

   A thank you page appears.

6. **Click the Click Here to Continue link.**

   A page appears that shows a list of posts from blogs you've associated with your account. If no blogs are associated yet, the page will look similar to Figure 2-2.

Figure 2-2:
A Networked
Blogs
account with
no feeds.

7. Click the Blogger Dashboard link at the top of the page.

Your NetworkedBlogs dashboard appears.

8. Click Grant permissions.

A page appears showing what permissions you're granting to the app. Essentially, you are allowing NetworkedBlogs to access your Page so your blog posts will update automatically on Facebook when they are published.

9. Click Allow in the bottom-right corner of the page.

The Welcome page appears, as shown in Figure 2-3.

Figure 2-3:
Networked
Blogs is
ready to go!

10. Click the Register a New Blog button at the bottom of the page.

The Register a New Blog page appears.

11. **Type the URL for the homepage of your blog in the Blog Link text box and click Next.**

The Register a New Blog page expands to allow you to complete more information about the blog you entered.

12. **Enter the following information as necessary:**

- Blog Name (required)
- Tagline (optional)
- Feed link (required; this is the link for your RSS feed)
- Topics (optional)
- Language (required)
- Description (optional)
- Your E-mail (required)

13. **(Optional) Click Show Advanced Options to enter a specific vanity URL for your blog.**

For example, `http://networkedblogs.com/blog/vanity` — where "vanity" is the title you choose to associate with your blog. You can leave this box blank, and the app will choose the URL for you.

14. **Click Next.**

The New Blog Registered page appears briefly, then forwards to a verification page, as shown in Figure 2-4.

Figure 2-4:
The
Networked
Blogs verifi-
cation page.

15. **Click the Yes button if you own this blog.**

The You've Claimed This Blog page appears, then quickly forward to the next confirmation step.

To confirm that you do indeed own the blog you've registered, you need to select one of two options:

- **Ask Friends to Confirm You Own the Blog:** Click this link and the Select Friends for NetworkedBlogs Request dialog box opens. Select at least five friends (and up to ten) who can verify that you own the blog you claimed. Then click the Send Requests button. The request will show up in your friends' right sidebar under the Ticker as well as in their notifications. When your friends view the notification, they see the verification page, as shown in Figure 2-5.

Figure 2-5:
Your friends need to verify you own the blog.

Author verification links

- **Choose Install the NetworkedBlogs Widget on Your Blog.** If you choose this option, a page appears with code you need to install on your blog. Copy the code and follow the NetworkedBlog instructions on how to place the code. Then click the Verify Now button.

Not having friends or followers verify your ownership isn't a deal-breaker. But Facebook isn't listing you as owner until enough people agree that you own your blog. You can still carry your blog's feed (and anyone's blog feed) on your personal and professional pages and you can still administrate that account.

Now it's time to add your blog feed to your Page — either as a tab or directly to your Timeline. I'll explain how to do both.

Publishing NetworkedBlogs as a tab

When you publish NetworkedBlogs as a tab, your blog updates don't appear on your Timeline; they appear in a Blog tab (under your Page's cover photo — see Figure 2-6). You direct your fans to the NetworkedBlogs tab on your Page by including the URL for the tab in updates.

Figure 2-6:
The
Networked
Blogs app
as a Page
tab.

To publish NetworkedBlogs as a tab, follow these steps:

1. **Return to your NetworkedBlogs dashboard** (`http://networkedblogs.com/dashboard`) **and click the Add to Facebook Page link (see Figure 2-7).**

The Add Page Tab dialog box appears.

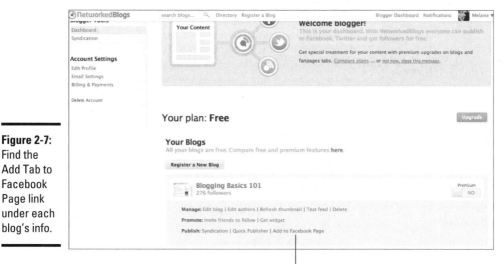

Figure 2-7:
Find the
Add Tab to
Facebook
Page link
under each
blog's info.

Add tab link

2. **Use the pull-down menu to choose which Page you want your blog updates to feed to and then click the Add Page Tab button.**

    You return to your NetworkedBlogs dashboard. Beneath the blog info, you see a list of the Page(s) you added to your blog feed, as shown in Figure 2-8.

Figure 2-8: Your dashboard shows the Pages you installed a Networked Blogs tab on.

    You can repeat this step to install your blog feed on multiple Pages.

3. **Select the Click to Edit link for the Page where you installed the tab.**

    You're taken to the canvas page for the NetworkedBlogs app on that page. It looks similar to Figure 2-9.

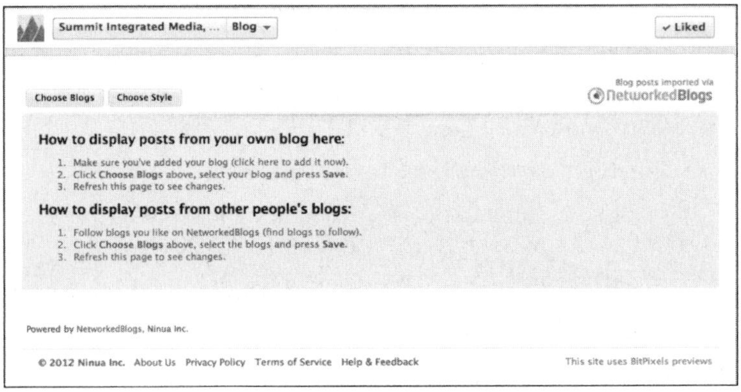

Figure 2-9: The Networked Blogs setup for your Page.

4. **Click the Choose Blogs button at the top of the page.**

    A new page appears showing all the blogs you installed or claimed. It's okay if you only see one blog — that may be all you've installed or claimed so far. Figure 2-10 shows a page whose admin has installed or claimed six blogs.

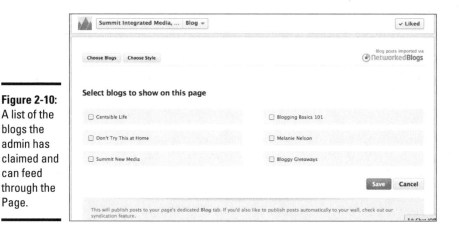

Figure 2-10: A list of the blogs the admin has claimed and can feed through the Page.

5. **Select the check box next to the blog(s) you want to feed through your Page and click Save.**

New blog posts will appear in the NetworkedBlogs tab on your Page (they will not show up on your Timeline).

Publishing NetworkedBlogs directly to your Timeline

To syndicate a blog (meaning, have it post directly to your Timeline and show in your fans' News Feed), head over to your NetworkedBlogs dashboard (http://networkedblogs.com/dashboard) and click the Syndication link in the left column. The Syndication page appears. From here:

1. **Use the pull-down menu to choose a claimed blog to feed to your Timeline.**

   More options appear.

2. **Click the Add Facebook Target button.**

   A dialog box appears with a list that includes your personal profile, all the Pages you're an Admin of, and the Facebook Groups you admin.

3. **Click the Add button next to each profile, Page, or Group you want your blog feed to appear on.**

4. **Click the Close button.**

   You see the confirmation that your NetworkedBlogs feed is set up (see Figure 2-11). New blog posts will appear as updates on your Page Timeline and in the News Feed.

Figure 2-11:
Your
Networked
Blogs feed
is set up!

After you set up the feed, other people can follow it on their Facebook Pages. They can find your blog using the NetworkedBlogs search function, or you can invite them to subscribe.

The benefits to following your blog on Timeline is that you and others won't have to leave Facebook to receive updates. If the headline, thumbnail image, and blurb are intriguing, folks will follow the link back to your blog and read the entire post. Most people agree Facebook is a great referrer of traffic to blogs.

Also, consider is how networked blogs may keep people from engaging on your blog itself as they may not want to leave Facebook. A trial run may be a good idea to measure both engagement and traffic after a month to see whether your network blog is worth the effort.

Sharing your tweets (or not)

You can set up your Facebook Timeline to include all your Twitter updates. So every time you tweet, your Facebook fans can see it, too. Sharing your tweets may sound like a fun way for folks to see another side of you, but the downsides may be stronger than the positives. (For more on marketing with Twitter, see Book IV.)

Most people don't want to see Twitter on Facebook. Before you make the decision to post your Twitter feed on Facebook, strongly consider why we don't recommend it. Introducing your Twitter feed to your Facebook fans is sort of a culture clash. They're used to seeing occasional updates from brands and friends, not a constant barrage of a one-sided conversation from Twitter.

If you're a heavy tweeter, each and every item you post appears on your Timeline. Your posts also appear on the status of everyone who likes you. However, most people don't want to receive a whole lot of updates from any one person or brand. If you tweet a lot, many people may opt to unfollow or hide your updates so that they don't have to see incessant updates. Moreover, you're only carrying your own feed, so if you have a conversation with someone, your Facebook community will see only your comments and not the person or people you're talking to.

Another downside is that if people are seeing all your updates on Facebook, they have no reason to follow and discuss on Twitter. If it's important to build up your Twitter community, you may want to share your tweets only there.

When you're posting on Twitter, you're using language that's native to Twitter. For example, if you're using *RT* for retweet or participating in a hashtag chat, many members of your Facebook community may have no idea what your tweets are about at all. Posting something to your Facebook Page makes no sense if your entire community doesn't understand what you're talking about.

There's no rule against posting your Twitter feed on Facebook, but some people do consider it an unwritten breach of etiquette. There's also no rule saying you can't share or repurpose some of your Twitter posts to appeal to your Facebook community. For example, if you're tweeting to invite your Twitter community to take part in a survey, you can post the same information on Facebook. However, do take care to not use the same abbreviations and language you use to fit Twitter's 140-character limit.

With all that said, it's not unheard of for brands and individuals to post Twitter feeds to their Facebook Pages, and there are certainly apps enabling you to do so. You can also share your Twitter feed without your updates appearing on your community's status pages.

After reading all the above, why would you want to post tweets to your Facebook Page?

✦ Not everyone uses Twitter. By allowing your Tweets to syndicate to your Facebook Page you're allowing more people to see them.

✦ Your message gets through to more people. For example, if you're sharing a discount code on Twitter, your Facebook fans can use it as well.

✦ Seeing your Twitter feed on Facebook may inspire others to follow you on both networks, which means your message sinks in twice.

You will find Facebook's Twitter app at `https://apps.facebook.com/twitter/`. When you click the Go to Your Twitter Profile Settings to Start button, the app asks for permission to access your Twitter account. After you grant permission, the updates appear in your feed.

A good solution is to investigate apps that appear as a tab on your Timeline so that interested parties can click to read your tweets rather than have all your tweets display on the Timeline. TwitterTab, shown in Figure 2-12, is one such app that can help: `https://apps.facebook.com/twittertab`.

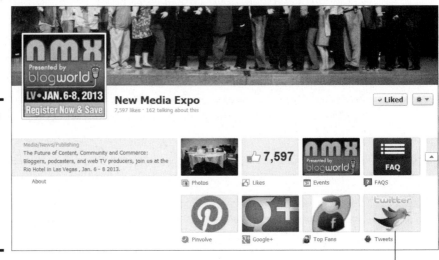

Figure 2-12: The TwitterTab app keeps Twitter updates in a tab and not on your Timeline.

Twitter tab

Advertising on Facebook

You can't deny Facebook is where the people are. In fact, Facebook contains the largest concentration of people interacting on the web than anywhere else. It stands to reason you can potentially reach more people with a Facebook ad than perhaps a television ad, and it's cheaper, too.

What follows are some benefits of advertising your brand on Facebook:

✦ **You have targeted advertising.** Facebook allows for you to choose your target audience rather than sending your message to people who have no interest in your brand. Because Facebook collects information about the people using the platform, it has a better ability to target advertisers to the people who can benefit from them the most. Your Facebook ad can even target by age or geographic location.

✦ **You can add new fans and Likes.** A Facebook ad campaign drives targeted traffic to your brand page for Likes and interaction.

✦ **You can change your ad around as needed.** Facebook ads allow you to change headlines, wording, and images, as well as track your campaigns to see what's working.

✦ **You can reach friends of fans.** Your ad will also show up in the sidebars of the friends of people who liked your page. So if you have 200 fans and they each have 100 friends, you can reach 20,000 people.

As with any campaign, before you start using Facebook advertising, first take the time to determine who you'll be targeting and what you want your end result to be. Is it to drive traffic to your website? Drive sales? More Likes? These are some of the things to think about before creating your Facebook ad.

Next, think of a variety of content for your ads. For example, different headlines, text, and images. You may be tempted to create an ad and leave it up all this time, but the same old ad gets boring. If you don't change around the content of your ad from time to time, not only will people become tired of it, but it can become invisible after a while.

People don't come to Facebook to read ads. They come to Facebook to share, interact, and play. So your ad has to catch their attention; otherwise, it'll just become sidebar noise. Your choice of headlines shouldn't be obnoxious, but it should be enough to catch the attention of someone who is on Facebook for other reasons. Also, because the image on your ad is something that people will see more than once, take some time to choose something pleasant over shock and awe. If you don't choose an image, Facebook will choose one for you. So do yourself a favor and choose an image that sets the right tone.

When you have a variety of ads worked out, test them and see which ones work best. Because you can change your ads any time you want and Facebook gives you the ability to check performance, you can play around with a variety of ads and stick with the ones that work best.

Another thing to keep in mind is that Facebook offers a variety of pricing for advertisements, so options are available for all budgets. Don't worry about spending a lot of money out of the gate. Instead, wait until you see how the ads are performing before investing a lot of money. You don't want to throw good money at poorly performing ads. After you find the text/title/image combinations that work best, you can raise the amount of money you want to spend, if you feel it's important.

Bringing Your Community into the Mix

Every tip you read about Facebook will come to nil if you don't have a positive, productive community. The more people who like your brand page, the more people you will have responding and commenting to your posts and campaigns. You want your community members to feel good about participating, and when they feel good, they share, and they buy.

The last thing you want is a Timeline filled with random updates. Take some time to explore the different apps to find out how to better interact with people. When you share in different, unique ways, your community will grow, and so will sales and brand recognition.

Selling on Facebook

Most of the people on Facebook aren't there because they want to buy or find a good bargain. They're there to visit with their friends. This mindset shouldn't discourage you from selling, however. With the right campaign, Facebook can become your community's equivalent of the supermarket impulse item aisle. Folks aren't there to buy, but it doesn't mean they can't be enticed to do so. While they may not have been interested in a sale, seeing that you have some products on display couldn't hurt. Facebook offers the perfect social shopping opportunity because people can socialize, shop, and share. In fact, people are more likely to buy something they see their friends buying.

Facebook has specific rules about what brands can present to their communities, especially when it comes to selling, promoting, and holding contests. If not kept in check, Facebook can become a haven for spammers, so regulations are necessary. It's a good idea to familiarize yourself with Facebook's Terms of Use for brands before selling in your Facebook updates. You can find the terms of use at `www.facebook.com/page_guidelines.php`.

Facebook requires the use of specific apps for selling and promotion to keep spammers out of the mix and ensure that all opportunities are legitimate. So, while it's absolutely possible to sell on Facebook, you have to do so the right way.

Here are a couple of apps to help you sell on Facebook:

✦ **Facebook Store:** This feature gives you the opportunity to create a shopping experience on your Timeline. The app appears as a tab and allows you to display merchandise or sell products and services. Your store can have as many items as you like.

✦ **Facebook Marketplace:** This app allows your advertisement to appear in classified advertising format. Because most Facebook users don't really know about this app, you may find it results in a low level of buying and engagement. However, some brands have found success.

Not all your selling on Facebook has to be via apps and widgets. You can also create action terms and phrases to post on your wall to lead your community to your website. Sharing news about a sale, new merchandise, or a discount is fine, as long as you're not spamming.

Looking at must-have apps for a brand Page

The best way to keep your community coming back at all is to offer a good mix of content. To make the most of your Facebook Timeline, do more than update with business items. Facebook allows you to be more than a place to drop the occasional comment. You can also take advantage of an amazing array of apps to use as tabs on your Timeline.

You can find apps for everything from highlighting your other social media brand pages to receiving feedback and highlighting your community.

You can find apps at Facebook's Apps section or a Facebook app website, such as `http://appbistro.com`. While many are free, just as many have a cost.

What follows is a list of apps to explore for your Timeline:

✦ **FAQ Tab:** Having a Frequently Asked Questions or FAQ tab on your Timeline gives you the ability to share plenty of details about your company. It's also a place where people can come for more information. Plus, the app allows users to ask their own questions, which you can answer. Find FAQ Tab at `www.facebook.com/faq.tab`. (See Figure 2-13.)

Figure 2-13: A Frequently Asked Questions tab allows for potential clients, customers, and community members to find out more about your brand.

✦ **Contact Me:** Enables you to create a contact form for community members to reach out and offer comments and feedback. Find Contact Me at `www.facebook.com/contactforms`.

✦ **Google+ Tab:** Allow your Facebook community to see your Google+ updates with this easy-to-install tab; see `www.facebook.com/googleplustopages`.

✦ **Pinvolve:** Allows your community to Pin to Pinterest any photos you upload to your Facebook Timeline; go to `https://apps.facebook.com/pinvolve/?ref=ts`.

✦ **Live Help:** Enables you to answer your community members' questions in real time. Find Live Help at `http://appbistro.com/facebook-business-app/products/live-help`.

✦ **EventBrite for Pages:** EventBrite enables you to create a registration and RSVP system for events, such as parties, conferences, and networking mixers. As EventBrite also enables you to share and promote your event, and doesn't cost a dime, it's one of the more popular event apps out there. Find EventBrite at `http://appbistro.com/facebook-business-app/products/eventbrite`.

✦ **UserVoice:** An app enabling you to collect customer feedback, UserVoice doesn't come cheap. It's $89 to use, but if learning from your community is important, it's well worth the price. `http://appbistro.com/facebook-business-app/products/uservoice`.

Take some time to browse the apps available to brands on Facebook and find those that create an interactive, engaging experience for your community. When you provide a fun, interesting environment, people will come back often.

Creating polls, quizzes, and contests

For a truly interactive experience, you have to give your Facebook community the tools to really get the party going. Asking questions or posting links is only a small part of growing your Facebook network. To truly tap into the power of the people, create some other fun experiences.

Polls can be fun and frivolous, or you can use them to collect information about the consumer. People like to participate in polls because they feel as if they're part of a campaign. Plus, creating a poll isn't a big time commitment; a simple click of the button, and you have their vote.

Facebook's poll app allows for participants to add comments about why they voted as they did, and you can also configure the poll to allow participants to add their own items for folks to vote on.

Polls are best advised for bigger Facebook communities. When smaller communities put out polls and have a poor showing, they may receive only a couple of responses. The last thing you want is to promote something publicly and have a poor showing.

For even more community interaction, try creating quizzes. Quizzes aren't necessarily a way to gather information from your community, but if they're entertaining, the people who take the quizzes will share them with others in the community.

Appbistro.com lists several quiz-building apps, and they're intuitive enough that even the most technically challenged people can create a quiz. See whether you can put something together representative of your brand. For example, if you're representing an Italian restaurant, create a quiz seeing how many Italian words and phrases your community recognizes. If yours is a car brand, list the parts of the car and see whether your community knows what each part does or where they're located. At the end of the quiz, have a ratings score for expertise. These quizzes are frivolous, but fun and extremely shareable. They're also great community-building tools.

Contests are another way to perform community outreach and raise awareness of your brand. However, like selling, Facebook has specific rules about contests. If you're going to give something away or feature another type of contest, you may only do so using a third-party app. Posting contests as a status update is against Facebook's Terms of Service. Facebook's app section and sites such as appbistro.com list many apps for brands wishing to host contests on their pages.

Before running a contest on Facebook, read Facebook's promotions policy. Check the policy each time you run a contest because the rules change now and then, and you don't want to be caught unaware. See Facebook's Terms of Use for Pages here:

`www.facebook.com/promotions_guidelines.php`

Offering discounts to your community

One of the main reasons people follow brands on Facebook is because they're interested in receiving bargains, freebies, or discounts. In fact, these types of perks are a terrific way to reward your community for their loyalty.

When you offer discounts and perks that are available only to your Facebook community, it makes people feel special and inclined to share your brand with others. Discounts are what fans share the most when it comes to brands.

You can offer discounts in a variety of ways:

✦ Set up a unique code for your Facebook community only.

✦ Link to discounts on your website.

✦ Use the Facebook Offers app, which enables you to post your discount and an image (and they then appear in your fans' News Feeds).

Do be careful not to spam your Facebook Page with discount codes and sales pitches. While your community is very interested in receiving bargains, they're not interested in reading spiel and jargon every time they see an update for you. Balance your discounts with other content and don't post sales or discounted items more than once per day.

Using Private or Secret Groups

Facebook enables users to create private Groups and secret Groups for more intimate discussion. Outside observers can view the messages in a private Group, but they can't participate unless they're invited or their membership requests are approved by administrators. Secret Groups are by invitation only, and only members can see them. Administrators for secret Groups can change the settings to determine whether members are allowed to invite friends or not.

Why set up a secret Group? Secret Groups can create exclusivity, for sure, but they also keep out spammers. Plus, your content isn't available for public search, and marketers can't hit up the members of your community. Secret Groups also enable the sharing of photos and documents without putting them out there to the whole world.

Brand Pages and Groups are different in that Pages are for fans to have conversations and learn about a brand, whereas Groups allow like-minded people to interact and have conversations on a more expansive basis. While you wouldn't have dozens of conversations going each day on your brand Page, in a Group, where members can opt in, you can have many conversations going at the same time. The downside to Groups is that Facebook caps the amount of people who can join to 5,000 members, whereas your Facebook brand Page can host millions.

To create a Facebook Group:

1. **Access the Facebook Groups page at www.facebook.com/about/ groups.**

2. **Click Create Group.**

   The Create New Group dialog box appears, as shown in Figure 2-14.

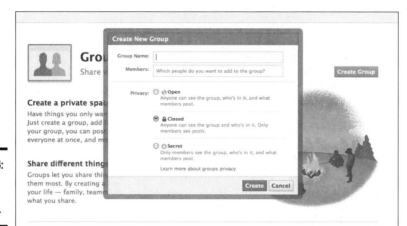

Figure 2-14:
Set up the
basics of
your group.

3. **Determine your Group name, invite members, and select your privacy options.**

4. **Click Create, and you're good to go.**

When creating separate discussion groups on Facebook, don't allow them to turn into cliques. If members feel excluded, they won't feel as strongly about your brand. Continue adding members to your Groups to keep the interaction fresh. See Book III, Chapter 2 for more on creating communities, not cliques.

Chapter 3: Gaining Insights about Your Facebook Community

In This Chapter

✔ Getting stats with Facebook Insights

✔ Looking over the numbers

*I*t's a great time to be on Facebook. The newly rolled out Timeline feature is perfect for brands. The cover photo allows for an eye-capturing image to give the right first impression, plenty of tabs and activities keep your fans engaged, and you now, more than ever, have the ability to learn about the people who make up your Facebook community thanks to Facebook's Insights.

By using the tools available to you, you can better interact with your Facebook community and learn more about the people who are supporting your brand. The more you know about them, the more you can tailor your content and campaigns to better suit their wants and needs.

Facebook's Timeline feature is perfect for any brand looking to grow its online presence and build up a community. Unlike blogs, the platform is already set up and you don't have to post 500 words every day. Though you'll have to stay close to monitor the conversation, you're able to enjoy the people who visit your Facebook Page and learn about their needs and habits. In fact, learning more about the people who use a product or service is one of the top reasons brands come to Facebook.

In this chapter, we look at how to analyze your Facebook Timeline in order to better promote and sell your brand. We also talk about how to handle some of the administrative tasks that come with having a Facebook Timeline.

The more you choose to do with your Timeline, the more your Facebook fan base will grow.

Getting the Scoop on Your Fans with Insights

Facebook Insights is an analytics tool for your brand Page, which allows you to see what your community is up to, as well as keep track of things like Likes, Unlikes, and comments. There are even downloadable reports for in-depth analysis. In short, Facebook Insights gives you a peek into what people are doing after they land on your Page.

Discovering info about your audience

Through Insights, you can determine your Facebook Page's success. Through your Insights, you find out

✦ **How many people like your Page each day, week, and month:** In addition to finding out how many people like your Page on a daily, weekly, and monthly, basis, Insights also breaks down the Likes by demographic (see Figure 3-1).

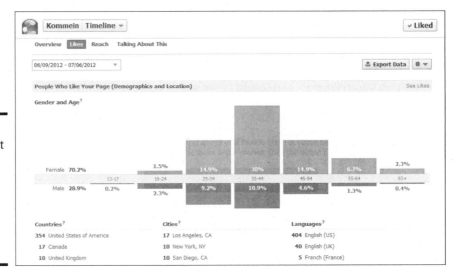

Figure 3-1: The amount of people who like your Page is broken down by demographic.

✦ **How many people unlike your Page:** Don't just measure Likes. Learning how many people unlike your Page is important, too. It helps you determine how your Facebook community is reacting to your content and the amount of updates you're serving up each day (see Figure 3-2).

Figure 3-2:
Unlikes help you to determine the most effective content strategy.

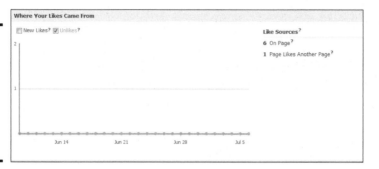

✦ **How many people are talking about or tagging your Page:** When you access the Talking About This option, you find out who is talking about or tagging your Page. In addition to discovering the demographic range of people talking about your brand on Facebook, you're also able to determine whether your Facebook campaign is paying off (see Figure 3-3).

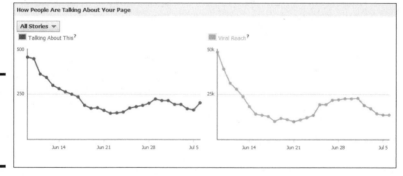

Figure 3-3:
Learn who is talking about you and why.

✦ **Which content gets the biggest (and lowest) reaction:** Your Insight's Overview section breaks down your Facebook community's reaction by content. Consider not posting, or posting less frequently, the types of content people respond to the least.

✦ **How people came to like your Page:** Knowing how many people like your Page is great, but that's only half the battle. It's also important to know where people are liking your Page. In the Likes section of your Insights, you can find out whether people are liking your Page by coming directly from your Timeline or from a different location.

+ **What are your total tab views:** Are your tabs working? Your total tab views shows you which tabs interest people the most, as shown in Figure 3-4.

+ **Information about external referrals:** Details which outside websites are sending people to your Facebook Page. See Figure 3-4.

Figure 3-4:
What sources outside of Facebook are sending people to your Page?

Total Tab Views[?]		External Referrers[?]	
1,326	timeline	44	blogworldexpo.com
73	Information	21	blogworld.com
52	Photos	8	t.co
24	Events	6	google.com
13	messages_inbox	5	hootsuite.com

+ **Details on demographics:** Facebook Insights offer a variety of demographics, including age, gender, and location.

Putting the info to good use

Now that you have all this information about your Facebook community, what are you going to do with it? The reason Facebook provides Insights for Pages is because they know how important it is for you to see if Facebook offers good ROI.

Take some time each week to check out your Facebook numbers:

+ If your Likes are going up: You're doing something right! When people like your Page it means they're interested in your brand. It also means the promotion your doing on behalf of your Facebook Page is working and you're creating the type of content folks are responding to and sharing. Continue doing what you're doing but don't be afraid to add different types of content to see what your Facebook community best responds to.

+ If your Likes are going down: If you're losing Facebook friends it can be for a variety of reasons. It might mean you're updating too many times in a day. Two to three times per day is optimal. Any more than that and people are going to tire of seeing you in their news feeds. It can also be that you're not offering the type of content they find interesting. Experiment with different types of content to see what they react to most.

✦ If your Likes aren't doing anything at all: This isn't a bad thing because people aren't unliking your Page, but it's not an ideal situation either. You want your Page to receive new Likes daily and if this isn't happening you have to step up your game. Try changing your Timeline photo to see if you can find one more appealing to your community. See what you can do to find the type of content or images that appeal at first glance to the people landing on your Page. To learn more about creating compelling content see Book V, Chapter 2.

✦ If people are talking about you: In a perfect world, your Facebook Page will be filled with other people's content too. This content is a good thing because it means people are writing about you and tagging your Facebook Page for all to see. The more people who see your name on Facebook, the better.

✦ If no one is talking about you: What good is a word-of-mouth marketing campaign if no words or coming out of anyone's mouth? If people aren't talking about you or sharing your content, you have to give them something to talk about. Maybe it's time to offer a Facebook only discount code, or give a special perk to everyone who likes your content. (For more on Facebook's guidelines regarding contests and promotions please see Book V, Chapter 2.) Also, you might want to work on special promotions and content outside of the Facebook Page. Create the types of content on your blog and website that entices people to share on Facebook.

✦ If people are responding well to certain types of content: Take note. If people are commenting, liking, and sharing certain content on your Facebook Page, this is the type of content you want to continue to provide. Do still create a good mix of different types of content, but give the people what they want as well.

✦ If no one is responding to certain types of content: If you post certain types of content and no one is responding, it means your community isn't interested. Avoid posting this type of content in the future.

Facebook provides Insights so that you can better learn about the people who are interacting on your Page or show interest in your brand. When you know how they react to your content, you can plan the types of campaigns they best respond to. Because you're given the additional benefit of demographics, you can also appeal to gender, age, and even locale.

Chapter 4: Finding the Facebook Sweet Spot

In This Chapter

✔ **Understanding Facebook's EdgeRank**

✔ **Timing your updates**

✔ **Finding out about consumers on Facebook**

✔ **Mixing up your content**

Facebook is an amazing marketing tool. If used properly, you can reach hundreds, if not thousands, of people. The key is in understanding how Facebook works. Posting random updates is fine if you just want to have a presence. However, if you want to have an engaging community and the type of interaction that leads to raving fans and customers, you have to go beyond posting random updates and do a little research into the inner workings of Facebook.

Facebook doesn't do things by accident, and neither should you. There's a rhyme and reason as to which updates are seen by your fans, and that's not always in their control. There are also right times to post content and even the right kinds of content to post. The more you discover about how Facebook works, and the best times and types of content, the better able you are to have the type of Page people are happy to support.

In this chapter, we explore Facebook's algorithm, EdgeRank, and find out how to use it to your advantage. We also talk about the best time to post content and the best types of content to post.

Understanding EdgeRank

EdgeRank is Facebook's algorithm, or Facebook's inner mechanics. In simple terms, the algorithm is how Facebook determines what people see in their News Feeds. Every action taken on Facebook — for example, comments, Likes, and tags — is called an *edge*. EdgeRank weighs your edges; if you're not an active participant on brand Pages or personal profiles, you won't see as many brand Pages or personal profile updates in your News Feed.

Something that surprises many people is how they don't see every update made by every friend or brand they subscribe to. If they don't show enough interest in a friend or brand's updates, they see only a selection of updates. In this chapter, we explore some ways to get around this.

Knowing what EdgeRank measures

EdgeRank is made up of three elements:

✦ **Affinity:** How much any one person engages with another individual or brand. For example, say that Person A engages with your brand on a daily basis. He comments on every update, gives his thumbs up to every photograph, and votes in ever poll. EdgeRank will ensure he sees all your updates. Person B, on the other hand, doesn't pay much attention to your updates and comments or reacts to your content only occasionally. EdgeRank won't show many of your updates on her News Feed at all.

✦ **Weight:** Each action people take on Facebook has a different weight. A comment weighs more than a Like, for example. Facebook takes these weights into account when determining how much someone participates on your brand page. If their interaction on your brand is low weight, they'll see fewer updates from your brand. If they're heavier commenters and participate often, they'll see more updates.

✦ **Time:** EdgeRank takes into account how old your content is. So while it's selecting who should see what content based on Affinity and Weight, it's also taking into account how old your content is. So someone's News Feed will see other people's newer content over your older content.

EdgeRank isn't a separate entity you can access on a control panel. It simply is. EdgeRank is what makes Facebook work, and you can't adjust it as you see fit. You can't see it or control it, but you can do some things to make EdgeRank work to your benefit.

Keeping your fans engaged

So now that you know a little bit about how the EdgeRank algorithm works, you want to work on keeping your fans so engaged that they all see your updates. In fact, if you want to keep your updates appearing in your fans' News Feeds, it's almost more important that they react to the content than read it.

To get more of a response from your Facebook fans, the trick is to make them do as little work as possible. Very few people want to invest a lot of time interacting with a brand. So if the update is long-winded, you lose a lot of people because they don't want to commit to reading huge blocks of text. If you can make your update in a sentence or two, they're more likely to read the whole thing.

This advice also goes with the type of response you're requesting. It takes no time to like an update, but it takes a lot of time for someone to type a heartfelt response. Most people don't want to spend all their Facebook time interacting on a brand page.

To get them to participate without committing a lot of their time,

✦ **Ask them to vote.** "Like this update if you agree peanut butter is better than jelly."

✦ **Request one-word answers.** "Give us one word to describe your day's to-do list."

✦ **Fill in the blanks.** "Walking is to running like _____ is to _____."

These types of posts are fun and open-ended, so they encourage participation. In fact, they encourage fans to check back to post again and see how other people are responding. This interaction helps EdgeRank decide to show them more of your updates. The more long-winded and antiseptic your updates, the less likely your fans are to engage — and see your content.

Knowing the Best Time to Post

Is there a right time to post your content? The short answer to this is "yes." Studies have analyzed brand page interaction, and there are definite times to post your content for the most engagement. For example, 6 a.m. probably isn't a good time to post because most families are getting ready for work and school and aren't paying attention to Facebook.

So at what times is it recommended you post your content? According to a study presented by Buddy Media, most brands post content between the hours of 10 a.m. and 4 p.m. — in other words, regular business hours. However, that doesn't mean that you should post only during these hours because the study also showed that brands that also engaged outside of business hours had 20 percent more engagement on their Facebook Pages than the brands that stuck to a strict business hour schedule.

Buddy Media also found brands that posted during business hours had more engagement toward the end of the week on Thursday and Friday than the beginning of the week. This trend may be because people find their attention waning as they get closer to the weekend and use Facebook as a distraction.

In fact, the best times for brand engagement on Facebook appear to be times when people are most looking for distractions. Coffee breaks, lunch times, and the end of the week, especially leading up to the end of the day, are the best times to interact.

Now, just because a study says it's so doesn't mean that this is the case for you. Each brand has to discover its own best time to interact. Experiment. Try your posts at certain times of the day to see where you have the most interaction. Try one time at, say, 10 a.m., and post at that time for one month. Log the engagement you receive — Likes, comments, shares, and so on — for each type of post, such as images, questions, polls, and discounts. After the month is over, try a different time and compare the level of engagement. It takes a little trial and error, but soon you'll find your own sweet spot.

By keeping track of the times, days of the week, and level of engagement, you can create the type of content that receives the best response and post it at a time when the level of engagement is sure to be high.

Using the Right Mix of Content

Take care when creating content for your brand Page. Even those who don't participate often are noticing what you post and how often. Presenting your Facebook community with the right mix of content means you're offering a variety of different types of updates and Timeline posts, while considering the time and even day for each time of post.

What follows are some best practices for finding the right mix:

+ **Don't make it about the sale.** If you make your Facebook community feel as if they're only there to be pitched to, they won't stick around long. Have a true community and make it about more than sales. Make it about engagement, interaction, and fun.

+ **Share things that catch attention in a good way.** Visual content always gets the best reaction. Photos and videos represent the content that is most shared, liked, commented on, and talked about on Facebook.

+ **Be mindful of how often you're posting each day.** Many brands only post once or twice per day. Try not to go more than three or four updates per day tops. If you post too often, you'll lose fans.

+ **Keep an editorial calendar.** Having an editorial calendar helps you space out the types of content you post and also allows for consistency.

+ **Make your community feel special**. Offer perks only available to your Facebook community.

+ **Don't overlook calls to action.** Encourage your Facebook fans to visit your website, check out deals, and follow you on other social networks.

Also consider the types of content to share with your community. Not everything is going to work for you. For example, some communities enjoy it when their hosts post informative news articles, but in other Facebook communities, these articles aren't always so well received. When you're starting out, consider it your trial period. Try a variety of content spread out through the day and see what works. This doesn't mean you try a specific type of content once, and if you receive no comments, you never post it again. Instead, it means to test out content over a series of days and times. Something you post on a Sunday may not have the same reaction as something you post on a Tuesday, and something you post at 10 a.m. may receive a different reaction than if you posted the same item at 6 p.m. Also, you may find you receive fewer reactions on Monday than on Friday. To try something once and give up would be a mistake.

With all that said, certain types of content are generally well received. Try these different types of content at a variety of dates and times and see what combinations work best for you:

✦ **Images:** Photos almost always do well on Facebook because they're so shareable.

✦ **Cartoons:** Like photos, cartoons are extremely shareable, especially if the people in your community can relate to them.

✦ **Video:** How-to videos, funny viral type videos, and touching scenes are shareable and lead to many comments.

✦ **Informative blog posts and articles:** People react well to a learning experience.

✦ **Fan highlights:** Bring your community into the mix. Call out fans who are doing good things, or share their content.

✦ **Discounts or other perks:** Rewarding fans for loyalty always goes over well.

✦ **Polls and quizzes:** In addition to adding an element of fun to your page, polls and quizzes also help you to gather feedback and information from your fans.

✦ **Questions and requests for feedback:** A mutually beneficial experience, when you request feedback, your community also feels as if they're helping out the brand.

Here are the ways to gauge your community's response:

✦ **Comments:** If you start to receive a lot of comments, it's a good indicator that your content is doing well, even if the comments disagree with a point. When you post and your community responds with their thoughts, it means they're reading and reacting.

✦ **Shares:** If your fans are sharing your content in their own news feeds, this tells you that they enjoy what you post and they want others to enjoy it as well.

✦ **Likes to content:** Are you receiving more Likes to the content your posting? If so, this is a good indication that you're doing something right.

✦ **New Likes to page:** New fans respond well to good content. If your community is sharing, it will lead to new likes on your page.

✦ **Lurker participation:** Every community has *lurkers,* or those who don't participate in discussions but read updates and enjoy the community in silence. A good indication that you're creating engaging content is that the lurkers will come out of hiding and start participating.

✦ **New fan participation:** If you notice a lot of new names becoming regular community members, this is a good indication your Facebook content strategy is working.

✦ **People talking about you:** If people are tagging you in their own posts and referring others to your page, it's because they like your content.

Book VI

Google+

Contents at a Glance

Chapter 1: Leaping into Google+

In This Chapter

✔ Determining whether Google+ is for you

✔ Getting the gist of Google+

✔ Bringing your Google+ page to life

✔ Creating a winning profile

✔ Choosing which notifications to receive

*I*n some ways, Google+ is a social network like many others: Your Google+ community can show approval for your content, share your content, join in video chats, and interact with people who have similar interests. However, Google+ is more than just another social network. Because you get to group friends and followers into Circles, it's easier to share with specific groups of people. Add in the extra search engine optimization value that comes with Google indexing any public updates, plus the ability to do video Hangouts, and Google+ has the ability to be a serious game changer.

Google+ launched in July 2011 to a selection of influential early adapters. After spending time interacting with their peers and testing the waters, many of the early adapters, especially those who work in social media, agreed that Google+ was a contender as a social network people could use every day.

You may not feel like dealing with yet another social network profile. When you create a page, you want to do it right, but maintaining it involves a time commitment. Is your time better spent cultivating the networks you're already a part of, or finding new ways to reach out to customers and clients and grow your online community?

Only you can determine whether you need Google+. Google+ hasn't replaced Facebook or Twitter as the social media weapon of choice for many brands, but companies such as ESPN, Cadbury, and Samsung have embraced Google+ in addition to other social networks, and they're finding success with it. You, too, may find that Google+ offers you a little something different than the usual social networks.

Check out Jesse Stay's *Google+ For Dummies,* Portable Edition, for a little more on Google+.

Determining whether Google+ Is Right for Your Brand

When marketing a brand, you really need to be careful of the content you put out in social media for the world to see. As important it is to have a strong social media presence, if you open an account with a social network, promote it, and then never use it, the resulting account quickly falls out of date. That doesn't look good for you or the brand — it looks like you either don't care about the account or can't find the time for it, and the brand appears to lack relevance and popularity. So before you take on Google+, be sure you have the time to devote to your web presence there and keep your page from becoming a virtual ghost town.

Here are several reasons to consider using Google+:

✦ **Do you want a better presence on the search engines?**

Being a part of the Google+ community means your brand is weighed heavier in the top-secret algorithm Google uses to determine where a company or site lands in search engine results. Using Google+ is an easy way to get closer to the top.

✦ **Do you want additional ways to interact with your existing customers and community?**

Sure, you may be on other social networking sites such as Facebook, Twitter, and LinkedIn, but if you have the time and resources, why not add another service to the mix? By trial and error, you'll find the social networks that produce the best results for your brand. And by best results, we mean more visibility and interaction with current and potential customers. Who wouldn't want that?

✦ **Do you want to interact in a space that isn't saturated with other brands?**

Although Google+ is a fantastic social networking resource, it is still very young. A huge number of companies haven't jumped on the bandwagon just yet because they're busy with other sites. Why not step outside of the box and build a strong presence on Google+? When you become a Google+ pro (by reading this minibook, of course), others may see you as a trailblazer, and chances are good they'll head to Google+, too. Who doesn't want to be seen as a person who is ahead of the curve?

✦ **Would you like to share engaging content or updates with your community without starting a blog?**

Google+ allows you to share your content with people who don't have a Google+ account by entering their e-mail address in the Share menu. You can also notify people in your Circles that you've added new content, much like an RSS (Really Simple Syndication) feed on a blog.

✦ **Do you need an easy way for customers and potential customers to contact you?**

Sure, your customers can access you via phone, e-mail, or your website, but Google+ adds yet another way they can communicate their thoughts by commenting on your posts or adding their own posts via the Join the Discussion box that you can add to the top of your page. The About section of your Google+ profile also allows you to add further contact information, so be sure to provide your customers plenty of ways to reach out to you.

Some obvious and not-so-obvious perks set Google+ apart from other social media services, as described in the following sections.

Recognizing the Google factor

Google is a search engine giant, and you want your brand front and center in the search engine race. Google+ can help you with that because public profiles and updates are indexed for search and appear in web searches of your brand. Therefore, someone using a search engine to seek more information on your brand could land on your Google+ page and see lots of engagement. And, keeping in line with Google's uncluttered look, Google+ has no ads running. In other words, there is nothing to pull your fans' attention away from your content!

Interacting via Google+ features

You have several ways to interact with the people you are connected with on Google+. When using the social network, the following features enhance your experience with your friends or fans:

✦ **Circles:** Your Circles are how you arrange the friends or fans who want to follow your brand on Google+. Circles are like lists you can use to direct content to specific people. For example, you can have separate Circles for team members, vendors, clients, and customers. This feature is great for ensuring the information you share with a specific Circle doesn't get seen by others for whom the content was not intended. You find more about Circles in Book VI, Chapter 2.

✦ **+1:** The +1 feature is a great way for users to find interesting content to read and share. Similar to a Facebook Like, the +1 says you like the content someone posted. When you click the +1 button, your picture will appear on the bottom right of the post for everyone in your Circles to see. When a post has a lot of +1s, more people are likely to read the post. We talk more about +1 in Book VI, Chapter 3.

✦ **Hangouts:** Google+ allows users to host *Hangouts* — video conversations with up to ten people at one time — so getting a group of people together for a video chat is easy. Maybe you want to hold a meeting of colleagues but a few are traveling. Hangouts are a great way to get some face time without having to be in the same location.

✦ **Hangouts on Air:** Hangouts on Air allow an unlimited amount of people to view your Hangout live. Hangouts on Air are excellent tools for discussion groups, focus groups, and reaching out to your community. We provide more information about Hangouts on Air in Book VI, Chapter 4.

✦ **Share:** You can share your content with the easy-to-use Share function.

   • *Sharing a link:* Click the link icon in your Share box and copy and paste your link in the box provided.

   • *Sharing photos:* Click the photo icon in your Share box to upload photos to share with your community.

   • *Sharing videos:* Click the video icon in your Share box to upload videos to share.

For a quicker way to share items, you can simply drag the links to photos, videos, and content into your Share box.

✦ **Tagging:** Unlike Facebook Pages, Google+ allows you to tag people even when they don't post in your thread. To tag people or brands, you add a + or an @ symbol in front of a person's name.

✦ **Edit status updates:** An extremely attractive element of Google+ is that you can edit your posts, even if you already hit Enter. Everyone makes a spelling error or wants to reword something at one point or another. On Google+, you can do so without having to delete the entire post.

✦ **Bumping up old posts:** When someone comments on an older post, it's brought back to the top of the page to add new life to the conversation.

Before getting started on Google+, take some time to get your bearings. Look around and see how other brands and individuals are using this network. Look at what people are sharing and what they're talking about and take some time to notice the posts that receive the most +1s and shares.

Creating Your Google+ Page

Google+ pages are spots on the Google+ social network where companies of all sizes and in all industries maintain a presence in order to share information and interact with their current and (hopefully) future customers. Whenever we reference a company's page, we're talking about its Google+ page.

If you already have a Google account, you're halfway to creating a Google+ page. If you use Gmail, Google Reader, Google Checkout, Google Calendar, Google Docs, or any other Google application, you have an account with Google. Don't worry that it's a personal account and you want to use it as a business page; you'll be able to do so.

If you don't have a Google account, you first have to create one to get started with Google+. Here's how:

1. **Go to** `https://plus.google.com.`

2. **Click the Create an Account link to the right of the Sign In button at the top of the screen, as shown in Figure 1-1.**

Google steers you to the Create a New Google Account page.

Create a new Google account

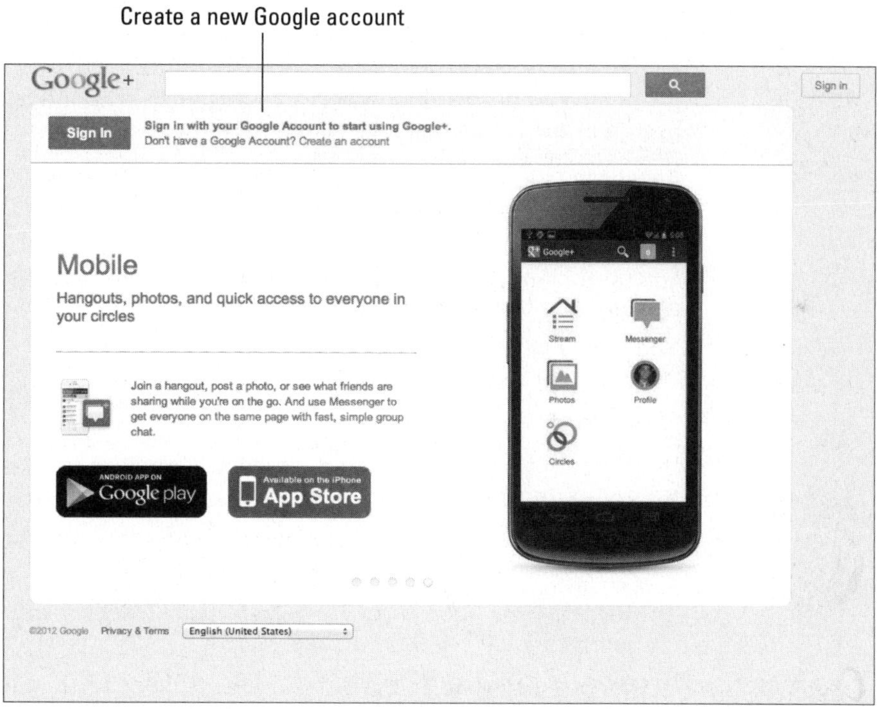

Figure 1-1:
Sign up for a Google account to access a ton of great features.

3. **Fill out the required information on the Create a New Google Account page.**

Google wants to know your name, desired username, account password, and your current (non-Gmail) e-mail address.

4. **Type the Captcha (the letters in the distorted text) to prove you're not a robot or about to spam the community**

You aren't a robot, right?

Sometimes the distorted words are difficult to read even for humans. If you can't make sense of the splotchy letters, click the Refresh icon (an arrow making a circle) to get a new word image.

5. **Select the check box labeled I Agree to the Google Terms of Service and Privacy Policy.**

As with all policy documents, I recommend you read these carefully to ensure you understand how Google will use your personal information and to know what you can and can't do with your Google account.

After you set up the required Google account, you're ready to set up your Google+ page:

1. **Go to** `http://plus.google.com/pages/create`.

If you haven't already signed in to your Google account, click the Sign In button at the top of the page. (Refer to Figure 1-1.)

If you aren't signed in, you see +You in the upper-left corner. If you are signed in, you see *+yourname,* where *yourname* is the name you provided when you created your Google account.

2. **Select the type of page you want to create by clicking the appropriate option from the list on the left, as shown in Figure 1-2.**

You have five options:

- *Local Business or Place:* Select this category if you have a physical location customers can go to.

- *Product or Brand:* Select this category if you provide a service that doesn't necessarily take place in only a brick-and-mortar location.

- *Company, Institution or Organization:* Select this category if you're a school or non-profit.

- *Arts, Entertainment or Sports:* Select this category if you run an entertainment-based company.

- *Other:* This broad category is for everything else that doesn't fit in the preceding categories.

Figure 1-2:
Select the
appropriate
category
from the
options on
the left.

Hover your mouse pointer on each category to see examples of the types
of entities each category is appropriate for, such as hotels, restaurants,
apparel, financial services, and so on.

After you click a category button, a sign-up form appears on the right, as
shown in Figure 1-3.

3. **Add your information to the sign up form.**

Type your page name into the first text box (we recommend your company name), add your website address in the text box below that, and
then select a category from the drop-down list. These categories break
down into exactly what industry your brand falls into, such as Financial
Services, Media, or Business and Industrial.

If your specific industry is not listed, scroll to the bottom of the drop-
down list, where you can select generic categories such as Brand,
Product, Service, or Other. See Figure 1-3.

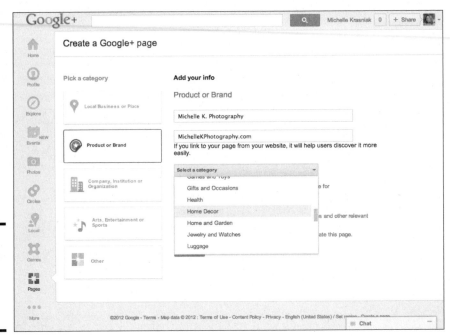

Figure 1-3:
Provide the details of what your page is about.

4. **Select which Google+ users your content is appropriate for.**

   These are age-related selections, so if you promote and sell alcoholic beverages, you would select the Alcohol Related option so Google+ knows not to make your page visible, to users who are not of legal drinking age. What this really means is only users who are of legal age can participate. Younger people can still view the content, however.

5. **Select the check box next to Yes, Please Keep Me Informed if you want to receive updates from Google+.**

6. **Select the I Agree check box to indicate that you agree to the Page Terms and are allowed to create this page.**

   As mentioned earlier, it's always a good idea to read through the fine print in these situations so you know how to stay within the usage guidelines. The last thing you want is to have your page shut down and lose all of your hard work because you've broken a rule.

7. **Click the Create button.**

   Congratulations! You officially have a Google+ page.

The next section covers what you have to do to populate your page with more information about your content and how to add engaging content for your fans.

Filling Out Your Google+ Profile

Your Google+ profile is an important resource. Because Google+ indexes pages for search, your profile is immediately available to those seeking more information about your products or services. Moreover, it's also an important first look at your brand by the people who are seeking you out on the search engine and Google+ itself.

In addition to entering your name, e-mail address, and other contact information, you should include a photo on your profile. For example, adding a company logo as your profile picture is a great idea. Or, if you're a service provider (such as a photographer), showing a picture of yourself doing what you do best is a great way for people to feel more connected to you or your business. It gives a face to the name, so to speak.

After you sign up for your Google+ page, Google deposits you on your home or landing page. You want to add information to your profile to give your fans a better idea of who you are and what you or your business can do for them.

Adding a profile picture

Your profile picture is the image you want people to see when they land on your Google+ page. The picture can be a personal picture if this is a personal account or your brand logo if you're creating a brand account.

Here's how to set up your profile photo:

1. **In your sidebar (the left menu), click the Profile icon to access your profile's details, as shown in Figure 1-4.**

   On the page that appears, you can change your profile picture; post text updates, videos, and photos; or add more information to your profile, such as a motto (tagline) and a short introduction about you or your business.

2. **Click the Change Profile Photo link beneath the large box on the right side of the page.**

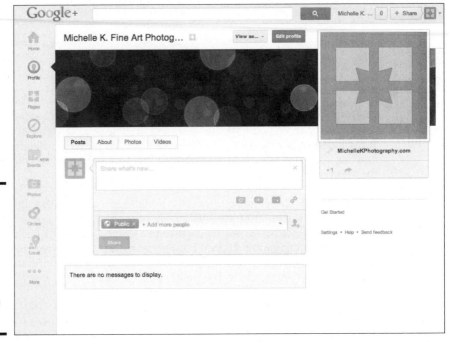

Figure 1-4:
Use your
logo or
an image
reflective
of your
brand for
your profile
photo.

3. **Click the Select a Photo from Your Computer button.**

   You can also use the links on the left side of the photo box, as shown in Figure 1-5, to select a photo you've already uploaded to your personal Google profile or a photo of you that someone else has taken. You can even take an entirely new picture by using your web camera.

   The image you choose must be at least 250 x 250 pixels large and be JPG, GIF, or PNG format.

   After your photo uploads, you can edit the image by clicking the Creative Kit that appears. From here you can crop, rotate, sharpen, resize, or add color to your photo. Decorating options that add doodles or cartoon bubbles are available, too, but we don't recommended these because they can make your image look unprofessional. Additionally, you can add a caption by clicking the Add Caption link.

4. **When you like what you see, click the Set as Profile Photo button.**

   After your profile photo is set, you can post a status update or comment about the image by entering text in the Add a Comment box and clicking the Share button. Your picture will be set whether or not you choose to add a comment.

Figure 1-5:
Choose a
photo from
a variety of
places.

Editing profile information

When you first sign up for a Google+ page, you aren't given the opportunity to give detailed information regarding you, your business, or your brand. Luckily, you can edit your page to fill in those blanks and round out your identity at any time. Just follow these steps:

1. **Sign in to your Google+ profile and click the Pages icon at the bottom of the left menu.**

This step lets you switch from using Google+ as your personal profile to using it as your page. You may have to click the More icon to reveal the Pages icon.

2. **Click the Switch to This Page button.**

You may be the administrator of more than one page. Be sure you click the button beneath the specific page you want to edit.

3. **On your page, click the Edit Profile button in the center of the page.**

The additional options you can edit to build your company's brand presence appear, as shown in Figure 1-6. The default tab you land on is the About tab.

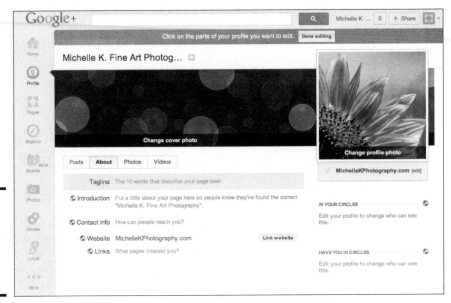

Figure 1-6:
Add brand
information
to your
Google+
profile.

You can customize these areas to personalize your page:

- *Tagline:* This is your company's motto, a one-line, succinct phrase that sums up what your brand is about. If you don't have a tagline already, brainstorm a couple of them to try or consider hiring a copywriter to write one for you.

- *Introduction:* Consider this the "About" of the About page; it's what you want fans and customers to know about your company right out of the gate. This section can also state how long you've been in business and special awards or accolades you've received for your work. You can dress up your text with different fonts and links, too, as shown in Figure 1-7.

Figure 1-7:
Make your
Introduction
eye-catching
by using a
different
font or a
bulleted list.

Introduction

B *I* **U** **Link**

Be sure to write something that catches your customer's attention here!

Some things to consider are:

- Reviews of your products or services
- Awards and accolades
- How long you've been in business

Public

Save   Cancel

- *Contact Info:* The ways people can contact you, including landline, cellular, and pager numbers; your e-mail address; chat program names; your physical address; and your fax number. You can also choose whom to make this information visible to. We recommend keeping the default Public setting because you want current and potential customers to be able to reach you.

- *Website:* This is where you provide, you guessed it, your website address. You're allowed to enter only one, however, so if you have more than one website, choose wisely. We recommend trying different websites for a month or so and checking your analytics to see which one sends you the most traffic.

  To the right of your web address is the Link Website button. You can click this button to get the HTML code to link your Google+ page to your website. Just copy and paste the code into the HTML code for your homepage. If you aren't familiar with HTML, we recommend you have your webmaster take care of it for you.

- *Links:* You can add other websites that are of interest to you. This is also a great place to add links to specific pages of your website that you want to draw attention to, without having them as your main website listing on your page.

  For example, if you were running a promotion, you could add the link to the promotion's page on your website. Or add a complimentary brand's site and ask for the same in return. This is a great way to get more exposure for your Google+ page and your company's website.

- *In Your Circles* and *Have You in Circles:* These sections on the right side of the page, as shown in Figure 1-8, allow you to change who sees the different people in your Circles, what Circles you share, and who can see what Circles you are a part of.

  You can make your Circles public so those who have you in their Circles whom you aren't following in return can view your content. You can also choose to show only particular Circles.

  Showing others which Circles you belong to shows your fans that you're actively engaged in your industry and community. No one likes an unsociable page on a social network.

4. **After you finish editing your page's information, click the Done Editing button in the menu bar at the top of the page.**

Figure 1-8:
Decide what
information
regarding
your Circles
you want to
share.

There you have it! Your Google+ page is set up and ready to go!

Adding managers

If you're not going to be the only person maintaining your Google+ page, you'll want to add others as managers. Google allows you to have up to 50 of them! There can be only one owner of the page, however. The owner is the only person who can delete the page or transfer ownership of the page to another individual.

Managers, on the other hand, are individuals who have permission to make changes to your account information such as updating your tagline or web address as well as post content. It's a good idea to have more than one manager just in case someone is not available to sign in for whatever reason. That way your Google+ page won't be silent!

Maintaining a social network for a brand is an important responsibility. Be sure the people you appoint for this task are up for the responsibility because everything they post on your behalf reflects you, your business, and your brand. Be sure your managers are aware of the type of comments and content you consider acceptable.

To add managers, follow these steps:

1. **Sign in to your Google+ profile and click the Pages icon in the left menu.**

   This step lets you switch from using Google+ as your personal profile to using it as your page. You may have to click the More icon to reveal the Pages icon.

2. **Beneath your profile picture, click the Settings link.**

   You arrive at your Google+ Settings page, which also happens to be the name of the default landing tab.

3. **Click the Managers tab at the top of the page.**

   You see a list of the managers you have and the role they play, as shown in Figure 1-9. Your profile is at the top of the list with the word *Owner* next to your name.

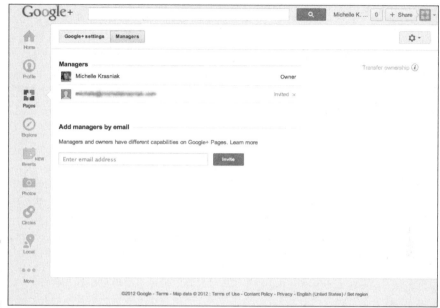

Figure 1-9:
Your current
Managers.

4. **Enter the e-mail address of the person you want to invite to be a manager of the page and click the Invite button.**

   You see a box that asks you to confirm your invite.

5. **Click the Invite button to send the invitation.**

   After you invite the person, he or she is automatically added to the Managers list. However, the page displays Invited next to the name until the invitation is accepted. At that point, *Invited* changes to *Manager*.

Setting Notifications

If you have an active Google+ stream, you don't necessarily want to receive notifications for every little thing that takes place. For example, if you don't adjust your notifications, you'll receive e-mail every time someone tags you, comments on your posts, comments on posts for which you clicked the +1 button, comments on posts you commented on, puts you in Circles, and more. If your role with your brand requires you to know about all community interaction and engagement, receiving notifications is important. Determine which notifications are most important to receive and set your notifications accordingly.

To avoid receiving so many notifications, take these steps:

1. **Sign in to your Google+ profile and click the Pages icon in the left menu.**

   This step lets you switch from using Google+ as your personal profile to using it as your page. You may have to click the More icon to reveal the Pages icon.

2. **Beneath your profile picture, click the Settings link.**

   Google whisks you away to your Google+ Settings page, which also happens to be the name of the default landing tab.

3. **Scroll through the notification options shown in Figure 1-10 and deselect the check boxes of the notifications you want to turn off.**

   To stay on top of what your followers are saying to and about you, we recommend keeping the Posts settings selected as well as any setting dealing with someone commenting on something you posted.

If you turn off all notifications, you still see activity. When you access any of your Google accounts, whether it's Gmail or Google+, your notification box on the top right of your screen shows the number of notifications available for you to view.

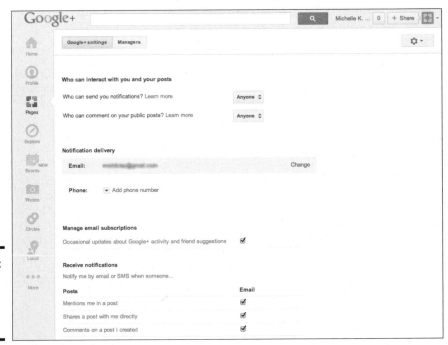

Figure 1-10: You can adjust your notification settings.

Navigating the Google+ stream and formatting your text

Hotkeys are small macros you can use as shortcuts to access some functions. Google+ offers some hotkeys that help you navigate your stream. Additionally, to better format your posts, Google+ offers some basic text formatting, which Facebook and Twitter do not.

✔ Press the spacebar to scroll down your page.

✔ Press Shift+spacebar to scroll up.

✔ Press the Enter key (Return key on a Mac) to start a comment

✔ Press the J key to scroll down to the next post in your stream.

✔ Press the K key to go to the previous post in your stream.

✔ To make text bold, put an asterisk before and after the text you wish to highlight.

✔ To make text italic, put an underscore before and after the text you wish to emphasize.

✔ To format text with strikethrough, put a hyphen (or dash) before or after the text you want to strike through.

**Book VI
Chapter 1**

**Leaping into
Google+**

Chapter 2: Socializing in Circles

In This Chapter

✔ Following and being followed

✔ Organizing followers

✔ Using Circles for sharing

✔ Creating private messages

The main reason to join Google+ is to interact with customers, clients, fans, and community members. Seemingly, Google+ has loyal members who prefer to interact on Google+ over other online communities. Therefore, you have the opportunity to reach entirely different groups of people than those on other social media networks.

On Google+, interaction occurs in *Circles,* which are user-created categories that hold friends, customers, clients, brands, and so on. For example, if someone follows your brand, he might add you to one of his personal Circles, which he might call something like "Brands I Like" or "Businesses I Follow." However, as a brand, you don't follow people the same way. You can't add anyone to your Circles unless they circle you first. So promoting your Google+ page, letting people know you have an account, and asking friends and fans to add your brand to their Circles is imperative.

One way to let people know about your presence on Google+ is by adding the snippet of HTML code to your website's homepage as discussed in Chapter 1 of this minibook.

To catch the attention of others, create compelling content. This way those who already have you in their Circles will be inclined to share and encourage others to follow you as well.

Creating Circles

Circles enable you to target who you share your content with. You have the ability to share it with the public, or you can target certain niches. For example, you can create circles for certain demographics, such as age groups, gender, and interests. If you're releasing a new product and it's geared toward Baby Boomers, you can create a "For Boomers Only" Circle so only those interested receive the content for the products. Because the Google+ community doesn't always release such info as age, many brands ask who would like to be put in a particular circle.

To get started, first create a Circle:

1. **In your sidebar menu, click the Circles icon, as shown in Figure 2-1.**

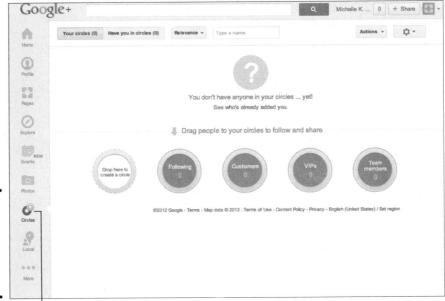

Figure 2-1:
Click the
Circles icon
located in
your left
sidebar.

Circles icon

Notice that Google has already populated your profile with some default Circles. Although Google+ suggests names for Circles, most Google+ users create their Circle names.

2. **Hover your mouse pointer on the words Drop Here to Create a Circle.**

When the Create Circle link appears, as shown in Figure 2-2, click the link.

The box that appears allows you to give your new Circle a name and decide who to add, as shown in Figure 2-3.

3. **Click inside the box at the top of the window that says Circle Name and type in an appropriate title.**

To create content specifically for different community, professions, demographics, or interest groups, give your Circle a name that makes it clear what this group is about. The more descriptive you are with your Circles, the less likely you are to share the wrong content with the wrong people.

Figure 2-2:
Click the
Create
Circle link
to, you
guessed
it, create a
Circle.

Figure 2-3:
Give your
Circle a
name.

4. **When your notifications let you know someone added your brand to their Circles, click the "Add" button next to that person's name and you'll see a Circles drop-down menu. Add the new person to the appropriate Circle.**

5. **Repeat Steps 2–4 as needed until you have a variety of Circles set up.**

   Some people choose to create many Circles right off the bat and then add people to them as they go along, whereas others create Circles as the need for new ones arises. There is no right or wrong way to do it. Circles are something you'll tweak as you go along. You may find you'll want to prune your Circles because the wrong people are added to the wrong groups, and you may find some Circles aren't relevant anymore. In this case you want to take the people in those Circles and add them to a more aptly titled Circle, or existing Circles, so you can still market to them.

Adding people to Circles

If you've had a presence on Google+ for a while, you may have already been added to other users' Circles. Lucky you! These individuals are a great place to start when you're looking for people to add to your Circles.

Here's how to add people to your circles who have already added you:

1. **In your sidebar menu, click the Circles icon.**

   The default landing tab is Your Circles. Here you see any Circles you've created and whether or not they have people in them. The number of people in the Circle appears underneath the Circle name.

2. **Click the Have You in Circles tab at the top of the window.**

   This tab can be found in the menu bar across from the Home icon on the left side of the screen. Here you see the people who have you in Circles.

3. **Click and drag the picture of the person you want to add and drop it over the icon of the Circle you want him to be in, as shown in Figure 2-4.**

   After you add him to your Circle, the number beneath the Circle's title increases, and that person receives a notification that he was added.

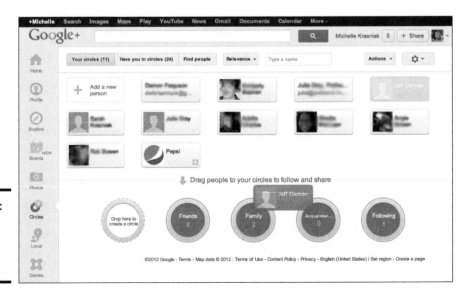

Figure 2-4:
To which Circle should I add him?

Finding people to circle

After you've added all the people that have connected to you, it's time to branch out to find new people.

As mentioned earlier, brands can't add people to their Circles unless those people have already added the brands to their own Circles first. It's sort of like opting in to a newsletter. Google wants to make sure no one is receiving brand updates unless she has given the brand explicit permission to send her those updates. So to start adding people to your Circles, you have to already be in someone else's Circle. Sometimes you miss notifications, so here are a few ways to learn who has you in their Circles so you can reciprocate.

✦ Set your e-mail notifications to inform you that others have added you to their Circles. Setting notifications is covered in detail in Chapter 1 of this minibook.

✦ Your notification button at the top right of your Google+ screen turns red and shows you the number of new notifications waiting. Be sure to check those frequently. You're just a click away from seeing — and getting — some new connections.

✦ Select the Circles function in your sidebar to see how many people have added you to their Circles.

Building your Circles might take you some time. The trick is to get on people's radars so they'll add you to their Circles, and you can circle them in return.

To get on people's radar, here's where to start:

✦ **Use your personal Google+ account.** If you have a personal Google+ account, use it to promote your business account. Tag or highlight your brand page by using the + symbol in front of the name used for your Google+ account. Also, share some posts from your brand Google+ page on your personal Google+ page. When people in your personal Circles see cool stuff shared from private Circles, they might be inclined to add your brand to their Circles as well.

✦ **Use your social networking accounts.** You can promote your Google+ account on your other social networking accounts. From time to time, encourage your other communities to join in on your discussions there. Let them know what you're talking about and how much you value their input. For example, "We're recommending books today on our Google+ page. Won't you come by and tell us about your favorites?" Don't forget to link to the page.

✦ **Include share buttons on your content.** Make sure to include Google +1 buttons on all your content. (See Figure 2-5.) Find out more about share buttons in Book III, Chapter 2.

Figure 2-5:
When
you add a
Google+
widget to
your blog or
website, it
encourages
others to
add you to
their Circles.

Comment 10   Like 67   Tweet 448   Share 28   +1 71

YouTube And Google+ Grow Closer: All Users Can Now Switch Their Usernames To Their Google+ Profiles

FREDERIC LARDINOIS

Friday, June 29th, 2012   10 Comments

✦ **Include buttons on your websites.** Your blog, website, and other channels should have a link or button that will lead your community to your brand's page on Google+. To learn more about share buttons, please see Book III, Chapter 2.

✦ **Ask.** Ask your friend and fans to help share your page. If they like what you do, they'll recommend it to their own friends and family.

✦ **Participate in as many conversations as possible.** As others add you to their Circles, you'll see their posts in your stream. Participate in as many of these discussions as possible. When people see a brand page actively engaged in the community, it reminds them to follow the page. Also, if you're productive in conversation, it will encourage others to add you to their Circles.

✦ **Optimize your brand updates for search.** When you use this technique, people searching for topics, products, or services similar to yours have a good chance of landing on your Google+ profile and adding you to their Circles. For more information on search engine optimization, see Book II, Chapter 2.

It may take a little time for others to add your brand page to their Circles at first. The important thing is to continue updating as if you already have a thriving community. Because Google+ is indexed for search, the more you update, the better it is for brand visibility.

Sharing Circles

Many individuals and brands like to share their Circles. That is, they're taking a Circle filled with names and inviting their communities to use that Circle as well. The people who are in the Circles appreciate being recommended as someone who is worthy of a follow, and those on the receiving end appreciate learning about interesting people and brands.

Here's how to share your Circles:

1. **Click the Circles icon on the right side of your page (refer to Figure 2-1).**

   You may have to click the More link at the bottom of the page in order to see the icon.

2. **Click the Circle you want so share.**

   The Circle turns gray and presents three icons: Edit Circle (the pencil), Share Circle (the dot with two arrows), or Delete Circle (the trash can), as shown in Figure 2-6.

Figure 2-6:
You can edit, share, or delete a selected Circle.

Circle icons

3. **Click the Share Circle icon.**

   In the box that appears, you can add a comment about why you want to share the Circle as well as decide whom you're going to share it with. The Public option, as opposed to your individual Circles, is the default setting.

4. **If you want to share the Circle with additional people or Circles, click the Add More People drop-down menu in the center of the screen to get the options shown in Figure 2-7.**

   You can choose to share the Circle with your other Circles, or you can click the Browse People icon on the right side of the Share box to select individuals to share with.

   If you select a Circle or people to share the Circle with and then change your mind before clicking the Share button, simply click the X next to the name of the people or group to remove them from the share list.

5. **When you're finished selecting the people you want to share with, click the Share button.**

   If you decide against sharing the Circle at this time, simply click the gray Cancel button instead.

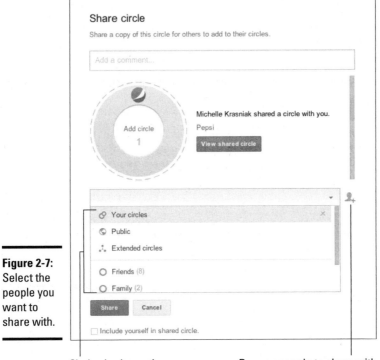

Figure 2-7:
Select the
people you
want to
share with.

Circle sharing options   Browse people to share with

Posting Publicly or Privately

Google+ is easy and intuitive to update with new content. If you spend time on other social networks, this is the same idea; post your content into the designated box on your screen called a Share box. You can share with specific Circles, to the public, or privately to one or more individuals at a time. There's no mistaking your Share box; it appears on the top of the page, as soon as you access Google+.

To post updates to specific Circles, click in the Share What's New box, which opens a drop-down list. From the drop-down list, select only the Circles you want to share with, as shown in Figure 2-8.

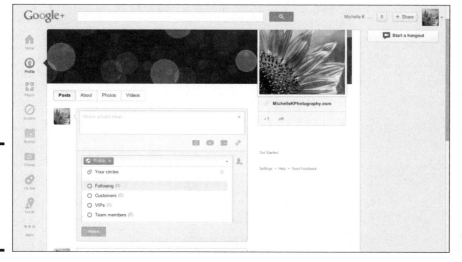

Figure 2-8:
Choose
only those
Circles you
want to
update.

To send a private message, as shown in Figure 2-9, choose only the person or people you want to send the message to by using their names with a + symbol in front of them, in the same way you do with tagging. Tagging specifically calls out a person or brand; the message appears in their steam and in their notifications.

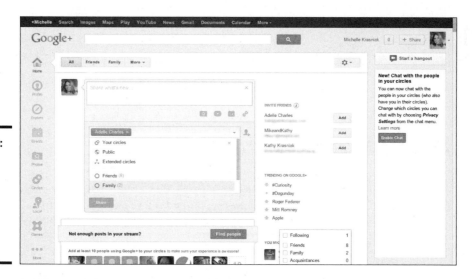

Figure 2-9:
You can
share a
private
message
with one
or more
people.

Chapter 3: Building Community through Pluses, Shares, and Comments

In This Chapter

✔ **Reaching people with Google+**

✔ **Sharing photos and videos**

✔ **Showing your appreciation for posts and comments**

✔ **Enjoying the conversation**

✔ **Commenting on other posts**

*G*oogle+ may be new and still gaining steam, but just because it's "quieter" doesn't mean it should be discounted as an important tool for marketing and growing community. Getting in at the beginning is a wonderful opportunity to cut through the noise some of the other social networks offer and truly reach people. Unlike Facebook, your Google+ updates are seen by everyone who has you in their Circles, and unlike Twitter, you can have a conversation using more than 140 characters.

Because many of the people who are using Google+ are on that social network to avoid some of the drama other social networks offer, they're more focused on a positive, intelligent conversation. Here's your chance to reach some old friends as well as a whole new audience.

In this chapter, we take a look at sharing content with your Google+ community, responding to content posted by others, and how to use the +1 feature to help you get your content noticed by others who aren't Google+ members yet.

Sticking to the Plan for Your Google+ Content

Everything brands do online must be strategic. If you don't map out a plan and follow a strategy, your presence on Google+ (and other social networks) is going to be a confusing mishmash rather than a series of well-thought-out, discussion-worthy posts. The outcome of everything you post should benefit your community and your brand. You want followers to become more likely to share your content or even add their two cents.

If you haven't refined your marketing plan for social media marketing purposes yet, check out Book I, Chapter 1. Book III, Chapter 1 provides information on choosing content that meets your needs.

Remember these strategies when sharing on any social media network:

✦ **Mix it up.** Use a variety of content so your community doesn't get bored. Ask questions, tell jokes, create short stories, or share photos and videos. People enjoy seeing beyond the same old, same old, so don't be afraid of originality.

✦ **Provoke intelligent discussion.** Although it's definitely important to keep your tone light, you also shouldn't be afraid of providing more thought-provoking questions or topics. Give your community a chance to weigh in. Ask open-ended questions, or encourage opinions. Make it clear that your followers' voices matter.

✦ **Establish a routine.** It's important to post as much as you can, but if you can't multiple times every day, at least keep a consistent schedule. For example, if you find that your Mondays and Wednesdays are the busiest days of your week, consider setting a schedule that runs Tuesday and Thursday. But make sure you stick with it, no matter what. The more they check back to see what you're up to, the better.

✦ **Participate often.** Community isn't a one-way street. You also have to get out among the people. Visit the people in your community and comment on their posts and updates. Not only will others view you as accessible, but it may encourage others who don't already follow you to add you.

✦ **Avoid hard selling.** Of course you want to drive sales, but if everything you post is perceived as a pressure tactic, your community will tire of it and no longer follow you.

✦ **Determine who will be posting and when.** If more than one person is running your account, coordinate efforts so they don't post the same things at the same time. Set up a schedule or follow an editorial calendar.

✦ **Use Search Engine Optimization (SEO).** A must when it comes to online content. People will have trouble finding your content if the search engines bury it in their search results pages because you didn't use enough or the correct keywords in your content. Book II, Chapter 2 has more information on SEO.

Your public Google+ posts have the ability to catch the attention of the search engines, most importantly Google, the top search engine in the world. To do so, make sure all content is optimized for search. Use search terms in your posts and when labeling your photographs or videos.

Building Relationships

If you're going to invest your time in yet another social network, it's because you're interested in reaching people to help you achieve your goals, whatever goals you may have. Google+ can help you reach people, but, because it's not as popular as Facebook or Twitter yet, it takes more work to build up your community. This isn't a negative at all. In fact, using Google+ is the perfect learning experience for all your relationship-building efforts. As the song goes, if you can make it there, you can make it anywhere.

Let's explore some of the ways you can use Google+ to reach people and build relationships.

Using the +1 feature

The Facebook Like button is one of that network's more popular features. Users like it because they can show their approval for content without having to commit to a comment or full-fledged discussion. Google+'s +1 feature works in a similar manner. Instead of a thumbs-up button, Google+ offers a +1 button next to every comment and under every post. Simply click the button to show off your approval. Plus, as you post content, your community will reciprocate by +1'ing the items they like best. The beautiful thing about this is you can use the amount of +1's on a given post to determine the type of content your community likes best.

The more useful and meaningful content you post, whether it's links to articles or text updates asking your community's opinions on a hot topic, the more likely you are to receive approval for your information in the form of the reader clicking the +1 button, as shown on the left side of the post in Figure 3-1. When a community member +1s your content, it will be shared in his activity stream for others to see.

Figure 3-1:
Show approval for posts and comments by using the +1 button.

This is an amazing way for your content to be shared with the Circles of others and will lead to you being able to expand your own Circles, which also increases your brand awareness. The more Circles you're added to, the more it shows that your content is trusted and worthwhile. See how it all comes full, er, Circle?

Clicking the +1 button doesn't have to happen on just your Google+ page, however. If someone stumbles across one of your blog posts, for example, if you have the +1 button code installed on your website, they can click it directly at the source. The best part? All of the +1s you've received on your content will show up in a Google search, as shown in Figure 3-2. This tells people that others really like the content, and more people are likely to check something out if they see others have approved of it.

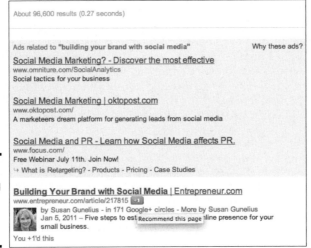

Figure 3-2:
+1s showing up in a Google search.

Don't forget to show approval for comments left on your posts or posts and comments left by other people. Use the +1 button to show others you appreciate their comments.

Sharing images

Images almost always receive a positive response on the social networks. When you post an image, whether it's staff photos, event photos, or something amusing, you bring a different element to your Google+ page because it's much more visual, not to mention personal.

When your community members can see a more personal element to your brand, such as pictures of your office or your latest employee of the month, they're more likely to feel as if they know you better. That familiarity in turn can lead to more meaningful interactions with them and even more sales down the line. After all, who would you rather do business with, a stranger or someone you know and trust? Someone you trust, of course, so don't be a stranger to your audience.

Although all photos that you post don't have to be personal in nature, if you do decide to upload personal or branded photos, it's a good idea to include a caption with them to let your community know what's going on. What's the point of posting company photos to give a glimpse into a different side of your business if everyone and everything in the photos are anonymous?

What photos should receive a caption:

✦ Anything that is not intuitive to look at. If the picture doesn't tell a story, you have to tell it.

✦ Anything with people in it, tag the photos or let your community know who it is you're showing, and why.

✦ Anything requiring further information, for example, if you post a picture of one of your products, you also want a descriptive caption that will send your community running to your sales page.

Also consider inviting your community to caption the photo themselves. Many brands do this with hysterical results.

Here's how to upload images to Google+:

1. **Click the Share box in the upper-right corner and then click the camera icon beneath the Share What's New box that appears. (See Figure 3-3.)**

The drop-down menu gives you three options:

- *Add Photos* to share a single photo

- *Create an Album* to add more than one picture at a time

- *Take a Photo* using your webcam

For the purpose of this example, we selected the Add Photos option.

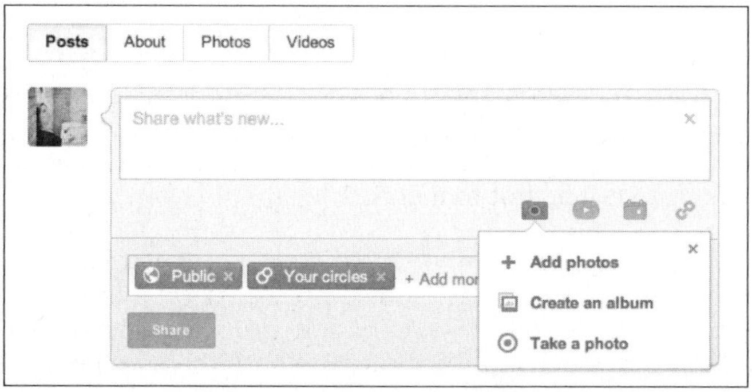

Figure 3-3:
Select the camera icon to see the drop-down menu.

2. **Select the Add Photos option and, in the box that appears, navigate to the photo you want to upload from your computer and then click the photo.**

   The photo uploads to the side and appears onscreen. You're then presented with the Edit Photos, Tag People, Add Text, Add More (photos), or Remove All (photos) options.

3. **Click the Edit Photos link underneath the picture to give it a caption or explanation, as shown in Figure 3-4.**

   The caption should be descriptive of what the photo shows. Under the link, you can also rotate your photos clockwise or counterclockwise or edit the photos themselves by using Picnik, Google's online photo editor.

Figure 3-4: Your photo may require editing before you publish.

4. **When you're finished adding a caption and editing your photo, click the Done button in the bottom-left corner of the box.**

   This step closes the box, and you return to your photo.

   You can continue to perform actions on your photo such as tagging any people in it or adding text to the photo. You can also add more photos or delete photos simply by clicking the corresponding blue link under your photo. There is a "tag photo" in the editing tool; to use it, just click on the person you wish to tag and type in their Google+ name.

To choose whom to share your photos with, take these steps:

1. **Click the Add More People link underneath the photo.**

    You see a drop-down menu of all the Circles you can share your photo with. You can also click the gray person icon to the right of this box in order to add specific individuals.

2. **After you've selected the people you want share your images with, click the Share button at the bottom.**

    Congratulations! You've shared a photo with your community.

For a quick way to upload a photo directly from your computer, click the Photos icon and then click the +Add Photos button.

Be sure to optimize your photos to appeal to the search engines. When you save photos, keep search engine optimization techniques in mind and use keywords and phrases, and do the same with any descriptive text. All your public posts have the ability to rank on Google. See Book II, Chapter 2 for more information on SEO.

Sharing video

You may want to upload video to your posts. Videos can be instructional, educational, or humorous. You can conduct interviews or product reviews or report live from an event. The possibilities are virtually endless and the most important part is that it's yet another way to get you and your brand in front of your community.

You can share videos in four different ways:

✦ **Copy and paste:** You can copy and paste the link to a video, such as one appearing on YouTube (www.youtube.com) or the mobile video-sharing site Viddy (www.viddy.com), by clicking the link icon shown in Figure 3-5.

    After you paste the link into the box, your video will automatically appear in the Share What's New box. At this point you can choose whom to share the video with in the same way you did with sharing photos in the previous section.

Figure 3-5:
Use the link option to share photos from a site such as YouTube.

✦ **Upload:** The second option for sharing video is to upload a video saved to your computer. To do so, click the video icon to the right of the camera icon in the Share What's New box and select Upload Video from the drop-down menu. Navigate to the location where the video resides on your computer and either drag and drop it into the box or click the Select Videos from Your Computer button. After you've located the file that you want, click the Add Videos button on the bottom right of the screen, as shown in Figure 3-6.

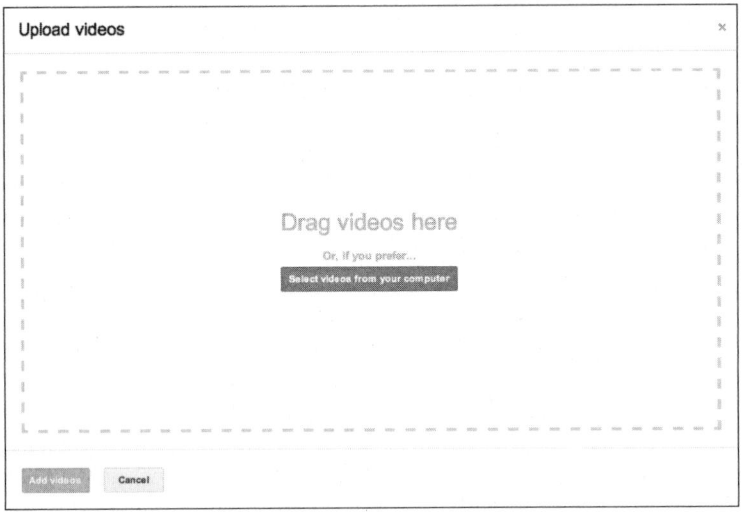

Figure 3-6:
You can upload a video in much the same way as you upload photos.

Upload videos   ×

Drag videos here

Or, if you prefer...

Select videos from your computer

Add videos   Cancel

✦ **YouTube:** This method for sharing videos is similar to the copy-and-paste method. If you click the video icon to the right of the camera in the Share What's New box, you see the YouTube option. Clicking that option brings up the screen shown in Figure 3-7, where you can search for a specific video by using search terms. To share the link from a YouTube video, click the Enter a URL link on the left of the window. You're presented with a box where you can paste in a URL in the same manner as discussed in the first bullet. When you've found the video you want, click the Add Video button.

✦ **Record:** The final method for adding a video is by recording it directly using your webcam. You do this by clicking the video icon to the right of the camera icon in the Share What's New box. Select Record Video from the drop-down menu. If you have either a built-in webcam or an external webcam, it will connect to the website and you will be able to start recording your video.

We don't recommend you record and upload a video this way, however. The video quality tends to be poor, and you do not have the ability to edit your video file as you would had you recorded it with a regular video camera. It also looks much more professional, and you want to put your company's best food forward, right?

Choose a YouTube video   ✕

Search
Enter a URL

You**Tube**   [   ]   🔍

Type your search in the box above to find videos.

Add video   Cancel

Figure 3-7:
You can
search
for the
right video
to share
directly on
YouTube.

For a quick way to upload a video directly from your computer, click the
Videos button above the Share What's New box and then click the Upload
New Videos button. This method takes you directly to the drag-and-drop
box mentioned in the Upload bullet in this section.

Moderating the Conversation

All this content, photo, and video sharing is for naught if you don't use the
content and media as tools for engaging your community. The purpose of
having a presence on Google+ and other networks is to build a community
of loyal followers, but it's also a great way to find out as much as possible
about the people who use your product or service. You can't do that unless
you're in the trenches among them, commenting on their posts, sharing
their images, and letting them know you're more than just a logo.

Being a good moderator

Moderating the conversation at your brand account is a delicate balance. On
the one hand, you want people to speak freely, but on the other, you don't
want any abusive language or behavior, and you definitely don't want spam.
For the most part, the people who occupy Google+ are respectful and drama-
free. From time to time, you'll encounter a few people who like stirring the
pot a little by name calling, swearing, or being mean.

Some of the things that might fly on a personal page (such as swearing)
would be considered offensive on a brand page. Make sure all comments are
appropriate for your entire community. To learn more about moderating
comments in detail, please see Book III, Chapter 2.

Deleting comments by users

As an owner or a manager of your brand page, you can delete comments you feel may be harmful to the conversation. To do so, follow these instructions:

1. **Click the X located to the right of each comment, as shown in Figure 3-8.**

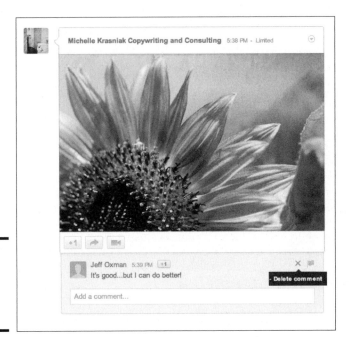

Figure 3-8: Click the X to delete comments or spam.

2. **In the box that appears, click the Delete button or the Delete and Block This User button.**

   Just selecting the Delete option will still allow the user to comment on your items; however, clicking the Delete and Block This User button kicks the commenter out of your Circle.

Next to the X is a flag you can use to report abuse to Google or block the user from commenting on your posts again.

Editing your own posts

Your own posts are under scrutiny because they make an impression on the brand. If you find you have made a typo or you're not sure your content sounds or looks right, you have the option to edit or delete the post. If you're an owner or moderator, you can edit any content posted by your brand account.

To make changes to a post on your brand page, do the following:

1. **Select the drop-down menu located to the right of the post, and choose one of the following options, as shown in Figure 3-9:**

   - *Edit This Post:* Make changes or corrections to your post such as fixing spelling errors or changing the caption on a photo or video.

   - *Delete This Post:* Remove the post altogether if you decide you no longer want to feature a certain article, for example.

   - *Link to This Post:* You can copy the link provided to you and send the update directly to people who may not be on Google+.

   - *Disable Comments:* If you don't want to give anyone the opportunity to weigh in on what you've posted by leaving a comment, yet you want them to be able to reshare or tag the post, choose this option.

   - *Lock This Post:* If you don't want others to reshare, mention, or tag your post, you can lock it. Posts are unlocked by default.

   - *View Ripples:* This option shows up only if your post has been shared. It shows you which community member shared the post and any comments made on it, how the post was shared (for example, directly or via URL), as well as some analytics on the sharing behavior (such as the language of the users, who shared the post, and how many people saw it as a result). All of this is in an interactive graphical form. It's a cool feature, so check it out!

Book VI Chapter 3

Building Community through Pluses, Shares, and Comments

Figure 3-9: Choose editing options from the drop-down menu located to the right of your post.

2. **Click Edit This Post, and your post (or caption if it's a photo or video) becomes editable.**

   Even if you delete all the text in the Share What's New box, clicking Save doesn't delete the comment. You have to use the drop-down menu mentioned in Step 1 in order to delete the comment.

3. **When you're finished making your desired changes, click the Save button at the bottom of the Share What's new box. (Or, if needed, click the X to the right of your editable comment to cancel the edit.)**

When you click the Save button, your comment remains in the same location in your activity feed; however, your changes have been made.

Note that if you click the X to cancel editing the comment, that action doesn't delete the comment. Click the X if you change your mind about editing the comment, and the comment box will no longer be changeable.

Commenting on the Conversation

As you put people in to your Circles, their updates appear in your stream. Sitting there and watching them go by is a missed opportunity. Each update is an opportunity to have a conversation with a potential customer, client, collaborator, or fan. The more you engage, the more others will trust your brand. Also, when others see you commenting in their friends' Circles, they're also going to put you in their own Circles. Commenting and participating is a great way to build your Google+ Community. Commenting is simple and intuitive. All you have to do is add your two cents in the Add a Comment field, as shown in Figure 3-10.

Figure 3-10: Adding a comment is easy and intuitive.

Here are some best practices for commenting on Google+:

✦ **Comment to connect with your community, not to sell.** Don't make a comment about you or your brand unless the conversation is about you or your brand or specific brand-related questions that are being raised. You're just another person in the conversation, not a salesperson.

✦ **Avoid using links.** Don't include links unless they're absolutely relevant to the conversation, and even then avoid links! Posting links to your content or sales pages is seen as self-serving and spammy.

✦ **Tag any people who you're replying to by putting a + symbol in front of their names.** If you're responding to a specific commenter or the original author of a post, or if you want to recommend or refer to another person on Google+, tag the appropriate people by using a + symbol before their names. These tags send a notification to the people you've tagged to alert them of the conversation, and they'll appreciate that they're being heard and you've taken the time to acknowledge them.

✦ **Add something of value to each conversation.** When you respond to a comment to say "LOL" or "I agree," you add nothing to the conversation. It's better to respectfully add your opinion for discussion purposes than to add a comment that brings nothing to the table.

✦ **Understand you're representing the brand.** Everything you say on Google+ is representative of your brand. Be careful when responding in anger or disagreeing in a defensive manner — you don't want to come off as confrontational. Always comment in a respectful manner, even if you disagree. Just because you're behind the computer, that doesn't mean you can act differently than you would if you were having a conversation with a colleague in person.

✦ **Stay on topic.** Don't talk about your Aunt Tilly's dentures in a conversation about peanut butter, unless the peanut butter has something to do with the dentures. If you're always off topic, people will ignore your posts or uncircle you altogether.

**Book VI
Chapter 3**

**Building Community
through Pluses,
Shares, and
Comments**

Chapter 4: Hanging with Your Google+ Community

Google+ allows its users to take their interaction to a more visual level with Hangouts. Hangouts are video chats involving two or more people. They're easy to set up and maintain, and you can record them to share on your website or a video sharing site. All you need is a webcam, a working internal or external microphone, and headphones or ear buds to minimize background noise, and you're ready to go!

In this chapter, we tell you what Google+ Hangouts are, why they're cool, and how to use them.

Why Hangout?

The benefits of Google+ Hangouts abound. Here are some things you can use Hangouts for:

✦ **Put a face to the brand.** Hangouts add a human element and personal touch to the brand name. This adds trust between you and the people who are your costumers or part of your community.

✦ **Receive feedback.** Hosting Hangouts to find out what people think of your brand is a terrific way to discover the wants and needs of your customers.

✦ **Interview guests.** Bring in experts to help your community learn, grow, and further benefit from interaction with your brand.

✦ **Give how-to presentations.** Use Hangouts to teach everyone how to use your product or service to its maximum potential.

✦ **Create focus groups.** Send active members of your community product samples and gather the members later to collect their thoughts.

✦ **Have a book or movie discussion.** Not everything has to be business related. Use Google+ for discussion groups having nothing to do with the brand. Off-topic Hangouts once in a while are not only acceptable, they're fun!

✦ **Answer questions from your community.** Host a town hall and invite your community to ask questions.

✦ **Share documents and slides.** Hangouts enable you to share more than your smiling face. Use them to host full-fledged presentations.

✦ **Share your screen with others.** Use live examples to illustrate a point by sharing your screen.

✦ **Show rather than tell.** Video allows you to add a new dimension to your content. When you offer video, people can see the expression on your face, hear the passion in your voice, and see exactly how to do whatever it is that you're sharing.

✦ **Talk live with people around the world.** Public Hangouts allow you to reach a bigger audience.

✦ **Hangout publicly or with only a few people.** Open your Hangouts to everyone or invite only a few people for a staff or client meeting.

If you're unfamiliar with Hangouts, sit in on a few first. See how they work and how others participate, and then you can decide whether it's something you'd like to try with your community.

To find a Hangout to sit in on, simply click the Hangouts icon in your left menu to access all the public Hangouts that are available.

Hanging with Google+ Hangout

It doesn't take much time to set up a Hangout, and no heavy equipment is required. All you need are these three things:

✦ A webcam

✦ A working internal or external microphone

✦ Headphones or ear buds to minimize background noise

You can host a Hangout whenever the urge hits. Hangouts aren't something you have to schedule in advance to use. Click the Hangout button and follow the instructions (which we cover here) for hosting your Hangout.

You can either invite people to your Hangout, which we cover in the upcoming "Creating Your Google+ Hangout," section or you can set up the Hangout without inviting people. If you don't invite people, your community will see that you have set up a Hangout and they can join if they so desire. The downside to not inviting people is that without an invitation, there's a chance no one may attend.

Don't wing it in a Hangout. Because you're using a brand account, it's not the same as if you're holding a Hangout with friends or family. Although it's okay to be off-the-cuff and ad-lib, it's best to have a plan in advance. Don't choose topics you know nothing about, or think you can fill an hour-long Hangout without printing out a list of talking points. You can't rely on others to fill the void.

The following sections give you the full scoop on using Google+ Hangouts.

Hangouts versus Hangouts on Air

Hangouts come in the following two flavors:

✦ **Hangouts:** Typical Hangouts allow for up to ten participants at a time, including the host. Anyone who doesn't make it in has to wait until someone leaves in order to view the Hangout. They can't view the Hangout, but they can see the comments. Those who don't make it in have to continue trying until someone leaves.

✦ **Hangouts on Air:** This variety of Hangout allows ten people to participate at a time, but an unlimited amount of people can watch the action. As with the traditional Hangout, as soon as a participant leaves the room, the next in line can take his place.

Many people who host Hangouts and Hangouts on Air choose to set Hangout for Extended Circles rather than Public. Many times when they set up a public Hangout, disruptive people come out of the woodwork and interrupt the Hangout or act rude.

Also, Hangouts on Air are recorded to YouTube so you can still share the video with anyone who couldn't make the live recording. This gives you the opportunity to share this content with people for years to come. If you don't already have an account with YouTube, it's a good idea to set one up before starting your Hangout.

Hangouts on Air weren't always available to everyone. Until mid-2012, only select power users were able to take advantage of this feature. The rest of the Google+ community held basic Hangouts. Now you have choices, but most people choose a Hangout on Air over a Hangout because more people can watch and participate.

Whether a circumstance calls for a Hangout as opposed to a Hangout on Air is up to you. You can make both options as public or private as you like. If you don't want to record your Hangout and want a more intimate session, it's probably better to use a Hangout. Hangouts on Air are perfect for having a large group discussion that you can record to share with the rest of your community later.

Creating a Google+ Hangout

Before you host a Hangout, determine whom you would like to invite. You might be inclined to invite the public, but that sometimes can come with a unique set of problems. Public Hangouts sometimes bring in people who like to disrupt Hangouts or act silly, ruining the discussion for many. It might be better to invite your *extended circles,* or friends of friends, in order to keep the discussion a pleasant experience for everyone.

Here's how to set up your own Google+ Hangout:

1. **Click the Start a Hangout button in the right pane of your Google+ stream, as shown in Figure 4-1.**

If this is your first Hangout, you may be prompted to install the Google Voice and Video plug-in. If that happens, click the Install Plugin button, let the download magic happen, and then do Step 1 again.

The Start a Hangout screen appears, as shown in Figure 4-2.

Click here to start a Hangout.

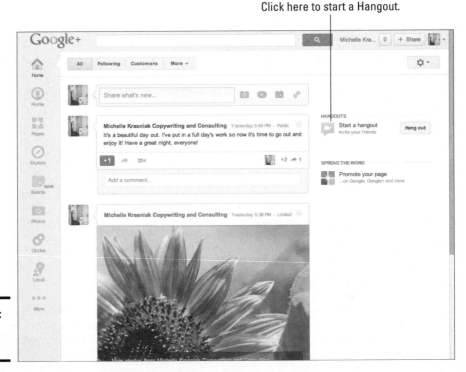

Figure 4-1:
Start your
Hangout.

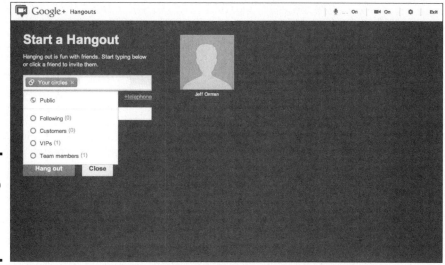

Figure 4-2:
Choose who
you want
to invite
to your
Hangout.

2. **Click the Invite People button to select whom to invite.**

   The next screen lets you invite people by entering their name, telephone number or e-mail address into the box at the top. To invite entire Circles, click inside the box and select the Circle you want to invite from the drop-down list, as shown in Figure 4-2.

   Before opening a Hangout to the people in your Circles, do a few trial runs by yourself or with a trusted friend or team member. Make sure you know how to handle the basics before going live.

3. **Name your Hangout by clicking inside the Name This Hangout box.**

   Make sure you name it something descriptive of the topic being discussed along with your business name. For example, if you are holding a how-to Hangout to show your community how to use your new product, you might name your Hangout, "XYZ Company presents How to Use the Tool-o-Matic."

   By default, the Enable Hangouts on Air check box is deselected. If you want to record and broadcast your Hangout, you need to host a Hangout on Air. I discuss how to do that option in the following section.

4. **Decide whether you want to restrict minors from watching and participating in your Hangout. If you do not want them to, select the Restrict Minors from Joining check box.**

   If your company produces products that are for the 18+ or 21+ year-old crowds, it's a good idea to check this box to make sure that the material remains for adult eyes only. Anyone who is younger will not be allowed to attend. You can find the Restrict Minors check box by clicking the Hangout Options box located directly under the Enable Hangouts on Air check box.

5. **When you're finished selecting these options, click the blue Hang Out button.**

   You then see a screen that displays "Waiting for people to enter this Hangout" until other people join you. You can also invite more people to your Hangout by clicking the Invite More button in the center of the screen.

As soon as others show up, you can start talking. Whoever is currently talking will have a larger image on display, one that's front and center. The rest of the participants are arranged at the bottom of the screen with a smaller display image showing.

The *Hangouts on Air* feature allows you to broadcast your Hangout live on your Google+ page, YouTube channel, and company website. You can also record it, and it will automatically be uploaded to your YouTube channel and Google+ page when the Hangout is complete.

To host a Hangout on Air, follow the instructions in the preceding section for hosting a Hangout, and in Step 3, select the Enable Hangouts on Air check box, as shown in Figure 4-3. You'll see a notice that your Hangouts on Air will broadcast on both YouTube and Google+. To agree to this, select OK. If you're not happy with this, you may exit and cancel your Hangout plans.

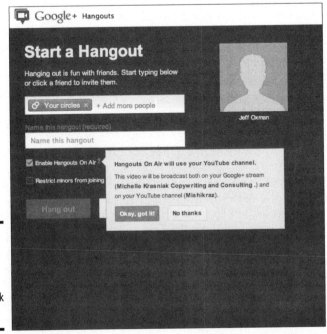

Figure 4-3: Select the Enable Hangouts on Air check box.

Now, you're not quite ready to get started yet because you have to agree to the terms. Yes, there are terms. You have to agree to allow Google to show your Hangout via YouTube and other Google owned apps, sites, and widgets. If this is still agreeable, check the box to indicate that you accept the terms.

If you invited special guests — for example, if you're interviewing someone — give them any necessary instructions for participating in the Hangout. Some people choose to do this via e-mail, and others give instructions on Skype, via phone or even a private Google+ message.

You may want to let the other party know the type of questions you're asking or whether you're going to be allowing a Q&A from others in the community. Make sure they know anyone who is in the Hangout can talk. When you're ready to set up the Hangout on Air, select the Start Broadcast button. You'll see a count down and after the number 1, you'll hear a chime, and you're live.

Running your Hangout

You're in control of your Hangout, so it's up to you to take the lead. In essence, as the host, you're a moderator for a discussion, and you're also there to pose topics and ensure there's no dead space or long pauses in the conversation. Here are some tips and best practices for hosting Google+ Hangouts:

✦ **Talk first.** As people file in to the Hangout, say, "Hello" and make small talk. When you feel it's time to begin, start. Don't wait for someone else to get the ball rolling if it's your Hangout.

✦ **Ask participants to introduce themselves.** When it's time to get started, encourage participants to introduce themselves. They'll participate more often if they also see it as a marketing opportunity.

✦ **Use the Mute button (shown in Figure 4-4) to silence background noise.** Sometimes you might hear unintentional background noise coming from someone's mic — for example, planes, trains, kids playing, and road noise. You can mute the participants with particularly noisy backgrounds while still enjoying the chat — simply click the Mute button under that person's name.

Figure 4-4:
Find Block
and Mute
buttons at
the top of
the screen.

✦ **Use the Block button (also shown in Figure 4-4) if someone is causing a disturbance.** Sometimes people forget their etiquette and play music or talk to others while a Hangout is going on. For those people who are creating a negative experience for everyone, the Block button comes in handy and deletes the offending party from your view.

✦ **Don't dominate the discussion.** Though it's your Hangout, don't dominate the entire discussion. Make sure everyone gets to participate so all points of view are represented.

✦ **Be prepared.** Before the Hangout, write out a list of what you plan to talk about so you don't lose track of the day's topic. Make a list of questions and comments geared toward provoking discussion.

✦ **Offer perks.** Surprise participants with coupon codes for discounts or free stuff. If word gets around that you offer perks or swag to the people who participate in your Hangouts, you'll attract more participants, and more people will add you to their Circles.

✦ **Minimize noise.** Using a headset or ear buds help to control background noise, feedback, and echoing.

Sharing documents and photos while hanging out

You can turn your Hangouts into full-fledged educational experiences by sharing documents with everyone in attendance. For example, host a Hangout for your social media marketing team members and show them graphs of a demographic breakdown as you discuss content strategies on Google+.

Follow these instructions to share a document:

1. **Click the Google Docs button, which appears on the menu bar at the top.**

   A Google Docs screen appears, as shown in Figure 4-5. The screen lists all the documents you have in Google Docs.

2. **Either select one or more documents from your list of Google Docs files or upload a new document from your computer.**

   If you just want to share a document that's already showing on the Google Docs tab, select its check box and move on to the Step 3.

   To upload a new document for sharing, click the Upload tab. This tab allows you to search your computer for your document if you haven't already loaded it into Google Docs.

   The Recently Selected tab just allows you to access a document that you have recently shared.

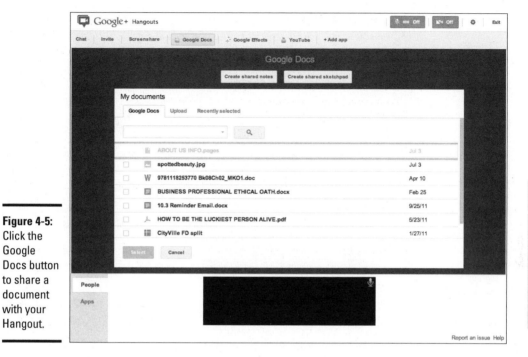

Figure 4-5:
Click the
Google
Docs button
to share a
document
with your
Hangout.

3. **After you've selected your document, click the Select button and then click the Upload button on the following screen.**

Your file, whether it's an image, Microsoft Word document, or PowerPoint presentation, for example, shows on your screen. However, the people in your Hangout won't automatically see your shared document, and you won't automatically see their shared documents, either.

4. **To view a shared Google Doc, click the Apps tab in the bottom-left corner of the screen, as shown in Figure 4-6.**

5. **Click the Google Docs icon.**

The shared documents are listed in the left pane, as shown in Figure 4-7, and the currently selected document appears to the right.

This feature is awesome for collaboration because it enables the host to edit a document onscreen, depending on the item you have shared. For example, you're able to edit a Word document and an Excel spreadsheet.

Figure 4-6:
Everyone
must be
viewing
the Apps
tab to see
a shared
document.

Click here to view a shared doc.

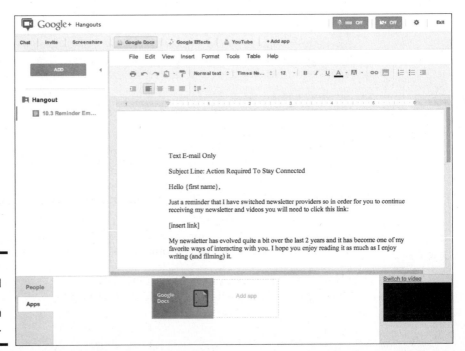

Figure 4-7:
The shared
document
appears on
the screen.

Sharing your screen while hanging out

You can also share what's in your screen at the moment with your Hangout attendees. This is handy for sharing a slide deck for a presentation or to show a website or online video, for example.

To share your screen:

1. **From inside a Hangout, click the Screenshare button on the menu bar at the top.**

A new window appears, as shown in Figure 4-8.

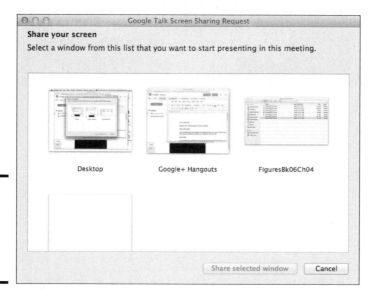

Figure 4-8: Determine which window you'll be sharing.

2. **Select the screen you want to share.**

You can share your desktop, your Hangout screen, a Google Doc you've uploaded, or an Internet window you have open. You'll have the opportunity to choose what you wish to share.

3. **Click the Share Selected Window button, and it opens in a new window.**

After you finish sharing, simply close the window of your shared screen, and you and your guests will automatically return to your Hangout screen.

Your Hangout attendees will see everything on your screen in real time, so make sure you have any sensitive information or Internet windows closed!

Book VII

Pinterest

Contents at a Glance

Chapter 1: Pinning Down Pinterest

*W*hat is it about Pinterest that's so attractive? Is it the mouth-watering food images, the inspiring island getaway shots, or the humorous jokes?

The answer is all of the above. Pinterest is a social network that enables you to share content, but there's a twist. You can't see the text beyond the caption that the "pinner" adds when "pinning" the image to his or her board. Because Pinterest pulls only images from blog posts and web articles, the site is more visually appealing. It's not an eye-catching headline that pulls you in, but rather colors and creativity.

One complaint people have about the various social networks is that everyone is sharing the same things across all the networks. They're making the same comments and sharing the same links and videos. Pinterest takes that sharing to a whole new level. It's not the same old, same old.

In this chapter, you find out about Pinterest, why it's so popular, and why this social network is so different from all the others.

What Is Pinterest?

Pinterest is a social network based on images. Users upload photos, called *pins,* to create *boards,* or groups of images centered on a common theme. Members of the Pinterest community use Pinterest for different reasons. Some just like to share pretty photos or recipes, while others share images in hopes that those viewing the photos will click through and drive traffic to their blog or website. Because it's a visual site, it's perfect for product-based retailers who are hoping to drive sales.

Pinterest is the perfect social network for clothing retailers, interior designers, foodies, landscapers, travel professionals, and any profession that can benefit from telling a story with an image. Though the U.S. user base is primarily female, men are also using Pinterest to share funny images, sports-related photos, gadgets, and the great outdoors. Knowing how the different demographics are using Pinterest is important, especially if you're reaching out to a global market.

Before you dive into the Pinterest deep end, be familiar with these common Pinterest terms:

✦ **Pin:** A pin is an image or video that you or someone else has uploaded to a board on Pinterest. When you enter a URL or upload an image to one of your boards, you are pinning to that board.

✦ **Boards:** Each time you add a pin, you assign it to a category of your creation called a *board.* In essence, you're creating virtual pin boards. For instance, you can create a board named Funny and pin images that make you laugh, or you can make a board named Knitting Patterns to Try and pin images from relevant how-to articles.

✦ **Pinner:** Someone who uses Pinterest.

✦ **Repin:** When someone shares one of your pins, or you share one of theirs. When you repin something, you add it to one of your boards. (The Repin button appears at the top of a pin when you hover your mouse pointer on the pin.)

✦ **Comment:** You can discuss pins by commenting in the area beneath the pin.

✦ **Like:** If you like someone's pin but don't necessarily want to repin it, you can show approval by liking it. Hover your mouse pointer on the pin and then click the center Like button (shown with a heart) to like the pin.

Getting Started

Before launching your Pinterest account, take some time to see what a few brands are doing on Pinterest. Whole Foods, shown in Figure 1-1, is a great example of a business that effectively uses Pinterest. Their boards tell the story of who they are, without being overly promotional.

Figure 1-1:
Whole
Foods pins
about food
as well as
cooking.

To search for a specific brand, follow these steps:

1. **Type any company name into the Search box in the top-left corner of the page.**

   You will see a results page with every pin using that search term.

2. **Beneath the search box are the Pins (selected by default), Boards, and People links, as shown in Figure 1-2.**

   • *Pins:* Shows all pins containing the search term.

   • *Boards:* Shows all boards titled with a name that includes the search term.

   • *People:* Shows all users who have that search term in their username or profile description.

Sort search results   Search box
with these links.

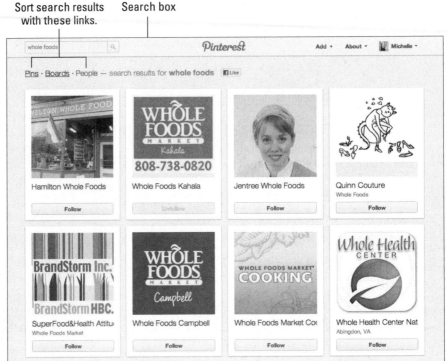

Figure 1-2:
The three
ways to sort
your search
results.

3. **Click the Boards link to see the boards and the pins they contain.**

   Check out boards that have a good variety of pins and start thinking of
   ways your brand can incorporate pinning.

   If it looks and sounds like Pinterest is a good fit for you, the following sections will have you pinning like a pro.

   Pinterest For Dummies, by Kelby Carr, is also a great resource for getting you
   up and running on Pinterest.

Joining Pinterest

You can create a Pinterest account much easier these days than you could when Pinterest arrived on the scene. You no longer need to request an invitation from Pinterest or ask a friend with a Pinterest account to invite you. Just head to `http://pinterest.com` and follow the steps to create an account:

1. **On the Pinterest home page, click the Join Pinterest button, as shown in Figure 1-3.**

    The Welcome to Pinterest page appears, and you see the options to sign up via Facebook, Twitter, or your e-mail address.

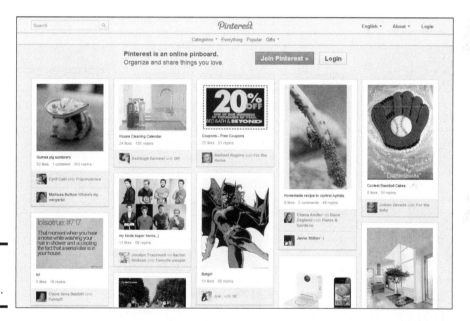

Figure 1-3: Pinterest's home page.

Book VII Chapter 1

Pinning Down Pinterest

2. **Click the Facebook button or the Twitter Button, as shown in Figure 1-4.**

    We suggest going with Facebook because you have the option to follow your friends from that network after you provide your profile details.

Figure 1-4:
Sign up for
Pinterest
with
Facebook,
Twitter, or
an e-mail
address.

3. **Enter your profile details, including your username, your e-mail
   address, and your password, as shown in Figure 1-5.**

   Your username becomes part of your profile's URL so consider whether
   you want to use your name or your company's name. Your profile's URL
   will look like `http://pinterest.com/`*yourname*.

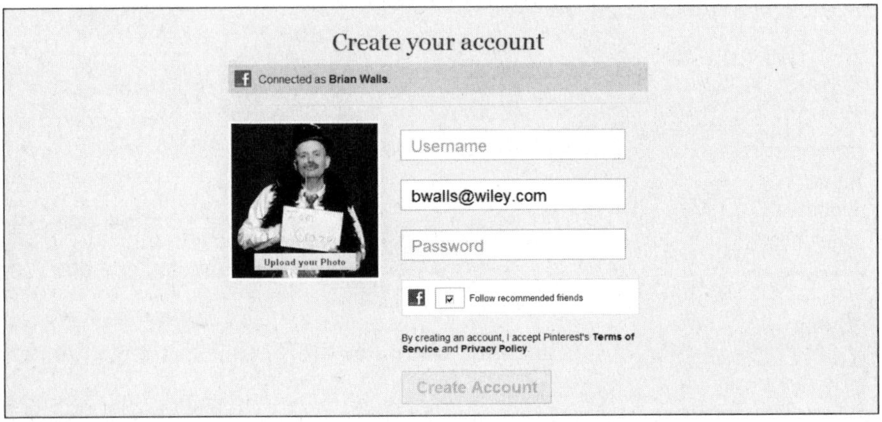

Figure 1-5:
Create your
Pinterest
profile.

4. Click Create Account.

Congratulations, you're the newest Pinterest member!

After you get an account, the easiest way to log in is by using the same method you used to create the account. Click either icon to sign in via one of these social networks (see Figure 1-6). You can also log in using your e-mail address. After you log in, you can get started.

You can choose to have your pins show up on Facebook. Many people who use Pinterest as a personal account enjoy sharing pins with their Facebook communities. However, it's different for a brand account. As we mention in Book V, Chapter 2, a brand's community doesn't want to receive as many updates and may become turned off if a brand's pins are showing up all day on their News Feeds.

Figure 1-6:
Log in using one of the social networks or your e-mail address.

Pinterest

f Login with Facebook

🐦 Login with Twitter

Email

Password

Navigating Pinterest

You have to know your way around Pinterest so you can pin like a pro. Whenever you log in, you see the most recent pins added to the boards you follow, as shown in Figure 1-7.

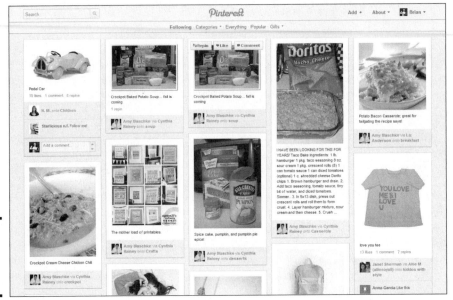

Figure 1-7:
Your
Pinterest
home page.

Your Pinterest home page is broken down as follows:

✦ **Search:** At the top-left is a Search box. Type a search term, and you'll be taken to a menu where you can search for that term or name among Pins, Boards, or People.

✦ **Following:** The images you see on your Pinterest page are from all Pinners who are your friends. For each Pinner, you can follow specific boards or all boards. When this section is bold, you are looking at the recent pins of all the users you follow.

✦ **Categories:** When you click the Categories link, a drop-down menu appears, listing the available categories, which range from Animals and Architecture to Women's Fashion and Videos. See Figure 1-8. Select a category that interests you to see the most recent pins in that category by anyone and everyone on Pinterest. This menu gives you a way to browse for specific types of pins.

Figure 1-8:
When you select Categories at the top of Pinterest, you see a list of categories to choose from.

✦ **Everything:** When you click the Everything link, you see the most recently pinned and repinned images made by anyone on Pinterest.

✦ **Popular:** When you click the Popular link, you're shown the most popular viral pins. That is, the pins that have the most people sharing, liking, and repinning them are considered popular pins.

✦ **Gifts:** Pinterest can also be used as a handy shopping tool. When you click the Gifts link, you go to a page of the most recently pinned images with price tags on them. We talk more about gifts in Chapter 3 of this minibook.

✦ **Add+:** Clicking this link in the top-right corner opens the Add box. You have the option to Add a Pin via a URL, Upload a Pin by locating an image file on your computer, or Create a new pin board to start adding stuff to.

✦ **About:** This menu exists to give you more information about Pinterest, and it includes the following options:

• *Help:* Need more help on Pinterest besides the information we have in this book? Click here.

• *Pin It Button:* Add a handy Pin It button to your browser's toolbar for instant pinning ability while surfing the web.

- *Careers:* Looking for a job and can't get enough of Pinterest? Maybe they have an opening for you!

- *Team:* The minds and faces behind your new (or soon-to-be new) obsession.

- *Blog:* Find out what's new and happening in the world of Pinterest.

- *Terms of Service:* This is legal stuff that tells you what you can and can't do while using the site. It's definitely worth a read to make sure you stay within the rules.

- *Privacy:* Here's more legal stuff worth a read. Find out how Pinterest safeguards your privacy.

- *Copyright and Trademark:* You find even more legal stuff, but this time it has to do with the intellectual property of both Pinterest and the items people are pinning. In short, don't claim to own anything that you don't.

✦ **You:** Clicking your username takes you to your profile page. Hovering your mouse pointer on your username opens a drop-down menu. Use this drop-down menu to invite and find friends; access your boards, pins, and likes; adjust your settings; or log out.

Creating your Pinterest profile

As with any social network, a first impression is important. It's especially important if you're using the social network as a marketing tool. Your Pinterest profile page is where pinners stop by to find out more about you. To get to this page, click your username in the top-right corner. The profile page, as shown in Figure 1-9, contains your profile image, a few words about you, and displays your boards. You can also add your website address (if you have one) and your Facebook profile page.

Before you get started on filling out your profile, you should get to know the elements of the Pinterest profile page:

✦ **Profile image:** This is the image you want to display that best represents your brand. Most brands use their logo or a photo of your product.

✦ **Repins From:** This box lists the most recent people to share your content.

✦ **Statistics:** You can see your total pins, likes, repins, and boards, as well as how many people you're following and how many are following you.

✦ **Boards:** All your boards are displayed. We talk about using boards to best share your message later in this chapter.

Profile image   Statistics

Figure 1-9:
Your profile
page is
where
people go
for more
information
about you.

Boards

Now it's time to make sure your profile gives a positive impression to your
Pinterest community as well as any potential community members or customers by filling out your profile information. Start with the general information first.

Take these steps to set up your profile page:

1. **Hover your mouse pointer on your name in the top-right corner of the
page and choose Settings from the drop-down menu.**

You arrive on the Edit Profile page, as shown in Figure 1-10.

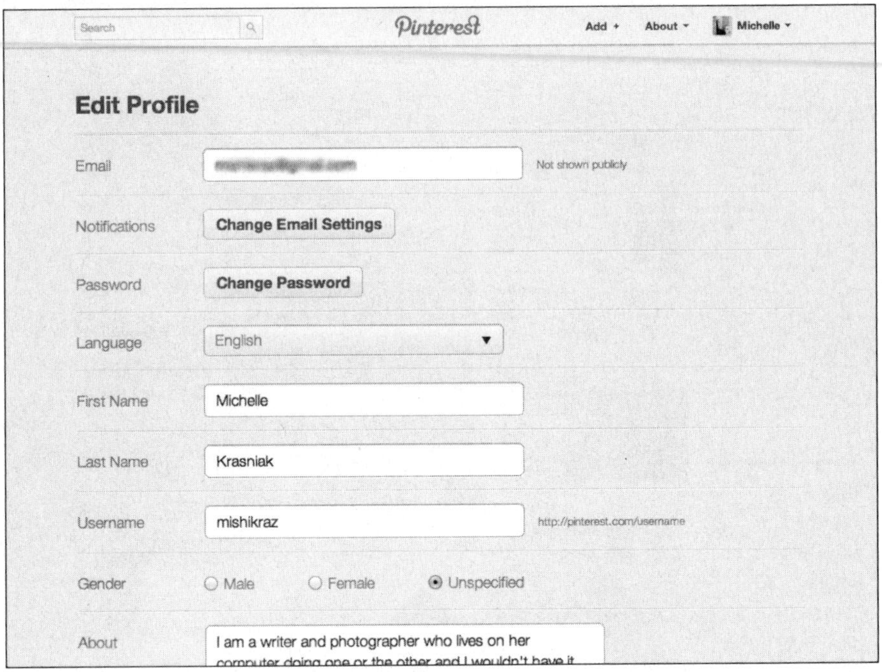

Figure 1-10:
Edit your
profile page
here.

The e-mail address you used to sign up for the account is automatically entered in the Email text box.

2. **If you need to change your e-mail address, simply click in the Email text box and enter the new e-mail address.**

   Don't worry; your e-mail address is not displayed publicly.

   Below the Email text box are several more options. For now, skip down to the Username text box.

3. **In the Username text box, enter the name you want to use for this account.**

   You can use your own name or the name of your brand. It has to be between 3 and 15 characters long. If the name is already in use, you see a `The username is already in use` message appear written in red on the right side of the box. If your desired name is not in use, the message says `Available` in green.

4. **Select gender if you want, or leave the option unspecified if you'd rather not.**

5. **In the About text box, add your bio or a few words about your business or brand.**

This is probably one of the most important parts of your Pinterest account (aside from what you pin, of course). Here's your chance to tell other pinners about you and/or your brand. When they click on your Pinterest page, this information appears right at the top of the screen, so make sure to put your best foot forward!

6. **In the Location text box, enter your city and state.**

   This is optional, but it's important to include this info if you have a physical location you want to drive people to.

7. **Add your website or blog URL in the Website text box.**

   Again, this is optional, but why would you be getting your brand involved with social networking if you didn't want to give out your website or blog address?

   Below the Website text box is an Image option. We cover that later on, in the section "Uploading a profile photo."

8. **Determine whether you want to add your pins to your Facebook Timeline or link to Twitter.**

   You can find more info on that in Chapter 3 of this minibook.

9. **Either select or deselect the Hide check box, which hides your Pinterest profile from search engines.**

   As Twitter is a marketing tool, it probably wouldn't make sense for you to hide your pins from the search engine. After all, the more people who land on your pins and click your links, the better, right? And all those backlinks to your home page or sales page couldn't hurt, either. However, sometimes when people are creating a new board they like to hide the pins until the board is complete. There are no hard and fast rules.

10. **Click the Save Profile button at the bottom of the screen.**

Now that your profile is filled out, you should determine what kind of e-mail notifications to receive.

Setting your e-mail notification preferences

By default, you'll receive notifications for every pin, repin, comment, and follow, and if your account is very active, that can add up to a lot of notifications.

To set e-mail notifications, do the following:

1. **Hover your mouse pointer on your name in the top-right corner of the page and choose Settings from the drop-down menu.**

The Edit Profile page appears. (Refer to Figure 1-10.)

2. **Click the Change Email Settings button.**

As you can see in Figure 1-11, you have a lot of options.

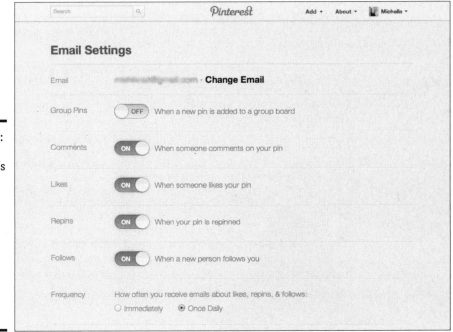

Figure 1-11: Set your notifications so you're not receiving e-mails every time there's activity on your Pinterest feed.

3. **Depending on your preferences, select or deselect the check boxes for Group Pins, Comments, Likes, Repins, and Follows.**

Think twice about opting-in to receive notifications every time someone repines, comments on, or follows you. If your Pinterest account is active, your inbox will become very full very quickly!

It's a good idea, at the very least, to be notified when someone comments on or repins what you've pinned. You can always test different settings out to see what works best for you.

4. **Decide on the frequency of the e-mails.**

You can have the e-mails sent to you as soon as an action takes place (immediately) or only once a day.

5. **Select or deselect the Digest and News check boxes, depending on your preferences.**

   If you select Digest, you receive notifications in a digest form on a weekly basis, as opposed to individual e-mails. If you select News, you receive news and updates from Pinterest. If you don't select Digest, you receive individual e-mails for each notification.

6. **When you're finished, click the Save Settings button to save your e-mail preferences.**

Uploading a profile photo

It's important to put a face to your Pinterest name by uploading a profile picture. To upload your profile image, do the following:

1. **Hover your mouse pointer on your name in the top-right corner of the page and choose Settings from the drop-down menu.**

   The Edit Profile page appears.

2. **Scroll down to the center of the page to where Image displays on the left side and click the Upload an Image button.**

   The button changes to a box, as shown in Figure 1-12. You can use the box to search your computer for the file you want to upload. After you select the file, Pinterest will upload it automatically.

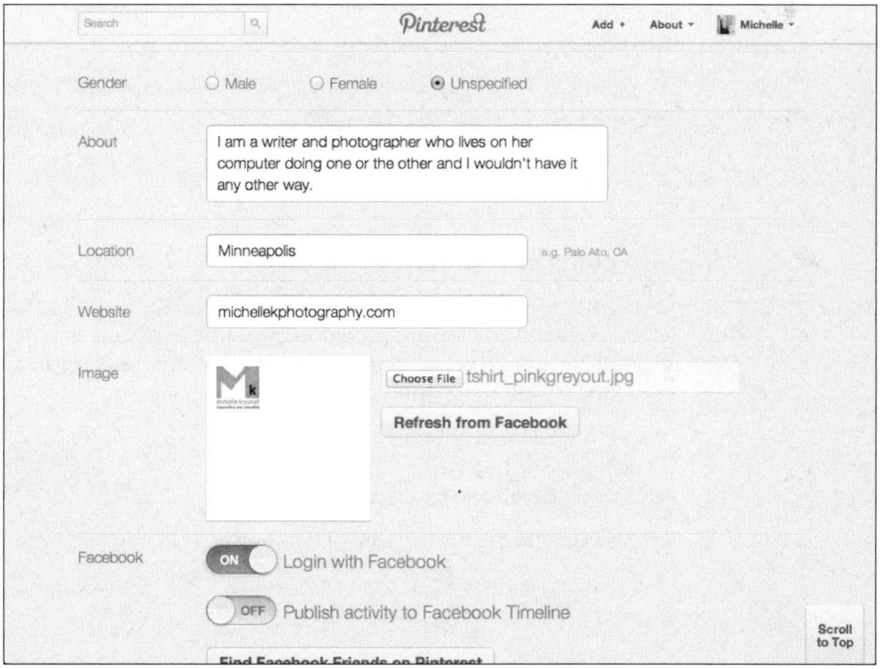

Figure 1-12:
Select
an image
that best
represents
your brand.

Book VII
Chapter 1

Pinning Down
Pinterest

3. **If you're happy with the image you select, click the Save Profile button at the bottom of your screen.**

    Congratulations! Your Pinterest account has a face!

Pinterest also offers the option to use your Facebook or Twitter photo for your Pinterest profile photo. This is a good idea if you want a consistent look among all the social networks.

Getting on Board

Boards are the way Pinterest organizes its users' content, in a manner that resembles a series of bulletin boards hanging on a wall, with each board having its own label. Boards organize your pins into categories of your choosing. However, if you treat your Pinterest boards as mere categories, you end up with a bunch of random, generic groupings. If you treat boards as a marketing tool for your product, brand, or business, you can create content that people want to follow that encourages them to find out more about what your brand is all about.

Basic boards can accomplish any number of goals, such as

✦ Showing steps in a process, say, creating a craft project and visually listing the instructions.

✦ Reflecting different elements of planning. For instance, for party or wedding planning, creating a board for food, drink, table settings, and theme ideas.

✦ Providing an industry overview; perhaps the clothing styles, designers, and fabrics of the fashion world.

✦ Highlighting the departments of a business, and including sales, marketing, engineering, and manufacturing.

Planning your initial boards

Before you start pinning, you want to have several boards in place. You'll create new boards while you progress on Pinterest, but do plan out the first few. What follows are some suggestions for your first boards:

✦ **History of your brand:** Go back to where you began and show how things have changed throughout the years. Pin promotional material or product labels from prior years to show how they've evolved.

✦ **History of your products:** Have your products received a makeover over the years? Has the packaging changed? Or maybe you have an archive of print ads spanning back through the decades. Use these items to create historic boards. When viewers see how long your product has been around, it tells them you have a product and a name worthy of their trust.

Kodak has a great example of how to feature your product in this manner at `http://pinterest.com/kodakcb/historic-photography` and Blockbuster's Old Hollywood board tempts viewers to rent an old black-and-white at `http://pinterest.com/blockbuster/old-hollywood`.

✦ **Showcase your brand:** Entice people into buying by showing them how they can use your product or service. You can even pin unusual or uncommon uses. Additionally, community members love it when they're highlighted on brand pages. Ask your community members to send photos of them using your product or service.

✦ **Who you are:** A Pinterest board can make a great About page. Use it to highlight team members, your location, your mission, and what you're selling. A couple of great examples of boards that tell about a brand can be found at New Media Expo's Pinterest account, where they feature team members at `http://pinterest.com/NewMediaExpo/meet-the-nmx-team`, and brief bios of all the speakers at their events `http://pinterest.com/NewMediaExpo/blogworld-ny-2012-speakers`.

✦ **Tips, how to's, and DIYs:** Use your pins to teach. For example, if you're a writer, give tips for creating headlines and hooks; if you're a carpenter, share tips for creating projects that don't look homemade.

A great example is Whole Foods. Their Kitchen Basics board includes food preparation instructions, such as prepping and storing strawberries, and recipes for things like homemade ranch dressing. Check them out at `http://pinterest.com/wholefoods`.

✦ **Gift ideas:** Product-oriented brands can benefit from pinning gift ideas. Take it even further by pinning a series of gift boards. We talk more about gift boards in Chapter 3 of this minibook.

✦ **Books:** Recommend books to your community that relate to your field. Lead a discussion in the comments section.

Creating your first board

To create a board, take these steps:

1. **Click the Add+ link located in the top-right corner of the Pinterest site.**

    The Add box appears, as shown in Figure 1-13, with three options: Add a Pin, Upload a Pin, and Create a Board.

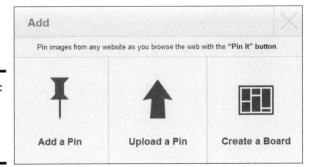

Figure 1-13: Options for adding content on Pinterest.

2. **Click the Create a Board button.**

    The Create a Board box appears, as shown in Figure 1-14.

3. **Fill in the Board Name text box.**

    Chose a name that will describe what your board is about, but in a way that catches the eye so other pinners will want to learn more.

4. **Select an option from the Board Category drop-down list.**

    Your category options range from Architecture to Photography, from Art to Wedding & Events. Choose the one most representative of your board and your brand. You can also choose Other if you don't see a suitable category on the menu. Do your best to choose a descriptive category, however. You want to be as specific as possible to catch the attention of people who are searching on Pinterest.

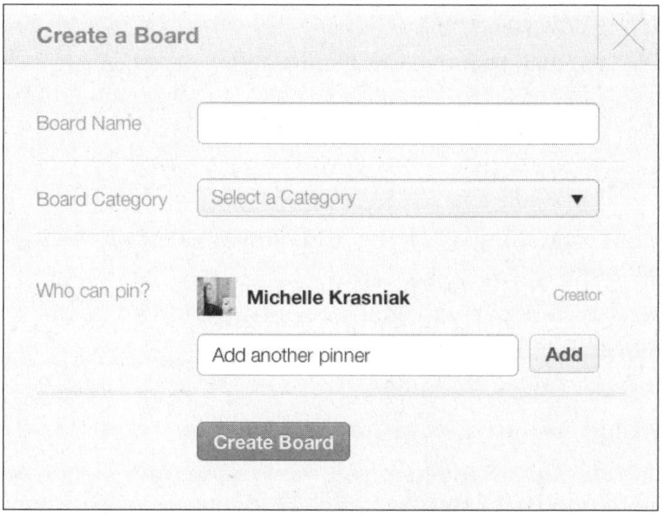

Create a Board   ✕

Board Name

Board Category   Select a Category   ▼

Who can pin?   **Michelle Krasniak**   Creator

Add another pinner   **Add**

Create Board

Figure 1-14: The Create a Board dialog box, where you provide your board's name and category.

5. Determine who can pin to the board.

If you want to be the only pinner, don't change a thing. If you want to invite other people you follow on Pinterest to add pins to this board, click in the Add Another Pinner text box and start typing a person you want to invite to the board. Click the Add button. Repeat to invite more people.

A collaborative board is a wonderful way to find out how others see your brand or niche and to get people excited about what you do. We talk more about collaborating on boards in Chapter 2 of this minibook.

6. Click the Create Board button.

You arrive at your newly created, and sadly empty, board. Go add some pins!

Pinning on Pinterest

Pinning can be addictive. Many pinners admit to spending hours pinning and finding items to like and repin. From a brand perspective, it may not look or feel like marketing because you're not doing something like creating eye-catching headlines. You *will* need a way with words for your descriptions, however. It's just that instead of those attention-grabbing headlines, you're capturing the attention of the Pinterest community with images and videos. That's why your content has to be appealing and colorful, and it needs to make folks want to learn more.

Pinning an image

Pinterest is a huge traffic driver. Funny and vivid images can capture the attention of thousands of people. To start, go ahead and pin something.

To pin an image from a blog or website (which, by the way, also pins a link back to the blog), take these steps:

1. **To pin something, click the Add+ link located on the top-right of your page.**

   You see a box pop up with three options: Add a Pin, Upload a Pin, and Create a Board.

2. **Click the Add a Pin button.**

   A dialog box with a space for a URL appears.

3. **Enter the URL of the item you want to pin (for example, an item you'd like to purchase) and then click Find Images, as shown in Figure 1-15.**

   Pinterest automatically pulls images from the website and displays them in the image box on the left side.

Figure 1-15: If you're linking to a blog post or web article, add the URL and find the images you wish to pin.

4. **Click the arrow to cycle through the images to choose the one you want to pin.**

   Make sure you select a photo that's eye-catching and properly show-cases what you're trying to show.

5. **Select the board you want to pin to, or create an appropriate board.**

   We discuss creating new boards in the earlier "Getting on Board" section.

6. **Create a description of up to 500 characters.**

   We talk more about creating meaningful descriptions for your pins in Chapter 2 of this minibook.

7. **Click the Pin It button at the bottom.**

   Your pin now appears in the feed on your main page as well as on the feeds of everyone who follows that particular board.

Some websites and blogs have blocked the ability to download or share their images because they don't want them reposted on Pinterest. If you have come across a photo that has sharing disabled, seek permission before pinning the image. The last thing you want is to be in copyright violation.

Pinning the right images

At first glance, Pinterest might seem like a random bunch of images. On a typical Pinterest feed, most users see dozens of photos, and many of the same pins are repinned over and over, as shown in Figure 1-16.

Being random and repetitive might be okay for personal users, but a brand must make sure its pins are well thought out. Keep these points in mind when selecting an image to pin:

✦ **Images shouldn't conflict with the message you're trying to send.** You want the viewer to be clear, not confused, about what you pin. For example, it wouldn't make sense for a ravioli manufacturer to post pictures of vehicles — unless they were delivery trucks, made out of ravioli.

✦ **Images should make people feel good or evoke emotion.** You want people to see the images and react with a comment, a like, or a repin. Just like with Facebook posts or Twitter tweets, you want to know your Pinterest community is paying attention.

✦ **Images must be eye-catching, engaging, and unique.** You want your content to stand out, and you only have a small number of seconds for your pin to catch someone's attention. If a viewer's response isn't positive and immediate, chances are your pin won't get a second look.

✦ **Images should support your goals.** If you want to drive sales, create pins with sales in mind. Create a board of images showing happy people using your product, or the end result of your service.

   If your goal is to drive traffic to a particular website, create one board with pins that link to the site. If every board you create and every image you pin is a link to your blog or website, you'll lose followers — fast.

   The rest of your boards should represent what you do without pushing sales or traffic.

Figure 1-16:
The same item pinned multiple times on a user's board.

Pinning the wrong images

Just as there are many ideas for what to pin, there are also plenty types of pins to avoid. Because Pinterest is visual and pins appeal to emotions, pinning one of the following can lead to unfollows:

✦ **Photos that are out of focus:** Images should be sharp and vivid.

✦ **Photos that have no rhyme, reason, or focus:** Though not every pin should be about your brand, if you have too many pins that are off topic, you might confuse your followers.

✦ **Repins that everyone is repinning:** If you pin the same things everyone else is pinning, there's no reason to follow you.

✦ **Photos that are rude and offensive:** Be considerate of your community. Leave swearing and vulgarity out of it, lest folks get the wrong message about you and your brand. If you wouldn't say something to a customer in person, don't say it on Pinterest.

✦ **Constantly spamming with sales messages:** Very few people use Pinterest to receive sales messages. Avoid pitching to the Pinterest community. Instead, let your images be your pitch. If you're known for making it all about the sale, no one will want to follow you.

✦ **Bait-and-switch images:** Don't mislead your followers. If you pin an image and it refers to an article called "10 Reasons to Paint Your Bedroom Purple," that's what people should see. Don't reference one thing on

Pinterest only to have users click through to something completely different, such as a sales page.

Whenever you repin someone else's pin, you should make sure the pin is legitimate: Test the pin by clicking through to the website. There is nothing worse than to repin something only to find out later that it's one of those bait-and-switch pins that are so hated.

Considering the use of watermarks

Watermarking is the act of putting your name or brand name on your original photos, as shown in Figure 1-17. Many photographers want to be sure they get credit for their photographs, which doesn't always happen when people repin a photo on Pinterest. By watermarking, photographers are also hoping people don't use their images without proper authorization.

Many people who watermark photos don't mind if the photo is shared on Pinterest as long as pinners can click through to the original source, but do check first. Sometimes it's just a matter of courtesy and asking the original source if you can use the photograph. The problem begins when folks don't link to the original source and instead upload the photo as their own original pin. Or, worse, they take the photo and add it to their own content, for example a blog post, without proper attribution. Passing off someone else's image as your own is completely unethical and a copyright violation.

Figure 1-17:
Some
people
watermark
photos to
protect their
intellectual
property
from
unauthorized
use.

Should you watermark your photos? Consider the following:

✦ **When you watermark, you'll receive proper credit for your photo.** Even though it's considered good Pinterest etiquette, people don't offer attribution. Many photos are repinned dozens of times, and the original photographer doesn't receive any credit for the image or the original pin. Watermarks ensure the original photographer receives the proper attribution, even though the images have been pinned many times over.

✦ **Watermarks can sometime distract or take away from the beauty of the image.** In watermarked photos, the eye is often drawn to the watermark rather than the subject of the image. There's no mistaking who the photographer is, but now the photo isn't as aesthetically pleasing. If watermarking, add to the lowest part of the image where it's less likely to be noticed.

If you decide to add watermarks to the bottom of images, the watermarks may still be cropped out using one of the many photo-editing programs out there. Keep that in mind when deciding where to place your watermark.

✦ **Watermarking helps to protect you from copyright theft.** When you watermark a photo, you're deterring others from passing your image off as their own. If they post the photo in their own content, your watermark will show. Also, if people enjoy your photos and see your watermark, they might search for more of your images.

Watermarking has its pros and cons. It provides protection, but it doesn't guarantee you'll receive credit for your photography.

Several tools are available that can help you watermark your photos. For instance, you can use photo-editing software, such as Photoshop Elements or PaintShop Pro. Each software comes with its own set of instructions, and you can also find tutorials online.

You can also find plenty of free photo-editing tools online, such as Pixlr Express (`http://pixlr.com/express`), Snipshot (`http://snipshot.com`), and FotoFlexer (`http://fotoflexer.com`).

Try using a semitransparent watermark so your name is still visible but less distracting than if you used a solid color.

Pinning a video

Pinterest isn't just for static images. You can also upload videos. Videos have their own category on the main Pinterest page so the people who are interested in finding in-depth experiences or how to's know exactly where to go.

To pin a video from a video site such as YouTube or Vimeo, do the following:

1. **Select the Add+ link located on the top right of the menu bar of your Pinterest page.**

You are presented with three choices: Add a pin, Upload a pin, and Create a board.

2. **Select Add a Pin.**

You are presented with a box where you can enter the URL of the item you want to pin.

3. **Navigate to the site hosting the video you want to upload, copy the URL from the top navigation bar, paste it into the URL box, and click the Find Images button.**

Your video will show up in the Add a Pin box as seen in Figure 1-18.

Figure 1-18: Copy and paste the video URL into the box.

Book VII Chapter 1

Pinning Down Pinterest

4. **If a snapshot of your video does not show up automatically in the image box on the left side, use the arrows underneath the box to locate it.**

The need to do this step depends on where you are uploading the video from. If it's from sites like YouTube or Vimeo, you typically don't have to do it. However if the video is from a blog or other website, you may have to pick the right image.

5. **Select a board and add a description.**

Properly categorizing it by choosing the correct board and writing a compelling description are important as they are what will entice the viewer to click on and watch your video.

6. Click the red Pin It button at the bottom of the box.

Pinterest automatically detects that the pin is a video and adds it to the main Video board as well as to your own board.

Be sure to use *video* in your description. This lets people know they're going to be viewing a video, and it also helps those who are searching specifically for videos.

Creating conversational pins

When you first start with Pinterest, it may be frustrating to wait for people to comment on your pins. It takes a while to grow a community and start receiving comments. With that said, there are ways to create the types of pins people feel inclined to comment on.

✦ **Appeal to emotion.** Whether it's laughing out loud or choking back tears, people talk about pins that inspire emotion. Before you pin something, ask yourself how you feel about it. If the answer is indifferent, consider finding something more thought-provoking.

✦ **Pin items your target audience can relate to.** It's important for you to stay on topic with your Pinterest community. For example, if you're marketing to parent bloggers, your pins should reflect items of interest to parents. If you're an automotive dealership, consider posting photos of cars or funny street signs. You want your community members to relate to you. If you go off topic, that will only serve to confuse people. If they're relating to your pins, they'll comment to tell you why.

✦ **Be different.** There may be times when you look at your feeds and notice that everyone is repinning the same thing. It's great for the original pinner to have something go viral, but after a while, seeing the same image over and over again gets boring. Go against the grain and find something different. Search Pinterest for pins that are compelling and unique, or create unique content and share that.

✦ **Find out what people are responding to.** Take a ride around Pinterest. Which types of pins are getting the most comments and why? Is it the type of pin? The types of friends? How is the pinner interacting? Take notes.

Tagging

Tagging on Pinterest is similar to tagging on Facebook or Twitter. You tag people to call their attention to your pins. For example, if they're in the photo you're pinning or if the topic is of interest to them. Tagging is important because when you call someone's attention to your photos, they might be inclined to share with their communities.

Here's how you tag someone on Pinterest: In the description area of the pin, put an @ symbol in front of the name of the person you want to tag, as shown in Figure 1-19. If that person is a friend (see the upcoming "Following on Pinterest" section), you'll see a menu of pinners' names to select from. If that person isn't a friend, you won't be able to tag her.

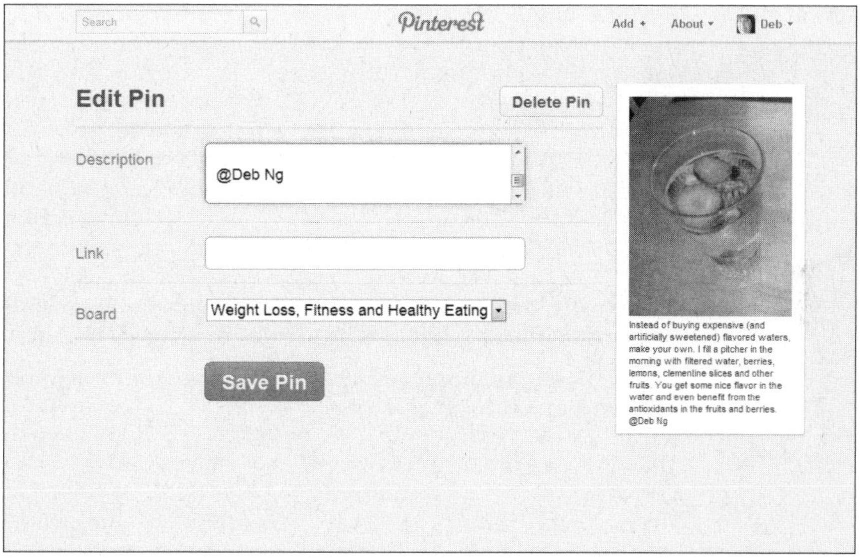

Figure 1-19:
Put the @ symbol in front of any name you wish to tag.

When tagged, that person will be notified that you've tagged her in a pin. Tagging is a great way to call a person's attention to a particular pin. For example, suppose you have a client who loves Italian food. If you're connected to her on Pinterest, you can let her know you posted a delicious recipe for her to consider. She'll appreciate that you were thinking about her!

Following on Pinterest

What fun is it to create boards and share pins when there's no one to share it with? To make friends, you have to first follow others. Following is similar to "friending" on Facebook. It means you're choosing to have someone's boards and pins show up in your feed, which will help you to find people you want to know more about, and inspire others to follow you in return.

Determining the types of people to follow and have follow you requires some strategy. Although your ultimate goal is to reach a wide variety of people, you also want to target the people who will do the most good. And by good, we mean those who will follow through with liking, commenting on, and repinning your content.

Following friends

Because you're representing a brand, you definitely want to appeal to the people who also follow your brand on Facebook, Twitter, and other social networks. However, you don't want to solely rely on your loyal, existing community to make up your Pinterest community. The reason you join any social network is to grow your community, and you can't grow it by following the same people every time.

Announcing on your blog, Twitter, Facebook, Google+, and other social media services that you've started a Pinterest page is great, but to build up the number of pinners you follow and who follow you, also contact friends directly and let them know you want to connect on Pinterest. You can invite friends by typing in their e-mail addresses, invite Facebook friends to connect with you, or Pinterest can search your Gmail or Yahoo! Mail accounts for contacts that are already on Pinterest. To invite your Facebook contacts:

1. **Hover your mouse pointer on your name in the top-right corner of the page and choose Invite Friends from the drop-down menu.**

2. **On the page that appears, select Facebook from the options on the left, as shown in Figure 1-20.**

Figure 1-20: Invite friends from your existing online communities.

3. **Click the Find Friends from Facebook button.**

A new page appears, and it shows your friends who have a Pinterest account and friends who don't.

For your friends who don't have a Pinterest account, you're given the opportunity to send them an invite through Facebook's private messaging system. Use this function sparingly. To receive invites from a brand via private message is likened to spam, and it's a good way to turn people off.

4. **For the friends who already have Pinterest accounts, a Follow button appears to the right of their photos.**

   Click Follow to add each new friend or click the Follow All button to add every friend in the list. You'll see their updates in your feed. However, they won't see yours unless they follow you in return.

5. **When you're finished, click the Pinterest logo at the top of the screen to return to your Pinterest home page.**

Following folks you don't know

After you've exhausted all your known contacts, it's time to branch out to make new friends to follow. The best way to find new friends that you aren't already connected to is to use the Search box located in the upper-left corner of your Pinterest page. You can also use the Categories drop-down menu located above the Pinterest feeds and then browse the categories that appear to find pins and pinners who you feel will be a good fit for your community.

Before randomly following everyone who pins, make sure you share common interests and that your brand page fits the types of pins they post and the interests discussed in their personal profiles.

If you're worried about being overwhelmed by too many images in your feed, you don't have to follow every board by a particular pinner. You have the option to follow only the boards that interest you.

Don't randomly follow people. Make a list of the types of people you wish to follow and the keywords and phrases used to find them, including the search engine optimization terms you use for your website or other social networking profiles. Search for existing customers so they can continue to support you by sharing your pins. And find new, potential customers by using search terms.

People follow your brand because they want to engage with you, learn more about what you do, or get a question answered.

Chapter 2: Marketing with Pinterest

In This Chapter

↙ **Sharing content on Pinterest**

↙ **Using keywords in your descriptions**

↙ **Building community**

↙ **Creating group boards**

*P*interest is more than a social network for people who like to share recipes or photos of their latest home improvement projects. On Pinterest, the marketing element is subtle — you can tell your brand's story and direct traffic to your business without using a single marketing term — but effective. Viewers don't see promotional copy or a sales spiel; instead, their eyes are drawn to images, and if the images are compelling, the viewer will want to learn more.

In this chapter, you find out how to effectively share content to drive traffic and grow community using Pinterest.

Sharing on Pinterest

Many marketers who were skeptical about Pinterest at first now admit it's a great source for sharing information about brands, products, and services. With the right image and the right descriptive text, a picture really is worth a thousand words.

Here are just a few of the ways brands are sharing their content on Pinterest:

✦ Wedding planners use Pinterest to pin images of flowers, gowns, table settings, and limousines in order to catch the attention of brides-to-be.

✦ Catering companies pin recipes with mouth-watering images of food.

✦ Yarn suppliers pin images of scarves, hats, and sweaters as well as supplies, such as needles and knitting bags.

✦ Travel agencies pin images of island getaways, luggage, and luxurious hotel suites.

✦ Fashion brands pin images of complete ensembles, including accessories and shoes.

✦ Businesses create boards featuring team members.

✦ Book publishers highlight books and authors.

What all these types of brands have in common is that they're not using their boards to post logos or product sales and information. In fact, many times their pins come from external sources. They're creating an appealing look into what they do. This is what helps them to gain more followers, more interest, and greater brand recognition.

Check out *Pinterest Marketing For Dummies,* by Kelby Carr, for more tips on building and nurturing a following on Pinterest.

Choosing what to share

What to share isn't a decision to take lightly. If you repin only the most popular pins, pins that everyone on Pinterest has already seen ad nausea, you're not giving any incentive for folks to follow you. If you share only obvious sales ploys, people are going to consider you to be a spammer. However, if you're known as someone who posts interesting, intriguing, shareable content, you'll have followers galore.

What sort of things you should share depends on your goal with Pinterest, the type of business you run, and who your customers are. Consider your brand and your message, and then brainstorm unique ways to share your brand's story. Before posting anything, ask yourself, "Is this image representative of my brand?"

Here are a few things to consider:

✦ **Make your content shareable.** Find images people will enjoy and talk about.

✦ **Images should appeal to the senses.** Make them mouth-watering, thought provoking, funny, or the stuff that inspires fantasy.

✦ **People prefer images to text.** Funny sayings and infographics are fun from time to time, but they can get old if that's all you post.

If you run a product-based company, consider putting a price tag on some of the items you sell, which places the items in the Gifts section. We cover the Gifts feature in Chapter 3 of this minibook.

Sharing other people's pins

When share another person's pin in your feed, you *repin* it. Similar to a Facebook share or Twitter retweet, a repin tells the original pinner you liked what she posted so much, you also wanted to share.

To repin a pin that you like, take these steps:

1. **Hover your mouse pointer on the pin that you want to share and click the Repin button.**

   It's the first button in the bar and it shows two pushpins.

   A window pops up with the pin, as shown in Figure 2-1. The comments section automatically populates with what the original pinner wrote.

Figure 2-1: Click the Repin button to share someone else's pin with your community.

2. **From the Boards drop-down list, select the board you want to repin the image to.**

   You have the option to select a board you already have or create a new board. We cover creating boards in Chapter 1 of this minibook.

3. **If you want to change the description, you may do so at this time.**

   If it's helpful information, such as the name of a particular food dish, we recommend leaving it as is. You can change the description to suit your community or leave the original description.

4. **Click the Pin It button.**

   The pin gets added to the board you selected, and it shows up in your feed and in the feeds of all the people who follow your board.

Note: You can also click the pin, which takes you to the pinner's page and to the pin itself. You can like the pin from there in the same manner.

Using share buttons

Ultimately, you want others to share your content on Pinterest. The ideal situation is for other people to read your blog or view one of your photographs and pin it, inspiring dozens of repins. However, you have to make it easy to do so.

Most people who read content online won't share the same content if sharing isn't made easy for them. Though it doesn't take more than a few seconds to cut a link and paste it into the Pinterest Add function, the truth is, it's too much trouble for most. They want to be able to share at the click of a button and not have to leave their current page.

Share buttons enable the people who consume your content to share it without even visiting Pinterest. All the user does is click the Pin It button, fill in the description, and choose a board, and then your content is pinned to their boards.

Here are a few features and plug-ins to look into:

+ **Pin It:** Available from Pinterest at (`http://pinterest.com/about/goodies`), the Pin It button enables you to embed code on your blog or website so others can pin your content. Pin It is available for WordPress blogs and even Flickr so you can share your photos with others.

  You can also place another type of Pin It button on your browser's toolbar, as shown in Figure 2-2, that lets you easily share others' content.

  Follow Me on Pinterest: You can add this button to your blog or website. Grab the code at `http://pinterest.com/about/goodies` and paste the code where you feel it will do the most good. Most people like pasting the code into their right sidebars at eye level. Share buttons should never be difficult to find.

+ **Digg Digg:** A WordPress plug-in (`http://wordpress.org/extend/plugins/digg-digg`) featuring a variety of share buttons for Twitter, Facebook, Google+, and many other social networks including Pinterest. When you install this plug-in, the share buttons appear on the side of your content so readers see it and share the content, if they're so inclined.

+ **ShareThis:** This is another plug-in that enables social share buttons. When you activate this plug-in, share buttons appear at the top or bottom of the page. You can find it here: `http://wordpress.org/extend/plugins/share-this`.

A Pin It button on the browser toolbar

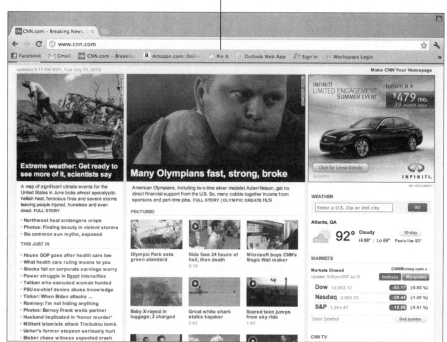

Figure 2-2:
Share content you like with the Pin It button in your browser's toolbar.

Although Digg Digg and ShareThis aren't specific to Pinterest, these popular share buttons are used to share content on Pinterest and other social networks. People who use one of these plug-ins have the option to tweet, pin, post on Facebook, and so on. Because Digg Digg and ShareThis feature all the social networks, the majority of bloggers who use share buttons on their content use these plug-ins rather than installing a bunch of individual ones.

Driving Traffic with Pinterest

Did you know that Pinterest drives more traffic to individual blogs and websites than YouTube, Google+, and LinkedIn combined? That's a force to be reckoned with, and it's why Pinterest, unlike some of the other emerging social networks, is something anyone marketing a brand needs to take seriously.

Here's how the traffic flow works. If you're following proper Pinterest etiquette, you're sharing a good mix of content (which can be both images and video). Some of that content is from your own sources, such as your blog or website. The rest of your content is from other content including repins, and other people's blog posts or videos. In fact, most of the items you pin shouldn't be your own content. Unless an image is uploaded directly, most images are links from external sources. Most people who are marketing with Pinterest do so because they want pinners to click their links.

However, it isn't as simple as sharing a link and hoping people visit your website — you have to be strategic about it.

What follows are a few things to consider when creating and sharing content on Pinterest:

+ **Select images with Pinterest in mind.** Your most important goal when creating pin-worthy content is to select an image that represents the article and entices others to click through to the originating site. Don't go through the motions and select some random stock photo. Use colorful, thought-provoking, and awe-inspiring photos. Pinterest automatically gives image options when you're preparing to pin something from a site, so take advantage of that opportunity to select the best pin! Photos that tell a story will inspire others to click to learn more.

+ **Be descriptive.** On Pinterest, brevity is essential. With that said, you should write a description worthy of the image. It's not exactly a headline but, similar to a headline, you want to use the description to capture attention. Share one or two sentences describing the image but leave most of the details to the imagination. The image shown in Figure 2-3 gives a good example of this technique. The strawberry slices might make the viewer click through to get more information, such as why the pinner wants you to drink water with berries in it. In addition to being cost-efficient, the pinner might be offering healthy tips on her website or promoting an article on the health benefits of water. Sometimes, the most important information isn't so obvious. We talk more about writing a description in the upcoming "Being descriptive but brief" section.

+ **Tag when at all possible.** There's really no reason to tag all your friends every time you post a pin; that gets kind of annoying. However, if a pin reminds you of someone or if you want to give credit to a particular pinner, do tag, as Figure 2-4 shows. The person being tagged, more often than not, will like or share your pin and that helps to get your brand on other peoples' radars.

Instead of buying expensive (and artificially sweetened) flavored waters, make your own. I fill a pitcher in the morning with filtered water, berries, lemons, clementine slices and other fruits. You get some nice flavor in the water and even benefit from the antioxidants in the fruits and berries.

1 like

Uploaded by user

Figure 2-3:
Describe what you're showing but leave room for users to learn more by clicking through.

✦ **Give others the opportunity to pin your content**. Use share buttons, like the one shown in Figure 2-5, on your blog posts, articles, images, and videos so others will share with their friends.

✦ **Take advantage of the Gifts option**. We cover ways to sell on Pinterest in Chapter 3 of this minibook, but the Gifts option is a way to sell without annoying people with spam or a sales pitch. You can add a price tag to a sales item, as shown in Figure 2-6, and it will appear on the Gifts page.

Add a Pin

http://www.potterybarn.com/products/wesley-kni   **Find Images**

Home. Style.   ▼

LOVE this throw! I bet @Dani could make one just like it. I'm still enjoying the one she made me! :)

Dani C.

← Prev   Next →

Figure 2-4:
Use tags in your descriptions to catch the attention of others.

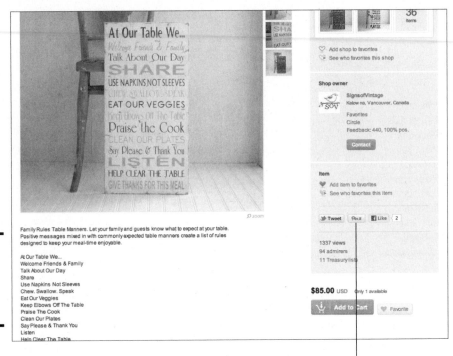

Figure 2-5:
Use share
buttons
on your
content.

Others can share this content by clicking this button.

Figure 2-6:
Turn your
pins into
items for
sale.

✦ **Use keywords and search terms.** Use the words and phrases in your descriptions that people are searching for. People also search for images online, so optimize your photos for search to help others find them.

✦ **Grow your community.** Keep finding new people to follow and interact with. As you grow your Pinterest community, you also grow traffic. We talk more about community later in this chapter, in the "Building Your Pinterest Community" section.

✦ **Be consistent.** Pin on a regular basis. If people never see anything new from you, they have no reason to continue to follow your pins.

✦ **Get nichey.** Cater to your niche. Appeal to the people who are most likely to use your products or services.

✦ **Use humor.** People love to share funny pins, and humor is a great way to break up the themes of your regular pins now and again.

✦ **Pay attention to your board categories.** Don't be generic. Your boards should be as eye-catching as your images. Take special care with the names you use for your boards. Pinterest suggests names, but those are only suggestions. Don't be afraid to change them, like the ones shown in Figure 2-7. Be creative and imaginative, and explore how other brands are using boards. We dive into how to use boards to your advantage in Chapter 1 of this minibook.

**Book VII
Chapter 2**

Marketing with Pinterest

Figure 2-7:
Create boards that are compelling and not generic.

✦ **Be strategic when arranging your boards.** Don't have a random mishmash of boards. Arrange them in an order that puts the most important boards first. If your goal is to sell, place the board with pins relating to your products or services first. To find more about planning boards, see Book VII, Chapter 1.

When we talk about sharing content and arranging boards, not every pin has to be your content or from you. You can use other people's content on your boards and in your pins.

Being descriptive but brief

The descriptions you include with pins are just as important as the images. It's not the image that brings in search traffic, but the words you use to describe the image.

If you're a travel agent and are posting a photo taken in Bora Bora, for example, you should let the viewer know where the image was taken, but you also need to tell the viewer that you can arrange vacations there. Write a description such as, "This gorgeous vista is Bora Bora. Now doesn't it make you want to plan your next tropical getaway there?" Now, you're also appearing in searches for Bora Bora, tropical, and getaway. Did you notice that we didn't state directly that we can plan the vacation for the viewer, though? The idea is to drive traffic with your pin, and you want to avoid the viewer seeing you as being too "selly." The idea is that you want the viewer to come to you.

Pinterest doesn't allow descriptions to break text into paragraphs, which means descriptions can become one long-winded block of text if you're not careful. Make sure your message comes across in a few clear, concise sentences.

Finding the right words

If you're using Pinterest as a sales or marketing tool, you want to be visible to search engines. You also want to create a description so enticing that pinners click through to the original location.

What follows are a few best practices for creating the best descriptions for your pins:

✦ **Use search engine optimization (SEO).** We talk about SEO a lot in this book because it's so important to catch the attention of the search engines. By all means, use search terms in your pin descriptions, but don't make it obvious. The terms you use should flow naturally. Think about what words people use, or words you would like to use, to land on your brand in Pinterest. Use those words or terms in a way that doesn't look silly.

✦ **Use words that paint a picture.** A description should, well, describe. If you pinned an image of a hen holding a flag, avoid stating the obvious. "This is a hen holding a flag" is descriptive but kind of boring. Calling the hen "patriotic" is less boring and describes the hen without insulting the intelligence of the reader.

✦ **Use words that stimulate discussion.** Try to string together words so they're open ended. When you ask questions, request more information, or make a statement that leaves room for interpretation, you're more likely to receive comments.

✦ **Use titles if they benefit you.** If you're pinning from a link to an article or a blog post, there's nothing wrong with using the original title as your description. However, there's also nothing wrong with not using the title and describing the image using words that benefit your brand and bring searchers to your board or pin.

✦ **Let your personality show.** Don't be afraid to be funny, perky, or anything else that helps you and your brand to shine. Avoid bland, general terminology and Internet slang, however. Use words that show your personality instead.

✦ **Avoid negativity.** Don't use words that evoke negative images or connotations. Always go for a positive point of view. But it's important to be appropriate and authentic. If your business sells Goth items, for example, "dark" words might be expected by the audience.

Finding pinners to emulate

You can also get help from the top pinners in your community to see which pins are receiving the most attention. Just click the Popular tab at the top of your page or simply look closely at your feed. Each pin shows how many likes and repins it receives. If a pin is going viral — you see the pin more than once — look for its original source.

Note the types of posts getting the best reactions in terms of the most repins and positive comments, too.

Additionally, several apps can help you find who the top pinners are

✦ **Pinreach** (`www.pinreach.com`): A Pinterest analytics tool measuring likes, repins, and follows

✦ **Pinpuff** (`www.pinpuff.com/about.php`): A tool measuring Pinterest influence

After you find the top pinners, read a sampling of their pins. Think about the descriptive words and phrases you would use to find them. Are they using the same keywords? For example, if a bedroom set has gone viral, read the description to note if it's a *"girl's bedroom set"* or a *"blue bedroom set."* Those descriptive terms are keyword phrases. Consider the words and phrases people are using to find pins and use those words and phrases in your own pins.

Building Your Pinterest Community

Even though you're using Pinterest as a marketing tool, make no mistake: Building up a community on any of the social networks is more about others than it is you. Your Pinterest community is made up of people who share like-minded interests. They visit Pinterest for their own reasons. They may be pinning to promote books, learn about particular topics, or market their own businesses. They want you to be part of their communities too. That's why interaction and participation are so important.

A variety of people make up your Pinterest community. As with the other social networks, you follow and are followed by friends, co-workers, family, new friends who you met online, and strangers. When you harness the power of your community, you're turning online friends into loyal customers and word-of-mouth marketing.

Driving traffic isn't about typing CLICK ON MY LINKS in big, bold letters. It's about giving people a reason to want to learn more about you. Driving traffic is more about creating the right types of content and building your community than it is using a sales pitch. You'll find when you take on a warm tone over marketing speech, you have a better chance of winning them over.

Collaborating with group boards

A great way to connect with your community is to collaborate on boards. Pinterest lets pinners participate in *group boards*, where like-minded people add pins around a common theme. For example, crafters can contribute to a board featuring current projects, or LEGO enthusiasts can pin their latest creations.

Here are a few reasons pinners are collaborating:

✦ **Exposure:** You're marketing your brand, and others are doing the same. Having pins on a collaborative board means more exposure. Moreover, some of the pins you're sharing will lead to your blogs and websites.

✦ **Grow community:** If you consistently posts intriguing pins, others will want to see more of your Pinterest pins and boards. Group boards are a terrific community building tool.

✦ **Camaraderie:** Some pinners just enjoy planning boards around a theme in the spirit of fun collaboration.

To create a group board, you essentially follow the steps to create a regular board as you did in Chapter 1 of this minibook:

1. **Click the Add+ button located in the top-right corner of any Pinterest page.**

2. **Click the Create a Board button.**

3. **Enter the board name and category, as described in Chapter 1 of this minibook.**

   Beneath those two options is the Who Can Pin? question. Your image appears next to it, and beneath that is a blank text box.

4. **In the text box, start typing the name of a pinner you want to invite to your group board.**

   Here's the first catch: The person has to be a member of Pinterest for you to invite her. And here's the second catch: You also have to be following the person before you can invite her to your group board.

   As you type, potential matches appear in a list below the text box.

5. **When you see your invitee listed, select the person's name and then click the Add button, as shown in Figure 2-8.**

   The person is added to a list below the Add button.

6. **Repeat Steps 4 and 5 to add all the people you want to invite to the group board.**

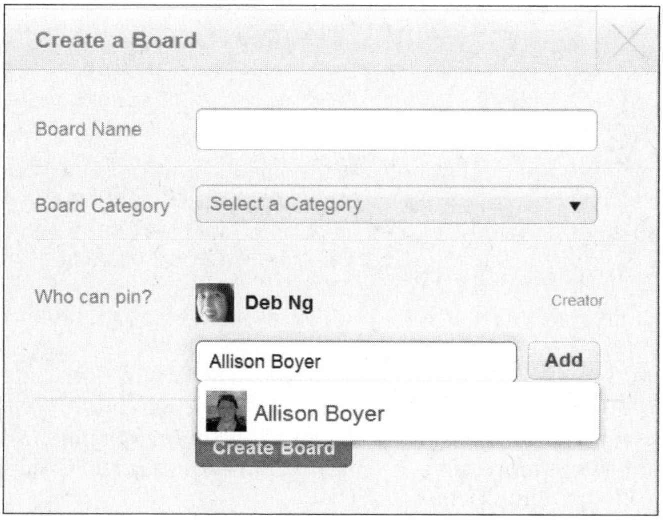

Figure 2-8:
Add the
names of
the people
you want to
collaborate
with.

Create a Board			✕
Board Name			
Board Category	Select a Category ▼		
Who can pin?	🖼 **Deb Ng**		Creator
	Allison Boyer	Add	
	🖼 Allison Boyer		
	Create Board		

7. **Click the Create Board button.**

> After the group board is created, those who are invited to collaborate receive a notification and can begin pinning immediately.

Here are some additional things to consider about group boards:

✦ **Invite people you trust.** Instead of inviting random pinners you don't know, invite friends. Be sure group pinners have your best interests at heart and won't spam the boards.

✦ **Invite people who are knowledgeable about the topic.** When you plan a board, choose people who know the subject matter. If you don't, your board will be a mish mash of items instead of a visually, informative resource.

✦ **Establish clear guidelines.** You want to establish some guidelines for pinning to your group board so there's no inappropriate content. This information can be provided in an e-mail— either a heads up that an invite is on the way or, better, a request asking whether it's okay to send the invite — that you send in advance.

✦ **Stay on topic.** If the board is meant to share the architecture of New York City and someone pins an image of the St. Louis's Gateway Arch, you'll probably want to alert the pinner to remove it unless it's germane to the discussion.

✦ **You can't remove pins or pinners.** As of this writing, anything someone else posts to your group board is there permanently unless the pinner decides to remove the pin or removes herself from the group board. Even as the group board's owner, you don't have the ability to moderate pins.

Liking pins

The fun isn't contained to only your boards. Showing approval for other people's boards and pins by "liking" them tells the pinner they're on the right track. And, if you like pins by people you don't know, they might want to look at your pins and subsequently follow you in return.

Likes show the Pinterest community you do more than pin and that you're not just on Pinterest to pimp out your own stuff. When others land on your page and see that you like a lot of images, they might be inclined to friend you so you can like their stuff too. When people see photos with a lot of likes to them, they want to see what all the fuss is about and click through for more information.

To like a pin, hover your mouse pointer on the pin's image. The Repin, Like, and Comment buttons appear, as shown in Figure 2-9. Click the Like button to show the pinner you like her pin.

Figure 2-9:
Mouse over
the pin to
access
these
buttons.

We cover the Repin button in the "Sharing other people's pins" section earlier in this chapter. You find out about the Comment button in the section that follows.

Commenting on pins

You may think the fun is in the pinning, but that's not it at all. The fun is in the conversation.

Don't wait for people to make remarks on your pins to engage with your community. Go ahead and comment on pins. Do you have an opinion on a particular image? Tell the pinner how you feel! Figure 2-10 shows a comment. Does an image evoke emotion? Share that emotion with the person who pinned. Do you have questions or concerns? Share those as well. You'll find that conversations ensue as others comment.

You can comment on a pin in two ways:

✦ **Quick-and-dirty method:** Hover your mouse pointer on a pin. Click the Comment button that appears in the top-right corner. A small comment box appears beneath the pin. Fill in your comment and press the Comment button.

✦ **Living-large method:** Click the pin. A window with a bigger image pops up. Below that image is the comment box. Say what you want to say and click the Post Comment button.

Always be polite in your comments. Some people on the Internet are looking to start fights by posting rude and negative comments. Don't give them the pleasure of knowing they've gotten under your skin by responding. Take the higher road.

How to make lavender oil at home

33 likes   1 comment   198 repins

Figure 2-10:
Take some
time to
comment
on pins.
When you
reach out
to others,
they often
reciprocate.

Playing nice

Every social network has its own set of etiquette rules, and Pinterest is no exception. Most social networking etiquette is in place so you don't annoy others, but most of it is common sense and courtesy.

What follows is a list of Pinterest etiquette tips. Keep in mind etiquette isn't made up of hard-and-fast rules; rather, it's a series of best practices most pinners follow to keep Pinterest free of spammers, trolls, and people who make the experience more difficult by causing arguments.

✦ **Give credit where credit is due.** If you're sharing another person's pin, always give a shout out to the original source. For example, if I upload a pin and you share it in your feed, type **via @debng** at the bottom of your description.

When sharing online content, some photographers or websites want you to ask permission before posting their images on Pinterest. You may feel you're doing a third party a favor by linking to their work, but since Pinterest pulls the image and you gave Pinterest permission to use your content, the original source may want compensation or recognition.

Be safe; follow the intellectual property rules laid out under the About menu on your top menu bar. And if you link to content someone else owns, be very sure they're okay with you doing so.

✦ **Fill out descriptions for all your pins.** It's not always easy to tell what the pin is about. For example, not everyone will know what a recipe is called or where an island scene is located. It's a nice courtesy to your friends to let them know what you're pinning.

✦ **Avoid over-pinning.** We know that pinning is addictive. However, don't flood your friends' streams with dozens of photos at once. Pace yourself. If they see only your pins all the time, and everyone else's pins are lost, your friends are going to stop following you.

✦ **Don't spam.** Mix up your pins so they provide a variety of content. For example, share other people's blog posts, web articles, and images (if you have permission). Don't make everything link back to your own website or sales page.

✦ **Keep your pin descriptions brief.** If your description is filled with all the details that are in the pin's original link, why would anyone click through to the pin's site for more information? See the earlier "Driving Traffic with Pinterest" section.

Most rules of etiquette are good common sense. If you think something you do might make others uncomfortable, it probably will.

Chapter 3: Driving Sales with Pinterest

In This Chapter

✓ Setting up shop

✓ Selling without annoying others

✓ Providing gift ideas

✓ Being honest about your affiliations

*P*interest offers a unique opportunity for brands to sell their products because not too many social networks allow you to display your products and pricing. Whether your brand is a product or a service, you can use Pinterest boards as catalogs, or gift guides, so that pinners can browse your wares and — we hope — buy. In this chapter, we talk about selling on Pinterest, using the Gifts feature to create sales, and selling ethically and responsibly.

Showing Off Your Wares

With all that said, you might be surprised to find out you can't set up an actual shop on Pinterest. Though it's the perfect social network for displaying your products, you can't use Pinterest as an online store. Pinterest is, first and foremost, a social network. Although many opportunities for sales exist, you can't actually hang an Open for Business banner in your storefront window.

Then how is Pinterest better at driving sales than Facebook or Twitter? There are several reasons:

✦ **Pinterest has a large female base.** Women make the buying decisions in most households.

✦ **Pinterest is a visual site.** Products and services are displayed in an esthetically pleasing manner. Pinners are enticed into buying because of the photos rather than a sales spiel.

✦ **Pinterest offers great product placement opportunities.** Because you're drawing in buyers via images rather than a written sales pitch, you can display your products in ways that best highlight their usefulness.

✦ **Images are shareable.** When pinners like what they see, they repin. Your products have the ability to reach thousands of people. It would cost thousands of dollars to reach so many people with traditional advertising methods.

According to a social shopping survey at www.steelhouse.com, 59 percent of Pinterest users have purchased an item they saw on the site, whereas only 33 percent of Facebook users purchase items they find on brand pages. Moreover, even though Facebook users are more likely to click on product images to learn more about them, the majority of them don't go much further than that. Pinners click and often buy.

Selling without Looking Like You're Selling

Here's the thing about selling on any social network: People get very touchy if they feel they're being pitched too. The majority of folks online are doing their social networking during their downtime as a way to relax. They don't want advertisements and spiels to be front and center. However, that doesn't mean they're not interested in buying. All you have to do is post the content that makes people say, "I want that."

What follows are some tips for selling on Pinterest:

✦ **Use images that paint the product or service in a positive light.** When adding any item directly to Pinterest, or even to a blog, website, sales page, or online catalog, use the best, most enticing shots possible. Remember that people can pin content from your blog and other web pages, so you want all your content to look good! If it's in your budget, consider getting a professional photographer to take the photos — he'll know the best lighting and setups to ensure your products shine.

✦ **Product placement counts for a lot.** Create boards and pins that aren't about selling but have your product in the shot. For example, if your brand sells organic fruit and you create a board with home design ideas, place bowls of fruit in the shot.

✦ **Make it easy for pinners to buy.** If you pin an enticing product, folks need to know where to go to buy it. If you can't lead to a sales page, make sure the page the pin does lead to offer details on where to find the product.

✦ **Create a gift guide.** Pinterest allows pinners to add prices to pins so the product is in the Pinterest Gifts section. We explore Gifts later in this chapter.

✦ **Pin shareable content.** Pin the types of images people like to share. Make sure they're pleasing to the eye and evoke emotion. Look around Pinterest at which pins are the most popular or viral. See whether you can "pin down" the common denominator among the most popular pins.

✦ **Use enticing words and phrases.** Be descriptive without selling. If you're pinning food, use words that make people hungry, such as *succulent* or *mouth-watering.* If you're pinning clothes, use words that make the potential wearer feel as if the style will look good on her, such as *flattering.*

✦ **Don't spam.** If you spam or push sales in a heavy way, you'll gain a bad reputation. Don't tag random people in your pins and say things like, "Hey! Have you checked out our great new thing-a-ma-bob?" The quickest way to lose followers is to be a spammer.

✦ **Share images of influential people using your product.** Do famous people use your product or service? Gather photographs and pin them. Nothing inspires people to buy more than knowing their heroes use a product.

✦ **Make sure pinners know where the original photo came from.** If possible, add the name of your brand to your pin. This way, folks can come to your website or research your brand for more information. Even better, link back to the product page on your website or blog.

Major brands are on Pinterest, and they're selling in a big way. They're able to do so because Pinterest offers a unique opportunity to sell using images instead of words. Most people will agree that marketing lingo and smarmy sales tactics are a turn-off. However, a strong visual can help viewers picture themselves using the product or service.

Pinterest gives you a chance to show, rather than tell. And everyone knows a picture is worth a thousand words.

Using Pricing in Your Images

One thing that sets Pinterest apart from other social networks is the ability to add prices to your pins. If you put a price in the pin's description, that same price appears in the upper-left corner of the pin, as shown in Figure 3-1.

To have a price appear on your pin, type the price in the description with either the dollar sign ($), as shown in Figure 3-2, or a British pound symbol (£). This method doesn't work for other currencies. The beautiful thing about having the price tag is that it's automatically added to the Pinterest Gift section, giving you the ability to reach a broader range of people.

Add a price to make your pin a gift suggestion.

Figure 3-1:
You can add prices to your pins to turn them into gift suggestions.

$16.99 Now on sale at Barnes & Noble.

Deb Ng onto Community Management

Figure 3-2:
After adding a currency symbol, a price appears in the pin's top-left corner.

It's important to note that it takes some time for pins to appear in the Gift section because so many people are adding pins. Also, if you add both the U.S. dollar amount and the U.K. pound amount to your description, the U.K. pound symbol will appear on your pin.

However, this quirk shouldn't stop you from creating your own gift guide, which we discuss further along in this chapter.

Using Your Gifts

When a pinner uses pricing in an image, as described earlier in this chapter, Pinterest collects all the items and places them in its Gifts section. Hover on the Gifts link in the menu bar, and a drop-down menu of specific price ranges appears, as shown in Figure 3-3. You can set any price you want, and your item will appear on that price point's page. To see one page that shows *all* Gifts, click the Gifts link.

Sort gift results by price.

Book VII Chapter 3

Driving Sales with Pinterest

Figure 3-3:
Pinterest categorizes gifts by price.

Price ranges are as follows:

+ $1–$20

+ $20–$50

+ $50–$100

+ $100–$200

+ $200–$500

+ $500+

At first, pinned gifts appear at the top of the Gifts section, but as more gifts are pinned, your pin falls farther down the page. Therefore, the likelihood of your gift being seen in the Gifts section decreases over time. Also, the Gifts section isn't independently searchable. Pinterest users can't, for instance, search for rings that have price tags on them.

Creating Gift Guides

As you can imagine, Gifts is a wonderful opportunity to reach a whole new consumer base. Although there's not much you can do to change the way the Pinterest Gifts section works, you can make it easier for your followers to check out your gifts by making gift guides on specific boards that separate your gift pins into categories. For example, here are just a few possibilities:

+ **Your catch-all gift guide:** Some brands don't sell a wide variety of items. If you sell just one type of thing, you might need only one gift guide for pinning gifts.

+ **Holiday gift guides:** This technique works especially well for brands that have particular holiday significance. For instance, are you marketing floral arrangements? Create separate boards to display Valentine's Day bouquets, Christmas arrangements, Thanksgiving centerpieces, and so on.

+ **Seasonal gift guides:** Create four boards, one for each season, and fill them with appropriate gifts. If you sell fashion wear, for example, you could pin the sundresses on the Summer Gifts board and the sweaters on the Winter Gifts board.

+ **Pricing gift guides:** You can divide your merchandise into your own preferred price ranges. For instance, if you sell children's toys, consider dividing categories by price so Uncle Fred can buy a gift that's in the $5–$10 range, and Grandma and Grandpa can find a deluxe toy in the $50–$100 range.

+ **And more:** You have a lot of options. Check out what other brands are doing for gift guides, particularly brands that you compete with.

Put your gifts into specific gift guide categories that make sense for how your followers want to shop.

We cover planning and creating boards in Chapter 1 of this minibook. The only difference in creating a gift board is that you want to make sure you reflect that in the title of the board — for instance, Easter Basket Gift Guide, Jewelry Gifts for Geeks, or Baby Dresses under $20.

It's not enough to create a gift guide and leave it at that. Find creative ways to promote your guide. For example, advertise it on your blog or website or share it on Twitter and your brand's Facebook Page. Don't wait for people to find it. Also, make sure you promote often enough that it gets fresh views, but not so often that you're spamming.

Disclosing Affiliates

If you're going to be selling on Pinterest as an affiliate for a brand, you have to disclose this information. The Federal Trade Commission (FTC) has strict rules for affiliate sales online, and if you're going to be earning money by selling someone else's products, you have to let people know.

According to the FTC, the following needs to be disclosed:

+ If someone gives you a free product in order for you to review said product, you must disclose.

+ If you receive money every time someone clicks a link, you must disclose.

+ If you write about a product and receive money in return, you must disclose.

+ If you push a product that belongs to someone who advertises on your blog or website, you must disclose.

Now, if you wrote up a product review and you're pinning the review to a Pinterest board, you might want to say in your description that you're reviewing a product. When people click through to the review to learn more about the product, they can read your disclosure there.

However, if you're directly selling a product on Pinterest (for example, as a gift), it's a good idea to let the Pinterest community know you're receiving money in exchange for that product. It's also misleading if you pin an affiliate or sales link without letting others know your intentions.

Some pinners simply type **affiliate link** or **sales page** at the bottom of their description. This satisfies the FTC guidelines and shows that you're honest about your intentions. People who want to find out more will click through.

When it comes to selling online, it's always a good idea to disclose your intentions. It keeps you out of trouble and builds trust between you and your customers and community.

Book VIII

Other Social Media Marketing Sites

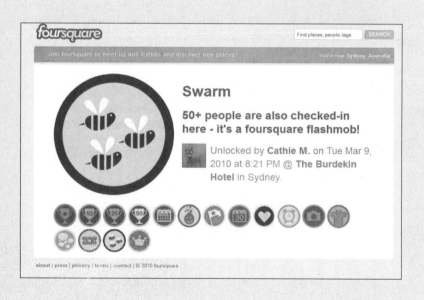

Contents at a Glance

Chapter 1: Weighing the Business Benefits of Minor Social Sites

In This Chapter

✔ Reviewing goals for social media marketing

✔ Conducting social media market research

✔ Assessing audience involvement

✔ Choosing minor social communities strategically

*W*ithout a doubt, Facebook, Twitter, LinkedIn, and Google+ are the elephants in the social marketing zoo, at least in terms of the largest number of visits per month. But this is one big zoo, as shown in Figure 1-1, which displays only 40 of more than 350 social sites. Among these, you'll find lions and tigers and bears, and more than a few turtles, trout, squirrels, and seagulls.

Figure 1-1: The zoo of social media sites is vast. Your time, however, is limited.

It's up to you to assess your business needs, research the options, and select which (if any) of these minor social marketing sites belongs in your personal petting zoo. In this chapter, we look at methods for doing just that.

With the exception of Ning and freestanding blogs (which can become your primary web presence if you use your own domain name), these smaller sites are best used to supplement your other social marketing efforts.

Reviewing Your Goals

In Book I, we suggest that you develop a strategic marketing plan. If you haven't done so yet, there's no time like the present. Otherwise, managing your social networks can quickly spin out of control, especially as you start to add multiple smaller sites for generating or distributing content.

Marketing is marketing, whether offline or online, whether for search engine ranking or social networking. Obviously, your primary business goal is to make a profit. However, your goals for a particular marketing campaign or social media technique may vary.

As we discuss in Book I, social media marketing can serve multiple goals. It can help you

✦ Cast a wide net to catch your target market

✦ Brand

✦ Build relationships

✦ Improve business processes

✦ Improve search engine rankings

✦ Sell when opportunity arises

✦ Save money on advertising

Your challenge is to decide which goal(s) applies to your business and then to quantify objectives for each one. Be sure that you can measure your achievements. You can find additional measurement information in Book IX.

Researching Minor Social Networks

Doing all the necessary research to pick the right mix of social networks may seem overwhelming, but, hey, this is the web — help is at your fingertips. Table 1-1 lists many resource websites with directories of social networking sites, usage statistics, demographic profiles, and valuable tips on how to use different sites. The selection process is straightforward, and the steps are quite similar to constructing a plan for paid online advertising.

Table 1-1	Social Network Research URLs	
Site Name	*URL*	*What It Does*
Alexa	www.alexa.com/siteinfo	Ranks traffic and demographic data by site
Experian Hitwise	www.hitwise.com/us/datacenter/main/dashboard-10133.html	Presents top ten social sites by visits per week
DoubleClick Ad Planner by Google	https://www.google.com/adplanner	Compiles traffic data by site
Google Toolbar	www.google.com/toolbar/ie/index.html	Install Google Toolbar with Google PageRank (not available for all browsers)
Ignite Social Media	www.ignitesocialmedia.com/social-media-stats/2011-social-network-analysis-report	Compiles traffic, demographic data
Mashable	http://mashable.com	Presents social media news, web tips
	http://mashable.com/follow/topics/social-media	Lists stories and resources about social media
	http://mashable.com/category/social-network-lists	Lists stories and resources about social networks
Practical eCommerce	www.practicalecommerce.com/articles/2932-18-Social-Networks-for-Entrepreneurs	Lists 18 social networks for entrepreneurs
Quantcast	www.quantcast.com	Compiles traffic and demographic data by site
SEOmoz	www.seomoz.org/article/social-media-marketing-tactics	Compares 101 business social networks
Social Media Today	http://socialmediatoday.com/amzini/306252/social-networking-growth-stats-and-patterns	Compiles statistical sources

**Book VIII
Chapter 1**

**Weighing the
Business Benefits of
Minor Social Sites**

(continued)

Table 1-1 *(continued)*

Site Name	URL	What It Does
Social Networking Watch	`www.socialnetworking watch.com/all_social_ networking_statistics/ index.html`	Aggregates social net news and stats
Toms Skyline Design	`www.tomsskylinedesign. com/2009/06/expand-your- social-media-vertical- markets`	Lists 17 vertical market sites
Traffikd	`http://traffikd.com/ social-media-websites`	Categorizes over 400 social media sites; regularly updated
Virgin Media	`www.virgin.com/media- and-mobile/news/ top-10-social-media- tools-generation-y`	Ranks top ten Gen-Y social networks
Yahoo! Voices	`http://voices.yahoo. com/top-10-best-senior- social-networking-sites- online-5491465.html`	Ranks ten senior social networks
Wikipedia	`http://en.wikipedia.org/ wiki/List_of_social_ networking_websites`	Provides directory of more than 160 social networking sites

Follow these general steps to get your research under way:

1. **Review the strategy, goals, and target markets for your social marketing campaign, as described in Book I.**

   If your B2B business needs to target particular individuals during the sales cycle, such as a CFO, buyer, or project engineer, be specific in your plan.

2. **Decide how much time (yours, staff, or third parties), and possibly budget, you want to commit to minor social networking sites.**

   Don't underestimate how much time social media marketing can take. After you're comfortable with Facebook and (if it fits) Twitter, it's okay to start with just one or two minor sites and slowly add services over time.

3. **Skim the directories and lists of social media in Table 1-1 to select possibilities that fit your goals.**

For more ideas, simply search using terms for your business area plus the words *social network* or *social media* (for example, *fashion social network*).

4. Review the demographics and traffic for each possibility by using a site such as Alexa, Google's double-click ad planner, or Quantcast as discussed in Book I, Chapter 3. Cull your list to keep only those that "fit."

Figure 1-2 displays the relative market share, according to StatCounter Global Stats (`http://gs.statcounter.com/#social_media-US-monthly-201201-201202-bar`), for the seven top-ranked social media services in the United States from January 2012 to February 2012. Market share is ranked not by traffic to the sites themselves but, rather, by "the amount of traffic they refer to other sites." This approach may be valuable for business analysis because it discounts personal users who stay on social media sites to communicate with their friends. The Other category encompasses sites such as Flickr, LinkedIn, Delicious, and Google+.

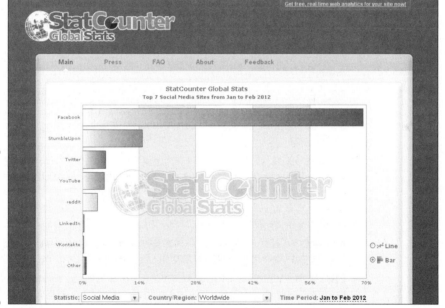

Figure 1-2: Factor in relative market share, using data such as that from StatCounter Global Stats.

Source: StatCounter Global Stats; http://gs.statcounter.com

5. Review each network (see suggestions in the following bullet list) to make sure you feel comfortable with its web presence, user interaction, Google PageRank, features, ease of use, and ability to provide key reports. Prioritize your sites accordingly.

6. **Enter your final selection in your Social Media Marketing Plan (described in Book I, Chapter 3) and set up a schedule for implementation and monitoring on your Social Media Activity Calendar (see Book I, Chapter 4).**

7. **Implement your plan. Modify it as needed after results come in.**

   Wait at least a month before you make changes; gaining visibility within some social network sites can take time.

For leads to other social networks that appeal to your audience, look for a section named Other Sites Visited (or similar wording) on one of the statistical sites.

Keep in mind these words of caution as you review statistics in Steps 3 and 4 for various minor social networks:

✦ **Not all directories or reports on market share define the universe of social media or social networks the same way.** Some include blogs, social bookmarking sites such as Delicious, or news aggregators. Small social networks may come and go so quickly that the universe is different even a few months later.

✦ **Confirm whether you're looking at global or U.S. data.** What you need depends on the submarkets you're trying to reach.

✦ **Determine whether the site displays data for unique visitors or visits.** A unique visitor may make multiple visits during the evaluation period. Results for market share vary significantly depending on what's being measured.

✦ **Repeat visits, pages per view, time on site, and number of visits per day or per visitor all reflect user engagement with the site.** Not all services provide this data, whose importance depends on your business goals.

✦ **Decide whether you're interested in a site's casual visitors or registered members.** Your implementation and message will vary according to the audience you're trying to reach.

✦ **Check the window of measurement (day, week, or month or longer) and the effective dates for the results.** These numbers are volatile, so be sure you're looking at current data.

Regarding social media or everything else, consider online statistics for relative value and trends, not for absolute numbers. Because every statistical service defines its terms and measurements differently, stick with one source to make the results comparable across all your possibilities.

Assessing the Involvement of Your Target Audience

After you finish the research process, you should have a good theoretical model of which minor social networks might be a good fit for your business. But there's nothing like being involved. Step 5 in the earlier section "Researching Minor Social Networks" includes visiting every site to assess a number of criteria, including user interaction. If you plan to engage your audience in comments, reviews, forums, or other user-generated content, you *must* understand how active participants on the network now interact.

Start by signing up and creating a personal profile of some sort so that you can access all member-related activities. The actual activities, of course, depend on the particular network.

Lurking

Spend time watching and reading what transpires in every interactive venue on the site, without participating. In the "olden days" of Internet forums and chat rooms, you were *lurking*. You make a number of qualitative assessments that will help you determine whether this site is a good fit for you:

✦ **Quality of dialog:** Do statements of any sort float in the ether, or does interaction take place? Does a moderator respond? The site owners? Other registered members? Is there one response, or continual back and forth? If you intend to establish an ongoing business relationship with other participants on the network, you want to select a site where ongoing dialog is already standard practice.

✦ **Quality of posts:** Are posts respectful or hostile? Do posts appear automatically, or is someone reviewing them before publication? Do they appear authentic? Because you're conducting business online, your standards may need to be higher than they would be for casual, personal interaction. Anger and profanity that might be acceptable from respondents on a political news site would be totally unacceptable on a site that engages biologists in discussion of an experiment.

✦ **Quantity of posts compared to the number of registered users:** On some sites, you may find that the same 20 people post or respond to everything, even though the site boasts 10,000 registered members. This situation signals a site that isn't successful as a social network, however successful it might be in other ways.

Responding

After you have a sense of the ethos of a site, try responding to a blog post, participating in a forum, or establishing yourself as an expert on a product review or e-zine listing. Assess what happens. Do others respond on the network? E-mail you offsite? Call the office?

Use this side of the lurk-and-response routine to gain a better understanding of what you, as a member and prospective customer, would expect. Will you or your staff be able to deliver?

If a site requires more care and feeding than you have the staff to support, consider dropping it from your list.

Quantifying market presence

In addition to assessing the number of unique visitors, visits, and registered members, you may want to assess additional components of audience engagement. Sites that provide quantitative information, such as Quantcast, help you better understand your audience's behavior, learn more about their lifestyle and brand preferences, and target your message. You can learn about these concepts:

✦ **Affinity:** A statistical correlation that shows the strength of a particular user behavior, such as visiting another site, relative to that of the U.S. Internet population as a whole — for instance, whether a Flickr user is more or less likely than the general Internet population to visit YouTube

✦ **Index:** The delivery of a specific audience segment, such as women or seniors, compared with their share of the overall Internet population

✦ **Composition:** The relative distribution of the audience for a site by audience segment, such as gender, age, or ethnicity

✦ **Addict:** The most loyal component of a site's audience, with 30 or more visits per month

✦ **Passer-by:** Casual visitor who visits a site only once per month

✦ **Regular:** A user partway between Addict and Passer-by; someone who visits more than once but fewer than 30 times per month

Choosing Social Sites Strategically

It may seem ridiculously time-consuming to select which minor social marketing sites are best for your business. Why not just throw a virtual dart at a list or choose randomly from social sites that your staff likes to visit? Ultimately, you save more time by planning and making strategic choices than by investing time in a social media site that doesn't pay off.

If you're short of time, select sites that meet your demographics requirement but on which you can easily reuse and syndicate content as described in Book II, Chapter 1. You can replicate blog postings, for instance, almost instantly on multiple sites.

If you truly have no time to select one of these sleek minor "critters," stick to one of the elephants and add others later.

MilkMade Ice Cream, shown in Figure 1-3 and described in the nearby sidebar, uses several social media channels to achieve its marketing goals.

Figure 1-3: MilkMade IceCream.com generates traffic to its website from a variety of social media that in turn lead back to the website.

Courtesy MilkMade Ice Cream

**Book VIII
Chapter 1**

Weighing the
Business Benefits of
Minor Social Sites

Even the smallest social network sites can be valuable if they have your target market. All the averages mean nothing. It's about *your* business and *your* audience. Niche marketing is always the effective use of your time. Fish where *your* fish are!

Milking social media for marketing gold

MilkMade Ice Cream is a craft ice cream company in New York City. Founded by owner Diana Hardeman in fall 2009 from her own desire for "a better pint," MilkMade hand-crafts and delivers two unique flavors of ice cream to members of its ice cream of the month club. It plans to soon begin shipping its artisanal pints to ice cream enthusiasts nationwide.

In spite of her own business background, Hardeman did not originally conceive MilkMade as a profit-making business. She's a bit bemused by MilkMade's success. "We accidentally received some press after serving 'scream' at a friend's party and found ourselves with hundreds of e-mails," she explains. Hardeman quickly set up a website (www.milkmadeicecream.com, Tumblr blog (http://blog.milkmadeicecream.com), and other social media outlets to communicate with members, waiting lists, friends, and anyone generally interested in following her progress.

She added Twitter, a Facebook group, Flickr to store photos, and Vimeo for videos, and later incorporated Instagram and Pinterest. "Setting up these accounts is simple," Hardeman notes, but "remembering and finding the time to maintain them regularly is a bit more difficult with our small team."

MilkMade doesn't actually target any market segment. "We make unique ice cream flavors that we think are delicious, with real, local ingredients, and use social media to share the process."

Their Tumblr blog remains MilkMade's most effective social media outlet. "We're shooting for 100,000 followers by summer 2012. Turns out, people love photos of ice cream! Since we gained popularity on Tumblr with our 'flavor of the day' photos, we've tried to keep that up as much as possible, with themes of the week."

MilkMade tweets as much as time allows, but constrains Facebook to one post a day to avoid offending fans. "Social media has definitely helped us gain new members," says Hardeman. "Luckily, our members often tweet how much they love the 'scream each month, serving as our word of mouth spokesmen."

To track success, they use Google Analytics and glance at intermediate performance measures (likes, retweets, repins), to see what interests people most.

Pinterest is MilkMade's latest social channel. They've opened eight boards. Consistent with Pinterest protocol, some boards are about their own "scream," and some about other ice cream shops around the country, their suppliers, and even about New York City. To gain more traffic from Pinterest, they plan to link it to their other social channels and add it to the social media buttons on their homepage.

Courtesy MilkMade Ice Cream

The company has been fortunate to have received a great deal of press, much of it online with a link to their website.

Hardeman remains enthusiastic about social media. "My best advice when using social media is to keep it real. Know the message and tone you want to convey to the world [and] make sure it's aligned with your brand. Put content out there that you love, and likely others will love it too."

MilkMade's web presence

www.milkmadeicecream.com

http://blog.milkmadeicecream.com

http://blog.milkmadeicecream.com/rss (RSS)

www.flickr.com/photos/42607293@N07

https://www.facebook.com/pages/MILKMADE-Ice-Cream/141607032309

http://pinterest.com/milkmadescream

https://twitter.com/#!/milkmadescream

http://web.stagram.com/n/milkmadescream

http://vimeo.com/user2627687

Chapter 2: Linking Up for B2B Success

In This Chapter

✔ Deciding whether LinkedIn is right for your business

✔ Putting the basics in place

✔ Making the most of LinkedIn features

✔ Advertising on LinkedIn

Social media marketing is, first and foremost, a method of networking online. From your own experience, you already know the importance of offline networking to find vendors, employees, and prospects; to learn about industry trends; and to hear the latest insider gossip. From tip networks to trade associations and chambers of commerce, networking is a mantra for business owners.

LinkedIn (www.linkedin.com) turns that offline mantra into a cybershout. LinkedIn, which successfully went public in spring 2011, has morphed into the primary professional networking site on the web. With 161 million members worldwide (62.8 million in the United States), LinkedIn claims (http://press.linkedin.com/about) that more than two users join every *second*.

More than 2 million businesses have created LinkedIn company pages; 1.3 million of those are small companies. In this chapter, we discuss why your business might very well want to be one of them, especially if you are a business-to-business (B2B) firm. We also discuss ways to get the most out of your LinkedIn presence.

For more information about LinkedIn, see *LinkedIn For Dummies,* 2nd Edition, by Joel Elad.

If you include LinkedIn as part of your social media activities, include it in your Social Media Marketing Plan, which you can find in Book I, Chapter 1 and at www.dummies.com/go/socialmediamarketingaio2e.

Deciding whether LinkedIn Is a Good Fit

Whether you're a business-to-consumer (B2C) firm or you sell to and buy from only other companies, you should know how LinkedIn can help your social media marketing efforts.

LinkedIn is used primarily for

+ Finding prospective clients and strategic partners
+ Locating and evaluating suppliers
+ Introducing dealmakers
+ Hiring people or searching for jobs
+ Establishing professional credibility
+ Improving service to existing customers
+ Enhancing your brand

Although LinkedIn is a great way to find *tips* (sales leads), it's not appropriate for direct sales. You can easily cross-promote between your website and LinkedIn, however.

Because you can receive 90 percent of the value of LinkedIn by using its free version, joining is a no-brainer. The three premium options may make sense for executive recruiters, human resources departments, purchasing agents, and individuals conducting an intensive job search.

Understanding user demographics

The demographic profile of LinkedIn users (see Figure 2-2) differs from users on other networking sites. LinkedIn users are slightly more likely to be male, older, Asian, more affluent, and better educated than Internet users in general.

For current demographics, see www.quantcast.com/linkedin.com/demographics#demo. The Quantcast statistics shown in Figure 2-1 have been *quantified* with directly measured data rather than estimates.

Forging connections

Relying on the theory of *six degrees of separation* (everyone is connected by a chain of no more than five others), LinkedIn helps you build a network of contacts online. You start with the people you already know, your *first-degree* connections. The people they're connected with are *second-degree* connections, and the people connected to them are *third-degree* connections.

Courtesy Quantcast.com

Figure 2-1:
The demo-graphics of LinkedIn users in April 2012.

When your first-degree connections introduce you to one of their contacts, you can ask their contacts to join your network. That's how your LinkedIn garden grows.

See helpful descriptions of the potential reach of your network by choosing Contacts⇨Network Statistics (www.linkedin.com/network).

Like other social networking sites, LinkedIn offers the opportunity to enter or import e-mail addresses so that you can invite people on your mailing list to connect with you on LinkedIn. Simply choose Contacts⇨Add Connections from the main menu drop-down or navigate to www.linkedin.com/fetch/importAndInvite.

After your network gets started, you will receive invitations to connect with other people you may or may not know. LinkedIn also suggests the names of people who know your direct connections (second-degree connections) that you may want to invite to connect with you. Accept invites from people you know or second-degree connections that you want to know. You *don't* need to accept every invitation you receive.

LinkedIn frowns on sending an invite to people you don't have a connection in common with. Be sure that you have someone in common before issuing an invitation.

Implementing LinkedIn Basics

Joining LinkedIn is simple: You set up a simple account with an e-mail username and password. Then complete your personal profile, which is sort of an online résumé (such as the one shown in Figure 2-2), followed with your company profile (shown in Figure 2-3).

Figure 2-2: A personal profile is often enough for freelancers and one-person professional companies, as well as for employees.

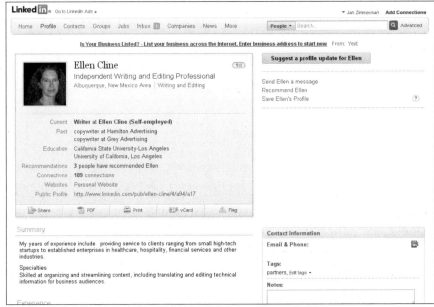

Courtesy Ellen Cline; www.ellenwrites.com

LinkedIn is well designed, with obvious prompts and a straightforward, step-by-step structure. Click the See Examples link on various fields for additional explanations and tips. Because LinkedIn is always evolving, options and directions may change at any time. LinkedIn is good about notifying members of changes, though.

Options for getting the most out of LinkedIn

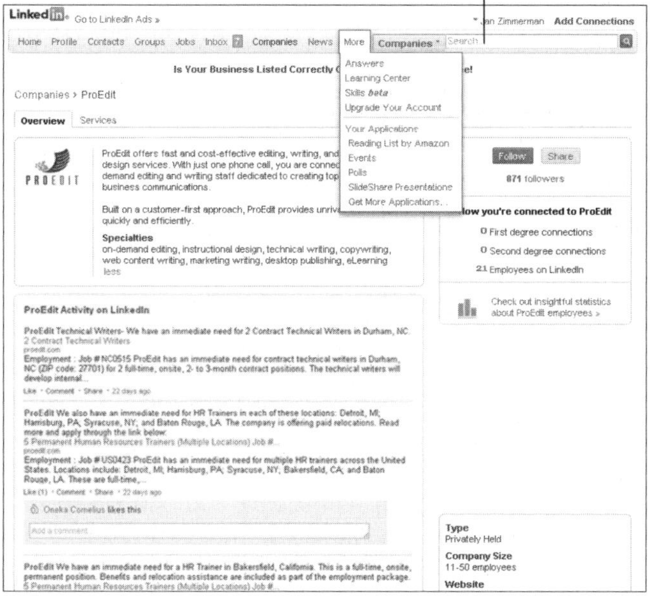

Figure 2-3:
ProEdit's
company
profile page.

Courtesy ProEdit, Inc.

If you have a business of any kind, but especially if you sell to or buy from other companies (that's just about everyone), establish a LinkedIn profile for your company and have each of your employees establish personal profiles, too.

Company profiles are visible to both members and nonmembers; LinkedIn members also see connections with staff and additional information.

You can search by people, jobs, companies, or groups under the drop-down menu next to the search box in the LinkedIn navigation bar. Take advantage of the Advanced Search link to filter results, too.

Write compelling and interesting profiles! Use descriptive words that point out your achievements rather than just list employers' names and job titles. You can include a creative, short narrative or story in the summary and write a headline with a benefit, such as *creative problem solver* or *zero defect addict.*

**Book VIII
Chapter 2**

Linking Up for B2B
Success

Optimizing your company profile

Adding a company profile is straightforward. After creating your personal profile, follow these steps:

1. **Log in and go to Home.**

2. **Click the Companies link on the menu at the top of the page.**

3. **In the upper-right area of the page, below the Search box, click the Add a Company link.**

4. **Enter your company name and your work e-mail address, verify that you're authorized to create the page, and then click Continue.**

   For more information, go to `http://help.linkedin.com/app/answers/detail/a_id/710`.

5. **Enter your company information and the click the Publish button (upper right).**

   You can have as many as three links on your profile; these links pass "link juice" (share their page rank with your site). Set one to your website, another to your blog, and a third to another component of your social media presence.

   For more information, see `http://marketing.linkedin.com/companypages`.

Look at the profiles of other companies in your industry to form an idea of what to include in your profile.

You can edit your company profile at any time. View your profile on the Companies tab. Click the Admin Tools link on the right and then select Edit. The screen that appears offers several valuable options:

+ **A customized link for your website:** Follow your company on LinkedIn. The link is hidden in the lower-right corner; you need to scroll down to see it.

+ **The Analytics tab:** Check out page views, clicks, and unique visitors for your company profile.

+ **The Careers tab:** Post job openings. You can choose whether to select one of the Premium options.

+ **The Products & Services tab:** Add multiple, detailed LinkedIn pages with additional links to your website.

✦ **The Share an Update field:** This option allows you to insert a message of up to 700 characters for distribution to your contacts and followers. To be efficient for space, use a link shortener like bit.ly (see Book II, Chapter 1) to include a link in your message. You can see updates from your network, and they can see yours, directly below the company overview (refer to Figure 2-1).

Try to post information at least once a week about new contracts, services, achievements, or trade shows that you'll be attending.

You can choose to cross-post (that is, simultaneously post on Twitter) the first 140 characters of updates created from your personal profile to Twitter; however, updates from your company profile cannot be "co-tweeted" at this time.

As you add information to your profile, a percentage of completion appears on the right side of your profile, along with a progress bar. As you add more information to your profile, it becomes an increasingly effective marketing tool.

Optimizing LinkedIn for search engines

As described in Book II, Chapter 2, start by including search terms within your profile text, within descriptions of any groups you start, and within postings. Just keep the terms gentle and unobtrusive. As always, include your standard page description metatag in the first paragraph of text on your profile.

Update your profile frequently. Every time you update content with events, products, or other activities, LinkedIn crawls your page and sends updates to search engines.

LinkedIn also sends out a weekly opt-in "update" e-mail notifying subscribers of your changes and changes made by your connections.

Garnering recommendations

LinkedIn suggests using recommendations for your products and services to "find new opportunities and reinforce your professional identity online." LinkedIn claims that "users with recommendations are three times as likely to get inquiries through LinkedIn searches." Now is the time to call in favors from your friends, colleagues, satisfied clients, and compatriots. You can review any recommendations you receive, so you can always decide whether to publish them.

People may use the Advanced Search feature to sort results by *relationship + recommendations,* so that profiles with the highest number of recommendations appear higher in search results. That's one of the reasons that garnering recommendations is so important.

Getting recommendations is a two-step process: asking and accepting.

Asking for recommendations

To get recommended, follow these steps:

1. **Log in to LinkedIn and then choose Recommendations from the Profile drop-down menu at the top.**

2. **Click Ask to Be Endorsed or select the Request Recommendations tab that appears.**

   Now is your chance to contact the people you've worked with and ask them to toot your horn. Fill out the form that appears.

3. **Fill in a name in the Your Connections text box and then click Finish.**

   Alternatively, you can click the LinkedIn icon to the right of the field, add as many connections as you need, and then click Finish.

4. **Accept or modify the default message and click Send.**

Accepting recommendations

Recommendations don't automatically show up on your profile. You have to accept them first, which gives you some control. When a contact sends you a recommendation, you're notified by e-mail. Click the button at the bottom of the message to display it. Then decide whether you want to accept or decline the recommendation.

If you receive a lukewarm recommendation, ask your contact to rephrase it. Or simply say thanks, ignore the recommendation, and publish another.

Using LinkedIn applications

LinkedIn applications offer options to create polls, add a reading list to your profile, create a link to your blog, and much more. Some applications require a fee and are created by third parties. From the More drop-down menu in the top navigation, select your desired application or select Get More Applications. Some of the more useful applications include

✦ **Polls:** Respond to posted polls in your field, or create your own poll to increase user interest.

✦ **Events:** Review events posted by others in your network or create ones of your own.

✦ **Blog Link:** Enhance your profile by automatically posting the latest news from your blog.

✦ **Slideshare:** Post slideshows about your services or products or presentations from professional conferences or tradeshows.

Following companies

You can easily identify companies to follow to keep up to date on their latest developments and industry news. Simply select Search Companies from the search box drop-down list. Then refine your selection by location, job opportunities, industry type, relationship, and other characteristics.

As you review the results, click the Follow Company link for competitors, prospects, industry leaders, and other companies of interest.

The entire LinkedIn member directory is available in alphabetical order for both individuals and companies.

When you follow a company, you're notified by e-mail when an event of your choice happens. You can choose Notification Settings that will trigger the timing of notifications from LinkedIn.

Exchanging network messages

You may receive messages from your contacts in a process is similar to e-mail, but within the LinkedIn network.

The tabs you see in your Inbox depend on your recent activity. For instance, you may see tabs for pending introductions, messages, introductions, questions and answers, and other topics.

Check LinkedIn daily for activity and respond within one business day, just as you would for any other form of communication.

Getting the Most from LinkedIn

Because you're competing for visibility against millions of other individuals and companies, you need to undertake some targeted activities to reach the people you want to reach. You have several alternatives for extending your presence: joining groups, reading *LinkedIn Today,* responding to Answers, and promoting your LinkedIn presence. For more information on LinkedIn options, visit the URLs in Table 2-1.

Table 2-1	Helpful LinkedIn URLs
To Find Out How to Do This	*See This URL*
Add a company page and read detailed information on setup	`www.linkedin.com/company/add/show`
	`http://marketing.linkedin.com/overviewtab`
	`http://learn.linkedin.com/company-pages/#how`
Advertise on LinkedIn	`http://partner.linkedin.com/ads/faqs`
	`www.linkedin.com/advertising`
	`http://partner.linkedin.com/ads/bestpractices/index.html`
	`http://partner.linkedin.com/ads/bestpractices/track.html`
	`http://marketing.linkedin.com/displayads`
Ask and answer questions to establish expertise	`www.linkedin.com/answers`
Participate in groups	`http://marketing.linkedin.com/customgroups`
Use the LinkedIn blog	`http://blog.linkedin.com`
Benefit from LinkedIn productivity tools	`www.linkedin.com/static?key=tools&trk=hb_ft_tools`
Read *LinkedIn Today* news	`www.linkedin.com/today`
Manage recommendations	`www.linkedin.com/references`

Participating in LinkedIn groups

LinkedIn groups, like Facebook groups (see Book V) and Twitter hashtags (see Book IV), give you the chance to identify users who share your interests and who might become potential clients, vendors, or helpful connections. The key, as always, is to monitor potential groups and then to offer helpful suggestions and comments, without overtly selling your products or services. Standard forum etiquette applies! To view potential groups, use the drop-down menu under the Groups tab in the top navigation.

Joining a group is easy. Here's the process.

1. **Log in to LinkedIn and then choose Groups Directory from the Groups drop-down menu.**

2. **In the Search Groups directory, enter some keywords in the text field.**

3. **Choose an option from the Categories drop-down list and click Search.**

   For example, you can choose from alumni, corporate, conference, or networking groups.

4. **Scroll through the group descriptions.**

   When you see a group you want to join, click the Join This Group link. A green box appears at the top, confirming you have joined the group and allowing you to change and save your group settings.

Many LinkedIn groups require membership approval from the group owner. To send the group owner a message explaining why you feel you would be an asset to the group, click the link that appears beneath the group in your My Groups section.

For most people, membership in three to five groups is plenty. As always, lurk (observe) for a while to decide whether the group really is a good fit for your business interests.

Another option is to create your own LinkedIn group. Creating a group, recruiting members, promoting the group, and moderating discussions can become very time-consuming, though.

Reading LinkedIn Today

Found on the drop-down menu under the News tab, *LinkedIn Today* aggregates business news from dozens of prime sources. You can customize your news selection by publication or industry, or both, by electing to follow various options in the Browse All section on the top menu. Early anecdotal evidence from LinkedIn members indicates that both profile views and referral links have increased since LinkedIn Today was introduced. To see how one company leveraged its LinkedIn presence for success, read the nearby sidebar and study their LinkedIn profile in Figure 2-4.

Book VIII
Chapter 2

Linking Up for B2B Success

Products tab

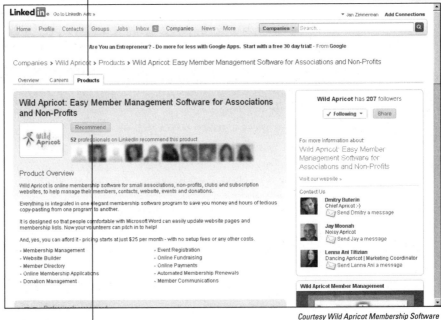

Figure 2-4:
Wild Apricot
features
recommend-
ations from
LinkedIn
users on the
Product tab
of its profile.

Courtesy Wild Apricot Membership Software

Recommend button

Wild Apricot links up with product reviews

Since 2006, Wild Apricot has offered membership software for local associations, nonprofits, and clubs. It currently has approximately 5,000 paid customers, with several thousand more using its free version.

Users of Wild Apricot software are usually either volunteers or part of a very small paid staff, says Jay Moonah, vice president of marketing. Most of their customers are older than 25, with a slight majority of women.

Wild Apricot set up its company page on LinkedIn as soon as the feature was offered. Recognizing the value of the LinkedIn user base, it quickly adopted an unusual strategy. "Our primary use of LinkedIn is to generate and leverage product reviews. We're lucky enough to have customers who regularly contact us with compliments about our software. When they do, we ask them to post a review on our LinkedIn page. We also feature some of these reviews directly on our own homepage, and visitors can click to LinkedIn to see further reviews," explains Moonah.

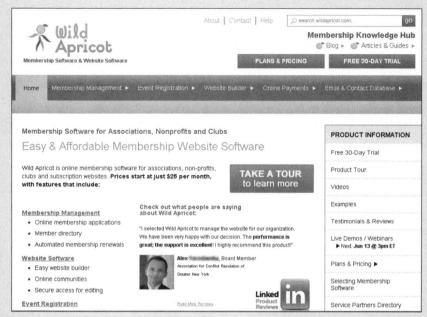

Courtesy Wild Apricot Membership Software

"Through testing, we've found that featuring [LinkedIn] reviews on our home page increases the likelihood of website visitors signing up for a free trial. We believe the LinkedIn reviews give them a sense that real people like them are using the product, and this gives them confidence about trying it for themselves."

Moonah measures sign-ups for free trials as a metric for success. "We specifically measured an increase in sign-ups when we featured the LinkedIn reviews on our homepage. For us, it's really all about having a reputable third-party place where people can see those reviews.

"We have a page dedicated to this at `www.wildapricot.com/membership-software-recommendation`. We direct users there in our e-mail communications, particularly if they contact us with compliments.

"For us, the biggest opportunity has to be leveraging the perception of LinkedIn as a trusted resource. Unlike the reviews and endorsements we post on our own site, I believe posts on LinkedIn and other social media sites are more trusted by many potential customers as they are seen as being more 'real' than the hand-picked and edited testimonials companies usually publish. It's that kind of social validation we find valuable. I believe many businesses could take advantage of this, assuming they have a good service and good reviews to highlight," Moonah adds.

(continued)

(continued)

Wild Apricot's web presence

```
www.wildapricot.com
www.linkedin.com/company/wild-apricot
www.facebook.com/wildapricot
www.wildapricot.com/blogs/newsblog
www.youtube.com/user/wildapricotcom
https://twitter.com/#!/WildApricot
https://plus.google.com/113345547999145227568
```

Gaining expertise with LinkedIn Answers

LinkedIn Answers is where you gain and share business knowledge with other LinkedIn users. You can even achieve expert status by providing the most insightful responses. To find LinkedIn Answers, click the More tab in the top navigation bar and then select Answers from the drop-down menu. (Refer to Figure 2-1.)

Asking questions

There can be strategic reasons to ask a question, as well as to answer one. If you are seeking a vendor or strategic partner, your question can become a quick qualifying filter. Or perhaps you are trying to evaluate various products or techniques, such as which social media service to select. Asking a question is a good way to solicit input from other businesses.

 Before you ask a question, search for similar questions that have already been asked. Click the Advanced Answers Search tab on the Answers page. On this tab, enter keywords and choose a category in which to search. You can also choose to show only unanswered questions. And sometimes it's worth exploring the Closed Questions tab to find answers to previously answered questions.

When you're ready to ask a question:

1. **Click the Ask a Question tab and enter your question in the box.**

   Keep your question short and specific.

2. **Select categories and subcategories for your inquiry.**

3. Select the connections you want to send the question to.

The form defaults to public sharing, but you can select only the connections you think are most likely to have the answer.

4. Click Finished and then click Send.

After your question is answered, you can close the question by choosing Answers from the More drop-down menu. Then click My Q&A, select the completed question, and click the Close button.

Answering questions

When someone asks a public question, all the asker's connections receive an update with the question. If the question is private, specific connections receive a private message.

You receive questions from your first-degree contacts directly. You should always respond to questions sent by your first-degree contacts; if you don't know the answer, thank the person for asking you the question, and offer to ask other colleagues to see if they can help.

To answer other questions:

1. Log in to LinkedIn, choose Answers from the More drop-down menu, and then click the Answer Questions tab.

The Browse Open Questions page appears. The answers are sorted by degree, with questions from your second-degree contacts appearing first.

2. Browse the questions.

Unfortunately, you have no easy way to search them, so you have to do it the old-fashioned way — question-by-question, page-by-page. Alternatively, you can narrow the focus of the questions to which you browse by clicking a link in the Browse section.

3. When you find a question you want to answer, click it.

In addition to seeing the question and detailed information, you see answers that have already been posted.

4. Click the Answer button, and type your response in the Answer field, adding any web resources that might be helpful.

5. Answer the question and add any web resources.

These resources can be web pages or blog posts. If they're your web pages or your blog posts, you've just directed more traffic to your site.

6. **(Optional) Click the Suggest Experts button.**

   If you don't have the answer, you can choose as many as three connections who might have expert knowledge regarding the question.

7. **Accept the default option to write a note with your answer.**

   This is a useful way to introduce yourself to the person asking the question.

8. **Click Submit.**

   Your answer is sent to the person who made the query and is added as an answer to the original question. Your answer appears in the asker's LinkedIn inbox and is sent to the associated e-mail address.

Answering questions makes you a "good LinkedIn citizen," while demonstrating your knowledge to potential customers. Also, you can invite viewers to visit your site or blog for additional information or to e-mail you for a more customized response.

Becoming an expert

One of the best ways to develop visibility on LinkedIn is to become an "expert" within LinkedIn Answers. When a LinkedIn user asks a question, the colleague can choose which answer is the "best." If your answer is selected as the best response, you gain a "point of expertise" in the category for that question. The more expertise points you have, the higher you rank. Keep in mind that you only receive points for publicly answered questions, though.

Click the Experts link under the Answers tab, below the new questions, to see a list of LinkedIn experts, categorized as Experts This Week or Experts All Time.

Promoting your LinkedIn presence

As always, cross-link between your website, other social media sites, and LinkedIn. Sign in and then visit these links to obtain code for buttons and widgets that you or your developer can install:

✦ **Share button for your web page:** The graphic link at `www.linkedin.com/publishers` makes it easy for viewers to share your website with their LinkedIn contacts.

✦ **Share button for browsers:** To share web pages and content with your LinkedIn connections when you're surfing the Web, head to `www.linkedin.com/static?key=browser_bookmarklet`.

✦ **Chicklets (graphic links to your own LinkedIn page): To add a link to your profile, group, or company page, grab a logo at** `http://developer.linkedin.com/documents/branding-guidelines#general-use`. You can even include your own call to action, preferably in black text next to the logo.

Networking with other business sites

LinkedIn isn't the only business social network. For the names of others that reach a more specific market, review the list of Business Networks in Book VIII, Chapter 3.

Focus on no more than one or two other networking sites that are specific to your industry, job function, or marketing goal, such as raising venture capital. Be sure to allow two hours per week on your Social Media Activity Calendar (see Book I, Chapter 2) for activities in this channel.

Advertising on LinkedIn

With its capability to segment a hard-to-reach B2B audience by industry, job title, and other categories, LinkedIn can deliver "eyeballs" that may be more difficult or expensive to achieve by using other paid advertising. For more information on LinkedIn advertising, see `www.linkedin.com/advertising` or `http://partner.linkedin.com/ads/faqs`.

A standard pay per click ad combines a small image with text in the rectangular ad unit in the right column of a page. These self-service ads offer a choice between PPC (pay per click) pricing with minimums of $2/click and $10/day or impression-based (CPM) pricing. The campaign structure is comparable with Google AdWords or Bing/Yahoo!.

To see examples of the block of ads on the right, refer to Figure 2-1. LinkedIn may choose to display a single line of text from a specific ad at the top of the page (refer to Figure 2-3). This is not space that you can purchase; selection is up to LinkedIn.

LinkedIn also offers *display* (banner) ads on specific pages. You must negotiate display ad costs separately with LinkedIn; display budgets start at $25,000 per month.

Setting up your LinkedIn advertising account

You can run ads from a personal account, but you'll probably want to use your business account because it can have multiple users. The steps are simple.

1. **Sign into your business account and click Go to LinkedIn Ads in the upper-left corner.**

2. **Click the New Ad Campaign link in the upper right.**

3. **Follow the steps on the screen to create an ad and upload a small (50 x 50 pixel) graphic.**

   LinkedIn requires a `.png`, `.jpeg`, or `.gif` file of no more than 2MB. LinkedIn will automatically resize images if the dimensions are too large, but you'll be happier with the quality if you upload a high-resolution image of the correct dimensions to start with.

4. **Insert the link to your landing page, enter a 25-character headline, and then ad text of up to 75 characters.**

   LinkedIn reviews ads before publishing them, which usually takes a day or less. If you have asked for notification in your Settings, you will receive a "canned" explanation of approval or disapproval. You can appeal a rejection, but there are no limits on how many times you can revise an ad.

5. **Create up to 15 variations of your ad for each campaign.**

   As with classifieds or other pay-per-click ads, you may want to test different headlines, benefits, and landing pages to determine your most effective ads.

   Use the Edit or Duplicate function on an individual ad to make this task easier.

6. **Click Next Step to set your geographic area and select options to define your target audience.**

   In the upper-right corner, LinkedIn estimates the size of your target audience as you change parameters for industry, job title, age, and gender. Generally, select the options to reach LinkedIn members on other websites, to collect leads, and to rotate ads. To reach a target audience with different characteristics, you'll need to set up a separate campaign. There are no limits on how many campaigns you can have.

7. **Set Your Budget.**

   Most companies select PPC rather than CPM (cost per thousand impressions) because it's more cost-effective. You can modify this at any time.

Interpreting your advertising results

PPC ads on LinkedIn don't usually perform as well in terms of click-through rate (CTR) as they do on Google, Yahoo!, or even Facebook, as shown in Table 2-2. The CTR partly depends on the size of the geographic range and the other selections (such as company characteristics and job titles) you make.

With LinkedIn's comparatively small audience, you might find that you need to enlarge the parameters for your target audience to get a reasonable response.

Table 2-2	Average CTR for PPC ads
Publisher	*Average CTR Q4 2011*
LinkedIn	0.025%
Facebook	0.051%
Google	2.36%
Yahoo!/Bing	1.61%
Banner ad	0.09%

LinkedIn provides advertising statistics for your campaigns, as shown in Figure 2-5.

Figure 2-5: LinkedIn provides easily accessible advertising results.

Courtesy Saybrook University, San Francisco, CA; www.saybrook.edu

Chapter 3: Maximizing Stratified Social Communities

In This Chapter

✔ **Valuing stratified social communities**

✔ **Making business connections online**

✔ **Searching for options by industry**

✔ **Searching for options by target market**

✔ **Searching for options by type of activity**

Social networking communities, like other marketing outlets, can be sliced and diced many ways. They can be sorted vertically by industry or horizontally by demographics, such as age, gender, ethnicity, education, or income. By doing a little research, you can *stratify* (classify) them according to other commonly used marketing segmentation parameters, such as geographical location, life stage (student, young married, family with kids, empty nester, retired), or *psychographics* (beliefs or behaviors).

In this chapter, we discuss how you can find these smaller, niche sites and then how you can get value from them.

Becoming a Big Fish in a Small Pond

Stratified sites may have much smaller audiences than sites such as Pinterest or Twitter. However, if you choose correctly, the users of these sites will closely resemble the profile of your typical client or customer, making them better prospects. Compare it to the difference between advertising at the Super Bowl versus distributing a flyer at a local high school football game. It all depends on where your audience is.

Your business can also make a much bigger splash on smaller sites. Frankly, it's so difficult to gain visibility and traction on a large social networking site that you almost need a marketing campaign just for that purpose (for instance, to acquire 2,000 Likes on Facebook).

On a smaller site, your business becomes a big fish in a small pond, quickly establishing itself as an expert resource or a source of great products or services.

The use of social media by business — blogs, social networks, social bookmarks, and news aggregators — is already in transition from trial stage to strategic implementation, even for small businesses.

This statement is confirmed by spending patterns: A 2012 survey conducted by Duke University's Furke School of Business found that businesses already spend 7.4 percent of their marketing budgets on social media marketing, with that figure predicted to grow to 10.8 percent in the next 12 months and to 19.5 percent in the next five years. To maintain your market share, you need to decide how you will communicate just as effectively across numerous platforms. Fortunately, all it takes is time.

Taking Networking to the Next Level

From your own experience, you know the importance of offline networking to find vendors, employees, and customers. From tip networks to trade associations, networking is a mantra for business owners. Social media marketing is, first and foremost, a method of networking online.

Business connection sites have proliferated in the past several years. These sites are generally appropriate for soft selling, not for hard-core marketing. Although referrals are used primarily for making business-to-business (B2B) connections, especially when targeting those with a specific job title, you never know when a referral will bring you a customer.

 Make a habit of including a link to your primary website on every profile and using some of your preferred search terms within your profile title and text. These techniques increase your inbound links and may help with search engine ranking, as described in Book II, Chapter 2.

Table 3-1 lists cross-industry directories. Visit the ones that seem appropriate, using the tactics described in Book VIII, Chapter 1 to make your selections.

Table 3-1	Business Networks	
Website	*URL*	*What It Is*
Biznik	`http://biznik.com`	Community of entrepreneurs and small businesses
Chief Financial Officer Network	`www.linkedin.com/ groups?home=&gid=51826`	Network of high-level CFOs, financial executives, and accounting leaders (requires LinkedIn membership)

Website	URL	What It Is
Doostang	www.doostang.com	Career community for professionals seeking new jobs
EFactor	www.efactor.com	Global network and virtual marketplace for entrepreneurs and investors
Entrepreneur Connect	http://econnect.entrepreneur.com	Community for entrepreneurial networking
Fast Company	www.fastcompany.com/company-of-friends	One of the first business social networks, organized by groups
Jigsaw	www.jigsaw.com	Business card networking directory
Meet the Boss	www.meettheboss.tv	Invitation-based network for executives and senior management, across industries
Naymz	www.naymz.com	Networking platform for professionals
PartnerUp	www.partnerup.com	Network for small-business owners
PROskore	www.proskore.com	An online business network that measures professional reputation
Ryze	http://ryze.com	Business connections for jobs, careers, and sales
Spoke	www.spoke.com	Worldwide professional business directory
StartupNation	www.startupnation.com	Entrepreneurial business advice and networking
Talkbiznow	www.talkbiznow.com	Business services and collaboration network
The Funded	http://thefunded.com	Community of entrepreneurs who rate and compare investors and funding sources

Book VIII Chapter 3

Maximizing Stratified Social Communities

(continued)

Table 3-1 *(continued)*

Website	URL	What It Is
XING	www.xing.com	Global networking for professionals
Women about Biz	www.womenaboutbiz.com	Businesswomen's online resource center
Yammer	www.yammer.com	Free networking tool for networking within a company

Be selective. Participating in multiple sites productively is time-consuming. Keep clear records of all sites that have your business profile. If your situation changes, you probably have to update your profiles individually. Figure 3-1 shows a networking profile for Arrayit, a company that makes micro-arrays for biotechnology, on ScienceStage.com. In this case, the company takes advantage of a vertically segmented scientific audience to showcase its products at `http://sciencestage.com/arrayit`. Its profile, under the About My Work section, links to its website and is loaded with keywords.

You can syndicate content postings (see Book II, Chapter 1), but you usually cannot syndicate profile entries.

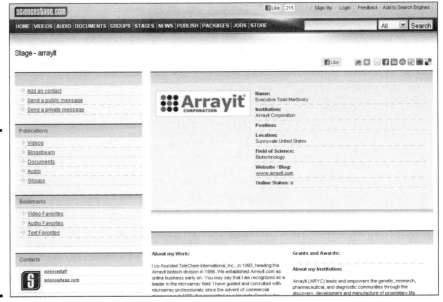

Figure 3-1: Arrayit uses the science network Science Stage.com to promote its biotechnology products.

Courtesy Todd J. Martinsky, Arrayit Corporation, Ticker: ARYC

Selecting Social Networks by Vertical Industry Sector

Whether you're marketing B2B or B2C (business-to-consumer), you can find dozens of industry- or interest-specific social networks. Search online for communities in your industry, using the strategies described in Book VIII, Chapter 1. As long as the social network is large enough to support your time investment, and continues to attract new users, you should enjoy enough of a payback to make your effort worthwhile.

Vertical industry sites, other than shopping, are particularly appealing for B2B marketers. If you use some adroit maneuvering, you can intersect with the sales cycle, reaching the appropriate decision-maker with the right message.

For the retail community, the growth of social shopping sites is a new avenue to reach consumers who want to spend after they see what everyone else is buying. Users flock to these sites for the latest product reviews, real-time deals, and news about the hottest items.

Track results so that you can decide which sites work best for you. If a site doesn't produce leads or sales after a few months, find another.

If you want to promote your products or services to more than one online community, customize your profiles and messages accordingly. For instance, a sporting goods store might promote camping gear on a social network for backpackers and running gear on one for joggers.

The list of vertical market social networks seems endless and ever changing. Table 3-2 provides a sample of some of these networks just to give you an idea of the range. This list includes no blog-only, bookmarking, or news aggregator sites.

Table 3-2	Vertical Market Social Networks	
Website	*URL*	*Description*
Art		
ArtSlant	www.artslant.com	Contemporary art network with profiles for artists, art professionals, art organizations, and art lovers
deviantART	www.deviantart.com	Post and share international art
Humble Voice	www.humblevoice.com	Virtual artistic space for "artists and those who appreciate them"

(continued)

Table 3-2 (continued)

Website	URL	Description
Art		
Imagekind	www.imagekind.com	CafePress-owned community for buying, selling, and creating art
Independent Collectors	www.independent-collectors.com	Online tool targeted at modern art collectors
Auto		
AutoSpies	http://autospies.com	Blogs about car care reviews; auto news aggregator
CarGurus	www.cargurus.com	Automobile community with reviews, photos, and share opinions
Motortopia	www.motortopia.com	Community for lovers of cars, motor bikes, planes, and boats
Books		
Goodreads	www.goodreads.com	Book recommendations to share
LibraryThing	www.librarything.com	Book recommendations and online catalog
The Mystery Reader	http://themystery reader.com	Mystery book reviews
Design		
Design Float	www.designfloat.com	Design-related content sharing, advertising, digital art, and branding
Decorati	http://decorati.com	Interior designer community enabling users to post items for sale and exchange
Environment		
TreeHugger	www.treehugger.com	Environmental topics at interactive community

Website	URL	Description
Entertainment, film, and music		
CreateSpace	www.createspace.com	Creation, collaboration, and distribution for writers, musicians, and filmmakers
Fanpop	www.fanpop.com	Network of fan clubs for fans of television, movies, music, and more
Flixster	www.flixster.com	Movie lovers community
Last.fm	www.last.fm	Music community
mediabistro.com	www.mediabistro.com	Careers and community for media professionals
Medical		
PatientsLikeMe	www.patientslikeme.com	Patients, healthcare professionals, and industry organizations making connections
Sermo	www.sermo.com	Largest online physician community in the United States
Legal		
The Lawyers Network	www.lawyrs.net	International social networking community for lawyers and law students
Philanthropy and nonprofits		
Care2	www.care2.com	Online community for people passionate about making a difference
ChangingThe Present	www.changingthepresent.org	Nonprofit fundraising community with membership of more than 400 nonprofits
Pets		
Uniteddogs	www.uniteddogs.com/en	Social networking for dogs and their owners

(continued)

Table 3-2 *(continued)*

Website	*URL*	*Description*
Shopping, fashion, and collecting		
Curiobot	www.curiobot.net	Collection of the most interesting items for sale on the Internet
iliketotally loveit.com	www.iliketotally loveit.com	Product recommendations with public link to online shops
Kaboodle	www.kaboodle.com	Product discovery, recommendations, and sharing
Multiply	http://multiply.com	Share photos and videos with friends and family; social shopping site popular in Southeast Asia
Polyvore	www.polyvore.com	Product mixing and matching from any online store
Rue La La	www.ruelala.com	Flash sales
Stylehive	www.stylehive.com	Stylish people connecting
ThisNext	www.thisnext.com	Product recommendation swaps
UsTrendy	www.ustrendy.com	Vote on and shop for new items from indie designers
Wists	http://wists.com	Create and share wishlists with products from any website
Sports		
beRecruited. com	www.berecruited.com	Connecting high school athletes and college coaches
Science and technology		
Lalisio	http://www.lalisio. com	Social network for scientists and academics
ResearchGate	http://www.research gate.net	Social network for scientists to connect and make their work more visible
ScienceStage. com	http://sciencestage. com	Hub for research scientists

As always, include a link to your primary website and use some of your preferred search terms within your postings and profiles. If these sites have blogs or accept photos, video, or music, you can syndicate that type of content to many sites simultaneously.

Selecting Social Networks by Demographics

No one ever has enough staff and time to do everything. You already know that the more tightly you focus your marketing efforts, the better the payoff from your investment. If you created a strategic plan in Book I, Chapter 1, return to it to analyze and segment your markets demographically into smaller, niche markets that you can reach with a coordinated campaign.

Think online guerrilla marketing. Go after one niche market online at a time. After you conquer one, go after the next. If you scatter your efforts across too many target markets at one time, your business won't have enough visibility in any of them to drive meaningful traffic your way.

Table 3-3 describes some sites that are primarily demographically and geographically stratified. You can find many, many more. As usual, qualify the sites for your business by following the concepts described in Book VIII, Chapter 1.

Table 3-3	Demographically and Geographically Stratified Sites	
Website	**URL**	**Description**
Ethnic		
Black Business Women Online	`http://mybbwo.com`	A social network for black women in business, women entrepreneurs, and bloggers
AsianTown.net	`http://my.asiantown.net/index.html`	Asian social community and news
BlackPlanet.com	`www.blackplanet.com`	African American professional network that includes job section by way of Monster.com
MiGente.com	`www.migente.com`	Largest Latin American community; includes job section by way of Monster.com

(continued)

Table 3-3 *(continued)*

Website	URL	Description
Ethnic		
MyTribalSpace. com	www.mytribalspace. com/tribal	Native American social network
High school and college		
Classmates	www.classmates.com	Networking with members of your graduating class at all levels
MeetMe (formerly myYearbook)	www.meetme.com	Networking site for high school and college students and grads
Reunion.com	www.reunion.com	Networking with members of your high school graduating class
Generational		
20 Something Bloggers	www.20sb.net	Ning community for 20-somethings
Brazen Careerist	www.brazencareerist. com	Career-building community for Gen-Y and Millennials (born 1982–2000)
Club Penguin	http://clubpenguin. com	Disney site for children under 12
Make Me Sustainable	http://makeme sustainable.com	Environmental community with Gen-Y appeal
More	www.more.com	Community for women over 40
Local		
Citysearch	www.citysearch.com	Localized directory with reviews and comments
DiscoverOurTown. com	www.discoverourtown. com	Comprehensive local city guide
HotFrog	www.hotfrog.com	Local business listings with maps

Website	URL	Description
Local		
Kudzu	www.kudzu.com	Local business directory with reviews and daily deals
Local.com	www.local.com	Local business directory with deals, events, and activities listings
Manta	www.manta.com	Local business directory for small businesses
MerchantCircle	www.merchantcircle.com	Find, review, and comment on local businesses
ThinkLocal	www.thinklocal.com	Local business search and directory
Tribe	www.tribe.net	Local-resident connections for advice and sharing about local resources
TripAdvisor	www.tripadvisor.com	Reviews of flights, hotels, and vacation rentals
Urbanspoon	www.urbanspoon.com	Restaurant listings and reviews from critics, food bloggers, and friends
Yelp	www.yelp.com	Local business reviews and comments
Yext	www.yext.com	Powerlistings across multiple websites all from one website
International		
Badoo	http://badoo.com	Popular European social networking site
Nexopia	www.nexopia.com	Canada's largest social networking site for young people

**Book VIII
Chapter 3**

**Maximizing
Stratified Social
Communities**

(continued)

Table 3-3 *(continued)*

Website	URL	Description
International		
Orkut	www.orkut.com/Main#Home	Google-owned alternative to Myspace and Facebook, now popular in Brazil
Sonico	www.sonico.com	Global Spanish language site with large U.S. membership
Zorpia	http://en.zorpia.com	International friendship network
Moms		
CafeMom	www.cafemom.com	Largest social networking and community site for moms and parenting
Mommysavers	http://mommysavers.com	Money-saving community and tips for moms
Lifetime Moms	www.lifetimemoms.com	Social network and parenting resource for moms
Seniors		
Grandparents.com	www.grandparents.com	Photo sharing and news site for grandparents
Senior Enquirer	www.seniorenquirer.com	Senior social network for people over 60
Tweens and young teens		
GirlSense	www.girlsense.com	Online dress-up games for girls
UGAME	http://ugame.com	Social network for video gamers
Wealthy		
ASMALLWORLD	www.asmallworld.net	Private international community of culturally influential people

As usual, customize your message and profile for the audience you're trying to reach. Be sure to include a link to your primary website and some of your key search terms in any profile or posting.

Figure 3-2 shows how businesses can take advantage of demographically targeted sites. Merchants and vendors who sell toys and gifts for children can send Grandparents.com their products for consideration. Selected products can be seen under the Toys & Gifts tab at `http://www.grand parents.com/gp/content/toys-gifts-gear/index.html`.

Figure 3-2:
Grand
parents.
com is an
example
of a demo-
graphically
targeted
social
network.

Courtesy Grandparents.com, Inc.

Selecting Social Networks by Activity Type

We can imagine what you're thinking. Why in the world would you want more than one service of a particular type, such as video sharing or blogging? The answer is simple: to improve search engine rankings and inbound links from high-ranking sites. When your content appears on multiple sites, such as those listed by activity in Table 3-4, you're simply casting a wider net and hoping to catch more fish.

Table 3-4   **Social Networks by Activity Type**

Website	URL	Description
Networking and profiles		
Bebo	www.bebo.com	Facebook-style site with global reach
FriendFeed	http://friendfeed.com	Create personal networks to share with friends, family, and co-workers
Friendster	www.friendster.com	Older global online social network; popular in Southeast Asia; emphasis on gaming
Gather	www.gather.com	Facebook-style social network for writers
hi5	http://hi5.com	Social entertainment for the youth market worldwide with Myspace-style profiles; bought by Tagged
MocoSpace	www.mocospace.com	Cellphone-compatible online community
Myspace	www.myspace.com	Now focused on entertainment, musicians, and comedians; attracts Gen-Y, ethnic audience
Image sharing		
Flickr	http://flickr.com	Well-known photo-sharing site
HoverSpot.com	http://hoverspot.com	Free social network with good photo sharing capabilities
Instagram	http://instagr.am	An image sharing and photo manipulation site, especially for images taken on smartphones
Photobucket	http://photobucket.com	Free image hosting and photo and video sharing
Picasa	http://picasa.google.com	Google's photo-sharing site
Pinterest	www.pinterest.com	Share and recommend photos for others
SlideShare	www.slideshare.net	Presentation sharing site

Website	URL	Description
Video sharing (YouTube alternatives)		
Dailymotion	www.dailymotion.com	Post videos, music, and movies
Jing	www.techsmith.com/jing.html	Video-sharing over web, IM, and e-mail
Ustream	www.ustream.tv	Platform for live, interactive, broadcast video
Vimeo	http://vimeo.com	Created by filmmakers and videographers to share creative work (noncommercial only)
Microblogging (Twitter alternatives)		
Plurk	www.plurk.com	A Twitter alternative for events with calendar display
Seesmic	http://seesmic.com	Twitter client that permits photo and video sharing on Twitter, Facebook, and LinkedIn
Unique services		
eHow	www.ehow.com	Squidoo-like site with content submissions on how to do things
HubPages	http://hubpages.com	Like Squidoo, allows users to publish expert content
Maholo	www.mahalo.com	Users with questions connecting with volunteers who write answers
Meetup	www.meetup.com	Local-group organizing for face-to-face meetings
Ning	www.ning.com	Build your own multifaceted community
QOOP	www.qoop.com	Build creative mash-ups to share or sell
Quora	www.quora.com	Group-sourced answers to questions
Squidoo	www.squidoo.com	Post your own "expert" content

**Book VIII
Chapter 3**

**Maximizing
Stratified Social
Communities**

The secret to keeping this situation manageable is syndication, via really simple syndication (RSS) or Ping.fm, or a similar service as discussed in Book II, Chapter 1. You post an image, a video, or a blog entry to your primary site and automatically update other services with the same content.

Even with syndication, use some common sense. It doesn't help to drive the "wrong" fish to your website and dilute your conversion rate. Of course, if you've monetized your site by showing ads by the impressions, then the more eyeballs, the merrier.

Because setting up multiple accounts can be time-consuming, you may want to stagger the process. Of course, by now you automatically include in any profile or posting a link to your primary website and some of your key search terms.

TravelLuggagePlus.com's Gather (www.gather.com) blog post "Stress Free Packing for Your Vacation: Travel Luggage Tips" (shown in Figure 3-3) includes a link to its own website in the author description at the end of the article. Check it out at

```
http://travel.gather.com/viewArticle.action?articleId=
    281474980689021
```

Figure 3-3: The end of this blog post links users to the Travel Luggage Plus website.

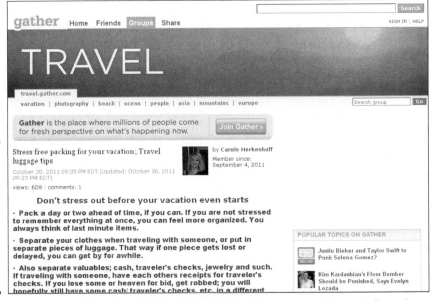

Written by Carol Herkenhoff, CDH Web Enterprises, LLC. Contact the author at her website www.travelluggageplus.com

Brooklyn Bowl scores a strike with Instagram

Even before Brooklyn Bowl opened in 2009, its creative/marketing team at Learned Evolution had decided to make Brooklyn Bowl the first-ever venue to be marketed almost exclusively using social/digital media. According to creative director Justin Bolognino, "Traditional marketing strategies such as ad buys in newspapers and magazines, radio, and broadcast were all set aside in favor of building an active social media following."

Five years later, Bolognino brags, "The numbers speak for themselves. In 2011, Brooklyn Bowl was the tenth-most searched keyword term in New York City on Google. It's the number one Nightlife check-in location on foursquare, and it has some of the highest social media engagement numbers of any venue in New York or the country."

Learned Evolution was able to leverage existing relationships to strengthen its marketing strategy. For instance, the company has produced an ongoing event series with Vimeo at Brooklyn Bowl called "Eye Candy for Strangers." Filmmakers from around the world submit their videos on Vimeo, where they are curated and premiered at Brooklyn Bowl.

"It was very important that Brooklyn Bowl was one of the first venues in the country to utilize Instagram," says Bolognino, "not only because it is such an amazing tool, but also because it fits the Bowl aesthetic so perfectly." The company launched its Instagram contest in early summer 2011. Each week, it selects the best Instagram taken at the Bowl and awards the winners with two tickets to the Bowl show of their choice. "As Instagram's popularity increases, and the word about our contest gets out, the number of entries increases each week," he enthuses.

In keeping with their leading use of Instagram, Learning Evolution created a new social media feature for Brooklyn Bowl. Bowlstagram (`http://bowlstagr.am`) is a three-tiered page with featured images at the top, weekly Instagram contest winners in the middle, and a feed at the bottom of every photo tagged #brooklynbowl or geo-tagged at Brooklyn Bowl.

Bolognino defines his strategy as allowing the Bowl community to promote the venue for them. Although the general market is music lovers, there isn't any focused target market; the segments vary from young to old, and all races and colors. "The mission is always simultaneity — using one resonant message to market to many different markets," he stresses. Just about everything they do drives users back to social media channels. "We have ads embedded in the newsletter that point to specific elements on our other social networks and website. We also host most of our contests on our social media networks."

HootSuite is Bolognino's go-to social management platform although it is limited in the number of portals for content syndication. At the beginning of each week, the team pre-schedules its "data-oriented" messages: show times and other basic objective information. They balance this with real-time, "improvised" tweets and direct interaction.

With so many social channels to monitor, they use Google Analytics to measure performance, as well as bit.ly, and internal statistical tools on Statigr.am, HootSuite, Facebook, and a new data service called Tracx, which helps them understand the way their social media efforts work together strategically. Learned Evolution sends the Bowl a weekly update that tracks all data.

**Book VIII
Chapter 3**

**Maximizing
Stratified Social
Communities**

(continued)

(continued)

Courtesy Learned Evolution: Growing Media for Growing Minds

"The biggest lesson we've learned is that every little word counts," explains Bolognino. "One night, we did a re-tweet campaign where we said something like: 'RT this for a free drink at the bar.' Within minutes, we had people lining up at the bar proving they had done what was asked. We meant to say 'RT this to enter to win a free drink at the bar.' Quite a huge difference — it cost us about 25 free drinks!

"I know it sounds clichéd," acknowledges Bolognino, "but at the end of the day, having an authentic voice and using it to actively engage with fans is the most vital strategy. It's all one big, never-ending conversation with your friends, after all."

Brooklyn Bowl's web presence

```
www.brooklynbowl.com
```

```
www.brooklynbowl.com/blog
```

```
http://www.brooklynbowl.com/win-tix-with-instagram
```

```
www.gramfeed.com/instagram/tags#brooklynbowl
```

```
www.youtube.com/BKBowl
```

```
http://vimeo.com/brooklynbowl
```

```
https://twitter.com/#!/brooklynbowl
```

```
www.facebook.com/BrooklynBowl
https://foursquare.com/v/brooklyn-bowl/4a1afeb7f964a520b77a1fe3
www.flickr.com/brooklynbowl
www.brooklynbowl.com/win-tix-with-instagram/feed (RSS)
https://twitter.com/statuses/user_timeline/brooklynbowl.rss (RSS)
http://flavorpill.com/brooklyn/venues/brooklyn-bowl
http://bowlstagr.am
```

Chapter 4: Geomarketing Services

In This Chapter

✔ Going geo or staying put

✔ Using geomarketing

✔ Playing foursquare

✔ Location apps on Twitter, Facebook, and Google

✔ Making money with meetups, tweetups, and cash mobs

*L*ocation, location, location: It's the mantra of real estate and yet another feature of successful social media marketing. The convergence of mobile devices (smartphones and tablets) with GPS and social media offers a great opportunity for marketers. You can inform potential customers that you offer exactly what they're looking for, when they're looking for it, and provide directions to get them there from their location.

In this book, we use the term *geomarketing tools* to refer to social media services that incorporate knowledge of users' locations or that bring people together in a specific, real-world space.

Several location-based services, including *social mapping* (identifying where people are) and location-based marketing games, are at the ready as you expand into geomarketing. Even though the freestanding geomarketing programs Gowalla and Loopt have been bought by other companies, foursquare remains a location-based loyalty-program offering rewards to consumers for patronizing particular retailers. Twitter, Google, and Facebook offer location-based options as well.

Going Geo

The techniques we describe in this chapter all apply to businesses that exist in the physical world with their own storefront, or that offer events that bring people together face-to-face. Pure cyber-businesses may not find these ideas as useful, but you never know what creative idea will hit you. Although geolocation services are particularly appropriate for business-to-consumer (B2C) businesses, we also offer some intriguing business-to-business (B2B) applications in this chapter.

Geomarketing for B2C

For most businesses, geomarketing involves a teaser deal that attracts residents or out-of-town visitors who "check in" online or with a mobile device when they arrive at the establishment. This concept is particularly attractive for events, tourist sites, restaurants, and entertainment venues. Almost all these services notify their subscribers by text message or on their mobile sites whenever an offer is available nearby.

Before you undertake one of these activities, follow the directions for local optimization in Book II, Chapter 2 to improve your success rate.

Each service operates a little differently, with some offering virtual badges as a reward, while others offer special discounts to repeat customers (those who check in most often) or first-timers.

Watching the rise of B2C geomarketing

Estimates show that locally targeted geomarketing techniques may produce results twice as high as untargeted advertising. For instance, The Breakfast Club in London has seen more than 1,600 check-ins since it started offering discounts for foursquare users.

According to a Microsoft survey conducted by Cross-Tab Marketing Services in December 2011, about 60 percent of Internet users are aware of check-in services, and more than half have used them.

In addition to being popular:

✦ Most geomarketing services work on multiple smartphone, tablet, and laptop platforms, so end-user device limitations aren't a concern.

✦ The rapid growth in mobile marketing (see Book VIII, Chapter 7) will accelerate the use of geomarketing.

✦ The audience for geomarketing skews heavily to young men, who also happen to be the early adopters of mobile technology. Only 22 percent of users are female; and of the men, 44 percent are 18–29 years old. If your product or service fits this demographic base well, B2C geomarketing might be up your alley.

✦ Some businesses may see only limited benefits, but the cost is also minimal. Unlike group coupons (see the next chapter), these offers are generally inexpensive, so merchants face no significant losses.

✦ Inbound links from services like foursquare can improve ranking in search results.

✦ Hospitality businesses, entertainment venues, and restaurants can create geomarketing offers for "slow" times of day or off-season occupancy. This approach can turn down-times into profitable opportunities.

Easy-to-use tools like PlacePunch (`http://placepunch.com`), a free-standing location marketing platform, help you manage multiple location check-in services or create your own. Although recently acquired by Silverpop, PlacePunch plans to continue operating across foursquare, Twitter, and Facebook location applications.

Considering geomarketing factors

Geomarketing isn't for every business. Whether you should use a geomarketing service depends on the nature of your business, whether your customer base already is using this option, and which location-based activities consume your prospective customers' time. Mull over these factors before you take the leap:

✦ **Don't reinvent the wheel.** Many cellphone apps already offer a location-specific tool — for example, a weather report, road conditions, a list of gas prices at stations around town — and then add a sponsor. If all you're trying to do is reach the on-the-go consumer who is ready to buy, do you need more than that? Maybe a pay-per-click (PPC) ad on a mobile search engine solves your needs.

✦ **Numbers matter.** Enough people living near or visiting your location have to use a particular geomarketing application to make it worth the effort. This issue is nontrivial because most services don't publicize this data. Try to research the number of users in your area with both the service provider and a third-party source, such as Alexa. The numbers can fluctuate widely and are difficult to find.

After you estimate the size of the potential audience (the *reach*), remember that only a small percentage of the audience is likely to become customers. Your best bet: Ask existing customers which location-based services, if any, that they use.

To get an idea of the number of members, try creating a user account. Then scan the list of places in your area (sometimes called *venues* or *spots*) for the inclusion of neighbors and competitors, and look at the maximum number of check-ins at those locations. Even if you don't ordinarily serve geolocation fanatics, a high-tech conference that draws a huge number of users may be a one-time opportunity worth taking advantage of.

✦ **Prospective customers must be willing to participate.** Some surveys have shown that 75 percent of women avoid location-based services partly out of fear of stalking and partly from lack of interest. You must take privacy issues into account.

✦ **Local is not always enough.** No matter the size of the total user base for a specific location tool in your neighborhood, you may draw a large audience of foursquare users only if you happen to own the pizza place across the street from the computer science building at the local college, not if you offer a badge to seniors at a local retirement community who show up for early-bird specials.

✦ **Demographics are fluid.** Be cautious: The demographics and statistics on these sites change quickly as they become more popular and move out of the early adopter stage.

✦ **The temptation is great to "go geo."** Don't jump into geomarketing just because it's cool or trendy.

For a summary of geolocation services, see Table 4-1.

Promote your geosocial participation in as many ways as possible on your other social media accounts and websites.

Table 4-1	Geolocation Services	
Geolocation	*Site URL for Businesses*	*Number of User Accounts*

Facebook Location	`https://www.`
	`facebook.com/`
	`about/location`
		200 million
		`http://www.zdnet.`
		`com/blog/btl/200-`
		`million-facebook-`
		`users-tagged-by-`
		`location-on-a-`
		`monthly-basis/73029`

foursquare	`https://foursquare.` `com/business/venues`	15 million
Google Latitude	`www.google.com/` `latitude/checkin`	10 million

Instagram	`http://help.`
	`instagram.com/`
	`customer/portal/`
	`topics/43530-`
	`instagram-for-`
	`businesses/articles`
		25 million; iPhone and Android app works with foursquare, Flickr, Facebook, and Twitter

PlacePunch (tool)	`http://place` `punch.com`	Not applicable; simplifies integration of multiple geo-marketing services into one campaign

Twitter Geolocation	`https://support.`
	`twitter.com/`
	`articles/78525-`
	`about-the-tweet`
	`location-feature`
		Not applicable; geotag available on all tweets (user option)

Yelp	`https://biz.yelp.` `com/support`	60 million

B2B geomarketing applications

Most users of social mapping are B2C businesses in hospitality, tourism, and recreation. HubSpot Internet Marketing, however, identified some potential applications of geomarketing for B2B) companies (`http://blog.hubspot.com/blog/tabid/6307/bid/31386/9-Ways-B2Bs-Can-Excel-With-Location-Based-Social-Media.aspx`), as listed below:

✦ **Location:** It will become part of search engine optimization (SEO) in the future, so you may as well reoptimize content now.

✦ **Trade show marketing:** Geomarketing may change how you exhibit or sponsor events. For example, the standard hospitality suite at the Consumer Electronics Show may be replaced with a foursquare "swarm," somewhat like a scheduled flash mob that rewards participants with a special virtual badge.

✦ **Customer relationship management (CRM) tools and databases:** Salespeople can more easily schedule visits to hot leads.

✦ **Identifying prospects and facilitating lead generation:** After you know where your target market "hangs out," you can easily connect with them.

Finding Yourself on foursquare

Foursquare (`www.foursquare.com`) is riding high at the moment, having reached 15 million users in three years of operation. This location-based game awards virtual badges or discounts to new visitors or frequent customers who check in at targeted locations using their smartphones, as shown in Figure 4-1. It's already compatible with the iPhone, Android, and BlackBerry, and third-party developers have developed apps for tablets.

You'll have to determine for yourself whether playing foursquare and similar games is a temporary geek-craze or will turn out to have long-term appeal to folks who simply needed a nudge (as in "discount") to try something new.

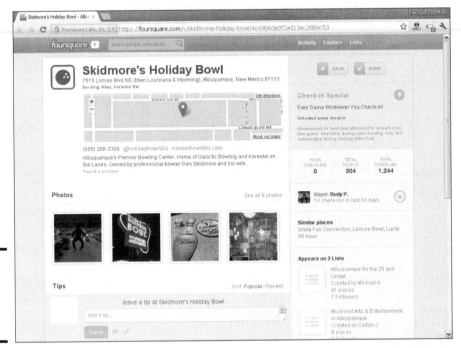

Figure 4-1:
A typical foursquare check-in page.

Courtesy Skidmore's Holiday Bowl; www.holidaybowlabq.com

Early adopters, mostly local restaurants and bars, have lined up in certain locations to offer discounts to new or repeat customers. For some of these businesses, foursquare acts like a loyalty program.

The foursquare merchant dashboard lets businesses monitor foursquare visitors who check in by number, gender, day of week, and time of day, as shown in Figure 4-2. You won't see a better service until cyber-psychics start offering their services.

Any business can easily "claim" its foursquare location. It's free, and it's another inbound link, even if you don't use it. Go to `http://foursquare.com/businesses` to create an account and log in. Then search for your listing (which comes from a mapping service) and click the Claim Here button. After you claim your venue, you can optimize it with your contact information and website. Anytime someone checks in, your location will be broadcast to all their friends on foursquare and may be published on their Twitter or Facebook pages as well.

Figure 4-2:
Foursquare allows you to monitor visitors who check in to your business.

Courtesy foursquare

Foursquare offers self-service tools for business owners to create, manage, and track how their offers perform at http://foursquare.com/businesses. You can choose to offer a variety of specials:

✦ **Mayor:** Can be used only by the *Mayor,* the user who has checked in most often in the past 60 days (refer to Figure 4-1).

✦ **Count-based:** Available after a user checks in a certain number of times.

✦ **Frequency-based:** Available multiple times after a certain number of check-ins per users.

✦ **Wildcard:** Always available, but the user has to meet certain conditions before receiving the special. For example, the Swarm badge, shown in Figure 4-3, is a badge awarded for participating in an event with 50 others.

Figure 4-3:
A foursquare
Swarm
badge.

Courtesy foursquare

Businesses promote their foursquare participation in many ways: on their own social media feeds, countercards at cash registers, and sandwich boards in the streets. Players who have requested notification can receive a text message whenever an offer is available nearby.

Page 1 Books takes a leaf from foursquare

Page 1 Books opened in 1981 as a newsstand and gradually expanded to include books, music, software, cards, and gifts. With a current staff of 18, Page 1 is trying to buck the trend to remain a freestanding, independent bookstore. It decided to start using Facebook in 2009, followed by Twitter.

The store added foursquare in February 2012, explains manager Melissa Jansen. "The twenty-somethings on our staff brought the technology to management's attention. One of the staff came in with his touchscreen phone and showed us how it worked. That staff member spearheaded the sign-up with foursquare and determined our offers. Our results are starting to build, with check-ins, and offers unlocked. And we have a Mayor."

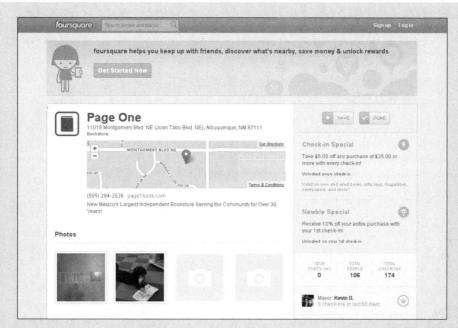

Courtesy Page One Bookstore

Jansen finds that Facebook works well for local branding and generating interest in their event calendar, especially with the 18–30 demographic, but finds it a little soon assess to foursquare.

In addition to linking to social media links on their website, Jansen used signage inside the store to drive traffic to its social media pages. She acknowledges some difficulties maintaining the bookstore's social media presence and figuring out the rules and technology.

"We had programming issues with Facebook early on when a staff member who didn't know what [he was] doing changed the site to Spanish and then deleted our Facebook page altogether, along with all the fans we had accumulated. Help from Facebook with this issue was nonexistent."

Jansen recommends that other business owners designate social media as a daily priority within the business. "Keeping content fresh and relevant is our greatest challenge," she acknowledges.

Page 1 Books' web presence

www.page1book.com

www.facebook.com/PageOneBookstore

https://twitter.com/#!/PageOneBooks

https://foursquare.com/v/page-one/4ba29a7cf964a520600838e3

**Book VIII
Chapter 4**

**Geomarketing
Services**

Spacing Out with Twitter, Facebook, and Google

The importance of integrating social media with location hasn't been lost on Twitter, Facebook, or many other applications.

Twitter

Twitter's Tweet with Your Location feature allows users' opt-in to include *geotags* (geolocation information) with their tweets, while developers can add Twitter functionality to other location-based apps. Twitter also uses geotagging within its Promoted Products to define and expand advertising opportunities.

Some third-party developers already offer apps based on the locations listed in user profiles. Twellowhood (www.twellow.com/twellowhood) locates a list of tweeters in a specified area; TwitterLocal.net, an Adobe AIR client, filters tweets by profile location; Twitter Nano (www.twitternano.com) shows you real-time tweets for a specified area on a map; What does it do? and Nearby Tweets (http://nearbytweets.com) sort tweets by topic within a specified region.

The local review site Yelp, at www.yelp.com, has a location-based, check-in feature on its smartphone version.

Facebook

Facebook phased out its Facebook Places as a standalone feature in favor of more fully integrating location options within its social networking service. Facebook's purchase of the geomarketing service Gowalla indicates that it intends to find new applications for location data, especially on smartphones.

Google Latitude

Although not yet fully launched, Google appears to be quietly expanding geomarketing with features like Leaderboard, which will allow users to earn points for checking into a location via its mobile app, Google Latitude. For more information, watch for updates at

www.google.com/latitude - or - http://mashable.
    com/2012/02/19/google-latitude-leaderboards

Making Real Connections in Virtual Space

Meetups, tweetups, and cash mobs bridge the gap between the cyberworld and the one we live in. They all make it easy for people with similar interests to organize meetings for fun, advocacy, learning, or simply to meet one another.

Meeting at a meetup

Meetup (www.meetup.com), which has been around since 2002, bills itself as "the world's largest network of local groups," claiming that more than 9 million monthly site visitors attend some 280,000 meetings held by 92,000 local groups located in 45,000 cities. The site reached great popularity as an organizing tool during the 2008 presidential election. Meetup charges organizers a fee ranging from $12 to $19 per month for using its platform.

Meetup technology (as shown in Figure 4-4) helps people find or start a group located near them. The system includes an easy-to-use interface to identify meetings within a certain distance and to reply by RSVP, find directions, and check out the history of a Meetup group. Meetup integrates nicely with Facebook events and RSVPs; it has an application for integrating Meetup with other applications.

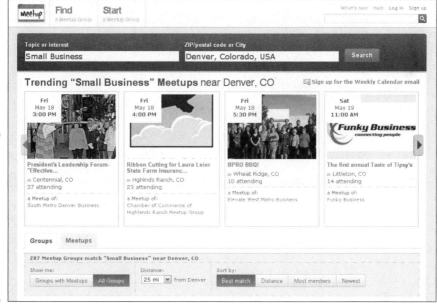

Figure 4-4: A Meetup search for small-business activities near Denver produces several results.

Courtesy MeetUp, Inc.

Book VIII
Chapter 4

Geomarketing
Services

In an inevitable mash-up, Meetup now allows Groupon fans (see the next chapter in this book) to hook up at "official" and self-organized events through `www.meetup.com/Groupon`.

What an easy way to find your target market in a location close to you!

Tweeting in real space

The term *tweetup* has been part of the Twitter lexicon for a long time to describe a live meeting of Twitter users or, more generally, any face-to-face event organized by way of social media.

Although there isn't yet a nationwide site that facilitates connections the way Meetup.com does, local sites exist. For example, in addition to its feed at `http://Twitter.com/BostonTweetUp` (shown in Figure 4-5), Boston Tweetup maintains a calendar and reviews technology-oriented events at its website `http://bostontweetup.com`.

Figure 4-5: Boston is serious about its tweetups.

Courtesy @BostonTweetUp, co-founded by @JoselinMane

Twitter is already influencing traditional gatherings, such as large conferences and seminars. Small groups with a particular interest or agenda can now more easily meet with each other socially or in a *rump session* (the "meeting" after the meeting). And many attendees have started tweeting questions and commentary during presentations, using the hashtag (#)

to mark tweets related to a particular session. This technique can either unnerve or energize presenters. Some tech-savvy people read the tweet stream as the session goes on and respond to questions on the fly.

In either case, a tweetup is definitely another way to take networking to the next level.

Marketing with meetups and tweetups

Meetups and tweetups offer you an exquisite opportunity to reach out to new customers, even if they're only complementary to your primary business. Contact meeting organizers to see whether you can

✦ Host an event at your restaurant or another event location: for example, a company selling kitchen countertops offering to hold cooking classes in its showroom

✦ Offer a discount to members or for the event

✦ Give a presentation or teach a class at a future meeting, which is an excellent way for a B2B or service provider to establish expertise in an area

✦ Provide information to members

Attending a meeting first is helpful (but not required) to make sure that the make-up of the group fits your target audience and to meet the leaders.

You can gauge interest by using Meetup to estimate the number of members in similar groups in your locations.

Organizing a meetup or tweetup

Nothing keeps you from organizing your own meetup or tweetup — just don't make it overtly self-serving. Creating a successful event can bring you recognition as a leader, enhance your credibility, attract media attention, and quickly bring new followers to your social media sites.

To ensure a successful event, promote it from your blog and e-mail newsletter and all your own social media channels, as well as by way of Meetup, Facebook events, Twitter, online calendars, and ordinary press releases. The more promotional channels, the better. You can find a set of helpful tools at www. rememberthemilk.com or www.twitip.com/planning-an-tweetup.

As with other location-dependent activities, make sure that a critical mass of local folks are interested in the event you're planning. In some cases, they may already need to be following you on the social networks you've identified as your promotion channels.

You can gauge interest by using Meetup to estimate the number of members in similar groups in your locations. Or take advantage of the following Twitter tools to help your planning:

✦ Geotagging makes it easier for people to find you. Log in to your Twitter account and open your settings. Select the Add a Location to Your Tweets check box. For each tweet, you can now choose to enter a specific location, a general area, or no location. For more information see `http://support.twitter.com/articles/78525-about-the-tweet-location-feature`.

✦ The search function can help you estimate the number of local Twitter users within a city or radius. Go to `http://search.twitter.com/advanced`. In the Places section, enter your city; then select the radius in miles or kilometers (for example, *Near: Albuquerque within 25 miles*). Because it only shows tweets, not users, this isn't a perfect system, but it's helpful.

At the event itself, do the basics:

✦ Check out the location ahead of time for size, lighting, quality, and service.

✦ Provide name tags and pens.

✦ Stay active, by facilitating discussions, resolving problems, making introductions, and generally acting as host.

You may want to take advantage of other event-planning tools, such as Eventbrite (`www.eventbrite.com`), Cvent (`www.cvent.com`), or Amiando (`www.amiando.com`) if you're expecting a large group. If you use Constant Contact for your e-mail newsletters, look at its Event Marketing tool at `www.constantcontact.com/event-marketing/index.jsp`.

Cashing in with cash mobs

One of the last twists on real-world social media interaction is the development of "cash mobs" instead of flash mobs. As described on `cashmob.wordpress.com`, the purpose of a cash mob is to support small, locally owned businesses.

In its own anarchic format, a random group of people establishes a target location, day, and time for the event and publicizes it using primarily Facebook and/or Twitter. The ground rules are simple: each person in the mob should try to spend at least $20 cash in the target store(s), and pay full price.

According to the blog site, almost 200 cash mobs have taken place in 35 states, some targeting a specific store and others a neighborhood shopping area. Those with experience recommend calling targeted businesses first to make sure they are willing and able to participate and ensure they have enough stock and staff to support a larger than usual number of customers.

Chapter 5: Attracting Customers with Daily Deal Coupons

In This Chapter

✔ Gaining customers by offering savings

✔ Learning about Groupon and Living Social

✔ Sharpening your edge with local daily deal sites

✔ Covering your back

A group of friends "hitting the mall" is the offline definition of *social shopping*. Online, though, social shopping means something quite different: An entire group of folks (sometimes, strangers) saves money by volume buying with a "group" coupon. The group coupon emerged several years ago as a way to aggregate new buyers, usually in specific cities, by offering a half-off, one-day promotion online or by e-mail. The underlying assumption was that by attracting a high volume of customers, a business could still make money on a highly discounted deal, "buy" goodwill and exposure, or fill their businesses during off-times or off-season.

The best-known and oldest of these coupon services are Groupon (www. groupon.com), which went public in fall 2011, and LivingSocial (www. livingsocial.com). Both companies have expanded to offer specific, tourism-related deals, as well as deals on goods and deals on national brands.

Seeing an opportunity for profit, dozens of other companies — some national, some regional or local — have entered the group coupon frenzy. The competition has had several consequences:

✦ With more coupon vendors to choose from, merchants have more leverage negotiating deals on favorable terms.

✦ Familiarity has taken the bloom off the discount rose.

✦ Some customers, who have come to expect major discounts as a matter of course, pressure merchants to "bend the rules" in their favor by threatening bad online reviews.

Using high-discount coupons can indeed bring new and repeat customers. On the downside, businesses may be exposed to significant financial risk and bad publicity. Many companies are now rethinking the shared coupon experiment or taking advantage of less costly local sites, offering daily deals.

In this chapter, which primarily addresses the needs of business-to-consumer (B2C) companies, you assess the risks and benefits of high-discount group deals. With this information, you can decide whether a deal strategy makes sense for your particular business.

Offering Savings, Gaining Customers

Offering a discount to attract customers is an obvious B2C technique used for ages by service and product companies: bars and restaurants, tourist destinations, health and beauty salons, events, recreation, personal services, and more.

Generally, customers who sign up for a deal service receive a daily e-mail offering some product or service for one-third to one-half off. For consumers to receive the "deal," a minimum number of deals must be purchased during a specific period, usually one to three days. If the minimum isn't reached, the deal doesn't go through and the consumer pays nothing.

Most, but not all daily deal sites are set up geographically, with users signing up to see deals near their homes or watching for deals they can use on their next vacation. For an example of a typical deal like this, GreatDealsNM.com offers high-discount deals weekly.

So that's how it works for users. To see how online coupons affect your end of the rope as a business, see the upcoming "Making an offer they can't refuse" section.

Consider these points while you decide whether to pursue a high-discount deal strategy:

+ **Ultimately, the coupon companies select which businesses participate at which time, and set the schedule for featuring offers.** You may not get the time frame that you want.

+ **A link to your site will appear in the offer.** In preparation, you should be willing to create a separate landing page on your website for the offer.

+ **Some sites offer national deals, particularly for large, web-based retailers.** For a national reach, you might target multiple, individual cities within your national audience with separate offers. This approach works for participating franchises or branches in several cities.

✦ **Confirm that the deal service you select reaches your city.** Because tourists and local residents are your primary audience, a service must have enough e-mail subscribers interested in a specific geographic area to make your deal workable.

You can make online couponing work for a business-to-business (B2B) audience, but it's a little more complicated. A successful B2B deal depends on the size and quality of the e-mail list that the coupon service maintains, an attractive offer on a product or service of wide interest (payroll services or office supplies, perhaps), and on recommendations from employees to employers. RapidBuyr (`www.rapidbuyr.com`), shown in Figure 5-1, and BizSaves (`www.bizsaves.com`) are two companies focused on the B2B deal market.

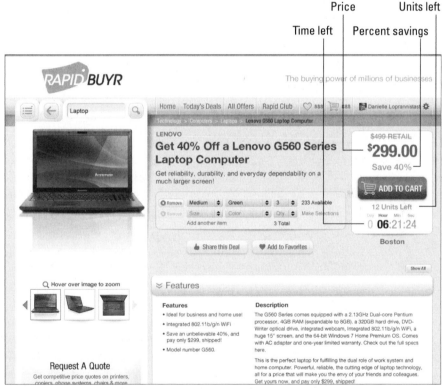

Figure 5-1: RapidBuyr deals are often capped by a maximum number of units available for purchase.

Courtesy RapidBuyr LLC

Book VIII
Chapter 5

Attracting
Customers with
Daily Deal Coupons

Making an offer they can't refuse

Sometimes, you just want people in your door, virtual or otherwise. If you offer a *loss leader* (a sale below cost), try not to sell too far below cost. Selling hundreds of $4 ice cream cones for half-price is one thing as long as you cover your cost of goods and service; on the other hand, discounting hundreds of $40 haircuts at half-price may leave you short on the rent.

If you're in a position to handle a potential loss, there are some viable reasons to consider online deals as a tool in your marketing arsenal:

+ **No upfront payments:** That's a good thing for your cash flow (if you get paid promptly by the coupon service).

+ **Backloaded payments:** The coupon company gets paid from revenues only if the minimum number of offers is purchased — and usually you can set the minimum and maximum number of coupons sold (more on that in a bit).

+ **Coupon deals often provide a stream of new customers in a relatively short length of time:** Compare the result to how long it takes other forms of advertising to produce new business. If you just opened a new business, coupons may be a good technique.

+ **Word-of-mouth works:** Buyers might bring their friends to share the experience.

+ **Factor estimated add-on purchases as well as lifetime customer value into your calculation:** Obviously, new customers who make multiple, repeat purchases are more valuable than customers who buy only once, say tourists. Try to make your offer something worth a repeat buy, or set the offer low enough that you can generate an up-sale from most buyers.

Setting some of the terms

You have many ways to refine and tailor your coupon campaign, within limits. You do want customers, but you don't want to lose your shirt, either. To limit your discount-exposure, you may be able to tweak the coupon vendor's share of revenue, the time frame during which the offer will be honored, the numbers of deals, and more.

Be sure to read the fine print before you sign with a coupon service. Each company has different rules.

The depth of the discount

Typically, the buyer receives 30–50 percent (or more) off the standard price. Then, the coupon service gets its slice: sometimes as high as an additional half of how much the buyer pays. So, as the merchant, you receive only 25 percent of your list price. For example:

30-minute parasailing adventure	$100
Customer coupon discount (50% off)	$50
Coupon service's cut	$25
Merchant's final take	$25

The percentages vary by company and by the nature of the offer, but thanks to the competition for deals, you may sometimes be able to negotiate better terms on the coupon service's cut, especially with some of the smaller deal companies (or if you're a huge multinational corporation).

The scope of the deal

Consider how you will establish the parameters of an offer to best meet your goals and objectives:

✦ **Min meets max:** Be sure to set the minimum number of sales high enough to mitigate your risk (bring in adequate volume), but the maximum number of sales low enough to keep from going broke (reduce your cost exposure).

If the minimum number of deals is sold, the coupon company takes its cut off the revenue first. The coupon firm collects payments from customers by credit card and sends you a check for your share afterward. The schedule of payments varies by coupon company.

Watch the schedule of payments carefully. Delayed payments from the coupon service can create a totally unnecessary cash flow crisis for your company.

✦ **Max meets max:** Set a maximum number of deals to limit both your financial and service exposure. A cap makes sense, especially for event organizers and service providers. For example, your small theater company may have a fixed number of seats, you may have room for only a certain number of people in a dance class, or you may have enough stylists to handle only a certain number of haircuts per day.

✦ **How long:** You specify the time frame over which buyers can exercise a deal, usually several months to a year. Plan ahead, keeping in mind how much product, space, and staff you'll need to fulfill your end of the deal.

✦ **Timing is everything:** Schedule the term of your offer so you don't have buyers showing up on your doorstep all at one time — unless the offer is for a scheduled event or you intentionally set a short period for redemption. Most merchants see a peak in redemptions the first 30 days after an offer and the last 30 days before expiration.

Grappling with the gotchas

Watch for landmines like these before signing up for a deal:

✦ **Fashionably late?** The fine print on some deals (and the law in some states) allows buyers to receive a discount equal to the amount they paid for their coupon — even if the deal itself has expired. For instance, suppose someone paid $6 for a pound of coffee costing $12 on a deal that expired on 12/31/11. Even if they come into your store a year later, you may have to give them $6 off a pound of coffee, whose price has now increased to $15. However, you don't have to honor the $12 price on the product that they buy.

✦ **Special package deals.** Many companies create a unique package or service just for their deal offer. You are usually not required to continue to offer that product or service beyond the term of the deal. For instance, say your company usually offers only hour-long dance lessons for couples and prices them at $40/hour. For the "deal" only, you offer a ½ hour dance lesson for couples valued at $20 but sold at $10. After the offer has expired, coupon buyers may be able to get $10 off the $40 price, but you aren't required to offer the ½ hour lesson any more.

✦ **Bookkeeping nightmares.** These deals can leave you with a record-keeping headache from tracking outstanding and redeemed offers at the register to holding potential entries on your books, even for expired coupons. Talk to your accountant about the impact on your financial statements for these ongoing liabilities.

✦ **Where's my money?** Payment isn't swift, either. Some coupon services divide your payments into three installments paid over 60 days, which could create cash flow problems for you if large numbers of buyers redeem their coupons quickly.

✦ **Be prepared.** If you can't provide high-quality service to meet the demand with the staff or space you have, you may lose not only the customer but also your reputation, if poor reviews appear online. Depending on the deal you're offering, protect yourself from unhappy customers by requiring appointments, stating "subject to availability" (say, for a massage or a haircut), and allowing adequate time to redeem the offer.

Measuring success

Good coupon sites offer detailed analytics, similar to newsletters, stating the number of offers e-mailed, number and percent of offers opened, number and percent of viewers who clicked for details, and the number and percent of viewers who purchased the deal. Additionally, they can provide how many viewers purchased more than one deal, total number of deals sold, and total dollar value received. Copy this information to a spreadsheet to:

✦ Assess whether the offer was financially successful for your business

✦ Obtain clues about what factors might have affected an offer that didn't succeed in meeting the minimum number of sales

✦ Compare the success and parameters of offers that you have sent out through the same company to see which offers are the most successful

✦ Compare what happens with the same offer distributed through different companies

If you can't figure out how to do this, ask your bookkeeper or accountant. They eat numbers for lunch.

Do the math. What percentage of customers might convert or upgrade their purchase? What is a reasonable "lifetime customer value" for each one? How does it compare to the cost of acquisition? Get help from your accountant if needed.

Seller beware! Small businesses with shallow pockets sometimes can't handle the pressure of serving so many customers. Many companies, especially restaurants, now report a loss in revenue whenever existing customers snap up their coupon deals. Receiving less than half the full price for a meal or service can turn coupon deals into an expensive loyalty program for existing clientele.

Further leveraging your deal

Many companies offer extra options to their coupon buyers in the hope that deals will go viral:

✦ **Opportunities to share opinions and photos:** Coupon buyers on Zozi. com or Yelp.com, for example, have the opportunity to enter comments about a company offering a deal. Other sites encourage participation in a social activity, such as ranking a service or posting photos. These actions are often perceived as testimonials by other prospective buyers and encourage them to purchase coupons. Almost all have share buttons to facilitate users sharing deals with others on their own social media pages.

✦ **Easy-to-share links to send deals to friends:** If three or more friends share a deal, the referrer receives a freebie. Include this element as an allowance in your revenue calculations. If someone organizes a share campaign, total revenues may decline.

This share-this-deal functionality encourages people who receive a daily coupon e-mail, or people who visit your site, to tell their friends about the deal on Facebook and Twitter and by e-mail.

✦ **Affiliate options:** Recommending a deal to others or signing up to promote offers on a commission basis usually generates internal "deal bucks" (not cash).

✦ **Easy integration with Facebook, Twitter, and e-mail to share deals:** Most services offer mobile apps for iPhone, iPad, Droid, and BlackBerry.

After the offer appears, you can promote the deal in your newsletter, on your social media outlets, and elsewhere, although you may not have much notice.

More upsides and downsides

As a merchant, you gain brand awareness, a direct appeal to locally targeted markets, word-of-mouth advertising, and high visibility to a new customer stream. The low-cost offer supposedly reduces customers' perceived risk of trying something new. It's your job to turn these one-time experimenters into loyal repeat customers.

In theory, compared with how long it takes other forms of advertising to produce new business, your business benefits from this approach by obtaining a stream of new customers in a relatively short length of time. The concept assumes (but this assumption doesn't always prove to be true) that when an offer brings prospects in the door, satisfied customers will proceed to spend more money through these avenues:

✦ **Impulse buys and add-ons:** Hey, you got them in the door, right? Time to exploit customers' good moods for your deal: See whether you can get them to come up off a little more cash. Say your buyers get 50 percent off a specialty burrito. You can then entice them to spend their "savings" on drinks, sides, or a take-home purchase: "This cupcake from the offer was so good that I'm buying a dozen to take home."

✦ **Repeat customers:** This is worth repeating (pun intended). Deliver quality on your discount deal, and you'll likely build a solid client base. One great massage and that client may be yours every two or three weeks for years.

✦ **Word-of-mouth:** Worth repeating, too. Buyers might bring friends.

Human nature being what it is, customers cashing in your deal don't always generate gold.

✦ **One-hit wonders:** Many people who use these deals are there only for the discount and have no intention of returning. That's life — and why you have to remember to price your deal with a profit margin/loss you can live with.

✦ **Cannibalizing existing customers:** Loyal patrons who would have paid full price or happily taken a 5 or 10 percent discount are now receiving a product or service at half-off, causing a loss in regular revenue.

✦ **Customer service versus aggressive customers:** Here's an ugly side of human nature. Regardless of conditions in the deal, some deal redeemers can be unreasonable and sometimes unpleasant. They demand to use more than one coupon per purchase, want to buy an item that's not on the offer, or otherwise take advantage of merchants who don't want to have a "scene" in their business.

✦ **Succumbing to greediness:** An overwhelmed business that can't meet the demand of a deal's sales are toast. When a business is pressured into selling more deals than it can manage, everyone — staff, customers, and business owners — has a bad experience. Unhappy customers threaten to post negative reviews on sites like Yelp, and some actually do.

If you want to read stories about other companies' experiences with group deals, check out

- ✦ Posies Café: `www.businessinsider.com/jesse-burke-groupon-nightmare`, `http://posiescafe.com/wp`, and `http://tech crunch.com/2011/06/09/groupon-single-worst-decision`

- ✦ Local Harvest Café & Catering: `www.riverfronttimes.com/2011-10-13/news/groupon-fail-st-louis-local-harvest-yelp`

- ✦ Brennan's Restaurant: `http://techcrunch.com/2011/10/19/a-restaurant-dive-shop-and-bakery-share-their-groupon-experience-tctv`

- ✦ Mission Minis Bakery: `http://techcrunch.com/2011/10/19/a-restaurant-dive-shop-and-bakery-share-their-groupon-experience-tctv`

Checking Out Groupon

With a unique copy style (see Figure 5-2) for the deals it features, Groupon (`www.groupon.com`) uses an advertising approach based on a "tipping point" and reaching a critical mass for social action or contributions. You can see The Point conceptualized at `www.thepoint.com`.

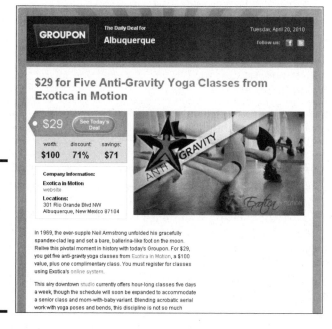

Figure 5-2: Groupon writes unusual (and often humorous) copy for the ads it features.

Like Don Vito Corleone in *The Godfather,* Groupon makes "an offer you can't refuse" to daily e-mail subscribers and site visitors in more than 190 cities in 45 countries. Groupon is far and away the largest of the group coupon sites. Groupon's press kit claims it sold more than 22 million Groupon deals in North America from its inception in 2008 through January 2011. The number of available deals is more than twice those offered by LivingSocial, its closest competitor.

In addition to its featured daily deal, Groupon offers a variety of auxiliary deals through Groupon Goods, Groupon Now, and Groupon Getaways (in partnership with travel site Expedia) and Kid-Friendly Deals. It also offers an affiliate program and in-house credits for referring deals to friends.

 After your offer appears, you can promote the deal in your own newsletter, blog, social media outlets and elsewhere, although you may not have much notice. The "share-this-deal" functionality encourages people who receive your daily Groupon e-mail, or those who visit your site, to tell their friends about the deal on Facebook and Twitter and by e-mail.

Demographics

According to studies by Forbes and comScore, Groupon users represent a coveted demographic profile: educated, young, single, working women who have a fair amount of discretionary income:

+ Female users outnumber males two-to-one.

+ Of recent 2012 users, 29 percent were Baby Boomers (born 1946–1964); 29 percent were GenXers (1965–1976), and 38 percent were Millenials (1977–1994).

+ Groupon users are more than twice as likely as nonusers to have a household income over $100,000.

+ Groupon users are 73 percent more likely to live in households whose net worth exceeds $1 million.

Merchant satisfaction

Groupon contends (on www.grouponworks.com) that its merchants are more than satisfied, with more than 97 percent of featured merchants wanting to make an offer again. According to Groupon, 91 percent of businesses report getting new customers, 90 percent claim customers spend more than the face value of their coupon, and 87 percent say the promotion increased their visibility.

Independent surveys don't necessarily agree. A report from Business Insider (www.businessinsider.com/groupon-survey-results-2011-7) had different findings:

✦ Only about 60 percent of businesses considered their Groupon experience a success.

✦ More than half of Groupon businesses didn't want to run another deal.

✦ Almost 40 percent of businesses thought their experience failed.

✦ Most businesses said only "a handful" of Groupon buyers became repeat customers.

✦ Half of the businesses polled said they would not recommend Groupon to another small business; the other half would.

To be fair, these complaints seem to apply to most daily deal sites. A professor at the Jones Graduate School of Business at Rice University surveyed 324 businesses that ran daily deals on five major sites in 23 U.S. markets between August 2009 and March 2011 (www.slideshare.net/p2045i/how-businesses-fare-with-daily-deals-a-multisite-analysis-of-groupon-livingsocial-opentable-travelzoo-and-buywithme-promotions).

The survey found that "55.5 percent of businesses reported making money, 26.6 percent lost money and 17.9 percent broke even. Furthermore, although close to 80 percent of deal users were new customers, significantly fewer users spent beyond the deal's value or returned to purchase at full price."

Once again, the results were mixed when it came to future use: "48.1percent of businesses indicated they would run another deal promotion; 19.8 percent said they would not, and 32.1percent said they were uncertain."

Speak with your accountant about how to handle revenue from Groupon and similar deals. Prepaid income is usually treated as a liability on your balance sheet until you fulfill the obligation or until the time expires to exercise the offer. (Think gift cards.) You may also encounter state-by-state issues regarding sales tax.

Vernon's Steakhouse finds Groupon a less than tasty dish

Named one of the "50 Most Romantic Restaurants in the Country" by Open Table Diners in both 2011 and 2012, Vernon's Hidden Valley Steakhouse (www.thehiddensteakhouse.com) in Los Ranchos de Albuquerque, New Mexico, opened in 2007 when four members of the Baird family built the Village Shops at Los Ranchos. After the Bairds took over the restaurant from its original owners in 2010, they expanded seating and offerings for the Steakhouse, expanded the Black Diamond Lounge as a jazz club and cigar bar, and opened PRIME by Vernon's as a sandwich deli, creating websites for both new venues, plus a portal site, www.yougottapassword.com.

According to owner Kim Baird, the restaurants started using social media immediately and quickly sought the help of a social media consultant. They now utilize Facebook, Twitter, YouTube, and Google+, with plans to add Flickr or Pinterest, as well as send e-newsletters through Constant Contact to a subscriber list of 12,000. "We invest a lot of money in other advertising including radio, radio endorsements, and some print," adds Baird. "We also give a lot to charity and schools and find that those avenues are fabulous mediums for advertising!"

"We did Groupon for both Vernon's and PRIME by Vernon's at the end of summer 2011 during our slow period," Baird explains. "We thought it would be a good way to increase customer flow, get the word out to more people, and entice people who might not come because of the cost. Groupon was fairly new and hot at the time."

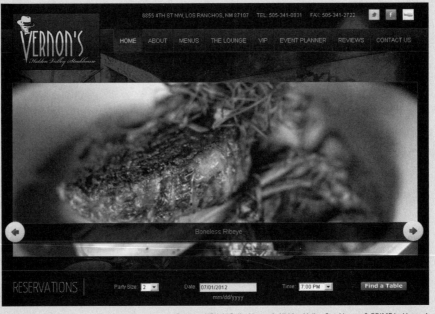

Courtesy VSH, LLC dba Vernon's Hidden Valley Steakhouse & PRIME by Vernon's

Selling more than 2,000 offers at $40 for an $80 value (www.groupon.com/deals/vernons-hidden-valley-steakhouse), Vernon's became one of Groupon's largest restaurant offers ever. Of the $80,000 generated, Groupon and Vernon's each made $40,000. However, the customers received $160,000 in food and service, leaving Vernon's upside down about $120,000 ($160,000–$40,000).

At first, the offer brought in new customers in a steady, manageable flow. Unfortunately, what sounded great initially later turned sour. "We got crushed in February, the month that the offer ended," Baird details. "We realized that a lot of our current customers bought Groupons, but they would have been in the restaurant at full price. Then we got an influx of a lot of new customers who really could not afford or did not want to spend the amount of money that an experience at Vernon's costs."

These customers began panning the award-winning restaurant on review sites about cost and value. Baird found this very frustrating because Vernon's is very open about the cost for an evening. "Our check average is usually about $70 a head; during the last month of Groupon in February 2012, our check average was less than $40. Furthermore, we cut into future customers for March and April because they all came in February."

While Baird is adamant that Groupon is not a good option for restaurants, she thinks it might make sense for hotels or other businesses that need to fill space that is not otherwise booked, or perhaps for a business with excess inventory to sell. While they may work for businesses with a high fixed over-head to cover, she doesn't recommend high-discount coupons for businesses with high variable costs.

"We will never do a Groupon again," she insists, noting that Vernon's has signed up for Restaurant. com, where it gets profit-sharing and can limit how many offers are sold for a given day, week, or month.

Her advice to other business owners is succinct: "You probably won't get the result you are looking for. Don't do it unless you have excess inventory [such as unused hotel rooms at a certain time of the year or an overstock of goods], or you are a service business selling your own time."

Vernon's Steakhouse's web presence

www.yougottapassword.com

www.thehiddensteakhouse.com

www.theblackdiamondlounge.com

www.cutofprime.com

https://plus.google.com/108641319164906519674 (Vernon's)

https://plus.google.com/110102347942052235037 (Prime)

https://twitter.com/#/vernonshidden

https://twitter.com/#!/VernonsPrime

https://twitter.com/#!/BDiamondLounge

www.facebook.com/thehiddensteakhouse

www.facebook.com/vernonsjazzclub

www.facebook.com/VernonsPrime

www.opentable.com/vernons-hidden-valley-steakhouse

http://itunes.apple.com/kz/app/prime-restaurant/id453575584?mt=8 (iPhone)

www.youtube.com/user/VernonsJazzClub

LivingSocial

The second-largest competitor to Groupon, LivingSocial (`http://living social.com`) offers enticing coupon deals, with a focus on local travel and events.

Launched in August 2009, LivingSocial says it now reaches more than 60 million subscribers in almost 200 cities in 20 countries worldwide.

The benefits are the same as with other deal sites: brand awareness, direct appeal to locally targeted markets, word-of-mouth advertising, high visibility to a new customer stream, no revenue sharing unless your minimum number is sold, and easy results tracking. LivingSocial, which already offers travel deals under LivingSocial Escapes, also has categories for family deals, nationwide deals, "at home" deals, and gifts.

LivingSocial integrates with Facebook, Twitter, and e-mail, and has apps for both the iPhone and Droid. Like Groupon, it offers an affiliate program and in-house rewards for referrals.

Comparing LivingSocial and Groupon

A recent comScore analysis (`http://blog.comscore.com/2011/06/groupon_livingsocial_grabbing.html`) found that these two major players actually reach different segments of the deal market and appeal to somewhat different users demographically.

While LivingSocial, founded in Washington, D.C., predominates in the eastern U.S., Groupon (headquartered in Chicago) focuses on the Midwest and Pacific regions. Groupon users skew younger and more female, while LivingSocial has more middle-aged users and roughly equal male and female users.

Diversifying Your Daily Deals

Many businesses have discovered smaller daily deal sites that are far less risky for the merchant. Some of these are local sites; some are national online opportunities targeting a particular product or market. Table 5-1 provides several examples. For sites in your area, try searching for "your city" or "your product" plus the words *daily deals* or *group coupons*.

Ask other local merchants about their experience before you sign up with any deal sites.

Table 5-1   Group Coupon and Daily Deal Sites

Name	URL for Media Kit and Advertising Information	Notes
BizSaves	`www.bizsaves.com/#vendorsignup`	Promotes weekly deals targeting the B2B market via e-mail

Bloomspot	`www.bloomspot.com/partners`
	
	`www.bloomspot.com/travel`
		Offers discounts on local attractions and to travel destinations

Facebook Offers	`www.facebook.com/help/offers`	Replaces Facebook Deals and Facebook Check-in Deals; created by page publishers; free; in beta
Gilt City	`https://vendornet.giltcity.com`	Offers local deals in selected cities
Google Offers	`www.google.com/offers/business`	Offers local deals in selected cities
Haute Look	`www.hautelook.com/about`	Daily discounts on top designer brands
LA Deals	`http://dailydeals.latimes.com/for-your-business`	Local deals from the *Los Angeles Times*
PopSugar City	`http://popsugarcity.com/get-featured`	Targets trend-setting women of Generation Y
RapidBuyr	`www.rapidbuyr.com/MerchantStreet/why-RapidBuyr.aspx`	Promotes one-day deal targeting the B2B market
Rue La La	`www.ruelala.com`	Invitation-only membership to high-style, short-lived, online, flash sale boutiques; runs nationwide
Tippr	`www.poweredbytippr.com/merchants`	Offers discounts by e-mail
Yelp for Business Owners	`https://biz.yelp.com/support/deals`	Deals promoted on Yelp, a consumer-rating site
Yipit	`www.yipit.com/about/businesses`	Custom discounts filtered by location and interest
Zozi	`www.zozi.com/businesses`	Focuses on outdoor activities
Zulily	`www.zulily.com/index.php/vendor`	Promotes daily deals targeting moms, babies, and kids

Book VIII Chapter 5

Attracting Customers with Daily Deal Coupons

Although the frenzy for deals may finally begin to slow as competitors saturate the coupon space, Facebook and Google have gotten into the "deal" game for competitive reasons. We describe their programs because these two companies can afford to offer businesses more attractive terms. Besides, no one can ever afford to ignore the gorillas in the room.

Google Offers

Google Offers (`www.google.com/offers/home`), which is in beta in certain areas, is Google's daily deal entry. Google will help you structure and design your offer and market it to subscribers in your area.

According to Google Offers' payment terms, it offers merchants a better alternative in terms of cash flow, claiming that merchants will receive 80 percent of their share of the revenue in four days. For more information, see `www.google.com/offers/business/how-it-works.html`.

Facebook Offers

Having given up on Facebook Deals and Facebook Check-in Deals, Facebook is now offering a feature for page administrators to create and share deals with people who Like their business pages (`www.facebook.com/help/offers`).

This program, which is still in beta for a limited number of local business pages, is easy to implement. From the Sharing Tool at the top of your Facebook timeline, click Offer, Event + and then click Offer again.

Unlike other deals, Facebook Offers merchants have total control over their offers and pay nothing to Facebook. For more suggestions on how to structure a Facebook Offer, see `www.ecommerce-guide.com/article.php/3939866`.

If Facebook Offers is not yet available for your business page and you don't want to wait, request to use the feature now by filling out an application form at `www.facebook.com/help/contact_us.php?id=367554259954235`.

Chapter 6: Social Gaming

In This Chapter

✔ **Considering social gaming as a marketing tool**

✔ **Understanding the surprising demographics of gamers**

✔ **Using social games and apps for marketing**

*I*n *social gaming,* video, online, and smartphone games are shifted to a social media paradigm, in which users play against each other (rather than against a machine). According to www.appdata.com/leaderboard/apps, at least 15 games on Facebook boast more than 10 million monthly players apiece, and FarmVille alone had more than 28.5 million Facebook players as of March 2012.

Social gaming enables people to play games with friends as well as strangers. This concept isn't new, but the extended combination with social networking is. It may portend a change in the entire sociology of gaming; it has already changed the demographics. And that's where your business opportunity arrives in the form of brand recognition, image-building, customer loyalty, and the viral spread of your message among gamers.

In this chapter, we show the options for integrating your marketing with the social gaming environment so you can decide whether it's cost-effective for your business.

Assessing the Marketing Value of Social Gaming

You have several promotional options with social games:

✦ Create your own game, like *SELF* magazine did with its "Workout in the Park" (www.selfworkoutinthepark.com) in March, 2012. Place the game on your website, social media pages, and/or on a gaming community site.

✦ Advertise on an existing game, the way Miracle-Gro does on FarmVille (see Figure 6-1), to leverage the game's popularity. In its more subtle manifestations, this "sponsorship" is similar to how a company sponsors a local show on public broadcasting.

Figure 6-1:
Advertising on a popular game like *FarmVille* is another way to take advantage of the social gaming population.

Courtesy Zynga, Inc.

✦ Take advantage of placement opportunities to promote your product or service, such as a billboard within a game.

✦ To increase visitor participation time, place a social gaming app on one of your social media pages or website to attract and hold visitors. The Animal Rescue Site does so for fundraising purposes on its Facebook page at `http://apps.facebook.com/arsgames`.

PlayFish and Zynga now offer the greatest number of social games on social media channels, but that's expected to change as other companies transfer their popular programs to social networking platforms. Some, but not all games, are available on standard web-based sites.

For instance, FarmVille, from Zynga (which went public in December 2011), is wildly successful in terms of Facebook users.

Table 6-1 lists some of the many popular social games and their creators. If you're interested in advertising, product placement, or sponsorship, investigate each one individually and contact the company.

Table 6-1	Companies That Create Social Games	
Company Name	*URL*	*Game Name*
Booyah!	`http://booyah.com`	MyTown 2, Early Bird!, PetTown
Heatwave Interactive	`www.platinumlife.com`	Platinum Life
Live Gamer	`www.livegamer.com`	Sid Meier's Civilization World
PlayFirst	`www.playfirst.com`	Diner Dash
Playfish	`www.playfish.com`	Restaurant City, Country Story, Pet Society, Crazy Planets, more
PopCap Games	`www.popcap.com`	Bejeweled Blitz, Zuma Blitz
Zynga	`http://company.zynga.com/about/advertise`	Café World, FarmVille, FishVille, Mafia Wars 2, PetVille, Treasure Isle, YoVille, Zynga Poker, and more

To view other games, try the Social Gaming App directory at `www.social-games-list.com`.

Before you decide to advertise on a gaming platform, observe and play a game for a while to make sure it will draw your target audience.

Tracking Who's Playing

Use Alexa or Quantcast to check user demographics, which may vary by game. If you plan to make a serious investment in social gaming, confirm that your target audience is actively participating.

A September 2011 survey of social gaming in the United States and UK, released by game-maker PopCap and Information Solutions Group, offers some fascinating insights:

```
www.infosolutionsgroup.com/pdfs/
    2011_PopCap_Social_Gaming_Research_Results.pdf
```

✦ Social gaming use is growing. Between June and August 2011, about 41 percent of Internet users in the United States and the UK played a social game for more than 15 minutes per week. In January 2010, only 24 percent of Internet users were that active in social gaming.

✦ Since January 2010, the average age of a social gamer has declined from 43 to 39 years.

✦ The number of players under 30 increased from 19 to 30 percent, while those over 50 years old declined from 38 to 32 percent.

✦ The proportion of male (45 percent) to female (55 percent) gamers remained stable between January 2010 and September 2011.

✦ Sixty-three percent of gamers play with personal (real-world) friends, 57 percent with online friends, and 37 percent with online strangers.

✦ Social gamers spend 56 percent of their time on social networking sites playing games, with 39 percent of their time playing social games with others.

✦ Ninety-one percent of social gamers go to Facebook to play, followed by Google+ (17 percent), Myspace (15 percent), and Bebo (7 percent).

✦ Social game selection is influenced by ads promoting games on social networking sites (50 percent), word of mouth (37 percent), alerts from an online friend (37 percent), and online searches (35 percent).

✦ The number of social game players who play at least six hours per week more than doubled from 7 percent in January 2010 to 15 percent in September 2011. Eighty-one million people play at least once a day, while 41 percent or 49 million people play multiple times a day.

✦ More than 25 percent of social gamers purchased virtual currency with real-world money: 36 percent of men and 28 percent of women. The 17 percent of current social gamers who are "newbies" are less likely to purchase virtual gifts.

✦ Among the games studied, Bejeweled Blitz and FarmVille remain two of the most popular, followed by Mafia Wars.

Demographics in the gaming world are fluid. They will vary significantly by game. Ask game publishers for user demographics and demographic trends by game; participate only in those that reach your target audience.

Changing the Game for Marketers

From a marketing point of view, you have several ways — generally limited only by your ingenuity and your budget — to take advantage of social gaming to reach these rather astonishingly large and devoted audiences.

Ah, that budget thing. We're not kidding. Many in-game advertising solutions are so expensive that only the largest companies can afford them.

The most expensive solution is developing your own game. Prepare to start with $100,000 to $300,000 to develop and launch a game, and then to allot a budget of tens to hundreds of thousands of dollars to market it, and that's just the beginning. Ongoing maintenance and content updates cost anywhere from $12,000 to $20,000 per month. For more information, try the resources at

```
http://developers.facebook.com/docs/guides/games
```

```
www.slideshare.net/Bitfold/social-facebook-game-space-at-
    a-glance
```

You can read about using a full-fledged game in the following section.

If you're not a tycoon, though, try these ideas:

✦ Advertise on games so your ads appear where characters would see them in reality: on billboards, signs, subway posters, street flags, or store signage. (Note how Miracle-Gro — a great fit for FarmVille — advertises on both a billboard and on the pop-up window in Figure 6-1.) According to Adparlor, a leading social game ad company, ads cost anywhere from 50 cents per install when a game is first launched to $3 per install in later stages of a game's life cycle.

✦ Let players "buy" your products with virtual currency, give them as virtual gifts, or win them as prizes. For example, Zynga's CaféWorld (`http://apps.facebook.com/cafeworld`), shown in Figure 6-2, allows players to purchase virtual currency or earn it by watching others' ads. Additionally, players can send "free gifts" to others and use the virtual currency to purchase items for their cafés.

Free gifts   Get coins & cash   Earn cafe cash

Figure 6-2:
CaféWorld
by Zynga
uses virtual
currency.

Courtesy Zynga, Inc.

✦ Give away points or virtual goods for clicking through to your online or
   video ads instead of ignoring them. The ads might appear as *interstitials*
   (between screens), as pop-ups or pop-unders, or between rounds of
   play. Dunkin' Donuts does something similar by giving away a Dunkin'
   Donuts Lawn Chair to players of The Sims Social who like their Facebook
   page. The first Sims Social branded virtual item, the lawn chair adds
   value to players' houses.

✦ Place your product so that it appears as a prop or part of the "stage set"
   for a game, just as it would in a movie, TV show, or video game. It can
   be a cereal box on a table, a book on a shelf, or branded running shoes
   worn by a character. The product reference can be hard-coded as the
   game is developed, or dynamically referenced so that the products that
   appear change based on users' demographics, date of use, or location.
   Sponsor branded items within the game that players can acquire, such
   as jobs or T-shirts. This is frequently done with console-style games, as
   you can see in the options at www.engageadvertising.com.

Integrating a Game App into Your Web Presence

For the truly ambitious (and well-funded), consider developing a game or app specifically about your product the way Malibu Rum did with its Facebook Beach Club Game in fall 2012 (`http://apps.facebook.com/beach-club-game`).

Trying to do all this yourself is worse than Lucy giving herself a home perm. Hire a game development company — Table 6-1 shows many — or search for *social game developers* on Google.

Most of the success with social gaming comes with increased brand recognition and customer loyalty. Traditional advertising methods for measuring these parameters can be found in *Advertising For Dummies,* 2nd Edition, by Gary Dahl. For more on integrating advertising metrics with your social media metrics, see Book IX, Chapter 6, or refer to Book I, Chapter 2 for estimating return on investment.

Chapter 7: Making Social Media Mobile

In This Chapter

✔ Understanding mobile media users

✔ Reaching people on the go

✔ Marketing with social media sites on smartphones

✔ Marketing with social media sites on tablets

Social media is no longer confined to a "standard" computer of any size. The proliferation of smartphones and apps, 4G networks, more affordable data plans, built-in web browsers, and mobile-ready websites have all contributed to the growth of mobile social activities. Most devices (except old feature phones) can use either a cellular network or Wi-Fi for wireless Internet access.

The integration of social media with mobile devices — from myriad smartphone forms to tablets and iPads — creates more opportunities to reach your target audience in addition to challenges for managing and integrating your marketing campaigns.

Mobile marketing can be implemented on standard feature-based cellphones, smartphones such as the iPhone and Android models, PDAs (personal digital assistants) such as the BlackBerry, and tablet computers.

As a social media marketer, try to tap the potential that these mobile devices offer: incredible marketing opportunities to reach both retail and business prospects at the moment they seek information about the product or service you offer, wherever they are. You don't have to wait for them to get back to their desktop computers. Of course, the social media marketing techniques you select may depend on the device(s) that your target market uses. In this chapter, we look at how rapidly advancing mobile technology allows you to use social media to reach people on the go.

Mobile social marketing gives you many new ways to "reach out and touch someone" with your message. The challenge, of course, is that everyone else is trying to do that, too. Your efforts have to cut through an increasing amount of clutter.

Understanding Today's Mobile Media Users

According to a comScore survey in August 2011, about one-third of all U.S. mobile users access social media services or blogs, a 37 percent jump from a year earlier. More than 72 million Americans accessed social networking sites or blogs via their mobile devices that month, with close to 40 million doing so almost daily. If you include other services, usage of mobile devices to browse the web, access applications, or download content grows to 116 million people by the end of August 2011.

```
www.comscore.com/Press_Events/Press_Releases/2011/10/
    Social_Networking_On-The-Go_U.S._Mobile_Social_Media_
    Audience_Grows_37_Percent_in_the_Past_Year
```

In a nutshell: Although more than twice as many people in 2011 used mobile apps via cellular networks to access social media than a year earlier, the mobile browser remains the most popular way to handle social networking — for the time being.

As you would expect, the increase in social mobile media meant that Facebook, Twitter, and LinkedIn all experienced a significant growth in monthly U.S. mobile usage. ComScore found that "Facebook's U.S. monthly mobile audience grew 50 percent year-over-year to 57 million, while Twitter's mobile user base skyrocketed 75 percent to 13.4 million users, and LinkedIn jumped 69 percent to 5.5 million users."

Measuring smartphone and tablet use

The shift of users from feature phones to smartphones has been stunningly fast. According to comScore, by July 2011, smartphones surpassed feature phones in the United States in terms of new mobile purchases.

Equally surprising is that the rate of use of mobile devices is surpassing use of desktops and laptops for web access, with rapidly increasing use of tablets and readers in the past year, as shown in Table 7-1. A recent Google study asserts that mobile usage had already surpassed desktop usage for Internet access by the end of 2011, although other studies project that milestone for 2014.

Table 7-1	Mobile Device Usage	
Device Usage	*Sept 2010*	*Feb 2012*
Mobile phone	85%	88%
Laptop	52%	57%
E-book reader	5%	19%
Tablet	4%	19%

Source: "Digital Differences" from the Pew Research Center; http://pewinternet.org/ Commentary/2012/February/Pew-Internet-Mobile.aspx

3G (third generation) and *4G* (fourth generation) refer to the speed and underlying technology of cellular networks by which mobile devices access the web. 3G supports voice and video and works well for people who download (at 14 Mbps) more than upload (at 5 Mbps); 4G (newer and more expensive) offers full Internet-style services at high connection speeds (100 Mbps to 1 Gbps), even from moving vehicles.

Generally speaking, Apple's and Android's market shares are increasing, BlackBerry's (RIM) share is decreasing, and Android phones are more popular than the iPhone among most recent buyers. Android led the market at 47.3 percent at the end of 2011. Symbian, an open source platform managed by Nokia, holds a small market share. Figure 7-1 shows the market share of smartphone operating systems from June 2010 to December 2011.

Book VIII
Chapter 7

Making Social
Media Mobile

Figure 7-1:
Market
share for
smart-
phones by
operating
system.

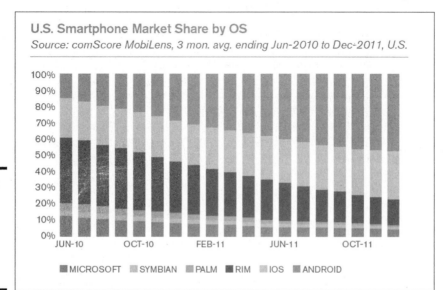

Courtesy comScore, Inc.

Why bother your marketing head with all this platform information? You need to get your social media message across on the specific platforms that your target audience uses. Not only must your content be technically compatible with different platforms, it should be optimized visually and for ease of use on mobile platforms.

Market share for smartphones is a highly competitive measurement that changes often. Check current statistics before you make a decision about targeting particular users.

Here are the demographics for smartphone users. A 2012 study by the Pew Center (www.internetretailer.com/mobile/2012/04/17/smartphone-owners-are-not-birds-feather) shows that 49 percent of U.S. adult men and 44 percent of women owned a smartphone in February 2012. The report also showed that the smartphone user population is racially diverse: 45 percent of whites, 49 percent of blacks, and 49 percent of Hispanics now use smartphones.

The biggest variation in smartphone use is by age, with 66 percent of those age 19–29 using smartphones, 59 percent of 30–49-year-olds, 34 percent of those age 50–64, and 13 percent of those 65 and older.

Household income is a second differentiator; 34 percent of households earning less than $30,000 annually have a smartphone. Smartphone usage also rises with income: 46 percent of those earning $30,000–$49,000; 49 percent of those earning $50,000–$74,000, and 68 percent of those earning more than $75,000.

Getting a handle on mobile activities

Mobile users check e-mail, weather, traffic, maps, directions, and headlines. They also search for companies and products (especially local ones), review entertainment schedules, access social media sites, watch videos, check review and ratings sites, sign up for alerts and coupons, and play games online. In other words, they are avid users of just about every social media channel. Table 7-2 shows the percentage of mobile users performing various activities online.

Table 7-2	What Mobile Users Do Online
Task	*Percentage of Mobile Users*
Sent text message	74.3%
Took photos	60.3%
Used e-mail	40.8%
Accessed social networking/blog	35.3%
Accessed weather	35.2%
Played games	31.4%
Accessed search	29.5%
Accessed maps	26.5%
Accessed news	25.5%
Listened to music	23.8%
Accessed sports information	21.8%
Accessed financial news or stock quotes	15.1%
Accessed online retail	12.2%

Source: comScore MobiLens; www.comscore.com/Press_Events/Presentations_Whiltepapers/2012/2012_Mobile_Future_in_Focus

Going mobile

With the rapid growth in the use of mobile media, you really don't have a choice. If you haven't already done so, have your programmer create a mobile site as part of your web presence. That mobile site should integrate seamlessly with your social media presence on mobile media.

As you can see by comparing the regular website for Taos.org (see Figure 7-2) with their mobile site (see Figure 7-3), the regular website has too many photos to load quickly in a mobile environment and would be difficult to navigate on a small screen. The mobile site focuses on fast, easy navigation.

**Book VIII
Chapter 7**

**Making Social
Media Mobile**

Figure 7-2:
Taos.org
standard
website as
it appears
in a desktop
environment.

Courtesy Webb Design, Inc.

If you need a custom solution, you can find $69 templates at www.webdesign
formobiledevices.com/wordpress-mobile-templates.php. Or try
Mobify (https://cloud.mobify.com/about/pricing), which is free
for one domain and up to 100,000 mobile page views per month. Table 7-3
lists some of the many tools and service providers available for developing a
mobile version of your website.

The best solution of all: Ask your developer for help developing your mobile
website.

When your mobile site is up and running, you can direct users from the
mobile site via chiclets to your social mobile pages or link to your primary
website for more information.

Figure 7-3:
The mobile website for Taos.org.

Courtesy Webb Design, Inc.

Table 7-3	Mobile Website Tools
Name	*URL*
MobGold (mobile advertising network)	`www.mobgold.com`
Mobify (free mobile web design for one domain)	`www.mobify.com`
MoveToDotMobi (custom mobile web design)	`www.movetodotmobi.com`
Wadja (mobile social networking service)	`www.wadja.com`
Web Design for Mobile Devices (templates for mobile web sites)	`www.webdesignformobiledevices.com/wordpress-mobile-templates.php`
Webhosting Search (mobile website tool resources)	`www.webhostingsearch.com/articles/30-best-tools-to-create-mobile-website.php`
Zinadoo (free mobile website tools)	`www.zinadoo.com`

Reaching People on the Move with Social Media

Almost all social media services now reconfigure their sites for mobile devices, as shown in Table 7-4. Generally, this reconfiguration happens automatically for client pages. All you have to worry about is how you can benefit from reaching people who are using mobile devices.

Table 7-4	Sites for Social Mobile Services
Name	*URL*
Blogger	`www.blogger.com/mobile-start.g`
Digg	`http://m.digg.com`
Facebook Mobile	`http://m.facebook.com`
Facebook for iPhone	`http://itunes.apple.com/us/app/facebook/id284882215?mt=8`
Flickr	`http://m.flickr.com`

Name	URL
foursquare	`https://foursquare.com/mobile/login?continue=%2Fmobile%2F`
Google+	`www.google.com/mobile/+`
Groupon	`www.groupon.com/mobile`
Kaboodle	`http://www.kaboodle.com/m#login`
LinkedIn Mobile	`http://touch.www.linkedin.com/mobile.html`
Myspace Mobile	`http://m.myspace.com/login.wap`
Oodle	`www.oodle.com/info/mobile`
Pinterest	`http://m.pinterest.com/`
Twitter Mobile	`https://twitter.com/#!/download`
WordPress	`http://wordpress.org/extend/mobile`
Yelp	`www.yelp.com/yelpmobile`
YouTube	`http://m.youtube.com/`

Source: http://socialmediatrader.com/38-social-networking-sites-for-your-mobile

For example, the mobile version of Facebook displays a stripped-down home page that focuses on interactivity. Users can view status updates and other messages and also post their own updates, comments, videos, and images. Even Twitter, which has cellphone DNA in its genes, has revamped its mobile applications with an app that gives the page a better, easier-to-use layout, including navigation icons at the top, @replies, a column for the message stream, and search functionality.

Figures 7-4 and 7-5 show the Weddings at Mountain Springs Lake Resort's Facebook Page in a mobile environment and on a standard desktop.

Check out your Facebook Page, LinkedIn profile, and Twitter stream on various phone and tablet operating systems to see how they appear, and then adjust them as needed.

**Book VIII
Chapter 7**

**Making Social
Media Mobile**

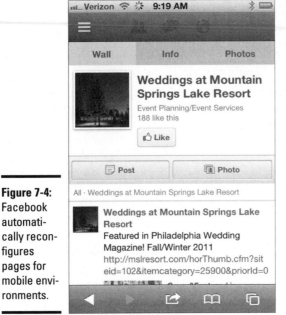

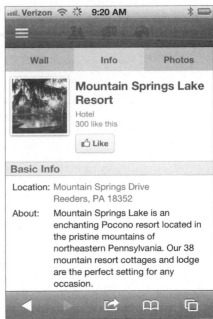

Figure 7-4:
Facebook automatically reconfigures pages for mobile environments.

Figure 7-5:
The desktop version of the Weddings at Mountain Springs Lake Resort Facebook Page.

Harvesting Leads and Sales from Social Mobile

You can find as many applications for marketing via mobile social media as you can imagine. Keep in mind the areas described in this list, whatever the device or market segment you target:

✦ **News and updates:** Distribute this type of information to your Twitter, Facebook, and LinkedIn customers, the people on your prospect list, and your newsletter subscribers. (See Figure 7-6 for some LinkedIn examples.)

✦ **Emergency information:** Warnings range from product recalls to weather hazard.

✦ **Comparison shopping:** Provide information so that Facebook, Twitter, and Pinterest shoppers can compare by price and feature and learn about sales.

✦ **Local business announcements:** Announce coupons, deals, and special offers across all your social media channels; see Figure 7-7 to see how a theatre lists its performances on social mobile sites.

✦ **Customer service improvements:** Use Twitter to let customers place a pick-up order and find out when their order is ready. Use QR codes so people can quickly determine your competitive products, features, and prices.

✦ **Event publicity:** On Twitter and Facebook, consider providing real-time logistical information.

✦ **Integration of mobile marketing and social media:** Post updates on the fly and use geomarketing services, such as foursquare (described in Book VIII, Chapter 4), especially if your business targets younger, local customers. (See Figure 7-8.)

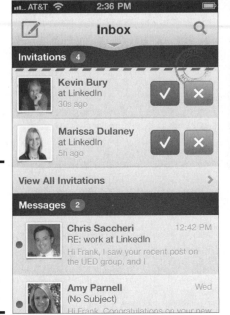

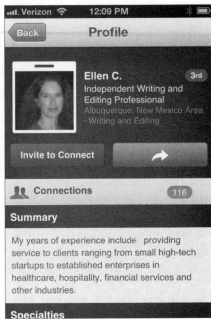

Figure 7-6:
LinkedIn
mobile
pages may
display
news,
contacts,
invitations,
or updates.

(Left) Courtesy LinkedIn (Right) Courtesy Ellen Cline

Figure 7-7:
The Roxy's
mobile
Twitter
pages
display
standard
information
(left) and
its tweet
stream
(right).

Courtesy The Roxy Theatre

Figure 7-8:
Foursquare mobile sites may display special offers (left) or a typical foursquare check-in screen (right).

Courtesy foursquare

Don't let the obvious business-to-customer (B2C) value of mobile devices blind you: Mobile marketing has a place in business-to-business (B2B) strategies as well. Some of the earliest adopters of new technology are businesses seeking improved productivity or a competitive edge. For example, sales people are using the technology for competitive research, tracking sales calls, and demonstrating their products and services to prospective customers.

Paysimple's 2012 survey

```
http://paysimple.com/blog/2012/04/11/infographic-how-
    small-business-owners-use-mobile-technology
```

shows that small businesses are getting ready to take advantage of mobile marketing options:

✦ 48 percent say it's very important to use a mobile device in small business.

✦ 83 percent believe mobile payments will be mainstream within the next four years.

✦ 37 percent of small business owners have smartphones.

✦ 34 percent of small businesses use iPads, four times the 2011 amount.

When mobile social media becomes the business

Kevin Zelko, owner of @MsBeerVendor.com, has been a beer vendor for more than seven years, working for vending companies at particular stadiums and teams, including the Seattle Mariners. He had long been using Twitter to make funny baseball-related comments when he and a friend had a brainstorm.

They realized that Twitter could be used to interact with other fans directly, and better yet, to sell them beer at their seats. In March 2011, they began tweeting about ordering beer at Mariners games. Their tweets quickly caught the attention of major sports networks and the press. "My idea really pointed to the interest of customers to be served directly at their seat, and their desire to use social media in everyday activities."

His Twitter customers use @msbeervendor on their smartphones, but Zelko realized that adding a website could assist with customer updates and help raise money for causes. With the help of a webmaster who built his WordPress site and optimized it for search, he can now update the website to let customers know which games he'll be working and which sections he'll be serving. He also set up a Facebook Page to expand interaction with customers. Other than that, says Zelko, "It's just good, old-fashioned connecting with people who can support your like business and personal interests. In my case, sports bars, beer companies, and soccer fans." A few local breweries and one big beer company have given him Mariners and beer promotional items to give out at pregame events to followers who tweet him then.

Most @msbeervendor followers come from the news stories on CNBC or ESPN, and also from the Mariners' Twitter community. He now has plenty of repeat customers and 1,470 followers on Twitter. "That's the best sign that people enjoy using the service. And because it's social media, you get to know your customers."

Zelko does see some limitations with the process. "I would love to take this a step further and be able to have payment processing instantly for a Twitter order so delivery can be that much quicker, and I can serve more customers. I have seen vendors use Square, but handing over an iPhone to the twelfth guy down and passing it back just isn't realistic.

"Be willing to take chances with Twitter, but realize it can really take off — and your company needs to be ready for that," Zelko reminds others. "When my story broke, there was no way I could cover the entire stadium with that many people tweeting me, so we had to adjust. Fun is a big part of social media, so make it fun and laughter-filled." Zelko has the true business-owner's optimism. "The more you interact, listen, and respond to the Twitter world, the better you will do. It's been such a wild ride — I can't wait to see where it goes next!"

MsBeerVendor's web presence

```
http://msbeervendor.com
```

```
https://twitter.com/msbeervendor
```

```
www.facebook.com/MsBeerVendor
```

```
http://msbeervendor.com/feed
```

Courtesy MsBeerVendor

Measuring Your Mobile Marketing Success

As with all analytics, which elements you measure depend on your goals and objectives. Of course, your choices depend on whether you're measuring intermediate performance indicators (the number of Likes on your Facebook Page comparing mobile versus desktop users) or the success of a mobile advertising campaign, the sales of a new mobile app, the number of visitors to your site, or the level of foot traffic to a brick-and-mortar store.

You can segment mobile visitors by using the available tools within Google Analytics, for example, to track their behavior on a mobile site or on your regular website (or both). You might want to set up a separate conversion funnel for mobile users. Watch for variations between mobile and web visitors on traffic to your social media pages, links to your mobile website, qualified prospects, and leads that turn into sales.

See Book IX, Chapter 5, for additional information about analyzing mobile social metrics and comparing them to metrics for social media in a standard environment.

Counting on Tablets

Use of e-readers, iPads, and other tablet computer models is exploding. CNBC reports that the rate of adoption of the iPad, in particular, positions it as "the most quickly adopted non-phone consumer electronics product in history." Given the convergence of high technology with usability, portability, mobility, and affordability, it may represent a true paradigm shift in computing.

According to the Nielsen Company, fewer than 5 percent of American consumers owned a tablet computer in May 2011 (compared with 36 percent who owned smartphones), but those consumers "watch more videos, read and pay for more books, are more willing to watch ads, and are more prone to buy an item after seeing an ad." In other words, businesses are already making money off them.

Within 18 months of the introduction of Apple's iPad, 11 percent of U.S. adults owned some type of tablet computer.

As with smartphones, tablet owners use their devices for many purposes: research, shopping, news, customer reviews, and yes, social media. Once again comScore comes through with interesting findings:

www.comscore.com/Press_Events/Press_Releases/2011/10/
    Smartphones_and_Tablets_Drive_Nearly_7_Percent_of_
    Total_U.S._Digital_Traffic

> *Tablets facilitate real-time social networking. Nearly three in five tablet owners updated their social networking status or commented on others' status on their device during September [2011], while slightly less than half shared their location using a location-sharing site during [that month].*

The demographics of iPad users are quite similar to those of the smartphone user base. They skew most heavily toward people who are between 25 and 34 years old (27 percent); more than 54 percent were male. Users initially trended toward very high levels of education and household income. As the more affordable Kindle Fire and Nook tablets become popular, users' average household income will also drop.

Making good social media use of the iPad

Obviously, the larger high-resolution iPad screen makes viewing videos more appealing than on smartphones, leading to even greater popularity for video-sharing sites like YouTube and Vimeo. Figure 7-9 shows how a Facebook site appears on an iPad.

Of course, all the major social media sites have their own apps for the iPad, as seen in Table 7-5.

Table 7-5	Inexpensive (or Free) iPad Apps for Social Mobile Services
App Name	*URL*
Facebook for iPad (created by a third party)	http://itunes.apple.com/us/app/friendly-for-facebook/id400169658
Flickr	http://itunes.apple.com/us/app/flickr/id328407587?mt=8
foursquare	http://itunes.apple.com/us/app/foursquare/id306934924?mt=8
Google+	http://itunes.apple.com/us/app/google+/id447119634?mt=8
Groupon	http://itunes.apple.com/us/app/groupon/id352683833?mt=8

Book VIII
Chapter 7

Making Social Media Mobile

(continued)

Table 7-5 *(continued)*

App Name	URL
LinkedIn	`http://itunes.apple.com/us/app/linkedin/id288429040?mt=8`
Myspace	`http://itunes.apple.com/us/app/myspace/id284792653?mt=8`
Pinterest	`http://itunes.apple.com/us/app/pinterest/id429047995?mt=8`
Twitter	`http://itunes.apple.com/us/app/twitter/id333903271?mt=8`
YouTube	`https://play.google.com/store/apps/details?id=com.google.android.youtube` for Android; built into iPad by Apple
Other marketing apps (some have fees)	www.warriorforum.com/internet-marketing-product-reviews-ratings/388242-best-ipad-apps-internet-marketers.html `http://blog.intuit.com/customers/7-must-have-ipad-apps-for-small-business-marketing` `http://mashable.com/2009/05/06/iphone-shopping-savings`

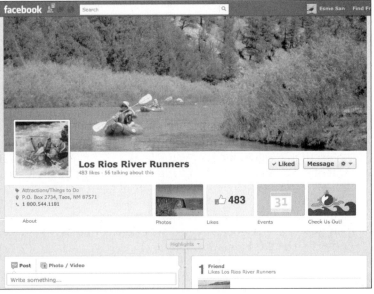

Figure 7-9:
Los Rios River Runners' Facebook Page on the iPad offers high-resolution imagery.

Courtesy Los Rios River Runners

Chapter 8: Multiplying Your Impact

In This Chapter

✔ Integrating social media with e-mail campaigns

✔ Incorporating social media, publicity, and public relations

✔ Combining social media with paid advertising

✔ Leveraging social media with website features

Social media has become such an essential way of "getting the word out" that it's now also a powerful tool for leveraging other forms of online marketing. All your marketing efforts can go viral when you take advantage of social media channels. Integration with social media can help you

✦ Increase newsletter subscriptions

✦ Broaden the audience for event announcements

✦ Maximize the distribution of press releases and other news

✦ Find additional paid online advertising opportunities

✦ Drive traffic to your hub website to encourage users to take advantage of special features

We discuss simple integration techniques in Book II, Chapter 3, such as displaying chiclets to invite people to follow your company on social media outlets and implementing share buttons to encourage viewers to share your pages with others. In this chapter, we discuss more advanced methods for integrating social media into your overall marketing plans.

Integration is generally easy and effective, but you'll need to invest in a little strategic planning beforehand and then some tactical execution. Eventually, though, these tactics become a matter of habit.

Include your integrated marketing tactics on your Social Media Marketing Plan (see Book I, Chapter 3) and schedule activities on your Social Media Activity Calendar (Book 1, Chapter 4).

Thinking Strategically

For many businesses, using social media marketing adds to the richness of a company's marketing mix. Others see it as a low-cost substitute for paid advertising, pay-per-click (PPC) campaigns, standard press release distribution, loyalty programs, or other forms of marketing.

If you're planning to swap tactics — replacing PPC campaigns or e-mail newsletters with social media, for instance — keep in mind that a social media campaign may take six months to a year to reach maturity. Don't stop using other tactics that now reach your target markets successfully. Wait for results from metrics showing that social media perform at least as well. And you can't know what to measure unless you first set goals for your integration efforts, which we discuss in Book I, Chapter 1. Sometimes you're after sales, sometimes leads, sometimes brand recognition, or sometimes just your 15 minutes of fame.

Whether you're planning to substitute or add social media to your other online marketing efforts, take advantage of the measurement tools we discuss in Book IX to establish baselines for traffic, click-through rate (CTR), conversion rates, and return on investment (ROI) for existing marketing methods so that you can detect any lift (or drop) that integration brings.

In its survey *The State of Marketing 2011,* Unica, an IBM Company, asked businesses whether they integrated their social media with other marketing techniques (`http://campaigns.unica.com/survey2011/Unica-s-Annual-Survey-of-Marketers-2011_v22.pdf`). Companies integrate social media with other marketing efforts about half the time. Businesses also reported that some forms of social media (social sharing links, ads, and widgets) were better integrated than others, as shown in Figure 8-1. Consider their experiences as you move forward with your own plans for integration.

Figure 8-1: How companies integrate social media with other marketing efforts.

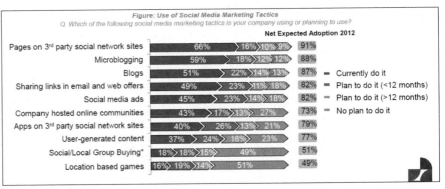

Source: IBM's State of Marketing 2012 Global Survey

To define the specific form your integration methods will take, who will execute them and when, and how you will measure the results, create a block diagram showing how content will flow as part of your integration plans (see Book I, Chapter 3).

Integrating with E-Mail

Recent studies show that people who use social media are more avid e-mail users than others. Given all the hype about social media, this might seem counterintuitive. Still, a June 2011 analysis from ShareThis.com states that although users share content via Facebook, the channel that they use depends on what they share. E-mail and LinkedIn, for instance, are most often the source of sharing informational content. Other sharing, such as bookmarks and blogs, have the highest level of engagement per click-through, as shown in Table 8-1.

Table 8-1	How Users Share Content	
Method	*Percent of Shared Links by Source*	*Average Number of Clicks by Source*
E-mail	17%	1.7 clicks
Facebook	38%	4.3 clicks
Twitter	11%	4.8 clicks
Other (blogs, bookmarks)	34%	5.3 clicks

Source: www.slideshare.net/ShareThisStudy/sharing-more-than-just-fans-friends-and-followers, Slides 4, 5, and 6

Confirming these observations, *The Social Habit 2011,* a study conducted by Edison Research, indicates that

✦ Forty-two percent of social networkers check their e-mail four or more times a day, compared with just 27 percent of those who don't use the current top social networking sites.

✦ Sixty-three percent of social networkers use the same e-mail account for their social networking messages and the majority of their permission (opt-in) e-mail.

✦ Twenty percent of Facebook, Myspace, and Twitter users have posted or shared something from permission e-mail to their social accounts by using a Share option.

With numbers like these, you have every reason to integrate e-mail with social media to attract new subscribers, promote your newsletter, obtain content ideas, and identify issues to address in your e-mail newsletters. For more information on e-mail marketing, see *E-Mail Marketing For Dummies*, 2nd Edition, by John Arnold.

Gaining more subscribers

Wherever and whenever prospects discover your presence on social media, try to provide them with other opportunities to find out how you might be able to solve their problems. Your online newsletter is certainly one of those opportunities. Follow these guidelines:

✦ **Include a link for newsletter subscription on your blog, all your other social media pages, and your e-mail signature block.** Constant Contact (`http://apps.facebook.com/ctctjmml`) and MailChimp (`www.mailchimp.com/campaign/getsocial`), among others, have apps you can add to your Facebook Page to allow Fans to sign up for your newsletter directly (see Figure 8-2). You never know — you might reach dozens, hundreds, maybe thousands of new prospects.

✦ **Treat your newsletter as an event on social media networks.** Add a preview of topics or tweet an announcement of your newsletter a day or so in advance. Include a linkable call to action to subscribe in both cases.

✦ **Post a teaser line in your social media outlets with a linkable call to action.** You might say, for example, "If you need to learn more about healthcare reform for small businesses, sign up for our newsletter."

✦ **Post newsworthy findings.** Use material from your newsletter on social news services like Digg and Reddit (see Book II, Chapter 3) to attract more readers.

✦ **Link to a sample newsletter or newsletter archive on your blog, website, or iFrame page on Facebook.** Prospective subscribers can see your newsletter's usefulness. Of course, you indicate the frequency with which you e-mail newsletters.

Finding more followers and connections

E-mail integration with social media works both ways: You can drive people from your newsletter to social media services or use social media services to gain subscribers:

✦ Use your newsletter to drive traffic to your social media outlets with social media chiclets. Independent record label The Mylene Sheath does so with its monthly newsletter. Along with Facebook, Twitter, and YouTube, The Mylene Sheath places chiclets for industry-specific social media sites, like Last.fm (an Internet radio site) and BandCamp.com, where artists can post samples of their music and links to The Mylene Sheath — where listeners can buy. (See Figure 8-3.)

✦ Include share buttons in every issue of your newsletter.

✦ Add options for signing up for social media on the e-mail registration page on your website (if possible).

✦ Use your e-newsletter to make an offer or run a contest for social media participants. For example, Bluefly.com (a retailer of discount designer apparel for women) runs an innovative contest in which participants "vote" on entries using the Like feature on Facebook.

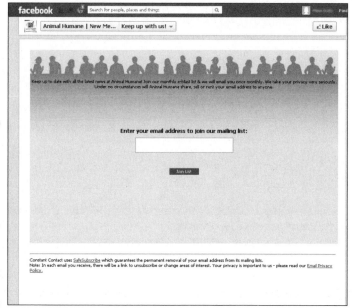

Figure 8-2: Animal Humane New Mexico solicits e-newsletter subscribers directly on its Facebook page.

Courtesy Animal Humane New Mexico

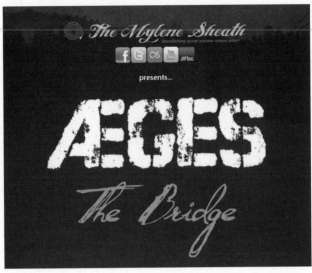

Figure 8-3:
Use chiclets on your newsletter to drive traffic to multiple social media outlets, as well as the home website.

Cross-promote your e-mail newsletter on all your social media channels. Remember to post all your social venues, not just your hub website, in your e-mail signature block.

Finding and sharing content

Writing content continuously for newsletters and social media is always a challenge. However, you can exploit the easy interaction between the two to lighten your writing burden:

✦ **Take advantage of social marketing capabilities from your e-mail service provider.** Many companies now let you easily send your e-mail directly to Facebook and other social networking pages.

✦ **Mine social media for content.** Read related information on social news sites, listen to hot topics that come up in LinkedIn and Facebook groups, and watch for trending topics. Pay attention to comments on your own and other people's forums, message boards, and social communities. They may clue you in to concerns, trends, or industry news.

✦ **Use Google Alerts, Social Mention, Twitter Search, and other search functions for mentions of your company.** You can turn positive comments into testimonial content on your newsletter, social media outlet, or website (with permission), or respond to many people at a time who may have read a negative comment.

- ✦ **Create a Q&A section in your regular newsletter.** Respond to questions that are common across social media venues.

- ✦ **Use keywords and tags to identify social news and content related to your industry.** In turn, be sure to include keywords in any newsletters or newsletter announcements that may be reposted on the web.

- ✦ **Pursue market intelligence even further by using the advanced Twitter search features.** Sort tweets geographically by search term. Then segment your mailing list accordingly, if appropriate. Visit `http://search.twitter.com/advanced`.

Use Google Insights (`www.google.com/insights/search/#`) to figure out the time of day, day of week, and time of year when users are most likely to use specific search terms, such as Christmas tree ornaments in November or December. Use that information to schedule your topical e-mail blasts. There's nothing like having information show up in someone's inbox just when they're looking for it! You'll be way beyond "top of mind."

Integrating with Public Relations and Press Releases

The reasons for dealing with public relations and press release distribution haven't changed since the explosion of social media — just the methodology. Where once you worried only about the care and feeding of a small covey of journalists, now you must nourish a veritable horde of bloggers, individual influencers, authors of e-zine articles, editors of online publications, and individuals who will recommend your article on a social news service.

In companies that view social media primarily as a public relations vehicle, the public or community relations person may be the one who coordinates the social media marketing strategy.

All these venues, not just standard media, now open a door to public attention. Take advantage them all as a cost-effective way to achieve these goals:

- ✦ **Broadcast announcements of products, appearances, and events.** Alerting target markets to new products and services is one of the most traditional uses of publicity.

- ✦ **Build brand recognition.** Whether it's acknowledgment of your participation in community events, awareness of your position within your industry, or simply the frequent repetition of your name in front of your audience, press coverage brings you publicity at a relatively low cost.

Book VIII Chapter 8

Multiplying Your Impact

✦ **Ask journalists, authors, or bloggers to write about your company.** Stories about your firm — at least the positive ones — boost your credibility, extend your reach, and provide you with "bragging" destinations for links from your site. Trade press is especially critical to business-to-business (B2B) companies.

✦ **Drive traffic to your website.** Online press releases almost always have at least one link to your central web presence, and often more. Social media offers a mechanism for distributing linkable press content around the web that others may embed. The accumulation of long-lasting inbound links obviously has a greater impact than a one-time release.

✦ **Improve search engine ranking.** You can gain many inbound links to your site when your release posts on multiple press outlets. Press sites generally transfer their high page rankings to your site; Google in particular weighs press mentions highly. Your visibility on preferred search terms may also rise, especially if you've optimized your press releases and headlines for keywords.

Setting up an online newsroom

If you haven't already done so, set up an online newsroom (media page) for the press on your primary website. Use this newsroom to present any press releases you create, provide writers with downloadable logos and images, link to articles and posts written about your company, and let writers sign up for really simple syndication (RSS) feeds for future release.

Also consider setting up this newsroom as a separate section in blog format (another way to integrate social media!) to aggregate queries, moderated posts, and trackbacks from individual releases. Give each release a unique URL and place your headline on the page title.

Cultivating influencers

Identifying influencers is one key way to get into a conversation. Influencers are people whose blogs, tweets, or Facebook pages drive much of the conversation in a particular topic area. They often have a loyal following of readers who engage in dialog, repeat, and amplify discussions the influencer began. In the olden days, press folks would cultivate public relations and press contacts the same way you now cultivate influencers.

Here's a quick checklist for finding these key figures to approach with a request for coverage:

✦ **Find conversations on blogs, Twitter, Facebook, forums, message boards, communities, and industry-specific social media by using keywords relevant to your company, brand, product, industry, and competitors.** You can find such searches on Bing Social Search (www.bing.com/social), Ice Rocket (www.icerocket.com), or Topsy (http://topsy.com).

✦ **Use search tools on particular networks and aggregator searches, such as Social Mention or WhosTalkin.** Those who post most often, or who have a lot of connections or followers, may be the experts or influencers you seek. Monitor the conversations for a while to be sure that you identified the right folks.

✦ **Use standard search techniques to locate trade publications or related newsletters.** Publication sites may include links to their own social media sites. Or, identify specific writers and editors whose interests sync with yours and search for their individual blogs and social networking accounts.

✦ **Become a contributor who answers questions on related subjects in various social media venues.** You can (and should) identify yourself, without promoting your company or products in your comments. Before you ask for anything, engage in the conversation and offer links to related posts and articles. Because links are the currency of social media, link from your site to influencers' sites, blogs, and tweets, and become a connection or follower.

To track your contacts, bookmark the conversations you find, organizing them in subfolders by the name of influencer.

Distributing your news

Frankly, the more sites, the merrier. Although you'll pay a penalty for duplicate content in search engines, press releases don't seem to suffer.

Place identifying tags on links in different press releases so that you can tell which releases generate click-throughs to your site. If you create only one release a month, this isn't essential; however, if you have an active campaign with numerous press mentions, or other types of postings on the same source sites, it's absolutely critical.

Table 8-2 shows a partial list of press and PR online resources.

Table 8-2	Publicity and PR Resources	
Name	*URL*	*Description*
BuzzStream	www.buzzstream.com/social-media	Fee-based social CRM and monitoring service
ClickPress	www.clickpress.com	Free press release posting on site
Free Press Release	www.free-press-release.com	Free press release distribution; includes social media
Help a Reporter Out	http://helpareporter.com	Matching reporters to sources
HubSpot	http://blog.hubspot.com/blog/tabid/6307/bid/29961/10-Ways-to-Rock-PR-Like-an-Inbound-Marketer.aspx www.slideshare.net/HubSpot/new-research-on-news-release-best-practices	Article and slide show about optimizing press releases and PR for SEO
Muck Rack	http://muckrack.com/gopro	Journalists on Twitter by beats
Muck Rack	http://muckrack.com/press_releases/submit	Fee-based Twitter pitch to journalists, $50 minimum
Page Trafic Buzz	http://www.pagetrafficbuzz.com/20-press-release-distribution-sites/6839/	List of 20 Press Release Distribution sites
PitchEngine	www.pitchengine.com	Social PR platform, social media release creation and distribution; free and paid versions
Press About	www.pressabout.com	Free press release distribution in form of blog

Name	URL	Description
PressDoc	www.pressdoc.com	Write, edit, publish and share social media releases online; €19 or $27.71 per release
PRWeb	http://service.prweb.com/learning/article/press-release-grader	Free press release–grader service
Reddit	www.reddit.com	Social news site that accepts links to releases
Shift Communications	http://www.shiftcomm.com/downloads/SMR_v1.5.pdf	Social media press release format
The Open Press	www.theopenpress.com	Free press release posting onsite

Posting on your own sites

Post your release, at minimum, on your own website and blog. You can, however, easily add releases to your other social networking profiles, if it's appropriate. For instance, an author might post a release for each book she writes, but wouldn't necessarily post a press release for everyone hired at her company.

To simplify your life, use syndication tools such as Seesmic Ping or Ping-o-matic, or RSS (see Book II, Chapter 1) to post both press release and newsletter content on your blog, Facebook Pages, and elsewhere. Of course, then the content will be identical.

Using standard press distribution sources

Many, many paid online press release distribution sources exist. Among the most well known are BusinessWire, Vocus, PR Newswire, PRWeb, and marketwire.com.

Sometimes, distribution services offer levels of service at different prices depending on the quantity and type of distribution, geographical distribution, and whether distribution includes social media, multimedia, offline publications, or other criteria.

Table 8-2, a little earlier in this chapter, includes several options for free distribution. Many free services don't distribute your releases — except perhaps to search engines — but, rather, simply post them on their sites for finite periods. Whether they're free or paid, be sure to read carefully what you're getting.

Perhaps the most straightforward example of integrating press releases with social media is the distribution of a release announcing your new social media presence. Preferred Market Solutions, LLC distributed the press release shown in Figure 8-4 through `www.24-7pressrelease.com`, one of many paid press release distribution services.

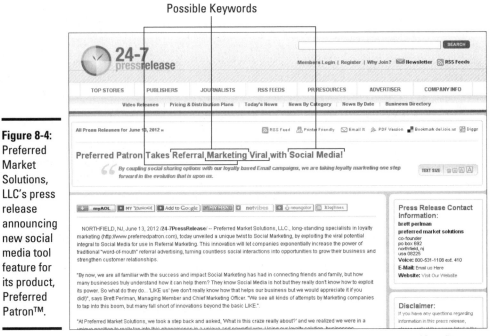

Figure 8-4: Preferred Market Solutions, LLC's press release announcing new social media tool feature for its product, Preferred Patron™.

Courtesy Preferred Market Solutions, LLC Preferred Patron™

Post linkable event announcements on calendars all over the web as well as event pages on Facebook, Myspace, and other social media. Calendars may be an "old-fashioned" pre–social media technique, but many high-ranking calendar pages feed page rank value until your event occurs and the listing expires.

Using bloggers as a distribution channel

You've laid the groundwork by identifying appropriate bloggers and other influencers and participated on their publications. The next step is to get them to post your news. The most discrete way is to e-mail it (or a link to it) with a cover note to see whether the recipient wants to share the article with readers or comment on its content.

Because you're "pitching" the bloggers, include in your cover note why you think readers of the blog would be interested and also a descriptive paragraph about your company. It's considered bad form to submit your press release as a post on most blogs — bad enough that a moderator probably would exclude it.

If you include a product sample with your release, implicitly asking for an independent review, the blogger now has to disclose that fact. In October 2009, the Federal Trade Commission published final guidelines for endorsement and testimonials. For more information, see `www.ftc.gov/opa/2009/10/endortest.shtm`.

Using social news services and other social networks

You can send similar e-mails to individuals and influencers you have identified as participating in key discussions about related products or issues, including a short notice about the press release on Twitter and a mention to groups and professionals on sites like Facebook and LinkedIn.

You can submit your release to the few social news services, such as reddit, that permit you to submit your own link to your press release. In other cases, you may need to submit to social news and bookmark services from another identity, or wait until the story appears on a blog and submit the blog post instead.

Of course, you can always link to press releases on your own site from your other social media, as new aggregator GreenAirOnline.com does with shortened URLs from its Twitter feed (see Figure 8-5).

Courtesy www.GreenAirOnline.com © Greenair Communications

Figure 8-5:
For extra mileage on press releases, link from your Twitter feed to releases on your website.

If your press release includes multimedia or you've created a video or audio release, be sure to submit it to relevant directories such as `www.blogtalk radio.com`, `www.digitalpodcast.com`, or `http://www.bloguniverse.com/video-blogs/`.

Emphasizing content

As always, content, tone, and interest level are the keys. Keep your release to about 400 words or fewer if you're including multimedia.

Keep your headline to about 80 characters and use an `<h1>` HTML header tag.

Combine anchor text (see Book II, Chapter 2) with the URL in parentheses right next to it (to cover all bases), but don't use the same anchor text twice. On some press distribution services — and of course on social media — you have a chance to submit keywords or tags, which is an essential process for leveraging your press release for search engine optimization (SEO) purposes. Be sure that some or all these keywords are included in the headline or first paragraph of the release. Try to use at least some of your primary set of search terms, as described in Book II, Chapter 2. For instance, in Figure 8-4 earlier, good keywords or tags appearing in the headline might have been *referral marketing, marketing viral,* or *social media.*

Rethinking the press release for social media

Over the past several years, users have debated the value of a new format for social media press releases. The biggest differences are that the social media release

+ Usually has three or four embedded links with anchor text for search engines, rather than URLs only (although you can mix the two)
+ May include embedded video and other multimedia options
+ Allows reports to "rip" content electronically and re-purpose it
+ May include tags and sharing options

In its *2009-10 B2B Marketing Benchmark Report,* Marketing Sherpa found the social media release roughly comparable to traditional releases in terms of the resulting quantity and quality of leads. The biggest difference noted was that businesses use the new format only about half as often as the traditional one. HubSpot, on the other hand, found that traditional releases were republished in full about 20 percent more often.

The choice is yours. The social media release is a convenient way to ensure that your master release format has all the elements you might need for various social media submissions.

You can find free templates for your press releases; Figure 8-6 shows one. You can pick and choose the bits and pieces to submit as appropriate to different services. If you're using a standard press release distribution service, you can easily extract the pure text version and adjust the URLs.

A sample of a prepared social media release is shown in Figure 8-7.

**Book VIII
Chapter 8**

**Multiplying Your
Impact**

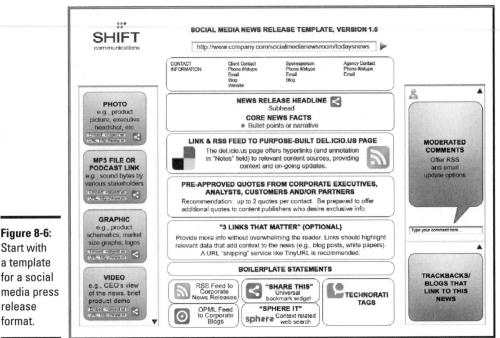

Figure 8-6: Start with a template for a social media press release format.

Courtesy SHIFT Communications PR

Figure 8-7: A press release in a social media format distributed through PitchEngine.

Courtesy Project Angel Heart

For more information on press releases, watch the HubSpot presentation at `www.hubspot.com/the-science-of-pr`.

Measuring results

The same social monitoring tools that you use to find influencers can be applied to track key performance indicators for your press efforts, such as Google Alerts, Social Mention, and `http://twitter.com/#!/search-home`. Assessing results from your publicity is a good place to use all that "qualitative" data, as well as advertising measurements for online brand awareness and equity. (See, for example, `http://www.questionpro.com/brand-awareness.html` or `www.businessknowhow.com/internet/social media.htm`.)

Measure baselines before you begin your press campaigns, and be sure that before-and-after results span comparable time frames. Here are a few key performance indicators that you might find relevant:

✦ Number of online mentions of company, brand, product or service line, and/or individual products or services anywhere online, including social media, during a specific time frame.

✦ Number and location of media placements: where and when mentions occurred, a press release was published, or an article about your company or product appeared on a recognized media outlet, whether online or offline.

✦ Site traffic generated from press releases and other linkable press-related mentions; see referrer logs in your web stats software for number of inbound links from each source. Include comparative CTRs and conversion rates, if available. To make this process easier, tag links with the identifiers related to the topic or date of the press release.

✦ Social media campaign participation and sentiment using monitoring tools; see Book II, Chapter 1.

✦ Average frequency of the product, company, or brand conversations related to the release compared to the frequency of conversations before the release.

✦ Estimated costs (hard dollars and labor) that were spent. Be sure to include costs for paid distribution, if used. To compare ROI for publicity to other methods, you compare costs to the value of sales that can be traced back to the release (if any). If you can't trace back sales, you might be able to compare brand engagement.

**Book VIII
Chapter 8**

Multiplying Your Impact

Integrating with Paid Advertising

Social media has the advertising world in ferment. As applications from social media companies mature, audiences grow, and technology improves, the companies expand their advertising opportunities to make money for their investors — everyone is just trying to make a buck. Over the past year, major advertising announcements have had the virtual world aflutter.

Facebook and Twitter have taken online advertising to the next level by extending their presence within the social stream of news or tweets where users' attention is focused, as well as by expanding advertising opportunities to their mobile environments.

These and other announcements indicate ways in which social media may affect your online marketing plans: First, they become additional destination opportunities for your own paid advertising; second, social media technology is fueling the growth of the new engagement ad.

Advertising on social media sites

Many social media sites, especially blogs, have long accepted advertising that you can incorporate into your plans for paid advertising (if any). Some (like Tumblr and YouTube) and many smaller social media venues display standard PPC, banner, and/or multimedia ads from Google AdSense. Flickr ads are served by Yahoo! Ad Solutions (`http://advertising.yahoo.com/advertisers`). A recent report by pivot on the "Rise of Social Advertising" (`www.briansolis.com/2011/08/report-the-rise-of-the-social-advertising`) summarizes the challenge of customizing advertising for different user preferences in different social environments.

The increased advertising offerings on social media channels can all be interpreted as attempts to overcome consumers' acquired "banner blindness" to ads appearing in predictable locations. For more information on online advertising, see *Advertising For Dummies,* 2nd Edition, by Gary Dahl.

Self-service ads

Larger sites, such as Myspace and Facebook, have long sold display ads using their onsite, self-service tools for ad creation and targeting. Table 8-3 lists popular social media sites offering paid advertising options.

Table 8-3	Social Media Sites That Offer Paid Advertising	
Name	*URL for Media Kit and Advertising Information*	*Notes*

Facebook	`www.facebook.com/advertising`
	
	`www.facebook.com/business/ads`
		Demographics information at `www.facebook.com/help/?page=863`

LinkedIn	`http://www.linkedin.com/advertising`	Demographics at `http://advertising.linkedin.com/audience`
Meebo	`https://www.meebo.com/advertisers/#Overview`	Demographics at `http://www.quantcast.com/meebo.com`
MySpace	`https://advertise.myspace.com` runs through third-party `www.myads.com`	Demographics at `www.myads.com/targetedadvertising.html`
reddit	`www.reddit.com/ad_inq`	Demographics at `www.quantcast.com/reddit.com`
Tagged	`http://about.tagged.com/advertising`	Demographics at `http://www.quantcast.com/tagged.com`

Twitter	`http://blog.twitter.com/2010/04/hello-world.html`
	
	`https://business.twitter.com/en/advertise/start`
	
	`https://support.twitter.com/articles/142101`
		Promoted tweets starting with selected advertisers

Twitter	`http://sponsoredtweets.com`	Third-party platform that connects advertisers with Tweeters willing to tweet about their products for a price
YouTube	`www.youtube.com/yt/advertise`	Demographics at `http://www.youtube.com/advertise/demographics.html`
Zynga	`http://company.zynga.com/about/advertise`	Demographics at `http://www.quantcast.com/zynga.com`

To be sure, some of these user-generated ads are plug-ugly, much like newsletters in the early days of desktop publishing. In the future, social networks may add prepackaged, preformatted ads to which you need to add only your text.

You can and should take advantage of targeting your audience as closely as the tools allow, selecting by geography, demographics, education, and interest area whenever possible. Some folks object to the targeting: Older women seem to receive a disproportionate number of ads for skin creams and diets; those who change their status to Engaged are quickly deluged with ads from wedding service providers.

You can evaluate advertising placements on these sites just as you would evaluate advertising placed anywhere else. Using the advertising metrics discussed in Book IX, Chapter 6, consider cost per click (CPC), cost per 1,000 impressions (CPM), CTR, and resulting conversions to decide whether any of these ads pay off for you.

Results so far indicate that ads appearing on social media pages generally perform slightly worse than banner ads on other publications. The average CTR on banners in 2011 was only 0.2 percent; on PPC ads, it was closer to 1 to 3 percent. However, so many variables affect CTR — ad size, placement, quality of the ad, match to audience, and value of the offer — that it's hard to generalize. Anecdotal evidence indicates that the CTR on Facebook display ads ran about half the average.

Averages are averages. The range at both ends may be extreme. Like so much material on the web, the only metrics that matter are your own.

Although you can test the same ad in several places at the same time to see which publishers yield the most bang for your advertising buck, also take into consideration whether the audiences on different social channels respond to a different message.

Targeting your market is primary. Spiceworks, a provider of free network management software, is so successful at delivering a target audience of highly coveted IT professionals on its forum pages (http://community. spiceworks.com) that paid advertising supports the company. With CTRs of 2 to 20 percent, it can charge a premium for its ads. Don't overlook small social sites that can deliver your audience directly to your site. They're worth it!

Facebook Sponsored Stories

Facebook has added Sponsored Stories (www.facebook.com/business/ads) to its standard PPC advertising repertoire, as shown in Figure 8-8. Businesses can now pay to highlight stories in a user's News Feed that appear from a Friend or Page that a user is already connected to.

Figure 8-8: Facebook Sponsored Stories appear within a Facebook feed.

Sponsored story

Courtesy 454 Creative

Generally, these sponsorships are based on specific activities related to a brand or product. For instance, a sponsored story can be created when another user likes a page, comments on a Page post, RSVPs to an event, votes on a question, checks into a place, uses an app, plays a game, or Likes or shares a website. By contrast, most Facebook PPC ads are targeted by user demographics and geography.

In addition to self-serve ads, you can take creative advantage of other Facebook features. For instance, you can use an iFrame page on Facebook to insert an entire page (or pages) of HTML advertising content, as BMW did with its interactive Make It Yours page at www.facebook.com/BMW/app_302638729751025.

Promoted Tweets

Twitter is expanding its Promoted Products to placements within the tweet stream, not just at the top of a page or as the result of search (see Figure 8-9). Twitter is also beginning to offer advertising options that are affordable for small businesses. Previously, Promoted Products were available only to companies able and willing to spend a minimum of $25,000 per month.

**Book VIII
Chapter 8**

Multiplying Your Impact

Promoted Tweets are currently in beta with a selected group of small advertisers, starting with an offer to American Express business card holders. Click the Notify Me button at `https://business.twitter.com/en/advertise/promoted-tweets` to receive an alert when Promoted Tweets are available to everyone.

Promoted tweet

Figure 8-9:
A Promoted Tweet is clearly identified within the Twitter stream.

According to Twitter (`https://support.twitter.com/articles/142101`), you need to understand a few important things about Promoted Tweets:

✦ Promoted Tweets are based on interests, phrases, or keywords that appear in the content of tweets.

✦ Because there is no "click" option in the traditional sense, you pay when a viewer does something specific: click, retweet, reply, or "favorite" your promoted tweet.

✦ Sponsors of Promoted Tweets are clearly identified. Otherwise, they act like regular tweets. They appear in the tweet stream of people already "following" your account. Because you can push your tweets toward the top of someone's feed when they login, these tweets receive extra attention.

✦ Twitter is adding options to target users whose characteristics match those of your existing followers. It is also allowing geographical targeting for local businesses and events.

✦ Twitter offers analytics to track performance, as well as other Promoted Product options for enhanced accounts, trends, and profiles.

User reaction to Promoted Tweets appearing in their tweet stream has not been positive; some users resent the intrusion of ads in their feed. Watch for changes in their advertising offerings if opposition continues to build.

As an advertiser, you need to maintain your communication effort with Twitter users; promoted tweets don't replace that. Put on your imagination thinking cap: You may need to revise your advertising creatives and offers to fit better with what the Twitter user expects and which promotion is most likely to be replied, retweeted, and otherwise spread around.

Some expect that promoted tweets will eventually end up redisplayed on other sites. Third-party sites can already redisplay promoted ads and split the revenue 50/50 with Twitter. One thing is certain: Lots of change is coming to the online advertising world. Stay up to date on promoted tweets at `http://blog.twitter.com`.

Engagement ads

Users have obviously started to tune out banner ads, even when the ads spill all over content and refuse to close, irritate eyeballs with annoying animation, or interrupt concentration with surprising bursts of unwanted sound.

The fuse was lit for innovation, and social media technologies ignited it, for good or ill. The marriage of advertising message with individual user information — with the potential of turning every viewer into a shill — has serious implications for privacy. Although the Interactive Advertising Bureau (IAB) has published best practices for user opt-in and privacy protection (`www.iab.net/socialads` and `www.iab.net/sm_buyers_guide`), it isn't clear how well they will be followed.

The IAB defines these engagement ads, sometimes called *social banners*, as

> *a type of banner that incorporates social or conversational functionality within it. . . . The key to success is for social banner ads to enable consumers to have a real interactive experience within the unit, as opposed to just passively viewing the content within the ad.*

**Book VIII
Chapter 8**

Multiplying Your
Impact

Comment-style ads seem to work well for entertainment, new products, cars, and clothes although virtual gift ads seem to attract consumer product and entertainment advertisers. Clicking the Like button on an ad now turns viewers into connections for that brand. This call to action ad works well for any established brand, luxury products, and products or entertainers with a passionate following.

More complex engagement ads draw content from a social network: the photo image and name from a profile (presuming an emotionally effective brand endorsement) or user-generated phrases from tweets, blogs, or RSS feeds. Users review the modified ads; if they agree to allow it, the ads are then distributed to their personal networks. For these complex ads to operate, the user must already be connected to her social network. (One could imagine using these ads to play an interesting game of rumor.)

Anyone can create a self-service display ad although having the assistance of an experienced graphic designer helps. However, these interactive engagement ads probably require involvement from tech support or your web developer.

Like the Promoted Tweets, engagement ads have an enhanced value based on how often others share them. If the sharing results in a cascading effect of recommended impressions to presumably qualified prospects, who just so happen to be friends, all the better for you. However, you need to watch for changes in pricing and business models as engagement ads take hold.

Integrating with Your Website

Any website can incorporate a myriad of features that integrate with social media, going well beyond the obvious and oft-repeated reminders to include Follow Us On and Share buttons everywhere, including product pages within stores. You can get clever: Include links to your Help forum or YouTube video tutorials as part of the automated purchase confirmation e-mail you send to buyers.

And, of course, this can work the other way: integrating your social media with your website. In Figure 8-10, Wesst (`www.wesst.org`) uses links throughout its Facebook Page to drive viewers to its website for additional information about services, workshops, events, news, and more.

In some cases, "old-fashioned" versions of social media — onsite forums, chat rooms, product reviews, and wikis — effectively draw repeat visitors to the hub site, avoiding any integration with third-party social media sites.

Figure 8-10:
Wesst
integrates
Facebook
with its
website
in multiple
ways.

Courtesy WESST New Mexico; www.wesst.org

More advanced sites have already implemented social media techniques onsite, including blogs and communities and other calls for user-generated content, photos and videos of people using your product or suggesting creative new designs and applications, and soliciting ratings.

Several strategic factors may affect your decision whether to implement such techniques onsite or off:

✦ The cost of development, storage, and support and ongoing maintenance versus costs offsite

✦ SEO and link strategies

✦ Plus-and-minus points of managing a more centralized and simplified web presence

A few onsite techniques, like loyalty programs, work just as well on social media (for example, special offers for those who "Like" you on Facebook). Three other popular methods practically cry out for integration: coupons, discounts, and freebies; games and contests; and microsites (more about these later in the chapter). For more information about onsite and other forms of online marketing, see *Web Marketing For Dummies,* 3rd Edition.

Brainstorm ways that an integrated media campaign might succeed for you. Diagram it and figure out what you'll measure to assess your accomplishments.

Martell's social media is greater than its parts

"Martell Home Builders believes in doing everything we can to turn an otherwise traditional industry on its ear," says Pierre Martell, CEO and President of Martell Home Builders. "By embracing the digital economy and communicating with our clients and trades in ways that are incredibly unique, we offer an experience like no other home builder. The success of 'The Martell Experience' can be measured via our rapid growth. We enjoy consistent growth in the range of 30 percent year-over-year."

The company launched its website in 2007, just one year after it was founded, and supplemented that site incrementally by adding YouTube, a blog, Twitter, and Facebook. This is part of Martell's strategic decision to sell its homes directly to buyers "so clients receive 'The Martell Experience' from start to finish," he explains. Martell Home Builders doesn't avoid realtors, but partners only with those who represent purchasers.

Courtesy Martell Home Builders

Given the company's wide range of social media activities, Martell uses different channels for different marketing functions. "While Facebook and Twitter are primarily used to connect with our network and leads, we use SmugMug to provide current clients with weekly photo updates on the construction of their homes. Clients are encouraged to share these branded photos via their own Facebook and Twitter pages with Share icons for each network," says Martell.

Their sales cycle has five steps:

Know→Like→Trust→Buy→Refer

"By using social media to make meaningful connections, we are often able to achieve Steps 1–3 before a face-to-face meeting." Martell looks at social media "less as a tool to drive traffic and more as a platform to engage with the community. Social media," she adds, "is not the place to sell, but rather to share and receive. Meaningful conversations and connections are the goals that enable us to build trust with our audience."

The Connect tab on the Martell website features live feeds from Twitter, Facebook, and its blog. It cross-promotes blog posts on Facebook or Twitter to further engage its audience. The company also publishes an e-newsletter and uses online retargeting ads to drive traffic to its website for comprehensive information.

Courtesy Martell Home Builders

(continued)

Book VIII
Chapter 8

Multiplying Your
Impact

(continued)

With social media guidelines specified in its operations manual, the company manages to keep everyone on staff engaged in the social media effort, according to Martell. Every employee has responsibilities tailored to her strengths, whether blogging versus tweeting, or on-camera versus video editing. Martell uses HootSuite to manage all these activities, schedules blog topics in advance on a calendar, and takes advantage of Google Analytics to measure traffic and the location of visitors.

Martell notes that the company uses offline marketing activities, too. It participates in trade shows and runs weekly open houses for potential clients to visit its model homes. "We have an installer put up more than 120 signs along major routes to funnel traffic directly to our location. We are known all over the city as the 'builders with the signs.'" The directional arrows, she claims, are more effective than any other form of advertising for Martell's open houses.

"Social media amplifies what you are already doing," Martell reminds business owners. "If you are working with integrity and connecting with clients in a positive way, social media will allow that information to be shared and create the same type of connection. Conversely, social media creates an opportunity for your audience to share negative experiences. It really puts integrity front and center."

Martell's web presence

`www.themartellexperience.com`

`www.themartellexperience.com/blog`

`www.facebook.com/martellhomebuilders`

`https://twitter.com/#!/martellhomes`

`http://martellhomes.smugmug.com`

`www.youtube.com/user/martellhomes`

`http://feeds2.feedburner.com/MartellHomeBuilders` (RSS)

Where's My Contractor? (app) `www.themartellexperience.com/connect`

Coupons, discounts, and freebies

It doesn't take much monitoring of Facebook and Twitter and social news, bookmarking, and shopping streams to see how frequently they're used to offer time-limited deals, coupons, special promotions, discounts, and free samples.

Certainly, longer-term offers can be made to LinkedIn and Plaxo members, to groups on Facebook or Flickr, or to members of a forum on any topic. However, the sense of urgency in certain social media environments catches viewers' interest. Just like the competitive energy of an auction may cause bidders to offer more than they intend, the ephemeral nature of real-time offers may inspire viewers to grab for a coupon they might otherwise have passed up.

Some user interest in savings and discounts may be encouraged by the recent recessionary mood, making people hyper-attentive to opportunities to save money. Getting "a deal" may also simply be human nature.

The upside and downside of real-time social media is precisely the immediacy of these offers and how quickly a chain of other posts extinguishes them from awareness. On one hand, you have a chance to move overstock quickly, bring in business on a slow day, or gain new prospects from a group you might not otherwise reach without making a long-term, and perhaps too-expensive, commitment.

On the other hand, you have to preplan and schedule your posts, repeating them frequently enough throughout the day to appear in real-time search results and near the top of chronologically organized posts on any social media site.

Always link back to your primary website or blog, not only to explain the details of the offer, but also to enjoy the inbound link value, offer additional goods and services, and capture prospect information. Be sure to use a unique promotion code for each offer, and tag your links with identifiers to track the source of click-throughs and conversions.

Most of the hundreds of online coupon sites already have a presence on Twitter, Facebook, Digg, and elsewhere. You can use their services or simply create a coupon of your own.

Whether you offer a discount through your website, social media, or any other form of advertising, be sure to include the impact of the discount in your cost analysis. Giving away a free soda may cost a business only 10 cents (mostly for the cup!), but if it gives away 1,000 drinks, the discount costs $100.

In the next chapter, we discuss a new model for coupons that is dependent on volume use reaching a critical mass.

Contests and games

Your imagination is the only limit to contests and games that you can post on your site and cross-promote via social media. As usual, make sure that viewers link back and forth among your sites, ensuring that an inbound link to your primary web presence exists. The goals of your contest may vary:

✦ Branding and name recognition

✦ Building relationships through entertainment

**Book VIII
Chapter 8**

Multiplying Your
Impact

✦ Obtaining feedback and building community through customer-generated content

✦ Locating hard-to-find resources, clients, or vendors

✦ Cross-promoting

✦ Acquiring testimonials

✦ Getting input into your own brainstorming process about where your product or service should go

As with special offers, be sure to include the cost of prizes and the labor involved in running the contest in your analysis of ROI. Depending on the goal of the contest, you may be looking for new visitors, repeat visitors, leads, or sales.

Figure 8-11 provides an example of a social media contest that helps draw traffic to a site. Luxefinds.com uses a Pinterest contest to encourage visitors to pin other images from its website on a special board to win a prize. They cross-promote their contests on their blog, Facebook, and other social media.

Figure 8-11: Luxefind's Pinterest contest drives traffic to its website to find images to pin.

Photo Courtesy of Luxefinds.com

You can find many more game ideas at the Social Media Eatery posting at `http://socialmediaeatery.com/social-network-powerful-contest-ideas`. The ideas range from simple to complex, but they will start your wheels turning.

Microsites

Microsites, which the Interactive Advertising Bureau also calls "brand conversation hubs," are branded environments specific to a particular product, line, or brand. Created like any other freestanding websites with their own domain names and only a few pages, microsites are usually dedicated to a specific product or service. Often used in conjunction with a new product introduction or special promotion, microsites may facilitate social media–style activities specific to that project. Often, user conversations or user-generated content contributions are incorporated into the site.

Figure 8-12 is an example of a microsite created for Lincoln College's Apprenticeships campaign. This college in England used a microsite to attract nontraditional students to its vocational programs.

Many microsites incorporate highly focused video presentations to launch a new product, turn a sale into an event, provide "how-to" instruction, or target specific demographic groups.

Figure 8-12: Use a microsite to attract a target audience.

Courtesy Lincoln College; www.lincolncollege.ac.uk

Book IX

Measuring Results; Building on Success

Contents at a Glance

Chapter 1: Delving into Data

In This Chapter

✔ Understanding the difference between monitoring and measuring

✔ Setting up your measurement plan

✔ Selecting analytics packages that meet your marketing objectives

✔ Learning to use Google Analytics

✔ Discovering Google Social Analytics

*W*eb analytics is the practice of analyzing performance and business statistics for a website, social media marketing, and other online marketing efforts to better understand user behavior and improve results. Some might call web analytics more art than science; to others, it's black magic.

The amount of data that can be acquired from online marketing efforts vastly exceeds the amount available using traditional offline methods. That statement alone makes online marketing, including social media, an attractive form of public relations and advertising.

In the best of all possible worlds, the results of your marketing efforts should appear as increased profits — in other words, as an improved bottom line with a nice return on investment (ROI). You're more likely to achieve this goal if you make analytics part of a process of continuous quality improvement.

For more information on measuring the performance of websites and online marketing campaigns, see *Web Analytics For Dummies,* by Pedro Sostre and Jennifer LeClaire.

Before getting mired in the swamp of online marketing data, assess the performance of your hub website. If you aren't making a profit from that core investment, it doesn't matter whether you fill the conversion funnel (see Book I, Chapter 1) with fantastic traffic from social media, exhibit a soaring click-through rate, or tally revenues through the roof. If you aren't sure how your hub site is performing, use the tools in this chapter and ask your web developer and bookkeeper for help.

Planning a Measurement Strategy

The basic principle "You can't manage what you don't measure" applies doubly to the online universe. Do you know whether Facebook or LinkedIn drives more traffic to your site? Whether more people buy after reading a blog posting about pets than from a blog posting about plants? If not, you're simply guessing at how to expend your precious marketing dollars and time.

To make the most of your effort, return to the goals and objectives you established on your Social Media Marketing Goals form (see Book I, Chapter 1 or download it from www.dummies.com/go/socialmediamarketingaio2e). Ask yourself what you need to measure to determine your accomplishments. Would interim measurements help you decide whether a particular aspect of a social media campaign is working?

For instance, if one of your goals is to substitute social media marketing for paid advertising, compare performance between the two. If you initiated social media activities to improve a ranking on Search Engine Results Pages (SERP), you must measure your standing by keywords at different times. In either case, of course, you might want to track visitors to the site who arrive from either a social media or natural search to see whether they continue to a purchase.

Fortunately, computers do one thing extremely well: count. Chances are good that if you have a question, you can find an answer.

Because computers count just about everything, you can quickly drown in so much data that you find it impossible to gather meaningful information, let alone make a decision. The last thing you need is a dozen reports that you don't have time to read.

Unless you have a very large site, monitoring statistics monthly or quarterly is usually sufficient. You might check more often when you first initiate a specific social media or another online marketing activity, if you invest significant amounts of money or effort into a new campaign, or if you support your site by way of advertising (in which case, monitoring traffic is the sine qua non of your existence).

On your Social Media Marketing Plan (see Book I, Chapter 3, or download it from www.dummies.com/go/socialmediamarketingaio2e), add your choice of measurement parameters and analytical tools and the names of the people who will be responsible for creating reports. Schedule the frequency of analytical review on your Social Media Activity Calendar (see Book I, Chapter 4).

Monitoring versus measuring

For the purposes of this book, we discuss only quantitative data as part of the measurement process. Use monitoring tools to review such qualitative data from social media as

✦ The degree of customer engagement

✦ The nature of customer dialogue, sometimes called *sentiment*

✦ Your brand reputation on a social network

✦ The quality of relationships with your target market

✦ The extent of participation in online conversations

✦ Positioning in your industry versus your competitors

If you have no monitoring tools in place yet, turn to Book II, Chapter 1.

"Real people" usually review subjective monitoring data to assess such ineffable qualities as the positive or negative characteristics of consumer posts, conversational tone, and brand acknowledgment. Notwithstanding Hal in the movie *2001: A Space Odyssey,* we don't yet have analytical software with the supple linguistic sophistication of the human brain.

Setting aside the "squishy" qualitative data, you still have two types of quantitative data to measure:

✦ **Internal performance measurements:** Measure the effectiveness of your social media, other marketing efforts, and website in achieving your objectives. Performance measurements include such parameters as traffic to your social pages or website, the number of people who click-through to your hub presence, which products sell best, and *conversion rate,* or the percentage of visitors who buy or become qualified leads.

✦ **Business measurements:** Primarily dollar-based parameters — costs, revenues, profits — that go directly to your business operations. Such financial items as the cost of customer or lead acquisition, average dollar value per sale, the value assigned to leads, break-even point, and ROI fall into this category. For more about measuring ROI, see Book I, Chapter 2.

Deciding what to measure

Most of the key performance indicators (KPI) and business criteria you measure fall into one of the following categories:

✦ **Traffic:** You must know the number and nature of visitors to any of the sites that are part of your web presence.

✦ **Leads:** Business-to-business (B2B) companies, service professionals, and companies that sell expensive, complex products often close their sales offline. Online efforts yield prospects, many of whom — you hope — will become qualified leads as they move down the conversion funnel.

✦ **Financials:** Costs, sales, revenue, and profits are the essential components of business success. Analytics let you track which sales arrive from which sources, and how much revenue they generate.

✦ **Search marketing:** As discussed in Book II, Chapter 2, optimizing social media can improve visibility in natural search. Not only do many social media sites appear in search results, but your hub site also gains valuable inbound links from direct and indirect referrals.

✦ **Other business objectives:** You may need customized analytics to track goals and objectives that don't fall into the other categories.

Book IX, Chapter 6 discusses KPIs in depth.

Don't plan on flying to the moon based on the accuracy of any statistical web data. For one thing, definitions of parameters differ by tool. Does a new visitor session start after someone has logged off for 24 minutes or 24 hours? For another, results in real-time tools sometimes oscillate unpredictably.

If a value seems "off," try running your analytics again later, or run them over a longer period to smooth out irregularities.

Relative numbers are more meaningful than absolute ones. Is your traffic growing or shrinking? Is your conversion rate increasing or decreasing? Focus on ratios or percentages to make the data more meaningful. Suppose that 10 percent of a small number of viewers to your site converted to buyers before you started a blog, compared to only 5 percent of a larger number of viewers afterward. What does that tell you?

Figure 1-1 shows what most businesses are measuring online. You can find lots of research about typical performance on different statistical parameters. Though it's nice to know industry averages for benchmarking purposes, the only statistics that matter are your own.

Regardless of how you go about the measurement process, you must define success before you begin. Without some sort of target value, you cannot know whether you've succeeded. Keep your handy, dandy Social Media Marketing Goals (see Book I, Chapter 1) accessible as you review this chapter.

A good measurement strategy determines how much data to leave out as well as how much to measure. Unless you have a huge site or quite a complex marketing campaign, you can focus on just a few parameters.

Figure 1-1:
This chart
shows
which
social media
metrics
most other
businesses
are
measuring
and
monitoring.

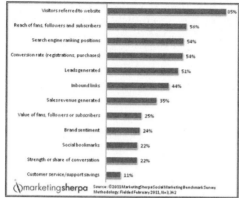

Source: MarketingSherpa.com

Establishing responsibility for analytics

Chances are good that your business isn't large enough to field an entire team whose sole responsibility is statistical analysis. Even if you aren't running an employment agency for statisticians, you can still take a few concrete steps to ensure that the right data is collected, analyzed, and acted on:

1. Ask your marketing person (is that you?) to take responsibility for defining what needs to be measured based on business objectives.

   Consult with your financial advisor, if necessary.

2. Have your programmer, web developer, or go-to IT person select and install the analytics tools that will provide the data you need.

   Make ease of use, flexibility, and customizability important factors in the decision.

3. If it isn't part of the analytical package, ask your IT person to set up a one-page *dashboard* (a graphical "executive summary" of key data).

   Try the Google Analytics dashboard, shown in Figure 1-2, or the Hub Spot dashboard for multiple media, shown in Figure 1-3. Dashboards display essential results quickly, preferably over easy-to-change time frames of your choice.

4. Let your marketing, IT, and content management folks work together to finalize the highest priority pages (usually landing pages and pages within your conversion funnels). When possible, set up tracking codes for links coming from social marketing pages. IT should test to ensure that the data collection system works and adjust it as needed.

5. Your marketing person can be responsible for regularly monitoring the results, adjusting marketing campaigns, and reporting to you and other stakeholders. Have your IT person validate the data and audit tracking tags at least twice a year — they can easily get out of sync.

6. Always integrate the results of your social media and online marketing efforts with offline marketing and financial results for a complete picture of what's happening with your business. Compare against your business goals and objectives and modify as needed.

Figure 1-2: A typical Google Analytics dashboard displays key web statistics.

Courtesy Hutton Broadcasting LLC

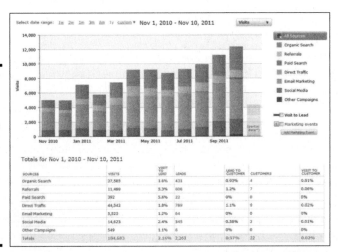

Figure 1-3: A HubSpot page showing the distribution of visits by source for Kuno Creative, a B2B company.

Courtesy HubSpot® www.HubSpot.com

Aggregate all analytics into one place. You're unlikely to find a premade dashboard that includes everything you need to measure for your specific campaigns. Your programmer may have to export data into Excel, PDF, or e-mail format; save it all in one place; and then build a custom spreadsheet to generate combined reports for your review.

Selecting Analytics Packages

Ask your developer or web host which statistical packages are available for your site. Unless you have a fairly large site or need real-time data, one of the free packages in Table 1-1 should work well. Review your choices to select the best fit for your needs. In many cases, Google Analytics is the best answer.

Table 1-1	Free Analytics Packages	
Name	*URL*	*Notes*
AddFreeStats	`www.addfreestats.com`	Graphical display; real-time, adjustable time frame
Analog and Report Magic	`www.analog.cx`	Displayed by `www.reportmagic.org`
AWStats	`http://awstats.org`	Log analysis tool
Clicky	`http://getclicky.com`	All the basics for small, single sites; data storage limited to 30 days; offers paid options
FeedBurner	`www.google.com/support/feedburner/bin/answer.py?hl=en&answer=78948`	Analytics for RSS and other forms of social media
GoingUp!	`www.goingup.com/features`	Customizable dashboard with graphs and charts
Google Analytics	`www.google.com/analytics`	Can include social media
Piwik	`http://piwik.org`	Open source analytics, including RSS
SiteTrail.com	`www.sitetrail.com`	Used for quick estimates on social media
StatCounter	`www.statcounter.com`	Accepts and analyzes traffic from many blogs and other social networking websites

(continued)

Table 1-1 *(continued)*

Name	URL	Notes
Webalizer	www.webalizer.org	Simple graphical display that works well with small sites
Woopra	www.woopra.com	Basic version, designed for blog analytics and social media
Yahoo! Web Analytics	http://web.analytics.yahoo.com	Can include social media (formerly IndexTools)

If your developer or web host tells you that you don't need statistics, find another provider. It's nearly impossible to measure success without easy access to statistics.

The specific suite of statistical results that a package offers may influence your choice of tools. Unfortunately, you can't count on getting comparable results when you mix and match different tools. Each one defines parameters differently (for example, what constitutes a repeat visitor). Consequently, you need to watch trends, not absolute numbers.

If you have a large site with heavy traffic or extensive reporting requirements, free packages — even Google Analytics — might not be enough. You can find dozens of paid statistical programs in an online search; Table 1-2 lists 14 of them. Several are fairly inexpensive, but the ones marked "Enterprise-level solution" in Column 3 can escalate into real money.

Table 1-2   **Paid Statistical Packages**

Name	URL	Cost
Campaign Commander Social	www.emailvision.com/products/social-edition	Analytics component of larger social media management tool
Chartbeat	http://chartbeat.com	$10 to $150 per month based on pages views, including blogs
eXTReME Tracking	http://extremetracking.com/?npt	$4.50 per month

Name	URL	Cost
IBM Enterprise Marketing Management	`www.ibm.com/software/products/us/en/category/SWX00`	Enterprise-level solution; includes social media
Kontagent	`www.kontagent.com`	Facebook and other social network analytics; contact for pricing
Log Rover	`www.logrover.com`	$99 to $499 flat fee
Lyris HQ	`www.lyris.com/solutions/lyris-hq`	$200 per month; enterprise-level solution; includes social media
Omniture Site Catalyst	`www.omniture.com`	Enterprise-level solution; includes social media
Sawmill LITE	`www.sawmill.net/lite.html`	From $99 flat fee
Site Stats Lite	`www.sitestats.com/home/home.php`	Cost varies by traffic; starts at $15 per month
Site Meter	`http://sitemeter.com`	Premium starts at $6.95 per month
uberVU	`www.ubervu.com`	Starts at $499 per month
VisitorVille	`www.visitorville.com`	Real-time 3D statistics; from $19.95 per month
Webtrends Social Measurement	`http://social.webtrends.com/packages.php`	Enterprise-level solution; includes social media

Not all marketing channels use the same yardstick — nor should they. Your business objectives drive your choice of channels and therefore your choice of yardsticks.

Some paid statistical packages are hosted on a third-party server. Others are designed for installation on your own server. Generally, higher-end paid statistical solutions offer several benefits:

✦ Real-time analytics (no waiting for results)

✦ Sophisticated reporting tools by domain or across multiple domains, departments, or enterprises

✦ Customizable data-mining filters

✦ Path-through-site analysis, tracking an individual user from entry to exit

+ Integrated traffic and store statistics

+ Integrated qualitative and quantitative analytics for multiple social media services

+ Analysis of downloaded PDF, video, audio, or another file type

+ Mapping of host addresses to company names and details

+ Clickstream analysis to show which sites visitors arrive from and go to

Don't collect information for information's sake. Stop when you have enough data to make essential business decisions.

Reviewing analytical options for social media

Depending on what you're trying to measure, you may need data from some of the analytical tools available internally from a particular social media channel, or statistics from social bookmarking sites such as AddThis (www. addthis.com) or from URL shorteners, which we discuss below.

Table 1-3 summarizes which social media services integrate with Google Analytics for traffic monitoring purposes and which also offer their own internal performance statistics. See Chapters 2 through 5 in this minibook for a detailed discussion of analytics on specific social media services.

Table 1-3	Social Media Specific Analytics		
Website	*URL*	*Integrates with Google Analytics?*	*Own Analytics Package?*
Facebook	www.facebook.com/ help/search/ ?q=insights	Yes	Yes
Google+	www.google.com/ analytics/features/ social-sharing.html	Yes	Yes
LinkedIn	http://linkedin.com/ network?trk=hb_tab_net	No	Yes
Meetup	www.meetup.com/help/ Can-I-get-page-view- statistics-about-my- Meetup-Group www.meetup.com/help/ What-are-Group-Stats/	Yes	Yes, for group organizers only

Website	URL	Integrates with Google Analytics?	Own Analytics Package?
Myspace	`http://myspace2.custhelp.com/app/answers/detail/a_id/412/kw/statistics`	Yes	Yes

Ning	`www.ning.com/help/?p=3314`
	
	`www.ning.com/help/?p=5484`
		Yes	No

Pinterest	`www.pinterest.com`	No	No, third-party only; `http://pinerly.com`, for example
Twitter	`www.twitter.com`	No	No, third party only; `http://twitalyzer.com`, for example

Register for free optional statistics whenever you can.

Selecting a URL shortening tool for statistics

One type of free optional statistics is particularly handy: traffic generated by shortened URLs, as described in Book II, Chapter 1. Be sure to select ones that offer analytics, including:

✦ **Bitly:** A free account (registration required) to track statistics from shortened links, as shown in Figure 1-4

✦ **Clicky.me:** A free account (registration required), which covers one site

✦ **Goo.gl:** Google's free URL shortener; requires logging into your Google account if you want a helpful URL history

✦ **Ow.ly:** HootSuite's free URL shortener

✦ **Su.pr:** From StumbleUpon; requires registration for a free account

✦ **Tiny.ly:** Free URL shortener with real-time traffic statistics

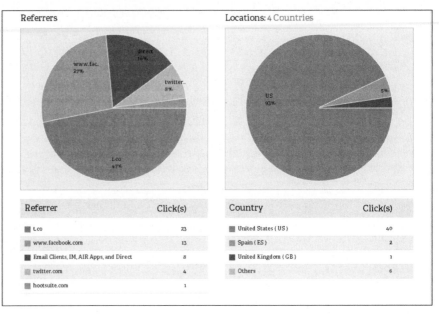

Figure 1-4:
Bitly offers
several
displays
for traffic
statistics for
a shortened
URL, bitly.
com/
uNxWSS+.

Courtesy Bitly

There's a shortcut to results for links shortened with bitly or su.pr. Paste the short URL into a browser, followed by the plus sign (+), to see how many clicks the short URL received.

You can use a dashboard tool like NetVibes.com to see all your stats in one convenient place. See Book I, Chapter 4 for more details about dashboards.

Getting Started with Google Analytics

Google Analytics is so popular that it justifies some additional discussion. It's popular because this free, high-quality analytics tool works well for most website owners. It now incorporates many social media services as part of its analysis and scales well from tiny sites to extremely large ones.

Start with the free Google Analytics and switch to an enterprise-level solution when and if your web effort demands it.

Among its many advantages, Google Analytics offers

✦ More in-depth analysis than most other free statistical packages

✦ Plenty of support, as shown in Table 1-4

✦ Easy-to-set specific time frames to compare results to other years

✦ Many of the more sophisticated features of expensive software, such as path-through-site

✦ Customization of the dashboard display

✦ Conversion funnel visualization, shown in Figure 1-5

✦ Analysis by *referrer* (where traffic to your site has linked from) or search term

✦ Tracking of such key performance indicators as returning visitors and *bounce rate* (percentage of visitors who leave without visiting a second page)

✦ Customizable reports to meet your needs and be e-mailed automatically

✦ New Social Analytics capabilities

✦ Seamless integration with AdWords, the Google pay-per-click program (although you don't need a paid AdWords campaign to take advantage of it)

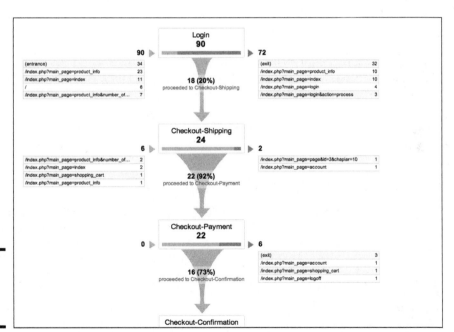

Figure 1-5:
A sample conversion funnel.

Courtesy WebReach Ireland Ltd.; www.webreach.ie

Google provides steps for installing Analytics at `www.google.com/analytics/sign_up.html`. This task definitely isn't for anyone who is faint-of-programming-heart. Get help from your developer. For detailed information on installing Google Analytics, refer to the help sites listed in Table 1-4 or go to `http://support.google.com/googleanalytics/bin/topic.py?hl=en&topic=10978`.

Table 1-4	Helpful Google Analytics Resource URLs	
Name	*URL*	*Description*
Analytics Blog	`http://analytics.blogspot.com`	Google blog for all things analytic
Analytics Goal-Setting	`http://analytics.blogspot.com/2009/05/how-to-setup-goals-in-google-analytics.html`	Setting up interim and final goals needed to track path to conversions
Analytics Guide	`www.smashingmagazine.com/2009/07/16/a-guide-to-google-analytics-and-useful-tools`	All-in-one guide for using Google Analytics
Analytics for Social Media	`www.google.com/analytics/features/social.html`	Guide to the features of Google's social media tools
Analytics Support	`www.google.com/support/analytics/?hl=en`	Google Analytics help center
Analytics for Video	`http://youtube-global.blogspot.com/2008/03/youtube-reveals-video-analytics-tool.html`	Analytics for YouTube channel
Garmahis.com Blog	`http://garmahis.com/tips/google-analytics`	Useful Google Analytics tips and tricks
IQ Lessons	`www.google.com/intl/en/analytics/iq.html`	Online Google Analytics training

You must tag each page of your website with a short piece of JavaScript. The tagging task isn't difficult. If your site uses a template or a common *server-side include* (for example, for a footer), you place the Analytics code once and it appears on all pages. You should start seeing results within 24 hours.

Integrating Google's Social Media Analytics

To be sure, you can still identify traffic arriving at your site from social media services simply by looking at Referrers under Traffic Sources in your Google Analytics account.

However, Google's new Social Media Analytics make it much easier to integrate statistical results from social media services into your reports and to assess the business value of social media. Take advantage of the new Social option to pre-filter for social site referrers only.

Start by clicking Traffic Sources in the left navigation as usual. Then click again to expand the Social option, as shown in Figure 1-6, and select Sources. As shown in Figure 1-6, Google Social Analytics compares combined visits from social media to all visits in the graphs and lists traffic from individual social media sources below the graphs.

Alternatively, beneath the Social options in the left navigation, click Social Visitors Flow. In the Select Segment drop-down box (at the top of the Social Visitors Overview page), select Referral Traffic. The resulting display, shown in Figure 1-7, appears.

Figure 1-6:
The Social Media section of Google Analytics makes it easy to collect and compare social media data.

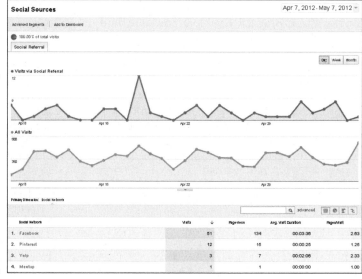

Courtesy Mountain Springs Lake, www.MSLresort.com

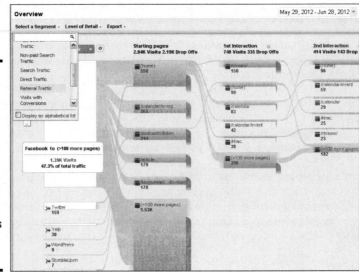

Figure 1-7:
The Social Visitors Overview page displays the path taken by visitors who arrive at your site from various social media.

Some social media services, such as Ning, Facebook, and Meetup, make it easy to integrate their data with Google Analytics by enabling you to place Google Analytics Tracking Code on your social media pages. Of course, the Google-owned Blogger, Google+, YouTube, and the RSS service FeedBurner are already compatible with Analytics.

Web analytics, from Google or anywhere else, are valuable only if you use them to improve users' experience on your site and your bottom line.

The URLs for funnel and goal pages don't need to have identical domain names, as long as the correct tracking code appears on the pages. The thank-you page for a purchase is sometimes on a third-party storefront, for instance. Or, perhaps you want to track how many people go from a particular page on your main website to post a comment on one of your social network sites or blog.

Social media is doggone hard work

Marcie Davis of Santa Fe, New Mexico, started International Assistance Dog Week (IADW), a project of the not-for-profit organization Soulful Presence, several years ago. Originally created to honor assistance dogs nationwide, the effort expanded internationally in 2011. The goal of the project is to inform more people about assistance dogs and help assistance dog organizations raise funds through the media focus the event can bring to their activities.

IADW started using Facebook and Twitter in February 2011 to reach people around the world even though the project has a very low budget. "I'm not sure we could have expanded without something as cost-effective as Facebook," observes Ellen Cline, publicist for IADW. With a part-time staff of two, Cline explains that she cross-posts for IADW automatically from Facebook to Twitter to save time yet still reach people who prefer Twitter.

Courtesy International Assistance Dog Week, a program of Soulful Presence. Inc.

The target audience is broad. "We want to talk to anyone who has an assistance dog, is interested in assistance dogs, is a puppy raiser, trainer, or member of an assistance dog organization," Cline says.

For IADW, which is supported by donations and grants, traffic statistics are critical. Cline uses Insights for the Facebook page and Google Analytics for its website, `www.assistance dogweek.org`. "The metrics and demographics are useful to potential sponsors to show them the audience we reach and that this audience is also one they want to reach. It helps convince them that they will receive value from their support of IADW."

(continued)

(continued)

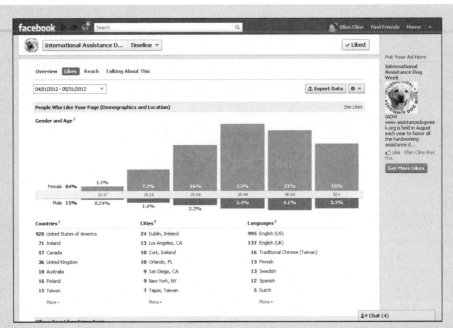

Courtesy International Assistance Dog Week, a program of Soulful Presence. Inc.

Cline also uses Google Alerts every day to keep up on assistance dog related news and to find news stories to post to the Facebook page. "We tag dog training organizations that are mentioned in the news stories and then they can share the news as well. We also share a lot of stories from dog organizations that we like on Facebook."

Their web developer added Facebook and Twitter chiclets to the website and customized their Constant Contact e-newsletter. "We now spend about an hour a day on two dog-related Facebook pages, IADW and Working like Dogs [a separate, but related organization also founded by Marcie Davis]."

As a publicist and copywriter, Cline takes advantage of multiple arrows in the publicity quiver. She uses e-newsletters, press releases, banner ads on media sponsors' sites, and public service announcements (PSAs) on radio and TV. She's also well aware of the value of integration. "We use the Constant Contact app on the Facebook page and the sign-up link on the website to increase e-newsletter subscriptions. The TV PSA that runs on TV stations and cable is also available on YouTube. There's also some crossover from the Working Like Dogs podcasts on Pet Life Radio, since some guests are from assistance dog organizations." Pet Life Radio is also a media sponsor for IADW and the podcasts are cross-linked from the IADW site and blog.

Cline is realistic about the limits of social media commitment for small businesses and non-profits. "It's never-ending and takes more time than you might think. Be prepared to allot some time to this every day. Decide if you can do it yourself; otherwise share the work with someone else."

International Assistance Dog Week's web presence

www.assistancedogweek.org

www.twitter.com/IADWeek

www.facebook.com/assistancedogweek

www.assistancedogweek.org/feed (RSS)

www.petliferadio.com/workingdogs.html (Podcast)

www.youtube.com/user/soulfulpresence

Chapter 2: Analyzing Content-Sharing Metrics

In This Chapter

✔ Using standard analytics to evaluate content-sharing success

✔ Evaluating internal metrics for blogs, videos, podcasts, and photos

✔ Checking iTunes subscribers

✔ Estimating ROI for content sharing

You've built a blog, updated hundreds of photos, created a podcast, or shot a series of videos. You've nurtured and fed your effort with multiple posts and episodes. You've promoted your creative endeavor, and now you want to know how many people have visited, how engaged they were, and most of all, whether they shared your content with others, giving your efforts maximum exposure.

Developing good content is hard work. As with any of your other marketing efforts, you need to understand your return on investment (ROI). In this chapter, we show you how to figure this out.

Measuring the Effectiveness of Content Sharing with Standard Analytics

If you have used content as a marketing tool, how do you know whether your message is getting out there? How do you measure your results? How viral is your content? Are viewers or readers recommending your content to people other than those you reached directly through your own efforts? Your website stats reveal the most information, but you can also glean effective information from specific statistics for each type of content sharing.

Maximizing website stats

You can find an amazing amount of information about the effectiveness of your content simply by using the program that tracks your website statistics, whether that is Google Analytics or any other program we mention in Book IX, Chapter 1. Table 2-1 summarizes which of the primary content-sharing sites integrate Google Analytics and/or offer their own.

Perhaps the easiest solution is to install Google Analytics on every content-sharing platform for which it's offered.

Table 2-1   Analytics Availability on Content-Sharing Sites

Website	URL	Description	Google Analytics Integration?	Own Analytics Package?
Image Sharing				
Flickr	`http://flickr.com`	Well-known photo-sharing site	No	Yes
Picasa	`http://picasa.google.com`	Google's photo-sharing site	Yes	Yes
Pinterest	`www.pinterest.com`	Share and recommend photos for others	No	No
Video sharing				
Ustream	`www.ustream.tv`	Platform for live, interactive, broadcast video	No	No
Vimeo	`http://vimeo.com`	Created by filmmakers and videographers to share creative work (non-commercial only)	No	Yes
YouTube	`www.youtube.com`	Well-known video sharing site	Yes	Yes
Blogs				
Blogger	`www.blogger.com`	Google's blog platform	Yes	Yes
TypePad	`www.typepad.com`	Free blog platform	Yes	Yes
WordPress	`www.wordpress.org`	Largest blog platform in the world	Yes	Yes

Review your general statistics to find the following types of information:

✦ **The number of visitors who land on the home page of your blog or other content site:** Watch for variations in the number and timing of visits as well.

✦ **The number of visitors seeking specific posts, videos, or podcasts:** This information tells you that visitors found the post through an external link, or perhaps a specific set of keywords in a search engine. Most analytics enable you to search Content results to the page level.

✦ **How visitors arrived at your content-sharing site:** Someone might have used a search engine, entered the URL for your social sharing presence, or linked from another website.

✦ **How long visitors remain on a specific post page:** If the duration of a visit is shorter than the potential length of time spent reading the post and pondering its contents, the post wasn't effective. You see this in the bounce rate.

Capitalize on effective posts by creating similar posts. When you analyze your web statistics, you'll know which posts are effective.

✦ **The number of unique visitors to your content-sharing site compared to the number of visitors to your website:** For instance, content posts can consist of unique information about your products or services. The more unique visitors you have to specific content posts, or to your content in general, the better your information is received. If your blog attracts more unique visitors than your site does, consider creating links in your blog posts to related information on your website. If your site receives more hits than your blog, add some links from the specific products or services you offer to blog posts about these specific items.

✦ **The number of people who linked to your website from one of your content-sharing pages.**

✦ **The geographical location of your content visitors:** If the majority of visitors are from a country or area other than your target market, change your message.

✦ **The direction of traffic:** Once you have an established content-sharing presence, your traffic rate and number of incoming links to your website should increase. If they aren't increasing, consider shaking things up a bit by offering different content. Look at which posts have been popular in the past. Expand on those topics or put a new spin on them, and carefully monitor the results.

✦ **Which pages are most frequently used to enter or leave the site:** If visitors are entering and exiting the home page and spending only a short length of time on your site, they're skimming only one or two posts before getting out of Dodge. If you're facing this situation, it's time to rethink your message. Visitors entering your site on a specific page, however, have honed in on a specific post from either a search engine result or an incoming link. If you have lots of these and visitors are spending a fair amount of time on your site and exiting from a different page, you have an effective content-sharing site.

Tracking comments

Beyond statistics, one of the most valuable ways to assess the success of your content-sharing sites is by tracking how many and what type of comments people leave. Look for the following information in the Comments section on blogs, YouTube, podcasts, and any other content-sharing sites that permit comments, reviews, rankings, or Likes/Dislikes.

Third-party social alert and monitoring sites may help you analyze comments for "sentiment." See Book II, Chapter 3 for helpful tools to use when the number of comments becomes overwhelming.

✦ **Number of comments on each blog post:** This information is important if your goal is to stimulate interaction with potential customers. If certain blog posts are drawing more comments than others, this information is more relevant to your subscribers.

✦ **Comment length:** If you've written a lengthy post and you receive lengthy comments, you've struck a chord with subscribers and presented useful information. If comments are sparse, however, indicating that you haven't given your user base food for thought, consider changing the nature of your posts or the type of information you post.

✦ **The tone of comments on your posts:** If comments on the majority of your posts sound positive and you have lots of comments, you're sending the right message. You can be somewhat controversial at times and stir up provocative comments, but unless you're a shock jock, make it the exception and not the rule. If, on the other hand, the comments aren't flattering, you know what you need to do.

If the number of comments for new posts is decreasing, you're losing your audience — and you probably need to review your messages. Be sure that you're inviting responses with an open question like "what do you think?" You may need to provide explicit directions about where to click to make a comment.

If you're receiving comments on individual podcast episodes, people are downloading the podcast from your website rather than using a subscription. Analyze which episodes reward you with the most comments — and then include that type of information in future podcasts.

✦ **Number of visitors versus the number of comments:** If you have a fairly high ratio of comments to visitors, you're creating interesting material that gets visitors thinking.

Evaluating Blog-Specific Metrics

Each of the primary blogging sites provides analytics information such as that seen in Figure 2-1. Blogger, WordPress, and TypePad all offer integration with Google Analytics. However, Blogger.com (which is owned by Google) enables you to use different third-party hit counters and stats if you want, and WordPress (http://wordpress.org/extend/plugins/stats as seen in Figure 2-1) and TypePad (www.typepad.com/features/smart-blog-stats) offer their own proprietary tools in addition, or as an alternative to Analytics.

If your blog is your only online effort, internal statistics may be enough. However, if you want to be able to compare and contrast multiple components of your web presence, Google Analytics or another package is required.

Of course, you'll watch for the number of incoming visitors in your blog dashboard. You also want to look at the number of people who have decided to "follow" you — by subscribing through the service, getting e-mail notifications, or using RSS.

Visualizing video success

When you've posted a video to a third-party site (such as YouTube or Vimeo), you can look there for some stats about these categories.

On YouTube, click My Channel, then click Channel Stats on the top right of the screen to see how many subscribers you have and how many views each of your videos received (see Figure 2-2). To view Comments on a video, click on the video link; the Comments appear below the video screen.

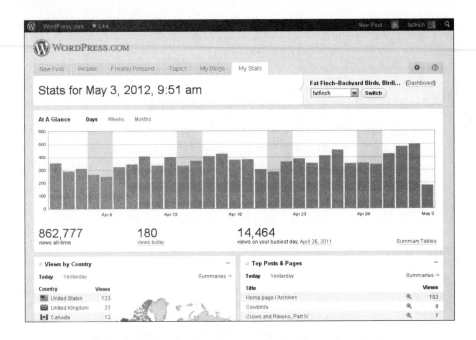

Figure 2-1:
WordPress
stats (top)
for the
FatFinch.
com blog
(bottom).

Courtesy The Fat Finch

On Vimeo, you need to subscribe to the premium (fee) option to see statistics. If you have the premium option, select Advanced Stats (`http://vimeo.com/stats/demo/geo`) to see a graph of comment quantity, Likes, total downloads, and total plays by date, as well as statistics for embedded videos.

✦ **Number of subscribers:** At YouTube, you find this information on your channel. If you're creating relevant videos, you should notice a steady increase in subscribers with each new video you upload.

✦ **Growth in the number of subscribers:** You should experience steady growth as you regularly add new videos to your channel. If you notice a significant spurt after you post a video, analyze its content to determine why the video caused the growth spurt. Chances are good that you did something different or found a topic of particular interest to your subscribers. If, on the other hand, you notice a decline in new subscribers or a decrease in subscribers after posting a video, figure out what you did wrong and refrain from posting similar videos.

✦ **Number of people viewing individual videos:** You can find this information by visiting your home page. On Vimeo, you see the number of plays for each video. On your YouTube channel, view your channel to see the number of plays for each video.

Figure 2-2:
Viewing
statistics
for YouTube
videos.

Courtesy Saybrook University, San Francisco, CA; www.saybrook.edu

Understanding Podcast Metrics

As with blogs, you need to watch several primary statistics on your podcasts:

✦ **The number of people listening to your live podcast:** This tells you how effective your marketing efforts are. When you have lots of visitors, you've created informative media that is in demand.

✦ **The number of unique page views for your podcast:** You can figure out which posts are being received well. Use this information for planning future episodes of your podcast.

✦ **The number of people who subscribe to follow your podcast.**

✦ **The number of people who rate your podcast highly and/or refer it to others.**

 Include a Social Sharing button (see Book II, Chapter 3) whenever possible to encourage your readers, viewers, and listeners to post the link to your material on their own social media pages.

Checking iTunes subscribers

When you make your podcast available from the iTunes store (whether free or fee), you're out there with the heavy hitters — and have access to additional analytical information. You have no way, at least for now, to find out how many iTunes users are subscribed to your podcast, but you can find out the popularity of your podcast by following the steps suggested by Podcast Advice (www.podcastadvice.co.uk/measuringyour-podcast stats). Here's how:

1. **Launch iTunes.**

The lovely iTunes interface graces your computer.

2. **Click Store.**

The iTunes Store appears.

3. **Click Podcasts.**

The most popular podcasts are listed. If yours is on this page, you've made the big leagues. If it isn't, you have to do a little more work to find out how popular your podcast is.

4. **Enter a keyword that's associated with your podcast.**

For example, if you're a photographer, *photography* is the keyword. After you enter the keyword, a list of podcasts appears.

5. **Analyze the list of podcasts to see where your brainchild appears.**

You can also sort podcasts by podcast name, episode name, release date, duration, popularity, or price. You're looking for popularity: When you see bars extending all the way across the Popularity column, you know that the episode is quite a popular one.

You can also use iTunes to determine which of your episodes are most popular. This information is useful in planning future episodes. To rank podcasts by popularity, follow these steps after you enter the iTunes Store and click Podcasts:

1. Enter the name of your podcast in the Search text field.

Your podcast description page appears.

2. Hover the cursor on the artwork representing the show.

An Information icon appears.

3. Click the Information icon.

Information about your show, including its ratings, appears in another window.

4. Click Go to This Podcast.

Your podcast appears; a list at the bottom contains any comments left about your podcast.

5. Click the Popularity icon.

Your episodes are sorted by popularity, as seen in Figure 2-3.

Figure 2-3:
Podcast statistics from iTunes can show which of your episodes are most popular.

Courtesy of The Bugle Podcast; www.thebuglepodcast.com

Measuring Your Image Results on Flickr

Most photo-sharing sites either integrate Google Analytics or provide their own internal metrics. For instance, basic statistical information about usage of your Flickr account is available in the free version; the Pro version offers additional detail. For more information, see www.flickr.com/help/stats.

Remember to look at referrers to your primary website to see how much traffic to your site comes from Flickr or other image-sharing sites, as compared to other websites, other social media, advertising, or search engines.

Reviewing free stats in Flickr

You can see either a quick snapshot of your Flickr activity for all time or somewhat more information for a specific time frame. For the snapshot, go to your photostream. Then click Popular, an option that only you — and not other viewers — can see. In addition to showing which of your photos is the most popular (viewed most often), the following options summarize activity on your photostream:

✦ **Interesting:** Provides the relative "interestingness" ranking of images within your photostream (and varies continually)

✦ **Views:** Measures every view of your photostream, except for the times you viewed it yourself

✦ **Favorites:** Tells you how many times other people have labeled one of your photos as a Favorite

✦ **Comments:** Totals how many comments others have left

For more data, choose You⇨Recent Activity⇨Custom View. This generates a column of choices on the right. In the drop-down menu, choose a time frame, which ranges from as recently as "the last hour" to as far back as "since the beginning" of your account. Then check all options that matter to you in terms of activities on your photos, replies you've made, or other people's actions related to you. Your home page then displays aggregate numbers for your photostream activity during the time frame you specified. The range of available statistics is seen in Figure 2-4.

Set a schedule for checking your stats. Unless you're tracking the impact of a specific marketing initiative or managing a huge online marketing budget, checking stats weekly or monthly is generally enough for Flickr and all your other social media marketing activities.

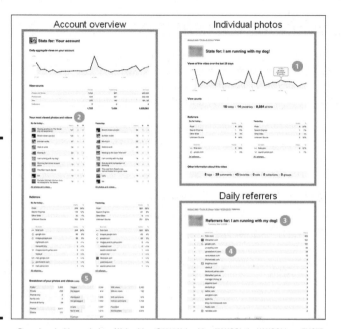

Figure 2-4:
Photo-
sharing
statistics
on Flickr
monitor
account,
group, and
individual
image
usage.

Reviewing Pro stats

For more detail by image or by sets for marketing purposes, purchase the
Pro version of Flickr for $24.95 per year. If Flickr is a major component of
your social media strategy, the detailed information may be worth it. For a
peek at the extended information and graphic displays in the Pro version,
see www.flickr.com/photos/me/stats. Flickr Pro provides the following
advantages:

✦ **Referrers:** List of where your Flickr visitors have come from

✦ **Statistics:** Page views broken down by individual image, sets, or
collections

✦ **Traffic:** Charts of visits over time

✦ **Popularity:** Rankings for individual photos and videos by number of views

Statistics offer valuable insight and feedback. Use your results to help guide
future uploads, to listen to your target audience, and to modify your Flickr
behavior. There's no point in looking at numbers for numbers' sake.

Comparing Hard and Soft Costs versus "Income"

Smart business people don't spin their wheels. If something doesn't gain traction, they do something else. After analyzing the number of visitors your content-sharing effort receives, consider your ROI to see if the effort is really worthwhile. For more on ROI, see Book I, Chapter 2.

Unless you are selling your content, this is a subtle number to figure out. You will need to derive sales results indirectly.

Remember to consider two types of costs in your evaluation:

✦ **Hard:** The number of man-hours needed to create content for your podcast, blog, photos, or videos. Next would be the cost to host any media online, which would be web hosting fees and any fees you pay to a designer to get your media online. If you're paying for premium video hosting such as Vimeo Plus, factor this cost in as well.

✦ **Soft:** This is the amount of time you personally spend creating content. Did that time take you away from any other profitable activities, such as hobnobbing with the rich and famous, or other potential clients?

Include a question at your online checkout that asks buyers which forms of social media they use. If you aren't using a social media network that attracts your customers, you may want to modify your social media efforts to see whether you can increase your business.

Chapter 3: Analyzing Twitter Metrics

In This Chapter

✔ Checking inbound website referrers and followers

✔ Comparing tweets to retweets

✔ Comparing mentions

✔ Measuring Twitter follower website visits

*A*fter your Twitter marketing campaign has been rolling for a while, it's time to check out both your performance metrics and the return on your time investment. You can do this in many ways: by looking at the information on your Twitter page; by using an app like TweetDeck.com; or by using an analytics program such as Google Analytics.

According to Network World (`www.networkworld.com`), in April 2012 Twitter acquired a team from an analytics company to develop its own analytics program, especially for its advertisers and publishers.

Tracking Website Referrals

If you use Google Analytics (as discussed in Book IX, Chapter 1), you can easily track the number of referrals from Twitter to your website or blog. This information is quite useful if one of your marketing goals is to drive more traffic to your website by way of Twitter.

By using Twitter's Web Intents JavaScript Events to measure user interaction, you can actually track far more than this, including the number of tweets and "follows" generated from your website. For more information on tracking and integration with Google Analytics, see `https://dev.twitter.com/docs/intents/events#the-events,https://developers.google.com/analytics/devguides/collection/gajs/gaTrackingSocial#twitter`, and `www.quora.com/How-can-I-integrate-Twitter-metrics-with-Google-Analytics`.

To see how much traffic comes to your website from Twitter using Google Social Analytics (discussed in Book IX, Chapter 1), simply log into your Analytics account and click on Traffic Sources in the left navigation as usual.

Choose Social⇨Sources. You'll see your Twitter numbers as part of Social Referrals, as shown in Figure 3-1.

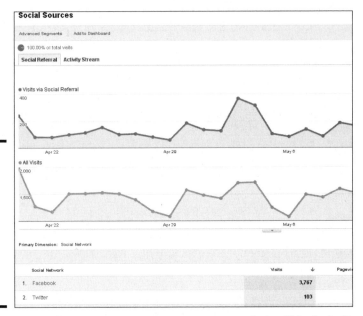

Figure 3-1: Referrers from social media are accessible through Google's social analytics feature.

Courtesy of Hutton Broadcasting

In Google Analytics, inbound links from Twitter are followed by the username, so you can sort to see how frequently account holders visit your site. If you're not sure who the follower is, click the inbound link to open the follower's Twitter page in a pop-up window.

Tracking Links

You can easily track shortened links from Twitter back to your website if you use bit.ly, su.pr, or Clicky.me to shorten your URLs, as we discuss in Book IX, Chapter 1.

Twitter is still working on analytics for its link-shortener (t.co), so it's best to use another for now. Watch the Twitter blogs (`http://blog.twitter.com` and `https://dev.twitter.com/blog`) for an announcement.

Using Third-Party Twitter Analytics Applications

Several good applications are devoted to Twitter analytics. Enter your username to find all sorts of information, such as the subjects you tweeted about, the hashtags you used, the number of tweets per day, and the extent of your reach. Here are a few analytic programs you might want to try:

✦ **TweetStats** (`http://tweetstats.com`) creates graphs showing what you've been up to on Twitter. See the number of tweets sent per hour, day, or month, a tweet timeline, reply statistics, a review of people you retweet, and more, as shown in Figure 3-2.

Figure 3-2:
Analytic programs like TweetStats. com can help you understand the value of Twitter.

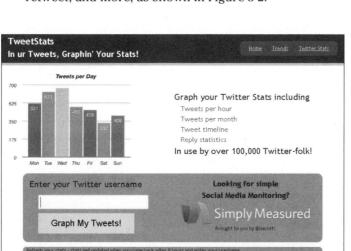

Courtesy Damon Cortesi, @dacort

✦ **TwitterGrader** (`http://tweet.grader.com`) shows how you stack up against other Twitter users. Enter your Twitter username and click Grade. In a few seconds — or longer, if you have lots of followers — you see your rank, and other information. You can also see Trend, a graph showing your pattern of adding followers compared to another site. Explore tabs for Twitter Elite and Tools to find out more about your Twitter life.

✦ **TwitterCounter** (`http://twittercounter.com`) claims to track more than 10 million Twitter users, providing information about the number of followers, following, tweets, top 100 Twitter users, and much more. You can set up your account to receive regular updates and notifications.

You'll find more Twitter tools at `http://twittertoolsbook.com/10-awesome-twitter-analytics-visualization-tools`.

Monitoring Retweets

One of the most important things to track is the number of messages that are retweeted compared to all the messages you've sent. That's the best metric for assessing whether your messages are going viral. No hard-and-fast rule applies to what constitutes a good ratio, but a high percentage of retweets means that you're sending the right stuff.

To monitor retweets within Twitter, log into your account and click @Connect in the top navigation on the left. (This was called @username in the previous version of Twitter.) From here, you have two choices: the Interactions tab and the Mentions tab.

On the Interactions tab, you can learn

✦ Who has retweeted a message and when

✦ Which of your tweets readers have designated as "Favorites"

✦ When you gained new followers and who they were

On the Mentions tab, you'll find key data in the resulting list:

✦ Recent retweets

✦ Recent tweets mentioning your @username

✦ Who has replied to one of your tweets

✦ Who has sent you a direct message

You can also use the TweetDeck application to find this information, including Mentions details.

To see another user's Mentions, search for all tweets mentioning his or her @username in the Search box.

Checking your retweet ranking

If you're adventurous, you can see your rank regarding retweets compared to all Twitter users by using a tool called Retweet Rank (`www.retweetrank.com`).

Enter your username in the Username box and click Go to see the results. If you log in with your Twitter handle, you can also see a variety of recent Twitter stats on a weekly dashboard. For longer-term records, you will need the paid version of Retweet Rank. The paid version also helps you see exactly which tweets strike a chord with your followers and which followers retweet most often.

Gleaning meaning from direct messages

Hmmm. We know what you're thinking: Why would you want to analyze your direct messages? After all, you know to whom you send direct messages — but which of your followers sent direct messages to you, and what was their subject matter? The answer to this two-part question tells you which followers are engaging you as a source of information and tells you the type of information they're requesting. If the same topic shows up in several direct messages, you can tweet about it and write blog posts about it.

Using one of the preceding methods, review your direct messages. Note which subjects prompted direct messages and expand on them in future tweets. Whenever you receive a direct message regarding one of your tweets, it's a good sign that the topic is worthy of further embellishment.

Using the Hashtag as a Measurement Mechanism

As we discuss in Book IV, when people want to make sure the word they're searching for is the main subject of the post and not just randomly added, they use the hashtag symbol.

The use of hashtags in conjunction with your Twitter username is another way to measure your popularity on Twitter. If lots of people, including those who don't follow you, take the time to precede your username with a hashtag, you're being directly referenced in a Twitter post. Finding out whether your username or brand is hashtagged is easy.

Go to `https://twitter.com/search` and enter #*yourusername* (where *yourusername* is your actual name) in the Search field. The Twitter search engine returns a list of tweets with your username preceded by the hashtag.

You'll probably see some usernames you recognize and some you don't. You may also see some bad press. Monitoring hashtags is a wonderful way of finding out who's talking about you and what they're saying. You may also find some people you want to follow.

FollowFriday, or #FF, is a Twitter hashtag tradition. Users incorporate this hashtag in their Friday tweets to give someone a "shout out" by recommending a company or individual that others might want to follow. Fridays are a good day to check the use of your name or brand as a hashtag.

Calculating a Following-to-Follower Ratio

The number of people you follow compared to the number of people following you is important information. So is the number of updates. This information is public for any Twitter user who stops by your piece of the Twitterverse. If you're following a lot of people and not many people are following you, it appears as though you're trying to sell something, especially if you have lots of updates.

As a marketer, your goal is to have at least three times the number of people following you as the number of people you follow. Remember to include linkable calls-to-action on your website and other social media to remind visitors to follow you on Twitter.

Chapter 4: Analyzing Facebook Metrics

In This Chapter

✔ Using Facebook Insights

✔ Using Facebook Insights for Platform Websites

✔ Monitoring comments for sentiment and distribution

✔ Comparing your Facebook performance to that of other companies

Y ou've created a spiffy Facebook Page, added a couple of bells and whistles, posted regularly to your Timeline, responded to comments, and recruited Likes. One of your goals was probably to drive more traffic to your website. But how do you calculate the fruits of your efforts? Almost all analytical packages provide this information — typically, in a section called Referrers or Traffic Sources.

In this chapter, we show you some ways to measure the effectiveness of your Facebook presence using Facebook's analytics package, called Insights, and other tools. For more information on Facebook for marketing, see Book V.

If you've enabled Google Analytics for your website, you can find more about incorporating Facebook metrics in Book IX, Chapter 1.

Monitoring Facebook Interaction with Insights

The three forms of Facebook analytics are *Facebook Insights*, which tracks activity internal to your Facebook pages, *Facebook Insights for (Facebook) Platform Applications*, which tracks interactions between Facebook and your primary website, and *Facebook Insights for Domains*, which consolidates key metrics for any website, regardless of whether it has implemented Facebook.

In the following sections we discuss only the first two, as they are less technical. For more information about *Insights for Domains*, send your programmer to http://developers.facebook.com/docs/insights or www.facebook.com/help/?page=120881494659811&ref=bc.

Using Facebook Page Insights

If you're looking for regular analytics for regular pages that you can do all by your lonesome self, the recently expanded Facebook Page Insights feature provides valuable, free, content-focused metrics.

Your Page must have 30 Likes before you can access Insights.

By analyzing user growth, demographics, and engagement with content, you can better focus on content that helps you hold onto your audience and that encourages them to share your material with their friends.

Gathering data for data's sake doesn't make sense. You need to take advantage of the data to modify your content stream. The principle is the same as with all marketing: If it works, keep doing it; if it doesn't work, stop.

Accessing Insights

As usual, Facebook provides multiple — and sometimes confusing — ways to accomplish a task. In this case, you have three options.

✦ Log in as administrator for your Page. In the left navigation, select the page you want to review (under Pages). The resulting Administration Panel for that page includes a snapshot of Insights. For more details, choose See All on the Insight Preview Box. The resulting display is shown in Figure 4-1.

✦ After logging in as administrator, type `www.facebook.com/insights` into the address bar of your browser and navigate to the page you want using the Select Insights drop-down menu located in the upper-left corner of the page. You'll reach the same Insights Dashboard Overview display, as shown in Figure 4-1.

✦ Choose View Insights on the menu that appears below the cover photo on your Page. Again, it will take you to the display in Figure 4-1.

All three methods take you to the same dashboard screen. For more information, see `www.facebook.com/help/?faq=116512998432353#What-are-Insights`.

Click these links to see stats   Click here to download Insights data

Figure 4-1:
The Overview page for Facebook Insights provides basic traffic information.

Courtesy Saybrook University, San Francisco, CA; www.saybrook.edu

Exporting Insights

To download the data in Insights, click the Export Data button in the top-right corner of the dashboard, as shown in Figure 4-1. (This may not work with all browsers.) According to Facebook, you can specify

✦ The date range for which you want to get data

✦ Whether you want data in Excel or CSV (comma-separated values) format

✦ Whether you want to see data at the Page level, or for each post

Making Sense of Insights

You can find the following information in your Page Insight results, even at the level of individual pages or posts:

✦ **A breakdown of activity over a one-month period:** Between the Overview page and the Likes page, you can see how many new Likes you have and how many people have Unliked your page.

✦ **The number of interactions per post, the breakdown of active fans, and much more:** To analyze a specific metric, select an option from the top navigation and scroll down.

✦ **A spike in the number of new Likes:** When you see this type of improvement, note the type of activity you posted on your Page that day. For more specific information, review the number of new Likes (or Unlikes) over a month span on the Likes tab. Then compare the post(s) for the specific date you saw a change on the Overview page.

For more information, check the Insight section on `www.seodigerati.com/the-marketers-guide-to-the-new-facebook-pages` or go to `www.facebook.com/help/search/?q=Insights`.

Monitoring comments and their distribution

Two of the best ways to know how well your messages are received are looking at the number of comments left in individual posts and seeing which posts your readers are passing along to their friends. Scroll down the Overview display in Insights to see a list of posts, as shown in Figure 4-2. In particular, you can find out the following for the 28-day period following a post:

✦ **Reach:** The number of unique users who have seen a post; equivalent to the concept of impressions in advertising.

✦ **Engaged Users:** The number of unique users who clicked on a post for more information.

✦ **Talking About This:** The number of unique users who created a "story" from a post; according to Facebook that means a user has liked, commented on, or shared a post, answered a question, or responded to an event.

According to Facebook, "Demographic data for *People Talking About This* is only available when more than 30 people were talking about this Page in the 7 days preceding the last day of your selected date range."

✦ **Virality:** The ratio of Talking About This to Reach; in other words, the percentage of people who "did something" after seeing your post. This is a measure of engagement.

Your goal is to have at least twice as many comments as you have posts. The higher the ratio of comments to posts, the better.

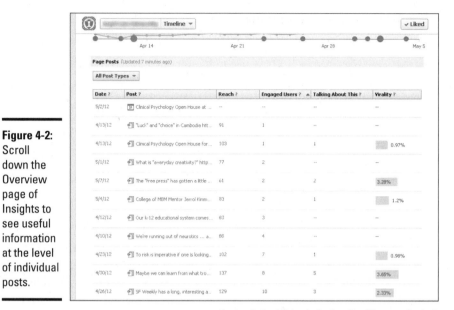

Figure 4-2:
Scroll
down the
Overview
page of
Insights to
see useful
information
at the level
of individual
posts.

Courtesy Saybrook University, San Francisco, CA; www.saybrook.edu

Drilling deeper

The Reach tab (refer to Figure 4-1) at the top of the Insights Page Dashboard
tells you how many people have seen your content, and how they may have
learned about your page through various Facebook internal channels. The
Reach chart shows you whether your page is visible on various internal
Facebook channels.

A Facebook post is limited to 500 characters. To keep your fans coming back
for more, break a popular subject into several small tidbits and use a URL
shortener with analytics, such as bitly. For more on shortener analytics, see
Book IX, Chapter 1.

Facebook defines these channels as organic, paid, or viral on `www.facebook.`
`com/help/search/?q=REACH`:

+ **Organic** reach means the number of unique people, fans or non-fans,
  who saw any content about your Page in their News Feed, Ticker, or on
  your Page.

+ **Paid** reach indicates the number of unique people who saw an ad or
  Sponsored Story that pointed to your Page.

+ **Viral** reach specifies the number of unique people who saw this post
  from a story published by a Friend.

Since people may see you in more than one place, the sum of Reach through these channels may exceed your total Page reach.

Scroll down to the very bottom of the Reach page to find external referrers to your Facebook Page.

Insights for Platform Applications

To monitor interaction between your Facebook presence and your primary website URL (such as how many people use Like or Follow icons on your website), there's Facebook's *Insights for Platform Applications*. This feature also allows you to monitor apps that you've implemented on your Facebook Pages.

For more on this option, see http://marketing.yell.com/web-design/facebook-insights-for-domain-explained.

First, you must "claim your domain" by associating it with a Facebook personal user account or application that you manage, preferably using your user ID:

1. **Click the green Insights for Your Domain link from the Insights Dashboard.**

2. **Fill out all the information in the form that appears.**

   Facebook will then generate a verification metatag (code) that appears in a field on the form.

3. **Add the metatag to the `<head>` section of the root web page for your domain.**

   This will connect your website to your Facebook account.

4. **Type your domain address into the text box and select the account to link it with.**

5. **Click the Get Insights button to complete the process.**

   Momentarily, your claimed domain will appear on the left-side navigation bar under the Websites section.

You need to implement Social Plug-ins from https://developers.facebook.com/docs/guides/web/#plugins. According to Facebook, "Social plugins let you see what your friends have liked, commented on, or shared on sites across the web." For a list of the many different plug-ins (each of which has different steps for implementation), see http://developers.facebook.com/docs/plugins.

Once implemented, referrals (inbound links) from Facebook-related Social Plug-ins will appear in Google Analytics, Facebook Insights, or other statistical programs using this format: www.facebook.com/plugins/*.This enables you to distinguish between referrals generated by Facebook plug-ins and referrals generated directly from your Facebook Page.

For more information, check out `https://developers.facebook.com/docs/guides/web/#insights`.

Chapter 5: Measuring Minor Social Media

In This Chapter

✔ **Tracking social plug-in results**

✔ **Analyzing Google+ metrics**

✔ **Making sense of Pinterest metrics**

✔ **Measuring LinkedIn success**

✔ **Mixing it all up with social mobile metrics**

At this point, social media performance metrics are probably dancing in your head, having replaced sugar plums as your object of desire. The newer and less popular sites have fewer metric options, but they are important if you've selected any of them as part of your social marketing mix. Therefore, in this chapter, we look at performance measurements for social plug-ins like share buttons and chiclets, as well as for Google+, Pinterest, LinkedIn, and the mobile versions of your social media pages.

Plugging into Social Media

The term *social plug-ins* refers to social media chiclets, share buttons, and other tools that allow your social media services to interact with your website and each other. You can find reports on the performance of plug-ins by going to Traffic Source➪Social➪Social Plug-ins in the left navigation of Google Analytics (see Figure 5-1).

The Social Plug-ins section offers three separate reports:

✦ **Social Actions Report:** Analyzes the number and type of social actions in one convenient location

✦ **Social Pages Report:** Shows which pages on your site drive the greatest number of social actions

✦ **Social Engagement Report:** Displays how site behavior changes if visitors click on Google +1 or other social buttons

After you have the +1 plug-in working — which Google will do for you automatically — it's easy to set up plug-ins for other social media. For more on the +1 plug-in, see the section below.

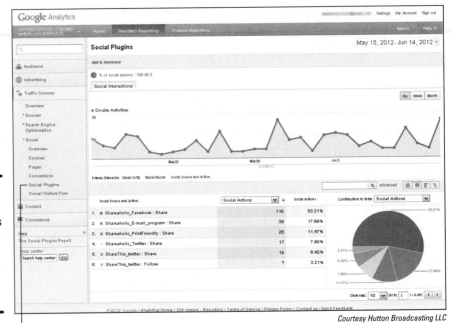

Figure 5-1:
Social Plug-
ins statistics
show how
your share
buttons and
chiclets
perform.

Courtesy Hutton Broadcasting LLC

Click here to find reports
on plug-in performance

Analyzing Google+ Success

Metrics for Google+ is, on some level, a no-brainer. Google+ is part of
Google's suite of tools, so of course Google has integrated statistics for
Google+ and the Plus One button into both Google Analytics and Google
Webmaster Tools.

Because Google Plus is search engine–based (unlike other social networks)
and because Google continues to knit Google+ into all its other services,
Google+ may eventually become more popular than it currently seems to
be. In any case, as discussed in Book VI, Google+ is useful for search engine
optimization (SEO) and should be part of your social media suite. Watch the
statistics for your site to see whether it produces traffic and sales.

You can see traffic for your Google+ profile and compare it to referrals from
other social media by going to Google Social Analytics and selecting Traffic
Sources⇨Social⇨Sources, as shown in Figure 5-2. For more on Google Social
Analytics, see Book IX, Chapter 1.

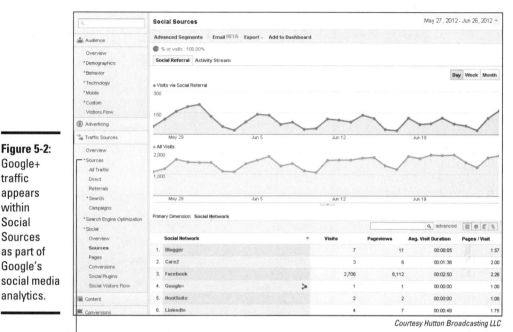

Figure 5-2:
Google+
traffic
appears
within
Social
Sources
as part of
Google's
social media
analytics.

Courtesy Hutton Broadcasting LLC

Click here for Google+ status

Plus One rankings

The whole point of Plus One rankings is to see which pages of your website and other pages of your web presence get the most votes (see Figure 5-3 for an example). In theory, if you write more pages and posts similar to those with the most +1 points, your site will perform better. We're a bit skeptical of that conclusion in all cases, but test it yourself.

As of July 2011, the automated social plug-in for +1 works only if you are using the default version of the latest Google Analytics tracking code.

Google Analytics and Webmaster Tools report Google +1 interactions somewhat differently, so the results may not match up. While Google Analytics includes only +1 interactions on your own site, Webmaster Tools reports +1 interactions for your content wherever they occur (for instance, on a search result). Analytics uses JavaScript for tracking social media; Tools doesn't. Finally, Analytics results are updated more often than Webmaster Tools.

Courtesy Hutton Broadcasting LLC

Figure 5-3:
Plus One statistics are available through Google Webmaster Tools.

Google has now made it possible to access Webmaster Tools search data, like +1 results, directly from Google Analytics — and vice versa. Your developer has to complete the geeky task of linking your Webmaster Tools account to a Google Analytics web property instead of linking it to a profile. Best approach is to direct her to `http://support.google.com/webmasters/bin/answer.py?hl=en&answer=1120006&topic=2370569&ctx=topic`.

No separate setup is needed to track Google +1 interactions that occur on your own site; Google Analytics does the setup for you.

Google+ internal performance metrics

For the most part, your Google+ profile performance can be analyzed using standard reports in Google Analytics. Just enter the URL for your profile in the Content section's search box. Drill down to In-Page Analytics to assist.

Google currently does not have separate internal statistics for Circles or Hangouts, but you can use one of the third-party packages, which we discuss in the next section. However, you can find a fascinating diagram showing the path your posts have traveled as they are shared with others. These are called *Google+ Ripples*.

Ripples help you visualize the ever-widening range of your content as people publicly refer it to others. You can also see who's doing the referring. After you post a publicly shared update on Google+, a diagram like the one in Figure 5-4 will be visible to everyone, as long you have a public Google+ profile.

To track the path of any publicly shared post, click the small down arrow at the top-right corner of a Google+ update. Privately shared posts are not included or visible in Ripples.

Figure 5-4:
The influence of the Dalai Lama ripples outward across the universe, even in cyberspace, through Google+ Ripples.

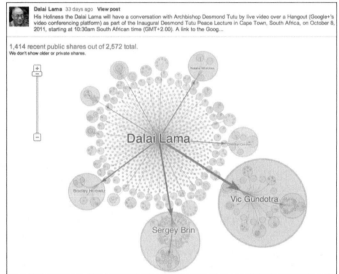

Screenshot © Google Inc. Used with permission.

External statistics sites for Google+

Several sites provide alternative or supplemental metrics for Google+. For example, www.plusya.com shortens the URL for your Google+ profile, and also produces free statistics on your profile traffic, including referrers and the geolocation of your visitors to your profile.

If you want to learn about Circles, try Google+ Social Statistics at www.socialstatistics.com, which tracks the top 100 Google+ users and posts. It not only ranks your Google+ site against others but also lets you see how many people add you to their Circles and how your own Circles grow over time.

Measuring Pinterest Success

Currently, Pinterest does not have its own analytics. Of course, you can see Pinterest in Google's Analytics tools, as discussed in Book IX, Chapter 1.

You can track Pinterest referrals by choosing Traffic Sources⇨Social⇨ Sources from the left navigation. If you have referrals from Pinterest, they will appear in the list of Social Sources in the lower section of the screen, along with those of Google+, Twitter, Facebook, and other services.

Pinterest offers basic information, such as how many people are following you and a summary of your posts. To see this information, select any of your pages from the navigation. Running across the page horizontally below your header image, you see your count of boards, pins, Likes, followers, and following (see Figure 5-5).

All other viewers, including your competitors, can also see these statistics, including followers and following. Of course, if you flip this warning around, you can see how your competitors perform on Pinterest, too.

See stats in this row

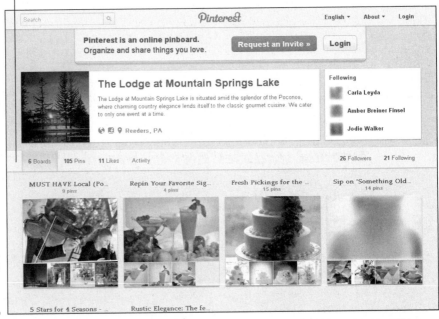

Figure 5-5: Pinterest provides very limited statistics in a row that runs across the top of your pages. These numbers are visible to all visitors.

Courtesy Mountain Springs Lake; www.MSLresort.com

TIP

The most important measure is the number of repins you have, because that shows which images are shared by others — their "viral" quality. Unfortunately, to see how many re-pins you have, you need to look at each pin separately or try one of the third-party solutions below. Ugh!

So far, there are only two helpful third-party analytics tools for Pinterest:

✦ **PinReach** (www.pinreach.com): PinReach scores Pinterest participation based on multiple factors, but primarily on the number of repins your material receives. It also compares your Pinterest score to other sites.

✦ **Pinerly** (www.pinerly.com/landing): Currently in beta with a waiting list, the Pinerly Dashboard promises to provide suggestions for pinners who share your interests, suggestions for which groups of people to unfollow, and current popular pins. It claims that it will also enable you to schedule pins and provide statistics on your Pinterest campaigns, including such items as clicks, repins, and Likes.

For more information on Pinterest, see Book VII.

Measuring LinkedIn Success

LinkedIn is a helpful place to meet professionals and extend your network. However, if you aren't getting referrals or if people aren't viewing your profile or asking you to connect to their networks, you're either doing something wrong or LinkedIn is the wrong social network for you.

One of your LinkedIn marketing goals is probably to drive more traffic to your website. As always, you can see how many people are coming to your site from LinkedIn by using Google's Social Analytics (refer to Figure 5-2).

A January 2012 study by HubSpot reported that "LinkedIn generates the highest conversion rate at 2.74%." (That is the percent of LinkedIn visitors who become qualified leads as they head down the conversion funnel shown in Book I, Chapter 1.)

To see if the results for your business-to-business (B2B) company bear out this conversion rate, look at the Social Value report in Google Analytics (see Figure 5-6), which you can find by scrolling down the Overview page. (Choose Traffic Sources⇨Social⇨Overview.)

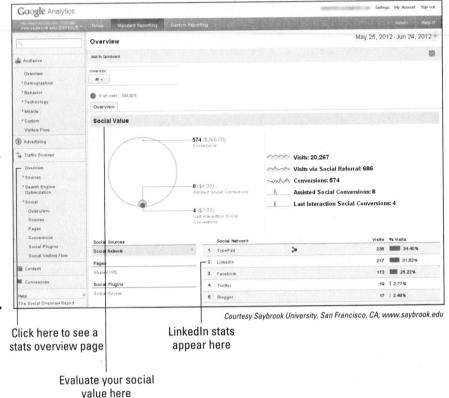

Figure 5-6:
The Social Value report appears on the Social Overview page of Google Analytics.

Click here to see a stats overview page

LinkedIn stats appear here

Evaluate your social value here

LinkedIn internal performance metrics

To see LinkedIn performance metrics, log in as an administrator and go to your Company Page (use the drop-down menu below Companies in the top navigation). On the Overview tab, you'll see the number of followers in the right column.

Then click the Page Statistics tab to see key performance metrics: Page Views, Visitor Demographics, Traffic Trends Over Time, and Product & Service Page results. You can drill down within these categories, as shown in Figure 5-7. These analytics, which are updated with about a 24-hour delay, will help you understand who your visitors are and what content they like.

The Page Statistics tab

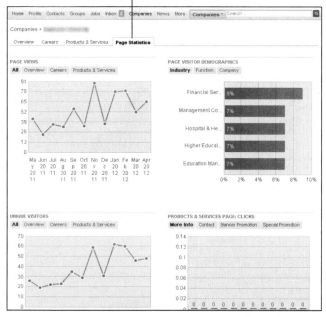

Figure 5-7:
Key internal
performance
metrics for
LinkedIn are
available
under
the Page
Statistics
tab.

Courtesy Saybrook University, San Francisco, CA; www.saybrook.edu

Tracking profile views

You can see the number of profile views you've received and the number of
searches for your company in the right column of your Profile page. Log into
your account, select Profile from the top navigation, and scroll down until
these numbers appear in the right column.

As you get more connections, the number of profile views should increase.
Additional views will come from second- and third-degree connections.

If you aren't attracting a lot of profile views, take a look at the first two sentences of your profile. Since people initially see only those lines, see if you
can make them more compelling. You may find that the page description
metatag you wrote for your website is just the ticket. (See Book II, Chapter 2
for more on metatags.)

Tracking comments

If you receive comments from several of your connections every time you post an update, you're posting the right kind of update. If you post an update and receive only a few replies, you haven't piqued the curiosity of your network members.

Unfortunately, you have to do this by eyeballing your posts; there is no internal data available. See which of your updates draw the largest response. Create new updates with similar information and see whether the trend of positive responses continues and you receive more replies on your updates.

As a paid LinkedIn subscriber of any level (see Book VIII, Chapter 2), you can view the number of profile visits you've received and the number of times you've appeared in search results, as well as the following additional statistics with Profile Stats Pro:

✦ The full list of people who have viewed your profile (as long as they didn't elect to remain anonymous)

✦ Trends (graphs for the past 12 weeks on a rolling basis; the graphs display how many visits you've had and how many times you have appeared in search results)

✦ Keywords used to find your profile

✦ Industries of people viewing your profile

Monitoring Social Mobile Impact

Measuring mobile analytics is a bit different because there are mobile applications for almost every social media service, as we discuss in Book VIII, Chapter 7. In this case, you are trying to compare the performance of social media by platform: web-based versus mobile.

The easiest way to do this is to segment visitors by using the Mobile menu within Google Analytics (choose Audience⇨Mobile⇨Overview, as shown in Figure 5-8). The Mobile Overview option compares mobile visits to regular computer visits, while the Devices option shows exactly which devices were used to access your site.

You might want to set up a separate conversion funnel for social mobile users.

As with all analytics, which elements you decide to measure and compare depend on your goals and objectives. Are you measuring the success of your own mobile or tablet site, the use of your social media pages on mobile devices, the number of visitors from social mobile pages to your primary website, or the level of foot traffic to a brick-and-mortar store? You can see some of these statistics in Figure 5-9, in a report provided by Apsalar, a vendor of mobile analytics services.

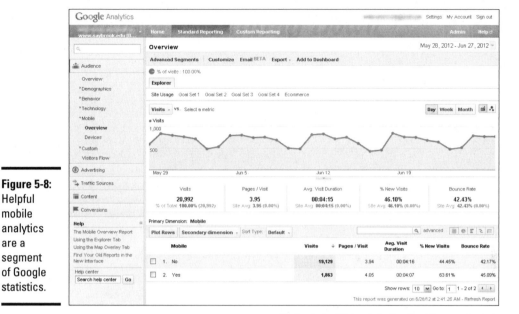

Figure 5-8:
Helpful
mobile
analytics
are a
segment
of Google
statistics.

Courtesy Saybrook University, San Francisco, CA; www.saybrook.edu

Standard site parameters, such as amount of social mobile traffic, click-through rate (CTR), number of impressions, number of page views, visit duration, and number of new versus repeat visitors still apply, of course.

Figure 5-9:
Apsalar
provides
helpful
mobile
statistics
to assess
performance
of your
mobile
social
pages.

Courtesy Apsalar

Watch for variations between mobile visitors and web visitors to your social media sites on conversion rates, newsletter subscriptions, and brand recall.

Naturally, you should watch for metrics specific to mobile use, such as

✦ Use of mobile phone versus tablet use and by operating system (iOS versus Droid, primarily) by choosing Overview➪Mobile➪Devices

✦ The use of mobile payment methods, codes, and coupons

✦ Click-throughs from a social mobile site to your regular, tablet, or mobile site

✦ Click-to-call rate versus actual clicks to your primary, mobile, or tablet-specific site

✦ Behavioral differences between users of your social media pages on the web versus on a mobile platform

Table 5-1 provides some third-party resources for mobile analytics.

Table 5-1		Mobile Analytics Resources	
Name	*URL*	*What You Can Find*	*Cost*
Apsalar	`http://apsalar.com`	Mobile app analytics including real-time daily cohorts and user-centric conversion funnels, cross-app analytics, and revenue and engagement data	Free
Bango	`http://bango.com`	Mobile marketing analytics for websites, mobile apps, campaigns, and payments from mobile devices	30-day free trial; starting from $49 per month
Flurry	`www.flurry.com`	Mobile app analytics for usage, category benchmarks, and audience segmentation	Free

Chapter 6: Comparing Metrics from Different Marketing Techniques

In This Chapter

✔ Comparing metrics among social media

✔ Integrating social media metrics with web metrics

✔ Analyzing social media with advertising metrics

✔ Juxtaposing social media with other online marketing

✔ Contrasting online with offline metrics

*B*y now, you may be asking yourself whether web *metrics* (the science of measurement) are worth the trouble. They certainly matter if you have a business with a finite amount of time, money, or staff — which covers just about every business.

Metrics aren't about determining whether your company is the "best" in any particular marketing or advertising channel. They're about deciding which channels offer your company the best value for achieving your business objectives. Not to denigrate your instinct, but metrics are simply the most objective way to optimize your marketing effort.

Marketing isn't rocket science. If your metrics show that a particular tactic is working, keep doing it. If they show it isn't working, try something else.

Establishing Key Performance Indicators

The most important items to measure — the ones that reflect your business goals and objectives — are *key performance indicators* (KPIs). They may vary by type of business, but after they're established, they should remain consistent over time.

An e-retailer, for instance, may be more interested in sales by product category or at different price points, though a business-to-business (B2B) service company might want to look at which sources produce the most qualified prospects. The trick is to select five to ten relevant metrics for your business.

If something isn't measured, it cannot be evaluated. If it cannot be evaluated, it isn't considered important.

As you read this chapter, you can establish your own KPIs. Then you can combine them with other information about how your various marketing efforts contribute to sales and leads, to your bottom line, and to the return on your investment (ROI). Armed with this information, you'll be in a position to make strategic business decisions about your marketing mix, no matter what size your company.

Enter at least one KPI for each business goal on your Social Media Marketing Plan (Book I, Chapter 2). Some business goals share the same KPI. Schedule a review of the comparative metrics on your Social Media Activity Calendar (Book I, Chapter 4) at least once per month, or more often if you're starting a new endeavor or running a brief, time-constrained effort or you handle a large volume of traffic.

Overcoming measurement challenges

Measuring success among forms of social media, let alone between social media and any other forms of marketing, is a challenge. You're likely to find yourself comparing apples to not only oranges but also mangoes, pineapples, kiwis, pears, and bananas. In the end, you have to settle for a fruit salad or smoothie.

Install the same statistical software, whether it's Google Analytics or another package, on all your sites. Your sites may not have identical goals (for instance, users may not be able to purchase from your LinkedIn profile or request a quote from your wiki), but using the same software will ensure that metrics are consistently defined. In fact, the availability of compatible analytics packages may influence your selection of a host, development platform, or even web developer.

Using A/B testing

You may want to apply *A/B testing* (comparing a control sample against other samples in which only one element has changed) to your forays into social media. Just as you might use A/B testing to evaluate landing pages or e-mails, you can compare results between two versions of a blog post or compare performance of two different headlines for an update on a social media service, while keeping all other content identical.

If you're comparing performance (click-throughs to your site) of content placed in different locations — for example, on several different social bookmarks or social news services — use identical content for greater accuracy.

Don't rely on "absolute" measurements from any online source. Take marketing metrics with a shaker full of salt; look more at the trends than at the exact numbers. Be forewarned, though, that the temptation to treat "numbers" as sacrosanct is hard to resist.

To no one's surprise, an entire business has grown up around web metrics. If you have a statistical bent, join or follow the discussions on the resource sites listed in Table 6-1.

Table 6-1	Online Metrics Resources	
Site Name	*URL*	*What It Offers*
Abtests.com	www.abtests.com	Help setting up A/B tests
BrianCray AB testing	http://briancray.com/2009/08/04/ultimate-ab-testing-resources	A/B testing resources
eMetrics	www.emetrics.org	Events and conferences on marketing optimization
Marketing Experiments	www.marketingexperiments.com/improving-website-conversion/ab-split-testing.html	Information on A/B split testing
Mashable	http://mashable.com/2012/02/09/social-media-analytics-spreadsheets	Helpful spreadsheet for social analytics
Omniture from Adobe	http://www.omniture.com/en/resources/guides	Best practice guides and white papers on analytics
Social Media Measurement Using Google Analytics	http://www.socialmediaexaminer.com/how-to-track-social-media-traffic-with-google-analytics	Helpful article about implementing social media in Google Analytics
Digital Analytics Association	http://www.digitalanalyticsassociation.org	Professional association for analytics practitioners
Web Analytics Demystified Blog	http://blog.webanalyticsdemystified.com	Digital measurement techniques
Web Analytics World Blog	www.webanalyticsworld.net	Current news on the web analytics and digital marketing front

(continued)

Table 6-1 *(continued)*

Site Name	URL	What It Offers
Webanalytics Forum	`http://tech.groups.yahoo.com/group/webanalytics`	Discussion forum hosted by the Digital Analytics Association
WebProNews	`www.webpronews.com`	Breaking news blog for web professionals, including analytics topics
Webtrends	`http://webtrends.com/expertise`	Resources for analytics and other marketing topics

Comparing Metrics across Social Media

We talk throughout this book about various genres of social media services. Each genre has its own, arcane measurements from hashtags to comments, from posts to ratings, from membership numbers to sentiment.

Use medium-specific metrics to gauge the efficacy of different campaigns within that medium or to compare results from one site within a genre to another.

However, to assess the overall effectiveness of social media efforts and your total marketing mix, you find common metrics that cross boundaries. Surprise! These common metrics look a lot like the statistics discussed in Book IX, Chapter 1. By using the right tools, or by downloading analytics to a spreadsheet and creating your own graphs, you can compare data for various social media.

Online traffic patterns may vary for all sorts of reasons and for different businesses. Watch for cyclical patterns across a week or by comparing the same time frames a year apart. Merchants often do this for same-store sales to compare how a store is performing compared to past years.

Carefully aggregate measurements over exactly the same time frame and dates. You obviously don't compare weekly data from a blog to monthly data for a website. But neither should you compare Tuesday traffic on one source to Saturday traffic on another, or compare November–December clicks for an e-commerce site selling gift items (which is probably quite high) to January–February clicks (which are probably low). Compare, instead, to the same time frames from the preceding year.

In most cases, these metrics become some of the KPIs on your list:

✦ **Traffic (visits):** The overall measure of the number of visits (not visitors) made to your site or to a particular social media presence over a set period. Facebook (see Figure 6-1) offers page administrators traffic data in its free analytics at www.facebook.com/help/?search=insights. Google Social Analytics enables you to compare traffic from different social media sources, as we discuss in Book IX, Chapter 1.

Figure 6-1:
Facebook's Insights analytics tool displays Facebook traffic over time.

Courtesy Saybrook University, San Francisco, CA; www.saybrook.edu

✦ **Unique users:** The number of different users (or, more specifically, IP addresses) who visited. Depending on your business model, you may want to know whether you have ten visits apiece from 100 ardent fans (multiple repeat users) or 1,000 users, each of whom drops in once. This type of detail is available for some, but not all, social media services.

✦ **Keywords:** The list of search terms or tags used to find a particular web posting. Phrases are often more useful than individual words.

✦ **Referrers:** A list of traffic sources that tells you how many visitors arrive at your web entities from such sources as search engines, other websites, paid searches, and many, but not all, other social media services.

Some even identify referrers from web-enabled cellphones. You can find this section in your analytics program. Track sources that include an identifying code in the link from the Entry Pages section. They can be aggregated and displayed graphically for easy review, as shown in Figure 6-2, in the traffic display from HubSpot.

Figure 6-2:
The HubSpot reporting system for inbound marketing provides a graphical display of traffic aggregated by source category.

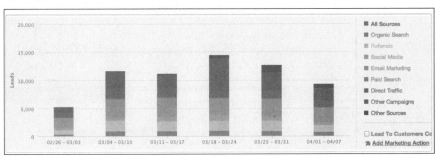

Courtesy HubSpot; www.hubspot.com

Keeping track of users' paths among many components of a complicated web presence isn't easy, but it's worth it. You may find that your marketing strategy takes B2B prospects from LinkedIn to your blog and then to a microsite. Or, you may watch business-to-consumer (B2C) clients follow your offers from a social news service to a store widget on Facebook before they conclude with a purchase on your site. We talk more about tracking your links in the following section.

✦ **Click-through rate (CTR):** The number of click-throughs to your site from a particular source divided by the number of visitors (traffic) that arrived at that source. If 40 people view your Facebook stream in one day, for instance, and 4 of them click-through to your primary site, the CTR is 10 percent. You may need to derive this data by combining traffic measurements from particular social media services with information from the Referrers or Entry Pages sections of your analytics program. In some cases, the CTR becomes the conversion measure for a particular social media service.

Table 6-2 lists the KPIs you can track by genre and social media platform.

Table 6-2	**Social Media by Genre and KPI**	
Social Genre	*Site Examples*	*Useful KPIs to Check*
Bookmarking	Delicious, StumbleUpon	traffic, keywords, CTR
Community	Forums, Ning, Google Groups, Yahoo! Groups	traffic, users, time, keywords, CTR
Information	Blogs, webinars, wikis	traffic, users, time, keywords, referrers, CTR
Media sharing	Flickr, podcasts, YouTube, Pinterest	traffic, users, time, keywords, CTR
Network	Facebook, LinkedIn, Google+, Twitter	traffic, users, time, keywords, CTR
News	Digg, reddit	traffic, keywords, CTR
Review	Angie's List, Epinions, TripAdvisor	traffic, CTR
Shopping	Kaboodle, ThisNext	traffic, keywords, CTR

Tagging links

Tagging your links with identifying code is especially helpful for tracking clicks that arrive from e-newsletters, e-mail, widgets, banner ads, and links from a phone because they otherwise aren't distinguishable in the referrer list. An unidentified referrer is usually displayed on a row with only a / (slash) in its name. This unspecified / category includes people who type your URL on the address bar of their browsers because they remembered it or were told about it or who have bookmarked your site.

If you have only a few such unspecified sources, simply tag the inbound link with additional information. Add `?src=` and the landing page URL. Follow that, in any order, with the source (where the link appeared, such as MerchantCircle), the medium (pay-per-click, banner, e-mail, and so forth), and campaign name (date, slogan, promo code, product name, and so on). Separate each variable with an ampersand (&). The tagged link will look something like `www.yoursite.com/landingpage?src=yahoo&banner&july12`.

Place enough information after the question mark to identify the source of the incoming link. For more information on tagging, see `http://support. google.com/analytics/bin/answer.py?hl=en&answer=1033863`.

As far as the user is concerned, the link automatically redirects to the correct landing page, but you can count each distinctive URL in the Entry Pages section or, in the case of Google Analytics, by choosing Traffic Sources⇨ Sources⇨Campaigns, as shown in Figure 6-3.

If you have a lot of links to tag for tracking purposes, use the URL builder at `http://support.google.com/analytics/bin/answer.py?hl=en&answer=1033867`. Enter the referrer name, medium, keywords, content, and campaign name. You end up with a link that looks something like `http://watermelonweb.com/?utm_source=google&utm_medium=031512_coupon&utm_campaign=spring_sale`.

UTM stands for Urchin Tracking Module, a leftover from the original source for Google Analytics, which Google bought from Urchin.

The process of tagging links may be time-consuming, but being able to monitor a particular campaign more accurately is worth your trouble.

Generate a separate, unique shortened link for tweets, LinkedIn updates, and mobile sites, if needed. *Always* test to ensure that the modified link works correctly.

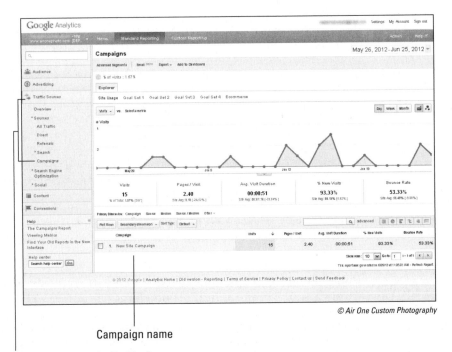

Figure 6-3:
It's easy to track campaign results in Google Analytics.

© Air One Custom Photography

Campaign name

Click Campaigns under Traffic Sources

Analyzing the clickstream

Clickstream analysis is a fancy name for tracking users' successive mouse clicks (the clickstream) to see how they surf the web. Clickstream analytics are usually monitored on an aggregate basis.

Server-based clickstream analysis provides valuable insight into visitor behavior. For instance, by learning which paths users most frequently take on a site and which routes lead to sales, you can make changes in content and calls to action, as well as identify ways to simplify navigation and paths to check out.

On a broader level, clickstream analysis gives you a good idea where your visitors were before they arrived at your website or social media service and where they went afterward.

Aggregated data about user behavior or industry usage is useful as you design your social media marketing strategy. This analysis may also help explain why a campaign is or isn't working.

In the end, however, the only data that truly matters is the data that shows what's happening with your business, your web presence, your customers, and your bottom line.

It's easy to see your upstream analysis (where visitors came from). That's the same as your referrers. What's harder to see is where visitors go when they leave your site.

Figure 6-4 displays a clickstream analysis of where visitors went by category after visiting Facebook in September 2011. Interestingly, less than 1 percent of Facebook users clicked through to wireless, sports, travel, health, or automotive websites. The implication is that Facebook may not be the best place to generate new traffic or prospects for certain types of businesses.

For specific URLS in the clickstream for social media services, try selecting the Clickstream tab for a site on alexa.com (for instance, at `www.alexa.com/siteinfo/twitter.com#`).

Clickstream data vary over time as users run hot and cold about a particular service, as the user population changes, or as a social media technique evolves.

You can find a free open source tool for clickstream analysis of users' paths through your website at http://sourceforge.net/projects/statviz.

You can also set up a clickstream analysis for sites in Google Analytics by choosing Conversions⇨Goals⇨Goal Flow. For more information, visit `http://support.google.com/analytics/bin/answer.py?hl=en&answer=2519989#segments`.

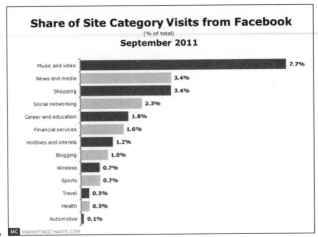

Figure 6-4:
Clickstream data from Marketing Charts shows where visitors went by category after using Facebook in September 2011.

Courtesy Compete, Inc.

Tracking your own outbound links

Google Analytics lets you track outbound, downstream clicks from your own pages. Your programmer must tag all outbound links you want to track, which involves some JavaScript customization. Send your programmer to http://support.google.com/analytics/bin/answer.py?hl=en&answer=1136920.

For additional help, visit Google's Event Tracking Guide at https://developers.google.com/analytics/devguides/collection/gajs/eventTrackerGuide. If you need to tag many external links, try the automated tagging solution at http://wptheming.com/2012/01/tracking-outbound-links-with-google-analytics.

To see the number of clicks to each external link in Google Analytics, choose Content⇨Events⇨Overview and look under whatever category name your programmer set up to track these external links.

Integrating Social Media with Web Metrics

In addition to creating your hub website, you may have developed sites either as subdomains within your primary domain name or with auxiliary domain names. These sites may take several forms:

✦ **Microsites:** These small, dedicated sites that have their own domain names are usually developed for a specific event, product or product line, service, or another promotion, or as specialized landing pages for an advertising campaign. Whether the microsite is permanent or temporary, you must make a strategic choice to create one, judging cost, branding needs, search engine optimization (SEO), and other marketing efforts against potential benefits.

✦ **Blogs:** All blogs and other information-sharing sites, such as webinars and wikis, can be fully tracked with analytical software. Some sites, such as Ning (`www.ning.com/help/cgi-bin/ning.cfg/php/enduser/std_adp.php?p_faqid=3003`) and Blogger (`www.blogger.com/blogger.g?blogID=4948549804114453926#othersettings`), offer Google Analytics integration, but not all hosted solutions do so. Though you can obtain statistics from certain hosted communities or third parties (for example, WordPress suggests that you use JetPack at `http://wordpress.org/extend/plugins/stats`), you may not be able to customize them or integrate them with your other statistics.

✦ **Communities:** All Ning communities, forums, chat rooms, and message boards fall into this category. Though they may have their own, internal statistics, also investigate whether you can customize those statistics to meet your needs before you select software or a hosted platform. For instance, Yahoo! (`http://groups.yahoo.com`) and Google Groups (`http://groups.google.com`) are inexpensive, user opt-in alternatives, but provide only limited statistics.

For statistical purposes as well as SEO, you should own the domain names of these sites rather than host them on another server (`http://myblog.wordpress.com`). Sites can almost always be tracked with your preferred analytics package if they are separately registered domains (`www.mymicrosite.com`), were created as subdirectories (`http://blog.yourdomain.com`), or live within a directory (`www.yourdomain.com/blog/blog-title`).

The use of KPIs at these additional sites makes it easier to integrate what happens with social media with what happens after users arrive at your primary website. To complete the analysis, add a few more comparative indicators, each of which you can analyze independently:

✦ **Conversion rate:** You're already computing the percentage of visitors who complete tangible goals on your primary website, whether they purchase a product or complete a request form. Now compare the conversion rate (for the same available goal) by traffic source to the average conversion rate across all sources for that goal. Figure 6-5 displays the Social Value option in Google Analytics, which analyzes conversion rate to assess the relative value of links from various social media. (Go to Traffic Sources⇨Social⇨Overview and scroll down.)

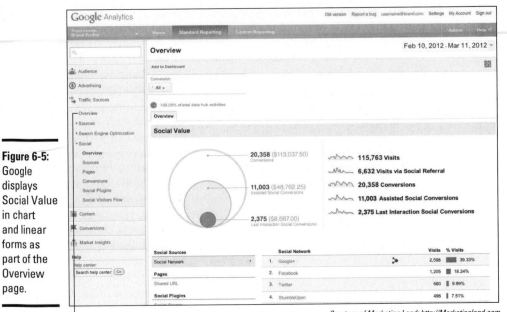

Figure 6-5:
Google
displays
Social Value
in chart
and linear
forms as
part of the
Overview
page.

Click here for the stats overview

✦ **Sales and lead generation:** These numbers may come from your storefront package or be based on measurements tracked offline. We discuss them in greater depth in Book I, Chapter 2.

✦ **Downloads:** Track the number of times users download video or audio files, slide show PDF files, white papers, or application forms from your sites.

To track downloads, use the same approach as tracking outbound links, as discussed above. Visit the event tracking guide for more information (`https://developers.google.com/analytics/devguides/collection/gajs/eventTrackerGuide`). If you have a lot of downloads, try the paid automated solution at `www.friendlywebguy.co.uk/post/How-to-automatically-track-file-downloads-in-Google-Analytics-without-javascript.aspx`.

✦ **Pages per view, pages viewed:** Microsites, communities, and blogs usually offer enough content to make these parameters reasonable to measure. Tracking this information by social source, however, as shown in Figure 6-5, can be valuable. Page views are available for most blogs and Ning sites, but not necessarily for all other services.

✦ **Time per visit:** The average length of time spent viewing material is a good, but not exact, proxy for the number of pages per view. Naturally, users spend less time reading a single tweet than they might spend on your blog or website, but fractions of a second are indications of trouble everywhere.

✦ **Bounce rate:** For another indication of interest in your content, determine the percentage of visitors who leave without visiting a second page (related to time per visit). As with pages per view or time per visit, the bounce rate may be a bit misleading. If many people have bookmarked a page so that they can immediately find the information they want, your bounce rate may be higher than expected, though pages per view or time per visit may be low. You may want to sort bounces by upstream source.

Using Advertising Metrics to Compare Social Media with Other Types of Marketing

Because you generally don't pay social media services, social media marketing is incredibly appealing as a cost-effective substitute for paid ads. You can convert the advertising metrics in the following sections to compare the cost effectiveness of your various social media efforts or to analyze social media outlets versus other forms of promotion, online and off.

Obtaining metrics for paid advertising

With the exception of pay-per-click advertising, which exists only online, the metrics used for paid advertising are the same whether you advertise online or offline. Most publishers offer advertisers a *media kit* that includes demographics, ad requirements, and ad rates based on one or more pricing models.

Advertising costs vary over time based on demand and availability and the overall economy. Ad prices are generally based on "what the market will bear." New, real-time bidding schemes for online advertising may make prices even more volatile. Life is negotiable in many advertising marketplaces, except for those that operate as self-service networks. It never hurts to ask for what you want. For more information, see *Google AdWords For Dummies,* Third Edition, by Howie Jacobson, PhD, Joel McDonald, and Kristie McDonald, or *Advertising For Dummies,* 2nd Edition, by Gary Dahl.

Many social media sites don't charge for posting content because their true goal is to sell either premium services or advertising. Your content generates what they sell: an audience. The more user "eyeballs" a social media service can deliver to its advertisers, the greater its own advertising revenue. In essence, you manufacture their product in exchange for getting some of that traffic for yourself.

CPM

Cost per thousand (CPM) impressions, one of the most consistently used metrics in advertising, work across all forms of media. CPM is based on the number of times an ad is viewed whether it's calculated for ads on TV, billboards, or in print magazines, received as dedicated e-mails, or viewed on web pages.

CPM is simple to calculate: Divide the cost by $\frac{1}{1000}$ (.001) of the number of impressions (views). The more narrowly defined the audience, the higher the CPM. You can find a handy CPM calculator at `www.clickz.com/cpm_ calculator`.

For instance, the CPM for a 30-second, broadcast Super Bowl ad in 2012 averaged about $35, but the actual dollar cost — $3.5 million — was high because the audience was 100 million TV viewers. By contrast, CPM for a small, highly targeted audience of CEOs in high-tech companies may run $100 or more.

Computing other factors given the CPM is easy. For example, for the total cost of the Super Bowl ad, multiply the CPM ($35) by the number of viewers divided by 1,000 (100 million worldwide viewers divided by 1,000 = 100,000) for an average cost of $3.5 million. That's roughly 3.5¢ per impression (divide CPM by 1,000) so you need deep pockets for a Super Bowl buy.

Because you may have difficulty tracking from impression to action in some channels, CPM models are often used to measure branding campaigns. Figure 6-6 shows the average CPM for a variety of media. CPM rates for online media vary widely; Advision Advertising estimated online advertising overall (including pay-per-click and display ads) at approximately $8 CPM in 2011.

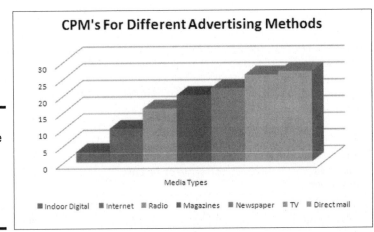

Figure 6-6: The relative CPM for various forms of advertising in 2011.

Courtesy Advision Advertising

CPA and CPC

Compare CPM with a *cost-per-action* (CPA) advertising model and its subset, *cost-per-click* (CPC) ads. CPA advertising triggers payment only when a user takes a specific action, such as downloads a white paper, signs up for a newsletter, registers for a conference, or becomes a fan, friend, or follower. At the far end of the CPA spectrum, when CPA is based on a user purchase, it approaches a sales commission model.

 In the classic definitions of CPA, CPC, and CPM, rates don't include the cost of producing an ad, the commission paid to an agency, or your own labor to research and review ad options. From a budget point of view, you need to include all these factors in your cost estimates.

A web-only metric, CPC (or sometimes *PPC*, for pay-per-click) falls within the CPA model because advertisers are charged only when a viewer clicks a link to a specified landing page. The CPC model is often used for ads in the right-most columns of search engines and also for clicks obtained from banner, video, and online classified ads and from shopping comparison sites and paid directory listings. For additional resources for paid online advertising, consult Table 6-3.

Table 6-3	Online Advertising Resources	
Name	*URL*	*What You Can Find*
Adotas	`http://research.adotas.com`	Online advertising research and news
AdRatesOnline	`www.adratesonline.com`	Sample rates for online advertising of various types and sizes

Internet Advertising Bureau	`www.iab.net/media/file/ GlossaryofInteractiv AdvertisingTerms.pdf`
	
	`www.onlineadvertising.net/ glossary.html`
		Glossary of interactive advertising terms

DoubleClick by Google	`www.google.com/doubleclick`	Ad management and solutions
Small Business Association	`www.sba.gov/content/ online-advertising`	Resources for online advertising
Internet Advertising Bureau	`www.iab.net/iab_products_ and_industry_services/ 1421/1443/1452`	List of standard online ad sizes

(continued)

Table 6-3 *(continued)*

Name	URL	What You Can Find
Internet Advertising Competition	www.iacaward.org	Annual Internet ad competition sponsored by the Web Marketing Association
The Webby Awards	www.webbyawards.com	Interactive ad competition
Word of Mouth Marketing Association	http://womma.org	Membership group, resources, events

Always ask which statistics a publisher provides to verify the results of your ads. Some confirm impressions as well as clicks or other actions (check against your own analytics program); some provide only impressions; and some publishers cannot — or will not — provide either one.

Even if you pay a flat fee, such as for an annual directory listing, you can compute CPC and CPM after the fact, as long as the publisher provides you with the number of impressions and you can identify click-throughs.

Reach

Reach is the estimated number of potential customers (qualified prospects) you can target in a specific advertising medium or campaign. You can apply the concept of reach, by extension, to specific social media channels, anticipated traffic on your website, or other populations, such as the addresses on your e-mail list. Reach is sometimes expressed as a fraction of the total audience for an advertising campaign (for example, potential customers divided by total audience).

The number of potential customers may be the total number of viewers in a highly targeted campaign, or only a segment of them. In the case of the Super Bowl example in the earlier section on CPM, for instance, a beer ad may be targeted at males ages 25 to 64; only that demographic percentage of the audience is calculated in reach. For the 2011 Super Bowl, 54 percent of viewers were male, 46 percent of who were in the target age group, out of 111.5 million viewers, making the worldwide reach about 28 million.

For the best results, identify advertising venues where the number of potential customers (reach) represents a large share of potential viewers (impressions). Return to your early market research for viewer demographics from Quantcast or Alexa.com, or review media kits to estimate the reach of each publication or social media site you're considering.

Applying advertising metrics to social media

Because publishers receive no payments for most social media appearances, comparing "free" social media marketing to paid advertising requires a little adjustment. How can you compare the CPM or CPC for something that's free versus something you pay for? Though you can acquire information about page views *(impressions)*, clicks, and other actions (conversion goals) from your analytics program, cost requires a little thought.

One possibility is to modify the cost of advertising to include labor and hard costs for production, management, and commission and any fees for services, such as press release distribution. Then estimate the hard costs and the amount of work in labor dollars required to create and maintain various elements of your social media presence. If you outsource the creation of ads or social media content to contractors such as copywriters, videographers, photographers, or graphic designers, include those expenses.

Don't go crazy trying to calculate exact dollar amounts. You simply estimate the relative costs of each medium or campaign to compare the cost-effectiveness of one form of promotion to another. Social media marketing may be relatively inexpensive, but if you see only one action or impression after 20 hours of labor, you need to decide whether it's worth it.

Juxtaposing Social Media Metrics with Other Online Marketing

Regardless of any other online techniques you use, you can combine links with source tags, analytics program results, and advertising metrics to compare social media results to results from other online techniques.

Refine your list of KPIs for these elements:

✦ **E-mail newsletters:** Whether you use your own mailing list or rent one, you measure

- *Bounces:* Bad e-mail addresses

- *Open rate:* The percentage of good addressees that open your newsletter, roughly equivalent to reach as a percentage of impressions

- *Click-through rate,* or *CTR:* The percentage of people who click through to a web page after opening a newsletter

- *Landing pages:* Where newsletter recipients "went"

Well-segmented, targeted lists result in better reach. If you rent lists, be sure to include the acquisition cost per thousand names, as well as the transmission cost, in your total cost for CPM comparison. Most newsletter services and list-rental houses provide all these metrics.

✦ **Coupons, promotion codes:** Online coupons can be tracked similarly to regular banner ads. However, for both promotion codes and coupons, track which offers produce the best results, which are almost always sales or registrations.

✦ **Press releases:** Sometimes press releases are hard to track online because many free press distribution services don't provide information on page views or click-throughs. By contrast, most paid distribution services tell you the click-through rate and the number of impressions (or number of times someone viewed your release) on their servers. Though these services can tell you where the release was distributed, they don't know what happened afterward. A press release is a good place to include an identifier in the links, as described earlier in the "Tagging links" section. The tag enables you to track entry pages. You may also see a spike in daily or hourly traffic to your site shortly after the distribution time.

✦ **Product placement in games and other programs:** Advertisers can now place the equivalent of banner ads or product images within online video games. If the ads are linkable, you can find the CTR and impressions to calculate CPM and CPC. Offline games with product placement must be treated as offline marketing elements.

✦ **Online events:** Track live concerts, chats, speeches, and webinars with KPIs for registration — request an e-mail address, at minimum — even if the event is free. Though not everyone who registers attends, this approach also provides a helpful set of leads and a built-in audience to notify of future events. Of course, you can also check referrers and entry pages.

✦ **Disaggregated components, such as third-party blogs, chat rooms, RSS feeds, regular e-mail, or instant messaging:** Tagged links that pass through from these forms of communication probably comprise your best bet.

You can incorporate a special tag for links forwarded by others, though you might not be able to tell how they completed the forwarding (for example, from a Share This feature versus e-mail) unless you have implemented Social Media Plug-ins). It all depends on what you're trying to measure.

Be sure to register for optional analytics when you install a Share function from sites such as AddThis or ShareThis, which integrate with Google Analytics. Then you can see where and how often users forward your link through these services.

Contrasting Word-of-Web with Word-of-Mouth

Word-of-mouth is, without a doubt, the most cost-effective form of advertising. Ultimately, that force powers all social media, with its peer-to-peer recommendations and referrals.

Research done by the Keller Fay Group in 2011 (`www.kellerfay.com/news-events/research-shows-positive-word-of-mouth-far-outweighs-negative`) is instructive. With 91 percent of interactions occurring in person or by phone, offline word-of-mouth is still far more prevalent than online.

However, the Keller Fay study finds that engagement on social media sites does help spark conversations. Keller Fay postulates that the Internet, followed by radio and then television, is the most "sociable in terms of generating conversations." The study presents several other interesting, and sometimes counterintuitive, findings:

✦ Positive experiences are more likely to generate word-of-mouth than negative by a 3:1 ratio.

✦ Highly satisfied customers can become brand ambassadors.

✦ The volume of criticism in online platforms is not as high as previously estimated, although this varies by topic and category.

Keep these points in mind as you consider the positive and negative impacts of participation in social media.

You can monitor mentions of your company online and the tone of those responses, as discussed in Book II.

Your analytical task here is to compare the efficacy of "word-of-web" by way of social media to its more traditional forms. Tracking visitors who arrive from offline is the trickiest part. These visitors type your URL in the address bar of their browsers either because they've heard of your company from someone else (word-of-mouth) or as a result of offline marketing.

Offline marketing may involve print, billboards, radio, television, loyalty-program keychain tags, promotional items, packaging, events, or any other great ideas you dream up.

By borrowing the following techniques from direct marketing, you can find ways, albeit imperfect, to identify referrals from offline sources or other individuals:

✦ **Use a slightly different URL to identify the offline source.** Make the URL simple and easy to remember, such as *yourdomain*.com/tv, *yourdomain*.com/wrapper, *yourdomain*.com/nyt, or *yourdomain*.com/radio4. These short URLs can show viewers a special landing page — perhaps one that details an offer or a contest encouraged by an offline teaser — or redirect them to an existing page on your site. Long, tagged URLs that are terrific for online sourcing and hard-to-remember shortened URLs are not helpful offline.

- ✦ **Identify referrals from various offline sources.** Use different response e-mail addresses, telephone numbers, extensions, or people's names.

- ✦ **Provide an incentive to the referring party.** "Tell a friend about us. Both of you will receive $10 off your next visit." This technique can be as simple as a business card for someone to bring in with the referring friend's name on the back. Of course, the card carries its own unique referral URL for tracking purposes.

- ✦ **Stick to the tried-and-true method.** Always ask, "May I ask how you heard about us?" Then tally the results.

You can then plug these numbers into a spreadsheet with your online referral statistics to compare offline methods with online social media.

HubSpot (www.hubspot.com) compared the subjective importance of various sources of B2B leads by marketing channel, including some offline activities, in its *2012 State of Inbound Marketing* survey. The results, shown in Figure 6-7, show that marketing professionals view online activities as more important sources of leads than traditional offline marketing venues, with social media and natural search seen as the most important, followed closely by blogs and paid search. Think about where you're spending your marketing dollars.

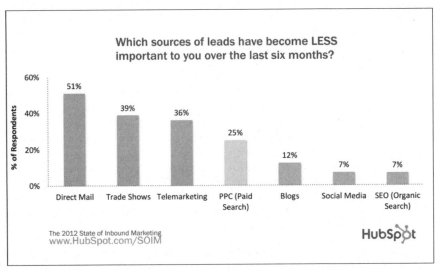

Figure 6-7: Businesses rate traditional marketing activities, like direct mail, trade shows, and telemarketing, less important than online marketing techniques.

Courtesy HubSpot; www.hubspot.com

Chapter 7: Making Decisions by the Numbers

In This Chapter

↙ **Using metrics to make decisions**

↙ **Diagnosing problem campaigns**

↙ **Returning to basics**

↙ **Reenergizing your creativity**

A 2012 survey from the Society for Human Resource Management (SHRM) showed that only 21 percent of professionals whose companies use social media said that they measure their return on investment (ROI). By using the tools for assessing qualitative and quantitative results, including ROI, you can certainly count yourself among those happy few who do! However, there's no point in collecting metrics just to save them in a virtual curio cabinet. The challenge is to figure out how to use the numbers to adjust your online marketing campaigns, whether they need fine-tuning or a major overhaul. In this chapter, we show you how to analyze problems, see what your data reveal, and then use the results to modify your marketing approach.

Using Metrics to Make Decisions

In spite of the hype, social media is, at its core, a form of strategic marketing communications. As a business owner, you must balance the subjective aspects of branding, sentiment, good will, and quality of leads with the objective performance metrics of traffic and click-through rate (CTR) and the business metrics of customer acquisition costs, conversion rate, sales value, and ROI. The balance point is unique to each business at a specific time. Alas, no fixed rules exist.

As part of your balancing act, you'll undoubtedly also tap your instincts, incorporating casual feedback from customers, the ever-changing evolution of your market, your budget, and your assessment of your own and your staff's available time and skills.

Even after you feel confident about your marketing program, keep watching your metrics as a reality check. Data has a funny way of surprising you.

Don't become complacent. Continue to check your performance and business metrics at least monthly. How do they compare to what your instinct is telling you?

Knowing When to Hold and When to Fold

There are a few things you'll watch for in your metrics. As always, you evaluate comparative results, not absolute numbers. Keep an eye on these characteristics:

✦ Negative and positive trends that last for several months

✦ Abrupt or unexpected changes

✦ "No change" in Key Performance Indicators (KPI) in spite of social media marketing activities

✦ Correlations between a peak in traffic or sales with a specific social marketing activity

Layering activity timelines with metrics, as shown in Figure 7-1, is a simple, graphical way to spot this type of correlation. Establishing baseline metrics for your hub presence first truly helps in this process. It also helps if you add social media techniques one at a time — preferably with tracking codes.

Figure 7-1: Correlating an activity timeline with key performance indicators provides useful information.

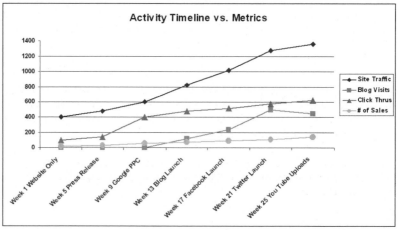

Copyright 2012 Watermelon Mountain Web Marketing; www.watermelonweb.com

Don't make *irreversible* decisions based on one event or from an analytical time frame that's too short for the marketing channel you're trying to implement. There are no rules for a time frame that is too short or too long. Your overall campaign may be designed to take off like a rocket in less than a week, or it may be set up to take 6 to 12 months to bear fruit. Be patient. Monitor your social media campaigns and rely on your business instincts.

You may find a time delay between the initiation of an effort and its impact on metrics, for these reasons:

✦ Viewers may wait to see a history of posts before engaging, let alone clicking through to your main hub.

✦ By definition, establishing a relationship with viewers or prospects takes time, just as it does in real life.

✦ Our brains haven't changed in spite of the Internet: As every brand marketer knows, most people still need to see something seven times to remember it.

✦ Many types of social media display a greater cumulative effect over time as viral marketing takes hold.

✦ Your mastery of a new medium usually improves as you climb the learning curve.

With positive results, the answer is simple: Keep doing what you're doing, and even more so. After you identify the elements responsible for your success, repeat them, amplify them, multiply them, and repurpose them.

Neutral or negative results force you to evaluate whether you should drop the activity or invest the effort needed to identify the problem and try to fix it. Ultimately, only you can decide whether you want to continue sinking time and effort into a social marketing method that doesn't produce results you want.

Make a chart for yourself like the one produced by the Robert H. Smith School of Business at the University of Maryland, shown in Figure 7-2. It shows how small businesses rank their accomplishments using social media. How do your efforts stack up?

The Fairmont Hotel & Resorts chain adjusts its marketing activity, as described in the nearby "Fairmont Hotels book success with social media" sidebar.

Figure 7-2:
With the exception of identifying new customers, small businesses became more positive about their social media accomplishments between 2009 and 2011.

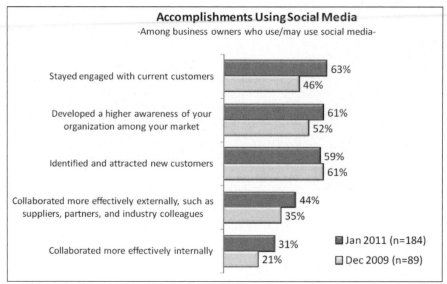

Accomplishments Using Social Media
-Among business owners who use/may use social media-

Stayed engaged with current customers	63% / 46%
Developed a higher awareness of your organization among your market	61% / 52%
Identified and attracted new customers	59% / 61%
Collaborated more effectively externally, such as suppliers, partners, and industry colleagues	44% / 35%
Collaborated more effectively internally	31% / 21%

■ Jan 2011 (n=184) □ Dec 2009 (n=89)

Fairmont Hotels book success with social media

In 1907, The Fairmont, San Francisco's grand dame of hotels, opened its doors. The iconic hotel soon became the city's venue of choice for glittering balls, presidential visits, and political gatherings, making the hotel synonymous with "place of occasion." With this auspicious beginning, the Fairmont Hotels & Resorts brand was born.

A privately held company, Fairmont is now a celebrated collection of more than 60 luxury properties, whose landmark addresses include Banff Springs, London, Quebec City, New York, Nairobi, and Shanghai.

According to Barbara Pezzi, director of Analytics & Search Optimization, Fairmont was an early adopter, seeing social media as a new and innovative way to reach its guests. It joined YouTube in 2007, Twitter in 2008, and Facebook in 2009. Fairmont also developed an online community site, `EveryonesAnOriginal.com` (EAO), where guests and colleagues can share photos, recipes, stories, advice, and more.

Pezzi says that content is used across multiple social media services as appropriate. For example, recipes on EAO are shared on Facebook, Facebook galleries are shared on Twitter, and YouTube videos are used across multiple platforms. But no matter what the content, the message is always platform-specific.

"Each social media channel," she explains, "is tailored to the different demographics and psychographics of its users. We monitor our social analytics and may take such information, such as geography, language, preferred content, and more into account when creating posts. When publicizing a specific campaign, we are careful to geo-target our social messaging to reach only those fans who may be eligible to participate."

Pezzi uses both Google Analytics and Omniture SiteCatalyst to analyze all this activity, utilizing tracking links to each post on Facebook, Twitter, and Google+. Both tools are set up in similar ways. "We add tracking links to each post and then analyze them accordingly," she notes. "This task is now automated in Excel."

(continued)

(continued)

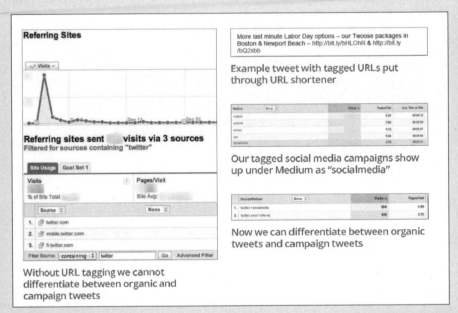

Courtesy Fairmont Raffles Hotels Intl.

The share of social traffic to the Fairmont site is still too small to alter the overall site dynamics and key metrics, Pezzi explains, even though it has been increasing exponentially over the past few years.

Apart from social networks, Fairmont takes advantage of social review sites like Tripadvisor.com and Yelp.com, which currently provide the highest percentage of bookers. However, Pezzi notes that all social services send a good percentage of qualified traffic, given that "qualified" varies by the goal of the site.

"Listening to what is being said about your brand is one of the most important roles in social media management," says Pezzi, "so we utilize a system of alerts to notify us of online mentions. We employ a paid monitoring tool, with a platform that we can log into at any time to see thousands of online mentions each day and to delve deeper into certain areas that we might like to investigate. We find that setting up alerts is a more efficient way to listen and monitor, without being tied to the platform. This allows us to be a first responder to mentions about our own brand, and chime in on conversations when appropriate, as well as stay in the loop on any issues that need attended to."

To maintain all these efforts, Fairmont has two full-time team members in the corporate Internet Marketing Department dedicated to social media, plus others in the PR Department. At each of its 60-plus properties, a social media champion is dedicated to managing and maintaining the hotel-level social networks and review sites.

Fairmont doesn't use social bookmarks on the main brand site, but does publicize its social links quite extensively on brand websites, in e-mail signatures, and in online promotions.

For Pezzi, it's all about content. "When using social media, we have found that developing diverse content that provides value for friends and followers is critical. The more you can do to add value for your fans through engaging, dynamic content, the more they will interact, respond, and promote your brand organically."

"The key," she emphasizes, "is to listen to your fans through likes, comments, analytics, and more to deliver the content they are interested in most. Our success depends on the reputation of our brand: Do people like to stay with us, will they return, and will they recommend us to others? Social media puts this reputation into the hands of the public, so every written review, opinion, and post matters. Do not underestimate the importance of listening, no matter how big or small your firm is. Having an attentive ear to your social media sources can also help you learn a lot about what you are doing well and what needs improvement."

The Fairmont Hotels & Resorts web presence

```
www.fairmont.com
```

```
www.everyonesanoriginal.com
```

```
http://rss.fairmont.com/p/subscribe (RSS)
```

```
https://plus.google.com/s/fairmont_hotels
```

```
https://twitter.com/#!/fairmonthotels
```

```
www.facebook.com/fairmonthotels
```

```
http://pinterest.com/fairmonthotels
```

```
www.youtube.com/fairmonthotels
```

```
www.linkedin.com/company/fairmont-hotels-and-resorts
```

Diagnosing Problems with Social Media Campaigns

Put on your business hat when you detect a problem. Some techniques may be worth modifying and trying again, while others should be dropped. Ultimately, it's a business decision, not a technological one.

Be patient when assessing cost of customer acquisition and ROI, though a few trend lines in your metrics might give you pause:

+ Traffic to a social media service never picks up, or falls and remains low after an initial burst.

+ Traffic to the social media site holds steady, but the CTR to your master hub or other sites is low.

+ Follow-through on intermediate calls-to-action is low in performance metrics.

+ Traffic and click-throughs increase, but the leads aren't well qualified.

+ Traffic and engagement, which had been increasing for quite a while, fall and continue to fall; small dips and rises are natural.

+ A conversion rate tracked back to a social media service is unintentionally lower than from other sources, and average sales value is lower. (Good strategic reasons for these results might exist, of course. You might deliberately target the younger student audience on foursquare with less expensive options than those offered to an older, more affluent audience on Facebook.)

+ The cost of customer or lead acquisition is much higher than for other channels, making the ROI unattractive. For example, a high-maintenance blog might generate a few leads but be relatively expensive compared to prescheduled tweets that drive more traffic successfully.

Fixing Problems

Underlying problems with low traffic on social media usually can be slotted into a few categories:

+ Problems locating your social media presence

+ Mismatch between channel and audience

+ Poor content

+ No audience engagement

+ Problems with the four P's of marketing: Product, price, placement or position (distribution), and promotion

After these problems are diagnosed, they can be handled in roughly the same way regardless of the social media venue used.

Before you panic, make sure that you have set reasonable expectations for performance and business metrics. Research the range of responses for similar companies, or view your competitors' social media sites to see how many responses, comments, and followers they have. Though you cannot foretell their ROI, you can assess their traffic and inbound links. Your results from social media may be just fine!

Use the social monitoring tools described in Book II, Chapter 3 to discover how your competitors are doing on social media compared to your business. Many of these tools enable you to check any domain name.

Be careful with interpretation, however; if your competitors began working on their social media campaigns long before you did, they are likely to have very different results.

Remember that the social media audience is quite fickle. A constant demand exists for changes in content, approach, tools, and tone to keep up.

Your social presence can't be found

Driving traffic to your social media presence is as challenging as driving people to your site. If traffic is still low after about four weeks, ensure that all your social media sites are optimized for external search engines such as Google and internal (on-site) search tools used by different social media services. Turn to Book II, Chapter 2 for optimization techniques.

The source of the problem may be poorly selected search terms or tags, a headline or description that contains no keywords, or content that hasn't been optimized. Unless your hub presence, whether it's a blog or website, is well optimized itself, your social media presence may suffer too.

Be sure that posts occur often enough for your social media page to appear in real-time search results.

Inappropriate match between channel and audience

The symptoms for a mismatch usually show up quickly: People take little or no interest in your social media postings, you suffer from low CTR, and your bounce rate is high whenever visitors click-through.

To start with, you may have chosen an inappropriate social media service or the "wrong" group within a network. For example, young tech males like Digg, but if you want a social site about cooking and gardening, try www. kirtsy.com instead.

The solution: Return to your Social Media Marketing Plan (see Book I, Chapter 3). Review the demographics and behavioral characteristics for the social media service you're using. They may have changed over time; for example, Facebook is still mostly popular with 18 to 24-year-olds, in spite of recent publicity about the growth in older users. Find a social venue that's a better fit, revise your plan, and try again.

Use Quantcast or Alexa to check demographics on social media sites if you aren't sure.

Poor content

Content problems are a little harder to diagnose than visibility problems, especially if the problem appears with your first posts. In that case, the problem may also look like a channel mismatch, with content that simply doesn't appeal to your target market or is inappropriate for the channel.

However, if you experience a persistent dip in traffic, comments, or CTR from your blog, Facebook stream, Flickr, podcast, or YouTube account, you have other difficulties. Perhaps the content has "aged," isn't updated frequently enough, or has degraded in quality and interest.

Content creators are commonly enthusiastic at the beginning of a project, or to start with a backlog of media that can be repurposed and posted initially. Later content may not be as valuable to your market, lack appropriate production values, or simply become boring.

Watch for burnout. After the backlog of media is used up, the insistent demands for new content can easily become a burden. It isn't surprising to have creators lose interest or focus on quantity rather than on quality.

Compare the individual posts that produced an increase in traffic, responses, or CTR to ones that are failing. Tally posts by the names of their creators and what they were about. Start by asking previously successful creators to develop new material along the lines of older, successful content. If that doesn't work, watch the "most popular" tags to see what interests visitors and try to tie new content into those topics, if appropriate.

Finally, try assigning fresh staff members, recruiting guest writers and producers, or hiring professionals for a while. If this change produces better results, you have indicators for a long-term solution.

Lack of audience engagement

If you see traffic to the social media service holding steady but lack follow-throughs from calls to action or you have an unusually low click-through rate to your hub site, you may not be engaging your audience. Watch especially for engagement parameters that never take off or that dip persistently.

Review user comments, retweets, and other interactions on each service. You can use the internal performance metrics for Twitter, Facebook, and your blog to assess numerical results of engagement. Then review the chain for interaction between social media visitors and your staff. Are visitor responses being acknowledged? Is there follow-up? One of the biggest challenges in social media is establishing a relationship with your visitors and maintaining a back-and-forth conversation. A lack of engagement may presage a lack of brand recognition, loss of customer loyalty, and reduced referrals from visitors to their friends or colleagues.

Use the tool from Forrester Research (`http://empowered.forrester.com/tool_consumer.html`), shown in Figure 7-3, to assess the level of engagement to expect from your market demographics. You can find the definitions for these consumer groups at `http://empowered.forrester.com/ladder2010`.

Figure 7-3:
The
Forrester
consumer
profile tool
offers a
yardstick
to predict
degrees of
social media
engagement
based
on the
demogra-
phics of
your target
market.

Courtesy Forrester Research, Inc.

The four P's of marketing

Perhaps you're getting traffic and click-throughs to your hub site and generating plenty of leads but still not closing or converting to sales. It might be
time to go back to basics.

Review a web analytics report generated before you started your social
media marketing efforts. Make sure your website is well optimized for
search, your online store (if you have one) is working well, and your conversion rate is solid. Fix any problems with your website before you try to
adjust your social media campaign.

Product, price, placement or position (distribution), and promotion — the
four P's — are considered the basic elements of traditional marketing. These
terms apply to social media and other forms of online marketing as well.

Product

Your *product* is whatever good or service you sell, regardless of whether the
transaction takes place online or off. Product also includes such elements as
performance, warranties, support, variety, and size. Review your competition to see which features, benefits, or services they offer, and which products they're featuring in social media. If you have an online store, look at

your entire product mix and merchandising, not just at individual products. Ask yourself these questions:

✦ Are you selling products that the people you're targeting with social media want to buy?

✦ Do you have enough products or services to compete successfully in this environment?

✦ Are you updating your offerings regularly and promoting new items often?

Price

Price comparison sites such as Shopping.com and discount stores online already put price pressure on small businesses. Now mobile social media shopping sites, with the rapid viral spread of news about special offers and price breaks, have put cost-conscious shoppers firmly in the driver's seat.

No longer can you check only competitors' websites and comparison-shopping sites for prices. Now you must check to see what they offer their Facebook, Twitter, LinkedIn, blog, e-newsletter, and social shopping visitors to gain new customers and hold onto them as loyal, repeat buyers. Any single product or service may now have multiple prices, depending on who's buying.

Use social shopping and other sites to assess your prices against your online competition. Are yours significantly higher or lower or price competitive?

Your small business can have difficulty competing in the market for standard manufactured goods such as baby clothes or DVDs unless you have excellent wholesale deals from manufacturers or distributors. But you can compete on price on customized goods or services or by offering unique benefits for buying from your company.

If you must charge higher prices than your social media competitors, review your value proposition so that people perceive an extra benefit. It might be a $5 promotional code for a discount on another purchase, a no-questions-asked return policy, exclusivity, or very accessible tech support.

Be careful not to trap yourself into matching prices against large companies with deep pockets. Make tactical financial decisions about loss leaders and discounts for users of particular social media. Consider a less-than-full-featured product or service package for social media users if needed (sometimes called the *freemium* business model).

Placement or position

Placement or position refers to how products and services are delivered to consumers (distribution channels). Where and how are your products and services available? Your website needs to serve as a 24/7 hub for customer research, support, and sales online, but social media offers brand-new opportunities to serve your clients. Best Buy, for example, has already become famous for its *twelpforce,* in which employees use Twitter to field customer support questions and make product recommendations.

With multiple social marketing outlets, watch for the effects of *channel cannibalization* (the use of multiple distribution channels that pull sales from each other). Products or services sold directly from social media outlets may depress the sales numbers on your website.

Promotion

Your online and social media marketing plans fall into the *promotion* category, which includes all the different ways you communicate with customers and prospects, both online and offline. This also includes making people aware of your multiple points of visibility online, almost as though you're marketing another product. Careful cross-promotion among all your online venues is now as critical as integrating online and offline advertising. Are people aware of all your social media pages? Are you using the right calls to action on those pages to get people to buy?

Don't continue investing in a social media technique just because everyone else is doing it.

Adjusting to Reality

Many times, expectations determine whether a marketing technique is seen as a success or a waste of time or something in between. It isn't possible for a particular social media service to produce extraordinary changes in traffic or conversions. In most cases, though, your victories will be hard-won, as you cobble together traffic from multiple social media sources to build enough of a critical mass to gain measurable sales.

Achieving that goal usually involves many people, each of whom may become a committed champion of the method she has been using. When you decide to pull the plug on one of your social media techniques — or just decide to leave it in a static state — try to still keep your employees engaged.

Unless social media participants have proved themselves to be nonperformers, try to shift them into another channel so that they can retain a direct relationship with customers.

Avoid the temptation to recentralize your social media marketing in one place, whether it's PR, marketing communications, management, or customer support. Instead, try to maintain the involvement of someone from each of those functional areas, as well as subject area experts from such diverse departments as manufacturing, sales, and research and development (R&D).

Marketing is only part of a company, but all of a company is marketing.

As wild a ride as social media may seem, it's more of a marathon than a sprint. Given that it may take months to see the return on your marketing efforts, you may need to nourish your social media sites for quite a while.

Feeding the hungry maw of the content monster week in and week out isn't easy. You need to not only keep your staff engaged and positive but also keep your content fresh. Take advantage of brainstorming techniques that involve your entire team to generate some new ideas each month. Here are a few suggestions to get you started:

✦ Create unique, themed campaigns that last one to three months. Find an interesting hook to recruit guest posts or writers, perhaps letting a few people try your product or service and write about it.

✦ Distribute short-term "deals" using some of the up-and-coming social media techniques described in Book VIII, Chapter 5, such as location-based coupons on cellphones or to meetup attendees.

✦ Write a Wikipedia entry about your product or business from a consumer's point of view.

✦ Make friends with Twitter by incorporating an interactive application, such as a poll or sweepstakes entry.

✦ Reach one or more of your discrete niche markets by using some of the smaller alternative social media services listed in Book VIII, Chapter 3, or in Book II, Chapter 3.

✦ If you aren't gaining traction with groups on Twitter or Facebook, post on an old-fashioned forum, message board, or chat room on a relevant topic.

✦ Tell a story about your product or service in pictures (not video — too easy!) and upload them to Flickr, Pinterest, or another photo service.

Every marketing problem has an infinite number of solutions. You have to find only one of them!

Index